Claims Handling Law and Practice

A Practitioner's Guide

To Fred and Kieron
with thanks for your wisdom and guidance.

Claims Handling Law and Practice

Law is accurate to the date of writing on 1 February 2018.

Claims Handling Law and Practice

A Practitioner's Guide

Lead author
Richard West

Authors and co-authors
Matt Andrews, Jenny Boldon, Marta Bozek, Marian Brennan, Will Brown, Mark Burton, Andrew Caplan, Christopher Chatfield, Cameron Clark, Dónal Clark, Justin Collins, Robert Corrigan, Martin Cox, Ian Davies, Niall Edwards, Jennifer Harris, Tracy Head, Louise Houliston, Felicity Ingram, Rory Jackson, Roger Jones, Christopher Malla, Charles Martin, Sam Mason, Joe McManus, Danny McShee, Rachel Moore, Paul Morris, Claire Mulligan, Deborah Newberry, Naomi North, Martina O'Mahoney, Karishma Paroha, Stephanie Power, Ron Ruston, Janet Sayers, Shane Sayers, Laura Siddall, Helen Snowball, Martin Stockdale, Lucy Suddaby, Katherine Totty, Carole Vernon, Mark Welbourn, Greg Woods, David Wright, Amanda Wylie

Third Edition 2018

Lead author
Richard West

Authors and co-authors
Matt Andrews, Jenny Boldon, Marta Bozek, Marian Brennan, Will Brown, Mark Burton, Andrew Caplan, Christopher Chatfield, Cameron Clark, Dónal Clark, Justin Collins, Robert Corrigan, Martin Cox, Ian Davies, Niall Edwards, Jennifer Harris, Tracy Head, Louise Houliston, Felicity Ingram, Rory Jackson, Roger Jones, Christopher Malla, Charles Martin, Sam Mason, Joe McManus, Danny McShee, Rachel Moore, Paul Morris, Claire Mulligan, Deborah Newberry, Naomi North, Martina O'Mahoney, Karishma Paroha, Stephanie Power, Ron Ruston, Janet Sayers, Shane Sayers, Laura Siddall, Helen Snowball, Martin Stockdale, Lucy Suddaby, Katherine Totty, Carole Vernon, Mark Welbourn, Greg Woods, David Wright, Amanda Wylie

2018

ISBN 978-1-910872-02-4

Published by
Kennedys Law LLP
25 Fenchurch Avenue
London EC3M 5AD, United Kingdom
www.kennedyslaw.com

Designed and typeset by
Clever Marketing Limited
Export House, Cawsey Way, Woking
Surrey GU21 6QX, United Kingdom
www.clevermarketing.co.uk

Printed and bound in Great Britain by L&S Printing

Foreword

This is effectively the fourth edition of this book. The first, and altogether much smaller, version was first published in 2000. In almost every way since the turn of the millennium, the legal and insurance world has changed beyond the predictions of all but the most wildly imaginative. The rise of the machine has maintained its trajectory with the continued advance and adjustment of Ministry of Justice (MoJ) online claims portals. A modern online court system is currently being developed by the MoJ with the express intent of allowing parties to litigate cases without necessarily needing a lawyer. Concepts that were science fiction back in 2000 are now a growing reality with the rapid advance of machine learning, predictive analytics and artificial intelligence.

One aspect that has thankfully not changed during the last 18-year period is the vision and drive demonstrated by Kennedys. That drive and vision has resulted in Kennedys now being a global insurance specialist, with (at the time of writing) almost 1,900 staff and 37 offices worldwide. In the months prior to the publication of this book, Kennedys was named 'UK Law Firm of the Year' at The British Legal Awards 2017 and won its second innovations prize for 'Technology Initiative of the Year 2017' at The London Market Awards.

That we have continued to grow successfully is also a result of our Core Principle – to help our clients to only use lawyers when they truly need to do so and to help break the twentieth-century 'addiction' to lawyers, peddled by some of our peers. This book, along with our technological innovations and broader global thought leadership, underpins that Core Principle.

This edition now spans 42 chapters. My colleagues and I have updated chapters covering important areas including road traffic accident and third-party liabilities, catastrophic injury, occupational disease, clinical negligence and professional indemnity. As a result of client demand, we have introduced new chapters on marine, aviation, property and environmental claims, as well as counter-fraud and crisis management. The aim of this book continues to be to support our clients and claims handlers on a day-to-day basis. It has been written to be both an aide memoire for the experienced and a training aid for the novice. It is our ambition that this edition will prove to be ever more beneficial and empower our readers to use lawyers less.

My thanks to the very large number of expert authors and editors from within Kennedys who have contributed to and promoted the publication of this now not-inconsiderable guide. We continue to welcome any and all suggestions that you may have as to how the book may be improved.

In the meantime, I look forward with genuine fascination to the next few years in the legal and insurance professions. We predict yet further consolidation in the legal sector, alongside the failure of any legal services provider who does not innovate and truly differentiate.

Richard West
Partner, Divisional Head and Head of Innovation
Kennedys

Foreword

(Reproduced from the 2008 edition)

Too often lawyers are guilty of clouding issues whilst attempting to provide explanations. That is something that we try not to do at Kennedys and in many ways I feel this book exemplifies our approach to providing legal services to our clients.

I am sure that all involved in claims have from time to time wished for access to a simple guide to the areas of law with which we most commonly deal, to ideally refer to one book only and not have to trek to a law library or open a number of tomes to find the answer. The practitioners' guide, written by a number of my colleagues at Kennedys, seeks to deliver such a book covering a wide variety of disciplines within one pair of covers.

This user-friendly guide covers fields as diverse as clinical negligence, health and safety, occupiers' liability, child abuse, manual handling, the Road Traffic Act, disease and highways law. In addition, reflecting the trend of insurers to turn to external cost providers to advise on the issue of third party costs, there are two chapters on funding.

The book's aim is to assist claims handlers with those areas of law with which they have to deal on a day-to-day basis. It is an aide memoire for the experienced but also sets out the basics for the novice. Our clients have told us that it is a helpful core text for in-house training.

The authors of this book are all leaders in their own fields but they and I would welcome any and all suggestions that you may have as to how the book may be improved for the fourth edition.

Nick Thomas
Senior Partner
Kennedys

September 2008

Introduction

Here is the latest, expanded edition of a work which I described as "achingly useful" in my introduction last time round.

If anything, that view is held with even greater fervour today, for the law refuses to settle down. On the contrary, vicarious liability, to take one specific example, has broken through earlier judicial constraints and runs amok, flattening hapless defendants.

I would like to say something about the mechanics of claims and how they are managed by the legal system. Within this fine work you will find a distillation of the applicable legal principles. However, we have an amazingly complex set of Court Rules and orders which dictate how those very legal rights and obligations are determined where a dispute arises.

The bible is 'The White Book'. It is indeed white but so complex that it occupies 6,373 pages (with the bulk of text set in minuscule print) and occupies not one book but two. If one were to stand upon the two volumes it is arguable that the Work at Height Regulations 2005 might come into play.

Given that it takes 51 editors to keep the blasted thing up to date you will forgive me if I do not attempt to summarise the contents. However, what I will do is point to a few major movements that every insurer or claims handler needs to be aware of. All are recent shifts.

Compliance with court orders given in a matter and the underlying Rules of Court is of the greatest importance today. In the not too distant past breach would provoke a yawn and a mild slap, if that. No more is that the case. The 2013 Jackson reforms enjoined everyone to comply and to behave.

Take *Gentry v Miller* [2016]. The defendant's insurer sadly dithered with handling a claim that had been issued. This enabled the claimant to secure a judgment in default of the requisite defence not having been delivered when due. The Court of Appeal refused to let the defendant off the hook – despite evidence that the claim might have been tainted by fraud. Astonishing. The Court made it abundantly clear that it expected insurers, who knew the ropes, to behave in accordance with the standards of lawyers.

Another frightener was *Eaglesham v Mod* [2016] where, in a difficult case for the claimant on liability, he secured a judgment without trial because the defendant had not disclosed key documents despite having been given one last chance to do so. Since the claim was worth arguably £6 million, one can see how exorbitantly expensive slippage can be.

Alternative dispute resolution (ADR) is adored by the most powerful judges within the civil process today. Their view is that, even if a case does not look promising, it is incumbent upon the parties to try and do some sort of deal. It is strange but true to say that judges do not want to try cases. They would much prefer them to be resolved quickly, cheaply and amicably. Reject ADR at your peril and do not think that if ultimately your stance was justified, as where the other side collapses at court, you will be lauded. More likely a costs sanction will be applied against you.

One welcome and evolving concept is proportionality. It is a matter of common sense that one ought to pursue a claim at a cost and in a manner commensurate with value. That wisdom has at last been enshrined in the Rules and should transform litigation activity. Quite how one actually arrives at a proportionate sum is still, as I write on a wet Sunday in January 2018, elusive. This is a bit of a blow since the new test has been with us since Easter 2013.

The hardest pill to swallow is the obligation to be nice and friendly to your opponent. Parties must cooperate and seek to agree as much as possible. Reasonable requests for more time should be granted. Cheap, technical challenges are now taboo. Litigation is not what it was.

Those are absolute principles which the reader of an earlier edition of this fine book would snigger at. Trust me, they have arrived and, like you and claims, are not going away.

Dominic Regan
Professor of Law and adviser to Lord Justice Jackson

Contents

Table of Legislation

Table of Cases

01 What is the law?

Richard West

- Enacting legislation
- Court structure
- European Union law
- Brexit

What is the law?

The law is a system of rules, enactments and decisions that set out rights and obligations within society.

The law is made up of the following:

- Acts of parliament (also known as legislation or statute)
- Previously decided case law (also known as common law or precedent)
- European Union law.

Acts of parliament

Parliament, through the House of Commons and the House of Lords, creates laws by enacting legislation.

> Examples of legislation that will be known to claims handlers include:
>
> - Road Traffic Act 1988
> - Occupiers' Liability Acts 1957 and 1984
> - Enterprise and Regulatory Reform Act 2013.

When enacting legislation, parliament sets out in some detail the laws that it wishes to bring into force.

Often, explanatory notes are provided with an Act. However, they are not legally binding.

A judge who is faced with a new piece of legislation is tasked with interpreting that legislation and will give their judgment based on that interpretation. The judicial interpretation of Acts of parliament is an important part of the law-making process. Judicial decisions are known as common law or precedent.

As an Act of parliament becomes older there will be more judicial decisions interpreting that legislation. The amount of precedent relating to that Act will therefore increase.

Previously decided case law

Previous decisions of the courts are known as precedent. Sometimes they have to be followed (binding precedent) and sometimes they can simply be taken into account by a judge when deciding a case (persuasive precedent).

Whether a previous decision binds a court or not will depend on the level of the court that reached the previous decision.

European Court of Justice

Decisions from the European Court of Justice on points of European law bind all English and Welsh courts. However, the European Court of Justice is not bound by its own previous decisions.

Supreme Court

The Supreme Court is the superior court of England and Wales. All decisions made by the Supreme Court are binding on inferior courts. The Supreme Court, however, is not bound by its own previous decisions.

The Constitutional Reform Act 2005 created the Supreme Court, replacing the House of Lords as the highest court in the land in October 2009.

Court of Appeal

The Court of Appeal is bound to follow previous decisions of the Supreme Court. It is also generally bound by its own previous decisions.

High Court

The High Court's decisions do not bind lower courts but are often considered to be highly persuasive.

The High Court is not bound by its own previous decisions, although it is bound by Court of Appeal and Supreme Court decisions. However, the High Court will consider carefully any of its previous decisions that are relevant to the case before it.

County courts

The county court judiciary must follow the previous decisions of the Supreme Court and Court of Appeal. They may find previous High Court decisions strongly persuasive and can often also be persuaded by other county court decisions.

It must be remembered that a persuasive precedent is an important part of the legal process. Courts will often follow previous decisions even if they do not bind them, if doing so ensures a common sense and consistent approach across the courts.

Distinguishing cases

It is possible for judges to 'distinguish' earlier cases. Judges can avoid a binding precedent by pointing out differences between past decisions and the case before them. They can argue, for example, that the facts of the case that they have to deal with are not 'on all fours' or precisely the same as those relating to an earlier decision that would otherwise be binding.

European Union legislation

Regulations, directives and decisions from the European Union constitute European Union legislation. They are all important:

- Regulations are directly applicable and binding on English courts. A regulation does not need to be enacted within separate legislation by the UK government. Regulations, once made, become part of English law.
- Directives must be implemented by parliament into English law within a specified period of time. Generally, they only bind English and Welsh courts once they have been enacted by parliament.
- As with Acts of parliament, regulations will be subject to judicial interpretation and may, therefore, generate a bank of precedent of their own.

Brexit

On 23 June 2016 the UK voted to leave the EU. The government triggered Article 50 of the Treaty of Lisbon on 29 March 2017.

EU Directives are turned in UK law as Statutory Instruments. When creating a new law, the law must reflect the minimum standard set out in European law. These laws will continue to be in force post exit from the EU, unless and until the government passes a new law to revoke these.

It is not yet clear when the UK will formally cease to be part of the EU or the impact that this will have on UK claims.

02 Negligence

Richard West

- Duty of care and breach of duty
- The meaning of damage
- Eggshell skull rule
- Causation and contributory negligence
- Vicarious liability and independent contractors
- Limitation

Negligence

Introduction

A negligent act or omission is a tort or a civil wrong. It is based mainly in common law.

The usual remedy to correct a civil wrong is to seek a sum of money to compensate the victim by way of damages. That is done through the courts.

Negligence is a tort that claims handlers will have to deal with almost every day.

A negligent act is an act (or omission) by one party that is inexcusable and that causes damage to another.

Negligence has three components. Each component must be proved before a claim in negligence can succeed:

- The defendant must have owed the claimant a duty of care.
- The defendant must have failed in, or breached, that duty of care.
- The claimant must have suffered damage or loss as a result.

Duty of care

Broadly, this is a matter of common sense. For example, a duty of care is owed by:

- Doctors to their patients
- Employers to their employees
- Motorists to other road users and pedestrians.

Whether a duty of care is owed will generally depend on whether a defendant could have reasonably foreseen that the claimant would be affected by their negligent act or omission.

> Lord Atkin gave the leading explanation of when such a duty of care exists in the case of *Donoghue v Stevenson* [1932]. He said:
>
> > "The rule that you are to love your neighbour becomes in law, you must not injure your neighbour; and the lawyer's question, Who is my neighbour? receives a restricted reply. You must take reasonable care to avoid acts or omissions which you can reasonably foresee would be likely to injure your neighbour. Who, then, in law, is my neighbour? The answer seems to be – persons who are so closely and directly affected by my act that I ought reasonably to have them in contemplation as being so affected when I am directing my mind to the acts or omissions which are called into question."

Breach of duty

The issue here is whether the defendant has done something that they should not have done or has not done something that they should have done. A party can breach their duty of care to another, therefore, either by an act or by an omission.

The courts will apply an objective test. Broadly, that test will be: "Has the defendant acted reasonably?" or "Would the reasonable man have done more?"

Whether a party has acted reasonably will depend upon the particular facts of each case. For example, a person driving a car at 75 miles per hour on a motorway, keeping up with the traffic flow, may be driving at a reasonable speed, albeit that they are driving in excess of the speed limit. However, the driving of a car at the same speed (75 miles per hour) in a built-up area within a speed limit of 30 miles per hour will almost certainly be found to be unreasonable.

Similarly, an employer may act reasonably in asking an appropriately experienced, trained and muscular employee to carry coal sacks without assistance. However, the same employer will probably act unreasonably in asking an inexperienced employee without the requisite training to do the same task.

When considering what is reasonable, the courts will tend to look at the following:

- The nature of the act or omission in question; for example could the act or omission have been easily avoided?
- The risks attached; for example, how serious was the risk and how much damage could have been caused?
- Who the defendant is; for example, are they in a position of responsibility – such as an employer, a doctor or a local authority?
- Who the claimant is; for example, are they in a class of persons who are particularly vulnerable – such as employees or patients?
- How easy it would have been to protect the claimant from the breach of duty; for example, how much would it have cost, what procedures would have been needed and the resources of that particular defendant?

Damage

Damage must not be too remote

The test here is whether the damage is of the kind that could reasonably have been foreseen. It is clearly foreseeable that driving a car at speed into the rear of another vehicle will cause damage to that car and injury to its occupants.

However, oil spilled from a ship into a harbour, which then ignites causing the destruction of a wharf by fire, has been found not to be foreseeable damage. In *The Wagon Mound No. 1* [1961], welding equipment ignited oil in the harbour, causing a fire. The Privy Council held that this was too remote a consequence of the oil spillage, which had arisen as a result of a breach of duty.

It can, therefore, be seen that even though damage may arise directly from a breach of duty, if that damage could not have been reasonably foreseen, a court will find it to be too remote for damages to be recovered.

Defendant must take claimant as they find them

This is the so-called eggshell skull rule. This principle generally arises in personal injury actions.

For example, if a minor blow causes an unexpected, but nevertheless genuinely severe, reaction because of the claimant's physiology, the defendant cannot say: "That is not reasonably foreseeable" or, "How was I to know that that would happen?"

The defendant, it has been decided by the courts, must take their victim as they find them.

In *Bourhill v Young* [1942], Lord Wright said:

> "It has long ago been stated and often restated that if the wrong is established the wrongdoer must take the victim as he finds him ... on the condition that the wrong has been established or admitted."

Lord Justice MacKinnon, in *Owens v Liverpool Corporation* [1938], stated that:

> "One who is guilty of negligence to another must put up with idiosyncrasies of his victim that increase the likelihood or extent of damage to him: it is no answer to a claim for a fractured skull that its owner had an unusually fragile one."

This situation often arises in claims involving psychiatric injury. There may have been a minor road traffic accident causing little physical injury. A claimant may claim, however, that they can no longer work, having been so traumatised by the accident that they can no longer cope with employment.

A defendant in such circumstances might obtain access to the claimant's medical records. These may show that the claimant had a pronounced psychiatric history for many years prior to the accident. What if such records show that the claimant was, before the accident, taking large periods of time off from work and had considerable difficulties domestically, socially and professionally because of their pre-accident personality?

The defendant in that situation could argue that the accident has not caused the claimant's problems, but that they were pre-existing.

If the court accepted that the accident caused a psychiatric injury, it would tend to reach one of two conclusions:

- The accident caused an increase in the pre-accident problems from which the claimant was suffering, and that the claimant had returned to their pre-accident state. In other words, that the accident had temporarily exacerbated or worsened the pre-existing psychiatric condition, or
- The accident, although minor, had, when combined with the claimant's pre-existing frailties, created a new and more serious condition that then prevented the claimant from working.

In the first case, the defendant would pay compensation for the loss that occurred during the period for which their negligence caused the claimant's condition to be temporarily worsened.

In the second case, the defendant cannot argue that the injury was not foreseeable, even though it may appear disproportionate. They must take their victim, frailties and all, as they find them. They must pay the claimant compensation for the loss that has occurred as a result of the new and more serious condition caused by their negligence.

Claims handlers will see, therefore, the importance of ensuring that their own experts are asked to deal carefully with this particular issue.

Causation

It must be the breach of duty that causes the damage.

Therefore, if the court finds, in the psychiatric example above, that the accident caused a temporary increase in the pre-existing condition, but that the ongoing problems are not accident related, the judge will make a finding that the claimant has not proved a causal link between the accident and the ongoing problems.

Consider also an example of an employer who has failed to carry out appropriate manual handling assessments for their employees. One of those employees visits a customer's premises to deliver a large, awkward and heavy item. In carrying the item from their van, they slip on some oil in the customer's car park, falling to the ground and injuring their back. That oil was recently deposited in a usually clean car park by an unknown vehicle.

If the employer can show that the slip was unconnected to their breach of duty (their failure to carry out proper manual handling assessments), they will escape liability. Although the employer breached the duty of care to their employee, they may be able to argue that the slip was not caused by that breach. There would, therefore, be a denial of causation.

For example, in *Clough v First Choice Holidays & Flights Ltd* [2006], the claimant was on holiday in Lanzarote and under the influence of alcohol when he slipped from a wall that divided two swimming pools and broke his neck. At first instance and on appeal, it was held that the defendant's failure to use non-slip paint on the wall was negligent but had not caused the accident. The Court of Appeal upheld the trial judge's decision that, on the balance of probabilities, the accident would not have been avoided had non-slip paint been used. It held that the increased risk caused by the absence of the non-slip paint had not caused or materially contributed to the accident.

Contributory negligence

As claims handlers will be aware, a court can find that one party or the other is entirely to blame; or that both parties are to blame.

The law is set out in s.1 of the Law Reform (Contributory Negligence) Act 1945, which states:

> Where any person suffers damage as the result partly of his own fault and partly of the fault of any other person or persons, a claim in respect of that damage shall not be defeated by reason of the fault of the person suffering the damage, but the damages recoverable in respect thereof shall be reduced to such extent as the court thinks just and equitable having regard to the claimant's share in the responsibility for the damage.

Lord Denning explained the concept of contributory negligence in two of his judgments.

In *Jones v Livox Quarries Ltd* [1952], he stated:

> “Although contributory negligence does not depend on a duty of care, it does depend on foreseeability. Just as actionable negligence requires the foreseeability of harm to others, so contributory negligence requires the foreseeability of harm to oneself. A person is guilty of contributory negligence if he ought reasonably to have foreseen that, if he did not act as a reasonable, prudent man, he might be hurt himself; and in his reckonings he must take into account the possibility of others being careless.”

In *Froom v Butcher* [1975], he stated:

> “Negligence depends on a breach of duty, whereas contributory negligence does not. Negligence is a man's carelessness in breach of duty to *others*. Contributory negligence is a man's carelessness in looking after *his own* safety.”

If a court finds that both parties are to blame, then liability will generally be apportioned between the parties on a percentage basis.

A defendant can, therefore, argue that the claimant has contributed towards their own damage by their own acts or omissions.
For example, a speeding motorist may suggest that the pedestrian they have run over, and who walked out into their path giving them no chance to stop, was partly responsible for the accident and is, therefore, contributorily negligent.

An employer may argue that their injured employee failed to use appropriate lifting equipment that they were trained to use and frequently told to use. The employer, if unable to defend the matter entirely, would, therefore, argue that their employee had been contributorily negligent.

Therefore, if a claimant has partially caused their own damage, they will receive less in damages from a defendant than they would had they not contributed to their own injury. For example, a claimant found to be 50% contributorily negligent will have the damages that they would have received, had they been blameless, reduced by one half.

100% contributory negligence?

A defendant's liability to a claimant cannot be entirely extinguished by that claimant's contributory negligence.

In *Anderson v Newham College of Further Education* [2002], the Court of Appeal decided that, whether a claim was in negligence or for breach of statutory duty, there could be no finding of 100% contributory negligence. The Court of Appeal held that either the claimant was wholly to blame for their injuries and there was no liability on the defendant, or the defendant was to blame subject to a degree of contributory negligence on the part of the claimant.

Negligence of joint tortfeasors

As well as finding a claimant and a defendant equally or partly to blame, a court can find that more than one party has contributed to the claimant's loss and damage.

For example, a speeding motorist may swerve to avoid a vehicle that has pulled out into their path without warning. The speeding vehicle may then collide with an oncoming vehicle, causing injury and loss to the occupant of that vehicle. In such a situation a court may find that the speeding motorist (for driving too fast) and the emerging motorist (for pulling out when it was unsafe to do so) are both to blame for the accident.

The court would apportion blame for the accident, on a percentage basis, between the two negligent motorists.

Vicarious liability

It can often be the case that an employee acting in the course of their employment for an enterprise or company personally commits a breach of duty.

For example, a driver of a van, in the course of their employment, collides with the rear of a stationary motor vehicle, causing injury to the claimant. It is the driver of the van and not their employer who was negligent. However, as the driver was driving in the course of their employment, the claimant can also sue the employer on the basis that it is vicariously liable for the negligent act of its employee.

Similarly, a local authority whose highway inspector fails to spot a defect in need of urgent repair could be held vicariously liable for the highway inspector's omission.

Employers will be held vicariously liable for the torts of their employees when torts are committed in the course of an employee's employment. Liability is imposed without the necessity for a primary breach of duty on the employer's part.

The law of vicarious liability has developed significantly over the past few years. As identified by the Supreme Court in *Various Claimants v Catholic Child Welfare Society and others* [2012], a number of important propositions have been established. It is now possible:

- For an unincorporated association to be vicariously liable for the wrongful acts of its members.
- For a defendant to be vicariously liable even if the wrongdoer's act is in breach of the duty they owe to the person liable, and even if the act was a criminal offence.
- For two or more defendants each to be vicariously liable for a single wrongful act.

When considering whether there should be a finding of vicarious liability, the courts have established a two-stage test:

- Stage one considers the nature of the relationship between the employer and employee. In *Cox v Ministry of Justice* [2014], the claimant was working as a catering manager at HM Prison Swansea. She was injured in an accident caused by the negligence of a prisoner carrying out paid work moving food supplies under her supervision. The Court of Appeal held that the defendant was vicariously liable for the negligent acts of the prisoner. Whilst there was some scope for debate, the relationship between the defendant and the prisoner was one akin to employment. The task being carried out by the prisoner was done on the defendant's behalf and for its benefit.

continued...

...continued

- Stage two considers the connection between that relationship and the act or omission. In *Mohamud v WM Morrison Supermarkets plc* [2014], the claimant was visiting the defendant's petrol station kiosk. He asked an employee if he could print off some documents. The employee was abusive to him. The claimant returned to his car. He was followed by the employee, who carried out a brutal and unprovoked attack on him for no apparent reason. The Court of Appeal upheld the first instance decision that the defendant was not vicariously liable for the actions of the employee. It held that there was no element that could bring this case within the close connection test so as to establish vicarious liability. Consideration was given to a number of previous decisions involving assaults by employees. In cases where vicariously liability was found to exist, the employee had been given duties involving the clear possibility of confrontation and the use of force, or the employee was placed in a situation where an outbreak of violence was likely.

Readers need to be alive to the fact that this area of law is rapidly developing. Courts are pushing the boundaries of this principle, even finding for example that situations, "akin to employment" may trigger a liability for the "employer" (*Cox v Ministry of Justice* (2016)). In the circumstances, and given that this area is so rapidly developing, readers are advised to also review recent case law whenever considering a possible vicarious liability.

Independent contractors

A person who hires an independent contractor will not generally be liable for the negligent acts or omissions of that independent contractor.

There are, however, circumstances in which the acts of an independent contractor can cause an employer to be primarily liable. In brief, this will depend upon whether or not, at the time that the independent contractor was working, the employer was also in breach of a duty of care to the claimant.

Liability can arise where the independent contractor has not been supervised properly or, indeed, where there is a strict duty on the part of the employer to ensure that no duty is breached. That will be a question of law and is largely outside the remit of this guide.

There are certain exceptional circumstances where a duty of care is non-delegable to an independent contractor.

Where there is potential liability for an independent contractor's acts or omissions, an employer can only be held liable if the negligent act in question falls within the contract for which the independent contractor was hired. Any negligent acts falling outside the scope of the contract (collateral negligence) will not impose a liability on the employer.

If an independent contractor's acts or omissions result in an employer being liable, the employer may be able to seek a contractual indemnity from the independent contractor (or their insurers) for any claims. This will be subject to the wording of the contract.

Non-delegable duty of care

In *Woodland v Essex County Council* [2013], the Supreme Court held that a local authority was liable for the negligence of an independent contractor, even though there was no fault on the local authority's part. There was a non-delegable duty of care.

Delivering the lead judgment, Lord Sumption acknowledged that non-delegable duties of care were inconsistent with the fault-based principles on which the law of negligence is based and that any erosion of those principles must, therefore, only be in exceptional circumstances.

The exceptional criteria to be satisfied are:

- The claimant is a patient, or child or otherwise vulnerable and dependent on the protection of the defendant against the risk of injury.
- There is a pre-existing relationship between the claimant and defendant that places the claimant in the actual custody or care of the defendant, and from which a positive duty to protect the claimant from harm can be imputed.
- The claimant has no control over how the defendant chooses to perform their obligations to the claimant.
- The defendant has delegated to a third party some function that is an integral part of a positive duty.
- The third party has been negligent in the performance of the very function of that duty delegated to them by the defendant.

Limitation

The limitation period for bringing any claim is governed by the Limitation Act 1980.

Limitation has become an important weapon in the armoury of a defendant and should be of equal consideration and importance as the issues of breach of duty and causation.

> A successful limitation defence alone can see a claim dismissed, even if breach and causation are admitted. Limitation requires the consideration of a claim from a different and distinct legal perspective. Therefore, it is advisable, if proceedings are issued, to seek to have the argument heard by way of a preliminary issue hearing.

Personal injury claims

In a normal personal injury action a claimant must commence an action (i.e. issue court proceedings) within three years. The primary three-year period begins to run on the date the cause of action accrued (i.e. the date of the accident) or the date of knowledge (if later) of the person injured.

Under s.14 of the 1980 Act, the date of knowledge is defined as being the date when a claimant first had knowledge of the following facts:

- That the injury was significant.
- That the injury was attributable in whole or in part to the act or omission that is alleged to constitute negligence, nuisance or breach of duty.
- The identity of the defendant.

Under s.14(2), an injury is deemed significant if the person whose date of knowledge is in question would reasonably have considered it sufficiently serious to justify their instituting proceedings for damages against a defendant who did not dispute liability and was able to satisfy a judgment.

A person's knowledge includes knowledge that they might reasonably be expected to acquire:

- From facts observable or ascertainable by them.
- From facts ascertainable by them with the help of medical or other appropriate expert advice that it is reasonable for them to seek.

If a court determines that a claimant's date of knowledge is more than three years prior to the date of issue, then the claim is statute barred. However, the claimant is entitled to a 'second bite at the cherry' and can apply for relief from sanction under s.33 of the 1980 Act. The court has discretionary powers to allow an action to proceed notwithstanding the fact that it was commenced outside the prescribed period should it consider it to be equitable to do so and after taking into account the relative prejudice to the claimant and the defendant. Section 33(3) contains a list of some of the matters the court must consider when deciding whether or not to exercise its discretionary powers. The list of matters is not exhaustive, but includes:

- The length of and reasons for the delay in bringing proceedings.
- The extent to which the delay has affected the cogency of the evidence.
- The conduct of the parties.
- The duration of any disability of the claimant after the date their cause of action accrued.
- The extent to which the claimant acted promptly and reasonably once they became aware that the defendant's act or omission giving rise to their injury might give rise to a claim for damages.
- The steps taken by the claimant to obtain expert advice and the nature of the advice received.

Checklist

- ✓ Did the defendant owe the claimant a duty of care?
- ✓ Could the defendant have reasonably foreseen that the claimant would be affected by their negligent act or omission?
- ✓ Was that duty of care breached by the defendant? Remember, this is an objective test and the courts tend to consider the following factors:
  - ✓ The nature of the act or omission in question; for example, could the act or omission be easily avoided?
  - ✓ The risks attached; for example, how serious is the risk and how much damage could be caused?

- ☑ Who the defendant is; for example, is the defendant in a position of responsibility, such as an employer, a doctor or a local authority?
- ☑ Who the claimant is; for example, is the claimant in a class of persons who are particularly vulnerable, such as employees or patients?
- ☑ How easy it would be to protect the claimant from the breach of duty; for example, how much would it cost, what procedures would need to be put in place and what are the resources of that particular defendant?

- ✓ Has the claimant suffered damage as a result of the breach? Claims handlers must consider three elements:
  - ☑ Was the damage too remote? Was it reasonably foreseeable that the damage would be caused?
  - ☑ The defendant must take their victim as they find them.
  - ☑ Causation – did the breach cause the damage claimed?
- ✓ Did the claimant act or fail to act in any way that contributed to their own damage?
- ✓ Is there any other third party who contributed to the claimant's loss or damage?
- ✓ What is the liability, if any, of any independent contractor retained by the defendant?

03 Nuisance

Richard West

- Definition
- Remedies: damages, injunction and abatement

Nuisance

- Nuisance, like negligence, is a tort or a civil wrong.
- Public nuisance and statutory nuisance are not dealt with within this text.
- Claims handlers will, however, need to deal with private nuisance.

Definition

A private nuisance is an unlawful interference with a person's use or enjoyment of land, or some right over or in connection with it.

> The courts have tended to find that an unlawful interference must be continuous. A noisy barbecue party in a neighbour's garden two or three times a year, a birthday party, or a smoky bonfire in the autumn are unlikely to constitute acts of private nuisance. They are not sufficiently continuous in nature.

However, continuous noise, smells or vibration, which interfere with private use of land, can all constitute a nuisance.

In *Butler v Standard Telephones and Cables Ltd* [1939], it was held that tree roots growing from one property under its boundary line and into another property, causing damage, could constitute a private nuisance.

Household insurers will often seek recovery of money paid to remedy damage caused to a policyholder's property by the roots of vegetation emanating from a neighbouring property. In these circumstances, they could seek, among other things, damages for nuisance.

Whether an act constitutes a nuisance cannot be determined by the act itself, but must be determined by all the surrounding circumstances of the particular case. Claims handlers should, therefore, consider some of the following circumstances that a court will take into consideration when making a decision as to whether a particular act constitutes a nuisance:

- Location of the act.
- Time (or times) of day it occurs.
- Whether it was completed in reasonable exercise of rights or maliciously.
- Effect of the act – e.g. is it transitory or permanent, occasional or continuous?

Remedies

There are three particular remedies that can be sought for private nuisance.

By way of example, a house owner whose property is subsiding because the roots of a neighbouring tree are extracting moisture from the soil under the foundations of their home could seek one or more of the following remedies.

Damages

These could include reimbursement of the costs of repairs and underpinning, additional accommodation costs and compensation for inconvenience caused by the encroaching roots.

This is a remedy that must be sought through the courts.

Injunction

An injunction could be obtained to compel a neighbour to maintain or remove the vegetation that constitutes the nuisance. The impact of the vegetation's roots would then be removed or diminished.

This is also a remedy that must be sought through the courts.

Abatement

The victim can seek to abate the nuisance, for example by having the roots cut back. This would be acceptable as long as the roots are only trimmed on the victim's land. There must be no trespass onto the neighbour's land. The roots that are trimmed and removed must be offered back to the neighbour.

Abatement is a self-help remedy that does not need court approval. It is, however, a remedy potentially fraught with difficulties. A neighbour whose tree has been pruned may claim that criminal damage has been committed to their property. If the tree dies the owner may sue for damages.

The courts dislike abatement. Judges have cautioned that it should only be adopted as a remedy of last resort, and then only when notice has been given.

04 Occupiers' liability

Andrew Caplan

- Meaning of key terms: occupier, premises and breach of duty
- Obvious risks and deliberate behaviour
- Children
- Defences, exclusions and warnings
- Restricting liability for death or personal injury

Occupiers' liability

Introduction

Prior to the Occupiers' Liability Act 1957 (the 1957 Act) and the Occupiers Liability Act 1984 (the 1984 Act), a person who was injured on another person's land had to rely on the tort of negligence.

Since the passing of the Acts, occupiers can be liable by statute for injuries suffered by those visiting or trespassing on their property. Therefore, if a claimant is injured in a shop, in a factory or school or on some other premises, they will often bring proceedings under these Acts.

Section 2(1) of the 1957 Act states:

> An occupier of premises owes the same duty, the "common duty of care", to all his visitors, except in so far as he is free to and does extend, restrict, modify or exclude his duty to any visitor or visitors by agreement or otherwise.

Section 2(2) states that the common duty of care is:

> a duty to take such care as in all the circumstances of the case is reasonable to see that the visitor will be reasonably safe in using the premises for the purposes for which he is invited or permitted by the occupier to be there.

This test, then, is very similar to the duty of care in the tort of negligence.

An occupier?

An occupier is more than just a person who owns or is in occupation of land. The definition of occupier extends to a person who exercises their control over the land (for example, somebody who permits or denies access to it).

An occupier must have a sufficient degree of control over premises to be able to ensure the safety of visitors and to appreciate that a failure to take reasonable care may result in an injury.

Control of the premises does not need to be entire or exclusive. There may be more than one occupier of the same premises, each under a duty to use care, dependent on their degree of control, and each liable to a visitor.

Clarification of the law in relation to ad hoc occupiers was provided in *Furmedge and others v Chester-le-Street District Council* [2011]. An interactive public art event took place in a park that was the responsibility of the local authority. The event included a large PVC inflatable structure that was open to the public and was erected by a company called Brouhaha International Ltd. A gust of wind caused the structure to break free from its anchorage and lifted it into the air, causing the death of two people.

The High Court held that Brouhaha had become an occupier of the structure within the meaning of the 1957 Act. This was based on a combination of factors. Through its employees it played an active and central role in the construction of the structure, it erected the structure, its employees acted as stewards and it should have appreciated that any failure to use care in relation to the structure could cause injury to people using it. The Court assessed Brouhaha's responsibility at 55%, with 45% attributed to the local authority.

> It is important to ensure that when an insured, be it a landowner or a tenant, invites a third party to hold an event on their land, they are clear who controls the running of the event, as this will affect an insured's potential liability as occupier under both Acts.

Premises

"Premises" are defined by s.1(3) of the 1957 Act and include "any fixed or moveable structure, including any vessel, vehicle or aircraft". They include land or buildings and can cover everything from offices and public buildings to shops and houses.

Furmedge illustrates that a large inflatable structure meets the definition of premises.

Breach of duty

Examples of incidents that can give rise to occupiers' liability claims include the supermarket customer who slipped on some produce that fell from one of the shelves; a restaurant staff member who slipped on a liquid spillage; and a schoolteacher who slipped on a recently polished floor.

In each case, the defendant would need to show that it had not breached its common duty of care to the claimant under the 1957 Act:

- The occupier of the supermarket would need to show that it had adequate procedures in place to clear up any produce that fell from shelves. If the produce had been on the floor for some time when the customer fell, it is unlikely that the defendant would be able to persuade the court that it had adequate procedures in place.
- The occupier of the restaurant would need to show that it had adequate procedures in place to clear up spills. Again, the length of time that the spill was left in position would be important.
- The defendant school would need to show that when cleaning the floor it had adequate procedures in place for ensuring the safety of staff, pupils and visitors. For example, did it have warning signs up, was the floor unusually slippery and had the cleaning process been carried out properly?

Increasingly, courts are placing emphasis on the need to have adequate systems in place and/or risk assessment procedures, particularly in the case of business and government institutions.

In *Hufton v Somerset County Council* [2011], the claimant, who was then a 15-year-old pupil at a school, slipped and fell on a small area of wet floor in the main assembly hall. The Court of Appeal held that there was no basis on which to interfere with the judge's conclusion that the defendant had a reasonable system in place to prevent the floor from becoming wet, even though that system failed on this occasion. The decision of the Court of Appeal in *Ward v Tesco Stores Ltd* [1975] was considered. However, in this case the evidence did not show that liquid gathering on the floor was a frequent problem. It was not realistic to say that the school should have had a system in place whereby a small area of water should have been spotted and mopped up during the brief period of time between its arrival and the moment when the claimant slipped.

Signs on the garden gates of domestic or other premises stating, for example, "no salesmen" or "no free newspapers" or "no tradesmen" are still fairly common. If someone then goes through the gate and on to the homeowner's property, the homeowner has a lesser duty to them under the 1957 Act as that person is a trespasser.

The 1957 Act

A duty of care to people with permission to be on the premises is imposed on occupiers of premises by the 1957 Act.

> It must be remembered by claims handlers that a strict liability will not arise simply because a claimant has been injured on premises occupied by the insured. In each case it is necessary to consider the common duty of care under the 1957 Act.

This duty also extends to negligent omissions. In determining whether the act or omission of an occupier was reasonable and, therefore, whether the visitor was reasonably safe, a court will consider all the circumstances, including the nature of the danger, the age of the visitor and the conduct expected of them, the state of knowledge of the occupier and whether there were any warnings, lighting, fencing, etc.

Obvious risks and deliberate behaviour

Since 2001, claimants who bring claims for injuries caused by their own behaviour have had less success before the courts than had previously been the case.

A Court of Appeal decision, in the case of *Darby v National Trust* [2001], started the new trend. The claimant and her family visited a park owned by the defendant. In the park was a pond that visitors regularly used for paddling. The pond was shallow at the edges but deepened towards the middle, at which point it became too deep to stand in. The claimant's husband swam towards the middle of the pond, but disappeared under water. He was dragged from the pond and, sadly, later died. The claimant sued the defendant under s.2 of the 1957 Act.

At first instance, the judge held that the defendant had failed to install adequate warning notices, failed to ensure that park wardens prevented people swimming and failed to have lifebuoys or other rescue devices. The Court of Appeal disagreed. It held that there was no duty on the defendant to warn against swimming in this pond where the dangers of drowning were no different or greater than those that were quite obvious to any adult.

In 2003, the Court of Appeal considered another water-based set of facts in *Donoghue v Folkestone Properties Ltd* [2003]. The defendants owned and occupied Folkestone harbour. Just after midnight on 27 December 1997, the claimant decided to go for a swim in the harbour. He jumped from the slipway, struck his head on an underwater obstruction and broke his neck. He was considered to be a trespasser as he had been in the harbour without permission.

The Court of Appeal held that when the claimant sustained his injury, the defendant had no reason to believe that anyone would be swimming from the slipway. The test to be applied when considering whether a duty of care arose under the 1984 Act had to be determined having regard to the circumstances prevailing at the time that it was alleged that the breach of duty had resulted in injury. In the circumstances, the claim was dismissed.

The House of Lords considered a similar set of facts in *Tomlinson v Congleton Borough Council and others* [2003], only five months after the Court of Appeal's decision in *Donoghue.* The defendant was the owner and occupier of Brereton Heath Country Park, within which was a lake that had formed in a derelict sand quarry. The claimant walked into the lake intending to swim there. When the water reached just above his knees, and while he could not see the bottom of the lake, he dove in. Tragically, he struck his head on the bottom and broke his neck, rendering him tetraplegic.

continued...

...continued

The claimant accepted in court that he knew that he should not have dived into shallow water and that he knew that there were notices in the park prohibiting swimming. The defendant had also distributed leaflets warning of the dangers of swimming in the lake. It was accepted that when he entered the water, the claimant became a trespasser by virtue of the prohibition on swimming. His claim was, therefore, pursued under the 1984 Act.

At first instance, the court found for the claimant on the basis that the notices displayed had been ignored by people and that they were, therefore, obviously ineffectual.

The House of Lords held that the lake did not present risks because of the state of the premises or anything done or omitted to be done on the premises as required by s.1(1)(a) of the 1984 Act. In addition, it was held that even if swimming had not been prohibited, and the defendant had owed a duty under s.2(2) of the 1957 Act, there would have been no requirement to take steps to prevent the claimant from diving or to warn him against dangers that were obvious.

The Court of Appeal once again considered the 1984 Act in *Higgs v WH Foster (t/a Avalon Coaches)* [2004]. The claimant was a policeman. He entered the defendant's premises in order to take up a surveillance position overlooking a neighbouring property. The defendant's premises were on open land on which the defendant parked coaches. The claimant searched around the coaches in case a suspect was hiding amongst them. The claimant had a torch with him but did not use it. In carrying out his search the claimant fell into an uncovered inspection pit at the rear of the defendant's premises. The claimant was a trespasser and so his claim was brought under the 1984 Act.

The Court of Appeal found for the defendant. It held that even if the defendant could be shown to have had reasonable grounds to believe that trespassers might enter its premises at night, there was no evidence to disclose reasonable grounds for believing that they might come into contact with the uncovered pit.

In 2005, the Court of Appeal decided the case of *Clare v Perry (t/a Widemouth Manor Hotel)* [2005]. The claimant was a visitor to the defendant's coastal hotel. The claimant attempted to leave the property with her partner by climbing down a retaining wall to the road. The route chosen was not a designated exit. There was a designated exit nearby. It was dark when the claimant jumped from the wall, and she was seriously injured. She argued that the defendant had not taken sufficient precautions to prevent an accidental fall from the site and that the site should have been fenced off.

The Court of Appeal found that deliberately choosing to jump from the wall was wholly different to an accidental fall. The claimant's actions could not have been foreseen or guarded against by the defendant. In addition, it was found that the claimant had been foolish.

> In *Keown v Coventry Healthcare NHS Trust* [2006], the Court of Appeal considered the actions of an 11-year-old child trespasser. The boy, who had climbed the outside of a fire escape, was held to have put himself at risk through his own choice to indulge in a dangerous activity. The child was aware that what he was doing was dangerous. His fall from the fire escape was not caused by a defect in the state of the premises. He was a trespasser and his claim failed. Although the defendant knew that the fire escape was unfenced (s.1(3)(a) of the 1984 Act) and knew that children played in the vicinity (s.1(3)(b) of the 1984 Act), it was not reasonable to expect it to offer protection from such a risk (s.1(3)(b) of the 1984 Act).

Finally, the Court of Appeal found for the defendant in *Cole v Davies-Gilbert and others* [2007]. The claimant stepped into an exposed hole on a village green and broke her leg. The hole had been dug so that a maypole could be erected for a village fete. It was found that the organisation responsible for digging the hole had neither been negligent nor breached a duty of care. It had previously sealed the hole and it was the unexplained removal of the infill, not the infill itself, that was the primary causative factor in the accident.

Recent developments

> More recent cases advocate the point that it is the premises themselves that must be shown to be unsafe and not that an unsafe activity has been undertaken on premises that are otherwise safe.

In *Poppleton v Trustees of the Portsmouth Youth Activities Committee* [2008], the claimant was at an indoor climbing centre. He was climbing without harness and ropes. He attempted a dangerous manoeuvre and suffered catastrophic injuries when the manoeuvre failed and he fell to the safety matting below. The Court of Appeal dismissed the claim. The safety matting was entirely adequate and appropriate. There were inherent and obvious risks in the activity, which the claimant was voluntarily undertaking. However, the law did not require the defendant to prevent him from undertaking it, or to train him or supervise him while he did it.

The principle was emphasised in *Geary v JD Wetherspoon plc* [2011]. A historic building was refurbished to become a pub. One of the original features of the building was a grand open staircase in the centre of the building with sweeping banisters on both sides. The banisters were below the minimum height allowed under Building Regulations at the time. On her way out, the claimant hoisted herself onto the left banister with the intention of sliding down it. Unfortunately, she fell backwards and landed on the marble floor, just less than four metres below. The High Court held that there was nothing unsafe about the premises. The danger was created by the decision to slide, not the banister itself. The claim failed.

Similarly, in *Grimes v Hawkins and another* [2011], an 18-year-old suffered severe spinal injuries when she dove into a private homeowner's swimming pool late at night after having a few drinks. The High Court dismissed her claim. The pool was not unsafe for diving. The duty owed to the claimant under the 1957 Act did not require the defendant to put the pool out of bounds that night. It was not incumbent on a householder with a private swimming pool to prohibit adults from diving into an ordinary pool, the dimensions and contours of which could clearly be seen.

At first instance, in *Clark v Bourne Leisure Ltd* [2011], the judge held that the premises were not reasonably safe for wheelchair users. The claimant had used her electric wheelchair to visit the bar on a holiday site and used the designated ramp. However, in error she left by the steps, which caused her to be tipped from her wheelchair.

The Court of Appeal overturned this decision and dismissed the claim. It held that the premises were reasonably safe for wheelchair users. The steps themselves were not safe for wheelchairs but they were clearly visible – any wheelchair user taking reasonable care for their own safety would avoid using them.

The law as set out in *Tomlinson v Congleton Borough Council and others* was applied in *Risk v Rose Bruford College* [2013]. At an annual event organised by the Student Ball Team, a 21-year-old dove headfirst into a small inflatable pool following a run of about 15 to 20 metres. He seriously injured his neck and was now tetraplegic. The High Court held that the pool itself was not dangerous; it was the claimant's actions that made it so. By acting as he did, the claimant created an obvious and serious risk that would not otherwise have existed. On the facts of this case, the claimant's arguments fell a long way short of establishing the necessary ingredients for an assumption of responsibility.

Other cases involving the need for and suitability of warnings to the public include the case of *English Heritage v Taylor* [2016] EWCA Civ 448:

- When upholding a decision that English Heritage was in breach of its common duty of care under s.2 of the Act by failing to provide a sign warning visitors to one of its sites of a sheer drop which was not obvious, the court reiterated the principle that adult visitors did not require warnings of obvious risk except where they did not have a genuine and informed choice.

More recent examples include the case of *Chris James Hood v Forestry Commission* [2017]:

- The Forestry Commission was not liable under the 1957 Act for injuries sustained by a mountain-biker who had fallen to the ground after his bike slipped on a boardwalk in a forest trial. The claimant was an experienced biker, the grooving appeared appropriate and slipping was not a hazard that had to be guarded against at all costs.

Children

> Although in general the common duty of care applies as in negligence, there is specific guidance given within the 1957 Act for certain types of visitor. Section 2(3)(a) states: "an occupier must be prepared for children to be less careful than adults." If the occupier allows a child to enter the premises then the premises must be reasonably safe for a child of that age.

The courts have had little sympathy for defendants who are faced with very young unsupervised children who are injured. For example, it is worth considering *Phipps v Rochester Corporation* [1955]. Although this case predates the 1957 Act, courts are likely to approach similar cases in the same way.

In *Phipps*, the defendant building company was aware that children were coming onto its land without its permission, but did nothing to stop them. The High Court found that the children were lawful visitors and that the defendant therefore owed them a duty of care. *Phipps* also stressed that the safety of little children must rest primarily with the parents, who should ensure they are not allowed to wander off and/or should satisfy themselves that any places they do allow their children to go unaccompanied are safe.

An occupier can expect a reasonable level of parental supervision and/or control, unless, for example, they are aware that children often go into an area unsupervised.

In *Marsden v Bourne Leisure Ltd (t/a British Holidays)* [2009], a two-and-a-half-year-old boy tragically drowned in a pond at a caravan park where he was on holiday with his parents. The boy drowned in the smallest of three ponds on the site, which was surrounded by wooden horizontal rails about two feet high and was fenced with wire mesh below the rails. While his mother was speaking to someone, the boy and his younger brother disappeared and, despite a desperate search, he was not found until it was too late.

At first instance, the judge found that Bourne Leisure, the operator and occupier of the site, should have instructed its staff to draw the attention of parents to the location of and access to the lakes and ponds and that, had it done so, the accident would have been avoided. However, the Court of Appeal held that the defendant was not under any obligation, in the exercise of reasonable care, to bring to the attention of parents the existence of the pathway or the precise location of the pond, when the danger they presented to small, unaccompanied children was obvious.

In *Pierce v West Sussex County Council* [2013], a nine-year-old schoolboy injured himself on a water fountain installed on the school premises. He was playing with his brother and accidentally caught his hand on the side of the water fountain, lacerating his thumb and damaging the tendons. The Court of Appeal considered that the question to be addressed was whether visitors to the school were reasonably safe in using the premises, including, for this purpose, the water fountain, bearing in mind that children do not behave like adults, and are inclined to lark around. The answer to that question was yes. The water fountain was reasonably safe. The school was not under a duty to safeguard children against harm in all circumstances. The underside edge of the water fountain could have been bevelled or padded. However, the school was no more obliged to take such steps in respect of the water fountain than it would be in respect of any of the other numerous ordinary edges and corners and surfaces against which children might accidentally injure themselves while on the premises.

These more recent cases show a common sense approach being adopted by the courts. Previously, the courts were quick to impose liability where a child was injured. However, it is unrealistic to expect occupiers to assess every activity and function, particularly those that are not foreseeable.

The adequacy of the supervision is often in dispute. Reasonable foreseeability is the standard applied by the courts. This is illustrated in two recent decisions. In the case of *Jamie Dyer v East Sussex County Council* [2016]:

- The local authority had not breached its duty to a school pupil who had suffered a significant head injury on school premises. His injury was caused by a metal gate that restricted access to an area which was out of bounds to pupils. On this occasion the gate been left unlocked and was kicked by another pupil causing injury to the claimant. The court held that the type of injury sustained was not reasonably foreseeable. Furthermore, the level of supervision was sufficient.

In the case of *Jack English v Burnt Mill Academy Trust* [2016]:

- The school was not liable under the 1957 Act to a pupil who had been injured after running into a bollard on school premises during horseplay. The bollard did not, before the accident, post an apparent risk of harm so as to impose a positive duty to remove it. The pupil was looking in the wrong direction at the time of the collision. The court was satisfied that in the normal course of events the bollard did not pose a hazard or risk. To impose a liability would be to raise the standard from reasonableness to something more akin to an absolute obligation to safeguard children from every possibility of harm.

Defences, exclusions and warnings

> Section 2(5) of the 1957 Act provides a statutory defence:
>
> > The common duty of care does not impose on an occupier any obligation to a visitor in respect of risks willingly accepted as his by the visitor (the question whether a risk was so accepted to be decided on the same principles as in other cases in which one person owes a duty of care to another).

Occupiers do not owe a duty of care to visitors in respect of risks willingly accepted by them (*volenti non fit injuria*). This defence may also be invoked under s.1(6) of the 1984 Act.

Occupiers may post notices/signs on premises to warn visitors of potential hazards in an attempt to discharge their duty of care. Examples include notices warning of a dangerous dog in a domestic property or of deep water in a boating lake.

However, a warning will not absolve the occupier of liability, unless in all the circumstances it was enough to enable the visitor to be reasonably safe (s.2(4) of the 1957 Act).

These types of warning notices are to be distinguished from those that are attempts by the occupier to exclude liability and avoid the duty of care: for example, signs stating "the owners accept no responsibility whatsoever for any death, personal injury or loss arising on these premises howsoever arising", or words to that effect.

> It is important that claims handlers remember that notices containing an exclusion clause are controlled by the Unfair Contract Terms Act 1977 (UCTA).

Section 2 of the UCTA states:

1) A person cannot by reference to any contract term or to a notice given to persons generally or to particular persons exclude or restrict his liability for death or personal injury resulting from negligence.

2) In the case of other loss or damage, a person cannot so exclude or restrict his liability for negligence except in so far as the term or notice satisfies the requirement of reasonableness.

The section applies only to business liability, i.e. liability for breach of obligations or duties arising from things done or to be done by a person in the course of a business or from the occupation of premises used for business purposes. This includes professions, government and local authority activities, e.g. hospitals, schools, shops, etc.

Restricting liability for death or personal injury

The "notice" referred to in s.2(1) of the UCTA includes signs at the entry to premises, in car parks, etc.

"Negligence" is specifically said by the Act to include breaches of the common duty of care imposed by the 1957 Act.

> Therefore, even if a sign that purports to exclude injury or death on premises is present, if the injury or death arose as a result of the negligence or breach of duty of the occupier, the occupier cannot rely upon the notice to avoid a finding of liability against them.

Other loss or damage

An occupier can rely upon a notice to exclude liability for negligence or loss or damage, but only if the contractual term or notice is reasonable. The sign must be in a prominent place, be large enough to be noticed and some steps must be taken to draw it to the attention of visitors.

Checklist

- ✓ Was the claimant a lawful visitor?
- ✓ If the claimant was a lawful visitor, consider whether the occupier has fulfilled the common duty of care under s.2(2) of the 1957 Act.
- ✓ If the claimant was a trespasser, consider the 1984 Act.
- ✓ Was the occupier aware of the danger or did the occupier have reasonable grounds to believe that the danger existed? If yes, then:
  - ✓ Did the occupier know, or should the occupier have reasonably believed, that there was a trespasser in the vicinity of the danger? If yes, then:
  - ✓ Is the danger one against which, in all the circumstances, the occupier may reasonably be expected to offer the trespasser some protection? If yes, then the occupier is primarily liable.
- ✓ Do not forget that visitors and trespassers can be contributorily negligent.
- ✓ Consider the effect and/or validity of the *volenti* defence and any warning or exclusion notices.

05 Employers' liability

Greg Woods

- Who is an employee?
- Common law duties: including ensuring competent staff, effective supervision and a safe place of work
- Statutory duties: including the 'six pack' of health and safety regulations
- Enterprise and Regulatory Reform Act 2013

Employers' liability

Introduction

Employers owe their employees particular duties. Those duties are imposed on the employer both by common law and by statute.

Who is an employee?

This needs to be considered because not all individuals who are paid to work are employees.

In most cases, the status of the individual claimant will be clear, but that is not always the case and may be a matter of dispute.

They may, for example, be independent contractors, agency workers or self-employed individuals.

The courts consider all of the circumstances and have developed a number of tests to decide whether an individual is an employee or not.

Manner in which the parties describe themselves

This is a starting point for the courts. However, simply because a person wishes to be paid on a gross basis and refers to themself as 'self-employed' does not mean that they are not an employee.

Does the individual have to provide personal service?

If the worker in question (A) does not have to provide personal service but can send along a substitute worker (B), that will be considered evidence in support of the conclusion that A is an independent contractor and not an employee.

If a worker provides personal service, that is a key indicator that that person is an employee. However, this test also must be considered in the light of the other tests above and below.

Control test

Does the employer control how much work the worker carries out and where and when that work is done? More importantly, does the employer decide how that work is to be carried out? If the employer controls the manner in which the work is done and provides that work, then it is likely that the worker will be considered to be an employee.

Business integration test

Does the worker actually form part of the organisation at which the work is being carried out? Do they work within the organisation or do they simply do work for it? If the former, they are likely to be an employee. If the latter, they may be an independent contractor.

Is the worker actually running a business of their own?

In other words, is the worker an independent contractor who attends and does work for a particular organisation, but who prepares their own tax assessment forms, keeps receipt books, and pays VAT, etc.? Such evidence would indicate that the worker was an independent contractor, not an employee.

Conversely, if the worker is paid their salary net, on a PAYE basis, that is good evidence that the worker is an employee.

What obligations do the employer and worker have to one another?

If the worker is obliged to be at work at a particular time every day and the employer is obliged to provide work to that employee, that is evidence that the worker is an employee. An independent contractor could arrange for a substitute worker to attend in their place to carry out the work. An employee is obliged to attend work personally to perform the duties given to them by the employer.

What about agency workers?

The position of agency workers has long proved problematic, with a considerable amount of case law devoted to considering the legal status of an agency worker.

There is a growing trend for certain types of worker to be contracted to an agency. Construction workers, nurses, secretaries and the like may sign up with an agency and agree to be placed at various types of business in order to supply labour. The agency will charge the business for supplying the labour. The business will provide the work. The agency will pay the worker for the hours worked at an agreed rate.

Is the agency worker an employee? If so, who employs them? Is the agency the worker's employer and sending them to work for another business? Alternatively, is the business the employer because it provides the actual work, instructs how it is done and controls the worker's day-to-day movements?

Agency workers have a contract with the agency that places them with an end user, i.e. the person for whom they work. The contract they have with the agency is, almost certainly, not a contract of employment. The contract between the agency and the end user is best described as a contract for the supply of the services of the agency worker. The agency worker is not a party to that contract and has no contract with the end user. There is, then, a tripartite relationship between worker, agency and end user, with agency workers, typically, having no contract of employment with either the agency or the business they are placed with. They are not, in most instances, the employee of anyone.

> The court may, in certain circumstances, imply a contract of employment with either the end user or the agency, or both, but the precise legal status of the agency worker remains uncertain.

When considering the health and safety obligations owed to agency workers by those for whom they work, however, a court is unlikely to conclude that an employer in control of a workplace and the health and safety systems operating in that workplace owes a lower level of duty towards agency workers in that workplace than it does to those with an employment contract with them.

Each case will, therefore, turn on its own facts.

If it is not certain that a policyholder is the employer of a claimant making a claim, the claims handler should obtain a detailed statement from the policyholder as to the role, obligations, methods of remuneration and working practices of the parties. Once that information has been gathered, a decision can be made as to whether or not the claimant would be likely to be found to be an employee of the policyholder.

Employers' liability: common law

> An employer has a duty at common law to take reasonable care for the health and safety of its employees while they are acting in the course of their employment. If an employer breaches that duty, it will be found negligent and liable to the employee for any foreseeable damage resulting from that breach.

It will be evident, then, that consideration of an employer's common law duty requires an understanding of the tort of negligence.

Beyond the statement of that general duty, the courts have considered how the outworking of that duty should manifest itself in practice in the workplace.

In *English v Wilsons and Clyde Coal Company Ltd* [1937], Lord Wright found that the employer's duty to his employees included:

> "the provision of a competent staff of men, adequate material and a proper system and effective supervision."

Wilson v Tyneside Window Cleaning Company [1958] extended the employer's duty of care to also provide a safe place of work:

> "If [the employer's premises] are dangerously in need of repair he can and must rectify the fault at once if he is to escape the censure of negligence."

It can be seen, therefore, that the employer's common law duty to their employees overlaps considerably with their duty of care to avoid negligently injuring their staff.

Competent staff

The employer must make sure that the staff that they employ are suitably qualified and experienced for the particular job. If they are to be trained, they must be given adequate training and supervision until they become sufficiently competent.

If the employer takes on an employee who is not appropriately competent or who is then not trained properly and that member of staff negligently injures a co-worker, then the employer may be liable.

An employer will also be **vicariously liable** for the negligent acts or omissions of an employee who injures a co-worker in the course of employment.

However, there are situations where an injured party cannot claim that their employer is vicariously liable for a co-worker's actions.

In *Hudson v Ridge Manufacturing Company Ltd* [1957], an employee, who was known to play practical jokes on co-workers, injured a co-worker in the course of a practical joke.

The injured person could not sue his employers under the principle of vicarious liability because the practical joke fell outside the scope of the course of the joker's employment.

However, the victim successfully sued the employer for failing to provide a competent co-worker. It was successfully argued that because the employer knew of the perpetrator's predisposition to play practical jokes, the joker should have been disciplined and prevented from conducting any further jokes. The employer's failure to discipline the joker rendered it liable in common law.

There are numerous cases involving injuries to employees as a consequence of "practical jokes" on the part of fellow employees, in each case the courts having to consider whether the actions leading to injury could be considered to be within the "course of employment" of the individual perpetrating them.

See, for example, *Smith v Crossley* [1951], a case involving apprentices injecting compressed air into a fellow apprentice; *Aldred v Nacanco* [1987], which involved an employee pushing a basin against the co-worker claimant to startle her; and *McReady v Securicor* [1991], in which an accident resulted from two employees playing together on trolleys. In each case, the employer was not vicariously liable as the acts were deemed **not** to be in the course of employment.

Contrast those authorities with *Chapman v Oakleigh* [1970] (men authorised to tell a boy what to do were acting in the course of their employment when they misused their authority to play a practical joke by telling him to put his hand in the aperture of a machine) and *Harrison v Michelin Tyre Co Ltd* [1985] (an employee who pushed a truck just a little off course to knock a claimant's duck-board as a practical joke was doing something that was not so divergent from his work that it ceased to be a part of it).

For further information about vicarious liability, see Chapter 2.

Adequate material

This includes the provision of adequate equipment.

Employers have a duty to take reasonable steps to provide their employees with adequate equipment. This includes protective clothing, appropriate tools, appropriate working materials, etc. This duty can also extend to obliging employers to train particular employees how to use particular equipment.

Paris v Stepney Borough Council [1950] emphasises this point. The claimant worked in a garage and carried out general mechanical duties. He was blind in one eye. During the course of his work he struck some metal and a metal splinter flew into his good eye. He was blinded in that eye. It was not, at the time, usual practice to supply goggles to mechanics.

The claimant claimed that his employer had breached its duty of care to him by allowing him to carry out the work without wearing goggles. He argued that his employer knew that he was blind in one eye and that he was, therefore, at more of a risk from this particular injury than his co-workers.

The claimant succeeded. The House of Lords decided that the employer's duty of care to employees could be a personal duty to each particular employee, taking into account each particular employee's circumstances.

Lord Simmons stated:

> “I will say at once that I do not dissent from the view that an employer owes a particular duty to each of his employees. His liability in tort arises from his failure to take reasonable care in regard to the particular employee and it is clear that, if so, all the circumstances relevant to that employee must be taken into consideration.”

Therefore, employers who take on employees with particular frailties may, depending on the type of work that they are carrying out, need to make special provision for them. A failure to do so could result in the employer being found liable if the employee is injured as a result of the employer's failure to take reasonable steps to protect that employee.

Proper system and effective supervision

If an employer fails to properly supervise employees and, as a result, an employee is injured, the employer can be found liable.

Similarly, if an employee is asked to carry out work in a manner that is dangerous and that causes injury, then the employer can be found negligent for breaching their duty of care to that employee.

> If equipment is provided, employers are also obliged to ensure that their employees use it appropriately and consistently.

In *Pape v Cumbria County Council* [1991], the claimant had to carry out cleaning duties. She developed a skin disorder as a result of coming into contact with various solvents and cleaning products. The defendant provided its employees with protective gloves, but had not told its staff to wear the gloves at all times. It did not tell its staff that, if they did not wear them, they might be injured.

In view of those omissions, the claimant succeeded in recovering damages for personal injury. The High Court found that the employer should have had procedures in place to ensure that its employees wore the equipment provided.

Safe place of work

As a general principle, the employer must ensure that the place at which its employees are working is safe and does not pose a risk to their health.

Therefore, a working environment that is too noisy and has damaged the hearing of employees, a mine that causes lung disease to miners working there, or a factory with an unsafe floor that causes an employee to trip and fall and be injured are all examples of premises that are unsafe. Again, liability will arise because the employer has breached the duty of care to its employees. It has acted negligently.

The employer may also be in breach of the Occupiers' Liability Acts 1957 and 1984. For further information see Chapter 4.

> *Andrews v Initial Cleaning Services Ltd and another* [1999] highlighted the particular difficulty that arises when an employer sends their staff to work at premises occupied by another party.

The Court of Appeal in *Andrews* found that the primary responsibility for an employee's safety rested with his employer. In that case, the employer was not the occupier of the building in which the claimant was injured. However, the employer had sent the claimant to work there. The following factors were relevant:

- The employer was aware of a defect at the premises and was aware that it was an actual and potential danger.
- The building owner/occupier was not aware of the defect.
- The building owner was not performing a site management role.
- The danger did not arise from the activities of the building owner.
- The employer had taken no steps to remove the potential danger or to remedy the defect.

The employer was found responsible, even though the injury occurred in premises that were neither owned nor occupied by them. The occupier was not without responsibility, however. The court apportioned liability 75% to the employer and 25% to the occupier.

It will be appreciated that in any given case a court will consider the relative culpability of the occupier and employer.

Employers' liability: statute

This section of this chapter should be read in conjunction with Chapter 10 on health and safety.

Health and safety regulations: 'the six pack'

Since the early 1990s, employers have been subject to a wide-ranging set of health and safety regulations, collectively described as the six pack, after the initial group of six sets of regulations.

Over the years, additional health and safety regulations have been introduced covering areas such as working at height and construction sites.

The regulations were designed to implement into English law a series of European directives, and were introduced under s.15 of the Health and Safety at Work etc. Act 1974 (the 1974 Act).

Until the introduction of s.69 of the Enterprise and Regulatory Reform Act 2013 (the Enterprise Act), breach of any duty imposed by the regulations could give rise to a civil claim for damages by an employee injured as a consequence of that breach.

This was provided for by s.47(2) of the 1974 Act, which stated:

> "Breach of a duty imposed by health and safety regulations shall, so far as it causes damage, be actionable except in so far as the regulations provide otherwise."

Until relatively recently, there was one set of regulations that expressly provided otherwise: Regulation 22 of the Management of Health and Safety at Work Regulations 1999 (the Management Regulations) excluded liability for breach of those Regulations.

Regulation 22 was subject to various revisions. From 6 April 2006 until the introduction of s.69 of the Enterprise Act, employees were entitled to bring a civil claim for breach of a duty imposed by the Management Regulations.

Enterprise and Regulatory Reform Act 2013

Section 69 of the Enterprise Act came into force on 1 October 2013. It applies in respect of any breach of a health and safety regulation occurring on or after that date.

It amended s.47(2) of the 1974 Act to provide that breach of a health and safety regulation shall not be actionable except to the extent that subsequent regulations might expressly provide.

...continued

> *...continued*
>
> The significance of s.69 should not be underestimated. It reversed, at a stroke, what had been the central underpinning of practically all employers' liability claims: breach of one or more of the health and safety regulations.
>
> The general effect of s.69 is to require employees to prove that the employer has been negligent.

The most obvious immediate impact is the removal of strict liability for breach of certain regulations, such as Regulation 5 of the Provision and Use of Work Equipment Regulations 1998 (duty to ensure that work equipment is maintained in an efficient state, efficient working order and good repair) and Regulation 12(1) of the Workplace (Health, Safety and Welfare) Regulations 1992 (duty to ensure that every floor in a workplace and the surface of every traffic route is of a construction such that it is suitable for the purpose for which it is used).

> It is important to recognise that the regulations have not been repealed. They remain in force and employers remain obliged to comply with those duties. Failure to do so may result in criminal sanctions. More particularly for the consideration of claims, failure to comply with long-established health and safety duties is routinely argued by claimants to indicate a failure on the part of the employer to take reasonable care for its employees. In other words, breach of a statutory duty is used as evidence of negligence.
>
> Even though s.69 of the Enterprise Act has been in force for several years, there is surprisingly little case law available illustrating the court's approach to references to breach of statutory duty in support of allegations of negligence.

Given that the regulations remain in force and given that s.69 of the Enterprise Act applies to breaches on or after 1 October 2013 only, the principal provisions of the main regulations are summarised below.

Management of Health and Safety at Work Regulations 1999

Since 27 October 2003 a breach of these Regulations has conferred a civil right of action on employees but not non-employees, bringing these Regulations in line with the rest of the six pack.

Key issues addressed in the Regulations include:

- Risk assessments – Regulation 3
- Health surveillance – Regulation 6
- Procedures for serious and imminent danger and for danger areas – Regulation 8
- Information for employees – Regulation 10
- Capabilities and training – Regulation 13.

Workplace (Health, Safety and Welfare) Regulations 1992

These Regulations cover particular aspects of the workplace, such as safety glass, doors, floors, stairs, ramps and falling objects.

- Workplace to be maintained in an efficient state, in efficient working order and in good repair – Regulation 5(1).
- Workplace should have suitable and efficient lighting – Regulation 8.
- Workstations shall be suitable for any person likely to work there and for the work to be done there – Regulation 11.

- Seats must be suitable for persons for whom they are provided as well as for operations to be performed, and a suitable footstool must be provided where necessary – Regulation 11.
- Suitability and repair and obstructions – Regulation 12.
- Traffic routes – Regulation 17.
- Windows and transparent or translucent doors, gates and walls – Regulation 14.

Provision and Use of Work Equipment Regulations 1998

These cover detailed examples such as leased equipment, defective or poorly maintained equipment, training and instruction, etc.

- Work equipment means "any machinery, appliance, apparatus, tool or installation for use at work" – Regulation 2.
- Work equipment must be suitable for the purpose for which it is used or provided in any respect which it is reasonably foreseeable will affect the health and safety of any person – Regulations 4(1) and 4(4).
- The employer must consider the working conditions under which the equipment is to be used and ensure that it is only used under conditions and for operations for which it is suitable – Regulation 4(3).
- Every employer shall ensure that work equipment is maintained in an efficient state, in efficient working order and in good repair – Regulation 5.
- When the use of equipment involves specific risks, there is a restriction as to who is to use and who is to maintain the work equipment – Regulation 7.
- Adequate training in the use of work equipment for health and safety purposes must be provided to users and supervisors – Regulation 9.

- Effective measures must be taken to prevent access to any dangerous part of machinery and to stop the movement of any dangerous part of the machinery before any part of a person enters a danger zone – Regulation 11.

Manual Handling Operations Regulations 1992

(See Chapter 6)

Health and Safety (Display Screen Equipment) Regulations 1992

- The employer must carry out an analysis of workstations in order to assess the health and safety risks to those using them – Regulation 2(1).
- The employer must reduce any risks identified to the lowest level that is reasonably practicable – Regulation 2(3).
- There are minimum requirements regarding the screen, keyboard, work surface, chair, the space available, lighting and reflection – Schedule 1.
- Activities must be planned so that there are periodic interruptions of work on display screens – Regulation 4.
- The employer must provide eyesight tests for users and special corrective appliances if needed – Regulation 5.
- The employer must provide adequate health and safety training – Regulation 6.

Personal Protective Equipment at Work Regulations 1992

- Employers have a duty to provide suitable personal protective equipment (PPE) to employees who may be exposed to a risk to their health and safety, except where the risk has been adequately controlled by other means that are equally or more effective – Regulation 4(1).

- PPE must be appropriate both for the risk and the individual user – Regulation 4(3).
- Employers must assess the suitability of PPE before providing it – Regulation 6.
- Employers shall ensure that PPE is maintained (which includes replacement and cleaning as appropriate) in an efficient state, in efficient working order and in good repair – Regulation 7.
- Employers must provide information, instruction and training on risks, purpose, use and maintenance of PPE – Regulation 9.
- Employers must take all reasonable steps to ensure that PPE is used – Regulation 10(1).
- Employees must use PPE in accordance with training and instruction given – Regulation 10(2).
- Employees must immediately report to their employer any loss or obvious defect in equipment – Regulation 11.

Strict liability?

Prior to the advent of s.69 of the Enterprise Act, the imposition of strict liability for breach of certain regulations was an important consideration. Breach of those regulations rendered the employer liable however "reasonable" its actions. The employer was not able to escape liability by proving that it did all that it reasonably could do to comply with the duty. Liability for breach was said to be "strict".

Such instances are increasingly rare as the number of claims arising from accidents prior to 1 October 2013 shrinks, but claims handlers still need to understand the issue. What follows examines the law that continues to apply in respect of pre 1 October 2013 accidents:

Stark v The Post Office [2000] concerned what is now Regulation 5(1) of the Provision and Use of Work Equipment Regulations 1998. The Regulation provided:

> "Every employer shall ensure that work equipment is maintained in an efficient state, in efficient working order and in good repair."

The Court of Appeal found that the Regulation imposed an absolute duty on the Post Office to ensure that the bicycle provided to the claimant for use in the course of his employment was in a state in which it worked efficiently at all times.

The claimant was riding his bicycle when, without warning, his front wheel locked and he was propelled over the handlebars, suffering serious injury. The Court of Appeal found that the claimant could, therefore, recover compensation as the Post Office was in breach of its statutory duty and that breach had caused the claimant's injuries. The Post Office was not permitted to succeed in its argument that it could not have known that there was a defect with the bicycle.

The same principle applies to a number of other regulations. The question in each case is: does the regulation provide that an employer must do all that is "reasonably practicable" or "practicable" to comply, or is compliance an absolute obligation, irrespective of the efforts of the employer?

If the regulation simply requires that a state of affairs exist, then, if it does not, the employer is in breach.

See also, for example, the following duties in the Workplace (Health, Safety and Welfare) Regulations 1992:

- Regulation 5(1): the workplace and equipment, devices and systems shall be maintained in an efficient state, efficient working order and in good repair.
- Regulation 12(1): every floor in a workplace and the surface of every traffic route is of a construction such that it is suitable for the purpose for which it is used.

> While there may be strict liability for a breach of some of the regulations, it is important to understand that in order to succeed in their claim, the claimant must still show that their injuries were caused by that breach. The claimant need not prove that the breach was the sole cause, merely that the breach made a material contribution to the incident causing the injuries.

Employer's Liability (Defective Equipment) Act 1969

If an employee is injured by defective equipment provided to them by their employer for use at work, an employer could argue, in their defence at common law, that it was a latent defect that they could not have known of and, therefore, could not be liable for. This would leave the employee in the difficult position of having to sue the manufacturer or supplier of the equipment.

The Employer's Liability (Defective Equipment) Act 1969 protects employees in such situations. It provides that an employer will be liable if:

- An employee suffers personal injury in the course of their employment in consequence of a defect in equipment provided by their employer for the purposes of the employer's business; and

- The defect is attributable wholly or partly to the fault of a third party (whether identified or not).

The Act has been largely ignored since the introduction of the Provision and Use of Work Equipment Regulations 1998, which imposed strict liability on employers in respect of work equipment.

It seems likely that the introduction of s.69 of the Enterprise Act will lead to claimants increasingly frequently seeking to rely on this Act.

Checklist

- ✓ Is the claimant an employee?
- ✓ What breach does the claimant allege – common law and/or statutory breach?
- ✓ If a common law breach is alleged, consider whether duty of care has been breached. What evidence do you need to prove that the employer took all reasonable care to keep the employee safe?
- ✓ If a statutory breach is alleged, which regulation applies? If the accident was before 1 October 2013, is there strict liability? Note: where a duty is imposed on an employer by a statutory regulation, the evidential burden is on the employer to prove compliance, not on the claimant to prove non-compliance.
- ✓ Consider the impact of s.69 of the Enterprise Act on statutory breaches on or after 1 October 2013. Could the claimant argue that breach of the statutory duty was evidence of negligence?
- ✓ Contributory negligence?

05 Employers' liability

06 Manual handling

Greg Woods

- Assessment of negligence and the Manual Handling Operations Regulations 1992
- Employers' duties: including avoiding manual handling and reducing the risk of injury
- Individual capability
- The impact of the EC Directive
- Practical Guidance for employers

Manual handling

Introduction

Manual handling relates to the moving of items by lifting, lowering, carrying, pushing or pulling. It is one of the most common causes of injury at work. Injuries caused by manual handling are part of a wider group of musculoskeletal injuries which, according to the Health and Safety Executive (HSE), account for over a third of all workplace injuries.

Since 1 January 1993, manual handling operations in the employment context have been governed by the Manual Handling Operations Regulations 1992 (the Regulations). These were introduced under s.15 of the Health and Safety at Work etc. Act 1974 and are intended to implement the EC Directive of 29 May 1990, 90/269/EEC (the EC Directive). They impose certain duties on employers designed to minimize the risk of injury to employees when undertaking manual handling operations at work.

As with all health and safety regulations, breach of the Regulations will no longer attract civil liability if the breach occurred on or after 1 October 2013 (see the comments on s.69 of the Enterprise and Regulatory Reform Act 2013 in Chapter 5). The claimant will have to prove that the defendant employer was negligent. That means proving, on the balance of probabilities, that:

- The manual handling operation gave rise to a reasonably foreseeable risk of injury.
- The defendant failed to take reasonable steps to protect the health and safety of the claimant by failing to take reasonable steps to reduce that risk.

The obligations imposed by the Regulations remain, however, and any employer in breach of the Regulations risks a finding of criminal liability.

Typically, claimants still refer to the Regulations when seeking to establish that the defendant was negligent. Alleged breaches of the

Regulations are often referred to in the particulars of claim. To the extent that an employer has breached them, it is argued that there was a failure on the part of the employer to take reasonable care for the health and safety of the claimant. Failure to comply with the Regulations, it is argued, demonstrates a failure to take reasonable steps to reduce the risk of injury and is thus evidence in support of a finding of negligence. Certainly, an employer that fails to assess the risk of injury that might arise from undertaking any manual handling task, and fails to take reasonably practicable steps to reduce that risk, is likely to be found negligent.

Unlike some other statutory regulations, the Manual Handling Operations Regulations do not impose strict liability. To apply, there must be a foreseeable risk of injury and the employer is required to take appropriate steps to reduce the risk of injury to the lowest level reasonably practicable, assuming that the avoidance of the task itself is not reasonably practicable. The duties therefore marry up rather neatly with the common law duty to take reasonable care for an employee's safety at work.

It is for this reason that claims handlers must still be familiar with the Regulations and consider the defendant's compliance with those regulations when assessing liability even if the alleged breach was after 1 October 2013.

Manual Handling Operations Regulations 1992

Who has a duty?

As already stated, the Regulations are principally concerned to establish a series of duties on employers to protect their employees from harm.

Regulation 5, however, places a duty on the employee to make full and proper use of any system of work provided for their use by their employer. Furthermore, the self-employed owe the duties set down under the Regulations to themselves.

By virtue of Regulation 3, the Regulations do not apply to the normal shipboard activities of the crew of a sea-going ship under the direction of the master, which are governed by separate merchant shipping legislation. They may apply to other manual handling activities on board ship, for example where a shore-based contractor carries out the work, provided the ship is within territorial waters.

They will apply to offshore activities carried out on, or associated with, oil and gas installations (Regulation 7).

The Regulations apply to servants of the Crown. However, the Secretary of State for Defence may, in the interests of national security, exempt any of the home forces, visiting forces or headquarters from the requirements of Regulations 4 and 5.

What are manual handling operations?

These are defined in Regulation 2 as:

> “any transporting or supporting of a load (including the lifting, putting down, pushing, pulling, carrying or moving thereof) by hand or by bodily force.”

A load includes any person or animal. The Regulations, therefore, have considerable importance for nursing and social service professions, as well as for the more obvious types of manual handling such as bin emptying or furniture removal. They do not, however, apply to every use of the hand. The task must include the moving or supporting of a load. Therefore, for example, they do not apply to typing or operating the controls of a machine, even though these tasks may involve a risk of injury.

Duties of employers

The Regulations impose a hierarchy of duties on employers.

> Under the Regulations, it is for the employee claimant to establish that the task in question involved a risk of injury. If they can do so, then the burden switches to the employer to prove compliance with the statutory duties.

Arguably, the position is different if the claimant must prove negligence to succeed, as is the case if the operation took place on or after 1 October 2013. To establish negligence, the burden is on the claimant to prove both that the risk was foreseeable and that the employer failed to take reasonably practicable steps to reduce the risk.

Under the Regulations, the first duty is, so far as is reasonably practicable, to avoid the need for employees to undertake any manual handling operations at work that involve a risk of their being injured.

It really cannot be stressed too strongly that this duty must be considered seriously. The employer will need to adduce evidence that it has complied with this duty when a possible breach of the Regulations is being considered.

If, and only if, the manual handling operation cannot be avoided within the limits of reasonable practicability, then consideration is given to the subsequent duties. These are, in summary:

- Make a suitable and sufficient assessment of the manual handling operation.
- Take appropriate steps to reduce the risk of injury to the lowest level reasonably practicable.
- Take appropriate steps to provide employees undertaking the operation with information regarding the weight of the load and the heaviest side of any load whose centre of gravity is not positioned centrally.

Avoiding the need for manual handling

Points that need to be considered in relation to this duty are:

- Is it a manual handling operation?
- Is the employee required to carry out the operation?
- Is there a risk of the employee being injured?
- What is meant by injury?
- Is it reasonably practicable to avoid this operation?

Is it a manual handling operation?

The Regulations are essentially concerned with the movement of loads. They do not, for example, apply to manually working on an object that is static and secured by non-manual means.

However it should not be overlooked that, although the main components of a task may not fall within the Regulations, the task may nevertheless have some components that do. For example, an employee who slipped while carrying out gritting was able to show this task was a manual handling operation because he was moving the grit in a barrow at the time of his accident. Consequently, the duties under the Regulations applied.

Employee?

The definition of employee is dealt with in Chapter 5.

Risk of injury?

It should be noted that "injury" for the purpose of the Regulations means injury to any part of the body, although the Regulations specifically exclude injury caused by any toxic or corrosive substance that has either leaked or spilled from the load, or is present on the surface of the load, or is a constituent part of the load. It is certainly not restricted to back injury, even though the EC Directive refers to avoiding or reducing the risk "particularly of back injury to workers".

The Regulations are relevant if the injury sustained is caused, for example, by the employee falling due to a restricted view caused by the load, or the employee being cut on part of the load or something adjacent while moving the load.

The question of whether the operations involve "a risk" of an employee being injured may be contentious:

- In *Anderson v Lothian Health Board* [1996], it was held that "for there to be a risk of injury, injury need be no more than a foreseeable possibility; it need not be a probability".
- In *Hawkes v London Borough of Southwark* [1998], a "slight" risk of falling was nonetheless held to be "a real risk".
- However, in *Hillhouse v South Ayrshire Council* [2000], the task of carrying tables about 86 yards was found not to involve a risk of injury, and in *Koonjul v Thameslink Healthcare Services* [2000], the Court of Appeal was similarly unimpressed by the risks of bed-making.
- In *Egan v Central Manchester and Manchester Children's University Hospitals NHS Trust* [2008], the Court of Appeal stated that, when assessing risk, the employer must take into account the risk of error by the employee: "Experience shows that, even when well trained, people can make mistakes due to inadvertence or because they are in a hurry or are distracted or simply because they are not concentrating as they should."

continued...

...continued

- In *Pattini v ICICI Bank UK PLC* [2014] the court concluded that the task of moving papers and files in the context of everyday office or clerical work gave rise to either no, or a very low, risk of injury. To require the defendant to carry out a precise evaluation of each and every such task would be beyond the realms of practicability. The defendant was not in breach of the Regulations in the circumstances.

There is unfortunately no alternative to looking at each task individually. Even the HSE risk assessment guidelines state that there are no "safe limits" for lifting. However, work outside the guidelines is likely to increase the risk of injury.

Is it reasonably practicable to avoid the operation?

If the task involves a risk of injury it is absolutely essential to show that it is not reasonably practicable to avoid the manual handling operation or the employer will fall at the first hurdle: see *King v RCO Support Services Ltd and another* [2000]; *Hall v Edinburgh City Council* [1998].

"Reasonably practicable" describes a step that is not just physically possible. It implies that a calculation is to be made by the employer, balancing the risk of injury against the cost, in time and money, that would need to be invested in eliminating that risk.

In the words of Lord Justice Asquith in *Edwards v National Coal Board* [1949]:

> "if it be shown that there is a gross disproportion between them – the risk being insignificant in relation to the sacrifice – the defendants discharge the onus on them."

In considering whether it is reasonably practicable to avoid a manual handling operation that involves a risk of injury, the employer should consider whether mechanical means could be used to move the load. If they could be, and if the cost of mechanising the task is not grossly disproportionate to risk, then they should be. If, for example, a load can be placed in a lorry using a forklift truck, rather than being lifted manually, then it should be. If a non-weight bearing patient can be transferred from bed to toilet using a hoist then the patient should be so moved.

An employer will need to be able to prove that it has applied its mind to the question of elimination of the manual handling operation.

Was it considered? What evidence is there to prove that it was?

Reducing the risk of injury to the lowest level reasonably practicable

Making an assessment

If an employee will have to manually handle a load with a risk of injury in doing so, an employer must carry out an assessment of that manual handling activity. Schedule 1 of the Regulations sets out what the assessment is required to deal with.

Failure to carry out an assessment will generally lead to a finding that the Regulations have been breached.

In *Ghaith v Indesit Company UK Ltd* [2012], the Court of Appeal upheld the claimant's appeal, finding the defendant liable where the claimant sustained an injury while carrying out a stocktake. Lord Justice Longmore held that there had not been any suitable or sufficient assessment of the relevant risk. Risk assessments relied on by the defendant did not deal with stocktaking at all.

The employer is also required to carry out a fresh assessment if there is reason to suspect that the original assessment is no longer valid or if there has been a significant change in the manual handling operations to which it relates.

The courts do, however, sometimes take the view that the making of an assessment is, in itself, not always reasonably practicable. For example, it may not be practicable to do so in an emergency. In *Fraser v Greater Glasgow Health Board* [1996], Scotland's Court of Session put forward the view that Regulation 4 did not apply to an emergency lift performed by a nurse and that Regulation 4.1(b) was only applicable to manual handling operations that were regularly undertaken.

At the other end of the scale is *Koonjul v Thameslink Healthcare Services* [2000]. This involved a care assistant having to pull a low bed away from the wall and bend low while making it. The Court of Appeal held that there had to be an element of realism. It was unrealistic, where a number of everyday tasks were undertaken, that the level of risk involved should be met by a precise evaluation of each task with a warning as to how each task was to be performed.

It has also been held that an assessment need not be formal: *Rowe v Swansea City and County Council* [1999]. Training can satisfy the need for an assessment: *Brown v East and Midlothian NHS Trust* [1999].

Taking appropriate steps to reduce the risk of injury to the lowest level reasonably practicable

> Having undertaken a suitable assessment of the task, the employer is able to consider, rationally and logically, what steps can be taken to reduce the risk of injury to the lowest level reasonably practicable.
>
> There are a number of steps that the employer can take when presented with a risky form of manual handling:

Systems of work

Even if it is not possible to eliminate manual handling, is it possible to reduce the amount of manual handling involved by introducing some mechanical assistance? For example, rather than an employee lifting a load from ground level and carrying it to another point in the factory, could a trolley be provided? The load may need to be manually handled onto the trolley, but the carrying element of the task would be eliminated.

Having regard to the nature of the load, is it possible to break it down into smaller, lighter components?

If that is not possible, would it be practicable to insist that two, three or more employees, as appropriate, should carry out the lift?

It is essential, where this is done, that everyone understands the manoeuvre they are undertaking and that someone coordinates their efforts. If a gang of four is carrying a heavy object, and three let go, things will not go well for the fourth.

Could the load container be designed better to make it easier to lift and carry?

Equipment

Another obvious solution would be to use some form of mechanical aid. For example, in caring for the sick and elderly it has become common to use hoists. These, unfortunately, can introduce new dangers, such as the patient falling out of the sling, and may cause employers to overlook that there can still be a manual handling risk when getting the patient in and out of the hoist and moving the hoist. These new risks must be assessed and dealt with and appropriate information, instruction and training given.

It must be borne in mind also that this equipment will be work equipment and will therefore fall under the Provision and Use of Work Equipment Regulations 1998.

Working environment

Where the problems relate to the working environment, the employer should be able to address additional hazards that increase the risks associated with the manual handling activity, such as uneven or slippery floors, poor lighting or ventilation problems.

Where the employer takes such steps, it must make sure that its employees are provided with proper instructions and proper supervision in order to ensure that they understand and carry out the steps necessary to reduce the risk.

This may be more difficult where the work is being carried out away from the employer's premises. A good example is home care workers working in private homes full of furniture which are not designed to accommodate large pieces of equipment like hoists, and with flooring that wheeled equipment will not traverse easily.

> Remember, in such cases, that the duty is to reduce the risk to the lowest level reasonably practicable. The employer must maximise space as much as possible and ensure that the care workers have proper instruction and systems of work to make the best use of the space available. However, the employer cannot eliminate all risk.

Training

Strangely, the Regulations contain no express requirement for training in manual handling operations. This is odd because the EC Directive at Article 6 requires that employers must ensure that workers receive proper training and information on how to handle loads correctly and the risk that they may be open to, particularly if these tasks are not performed correctly.

Despite this omission, an employer would not be able to argue successfully that it had taken appropriate steps to reduce the risk of injury to the lowest level reasonably practicable if it could not prove that it had provided appropriate training for all employees required to carry out the work.

The courts find training to be an essential element in reducing the risk of injury, e.g. *Peck v Chief Constable of Avon and Somerset* [1999]; and, as stated above, good training can on occasion replace the need for a risk assessment.

The level of training necessary would obviously vary according to the variety and complexity of tasks that an employee is required to carry out.

If there is a risk of injury in a manual handling operation, and the employer has decided on the safest way of carrying out the operation to reduce that risk to the minimum, then, clearly, this must be shown to the employee. The employee must also be warned of the incorrect ways of carrying out that operation and the inherent dangers of doing it in an incorrect manner.

The employer must ensure that the training is done in such a way that the employee understands it. Training must also be reinforced by proper supervision. It will not help if the employer claims that adequate training has been given but subsequent bad practice has been tolerated.

Failure to provide suitable training or to document training in a suitable log (preferably signed and dated by the employee and including a description of the training provided) will almost invariably be fatal to any defence to a manual handling claim.

As with any training, care should be taken in cases involving claimants who do not speak English as a first language. Can the employer prove that, despite the language difficulties, the training was delivered in such a way that it could be understood by the employee?

Further examples of cases that have considered the duty to reduce the risk of injury to the lowest level reasonably practicable include:

- *Egan v Central Manchester and Manchester Children's University Hospitals NHS Trust* [2008]: the Court of Appeal upheld the appeal of a nurse who was transferring a patient into a bath using a hoist. The hoist suddenly stopped because of a plinth under the bath, causing a jerking injury. The defendant could, at a modest cost, have reduced the risk of injury, for example, by making the plinth visible or placing markings on the floor to enable the operator to align the hoist.
- *Ghaith v Indesit Company UK Ltd* [2012]: this case is mentioned above in the context of making an assessment. The Court of Appeal also held that the defendant had not taken appropriate steps to reduce the risk of injury to the lowest reasonable practicable level. The most obvious precaution was that there should be regular breaks of reasonable length in the stocktaking operation.
- *Sloan v The Governors of Rastrick High School* [2014]: a learning support assistant failed in her claim for injury sustained while pushing a student in a wheelchair. The Court of Appeal upheld a decision that the school had taken appropriate steps to reduce the risk of injury to the lowest level reasonable practicable. These included training, regular rotation of staff and the requirement to only push the wheelchairs for short periods.

Individual capability

The checklist for manual handling assessment, contained in Schedule 1 of the Regulations, requires the employer to consider the individual capability of the employee in the following terms.

Does the job:

- Require unusual strength, height, etc.?
- Create a hazard to those who might reasonably be considered to be pregnant or have a health problem?
- Require special information or training for its safe performance?

The EC Directive, in Annex 2, puts the question more broadly and requires the employer to consider whether the employee is physically unsuited to carry out the task in question. One suspects that in this respect the Regulations would be interpreted in line with the EC Directive. *Wells v West Hertfordshire Health Authority* [2000] and *Wiles v Bedfordshire County Council* [2001] are examples of cases where workers with particular health problems succeeded where others might have failed.

Note, however, that special training can be a reasonable answer to a particularly hazardous task. That might well be particularly true in respect of the emergency services.

The impact of the EC Directive

With s.69 of the Enterprise and Regulatory Reform Act 2013 making it impossible to found a civil claim on alleged breaches of health and safety Regulations where the event took place on or after 1 October 2013, consideration of the extent to which the Regulations fail to fully implement the EC Directive, and the implications of any such differences, is increasingly of historical interest only.

There are a number of respects in which the Regulations do not fully implement the EC Directive. They do not appear to apply to temporary agency workers. Reference to reasonable practicability in Regulation 4(1) is not contained in Article 3 of the EC Directive. In addition, the consideration of the personal limitations of the employee is more restricted in the Regulations than in the EC Directive.

Where regulations are intended to implement an EC Directive, as is the case here, they must be construed 'purposively'. That is, they must be interpreted in such a way that they will bring about the results envisaged by the directive.

The judgment of the European Court of Justice in *Marleasing SA v La Comercial Internacional de Alimentacion SA* [1990] stated:

> “in applying national law, whether the provisions in question were adopted before or after the directive, the national court called upon to interpret it is required to do so, so far as possible, in the light of the wording and the purpose of the directive in order to achieve the result pursued by the latter and thereby comply with the third paragraph of Article 189 EEC.”

If the regulations cannot be interpreted in order to achieve the purpose of the particular directive they were designed to implement, the directive will apply directly where the employer is an emanation of the state. This would include central government and local government bodies, health authorities, police authorities and even privatised utilities. It does not follow, however, that the court would find that the duty imposed by the directive is greater than that by the regulations. What this does mean however, is that those employed by emanations of the state may be entitled to bring a civil claim for breach of the directive, even if the manual handling operation was on or after 1 October 2013.

Practical guidance

The HSE has produced some guidelines dealing with weights of loads being:

- lifted and lowered
- pushed and pulled
- handled while seated.

The guidelines take into account such factors as handling the load away from the body, twisting and frequency of effort. The aim of the guidelines is to establish an initial filter. If the load exceeds the suggested guidelines, the HSE does not say that that operation is dangerous, but rather that it merits a more detailed assessment.

> Please bear in mind, however, what is said above about what the courts consider to be a real risk of injury. In particular, we refer again to the judgment in *Anderson v Lothian Health Board* [1996]:
>
> > "for there to be a risk of injury, injury need be no more than a foreseeable possibility; it need not be a probability."

The HSE guidelines are useful, however, when considering the approximate parameters of risk involved in a manual handling task. If a task fell beyond the guidelines, and there had been no assessment, an employer would be likely to be found in breach of the Regulations and, arguably, would be found to be negligent.

Checklist

Where the manual handling operation took place on or after 1 October 2013, a claimant cannot found a civil claim on alleged breaches of the Regulations; negligence must be proven, i.e. that the activity undertaken gave rise to a foreseeable risk of injury and the employer failed to take all reasonably practicable steps to reduce that risk. Breach of the Regulations will, however, be cited as evidence supporting the contention that the employer was negligent. It therefore remains relevant to consider whether the Regulations have been complied with.

The following checklist should help a claims handler to consider, in a structured way, whether there has been a breach of the Regulations:

- ✓ Are the parties involved an employee and an employer? If not, then the Regulations do not apply.
- ✓ Was the activity genuinely a manual handling operation?
- ✓ Was the manual handling of a type that would carry a foreseeable risk of injury?
- ✓ Could the need for manual handling have been avoided entirely by reorganising the work process or by the use of mechanical assistance, within the limits of reasonable practicability?
- ✓ If not, has a manual handling assessment been carried out?
- ✓ If an assessment has been carried out, is the assessment adequate? Consider here the requirements of Schedule 1 of the Regulations.
- ✓ What steps have been taken to reduce the risk of injury in terms of equipment, system of work and training?
- ✓ Do the equipment, system and training reduce the risk to the lowest level reasonably practicable? Some might consider them adequate, but if it is reasonably practicable to reduce the risk even further, then they do not comply with the Regulations.

07 Quantum

Richard West

- Determining value: liability, quantum and interest
- General damages
- Orthopaedic injuries: instructing an expert and points to consider
- Peronal injury reforms
- Psychiatric inquiries: criteria for compensation
- Handicap on the open labour market: *Smith v Manchester* award
- Special damages
- Loss of earnings and employed, including self-employed, claimants
- Calculating care: gratuitous and professional

Quantum

Introduction

Three main aspects determine the value of any claim for compensation:

- Liability
- Quantum
- Interest

Liability

A party can be found to be responsible (and therefore liable) for an accident if they have committed a tort or have breached a statutory duty.

Liability will sometimes rest solely with one party. Liability, however, can be apportioned between the parties. If liability is apportioned between the parties, (e.g. more than one defendant is found liable or the claimant is found to have been contributorily negligent in some way), this will reduce the amount that each defendant has to pay or, if there is only one defendant and the claimant is found to have contributed to their own loss, the value of the claim for the claimant.

Quantum

The value of the claim is known as quantum.

Quantum comprises the various elements of the claimant's entitlement to damages. These include compensation for injuries or for damage to property, as well as financial losses, such as lost earnings, the cost of repairs to motor vehicles or the cost of underpinning homes.

In practice, lawyers and the courts define general damages as compensation for personal injury, and special damages as compensation for financial losses.

The combination of general damages and special damages awarded by a court to a claimant is the quantum of a case.

Interest

The third aspect of any claim's value is the interest that the claimant receives on general and on special damages. The rate of interest will vary depending on the claim.

General damages

The key elements of a general damages claim are:

- Compensation for pain, suffering and loss of amenity.
- Compensation for handicap on the labour market, also known as disadvantage on the labour market or a *Smith v Manchester* claim.

A court will award the claimant compensation for past and future pain and suffering attributable to the incident in question. Psychiatric injury is also compensated. The severity and type of a claimant's injuries, together with the claimant's age and sex, are factors that must be considered when assessing the level of a general damages award.

The *Judicial College Guidelines for the Assessment of General Damages in Personal Injury Cases* (the *JC Guidelines*) are now in their 14th edition, and act as a ready reckoner for the appropriate compensation bracket for any given injury.

In order to refine the likely level of an award of compensation for any given injury, it is recommended that a claims handler considers past judicial decisions (precedent) that deal with similar injuries. Publications such as *Current Law* and *Kemp and Kemp* provide quantum reports that can be useful for comparison of like-for-like injuries and for valuation purposes.

General damages: checklist

- ✓ Will the claimant recover fully from the injuries? If the answer to that question is no, then the claimant will recover a higher level of damages because a permanent disability has been suffered.

- ✓ What is the age of the claimant? If the claimant has suffered a permanent disability, the number of years for which the claimant will have to suffer from that disability will affect the level of compensation that can be expected.

- ✓ What sex is the claimant? Certain types of injury may give rise to greater compensation for one sex or another. For example, facial scarring on a young female claimant may attract a higher compensation award than identical scarring in a similarly aged male claimant. However, it should be noted that the 12th edition of the *JC Guidelines* questions whether gender can be a proper factor in determining the level of general damages.

- ✓ Did the claimant have any relevant pre-existing medical conditions? If so, an expert opinion will be needed to determine whether or not the injury in question has permanently worsened the condition, whether it has caused a temporary flare-up or exacerbation of the condition or whether it has accelerated the condition by a particular period of time. The effect of the injury on the pre-existing condition will affect the level of compensation that can be expected.

- ✓ What effect does the injury have on the claimant's everyday life? If the claimant has suffered a permanent disability but it is minor and does not affect the claimant's way of life unduly, then the compensation would be less than, for example, a professional sportsperson who has been injured and who can no longer participate in their sport or an avid hiker who can no longer walk long distances.

10% uplift on general damages

Following the Court of Appeal's revisiting of the decision in *Simmons v Castle* [2012], a 10% increase in general damages will be applied at trial in all cases where:

- Judgment is given after 1 April 2013
- The claimant has not entered into a conditional fee agreement (CFA)/collective conditional fee agreement (CCFA) before that date.

Interest on general damages

Interest on general damages runs at 2% per annum from the date of issue of proceedings.

Orthopaedic injuries: an outline

The most common personal injury claims are for orthopaedic injuries.

Of claims made for orthopaedic injuries, the most common are for whiplash injuries. Most whiplash injuries occur when one vehicle collides into the rear of another. An occupant of the front vehicle may, in such circumstances, be injured.

A 'rear shunt' has an effect on the neck of the occupant of the vehicle in front. That occupant will be thrown forward by the impact and then thrown backwards in a very short space of time. This movement can cause a tearing of muscles and ligaments in the neck and back.

Whiplash symptoms can develop a day or so after the accident. This is because torn muscles swell and become painful, often overnight or on the day following the accident.

Most whiplash injuries are treated by a general practitioner or by the accident and emergency department of a hospital. Treatment is usually limited to the taking of anti-inflammatory tablets or possibly the use of a supportive neck collar.

Anterior anatomy

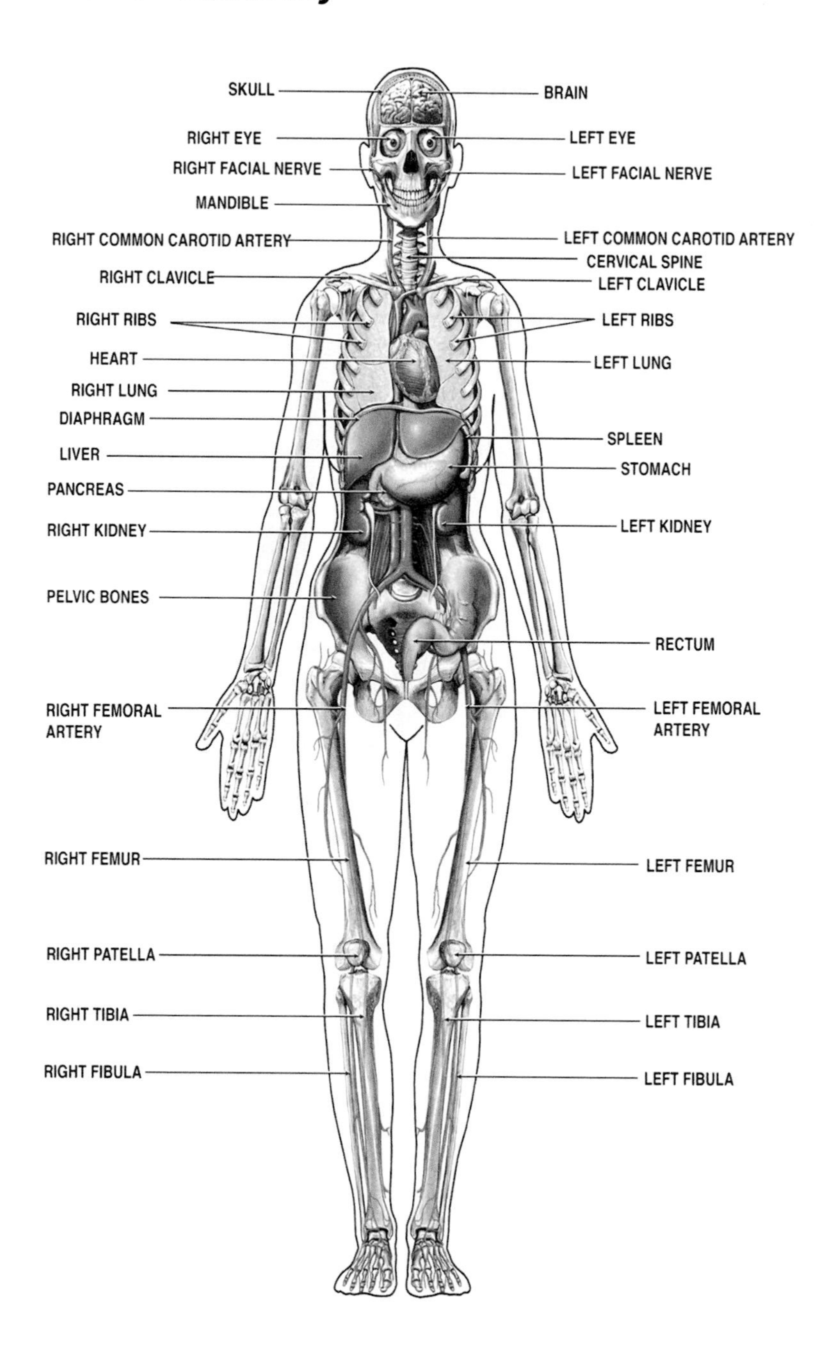

Posterior anatomy

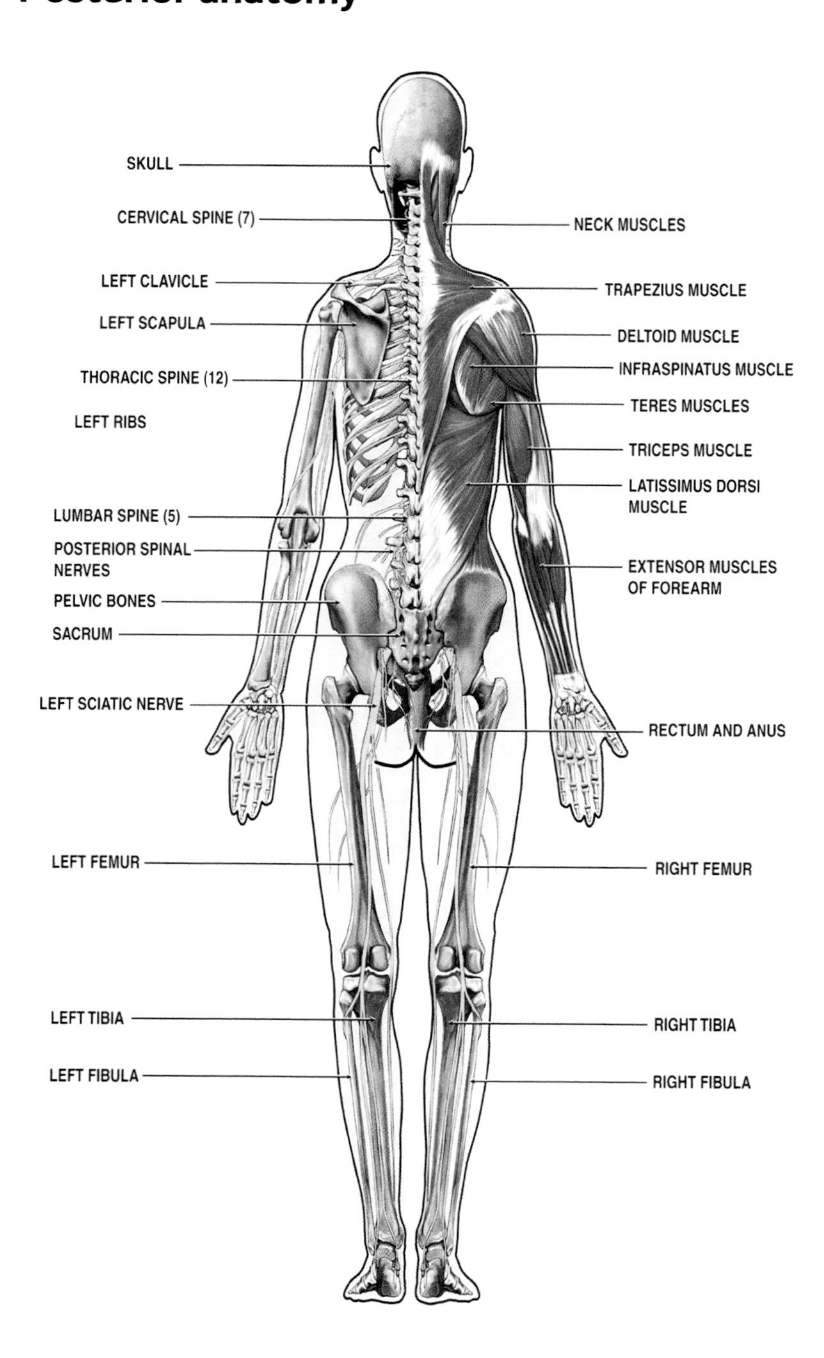
SKULL
CERVICAL SPINE (7)
NECK MUSCLES
LEFT CLAVICLE
TRAPEZIUS MUSCLE
LEFT SCAPULA
DELTOID MUSCLE
INFRASPINATUS MUSCLE
THORACIC SPINE (12)
TERES MUSCLES
LEFT RIBS
TRICEPS MUSCLE
LATISSIMUS DORSI MUSCLE
LUMBAR SPINE (5)
POSTERIOR SPINAL NERVES
EXTENSOR MUSCLES OF FOREARM
PELVIC BONES
SACRUM
LEFT SCIATIC NERVE
RECTUM AND ANUS
LEFT FEMUR
RIGHT FEMUR
LEFT TIBIA
RIGHT TIBIA
LEFT FIBULA
RIGHT FIBULA

Symptoms usually resolve in a week or so. Usually no, or very little time is lost from work. However, symptoms can last for a number of months and in relatively serious cases symptoms can last for a year or more.

Most whiplash sufferers recover completely, unless the injured party was particularly susceptible to a neck injury. A claimant may be susceptible to a neck injury because they already have a pre-existing orthopaedic condition such as arthritis in the neck (cervical spondylosis) or some pre-existing injury.

> It is important to remember that a claimant who has a pre-existing weakness that is made worse by an accident can expect compensation for that worsened condition. This is known as the 'eggshell skull' principle. This means that a defendant who is negligent and who causes injury must take their victim as they find them. It is not a defence to argue that the injury could not have been foreseen or that it is not proportionate to the foreseeable consequences of the negligence.

If a claimant has suffered an orthopaedic injury that appears to be disproportionate to the accident circumstances, the defendant should consider obtaining its own medical report on the claimant's condition, on a joint or agreed basis if appropriate.

Instructing an expert

It is important that an expert has access to all the claimant's medical records, not just those relating to the accident. In that way, any relevant pre-existing medical conditions can be considered by the expert and commented on.

The expert should be asked:

- What are the effects of the accident?
- Is there a relevant pre-existing condition? If so, what have been the effects of the accident on the pre-existing condition, if any?
- How long will the claimant take to recover, if a recovery has not yet taken place?
- Is there any treatment that the claimant can have to speed the recovery? If so, what is the cost of the treatment and how long will it last? With such treatment, when and to what extent can the claimant expect to improve or recover?
- If the accident has had an effect on a pre-existing condition, has the accident caused:
    - A permanent worsening of the pre-existing condition?
    - A temporary flare-up that will in due course return to the pre-existing normal? If yes, when will that recovery take place?
    - Any pre-existing condition to be accelerated in some way? If so, by how much or by how long?
- With treatment, what is the best recovery that the claimant can hope to achieve, and when will that recovery take place?
- If the claimant will not recover fully, what will the effect of the ongoing symptoms be on the claimant's professional and personal life?

Points to consider in relation to orthopaedic injuries

- When did the claimant first seek medical help for the injury? If it was very soon after the accident, all things being equal, a court will believe that the claimant has been injured.

- If the claim has not been presented for some time and treatment has been ongoing, obtain the claimant's pre-accident medical records and also all those relating to the claimant's treatment. These will need to be seen by the expert who can consider whether the treatment given is consistent with the alleged injury, or some pre-existing condition unrelated to the index event.

- Once the medical report has been obtained, assess the appropriate valuation for the injuries in question.

- Ensure the claim is registered with the Compensation Recovery Unit. Take into account relevant deductible benefits before making any offer.

- If you are concerned that the claim is not a genuine one, consider instructing an experienced investigator to place the claimant under surveillance for a period. If this is to be considered, bear in mind the following:

    - The cost of surveillance.

    - Do not tell your medical expert that the claimant is under surveillance until they have examined the claimant. If your expert knows of the surveillance before they do so, they may feel professionally compromised.

    - The timing of service of the surveillance evidence. If you obtain video footage of the claimant doing something they have said they cannot do, that may suggest that the claim is not genuine. However, if the surveillance is served immediately the claimant will have an opportunity to suggest that they were caught on a 'good day' or that they have started to recover. It may, therefore, be preferable to hold the surveillance in reserve until after medical reports and witness statements have been provided and/or exchanged. It may not be possible to assess the value of the surveillance evidence until this point in any event.

If the claimant has told the medical experts in the case, for example, that they have not had a good day since the accident, and cannot walk more than 500 metres, and you have surveillance evidence of them walking further without apparent difficulty, the claimant will have great difficulty in explaining away the surveillance. That will particularly be the case if the claimant gave similar evidence in their witness statement.

Correctly timing the service of good surveillance evidence is crucial. It is equally important to serve it in good time, once it has been possible to properly evaluate the footage. A delay beyond that point may result in a court denying a defendant the opportunity to rely on it.

Personal injury reforms

On the 17 November 2016, the Ministry of Justice launched a consultation on proposals to scrap the right to compensation or put a cap on the amount that people can claim for whiplash injuries.

The outcome of the consultation was announced in February 2017. The government stepped away from a ban on whiplash that it had originally proposed and recommended the following reforms:

- A definition of RTA-related whiplash claims and minor psychological claims (not covering serious psychological injuries).
- The introduction of a damages based-tariff for whiplash and minor psychological claims with an injury duration of 0–24 months. Judges to have power to depart from these tariffs by 20% either way.
- Smalls claims limit for pain, suffering and loss of amenity to rise to £5,000 for RTA claims and £2,000 for non-RTA.
- A ban on offers in RTA whiplash claims only prior to expert medical evidence being obtained.

These reforms are expected to be contained within the anticipated Civil Liability Bill which was included in the government's Legislative Programme 2017–19 but, at the time of going to press, has not yet been presented to parliament.

Psychiatric injuries: an outline

As a general rule, compensation will only be payable to a claimant who has suffered a genuine and recognised psychiatric illness arising out of an accident. It matters not whether an accident has caused post-traumatic stress disorder (PTSD), reactive depression, phobic anxiety or some other type of psychiatric illness as all can be compensated for. Different levels of compensation will, however, be awarded for different levels of psychiatric illnesses.

Some can be treated easily, while others will require more prolonged treatment. It is therefore important to obtain an accurate diagnosis from an appropriately qualified expert.

In some cases no psychiatric illness will have developed, notwithstanding the diagnosis made by the claimant's medical expert.

Psychiatrist vs psychologist?

It is particularly important to note the difference between psychiatrists and psychologists.

A psychiatrist is a medically qualified doctor, who has subsequently specialised in the field of psychiatry. Psychiatry can be defined as the study and treatment of mental health conditions.

Psychologists generally have no medical qualification. They have a psychology degree. Those who call themselves doctors are entitled to do so by virtue of having obtained a doctorate in psychology. Psychologists, who are not medically qualified, have no authority to make a medical diagnosis of psychiatric conditions. Psychology can be defined as the science of the nature, functions and phenomena of the human mind.

> In medical practice, psychiatrists diagnose psychiatric conditions and will often then refer a patient to a psychologist for treatment.
>
> If a claimant relies on a psychologist's report, be wary of accepting a diagnosis of a serious mental illness made within that report.

When can a claimant seek compensation for a psychiatric injury?

> The House of Lords set out the position in the case of *White and others v Chief Constable of South Yorkshire and others* [1998].
>
> The claimant must show that the injury is a recognised psychiatric disorder or illness. Compensation is not awarded for claims for 'shock and shaking' following a road traffic accident.

If the claimant is a bystander who witnesses an accident or its aftermath, they can claim compensation if they develop a recognised psychiatric condition, but only if:

- They have a sufficiently close relationship with the victim (husband, wife, parent or child).
- They were close enough to the accident to be affected by it. They must, therefore, have actually witnessed the accident or its immediate aftermath. If, a day after an accident, they saw the highlights of the accident on the television or were affected by having to identify a loved one at a mortuary, they would not be able to recover compensation.

See *Alcock and others v Chief Constable of South Yorkshire* [1991] and *Page v Smith* [1996].

A claimant who is a rescuer and suffers no physical injury but goes on to develop a recognised psychiatric condition can recover only if the claimant was in actual danger or believed that they were in actual danger.

Points to consider in relation to psychiatric injuries

- Does the claimant fall into a class that allows them to claim compensation for a psychiatric injury?
- Does the claimant have a recognised psychiatric illness?
- Are you prepared to accept the claimant's medical report? Has a diagnosis been provided by an appropriately qualified medical doctor? Does it refer to the claimant's medical records? The reporting expert should rely on those records as well as their examination of the claimant to support their conclusions. If there appears to be over-reliance by the expert on tests given during the examination, consider whether those tests were appropriate and/or whether the claimant could have manipulated them.
- If you are to obtain your own report, instruct a consultant psychiatrist.
- Make sure that your expert has sight of the claimant's previous medical records. The claimant may have a relevant pre-existing psychiatric medical history.
- Make sure that the expert has the claimant's medical records post-dating the accident. When did the claimant first report to a doctor that they were suffering from the symptoms that have been diagnosed as a psychiatric condition? The symptoms of any psychiatric condition are likely to be at their worst a short time after the accident. If there is a delay in the onset of the symptoms, can that be explained?

- Consider obtaining appropriate surveillance evidence if you feel the claim is not genuine. For example, if the claimant alleges that they cannot drive (because they are so traumatised) can you obtain video evidence of them doing just that?
- If the claimant has been to see their GP complaining of physical symptoms arising from an accident, but for some considerable time failed to report any psychiatric symptoms, the claim should be regarded cautiously. Your own expert can consider whether the claimant had a legitimate reason for failing to promptly report psychiatric symptoms. Late reporting may be genuine and the claimant may have had legitimate concerns about reporting such symptoms. However, such a history can equally be evidence of a claim that is less than genuine.

Handicap on the open labour market

A claimant is entitled to compensation if, as a result of injuries, they would be at a disadvantage if they had to compete in the open labour market.

Claims under this head can arise even when the claimant remains in their pre-accident employment and where there is no sign of that employment ending.

Broadly, the courts have to decide whether the claimant, if they were to lose their job, would find it more difficult to find another suitable job because of their injuries than they would have done had the injuries not occurred.

> *Smith v Manchester Corporation* [1974] confirmed that compensation could be given for a handicap on the open labour market.
>
> The court must first consider whether a claimant would be at a disadvantage because of the injury if they were placed back into the job market. The court must then consider what is the risk of that claimant being thrown back into the job market. The Court of Appeal suggested a dual-test approach to the issue of when compensation should be paid in the case of *Moeliker v A Reyrolle & Co Ltd* [1976].

The test is:

1) Is the claimant in work at risk at some time before retirement of losing their job and finding themself on the labour market?

2) If so, what is that risk?

There has to be a real risk that this will occur. However, it would seem that if there is a real risk, albeit a slight one, that would suffice.

The court will look at the following matters:

- The age of the claimant.
- The type of work undertaken by the claimant.
- The claimant's employer's business.
- The nature of the injuries and their effect on the claimant's employment and employability.
- Any comments made by the claimant's employer as to future employment prospects.

If there is a substantial or a real risk then the court will have to place a monetary value on that risk. There is no rule of thumb that can be adopted in assessing how much should be awarded and no limit on the amount that can be awarded. Assessing an award very much comes down to experience, looking at the facts of the case and considering the factors listed above.

The position was set out by Lord Justice Lloyd in the case of *Foster v Tyne and Wear County Council* [1985]:

> “[T]here is no rule of thumb which can be applied. It would be so much easier if there were. But there is not. In each case the trial judge has to do his best to assess the plaintiff's handicap, as an existing disability, by reference to what may happen in the future. As has been said so often, that is necessarily a matter of speculation; it is necessarily a matter of weighing up risks and chances in all the circumstances of a particular case.”

Special damages

Special damages are the financial losses arising out of the claim. These include past and future lost earnings, claims for care, accommodation costs, travel expenses, etc.

Claims for future losses are considered in Chapter 14.

Loss of earnings

There is no magic or mystery to examining a loss of earnings claim. There are two types of loss of earnings claim. These are:

- **Past loss of earnings:** those losses that have been incurred from the date of the injury to the date of the assessment, settlement or trial.
- **Future loss of earnings:** those earnings that will be lost as a result of the injury from the date of the assessment, settlement or trial into the future.

Claimants can also broadly be divided into two types:

- Employed, who pay tax via the Pay As You Earn (PAYE) scheme or, if they are higher rate taxpayers, by completing a tax assessment form.
- Self-employed, who complete tax assessment forms annually, if they have a tax liability.

A court's overriding objective when awarding compensation is to put a claimant back into the position that they would have been in if the injuries in question had not occurred. Claimants are not entitled to make a profit or to receive a benefit as a result of the accident. However, claimants should not be expected to suffer a loss.

Employed claimants

Past loss of earnings

Employed claimants will generally pay tax directly out of their salary under the PAYE scheme. They are entitled to claim their lost net pay (i.e. take home pay net of tax and national insurance). Payslips must therefore be checked to confirm the following:

- The net salary received prior to the date of the injury.
- The net level of earnings received for three calendar months (13 weeks) prior to the injury.
- The net level of earnings received after the accident (if any).

It is important to check the level of earnings received by a claimant in the three calendar months prior to the injury and, if necessary, for a longer period. In that way, it is possible to confirm whether there are any seasonal variations in the level of the claimant's income and/or any variations in the level of any commission paid.

For example, consider a claimant who is an estate agent and who is injured in October. They may have received relatively high commission for sales through the three months prior to the injury. This is because, traditionally, the housing market is buoyant throughout the summer months. If that claimant is then kept away from work for the following three months, claims handlers should be alive to the argument that the claimant's commission would drop over the winter months as the housing market dips.

It is important, therefore, to be conscious of the particularities of the claimant's employment and consider whether that employment is subject to fluctuations in income levels. Of course, the claimant's solicitors will also be alive to those arguments and will try to use them to their client's advantage.

If the claimant has changed jobs since the accident occurred, then ask for a P45. That is a tax document provided by an employer to individuals on the termination of their employment. It sets out the total income paid to the employee in the tax year to the date of the termination.

If past tax years need to be considered (perhaps because a claim has not been intimated for some time following an accident date), then ask for copies of P60s. Employers provide these to their employees at the end of each tax year. P60s confirm the total level of income received by an employee within each tax year.

Employees' contractual obligations to their employers to recover monies

The claimant's employer may have paid them during the period when they were unable to work. It can often be the case that an employer will remunerate on a full pay basis a member of staff who is away from work because of illness or injury for a few weeks or months.

> If the employer has paid the claimant's salary in full while the claimant was away from work, then, on the face of it, the claimant has suffered no loss and cannot make a loss of earnings claim.

However, some employers will ensure within the contract of employment with the claimant that the claimant is obliged to recover from the person who has caused the injury (and who has, therefore, caused the absence from work) any monies paid by the employer. That is a contractual obligation and can be exercised by a claimant. In such circumstances the claimant can seek repayment of such monies from the defendant. Therefore, if a claimant alleges that they are making a claim pursuant to that contractual obligation, ask for a copy of the contract of employment. Do not be satisfied with a letter from an employer simply stating that the employee is obliged to recover those monies. Ask for a copy of the contract itself and make sure that the claimant entered into it before the accident/injury date.

As stated above, the claimant is only entitled to be put back into the position that they would have been in had the accident not happened. Therefore, if the employer paid the claimant while they were away from work, the claimant did not suffer any loss and, therefore, cannot claim for a loss of earnings. However, they can do so if there is a contractual obligation, as mentioned above.

Finally, always ask for a letter from the claimant's employer confirming the claimant's time away from work. The employer can also confirm the level of lost pay but, as recommended above, claims handlers should always ask for payslips too.

Commission and overtime

If lost commission is claimed, ask for details of the commission paid to other employees who are in a similar position to the claimant. Comparable figures will show the level of commission paid while the claimant was away from work, and will, therefore, reflect any seasonal variations in commission income.

Be careful in case those employees have received extra commission while the claimant was away from work by doing the claimant's work for them. In such a situation the figures may be distorted in the claimant's favour as they may suggest a higher level of commission than would have been earned by the claimant. The same principle applies for overtime.

Remember that overtime and commission are both taxable.

Again, check past payslips to confirm the pre-injury net level of commission and overtime (if any) received by the claimant.

Past loss of earnings: checklist

- ✓ Is the claimant employed or self-employed?
- ✓ What was the level of their pre-injury income (including commission and overtime)?
  - ☑ Ask for payslips for 13 weeks (three months) prior to the injury.
  - ☑ Ask for copies of self-assessment forms for a higher rate taxpayer if the lost earnings arise in past tax years.
  - ☑ Calculate the claimant's average net weekly income over those 13 weeks.
  - ☑ Carry out the same calculation for commission and overtime, bearing in mind seasonal variations of income.
- ✓ Has the claimant received any income while away from work, for example, Statutory Sick Pay, etc.? Ask for copies of all payslips since the accident occurred.
- ✓ Is it the injury that is keeping the claimant away from work? Check medical evidence/employment records for any other cause.
- ✓ For how long was the claimant away from work? Ask for details from the claimant's employer.
- ✓ Make sure that the sums claimed are net of tax and national insurance and not gross. If the claimant is employed, they are only entitled to be put back into the position they would have been in had the injury not occurred. If the claimant has suffered a loss of earnings as a result of an injury, their compensation will be their net lost pay. You are entitled to deduct tax and national insurance from the claimant's gross pay.

✓ If the claimant seeks to recover monies on behalf of an employer pursuant to a contractual obligation, ask for a copy of the contract. Ensure the contract was signed and dated before the date of the accident. Do not accept a contract that post-dates the accident. Do not simply accept a letter from an employer that purports to confirm the claimant's contractual obligations.

Self-employed claimants

Self-employed claimants, rather than paying taxes on a monthly basis out of their earnings, have to complete a self-assessment tax form once, and occasionally twice, every financial year.

Claims handlers should ask for the following documentation when dealing with a claim for loss of earnings by a self-employed claimant:

- A copy of the claimant's self-assessment form for the full tax year prior to the injury.
- A copy of the claimant's self-assessment form covering the year of the injury (if/when one has been prepared).
- Copies of profit and loss accounts for the year prior to the injury and for the year including the injury. It may be necessary to obtain these from the claimant's accountant.
- Copies of any correspondence between the claimant/their accountant and the Inland Revenue in relation to the tax position.

A self-employed claimant is not entitled to claim for loss of turnover. They are, however, entitled to claim for a loss of net profit. The loss of net profit is as follows:

> Loss of net profit = monies received by the business less expenses and overheads

Claims handlers are entitled to deduct tax and national insurance from a self-employed claimant's compensation for lost earnings. Payments should, therefore, be made net.

Care

If a claimant has been injured and genuinely requires help with day-to-day activities as a result of their injuries, the reasonable cost of obtaining that help can be sought by way of compensation. Such compensation is usually calculated on a cost per hour of care basis.

Care claims will fall broadly into two types:

- Care provided by family and friends (gratuitous care)
- Professional care.

Gratuitous care

In a range of cases, family members may give a claimant care. For example, if a claimant is bedridden for a week following a car accident, claims for care provided by a spouse or other family members can be made. Similarly, a seriously injured claimant may receive gratuitous care until such time as a formal care package can be arranged privately. This may arise when liability for an accident is in dispute and there are no funds available to pay for privately provided care.

In *Cunningham v Harrison* [1973], Lord Denning MR stated: "[I]t is only right and just that, if his wife renders services to him, instead of a nurse, he should recover compensation for the value of the services that his wife has rendered."

In *Mills v British Rail Engineering Ltd* [1992], Lord Justice Staughton stated that the care provided should go "distinctly beyond that which is part of the ordinary regime of family life".

When claims for gratuitous care are made, claims handlers should not pay for such care at a commercial rate. Commercial rates are appropriate for commercial carers where overheads are to be borne and tax and national insurance to be paid by those carers.

A reduced rate is, therefore, appropriate if a family member or friend provides the care. It is suggested that a reduction of 25% to 33% from a commercial care rate should be made in order to reflect the non-payment of tax and national insurance.

A claim for care by a family member is inappropriate if it is that family member who caused the injury in question (*Hunt v Severs* [1994]).

Claims handlers should also be alive to the fact that in some cases involving claimants who are very young or infirm, some care may have been given by a family member even had the accident not happened. That element of the care should be deducted from any care claim presented.

Gratuitous care: checklist

- ✓ Is care necessary? Consider the medical evidence, type of injury and description of care given.
- ✓ Who has provided the care? Is it the person who caused the injury? Could anybody else have reasonably given the care more cheaply?
- ✓ Is the family carer, in giving the care, going “distinctly beyond that which is part of the ordinary regime of family life”?
- ✓ How much care should have been necessary per day, bearing in mind the level of the injury or incapacity? You may need an expert medical opinion on this point.
- ✓ What is the appropriate hourly rate for that care? If a family member gave the care, then a commercial rate is not appropriate.
- ✓ Multiply the number of hours per day for an appropriate level of care by the appropriate hourly rate. That will be the daily cost of care.
- ✓ How long did or will the care reasonably last for?
- ✓ Build into your calculations/offer the fact that the care being given should normally diminish as the claimant recovers.

Professional care

In serious injury cases professional care, both past and future, may be appropriate. Such care may be necessary indefinitely.

The appropriate type and level of care will need to be investigated. It is usual to commission a care consultant's report for this. Such a report will assess the injury, the claimant and any needs that arise, together with the likely level of care to be needed in the future. The report will take into account any prognosis provided by medical experts. Based on that, it sets out the cost of the care that will be necessary into the future.

For further detail see Chapter 14.

Interest on special damages

Interest on past special damages that have ceased to accrue is calculated at the court special account rate from the date of the loss to the date of assessment of the loss. The special account rate is currently 0.5%, and has been at this level since 1 July 2009.

Interest on special damages will only begin to run when a loss has been suffered (payment made or sum lost). Therefore, interest will not run on the cost of repairs to a motor vehicle until those repairs are paid for; and may never run on the sum claimed for credit hire.

If a loss is continuing, the general principle is that interest is calculated at half the special account rate on the total amount over the period from the date of the accident to the date of trial.

08 The Civil Procedure Rules 1998

Marta Bozek and Deborah Newberry

- Overriding objective: a strict approach
- Costs management: proportionality and budgets
- Part 36: costs consequences and sanctions
- The Personal Injury Pre-Action Protocol: steps and investigation
- Pre-action disclosure

The Civil Procedure Rules 1998

Introduction

The Civil Procedure Rules 1998 (CPR) came into force on 26 April 1999 with the intention of providing a new code of civil procedure for the civil courts aimed at achieving greater efficiency and better cost management.

Despite best intentions for improving the civil justice system, civil litigation costs continued to increase and prompted a further review by Lord Justice Jackson, who published his final report in January 2010.

Jackson LJ found that the costs of civil litigation were too high and were fuelled by the operation of 'no win no fee' conditional fee agreements (CFAs).

Jackson LJ's report contained extensive recommendations for wholesale reform of the civil justice system. It prompted a government-led consultation between November 2010 and February 2011 and resulted in the implementation of the 'Jackson CFA reforms' by virtue of Part 2 of the Legal Aid, Sentencing and Punishment of Offenders Act 2012 (LASPO). The relevant provisions in Part 2 of LASPO came into effect on 1 April 2013.

The key changes brought in by LASPO and the corresponding amendments made to the CPR include:

- **Abolition of recoverability of additional liabilities:** CFA success fees and after-the-event insurance premiums are no longer recoverable from the losing party. Any success fee sought from the claimant is capped at 25% of damages (future losses ringfenced).
- **General damages uplift of 10%:** where a claimant has entered into a CFA on or after 1 April 2013.

- **Change to Part 36 regime:** an additional sanction permitted in all claims where the defendant's offer is beaten, calculated as a percentage of the amount awarded by the court up to a maximum award of £75,000.
- **Introduction of qualified one-way costs shifting (QOCS):** an introduction that applies to funding arrangements entered into on or after 1 April 2013, meaning that in most cases, defendants, whether they win or lose at trial, will almost always have to pay their own costs.
- **Permission to use damages-based agreements (DBAs):** subject to a cap of 25% of damages (future losses ringfenced); this applies in all types of civil litigation.
- **Horizontal and vertical extension of the Pre-Action Protocol for Low Value Personal Injury Claims in Road Traffic Accidents:** to include most employers' and public liability claims up to the value of £25,000, with corresponding fixed recoverable costs regimes.

Part 36 of the CPR and QOCS are considered in further detail below.

The CPR are, to a great extent, the domain of lawyers. That said, a clear theme of the Jackson reforms is to encourage all parties to litigation to take a much greater interest in the costs generated – responsible litigation is now the order of the day.

While it may be too soon to reach a balanced conclusion about the full impact of the reforms, a positive shift in the litigation experience is already being seen.

The aim of the CPR is:

- To provide alternative dispute resolution methods to potential litigants so that they might avoid litigation. Alternative dispute resolution may take the form of mediation or conciliation, which are less formal and confrontational than litigation.

- If litigation is unavoidable, to put in place protocols for both parties to comply with before proceedings are issued. The aim is to encourage the parties to give greater disclosure of their respective cases in evidence in an effort to avoid litigation.
- To shorten, where appropriate, the litigation process by allocating cases to an appropriate 'track'.
- To place the management of cases in the hands of the court in an effort to speed up and control the costs of the litigation process.
- To put in place a new costs regime, the mainstay of which is proportionality.

Overriding objective

The aim of the CPR is encapsulated in the overriding objective. The purpose of the overriding objective is to assist with the application of specific provisions of the CPR and to guide the behaviour of those contemplating or involved in litigation in situations where no specific rule applies.

The overriding objective demands a strict approach:

> These Rules are a new procedural code with the overriding objective of enabling the court to deal with cases justly and at proportionate cost.

Part 1.1(2) of the CPR defines what is meant by dealing with a case justly and at proportionate cost:

a) ensuring that the parties are on an equal footing;

b) saving expense;

...continued

...continued

c) dealing with the case in ways which are proportionate:

    i) to the amount of money involved;

    ii) to the importance of the case;

    iii) to the complexity of the issues; and

    iv) to the financial position of each party;

d) ensuring that it is dealt with expeditiously and fairly;

e) allotting to it an appropriate share of the court's resources, while taking into account the need to allot resources to other cases; and

f) enforcing compliance with rules, practice directions and orders.

The overriding objective – especially the new rules in respect of proportionality – sets the foundation for all other changes contained within the CPR. It applies to any action, on any case, regardless of date of issue. As stated by Jackson LJ, "proportionality is the new king of trumps".

Although, as stated above, the CPR will usually be the territory of the parties' legal representatives, claim handlers must be aware of a number of particularly important areas under the rules.

Costs management

A new costs management section is included in Part 3 of the CPR, which provides the court with greater powers to manage the costs to be incurred in any proceedings. The rules confirm that the court should manage both the steps to be taken and the costs to be incurred by the parties so as to further the overriding objective.

> In practice, this means that the courts will place greater emphasis on the proportionality of global costs than on either reasonableness or necessity.

Subject to some exceptions, including proceedings commenced on or after 6 April 2016 by or on behalf of a child or where the proceedings are the subject of fixed or scale costs, for all multi-track cases commenced on or after 1 April 2013, all parties (except litigants in person) must file and exchange budgets with their directions questionnaires (if the stated value of the claim on the claim form is less than £50,000) or not later than 21 days before the first case management conference (in any other case) unless the court orders otherwise.

Failure to do so allows the court to treat the 'offending' party's budget as containing applicable court fees only.

Where a budget does not exceed £25,000 or the value of the claim on the claim form is less than £50,000, the parties must only use the first page of Precedent H. Otherwise, a full document is required.

In addition, parties are required to file an agreed budget discussion report at least seven days before the first claims management conference.

Where costs budgets have been filed and exchanged, the court will make a costs management order to record the:

- Extent to which budgets are agreed between the parties.
- Court's approval of the budget/parts of the budget that required revision.

Once a costs management order has been made, the court will continue to control the parties' budgets in respect of recoverable costs. When making any case management decision, the court is required to have regard to agreed (or available) budgets and the costs involved in each procedural step.

In practice, the court will not depart from an approved budget unless satisfied there is good reason to do so. While a court should allow a party to correct an irregularity that has not prejudiced the other party or the litigation in general, costs budgets should be given the respect they deserve.

In turn, costs budgets are viewed as a useful tool that enable greater clarity in the prediction of total costs, thereby assisting in achieving settlement. Costs budgets help compensators to properly assess their reserves at an earlier point in the claim life cycle. They can then be proactive in managing costs at different stages rather than having to wait until the conclusion of a claim.

Relief from sanction

The overriding objective requires the court to place greater weight than it might have done previously on enforcing compliance with the rules, practice directions and court orders. Procedural defaults can now have serious consequences upon evidence and issues.

Part 3.9 of the CPR provides the stricter approach to default. On an application for relief from any sanction imposed for a failure to comply with any rule, practice direction or court order, the court will consider all the circumstances of the case, including the need:

- For litigation to be conducted efficiently and at proportionate cost; and
- To enforce compliance with rules, practice directions and orders.

Mitchell v News Group Newspapers [2013]

Initially, the tougher, more robust approach to rule compliance sent shock waves through the industry. *Mitchell* signalled that where non-compliance is neither minor nor trivial, and in the absence of good reason for any default, relief from sanctions was unlikely to be granted.

The situation was partly addressed by the introduction of Part 3.8(4) of the CPR – the 'buffer rule' – which allows deadlines to be extended by up to 28 days, provided both parties agree and it does not put any hearing date at risk.

Denton and others v TH White Ltd and others [2014]

The decision in *Denton* signalled a fresh approach to applications for relief from sanctions, softening the extremes of *Mitchell* by attaching greater weight to the overall circumstances of the case.

While some calm has been restored, the default position must remain: comply with ordered directions. Reliance on the buffer rule is not ideal, and best practice still means that parties need to liaise closely with experts and witnesses to ensure that deadlines imposed can be complied with.

Part 36

A well-judged Part 36 offer will apply pressure on a claimant to settle a claim. However, since the April 2013 rule changes, even an early Part 36 offer may not provide the saving for a defendant that it might have done previously.

Part 36 of the CPR allows either party to make a written offer of settlement of the claim. A settlement offer can be made at any stage of the proceedings, including pre-action, and can be made in respect of individual parts of a claim, for example, general damages only.

Defendants should also consider making an offer while an up-to- date certificate of recoverable benefits (Compensation Recovery Unit (CRU) certificate) is awaited from the Department for Work and Pensions (DWP). Part 36.22(7) of the CPR specifically provides for this.

Claims handlers will be used to seeing claimants' Part 36 offers to settle. The terms of any offer made by the claimant must be considered carefully.

Equally, there are a number of considerations to be alive to when making an offer – the consequences for getting them wrong can mean the offer is ineffective and/or does not carry the intended costs consequences.

By way of guidance only, it is expected that a Part 36 offer to settle letter will typically cover the elements listed below – the detail of which will vary in practice depending on the type of offer to be made.

The precise wording of a Part 36 letter will depend on, in particular, whether:

- The offer is made by one defendant or multiple defendants.
- The offer to settle relates to the whole of the claim or part of the claim only.
- An interim payment(s) has been made.
- Deductible benefits have been paid, that is the CRU position.
- A counterclaim has been made that is relevant to the offer.
- The offer is made less than 21 days before the start of trial.

Deductible benefits

Before making a Part 36 offer, a CRU certificate should be applied for and if available, the certificate should accompany the letter.

It is prudent to be clear that in the event that the claimant's CRU certificate is appealed or reviewed (or for any other reason there is a refund of recoverable benefits), the refund will be payable to the defendant and not to the claimant.

For further detail on CRU see Chapter 17.

Additional points

It is sensible to allow for the possibility that further benefits are paid to the claimant after the date of the offer. It is usual to require the claimant to seek the court's permission to accept the offer after expiry of the relevant period (pursuant to CPR 36.11(3)(b)).

Payment of damages should also be stated in the letter, for example, agreement by the defendant to pay any damages due within 14 days of the date of service of notice of acceptance of the offer.

Costs consequences

While the costs consequences of acceptance of a Part 36 offer are stipulated in the CPR, it is vital to specify the liability for costs in the offer to settle letter. Potential consequences are far-reaching – requiring substantial cross-referencing when reading the rules – and demand clarity in drafting.

Defendant accepts claimant's offer

If the defendant accepts the claimant's offer within 21 days, then subject to the appropriate costs rules, the claimant's costs will also become payable on a standard basis. The defendant must pay the damages within 14 days of acceptance of the claimant's offer.

Claimant accepts defendant's offer

If a claimant accepts the defendant's offer within 21 days, then, again, subject to the appropriate costs rules, the defendant will pay the claimant's costs on a standard basis until the date of acceptance. The defendant must pay the claimant the damages due within 14 days of the claimant's acceptance.

Claimant fails to beat the defendant's offer

In cases where funding is entered after 1 April 2013 and QOCS applies, recovery of any successful order for costs against a claimant will be limited as set out within appropriate costs rules. QOCS applies to proceedings that include a claim for personal injuries, under the Fatal Accidents Act 1976, or one that arises out of a death (for the purposes of the Law Reform (Miscellaneous Provisions) Act 1934).

Where QOCS applies, unless the claimant's action is struck out (for example, due to reasons of conduct or an abuse of process) or is found to be fundamentally dishonest, the defendant will not recover costs in cases where the claimant fails entirely at trial.

Enforcement against the claimant without court permission for the full amount of costs is possible in certain cases where the claim is struck out.

Enforcement for the full amount because of a finding of fundamental dishonesty may only be ordered by a court.

Part 44.14 of the CPR sets out when a costs order against a claimant may be enforced without permission of the court but only to the extent that the aggregate amount in money terms of such orders does not exceed the aggregate amount in money terms of any order awarding the claimant damages and interest. They can only be enforced after the proceedings are concluded.

For example:

> The claimant's funding agreement is entered into after 1 April 2013 and QOCS applies. The defendant makes a Part 36 offer of £29,000, and at trial the claimant fails to obtain a more advantageous judgment and is awarded £26,000.
>
> The claimant has, therefore, failed to beat the defendant's Part 36 offer.
>
> The total of the defendant's costs incurred since the date of the Part 36 offer are £30,000. Under Part 44.14 of the CPR, the defendant would be able to enforce without permission of the court up to the aggregate amount of damages awarded (i.e. £26,000) but only after the costs are concluded. The court may order set-off on costs in any event.

Defendant fails to do better than claimant's offer

If the claimant makes an offer that is not accepted by the defendant and that the claimant subsequently matches or beats, the claimant can seek a number of sanctions against the defendant.

The relevant provision is Part 36.17(4) of the CPR:

> the court must, unless it considers it unjust to do so, order that the claimant is entitled to–
>
> a) interest on the whole or part of any sum of money (excluding interest) awarded, at a rate not exceeding 10% above base rate for some or all of the period starting with the date on which the relevant period expired;
>
> b) costs on the indemnity basis from the date on which the relevant period expired;

c) interest on those costs at a rate not exceeding 10% above base rate; and

d) an additional amount, which shall not exceed £75,000, calculated by applying the prescribed percentage set out below to an amount which is–

   i) where the claim is or includes a money claim, the sum awarded to the claimant by the court; or

   ii) where the claim is only a non-monetary claim the sum awarded to the claimant by the court in respect of costs–

Amount awarded by the court	Prescribed percentage
up to £500,000	10% of the amount awarded
above £500,000 up to £1,000,000	10% of the first £500,000 and (subject to the limit of £75,000) 5% of any amount above that figure

The new rule 36.17(4), as highlighted above, only applies to offers made on or after 1 April 2013. Therefore, for offers made after 1 April 2013, where judgment against the defendant is at least as advantageous to the claimant as the proposals contained in the claimant's Part 36 offer, the claimant can now claim the additional sanction – up to a maximum amount of £75,000 – as set out at sub-paragraph (d) above. This sanction is in addition to the usual costs consequences in relation to indemnity costs.

Genuine attempt to settle

When deciding whether it would be just to apply the usual cost consequences, a court will consider whether a Part 36 offer was a genuine attempt to settle.

There is no set rule as to what constitutes a genuine attempt to settle. Each case will be considered on its own facts. However, the following general principles are likely to apply:

- An offer that is all take and no give is unlikely to be viewed as a genuine attempt to settle. Thus an offer to take 100% is unlikely to be considered a valid offer. Some element of discount will be necessary.
- A claimant with a very strong claim who has made a Part 36 liability offer with a small concession is likely to be in a better position to argue that their offer was a genuine attempt to settle than a claimant with a weaker claim.

In particular, when deciding whether to make a punitive costs order against the defendant, the court will look at what information was available to the defendant at the time that the offer was made and whether or not the defendant could have assessed the worth of the claim at the time that the offer was made with the information that was to hand.

It is anticipated that, given the potential uncertainty here, case law is likely to be generated as a result.

It should also be noted that truly speculative offers made by a claimant's solicitor as soon as a claim is intimated can arguably be ignored; save that they give a claims handler an indication of the claimant's solicitor's expectations.

Part 36 in respect of costs

A further key change is that Part 36 offers are introduced into detailed assessment proceedings (i.e. a notice of commencement) commenced after 1 April 2013. The details of the provision are found in Parts 44 to 48 of the CPR.

Therefore, where a bill of costs is served after 1 April 2013, or where the bill of costs has not yet been served, making a Part 36 offer should be considered.

Further changes

Additional key changes to Part 36 are anticipated to apply to Part 36 offers made on or after 6 April 2015. These are summarised as follows:

- **Time limited offers:** a party can make a time limited Part 36 offer, provided the offer remains open for at least 21 days. The offer will be treated as having been automatically withdrawn in accordance with its written terms. It will no longer be necessary to send a separate, later, letter formally withdrawing the offer.

  For low-value, straightforward claims there are unlikely to be many advantages to time limiting a Part 36 offer. However, it could apply extra pressure to consider an offer promptly. Alternatively, it could be used to highlight a risk to an opponent. For example, a Part 36 offer could be time limited to expire on the date medical evidence is due to be served.

- **Varying offers:** provided a Part 36 offer has not been accepted, it can be withdrawn or its terms varied. However, once the offer is withdrawn, it will not attract Part 36 consequences.

  If a Part 36 offer is varied to make it more favourable to an opponent, this will be treated as making a new Part 36 offer with a fresh relevant period for acceptance.

  Where a Part 36 offer is varied to be less advantageous, while not explicit in the rules, the position appears to be that this does not create a new relevant period for acceptance.

- **Late acceptance:** where there is late acceptance of a Part 36 offer, a court must make the usual costs order, unless it considers it unjust to do so. This removes some of the previous uncertainty in this regard.

- **Failure to file a costs budget:** the new rules allow a party who would normally be restricted to recovering only court fees to still recover 50% of their costs, from expiry of the relevant period to judgment, where their opponent has failed to beat their Part 36 offer. The purpose of this is to discourage a party from taking advantage of their opponent's cost predicament and refusing reasonable settlement offers.
- **Counterclaims:** a counterclaiming defendant will be able to make a Part 36 offer in respect of their counterclaim, as if they were the claimant.
- **Appeals:** a Part 36 offer will only have cost consequences in relation to the proceedings in which it is made. If an appeal is brought, a fresh Part 36 offer must be made, if the offeror wishes to have costs protection in the appeal.
- **Split trials:** previously, Part 36 offers could not be brought to the attention of a trial judge until the final conclusion of the claim. This caused difficulties where there was a split trial and the court had to make a costs order without being aware of the Part 36 liability offers exchanged between the parties.

  Where a Part 36 offer was made before 6 April 2015 but the trial takes place on or after that date a Part 36 offer can be brought to the attention of the court where the offer concerns a part of the claim which has been decided. Unless the parties agree, any other Part 36 offer cannot be accepted within seven clear days after judgment has been given or handed down.

The Personal Injury Pre-Action Protocol

To support the ethos of narrowing the issues prior to the use of proceedings and to encourage best practice, the CPR introduced pre-action protocols. The objective of the protocols is often referred to as a 'cards on the table' approach.

The Personal Injury Pre-Action Protocol (PIPAP) is one of 14 pre-action protocols now in force. Other protocols cover construction disputes, judicial review, housing disrepair, rent arrears, defamation, clinical negligence, disease and illness claims, professional negligence, debt claims, low-value claims in road traffic accidents (RTA), and employers' and public liability (EL and PL) claims.

For the purposes of this chapter the focus is on the PIPAP. (Please see Chapters 12, 24 and 25 for clinical negligence, low-value RTA claims, and low-value EL/PL claims, respectively.)

The overall aim of the PIPAP is to avoid proceedings if at all possible and encourage early settlement. If proceedings are inevitable, it will assist the parties to identify, prior to the issue of proceedings, those issues that will need to be concentrated upon in litigation.

The PIPAP and its annexes are available on the Justice website at: http://www.justice.gov.uk/courts/procedure-rules/civil/protocol/prot_pic

The steps of the PIPAP are:

Step 1: early notification

The claimant is encouraged to notify the proposed defendant as soon as they know a claim is likely, even if they are unable to send a letter of claim. This can be useful, especially where the defendant has little or no knowledge of the potential claim or where the claimant is already incurring significant expenditure. Early notification will not cause the timetable for a response to start to run.

Step 2: letter of claim

The claimant must send to the proposed defendant a letter of claim that contains sufficient information for the defendant or their insurer to commence full investigations and to assess a reserve figure. It should contain a clear summary of the facts, the nature of the injuries and details of any financial loss incurred. Once sent, the claimant should not carry out any further investigations until a response is received. The letter does not have to be set out as a pleading, nor does it have the same status as a pleading.

If the claimant nominates an expert, the defendant has 14 days to object (see Step 7 below) after the expiration of the 21-day period within which to reply to the letter of claim (see Step 3 below).

Step 3: reply

The defendant (or their insurer) should reply within 21 days of the date of the posting of the letter of claim, identifying the insurer if there is one. The party replying should at this stage identify any significant omissions from the letter of claim. It is suggested in such circumstances that the defendant's time to investigate the claim (see Step 4 below) should not be triggered until the claimant has provided that information. If there is no response to the letter of claim within the 21-day period the claimant is entitled to issue proceedings.

Step 4: response

The defendant, or their insurers, has a maximum of three months from the date of the acknowledgment of the claim to investigate matters. At or before the end of that period the defendant must reply stating whether liability is denied and, if so, giving full reasons for the denial of liability including any alternative version of events.

> If the defendant admits liability the presumption is that the defendant will be bound by that admission. If the defendant subsequently becomes aware of fresh facts that cause it to change its mind as to liability, those new facts and a repudiation of liability should be communicated to the claimant's advisors immediately. It is unlikely that a defendant will be able to resile from any earlier admission, and so it is crucial that liability is only admitted when proper investigations have been carried out and completed.

Step 5: documents

If the defendant denies liability, with their letter of response they should include documents in their possession that are material to the issues between the parties. Such documents are likely to be those that will be ordered to be disclosed by the court, be it on an application for pre-action disclosure or by virtue of a direction for disclosure during proceedings. A claimant is likely to issue an application for pre-action disclosure (see below) if incomplete disclosure is given.

The PIPAP provides specimen lists of documents that are likely to be relevant in different types of claims, for example, records of inspection for the relevant stretch of highway in a highway tripping claim.

Step 6: special damages

A schedule of special damages with supporting documentation should be prepared and served by the claimant upon the defendant's insurers (or solicitors, if appointed) as soon as is practicable, particularly where an admission of liability has been made.

Step 7: experts

Before either party instructs an expert the other party must be shown a list of the name(s) of one or more experts to whom it is intended instructions are sent. The claimant must obtain access to relevant medical records (see Step 8 below).

Within 14 days of receipt of the list the other party may indicate an objection to one or more of the experts. The first party should then instruct a mutually acceptable expert.

If the other party objects to all of the experts on the list then the parties can instruct experts of their own choice. However, the court may impose costs sanctions if the instruction of two experts is, in the court's opinion, unnecessary.

Unless the second party objects to a nominated expert they will not be entitled to rely upon their own expert evidence unless:

- The first party agrees;
- The court so directs; or
- The first party's expert report has been amended and the first party is not prepared to disclose the original report.

> It should be understood that the claimant has an advantage here. If experts are not agreed under the PIPAP it is very likely that the claimant will press on to obtain a unilateral report while refusing to consent to being examined or interviewed by the defendant's proposed expert. There is nothing that the defendant can do in such circumstances other than to request in writing that the claimant submit to a medical examination by the defendant's expert.

In such circumstances the defendant must then wait for the claimant's expert's report to be served. Of course, the report may be acceptable, in which case settlement should be possible. There are occasions, however, when the report will not be acceptable. Examples for that unacceptability are often as follows:

- The claimant's expert has not had access to the claimant's pre- and post-accident medical or other records.
- The expert is not properly qualified or experienced to provide the opinion in question.
- The expert has failed to set out a range of possible alternative opinions that other experts may reasonably hold.
- The expert has unreasonably failed to reach any firm conclusions.

If the claimant's expert's report is unacceptable to the defendant, the defendant may be able to move matters forward pragmatically by putting questions in writing to the expert, where the answers may solve what the defendant perceives to be the problems with the report. The replies may be acceptable and make a settlement possible.

If they are not, the defendant may wish to repeat the request to have the claimant examined by an alternative expert. If the claimant again refuses the request and settlement cannot be achieved, the defendant will have to wait for the claimant to issue proceedings and apply to the court for permission to rely upon fresh medical evidence (and, if appropriate, seek costs of the application).

> The court should have sympathy for the defendant if the earlier examination has been unreasonably refused. If the claimant's conduct is called into question, the court may not only consider awarding costs against the claimant, but also a stay of the proceedings to allow the defendant to obtain their report.

Step 8: medical records

The claimant will obtain access to relevant medical records with the instruction of an expert.

In addition, and if necessary, the court has power under Part 35.9 of the CPR to direct a party to provide information to the other party:

> Where a party has access to information which is not reasonably available to another party, the court may direct the party who has access to the information to:
>
> - prepare and file a document recording the information; and
> - serve a copy of that document on the other party.

Step 9: written questions

Either party may send written questions on the report, which are relevant to the issues, to the expert via the instructing party's solicitors.

The expert should send answers to the questions separately and directly to each party.

If liability has been admitted the claimant should wait 21 days before issuing proceedings in order to allow the parties to attempt to settle the case.

Step 10: rehabilitation

Traditionally, insurers have tended to focus on rehabilitation in the most serious injury cases. The PIPAP now requires both parties to consider "as early as possible whether the claimant has reasonable needs that could be met by rehabilitation treatment or other measures".

The parties are required to consider the Rehabilitation Code. Any report obtained in order to consider rehabilitation can only be used within the litigation by the consent of both parties.

Step 11: Part 36

Part 36 of the CPR permits both parties to make offers to settle matters pre-proceedings, and it is actively encouraged that parties do so. The party making the offer must always supply sufficient evidence to enable proper consideration of the offer.

General

A failure to comply with any of the protocols may lead the court to refuse to extend any period for the serving of a statement of case and penalise a party in costs at any stage of the proceedings. Indeed, Part 44.2(5)(a) of the CPR specifically requires the court to have regard to the conduct before proceedings and the extent to which the protocols were followed.

When awarding costs, the court will also take into account an unreasonable refusal by either party to attempt to settle a case before litigation.

Claims handlers' investigations under the PIPAP

In accordance with the PIPAP and its disclosure lists, it is important that claims handlers seek from their clients:

- A fully completed incident report form, if possible, handwritten by the driver (in a motor claim) or the appropriate officer (if an EL/PL claim).
- Full documentation in accordance with the PIPAP disclosure lists (see below).
- Where appropriate, witness statements – properly set out with a statement of truth.
- Where appropriate, plans of the scene of the incident together with photographs.

If the first letter received from the claimant does not contain sufficient information to allow the claim to be investigated fully, seek the additional information required.

Pre-action disclosure

Part 31.16 of the CPR allows a party to seek, by way of application, disclosure of relevant documents before proceedings have started.

The court will make such an order where:

- The respondent is likely to be a party to subsequent proceedings.
- The applicant is also likely to be a party to those proceedings.
- If proceedings have started, the respondent's duty by way of standard disclosure will extend to the documents or classes of documents of which the applicant seeks disclosure.
- Disclosure before proceedings have started is desirable in order to:

  i) dispose fairly of the anticipated proceedings

ii) assist the dispute to be resolved without proceedings, or

iii) save costs.

If any relevant documents are no longer in control of the respondent, they may well be required by the court to state what has happened to them.

Therefore, if a defendant under the PIPAP gives incomplete disclosure, a court may not only impose sanctions at a later stage, but the claimant may seek an order under Part 31.16 of the CPR.

However, if a case is started under the EL/PL or RTA Protocol for Low Value Personal Injury Claims a successful claimant is likely to be awarded fixed costs of the action.

09 Occupational disease

Cameron Clark

- Nature and characteristics of disease claims
- History of disease claims
- Types of diseases:
  - Chest and skin conditions
  - Noise-induced hearing loss
  - Vibration white finger
  - Work-related upper limb disorder
- Pre-Action Protocol for Disease and Illness Claims
- Main features of the Pre-Action Protocol for Disease and Illness Claims
- Investigating and defending a disease claim

Occupational disease

Introduction

It is a sad indictment of our industrial development that work-related diseases have blighted and, in some cases, taken the lives of workers in countless occupations.

Moreover, despite statutory regulation and improved industrial hygiene, newer work-related illnesses and medical conditions have occurred in environments not previously considered to be hazardous, such as offices, shops and hospitals. Asbestos was once thought of as a wondrous product, but little did employers know of the horrors that it would unleash. As technology and medical science develop, only in future years shall we fully appreciate the disease legacies we are currently creating.

It is not possible to deal with each and every occupational disease or work-related illness in a single chapter. This chapter is heavily biased towards asbestos-induced disease claims because the case law in that area has given rise to some of the leading authorities in disease litigation. Nevertheless, much of what is said relative to investigating and defending an asbestos-attributable disease claim should be useful to a claims handler who finds themself dealing with a claim for, say, occupational deafness, vibration white finger or a repetitive strain injury.

Nature of disease claims

Disease claims arise from a claimant's culpable exposure to a toxic or dangerous substance or to an activity that induces injury by a defendant.

Commonly, disease claims are employers' liability (EL) claims in that the culpable exposure to the toxic or dangerous substance occurred during the course of the claimant's employment.

Disease claims may, however, be public liability (PL) claims, for example where a claimant's exposure stems neither from the negligence nor breach of statutory duty on the part of their own employer, but from the activities of other trades they worked alongside. A further example of a PL disease claim is where a factory or installation allows a toxic or dangerous disease-causing substance to escape from its premises thus exposing local inhabitants.

Disease claims can also fall into the category of product liability claims where, for example, a claimant claims compensation from a manufacturer or supplier of a product containing a toxic or dangerous substance with no warning as to the product's toxicity/danger and where exposure caused the claimant to contract a disease.

Disease claims can be classified as either divisible or indivisible conditions.

A divisible condition is one in which, following contraction of the disease, further exposure to the hazardous agent aggravates or worsens the condition, for example:

- Industrial deafness
- Hand-arm vibration syndrome (HAVS)
- Asbestosis
- Pleural thickening.

Alternatively, an indivisible condition refers to the fact that following commencement of the disease subsequent exposure to the hazardous agent does not affect the progress of the disease, for example:

- Mesothelioma
- Lung cancer.

Equally, disease claims can also be classified as either long-tail or short-tail conditions.

A long-tail disease is gradual in operation, usually arising from cumulative exposure and where there is an insidious manifestation of symptoms. The most common examples are:

- Asbestos-related diseases
- Industrial deafness
- HAVS
- Chronic obstructive pulmonary disease (COPD)
- Cancers
- Vibration-induced carpal tunnel syndrome (CTS).

Where there is a single defendant, the last insurer on risk for the period of culpable exposure usually handles the claim unless the insurer with the greatest contribution (i.e. who has to pay the largest proportion of damages) would prefer to assume the role of handling insurer. Where there are multiple defendants, the handling insurer for the defendant with the greatest exposure (as between defendants) should become the coordinating insurer.

> Claims should be apportioned between insurers on a culpable time on risk basis. The onus is on any insurer to demonstrate a cut-off date of culpable exposure during their period of risk. If the handling insurer can demonstrate that there was no culpable exposure during their time on risk then the claim can be passed back to the relevant previous insurer. Where there is continuing culpable exposure then the cut-off date, for the purposes of apportionment between insurers, is usually taken as the date of the letter of claim to the last culpable defendant.

It may be possible to argue that for certain disease claims, such as industrial deafness, any period of culpable exposure of less than three months with a single employer, and also less than 5% of the total overall exposure, is *de minimis* and should be ignored for the purposes of apportionment.

Short-tail diseases have a close temporal association between the work activity (culpable exposure) and the onset of symptoms. Common examples are:

- Dermatitis
- Asthma
- Work-related upper limb disorders/repetitive stress injury (RSI)
- Stress
- RSI-induced CTS.

When handling short-tail claims the date of manifestation of symptoms should be the trigger. Where culpable exposure continues then an apportionment forward in time may be appropriate.

Unusual characteristics of a disease claim

Most EL and PL personal injury claims result from an accident that occurred on a specific date. Commonly, there are witnesses to the accident and there is usually little doubt that the claimant's injury was sustained in the index event.

Many occupational diseases are latent and arise long after the culpable exposure to a toxic or dangerous substance has ceased. Industrial diseases may be attributable to short, prolonged or intermittent exposure by one or several sources. By the time the claimant has developed the first symptoms of their disease there may be no independent witness evidence available to corroborate or controvert their alleged employment (in the case of an EL claim) or their culpable exposure by the defendant. In an asbestos-induced mesothelioma claim the disease may not manifest itself until 30 years or more after the claimant was first exposed to the toxic or dangerous agent (asbestos dust and fibres). By the time those first symptoms arise, the claimant may have a life expectancy of only a few months.

The issue of medical causation comes into play more frequently in a disease claim because the symptoms of some industrial diseases (e.g. impaired lung function) may be caused or contributed to by some other unrelated medical condition.

In a typical accident at work claim the defendant will usually (a) be aware that the accident occurred and (b) will know something of the circumstances. Also, the defendant will usually receive an intimation of any claim relatively soon after the incident occurred.

A defendant in a disease claim, however, has no specific incident on which they can focus. There will be no entry in the accident report book. The culpable exposure may have occurred many years ago at a time when the defendant company had different owners. The liabilities (realised or otherwise) as well as the assets of a defendant company may have passed to the current proprietors on the purchase of the company. Further, the new proprietors may never have used the toxic or dangerous substance that caused the claimant's disease during the period of their proprietorship, and yet they may still be liable because they may have acquired the company's liabilities as well as its assets.

When defending a disease claim the defendant often finds itself in the position of having to prove a negative. The claimant may claim that the defendant culpably exposed them to a toxic or dangerous substance during the course of their employment many years earlier. The defendant may not have old employment records. It is very unlikely to have kept records that show whether they were using the toxic or dangerous substances at the time of the claimant's alleged exposure. The defendant may not have kept records from which it may establish who its insurers were at the time of the alleged culpable exposure. The claimant may (in the absence of any documentary evidence) establish, simply by giving oral evidence, that the defendant once employed them.

There is little a defendant can do in the absence of contemporaneous records to contradict the claimant's evidence of employment. If the claimant appears to be a truthful witness and a reasonable historian, then their evidence is likely to be accepted by the court.

Defending a disease claim can feel akin to boxing with one arm tied behind one's back. Once a claim is intimated, a defendant has a lot of ground to make up. The claimant's solicitor will already have carried out their investigation and be eager to pursue their client's claim as quickly as possible.

In the case of a serious and life-threatening industrial disease the claimant's solicitor will be unable to grant a defendant much indulgence and it is not uncommon for such a case to be the subject of an order for a quick trial. Speedy directions in mesothelioma claims, where the life expectancy of the victim is very short, have resulted in trials only six weeks or so after the letters intimating those claims were written.

History of disease claims

Historically, disease claims have resulted from poor levels of industrial hygiene, ignorance and even exploitation.

Until the latter third of the 20th century, the attitude of employers and employees alike to health and safety in the workplace was at best indifferent and at worst reckless. Up until the 1960s it was not uncommon for machinery to be operated without guards or other safety features. Airborne dust of many types was common in the workplace and the provision of effective respirators and/or dust-extracting systems was inadequate or non-existent. Likewise, the provision of proper training and the enforcement of safe working practices did not feature in the workplace.

Legislation going back to the beginning of the last century imposed duties on owners and operators of factories to use all practicable steps to suppress and, where possible, to remove from working areas, "gases, vapours, dust, or other impurities ... that may be injurious to health" (s.1(1)(d) of the Factory and Workshop Act 1901).

As a result of the latent effect of many industrial diseases, and because of the law on limitation, most industrial disease claims were, until the 1960s, confined to claims under the Workmen's Compensation Acts of 1897 and 1925. These Acts enabled a victim of an injury resulting from a breach of the Factories Acts or any similar legislation (e.g. the Asbestos Industry Regulations 1931) to obtain compensation without having to prove negligence on the part of their employer. An employer was able to insure against Workmen's Compensation Act liability (although there was no obligation to do so).

Workmen's compensation was confined to lost earnings up to specific limits. There was no compensation for pain, suffering and loss of amenity. Although a victim of an industrial disease could bring a common law claim for damages against their employer prior to the 1960s, there were difficulties. Many manual workers were poorly educated and were unaware of their rights. Prior to the introduction of legal aid, many manual workers, particularly those who were not members of a trade union, neither had the means to sue their employers nor the comfort of the employment protection laws that exist today.

> Of all the difficulties that beset a claimant with an industrial disease, it was probably the law on limitation that caused the biggest problem. Under the Limitation Act 1939 a claimant in an action founded in tort could not bring an action after the expiration of six years from the date the cause of action accrued. The cause of action was deemed to have accrued once the damage had occurred. Therefore, in the case of a claimant suffering from asbestosis, they may have sustained a significant injury to their lungs more than six years before they were diagnosed as having the condition. In such a case, the 1939 Act would have prevented them from bringing a civil action.

Matters were subsequently made worse for claimants. Under the Limitation Act 1954 the limitation period in personal injury claims was reduced to three years from the date that damage occurred.

This obvious injustice was only temporary. Under the Limitation Act 1963 the primary three-year period for bringing a personal injury claim could be extended by the court, provided the claimant was able to show that certain material facts remained outside their knowledge (actual or constructive) until after the expiration of the primary three-year period.

It was the 1963 Act, coupled with the introduction of legal aid, that led to an increase in civil claims and a decline in workmen's compensation claims. The Limitation Acts 1975 and 1980 (particularly the latter with its discretionary provisions under s.33) have further assisted claimants in disease claims.

Types of industrial disease

It is not possible to deal with the many types of industrial disease in a single chapter. The following list of occupational diseases comprises a small but relevant selection.

Chest diseases

a) Pneumoconiosis

Pneumoconiosis is a generic term for a group of diseases that result in the fibrosing (scarring) of the lung tissue following the inhalation of harmful dusts. The most common of these diseases are:

- Asbestosis – from the inhalation of asbestos dust and fibres
- Silicosis – from the inhalation of silica (rock dust)
- Berylliosis – from the inhalation of beryllium
- Byssinosis – from the inhalation of cotton fibre or hemp dust
- Farmer's lung – from the inhalation of fungal spores from rotting hay or straw.

b) Allergic chest conditions

Allergic chest conditions include occupationally induced:

- Asthma – an allergic reaction to numerous substances found in the workplace, such as dust and fumes that cause symptoms such as wheezing, coughing and breathlessness.
- Hard metal disease – an allergic condition contracted by workers engaged in the manufacture of certain metals and, in particular, cobalt and tungsten carbide. Minor symptoms include asthma-like symptoms. The more serious cases can result in permanent pulmonary disease.
- Welder's lung – a generic term commonly used to describe respiratory conditions caused by exposure to the fumes given off in welding. Symptoms include breathlessness, chronic bronchitis, emphysema and lung inflammation with reduced lung function.

Skin conditions

These include:

- Dermatitis – inflammation of the skin caused by exposure to numerous substances, most commonly, cement, detergents, solvents, hairdressing materials and bitumen. Dermatitis can be either irritant contact dermatitis or allergic contact dermatitis. The former is by far the most common.
- Skin cancer – caused by exposure to radiation, certain mineral oils, tar, pitch and arsenic.

Industrial deafness/noise-induced hearing loss

Industrial deafness arises as a result of being exposed to excessive noise in the workplace. It is a cumulative condition, gradual and insidious in nature, and consequently classified as a long-tail disease.

A claimant in an industrial deafness claim must establish:

- They have sustained a hearing loss.
- The loss of hearing was caused by them being exposed to excessive noise in their workplace.
- The level of noise to which they were exposed constituted a breach of duty on the part of their employer.

Prior to the introduction of the Noise at Work Regulations 1989 on 1 January 1990 there was no statutory regulation that dealt expressly with noise in the workplace. Claimants had to either establish common law negligence or a breach of s.29(1) of the Factories Act 1961, which imposed a general duty on an employer to make and keep a workplace safe.

> The decision of the Supreme Court in *Baker v Quantum Clothing Group Ltd and others* [2011] (the final instalment of the Nottinghamshire and Derbyshire textile industry industrial deafness litigation) confirmed that s.29(1) did not add to the common law duties owed by an employer. Whether a workplace was safe involved a judgment that was objectively assessed by reference to the knowledge and standard of the time.

In 1963, the Ministry of Labour published "Noise and the Worker", which was adopted as the date of 'guilty' knowledge by which employers are judged for deafness claims (see *Thompson v Smiths Shiprepairers (North Shields) Ltd* [1983]).

In 1972, the Department of Employment published the "Code of Practice for Reducing the Exposure of Employed Persons to Noise". This provided that the upper level for daily exposure equivalent to eight hours' continuous sound (leq) was 90dB(A). This action level has been retrospectively applied to 1963. Employers should not, therefore, have exposed employees to noise levels in excess of 90dB(A) from 1 January 1963 to 31 December 1989, otherwise such exposure was a breach of the common law action level.

Attempts have been made by claimants to reduce the common law actionable noise threshold to 85dB(A) or lower. The Supreme Court ultimately clarified the issue in *Baker*, where the rationale, arising from the case of *Harris v BRB (Residuary) Ltd and another* [2005], of an employer having "greater than average knowledge" was considered.

Mrs Baker worked for Quantum as a machinist between 1971 and 2001. She was exposed to noise levels within the factory of between 85 and 90dB(A). The Supreme Court held that Quantum had "average knowledge" as to the risks of noise exposure below 90dB(A). A consultative document on the EC draft directive (which was later to become the Noise at Work Regulations 1989) was published in 1988. It was held that from this date in 1988 an "average employer" should have been aware of the risks of noise exposure below 90dB. The Supreme Court allowed a period of two years for Quantum to implement protective measures, meaning that an "average employer" had no common law liability for noise levels below 90dB(A) before 1 January 1990.

It is a question of fact for the court to determine the extent of an employer's knowledge as to the risks associated with hearing loss at exposure levels below 90dB(A) prior to the introduction of the 1989 Regulations. In the textile litigation, both Courtaulds and Pretty Polly were found to have had "greater than average knowledge" due to the size of the organisations and the involvement their occupational health departments had with the EC draft directive. It was found that by the beginning of 1983 these employers had an understanding of the risk that some workers would suffer damage from exposure to noise at levels below 90dB(A). Allowing a further two years for

Courtaulds and Pretty Polly to implement protective measures, they were potentially liable at common law from 1985 for exposure levels above 85dB(A).

The action level was reduced by the Noise at Work Regulations 1989. The Regulations introduced a first action level of 85dB(A), a level from which an employer was required to make hearing protection available on request, carry out and review noise assessments and also to provide instruction on the use of ear protection and on the dangers of excessive noise exposure. A second action level was created at 90dB(A) from which the provision of hearing protection became compulsory, the need to create ear protection zones arose, a system of health surveillance was to be introduced and technical measures were to be adopted to reduce noise exposure at source.

The downward trend in the action level continued when the Control of Noise at Work Regulations 2005 were introduced on 6 April 2006. Under the revised Regulations, the lower exposure action value was reduced to 80dB(A) and the upper exposure action value was reduced to 85dB(A). A new exposure limit value of 87dB(A) was created, taking into account the benefit of an employee wearing ear protection.

It is commonplace for an acoustic engineer to be instructed in deafness claims to determine the claimant's average noise exposure with a particular employer so as to ascertain whether the various action levels applicable at the time of employment were breached. The engineer will make this assessment based on any noise surveys provided by the employer, witness evidence or any experience they may have of a similar working environment. It does not have to be the case that a factory still needs to be in operation for the noise calculation to be completed.

> The medical expert instructed in a deafness claim is a consultant ear, nose and throat (ENT) surgeon (or *otorhinolaryngologist.*) There is no definitive test to prove that a claimant's hearing has been damaged by noise, let alone how much of the hearing loss is due to noise. The diagnosis by the medical expert is one of exclusion and probability.

Causation

Causation is often a complex issue in industrial deafness claims because it is not just noise damage that can cause hearing loss. The natural ageing process, known as presbycusis, leads to increasing levels of hearing loss. The characteristics of age-associated hearing loss are very similar to and often indistinguishable from noise-induced hearing loss. A medical expert will need to deduct from the overall hearing loss an element for age-associated loss appropriate for the claimant's sex and age. This is done by reference to various statistical age associated hearing-loss data such as the NPL Tables, ISO 1999 or ISO 7029 tables. Comparing a claimant's hearing loss with this data can reveal whether the loss is entirely attributable to age. If so, then the cause cannot be noise damage. The hearing threshold levels at 1kHz and 8kHz are taken from an audiogram and used as anchor points. From these anchors the statistical data is applied to assess the percentile (either 25th, 50th or 75th) comparable to a claimant's age and sex. These readings are applied across the remaining frequencies. The difference between the anchor points and the percentile values are calculated and the misfit is interpolated to provide for adjusted age-associated loss values at each frequency. Once deducted from the audiogram readings, any loss in excess of the adjusted age value is likely to be attributable to noise.

Hearing loss may also be due to other medical factors, including a head injury/whiplash, genetic damage, meningitis, tuberculosis, malaria, gout, use of ototoxic drugs, hypertension, alcohol, smoking, diabetes and ischaemic heart disease. It may also be due to social causes (known as socioacusis), such as shooting, motorcycling, use of lawnmowers, clubbing or even the use of iPods.

> The use of an audiogram is the gold standard test for diagnosing noise-induced hearing loss, but it is not conclusive. It is possible that the readings taken during audiometry can be manipulated by a claimant or be subject to user error on the part of the audiometrist. The audiogram should ideally plot a bilateral 4kHz notch because this is the classic pattern associated with noise damage.

A medical expert should take into consideration the Coles guidelines ("Guidelines on the diagnosis of noise-induced hearing loss for medicolegal purposes" – Coles, Lutman and Buffin (2000)) when either making or excluding a diagnosis of noise-induced hearing loss, because this criterion is the mostly commonly used. These guidelines have been added to by a further paper in 2015, principally from Professor Lutman, which addresses the quantification of noise-induced hearing loss in a medico-legal context which was absent from the earlier study. The new guidelines consider that the 1 and 8kHz frequencies overestimate age-associated loss (due to there being some noise damage at these anchor points) and recommend that a logarithmic modification is made to the anchor points to more accurately reflect the characteristics of the individual being tested. This revised calculation (known as Pass 2) effectively reduces the age-associated loss deduction from the total hearing loss which consequently is more likely to increase the noise component.

Under the guidelines a medical expert should also take into account the following factors for the purposes of diagnosis of noise-induced hearing loss:

- Requirement R1 is a sensorineural and high-frequency hearing loss; this is where the hearing threshold level (HTL) between 3 and 6kHz is at least 10dB greater than the HTL at 1 or 2kHZ.

- Requirement R2 is a credible history of potentially hazardous noise exposure. A claimant is required to prove exposure to a noise immission level (NIL) of at least 100dB(A) with the notch being 10dB deep. It is 'however' possible for a diagnosis to be made where the NIL is between 90 and 99dB(A) if the notch is 20dB deep.
- Requirement R3 is the presence of a high-frequency audiometric notch or bulge of at least 10dB, greater at 3 to 6kHz than at 1 or 2kHz and at 6 or 8kHz. The classic indication of noise-induced hearing loss is a 4kHz downward notch; however, with an older claimant the additional presence of age-associated hearing loss flattens this notch into a bulge, with the shape of the audiogram still compatible with a diagnosis of noise-induced hearing loss.
- The level of hearing impairment recorded should be consistent with the level of noise exposure.
- The onset of hearing loss should not be acute (because industrial deafness is gradual).
- The audiograms are symmetrical in pattern.
- There should be a conformity of the audiograms, i.e. that the pattern is replicated on the audiograms if they were taken at a similar time.
- The hearing loss should be bilateral.
- Looking at the clinical picture, there are no other competing causes to explain the hearing loss.

Even if a claimant is found to suffer from noise-induced hearing loss, an argument arises that they must establish an appreciable loss or disability to be entitled to compensation. This legal maxim of *'de minimis non curat lex'* was applied in *Hughes v Rhondda Cynon Taff County Council* [2012] and more recently in *Holloway v Tyne Thames Technology Ltd* [2015.] In Holloway it was held that a noise loss of 3dB was not an appreciable loss. In *Lomas v London Electric*

Wire Company [2015] the claimant was awarded compensation for tinnitus despite his noise-induced hearing loss being found *de minimis*.

A claimant may complain of tinnitus (a buzzing or ringing in the ears) related to the noise exposure. Tinnitus is a subjective condition and the severity of symptoms can be disproportionate to the amount of hearing loss. It is thought that there is a substantial element of psychological overlay associated with the condition. Although tinnitus is considered to be permanent once it has developed, it is possible to offer a claimant tinnitus retraining therapy as a coping mechanism for the condition.

It has become increasingly common for a claimant to seek the cost of hearing aids following a diagnosis of noise-induced hearing loss. A claimant needs to establish that the need for hearing aids is not due to age-associated loss alone or that the hearing disability is such that the need for aids is warranted.

It should be noted that a claimant does not qualify for industrial injury benefits until the total hearing loss exceeds 50dB. It may be that the noise damage has only accelerated the need for aids, in which case the claim is limited to a number of years and not for life. This issue needs to be addressed by the medical expert.

It is arguable that a claimant should obtain any hearing aids from the NHS free of charge, but this argument is difficult to sustain as aids on the open market are of better design and quality. In *Coffin and Tarrant v Ford Motor Company Ltd* [2008], it was held that the claimants were entitled to the reasonable costs of purchasing private hearing aids, assessed at £1,000 per set and £500 for 10 years of batteries.

Finally, if a claimant is able to establish both breach of duty and causation then it should be remembered that noise-induced hearing loss is a divisible condition. The liability of an employer is based only on the extent to which it negligently contributed to the injury.

Deducted from the claim for damages can be either any excessive exposure prior to the 1963 date of knowledge, i.e. non-negligent exposure, any negligent exposure by other employers (even if not named within the proceedings) or any excessive exposure arising from a claimant's hobbies, e.g. clay pigeon shooting. These deductions are apportioned upon a time on risk basis.

Vibration white finger/hand-arm vibration syndrome

Vibration white finger (VWF) occurs in some workers whose hands are regularly exposed to high vibration from the use of vibratory tools and machinery. There is no cure. Many months (even years) of exposure may be required, depending on the exposure levels and an individual's susceptibility, before symptoms first occur. Initial symptoms are tingling and numbness, which may result in a loss of dexterity. Episodic blanching is commonly precipitated by cold weather. There is no effective treatment.

In 1970, the Industrial Injuries Advisory Council produced an interim report on the subject of vibration syndrome. The report concluded that further research should be undertaken.

In 1974, a study by Taylor and others, "Vibration White Finger in Industry", was published.

In February 1975, the British Standards Institution (BSI) published a draft for development (DD 43) – "Guide to the evaluation of exposure of the human hand-arm system to vibration". The guide recommended maximum vibration levels beyond which vibration was considered to have an adverse effect on the hand/arm.

Since April 1986, VWF has been a reportable disease under Reporting of Injuries, Diseases and Dangerous Occurences Regulations 2013 (RIDDOR).

In October 1987, a British Standard BS 6842:1987 titled "Guide to measurement and evaluation of human exposure to vibration transmitted to the hand" was published. This set out recommended preventative measures where exposure to vibration regularly exceeded a certain level. It introduced a method for calculating daily exposure, giving rise to the A(8) formula (an eight hour energy-equivalent frequency-weighted acceleration).

In 1994, the Health and Safety Executive (HSE) published a guidance booklet, HSG 88, which provided a standard that was considered reasonable for a prudent employer to employ when considering the appropriate level of permissible exposure. The document gave rise to the action level of $2.8 m/s^2 A(8)$, which has been retrospectively applied to the date of 'guilty' knowledge. The guidance drew on research arising from BS 6842:1987, which indicated that there was evidence suggesting that exposure at $2.8 m/s^2$ may cause finger blanching in about 10% of the vibration-exposed population after eight years.

> As to the date of 'guilty' knowledge for a HAVS claim, it is very much dependent on the industry awareness of the risks posed when an employer requires excessive vibratory tool use by its employees. The risks would be more obvious to a firm of shipbuilders than a small local garage, and hence case law has shown differing dates to be applicable. *Brookes v South Yorkshire Passenger Transport Executive and another* [2005] found 1973 to be the date for the coal and rail industries, but 1987 for a medium-sized transport company.

HAVS is caused by excessive vibration exposure from the use of vibratory tools. Factors to consider when determining whether exposure was excessive include the vibration magnitude of the tool used, frequency of use, force exerted, posture, state of repair of the tool, clothing worn and the climatic conditions.

There is often a disparity between the claimant's estimate of vibratory tool usage time and the actual time when their fingers were operating the machinery, known as 'anger time'. An HSE research paper in 1991 assessed this overestimate between 50% and 75%.

An engineer can assess the level of vibration produced by each tool and calculate the likely total exposure to determine whether action levels were breached.

The preventative measures expected to be seen are the measurement of vibration levels emitted from tools, minimising exposure, maintenance of tools, job rotation, advice on the risks of exposure, training on the proper use of equipment and medical surveillance.

Although the common law action level is often taken as $2.8m/s^2A(8)$, the argument that breach of duty can only arise at this action level was rejected in *Doherty and others v Rugby Joinery (UK) Ltd* [2004]. The Court of Appeal held that it is only at vibration levels below $1m/s^2A(8)$ that exposure can be said to be safe in the absence of HAVS awareness training provided to a claimant by their employer. The rationale by the Court was that an employer who did nothing to address the risk of HAVS should not escape liability by default, but should be taking conscious action for the safety of its employees.

> Surprisingly, statutory regulation was only introduced on 6 July 2005 in the Control of Vibration at Work Regulations 2005. An exposure action value of $2.5m/s^2A(8)$ was introduced, the daily amount above which employers are required to take action to control exposure. In addition, an exposure limit value of $5m/s^2A(8)$ was created, the maximum amount of vibration to which an employee may be exposed on any single day. The Regulations require employers to assess the risk to health created by vibration in the workplace. If an employee is assessed as being at risk then an employer should take measures to eliminate or control exposure, provide health surveillance and provide information, instruction and training on the risks arising from the use of vibratory tools.

The excessive use of vibratory tools can give rise to three types of symptoms.

- Vascular injury or circulatory disturbance. VWF refers only to the blanching of the fingers known as Raynaud's phenomenon (which can also be a constitutional condition). The vascular condition causes symptoms of tingling, numbness and whiteness of the fingers. It is very rare that a claimant experiences blanching symptoms during a medical examination, so the medico-legal expert has to rely on the claimant's account of their symptoms. For a diagnosis of HAVS there should be a description of candle-white blanching around the entire circumference of the tips of the finger, with a clear demarcation. The description should be of blanching, redness (as the blood returns to the fingers) and then pain and tingling, in that order.
- Sensorineurological disturbances, causing tingling and numbness of the fingers and problems with dexterity.
- Musculoskeletal complaints. There is a significantly higher prevalence of upper limb pain and CTS reported in workers exposed to vibration, although the pathology is not fully understood and is subject to differing medical opinion. Vibration-induced CTS became a prescribed disease in 1992 on the basis that the use of vibratory tools doubled the risk of developing the condition.

Diagnosis

A HAVS diagnosis is a subjective assessment by the medical expert, a consultant vascular surgeon or a hand surgeon, who relies heavily upon the history of exposure and symptoms given to them by the claimant. In the absence of any other explanation of the cause of the symptoms a diagnosis is often made. Since 1986, both vascular and neurological symptoms are graded in severity on the Stockholm Workshop scale from stage 0 (no symptoms) to 4 (very severe symptoms.) It is very rare for a stage 4 diagnosis to be made.

The latency period for vascular symptoms between the last exposure to vibration and the development of symptoms is usually 12 to 18 months. There is no such timescale limitation for the sensorineural element of the condition.

Apportionment

HAVS claims are usually apportioned upon a time on risk basis between all negligent employers who have exposed a claimant to excessive vibration. In addition, deduction is made for any exposure prior to an employer's date of 'guilty' knowledge or any non-negligent exposure.

> There is a potential argument that the employer at the time symptoms developed should be fully liable. In *Smith v Wright & Beyer Ltd* [2001], the Court of Appeal held that in a total dosage situation, the fact that some of the exposure was before a supposed date of knowledge did not prevent the claimant recovering full compensation from the defendant for the total loss sustained. The rationale was if the defendant had not been in breach of duty then the critical dose might not have been reached to cause the claimant to suffer HAVS symptoms. It was the exposure with the last employer that overflowed "the reservoir of tolerance".

Work-related upper limb disorder

Work-related upper limb disorder (WRULD) is a generic term that describes pain, swelling and other discomfort occurring in the soft tissues of the fingers, hand, wrist, arm and shoulder. These symptoms are caused by prolonged repetitive work and are exacerbated by poor posture. The condition is commonly found in assembly line workers, supermarket cashiers and secretaries and other persons using computer equipment.

A successful claimant must establish that their employer ought reasonably to have foreseen the risk of injury from the activity the claimant was required to carry out. They must also establish that there were steps the employer could and should have taken to avoid the risk and that the employer failed to take adequate steps to do so.

In November 1972, the Department of Employment published a guidance note that dealt specifically with tenosynovitis, which was said to occur in certain industries as a result of repetitive activities.

In 1983, the HSE published a guide, "Visual Display Units", that made recommendations in relation to employees using computer keyboards and visual display units (VDUs). This guide was followed in 1986 by another HSE publication, "Working with VDUs".

In 1990, a further guidance note was published, "Work-related upper limb disorders: A guide to prevention". As its title suggests, this contained guidance on the measures to be adopted by employers to prevent their employees contracting upper limb disorders. These measures included carrying out risk assessments on work equipment, and postural changes and appropriate training.

In 1992, the HSE produced a further guidance booklet relating to the Health and Safety (Display Screen Equipment) Regulations 1992. This set out in unequivocal terms the risks associated with the use of VDUs.

> For a claimant to succeed in an action concerning an upper limb disorder they will need to establish that the injury was reasonably foreseeable; that their employers were in breach of duty by failing to take the appropriate measures to minimise the risk of injury; and that it was the employer's breach that caused the injury.

In *Fifield v Denton Hall Legal Services and others* [2006], a secretary with an upper limb disorder brought proceedings against her employers, alleging negligence and breaches of the Health and Safety (Display Screen Equipment) Regulations 1992. The claimant alleged that there was a causal link between a significant increase in her workload and the onset of symptoms. The defendant denied that the claimant's symptoms were work related and in the alternative contended that even if they were, they were not caused by any negligence or breach of duty on their part. The judge at first instance rejected the defendant's defence.

The Court of Appeal upheld the first instance decision. The Court of Appeal considered the evidence that established that the claimant's symptoms were work related to have been overwhelming. It also held that it was for the employer to intervene and alter work practices if changes were necessary. An employer could not rely on an employee who may not (in the absence of proper training) appreciate the importance of taking breaks and varying working routines.

Prescribed diseases and the obligation to report

Schedule 1 Part 1 to the Social Security (Industrial Injuries) (Prescribed Diseases) Regulations 1985, as amended, provides a comprehensive list of occupational diseases and medical conditions, the attributable occupations and the symptoms caused.

Likewise, the Reporting of Injuries, Diseases and Dangerous Occurrences Regulations 2013 provides a list of medical conditions contracted by employees that employers are required to report. The list specifies the type of medical condition and its cause.

Defending a disease claim

Previously, the first intimation a defendant received of a disease claim was a letter of claim from the claimant's solicitor containing minimal information and alleging negligence on the part of the defendant for exposure that may have been sustained many years, if not decades, earlier. It is fair to say that in disease claims a defendant is more likely to be 'on the back foot' in terms of defending claims than other areas of personal injury litigation. The defendant's cause has not been helped by the extension of the portal.

Pre-Action Protocol for Low Value Personal Injury Claims/the portal

From 31 July 2013, the portal was extended to include EL and PL claims valued between £1,000 and £25,000.

For a disease claim to qualify under the portal, no letter of claim will have been sent to the defendant prior to 31 July 2013. Although the extension of the portal does not affect higher value disease claims, the portal will encompass the majority of disease claims because most industrial deafness and HAVS claims attract awards below £25,000.

The portal, however, provides for circumstances of automatic exclusion from the new regime. Paragraph 4.3(6) of the Protocol specifically excludes a disease claim where there is more than one employer defendant. Paragraph 4.3(10) also excludes a claim for mesothelioma.

Claimants' solicitors with disease claims excluded from the portal are permitted to recover costs on an hourly rate basis as opposed to the fixed recoverable costs that apply to other types of low value injury claims that exit the portal.

The benefit to a defendant in keeping a disease claim within the portal is the fixed recoverable costs regime to which the claimant's solicitor is subject. However, the reality is it may be difficult for a defendant to comply with the tight portal timescales.

Under the portal, a defendant has 30 days in which to respond to a claims notification form (CNF) with a decision on liability. However, under the Data Protection Act 1998, it can take up to 40 days to obtain documents such as GP or occupational health records. In addition, in a disease claim it may often be problematic and prolonged to either trace a defendant's insurance history or investigate whether there are other potential defendants.

Main features of the Pre-Action Protocol for Disease and Illness Claims

If a claim is ejected or does not qualify for the portal then the claim should be subject to the Pre-Action Protocol for Disease and Illness Claims (PAP).

> The PAP applies to all personal injury claims where the injury complained of arises not from an accident or a single event but where it takes the form of an illness or disease. 'Disease' covers any illness, physical or psychological, any disorder, ailment, affliction, complaint, malady or derangement other than a physical or psychological injury solely caused by an accident or other single event. The PAP is not limited to diseases occurring in the workplace.

The aim of the PAP is to try to resolve claims without litigation or, where a claim cannot be resolved, to identify the relevant issues that remain in dispute.

Early communication between the parties is encouraged, as is the early and voluntary exchange of information and documents.

In an appropriate case, a potential claimant may request certain documents (e.g. occupational health records) before sending a formal letter of claim. Such records should, except in exceptional circumstances, be supplied by a defendant (without cost) within 40 days. If a defendant fails to comply then a claimant may seek an order for pre-action disclosure.

Once a claimant decides to make a claim, they must send the defendant a letter of claim in the prescribed form, plus a copy of the same. The letter should provide a chronology of relevant events (e.g. dates or periods of exposure) and an employment history, particularly when the claimant has been employed by a number of employers and the illness complained of has a long latency period. The letter of claim must identify relevant documents not already in the defendant's possession, e.g. GP records. In the case of claims under the Law Reform (Miscellaneous Provisions) Act 1934 or Fatal Accidents Act 1976, the relevant documents will include the death certificate, post-mortem report, inquest depositions and any grant of probate. The letter of claim should state whether a claim is being made against any other party.

A claimant should not normally commence proceedings until after three months from the date a defendant acknowledges the letter of claim.

Under the PAP, a defendant should acknowledge a letter of claim within 21 days (identifying their insurers), but if it fails to acknowledge the letter then the claimant is permitted to commence proceedings.

> A defendant's formal response to the claim should be written within three months of the date of the acknowledgment letter. The response should indicate whether liability is admitted wholly or in part. Where liability is not admitted the response should enclose copies of relevant documents on which the defendant's denial is based.
>
> Where it is not practicable for a defendant to complete its investigations into liability within three months, it should request an extension, stating the reasons why this is required. A claimant should agree to an extension where justifiable reasons have been provided.

Under the PAP, a claimant must serve a schedule of loss together with supporting documents as soon as practicable. It also encourages the joint instruction of experts, but recognises the need for flexibility, as in many cases it will be necessary for a claimant to commission a medical report before writing a letter of claim. In such cases, a defendant will be entitled to instruct its own medical expert.

In a matter where the joint instruction of an expert is considered appropriate, the party proposing joint instruction should provide the other party with a list of one or more experts in the required discipline. Within 14 days the other party should indicate its acceptance or otherwise of the invitation to participate in a joint instruction of one of the experts proposed. If a claimant proposes joint instruction of an expert in the letter of claim, then the 14-day period is treated as being in addition to the 21 days for acknowledging the letter of claim.

If the party who is invited to agree to the joint instruction of an expert expressly objects to the proposed joint instruction, then the parties will be entitled to instruct experts of their own choice. If the party who is being invited to agree a joint instruction does not expressly object to one of the suggested experts, then they will not be entitled to rely on their own expert evidence without either the other party's agreement or the court's permission. Either party may send written questions to an agreed joint expert.

> Where a defendant admits liability, in whole or in part, before a medical report is obtained under the PAP, the report should be disclosed once it becomes available. Likewise, where a defendant admits liability, in whole or in part, before proceedings are issued, they should disclose any medical report they have obtained under the PAP and on which they intend to rely.

The parties are encouraged to disclose experts' reports relative to liability and causation before proceedings are issued. Indeed, claimants are encouraged to delay issuing proceedings for 21 days from disclosure of such reports.

Under paragraph 2.5 of the PAP, a claimant may commence proceedings without complying with the PAP if (a) by complying, their claim would become time barred under any provision in the Limitation Act 1980, or (b) the claimant has a terminal illness and their life expectancy is short.

If court proceedings are issued without complying with the terms of the PAP, then the claimant faces potential adverse costs consequences, even if the claim is successful. The defendant should bring the circumstances of the claimant's breach to the attention of the judge, who is able to exercise their discretion to make such a costs order as they deem appropriate.

Limitation

For an overview of issues relating to limitation, see the '*History of disease claims*' earlier in this chapter.

In a disease claim it can be difficult to establish with precision when the damage occurred. Time does not begin to run against a claimant until a significant injury actually occurs and the claimant attributes this to his employment. It is favourable to a defendant that the claimant's knowledge in this regard is assessed by the court objectively.

One of the leading authorities on limitation is the Court of Appeal decision in *Johnson v Ministry of Defence and Hobourn Eaton Ltd* [2012], where Kennedys represented the first defendant. The claimant worked at Chatham Dockyard for the Ministry of Defence (MoD) from 1965 to 1970 and from 1974 to 1979. He was exposed to loud noise and the MoD admitted breach of duty. The claimant alleged that he noticed hearing loss symptoms in 2001 but it was not until he approached a claims company in 2007 that he thought about making a claim. He was examined by an ENT surgeon in 2009 and diagnosed with industrial deafness and, therefore, argued for a date of knowledge from that date.

continued...

...continued

The Court of Appeal said that an objective approach was required to assess the claimant's date of knowledge. The test was what a person with the essential characteristics of the claimant, such as their age and mental capacity, would do if acting reasonably. There would be an assumption that a person who had suffered a significant injury would be sufficiently curious to seek medical advice. In the claimant's case, a reasonable person would have consulted their GP by 2002, allowing a year's 'thinking time' between when they realised that they had a significant condition and the date on which they ought reasonably to have taken expert advice. It followed that by the end of 2002 the claimant had knowledge that his deafness might be attributable to his exposure to noise while in the employment of the defendant. Primary limitation therefore expired by the end of 2005 and the claim was dismissed.

A claim under the Law Reform (Miscellaneous Provisions Act) 1934, on the part of the disease victim's estate, will be statute barred if at the date of the deceased's death they could not for reasons of limitation have maintained a claim in their own right. If, however, a disease victim dies before the period for them bringing a claim expires, then their cause of action will survive and their estate may bring a claim in respect of the deceased's injuries within three years of (a) the deceased's death or (b) the date of the personal representatives' knowledge (whichever is later).

Under s.12 of the Limitation Act 1980, a claim for dependency under the Fatal Accidents Act 1976 may be brought within three years from (a) the date of death or (b) the date of knowledge of the person for whose benefit the action is brought (whichever is later). If an action under the Fatal Accidents Act 1976 is statute barred by reason of the expiry of the three-year period, then the dependants may seek the court's discretion under s.33 of the 1980 Act.

Investigating a claim

The first notification of a claim a defendant is likely to receive is a letter of claim or CNF. The notification letter may relate to a current or ex-employee of the defendant or to a person who has never been employed by the defendant but whose disease is allegedly attributable to the negligent acts and omissions of the defendant which occurred many years ago.

Because companies can have similar names (particularly companies within the same group) and companies can cease to exist by reason of liquidation or acquisition, it is important to establish whether or not the letter of claim is addressed (a) to the correct company and (b) to one that remains in existence. This can be established by a Companies House search (https://beta.companieshouse.gov.uk). It is also important to establish whether there was any valid liability insurance cover in place at the time of the negligent acts or omissions complained of. A search can be made with the ELTO (Employers Liability Tracing Office).

Hopefully, the letter of claim or CNF will contain specific allegations of exposure, including the exact location where the exposure is alleged to have occurred, the nature of the alleged exposure and the period involved. If this information is not provided, then the defendant should request it. In an EL claim, the claimant should be asked to provide some evidence of their employment by the defendant, such as a letter of appointment, redundancy notice or payslips.

A defendant may or may not have employment records dating back to the time of the alleged exposure. This should be checked. Whether or not the defendant's old employment records survive, the claimant should be asked to obtain and disclose an HM Revenue and Customs schedule of employment. Such a schedule will identify all of the claimant's employers, beginning with tax year 1961/1962, to date. It will not, however, provide confirmation of the exact dates upon which any employment began or ceased.

If no employment records survive, the defendant should consider asking the claimant to identify their immediate superior and any other work colleagues during the period of their alleged employment. If the claimant is able to identify former colleagues and if those former work colleagues can be identified in the defendant's old employment records, then this will be fairly persuasive evidence that the claimant's alleged employment is genuine.

> Besides seeking to verify the claimant's alleged employment, the defendant also needs to establish whether the culpable exposure alleged against it was the claimant's only material exposure, or whether there was culpable exposure elsewhere. Therefore, the defendant should press the claimant for a comprehensive employment history going back to the date they left school, particularly in those cases where the claimant entered the labour market before tax year 1961/1962. The HM Revenue and Customs schedule of employment may provide an insight into whether the claimant is likely to have had culpable exposure elsewhere.

With a view to expediting the defendant's investigations and decision on liability, the claimant should be invited to make early disclosure of witness statements on a without prejudice basis.

Once a full employment history is available, this should enable a defendant to determine whether there is some other potential source of culpable exposure from which an indemnity, contribution or 'Holtby' discount may be sought (see page 191), or whether it alone must bear the full burden of any damages and costs the claimant may ultimately be awarded.

Each disease claim needs to be considered on its own merits. However, it may be that the defendant has a previous claims history in relation to the disease about which a claimant complains. Insurers may have settled similar claims on behalf of the defendant. For example, in a claim against an asbestos manufacturing company that has faced numerous other similar claims, it may be unnecessary to carry out extensive enquiries to determine whether or not the company used asbestos during the relevant period or whether conditions inside their factory premises were such that it was negligent or in breach of its statutory duty. In such a case the defendant will simply wish to:

- Verify the claimant's alleged employment.
- Determine whether there is another employer from whom a contribution may be sought.
- Consider whether the symptoms the claimant exhibits are attributable wholly or in part to the industrial disease complained of or to some other non-related medical condition.

Where a defendant is facing a disease claim for the first time, it will be necessary to ascertain whether the defendant used the toxic or dangerous substance complained of during the period of the claimant's employment. If they did, it will be necessary to determine:

- Whether the defendant knew or ought reasonably to have known of the toxicity or dangers associated with that substance.
- If so, what precautionary steps were taken to avoid or reduce exposure.
- Whether, in the light of such knowledge, they took all reasonable steps to protect the claimant from harm.

In *Margereson and Hancock v J W Roberts Ltd* [1996], the defendant maintained a 'knowledge' defence. These claims concerned two individuals who, as children, had lived and played in close proximity to an asbestos factory and who many years later contracted mesothelioma. It was asserted by the defendant that no one within the industrialised world was likely to have known during the period 1925 to 1965 that residents living in close proximity to an asbestos factory were at risk of injury. In rejecting the defence, the Court of Appeal held that conditions on a loading bay immediately outside the factory, and where children (including the claimants) played, effectively replicated the appalling conditions inside the factory.

However, in a similar case, *Pinder v Cape Plc* [2006], the defendant's 'knowledge' defence succeeded. During the 1950s, Mr Pinder played as a child on a local rubbish tip where the defendant disposed of their asbestos waste. The tip was some five miles from the defendant's factory. It was alleged that the defendant was under an obligation to dispose of the waste asbestos safely and that it had a duty to ensure that it did not replicate the risk of exposure to which its employees were exposed. Despite finding that the claimant's material exposure resulted from playing on the waste tip, the High Court held that it would not have been until a decade later that there was a foreseeable risk of injury from low and intermittent exposure to asbestos. Further, there was no evidence that the defendant knew that children played on the waste tip.

There are two other cases where a 'knowledge' defence has succeeded. In *Gunn v Wallsend Slipway and Engineering Company Ltd* [1988], Mrs Gunn had, between 1948 and early 1965, laundered her husband's work clothes that were contaminated by asbestos dust and fibres. Before laundering them by hand, it was her practice to shake the clothing in the back yard. In doing so, she inhaled asbestos dust and fibres. Towards the end of 1984, Mrs Gunn became ill. About two months before her death she was diagnosed as having a malignant mesothelioma. Numerous medical and scientific papers were analysed in an attempt to establish the extent of the knowledge a prudent employer should have had of the hazards of asbestos exposure during the period of Mrs Gunn's exposure. Mr Justice Waterhouse found, on the evidence before him, that no one in the industrial world had, before the publication of a paper by Newhouse and Thompson in October 1965, directed their mind to the risk of physical injury from domestic exposure to asbestos dust and, in particular, to the risk of injury to anyone coming into contact with asbestos dust on work clothes. Accordingly, judgment was entered for the defendant.

> In 2004, the very similar case of *Maguire v Harland & Wolff plc* [2004] fell to be determined by Mr Justice Morland. Mrs Maguire had laundered her husband's work clothes that had been contaminated by asbestos dust and fibres. The defendant denied that it owed Mrs Maguire any duty of care because it was unforeseeable that she was at risk, having regard to the nature of her exposure and the state of knowledge at the time. Morland J refused to follow Waterhouse J in the *Gunn* case. Instead, he held that the defendant had not needed prophetic vision to foresee that the wives of its workers were exposed to substantial quantities of asbestos dust on their husbands' work clothes and that the attendant risks of serious injury to health were well known at the time of Mr Maguire's exposure. Further, he considered the risk to Mrs Maguire's health was not only foreseeable but also obvious. The defendant appealed. In 2005, by a majority of two to one, the Court of Appeal held that on the basis of the contemporary literature available to an employer on the potential risk to spouses of employees, the date of knowledge was late 1965. Because Mrs Maguire's exposure had ceased by April 1965, her claim failed.

It would appear from the *Maguire* case that the imputed date of knowledge in 'household' or secondary exposure claims is considered to be much later than in the case of claims concerning direct exposure.

Breach of duty

So when will a defendant be found to be culpable and therefore liable to a claimant in a disease claim? In terms of negligence, the same essential components apply to a disease case as apply to any other injury claim and the claimant must establish:

- The defendant owed them a duty to take care
- The defendant breached that duty
- Damage resulted that was causally connected to the breach.

In an EL disease claim, the defendant employer will be considered to have been under a non-delegable common law and statutory duty not to expose their employee to the risk of harm during the course of their employment. Therefore, if an employee was deployed to carry out work at an asbestos manufacturing factory where they were subjected to airborne asbestos dust and fibres without adequate respiratory protection, their employer is likely to be found to have been in breach of their duty.

The employer may have a right of an indemnity or contribution against the asbestos manufacturer but that will not affect their primary liability to their employee. If the employee pursued a claim against the asbestos manufacturer, then to succeed, they would have to establish that the asbestos manufacturer owed them a duty of care and that it committed a breach of that duty. It is, therefore, easier for a claimant to pursue a claim against their employer than against some other party because the duty on an employer is an onerous one.

> It should be borne in mind that the burden of proving a breach of duty still rests with the claimant. In *Brett v University of Reading* [2007], a claim arising out of the deceased's contraction of mesothelioma was brought against Reading University. The Court of Appeal emphasised the necessity for the claimant to establish that the defendant had failed to take all necessary precautions to ensure that it had not exposed the deceased to respirable asbestos fibres. It did not fall to the defendant to establish that all precautions had been taken.

In determining whether an employer was in breach of its common law duty in a disease claim, a claimant may rely on published literature that highlights the risk associated with the toxic/dangerous substance or activity complained of and of which the employer was or ought reasonably to have been aware. Such literature may consist of medical or other scientific papers or HSE publications and circulars. A claimant may also establish liability on the part of the defendant by demonstrating that the defendant was in breach of a statutory duty.

It is impossible to identify and discuss in a single chapter all the statutory regulations a defendant can fall foul of in relation to a disease claim. However, the following are some examples.

Asbestos-attributable disease claims

- Asbestos Industry Regulations 1931
- Factories Acts 1937, 1948 and 1961
- Building (Safety, Health and Welfare) Regulations 1948
- Construction (Working Places) Regulations 1966
- Asbestos Regulations 1969
- Asbestos (Licensing) Regulations 1983
- Asbestos Products (Safety) Regulations 1985
- Asbestos (Prohibitions) Regulations 1992
- Control of Asbestos at Work Regulations 1987 and 2002
- Control of Asbestos Regulations 2002 and 2012

Silicosis

- Grinding of Metals (Miscellaneous Industries) Regulations 1925
- Factories Act 1961
- Control of Substances Hazardous to Health Regulations 1999, 2002 and 2004

Industrial deafness

- Factories Act 1961
- Noise at Work Regulations 1989
- Control of Noise at Work Regulations 2005

VWF

- Factories Act 1961
- Employer's Liability (Defective Equipment) Act 1969
- Personal Protective Equipment at Work Regulations 1992
- Manual Handling Operations Regulations 1992
- Provision and Use of Work Equipment Regulations 1998
- Control of Vibration at Work Regulations 2005

Occupational dermatitis

- Factories Act 1961
- Offices, Shops and Railway Premises Act 1963
- Employer's Liability (Defective Equipment) Act 1969
- Personal Protective Equipment at Work Regulations 1992
- Workplace (Health, Safety and Welfare) Regulations 1992
- Control of Substances Hazardous to Health Regulations 1999, 2002 and 2004

WRULD

- Manual Handling Operations Regulations 1992
- Workplace (Health, Safety and Welfare) Regulations 1992
- Provision and Use of Work Equipment Regulations 1998
- Management of Health and Safety at Work Regulations 1999

Section 69 of the Enterprise and Regulatory Reform Act 2013 has removed the right of civil action against employers for breach of Regulations that do not specifically provide for such action where the breach occurred on or after 1 October 2013.

Causation

As well as establishing that the defendant owed them a duty of care and that the defendant breached that duty, a claimant must also establish that any injury and loss they suffered was caused by that breach.

> Generally speaking, where a claimant succeeds in establishing that a defendant owed them a duty of care that was breached, and where they have adduced medical evidence attributing the occupational disease complained of to that breach of duty, the claim will succeed.

However, the issue of causation in a mesothelioma case required careful analysis by the House of Lords in the case of *Fairchild v Glenhaven Funeral Services Ltd and others* [2002].

The brief facts of this case were that the deceased was employed at different times by two employers who negligently exposed him to asbestos dust and fibres during the course of his employment. As a result, he contracted malignant mesothelioma, an invariably fatal asbestos-induced cancer of the pleura (lining of the lung) or peritoneum. Mesothelioma is a latent condition and, frequently, first symptoms of the disease do not appear until 30 years or more after first exposure. Unlike some asbestos-attributable conditions, mesothelioma can result from relatively light exposure to asbestos fibres, although the greater the exposure the greater is the risk of contracting the disease. The medical experts were unable to say with any certainty whether the claimant's mesothelioma was attributable to his exposure by either or both defendants. As a result, the claimant's claim failed at first instance because he was unable to establish who his employer was at the date he ingested the fibres that actually led to the mutation of his fatal illness. The first instance decision was upheld in the Court of Appeal.

On appeal, the House of Lords was concerned by the obvious injustice the conventional approach to the issue of causation had caused the claimant. There was no doubt that both defendants had negligently exposed the claimant to asbestos dust and fibres; and, further, that negligent exposure had, on a balance of probabilities, led to the claimant ingesting the fibres that caused the mutation of a cancerous cell within the claimant's pleural cavity. Justice and common sense led the court to conclude that the claimant's inability to prove which of the defendants had exposed him to the offending fibre should not defeat his otherwise worthy claim. It was, therefore, held that if a breach of duty contributed substantially to the increased risk of the claimant contracting a disease, then there was a causal connection between the breach of duty complained of and the injury sustained.

For a claimant to succeed it need only be established that the exposure to asbestos materially contributed to the risk of the disease developing.

Fairchild was not the end of the story because it remained unclear whether a defendant's liability in a mesothelioma case was joint and several or whether there were limits to the extent of a defendant's liability.

On 13 May 2006, the House of Lords handed down its judgment in the mesothelioma case of *Barker v Corus (UK) plc* [2006]. The issues the House of Lords had to resolve were:

- What were the limits of the exception to causation under *Fairchild*?
- The extent of a defendant's liability in the light of *Fairchild*.

Unlike Mr Fairchild, who was the innocent victim of someone else's negligent acts and omissions, Mr Barker had himself been negligent by exposing himself to asbestos dust and fibres during a seven-year period when he worked as a self-employed plasterer. The defendant had culpably exposed Mr Barker for about six months and it was its contention that the *Fairchild* exception should not apply in a case where the claimant had himself also been guilty of negligence. It went on to argue that the law relating to causation had been modified in *Fairchild* on public policy grounds to prevent the culpable defendants from avoiding liability simply because a claimant could not establish which asbestos fibres, of more than one source of culpable exposure, triggered his illness. It would push the bounds of tortious liability too far to extend the *Fairchild* exception to a claimant who had negligently and significantly exposed himself to asbestos. The defendant also contended that in the event of it being found liable, then its liability should be apportioned to reflect the period that Mr Barker had been culpably exposed elsewhere.

In the Court of Appeal the first instance decision of Mr Justice Moses was upheld. Moses J had held that the defendant's liability was joint and several and that the deceased's status as an innocent victim in *Fairchild* was not a prerequisite for establishing causation. He also found that there was no good reason for finding that Mr Barker's negligence should deprive his widow of all compensation. Justice could be met by reducing damages under the Law Reform (Contributory Negligence) Act 1945. He reduced the damages payable by 20%.

In the House of Lords it was held that the *Fairchild* exception applied even though not all periods of exposure were tortious. The source of the deceased's other exposure was irrelevant, even if it resulted from his own negligence. However, in relation to apportionment, the House of Lords sought to balance any injustice caused to the defendant by its earlier decision in *Fairchild* by finding that a defendant was only liable to pay a mesothelioma victim damages to the extent that its breach of duty had contributed to the risk of the claimant contracting the disease.

> The defendant's success in *Barker* was short lived because the protestations of claimant lawyers, trade unions and certain politicians led to the government tagging on to the Compensation Bill (which was passing through parliament at the same time) a new clause designed to negate the House of Lords' decision.
>
> Section 3 of the Compensation Act 2006 now provides that each negligent employer who has contributed towards a mesothelioma victim's illness shall have joint and several liability and, therefore, shall be liable for all the damage caused to that person. This statutory provision will not affect the right of a defendant to seek contribution from a joint tortfeasor. However, in the event of them being a defunct and uninsured joint tortfeasor, the surviving defendant will be liable to pay the claimant all their damages and costs. A defendant is, though, permitted to seek a reduction of their liability to reflect the claimant's contributory negligence under s.3(3)(b).

As can be seen from the government's intervention following the House of Lords' decision in *Barker*, the law in the field of mesothelioma claims is subject to political interference. Mesothelioma is a terrible disease, resulting in a painful and distressing death. In a desire to see victims fully compensated, the normal laws on causation have been tweaked.

The Court of Appeal considered whether the *Fairchild* principle should apply to lung cancer cases in *Heneghan v Manchester Dry Docks Ltd* [2016]. Mr Heneghan died from lung cancer in 2013. He had been exposed to asbestos by multiple employers. The total exposure dose was assessed at 133 fibre/ml years. Under the Helsinki criteria a cumulative exposure of 25 fibre/ml years is sufficient to infer that lung cancer is attributable to asbestos. Proceedings were issued against six defendants. Their combined exposure was 46.9 fibre/ml years or 35.2% of the total dose. The individual doses for each defendant ranged from 2.5% to 10.1%. Biological evidence could not establish which, if any, of the exposures triggered the cancer; however, epidemiological evidence could establish each defendant had increased the risk of contracting the disease. The defendants admitted breach of duty. The claimant argued that each defendant was liable in full on the basis that each had materially contributed to the cancer.

The Court of Appeal held that a two-stage approach to causation should be taken. Firstly, to ask what had caused the lung cancer? Was it asbestos, smoking or something else? This question was answered by the doubling of risk test. In *Heneghan* this was satisfied as the asbestos exposure with the defendants was five times in excess of the Helsinki criteria. The second question was who caused the lung cancer (in cases of multiple tortfeasors)? The court accepted that due to the state of medical science, in cases like mesothelioma it was not possible to identify which exposure caused the disease to develop. It could not be proven that any individual defendant had doubled the risk and under the normal rules of causation the claim would have failed.

Accordingly it was appropriate to apply the *Fairchild* exception and to apportion liability on the basis that each defendant had materially increased the risk of the claimant contracting the disease. Section 3 of the Compensation Act 2006, however, only applies to mesothelioma claims and therefore lung cancer is treated as an indivisible disease with divisible damages. The claimant therefore received damages of £61,600 (which was 35.2% of the £175,000 awarded.) The Court of Appeal was not prepared to address the issue of an employer who was responsible for 51% of a claimant's total asbestos exposure and whether such a defendant was fully liable on the balance of probabilities test or whether a 51% contribution to risk was the appropriate apportionment.

Other culpable exposure

A claimant may intimate a claim against one or all of the entities that have culpably exposed them to the toxic or dangerous substance complained of.

> If a claimant intimates a claim against all the entities concerned, then it will be important to establish the identity of those other entities and their insurers. It may be that one or more of the other defendants were insured by more than one insurer during the period of the alleged exposure. It is, therefore, important to establish which insurers are involved for each defendant and the period that each insurer was on cover.

Having established the insurance position, the next step is to ascertain what each defendant's attitude is to the claim. Assuming none of the defendants is able to assert a positive defence, then it should be ascertained whether each defendant/insurer is prepared to make a voluntary contribution towards the burden of the claimant's claim and costs. If a defendant cannot identify their insurers or if that defendant is no longer in existence, it may be possible to ascertain which insurers were on cover for that particular defendant during the requisite period by carrying out a search with the Employers' Liability Tracing Office.

Once all interested insurers have been identified, it is usual for the defendant with the largest potential interest, in terms of a time on risk basis, to coordinate the defence and produce a provisional contribution schedule, identifying each defendant and the period of culpable exposure attributed to them. It will then be possible to express the apportionment in percentage terms, showing the percentage contribution each defendant should be making.

> In a case where one or more of the defendants were uninsured during any period during which they are alleged to have culpably exposed the claimant, those defendants will be personally liable to contribute in respect of the uninsured period.

Where a defendant is no longer in existence and no valid liability insurance can be traced, the remaining defendants will, unless a *Holtby* situation exists (see below), agree to absorb the burden of the defunct defendant's liability on the basis of their agreed contributions.

Where a claim is intimated against more than one defendant and one of those defendants refuses to contribute voluntarily towards the claim and costs, then the remaining defendant or defendants may seek to protect their position by making a joint Civil Procedure Rules (CPR) Part 36 offer of contribution to the claimant and, if necessary, bring Part 20 proceedings against that defendant.

For a disease that is an indivisible condition, such as mesothelioma, a claimant may decide not to intimate a claim against all culpable parties but instead choose to pursue a claim against only one defendant. There is no reason why that defendant should not seek a voluntary contribution from another culpable employer on the basis that if it agrees to do so, it will not be necessary to begin Part 20 proceedings against it. However, if the disease is a divisible condition, such as industrial deafness, then it is open for a defendant to settle or make a Part 36 offer for just its share of the claimant's damages and costs.

Extent of a defendant's liability

Where a claimant sustained injury by reason of their negligent exposure to a toxic or dangerous substance by two or more former employers, is one of those former employers liable for the entirety of the claimant's loss and damage, or is its liability limited to that part of the loss and damage it actually caused? This is a question that was determined by the House of Lords in *Fairchild* (see above).

In the earlier case of *Holtby v Brigham & Cowan (Hull) Ltd* [2000], which was determined by the Court of Appeal, the claimant had contracted asbestosis as a result of his negligent exposure to asbestos by the defendant and by other former employers who were not implicated in the action. At first instance, the trial judge heard medical evidence to the effect that the degree of exposure to asbestos dust determines the extent to which a person will contract and suffer from asbestosis. Cumulative exposure causes and aggravates the condition. The trial judge went on to find that the defendant was only liable for the damage that it had caused. Because it was impossible to make a mathematical apportionment based purely on the available medical evidence, it was held that the amount of damages the claimant should recover from the defendant should be discounted by 25%.

The claimant appealed to the Court of Appeal. The appeal was dismissed. Because asbestosis was a divisible condition (i.e. one that was made worse by further exposures) it was held that the defendant was only liable to the extent of the disability it had caused and that the Court should do the best it could to achieve justice between the parties. Had the claimant suffered mesothelioma (an indivisible condition), then he would have succeeded in full against the defendant.

The term Holtby discount is therefore applied where a claimant has worked for multiple tortious employers but has not claimed against them all. The employer who has been pursued can therefore offer apportioned damages, deducting the claimant's periods of exposure with the other tortfeasors (however, costs are only apportioned between those employers pursued).

It can be seen that it is important to draw a distinction between divisible and indivisible conditions. If the extent of a claimant's injury can be attributed to the acts and omissions of a particular defendant, that defendant's liability should be limited to the extent of the damage they caused. Therefore, in an asbestosis claim or an industrial deafness claim where the condition is divisible, and may be attributed to exposure by different employers, each employer's liability should be limited to the amount of damage they actually caused.

But what is the extent of a defendant's liability in a disease claim where the claimant has, by reason of their own acts and omissions, contributed towards the contraction of the disease?

Mr Justice Stanley Burton considered this issue in *Badger v Ministry of Defence* [2005]. The deceased was employed by the MoD as a boilermaker between 1954 and 1987. During the course of his employment he was exposed to asbestos, and died of lung cancer at the age of 63. Primary liability was admitted. It was further admitted that the deceased's exposure to asbestos had made a material contribution to the risk of him contracting lung cancer. It was, however, contended by the defendant that the deceased's smoking had also made a material contribution to the deceased's contraction of lung cancer and that damages should be reduced to reflect his contributory negligence.

continued...

...continued

In his judgment, Stanley Burton J referred to s.1(1) of the Law Reform (Contributory Negligence) Act 1945, which provides that where a person sustains damage in part because of their own fault, the damages recoverable will be reduced to reflect the share of their own culpability. The judge went on to find that since health warnings first appeared on cigarette packets in 1971, by the mid 1970s it was reasonably foreseeable by a reasonably prudent man that if he continued to smoke he was putting his health in jeopardy. Accordingly, the deceased's continued smoking of 20 cigarettes per day after 1975 constituted contributory negligence on his part and the damages payable should be reduced by 20%.

Medical causation

In addition to considering the issues of liability and contribution, it will be necessary for the claims handler to consider the issue of medical causation.

Whereas in a tripping accident there can be little doubt that the victim's broken wrist can be directly attributable to the accident itself, in a disease claim, closer analysis of the claimant's symptoms and medical history will be necessary. For example:

- Is the claimant's deafness attributable to them having worked for the defendant in a noisy workshop, or is it in fact attributable in whole or in part to them being a member of a heavy rock band?
- Is the claimant's breathlessness attributable to them having been exposed to airborne dust or fumes while in the defendant's employment or do they in fact suffer from an unrelated pulmonary or cardiac condition?

For a claimant to recover damages in a disease claim, they must not only establish that the defendant was negligent or in breach of its statutory duty, but must also establish that the medical symptoms of which they complain are directly attributable, in whole or in part, to each breach of duty complained of. To the extent that the symptoms complained of do not relate to the disease, the claimant's damages should be reduced or extinguished to reflect other unrelated causes.

Medical and other records

The defendant needs to call for early disclosure of all general practitioner (GP) and hospital records. When requesting the hospital records the defendant should emphasise that they wish to see not only the claimant's hospital records attributable to the disease complained of, but all hospital records. Also, the defendant should ask to see copies of all pathology and histology reports.

Check with the defendant whether it is in possession of the claimant's occupational health and personnel records and, if it is, obtain the claimant's signed authority for their disclosure.

If the claimant is no longer in the defendant's employment but is now employed by someone else, it might prove useful to see copies of any occupational health records kept by that employer or indeed any prior employer.

Where the victim of the industrial disease has died, the defendant should call for copies of the inquest depositions (including the post-mortem report) and any histology reports relative to the post-mortem. It may also be necessary to obtain the defendant's GP and hospital records to investigate any comorbid conditions because these are relevant to life expectancy and future loss claims.

Where the claimant is in receipt of state benefits that are attributable to the disease complained of, the defendant should request a copy of the claimant's application for benefits and any correspondence with the medical boarding centre (MBC) as well as the MBC's diagnosis and all assessments. These frequently contain useful information that is relevant to the issue of limitation. They also frequently contain information about the nature and extent of culpable exposure by other employers.

All these records should inform a defendant about when the claimant first began to suffer the symptoms they attribute to their alleged occupationally induced condition and when that condition was first diagnosed. Such information is essential to a defendant in determining whether the claim is being made within the limitation period. The medical records should also reveal whether the claimant has some other medical condition that may be the cause (in whole or in part) of the symptoms complained of.

> In some cases it is particularly important to establish when the claimant's first symptoms occurred. For example, in a mesothelioma case any exposure to asbestos dust less than 10 years prior to the development of symptoms can be disregarded as causative of the condition.

It also helps to know something about the clinical presentation of the industrial disease the claimant is alleged to have contracted. For example, asbestosis is the fibrosing or scarring of the lungs caused by the inhalation of asbestos dust and fibres. The lungs' capacity to expand is restricted and, thus, the victim becomes breathless. The condition is progressive, incurable and can be fatal. To contract asbestosis the claimant will have had to have very substantial exposure, usually over a long period. Therefore, if the claimant's alleged exposure was minimal and over a short period, a defendant should be dubious of any assertion that they have asbestosis. Further, asbestosis is a slow, progressive and insidious disease. If a claimant has gone from being reasonably well to having severe and disabling fibrosis of their lungs within a short period of time, a defendant should again be dubious of a diagnosis of asbestosis. In such a case, any fibrosing of the lungs is likely to be idiopathic fibrosis (formally known as cryptogenic fibrosing alveolitis), which is not asbestos attributable.

In a pneumoconiosis claim (which includes an asbestos claim), enquire whether the claimant (or their spouse in the case of a fatal injury) has received a lump sum payment under either the Pneumoconiosis etc. (Workers' Compensation) Act 1979 (PWCA) or the 2008 Diffuse Mesothelioma Scheme (introduced from 1 October 2008).

In *Ballantine v Newalls Insulation Company Ltd* [2000], the Court of Appeal held that compensatory awards under the PWCA were deductible from the whole of the claimant's damages, otherwise a claimant stood to make a double recovery. Similar to a Compensation Recovery Unit (CRU) certificate, the payment is recouped from compensators by the Department for Work and Pensions (DWP) (assuming damages are required to be paid). Therefore, it is important for a defendant to set off a mesothelioma victim's lump sum payment against any claim for damages, otherwise the defendant will end up paying twice, once to the claimant and again to the DWP.

Medical experts

Depending on what a defendant may find in the claimant's medical notes and the severity of the condition complained of, it may decide to commission medical evidence of its own, subject to the claimant's solicitors' consent or with the permission of the court. Such evidence will establish whether the medical condition of which the claimant complains has been accurately diagnosed and, if so, whether it is the sole or partial cause of the claimant's symptoms. A medical report will also enable a defendant to establish the extent of the claimant's incapacity and ascertain a prognosis. A defendant will want its expert to consider whether there is anything in the claimant's medical history that impacts on their present condition or prognosis. If the claimant has a comorbid cardiac condition, is it contributing towards their breathlessness? If so, will that cardiac condition adversely affect the claimant's working and/or normal life expectancy? Such information is very important where there is a continuing loss claim.

It is also important that a defendant retains a medical expert in the applicable medical discipline. It is worth taking time to find an expert who is suitably qualified to comment upon the particular disease, and who is experienced in preparing medico-legal reports and giving evidence in the witness box at court.

In a Fatal Accidents Act 1976 claim it may be appropriate for a defendant to have the deceased's pathology and histology samples examined by an independent consultant pathologist. As a result of what is said in the post-mortem report, it may be appropriate for a defendant to seek a medical opinion elsewhere on the question of life expectancy. Although the claimant may have died from an industrial disease, the post-mortem report may suggest that their life expectancy was severely impaired in any event by reason of some other medical condition, i.e. a comorbid condition. If this is so, then the defendant will be able to contend for a lower multiplier.

Types of medical expert

It is not possible to provide a comprehensive list of the applicable medical experts in every occupational disease claim. However, the following may prove to be of assistance:

- Lung disease – consultant chest physician
- HAVS – consultant vascular or hand surgeon
- Industrial deafness – consultant ENT surgeon
- WRULD – consultant hand surgeon or rheumatologist
- Occupational stress – consultant psychiatrist
- Occupational cancers – consultant epidemiologist or histopathologist.

Settlement – final or provisional damages?

As in the case of other personal injury claims, the claimant in most disease claims will be compensated on a full and final basis. However, where there is a chance that the claimant may at some future date develop another and perhaps more serious medical condition, they may elect to be compensated on the assumption that the more serious medical condition will not develop, but that they will be entitled to seek further damages if, at some future date, they succumb to the other medical condition.

> It is best practice for any settlement on a provisional damages basis to be recorded in a consent order and registered with the court. The order should expressly record the fact that the claimant is being compensated on a provisional damages basis and should state with precision the medical condition or conditions in respect of which the claimant will be permitted to seek further damages. It is also best practice for a case file containing the particulars of claim, medical reports and a copy of the order for provisional damages to be lodged with the court.

A good example of where provisional damages were (until the case of *Rothwell v Chemical & Insulating Co Ltd and another* [2006]) considered appropriate is asbestos-attributable pleural plaques claims. Although pleural plaques are usually benign and symptomless, they carry a lifetime risk of developing into a malignant mesothelioma and, depending on the extent of exposure, asbestosis, lung cancer and diffuse pleural thickening. Such conditions will (depending on the medical evidence) frequently feature as 'return' conditions in judgments for provisional damages. It is recommended that whenever lung cancer is a 'return' condition it be qualified by adding the phrase "which is asbestos attributable".

In the case of an elderly claimant where the risk of future injury or deterioration is small, they may elect to be compensated on a full and final rather than on a provisional damages basis. By doing so, they will be entitled to be compensated to reflect the percentage risk of them succumbing to further injury.

It should be noted that it is the claimant's prerogative to decide whether they should be compensated on a full and final or on a provisional damages basis.

Insurance policy coverage in a mesothelioma claim

In respect of mesothelioma claims, an interesting distinction has arisen between PL and EL policies as to the basis on which the insurer on risk is determined.

The story starts with the case of *Bolton Metropolitan Borough Council v Municipal Mutual Insurance and another* [2006].

The Court of Appeal was required to interpret, in the context of a claim for personal injuries, the insuring clauses in two PL policies that Bolton had taken out with Municipal Mutual Insurance (MMI) and Commercial Union (CU). Bolton's claim for an indemnity from its PL insurers arose as a result of settling a PL claim of a mesothelioma victim who died in November 1991, having been diagnosed with the illness in January 1991. All the medical experts involved agreed that the deceased's mesothelioma probably began to mutate about 10 years before his first physical symptoms manifested, commonly known as 'the 10 year rule'. His first physical symptoms occurred during 1990 and so, therefore, the injury was deemed to have occurred in 1980.

From 1960 to 1965, Bolton had PL cover with CU. At the date the deceased's mesothelioma began to mutate up until the date of his death, MMI were on risk for Bolton's PL claims, i.e. between 1979 and 1991.

MMI blamed CU, which was on risk at the time the deceased was negligently exposed to asbestos between 1960 and 1963 and when the fibres were inhaled. During this time the deceased was working for a firm of electrical contractors helping to build a college for Bolton.

The MMI policy wording provided an indemnity for "accidental bodily injury" when such injury "occurred" during the currency of the policy. The CU policy wording was similar. The judge at first instance found that mesothelioma was an accidental bodily injury (in the sense of being unintended), but that the injury itself did not occur when the asbestos fibres were inhaled but rather the occurrence of the injury was only when the physical symptoms began to manifest several years, if not decades, later. The mere exposure to asbestos is not an injury within the meaning of a PL policy. That being the case, the judge exonerated CU from any liability to indemnify Bolton. The Court of Appeal upheld the first instance decision and dismissed MMI's appeal.

It was not necessary for the Court of Appeal to decide whether the injury occurred when the malignant tumour was first created in 1980 (i.e. the 10 year rule) or when identifiable symptoms first occurred in 1990 as MMI's period on risk covered both alternatives. It would have been helpful for practitioners had guidance been given upon this issue.

> The decision, therefore, means that detailed consideration is needed of the wording of a PL policy and whether it was written on an 'occurring' basis. If so, it may leave an insured potentially exposed. An insured may have had PL cover in place during the period a claimant was exposed to asbestos dust but such policy ceased by the time the symptoms occurred many years later, leaving it uninsured against the claim.

Unsurprisingly, the decision in *Bolton* led some run-off insurers to seek a similar ruling on the wording of EL policies. The same finding as for PL policies in respect of EL policies could save these insurers millions of pounds on mesothelioma claims because they ceased to write current business many years previously (as the name run-off implies).

The Supreme Court resolved the position in *Durham v BAI (Run Off) Ltd* [2012], known as the EL policy trigger litigation. The litigation consisted of six separate actions by run-off insurers who sought declarations to the effect that they were entitled to repudiate mesothelioma claims by the victims or by their employers that had taken out EL insurance covering the period of the victims' culpable occupational exposure. The clauses in the EL policies were variously written with wordings that provided indemnity in respect of injury or disease "contracted", "sustained" or "caused" within the currency of the policy.

The Supreme Court was unanimous in its interpretation of the policy wordings that it is the EL insurer at the time the claimant is exposed to asbestos dust that is on risk and must respond to the claim.

An issue arising for the High Court decision, but not explored further in either the Court of Appeal or Supreme Court, was that Mr Justice Burton found, based on the medical evidence he heard, the deemed date of injury in a mesothelioma claim was the date of angiogenesis, namely when the tumour developed its own independent blood supply, which was about five years before the manifestation of first physical symptoms. This is in direct conflict with the 10-year rule arising from *Bolton*.

Finally, in *International Energy Group Ltd v Zurich Insurance plc* [2013], the Court of Appeal decided that an EL insurer was liable to indemnify an employer for the whole of a mesothelioma claim and not just the proportion relating to its insurance period. In the claim, the deceased was exposed to asbestos while employed by the employer for 27 years from 1961 to 1988. The employer settled the deceased's claim for damages and then sought to recover its outlay from Zurich, with whom it had EL cover for a six-year period between 1982 and 1988. The Court of Appeal found that, following *Fairchild*, a more relaxed view on causation was to be taken towards mesothelioma claims. As far as the law was concerned, the claimant had established causation in each and every policy year and was entitled to 100% liability in each year. In turn, the employer was entitled to an indemnity in each of the six policy years. The case proceeded to the Supreme Court in 2015 and it was held that an insurer has an equitable right of recoupment from a solvent policyholder. Calculated upon a time on risk basis for the period of exposure, the policyholder was required to reimburse for the uninsured period. Where the policyholder is insolvent then the insurer is required to pay the whole claim thereby safeguarding a claimant's entitlement to full compensation.

Defending a disease claim: checklist

- ✓ Consider the nature of the disease – is it short- or long-tail? Is it a divisible or indivisible condition?
- ✓ Does the claim qualify under the portal? Note that, even where a disease claim does qualify, it will be challenging to keep it within the tight portal timescales.
- ✓ Be alert to the requirements of the disease pre-action protocol, in particular the timescales for acknowledging a claim, providing a response on liability and expert evidence.
- ✓ Is there a limitation defence? What was the date of knowledge? Would a court exercise its discretion under s.33 of the Limitation Act to allow the claim to proceed?
- ✓ Was there valid liability insurance in place at the time of the negligent acts complained of? Does this cover the entire period of exposure? Should you be coordinating the claim either as the last insurer on risk or as the insurer with the largest potential apportionment?

- ✓ Carry out investigations. In an EL claim, is there evidence that the claimant was employed? Was there some other potential source of culpable exposure from which an indemnity, contribution or Holtby discount may be sought? Does the defendant have a previous relevant claims history?
- ✓ Consider the defendant's state of knowledge. Can a 'knowledge' defence be put forward?
- ✓ Was the defendant in breach of their common law or statutory duty to the claimant?
- ✓ In a mesothelioma case, be aware of the impact of the Compensation Act 2006 on the issue of joint and several liability.
- ✓ Will the claimant succeed in establishing medical causation? Consider whether there may be unrelated causes. Obtain copies of the claimant's medical, occupational health and DWP records. Consider whether expert medical evidence should be obtained.
- ✓ Consider the potential impact of a provisional damages claim on the amount of general damages to be awarded and the wording of the return conditions.

10 Health and safety enforcement

Danny McShee

Co-author: Stephanie Power

- The context of health and safety law
- Who investigates and what do they investigate?
- Stages of a criminal investigation:
  - Information gathering and investigation
  - Interviews under caution
  - Decision making
  - Criminal court procedure
- Penalties for health and safety offences

Health and safety enforcement

Introduction

This chapter covers the criminal aspects of health and safety law. It is a strange area for a claims handler in that, because decisions have to be made by the insured company, the claims handler can feel as if they have little control over the claim despite the fact that defence costs can be extremely significant. In addition, claims for criminal investigations, whether they be by the police, Health and Safety Executive (HSE), Environment Agency (EA) or some other organisation, will not come before the claims handler as commonly as civil claims for which they will be responsible for themselves.

However, given the increasingly detailed nature of criminal investigations and the potential for large claims for defence costs, it is important to have an overview and understanding of criminal investigations and criminal court procedure.

The context of health and safety law

Health and safety investigations are conducted within the criminal law. The police and the HSE (as well as other agencies like the EA) are enforcement agencies with powers under the criminal law. The police operate within the powers of the Police and Criminal Evidence Act 1984 (PACE) and health and safety inspectors have powers under s.20 of the Health and Safety at Work etc. Act 1974 (HSWA). The police are able to arrest persons who they have a reasonable suspicion have committed an offence, and both the police and the HSE are in a position to take witness statements, seize documents, download emails, take computers, etc. It is not uncommon for investigations following a fatal incident to be conducted by the homicide division of a police force.

There is no doubt that the process has become more 'criminal' in recent years, since the introduction of the Corporate Manslaughter and Corporate Homicide Act 2007 (CMCHA), with greater involvement of the police and wider use of the powers available to them. This has been clearly evidenced in recent times, for example, by the police's public pronouncement that they have "reasonable suspicion" that organisations have committed corporate manslaughter in connection with the Grenfell Tower tragedy, at a time when members of those organisations have not been interviewed and the investigation is at a very early stage.

In addition, the area of health and safety sentencing has been revolutionised by the introduction of the Definitive Sentencing Guideline in February 2016, which has seen £1 million plus fines become the norm for large companies convicted of health and safety offences. The Guideline is having a dramatic effect in terms of the size of sentences being imposed upon companies and an increase in custodial sentences for individuals. Recent months have shown a continuing trend in that direction. By way of example, there were no £1 million fines in 2014 compared to 21 in the first year of the Guideline. There were only a very small number of custodial sentences compared to 26 during the same period. This development continues to dominate the regulatory world with similar increased fines for environmental offences. Although the development itself is one that has taken place, we believe that its ongoing effect should not be underestimated and that companies will continue to want to explore ways to defend themselves or to seek to attack the levels of culpability and harm categories alleged by the HSE or EA.

It should be emphasised that the process of health and safety law has nothing to do with the civil system for compensation for personal injuries, which is dealt with in an entirely different system and set of rules. Criminal law has its own courts (magistrates' and Crown Court) and its own Criminal Procedure Rules.

Who investigates and what do they investigate?

The answers to these questions will depend upon the outcome of the incident under investigation. Where the event is a fatal incident, a protocol, "Work-related deaths: A protocol for liaison", applies; the signatories to the protocol include the Crown Prosecution Service, Association of Police Constables and the HSE. This protocol requires the police to lead investigations following a fatal incident where there is suspicion of gross negligence, which would justify a manslaughter investigation. What commonly happens is that the police and HSE both attend the site of a fatal incident and, under the protocol, the police take the lead, or primacy, of the investigation.

Where, at any time during the investigation, a decision is made that gross negligence is no longer suspected then the primacy will be passed to the HSE (or the environmental health office (EHO) if it is not an HSE-regulated area). The transfer of primacy can take place on the day of an incident, some months after or even years later, and can be transferred back and forth between the police and the HSE on a number of occasions in complex investigations and/or where new evidence is identified. As a consequence, while it is always good news when primacy is passed to the HSE, it does not mean that the police cannot take back primacy if circumstances dictate and new evidence of gross negligence emerges.

> The HSE (or EHO) will lead non-fatal investigations. The police do not have jurisdiction to investigate non-fatal health and safety matters.

Which offences are investigated will depend upon the views of the investigators as to the seriousness of the case in question. Investigations will look at manslaughter involving gross negligence where there is a suspicion that a breach of duty may have been so serious as to be gross.

> Either a company or an individual can commit manslaughter. An individual can commit manslaughter by gross negligence where they owe a duty of care to another, breach that duty and the breach of duty is so serious as to constitute gross negligence and was a cause of the person's death. There have been increasing numbers of manslaughter investigations against individuals in recent years, with the police retaining primacy of investigations for longer. While many of these will not turn into manslaughter prosecutions, there are still more prosecutions than there were some years ago. A person investigated and prosecuted for manslaughter and subsequently convicted is likely to receive a prison sentence.

Under the CMCHA, a company commits corporate manslaughter where it is proven that the way in which its activities are organised or managed caused a person's death and the breach of its duty was so serious as to be classified as gross negligence. However, for the company to be convicted, a substantial element of the breach of duty must involve the conduct of senior management. In effect, the CMCHA allows the prosecuting agencies to aggregate the negligence, leading to an overall assessment of gross negligence of a number of persons within the company where senior management played a role in the breach of duty by the company. This is a change from the common law in place up to 2008.

An organisation convicted of corporate manslaughter can expect a fine of many hundreds of thousands of pounds, possibly millions, depending on the size of the company and its financial situation.

The investigating agencies can also investigate possible breaches of health and safety legislation. The main provisions usually investigated and prosecuted in relation to employers are s.2 and s.3 of the HSWA. Section 2 imposes the duty on an employer to ensure the health, safety and welfare of its employees so far as is reasonably practicable. Section 3 creates a similar duty in relation to those persons who are not employees, such as members of the public or contractors, for example.

In addition, individuals can be prosecuted for breaches of s.7 or s.37 of the HSWA, depending on their position in the hierarchy of the company. All employees of a company have a duty to take reasonable care of themselves and other people affected by their work. Employees can be prosecuted for breach of s.7 where it is alleged they have breached that duty.

Officers of the company, including directors, the company secretary or other senior officer, have a potential liability under s.37 of the HSWA where it can be shown that any failure by their company was committed with their consent, connivance or was attributable to any neglect on their part.

There are also numerous regulations made under the HSWA, including the Management of Health and Safety at Work Regulations 1999, Provision and Use of Work Equipment Regulations 1998, Work at Height Regulations 2005, Construction (Design and Management) Regulations 2007 etc., and the HSE will often prosecute companies for breach of these regulations.

Stages of a criminal investigation

There are four stages to a criminal investigation and prosecution from the date of an incident until a company (or individual) is dealt with in court for a breach of health and safety legislation or for manslaughter.

First stage: information gathering and investigation

This immediately follows an incident and usually lasts for some months until the police/HSE are in a position to identify whether any individual or company may have committed an offence and should, therefore, be treated as a suspect.

What happens in practice is that both the police and the HSE investigate in a similar way following an incident by requesting documents and obtaining witness statements.

As indicated above, the police have powers to seize documents, take computers, download emails, etc., under PACE. The HSE has similar powers under s.20 of the HSWA. In practice, both will request that companies under investigation provide documents and information voluntarily without the need for either authority to resort to their formal powers to seize them. Generally, it is in a company's interest to cooperate with the police or HSE and avoid any need for witness summonses, production orders, etc.

> However, it is important to have systems in place to ensure that the police and/or HSE will only be provided with documentation to which they are legally entitled. In most cases, the documentation that the police or HSE will later rely on will be documentation that has been taken from the company. It is very common when cases go to prosecution for exhibits in a prosecution bundle to contain the company's own pre-incident documents, policies, procedures, risk assessments, method statements, etc.

The police and the HSE are also entitled to take documents that are created following the incident, unless the documentation has the benefit of legal privilege. Accordingly, it is very important that any organisation under investigation following an incident has a protocol in place whereby it can properly control what documentation is created following an incident and for what purpose. There have been numerous cases where, for example, unhelpful emails have been produced including language that assists the police and the HSE and that are seized by them for use in a prosecution. However, it is an offence to destroy, delete or otherwise withhold evidence relating to the incident which is not subject to legal privilege and so it ought to be made very clear to an insured that this ought not to happen.

Insurers and the company under investigation will have a strong common interest in most cases. Ultimately, protecting a company's interest is likely to save an insurer costs. Accordingly, the first trigger point in any serious case for an insurer is notification of the incident. It is then necessary to consider what legal advice should be obtained at that stage.

The first few days after an incident are vital in terms of document management and ensuring that the investigating authorities only receive those documents to which they are entitled. Companies will need advice on subjects such as legal privilege. There is an implied legal duty on companies under the Management of Health and Safety at Work Regulations 1999 to investigate accidents. The HSE will normally expect companies to investigate a serious incident themselves regardless of whether the HSE is formally investigating. Therefore, a very important early consideration is the company's internal accident investigation. It is imperative that early legal advice is taken on the nature of a company's own accident investigation. Specifically, it is important that any report produced should be factual and concise and not use language that is provocative or inflammatory. Language should not contain statements that might suggest some form of legal liability. Words such as negligence, gross, failure, etc., should be avoided.

In a recent high-profile case, *The Director of the Serious Fraud Office (SFO) v Eurasian Natural Resources Corporation (ENRC)* [2017], the High Court held that documents prepared during an internal corporate investigation may not be protected by legal privilege.

In December 2010 ENRC received a 'whistle-blower' report alleging financial irregularity at a subsidiary company. ENRC instructed solicitors and forensic accountants to conduct an internal investigation. In 2013 the SFO commenced a criminal investigation and demanded disclosure of all documents produced during the internal investigation on the basis that they were subject neither to legal advice privilege, which protects advice given by lawyers to their clients, nor to litigation privilege, which protects client, lawyer and third-party communications if litigation or adversarial proceedings have commenced or are anticipated. With minor exceptions the court agreed.

It is unclear currently what impact the *ENRC* case will have on other areas beyond the types of corporate investigations that are common in SFO cases, and whether it will be subject to appeal, being a first instance decision, but the case is potentially concerning. In the context of workplace manslaughter, health and safety, environmental and other investigations, it is possible that the police and regulatory bodies may now seek production of investigatory documents which might previously have been considered, rightly or wrongly, privileged. These documents may include statements, draft statements, notes of discussions with witnesses and written records of interviews created for the purpose of internal investigations and fact finding.

This means that extra caution is required when conducting internal investigations to ensure that any claim to legal privilege is justified because *ENRC* may embolden the authorities to make more challenges and press disclosure demands more keenly. The requirement to produce documents that were generated in the mistaken belief that they were privileged may be very damaging.

A second point in an investigation that insurers need to be aware of is when the investigating agencies start taking witness statements. This process can take place very soon after an incident – sometimes on the same day. It reinforces the need to respond quickly to an incident.

Individuals giving witness statements will often require advice and assistance on their rights and the process of giving statements to the investigating agencies. In many cases, the agencies will not explain to the person being interviewed the nature of the statement they are giving and what it means in relation to them personally. The statement is a legal statement that may be used in criminal court proceedings,

Sometimes a person gives a witness statement believing that they are in a blame-free environment, only to find themselves later invited to an interview under caution as a suspect. Accordingly, it is important that companies take advice on the process of their employees giving witnesses statements and, if appropriate, those employees should be given advice and assistance personally.

Guidance from the Solicitors Regulation Authority imposes a duty on a solicitor to take care not to put themselves into a conflict of interest situation when they are giving assistance to employees at the same time as to an employer. In many cases there will be no conflict, but there is a duty on the solicitor to explore the circumstances of the case and the facts known and likely to come out.

> On some occasions where a solicitor feels that they cannot give assistance to the company as well to employees, insurers will be asked to fund a second firm in order to give advice solely to the employees. This can easily lead to a significant escalation of costs and insurers should ask the solicitor to justify why a second firm should be instructed. In addition, the insurer should ask why employees need to have a lawyer with them at a witness statement interview in any event. There will be circumstances where it is clearly appropriate for that to be the case, but many do not necessarily require a solicitor to be present when an employee is interviewed.

One area that causes considerable concern to companies for which they often seek assistance from their solicitors and insurers is the HSE's scheme Fee for Intervention. In October 2012, a new system was introduced whereby the HSE can charge for its time where it considers there to have been a material breach of duty. The HSE was charged at the time with introducing a process for disputing/appealing the findings of the inspectors involved. To date this has involved the HSE in effect being the arbiter of their own decisions. This led to a judicial review of the system, which was due to be heard last year. Prior to that hearing taking place, the HSE conceded and said that it would look again at the process for dealing with disputes/appeals. Since then it has produced a further proposal, which most defence organisations consider still involves the HSE having to create a say in the appeal of its own decisions.

We believe that there will be a further challenge to this and that a new system is inevitable based upon a truly independent assessment of the HSE's decision. This in turn is likely to lead to more challenge by organisations.

Second stage: interviews under caution

The police and/or the HSE have powers to invite an individual and/or a company to an interview under caution when they suspect they may have committed an offence. As indicated above, it can take many months, even years, for this stage of the process to be reached.

It is likely that the police/HSE will write to the individual or company and ask them to attend an interview. The letter should indicate that it is for an interview under caution to be held in accordance with the Codes of Practice made under PACE. The letter should urge the individual and/or company to take legal advice.

Sometimes arrangements for interviews can be made between the police/HSE and the individual or company's lawyer direct. Either way the police/HSE should be pressed to set out in writing the basis for their belief that the individual and/or company may have committed an offence and to identify in writing what legislation and offences are being investigated. Solicitors should urge the investigating agencies to explain the grounds for an interview under caution. They should also seek pre-interview disclosure in the form of any documents that the police/HSE may wish to put to the interviewee.

The receipt by a company or individual of a letter inviting them to interview under caution is another trigger point for insurers to look out for. No company or individual should ever attend an interview under caution without having received legal advice and taking the steps outlined above to establish the justification for the interview and the subjects to be covered.

It is absolutely crucial to prepare for such interviews and to take advice on the best form of response. While interviews under caution are often a precursor to prosecution, that is not always the case and it is an important stage where the individual and/or company may be able to persuade the investigating authorities not to prosecute. Alternatively, where prosecution does follow, the prosecution will often heavily rely on the information provided at the interview under caution stage.

While it can take a long time for the investigating agencies to reach the point of inviting individuals and/or companies to interviews under caution, where death has occurred an initial interview under caution of individuals directly involved (for example the driver of a piece of plant involved in the incident) may take place on the day of an incident.

There is no bar to the number of times a person can be invited to an interview under caution, although if multiple or repeated interviews are requested this is likely to be oppressive and should be refused.

When manslaughter is being investigated the police will usually invite individuals to attend a police station voluntarily to be interviewed under caution. Where an individual refuses to attend voluntarily, the police may have the power in appropriate cases to compel the individual's attendance by arresting them. However, an arrest should only take place where it is "necessary". There is guidance that suggests that police officers should only use arrest where absolutely necessary and if the individual is willing to attend voluntarily then they should not be arrested.

The police do not have the power to compel a company to attend an interview under caution in relation to corporate manslaughter. The HSE does not have the power to compel either a company or an individual to attend an interview under caution.

There are essentially four choices open to a person in connection with a voluntary interview under caution:

1) Attend the interview and answer questions.
2) Decline to assist at all.
3) Provide a prepared written statement incorporating the suspect's position and do no more.
4) Provide a prepared written statement and attend an interview to answer any questions that may arise from that statement.

There is no right or wrong answer as to which option is appropriate in any particular case. It is a matter of judgement and experience and/or the suspect's decision in relation to that interview.

For example, while option (2) might appear to be an unattractive option in many cases, there are circumstances where it is clear that the investigating agencies are on a 'fishing expedition' and, accordingly, declining to assist becomes the preferred option. In other cases it may well be apparent that this option is inappropriate. In particular, with companies, care needs to be taken to ensure that an appropriate response is given on behalf of the company as a whole.

Interviews under caution with nominated representatives of the company are in many ways artificial, in that the company's position is dictated on its behalf by answers from one individual. While in a very small company that might be acceptable, in a very big company there are dangers in relying on one person to give the company's response. The nominated representative's opinion will bind the company in law.

For an interview under caution, the interviewee will attend either a police station, if the interview is being conducted by the police, or the relevant office of the HSE, if it is an HSE-led investigation. The interviews are recorded and later transcribed. Interviews will usually now be recorded on compact disc (CD), although some authorities still rely upon a tape deck. If it is a CD, then three CDs will be inserted into a machine to record simultaneously throughout the interview. One recording is later sealed and becomes the 'master copy'. It remains sealed and can only be opened in the event of a challenge to the accuracy of any transcript produced, or if either of the other copies become damaged. The second disc is a working disc used to produce a transcript. The third disc is usually given to the person being interviewed.

The investigating agency will start the interview by making it clear that it is under caution and will administer the criminal caution, which is "You do not have to say anything but it may harm your defence if you do not mention when questioned something you later rely on in court. Anything you do say may be given in evidence."

The effect of the caution is that an individual/company retains the right to remain silent at an interview under caution. However, the second part of the caution allows a court, in appropriate circumstances, later to draw an adverse inference from the fact that answers were not given at the interview under caution. In addition, where a person interviewed later gives a defence to a charge that is different from that given at the interview under caution, then the court may permit the magistrates or jury to draw an adverse inference from the change in the substance of the defence.

> The key aspect of any interview under caution is that "anything you do say may be given in evidence". This is crucial, and careful preparation for an interview is necessary. Preparation would normally involve a meeting between the solicitor and client in advance of the interview to discuss the type of questions likely to be asked so that the interviewee has time to think about their position and formulate their responses.

Third stage: decision-making process

This is when the authorities decide whether to prosecute an individual and/or company. Despite what is often said at an interview by the interviewing officer, it can take several months for a decision to be made. As it is not uncommon for there to be little activity between the interview under caution and the decision being made to prosecute, it can be a particularly difficult period for the potential defendant who must wait and is powerless to influence the decision. Regrettably, there is no practical mechanism to force the authorities to make their decision other than to keep pressing them.

If the authorities decide not to prosecute, that is usually the end of the case for the individual and/or company. If the police decide not to prosecute for manslaughter, then the case may transfer to the HSE under the protocol for further investigation. A decision not to prosecute at all is often colloquially called an 'NFA' (no further action).

Prosecutors follow a code when making decisions on whether or not to prosecute. The code requires that the decision be based on the evidence and whether it justifies a charge, which means that the prosecutor needs to be confident that there is a realistic prospect of conviction. In addition, there must be a public interest to prosecute. The HSE has its own Enforcement Guide that gives further criteria as to when a prosecution may be justified. In the event of a very serious incident it will usually be difficult to argue that the public interest will not be served by a decision to prosecute if there is sufficient evidence. However, where incidents are minor in terms of their consequence(s), it may be possible to argue that the public interest is not served by prosecuting.

Fourth stage: criminal court procedure

If a decision is made to prosecute then the individual and/or company will normally be summoned to appear before a magistrates' court.

The offences of manslaughter and corporate manslaughter can only be heard in the Crown Court and will be sent there after a very short hearing in the magistrates' court almost immediately after the charge. A hearing is then required in the Crown Court within seven days, when directions will be given for the trial of the matter.

All other health and safety offences can be heard by either the magistrates' or the Crown Court, depending upon their severity, and are known as 'triable either way offences'. These cases will start in the magistrates' court. There will be a hearing called a 'plea before venue' or a 'mode of trial' hearing to decide in which court the substantive hearing will be held. At the plea before venue hearing, the defendant will be asked to indicate their plea:

- Where the plea is 'guilty', the magistrates will make the decision whether or not to retain the case or to commit it to the Crown Court for sentence. They will do this if they feel their sentencing powers are inadequate.
- Where the plea is 'not guilty', or no plea is indicated, the magistrates will again decide where the case should be heard. The defendant has the right to elect a Crown Court trial to be heard by a jury even if the magistrates accept jurisdiction of the case.
- There will be many cases when a defendant is not in a position to indicate its plea by the plea before venue hearing and it is not unusual for a defendant at that hearing not to enter a plea. The court is then obliged to treat the no plea as if it was a not guilty plea and to make a decision as to whether the matter should be heard in the magistrates' court or the Crown Court. Obviously, at some point the defendant will be pressed to enter their plea.

There is firm guidance to the effect that cases involving death will normally be heard in the Crown Court.

It is important to emphasise that both the magistrates' and Crown Court are criminal courts. They are not civil county courts. Therefore, health and safety cases will rarely deal with compensation, which is considered by the magistrates and judges to be entirely separate.

The prosecution will normally serve a case summary and supply supporting evidence, which is called the initial details process. The evidence received by the defendant needs to be carefully reviewed. The case summary will usually set out the facts from the HSE's perspective and identify why it is alleged that breaches of duty have occurred. The prosecutor will set out the aggravating features alleged to be present in the case. This is called the '*Friskies* process', after *R v Friskies Petcare UK Ltd* [2000]. The prosecution will produce a document that outlines any features that allegedly aggravate the case, and on the basis of which a higher sentence should be imposed.

It is not uncommon for the defence to consider the *Friskies* schedule to be highly contentious. It may often seem that the HSE has 'overcharged' a defendant, anticipating some form of negotiation with the defendant to reach a middle ground. This can be a sensitive part of the process because any employer and/or individual will be sensitive to prosecution allegations that they consider to be scurrilous, for example, putting profit before safety, a situation that is, in reality, rare, yet the HSE often alleges it.

The guidance in *Friskies* states that a defendant should respond to the *Friskies* schedule in writing. The defendant's *Friskies* response should also contain details of what it considers to be the mitigating features of the case. *R v F Howe & Son (Engineers) Ltd* [1998] is helpful when identifying the type of mitigating features common in health and safety cases. Mitigating features include factors such as the breach was isolated, it only lasted for a very short time, immediate steps were taken to prevent a recurrence and the defendant has no previous convictions or limited enforcement history.

> It may sound obvious, but there is a significant difference between the conduct of a criminal case and a civil case where insurers will be familiar with joint settlement meetings, mediations, etc. While there can be a process of discussion between the parties in a criminal case regarding the nature of the offences, it is not possible to 'settle' a criminal case by, for example, offering to pay a certain amount of money if the prosecution withdraws.

The options open to a company charged with an offence are:

- Plead not guilty and have a trial, to be decided either by magistrates or in the Crown Court by a jury.
- Plead guilty as charged on the basis of the prosecution's case summary and *Friskies* schedule. Given the nature of such documents, it is almost unheard of for a defendant to accept a prosecution's case in its entirety.

- Plead guilty, but in doing so not accept all of the allegations being made. This is often called pleading guilty on a basis. As part of the *Friskies* process, a defendant is expected to set out the nature of its basis of plea in writing. In its simplest form, this means explaining to what extent the defendant accepts that it has committed an offence and highlighting those parts of the prosecution's case that are not accepted.

Despite efforts to increase the pace of cases before criminal courts, the process remains laborious. It can often take the HSE/police several years to bring a case, and the defendant is required to attend a plea before venue within a matter of only three to four weeks of receipt of notice that charges are being laid. This can seem even less fair when one considers that courts are demanding a plea be entered on the first date of hearing and will look to sentence immediately thereafter. A date for trial is likely to be fixed on that first date of hearing if the matter is to remain in the magistrates' court or will be sent directly to the Crown Court if jurisdiction is declined.

If the individual or company pleads not guilty, then the matter will proceed to trial. Trials in the Crown Court are heard by judge and jury. Cases involving serious injury or death can be highly complex and, as a result, trials can take many weeks, sometimes months. This is because the evidence can often be highly technical in health and safety cases, involving specialist inspectors from the HSE and defendant experts who are often specialist technical engineers. An example of a lengthy trial is the corporate manslaughter case relating to the Welsh mine at Gleision where four miners died in September 2011, which lasted for nearly three months.

In addition, the offences themselves are also not as black and white as other criminal offences, like burglary or handling stolen goods, etc.

> The question of reasonable practicability under HSWA involves an element of judgement as to how reasonably an individual or company may have acted. Similarly, the test for gross negligence in manslaughter cases is a question of judgement for a jury. In the leading manslaughter case, *R v Adomako* [1994], Lord Mackay said that the question of grossness was "supremely a jury question". In effect, a judgement will need to be made as to whether conduct fell below a certain level.

Another time for insurers to become involved is when a defendant is being advised on their plea. Insurers will have their own priorities and decision-making processes internally, but as a general rule should be entitled to consider their ongoing coverage where the legal advice is that the prospects of success at trial are extremely low. There will, of course, be occasions when a defendant will want to 'take a punt' and defend the case, but an insurer may decide not to continue funding a defence where the prospects of an acquittal are low.

Penalties for health and safety offences

Background

Companies can face unlimited fines for breaches of health and safety legislation and corporate manslaughter. In general, fines are increasing and can often be in the many hundreds of thousands of pounds, and sometimes in the millions. Fines, of course, cannot be indemnified by an insurer as to do so would be contrary to public policy: the company or individual must pay any fine.

For offences committed on or after 12 March 2015, when s.85 of the Legal Aid, Sentencing and Punishment of Offenders Act (LASPO) 2012 came into force, the maximum level of fine available to magistrates' courts has been increased from £20,000 per offence to an unlimited fine. Where a matter is committed to the Crown Court for sentence or where a trial heard in the Crown Court returns a guilty verdict, the fine can also be unlimited. Since the introduction of the Health and Safety (Offences) Act 2008 (which came into force in January 2009) individuals can be imprisoned for breaches of health and safety legislation, as well as for manslaughter.

Aside from the penalties, a company or individual will be concerned at the prospect of a criminal conviction and the devastating effect on their reputation. Insurers will know of cases where a company wishes to take a matter to trial over the principle of a criminal conviction and the effect that it is likely to have on its reputation and the effect that publicity will have in relation to future tenders, etc. This can lead to a desire for the defendant to defend the case, even where the actual penalty in financial terms is likely to be very small. However, health and safety and manslaughter cases are regularly reported in local and national media and the effect on reputation cannot be overstated.

If a company decides to plead guilty, then while it can still face significant fines, it is entitled to a credit of a one-third reduction in sentence where the plea is entered at the first available opportunity. This credit will reduce the closer to trial that the guilty plea is entered. In general terms, a defendant that pleads guilty immediately before the trial, but saves the trial from taking place, will receive a credit of one-tenth. Both companies and individuals are entitled to credit. A credit will still be applicable even where a custodial sentence is being considered.

> If a company or individual is convicted following a trial or pleads guilty, then they will usually be required to pay the prosecution's costs. There are some insurance policies that indemnify defendants for prosecution costs, but, on the whole, defendants' costs are not indemnified and will, therefore, be paid by the defendants themselves.

Sentencing guidelines

For many years, the leading case on sentencing in cases involving health and safety offences has been *R v F Howe and Son (Engineers) Ltd* [1998]. *Howe* set out the factors that a court should consider when imposing a penalty. The case applied to cases in both the magistrates' courts and Crown Court.

In 2010, further guidelines were given by the Sentencing Council for health and safety offences causing death and corporate manslaughter. The guidelines indicate that a fine for a health and safety offence causing death should seldom be less than £100,000. A fine for corporate manslaughter should seldom be less than £500,000.

Paying the penalty: a new era of sentencing

The Sentencing Council's Health and Safety Offences, Corporate Manslaughter and Food Safety and Hygiene Offences Definitive Guideline (the Guideline) came into effect on 1 February 2016.

One of the main aims of the Guideline was to achieve greater consistency in the sentencing of health and safety cases and also to subject larger companies to more significant financial penalties. Pre-Guideline, fines in the millions of pounds were reserved for the most serious health and safety cases, usually involving multiple fatalities or matters of public interest (for example, rail disasters or the Buncefield explosion). That is no longer the case.

Post-Guideline, large companies are regularly attracting fines of that magnitude, even in cases where there has been little or no injury suffered.

Even more important, many will think, is the effect that the Guideline has had on individuals who fall foul of health and safety law.

Following the implementation of the Guideline, even where a court assesses a person's culpability to be "low", there is the real risk of a custodial sentence being imposed. The harsh reality is that even where the failings of an individual are found to be minor, or significant efforts were made to address the risk, an individual, be it a site labourer or a director, could still be imprisoned.

In addition, at the time of writing this chapter, there are yet further proposals to reform this area of the law with a consultation to consider introducing a Guideline for those convicted of gross negligence manslaughter that could lead to vastly increased prison sentences. The aim of that consultation is to entrench long prison sentences for those convicted of gross negligence manslaughter. Again, this is likely to have an ongoing effect on cases where gross negligence manslaughter is alleged, as individuals will be still more determined to avoid such prosecutions or, where they are brought, to robustly defend themselves from the possibility of such penalties.

Company turnover is key

The Guideline requires the court to consider the turnover of the company to decide whether it is a very large, large, medium, small or micro organisation. Next follows an assessment of the level of culpability of the organisation and the likelihood of the harm risked by the failings and the severity of the harm risked.

The Guideline also states that where the turnover of an organisation "very greatly exceeds" £50 million (which is the threshold for a large organisation) it may be necessary to move outside the suggested range to achieve a proportionate sentence. Since the introduction of the Guideline, there has not been a health and safety case in the Court of Appeal to clarify exactly what a "very large" organisation is for the purposes of the Guideline.

That said, the issue of a "very large company" was considered by the Court of Appeal in *R v Ineos ChlorVinyls Limited* [2016], an environmental case in which the company's turnover was in the region of £900 million. In that case the court noted that the turnover of the company was "vastly larger" than the indicative figure given for a "large" organisation and the court found that the sentencing judge in that case had been fully entitled to go outside the bracket concerned for that reason.

Application

Given that the sentencing guideline for environmental offences is very similar to the Guideline for health and safety matters, it serves as a strong indicator as to how the Court of Appeal might approach the same analysis in a health and safety case. In essence it seems that if £900 million is "vastly larger" than £50 million then £400 million or even less could be held to "greatly exceed" it. In fact, the courts at first instance have indicated that turnovers of that value might indeed pass the threshold into "very large".

By way of example, we have reviewed two of our recent cases involving large companies:

1) *R v Network Rail Infrastructure Limited* [2016]
   This concerned an incident at a footpath crossing over the railway near Needham Market in Suffolk where an elderly member of the public suffered fatal injuries when she was hit by a train while she was traversing the crossing.

   In applying the Guideline, the judge remarked that the turnover of the company was well in excess of the £50 million threshold but, having regard to the company's acceptance of its breach and the fact it had acted immediately and extensively to improve protection for others, he concluded it was not necessary or proportionate to move outside the range of fines for a large organisation. The judge did not accept the contention by both prosecution and defence that this was a case involving medium likelihood of harm since the crossing exposed a number of members of the public to risk and the breaches were a significant cause of death, and instead proceeded on the basis of high likelihood of harm arising at this particular crossing. The judge concluded that this was a high culpability, harm category 1 case, having allowed maximum credit of one third for early plea and following substantial mitigation.

2) *R v Merlin Attractions Operations Limited* [2016]
   The prosecution of Merlin Attractions Operations Limited [2016] in relation to a collision on a rollercoaster ride at Alton Towers (which led to serious injuries being sustained by 16 individuals) is

another example of the courts considering the "very large" issue for the purposes of sentencing. The turnover of the company was £400 million and the court could have taken the decision to impose a fine well outside of the £1.6 million to £6 million range set out in the Guideline, in fact the submission was made by the prosecution that it should do. The judge commented that while a £400 million turnover is one that would justify moving out of the range pursuant to what was said in the environmental case of *R v Ineos ChlorVinyls Limited* [2016], the court on this occasion could reach a proportionate sentence without moving outside of the offence range for a large organisation. Merlin Attractions Operations Limited was fined £5 million.

Rising fines

The cases sentenced since the introduction of the Guideline have also confirmed our prediction that the fines involving cases where no injuries have been sustained would rise. This includes the sentencing of ConocoPhillips and G4S Cash Solutions where fines of £3 million and £1.8 million respectively were imposed even though there was no evidence of actual harm being sustained as a result of the health and safety failings. The sentences were based on the assessment of the harm *risked*, a significant departure from the position pre-February 2016.

Other cases worthy of a mention include the very recent case of *R v Kentucky Fried Chicken (KFC) (Great Britain) Limited* [2017]. KFC received a fine of £950,000 when a worker suffered burns when he spilled a tub of gravy on to himself as he performed the everyday task of taking gravy out of a microwave oven. This is a long way away from the type of multiple fatality national disaster case that would have attracted a colossal fine such as this pre-Guideline.

Volvo Group UK Ltd has also recently been sentenced for an incident where a worker fell from a stepladder. Volvo was fined a similar sum to KFC, of £900,000. Interestingly this case was heard and sentenced by a district judge in Westminster Magistrates' Court. When LASPO 2012 came into force in relation to offences committed after 12 March 2015 (which increased the maximum level of fine available to magistrates' courts to an unlimited fine – previously £20,000 per offence for most health and safety offences) there would not have been many who would have anticipated district judges in the magistrates' courts handing down fines close to £1 million. Magistrates' courts are increasingly accepting jurisdiction for cases where companies are facing fines in the hundreds of thousands of pounds.

A report published by Institution of Occupational Safety and Health (IOSH) in January 2017 sets out the stark reality for businesses in this post-Guideline era. IOSH conducted an analysis of fines showing the fundamental shift that has occurred in the 'top 20' fines from 2014 through to 2016. In 2014 all 20 of the highest fines were below the £1 million mark, with two thirds of those being below £250,000. Shift to 2016, and all but one of the highest 20 fines were more than £1 million, with four of those cases attracting fines of £3 million plus.

National safety agenda?

The question this poses is: are these huge fines necessary to drive the national safety agenda?

By the HSE's own analysis, the UK consistently has one of the lowest fatality rates across the EU and with European surveys demonstrating that the majority of UK workers are confident that their job does not put their health and safety at risk. Why should UK big businesses be punished for creating a health and safety record the country should be proud of and a health and safety reputation that has set the benchmark for Europe?

Big business

It has been suggested that the Guideline is merely a convenient vehicle to generate multi-millions for the Treasury, and to demonstrate to the disenchanted that the government is tough on big business.

The reality is that the vast majority of large corporate organisations have extensive safety management systems and resources in place and their commitment to the safety agenda is generally far stronger than smaller companies. Admittedly part of that is down to the fact they can better afford the commitment. And equally, they are usually better able to bear these big fines. But it follows, the bigger the operation the more chance there will be a safety incident.

Of course large fines can sometimes be necessary to bring home the message that safety should be taken seriously, but the question remains whether penalising large companies for comparatively minor offences, against an excellent background of safety, may lead to many big businesses moving elsewhere.

Individuals

One of the main concerns following the introduction of the Guideline was the lowering of the custody threshold for individuals charged with health and safety offences. For many years it has been possible for individuals to be imprisoned for up to two years for breaches of health and safety legislation. However, the courts reserved such sentences for the most serious cases, usually those involving a number of aggravating features.

The Guideline introduced the possibility of imprisonment for a low culpability harm category 1 offence. This means those who had made significant efforts to address and manage risks could face a custodial sentence where the seriousness of the harm risked was in the highest category. This was potentially one of the most troubling aspects of the new regime, especially given the substantial increase we have seen in company directors and senior managers being prosecuted in their personal capacity for safety offences during 2015 to 2016, as compared with previous years.

Prosecutions

Over the last 12 months, there have been far fewer prosecutions against individuals than organisations. Therefore it is more difficult to map any trends in terms of the way that the courts are applying the Guideline, and there is also limited statistical data available.

However it appears the courts are demonstrating a continued reluctance to impose immediate custodial sentences in all but the most serious of cases.

In August 2016, Kenneth Thelwall, company director of Thorn Warehousing Ltd, was charged under s.37 of the Health and Safety at Work Act 1974. This resulted from an incident where one of his employees was crushed to death by a remote controlled Mobile Elevated Working Platform. Mr Thelwall was sentenced to 12 months in prison, disqualified from being a company directory for seven years and ordered to pay prosecution costs. His subsequent appeal against his sentence to the Court of Appeal was dismissed. It is likely that even if this case had appeared before the courts prior to the introduction of the Guideline, the outcome would have been very similar. The court heard that there was no risk assessment or safe system of work in place for the equipment and that the employee had not been properly trained. The court was also highly critical of the poor health and safety record of the business and the fact that Mr Thelwall had a previous prosecution following the death of another employee.

In Scotland, Sheriff Collins recently sentenced the manager of Craig Services and Access, Donald Craig, to two years' imprisonment following the collapse of a 'cherry picker' working platform. The court had regard to the Guideline in passing sentence and was highly critical of the personal assurances Mr Craig had given to others about the use and load-bearing qualities of the cherry picker. It would appear that Mr Craig was instrumental in a decision to select a cheaper method of repairing the cherry picker in question, which left it in an unsafe condition and ultimately led to the death of a worker. Again, evidence of this level of disregard for safety in a management position would have been likely to attract a custodial sentence even before the introduction of the Guideline.

Comment

There has been a marked change in the approach taken by defence lawyers to cases where charges are brought against individuals in their personal capacity. Where a custodial sentence is a real possibility, the importance of an early guilty plea in order to obtain the maximum discount on the sentence should be weighed against the risk that a finding of guilt following a trial could tip the case over the custodial threshold.

While each case must be assessed on its own merits, there may be value in looking to reach agreement with the prosecution that a case does not reach the custody threshold and asking the court for a formal indication that an immediate custodial sentence is not likely to happen (referred to as a 'Goodyear indication').

Therefore, while the effects of the Guideline have so far been felt the most by large companies facing much higher and more consistent fines for health and safety breaches, longer-term concerns remain with those who are facing prosecution in their personal capacity.

11 Professional liability

Matt Andrews

Co-author: Lucy Suddaby

- Basis of claim
- Duty of care and breach of duty
- Causation and damages
- Proceedings: including pre-action protocols and limitation
- Coverage issues: including pre-inception, insuring clause and exclusions

Professional liability

Introduction

This chapter looks at claims made against professionals for damages arising out of an act or omission on their part.

The claimant is traditionally a client. The complaint is usually that the claimant's position has been harmed as a result of the professional's failure to advise them correctly or to achieve a specific outcome. The traditional professions that fall within this type of liability include solicitors, surveyors, accountants, brokers and construction professionals. However, more recently, claims against financial practitioners and other 'new' professionals, such as IT consultants, have been considered as falling within the scope of the professional liability umbrella.

This chapter provides an overview of the key issues that arise when dealing with professional liability claims generally (in terms of both defence and coverage). It does not provide an in-depth analysis of the nuances and particularities of claims made against each of the professions.

Basis of claim

Contract

In the majority of cases, there is a contract between the professional and their client that sets out certain express terms and conditions to which the retainer is subject.

It is important to consider the terms of a professional's retainer at the outset in order to determine the exact scope and nature of the professional's obligations. In particular, it is important to determine whether or not the contract governs the whole, or only part, of the relationship between parties. If the latter, it will be necessary to consider whether a tortious duty exists in respect of other parts of the retainer and, if so, whether the tortious duty is consequently wider in scope than the contractual obligations.

It is usual for the courts to find that there is an implied term that the professional will act with reasonable care and skill in achieving a specific outcome or in carrying out a specific task. However, it will be a matter of construction of the contract as to whether express terms confer a more onerous obligation on the professional.

Negligence

In addition to duties imposed by contract, a professional may owe a tortious duty of care to their client, which, if breached, may lead to a finding of negligence against them.

As with all types of negligence cases, to succeed in a claim against a professional, a claimant will have to prove, on the balance of probabilities, that:

- The professional owed the claimant a duty of care
- The professional breached that duty of care
- The claimant has suffered a loss as a result of that breach.

Unless a claimant is able to satisfy all three strands, a claim in negligence will fail.

Duty of care

A tortious duty arises out of, and is defined by, the assumption of responsibility to carry out a specific task and/or provide a particular service.

While it is often the case that a professional will owe their client both contractual and tortious duties, the professional will not owe a concurrent duty of care in tort to their client merely due to the fact that there is a contractual relationship between them.

It is generally accepted that professionals such as solicitors, accountants and surveyors will owe a concurrent duty of care to their clients on the basis that the nature of the services they provide usually involves reliance by their clients upon their advice and/or their expertise. The test for determining whether such a relationship exists between two parties was set out in *Hedley Byrne & Company Ltd v Heller & Partners Ltd* [1963].

> In view of the above, as a general rule, professionals will owe a duty of care to their clients in tort as well as in contract. This is not, however, without exception and much will depend on the facts of each case. By way of example, building contractors will not generally owe a duty of care in tort to their client (unless the facts indicate that they have assumed a wider duty) merely because they have contracted to carry out works on their behalf.

Particular attention should, therefore, be paid to the nature and scope of service provided to the client, and consideration should be given to whether a *Hedley Byrne* relationship exists between the parties.

Breach of duty: standard of care

The general standard of care against which a professional is to be judged is the same test that is applied in clinical negligence cases (see Chapter 12). *Bolam v Friern Hospital Management Committee* [1957] laid down the test, which is, essentially, whether the professional acted in accordance with a "responsible body of opinion". In other words, the question that should be asked is "what degree of care and skill would be expected of a competent professional in the relevant field?"

When considering the appropriate standard of care to be expected of a professional, a number of factors will be taken into consideration. However, a key issue will be whether the professional holds themselves out as having particular expertise and skill, or as a specialist in their field. In those circumstances, the professional will be judged against the standards in that specialist field, regardless of whether or not the professional is actually a specialist.

It is usual for the question of breach to be determined by expert evidence. However, in recent times the development of professional standards and regulation (either statutory or imposed by professional governing bodies) has assisted in the determination of the question of breach. Such rules or regulations provide guidance on what is to be expected of a professional in discharging their duty of care and skill. A breach of these rules will often be persuasive evidence that a breach has occurred. It is, therefore, important for a practitioner to consider any guidance or professional standards published by the professional body in question and/or their governing body (for example the Solicitors Professional Conduct Rules, the Financial Services Authority Handbook, etc.).

Causation

Even if a claimant is able to prove that a professional's conduct fell below what was to be expected of their reasonably competent peers, in order to succeed in their claim, the claimant will have to prove that the professional's negligent act or omission has caused them to suffer loss.

> The test to be applied is the 'but for' test, that is, but for the negligence of the professional would the claimant have suffered the loss claimed? In order to answer this question, practitioners (and ultimately the courts) need to consider what, hypothetically, the claimant would have done had the professional provided the correct advice, acted competently or achieved a specific outcome.

This question will often come down to witness evidence and will be assessed by the court on the balance of probabilities. Should the claimant be able to overcome that hurdle, the court will not apply any discount to the damages claimed (other than in respect of contributory negligence).

Where the potential outcome depends upon what a third party would have done (rather than the claimant), the court will assess damages on a 'loss of a chance' basis.

In loss of chance cases, the initial question of whether a third party would have acted in a particular way is not assessed on the balance of probabilities. A claimant merely has to show that there was a real and substantial chance that a third party would have done something.

This means that the court must consider what the chances were of a third party acting in a certain way. Once this has been determined, the court will reduce the amount of damages claimed (on a percentage basis) to reflect the lost chance. The leading case on loss of chance is *Allied Maples Group Ltd v Simmons & Simmons* [1995].

Damages

The overriding principle in relation to the recoverability of damages is that the claimant should be put in the position they would have been in 'but for' the professional's negligence. This will, however, be subject to rules in respect of remoteness and mitigation.

Damages will also be reduced where it can be shown that the claimant was contributorily negligent. However, the availability of this 'defence' is limited to tortious claims. In addition, it cannot be used to reduce damages in relation to equitable remedies, for example claims for breach of trust, fiduciary duty and/or fraud.

The rules in relation to remoteness of damage, mitigation of loss and contributory negligence are beyond the scope of this chapter.

South Australia Asset Management Corporation v York Montague Ltd [1996] introduced a further consideration in respect of the assessment of damages. The case confirmed that the scope of the duty that has been breached must be determined before issues of causation and remoteness can be considered. In particular, the House of Lords drew a distinction between 'information' and 'advice' such that it was held that, in respect of the former, the defendant will only be responsible for all the foreseeable consequences of the information being wrong.

Distress and inconvenience

A claimant will often claim damages for distress and inconvenience resulting from the professional's negligence. Such damages will generally only be recoverable from the professional if the claimant is able to show that the main purpose of the contract was to ensure peace of mind for the claimant. While there will be circumstances in which such damages are recoverable from a professional, they will be limited and only nominal damages should be awarded. The leading authority in this area is *Farley v Skinner (No. 2)* [2001].

Economic loss

Donoghue v Stevenson [1932] established that where a manufacturer supplies a product containing a latent defect that renders it dangerous to persons or property other than the product itself, they will be liable to pay compensation in tort for any bodily injury to those persons or physical damage caused to 'other' property. If, however, damage is caused to the product itself, the product is either capable of repair (at cost) or is irreparable and must be thrown away. Either way, the loss suffered is purely economic.

It is generally accepted that where a *Hedley Byrne* relationship exists between the parties, economic loss is recoverable. Therefore, it is usual for economic loss to be recoverable in claims against solicitors, accountants, etc., where it can be shown that the client relied on the professional's expertise.

However, in the absence of such a relationship, a claimant will have to prove that damage has been caused to other property (in the *Donoghue v Stevenson* sense) in order to recover their losses.

In relation to building contracts, the House of Lords, in *Anns and others v London Borough of Merton* [1977], was prepared to treat building defects as "material, physical damage" in the *Donoghue v Stevenson* sense, where those defects posed an imminent danger to health and safety. This caused confusion and argument as it appeared to support the proposition that economic loss was recoverable in the absence of a *Hedley Byrne* relationship and/or contract between the parties.

The leading case of *Murphy v Brentwood District Council* [1990] is thought to clarify the position in respect of economic loss. The House of Lords considered that *Anns* had been decided on the basis that in complex structures of products (such as a house or building) one part of the structure might, when it caused damage to another part of the same structure, be considered to have caused damage to other property. This is generally known as the 'complex structure theory'. However, the House of Lords stated that they did not support this theory; rather it was a rationale for the decision in *Anns*.

In view of the above, it appears that a claimant will only be able to succeed in a claim for damages against a construction professional for economic loss if either:

- There is a *Hedley Byrne* relationship between the parties; or
- The construction professional has assumed responsibility towards the claimant that would give rise to a concurrent duty of care to guard against economic loss.

If, of course, the defect is a question which can properly be considered to be separate to the property to which damage is caused, and which would, therefore, mean that it should be categorised as damage to other property (in the *Donoghue v Stevenson* sense), then this would not be categorised as economic loss in any event and would be recoverable.

Proceedings

Pre-action protocols

Before issuing proceedings, parties are expected to comply with the pre-action protocol that applies to the particular claim in question. The protocols form part of the Civil Procedure Rules (CPR) 1998, which govern the conduct of all civil claims.

The overriding objective of all the protocols is to ensure that the parties exchange information at an early stage and engage in a constructive dialogue, with the aim of resolving the dispute without the need to issue proceedings. If a party fails to comply with the requirements of the relevant protocol, the court has specific powers to impose sanctions, usually by way of an adverse costs award.

Those protocols relevant to claims against professionals are:

- Pre-Action Protocol for Professional Negligence
- Pre-Action Protocol for Construction and Engineering Disputes.

The majority of claims against professionals will fall within the first one. It is, however, important to consider which protocol applies in each particular case, not least because different timescales for compliance will apply. For example, a defendant is usually allowed up to three months to provide a letter of response under the Pre-Action Protocol for Professional Negligence, whereas this is reduced to one month under the Pre-Action Protocol for Construction and Engineering Disputes. In respect of the latter, the parties will also be expected to attend an early site meeting and will have to justify (on the grounds of proportionality and/or reasonableness) any refusal to do so.

Limitation

Claimants will often bring claims against a professional in both contract and tort, and claim damages on alternative bases. While claimants will often do so in order to get around the limits on remedies or damages that one particular cause of action may impose, another reason will be to take advantage of the different limitation rules that apply.

While this chapter does not consider the rules of limitation in any detail, it is important to remember that in contract the six-year limitation period begins to run from the date of breach, whereas in tort the six-year period begins to run from the date the loss is suffered. In respect of both, the question of when the breach and/or loss occurred, or is sustained, can be complicated and is highly fact dependent.

In addition, it is significant to note that a claimant will often seek to rely on s.14A of the Limitation Act 1980. This provides that a claimant has three years from the date that they became aware of the professional's negligence in which to bring a claim.

If this three-year period expires later than the six-year period which normally applies to claims brought in tort, the claimant will be able to bring a claim against a professional even though the claim would otherwise be statute barred. Again, the date of knowledge is both fact dependent and complex.

Except in cases of fraud, the s.14A period is subject to a 'long stop' of 15 years.

Civil Procedure Rules 1998

As with all civil claims, the procedure and management of claims brought against professionals are governed by the CPR. It is, therefore, important to consult the CPR at all stages of a claim to ensure compliance. A failure to do so could result in an adverse costs award and potentially a claim against the practitioner themselves for negligence.

Further detail is included in Chapter 8.

It is worth noting that parties are expected to comply with the following guides relating to specific types of claims:

- Queen's Bench Guide
- Admiralty and Commercial Courts Guide
- Mercantile Court Guide
- Chancery Guide
- Technology and Construction Court Guide.

Coverage

Coverage issues generally are considered in Chapter 35. We consider below matters of particular relevance to professional liability policies.

> Professional liability policies are generally written on a 'claims made' basis. Subject to the insured's compliance with provisions regarding notification, they respond to claims made against a professional during the particular policy year. Unlike 'occurrence' policies, the date of the insured's negligence/breach of contract, or the date of the claimant's damage does not determine the policy year under which the claim falls to be considered.

Claims made policies also contain an extension to cover. An insured is entitled/obliged to notify circumstances that "may" or "are likely to" – depending upon the wording of the policy – give rise to a claim. If such circumstances are notified, and all other terms and conditions of the policy are complied with, then any claim that is made arising from those circumstances, but subsequent to the expiration of the policy period, will be deemed to have been made during that policy year.

When considering coverage under a claims made policy, there are a number of issues to consider.

Pre-inception issues

Like all insurance contracts, claims made policies are contracts of utmost good faith.

Prior to the enactment of the Insurance Act 2015, an insured was under a duty to disclose every material circumstance known to them before the contract was concluded, i.e. every circumstance that would affect the underwriting judgement of a prudent insurer. The insured would usually complete a proposal form that concluded with a declaration that the contents of the proposal form are true, and that they form the "basis of the contract".

In the event of an untrue statement in the proposal form, the insured was likely to have misrepresented information to insurers and/or be in breach of the basis of contract clause. If the misrepresentation or failure to disclose related to information material to the underwriting of the risk and that induced the actual insurer to enter the contract, then insurers may have been entitled to avoid the contract and treat the policy as having never existed.

With the enactment of the Insurance Act 2015, insureds under non-consumer policies which incept after 12 August 2016 are now under a duty to make a fair presentation of the risk. This requires disclosure of every material circumstance that the insured knows or ought to know, or sufficient information to put the prudent insurer on enquiry. In addition, basis of contract clauses are abolished.

Remedies are only available if the insurer can show that but for the misrepresentation, they would not have entered into the contract or would have done so on different terms. Significantly, unless the breach is deliberate or reckless (in which case the policy can be avoided), remedies are available proportionate to the action which would have been taken but for the misrepresentation.

In some policies the right to avoid is specifically constrained by an "innocent non-disclosure" clause. These usually provide that insurers may avoid only if there has been a fraudulent misrepresentation, non-disclosure or intent to deceive.

Insuring clause

Assuming there are no pre-inception issues that call into question the existence of the policy, the first policy issue to look at is whether the allegations against the professional fall within the terms of the insuring clause. Many insuring clauses insure the insured against "civil liability". Some are more limited, insuring only against legal liabilities to pay "compensatory damages" or "in respect of negligence".

If an allegation, or a head of loss, does not fall within the insuring clause, the policy will not respond.

Exclusions

The policy will also itemise either causes of, or categories of, loss that are expressly excluded. For example, one common exclusion in professional liability policies is any liability assumed under a contract or agreement that would not have existed but for that contract or agreement. Another common exclusion is claims or circumstances known to the insured prior to the policy, or notified to prior insurers.

Insurers will bear the onus of proving that an exclusion applies, unless the policy specifically provides that the insured bears the onus of proving that an exclusion does not apply.

General conditions

The policy will provide various things the insured must do in order to be entitled to an indemnity under the policy. Many of these conditions relate to the insured's obligation in the event of becoming aware of circumstances that may lead to a claim or becoming aware of a claim. They may impose obligations as to when the claim or circumstance must be notified. It is common for policies to require notification "as soon as practicable". The question of what is as soon as practicable or as soon as possible will be fact dependent.

Other general conditions may relate to what level of assistance the insured must give insurers, or how disputes between insureds and insurers are to be resolved.

The general conditions will also usually specify the applicable governing law of the insurance.

> The consequences of a breach of a condition of the policy will depend on whether the condition is a condition precedent to indemnity or a mere condition. For policies which incepted before 12 August 2016 breach of a condition precedent means that the insured has no entitlement to an indemnity under the policy. Breach of a condition, however, only entitles the insurer to make a counterclaim for damages equivalent to its prejudice suffered as a result of the breach. For policies which incepted after 12 August 2016, breach of a condition precedent will suspend cover until the breach is remedied. If the breach is not remedied but it has not increased the risk of the particular loss occurring, the claim cannot be declined.

Conditions precedent will usually be specifically identified in the policy. If a condition specifies the consequences of a breach, e.g. "we will not pay unless ...", it may still be held to be a condition precedent, even though the words 'condition precedent' are not used.

Aggregation

Where there is more than one claim against an insured it will be necessary to consider whether all claims (or any of them) aggregate for the purposes of limits of indemnity or the application of policy excesses or deductibles. There are many different forms of aggregation wording and the law in relation to aggregation is complex. Aggregation wordings range from those considered to be narrow, such as "all claims arising from a single act, error or omission", to those that are regarded as being very broad, for example "all claims arising out of the same source or original cause".

Particular complexity arises where aggregation clauses contain the words "related", "related series", or "series of related" in conjunction with other terms.

Defence costs

In addition to indemnifying an insured against its legal liability, professional liability policies generally also insure defence costs.

> It is important to determine whether there is a stand-alone insuring clause in respect of defence costs, or whether the promise to indemnify defence costs appears in the same clause that deals with the promise to indemnify against legal liability. The rules regarding payment of defence costs are different in each instance.

In simple terms:

- If the promise to indemnify against legal liability and the promise to indemnify defence costs are in the same clause, there is no obligation to pay defence costs unless and until a legal liability to a third party has been established.

- By contrast, if there is a stand-alone insuring clause in respect of defence costs then, provided the allegations (if proven) would fall to be indemnified by the policy, there is an obligation to advance defence costs irrespective of whether legal liability is ultimately established.

It is important to consider whether the defence costs are subject to an excess or deductible and whether they are part of an all-inclusive limit of indemnity or 'in addition' to the limit of indemnity.

Policies usually require that an insurer provides written consent prior to the defence costs being incurred. That requirement will be subject to an implied term that consent cannot be unreasonably withheld, even if the policy is silent on that issue.

12 Clinical negligence claims

Janet Sayers

- Who is the defendant?
- A claimant's right of action: contract or tort
- Negligence:
  - Duty of care
  - Standard of care
  - Causation
  - Loss of chance
  - Apportionment
- Duty of candour
- Consent to treatment and confidentiality
- Disclosure of medical records
  - Limitation
  - Pre-action Protocol for the Resolution of Clinical Disputes
  - Proceedings

Clinical negligence claims

Introduction

Clinical negligence claims are generally claims for damages for personal injury. In that respect, clinical negligence claims are dealt with in the same way as any claim for personal injury. However, this chapter deals with clinical negligence claims separately as some areas differ from personal injury cases. It does not discuss quantum as clinical negligence claims are quantified in the same way as other claims for damages for personal injury.

Defendants

National Health Service (NHS)

Since January 1990, health authorities and trusts have been vicariously liable for the negligent acts and omissions of their employees (doctors, nurses and other clinicians, etc.) and so it is usually the NHS trust or health authority that will be named in any proceedings. As with any employers' liability claim, there is no need to join an individual as a defendant to proceedings. It is usual to name their employer only.

In 1995, the NHS Litigation Authority was established (as of 1 April 2017 it has changed its name to NHS Resolution). It is a Special Health Authority and, therefore, part of the NHS. It is responsible for handling clinical negligence claims made against NHS bodies in England.

The Existing Liabilities Scheme (ELS) applies to claims that occurred before 1 April 1995. The Clinical Negligence Scheme for Trusts (CNST) deals with claims that occurred after this date.

NHS Resolution manages claims through a panel of solicitors (including Kennedys) and is responsible for payment of any damages and legal costs.

Private healthcare sector

Private hospitals and clinics are insured by medical malpractice underwriters in the open insurance market. The insurance cover is for employees of the healthcare establishment (it might be a private hospital, private fertility clinic or perhaps a private clinic conducting MRI scans). The policy will only cover employees of the establishment.

Consultants working on a private basis in a private hospital are obliged to make their own funding arrangements. They are independent contractors and not employees of the establishment.

Most consultants acting in a private capacity, and also the majority of general practitioners, will belong to one of two medical defence organisations, either the Medical Defence Union (MDU) or Medical Protection Society (MPS). A small number may obtain insurance on the open market.

There are some instances now in which private hospitals are indemnified under the CNST where they have contracted to provide services to the NHS.

A claimant's right of action: contract or tort?

There is probably no contractual relationship between a patient and the NHS, although there is no case law on this either way. For this reason, a claimant will bring their claim against the NHS for the civil wrong, or tort, of negligence.

Where a claimant is basing their claim on an issue of consent they may also consider the tort of battery or assault. In extreme cases, criminal law may apply and the police may be asked to investigate an alleged wrongful killing or possibly charges of grievous bodily harm.

In the private healthcare sector a patient may enter into a contract with the private hospital. They may bring a claim in both contract and tort.

Negligence

To prove negligence a patient will have to satisfy a court that:

- They were owed a duty of care by the defendant (hospital/consultant).
- The defendant was in breach of that duty.
- The patient has suffered a loss as a result of that breach.

If one of these criteria is not established, then any claim for clinical negligence will fail.

Duty of care

The House of Lords gave guidance in the case of *Caparo Industries plc v Dickman and others* [1990] on determining the existence of a duty of care, indicating that it must be "fair, just and reasonable" to impose such a duty.

In the case of *Darnley v Croydon Health Care Services NHS Trust* [2017] the Court of Appeal indicated that it must also be considered in the context of the scope of the duty and the range of consequences flowing from it. In that particular case the Court of Appeal found that it was not "fair, just or reasonable" to impose a duty of care upon a hospital receptionist to provide accurate information regarding waiting times in hospitals.

Standard of care

Assuming a duty does exist, where doctors and other medical personnel are concerned, the law imposes a duty of care where the standard of care is one of medical, not legal, judgement. It is the medical profession that determines the standards of proper medical practice. A doctor treating a patient in accordance with approved medical practice, even a practice approved and followed by only a minority of the profession, will not be found negligent/in breach of duty.

The standard for 'reasonable care' depends on the nature of the activity undertaken, the risk being created and the seriousness of the consequences if due care is not exercised. The test for negligence was set out in *Bolam v Friern Hospital Management Committee* [1957], widely viewed as the case setting out the basis for the standard of care in clinical negligence claims.

> The *Bolam* test:
>
> "The test is the standard of the ordinary skilled man exercising and professing to have that special skill ... a doctor is not guilty of negligence if he has acted in accordance with the practice accepted as proper by a responsible body of medical men skilled in that particular art."

Essentially, the doctor must have acted in accordance with a responsible body of opinion. So, for example, a consultant anaesthetist who allegedly treats a patient negligently will be judged by the standard of a responsible body of consultant anaesthetists' opinion. It suffices if the consultant anaesthetist only finds one other expert to support their actions. Whether a lawyer or claims handler would want to rely on one opinion, at complete odds to other experts, is another matter.

A doctor must, however, always exercise ordinary skill and be ready to accept that a commonly used practice may be considered negligent in some circumstances.

The clinical standard is judged by the practice at the time of the alleged negligence (rather than at the time the matter is investigated).

Causation

A claimant may be able to prove that a hospital was negligent. However, to establish liability it is essential for the claimant to show that the hospital's negligence caused the claimant's loss or damage.

The burden of proof is on the claimant to show that, on the balance of probabilities, the defendant's negligent act or omission caused their harm or loss. If the claimant is unable to prove this, their claim will fail.

The test that the courts consider in relation to causation is the 'but for' test, i.e. but for the negligence of the defendant, would the claimant have suffered their injuries, loss or damage? If the claimant would have suffered loss or damage in any event then they are unable to prove the second element of a claim, i.e. the defendant's negligence is not causative of the claimant's loss or damage.

When it is impossible to answer the 'but for' test the claimant may rely on 'material contribution', i.e. causation will be established if the claimant can show the breach of duty materially contributed to their loss or damage.

Loss of chance

When considering the circumstances of a claimant who has undergone medical treatment to improve or cure their illness it is necessary to consider their underlying condition and whether that would have prevented a full recovery in any event.

A loss of chance occurs where the claimant has lost an opportunity to make a better or full recovery (possibly through a delay in treatment of cancer) or for the condition to improve as might have been expected. The House of Lords' decision in *Gregg v Scott* [2005] is the leading case on this.

Apportionment

Where the claimant brings a claim against more than one medical organisation (e.g. a number of hospitals and/or doctors or GPs), apportionment of liability should be established between them so as to quantify the damages each defendant will be responsible for.

The Medical Defence Organisations' Protocol is a protocol between the medical defence organisations (MDO), which sets out guidance for the resolution of apportionment issues between these defendants.

Duty of candour

The Francis Inquiry into Mid Staffordshire NHS Foundation Trust recommended the introduction of a statutory duty of candour in order to reduce avoidable harm.

A statutory duty of candour came into force in November 2014. It places a legal duty on NHS trusts, NHS foundation trusts and special health authorities to inform and apologise to patients if there have been mistakes in their care that have led to significant harm.

The guidance issued by the Care Quality Commission in November 2014 states that, to fulfil this duty, an NHS organisation must:

- In carrying on a regulated activity, make sure it acts in an open and transparent way with relevant persons in relation to care and treatment provided to people who use services.
- Tell the relevant person in person as soon as reasonably practicable after becoming aware that a notifiable safety incident has occurred, and provide support to them in relation to the incident, including when giving the notification.
- Provide an account of the incident that, to the best of the health service body's knowledge, is true, and of all the facts the body knows about the incident at the date of the notification.
- Advise the relevant person what further enquiries the health service body believes are appropriate.
- Offer an apology.
- Follow this up by giving the same information in writing, and providing an update on any enquiries.
- Keep a written record of all communication with the relevant person.

Consent to treatment

Consent is required for any medical treatment. It is now well established and accepted that all medical practitioners (doctors, midwives and dentists, etc.) should seek their patient's consent before commencing any treatment (except in emergencies or where the patient lacks capacity), otherwise they may face civil or even criminal proceedings for assault.

Consent is the voluntary and continuing permission of a patient to receive a particular treatment. It can be implied or expressed, verbal or in writing. It must be based on adequate knowledge of the purpose, nature and likely effects and risks of the treatment, including the likelihood of its success and any alternatives to it. Consent is given by patients with the capacity to do so.

Form of consent

Written consent provides the clearest evidence that the patient has been provided with details of what is proposed and has consented to it. The NHS Executive has provided a series of model consent forms for health authorities and trusts. However, the existence of a written consent form is not proof that consent has in fact been obtained. It may, for example, have been signed without being read or without adequate explanation being given or under duress. If a patient has not given proper consent, any treatment will be unlawful, even where they have signed a consent form. The reality prevails over the writing.

It is not always necessary for consent to be expressed in writing. Consent may be implied if it is clear from the circumstances that the patient has accepted and consented to the treatment. If a patient has been asked to undress to enable a doctor to perform an examination, the act of undressing indicates the patient's agreement to the examination. When patients roll up their sleeves to receive an injection (having first been informed by the doctor of the benefits and risks) this is an indication of their consent to it.

Valid consent

The validity of a patient's consent depends on a number of factors. To be valid, consent must be 'real' and this means that patients must be competent or able to give their consent. They must know in broad terms what they are consenting to and they must give their consent freely and without being deliberately misled.

The basic rule is that a medical practitioner is entitled to assume that their patient is able to consent to or refuse treatment. The fact that a patient does not appear to the professional to make a wise choice is not itself evidence of incapacity.

The leading case on adult competency is *F v West Berkshire Health Authority* [1989], where the House of Lords said a patient should be able to: appreciate what will be done to them if they accept treatment; understand the likely consequences of leaving their condition untreated; and understand the risks and side effects that the health professionals explain to them.

Informed consent

The case of *Montgomery v Lanarkshire Health Board* [2015] changed the issue of consent as previously understood by overturning the case of *Sidaway v Board of Governors of the Bethlem Royal Hospital and the Maudsley Hospital and others* [1985], which applied the *Bolam* test to consent. The Supreme Court: "An adult person of sound mind is entitled to decide which, if any, of the available forms of treatment to undergo, and ... consent must be obtained before treatment interfering with ... bodily integrity is undertaken. The doctor is therefore under a duty to take reasonable care to ensure that the patient is aware of any material risks involved in any recommended treatment, and of any reasonable alternative or variant treatments. The test of materiality is whether, in the circumstances of the particular case, a reasonable person in the patient's position would be likely to attach significant risk, or the doctor should have been reasonably aware that the particular patient would be likely to attach significance to it".

It is therefore no longer a defence to point to a reasonable body of medical opinion when considering consent. The test of materiality is now subjective to the actual patient. The doctor must now not only consider those risks which a reasonable patient in the patient's position would have considered significant, but also the risks that the actual patient would consider significant. The onus is now on doctors to show they have engaged the patient in dialogue with an aim of ensuring the patient understands the seriousness of their condition, the risk and benefits of proposed treatment and any alternative treatment before it can be said they have taken informed consent. Simply handing over a leaflet or obtaining a signature on a consent form is not enough.

Article 3 of the European Convention on Human Rights 1968 states that no one shall be subjected to torture or inhumane or degrading treatment or punishment. Article 8 indicates that "Everyone has the right to respect for private and family life", which has been held to extend to protecting bodily integrity and a right to self-autonomy. Treatment given without consent may also fall within the ambit of Article 3.

Capacity

Mental capacity is the ability to make decisions and it is presumed that a patient has mental capacity unless otherwise established.

Medical practitioners are obliged to treat patients lacking capacity in accordance with the 'best interests' principle:

- Mental incapacity – generally, if a patient is unable to make a decision then their medical practitioner must act in their best interests. Treatment will be lawful in such circumstances, providing a responsible body of professional opinion would accept that it was in the patient's best interests. The statutory test of incapacity under s.2(1) of the Mental Capacity Act (MCA) 2005 is that, at the material time, the patient is unable to make a decision for themselves in relation to a matter because of an impairment of, or disturbance in the functioning of, the mind or brain. However, while a patient may be described as not having capacity, they may have some capacity to make certain decisions. In *Re SB* [2013], Mr Justice Holman held that while a patient was detained under s.2 of the Mental Health Act 1983, she nevertheless had capacity to consent to termination of pregnancy at 23 weeks. He considered that she had capacity to make this decision for which she had a range of rational and genuinely held reasons.

- Minors – parents may provide consent on behalf of their children until they reach the age of 18. Following *Gillick v West Norfolk and Wisbech Area Health Authority and another* [1984], a child under 18 may be competent to consent if they have sufficient understanding and intelligence to understand fully what is proposed.

If there is time, however, reasonable effort should be made to find out if there is a valid lasting power of attorney and/or advanced decision. Treatment can be provided with the consent of the attorney if it is in the patient's best interests. If there is an advanced decision in place then it should be respected when considering treatment.

Undue influence

Consent or refusal of consent may be the result of undue influence. If that is the case, consent would not be voluntary and would be invalid. This was considered by the Court of Appeal in *Re T* [1992]. In that case an adult patient told hospital staff, when admitted to hospital after a car accident, that she did not wish to have a blood transfusion. She made that decision after speaking to her mother who was a Jehovah's Witness. The Court of Appeal decided that while it was to be expected a patient will seek advice before deciding whether to accept treatment, it was possible that their will might be overborne by pressure brought by others, in this case, the patient's mother. The refusal of consent to treatment was, therefore, invalid.

Obtaining a court declaration to treat

The Court of Protection has jurisdiction on matters relating to capacity,

In *A NHS Trust v K and another* [2012], Kennedys obtained a declaration to treat K, a morbidly obese woman in need of a hysterectomy. K lacked capacity to make an informed decision. Without surgery, there was a likelihood she would die of cancer. With surgery, her chance of death was also over 50%. The High Court granted the declaration requested by the hospital to treat *K* in her best interests, despite opposition from the Official Solicitor acting on *K*'s behalf. Although extremely risky, sufficient safeguards assured the judge that complications would be managed effectively, minimising the chance of death.

If a clinician considers that a patient lacks capacity and wishes to treat in the patient's best interests but the patient's relatives disagree with the treatment, then it is advisable that an application to court be made.

However, where a patient with capacity refuses treatment, their wishes must be respected, regardless of the consequences.

Withholding or withdrawing treatment

The MCA Code of Practice provides that it may be in the best interest of a patient in a limited number of cases not to give life-sustaining treatment "where treatment is futile, overly burdensome to the patient or where there is no prospect of recovery ... even if this may result in the person's death".

In *Aintree University Hospitals NHS Foundation Trust v James* [2013], the Supreme Court clarified the term 'futility' in the context of medical treatment. It is correct to consider whether the proposed treatment would be futile in the sense of being 'ineffective' or being 'of no benefit to the patient'. Treatment is not futile if it enables a patient to resume a quality of life that the patient would regard as worthwhile.

The Supreme Court considered that the Court of Appeal had been "setting the goal too high" in finding that treatment is futile unless it has a real prospect of curing or at least providing palliative care for a life-threatening disease or illness. It is not for others to say that a life that the patient would regard as worthwhile is not worth living.

Hospitals and clinicians can do no better than keep relatives closely advised of any decision and their reasons for that decision. If it is clear that the patient's relatives do not agree with the decision then legal advice must be sought. As always, the clinicians must be able to show that the decision is in the best interests of the patient.

Emergencies

Emergencies justify treatment without consent as long as the treatment is in the patient's best interests. Emergencies are, in essence, an example of implied consent.

Confidentiality

There is a general duty of confidentiality between a patient and those treating them. Confidentiality is necessary so as to generate trust between a patient and the treating doctor. There are, however, exceptional circumstances that may arise that allow this duty to be breached:

- In civil procedure there is a legal duty to provide disclosure. If a patient makes complaints or brings proceedings, they have impliedly consented to their medical records and details being disclosed to lawyers representing the hospital/ healthcare professional.
- Statutory provision is made for doctors to report details of notifiable diseases to a "Proper Officer" of the local authority or local Health Protection Unit.
- Sharing information within a team of healthcare workers is allowed. For example, where they work within a practice, partnership or within a team in hospital.

Disclosure

Medical records

When a clinical negligence claim is first investigated the claimant will be asked to sign a form of authority giving their authority for the disclosure of all relevant medical notes and records to their legal advisor and to those representing the defendant. Any individual can request access to their medical records under the Access to Health

Records Act 1990. A request cannot reasonably be refused unless the material contained in the notes is likely to harm the patient. This is a common concern, for example, when the patient's notes may relate to mental health issues. Disclosure will generally be to a limited number of individuals, for example, lawyers for the parties and medical experts.

During the course of litigation if a doctor wishes to withhold medical records then they may be released to certain specified named experts to allow the matter to proceed and the allegations to be considered properly.

Documents

When a claim is initiated, it is important to establish whether the defendant has any correspondence or documentation relating to the matter in issue. For example, a hospital may have investigated the matter internally in response to a letter of complaint sent by the patient or as part of an internal 'Serious Incident Investigation'. In these instances such documents are likely to be disclosable to the claimant (including internal emails and comments from doctors) as they cannot be said to have been prepared in contemplation of litigation and therefore privileged from production.

If comments or communications etc. are prepared or obtained by the defendant in respect of a contemplated claim then they are arguably privileged and not subject to disclosure. For example if they are prepared following a letter from the claimant's solicitor, this would be good evidence that they were prepared in contemplation of litigation.

Sometimes comments made by doctors are critical of the care given by a defendant and are not privileged from disclosure. This should be considered when determining whether liability should be contested. If liability is contested these documents will need to be disclosed and explained unless they are not relevant to the issues in the case.

If an inquest has taken place into the death of a patient and a claim is subsequently brought by the family of the deceased, the documents relating to the inquest will also be disclosable in any claim. This is because the purpose of the inquest is to establish the narrow issues of how, when and where the deceased came by his death. It is not to attribute blame for the death. It is therefore difficult to argue privilege in respect of documents relating solely to an inquest.

Continuing duty of disclosure

A claims handler or lawyer investigating a claim will be hampered in the course of their work unless there is unfettered access to the claimant's records. Under the Civil Procedural Rules (CPR) the duty of disclosure is an ongoing one throughout the course of proceedings. The defendant hospital or medical practitioner is entitled to see all the material that the claimant has seen and vice versa.

Limitation

The Limitation Act 1980 does not make specific provision for clinical negligence claims, although there are specific rules relating to cases of personal injury or death and, as said before, in practice, most clinical negligence claims will be for damages for personal injury or death.

In most cases, the patient has three years from the date their cause of action arises (usually the date when the accident or incident occurred) or three years from their 'date of knowledge' in which to issue proceedings. So, for example, in a case where a claimant is alleging that she is now permanently paralysed as a result of an epidural not being properly administered during labour, time will start to run from the date when the anaesthetic was administered or, alternatively, three years from when the claimant discovered that the reason for her paralysis can be attributed to the administration of the anaesthetic.

But what if:

- The patient dies before the limitation period expires? Their estate has three years from their death or the date of their personal representative's knowledge in which to commence the claim.
- The alleged negligent act proves fatal? The deceased's dependants have three years from the date of death to bring an action or three years from their date of knowledge or that of the personal representative of the deceased.
- The claimant is under a disability (i.e. minors or those who lack capacity to conduct legal proceedings)? The limitation period does not begin to run until the disability ceases. In the case of a minor, they cease to be under a disability when they reach the age of 18 and time will only begin to run from then, assuming they have the relevant knowledge. If they do not have the necessary knowledge, the period will only begin to run when they acquire that knowledge. Parents or representatives of a minor (or person under a disability) can commence an action on the child's behalf before the child attains majority. If the patient lacks capacity within the meaning of the MCA 2005, and is incapable of managing their own affairs, time will not run until they cease to be under a disability. If the patient's condition is permanent, time will only start to run on their death.

The limitation period, therefore, does not necessarily start to run from the date of the alleged negligent act or omission. While a hospital or medical practitioner may investigate an incident that may lead to a claim soon after the negligent act or omission has occurred, it could be many years before any claim is made, which may not be statute barred, i.e. brought outside the limitation period. Even if the claim is statute barred, the court has a discretion to disapply the time limits for personal injury and death cases and allow the case to proceed.

> It is for these reasons that records belonging to hospitals and medical practitioners must be retained for a number of years. As time does not run in respect of any claim a child may have until they reach their majority, their notes and records should be retained until at least their 21st birthday, i.e. up to the age of majority and three years thereafter.

As regards those who lack capacity to conduct legal proceedings, there is no limitation period and for that reason a hospital, particularly a mental health hospital, is under an obligation to retain those patients' notes and records for as long as is reasonably practicable.

What knowledge is required?

The extent of knowledge necessary to start limitation running against a patient is defined in s.14 of the Limitation Act 1980. There must be knowledge, not just reasonable belief or suspicion, of the following:

- The injury complained of is significant.
- The injury was attributable in whole or in part to the act or omission that is alleged to constitute negligence or a breach of duty.
- The identity of the defendant.

Pre-action Protocol for the Resolution of Clinical Disputes

The CPR make provision for the use of a pre-action protocol for the resolution of clinical disputes. There is also a protocol for obtaining hospital medical records.

The protocol requires early disclosure of medical records (within 40 days of a request). When such a request is received from a claimant solicitor it may be an indication that litigation is being contemplated and the defendant should commence investigation and consider notifying their insurers/MDO/NHS Resolution of the potential claim.

Before issuing proceedings, the claimant must prepare a letter of claim, which should follow a prescribed format as set out in the Protocol. It should include the following:

1) Patient's name, address and date of birth
2) Date or dates of allegedly negligent treatment
3) Events giving rise to the claim
4) As much detail as possible on the allegations of negligence and causal link to injuries
5) Details of the injuries sustained
6) Details of the claim for damages e.g., likely heads of loss and likely value of claim.

All this information will enable the defendant to assess the claim against it and respond accordingly.

Upon receipt of a letter of claim, a defendant has four months from the date of receipt of the letter of claim to investigate and serve a letter of response.

The letter of response should also be detailed and provide information obtained from the defendant's investigation and/or independent medical expert evidence. The letter of response must specifically state whether a claim or any part of it is admitted or denied. A denial should be supported by an explanation for that denial.

Proceedings

To issue proceedings, a claimant must file and serve a claim form, Particulars of Claim and supporting condition and prognosis medical evidence within the relevant time dictated by the CPR. A personal injury claim worth less than £50,000 should not be issued in the High Court of Justice but in a county court.

If the proceedings are the first notification of the claim, the defendant should seek an extension of time for service of its defence for four months, which is the time that would have been afforded for investigation under the pre-action protocol if a letter of claim had been served.

Once the defence is served, clinical negligence claims are generally allotted to the multi-track, as evidence is rarely straightforward.

In the county court, the claim is dealt with by a district judge through interlocutory stages.

In the High Court, clinical negligence masters are allotted to clinical negligence claims and oversee the initial interlocutory stages.

A case management hearing (CMC) will be listed shortly after allocation and the parties are encouraged to agree directions and set a timetable as far as possible. The parties will discuss the types of experts that the case requires and any disagreement will need to be determined by the judge/master at the hearing. How long is required between directions is likely to depend on the complexity of the case and the availability of the experts to examine and provide a report.

If the case is not excluded from cost budgeting then each party must prepare a budget of costs to include costs incurred to date and those anticipated. Prior to the hearing these must be agreed as far as possible. The judge/master will rule on any outstanding issues and approve costs budgets at the CMC.

Witnesses of fact

When a patient first intimates a claim, initial investigations should include identification of those involved in their care. Witness statements should be taken from them as soon as possible. Sometimes it can be difficult to identify all the relevant staff from the medical records and they may only be identified once other witnesses are interviewed. It is important to trace and make contact with all witnesses involved, however minor their role.

Expert witnesses

Independent medical experts are crucial to a clinical negligence claim. If proceedings are issued, court rules provide that the claimant must serve with their proceedings (among other documents) a medical report relating to their condition and prognosis. It follows that the claimant's medical expert will want to see at an early stage the claimant's medical notes and records. This will enable the claimant's medical expert to evaluate whether the claimant has a claim and to prepare a report to serve with proceedings.

By the same token, the defendant will need to instruct an independent medical expert at an early stage to assist in the drafting of the letter of response.

Often, numerous experts will be required to comment on breach of duty and causation and this will have been determined at the CMC.

Single joint experts are less common in clinical negligence cases but may be ordered to report on some quantum issues.

It is common for all experts involved in a case to have permission to give oral evidence at trial, where issues remain in dispute.

Settlement

If liability is admitted, the defendant should press the claimant to provide a schedule of loss and, if possible, expert quantum evidence (even on a without prejudice basis). This allows the defendant to consider whether an early offer can be advanced and what level that offer should be. It may be that due to complexities of the case, or disagreement regarding the reasonableness of the claimant's evidence that the defendant may obtain its own quantum evidence before advancing an offer of settlement.

CRU

Before settlement is agreed the defendant should apply to the Department of Work and Pensions (DWP) for a Compensation Recovery Unit (CRU) certificate. This is because when a defendant pays damages to a claimant following a personal injury claim, benefits paid to the claimant (which are attributable to the injury) can be recovered by the DWP from the defendant. If there are any such sums to be repaid then the defendant can seek to deduct these sums from the gross offer of settlement.

Also, if the NHS provides treatment to an injured claimant (at a hospital not named as a defendant) which is attributable to the injury then the cost of this treatment is also recoverable from the defendant. These sums are not deducted from any damages but must be paid in addition to any settlement. It is important that an NHS charges certificate is also obtained from the DWP so the defendant knows its full liability before agreeing any settlement.

On payment of damages to the claimant the defendant must repay the total shown on both the CRU and NHS charges certificates. It would be negligent to settle a claim without valid and up-to-date certificates.

Mediation/ADR

Under the CPR the parties are encouraged to use Alternative Dispute Resolution (ADR) and the court has the power to order a one-month stay, with the parties' agreement, to allow for this. It can be useful not only in disputes over quantum but also in discussing and narrowing issues between the parties. The court also has the power to consider the parties' attitude towards ADR when considering costs.

Trial

For claims in the High Court of Justice, trial will be by judge sitting on their own without a jury, as in personal injury claims. The judge does not have to have experience of clinical negligence claims or indeed personal injury claims.

For claims in the county courts, the trial is sent to a trial centre for hearing and is usually heard by a circuit judge.

Obstetric cases

A healthcare provider owes a duty of care to an expectant mother and her baby not to cause harm to either of them before, during or after labour. Claims commonly brought by children relate to brain damage caused during delivery (a condition known as cerebral palsy) and brachial plexus injuries caused by shoulder dystocia (known as Erb's palsy). Claims may also be brought arising from the death of a baby during labour.

Claims brought in respect of cerebral palsy are commonly the most expensive claims.

Allegations of negligence commonly found in cerebral palsy claims relate to a failure to properly monitor the foetal heart rate, respond to signs of foetal distress and delay in delivering the baby. To succeed in proving causation, it must be shown that the negligence caused or materially contributed towards the brain damage. It is considered that a foetus can withstand 10 minutes of oxygen starvation before brain damage starts. Death will usually result at around 25 minutes if the lack of oxygen continues, though the foetus may survive longer if there is only partial lack of oxygen. Timing of any negligent act or omission is therefore key in the consideration of causation in cerebral palsy claims. It is also important to consider whether there may be any other cause of the brain damage (e.g. genetic abnormality) and whether some or all of the brain damage would have occurred in any event.

The future

Governments across the world are understandably concerned about the rising cost of clinical negligence claims. It was for this reason that the NHS Litigation Authority (now NHS Resolution) was established in 1995 and the ELS and CNST schemes created so as to streamline management of these claims and reduce legal costs.

The introduction of the Jackson reforms from April 2013 saw the abolition of conditional fee agreements and success fees and introduction of one way costs shifting and, more recently, fixed fees for lower value claims in the hope of containing the rising legal costs associated with these type of claims.

The amendment to the discount rate introduced by the Lord Chancellor in February 2017 saw the discount rate change from 2.5% to –0.75%. This has seen a significant rise in the level of damages awarded for future losses. At the time of writing the government is undertaking a response to the discount rate consultation and the position remains uncertain.

13 Catastrophic injury

Charles Martin and Mark Burton

- Defining catastrophic injury
- Traumatic brain injury, spinal cord injury, amputation and pain disorders
- Life expectancy: impaired lives, resources and methodology
- Assessing capacity and the Court of Protection
- Experts, case management and rehabilitation
- Interim payments, provisional damages and tactical claims handling

Catastrophic injury

Introduction

Catastrophic injury claims are often at the forefront of developments in personal injury law. Developments are rapid, reflecting the high financial and human cost involved when an accident results in catastrophic injury. While such claims represent a relatively small proportion of any insurer's claims volumes, they make up a large proportion of overall reserves.

What constitutes a catastrophic injury claim? Different stakeholders have their own financial criteria, with the entry level typically ranging from £250,000 to £1 million. From the medical standpoint, the claimant's injuries will normally include one or more of the following:

- Serious head injury or brain injury
- Spinal cord injury resulting in complete or incomplete quadriplegia, tetraplegia or paraplegia
- Amputation of upper or lower limbs
- Blindness
- Multiple orthopaedic trauma
- Serious pain disorders

> The catastrophic injury claims handler faces a range of technical challenges, such as periodical payments, mental capacity, life expectancy and computation of care packages, and will need to rely on a team of experts from different medical and non-medical disciplines.

Serious accidents have a devastating impact on the victim and their family and, at the same time as progressing the claim, the parties may engage in rehabilitation initiatives to restore function and maximise quality of life. The claims handler may have to make life-changing decisions regarding rehabilitation funding, including for large purchases such as specially adapted housing.

These claims can take many years to resolve, especially in infant cases, and consequently the legal costs can be high and may themselves run into seven figures in utmost severity cases. A sophisticated claims handling approach is required to unlock settlement outside the traditional litigation timetable.

From 20 March 2017 the discount rate was reduced from 2.5% to –0.75%. As a consequence multipliers for heads of future loss have increased and the impact of this will be seen most significantly in catastrophic claims.

On 7 September 2017 the Lord Chancellor announced reforms of the current discount rate methodology following market consultation. He indicated that if a single rate was being set according to the proposed reforms it would be between 0% and 1% at this time. The predicted timescale is fairly slow and the rate may not change until early 2019, depending on parliamentary capacity for the enabling legislation.

This chapter explores the legal, medical and tactical issues that arise when dealing with catastrophic injury claims and offers practical guidance on claims handling best practice. For a broader analysis of matters affecting catastrophic injury claims, including quantum issues, see the Kennedys Catastrophic Injury Claims Guide.

Traumatic brain injury

Traumatic brain injury (TBI) is damage to the brain resulting from external mechanical force such as rapid acceleration or deceleration, impact or penetration by an object. The severity and effects of a brain injury can vary significantly and can result in substantial claims for damages. Expert evidence will be required to assess the extent of the injury sustained and the claimant's immediate and long-term needs.

Anatomy of the brain

The brain is divided into a number of different areas and the area and severity of damage will determine the level of disability.

The largest part of the brain is the cerebrum, which consists of four lobes:

- **Frontal lobe:** controls a person's emotions and personality. It is involved in executive and cognitive functions, problem solving, memory, language, judgement, social and sexual behaviour.
- **Temporal lobe:** deals with hearing, memory acquisition, some visual perceptions and categorisation of objects
- **Parietal lobe:** deals with visual attention, touch perception, goal-directed voluntary movement, manipulation of objects and the integration of senses.
- **Occipital lobe:** controls vision.

The second largest part of the brain is the cerebellum, which controls unconscious motor function, coordinated voluntary movement and balance.

There are three membranes surrounding the brain (and the spinal cord) located between the skull and the brain:

- **Dura:** the outermost and thickest of the three membranes.
- **Arachnoid:** the central membrane.
- **Pia mater:** the innermost and thinnest membrane.

Other significant areas of the brain are the hypothalamus, thalamus, pineal body, pons, medulla oblongata and pituitary gland.

Classification of a brain injury

The terms 'head injury' and 'brain injury' are often used interchangeably. However, a head injury normally denotes an injury that causes no or very minor injury to the brain, but which can involve damage to the scalp and skull.

TBI is usually classified based on the mechanism, pathological features and severity of the injury.

Mechanism

TBI can be caused in a number of ways, including road traffic accidents, falls and during birth. The mechanism of a TBI can be divided between closed and open head injuries. A closed injury occurs when there is no penetration of the skull and the brain is not exposed. An open (or penetrating) injury occurs when an object pierces the skull.

Damage may occur to the part of the brain located at the site of impact or on the side opposite the impact (coup and contrecoup injury). Coup injuries are more likely when the stationary head is struck by a moving object, whereas contrecoup injuries are usual when the moving head strikes a stationary object, for example in a road traffic accident.

Pathological features

The type of TBI sustained can be defined by its pathological features. Lesions can occur within the skull but outside the brain (extra-cerebral) or within the brain tissue (intra-cerebral).

Damage from TBI can be focal (i.e. confined to specific areas) and/or diffuse. Focal injuries include those to the frontal and temporal lobes, cerebral lacerations and haematomas. Diffuse injuries include swelling (oedema) and concussion.

Haemorrhage with bleeding in the brain tissue itself is an intracerebral lesion. Extra-cerebral lesions include haemorrhages involving membranes surrounding the brain (dura, arachnoid and pia mater), epidural (between the dura and skull), subdural (between the dura and the arachnoid) and subarachnoid haematomas (between the arachnoid and the pia mater).

Brain injuries are classified as either primary or secondary injuries. Primary brain injury is caused at the moment of trauma when blood vessels are ruptured or haemorrhage and brain tissue is damaged (contusions). There can then follow secondary injury when complications arise out of the primary injury due to problems such as swelling, blood clots and lack of oxygen.

Types of primary brain injury

- **Diffuse axonal injury:** results from shearing of the brain tissue. Most people will lose consciousness for a period of time depending on the severity of the injury.
- **Contusions:** usually caused by a direct blow to the head or whiplash-type injury where the brain impacts the skull. Symptoms may include weakness, lack of motor coordination, and memory and cognitive problems.
- **Concussion:** is the most common type of brain injury. The term concussion has no clear definition and no pathological meaning. It is defined by its symptoms. Symptoms are highly variable in extent and duration although most symptoms resolve within a short period. Symptoms include headaches, dizziness, nausea and cognitive problems. A person can develop post-concussion syndrome (PCS) where symptoms can mirror a more serious organic brain injury.

  Concussion in sport has become the focus of a great deal of recent attention particularly in the US where there is significant high profile litigation. Injuries are diagnosed as either Sport Related Concussion (SRC) or Chronic Traumatic Encephalopathy (CTE):

SRC – this is a closed head injury resulting from a direct blow to the head. Symptoms are generally acute resulting from a single event and largely reflect a functional disturbance rather than organic injury.

CTE – this is a progressive chronic degenerative brain disorder. Technically CTE can only be identified post-mortem.

Causation between SRC and CTE, and other long term neurocognitive conditions, is not scientifically proven.

Types of secondary brain injury

- Epidural, subdural and subarachnoid haematomas
- Insufficient blood flow (ischaemia)
- Insufficient oxygen to the brain (anoxia and hypoxia)
- Swelling to the brain (cerebral oedema)
- Pressure within the skull (intracranial pressure).

Effects include headaches, confusion, seizures, paralysis and loss of consciousness.

Severity

The most commonly used system for classifying TBI is the Glasgow Coma Scale (GCS) which grades a person's consciousness on a scale of 3 to 15 based on verbal response, motor response and eye opening reaction to stimuli.

Glasgow Coma Scale

Total score	TBI
13 or above	mild
9 to 12	moderate
8 or below	severe

The GCS classification is used in the Judicial College Guidelines. It does, however, have limited application to children.

The other objective indicators of the severity of a TBI are the existence and duration of loss of consciousness (LOC) and the presence of post-traumatic amnesia (PTA), although the PTA history can be an unreliable diagnostic tool where an accident victim has been medicated in hospital.

Post-traumatic amnesia

Severity of brain injury	Length of PTA
Minor	less than one hour
Moderate	one to 24 hours
Severe	24 hours to seven days
Very severe	more than seven days

Mild/subtle brain injury

Where it is alleged that the claimant has suffered a mild or subtle brain injury there may nevertheless be a claim for significant damages. It can be difficult to determine whether the claimant has suffered organic damage to the brain or has psychological symptoms, which often mirror those caused by injury to the brain, or both. Significant resources, including numerous experts reports, may be required to determine the true position. Cases such as these often litigate.

As with sport related concussion, causation will be an important issue. It can be alleged, on behalf of the claimant, that there is a risk of the onset of dementia, or other neurodegenerative conditions, later in life. However, the relationship between the two remains subject to scientific proof.

Symptoms

TBI can result in a wide range of symptoms that are largely dependent on the type of TBI sustained, the part of the brain affected and the severity of the injury.

Symptoms include:

- Prolonged or permanent effects on consciousness, e.g. coma, brain death and persistent vegetative state (PVS). The characteristics of PVS are continuing state of coma, inability to communicate in any form and ability to breathe without mechanical assistance. Alternatively, a person may be described as 'walking wounded' where they appear physically normal but continue to suffer the mental effects of their brain injury.
- Movement disorders, e.g. tremor, ataxia (uncoordinated muscle movements) and myoclonus (contractions of muscles).
- Altered vision, smell, taste, speech, hearing, dizziness and nausea.
- Cognitive deficits, e.g. impaired attention, insight, intellect and executive function, i.e. problem solving, multitasking and problems with memory and concentration.
- Emotional, behavioural and personality problems, e.g. disinhibition, hypomania, sleep disturbance, fatigue, anger and aggression. There may also follow psychiatric problems including depression, phobias and obsessive behaviour.

Quantum

Damages for pain, suffering and loss of amenity (PSLA) will reflect the severity of the injury and the symptoms present. Ranges of awards for general damages are set out in the Judicial College Guidelines (JC Guidelines). The level of award largely depends on the extent of symptoms.

The assessment of most heads of loss follows usual quantum principles. The main departure point in TBI claims is that the claimant may lack capacity to manage the litigation and/or their finances, which has various implications, including:

- The claimant may claim damages for the expense of a professional deputy and Court of Protection fees.
- Any settlement will require court approval.
- Many claimants' solicitors assert that periodical payments are the only appropriate form of damages for a brain-injured client.
- Many TBIs cause epilepsy or carry a future risk of developing epilepsy. Some claimants will, therefore, seek a provisional damages award with a return condition for further damages and/or a variable periodical payments order in the event of uncontrollable epilepsy. The qualification "uncontrollable" is important because many forms of epilepsy can be successfully controlled with anticonvulsant medication.

Spinal cord injury

Anatomy

The spinal cord is part of the central nervous system (CNS), which runs from the brain, down the back, and is surrounded and protected by vertebrae. Spinal nerves come off the spinal cord and pass between the vertebrae to carry information from the spinal cord to the rest of the body.

Spinal nerve categories

Nerve type	Location	Supply function	Vertebrae classification
Cervical	neck	movement and feeling to arms, neck and upper trunk	C1 to C8
Thoracic	upper back	trunk and abdomen	T1 to T12
Lumbar and sacral	lower back	legs, bladder, bowel and sexual organs	L1 to L5

Spinal cord injury leading to paralysis

With spinal cord injury, the spinal nerves joining the spinal cord below the level of injury will either be completely or partially cut off from the brain resulting in quadriplegia, tetraplegia or paraplegia.

- **Quadriplegia/tetraplegia:** a spinal cord injury above the first thoracic vertebra, which usually causes paralysis of all four limbs. The abdominal and chest muscles will also be affected, resulting in weakened breathing and the inability to properly cough and clear the chest.
- **Paraplegia:** a spinal cord injury below the first thoracic vertebra. The extent of the injury can vary from impairment of leg movement to complete paralysis of the legs and abdomen up to the nipple line. The individual retains the use of their arms and hands.

Extent of paralysis

C1 to C3	tetraplegia	Complete paralysis of all limbs and in many cases ventilation required to aid breathing. C3 patients may be able to breathe unaided.
C4 to C5	tetraplegia	Complete paralysis below chest level. Limited shoulder and arm movement including lack of tricep muscles, wrist extensors and finger movement.
C6 to C7	tetraplegia	Partial paralysis of hands and arms and lower body.
T4	paraplegia	Paralysis below the chest.
L1	paraplegia	Paralysis below the waist.

Incomplete spinal cord injuries

These occur where the spinal nerves are only partially cut off from the brain. The location of the damage dictates the type of paralysis/level of sensation.

- **Anterior cord syndrome:** damage towards the front of the spinal cord can result in the loss or impaired ability to sense pain, temperature or touch below the level of injury. Pressure and joint sensation may be preserved and some patients with this form of injury may recover some movement.

- **Central cord syndrome:** damage to the centre of the spinal cord, which can result in loss of function in the arms. Some leg movement and control over the bowel and bladder may be preserved. Some recovery may be possible, usually starting in the legs and moving upwards.
- **Posterior cord syndrome:** damage is towards the back of the spinal cord and may leave the patient with good muscle power, and pain and temperature sensation. Difficulty in the coordination of limbs may occur.
- **Cauda equina lesion:** cauda equina is a mass of nerves, which fan out of the spinal cord between the first and second lumbar region of the spine. Injury to these nerves will cause partial or complete loss of movement and sensation. If the nerves are not too badly damaged, nerve regrowth and recovered function is possible.
- **Cervical stenosis and myelopathy:** cervical stenosis is the progressive narrowing of the spinal canal. This can lead to a cervical myelopathy or compression of the spinal cord. In turn, this can lead to incomplete paraplegia or incomplete tetraplegia.

Life expectancy

Due to the availability of improved housing and care the general life expectancy of a spinal patient is continuing to improve. It has been calculated the average life expectancy of a paraplegic is 70 to 85% of normal life expectancy, depending on other factors such as the individual's smoking history.

Quantum

PSLA

Ranges of awards for general damages are set out in the JC Guidelines.

The level of the award within each of the above brackets will be affected by the extent of any residual movement, the presence and extent of pain, the degree of independence, depression, age, other complications and life expectancy.

Special damages

The level of injury and extent of paralysis will determine the heads of loss. The heads of damage likely to be claimed are:

- Care and case management (likely to be substantial)
- Aids and equipment
- Therapies (often including the cost and maintenance of a hydrotherapy pool)
- Accommodation (likely requirement for single level accommodation)
- Holidays
- Transport
- Medical costs
- Increased heating and laundry costs
- Loss of earnings

A recent innovation is the powered exoskeleton or 'robot suit', which enables paralysed patients to walk again. The current cost is approximately £50,000 over a seven-to-ten-year replacement cycle. The reported benefits include an improvement in general health and life expectancy due to restoration of mobility, as well as the mental health gains from being able to stand and walk.

Claims for hydrotherapy pools have often been disputed on the basis that appropriate facilities are situated close to the claimant, thus removing the need for their own pool. Another defence argument relates to the expertise required to maintain the pool temperature and the danger of worsening symptoms if this is not done correctly.

Provisional damages

Spinal cord injury claims increasingly include a claim for provisional damages. If the injury is expected to get worse in the future, the court may make an order allowing the claimant to return to court to seek further damages should they suffer a "serious deterioration".

The most common cause of serious deterioration in spinal cord injury patients is the development of a syrinx or syringomyelia. This occurs in approximately 1% to 3% of spinal cord injury patients. The risk associated with syringomyelia is a loss of function above the level of the original spinal cord injury. The condition will progress with time and require surgical decompression and surgical drainage.

Other considerations

Common issues affecting spinal cord injury patients are bladder dysfunction, bony dysfunction, cardiovascular disease, deep vein thrombosis, hypothermia/hyperthermia, neuropathic pain, osteoporosis and fractures, pneumonia, hypertension, spasticity and vascular dysfunction.

There are also other conditions that are directly related to spinal cord injury and can affect quality of life. These include pressure sores, chest infections, urinary tract infections and ill health associated with poor/no mobility.

Expert evidence will need to be obtained to deal with these issues.

Amputation

Types of injury

Approximately 6,000 major limb amputations take place in the UK each year.

There are two main types of amputation:

- Lower limb amputation where the foot and/or part of the leg is removed.
- Upper limb amputation where the hand and/or part of the arm is removed.

The most common type of amputation, accounting for more than half of all cases in the UK, is a type of lower limb amputation known as a transtibial amputation. This is where the bottom section of a leg is amputated beneath the knee. It is also known as a below-the-knee amputation.

Other types of lower limb amputation in order of how commonly they are performed in the UK are:

- Lower digit, where one or more of the toes are amputated.
- Transfemoral, where both the bottom half of the leg and part of the thigh above the knee are amputated, also known as an above-knee amputation.

For upper limb amputations, the main types are:

- Upper digit amputation, where the thumb or one or more of the fingers are amputated.
- Transhumeral, where the hand and a section of the arm are amputated above the elbow.
- Transradial, where the hand and a section of the arm are amputated below the elbow.

Quantum

PSLA

Compensation awards for amputations reflect the very serious effect on an individual's lifestyle and ability to work caused by the partial or complete loss of a limb.

The amount of the award will depend on:

- The severity of ongoing organic and phantom pains
- Whether or not the amputation was of a dominant arm/limb
- The existence of any problems with the prosthesis
- Psychological issues arising from the injury.

Loss of earnings

There is likely to be a claim for both past and future loss of earnings. When using the Ogden tables, most (if not all) amputees are likely to be categorised as disabled.

Nursing care

As a result of an amputation, the injured party is likely to need assistance. Care needs will depend on the remaining function of the limb and the type of prosthesis fitted. With upper limbs, more care will be required following the loss of a dominant limb. The loss of a thumb may also attract a care claim, given that many tasks depend on an adequate pinch grip between finger and thumb.

With leg amputations, the higher the level of amputation the greater the claimant's care needs will be, because of the corresponding reduction in power and control from the residual limb and the inevitable consequences for prosthetic function and overall mobility.

Prosthetics

An artificial limb or part of it is known as a prosthesis.

Many upper limb prostheses are mainly cosmetic, although technological advances have led to a significant increase in the degree of functional capabilities.

Lower limb prostheses are generally functional, but their effectiveness depends on the level of amputation and the person's age, build and motivation. While the NHS provision of prosthesis has improved, service is variable and future budgets are uncertain. Most claimants, therefore, elect for private prosthetics. Such claims are normally for two to three limbs, including the main daily limb, a spare, and any specialist activity limbs. The daily limbs are usually replaced at approximately five-year intervals and will need servicing and maintenance during that period.

The number of limbs, the frequency of replacement and the cost of maintenance are often the subject of dispute between the parties, and expert evidence from prosthetists is crucial.

It is important to consider an amputee's physical make-up including age and weight when considering the suitability of prosthetics. Prosthetics are inappropriate for some amputees including those with:

- Neurological conditions, who may not have the capacity to make use of prosthetics.
- Renal conditions, who can have problems with sockets because of the effects of dialysis.

The quantum of this head of loss is increasing. This is because of the increase in capability of bionic limbs, whether it is a Genium knee or a Michelangelo hand. Technology is continually improving and this brings increased costs.

Accommodation

It is not unusual to see claims for accommodation being advanced in lower limb amputation claims on the basis that the amputee needs access to a downstairs toilet. Even with a prosthesis, there may be a need for occasional wheelchair use, requiring wider doors, etc.

From a defendant's perspective, it is useful to seek the advice of medical and nursing care experts to establish if there is a genuine need for a new property or whether adaptations could be made to an existing property.

Aids and appliances

Claims in relation to aids and appliances can be sizeable in a typical amputation claim. Recommendations will often include both manual and electric wheelchairs, recliner chairs, and kitchen and household equipment.

A larger car may also be required to facilitate wheelchair access and movement.

Again, advice from medical experts should be sought. Additional expertise may also be necessary in the form of an occupational therapist (although aids and equipment can often be dealt with by the care expert).

The future

We are likely to continue to see further advances in prosthetics and surgical procedures, driven in part by the volume of military amputees who have suffered combat injuries.

One such development is known as osseointegration, which enables a prosthesis to be attached directly to the body via a surgically implanted metal pin.

This enables a very sophisticated microprocessor-controlled prosthesis to be fitted directly to the bone, negating the need for a socket/stump interface. The results have been dramatic regarding level of function, comfort and gait. The downside is that it does increase the risk of infection.

Another surgical development is the process known as targeted muscle reinnervation (TMR). TMR is a surgical technique in which nerves, which previously controlled muscles of an amputated limb, are surgically rerouted so that they reinnervate a small region of a large intact muscle. As a result, when a patient thinks about moving the thumb or a missing finger, for example, a small area of muscle on their chest will contract, and a considerable number of sensors are then placed over the area of reinnervated muscle that can control multi-segmented robotic limbs.

There are also a number of new developments in prosthetic technology, including the Michelangelo hand and the next generation of microprocessor-controlled limbs: the Ottobock Genium knee and the Ossur Power Knee. They offer users even greater stability and control, with variable settings for different activities, such as climbing stairs, walking backwards and even cycling or golf. They are commensurately more expensive than older products and many claims are compromised on the basis of a state-of-the-art daily limb from the latest range with a lower specification spare limb.

Summary

Amputation claims need to be handled sensitively. Careful consideration needs to be given to valuing these claims, which on occasion can be worth seven figures. In the case of a well-motivated claimant, it should be possible for them to make a good recovery from an amputation and consideration should be given, at the outset, to rehabilitation where appropriate.

Pain disorders

Pain disorders can have a significant impact on function and mobility. This, in turn, can result in claims for substantial damages. It can be difficult to recognise cases such as this as potentially catastrophic, given the slow-burn effect of the symptoms.

A greater recognition of these conditions is illustrated by a change in the 11th edition of the JC Guidelines, published in 2012, where pain disorders were featured for the first time in a separate chapter in their own right. Prior to this they had been included in the psychiatric damage chapter.

Common disorders

Although each disorder has its own specific symptoms and diagnostic criteria, there is a great deal of overlap, so specific diagnosis can be difficult (and controversial). The general theme is the presence of subjective pain without any clear organic basis. However, if one of the disorders is diagnosed it is important to check that the correct diagnostic criteria have been applied.

The most commonly seen disorders are set out below.

- Fibromyalgia
- Complex regional pain syndrome (CRPS)
- Chronic fatigue syndrome (also known as myalgic encephalopathy (ME))
- Somatoform pain disorders
- Conversion disorders (also known as dissociative disorders)
- Chronic pain syndrome (CPS)

Symptoms

Symptoms can include: pain, hypersensitivity to touch, numbness, pins and needles, memory/concentration problems, insomnia, changes to hair/skin/nails (particularly with CRPS), IBS, fatigue, nausea and psychological symptoms.

Identifying claims

Pain disorders are not always well understood within the medical profession. This makes it all the more difficult for the claimant, insurers, lawyers and the judiciary.

The fact that these disorders are not immediately obvious can be both positive and negative as far as claims handling is concerned:

- If a potential pain disorder claim is identified early on, then it may be possible to settle it relatively quickly and economically before the claim starts to escalate in value. Crucial in identifying these claims is a consistent and rigorous referral process within the claims team where the claims will often begin.
- However, it can often be difficult to accept that the claimant is as disabled as suggested. At an early stage, the claimant's solicitor may not even be aware of the potential value of the claim. The deterioration over time from what initially seemed a minor accident/injury can mean that these claims are initially under reserved.

More often than not there are significant causation arguments. This can mean a host of experts being instructed on both sides:

- Orthopaedic surgeons
- Neurologists
- Rheumatologists
- Psychologists
- Psychiatrists
- Pain management experts

As always, choosing the right expert, in terms of discipline, expertise and medico-legal experience, is vital. It is also essential that full disclosure of all relevant records (GP, hospital, treatment, employment and Department for Work and Pensions) is obtained, so that a full history can be established and investigated.

Treatment/rehabilitation

By definition these disorders do not always emanate from an organic cause. They are therefore difficult to treat in the sense of resolving the problem completely.

The disorders are often diagnosed after the passage of several months, if not years. By that time the claimant may have become trapped in a 'pain circle'. They have pain, so they reduce activity. This leads to psychological problems, which in turn leads to increased pain perception and further reduction in activity, and so on.

Early treatment is crucial, with the aim of stopping the pain circle before it takes hold. Conventional treatment, such as physiotherapy, should be provided in the first instance. It is wise to avoid, if possible, mention of 'chronic pain' in the early stages, as the label can then take a firm hold in the claimant's mind. If early intervention has not been possible then the timing of treatment needs to be carefully considered. The litigation will be a maintaining factor for the pain and delaying treatment until after the claim may have to be considered.

If conventional treatment does not work, and a pain disorder is recognised, then the normal course of events is referral to a pain management programme. This can be undertaken as an outpatient, but there are now several specialist centres offering inpatient focused rehabilitation, which can be more successful. As most, if not all, of the disorders have a psychological element, psychological treatment will almost certainly form part of the overall package. The focus of the rehabilitation is often on functional restoration rather than cure. This treatment can be quite expensive but, if successful in improving function, can reduce the value of the claim significantly.

If the problem is more psychologically based (somatoform or conversion disorders) then it may be more amenable to treatment, but success is by no means guaranteed.

Claims handling

The instruction of various experts and the detailed enquiries that are involved in these cases inevitably increases costs to a potentially significant level. It is therefore important to undertake appropriate investigations early and make informed decisions.

If the indications are that the claimant is developing a pain disorder, then an early commercially focused Part 36 offer can prove effective, either disposing of the claim (and managing costs) or providing costs protection and applying tactical pressure later in the claim.

As pain disorder cases are largely related to subjective pain perception, and the resulting functional limitations, early covert surveillance can also be effective, as can claimant profiling and social media checks.

Quantum

Ranges of awards for general damages are set out in the JC Guidelines.

Life expectancy

A reduction in life expectancy can have a major impact on the appropriate multiplier and the level of lump sum damages awarded. It will not be a factor in periodical payments cases because these are guaranteed for the claimant's lifetime, however long that may be. Any claimant with uncertain life expectancy is, therefore, likely to strongly consider a periodical payments order to avoid the undercompensation risk attaching to lump sum damages. This section will, therefore, be of most interest in lump sum cases or to insurers handling periodical payments cases and who must nonetheless fix a claim reserve based on the available evidence regarding life expectancy.

Impaired lives

Health issues that can reduce life expectancy, whether related to or consequential to the accident or not, can include:

- Smoking
- Asthma
- Drug abuse
- Diabetes
- Obesity
- Epilepsy
- Heart problems or high blood pressure.

In addition, many studies show that individuals who lack mobility, or have reduced mobility, are at greater risk of mortality, for example as a result of loss of muscle tissue, decline in lung function, pressure sores that lead to infection and sepsis, and increased risk of clots through poorer circulation. Many of these problems also reduce the body's ability to fight off routine chest infections and urinary tract infections, which can further increase the risk of mortality.

If a claimant has suffered a spinal cord injury, there is a risk that they will develop a syrinx (a fluid-filled cavity within the spinal cord or brain stem), which can cause a loss of strength, function and sensation in the body systems and can reduce life expectancy further.

Resources

The Ogden tables use mortality assumptions based on the general population, and arguably take account of someone who is an average smoker, for example. Therefore, unless there is clear evidence that the claimant is atypical and will experience a shorter or longer than average life, no adjustment may be required. However, an atypical individual might be a heavy smoker or someone suffering a head injury or spinal injury, and in those cases the multiplier might need adjusting to reflect a lower life expectancy.

The Life Expectancy Project at the University of California, whose Director is Professor Strauss, is the leading resource on impaired lives and provides statistical evidence on life expectancy in different types of catastrophic injury cases, including cerebral palsy, vegetative state, spinal cord injury and TBI. It has an excellent website with links to data and articles published by the research team: http://www.lifeexpectancy.org/index.shtml

Methodology

The courts have previously considered the question of whether a statistical or clinical approach is preferable when determining life expectancy. It is usually the clinical experts who provide leadership, including by drawing on the statistical research as appropriate (see *Royal Victoria Infirmary & Associated Hospitals NHS Trust v B (Child)* [2002], *Arden v Malcolm* [2002]).

Another important question is which of the Ogden tables should be used. On the one hand, Table 1 provides life multipliers based on mortality risks in the general population. On the other hand, Table 28 provides a multiplier for a fixed period or term certain.

There have been conflicting judgments. *Sarwar v Ali* [2007] and *Burton v Kingsbury* [2007] suggest the application of Table 28, whereas *Crofts v Murton* [2008] and *Smith v LC Window Fashions Ltd* [2009] suggest Table 1. The editors of the Ogden tables, at paragraph 20 of the explanatory note to the 7th edition, also advocated the use of Table 1 rather than 28. Defendants should argue for Table 1 because this rightly takes account of mortality risks in the general population and produces a lower but more accurate multiplier.

Capacity

Individuals who have suffered a severe brain injury may suffer from a loss of mental capacity. This may be temporary or permanent. It may affect their ability to conduct litigation, manage their own financial affairs and make decisions in relation to their welfare. Mental health problems, strokes, and alcohol or substance misuse can also affect capacity.

Capacity is both time and function specific: an individual may lack capacity to make a particular decision at a particular time. They may have capacity to make some decisions but not others. Accordingly, capacity is to be determined at the time the decision is to be made.

> An individual's capacity should be assessed to establish whether the Official Solicitor or a litigation friend should be appointed. The Official Solicitor may be appointed to represent adults who lack capacity to conduct litigation and who have no litigation friend available.

Statutory definition

The Mental Capacity Act 2005 provides a statutory framework to empower and protect vulnerable people who may not be able to make their own decisions. The Act makes it clear who can take decisions in which situations and how they should go about this. It also enables people to plan for a time when they may lose capacity.

Section 2(1) states that "a person lacks capacity in relation to a matter if at the material time he is unable to make a decision for himself in relation to the matter because of an impairment of, or a disturbance in the functioning of, the mind or brain."

The key statutory principles are:

- There is an assumption of capacity.
- All practicable steps must be taken to help a person to make their own decision before concluding they are unable to do so.
- A person should not be treated as unable to make a decision merely because they make an unwise decision.
- Decisions made on behalf of the person who lacks capacity must be made in their best interests.
- The decision should be the least restrictive of an individual's rights.

- A diagnosis that an individual lacks the capacity to make a particular decision should be based on the balance of probabilities.

Assessing capacity

The Code of Practice supporting the Act outlines a two-stage test to assess capacity:

- Does the person have an impairment of, or disturbance in, the functioning of their mind or brain?
- If so, does the impairment or disturbance mean that the person is unable to make a specific decision when they need to?

The Act sets out (in s.3) the test for assessing whether a person is unable to make a decision and, therefore, lacks capacity. Four reasons are given as to why a person may be unable to make a decision. A person needs to be able to:

- Understand the information relevant to the decision
- Retain that information
- Use or weigh that information as part of the decision-making process
- Communicate their decision.

The first three criteria should be applied together. If a person cannot do any of these three things, they will be treated as unable to make a decision. The fourth criterion only applies in situations where people cannot communicate their decision in any way (for example, when in a coma).

Assessing the ability to make complex or serious decisions may require a formal assessment and expert guidance may be sought, e.g. from a neurologist, a psychiatrist, a neuropsychiatrist, a psychologist or a neuropsychologist. Where there is concern about a person's ability to communicate, it is important to make all practical efforts to help them communicate. This may mean the involvement of speech and language therapists or specialists in non-verbal communication.

There are also many practical ways that should be considered to help someone make a decision for themselves; for instance, with regard to location, timing and seeking support from other people such as family.

Many medico-legal experts are quick to find that a claimant lacks litigation capacity following their examination, but without necessarily adequately considering the presumption of capacity or the fallback option of the claimant being supported (e.g. by their family, or solicitor, or case manager, or carers) to make decisions. Defendant practitioners should be alert to challenging the claimant's experts via Part 35 of the Civil Procedure Rules (CPR) questions, especially in borderline cases where a finding of capacity offers significant gains, such as extinguishing potential claims for Court of Protection and deputy fees.

Capacity should always be reviewed:

- Whenever a care plan is being developed or reviewed
- At other relevant stages of the care planning process
- As particular decisions need to be made, especially in relation to final settlement of the claim.

Who should assess capacity?

The person who assesses an individual's capacity to make a decision will normally be the person who is directly concerned with the individual at the time the decision needs to be made. This is often the individual's carer. In settings such as a hospital, this is likely to involve the multidisciplinary team.

More complex decisions are likely to need more formal assessments, such as seeking a professional opinion from, say, a psychiatrist. However, the final decision about capacity must be made by the person intending to make the decision or carry out the action on behalf of the person who lacks capacity.

In all cases, the findings should be recorded clearly and comprehensively in the relevant medical records.

Court of Protection

The Court of Protection is a specialist court which follows the practice and procedure set out in the Court of Protection Rules 2007.

The Court of Protection may:

- Decide whether the person has capacity to make a particular decision.
- Make a decision on financial or welfare matters affecting a person who lacks capacity, including in relation to creating a personal injury trust where income derived from a damages award is disregarded for the purposes of means testing for benefits or local authority care.
- Appoint a deputy, who may be a friend, relative or professional, to make decisions in relation to welfare or finance as specified by the court.

The fees of the Court of Protection and deputy will form part of the claimant's damages and will often be substantial. A professional deputy (who is frequently a solicitor) will carry out work charged at an hourly rate. Initial commencement fees are charged on the appointment of a deputy and the involvement of the Court of Protection. Thereafter, an annual fee is charged.

The annual costs of a deputy are increasing. Care should be taken to ensure that there is not an overlap/duplication of costs in terms of the work carried out by the claimant's solicitor and their deputy.

Compromise of claims

As provided for under CPR Part 21.10, no settlement or compromise of a claim by a party who lacks capacity will be valid without the approval of the Court. Where a settlement or compromise is agreed at the pre-litigation stage the parties must, therefore, issue Part 8 proceedings for the sole purpose of seeking approval.

The importance of Part 21.10 was highlighted by the Supreme Court judgment in *Dunhill (a protected party by her litigation friend Tasker) v Burgin* [2014], where a previous settlement was set aside because the claimant did not have capacity at the time.

The claim arose out of a road traffic accident in 1999. The defendant, who was riding a motorbike, struck the claimant, who was crossing the road. The claimant suffered a severe closed head injury.

The claimant issued a claim on 13 May 2002, limited to £50,000. Liability was disputed. A compromise settlement was achieved on the day of the trial on 7 January 2003 for £12,500 plus costs, partly because one the claimant's main witnesses did not show up. On any view this was a gross undervaluation of her claim, if she could establish negligence. Her advisors at the time of the Supreme Court hearing put her claim at over £2 million on a full liability basis, with the defendant accepting it was worth around £800,000.

In July 2006, the claimant sought the advice of new solicitors. In February 2009, her litigation friend issued the proceedings in question. These took the form of an application in the original action, seeking a declaration that the claimant did not have capacity at the time of the settlement in January 2003 and that the consent order should be set aside. Giving judgment on behalf of the Supreme Court, Lady Hale held as follows:

- **Test for capacity:** the test for capacity to conduct proceedings for the purpose of Part 21 is the capacity to conduct the claim or cause of action that the claimant in fact has, rather than to conduct the claim as formulated by their lawyers. Judged by that test, it was common ground that the claimant did not have the capacity to conduct this claim.
- **Effect of incapacity:** given this finding, in accordance with Part 21.10(1) the settlement and court order were of no effect. No external check on the propriety of the settlement had been carried out by the court.

- **Policy issues:** although there was a need for finality in litigation, and the difficulty of reopening cases long after the event was recognised, the policy underlying the Civil Procedure Rules was clear. Those lacking capacity require and deserve protection, not only from themselves but also from their legal advisors.

Dunhill allows cases that settled long ago without court approval to be reopened where it is later discovered that the claimant lacked the mental capacity to enter a settlement agreement. This may be through no fault of the defendant, who may not ever have met the claimant in the course of the legal action before settling the case.

A claimant could still seek to make a claim against their legal advisors via the professional negligence route, but a periodical payment order would not then be available and that might disadvantage a claimant in a high-value claim.

It is, therefore, prudent for defendants to take protective steps. Where the medical records or pleadings suggest an element of cognitive compromise, the claimant should be assessed for mental capacity to conduct the claim before any settlement agreement is reached. It is not necessary to instruct a psychiatrist or psychologist to do this, unless such an expert is required for other aspects of the claim. Any medical expert instructed ought to know how to test whether the claimant is suffering a disturbance of the mind or brain that is rendering them incapable of making a particular decision (in this case, a decision concerning the claim itself). If there is any concern over capacity, either party should apply for court approval of any future settlement.

Experts

Use of experts in catastrophic injury cases is vital. Experts are required to assess the technical issues in the case and provide the information needed to undertake an informed valuation and then to persuade an opponent (and ultimately the court) that your case is stronger than theirs. Medical experts will also often be required to give careful consideration to causation.

Case management

The court will only give permission to rely on an expert if a particular issue indicates the need for professional expertise beyond already available expert evidence or inferences the court can reasonably draw from the available evidence. Courts often give the parties a great deal of latitude in relation to the number of experts appointed in catastrophic cases but the general trend, particularly following the Jackson reforms, is to limit the number and cost of experts. That should help to prevent the escalation of damages and limit costs, provided the parties are still allowed to instruct the minimum experts required to deal with the claim on an informed basis.

When considering whether to give permission for the parties to rely on expert evidence the court may order the parties to instruct a single joint expert (SJE). In catastrophic claims it is possible that a SJE will be appointed to address an issue relating to liability, causation or quantum where the expert evidence falls within a substantially established area of knowledge that is unlikely to be in dispute or about which there is unlikely to be a range of expert opinion.

Once the experts have reported, it is now common practice for the court to order experts from like disciplines to prepare a joint statement. The purpose is to narrow the issues between them and identify areas of agreement and disagreement with reasons why.

CPR Practice Direction 35.11 deals with concurrent expert evidence, also known as hot-tubbing. This is where, during the trial, experts from like disciplines give evidence at the same time in accordance with an agreed agenda. The judge will ask questions followed by questions from counsel. However, a full cross-examination is neither necessary nor appropriate.

Types of expert

A combination of medical and non-medical experts will be needed to enable the parties to obtain a detailed picture of the injuries sustained, the claimant's immediate and long-term needs and their cost.

Catastrophic injury cases can often require the appointment of numerous experts in different disciplines. Care must be taken to ensure that the correct areas of expertise are identified for the injuries sustained. The experts already appointed by the claimant will often influence what type of experts the defendant instructs. However, that should only be one factor in determining what experts are needed.

Brain injury cases

- **Neurologist:** a physician who specialises in the diagnosis and treatment of disorders of the nervous system, including the brain.
- **Neurosurgeon:** a surgeon who specialises in carrying out surgical procedures on the nervous system.
- **Neuropsychiatrist:** a psychiatrist is a medically qualified doctor who, having qualified, has subsequently specialised in the field of psychiatry. A psychiatrist specialises in the diagnosis, treatment and prevention of mental illness. A neuropsychiatrist deals with the diagnosis, treatment and prevention of mental and emotional disorders arising out of illness or injury to the nervous system, including the brain.
- **Psychologist:** a psychologist is a scientist who deals with mental processes and behaviour. Psychologists are not necessarily medically qualified. They have a psychology degree. Those that call themselves doctors are entitled to do

so generally by having obtained a doctorate in psychology. Psychologists who are not medically qualified have no authority to make a medical diagnosis of psychiatric conditions or dispense medicines.

- **Neuropsychologist:** A neuropsychologist diagnoses changes in cognitive function and behaviour following a known or suspected brain injury. Neuropsychologists carry out cognitive/psychometric testing to assess global function and mood status, intellectual function, memory, attention and learning, language, psychomotor speed and executive function, and emotional judgement.
- **Neuroradiologist:** a neuroradiologist is a specialist radiologist who focuses on the diagnosis and characterisation of abnormalities of the nervous system using neuroimaging techniques such as computed tomography (CT) and magnetic resonance imaging (MRI) scans.

Practical considerations – brain injury claims

Whether to instruct a neurologist, neurosurgeon, neuropsychiatrist, neuropsychologist, neuroradiologist, or a combination of all five, in a brain injury case will often be determined by the severity of the injury sustained.

> In a case where there is no real dispute as to whether or not there has been a brain injury and where the claimant's presentation is clearly due to having sustained a brain injury, then the choice may be limited to the appointment of either a neurosurgeon or neurologist and a neuropsychologist. A neurosurgeon will be preferred if there has been surgery post-accident to the brain, otherwise a neurologist might be preferred. They will assess the position of the injury within the brain and the extent of the injury. A neuropsychologist can then assess the cognitive, behavioural and emotional consequences of the injury.

Where the injury is less severe the position may be more complicated. Experts will need to assess whether there has only been a head injury or mild brain injury and if the claimant's presentation is due to an organic injury or is non-organic/psychological. In the latter case, the lead expert is likely to be a neuropsychiatrist.

A neuroradiologist is probably the least often used expert amongst these disciplines. The neurologist or neurosurgeon will usually be confident about interpreting the radiology, but may sometimes indicate in their report if they require the assistance of a neuroradiologist. This will be to assist them to interpret the neuroradiology in order to assess whether an injury to the brain has occurred, where within the brain it has occurred and the extent of the injury. They may also be asked to consider whether there has been a previous injury.

Spinal injury claims

- **Spinal surgeon:** a spinal surgeon is an orthopaedic surgeon who specialises in spine surgery. Spine surgery is also undertaken by neurosurgeons. However, when dealing with claims involving paralysis due to a spinal cord injury (tetraplegia and paraplegia) the preference is, generally, to instruct a consultant in spinal cord injury who practises at one of the recognised spinal injury centres. These centres provide rehabilitation care for patients with spinal cord injuries and, therefore, the expert is able to deal with a wide range of issues, including the diagnosis, treatment and rehabilitation of the claimant. Issues relating to causation should be dealt with by a spinal surgeon.

Amputation claims

- **Prosthetist and orthotist:** a prosthetist and orthotist provide care for anyone requiring an artificial limb (prosthesis) or a device to support or control part of the body (orthosis). In amputation cases it is usual to instruct a prosthetist and/or a consultant in rehabilitation medicine working at a prosthetic rehabilitation unit that provides treatment and care to people who have undergone amputation.

Other experts

A combination of medical and non-medical experts will need to be appointed in a catastrophic injury claim. Medical and non-medical experts must work in partnership and tend to be instructed sequentially so that, for example, a care expert is provided with the medical evidence in order to properly assess a claimant's care requirements.

Other medical experts include:

- Urologist
- Gastroenterologist or colorectal surgeon
- Cardiologist (heart)
- Chest physician or thoracic surgeon (lungs/chest injuries)
- Plastic surgeon (usually in relation to scarring)
- Pain management consultant
- Rheumatologist (musculoskeletal or autoimmune disorders of the bones, joints and muscles)
- Ophthalmologist
- Speech and language therapist
- Physiotherapist.

Other non-medical experts include those specialising in:

- Care
- Occupational therapy (aids and equipment)
- Accommodation
- Employment
- Assistive technology
- Court of Protection fees/deputy costs
- Life expectancy (statistician)
- Forensic accountancy.

Rehabilitation

Catastrophic claims are nearly always appropriate for rehabilitation intervention because of their devastating effect on the claimant's health and lifestyle.

The usual starting point is to jointly select and instruct a specialist case manager to undertake an initial needs assessment (INA) pursuant to the Rehabilitation Code. The Code aims to ensure that the management of rehabilitation is a collaborative process.

The main role of the case manager is to coordinate the available services. Rehabilitation can take many forms, including arranging private medical referrals or treatment, securing benefits or other public funding, purchasing aids and equipment, adapting the claimant's home, organising transport solutions, coordinating a carer regime or seeking alternative job opportunities accommodating the acquired disability.

Choice of case manager

There is a growing choice of case management companies offering a panel of case managers, although some geographical areas are better served than others.

It is preferable to select a case manager on a case-by-case basis. The main criteria are:

- Availability and waiting time for an INA
- The right qualifications and experience for the injuries concerned
- Geographical proximity and ease of travel for home visits
- Charging rates.

The Code provides that neither party can impose their choice of case manager if the other objects on reasonable grounds.

Funding

The main barrier to rehabilitation funding is a complete denial of liability. In cases where the defendant's denial is necessarily motivated by a lack of liability evidence and the need for further investigations, one interim option for the parties to consider is for the defendant to fund a case manager to maximise public funding and health services.

The Code envisages that in most cases the defendant will provide funding for the case manager and for implementing their recommendations. The defendant will have to justify any refusal to fund the recommendations. Once funding is agreed, the defendant should neither dispute the expenditure nor seek to recover this from the claimant.

In cases where the defendant accepts full liability, the claimant's solicitor may seek an interim payment to privately fund unilateral rehabilitation outside the Code. This can build mistrust between the parties and lead to later challenges regarding the reasonableness of the expenditure.

The position is more complicated in split liability cases because the Code ignores any contributory negligence and still envisages 100% funding, notwithstanding that the claimant is making a lower percentage recovery in the claim. If the parties are unable to agree major items of expenditure or the defendant has serious concerns regarding overprovision, the other option is to make interim payments for unilateral rehabilitation. In that way, the claimant takes the burden of partly irrecoverable expenditure due to the liability shortfall and is more likely to be more careful with their money.

Assessment

The INA should generally be carried out as soon as possible following the accident, although in some cases it may still be beneficial years later. The case manager should report on the injuries sustained, their effect on lifestyle, the claimant's domestic and family circumstances, the recommended intervention and its likely cost, the availability of public funding and state benefits, and the rehabilitation objectives.

> The main complaint by defendants relates to exaggerated recommendations or occasional abuse of agreed funding. To safeguard against this and to put the INA in its proper context, the defendant is entitled to sufficient information from the claimant to reach a proper decision about funding.

The case manager is unlikely to be an expert in all the relevant disciplines and the parties may sometimes require a second opinion. For example, the parties may consult a treating practitioner or medico-legal expert about very costly items such as home adaptations or vehicle purchases, or refer employment issues to a vocational rehabilitation specialist.

Claim implications

The INA itself is privileged from disclosure in any subsequent litigation, unless the parties agree otherwise, whereas by comparison all subsequent case manager updates and other rehabilitation materials are not privileged and should be disclosed.

Some claimant solicitors seek to extend the case manager role into supporting their litigation aims. This can include serving a statement from the case manager and inviting them to privileged conferences with the litigation team. The code now expressly provides that the case manager's retainer should solely be therapeutic. As a safeguard, the defendant can write to the claimant's solicitor confirming that a one paragraph statement from the case manager exhibiting the relevant reports will suffice for the purposes of the claim.

The items funded directly by the defendant should be excluded from the claim. When a claim is eventually settled, the usual arrangement is for the defendant to stop payments and for the claimant to fund rehabilitation directly, using damages specifically awarded for that purpose.

Interim payments

The making of an interim payment by a defendant to a claimant can be an important tactical step with various practical consequences for future case handling, including:

- The court must approve interim payments to a child or a protected party, which means that proceedings will have to be commenced in those cases.
- It can unfairly upset the status quo and tie the hands of the trial judge in relation to major issues such as future care and accommodation if, by the trial date, the claimant has already established the regime contended for by their expert team.
- It can limit the trial judge's discretion in relation to the form of award if the amount of previous interim payments leaves insufficient funds for periodical payments.

- It triggers liability for repayment of deductible benefits and NHS charges to the Compensation Recovery Unit (CRU).

Procedure

The general procedure is set out in Part 25.6 to 25.9 of the CPR and the accompanying Practice Direction 25B.

> The main precondition for entitlement to an interim payment is that liability must have been admitted or judgment entered, failing which it is for the claimant to prove that, if the case went to trial, they would obtain judgment for a substantial amount of money from a specific defendant, or from one of a group of secure defendants backed by insurance, the Motor Insurers' Bureau (MIB) or public funds. That exercise can involve a mini-trial of liability issues.

In all other cases, interim payments are at the defendant's discretion. The defendant is at an especial disadvantage during the pre-litigation phase when, by and large, the claimant controls what information is shared. A request for an interim payment, therefore, provides a valuable opportunity for the defendant to trade funding for missing information, such as a preliminary schedule of loss, medical records or even meeting the claimant face-to-face where appropriate.
In most cases, the claimant's solicitor will cooperate because they know that, if nothing can be agreed and a contested application is required, they are obliged to file supporting evidence in any event.

The amount available to the claimant by way of interim payment is limited to a reasonable proportion of the likely amount of the final judgment, net of contributory negligence, any relevant set-off or counterclaim and whatever deductible benefits are shown on the CRU certificate.

The *Eeles* criteria

In practice, a high proportion of interim payments are negotiated according to the criteria defined by *Eeles v Cobham Hire Services Ltd* [2009], where the Court of Appeal set out the approach to be followed in cases where the trial judge might wish to award periodical payments – known by many practitioners as the 'first limb' and 'second limb' of *Eeles*:

- The first limb is to assess the likely amount of the final judgment, excluding the heads of future loss that are potentially suitable for periodical payments. This usually leaves damages for PSLA, past special damages, interest on past losses, and future accommodation and running costs. The assessment must be carried out on a conservative basis and may, therefore, be closer to the defendant's estimate. The court is then entitled to award a reasonable proportion (which may be a high proportion) of the conservative assessment.
- In relation to the optional second limb, the court can award additional elements of the final judgment as an interim payment where it is satisfied, to a high degree of confidence, that the trial judge will award this as a lump sum because of immediate needs.

If the interim payment is to buy a house, the judge does not need to decide whether the particular house proposed is suitable; that is a matter for the Court of Protection in cases where it is involved.

The *Eeles* criteria have been refined as follows by later cases:

- The past losses should be assessed as at the future trial date, not just up to the date of the present application.
- A reasonable proportion of the conservative assessment has generally been fixed at a high proportion, typically about 75% and in some cases as much as 90%.

- Future accommodation has been excluded from the analysis where there was a genuine dispute over home versus residential care, and where the case was close to trial and the trial judge would be resolving this soon.
- A higher interim payment has been awarded where the court was persuaded that periodical payments were unsuitable due to high contributory negligence, variable future care requiring the flexibility of a lump sum or where the claimant's strong preference was for a lump sum.
- A lower interim payment has been awarded where the court was persuaded that periodical payments offered greater security due to low investment returns from a lump sum.

The criteria can be misunderstood as applying to all cases whereas in fact they should only be applied to those cases where periodical payments are a possibility. The defendant is usually keen to know whether the claimant is likely to elect for periodical payments, and the exercise of negotiating interim payments offers a useful opportunity to flush this out.

In periodical payment cases, the criteria have arguably set a higher threshold test for claimants seeking large interim payments and by doing so have placed the parties on a more equal footing. However, properly prepared and deserving cases should still qualify, and most applications substantially succeed unless there is a major point of principle, such as uncertain liability or a genuine dispute regarding future lifestyle.

The editors of *Kemp & Kemp* suggest that claimants can sidestep the criteria entirely by invoking the rarely used provision in Part 25.6(7) of the CPR for the court to order an interim payment in instalments. They even interpret this as encompassing an interim order for periodical payments and give the example of a seriously injured infant with an uncertain prognosis where such an order would provide continuity of funding for interim care needs. However, they recognise that there have not yet been any reported examples of that approach succeeding before the courts.

A lower discount rate may limit a claimant's entitlement under *Eeles* 1. Firstly, the defendant may argue, in order to mitigate the higher lump sum otherwise payable, that more or all future heads should now be awarded as periodical payments.

Secondly, the future accommodation claims may be nil under the old *Roberts v Johnstone* formula, pending any reform of the methodology.

Conversely, a lower discount rate may then strengthen any application under *Eeles* 2 because, if the court is satisfied that a trial judge will award certain heads as a lump sum for immediate needs, the corresponding amounts will be higher and the capital required for any property purchase will more frequently be achievable from the interim payment.

Tactical considerations

In extreme cases where an adversarial claimant's solicitor is taking full advantage of their pre-litigation control and refusing to collaborate, one option for the defendant is to refuse an interim payment and effectively force the claimant to commence proceedings. This means the claim can be properly case managed and the defendant can have a significant input.

At the other pre-litigation extreme, where court approval is required but experienced practitioners have good working relations and there are no limitation issues, procedural costs can be minimised by agreeing that the claimant will only commence streamlined proceedings via the alternative Part 8 procedure, which can then be stayed following approval. This does not stop the court from later ordering that the claim should continue as though Part 8 was not used or from giving directions.

Alternatively, where the interim payment is required for rehabilitation expenditure such as case management or therapies, it is arguable that court approval is not required if such payments are made according to the Rehabilitation Code and, therefore, outside the litigation.

In the middle category of cases where the parties agree in principle that an interim payment should be made, but are disputing the amount and an application seems likely to be required to decide the point, case handlers might wish to seek a legal second opinion on its merits because a wrong move can result in the double expense of proceedings and application costs.

A contested interim payment application in a catastrophic injury claim can be an expensive exercise and costs frequently exceed £10,000. It is, therefore, vital for the defendant to attempt to protect its position on costs by offering a reasonable amount in writing before the hearing, which can be shown to the judge in the event the claimant fails exceed this sum.

Many interim payment applications seek a specific amount targeted by the claimant's team. If the court awards a lower amount then it is strongly arguable that the application as drafted has been unsuccessful and that a costs order should be made in favour of the defendant. For that reason, many such applications now ask the court in the alternative for the higher amount or such other award as it sees fit.

> Interim payments obviously mitigate the defendant's liability for interest on the claim. It is, therefore, good financial practice to specify that they be applied first to whichever losses attract the highest interest rates. At present, that is the 2% payable on general damages for PSLA, rather than the 0.25% (half the special account rate) payable on continuing special damages.

Provisional damages

The right to seek provisional damages arises from s.6 Administration of Justice Act 1982, which introduced s.32A into the Senior Courts Act 1981. The power of county courts to award provisional damages can be found in s.51 County Courts Act 1984.

Before provisional damages were introduced, the courts applied the traditional final lump sum assessment method for assessing the entirety of a claimant's award of damages. This either did not take into account the possibility of future losses arising from a future deterioration in the claimant's condition or, if it did, risked an unfair result.

Grounds for an award

Provisional damages allow a claimant to seek a lump sum award on the basis that their condition will not deteriorate in the future. If, however, the claimant does suffer a deterioration, the order allows the claimant to return to court for further damages. This is subject to satisfying the grounds for a further award, including persuading the court to exercise its discretion in the claimant's favour.

Section 32A of the Senior Courts Act 1981/s.51 County Courts Act 1984 states as follows:

> “ 1) This section applies to an action for damages for personal injuries in which there is proved or admitted to be a chance that at some definite or indefinite time in the future the injured person will, as a result of the act or omission which gave rise to the cause of action, develop some serious disease or suffer some serious deterioration in his physical or mental condition.
>
> 2) Subject to subsection (4) below, as regards any action for damages to which this section applies in which a judgment is given in the High Court/County Court, provision may be made by rules of court for enabling the court, in such circumstances as may be prescribed, to award the injured person –
>
> a) damages assessed on the assumption that the injured person will not develop the disease or suffer the deterioration in his condition; and
>
> b) further damages at a future date if he develops the disease or suffers the deterioration. ”

Part 41.2 of the Civil Procedure Rules 1998 (CPR), supplemented by Practice Direction 41A, sets out steps to be taken when seeking an award for provisional damages:

> “41.2(1) The court may make an order for an award of provisional damages if –
>
> a) the particulars of claim include a claim for provisional damages; and
>
> b) the court is satisfied that SCA s.32A or CCA s.51 applies.
>
> 2) An order for an award of provisional damages -
>
> a) must specify the disease or type of deterioration in respect of which an application may be made at a future date;
>
> b) must specify the period within which such an application may be made; and
>
> c) may be made in respect of more than one disease or type of deterioration and may, in respect of each disease or type of deterioration, specify a different period within which a subsequent application may be made.
>
> (2) (3) The claimant may make more than one application to extend the period specified under paragraph (2)(b) or (2) (c).”

Level of chance or risk

The claimant must satisfy the court that the chance of developing the disease or deterioration in a physical or mental condition is measurable and more than fanciful (*Wilson v Ministry of Defence* [1990]).

Based on the judgment of Lord Justice Roch in *Curi v Colina* [1998] if a risk is certain or likely to occur, i.e. between 50 and 90%, then a lump sum final award is appropriate.

An award of provisional damages is fundamentally at the discretion of the court and, unsurprisingly, this can produce inconsistent results. It appears that an award for provisional damages is likely to be made if the risk of deterioration is between 2% and 20%.

However, awards have been made in cases where the risk of serious deterioration is measured at 1% or less. *Mitchell v Royal Liverpool & Broadgreen University Hospitals NHS Trust* [2006] and *Kotula v EDF Energy Networks (EPN) PLC* [2011] both dealt with the risk of the claimants developing syringomyelia arising from severe spinal injuries. Both judges concluded that the risks in those cases, measured at 0.15% and 1%, were measurable, as opposed to fanciful. In *Mitchell*, Mr Justice Beatson quoted from the judgment in *Wilson*:

> “However slim those chances may be, I think that they are measurable within the meaning of this section.”

Conversely, in *Davies v Bradshaw* [2008] the court declined to award provisional damages for the risk of the claimant, who suffered incomplete tetraplegia, developing syringomyelia, despite this risk being assessed at 3%. The court considered that, if the condition was caught early, surgery would be likely to be successful and therefore the risk of deterioration was not sufficiently clear to warrant a provisional damages award.

Serious disease or deterioration

The court will assess the weight of the combination of the level of risk and the seriousness of the disease or deterioration. A very small risk of a very serious condition will trigger an award for provisional damages.

In *Patterson v Ministry of Defence* [2012] it was held that a 5% risk of further pleural thickening in an asbestos case was a risk insufficiently serious to trigger provisional damages. However, a 2% to 3% risk of mesothelioma was sufficiently serious to merit a provisional award.

Gradual deterioration, and failure to improve, are not generally considered to be serious deterioration that would trigger an award for provisional damages.

Discretion

The power to award provisional damages is discretionary, so a court may refuse an award even if the other grounds are met. The paramount consideration for the court is justice and whether this is best served by a final award or by provisional damages.

Practical considerations

- If the claimant seeks an order for provisional damages this must be pleaded in the particulars of claim.
- Where a claimant seeks an award for provisional damages in the particulars of claim, the claimant is then barred from seeking judgment in default of a defence being filed unless they abandon the claim for provisional damages.
- An order for provisional damages must specify the period (or periods) within which an application for further damages may be made in respect of each disease or type of deterioration. The claimant may apply to extend the period.
- The claimant is only entitled to make one application for further damages as a result of the occurrence of each trigger disease or deterioration. They must give the defendant and their insurers 28 days' notice of their intention. The claimant then has 21 days after the expiration of the notice to make the application.

Tactical claims handling: cooperation, collaboration and consensus

It is in the interests of the parties and their insurers to achieve a fair settlement as soon as reasonably possible.

The objective is to proceed consensually. A constructive relationship with the claimant's solicitor is essential to enable the parties to work together to achieve a settlement. Such a relationship is of particular importance where a lower discount rate increases potential damages in many cases to levels not previously seen.

Where liability is not going to be in serious issue, the ideal arrangement is for the insurer or its solicitor to secure a face-to-face meeting with the claimant and their family as soon as possible.

The best opportunity to achieve this will usually be during discussion about immediate needs/rehabilitation, before discharge from hospital.

An early meeting between the parties, including the claimant and their family, should assist in removing any suspicions that the claimant/their family may have regarding the 'faceless' insurer behind the defendant. Where a direct relationship is achieved, it is much easier to proceed on a basis of mutual understanding, which in turn will allow agreement on the most contentious issues when they arise. The risk of the traditional adversarial exchange of ambitious schedules and counter-schedules of loss during litigation can also be reduced.

Working together should assist in limiting the escalation of the claimant's costs.

The key to unlocking settlement

Usually the single defining feature of catastrophic claims is the assessment of the lifelong professional care regime.

Under a standard litigation timetable, this will not usually be formally discussed/quantified until exchange of final schedules/ counter-schedules of loss. This can be four to five years post-accident, with the parties following directions towards trial, or consensually working towards a distant joint settlement or round table meeting (JSM/RTM). Insurers are, quite reasonably, concerned at the damages and costs inflation inherent in such a timetable.

While the experienced catastrophic practitioner (whether for the claimant or defendant) can estimate accurately at an early stage the likely final award for standard catastrophic injuries, the advice given to a claimant will always be against final settlement until they are confident that the appropriate care regime will be put in place and maintained for life. It is difficult to challenge such advice.

So, if settlement of a catastrophic claim is going to be achieved at an earlier stage, cooperation, collaboration and consensus will need to be promoted from the outset.

Tactics

Immediate tactics (incidental to rehabilitation)

- Immediate notification of incident to insurer.
- Reach earliest possible decision on liability, even before claim.
- If liability is clear, insurer to decide whether to invite claim, to avoid consequences of delay where claim inevitable.
- Make earliest telephone contact (ideally before discharge from hospital) with the claimant, family and representatives. This should be used as a means of arranging a face-to-face meeting and as a fact-gathering exercise.
- Suggest an INA.
- Fund and implement recommendations set out in INA.
- Schedule rehabilitation review meetings with case manager and the claimant/their solicitor.
- Where liability is to be contested, consider application for negative declaratory relief: see *Toropdar v D* [2009].

- Where it is apparent that a collaborative approach will not be possible, e.g. where there is a significant liability dispute and/or an obstructive or cost-driven solicitor, inviting proceedings and an application for an interim payment may be the best option to promote a level playing field in the rehabilitation and early investigation process.

Post-claim/investigation (rehabilitation to investigation)

- Agree and keep under review disposal timetable.
- Identify fields of expertise for expert assessment. Where possible for less contentious issues, agree a SJE.
- Volunteer direct funding by insurer of rehabilitation and interim care arrangements.
- Be flexible where rehabilitation initiatives offer potential results as opposed to increasing ultimate schedule, but at the same time keep a rein on unnecessary recommendations, such as excessive case management.
- Be flexible on interim payments.
- Be prepared to be flexible on equipment and accommodation in return for cooperation in relation to benefits.
- Identify statutory obligations owed to the claimant.
- Approach (tactfully) potential involvement of NHS agencies and social services. The claimant will not usually entertain such involvement unless liability is in issue or there is a significant level of contributory negligence.
- Offer to jointly instruct an individual with statutory funding know-how to work outside the litigation process to identify what is available and best for the claimant.

The cases that settle most effectively for all parties will usually be those where quantum investigation has been undertaken consensually outside litigation.

Negotiation/disposal

- Consider early neutral evaluation of specific heads of loss.
- Invite experts on each side to attempt joint determination of specific heads of loss.
- Consider early neutral evaluation of whole claim, even if not legally binding.
- Consider mediation. This is most effective where liability is in issue and/or three or more parties are involved.
- Consider without prejudice meetings without counsel, but ideally with the claimant present, to resolve individual heads of loss.
- Be willing to reach agreement on less substantial/ contentious heads of damage, to concentrate the parties on the more substantial heads of loss and complex issues such as statutory funding.
- Resolve the issue/role of statutory funding before the parties convene for an RTM/JSM. The involvement of local authorities can often slow a matter down.
- Plan for an RTM/JSM. These are of most use if arranged as a means to settlement outside the litigation process. Do not fall into the trap of agreeing a directions timetable geared to an RTM/JSM slotting in between schedules and trial.
- Offer staged payments of costs on account, in full settlement of costs incurred to payment date (excluding success fee).
- Always invite the claimant to include costs as part of the agenda for any RTM/JSM.

14 Calculating future losses

Jennifer Harris

Calculating future losses

Introduction

If a claimant has suffered a financial loss as a result of an accident, they are entitled to be put back in the position they would have been in had the accident not occurred.

It is relatively straightforward to calculate past losses. However, different principles have to be applied when calculating future losses.

For example, consider a 40-year-old man who is unable to work again and has no residual earning capacity. If he intended to retire at 67 he has been denied the opportunity of 27 years' salary. However, it does not follow that he is entitled to receive a lump sum equivalent to 27 years' salary as compensation for his future loss of earnings. He would be able to invest that sum and, as a consequence, receive a benefit greater than that he would have received had the accident not happened.

What of the retirement age? Claimants will often argue for a retirement age beyond 65 as the state pension age is increasing as follows:

- For women – from 60 to 65 by 2018.
- For women and men – from 65 to 66 by 2020.
- Further rises planned for women and men to 68 by the mid 2030s.
- Future rises to 70 are predicted. The government plans to create a solid link between the state pension age and rising life expectancy.

Starting point

The actual types of loss must be identified. For example, is there a claim for a future loss of earnings, the future cost of care and/or the future cost of gardening, etc.?

> To ensure that the future loss claimed is valid, it is important to cross reference all evidence with each head of claim. Particularly relevant are medical records, care or employment reports (where available) and witness statements. The claimant's records from the Department for Work and Pensions will also be useful.

For example, a claimant's injuries may prevent them from returning to their pre-accident employment because they are unable to perform precisely the same job. However, the claimant may still have some residual earning capacity in that they can still carry out some form of employment, even if it is less well paid.

The loss suffered in that situation would be the claimant's pre-accident earnings figure, less their residual earning capacity. A residual earning capacity will reduce a potential future loss of earnings claim.

A claimant must take steps to mitigate their losses by taking such employment as is available and that they could reasonably be expected to do given their physical condition.

In relation to a care claim, there may be a great deal of care necessary immediately after the accident. In the most serious cases, this care will last for the rest of the claimant's life. However, in most cases the amount of care will generally decrease or plateau as time goes on and the claimant's recovery progresses. It is necessary to identify how much care will be required into the future. Does that care arise out of the defendant's breach of duty or would it have been required anyway had the accident not occurred? Medical or care evidence will be useful in determining the amount of care that a claimant will require in the future and the cause of that requirement.

Claims handlers will need to identify the annual net loss or cost to the claimant. That annual net loss or cost is known as the multiplicand.

Second stage

Claims handlers must then consider the individual claimant:

- Are they male or female?
- How badly injured?
- How old?
- How well educated?
- Do they have any unrelated medical conditions that may affect life expectancy or ability to work in their pre-accident career?
- Are they now considered disabled as a consequence of the accident?
- In the case of a future loss of earnings claim, had the accident not happened, for how much longer would the claimant have continued to work? Consider here the usual retirement age in the claimant's type of work, the claimant's own wishes and the risk of earlier redundancy or retirement in the claimant's particular profession.

Consider requesting the claimant's human resources records and contacting their employers/former employers. Disclosure of their pension records or personnel file may reveal details of their intended plan for retirement.

Calculating the future loss claim

Consider a 40-year-old employed male claimant who, before the accident, earned £20,000 a year net of tax and national insurance.

- He claims that, had the accident not occurred, he would have worked until the age of 67. He has no residual earning capacity.
- He has, therefore, been deprived of 27 years' salary at £20,000 a year net. His loss of earnings multiplicand is, therefore, £20,000.

- It would not be appropriate to pay him 27 years of lost salary of £20,000 a year net, a total of £540,000. He is only entitled to be put back into the position he would have been in had the accident not happened. That is because he would be able to invest the capital sum of £540,000 and, over the subsequent 27 years, he would earn interest on this. He would, therefore, do rather better than he would have done had he remained at work.

The courts have avoided this problem of potential overcompensation by reducing the number of years' earnings to be paid to claimants for future losses. Claimants receive less by way of a lump sum because of the accelerated receipt of the capital sum. The number of years by which the multiplicand is to be multiplied by is known as the multiplier.

In *Wells v Wells* [1998], the House of Lords held:

- The multiplier must be based on the assumption that a claimant who prudently invests his compensation receives income from the capital investment at a particular percentage rate per annum.
- The aim of the court is to ensure that a claimant who receives compensation for future lost earnings will have a sum which, when invested, will run out on the date of the previously anticipated retirement.
- The use of actuarial tables should be recognised and encouraged.

The 'Actuarial Tables with explanatory notes for use in Personal Injury and Fatal Accident Cases' are more familiarly known as the Ogden tables. Sir Michael Ogden QC was the chairman of a working party, involving accountants, lawyers, insurers and actuaries, that produced the first tables in 1984. The tables are now in their 7th edition. They are a set of statistical tables with other information and guidance for use in calculating the appropriate lump sum for future losses.

The multipliers in the tables take into account:

- **Mortality:** the prospect of the death of the claimant before the end of the period of the loss or expense, or, where the loss is for life, death before or after the average. However, note that Tables 27 and 28 take no account of mortality.
- **Early receipt:** that the claimant is receiving a lump sum. It is assumed that the claimant will invest the lump sum and that investment will create income.

The columns in each table represent different rates of return on investment, which now range from –2.0% to plus 3.0%. These are known as the discount rates. The appropriate multiplier to use will change subject to the discount rate.

The discount rate is fixed by the Lord Chancellor pursuant to s.1 of the Damages Act 1996. It is currently, minus 0.75%.

It should be noted that the Ogden tables are not legislation and are only a guide, albeit a commonly used one. They are admissible in evidence by virtue of s.10 of the Civil Evidence Act 1995.

Useful formulae

The Ogden tables are to be used when calculating any item of future monetary loss or expense, whether one-off or continuous.

Put simply, the calculation is: multiplicand x multiplier.

There are 28 tables:

- **Table 1 (males) and Table 2 (females):** life expectancy and loss for life.
- **Tables 3 to 14:** loss of earnings up to various retirement ages.
- **Tables 15 to 26:** loss of pension from various retirement ages.
- **Table 27:** discounting to a date in the future.
- **Table 28:** a recurring loss over a period of time.

For future loss of earnings claims the approach should be:

- Multiplicand = net annual loss less any residual earning capacity.
- Multiplier = anticipated retirement date, less age of claimant, subject to Ogden tables.

Other future losses are treated slightly differently. Non-earnings-related future losses often run for the rest of the claimant's life. Life expectancy is, therefore, more important than the anticipated date of retirement:

- Mutliplicand = net annual loss/cost.
- Multiplier = life expectancy of claimant less age of claimant, subject to Ogden tables.

Contingencies other than mortality

Multipliers however can, and should where necessary, be adjusted to reflect contingencies other than mortality. This may include periods when the claimant might not have been earning in any event as a result of ill health (unrelated to the injuries), career break, redundancy, etc.

The 7th edition of the Ogden tables and the explanatory notes are based on the outcome of research that demonstrated that the key issues affecting a person's future working life are:

- Employment status
- Disability status
- Educational attainment.

It was felt by the Ogden working party that it was appropriate to include these risks in the Ogden approach to calculating future loss of earnings. Accordingly, additional Tables A to D were included from the 6th edition to take account of risks of periods of non-employment and absence from the workforce because of sickness.

Claims handlers should use Tables A to D as a ready reckoner in future loss of earnings calculations to take account of these risks. However, they should be alive to the particular facts of the case to see whether there are any arguments for lower adjustments. For example, a particular pre-accident disposition to periods of depression may have affected the claimant's future employment in any event.

An important contingency is whether the claimant is disabled. The explanatory notes to the Ogden tables state that a person is classified as disabled if all three of the following conditions are met:

- An illness or disability that has or is expected to last for over a year or is a progressive illness.
- The impact of the disability substantially limits the person's ability to carry out normal day-to-day activities.
- The condition affects either the kind or the amount of paid work the person can do.

Worked examples

Example 1 – loss of future earnings/future care

The following example is based on one within the explanatory notes of the 7th edition of the Ogden tables. However, the revised discount rate has been applied.

The claimant is female, aged 35 at the date of trial. She has three A levels, but not a degree, and was in employment at the date of the accident at a salary of £25,000 a year net of tax. She was not disabled before the accident. As a result of her injuries, she is now disabled and has lost her job but has found part-time employment at a salary of £5,000 a year net of tax. She anticipated that she would retire at age 60. Her cost of future care is £5,000 a year.

- **Step 1:** identify the multiplicand figures and consider relevant facts. We know that the claimant is 35 years old, female and intended to work until the age of 60. Her multiplicand for earnings is £25,000. Her multiplicand for cost of care is £5,000.
- **Step 2:** future loss of earnings multiplier. As the claimant is female and due to retire at age 60, the appropriate Ogden table is Table 8. The row to look at is that marked as age 35. The column to look at is that marked as the rate of return at –0.75%. Accordingly, the multiplier for loss of earnings is 27.10. Before any adjustments are made, the loss of earnings claim would be calculated as £25,000 × 27.10 = £677,500.
- **Step 3:** deductions for risks other than mortality. The claimant has A levels and was not disabled before the injury. Therefore, the table to use to account for this deduction is Table C. The appropriate column is 'Employed GE-A'. This provides that the multiplier of 27.10 should be multiplied by 0.86, which results in a revised multiplier of 23.306. The damages for loss of earnings are then calculated as £582,650 (23.306 × £25,000).
- **Step 4:** take account of mitigation of loss of earnings. Table 8 shows that, on the basis of a –0.75% rate of return, the correct multiplier for a female aged 35 is 27.10. We then apply the deductions, taking into account risks other than mortality and allowing for the claimant being employed, having A levels and being disabled as a result of the injuries. Table D and column 'Employed GE-A' give a multiplier of 0.48. The multiplier of 27.10 should be multiplied by 0.48, resulting in a revised multiplier of 13.008. The amount of mitigation for post-injury earnings is assessed as £65,040 (13.008 × £5,000).
- **Step 5:** subtract the mitigation figure from the loss of earnings figure to give a total loss of earnings figure. The award for loss of earnings after allowing for mitigation is £582,650 – £65,040 = £517,610.

- **Step 6:** calculate care. Look at Table 2, 'Multipliers for pecuniary loss for life (females)', for the appropriate multiplier for the claimant's age of 35. At a rate of return of –0.75% the multiplier is 68.54. No further adjustment is made for risks other than mortality. The future cost of care claim would be calculated as £5,000 × 68.54 = £342,700.

Example 2 – variable future loss of earnings

A more complicated example from the explanatory notes includes variable future probable earnings but for the accident.

The claimant is female with a degree. She is aged 25 at the date of the trial. Her probable career progression, in the absence of injury, would have provided her with salary increases at ages 30, 35 and 40. She would then have continued at the same salary to age 60, when she would have stepped down from full-time work to part-time until 70. As a result of the accident she is now incapable of working.

Her future net loss of earnings were projected as:

Age 25–30: £16,000 a year

Age 30–35: £25,000 a year

Age 35–40: £35,000 a year

Age 40–60: £40,000 a year

Age 60–70: £20,000 a year

- **Step 1:** identify the multiplicand figures and consider relevant facts. From the above information we know that the claimant is 25 years old, female and intended to work until the age of 70. The multiplicands for lost future earnings are as above.
- **Step 2:** future loss of earnings multiplier. As the claimant is female and was due to retire at age 70, the appropriate Ogden table is Table 12. The row to look at is that marked as age 25. The column to look at is that marked as the rate of return at –0.75%. Accordingly, the multiplier for loss of earnings taking into account mortality, but without any discounts for any other contingencies, is 52.25.

- **Step 3:** determine the working life multiplier. The working life will be 45 years (70 – 25) and the multiplier for a term certain of 45 years (ignoring mortality risks) from Table 28 is 53.56.
- **Step 4:** split the working life multiplier into segmented multipliers to correspond with the variable earnings.
  The multiplier of 53.56 should be split so that each individual segment of the whole working life period (45 years) is represented by a figure. Claims handlers should refer to Table 28 for each corresponding period. The figures are:

25–30	5.10 (multiplier for a term certain of five years)
30–35	5.29 (figure for a term certain of 10 years, 10.39 less 5.10)
35–40	5.49 (15-year figure of 15.88 less 10.39)
40–60	24.16 (35-year figure of 40.04 less 15.88)
60–70	13.52 (53.56 less 40.04)

- **Step 5:** calculate each of the working life segmented multipliers as a percentage of the total multiplier.
  For example, the first five years' segmented multiplier of 5.10 is 9.52% of the whole figure of 53.56:

25–30	9.52%
30–35	9.88%
35–40	10.25%
40–60	45.11%
60–70	25.24%

- **Step 6:** recalculate the future loss of earnings multiplier for each segment of the claimant's working life (to take account of mortality). This is done by working out the percentage figure for each segment of the working life multiplier from the total loss of earnings multiplier from Table 12 (52.25). The new figures are:

  25–30 4.97 (9.52% of 52.25)

  30–35 5.16 (9.88% of 52.25)

  35–40 5.36 (10.25% of 52.25)

  40–60 23.57 (45.11% of 52.25)

  60–70 13.19 (25.24% of 52.25)

- **Step 7:** deductions for risks other than mortality. The correct table to use is Table C (as she was not disabled, and is female), the row is 25–29 and the column is D (as she is educated to degree level). The applicable discount factor is 0.89. Multiply each of the loss of earnings multiplier segments by 0.89 to provide the correct discounted multipliers:

  25–30 4.42 (4.97 × 0.89)

  30–35 4.60 (5.16 × 0.89)

  35–40 4.77 (5.36 × 0.89)

  40–60 20.98 (23.57 × 0.89)

  60–70 11.73 (13.19 × 0.89)

- **Step 8:** multiply each discounted multiplier loss of earnings segment by the applicable multiplicand for each segment. These periods should then be added together to provide the full sum for loss of future earnings. This totals £1,426,470.

- **Step 9:** take into account mitigation of loss of earnings. In this example there is no mitigation of loss of earnings as the claimant is unable to work. However, at this stage, claims handlers would, if there was any mitigation of loss, calculate this as for Example 1 and then subtract this figure from the total loss of earnings figure.

Table 14.1: Breakdown of calculation

Ages	Period (years)	Table 28: multipliers working life term certain (not taking into account mortality)	% split of total multiplier	Table 12: multipliers loss of earnings (taking into account mortality)	Discounted multipliers to take into account contingencies other than mortality (Table 12 multiplier x Table C multiplier of 0.89)	Net annual earnings/ multiplicand	£ loss
25–30	5	5.10	9.52	4.97	4.42	16,000	70,720
30–35	5	5.29	9.88	5.16	4.60	25,000	115,000
35–40	5	5.49	10.25	5.36	4.77	35,000	166,950
40–60	20	24.16	45.11	23.57	20.98	40,000	839,200
60–70	10	13.52	25.24	13.19	11.73	20,000	234,600
Totals	45	53.56	100.0	52.25	46.5		**1,426,470**

Please see Table 14.1 for the purposes of the entire calculation.

Discount rate

In 2001, the then Lord Chancellor set the discount rate at 2.5% by reference to index-linked government stocks (ILGS). However, due to the low rate of return over recent years, claimants called for the discount rate to be cut, in order to increase the amount of damages they would receive.

On 27 February 2017, the Lord Chancellor announced a change in the Ogden discount rate from 2.5% to –0.75%, resulting in a significant impact on the value of the most serious personal injury claims.

Can a court depart from the discount rate set by the Lord Chancellor? Under s.1(2) of the Damages Act 1996, a court theoretically has the power to use a different discount rate if a party "shows that it is more appropriate in the case in question". The Lord Chancellor in his initial announcement of the discount rate commented that he had borne in mind departing from the prescribed rate of return "if there were exceptional circumstances which justify that".

In *Love v Dewsbury* [2010], a case in which Kennedys acted, the claimant argued that it was appropriate to deviate from the rate of 2.5%; alternatively to defer the assessment of certain heads of loss pending the outcome of the Lord Chancellor's review. The court held that it was inappropriate to adjourn the computation of damages. The court was required to apply the law as it stood and a discount rate of 2.5% was applied. We are unaware of any cases in English law where another discount rate has been awarded, despite it being regularly argued.

However, claims handlers should be aware of the impact of *Helmot v Simon* [2012]. This was a Guernsey Privy Council decision, so the case is persuasive but creates no precedent in English law.

Section 1(1) of the Damages Act 1996 and, consequently, the then 2.5% discount rate does not apply in Guernsey. However, the court at first instance used a single discount rate of 1% for all future losses and awarded damages of £9.3 million. The claimant argued successfully on appeal for different rates than those applicable in the UK. Actuarial evidence was adduced that the rate should be 0.5% for non-earnings-related losses and –1.5% for earnings-related losses. As a result, the final amount of the award was increased to over £14 million. The decision to alter the discount rate for different heads of loss was upheld on appeal to the Privy Council.

Ogden 8

Due to the recent change to the discount rate, it is anticipated that Ogden 8 will be published shortly. In the meantime, a supplemental Ogden 7 table has been released with the inclusion of a –0.75% column (with effect from 20 March 2017).

Updated versions of Ogden 27 and 28 have been created and Tables A1 and A5 have also been updated.

We have included a copy of the updated versions after the Ogden tables, which appear at the end of this chapter.

Ogden 8 is expected to include updated explanatory notes, updated tables to reflect updated mortality rates, greater guidance on disability discounts and also, possibly, an increased number of tables to reflect different possible retirement ages.

Local authority care provision

The decision in *Sowden v Lodge* [2004] is important when considering the cost of future care and accommodation, which is generally an issue in the most serious personal injury cases. The Court of Appeal decided that an award of damages for personal injury could, in principle, be made on the basis that residential care and accommodation provided by the local authority would be topped up by a payment for the provision of further care. This was on the basis that the feasibility of the proposed topping up had to be proved by evidence.

The claimant was seriously injured. Prior to trial she was a resident in a local authority residential home. The court decided that the correct test to be applied was what was required to meet the claimant's reasonable needs.

This decision was followed in *Crofton v NHS Litigation Authority* [2007] and *Sklair v Haycock* [2009].

A further example is *Peters v East Midlands Strategic Health Authority and others* [2009]. The defendants joined the local authority as Part 20 defendant. They sought a declaration that the local authority was not entitled to charge the claimant for her care. The local authority asserted that it should be able to recover a contribution from the claimant's award of damages.

The Court of Appeal held that an award of damages, or income produced from that award, was not to be taken into account when assessing a person's assets for the purposes of contribution toward their care costs. In addition, in this particular case, the claimant's disability was so severe that she would never have any assets other than those awarded by way of damages and it was unlikely that the local authority would be able to accommodate the level of care to which the claimant was accustomed. The defendant was, therefore, liable to pay the claimant's past and future care costs.

continued ...

... continued

On 7 April 2008, the National Assistance (Sums for Personal Requirements and Assessment of Resources) Amendment (England) Regulations 2008 (SI 2008/593) came into force, bringing about a major change in the way local authorities assess a person's entitlement to care provisions. The Regulations provide that where an award of damages for personal injury is placed into a trust any amount awarded in respect of care will no longer be disregarded by the local authority. This means that significantly more claimants are deemed as self-funders for the purposes of residential and domiciliary care. It should be noted, however, that this provision does not apply to funds administered by the Court of Protection, which are still disregarded.

Accommodation

Seriously injured claimants will often need alterations to their home to promote their independence and mobility and/or to assist their carers. The cost of alterations will form part of the claim for special damages if those alterations are a necessary consequence of the disability.

In addition, it is usually more expensive to run and maintain a home with a disabled person in a wheelchair or requiring other aids and equipment and/or carers. Consequently, claims will be made for additional wear and tear on carpets and floor surfaces, additional heating and extra insurance.

In the more serious cases, extensive equipment may be needed that requires additional space beyond that available in the claimant's existing home. Resident carers may be necessary, making additional rooms essential. This raises the necessity for either an extension to an existing property or an alternative and more expensive house/bungalow.

If the existing house can be adapted by way of an extension to accommodate the claimant, their aids and equipment and their carers, claims will be made for surveys/architects' fees for adaptations, building costs for the adaptations and extensions, and costs of additional furnishings and fittings for the extension.

Alternative accommodation

The capital cost of purchasing alternative accommodation does not form part of the claim for special damage as it is an asset with value rather than an expense. *Roberts v Johnstone* [1988] provides a formula to enable a claimant to purchase suitably enhanced accommodation while depriving their estate of any windfall element on death.

The formula treats the loss to the claimant as an annual sum representing "the net additional capital cost of the suitable enhanced alternative accommodation".

Example

A paraplegic claimant lives in an unsuitable house with a market value of £100,000. A more suitable bungalow has a price of £150,000. Alterations costing £50,000 are required. The alterations will increase the value by £15,000. The claimant will live in the adapted house for the rest of her life. The agreed life multiplier is 10.

	Value of new property, including value added by alterations:	£165,000
	Less value of former house (if any):	£100,000
	Additional capital cost:	£65,000
	Annual cost of loss of use of capital is £65,000 × 2.5% = £1,625 p.a. This is a continuing loss for the rest of the claimant's life, so the agreed multiplier of 10 is applied:	£16,250
Add:	Cost of extension and adaptations:	£50,000

Add:	Cost of moving (recovered in full if claimant would not have moved house but for the accident):	£7,500
Add:	Extra annual cost of living in larger more expensive house (£500 × 10), e.g. higher council tax, decorating:	£5,000
Less:	Value added by adaptations and extension:	£15,000
		£78,750
	Accommodation loss is:	£63,750

Time for a change?

Roberts v Johnstone has been under scrutiny for many years by claimant lawyers because of the hardship that can arise; for example, where there is contributory negligence or the claimant has a greatly reduced life expectancy. With increasingly higher house prices, the calculation may produce only a small proportion of the sum required to purchase/adapt a property. In such cases, a claimant has to apply sums allocated to other heads of loss such as earnings, therapies or care.

There have been a few (unreported) cases where the defendant/insurer has been prepared to innovate by purchasing a property and granting a life interest to the claimant. At present, such arrangements have been possible only where there is a consensual approach and a defendant volunteers to fund. There is a place, therefore, for defendants to work together with the claimant and their advisors to find innovative solutions that suit all parties concerned.

Some claimant lawyers believe that arguments can be advanced that will enable courts to order full funding, subject to a charge over the property, so that the sum advanced reverts to the defendant on the claimant's death. As an alternative, claimant lawyers are also exploring the legal scope to widen the rules on periodical payments and indexation of these to allow for an order for annual periodical payments to cover interest on a bank loan applied to purchase suitable accommodation.

The confusion around *Roberts v Johnstone* persists because of the uncertainty created by the dramatic change in the discount rate.

At the time of preparing this chapter, what is believed to be the first decision on the approach to *Roberts* in the era of a negative discount rate is *JR v Sheffield Teaching Hospitals NHS Trust* [2017]. The judge found the court was bound by *Roberts* and, given the negative discount rate, he had to consider the return on a risk-free investment as representing the claimant's loss. However, on the evidence (and discount rates) there was no loss.

Pending *JR v Sheffield* going to the Court of Appeal (which is likely) – and/or pending certainty around the ongoing review of the discount rate – it seems likely that claimants will seek evidence on the cost of funding properties.

Defendants have found pragmatic solutions to the problem by offering sensible lump sums for claims for accommodation costs that reflect need arising out of the injuries sustained and disability suffered.

There are other alternatively pragmatic, perhaps novel, approaches including offering the interest cost of the relevant mortgage.

We will update this section once the discount rate review has been concluded, which is difficult to predict following the Justice Committee's report published on 30 November 2017 referring the matter back to the government for further evidence and consideration.

Overall, legal challenges to *Roberts v Johnstone* should be anticipated.

Checklist

- ✓ What future losses are being claimed?
- ✓ Does the evidence support the future loss? Consider medical reports, medical records, personnel records, employment reports, care reports, pension documents, Department for Work and Pensions records, etc.
- ✓ In the case of loss of earnings, does the claimant have a residual earning capacity? In other words, even if it is

accepted that the claimant cannot return to their pre-accident employment, can they usefully carry out some other form of paid employment? If they can, this will reduce the loss of earnings multiplicand. Remember that the claimant is under an obligation to mitigate their losses and cannot simply say, "I have been injured, I need not work at all". If they are capable of some form of paid work, and work is available, they must accept it.

- ✓ For other future cost or loss claims (such as care, gardening, decorating, car maintenance), what is the actual cost to the claimant? Is this supported by evidence? Consider the evidence you have in order to apply the correct multiplicand for each head of claim. Ensure that the claimant has suffered a loss and was not paying for the items claimed for before the accident.
- ✓ Consider the Ogden tables, taking into account the age, sex, health and education of the claimant, and in the case of earnings, their anticipated retirement date. Adopt the appropriate discount rate. Make appropriate adjustments to the multiplier.
- ✓ Remember that some future loss claims should not be allowed for the rest of the claimant's life. It is unlikely that the claimant would have decorated their own home for the rest of their life. At some point, their age would have prevented them from doing so in any event. Such future claims should be limited and paid up to a reasonable age.
- ✓ Having assessed the future claims, consider the impact of recoverable benefits. You will have to withhold appropriate benefits from appropriate damages. You should do so before paying the claimant their compensation. (See Chapter 17 on the Compensation Recovery Unit).
- ✓ Consider the operation of the Courts Act 2003 and the potential for a periodical payment order (see Chapter 16 on Periodical payments).

INTRODUCTION to the 7th Edition of the OGDEN TABLES

"When it comes to the explanatory notes we must make sure that they are readily comprehensible. We must assume the most stupid circuit judge in the country and before him are the two most stupid advocates. All three of them must be able to understand what we are saying".

Sir Michael Ogden, QC,
on his explanatory notes to the
First Edition of the Ogden Tables[1].

1. The Working Party has been eager to see a new set of these Tables published, as there have been changes in the official projections of future mortality rates for the UK since the previous, sixth, edition was published which produce significant changes in the values of some of the multipliers. The Working Party is grateful that the Ministry of Justice has agreed to fund the production of this edition of the Ogden Tables.

Purpose of the tables

2. These tables are designed to assist those concerned with calculating lump sum damages for future losses in personal injury and fatal accident cases in the UK.

3. The methodology is long-established whereby multipliers are applied to the present day value of a future annual loss (net of tax in the case of a loss of earnings and pension) with the aim of producing a lump sum equivalent to the capitalised value of the future losses. In essence, the multiplier is the figure by which an annual loss is multiplied in order to calculate a capitalised sum, taking into account accelerated receipt, mortality risks and, in relation to claims for loss of earnings and pension, discounts for contingencies other than mortality.

4. This methodology was endorsed by the House of Lords in the famous case of **Wells v Wells [1999] 1 AC 345**. In that case the Court determined that the discount rate should be based on the yields on Index Linked Government Stock. The discount rate is now fixed by the Lord Chancellor of the day pursuant to his powers under the Damages Act 1996. The above method was further endorsed by Lord Chancellor Irvine in his decision of July 2001, when he fixed the Discount Rate as being 2.5%. He also gave his reasons for his decision, which reasons appear now to be less than happy in the light of the financial turmoil which has since occurred. I will deal with this below. In my view, this present rate is long out of date and does not reflect the substantial reduction in yields on Index Linked Government Stocks since 2001. The present Lord Chancellor Clarke has agreed to review it although his decision may not be available for several months.

First decision of the Working Party

5. It was decided that, with funding now obtained, a new set of Tables, based on the most recent mortality rates produced by the Office for National Statistics (ONS), with as few other revisions as possible, should be issued as quickly as was realistically achievable.

Second decision of the Working Party

6. It was decided that, due to the passage of time and the changed circumstances since the Tables were first produced, the text of the Explanatory Notes will require a substantial re-write in order to bolster its usefulness to practitioners. Not only is there a need to change the language, but the effect of other decided cases has made this a task of importance. The intention of the Working party is to accomplish this re-writing in the next (eighth) Edition, which will rely on the further updated mortality projections due to be produced by the ONS later in 2011. It is hoped that the eighth edition will be available in autumn 2012.

Third decision of the Working Party

7. Developments in Guernsey and the review of the discount rate currently being carried out by the Lord Chancellor (see further below in respect of both matters) caused the Working Party to decide to include in this Edition tables with discount rate columns which range between minus 2 per cent and plus 3 per cent.

8. It is not, we believe, the purpose of these Tables or the role of the Working Party to advocate a discount rate, but merely to provide the tools so that, whatever the rate should be, personal injury and fatal accident claims may be quantified.

9. The revised spread of discount rates will assist comparison between lump sums and periodical payments, a process required by the Damages Act 1996, to be more accurately appreciated. The present value of periodical payments is substantially higher than lump sums calculated using the current discount rate of 2.5%. Brooke LJ remarked in paragraph 34 of the **Flora v Wakom [2006] EWCA Civ 1103, [2007] 1 WLR 282** judgment: 'The fact that these two quite different

[1] Memoirs of Sir Michael Ogden, QC, 'Variety is the Spice of Legal Life', p.182; The Book Guild, 2002

mechanisms now sit side by side in the same Act of Parliament does not in my judgment mean that the problems that infected the operation of the one should be allowed to infect the operation of the other.' This imbalance is a factor which any Lord Chancellor ought to take into account.

Fourth decision of the Working Party

10. The Working Party decided not to increase further the number of tables to reflect different possible retirement ages. The multipliers for retirement ages which do not conform strictly with the 5 yearly intervals between 50 and 75 can be calculated with reasonable accuracy by interpolation. We would be interested to learn of other views on this decision which might cause us to think again.

Helmot v Simon

11. The judgment in **Helmot v Simon [2009-10] GLR 465** in the Court of Appeal of the Island of Guernsey (14th September 2010), presided over by Sumption J.A., could be truly described as a decision which has had after-effects. The results have rippled the waters within the English legal establishment, even though the decision creates no precedent in England.

12. The first point to make about the case is that the Damages Act 1996 (as amended) does not apply in Guernsey. Consequentally, neither the 2.5% discount rate prescribed under the power provided by section 1 applies nor is there any power to make an award by way of a periodical payment.

13. The original lump sum award made at first instance on 14 January 2010 was for damages in the sum of £9.3 million plus interest. The court used a single discount rate of 1% for all future losses. The claimant had argued for differential rates of 0.5% for non-earnings-related losses and of minus 1.5% for earnings-related losses. Some eight months later these arguments succeeded on appeal and the final amount of the award was increased to more than £14 million. Permission has been granted to appeal the decision to the Privy Council.

14. The consequences in England and Wales have been profound. The Lord Chancellor has indicated his intention to reconsider the discount rate and at the time of writing is in the process of doing so. It has also emphasised the disparity between lump sum awards and the provision of periodical payments, to the detriment of lump sum awards, when the discount rate is inappropriate, it not having been revised for a period of 10 years.

Mortality data

15. Projections of future mortality rates are usually produced on a two-yearly basis by the ONS as part of the production of national population projections for the United Kingdom and its constituent countries. Multipliers published in the sixth edition of the Ogden Tables were calculated using mortality rates from the 2004-based projections; this new edition provides multipliers based on mortality rates from the most recent, 2008-based, projections. The 2006-based projections showed rather higher projected life expectancies at many ages than those in the 2004-based projections. The 2008-based projections suggest slightly higher projected life expectancies than those in the 2006-based projections, but which are of relatively little significance in terms of the values of the multipliers at most ages.

16. There is much debate among demographers about whether the factors that have led to the significant improvements in mortality in recent years can continue unabated, thus adding some uncertainty to any projections of future mortality. While the Working Party has continued to use the official projections made by the ONS of future mortality rates in the UK, we propose to monitor developments as new evidence becomes available.

Contingencies other than mortality

17. We have persuaded Dr Victoria Wass to join the Working Party. She has suggested changes to the definition of 'disabled' and also clarified some of the language in the Explanatory Notes. We anticipate some further suggestions for amendment in the eighth Edition.

18. The Working Party notes that there have been a number of cases in which judges have made significant adjustments to the suggested discount factors. In particular the approach of the trial judges to the calculation of future loss of earnings in **Conner v Bradman [2007] EWHC 2789 (QB)** and **Clarke v Maltby [2010] EWHC 1201 (QB)** has generated some debate. These issues will be discussed in detail when drafting the eighth Edition and consideration given to whether or not the Explanatory Notes need amendment, especially as regards the circumstances in which it might be appropriate to depart from the suggested non-mortality reduction factors and the size of any adjustments that are made. In the meantime, practitioners performing such calculations are referred to the helpful article by Dr Wass, *"Discretion in the Application of the New Ogden Six Multipliers: The Case of Conner v Bradman and Company"*, published in JPIL Issue 2/2008 pp 154-163 which highlights some of the relevant issues.

Fatal Accidents Act calculations and the 'Actuarially Recommended Approach'

19. This is dealt with in detail in Section D of the Explanatory Notes. To those comments I would add one qualification which is that the Court of Appeal in **Fletcher v A Train & Sons Ltd [2008] EWCA Civ 413, [2008] 4 All ER 699** was sufficiently concerned with the consequence of following the reasoning of the House of Lords in **Cookson v Knowles [1979] AC 566** that it unanimously gave the unsuccessful Appellant permission to appeal to the House of Lords on the point; the appeal was subsequently compromised.

20. The Scottish Parliament has since enacted the Damages (Scotland) Act 2011 dealing with the same point and in so doing has demonstrated that it agrees with the point that our predecessors had made on this topic.

21. Section 7(1)(d) of the Damages (Scotland) Act 2011 provides for the multiplier to be calculated at the date of the proof (trial) and the losses over the period between the fatal accident and the proof to be calculated separately, subject to a factor for possible early death, with interest added. Multipliers are determined from the tables based on the age of the deceased had he/she survived to the date of proof. This is the same as our actuarially recommended approach.

Concluding Remarks

22. The changes to the Explanatory Notes in this Edition are minor; it is the figures that have been updated.

23. As I have previously stated, the figures for the Tables themselves are produced by the Government Actuary's Department according to long-established principles.

24. The other matters discussed are the subject of careful and detailed analysis by the members of the Working Party. Its discussions are never less than uninhibited and I am grateful to those members of the Working Party (listed inside the front cover) who give their time and energy to attend the meetings and ensure that all is done which ought to be done.

25. I begin to believe that the journey made by Jason and the Argonauts in search of the Golden Fleece is as nothing in comparison with the desire of those involved in these Tables to make the assessment of future losses as simple and accurate as they possibly can be, whilst remaining as clear as we can be in explaining the actual process of calculating the figures. I am conscious that we may not always succeed in that ambition.

1 August 2011

Robin de Wilde, Q.C.

EXPLANATORY NOTES

SECTION A: GENERAL

Purpose of tables

1. The tables have been prepared by the Government Actuary's Department. They provide an aid for those assessing the lump sum appropriate as compensation for a continuing future pecuniary loss or consequential expense or cost of care in personal injury and fatal accident cases.

Application of tables

2. The tables set out multipliers. These multipliers enable the user to assess the present capital value of future annual loss (net of tax) or annual expense calculated on the basis of various assumptions which are explained below. Accordingly, to find the present capital value of a given annual loss or expense, it is necessary to select the appropriate table, find the appropriate multiplier and then multiply the amount of the annual loss or expense by that figure.

3. Tables 1 to 26 deal with annual loss or annual expense extending over three different periods of time. In each case there are separate tables for men and women.

- In Tables 1 and 2 the loss or expense is assumed to begin immediately and to continue for the whole of the rest of the claimant's life
- In Tables 3 to 14 the loss or expense is assumed to begin immediately but to continue only until the claimant's retirement or earlier death.
- In Tables 15 to 26 it is assumed that the annual loss or annual expense will not begin until the claimant reaches retirement but will then continue for the whole of the rest of his or her life. These tables all make due allowance for the chance that the claimant may not live to reach the age of retirement.

Mortality assumptions

4. The tables are based on a reasonable estimate of the future mortality likely to be experienced by average members of the population alive today and are based on projected mortality rates for the United Kingdom as a whole. The Office for National Statistics publishes population projections on a regular basis which include estimates of the extent of future improvements in mortality. Tables 1 to 26 in this edition show the multipliers which result from the application of these projected mortality rates which were derived from the principal 2008-based population projections for the United Kingdom, which were published in October 2009. (Further details of these projections can be found on the ONS website at http://www.ons.gov.uk/ons/rel/npp/national-population-projections/2008-based-projections/index.html.)

5. The tables do not assume that the claimant dies after a period equating to the expectation of life, but take account of the possibilities that the claimant will live for different periods, e.g. die soon or live to be very old. The mortality assumptions relate to the general population of the United Kingdom. However, unless there is clear evidence in an individual case to support the view that the individual is atypical and will enjoy longer or shorter expectation of life, no further increase or reduction is required for mortality alone.

Use of tables

6. To find the appropriate figure for the present value of a particular loss or expense, the user must first choose that table which relates to the period of loss or expense for which the individual claimant is to be compensated and to the gender of the claimant, or, where appropriate, the claimant's dependants.

7. If, for some reason, the facts in a particular case do not correspond with the assumptions on which one of the tables is based (e.g. it is known that the claimant will have a different retiring age from that assumed in the tables), then the tables can only be used if an appropriate allowance is made for this difference; for this purpose the assistance of an actuary should be sought, except for situations where specific guidance is given in these explanatory notes.

Rate of return

8. The basis of the multipliers set out in the tables is that the lump sum will be invested and yield income (but that over the period in question the claimant will gradually reduce the capital sum, so that at the end of the period it is exhausted). Accordingly, an essential factor in arriving at the right figure is the choice of the appropriate rate of return.

9. The annual rate of return currently to be applied is 2½% (net of tax), as fixed by the Lord Chancellor on 25 June 2001, and reassessed on 27 July 2001, under the provisions of the Damages Act 1996 Section 1. An annual rate of return

of 2½% was also set for Scotland by the Scottish Ministers on 8 February 2002. The Lord Chancellor may make a fresh determination of this rate, after receiving advice from the Government Actuary and the Treasury (and, in Scotland, the Scottish Ministers after consultation with the Government Actuary). In order to allow the Tables to continue to be used should a new discount rate be specified, the tables are accordingly shown for a range of possible annual rates of return ranging from –2% to 3%, in steps of 0.5%, rather than the range 0.0% to 5.0% as in the 6th edition. This change has been made because multipliers at negative rates are useful for the financial evaluation of periodical payments in the exercise which is required by the Damages Act in all cases for comparison with lump sums. In addition, it is recognised that multipliers based on discount rates of more than 3% are currently not generally required, and a recent case heard in the Channel Islands (**Helmot v Simon [2009-10] GLR 465**) has made an award based on negative discount rates.

10. The figures in the 0% column show the multiplier without any discount for interest and provide the expectations of life (Tables 1 and 2) or the expected period over which a person would have provided a dependency (up to retirement age Tables 3 to 14 or from pension age Tables 15 to 26). These are supplied to assist in the calculation of multipliers in Fatal Accidents Act cases (see Section D).

11. Section 1(2) of the Damages Act 1996 makes provision for the Courts to make variations to the discount rate if any party to the proceedings shows that it is more appropriate in the case in question. Variations to the discount rate under this provision have, however, been rejected by the Court of Appeal in the cases of **Warriner v Warriner [2002] EWCA Civ 81, [2002] 1 WLR 1703** and **Cooke & Others v United Bristol Health Care & Others [2003] EWCA Civ 1370, [2004] 1 WLR 251**.

12. Previous editions of these tables explained how the current yields on index-linked government bonds could be used as an indicator of the appropriate real rate of return for valuing future income streams. Such considerations were endorsed by the House of Lords in **Wells v Wells** and the same argumentation was adopted by the Lord Chancellor when he set the rate on commencement of Section 1 of the Damages Act 1996. In cases outwith the scope of these tables, the advice of an actuary should be sought.

Different retirement ages

13. In paragraph 7 above, reference was made to the problem that will arise when the claimant's retiring age is different from that assumed in the tables. Such a problem may arise in valuing a loss or expense beginning immediately but ending at retirement; or in valuing a loss or expense which will not begin until the claimant reaches retirement but will then continue until death. Tables are provided for retirement ages of 50, 55, 60, 65, 70 and 75. Where the claimant's actual retiring age would have been between two of the retirement ages for which tables are provided, the correct multiplier can be obtained by consideration of the tables for retirement age immediately above and below the actual retirement age, keeping the period to retirement age the same. Thus a woman of 42 who would have retired at 58 can be considered as being in between the cases of a woman of 39 with a retirement age of 55 and a woman of 44 with a retirement age of 60. The steps to take are as follows:

(1) Determine between which retirement ages, for which tables are provided, the claimant's actual retirement age R lies. Let the lower of these ages be A and the higher be B.

(2) Determine how many years must be subtracted from the claimant's actual retirement age to get to A and subtract that period from the claimant's age. If the claimant's age is x, the result of this calculation is $(x+A-R)$.

(3) Look up this new reduced age in the Table corresponding to retirement age A at the appropriate rate of return. Let the resulting multiplier be M.

(4) Determine how many years must be added to the claimant's actual retirement age to get to B and add that period to the claimant's age. The result of this calculation is $(x+B-R)$.

(5) Look up this new increased age in the Table corresponding to retirement age B at the appropriate rate of return. Let the resulting multiplier be N.

(6) Interpolate between M and N. In other words, calculate:

$(B-R) \times M + (R-A) \times N$

and divide the result by $[(B-R) + (R-A)]$, (or equivalently $[B-A]$).

14. In the example given in paragraph 13, the steps would be as follows:

(1) R is 58, A is 55 and B is 60.

(2) Subtracting 3 years from the claimant's age gives 39.

(3) Looking up age 39 in Table 6 (for retirement age 55) gives 13.10 at a rate of return of 2½%.

(4) Adding 2 years to the claimant's age gives 44.

(5) Looking up age 44 in Table 8 (for retirement age 60) gives 13.03 at a rate of return of 2½%.

(6) Calculating 2 x 13.10 + 3 x 13.03 and dividing by (60-58) + (58-55) [equals 5] gives 13.06 as the multiplier.

15. When the loss or expense to be valued is that from the date of retirement to death, and the claimant's date of retirement differs from that assumed in the tables, a different approach is necessary, involving the following three steps.

(1) Assume that there is a present loss which will continue for the rest of the claimant's life and from Table 1 or 2 establish the value of that loss or expense over the whole period from the date of assessment until the claimant's death.

(2) Establish the value of such loss or expense over the period from the date of assessment until the claimant's expected date of retirement following the procedure explained in paragraphs 13 and 14 above.

(3) Subtract the second figure from the first. The balance remaining represents the present value of the claimant's loss or expense between retirement and death.

16. If the claimant's actual retiring age would have been earlier than 50, or later than 75, the advice of an actuary should be sought.

Younger ages

17. Tables 1 and 2, which concern pecuniary loss for life, and Tables 15 to 26, which concern loss of pension from retirement age, have been extended down to age 0. In some circumstances the multiplier at age 0 is slightly lower than that at age 1; this arises because of the relatively high incidence of deaths immediately after birth.

18. Tables for multipliers for loss of earnings (Tables 3 to 14) have not been extended below age 16. In order to determine the multiplier for loss of earnings for someone who has not yet started work, it is first necessary to determine an assumed age at which the claimant would have commenced work and to find the appropriate multiplier for that age from Tables 3 to 14, according to the assumed retirement age. This multiplier should then be multiplied by the deferment factor from Table 27 which corresponds to the appropriate rate of return and the period from the date of the trial to the date on which it is assumed that the claimant would have started work. A similar approach can be used for determining a multiplier for pecuniary loss for life where the loss is assumed to commence a fixed period of years from the date of the trial. For simplicity the factors in Table 27 relate purely to the impact of compound interest and ignore mortality. At ages below 30 this is a reasonable approximation but at higher ages it would normally be appropriate to allow explicitly for mortality and the advice of an actuary should be sought.

Contingencies

19. Tables 1 to 26 make reasonable provision for the levels of mortality which members of the population of the United Kingdom alive today may expect to experience in future. The tables do not take account of the other risks and vicissitudes of life, such as the possibility that the claimant would for periods have ceased to earn due to ill-health or loss of employment. Nor do they take account of the fact that many people cease work for substantial periods to care for children or other dependants. Section B suggests ways in which allowance may be made to the multipliers for loss of earnings, to allow for certain risks other than mortality.

Impaired lives

20. In some cases, medical evidence may be available which asserts that a claimant's health impairments are equivalent to adding a certain number of years to their current age, or to treating the individual as having a specific age different from their actual age. In such cases, Tables 1 and 2 can be used with respect to the deemed higher age. For the other tables the adjustment is not so straightforward, as adjusting the age will also affect the assumed retirement age, but the procedures described in paragraphs 13 to 15 may be followed, or the advice of an actuary should be sought. In other cases, the medical evidence may state that the claimant is likely to live for a stated number of years. This is often then treated as requiring payment to be made for a fixed period equal to the stated life expectancy and using Table 28 to ascertain the value of the multiplier. In general, this is likely to give a multiplier which is too high since this approach does not allow for the distribution of deaths around the expected length of life. For a group of similarly impaired lives of the same age, some will die before the average life expectancy and some after; allowing for this spread of deaths results in a lower multiplier than assuming payment for a term certain equal to the life expectancy. In such cases, it is preferable to look up the age in the 0% column in Table 1 or 2 for which the value of the multiplier at 0% is equal to the stated life expectancy. The relevant multipliers are then obtained from the relevant tables using this age. Take, for example, an impaired male life which is

stated to have a life expectancy of 20 years. By interpolation, the age for which the multiplier in the 0% column in Table 1 is 20 is:

(20 – 19.74)/(20.57 – 19.74) x 66 + (20.57 – 20)/(20.57 – 19.74) x 67

which equals 66.7 years.

The value of the whole of life multiplier is then obtained from the 2.5% column of Table 1 for age 66.7 years:

(67 – 66.7) x 15.38 + (66.7 – 66) x 14.90

which equals 15.04 (compared to 15.78 for the value for a term certain of 20 years using the 2.5% column of Table 28).

Fixed periods

21. In cases where pecuniary loss is to be valued for a fixed period, the multipliers in Table 28 may be used. These make no allowance for mortality or any other contingency but assume that regular frequent payments (e.g. weekly or monthly) will continue throughout the period. These figures should in principle be adjusted if the periodicity of payment is less frequent, especially if the payments in question are annually in advance or in arrears.

Variable future losses or expenses

22. The tables do not provide an immediate answer when the annual future loss or expense is likely to change at given points in time in the future. The most common examples will be where:

(a) the claimant's lost earnings would have increased on a sliding scale or changed due to promotion; or

(b) the claimant's future care needs are likely to change in the future, perhaps because it is anticipated that a family carer will not be able to continue to provide help.

In such situations it is usually necessary to split the overall multiplier, whether for working life or whole of life, into segments, and then to apply those smaller segmented multipliers to the multiplicand appropriate for each period.

There are a variety of methods which could be used for splitting a multiplier, especially where the age at which a payment is increased or decreased, or stops or begins, is one which is tabulated in Tables 1 to 26. The following examples serve to illustrate how multipliers might be split using the "apportionment method". This method can be extended for use in cases where none of the ages at which payments change are tabulated.

Example 1 – Variable future earnings

23. The claimant is female, a graduate with a degree, aged 25 at date of settlement/trial. Her probable career progression, in the absence of injury, would have provided her with salary increases at ages 30, 35 and 40; thereafter she would have continued at the same level to age 60, when she would have stepped down from full-time work to work part-time until 70. Post accident she is now incapable of working.

The multiplicands for lost future earnings are:

Age 25 to 30:	£16,000 a year
Age 30 to 35:	£25,000 a year
Age 35 to 40:	£35,000 a year
Age 40 to 60:	£40,000 a year
Age 60 to 70:	£20,000 a year

The multipliers for each stage of her career are calculated as follows:

(1) The working-life will be 45 years and the Multiplier from Table 12 for that period taking into account mortality risks but without any discounts for any other contingencies will be 26.73.

(2) The multiplier for a term certain of 45 years (ignoring mortality risks) from Table 28 is 27.17.

(3) The multiplier from Table 28 should be split so that each individual segment of the whole working life period (45 years) is represented by a figure. So, the first 5 years is represented by a multiplier for a term certain of 5 years, namely 4.70; the next 5 years is represented by a multiplier of 4.16 (being the difference between the figure for a term certain of 10 years, namely 8.86 and the figure for a term certain of 5 years, namely 4.70); the

next 5 years by 3.68 (i.e. the 15 year figure of 12.54 less the 10 year figure of 8.86); the next 20 years by 10.89 (i.e. the difference between the 35 year figure which is 23.43 and the 15 year figure of 12.54); then, the final 10 years by the balance of 3.74 (the residual figure being 27.17 less 23.43).

(4) Each of those smaller segmented multipliers can be shown as a percentage or fraction of the whole: so, for the first 5 years the segmented multiplier of 4.70 is 17.30% of the whole figure of 27.17, and so on for each segment of the 45 year period.

(5) The working life multiplier from Table 12 can now be split up in identical proportions to the way in which the Table 28 multiplier has been treated above: thus the first 5 year period is now represented by a multiplier of 4.62, which is calculated by taking 17.30% of 26.73. Each segmented multiplier is calculated in the same way.

(6) Having now obtained multipliers for each segment of working life, taking into account mortality risks, it is then necessary to discount those figures for "contingencies other than mortality". The discount factor from Table C (using the column for a female, not disabled, with degree level education) is 0.89. So, the figure of 4.62 for the first 5 year period now becomes 4.11 (i.e. 4.62 x 0.89). Again, treat each segmented multiplier in the same way.

(7) The multiplicand for each segment of working life is now multiplied by the appropriate segmented multiplier to calculate the loss for that period. The sum total of those losses represents the full sum for loss of future earnings (ignoring any mitigation).

(8) The figures are set out in tabular form below and give a total lump sum award of £716,260:

Ages	Period (years)	Table 28	% Split	Table 12	Discounted Multipliers (Table C) (x 0.89)	Net Annual Earnings £	£ Loss
25 – 30	5	4.70	17.30	4.62	4.11	16,000	65,760
30 – 35	5	4.16	15.31	4.09	3.64	25,000	91,000
35 – 40	5	3.68	13.54	3.62	3.22	35,000	112,700
40 – 60	20	10.89	40.08	10.71	9.53	40,000	381,200
60 – 70	10	3.74	13.77	3.68	3.28	20,000	65,600
Totals:	45 years	27.17	100.0	26.73	23.79		**716,260**

N.B. the figures in the above table have been rounded at each step of the calculation so the totals shown are not necessarily the sum of the individual multipliers in the columns

Example 2 – Variable future care costs

24. A male aged 20 years at the date of settlement/trial requires personal care support for life. He has a normal life expectation for his age. Significant changes in his care regime are anticipated at age 30 and again at age 50.

The multiplicands for care costs are:

Age 20 to 30:	£30,000 a year
Age 30 to 50:	£60,000 a year
Age 50 for rest of life:	£80,000 a year

The multipliers for each stage of the care regime are calculated as follows:

(1) The life expectation will be 67.22 years (from the 0% column of Table 1) and the multiplier for that period taking into account mortality risks (from Table 1) will be 32.10.

(2) The multiplier for a term certain of 67.22 years (ignoring mortality risks) from Table 28 lies between 32.75 (for 67 years) and 32.94 (for 68 years) and is calculated thus:

(68 – 67.22) x 32.75 + (67.22 – 67) x 32.94 = 32.79.

(3) The multiplier from Table 28 should be split so that each individual segment of the whole period of life expectation is represented by a figure. So, the first 10 years (20-30) are represented by a multiplier of 8.86; the next 20 years (30-50) are represented by a multiplier of 12.33 (being the difference between the 30 year figure of 21.19 and the 10 year figure of 8.86); then, the final years (50 to death) are represented by the balance of 11.60 (being the difference between the term certain multiplier of 32.79 and the 30 year figure of 21.19).

(4) Each of those smaller segmented multipliers can be shown as a percentage or fraction of the whole: so, for the first 10 years the segmented multiplier of 8.86 is 27.02% of the whole figure of 32.79, and so on for each segment of the life period.

(5) The life multiplier from Table 1 can now be split up in the way in which the Table 28 multiplier was treated above and in identical proportions: thus the first 10 year period is now represented by a multiplier of 8.67 which is calculated by taking 27.02% of 32.10.

(6) The figures are set out in tabular form below and give a total lump sum award of £1,893,100:

Age (years)	Table 28 (67.22 years) Split multipliers	% Split (of Table 28 figure)	Table 1 (multiplier allowing for mortality)	Care costs £ a year	Total £
20 – 30	8.86	27.02%	8.67	30,000	260,100
30 – 50	12.33	37.60%	12.07	60,000	724,200
50 till death	11.60	35.38%	11.36	80,000	908,800
Totals	32.79 (no mortality discount)	100.00%	32.10 life multiplier		**1,893,100**

N.B. the figures in the above table have been rounded at each step of the calculation

Spouses' pensions

25. If doubt exists whether the tables are appropriate to a particular case which appears to present significant difficulties of substance, it would be prudent to take actuarial advice. This might be appropriate in relation to the level of spouses' benefits, if these are to be assessed, since these are not readily valued using Tables 1 to 26. As a rough rule of thumb, if spouses' benefits are to be included when valuing pension loss from normal pension age, the multipliers in Tables 15 to 26 should be increased by 5% for a female claimant (i.e. benefits to the male spouse) and by 14% for a male claimant if the spouse's pension would be half of the pension that the member was receiving at death. If the spouse's pension would be payable at a rate of two-thirds the member's pension at death the multipliers should be increased by 7% for a female claimant and by 18% for a male claimant.

SECTION B: CONTINGENCIES OTHER THAN MORTALITY

26. As stated in paragraph 19, the tables for loss of earnings (Tables 3 to 14) take no account of risks other than mortality. This section shows how the multipliers in these tables may be reduced to take account of these risks.

27. Tables of factors to be applied to the existing multipliers were first introduced in the Second Edition of the Ogden Tables. These factors were based on work commissioned by the Institute of Actuaries and carried out by Professor S Haberman and Mrs D S F Bloomfield (*Work time lost to sickness, unemployment and stoppages: measurement and application* (1990), Journal of the Institute of Actuaries 117, 533-595). Although there was some debate within the actuarial profession about the details of the work, and in particular about the scope for developing it further, the findings were broadly accepted and were adopted by the Government Actuary and the other actuaries who were members of the Working Party when the Second Edition of the Tables was published and remained unchanged until the 6th edition.

28. Some related work was published in 2002 by Lewis, McNabb and Wass (*Methods of calculating damages for loss of future earnings*, Journal of Personal Injury Law, 2002 Number 2). For the publication of the 6th Edition of the Ogden Tables, the Ogden Working Party was involved in further research into the impact of contingencies other than mortality carried out by Professor Richard Verrall, Professor Steven Haberman and Mr Zoltan Butt of City University, London and, in a separate exercise, by Dr Victoria Wass of Cardiff University. Their findings were combined to produce the tables of factors given in section B of the 6th edition and repeated here.

29. The Haberman and Bloomfield paper relied on data from the Labour Force Surveys for 1973, 1977, 1981 and 1985 and English Life Tables No. 14 (1980-82). The Labour Force Survey (LFS) was originally designed to produce a periodic cross-sectional snapshot of the working age population and collects information on an extensive range of socio-economic and labour force characteristics. Since the winter of 1992/3, the LFS has been carried out on a quarterly basis, with respondents being included in the survey over 5 successive quarters. The research of Professor Verrall *et al* and Dr Wass used data from the Labour Force Surveys conducted from 1998 to 2003 to estimate the probabilities of movement of males and females between different states of economic activity, dependent on age, sex, employment activity and level of disability. These probabilities permit the calculation of the expected periods in employment until retirement age, dependent on the initial starting state of economic activity, disability and educational attainment. These can then be discounted at the same discount rate that is used for obtaining the relevant multiplier from Tables 3 to 14, in order to give a multiplier which takes into account only those periods the claimant would be expected, on average, to be in work. These discounted working life expectancy multipliers can be compared to those obtained assuming the person remained in work throughout, to obtain reduction factors which give the expected proportion of time to retirement age which will be spent in employment.

30. The factors described in subsequent paragraphs are for use in calculating loss of earnings up to retirement age. The research work did not investigate the impact of contingencies other than mortality on the value of future pension rights. Some reduction to the multiplier for loss of pension would often be appropriate when a reduction is being applied for loss of earnings. This may be a smaller reduction than in the case of loss of earnings because the ill-health contingency (as opposed to the unemployment contingency) may give rise to significant ill-health retirement pension rights. A bigger reduction may be necessary in cases where there is significant doubt whether pension rights would have continued to accrue (to the extent not already allowed for in the post-retirement multiplier) or in cases where there may be doubt over the ability of the pension fund to pay promised benefits. In the case of a defined contribution pension scheme, loss of pension rights may be allowed for simply by increasing the future earnings loss (adjusted for contingencies other than mortality) by the percentage of earnings which the employer contributions to the scheme represent.

31. The methodology proposed in paragraphs 33 to 42 describes one method for dealing with contingencies other than mortality. If this methodology is followed, in many cases it will be appropriate to increase or reduce the discount in the tables to take account of the nature of a particular claimant's disabilities. It should be noted that the methodology does not take into account the pre-accident employment history. The methodology also provides for the possibility of valuing more appropriately the possible mitigation of loss of earnings in cases where the claimant is employed after the accident or is considered capable of being employed. This will in many cases enable a more accurate assessment to be made of the mitigation of loss. However, there may be some cases when the *Smith v Manchester Corporation* or *Blamire* approach remains applicable or otherwise where a precise mathematical approach is inapplicable.

32. The suggestions which follow are intended as a 'ready reckoner' which provides an initial adjustment to the multipliers according to the employment status, disability status and educational attainment of the claimant when calculating awards for loss of earnings and for any mitigation of this loss in respect of potential future post-injury earnings. Such a ready reckoner cannot take into account all circumstances and it may be appropriate to argue for higher or lower adjustments in particular cases. In particular, it can be difficult to place a value on the possible mitigating income when considering the potential range of disabilities and their effect on post work capability, even within the interpretation of disability set out in paragraph 35. However, the methodology does offer a framework for consideration of a range of possible figures with the maximum being effectively provided by the post injury multiplier assuming the claimant was not disabled and the minimum being the case where there is no realistic prospect of post injury employment.

The deduction for contingencies other than mortality

33. Under this method, multipliers for loss of earnings obtained from Tables 3 to 14 are multiplied by factors to allow for the risk of periods of non-employment and absence from the workforce because of sickness.

34. The research by Professor Verrall *et al* and Dr Wass referred to in paragraphs 28 and 29 demonstrated that the key issues affecting a person's future working life are employment status, disability status and educational attainment.

35. The definitions of employed/not employed, disabled/not disabled and educational attainment used in this analysis and which should be used for determining which factors to apply to the multipliers to allow for contingencies other than mortality are as follows:

Employed — Those who at the time of the accident are employed, self-employed or on a government training scheme

Not employed — All others (including those temporarily out of work, full-time students and unpaid family workers)

Disabled — A person is classified as being disabled if all three of the following conditions in relation to the ill-health or disability are met:

(i) has an illness or a disability which has or is expected to last for over a year or is a progressive illness

(ii) satisfies the Equality Act 2010 definition that the impact of the disability substantially limits the person's ability to carry out normal day-to-day activities

(iii) their condition affects either the kind or the amount of paid work they can do

Not disabled — All others

Normal day-to-day activities are those which are carried out by most people on a daily basis, and we are interested in disabilities/health problems which have a substantial adverse effect on respondent's ability to carry out these activities.

There are several ways in which a disability or health problem may affect the respondent's day to day activities:

Mobility – for example, unable to travel short journeys as a passenger in a car, unable to walk other than at a slow pace or with jerky movements, difficulty in negotiating stairs, unable to use one or more forms of public transport, unable to go out of doors unaccompanied.

Manual dexterity – for example, loss of functioning in one or both hands, inability to use a knife and fork at the same time, or difficulty in pressing buttons on a keyboard

Physical co-ordination – for example, the inability to feed or dress oneself; or to pour liquid from one vessel to another except with unusual slowness or concentration.

Problems with bowel/bladder control – for example, frequent or regular loss of control of the bladder or bowel. Occasional bedwetting is not considered a disability.

Ability to lift, carry or otherwise move everyday objects (for example, books, kettles, light furniture) – for example, inability to pick up a weight with one hand but not the other, or to carry a tray steadily.

Speech – for example, unable to communicate (clearly) orally with others, taking significantly longer to say things. A minor stutter, difficulty in speaking in front of an audience, or inability to speak a foreign language would not be considered impairments.

Hearing – for example, not being able to hear without the use of a hearing aid, the inability to understand speech under normal conditions or over the telephone.

Eyesight – for example, while wearing spectacles or contact lenses – being unable to pass the standard driving eyesight test, total inability to distinguish colours (excluding ordinary red/green colour blindness), or inability to read newsprint.

Memory or ability to concentrate, learn or understand – for example, intermittent loss of consciousness or confused behaviour, inability to remember names of family or friends, unable to write a cheque without assistance, or an inability to follow a recipe.

Perception of risk of physical danger – for example, reckless behaviour putting oneself or others at risk, mobility to cross the road safely. This excludes (significant) fear of heights or underestimating risk of dangerous hobbies.

Three levels of educational attainment are defined for the purposes of the tables as follows:

D Degree or equivalent or higher

GE-A GCSE grades A to C up to A levels or equivalents

O Below GCSE C or CSE 1 or equivalent or no qualifications

The following table gives a more detailed breakdown of the allocation of various types of educational qualification to each of the three categories above and are based on the allocations used in the research by Professor Verrall *et al* and Dr Wass.

Categories of highest educational attainment

D **Degree or equivalent or higher**	**GE-A** **GCSE grades A to C up to A levels or equivalent**	**O** **Below GCSE C or CSE 1 or equivalent or no qualifications**
Any degree (first or higher)	A or AS level or equivalent	CSE below grade 1
Other higher education qualification below degree level	O level, GCSE grade A-C or equivalent	GCSE below grade C
Diploma in higher education		
NVQ level 4 or 5	NVQ level 2 or 3	NVQ level 1 or equivalent
HNC/HND, BTEC higher etc	BTEC/SCOTVEC first or general diploma	BTEC first or general certificate
	OND/ONC, BTEC/SCOTVEC national	SCOTVEC modules or equivalent
RSA higher diploma	RSA diploma, advanced diploma or certificate	RSA other
Teaching, Nursing etc	GNVQ intermediate or advanced	GNVQ/ GVSQ foundation level
	City and Guilds craft or advanced craft	City and Guilds other
	SCE higher or equivalent Trade apprenticeship	YT/ YTP certificate
	Scottish 6th year certificate (CSYS)	Other qualifications
		No qualification
		Don't know

Note: "educational attainment" is used here as a proxy for skill level, so that those in professional occupations such as law, accountancy, nursing etc who do not have a degree ought to be treated as if they do have one.

36. The research also considered the extent to which a person's future working life expectancy is affected by individual circumstances such as occupation and industrial sector, geographical region and education. The researchers concluded that the most significant consideration was the highest level of education achieved by the claimant and that, if this was allowed for, the effect of the other factors was relatively small. As a result, the Working Party decided to propose adjustment factors which allow for employment status, disability status and educational attainment only. This is a change from earlier editions of the Ogden Tables where adjustments were made for types of occupation and for geographical region.

37. A separate assessment is made for (a) the value of earnings the claimant would have received if the injury had not been suffered and (b) the value of the claimant's earnings (if any) taking account of the injuries sustained. The risk of non-employment is significantly higher post-injury due to the impairment. The loss is arrived at by deducting (b) from (a).

38. In order to calculate the value of the earnings the claimant would have received, if the injury had not been suffered, the claimant's employment status and the disability status need to be determined as at the date of the accident (or the onset of the medical condition) giving rise to the claim, so that the correct table can be applied. For the calculation of future loss of earnings (based on actual pre-accident earnings and also future employment prospects), Tables A and C should be used for claimants who were not disabled at the time of the accident, and Tables B and D should be used for those with a pre-existing disability. In all of these tables the three left hand columns are for those who were employed at the time of the accident and the three right hand columns are for those who were not.

39. In order to calculate the value of the actual earnings that a claimant is likely to receive in the future (i.e. after settlement or trial), the employment status and the disability status need to be determined as at the date of settlement or trial. For claimants with a work-affecting disability at that point in time, Tables B and D should be used. The three left hand columns will apply in respect of claimants actually in employment at date of settlement or trial and the three right hand columns will apply in respect of those who remain non-employed at that point in time.

40. The factors in Tables A to D allow for the interruption of employment for bringing up children and caring for other dependants.

41. In the case of those who at the date of the accident have not yet reached the age at which it is likely they would have started work, the relevant factor will be chosen based on a number of assessments of the claimant's likely employment had the injury not occurred. The relevant factor from the tables would be chosen on the basis of the level of education the claimant would have been expected to have attained, the age at which it is likely the claimant would have started work, together with an assessment as to whether the claimant would have become employed or not. The work multiplier will also have to be discounted for early receipt using the appropriate factor from Table 27 for the number of years between the claimant's age at the date of trial and the age at which it is likely that he/she would have started work.

42. Tables A to D include factors up to age 54 only. For older ages the reduction factors increase towards 1 at retirement age for those who are employed and fall towards 0 for those who are not employed. However, where the claimant is older than 54, it is anticipated that the likely future course of employment status will be particularly dependent on individual circumstances, so that the use of factors based on averages would not be appropriate. Hence reduction factors are not provided for these older ages.

Table A
Loss of Earnings to pension Age 65 (Males – Not disabled)

Age at date of trial	Employed			Not employed		
	D	GE-A	O	D	GE-A	O
16-19		0.90	0.85		0.85	0.82
20-24	0.92	0.92	0.87	0.89	0.88	0.83
25-29	0.93	0.92	0.89	0.89	0.88	0.82
30-34	0.92	0.91	0.89	0.87	0.86	0.81
35-39	0.90	0.90	0.89	0.85	0.84	0.80
40-44	0.88	0.88	0.88	0.82	0.81	0.78
45-49	0.86	0.86	0.86	0.77	0.77	0.74
50	0.83	0.83	0.83	0.72	0.72	0.70
51	0.82	0.82	0.82	0.70	0.70	0.68
52	0.81	0.81	0.81	0.67	0.67	0.66
53	0.80	0.80	0.80	0.63	0.63	0.63
54	0.79	0.79	0.79	0.59	0.59	0.59

Table B
Loss of Earnings to pension Age 65 (Males – Disabled)

Age at date of trial	D	Employed GE-A	O	D	Not employed GE-A	O
16-19		0.55	0.32		0.49	0.25
20-24	0.61	0.55	0.38	0.53	0.46	0.24
25-29	0.60	0.54	0.42	0.48	0.41	0.24
30-34	0.59	0.52	0.40	0.43	0.34	0.23
35-39	0.58	0.48	0.39	0.38	0.28	0.20
40-44	0.57	0.48	0.39	0.33	0.23	0.15
45-49	0.55	0.48	0.39	0.26	0.20	0.11
50	0.53	0.49	0.40	0.24	0.18	0.10
51	0.53	0.49	0.41	0.23	0.17	0.09
52	0.54	0.49	0.41	0.22	0.16	0.08
53	0.54	0.49	0.42	0.21	0.15	0.07
54	0.54	0.50	0.43	0.20	0.14	0.06

Table C
Loss of Earnings to Pension Age 60 (Females – Not disabled)

Age at date of trial	D	Employed GE-A	O	D	Not employed GE-A	O
16-19		0.81	0.64		0.77	0.59
20-24	0.89	0.82	0.68	0.84	0.76	0.60
25-29	0.89	0.84	0.72	0.83	0.75	0.61
30-34	0.89	0.85	0.75	0.81	0.75	0.63
35-39	0.89	0.86	0.78	0.80	0.74	0.63
40-44	0.89	0.86	0.80	0.78	0.72	0.60
45-49	0.87	0.85	0.81	0.72	0.64	0.52
50	0.86	0.84	0.81	0.64	0.55	0.43
51	0.85	0.84	0.81	0.60	0.51	0.40
52	0.84	0.84	0.81	0.56	0.46	0.36
53	0.83	0.83	0.81	0.50	0.41	0.32
54	0.83	0.83	0.82	0.44	0.35	0.27

Table D
Loss of Earnings to Pension Age 60 (Females – Disabled)

Age at date of trial	Employed			Not employed		
	D	GE-A	O	D	GE-A	O
16-19		0.43	0.25		0.35	0.19
20-24	0.64	0.44	0.25	0.58	0.33	0.17
25-29	0.63	0.45	0.25	0.50	0.32	0.16
30-34	0.62	0.46	0.30	0.44	0.31	0.15
35-39	0.61	0.48	0.34	0.42	0.28	0.14
40-44	0.60	0.51	0.38	0.38	0.23	0.13
45-49	0.60	0.54	0.42	0.28	0.18	0.11
50	0.60	0.56	0.47	0.23	0.15	0.10
51	0.61	0.58	0.49	0.21	0.14	0.09
52	0.61	0.60	0.51	0.20	0.13	0.08
53	0.62	0.62	0.54	0.18	0.11	0.07
54	0.63	0.66	0.57	0.16	0.09	0.06

The factors in Tables A to D will need to be reviewed if the discount rate changes.

Different pension ages

43. The factors in the preceding tables assume retirement at age 65 for males and age 60 for females. It is not possible to calculate expected working life times assuming alternative retirement ages from the LFS data, since the employment data in the LFS are collected only for the working population, assumed aged between 16 and 64 for males and between 16 and 59 for females. Where the retirement age is different from age 65 for males or age 60 for females, it is suggested that this should be ignored and the reduction factor and the adjustments thereto be taken from the above tables for the age of the claimant as at the date of trial with no adjustment i.e. assume that the retirement age is age 65 for males and age 60 for females. However, if the retirement age is close to the age at the date of trial, then it may be more appropriate to take into account the circumstances of the individual case.

44. It should be noted that the reduction factors in Tables A, B, C and D are based on data for the period 1998 to 2003. Whilst the reduction factors and adjustments allow for the age-specific probabilities of moving into, or out of, employment over future working life time, based on data for the period 1998-2003, the methodology assumes that these probabilities remain constant over time; there is no allowance for changes in these age-specific probabilities beyond this period. It is also assumed that there will be no change in disability status or educational achievement after the date of the accident. Future changes in the probabilities of moving into, and out of, employment are especially difficult to predict with any certainty. It is the intention that the factors should be reassessed from time to time as new data become available.

SECTION C: SUMMARY OF PERSONAL INJURY APPLICATIONS

45. To use the tables the guidance below should be followed:

(1) Choose the table relating to the appropriate sex of the claimant and period of loss or expense (e.g. loss for life, or loss of earnings to a set retirement age). Where loss of earnings is concerned, and none of the tables is relevant because the claimant's expected age of retirement differs from that assumed in the tables, the procedure in paragraphs 13 to 16 of the explanatory notes should be followed.

(2) Choose the appropriate discount column (currently 2½%).

(3) In that column find the appropriate figure for the claimant's age at trial ("the basic multiplier").

Loss of earnings

(4) When calculating **loss of earnings**, the tables should be used when a multiplier/multiplicand approach is appropriate. If it is, the basic multiplier should be adjusted to take account of contingencies other than mortality. These contingencies include the claimant's employment and disability status and educational qualifications. The basic multiplier should be multiplied by the appropriate figure taken from Tables A to D. It may be necessary at this stage to modify the resulting figure further to allow for circumstances specific to the claimant.

This process gives "the adjusted table multiplier".

(5) Multiply the net annual loss (the multiplicand) by the adjusted table multiplier to arrive at a figure which represents the capitalised value of the future loss of earnings.

(6) If the claimant has a residual earning capacity, allowance should be made for any post-accident vulnerability on the labour market: the following paragraphs show one way of doing this, although there may still be cases where a conventional **Smith v City of Manchester** award is appropriate.

Where it is appropriate to do so, repeat steps 1 to 5 above, replacing the pre-accident employment and disability status with the post-accident employment and disability status in step 4 and replacing the net annual loss by the assumed new level of net earnings at step 5. It will only be necessary to reconsider the claimant's educational attainments if these have changed between the accident and the date of trial or settlements.

The result will represent the capitalised value of the claimant's likely post-accident earnings. It is important to note that, when carrying out this exercise, the *degree* of residual disability may have a different effect on residual earnings depending on its relevance to the claimant's likely field of work. For example, the loss of a leg may have less effect on a sedentary worker's earnings than on a manual worker's.

(7) Deduct the sum yielded by step 6 from that yielded by step 5 to obtain the net amount of loss of earnings allowing for residual earning capacity. Where the above methodology is used there will usually be no need for a separate **Smith v City of Manchester** award.

Life time losses

(8) Where a **loss** will continue **for life**, follow steps 1 to 3 above to find the appropriate multiplier in the table.

Where the normal life expectancy given by the table is inapplicable the approach set out in paragraph 20, using the lifetime tables rather than Table 28, is the correct approach.

(9) This figure may need adjustment to allow for the particular circumstances of the claimant.

(10) Multiply the annual loss or expense by the multiplier as adjusted

Variable annual losses

(11) In cases where there will be different losses at different periods it may be necessary to split the multiplier. The approach set out at paragraphs 22 to 24 should be followed.

Fixed period and Deferred losses

(12) Where a loss will continue over a fixed period, the appropriate multiplier can be found in Table 28.

(13) Where a loss will not commence until some future date, multiply the appropriate multiplier by a discount figure taken from Table 27 (the use of which is explained in paragraph 18). This paragraph does not apply to loss of pensions, which have their own tables.

Examples

46. The following are examples of the use of the tables in illustrative personal injury cases with simplified assumptions.

Example 3

47. The claimant is female, aged 35 at the date of the trial. She has three A levels, but not a degree, and was in employment at the date of the accident at a salary of £25,000 a year net of tax. She was not disabled before the accident. As a result of her injuries, she is now disabled and has lost her job but has found part-time employment at a salary of £5,000 a year net of tax. Her loss of earnings to retirement age of 60 is assessed as follows:

(1) Look up Table 8 for loss of earnings to pension age 60 for females.

(2) The appropriate rate of return is determined to be 2½% (the rate currently set under Section 1 of the Damages Act 1996).

(3) Table 8 shows that, on the basis of a 2½% rate of return, the multiplier for a female aged 35 is 18.43.

(4) Now take account of risks other than mortality. Allowing for the claimant being employed, not disabled and having achieved A levels at the date of trial, Table C would require 18.43 to be multiplied by 0.86, resulting in a revised multiplier of 15.85.

(5) The damages for loss of earnings are assessed as £396,250 (15.85 x £25,000).

(6) Allow for mitigation of loss of earnings in respect of post-injury earnings. As before, Table 8 shows that, on the basis of a 2½% rate of return, the multiplier for a female aged 35 is 18.43.

(7) Now take account of risks other than mortality. Allowing for the claimant being employed, disabled and having achieved A levels at the date of trial, Table D would require 18.43 to be multiplied by 0.48, resulting in a revised multiplier of 8.85.

(8) The amount of mitigation for post-injury earnings is assessed as £44,250 (8.85 x £5,000).

(9) Hence award for loss of earnings after allowing for mitigation is £396,250 – £44,250 = £352,000.

Example 4

48. The claimant is male, aged 48 at the date of the trial. He has no educational qualifications. His retirement age was 65, he was employed at the time of the accident and his pre-retirement multiplicand has been determined as £20,000 a year net of tax. He was not disabled before the accident. As a result of his injuries, he is now disabled and has lost his job. The multiplicand for costs of care is deemed to be £50,000 a year. He is unemployed at the date of trial but has been assessed as capable of finding work with possible future earnings of £5,000 a year net of tax. His loss of earnings to retirement age of 65 is assessed as follows:

(1) Look up Table 9 for loss of earnings to pension age 65 for males.

(2) The appropriate rate of return is determined to be 2½% (the rate currently set under Section 1 of the Damages Act 1996).

(3) Table 9 shows that, on the basis of a 2½% rate of return, the multiplier for a male aged 48 is 13.42.

(4) Now take account of risks other than mortality. Allowing for the claimant being employed, not disabled and having no educational qualifications at the date of trial, Table A would require 13.42 to be multiplied by 0.86, resulting in a revised multiplier of 11.54.

(5) The damages for loss of earnings are assessed as £230,800 (11.54 x £20,000).

(6) Allow for mitigation of loss of earnings in respect of post-injury earnings. As before, Table 9 shows that, on the basis of a 2½% rate of return, the multiplier for a male aged 48 is 13.42.

(7) Now take account of risks other than mortality. Allowing for the claimant being unemployed and disabled with no educational qualifications at the date of trial, Table B would require 13.42 to be multiplied by 0.11, resulting in a revised multiplier of 1.48.

(8) The amount of mitigation for post-injury earnings is assessed as £7,400 (1.48 x £5,000).

(9) Hence award for loss of earnings after allowing for mitigation is £230,800 – £7,400 = £223,400.

49. The damages for cost of care are assessed as follows:

(1) Look up Table 1 for the multiplier at age 48.

(2) The appropriate rate of return is 2½%.

(3) Table 1 shows that, on the basis of a 2½% rate of return, the multiplier at age 48 is 23.51.

(4) No adjustment is made for risks other than mortality.

(5) The damages for cost of care are assessed at £1,175,500 (23.51 x £50,000).

Example 5

50. The claimant is female, aged 14 at the date of the trial. She is expected to achieve a degree and to be in employment thereafter on a salary, in current terms, of £30,000 a year net of tax. She was not disabled before the accident. As a result of her injuries, she is now disabled – she is still expected to achieve a degree and to be in employment, but with an average salary in current terms of £20,000 net of tax. She will be aged 21 when she completes her degree. Her loss of earnings to retirement age of 60 is assessed as follows:

(1) Look up Table 8 for loss of earnings to pension age 60 for females.

(2) The appropriate rate of return is determined to be 2½% (the rate currently set under Section 1 of the Damages Act 1996).

(3) Table 8 shows that, on the basis of a 2½% rate of return, the multiplier for a female graduate aged 21 is 24.83. This needs to be discounted back to age 14. The factor at 2½% for a period for deferment for seven years is 0.8413 from Table 27, giving a total multiplier of 24.83 x 0.8413 = 20.89.

(4) Now take account of risks other than mortality. Allowing for the claimant at age 21 assessed as achieving a degree, being employed and not disabled, Table C would require 20.89 to be multiplied by 0.89, resulting in a revised multiplier of 18.59.

(5) The damages for loss of earnings are assessed as £557,700 (18.59 x £30,000).

(6) Allow for mitigation of loss of earnings in respect of post-injury earnings. As before, Table 8 shows that, on the basis of a 2½% rate of return, the multiplier for a female graduate aged 21 is 24.83. As before, after discounting for seven years to age 14 the multiplier is reduced to 24.83 x 0.8413 = 20.89.

(7) Now take account of risks other than mortality. Allowing for the claimant at age 21 assessed as achieving a degree, being employed and disabled, Table D would require 20.89 to be multiplied by 0.64, resulting in a revised multiplier of 13.37.

(8) The amount of mitigation for post-injury earnings is assessed as £267,400 (13.37 x £20,000).

(9) Hence award for loss of earnings after allowing for mitigation is £557,700 – £267,400 = £290,300.

Example 6

51. The claimant is male, aged 40 at the date of the trial. He has achieved O levels. He was unemployed at the time of the accident. His potential pre-retirement multiplicand has been determined as £15,000 a year net of tax. He was disabled before the accident. As a result of his injuries, he has been assessed as having no future prospect of employment. His loss of earnings to retirement age of 65 is assessed as follows:

(1) Look up Table 9 for loss of earnings to pension age 65 for males.

(2) The appropriate rate of return is determined to be 2½% (the rate currently set under Section 1 of the Damages Act 1996).

(3) Table 9 shows that, on the basis of a 2½% rate of return, the multiplier for a male aged 40 is 18.09.

(4) Now take account of risks other than mortality. Allowing for the claimant being unemployed, disabled and having achieved O levels at the date of trial, Table A would require 18.09 to be multiplied by 0.23, resulting in a revised multiplier of 4.16.

(5) The damages for loss of earnings are assessed as £62,400 (4.16 x £15,000).

(6) As the claimant has been assessed as having no future prospect of employment following the accident, there is no mitigation of loss of earnings in respect of post-injury earnings.

(7) Hence award for loss of earnings after allowing for mitigation is £62,400.

SECTION D: APPLICATION OF TABLES TO FATAL ACCIDENT CASES

52. The current approach of the courts, except in Scotland, is to assess the multiplier as at the date of death (**Cookson v Knowles [1979] AC 556**).

53. That approach was criticised by the Law Commission in their Report 263 (*Claims for Wrongful Death*). The Law Commission recommended that multipliers should be assessed as at the date of trial and that the multipliers derived from the Ogden Tables should only take effect from the date of trial. The Law Commission stressed that the current approach incorporates an actuarial flaw in that it incorporates a discount for early receipt in the period prior to trial or assessment.

54. The Working Party, then under the Chairmanship of the late Sir Michael Ogden QC, considered that the Law Commission's criticism was valid. In the Fourth Edition of the Tables published in August 2000, the Working Party set out guidance in Section D of the Explanatory Notes on how damages should be calculated in such cases. We refer to that guidance below as the actuarially recommended approach. We note that the actuarially recommended approach has been adopted in the Damages (Scotland) Act 2011. For further details see paragraphs 20-21 in the Introduction.

55. However the courts have considered themselves bound by **Cookson v Knowles** and hence have not followed the actuarially recommended approach (**White v Esab [2002] PIQR Q6, H v S [2002] EWCA Civ 792, [2003] QB 965** and **Fletcher v A Train & Sons Ltd [2008] EWCA Civ 413, [2008] 4 All ER 699**).

The Basic Law in England and Wales

56. Under the Fatal Accidents Act the loss is that of the dependants, i.e. those who relied upon the deceased for support. They may claim that part of the deceased's income (whether earnings, pension, unearned income or state benefits) that the deceased would have spent on them. They may also claim the loss of the services such as DIY, domestic/household or childcare which the deceased would have undertaken and from which they would have benefited. The position of each dependant must be considered separately.

57. Each head of dependency must be considered separately. For each head of claim for each dependant the court calculates a multiplicand. This is calculated on the basis of what is known at the date of trial. For pre-trial losses, the actual loss to date of trial is calculated. Interest is added. For post-trial losses the multiplicand is calculated as at the date of trial.

58. A multiplier for the period of dependency is applied to the multiplicand to arrive at an overall lump sum for each head of dependency.

59. The remainder of Section D deals with how to approach the calculations in fatal accident claims. Three approaches are put forward. Paragraphs 60 to 63 set out the current approach. The actuarially recommended approach is then set out at paragraphs 64 to 81. Example 7 illustrates the application of both these approaches whilst Examples 8 and 9 show the actuarially recommended approach applied to more complex situations – these examples make up paragraphs 82 to 87. The final paragraphs of section D, 88 to 90, offer an alternative approach using multipliers selected from the date of death.

The Current approach

60. Under the approach currently followed by the courts, the multiplier is calculated as at the date of death. However, when making that calculation the court is entitled to take into account matters that have arisen between death and trial. For example, **Williamson v Thorneycroft [1940] 2 KB 658** in which the deceased's widow died after her husband but before trial, her dependency terminated at her death. See also **Corbett v Barking, Havering & Brentwood HA [1991] 2 QB 408**.

61. There are two periods to be determined:–

(i) The expected period from date of death in which the deceased would have been capable of providing the dependency;

(ii) The expected period from the date of the death in which the dependant would have been able to receive the dependency.

The shorter of those two periods provides the basis for the multiplier.

62. In respect of each of those periods consideration must be given as to what discount should be made for contingencies other than mortality. The most obvious contingencies other than mortality fall into the following three categories:–

(i) Factors relating to the deceased. For example, the deceased's health may have been such as to seriously affect his ability to provide services or work until retirement age. In relation to earnings the starting point for the adjustment factor should be the figures contained in Tables A to D.

(ii) Factors relating to the dependant. For example, at trial it may be proved that a dependant has a significantly reduced life expectancy.

(iii) Factors relating to the relationship of the deceased and the dependant. For example, an unmarried couple who were on the point of separation before the deceased died. See also section 3 (4) of the Act and **Drew v Abassi**, Court of Appeal 24 May 1995.

63. The assessment of the multiplier involves the following steps:–

(1) Determine the expected period from the date of death for which the deceased would have been capable of providing the dependency.

(2) Discount that period for early receipt using the appropriate Table as at the date of death and a discount rate of 2½%.

(3) Apply any adjustment to the above figure to reflect contingencies other than mortality.

(4) Determine the expected period from date of death for which the dependant would have been able to receive the dependency.

(5) Discount that period for early receipt using the appropriate Table as at the date of death at a discount rate of 2½%.

(6) Apply any adjustment to the figure in (5) to reflect contingencies other than mortality.

(7) Take the lower of the figures in (3) and (6) above. That is the overall multiplier from date of death.

(8) Subtract the period elapsed from date of death to date of trial. Losses in this period will be treated as in effect special damages and will attract an award of interest.

(9) The balance of the multiplier will be the multiplier for the post trial multiplicand.

The Actuarially Recommended approach

64. Whereas in personal injury cases the problem to be solved is that of setting a value on an income stream during the potential life of one person (the claimant), the situation is generally more complicated in fatal accident cases. Here the compensation is intended to reflect the value of an income stream during the lifetime of one or more dependants of the deceased (or the expected period for which the dependants would have expected to receive the dependency, if shorter) but limited according to the expectation of how long the deceased would have been able to provide the financial support, had he or she not been involved in the fatal accident.

65. In principle, therefore, the compensation for post-trial dependency should be based on the present value at the date of the trial of the dependency during the expected future joint lifetime of the deceased and the dependant or claimant (had the deceased survived naturally to the date of the trial), subject to any limitations on the period of dependency and any expected future changes in the level of dependency, for example, on attaining retirement age. In addition there should be compensation for the period between the date of accident and the date of trial.

66. A set of actuarial tables to make such calculations accurately would require tables similar to Tables 1 to 26 but for each combination of ages as at the date of the trial of the deceased and the dependant to whom compensation is to be paid. The Working Party concluded that this would not meet the criterion of simplicity of application which was a central objective of these tables and recommends that, in complex cases, or cases where the accuracy of the multiplier is thought by the parties to be of critical importance and material to the resulting amount of compensation (for example in cases potentially involving very large claims where the level of the multiplicand is unambiguously established), the advice of a professionally qualified actuary should be sought. However, for the majority of cases, a certain amount of approximation will be appropriate, bearing in mind the need for a simple and streamlined process, and taking into consideration the other uncertainties in the determination of an appropriate level of compensation. The following paragraphs describe a methodology using Tables 1 to 26 which can be expected to yield satisfactory answers.

(i) Damages for the period from the fatal accident to the date of trial

67. The period of pre-trial dependency will normally be equal to the period between the date of the fatal accident and the date of the trial, substituting where appropriate the lower figure of the expected period for which the deceased would have provided the dependency, had he or she not been killed in the accident, or if the period of dependency would have been limited in some way, for example, if the dependant is a child.

68. A deduction may be made for the risk that the deceased might have died anyway, in the period between the date of the fatal accident and the date at which the trial takes place. In many cases this deduction will be small and could usually be regarded as *de minimis*. The need for a deduction becomes more necessary the longer the period from the date of accident to the date of trial and the older the deceased at the date of death. As an illustration of the order of magnitude of the deduction, Table E shows some examples of factors by which the multiplier should be multiplied for different ages of the deceased and for different periods from the date of accident to the date of the trial.

TABLE E

Factor by which pre-trial damages should be multiplied to allow for the likelihood that the deceased would not in any case have survived to provide the dependency for the full period to the date of trial.

Age of deceased at date of accident	Period from date of accident to date of trial or date of cessation of dependency, if earlier (years)					
	Male deceased			Female deceased		
	3	6	9	3	6	9
10	1.00	1.00	1.00	1.00	1.00	1.00
20	1.00	1.00	1.00	1.00	1.00	1.00
30	1.00	1.00	0.99	1.00	1.00	1.00
40	1.00	0.99	0.99	1.00	1.00	0.99
50	0.99	0.99	0.98	1.00	0.99	0.99
60	0.99	0.97	0.94	0.99	0.98	0.97
65	0.98	0.95	0.91	0.99	0.97	0.95
70	0.97	0.92	0.86	0.98	0.95	0.91
75	0.94	0.87	0.78	0.96	0.91	0.84
80	0.90	0.79	0.67	0.93	0.84	0.75

N.B. The factor for a period of zero years is clearly 1.00. Factors for other ages and periods not shown in the table may be obtained approximately by interpolation.

69. The resultant multiplier, after application of any discount for the possibility of early death of the deceased before the date of trial, even had the accident not taken place, is to be applied to the multiplicand, which is determined in the usual way. Interest will then be added up to the date of trial on the basis of special damages.

(ii) Damages from the date of trial to retirement age

70. The assessment of the multiplier involves the following steps:

(1) Determine the expected period from the date of the trial for which the deceased would have been able to provide the dependency (see paragraph 71).

(2) Determine the expected period for which the dependant would have been able to receive the dependency (see paragraphs 71 and 72).

(3) Take the lesser of the two periods.

(4) Treat the resulting period as a term certain for which the multiplier is to be determined and look up the figure in Table 28 for this period at the appropriate rate of interest.

(5) Apply any adjustment for contingencies other than mortality in accordance with Section B.

(6) If necessary, make an allowance for the risk that the deceased might have died anyway before the date of the trial (see paragraph 73).

71. The expected periods at (1) and (2) of paragraph 70 may be obtained from the 0% column of the appropriate table at the back of this booklet. For (1), Tables 3 to 14 will be relevant, according to the sex of the deceased and the expected age of retirement. The age at which the table should be entered is the age which the deceased would have been at the date of the trial. For (2) Tables 1 and 2 can be used, according to the sex of the dependant and looking up the table at the age of the dependant at the date of the trial.

72. If the period for which the dependency would have continued is a short fixed period, as in the case of a child, the figure at (2) would be the outstanding period at the date of the trial.

73. A deduction may be made for the risk that the deceased might have died anyway before the date of trial. The need for such a deduction becomes more necessary the longer the period from the date of accident to the date of trial and the older the deceased at the date of death. As an illustration of the order of magnitude of the deduction, Table F shows some examples of the factor by which the multiplier, determined as above, should be multiplied for different ages of the deceased and for different periods from the date of accident to the date of the trial.

TABLE F

Factor by which post-trial damages should be multiplied to allow for the likelihood that the deceased would not in any case have survived to the date of trial in order to provide any post-trial dependency.

Age of deceased at date of accident	Period from date of accident to date of trial (years)					
	Male deceased			Female deceased		
	3	6	9	3	6	9
10	1.00	1.00	1.00	1.00	1.00	1.00
20	1.00	1.00	0.99	1.00	1.00	1.00
30	1.00	0.99	0.99	1.00	1.00	0.99
40	0.99	0.99	0.98	1.00	0.99	0.99
50	0.99	0.97	0.95	0.99	0.98	0.97
60	0.97	0.93	0.88	0.98	0.96	0.92
65	0.96	0.90	0.82	0.97	0.93	0.88
70	0.93	0.84	0.71	0.96	0.89	0.80
75	0.88	0.73	0.55	0.92	0.81	0.66
80	0.83	0.59	0.37	0.86	0.68	0.48

N.B. The factor for a period of zero years is clearly 1.00. Factors for other ages and periods not shown in the table may be obtained approximately by interpolation.

74. The resulting multiplier, after application of any discount for the possibility of early death of the deceased before the date of trial, even had the accident not taken place, is to be applied to the appropriate multiplicand, determined in relation to dependency as assessed for the period up to retirement age.

75. If there are several dependants, to whom damages are to be paid in respect of their own particular lifetime (or for a fixed period of dependency), separate multipliers should be determined for each and multiplied by the appropriate multiplicand using the procedure in paragraphs 70 to 74. The total amount of damages is then obtained by adding the separate components. If a single multiplicand is determined, but the damages are to be shared among two or more dependants so long as they are each alive, or during a period of common dependency, then the multiplier will be calculated using the procedure in paragraphs 70 to 74. However, at step (2) of paragraph 70 the expected period will be the longest of the expected periods for which the dependency might last.

(iii) Damages for the period of dependency after retirement age

76. The method described in paragraphs 70 to 75 for pre-retirement age dependency cannot satisfactorily be applied directly to post-retirement age dependency with a sufficient degree of accuracy. We therefore propose a method which

involves determining the multiplier by looking at dependency for the rest of life from the date of trial and then subtracting the multiplier for dependency up to retirement age.

77. The assessment of the multiplier for whole of life dependency involves the following steps:

(1) Determine the expectation of life which the deceased would have had as at the date of trial, or such lesser period for which the deceased would have been able to provide the dependency (see paragraph 78).

(2) Determine the expected period for which the dependant would have been able to receive the dependency (see paragraph 78).

(3) Take the lesser of the two periods.

(4) Treat the resulting period as a term certain for which the multiplier is to be determined and look up the figure in Table 28 for this period at the appropriate rate of interest.

78. The expected periods at (1) and (2) of paragraph 77 may be obtained from the 0% column of the appropriate table at the back of this booklet. For (1) Tables 1 or 2 will be relevant, according to the sex of the deceased. The age at which the table should be entered is the age which the deceased would have attained at the date of the trial. For (2) Tables 1 and 2 can be used, according to the sex of the dependant and looking up the table at the age of the dependant at the date of the trial.

79. Deduct the corresponding multiplier for post-trial pre-retirement dependency, as determined in paragraphs 70 to 75, but without any adjustment for contingencies other than mortality, or that the deceased may have died anyway before the date of trial. The result is the multiplier for post-retirement dependency, which must then be applied to the appropriate multiplicand, assessed in relation to dependency after retirement age. The adjustment for contingencies other than mortality in respect of the damages for the period of dependency after retirement age will often be less than that required for pre-retirement age damages (see paragraph 30).

80. A deduction may finally be made for the risk that the deceased might have died anyway before the date of trial. The need for such a deduction becomes more necessary the longer the period from the date of accident to the date of trial and the older the deceased at the date of death. As an illustration of the order of magnitude of the deduction, Table F shows some examples of the factor by which the multiplier, determined as above, should be multiplied for different ages of the deceased and for different periods from the date of accident to the date of the trial. The factors for this purpose are exactly the same deductions as used in the calculation at paragraphs 70 to 75.

81. The layout of paragraphs 70 to 80 is based on the assumption that the dependency provided by the deceased would have changed at retirement age. This may not be appropriate in some cases, particularly in the important case of the deceased wife and mother whose contribution has been solely in the home or in the case of an adult child caring for an elderly parent or parents. In cases like this, where the deceased might have provided the dependency throughout their lifetime, paragraphs 76 to 80 should be ignored and paragraphs 70 to 75 used, with the difference that the expected period required at step (1) of paragraph 70 should be a whole of life expectancy, taken from Tables 1 and 2. This is also the approach to use when the deceased was already a pensioner

Examples

82. Paragraphs 83 and 84 give calculations of damages awards for Example 7, calculated using first the current approach and then the actuarially recommended approach.

Example 7

83. The dependant is female, aged 38 at the date of the trial, which is taking place 3 years after the date of the fatal accident which killed her husband, at that time aged 37, on whom she was financially dependent. The deceased had A levels, was in employment and in good health with no disability at the time of the fatal accident. The dependant was, at the date of death, and is at the date of trial, in good health. Their relationship was stable. The Court has determined a multiplicand of £30,000 up to the deceased's normal retirement age of 65 with no financial dependency post age 65, nor any services dependency. The damages are to be calculated as follows:

The Current approach

(1) The deceased would have been capable of providing the financial dependency to the dependant for the period of 28 years from the date of his death aged 37 to his 65th birthday.

(2) The appropriate Table is 9. Using the 2.5% column the multiplier = 19.64.

(3) Adjustment factor for contingencies other than mortality (in accordance with Section B) for an employed male aged 37 with A levels and who is not disabled = 0.9 to give a multiplier of 19.64 x 0.9 = 17.68.

(4) The expected period for which the dependant would have been able to receive the dependency was between the ages of 35 and 63.

(5) The appropriate Tables are 8 and 10, and using the 2.5% column the multiplier = 19.91.

(6) The parties were married so section 3 (4) does not apply. The relationship was stable. The dependant was and is in good health. The court is unlikely to make much of an adjustment to the figure in (5) above to reflect contingencies other than mortality.

(7) The lower of the two figures is that in (3) above, namely 17.68.

(8) The period that has elapsed between date of death and date of trial is 3 years. The pre-trial loss is therefore £30,000 x 3 = £90,000.

(9) Interest at half rate from date of death to date of trial: 3 years at 3% a year = 9%.
£90,000 x 9% = £8,100.

(10) The post trial multiplier is 14.68 (17.68 – 3).

(11) The post trial loss is therefore 14.68 x £30,000 = £440,400.

(12) Total financial dependency is therefore £90,000 + £8,100 + £440,400 = £538,500.

The Actuarially Recommended approach

84. Applying this approach to Example 7 set out above:

Pre-trial damages:

(1) Period between fatal accident and trial: 3 years.

(2) Factor for possible early death (Table E for male aged 37 and 3 years) = 1.00.

(3) Pre-trial damages = 3 x 1.00 x £30,000 = £90,000 (plus interest as special damages).

(4) Interest at half rate from date of death to date of trial: 3 years at 3% a year = 9%.
£90,000 x 9% = £8,100.

Post-trial damages:

(1) Expected period for which the deceased would have provided the dependency (Table 9 at 0% for male aged 40, the age as at the date of trial): 24.13.

(2) Expected period for which the dependant would have been able to receive the dependency (Table 2 at 0% for female aged 38): 51.38.

(3) Lesser of two periods at (1) and (2) = 24.13.

(4) Multiplier for term certain of 24.13 years at 2½% rate of return = 18.18.

(5) Adjustment factor for contingencies other than mortality (in accordance with Section B) for an employed male aged 40 with A levels and who was not disabled = 0.88 to give a multiplier of 18.18 x 0.88 = 16.00.

(6) Adjustment factor for the risk that the deceased might have died anyway before the date of trial (Table F for male aged 37 and 3 years): 0.99 to give a multiplier of 16.00 x 0.99 = 15.84.

(7) Post-trial damages = 15.84 x £30,000 = £475,200.

(8) Total financial dependency is therefore £90,000 + £8,100 + £475,200 = £573,300.

85. Examples 8 and 9 in the following paragraphs set out two further examples to show the application of the actuarially recommended approach to more complex examples.

Example 8

86. The dependant is female, aged 50 at the date of the trial, which is taking place 4 years after the date of the fatal accident which killed the man, at that time aged 47, on whom she was financially dependent. The deceased was in employment at the time of the fatal accident, was not disabled and had achieved A levels. The Court has determined a multiplicand, up to the deceased's normal retirement age of 60, of £50,000 and has decided that post-retirement damages should be payable based on a multiplicand of £30,000. The damages are to be calculated as follows:

Pre-trial damages:

(1) Period between fatal accident and trial: 4 years.

(2) Factor for possible early death (Table E for male aged 47 and 4 years): 0.99.

(3) Pre-trial damages = 4 x 0.99 x £50,000 = £198,000 (plus interest as special damages).

Post-trial pre-retirement damages:

(1) Expected period for which the deceased would have provided the dependency (Table 7 at 0% for male aged 51, the age as at the date of trial): 8.81.

(2) Expected period for which the dependant would have been able to receive the dependency (Table 2 at 0% for female aged 50): 38.73.

(3) Lesser of two periods at (1) and (2) = 8.81.

(4) Multiplier for term certain of 8.81 years at 2½% rate of return (interpolating between the values for 8 and 9 in Table 28) = (9 – 8.81) x 7.26 + (8.81 – 8) x 8.07 = 7.92.

(5) Adjustment factor for contingencies other than mortality (in accordance with Section B) for an employed male aged 51 with A levels and who was not disabled = 0.82 to give a multiplier of 7.92 x 0.82 = 6.49.

(6) Adjustment factor for the risk that the deceased might have died anyway before the date of trial (Table F for male aged 47 and 4 years): 0.99 to give a multiplier of 6.49 x 0.99 = 6.43.

(7) Post-trial pre-retirement damages = 6.43 x £50,000 = £321,500.

Post-retirement damages:

(1) Expectation of life of deceased at date of trial (Table 1 at 0% for male aged 51): 34.45.

(2) Expected period for which the dependant would have been able to receive the dependency (Table 2 at 0% for female aged 50): 38.73.

(3) Lesser of two periods at (1) and (2) = 34.45.

(4) Multiplier for term certain of 34.45 years at 2½% rate of return (interpolating between the values for 34 and 35 in Table 28) = (35 – 34.45) x 23.01 + (34.45 – 34) x 23.43 = 23.20.

(5) Deduct multiplier for post-trial pre-retirement damages before application of adjustment factors for contingencies other than mortality and for the risk that the deceased might have died anyway before the date of trial: 23.20 – 7.92 = 15.28.

(6) Adjustment factor for the risk that the deceased might have died anyway before the date of trial (Table F for male aged 47 and 4 years): 0.99 to give a multiplier of 15.28 x 0.99 = 15.13.

(7) Post-retirement damages = 15.13 x £30,000 = £453,900.

Example 9

87. There are two dependants, respectively a child aged 10 and a male aged 41 at the date of the trial, which is taking place 3 years after the date of the fatal accident which killed the woman, at that time aged 35, on whom both were financially dependent. She had a degree and worked in London for a computer company. The Court has determined a multiplicand, up to the deceased's normal retirement age of 62, of £50,000 for the male dependant and £10,000 for the child, up to the age of 21, and has decided that post-retirement damages should be payable based on a multiplicand of £20,000. The damages are to be calculated as follows:

Pre-trial damages:

(1) Period between fatal accident and trial: 3 years.

(2) Factor for possible early death (Table E for female aged 35 and 3 years): 1.00.

(3) Pre-trial damages = 3 x 1.00 x (£50,000 + £10,000) = £180,000 (plus interest as special damages).

Post-trial pre-retirement damages:

(1) Expected period for which the deceased would have provided the dependency should be based on female aged 38 at the date of trial with retirement age of 62. First calculate as though deceased were aged 36 and had retirement age of 60 (Table 8 at 0% for female aged 36): 23.66.

Then calculate as though deceased were aged 41 and had retirement age of 65 (Table 10 at 0% for female aged 41): 23.47.

Interpolate for age 38 with retirement age of 62 = (3 x 23.66 + 2 x 23.47)/5 = 23.58.

(2) Expected period for which the male dependant would have been able to receive the dependency (Table 1 at 0% for male aged 41): 44.71.

Expected period for which child would have been able to receive the dependency = 11.00.

(3) Lesser of two periods at (1) and (2) = 11.00 (in case of child)
= 23.58 (in case of man).

(4) Multiplier for term certain of 11 years at 2½% (Table 28): 9.63.

Multiplier for term certain of 23.58 years at 2½% rate of return (interpolating between the values for 23 and 24 in Table 28)

= (24 – 23.58) x 17.55 + (23.58 – 23) x 18.11= 17.87.

(5) Adjustment factor for contingencies other than mortality (in accordance with Section B) for an employed female aged 38 with a degree and who was not disabled = 0.89 (does not apply to child) to give a multiplier of 17.87 x 0.89 = 15.90.

(6) Adjustment factor for the risk that the deceased might have died anyway before the date of trial (Table F for female aged 35 and 3 years): 1.00, so multipliers are 9.63 and 15.90 respectively.

(7) Pre-retirement damages = 9.63 x £10,000 + 15.90 x £50,000
= £96,300 + £795,000 = £891,300.

Post-retirement damages:

(1) Expectation of life of deceased at date of trial (Table 2 at 0% for female aged 38): 51.38.

(2) Expected period for which the dependant would have been able to receive the dependency (Table 1 at 0% for male aged 41): 44.71 (no post retirement dependency for child).

(3) Lesser of two periods at (1) and (2) = 44.71.

(4) Multiplier for term certain of 44.71 years at 2½% rate of return (interpolating between the values for 42 and 43 in Table 28)

= (45 – 44.71) x 26.83 + (44.71 – 44) x 27.17 = 27.07.

(5) Deduct multiplier for post-trial pre-retirement damages before application of adjustment factors for contingencies other than mortality and for the risk that the deceased might have died anyway before the date of trial: 27.07 – 17.87 = 9.20.

(6) Adjustment factor for the risk that the deceased might have died anyway before the date of trial (Table F for female aged 35 and 3 years) = 1.00, so multiplier is 9.20 x 1.00 = 9.20.

(7) Post-retirement damages = 9.20 x £20,000 = £184,000.

An Alternative approach

88. If the court wishes to select multipliers from the date of death, it is essential to ensure that the period before the trial does not include a discount for early receipt. This could be achieved by selecting multipliers from the 0% columns of the appropriate tables and then applying the discount for early receipt to the period after the trial (using the discount rate set under Section 1 of the Damages Act 1996). The calculation of the multiplier involves the following steps:

(1) Determine the expected period for which the deceased would have provided the dependency at the date of death.

(2) Deduct the period between accidental death and date of trial to give post-trial period.

(3) Determine the expected post-trial period for which the dependant would have been able to receive the dependency.

(4) Take the lesser of two periods at (2) and (3).

(5) Take the multiplier for term certain for the period calculated at (4) at 2½% rate of return (from Table 28).

(6) Apply any adjustment factor to the figure in (5) to reflect contingencies other than mortality (in accordance with Section B) . This will give the multiplier for the post-trial multiplicand.

89. Applying this approach to Example 7 set out above:

(1) Expected period for which the deceased would have provided the dependency (Table 9 at 0% for male aged 37, the age as at the date of death): 27.06.

(2) Deduct period between accidental death and date of trial of 3 years to give post-trial period: 24.06.

(3) Expected post-trial period for which the dependant would have been able to receive the dependency (Table 2 at 0% for female aged 38): 51.38.

(4) Lesser of two periods at (2) and (3) = 24.06.

(5) Multiplier for term certain of 24.06 years at 2½% rate of return (Table 28) = 18.14.

(6) Adjustment factor for contingencies other than mortality (in accordance with Section B) for an employed male aged 37 with A levels and who was not disabled = 0.90 to give a multiplier of 18.14 x 0.90 = 16.33.

(7) Pre-trial damages = 3 x £30,000 = £90,000 (plus interest as special damages of £8,100).

(8) Post-trial damages = 16.33 x £30,000 = £489,900.

(9) Total financial dependency therefore £90,000 + £8,100 + £489,900 = £588,000.

90. As can be seen the three methodologies (the current approach, the actuarially recommended approach and this alternative approach) give three different amounts of damages in relation to Example 7, namely £538,500 for the current approach used by the courts, £573,300 using the actuarially recommended approach and £588,000 using this alternative approach. The size of the disparities between the three methods depends on the length of the period between the date of death and the date of trial; if the example had assumed a period of 6 years the differences would have been greater.

SECTION E: CONCLUDING REMARKS

91. These tables are designed to assist the courts to arrive at suitable multipliers in a range of possible situations. However, they do not cover all possibilities and in more complex situations, such as where there are significant pension rights, advice should be sought from a Fellow of the Institute and Faculty of Actuaries.

GEORGE RUSSELL FIA
Deputy Government Actuary
London
August 2011

Table 1 Multipliers for pecuniary loss for life (males)

Age at date of trial	Multiplier calculated with allowance for projected mortality from the 2008-based population projections and rate of return of											Age at date of trial
	–2.0%	–1.5%	–1.0%	–0.5%	0.0%	0.5%	1.0%	1.5%	2.0%	2.5%	3.0%	
0	264.76	195.32	147.14	113.22	88.96	71.35	58.34	48.60	41.17	35.41	30.89	0
1	259.11	191.95	145.15	112.06	88.31	71.00	58.18	48.54	41.18	35.46	30.96	1
2	252.28	187.68	142.46	110.35	87.22	70.30	57.73	48.24	40.98	35.33	30.87	2
3	245.58	183.46	139.78	108.64	86.12	69.58	57.26	47.94	40.78	35.19	30.78	3
4	239.02	179.29	137.12	106.93	85.01	68.86	56.78	47.62	40.56	35.05	30.68	4
5	232.59	175.19	134.48	105.22	83.89	68.12	56.30	47.29	40.34	34.90	30.58	5
6	226.29	171.15	131.87	103.52	82.78	67.39	55.80	46.96	40.12	34.75	30.47	6
7	220.14	167.18	129.29	101.83	81.66	66.65	55.31	46.63	39.89	34.59	30.36	7
8	214.13	163.28	126.74	100.15	80.55	65.90	54.80	46.28	39.65	34.42	30.24	8
9	208.23	159.43	124.21	98.48	79.43	65.15	54.29	45.93	39.41	34.25	30.13	9
10	202.47	155.64	121.71	96.81	78.31	64.39	53.78	45.58	39.16	34.08	30.00	10
11	196.83	151.92	119.23	95.15	77.19	63.63	53.25	45.22	38.91	33.90	29.87	11
12	191.33	148.26	116.79	93.50	76.07	62.86	52.72	44.85	38.65	33.72	29.74	12
13	185.95	144.67	114.37	91.87	74.96	62.09	52.19	44.47	38.39	33.53	29.61	13
14	180.69	141.14	111.98	90.24	73.84	61.32	51.65	44.10	38.12	33.34	29.47	14
15	175.56	137.67	109.62	88.63	72.73	60.55	51.11	43.71	37.84	33.14	29.32	15
16	170.55	134.27	107.30	87.02	71.61	59.77	50.56	43.32	37.57	32.94	29.17	16
17	165.66	130.93	105.00	85.44	70.51	58.99	50.01	42.93	37.28	32.73	29.02	17
18	160.89	127.66	102.74	83.86	69.41	58.22	49.46	42.53	37.00	32.52	28.87	18
19	156.25	124.45	100.52	82.31	68.31	57.44	48.91	42.14	36.71	32.31	28.71	19
20	151.72	121.31	98.32	80.76	67.22	56.66	48.35	41.73	36.41	32.10	28.55	20
21	147.28	118.22	96.15	79.23	66.13	55.88	47.78	41.32	36.11	31.87	28.39	21
22	142.94	115.17	94.00	77.70	65.04	55.09	47.21	40.90	35.81	31.64	28.22	22
23	138.69	112.17	91.87	76.18	63.94	54.30	46.63	40.48	35.49	31.41	28.04	23
24	134.54	109.22	89.77	74.67	62.85	53.51	46.05	40.05	35.17	31.17	27.86	24
25	130.49	106.33	87.69	73.17	61.76	52.71	45.46	39.61	34.85	30.92	27.67	25
26	126.54	103.50	85.65	71.69	60.68	51.91	44.87	39.17	34.51	30.67	27.48	26
27	122.69	100.72	83.63	70.22	59.59	51.11	44.28	38.73	34.18	30.42	27.28	27
28	118.90	97.98	81.63	68.74	58.51	50.30	43.67	38.27	33.83	30.15	27.08	28
29	115.20	95.28	79.64	67.28	57.42	49.49	43.06	37.81	33.48	29.88	26.87	29
30	111.59	92.63	77.69	65.83	56.34	48.68	42.45	37.34	33.12	29.60	26.65	30
31	108.09	90.04	75.78	64.40	55.27	47.87	41.83	36.87	32.76	29.32	26.44	31
32	104.68	87.52	73.89	62.99	54.20	47.06	41.22	36.40	32.39	29.04	26.21	32
33	101.36	85.04	72.04	61.60	53.15	46.26	40.60	35.92	32.02	28.75	25.99	33
34	98.10	82.61	70.21	60.21	52.09	45.45	39.98	35.44	31.65	28.46	25.75	34
35	94.92	80.21	68.39	58.83	51.03	44.63	39.35	34.95	31.26	28.15	25.51	35
36	91.82	77.86	66.60	57.46	49.98	43.82	38.71	34.45	30.87	27.84	25.27	36
37	88.78	75.55	64.83	56.10	48.93	43.00	38.07	33.95	30.47	27.53	25.01	37
38	85.81	73.27	63.08	54.74	47.87	42.18	37.42	33.44	30.06	27.20	24.75	38
39	82.89	71.03	61.35	53.39	46.82	41.35	36.77	32.91	29.65	26.86	24.48	39
40	80.05	68.83	59.63	52.05	45.76	40.51	36.11	32.39	29.22	26.52	24.20	40
41	77.27	66.67	57.94	50.72	44.71	39.68	35.44	31.85	28.79	26.17	23.91	41
42	74.56	64.55	56.28	49.41	43.67	38.84	34.77	31.31	28.35	25.81	23.62	42
43	71.92	62.47	54.63	48.10	42.62	38.01	34.10	30.76	27.91	25.45	23.32	43
44	69.34	60.43	53.01	46.81	41.59	37.17	33.42	30.21	27.45	25.08	23.01	44
45	66.82	58.43	51.41	45.52	40.55	36.33	32.73	29.65	26.99	24.70	22.69	45
46	64.36	56.46	49.83	44.25	39.52	35.49	32.05	29.08	26.53	24.31	22.37	46
47	61.96	54.53	48.28	42.99	38.49	34.65	31.35	28.51	26.05	23.91	22.04	47
48	59.63	52.64	46.74	41.74	37.47	33.81	30.66	27.94	25.57	23.51	21.70	48
49	57.35	50.79	45.24	40.50	36.45	32.97	29.97	27.36	25.09	23.10	21.36	49
50	55.14	48.99	43.76	39.29	35.45	32.14	29.27	26.78	24.60	22.69	21.01	50
51	52.99	47.23	42.31	38.09	34.45	31.31	28.58	26.19	24.11	22.27	20.65	51
52	50.90	45.51	40.89	36.91	33.47	30.48	27.88	25.61	23.61	21.85	20.29	52
53	48.87	43.83	39.49	35.74	32.49	29.67	27.19	25.02	23.11	21.42	19.92	53
54	46.90	42.19	38.12	34.60	31.53	28.85	26.50	24.43	22.61	20.99	19.55	54
55	44.99	40.60	36.79	33.47	30.58	28.04	25.81	23.85	22.11	20.56	19.18	55
56	43.15	39.04	35.48	32.37	29.64	27.25	25.13	23.26	21.60	20.12	18.80	56
57	41.35	37.53	34.19	31.28	28.71	26.45	24.45	22.67	21.09	19.68	18.42	57
58	39.59	36.04	32.93	30.19	27.78	25.65	23.76	22.08	20.58	19.23	18.02	58
59	37.87	34.57	31.67	29.11	26.85	24.85	23.07	21.47	20.05	18.77	17.62	59
60	36.17	33.12	30.42	28.04	25.92	24.04	22.36	20.86	19.51	18.30	17.20	60
61	34.52	31.69	29.19	26.97	25.00	23.23	21.65	20.24	18.96	17.81	16.77	61
62	32.91	30.30	27.98	25.92	24.08	22.43	20.95	19.62	18.41	17.33	16.34	62
63	31.36	28.95	26.80	24.89	23.17	21.63	20.25	19.00	17.86	16.84	15.90	63
64	29.85	27.63	25.65	23.88	22.28	20.85	19.55	18.38	17.31	16.35	15.47	64
65	28.40	26.37	24.54	22.90	21.42	20.08	18.87	17.77	16.77	15.86	15.03	65
66	27.02	25.14	23.46	21.94	20.57	19.33	18.20	17.17	16.24	15.38	14.60	66
67	25.68	23.96	22.41	21.01	19.74	18.59	17.54	16.58	15.70	14.90	14.16	67
68	24.38	22.81	21.39	20.10	18.93	17.86	16.88	15.99	15.17	14.42	13.73	68
69	23.13	21.69	20.39	19.21	18.12	17.14	16.23	15.40	14.64	13.93	13.29	69

continued

Table 1 Multipliers for pecuniary loss for life (males) ***continued***

Age at date of trial	Multiplier calculated with allowance for projected mortality from the 2008-based population projections and rate of return of											Age at date of trial
	–2.0%	–1.5%	–1.0%	–0.5%	0.0%	0.5%	1.0%	1.5%	2.0%	2.5%	3.0%	
70	21.91	20.60	19.41	18.32	17.32	16.41	15.58	14.81	14.10	13.44	12.84	70
71	20.70	19.52	18.43	17.44	16.53	15.69	14.92	14.21	13.55	12.94	12.38	71
72	19.52	18.44	17.46	16.56	15.72	14.96	14.25	13.60	12.99	12.43	11.91	72
73	18.34	17.38	16.49	15.67	14.92	14.22	13.57	12.97	12.42	11.90	11.42	73
74	17.18	16.32	15.52	14.79	14.10	13.47	12.89	12.34	11.83	11.36	10.92	74
75	16.04	15.27	14.56	13.90	13.29	12.72	12.19	11.70	11.24	10.81	10.40	75
76	14.93	14.25	13.62	13.03	12.48	11.97	11.50	11.05	10.64	10.25	9.88	76
77	13.86	13.26	12.70	12.18	11.70	11.24	10.82	10.42	10.05	9.69	9.36	77
78	12.83	12.31	11.82	11.36	10.93	10.53	10.15	9.79	9.46	9.15	8.85	78
79	11.86	11.40	10.97	10.57	10.19	9.84	9.50	9.19	8.89	8.61	8.34	79
80	10.94	10.55	10.17	9.82	9.49	9.18	8.88	8.60	8.34	8.09	7.85	80
81	10.10	9.75	9.43	9.12	8.83	8.56	8.30	8.05	7.82	7.60	7.38	81
82	9.33	9.03	8.74	8.47	8.22	7.98	7.75	7.53	7.33	7.13	6.94	82
83	8.62	8.36	8.11	7.88	7.65	7.44	7.24	7.05	6.87	6.69	6.53	83
84	7.97	7.74	7.53	7.32	7.13	6.94	6.76	6.59	6.43	6.28	6.13	84
85	7.36	7.16	6.98	6.80	6.63	6.47	6.31	6.16	6.02	5.88	5.75	85
86	6.79	6.62	6.46	6.31	6.16	6.02	5.88	5.75	5.62	5.50	5.39	86
87	6.25	6.11	5.97	5.83	5.71	5.58	5.46	5.35	5.24	5.14	5.04	87
88	5.74	5.62	5.50	5.38	5.27	5.16	5.06	4.96	4.87	4.78	4.69	88
89	5.26	5.15	5.05	4.95	4.86	4.76	4.68	4.59	4.51	4.43	4.35	89
90	4.81	4.72	4.64	4.55	4.47	4.39	4.31	4.24	4.17	4.10	4.03	90
91	4.40	4.32	4.25	4.17	4.10	4.04	3.97	3.91	3.85	3.79	3.73	91
92	4.01	3.94	3.88	3.82	3.76	3.70	3.65	3.59	3.54	3.49	3.44	92
93	3.65	3.59	3.54	3.49	3.44	3.39	3.34	3.30	3.25	3.21	3.17	93
94	3.33	3.29	3.24	3.20	3.16	3.11	3.07	3.03	2.99	2.96	2.92	94
95	3.06	3.02	2.98	2.94	2.91	2.87	2.84	2.80	2.77	2.74	2.71	95
96	2.83	2.79	2.76	2.72	2.69	2.66	2.63	2.60	2.57	2.54	2.52	96
97	2.62	2.59	2.56	2.53	2.50	2.48	2.45	2.42	2.40	2.37	2.35	97
98	2.44	2.41	2.38	2.36	2.34	2.31	2.29	2.27	2.24	2.22	2.20	98
99	2.27	2.25	2.22	2.20	2.18	2.16	2.14	2.12	2.10	2.08	2.06	99
100	2.11	2.09	2.07	2.06	2.04	2.02	2.00	1.98	1.97	1.95	1.93	100

Table 2 Multipliers for pecuniary loss for life (females)

Age at date of trial	Multiplier calculated with allowance for projected mortality from the 2008-based population projections and rate of return of											Age at date of trial
	−2.0%	−1.5%	−1.0%	−0.5%	0.0%	0.5%	1.0%	1.5%	2.0%	2.5%	3.0%	
0	285.20	208.39	155.57	118.70	92.57	73.74	59.95	49.69	41.92	35.94	31.26	0
1	279.01	204.72	153.41	117.45	91.86	73.36	59.76	49.62	41.91	35.97	31.32	1
2	271.81	200.28	150.65	115.73	90.77	72.67	59.33	49.34	41.73	35.86	31.24	2
3	264.75	195.89	147.91	114.00	89.68	71.97	58.88	49.05	41.55	35.73	31.16	3
4	257.83	191.56	145.19	112.28	88.58	71.27	58.43	48.75	41.35	35.60	31.08	4
5	251.06	187.30	142.49	110.56	87.49	70.56	57.97	48.45	41.15	35.47	30.99	5
6	244.43	183.11	139.83	108.85	86.38	69.85	57.50	48.14	40.95	35.34	30.89	6
7	237.94	178.98	137.18	107.15	85.28	69.13	57.03	47.83	40.74	35.19	30.80	7
8	231.59	174.92	134.57	105.46	84.18	68.40	56.55	47.51	40.52	35.05	30.70	8
9	225.38	170.93	131.98	103.77	83.07	67.67	56.06	47.18	40.30	34.90	30.60	9
10	219.31	167.00	129.43	102.10	81.97	66.94	55.57	46.85	40.08	34.75	30.49	10
11	213.37	163.14	126.90	100.43	80.86	66.20	55.07	46.52	39.85	34.59	30.38	11
12	207.57	159.34	124.40	98.78	79.76	65.46	54.57	46.18	39.62	34.42	30.27	12
13	201.89	155.60	121.92	97.13	78.65	64.71	54.07	45.83	39.38	34.26	30.15	13
14	196.33	151.93	119.48	95.49	77.55	63.96	53.55	45.47	39.13	34.09	30.03	14
15	190.91	148.32	117.06	93.86	76.44	63.21	53.03	45.12	38.88	33.91	29.90	15
16	185.61	144.77	114.67	92.25	75.34	62.45	52.51	44.75	38.62	33.73	29.77	16
17	180.42	141.28	112.31	90.64	74.24	61.70	51.99	44.38	38.37	33.55	29.64	17
18	175.36	137.86	109.98	89.05	73.14	60.94	51.46	44.01	38.10	33.36	29.51	18
19	170.42	134.50	107.68	87.46	72.05	60.17	50.92	43.63	37.83	33.16	29.37	19
20	165.60	131.20	105.42	85.89	70.96	59.41	50.38	43.25	37.56	32.97	29.22	20
21	160.88	127.95	103.17	84.33	69.86	58.64	49.84	42.86	37.28	32.76	29.08	21
22	156.26	124.76	100.95	82.78	68.77	57.86	49.28	42.47	36.99	32.56	28.92	22
23	151.72	121.60	98.74	81.22	67.67	57.08	48.72	42.06	36.70	32.34	28.76	23
24	147.29	118.50	96.56	79.68	66.57	56.29	48.16	41.65	36.40	32.12	28.60	24
25	142.97	115.46	94.41	78.15	65.48	55.50	47.58	41.23	36.09	31.89	28.43	25
26	138.74	112.47	92.28	76.63	64.38	54.71	47.01	40.81	35.78	31.66	28.26	26
27	134.61	109.53	90.18	75.12	63.29	53.92	46.43	40.38	35.46	31.42	28.08	27
28	130.57	106.65	88.11	73.62	62.20	53.12	45.84	39.95	35.14	31.18	27.90	28
29	126.63	103.81	86.05	72.13	61.11	52.32	45.25	39.51	34.81	30.93	27.71	29
30	122.78	101.02	84.03	70.65	60.02	51.52	44.65	39.06	34.47	30.68	27.51	30
31	119.02	98.29	82.03	69.18	58.94	50.71	44.05	38.61	34.13	30.41	27.31	31
32	115.34	95.60	80.06	67.72	57.86	49.90	43.44	38.15	33.78	30.15	27.11	32
33	111.75	92.97	78.11	66.27	56.77	49.09	42.83	37.68	33.42	29.87	26.89	33
34	108.24	90.37	76.18	64.83	55.69	48.27	42.21	37.21	33.06	29.59	26.67	34
35	104.80	87.81	74.27	63.40	54.61	47.45	41.58	36.73	32.69	29.31	26.45	35
36	101.45	85.31	72.39	61.98	53.53	46.63	40.95	36.24	32.31	29.01	26.22	36
37	98.17	82.84	70.53	60.57	52.46	45.81	40.31	35.75	31.93	28.71	25.98	37
38	94.97	80.42	68.69	59.17	51.38	44.98	39.67	35.25	31.54	28.40	25.74	38
39	91.83	78.04	66.88	57.78	50.31	44.15	39.03	34.74	31.14	28.09	25.48	39
40	88.77	75.71	65.08	56.39	49.24	43.31	38.37	34.23	30.73	27.76	25.23	40
41	85.78	73.41	63.31	55.02	48.17	42.48	37.71	33.71	30.32	27.43	24.96	41
42	82.86	71.16	61.56	53.66	47.10	41.64	37.05	33.18	29.90	27.09	24.69	42
43	80.01	68.94	59.84	52.31	46.04	40.80	36.38	32.65	29.47	26.75	24.41	43
44	77.23	66.77	58.14	50.97	44.98	39.95	35.71	32.11	29.03	26.39	24.12	44
45	74.52	64.65	56.46	49.64	43.93	39.11	35.03	31.56	28.59	26.03	23.82	45
46	71.87	62.56	54.81	48.32	42.87	38.27	34.35	31.01	28.14	25.67	23.52	46
47	69.28	60.51	53.17	47.02	41.83	37.42	33.67	30.45	27.69	25.29	23.21	47
48	66.77	58.50	51.57	45.73	40.79	36.58	32.98	29.89	27.23	24.91	22.90	48
49	64.32	56.54	50.00	44.46	39.76	35.74	32.30	29.33	26.76	24.53	22.58	49
50	61.93	54.62	48.44	43.20	38.73	34.90	31.61	28.76	26.29	24.14	22.25	50
51	59.60	52.73	46.91	41.95	37.71	34.06	30.91	28.19	25.81	23.74	21.92	51
52	57.33	50.88	45.40	40.71	36.69	33.22	30.22	27.61	25.33	23.33	21.57	52
53	55.11	49.07	43.92	39.49	35.68	32.38	29.52	27.02	24.84	22.92	21.22	53
54	52.96	47.30	42.46	38.28	34.68	31.55	28.82	26.44	24.34	22.50	20.87	54
55	50.86	45.57	41.02	37.09	33.68	30.71	28.12	25.84	23.84	22.07	20.51	55
56	48.83	43.88	39.61	35.91	32.69	29.88	27.42	25.25	23.34	21.64	20.14	56
57	46.84	42.22	38.23	34.75	31.71	29.05	26.72	24.65	22.83	21.21	19.76	57
58	44.89	40.60	36.86	33.59	30.74	28.22	26.01	24.05	22.31	20.76	19.37	58
59	42.99	38.99	35.50	32.44	29.76	27.39	25.29	23.43	21.78	20.30	18.98	59
60	41.12	37.41	34.16	31.30	28.78	26.55	24.57	22.81	21.24	19.83	18.57	60
61	39.30	35.86	32.83	30.16	27.80	25.70	23.84	22.18	20.69	19.35	18.15	61
62	37.52	34.33	31.52	29.03	26.83	24.86	23.11	21.54	20.13	18.86	17.72	62
63	35.79	32.84	30.24	27.92	25.86	24.02	22.38	20.90	19.57	18.37	17.28	63
64	34.11	31.39	28.98	26.83	24.91	23.19	21.65	20.26	19.01	17.87	16.84	64
65	32.50	29.99	27.76	25.77	23.98	22.38	20.93	19.63	18.45	17.38	16.40	65
66	30.94	28.64	26.58	24.73	23.07	21.58	20.23	19.00	17.89	16.88	15.96	66
67	29.44	27.32	25.43	23.72	22.18	20.78	19.52	18.38	17.34	16.39	15.52	67
68	27.99	26.05	24.30	22.72	21.29	20.00	18.83	17.76	16.78	15.89	15.07	68
69	26.57	24.80	23.19	21.74	20.42	19.22	18.13	17.13	16.22	15.39	14.62	69

continued

Table 2 Multipliers for pecuniary loss for life (females) ***continued***

Age at date of trial	Multiplier calculated with allowance for projected mortality from the 2008-based population projections and rate of return of											Age at date of trial
	–2.0%	–1.5%	–1.0%	–0.5%	0.0%	0.5%	1.0%	1.5%	2.0%	2.5%	3.0%	
70	25.19	23.57	22.10	20.76	19.55	18.44	17.43	16.50	15.65	14.87	14.15	70
71	23.83	22.35	21.01	19.79	18.67	17.65	16.72	15.86	15.07	14.35	13.68	71
72	22.47	21.14	19.92	18.81	17.79	16.85	16.00	15.20	14.48	13.80	13.18	72
73	21.13	19.93	18.83	17.82	16.89	16.04	15.25	14.53	13.86	13.24	12.66	73
74	19.80	18.72	17.73	16.82	15.99	15.21	14.50	13.84	13.23	12.66	12.13	74
75	18.48	17.53	16.64	15.83	15.08	14.38	13.74	13.14	12.58	12.06	11.58	75
76	17.20	16.35	15.57	14.84	14.17	13.55	12.97	12.43	11.92	11.45	11.01	76
77	15.95	15.21	14.51	13.87	13.28	12.72	12.20	11.72	11.27	10.84	10.45	77
78	14.75	14.10	13.50	12.93	12.40	11.91	11.45	11.02	10.62	10.24	9.88	78
79	13.62	13.05	12.52	12.03	11.56	11.13	10.72	10.34	9.98	9.64	9.32	79
80	12.56	12.07	11.61	11.17	10.77	10.38	10.02	9.69	9.37	9.07	8.78	80
81	11.58	11.15	10.75	10.37	10.02	9.68	9.36	9.06	8.78	8.51	8.26	81
82	10.67	10.30	9.95	9.62	9.31	9.02	8.74	8.48	8.23	7.99	7.76	82
83	9.83	9.51	9.21	8.92	8.65	8.39	8.15	7.92	7.70	7.49	7.29	83
84	9.06	8.78	8.52	8.27	8.03	7.81	7.59	7.39	7.19	7.01	6.83	84
85	8.34	8.10	7.87	7.65	7.45	7.25	7.06	6.88	6.71	6.55	6.40	85
86	7.66	7.45	7.25	7.07	6.89	6.72	6.56	6.40	6.25	6.11	5.97	86
87	7.01	6.84	6.67	6.51	6.36	6.21	6.07	5.93	5.80	5.68	5.56	87
88	6.41	6.26	6.11	5.98	5.85	5.72	5.60	5.48	5.37	5.26	5.16	88
89	5.84	5.71	5.59	5.47	5.36	5.25	5.15	5.05	4.95	4.86	4.77	89
90	5.31	5.20	5.10	5.00	4.90	4.81	4.72	4.64	4.55	4.47	4.40	90
91	4.82	4.73	4.64	4.55	4.47	4.40	4.32	4.25	4.18	4.11	4.04	91
92	4.37	4.29	4.22	4.15	4.08	4.01	3.95	3.89	3.83	3.77	3.71	92
93	3.97	3.90	3.84	3.78	3.72	3.67	3.61	3.56	3.51	3.46	3.41	93
94	3.62	3.56	3.51	3.46	3.41	3.36	3.31	3.27	3.22	3.18	3.14	94
95	3.32	3.27	3.23	3.18	3.14	3.10	3.06	3.02	2.98	2.94	2.91	95
96	3.06	3.02	2.98	2.94	2.91	2.87	2.84	2.80	2.77	2.74	2.71	96
97	2.84	2.80	2.77	2.74	2.70	2.67	2.64	2.61	2.58	2.56	2.53	97
98	2.64	2.61	2.58	2.55	2.52	2.49	2.47	2.44	2.42	2.39	2.37	98
99	2.45	2.42	2.40	2.37	2.35	2.32	2.30	2.28	2.26	2.23	2.21	99
100	2.27	2.25	2.22	2.20	2.18	2.16	2.14	2.12	2.10	2.08	2.06	100

Table 3 Multipliers for loss of earnings to pension age 50 (males)

Age at date of trial	Multiplier calculated with allowance for projected mortality from the 2008-based population projections and rate of return of											Age at date of trial
	−2.0%	−1.5%	−1.0%	−0.5%	0.0%	0.5%	1.0%	1.5%	2.0%	2.5%	3.0%	
16	48.26	43.90	40.05	36.65	33.63	30.94	28.55	26.42	24.51	22.80	21.26	16
17	46.31	42.26	38.66	35.47	32.63	30.10	27.84	25.81	24.00	22.36	20.89	17
18	44.40	40.64	37.29	34.30	31.64	29.25	27.12	25.20	23.47	21.91	20.51	18
19	42.54	39.04	35.93	33.14	30.65	28.41	26.39	24.57	22.94	21.45	20.11	19
20	40.71	37.48	34.58	31.99	29.66	27.55	25.66	23.94	22.39	20.99	19.71	20
21	38.91	35.93	33.25	30.84	28.66	26.70	24.92	23.30	21.84	20.50	19.29	21
22	37.16	34.41	31.94	29.70	27.67	25.84	24.17	22.65	21.27	20.01	18.86	22
23	35.44	32.92	30.63	28.56	26.68	24.97	23.41	21.99	20.69	19.51	18.42	23
24	33.75	31.44	29.34	27.43	25.69	24.10	22.65	21.32	20.11	18.99	17.96	24
25	32.10	29.99	28.06	26.31	24.70	23.23	21.88	20.65	19.51	18.46	17.49	25
26	30.48	28.56	26.80	25.19	23.71	22.36	21.11	19.96	18.90	17.92	17.01	26
27	28.89	27.15	25.55	24.08	22.72	21.47	20.32	19.26	18.27	17.36	16.52	27
28	27.34	25.76	24.31	22.97	21.73	20.59	19.53	18.55	17.64	16.79	16.00	28
29	25.81	24.40	23.08	21.87	20.74	19.70	18.73	17.83	16.99	16.21	15.48	29
30	24.32	23.05	21.87	20.78	19.76	18.81	17.92	17.10	16.33	15.61	14.94	30
31	22.86	21.73	20.67	19.69	18.77	17.91	17.11	16.36	15.66	15.00	14.38	31
32	21.43	20.43	19.49	18.61	17.78	17.01	16.29	15.61	14.97	14.37	13.81	32
33	20.03	19.15	18.31	17.53	16.80	16.11	15.46	14.85	14.28	13.73	13.22	33
34	18.66	17.88	17.15	16.47	15.82	15.20	14.63	14.08	13.57	13.08	12.62	34
35	17.31	16.64	16.00	15.40	14.83	14.29	13.78	13.30	12.84	12.41	11.99	35
36	16.00	15.42	14.87	14.34	13.85	13.38	12.93	12.51	12.10	11.72	11.35	36
37	14.70	14.21	13.74	13.29	12.86	12.46	12.07	11.70	11.35	11.01	10.69	37
38	13.44	13.02	12.62	12.24	11.88	11.53	11.20	10.88	10.58	10.29	10.01	38
39	12.19	11.85	11.52	11.20	10.89	10.60	10.32	10.05	9.79	9.54	9.31	39
40	10.98	10.69	10.42	10.16	9.91	9.67	9.43	9.21	8.99	8.78	8.58	40
41	9.78	9.55	9.34	9.13	8.92	8.72	8.53	8.35	8.17	8.00	7.84	41
42	8.61	8.43	8.26	8.10	7.93	7.78	7.63	7.48	7.34	7.20	7.07	42
43	7.46	7.33	7.20	7.07	6.95	6.83	6.71	6.60	6.49	6.38	6.28	43
44	6.33	6.24	6.14	6.05	5.96	5.87	5.78	5.70	5.62	5.54	5.46	44
45	5.23	5.16	5.10	5.03	4.97	4.91	4.85	4.79	4.73	4.68	4.62	45
46	4.14	4.10	4.06	4.02	3.98	3.94	3.90	3.86	3.83	3.79	3.75	46
47	3.08	3.06	3.03	3.01	2.99	2.97	2.94	2.92	2.90	2.88	2.86	47
48	2.03	2.02	2.01	2.00	1.99	1.98	1.97	1.96	1.96	1.95	1.94	48
49	1.01	1.01	1.00	1.00	1.00	1.00	0.99	0.99	0.99	0.99	0.98	49

Table 4 Multipliers for loss of earnings to pension age 50 (females)

Age at date of trial	Multiplier calculated with allowance for projected mortality from the 2008-based population projections and rate of return of											Age at date of trial
	–2.0%	–1.5%	–1.0%	–0.5%	0.0%	0.5%	1.0%	1.5%	2.0%	2.5%	3.0%	
16	48.58	44.19	40.30	36.87	33.82	31.12	28.71	26.56	24.63	22.91	21.36	16
17	46.62	42.53	38.91	35.69	32.82	30.27	27.99	25.95	24.12	22.47	20.99	17
18	44.71	40.91	37.53	34.52	31.83	29.42	27.27	25.33	23.59	22.02	20.60	18
19	42.83	39.30	36.16	33.35	30.83	28.57	26.54	24.71	23.06	21.56	20.21	19
20	40.98	37.73	34.81	32.19	29.83	27.72	25.80	24.08	22.51	21.09	19.80	20
21	39.18	36.17	33.47	31.03	28.84	26.85	25.06	23.43	21.96	20.61	19.39	21
22	37.41	34.64	32.14	29.89	27.84	25.99	24.31	22.78	21.39	20.12	18.96	22
23	35.68	33.13	30.83	28.74	26.85	25.12	23.55	22.12	20.81	19.61	18.51	23
24	33.98	31.65	29.53	27.60	25.85	24.25	22.78	21.44	20.22	19.09	18.06	24
25	32.31	30.18	28.24	26.47	24.85	23.37	22.01	20.76	19.61	18.56	17.59	25
26	30.68	28.74	26.97	25.35	23.86	22.49	21.23	20.07	19.00	18.01	17.10	26
27	29.08	27.33	25.71	24.23	22.86	21.60	20.44	19.37	18.37	17.45	16.60	27
28	27.52	25.93	24.46	23.11	21.87	20.71	19.64	18.65	17.74	16.88	16.09	28
29	25.98	24.55	23.23	22.01	20.87	19.82	18.84	17.93	17.08	16.30	15.56	29
30	24.48	23.20	22.01	20.90	19.88	18.92	18.03	17.20	16.42	15.70	15.02	30
31	23.01	21.86	20.80	19.81	18.88	18.02	17.21	16.45	15.74	15.08	14.46	31
32	21.56	20.55	19.60	18.72	17.89	17.11	16.38	15.70	15.05	14.45	13.88	32
33	20.15	19.26	18.42	17.63	16.89	16.20	15.55	14.93	14.35	13.80	13.29	33
34	18.76	17.98	17.25	16.55	15.90	15.28	14.70	14.15	13.63	13.14	12.68	34
35	17.41	16.73	16.09	15.48	14.91	14.37	13.85	13.36	12.90	12.46	12.05	35
36	16.08	15.49	14.94	14.41	13.92	13.44	12.99	12.56	12.16	11.77	11.40	36
37	14.77	14.28	13.80	13.35	12.92	12.51	12.12	11.75	11.40	11.06	10.73	37
38	13.50	13.08	12.68	12.30	11.93	11.58	11.25	10.93	10.62	10.33	10.05	38
39	12.25	11.90	11.56	11.24	10.94	10.64	10.36	10.09	9.83	9.58	9.34	39
40	11.02	10.73	10.46	10.20	9.95	9.70	9.47	9.24	9.02	8.82	8.61	40
41	9.82	9.59	9.37	9.16	8.95	8.76	8.56	8.38	8.20	8.03	7.86	41
42	8.64	8.46	8.29	8.12	7.96	7.80	7.65	7.51	7.36	7.22	7.09	42
43	7.48	7.35	7.22	7.09	6.97	6.85	6.73	6.62	6.51	6.40	6.29	43
44	6.35	6.25	6.16	6.06	5.97	5.89	5.80	5.72	5.63	5.55	5.48	44
45	5.24	5.17	5.11	5.04	4.98	4.92	4.86	4.80	4.74	4.69	4.63	45
46	4.15	4.11	4.07	4.03	3.99	3.95	3.91	3.87	3.83	3.80	3.76	46
47	3.08	3.06	3.04	3.01	2.99	2.97	2.95	2.93	2.90	2.88	2.86	47
48	2.04	2.03	2.02	2.01	2.00	1.99	1.98	1.97	1.96	1.95	1.94	48
49	1.01	1.01	1.00	1.00	1.00	1.00	0.99	0.99	0.99	0.99	0.98	49

Table 5 Multipliers for loss of earnings to pension age 55 (males)

Age at date of trial	Multiplier calculated with allowance for projected mortality from the 2008-based population projections and rate of return of											Age at date of trial
	-2.0%	-1.5%	-1.0%	-0.5%	0.0%	0.5%	1.0%	1.5%	2.0%	2.5%	3.0%	
16	58.33	52.26	47.00	42.43	38.44	34.96	31.90	29.22	26.85	24.76	22.90	16
17	56.17	50.49	45.54	41.22	37.44	34.13	31.22	28.65	26.38	24.37	22.58	17
18	54.07	48.74	44.09	40.02	36.45	33.30	30.53	28.08	25.90	23.97	22.24	18
19	52.00	47.03	42.67	38.83	35.46	32.48	29.84	27.50	25.42	23.56	21.90	19
20	49.99	45.34	41.26	37.65	34.47	31.65	29.14	26.91	24.92	23.14	21.55	20
21	48.01	43.68	39.86	36.48	33.48	30.81	28.44	26.31	24.42	22.72	21.19	21
22	46.07	42.04	38.47	35.31	32.49	29.97	27.72	25.71	23.90	22.28	20.82	22
23	44.17	40.43	37.11	34.14	31.49	29.13	27.00	25.10	23.38	21.83	20.43	23
24	42.31	38.84	35.75	32.98	30.50	28.28	26.28	24.47	22.85	21.37	20.04	24
25	40.49	37.28	34.41	31.83	29.52	27.43	25.54	23.84	22.30	20.90	19.63	25
26	38.70	35.74	33.08	30.69	28.53	26.57	24.81	23.20	21.75	20.42	19.21	26
27	36.95	34.23	31.77	29.55	27.54	25.71	24.06	22.55	21.18	19.93	18.78	27
28	35.24	32.74	30.47	28.42	26.55	24.85	23.30	21.89	20.60	19.42	18.34	28
29	33.56	31.27	29.18	27.29	25.56	23.98	22.54	21.22	20.01	18.91	17.89	29
30	31.91	29.82	27.91	26.17	24.57	23.11	21.78	20.55	19.42	18.38	17.42	30
31	30.30	28.40	26.66	25.06	23.59	22.24	21.00	19.86	18.81	17.83	16.94	31
32	28.73	27.00	25.41	23.95	22.61	21.37	20.22	19.17	18.19	17.28	16.44	32
33	27.19	25.63	24.19	22.86	21.63	20.49	19.44	18.46	17.56	16.72	15.94	33
34	25.68	24.27	22.97	21.76	20.65	19.61	18.65	17.75	16.92	16.14	15.41	34
35	24.20	22.94	21.77	20.68	19.67	18.72	17.85	17.03	16.26	15.55	14.88	35
36	22.75	21.63	20.58	19.60	18.69	17.83	17.04	16.29	15.59	14.94	14.32	36
37	21.33	20.33	19.40	18.52	17.71	16.94	16.22	15.55	14.91	14.32	13.76	37
38	19.94	19.06	18.23	17.46	16.73	16.04	15.40	14.79	14.22	13.68	13.17	38
39	18.57	17.80	17.07	16.39	15.75	15.14	14.56	14.02	13.51	13.02	12.56	39
40	17.23	16.56	15.93	15.33	14.76	14.23	13.72	13.24	12.79	12.35	11.94	40
41	15.92	15.34	14.79	14.28	13.78	13.32	12.87	12.45	12.05	11.67	11.30	41
42	14.63	14.14	13.67	13.23	12.80	12.40	12.01	11.65	11.30	10.96	10.64	42
43	13.37	12.96	12.56	12.18	11.82	11.48	11.15	10.83	10.53	10.24	9.96	43
44	12.13	11.79	11.46	11.14	10.84	10.55	10.27	10.01	9.75	9.50	9.26	44
45	10.92	10.64	10.37	10.11	9.86	9.62	9.39	9.17	8.95	8.74	8.54	45
46	9.73	9.51	9.29	9.08	8.88	8.68	8.50	8.31	8.14	7.97	7.80	46
47	8.57	8.39	8.22	8.06	7.90	7.74	7.59	7.45	7.31	7.17	7.04	47
48	7.43	7.29	7.17	7.04	6.92	6.80	6.68	6.57	6.46	6.35	6.25	48
49	6.31	6.21	6.12	6.02	5.93	5.85	5.76	5.68	5.60	5.52	5.44	49
50	5.21	5.14	5.08	5.01	4.95	4.89	4.83	4.77	4.72	4.66	4.60	50
51	4.13	4.09	4.05	4.01	3.97	3.93	3.89	3.85	3.81	3.78	3.74	51
52	3.07	3.05	3.03	3.00	2.98	2.96	2.94	2.91	2.89	2.87	2.85	52
53	2.03	2.02	2.01	2.00	1.99	1.98	1.97	1.96	1.95	1.94	1.93	53
54	1.01	1.01	1.00	1.00	1.00	1.00	0.99	0.99	0.99	0.99	0.98	54

Table 6 Multipliers for loss of earnings to pension age 55 (females)

Age at date of trial	Multiplier calculated with allowance for projected mortality from the 2008-based population projections and rate of return of											Age at date of trial
	–2.0%	–1.5%	–1.0%	–0.5%	0.0%	0.5%	1.0%	1.5%	2.0%	2.5%	3.0%	
16	58.83	52.69	47.37	42.75	38.72	35.20	32.11	29.40	27.01	24.90	23.03	16
17	56.66	50.91	45.90	41.54	37.72	34.37	31.43	28.84	26.54	24.51	22.70	17
18	54.54	49.15	44.45	40.34	36.72	33.55	30.74	28.26	26.07	24.11	22.37	18
19	52.46	47.43	43.02	39.14	35.73	32.71	30.05	27.68	25.58	23.71	22.03	19
20	50.43	45.73	41.60	37.95	34.73	31.88	29.35	27.09	25.09	23.29	21.68	20
21	48.43	44.05	40.19	36.77	33.73	31.04	28.64	26.50	24.58	22.86	21.32	21
22	46.48	42.41	38.80	35.59	32.74	30.20	27.92	25.89	24.06	22.42	20.95	22
23	44.56	40.78	37.42	34.42	31.74	29.35	27.20	25.27	23.54	21.97	20.56	23
24	42.69	39.18	36.05	33.25	30.74	28.49	26.47	24.65	23.00	21.51	20.17	24
25	40.85	37.60	34.70	32.09	29.75	27.64	25.73	24.01	22.46	21.04	19.76	25
26	39.04	36.05	33.36	30.94	28.75	26.78	24.99	23.37	21.90	20.56	19.34	26
27	37.28	34.52	32.04	29.79	27.76	25.91	24.24	22.72	21.33	20.06	18.91	27
28	35.55	33.02	30.73	28.65	26.76	25.04	23.48	22.05	20.75	19.56	18.46	28
29	33.86	31.54	29.43	27.51	25.77	24.17	22.72	21.38	20.16	19.04	18.01	29
30	32.20	30.08	28.15	26.38	24.77	23.30	21.94	20.70	19.56	18.51	17.54	30
31	30.57	28.64	26.88	25.26	23.78	22.42	21.16	20.01	18.94	17.96	17.05	31
32	28.98	27.23	25.62	24.15	22.79	21.53	20.38	19.31	18.32	17.40	16.56	32
33	27.42	25.84	24.38	23.03	21.79	20.64	19.58	18.60	17.68	16.83	16.04	33
34	25.89	24.46	23.15	21.93	20.80	19.75	18.78	17.87	17.03	16.25	15.52	34
35	24.39	23.11	21.93	20.83	19.81	18.86	17.97	17.14	16.37	15.65	14.97	35
36	22.92	21.78	20.73	19.74	18.82	17.96	17.15	16.40	15.69	15.03	14.41	36
37	21.48	20.48	19.53	18.65	17.83	17.05	16.33	15.65	15.01	14.40	13.84	37
38	20.07	19.19	18.35	17.57	16.84	16.14	15.49	14.88	14.30	13.76	13.25	38
39	18.69	17.92	17.19	16.50	15.85	15.23	14.65	14.11	13.59	13.10	12.64	39
40	17.34	16.67	16.03	15.43	14.86	14.32	13.80	13.32	12.86	12.42	12.01	40
41	16.02	15.44	14.89	14.36	13.87	13.40	12.95	12.52	12.12	11.73	11.36	41
42	14.72	14.22	13.75	13.30	12.88	12.47	12.08	11.71	11.36	11.02	10.70	42
43	13.45	13.03	12.63	12.25	11.89	11.54	11.21	10.89	10.59	10.29	10.01	43
44	12.20	11.85	11.52	11.20	10.90	10.61	10.33	10.06	9.80	9.55	9.31	44
45	10.98	10.70	10.42	10.16	9.91	9.67	9.43	9.21	8.99	8.79	8.58	45
46	9.78	9.56	9.34	9.13	8.92	8.73	8.54	8.35	8.17	8.00	7.84	46
47	8.61	8.43	8.26	8.09	7.93	7.78	7.63	7.48	7.34	7.20	7.07	47
48	7.46	7.33	7.20	7.07	6.95	6.83	6.71	6.60	6.49	6.38	6.28	48
49	6.33	6.24	6.14	6.05	5.96	5.87	5.78	5.70	5.62	5.54	5.46	49
50	5.23	5.16	5.10	5.03	4.97	4.91	4.85	4.79	4.73	4.68	4.62	50
51	4.14	4.10	4.06	4.02	3.98	3.94	3.90	3.86	3.83	3.79	3.75	51
52	3.08	3.06	3.03	3.01	2.99	2.97	2.94	2.92	2.90	2.88	2.86	52
53	2.03	2.02	2.01	2.00	1.99	1.98	1.97	1.96	1.96	1.95	1.94	53
54	1.01	1.01	1.00	1.00	1.00	1.00	0.99	0.99	0.99	0.99	0.98	54

Table 7 Multipliers for loss of earnings to pension age 60 (males)

Age at date of trial	Multiplier calculated with allowance for projected mortality from the 2008-based population projections and rate of return of											Age at date of trial
	−2.0%	−1.5%	−1.0%	−0.5%	0.0%	0.5%	1.0%	1.5%	2.0%	2.5%	3.0%	
16	69.28	61.13	54.18	48.26	43.18	38.81	35.03	31.77	28.93	26.46	24.29	16
17	66.90	59.22	52.65	47.02	42.18	38.00	34.38	31.24	28.50	26.11	24.01	17
18	64.58	57.34	51.13	45.79	41.18	37.19	33.73	30.71	28.07	25.75	23.72	18
19	62.30	55.49	49.63	44.57	40.19	36.38	33.06	30.17	27.62	25.39	23.42	19
20	60.08	53.68	48.15	43.36	39.20	35.57	32.40	29.62	27.17	25.02	23.11	20
21	57.90	51.89	46.68	42.15	38.21	34.75	31.72	29.06	26.71	24.64	22.80	21
22	55.76	50.13	45.23	40.95	37.21	33.93	31.04	28.50	26.25	24.25	22.47	22
23	53.66	48.40	43.79	39.76	36.22	33.11	30.36	27.93	25.77	23.85	22.14	23
24	51.61	46.69	42.37	38.57	35.23	32.28	29.66	27.35	25.28	23.44	21.80	24
25	49.60	45.01	40.96	37.40	34.24	31.45	28.97	26.76	24.79	23.02	21.44	25
26	47.64	43.35	39.57	36.22	33.25	30.61	28.26	26.16	24.28	22.59	21.08	26
27	45.71	41.72	38.19	35.06	32.27	29.77	27.55	25.56	23.77	22.16	20.71	27
28	43.82	40.12	36.83	33.90	31.28	28.93	26.83	24.94	23.24	21.71	20.32	28
29	41.97	38.54	35.48	32.74	30.29	28.09	26.10	24.32	22.70	21.25	19.92	29
30	40.15	36.99	34.14	31.59	29.30	27.24	25.37	23.69	22.16	20.78	19.52	30
31	38.38	35.46	32.83	30.46	28.32	26.39	24.64	23.05	21.61	20.29	19.10	31
32	36.65	33.96	31.53	29.33	27.34	25.53	23.89	22.40	21.04	19.80	18.67	32
33	34.96	32.48	30.24	28.21	26.36	24.68	23.15	21.75	20.47	19.30	18.23	33
34	33.30	31.03	28.97	27.09	25.38	23.82	22.39	21.09	19.89	18.79	17.78	34
35	31.67	29.60	27.71	25.98	24.40	22.96	21.63	20.42	19.30	18.27	17.32	35
36	30.07	28.19	26.46	24.88	23.43	22.09	20.87	19.74	18.69	17.73	16.84	36
37	28.51	26.80	25.23	23.78	22.45	21.22	20.09	19.04	18.08	17.18	16.35	37
38	26.98	25.43	24.01	22.69	21.48	20.35	19.31	18.34	17.45	16.61	15.84	38
39	25.48	24.08	22.80	21.60	20.50	19.47	18.52	17.63	16.81	16.04	15.32	39
40	24.00	22.76	21.60	20.52	19.52	18.59	17.72	16.91	16.15	15.44	14.78	40
41	22.56	21.45	20.41	19.45	18.54	17.70	16.91	16.17	15.48	14.84	14.23	41
42	21.15	20.16	19.24	18.38	17.57	16.81	16.10	15.43	14.80	14.21	13.66	42
43	19.76	18.90	18.08	17.31	16.59	15.92	15.28	14.68	14.11	13.58	13.07	43
44	18.41	17.65	16.93	16.26	15.62	15.02	14.45	13.91	13.41	12.93	12.47	44
45	17.08	16.42	15.79	15.20	14.64	14.12	13.61	13.14	12.69	12.26	11.85	45
46	15.78	15.21	14.67	14.16	13.67	13.21	12.77	12.35	11.95	11.58	11.22	46
47	14.50	14.02	13.56	13.12	12.70	12.30	11.92	11.55	11.21	10.88	10.56	47
48	13.26	12.85	12.46	12.08	11.73	11.38	11.06	10.75	10.45	10.16	9.89	48
49	12.03	11.69	11.37	11.05	10.75	10.47	10.19	9.93	9.67	9.43	9.19	49
50	10.83	10.56	10.29	10.03	9.78	9.55	9.32	9.10	8.88	8.68	8.48	50
51	9.66	9.44	9.22	9.01	8.81	8.62	8.43	8.25	8.08	7.91	7.75	51
52	8.51	8.34	8.17	8.00	7.84	7.69	7.54	7.40	7.26	7.12	6.99	52
53	7.38	7.25	7.12	7.00	6.87	6.76	6.64	6.53	6.42	6.32	6.21	53
54	6.27	6.18	6.08	5.99	5.90	5.82	5.73	5.65	5.57	5.49	5.41	54
55	5.18	5.12	5.05	4.99	4.93	4.87	4.81	4.75	4.69	4.64	4.58	55
56	4.12	4.07	4.03	3.99	3.95	3.91	3.87	3.84	3.80	3.76	3.73	56
57	3.06	3.04	3.02	2.99	2.97	2.95	2.93	2.91	2.89	2.86	2.84	57
58	2.03	2.02	2.01	2.00	1.99	1.98	1.97	1.96	1.95	1.94	1.93	58
59	1.01	1.00	1.00	1.00	1.00	0.99	0.99	0.99	0.99	0.98	0.98	59

Table 8 Multipliers for loss of earnings to pension age 60 (females)

Age at date of trial	Multiplier calculated with allowance for projected mortality from the 2008-based population projections and rate of return of											Age at date of trial
	–2.0%	–1.5%	–1.0%	–0.5%	0.0%	0.5%	1.0%	1.5%	2.0%	2.5%	3.0%	
16	70.04	61.77	54.73	48.72	43.57	39.14	35.32	32.02	29.14	26.64	24.45	16
17	67.65	59.85	53.18	47.48	42.57	38.33	34.67	31.49	28.72	26.29	24.17	17
18	65.30	57.96	51.66	46.24	41.57	37.52	34.01	30.96	28.28	25.94	23.88	18
19	63.01	56.10	50.15	45.02	40.57	36.71	33.35	30.41	27.84	25.58	23.59	19
20	60.76	54.27	48.66	43.80	39.57	35.90	32.68	29.87	27.39	25.21	23.28	20
21	58.56	52.46	47.18	42.58	38.58	35.08	32.01	29.31	26.93	24.83	22.97	21
22	56.40	50.69	45.71	41.37	37.58	34.25	31.32	28.74	26.46	24.44	22.64	22
23	54.29	48.94	44.26	40.17	36.58	33.42	30.64	28.17	25.98	24.04	22.31	23
24	52.21	47.21	42.83	38.98	35.58	32.59	29.94	27.59	25.50	23.63	21.97	24
25	50.18	45.51	41.41	37.79	34.59	31.75	29.24	27.00	25.00	23.21	21.61	25
26	48.19	43.84	40.00	36.60	33.59	30.91	28.53	26.40	24.49	22.78	21.25	26
27	46.24	42.20	38.61	35.43	32.59	30.07	27.81	25.79	23.98	22.34	20.87	27
28	44.33	40.58	37.24	34.26	31.60	29.22	27.09	25.17	23.45	21.89	20.49	28
29	42.46	38.98	35.87	33.09	30.60	28.37	26.36	24.55	22.91	21.43	20.09	29
30	40.63	37.41	34.53	31.94	29.61	27.51	25.62	23.91	22.37	20.96	19.69	30
31	38.83	35.86	33.19	30.79	28.62	26.65	24.88	23.27	21.81	20.48	19.27	31
32	37.08	34.34	31.87	29.64	27.62	25.79	24.13	22.62	21.24	19.98	18.83	32
33	35.35	32.84	30.57	28.50	26.63	24.93	23.37	21.96	20.66	19.48	18.39	33
34	33.67	31.37	29.28	27.37	25.64	24.06	22.61	21.29	20.07	18.96	17.93	34
35	32.01	29.91	28.00	26.25	24.65	23.18	21.84	20.60	19.47	18.43	17.46	35
36	30.40	28.48	26.73	25.13	23.66	22.30	21.06	19.91	18.86	17.88	16.98	36
37	28.81	27.08	25.48	24.02	22.67	21.42	20.28	19.21	18.23	17.32	16.48	37
38	27.26	25.69	24.24	22.91	21.68	20.54	19.48	18.50	17.60	16.75	15.97	38
39	25.73	24.32	23.02	21.81	20.69	19.65	18.68	17.78	16.95	16.17	15.44	39
40	24.24	22.98	21.81	20.72	19.70	18.76	17.88	17.05	16.29	15.57	14.90	40
41	22.78	21.66	20.61	19.63	18.71	17.86	17.06	16.31	15.61	14.96	14.34	41
42	21.35	20.35	19.42	18.55	17.73	16.96	16.24	15.56	14.93	14.33	13.77	42
43	19.95	19.07	18.24	17.47	16.74	16.05	15.41	14.80	14.23	13.69	13.18	43
44	18.58	17.81	17.08	16.40	15.75	15.15	14.57	14.03	13.52	13.03	12.57	44
45	17.24	16.57	15.93	15.33	14.77	14.23	13.73	13.25	12.79	12.36	11.95	45
46	15.92	15.34	14.80	14.28	13.79	13.32	12.87	12.45	12.05	11.67	11.30	46
47	14.63	14.14	13.67	13.23	12.80	12.40	12.01	11.65	11.30	10.96	10.64	47
48	13.37	12.95	12.56	12.18	11.82	11.48	11.15	10.83	10.53	10.24	9.96	48
49	12.13	11.79	11.46	11.14	10.84	10.55	10.27	10.00	9.75	9.50	9.26	49
50	10.92	10.64	10.37	10.11	9.86	9.62	9.39	9.17	8.95	8.74	8.54	50
51	9.73	9.51	9.29	9.08	8.88	8.69	8.50	8.31	8.14	7.97	7.80	51
52	8.57	8.39	8.22	8.06	7.90	7.75	7.60	7.45	7.31	7.17	7.04	52
53	7.43	7.30	7.17	7.04	6.92	6.80	6.68	6.57	6.46	6.36	6.25	53
54	6.31	6.21	6.12	6.03	5.94	5.85	5.76	5.68	5.60	5.52	5.44	54
55	5.21	5.14	5.08	5.02	4.95	4.89	4.83	4.77	4.72	4.66	4.61	55
56	4.13	4.09	4.05	4.01	3.97	3.93	3.89	3.85	3.82	3.78	3.74	56
57	3.07	3.05	3.03	3.00	2.98	2.96	2.94	2.92	2.89	2.87	2.85	57
58	2.03	2.02	2.01	2.00	1.99	1.98	1.97	1.96	1.95	1.94	1.93	58
59	1.01	1.01	1.00	1.00	1.00	1.00	0.99	0.99	0.99	0.99	0.98	59

Table 9 Multipliers for loss of earnings to pension age 65 (males)

Age at date of trial	Multiplier calculated with allowance for projected mortality from the 2008-based population projections and rate of return of											Age at date of trial
	–2.0%	–1.5%	–1.0%	–0.5%	0.0%	0.5%	1.0%	1.5%	2.0%	2.5%	3.0%	
16	81.11	70.46	61.56	54.09	47.80	42.47	37.95	34.08	30.77	27.92	25.46	16
17	78.49	68.41	59.95	52.82	46.80	41.68	37.32	33.59	30.38	27.61	25.21	17
18	75.93	66.39	58.35	51.56	45.80	40.89	36.69	33.09	29.98	27.29	24.96	18
19	73.42	64.40	56.78	50.31	44.80	40.10	36.06	32.58	29.58	26.97	24.70	19
20	70.97	62.45	55.22	49.07	43.81	39.30	35.42	32.07	29.16	26.64	24.43	20
21	68.57	60.53	53.68	47.83	42.82	38.50	34.78	31.55	28.74	26.30	24.15	21
22	66.21	58.63	52.16	46.60	41.82	37.70	34.13	31.02	28.31	25.95	23.87	22
23	63.90	56.77	50.65	45.38	40.83	36.89	33.47	30.49	27.88	25.59	23.57	23
24	61.64	54.93	49.15	44.16	39.84	36.08	32.81	29.94	27.43	25.22	23.27	24
25	59.43	53.12	47.68	42.95	38.85	35.27	32.14	29.39	26.98	24.85	22.96	25
26	57.26	51.35	46.22	41.75	37.86	34.45	31.46	28.84	26.52	24.47	22.65	26
27	55.14	49.60	44.77	40.56	36.87	33.63	30.78	28.27	26.05	24.07	22.32	27
28	53.06	47.87	43.34	39.37	35.88	32.81	30.10	27.70	25.57	23.67	21.98	28
29	51.02	46.17	41.92	38.18	34.89	31.98	29.40	27.11	25.08	23.26	21.63	29
30	49.03	44.50	40.52	37.01	33.90	31.15	28.70	26.52	24.58	22.84	21.28	30
31	47.08	42.86	39.14	35.84	32.92	30.32	28.00	25.93	24.07	22.41	20.91	31
32	45.17	41.25	37.78	34.69	31.94	29.49	27.29	25.33	23.56	21.97	20.54	32
33	43.31	39.67	36.43	33.54	30.96	28.65	26.58	24.72	23.04	21.53	20.16	33
34	41.48	38.11	35.10	32.40	29.99	27.81	25.86	24.10	22.51	21.07	19.77	34
35	39.69	36.57	33.78	31.27	29.01	26.97	25.14	23.48	21.97	20.60	19.36	35
36	37.94	35.06	32.47	30.14	28.03	26.13	24.41	22.84	21.42	20.13	18.95	36
37	36.22	33.57	31.18	29.02	27.06	25.28	23.67	22.20	20.86	19.64	18.52	37
38	34.54	32.11	29.90	27.90	26.08	24.43	22.92	21.55	20.29	19.13	18.08	38
39	32.89	30.66	28.64	26.79	25.11	23.57	22.17	20.88	19.70	18.62	17.62	39
40	31.27	29.24	27.38	25.69	24.13	22.71	21.41	20.21	19.11	18.09	17.16	40
41	29.69	27.84	26.14	24.59	23.16	21.85	20.64	19.53	18.50	17.55	16.68	41
42	28.14	26.46	24.92	23.50	22.19	20.98	19.87	18.84	17.88	17.00	16.18	42
43	26.62	25.10	23.70	22.41	21.22	20.11	19.09	18.14	17.26	16.44	15.68	43
44	25.13	23.77	22.50	21.33	20.25	19.24	18.30	17.43	16.62	15.86	15.16	44
45	23.68	22.45	21.32	20.26	19.28	18.36	17.51	16.71	15.97	15.27	14.62	45
46	22.25	21.16	20.14	19.19	18.31	17.48	16.71	15.98	15.30	14.67	14.07	46
47	20.86	19.89	18.98	18.14	17.34	16.60	15.90	15.24	14.63	14.05	13.50	47
48	19.49	18.64	17.84	17.08	16.38	15.71	15.09	14.50	13.94	13.42	12.92	48
49	18.15	17.41	16.70	16.04	15.41	14.82	14.27	13.74	13.24	12.77	12.33	49
50	16.85	16.20	15.58	15.00	14.46	13.94	13.44	12.98	12.53	12.11	11.71	50
51	15.57	15.01	14.48	13.98	13.50	13.04	12.61	12.20	11.81	11.44	11.09	51
52	14.32	13.84	13.39	12.95	12.54	12.15	11.77	11.42	11.08	10.75	10.44	52
53	13.09	12.69	12.30	11.94	11.59	11.25	10.93	10.62	10.33	10.05	9.78	53
54	11.89	11.56	11.24	10.93	10.63	10.35	10.08	9.82	9.57	9.33	9.10	54
55	10.71	10.44	10.18	9.92	9.68	9.45	9.22	9.00	8.79	8.59	8.40	55
56	9.56	9.34	9.13	8.93	8.73	8.54	8.35	8.17	8.00	7.84	7.67	56
57	8.43	8.26	8.09	7.93	7.77	7.62	7.47	7.33	7.19	7.06	6.93	57
58	7.32	7.19	7.06	6.94	6.82	6.70	6.59	6.48	6.37	6.26	6.16	58
59	6.22	6.13	6.03	5.94	5.85	5.77	5.68	5.60	5.52	5.45	5.37	59
60	5.14	5.08	5.01	4.95	4.89	4.83	4.77	4.71	4.66	4.60	4.55	60
61	4.09	4.04	4.00	3.96	3.92	3.89	3.85	3.81	3.77	3.74	3.70	61
62	3.04	3.02	3.00	2.98	2.95	2.93	2.91	2.89	2.87	2.85	2.83	62
63	2.02	2.01	2.00	1.99	1.98	1.97	1.96	1.95	1.94	1.93	1.92	63
64	1.00	1.00	1.00	1.00	0.99	0.99	0.99	0.99	0.98	0.98	0.98	64

Table 10 Multipliers for loss of earnings to pension age 65 (females)

Age at date of trial	Multiplier calculated with allowance for projected mortality from the 2008-based population projections and rate of return of											Age at date of trial
	–2.0%	–1.5%	–1.0%	–0.5%	0.0%	0.5%	1.0%	1.5%	2.0%	2.5%	3.0%	
16	82.26	71.41	62.34	54.74	48.34	42.93	38.33	34.41	31.05	28.16	25.66	16
17	79.62	69.34	60.72	53.47	47.34	42.14	37.71	33.91	30.66	27.85	25.41	17
18	77.03	67.31	59.12	52.20	46.34	41.35	37.08	33.42	30.26	27.53	25.16	18
19	74.50	65.30	57.53	50.95	45.34	40.55	36.45	32.91	29.86	27.21	24.91	19
20	72.02	63.33	55.96	49.70	44.34	39.75	35.81	32.40	29.45	26.88	24.64	20
21	69.59	61.39	54.41	48.45	43.34	38.95	35.16	31.88	29.03	26.54	24.37	21
22	67.20	59.48	52.87	47.21	42.34	38.15	34.51	31.35	28.60	26.20	24.08	22
23	64.87	57.59	51.35	45.98	41.35	37.33	33.85	30.82	28.16	25.84	23.79	23
24	62.58	55.73	49.84	44.75	40.35	36.52	33.19	30.27	27.72	25.47	23.49	24
25	60.34	53.91	48.35	43.53	39.35	35.70	32.51	29.72	27.27	25.10	23.19	25
26	58.14	52.11	46.87	42.32	38.35	34.88	31.84	29.16	26.80	24.72	22.87	26
27	55.99	50.33	45.41	41.11	37.35	34.05	31.15	28.60	26.33	24.33	22.54	27
28	53.88	48.59	43.96	39.91	36.36	33.23	30.46	28.02	25.85	23.93	22.21	28
29	51.82	46.87	42.53	38.72	35.36	32.39	29.77	27.44	25.36	23.51	21.86	29
30	49.80	45.18	41.12	37.53	34.36	31.56	29.06	26.84	24.87	23.09	21.51	30
31	47.82	43.52	39.72	36.35	33.37	30.72	28.35	26.25	24.36	22.66	21.14	31
32	45.88	41.88	38.33	35.18	32.38	29.87	27.64	25.64	23.84	22.22	20.77	32
33	43.98	40.27	36.96	34.01	31.38	29.03	26.92	25.02	23.31	21.77	20.38	33
34	42.12	38.68	35.60	32.85	30.39	28.18	26.19	24.39	22.78	21.31	19.98	34
35	40.30	37.11	34.26	31.70	29.40	27.32	25.45	23.76	22.23	20.84	19.57	35
36	38.51	35.58	32.93	30.56	28.41	26.47	24.71	23.12	21.67	20.35	19.15	36
37	36.76	34.06	31.62	29.42	27.42	25.61	23.96	22.47	21.10	19.86	18.72	37
38	35.05	32.57	30.32	28.28	26.43	24.74	23.21	21.81	20.52	19.35	18.28	38
39	33.38	31.10	29.04	27.16	25.44	23.88	22.44	21.14	19.93	18.83	17.82	39
40	31.73	29.66	27.76	26.04	24.45	23.00	21.68	20.46	19.33	18.30	17.35	40
41	30.12	28.24	26.51	24.92	23.47	22.13	20.90	19.77	18.72	17.76	16.86	41
42	28.55	26.84	25.26	23.81	22.48	21.25	20.12	19.07	18.10	17.20	16.37	42
43	27.01	25.46	24.03	22.71	21.50	20.37	19.33	18.36	17.46	16.63	15.85	43
44	25.49	24.10	22.81	21.62	20.51	19.48	18.53	17.64	16.82	16.05	15.33	44
45	24.02	22.77	21.61	20.53	19.53	18.60	17.73	16.92	16.16	15.45	14.79	45
46	22.57	21.46	20.42	19.45	18.55	17.71	16.92	16.18	15.49	14.84	14.23	46
47	21.15	20.17	19.24	18.38	17.57	16.81	16.10	15.43	14.81	14.22	13.66	47
48	19.77	18.90	18.08	17.31	16.59	15.92	15.28	14.68	14.11	13.58	13.08	48
49	18.41	17.65	16.93	16.26	15.62	15.02	14.45	13.91	13.41	12.93	12.47	49
50	17.08	16.42	15.80	15.21	14.65	14.12	13.62	13.14	12.69	12.26	11.85	50
51	15.78	15.21	14.67	14.16	13.67	13.21	12.77	12.35	11.96	11.58	11.22	51
52	14.51	14.02	13.56	13.12	12.70	12.30	11.92	11.56	11.21	10.88	10.56	52
53	13.26	12.85	12.46	12.09	11.73	11.39	11.06	10.75	10.45	10.17	9.89	53
54	12.04	11.70	11.37	11.06	10.76	10.47	10.20	9.93	9.68	9.43	9.20	54
55	10.84	10.56	10.30	10.04	9.79	9.55	9.32	9.10	8.89	8.68	8.49	55
56	9.67	9.44	9.23	9.02	8.82	8.63	8.44	8.26	8.09	7.92	7.75	56
57	8.52	8.34	8.17	8.01	7.85	7.70	7.55	7.40	7.26	7.13	7.00	57
58	7.39	7.25	7.13	7.00	6.88	6.76	6.65	6.53	6.43	6.32	6.22	58
59	6.28	6.18	6.09	5.99	5.91	5.82	5.73	5.65	5.57	5.49	5.41	59
60	5.19	5.12	5.05	4.99	4.93	4.87	4.81	4.75	4.69	4.64	4.58	60
61	4.11	4.07	4.03	3.99	3.95	3.91	3.87	3.84	3.80	3.76	3.73	61
62	3.06	3.04	3.02	2.99	2.97	2.95	2.93	2.91	2.88	2.86	2.84	62
63	2.03	2.02	2.01	2.00	1.99	1.98	1.97	1.96	1.95	1.94	1.93	63
64	1.01	1.00	1.00	1.00	1.00	0.99	0.99	0.99	0.99	0.98	0.98	64

Table 11 Multipliers for loss of earnings to pension age 70 (males)

Age at date of trial	Multiplier calculated with allowance for projected mortality from the 2008-based population projections and rate of return of											Age at date of trial
	–2.0%	–1.5%	–1.0%	–0.5%	0.0%	0.5%	1.0%	1.5%	2.0%	2.5%	3.0%	
16	93.75	80.18	69.05	59.87	52.26	45.93	40.62	36.16	32.38	29.18	26.44	16
17	90.86	77.97	67.35	58.57	51.26	45.15	40.02	35.69	32.02	28.89	26.22	17
18	88.04	75.80	65.68	57.27	50.25	44.37	39.41	35.22	31.65	28.61	25.99	18
19	85.28	73.67	64.03	55.99	49.26	43.59	38.81	34.74	31.28	28.31	25.76	19
20	82.58	71.57	62.39	54.71	48.26	42.81	38.19	34.26	30.90	28.01	25.52	20
21	79.94	69.50	60.78	53.44	47.26	42.03	37.58	33.78	30.52	27.71	25.28	21
22	77.35	67.47	59.17	52.18	46.27	41.24	36.95	33.28	30.12	27.39	25.03	22
23	74.81	65.46	57.59	50.93	45.27	40.45	36.32	32.78	29.72	27.07	24.77	23
24	72.32	63.49	56.02	49.68	44.27	39.65	35.68	32.26	29.31	26.74	24.50	24
25	69.89	61.55	54.47	48.44	43.28	38.85	35.04	31.75	28.89	26.40	24.23	25
26	67.50	59.64	52.93	47.20	42.29	38.05	34.39	31.22	28.47	26.06	23.95	26
27	65.17	57.76	51.42	45.98	41.29	37.25	33.74	30.69	28.03	25.70	23.66	27
28	62.88	55.91	49.92	44.76	40.30	36.44	33.08	30.15	27.59	25.34	23.36	28
29	60.64	54.08	48.43	43.54	39.31	35.63	32.41	29.61	27.14	24.97	23.05	29
30	58.45	52.29	46.96	42.34	38.32	34.81	31.74	29.05	26.68	24.59	22.74	30
31	56.31	50.53	45.51	41.14	37.33	34.00	31.07	28.49	26.22	24.20	22.42	31
32	54.21	48.80	44.08	39.96	36.35	33.18	30.39	27.93	25.75	23.81	22.09	32
33	52.17	47.10	42.67	38.79	35.37	32.37	29.71	27.36	25.27	23.41	21.75	33
34	50.16	45.43	41.28	37.62	34.40	31.55	29.02	26.78	24.79	23.00	21.41	34
35	48.20	43.78	39.89	36.46	33.42	30.73	28.33	26.20	24.29	22.58	21.05	35
36	46.28	42.16	38.53	35.31	32.45	29.90	27.63	25.60	23.79	22.15	20.69	36
37	44.39	40.57	37.18	34.16	31.47	29.07	26.93	25.00	23.27	21.72	20.31	37
38	42.55	39.00	35.84	33.02	30.50	28.24	26.21	24.39	22.75	21.27	19.93	38
39	40.74	37.45	34.51	31.88	29.52	27.40	25.49	23.77	22.21	20.80	19.53	39
40	38.96	35.92	33.20	30.75	28.55	26.56	24.76	23.14	21.67	20.33	19.12	40
41	37.23	34.42	31.90	29.63	27.57	25.71	24.03	22.50	21.11	19.85	18.70	41
42	35.53	32.95	30.62	28.51	26.60	24.87	23.29	21.86	20.55	19.36	18.26	42
43	33.86	31.50	29.35	27.40	25.63	24.02	22.55	21.20	19.98	18.85	17.82	43
44	32.23	30.07	28.10	26.30	24.66	23.17	21.80	20.54	19.39	18.34	17.36	44
45	30.64	28.66	26.86	25.21	23.70	22.31	21.04	19.87	18.80	17.81	16.90	45
46	29.08	27.28	25.63	24.12	22.73	21.45	20.28	19.19	18.19	17.27	16.41	46
47	27.55	25.92	24.42	23.04	21.77	20.59	19.51	18.51	17.58	16.72	15.92	47
48	26.06	24.58	23.22	21.97	20.81	19.73	18.74	17.81	16.95	16.16	15.41	48
49	24.60	23.27	22.04	20.91	19.85	18.87	17.96	17.11	16.32	15.58	14.90	49
50	23.17	21.98	20.88	19.85	18.90	18.01	17.18	16.40	15.68	15.00	14.37	50
51	21.78	20.72	19.73	18.81	17.95	17.14	16.39	15.69	15.02	14.40	13.82	51
52	20.42	19.48	18.60	17.78	17.00	16.28	15.60	14.96	14.36	13.80	13.27	52
53	19.09	18.26	17.48	16.75	16.06	15.41	14.81	14.23	13.69	13.18	12.70	53
54	17.79	17.06	16.38	15.73	15.12	14.55	14.01	13.49	13.01	12.55	12.11	54
55	16.51	15.88	15.29	14.72	14.19	13.68	13.20	12.75	12.31	11.90	11.52	55
56	15.27	14.73	14.21	13.72	13.25	12.81	12.39	11.99	11.61	11.25	10.90	56
57	14.05	13.59	13.14	12.72	12.32	11.94	11.57	11.22	10.89	10.57	10.27	57
58	12.85	12.46	12.09	11.73	11.39	11.06	10.75	10.45	10.16	9.88	9.62	58
59	11.68	11.35	11.04	10.74	10.45	10.17	9.91	9.66	9.41	9.18	8.95	59
60	10.52	10.26	10.00	9.75	9.51	9.28	9.06	8.85	8.65	8.45	8.26	60
61	9.39	9.18	8.97	8.77	8.58	8.39	8.21	8.04	7.87	7.71	7.55	61
62	8.28	8.11	7.95	7.79	7.64	7.49	7.35	7.21	7.07	6.94	6.82	62
63	7.19	7.06	6.94	6.82	6.70	6.59	6.48	6.37	6.27	6.16	6.06	63
64	6.12	6.03	5.94	5.85	5.77	5.68	5.60	5.52	5.44	5.36	5.29	64
65	5.07	5.01	4.95	4.89	4.83	4.77	4.71	4.65	4.60	4.54	4.49	65
66	4.04	4.00	3.96	3.92	3.88	3.84	3.81	3.77	3.73	3.70	3.66	66
67	3.02	3.00	2.97	2.95	2.93	2.91	2.89	2.86	2.84	2.82	2.80	67
68	2.01	2.00	1.99	1.98	1.97	1.96	1.95	1.94	1.93	1.92	1.91	68
69	1.00	1.00	1.00	0.99	0.99	0.99	0.99	0.98	0.98	0.98	0.98	69

Table 12 Multipliers for loss of earnings to pension age 70 (females)

Age at date of trial	Multiplier calculated with allowance for projected mortality from the 2008-based population projections and rate of return of											Age at date of trial
	−2.0%	−1.5%	−1.0%	−0.5%	0.0%	0.5%	1.0%	1.5%	2.0%	2.5%	3.0%	
16	95.47	81.58	70.18	60.79	53.01	46.54	41.12	36.57	32.73	29.47	26.68	16
17	92.56	79.35	68.47	59.48	52.01	45.76	40.53	36.11	32.37	29.19	26.46	17
18	89.71	77.16	66.79	58.18	51.00	44.99	39.93	35.65	32.01	28.91	26.24	18
19	86.92	75.00	65.12	56.89	50.00	44.21	39.32	35.18	31.64	28.62	26.02	19
20	84.18	72.88	63.47	55.61	49.00	43.43	38.71	34.70	31.27	28.32	25.79	20
21	81.50	70.79	61.84	54.33	48.00	42.64	38.09	34.21	30.88	28.02	25.55	21
22	78.87	68.73	60.22	53.06	47.00	41.85	37.47	33.72	30.49	27.71	25.30	22
23	76.30	66.70	58.62	51.79	46.00	41.06	36.84	33.22	30.09	27.39	25.04	23
24	73.77	64.70	57.04	50.53	44.99	40.26	36.20	32.71	29.68	27.06	24.78	24
25	71.30	62.73	55.47	49.28	43.99	39.46	35.56	32.19	29.27	26.73	24.51	25
26	68.88	60.80	53.91	48.03	42.99	38.65	34.91	31.67	28.85	26.39	24.23	26
27	66.51	58.89	52.38	46.80	41.99	37.85	34.26	31.13	28.41	26.03	23.95	27
28	64.19	57.01	50.86	45.56	40.99	37.03	33.59	30.60	27.98	25.68	23.65	28
29	61.91	55.17	49.36	44.34	39.99	36.22	32.93	30.05	27.53	25.31	23.35	29
30	59.68	53.35	47.87	43.12	39.00	35.40	32.25	29.50	27.07	24.93	23.04	30
31	57.50	51.56	46.40	41.91	38.00	34.58	31.58	28.94	26.61	24.55	22.72	31
32	55.37	49.79	44.94	40.71	37.01	33.75	30.89	28.37	26.13	24.15	22.39	32
33	53.27	48.06	43.51	39.52	36.01	32.92	30.20	27.79	25.65	23.75	22.05	33
34	51.22	46.35	42.08	38.33	35.02	32.09	29.50	27.21	25.16	23.34	21.70	34
35	49.22	44.67	40.67	37.14	34.02	31.26	28.80	26.61	24.66	22.91	21.35	35
36	47.25	43.02	39.28	35.97	33.03	30.42	28.09	26.01	24.15	22.48	20.98	36
37	45.32	41.39	37.90	34.80	32.04	29.58	27.37	25.40	23.63	22.04	20.60	37
38	43.44	39.79	36.54	33.64	31.05	28.73	26.65	24.78	23.10	21.58	20.21	38
39	41.59	38.21	35.19	32.48	30.06	27.88	25.92	24.16	22.56	21.12	19.81	39
40	39.78	36.66	33.85	31.34	29.07	27.03	25.19	23.52	22.01	20.65	19.40	40
41	38.01	35.13	32.53	30.20	28.08	26.18	24.45	22.88	21.46	20.16	18.98	41
42	36.28	33.62	31.23	29.06	27.10	25.32	23.70	22.23	20.89	19.66	18.54	42
43	34.58	32.14	29.94	27.93	26.11	24.46	22.95	21.57	20.31	19.15	18.10	43
44	32.92	30.69	28.66	26.81	25.13	23.59	22.19	20.90	19.72	18.63	17.64	44
45	31.29	29.26	27.40	25.70	24.15	22.73	21.42	20.22	19.12	18.10	17.17	45
46	29.70	27.85	26.15	24.60	23.17	21.86	20.65	19.54	18.51	17.56	16.68	46
47	28.15	26.47	24.92	23.50	22.19	20.99	19.87	18.84	17.89	17.01	16.19	47
48	26.63	25.11	23.71	22.41	21.22	20.11	19.09	18.14	17.26	16.44	15.68	48
49	25.14	23.77	22.51	21.34	20.25	19.24	18.30	17.43	16.62	15.86	15.16	49
50	23.68	22.46	21.32	20.27	19.28	18.36	17.51	16.71	15.97	15.27	14.62	50
51	22.26	21.17	20.15	19.20	18.31	17.49	16.71	15.99	15.31	14.67	14.07	51
52	20.87	19.90	18.99	18.14	17.35	16.60	15.91	15.25	14.63	14.05	13.51	52
53	19.50	18.65	17.85	17.09	16.39	15.72	15.09	14.50	13.95	13.42	12.93	53
54	18.17	17.42	16.72	16.05	15.43	14.83	14.28	13.75	13.25	12.78	12.33	54
55	16.86	16.21	15.60	15.02	14.47	13.95	13.45	12.99	12.54	12.12	11.72	55
56	15.58	15.02	14.49	13.99	13.51	13.05	12.62	12.21	11.82	11.45	11.09	56
57	14.33	13.85	13.40	12.96	12.55	12.16	11.78	11.43	11.09	10.76	10.45	57
58	13.10	12.70	12.31	11.95	11.59	11.26	10.94	10.63	10.34	10.05	9.78	58
59	11.89	11.56	11.24	10.93	10.64	10.35	10.08	9.82	9.57	9.33	9.10	59
60	10.71	10.44	10.18	9.92	9.68	9.44	9.22	9.00	8.79	8.59	8.39	60
61	9.55	9.33	9.12	8.92	8.72	8.53	8.35	8.17	8.00	7.83	7.67	61
62	8.42	8.25	8.08	7.92	7.76	7.61	7.46	7.32	7.18	7.05	6.92	62
63	7.30	7.17	7.05	6.92	6.80	6.69	6.57	6.47	6.36	6.25	6.15	63
64	6.21	6.12	6.02	5.93	5.85	5.76	5.68	5.59	5.51	5.44	5.36	64
65	5.14	5.07	5.01	4.95	4.89	4.83	4.77	4.71	4.65	4.60	4.54	65
66	4.08	4.04	4.00	3.96	3.92	3.88	3.85	3.81	3.77	3.74	3.70	66
67	3.04	3.02	3.00	2.98	2.95	2.93	2.91	2.89	2.87	2.85	2.83	67
68	2.02	2.01	2.00	1.99	1.98	1.97	1.96	1.95	1.94	1.93	1.92	68
69	1.00	1.00	1.00	1.00	0.99	0.99	0.99	0.99	0.98	0.98	0.98	69

Table 13 Multipliers for loss of earnings to pension age 75 (males)

Age at date of trial	Multiplier calculated with allowance for projected mortality from the 2008-based population projections and rate of return of											Age at date of trial
	−2.0%	−1.5%	−1.0%	−0.5%	0.0%	0.5%	1.0%	1.5%	2.0%	2.5%	3.0%	
16	107.05	90.16	76.55	65.51	56.51	49.13	43.04	37.99	33.77	30.23	27.24	16
17	103.88	87.79	74.76	64.17	55.50	48.37	42.46	37.55	33.44	29.97	27.04	17
18	100.78	85.45	73.01	62.84	54.49	47.60	41.88	37.10	33.10	29.71	26.84	18
19	97.75	83.16	71.27	61.52	53.49	46.83	41.29	36.65	32.75	29.44	26.63	19
20	94.79	80.91	69.55	60.21	52.48	46.06	40.70	36.20	32.40	29.17	26.42	20
21	91.89	78.69	67.86	58.91	51.48	45.29	40.11	35.74	32.04	28.89	26.20	21
22	89.04	76.51	66.17	57.61	50.48	44.52	39.50	35.27	31.67	28.61	25.98	22
23	86.25	74.36	64.51	56.32	49.48	43.74	38.89	34.79	31.30	28.31	25.74	23
24	83.52	72.24	62.86	55.04	48.48	42.95	38.28	34.31	30.92	28.01	25.51	24
25	80.85	70.15	61.23	53.76	47.48	42.17	37.66	33.82	30.53	27.70	25.26	25
26	78.23	68.10	59.63	52.50	46.48	41.38	37.04	33.32	30.14	27.39	25.01	26
27	75.67	66.09	58.03	51.24	45.48	40.59	36.41	32.82	29.74	27.07	24.75	27
28	73.16	64.10	56.46	49.99	44.48	39.79	35.77	32.31	29.32	26.74	24.48	28
29	70.70	62.14	54.90	48.74	43.49	38.99	35.13	31.79	28.91	26.40	24.21	29
30	68.29	60.22	53.35	47.50	42.49	38.19	34.48	31.27	28.48	26.05	23.93	30
31	65.95	58.33	51.84	46.28	41.50	37.39	33.83	30.74	28.05	25.70	23.64	31
32	63.65	56.48	50.34	45.06	40.52	36.59	33.18	30.21	27.62	25.35	23.35	32
33	61.41	54.66	48.86	43.86	39.54	35.79	32.52	29.67	27.18	24.98	23.05	33
34	59.22	52.87	47.40	42.66	38.56	34.98	31.86	29.13	26.73	24.61	22.74	34
35	57.06	51.11	45.95	41.47	37.58	34.17	31.19	28.58	26.27	24.23	22.43	35
36	54.96	49.37	44.52	40.29	36.60	33.36	30.52	28.02	25.80	23.84	22.10	36
37	52.90	47.67	43.11	39.12	35.62	32.55	29.84	27.45	25.33	23.45	21.77	37
38	50.87	45.98	41.70	37.95	34.64	31.73	29.16	26.87	24.85	23.04	21.42	38
39	48.89	44.33	40.31	36.78	33.67	30.91	28.46	26.29	24.35	22.62	21.07	39
40	46.95	42.69	38.94	35.62	32.69	30.08	27.76	25.70	23.85	22.19	20.70	40
41	45.05	41.09	37.58	34.47	31.71	29.25	27.06	25.10	23.34	21.75	20.33	41
42	43.19	39.51	36.24	33.33	30.74	28.42	26.35	24.49	22.81	21.31	19.95	42
43	41.37	37.96	34.91	32.20	29.77	27.59	25.63	23.87	22.29	20.85	19.55	43
44	39.59	36.43	33.60	31.07	28.80	26.76	24.91	23.25	21.75	20.39	19.15	44
45	37.85	34.93	32.31	29.95	27.83	25.92	24.19	22.62	21.20	19.91	18.73	45
46	36.14	33.45	31.03	28.84	26.87	25.08	23.46	21.98	20.64	19.42	18.31	46
47	34.47	32.00	29.76	27.74	25.90	24.24	22.72	21.34	20.08	18.93	17.87	47
48	32.84	30.58	28.52	26.65	24.95	23.39	21.98	20.69	19.50	18.42	17.42	48
49	31.25	29.18	27.29	25.56	23.99	22.55	21.24	20.03	18.92	17.90	16.97	49
50	29.70	27.81	26.07	24.49	23.04	21.71	20.49	19.37	18.33	17.38	16.50	50
51	28.18	26.46	24.88	23.43	22.10	20.87	19.74	18.70	17.74	16.85	16.03	51
52	26.70	25.14	23.70	22.38	21.16	20.03	18.99	18.03	17.13	16.31	15.54	52
53	25.26	23.85	22.54	21.34	20.23	19.19	18.24	17.35	16.52	15.76	15.04	53
54	23.85	22.58	21.40	20.31	19.30	18.35	17.48	16.66	15.90	15.20	14.53	54
55	22.48	21.34	20.28	19.29	18.37	17.52	16.72	15.98	15.28	14.63	14.02	55
56	21.13	20.12	19.17	18.28	17.46	16.68	15.96	15.28	14.64	14.05	13.49	56
57	19.82	18.92	18.07	17.28	16.54	15.85	15.19	14.58	14.00	13.46	12.95	57
58	18.53	17.74	16.99	16.29	15.63	15.00	14.42	13.86	13.34	12.85	12.39	58
59	17.27	16.57	15.91	15.29	14.71	14.16	13.63	13.14	12.67	12.23	11.81	59
60	16.03	15.42	14.85	14.30	13.79	13.30	12.84	12.40	11.99	11.60	11.22	60
61	14.81	14.29	13.79	13.32	12.87	12.45	12.04	11.66	11.29	10.95	10.61	61
62	13.62	13.18	12.75	12.35	11.96	11.59	11.24	10.91	10.59	10.28	9.99	62
63	12.46	12.09	11.73	11.38	11.05	10.74	10.44	10.15	9.88	9.61	9.36	63
64	11.33	11.02	10.72	10.43	10.15	9.89	9.63	9.39	9.15	8.93	8.71	64
65	10.22	9.97	9.72	9.48	9.25	9.03	8.82	8.61	8.42	8.23	8.04	65
66	9.14	8.93	8.73	8.54	8.36	8.18	8.00	7.83	7.67	7.52	7.36	66
67	8.08	7.92	7.76	7.61	7.46	7.32	7.18	7.04	6.91	6.79	6.66	67
68	7.04	6.91	6.79	6.67	6.56	6.45	6.34	6.24	6.14	6.04	5.94	68
69	6.01	5.92	5.83	5.74	5.66	5.58	5.50	5.42	5.34	5.27	5.19	69
70	4.99	4.93	4.87	4.81	4.75	4.69	4.63	4.58	4.52	4.47	4.42	70
71	3.98	3.94	3.90	3.86	3.83	3.79	3.75	3.72	3.68	3.65	3.61	71
72	2.98	2.96	2.94	2.92	2.89	2.87	2.85	2.83	2.81	2.79	2.77	72
73	1.99	1.98	1.97	1.96	1.95	1.94	1.93	1.92	1.91	1.90	1.89	73
74	1.00	0.99	0.99	0.99	0.99	0.98	0.98	0.98	0.98	0.97	0.97	74

Table 14 Multipliers for loss of earnings to pension age 75 (females)

Age at date of trial	Multiplier calculated with allowance for projected mortality from the 2008-based population projections and rate of return of											Age at date of trial
	–2.0%	–1.5%	–1.0%	–0.5%	0.0%	0.5%	1.0%	1.5%	2.0%	2.5%	3.0%	
16	109.63	92.19	78.15	66.79	57.53	49.95	43.70	38.52	34.21	30.59	27.53	16
17	106.42	89.80	76.36	65.44	56.52	49.19	43.13	38.09	33.88	30.34	27.34	17
18	103.28	87.44	74.59	64.11	55.51	48.43	42.55	37.65	33.55	30.08	27.15	18
19	100.20	85.12	72.84	62.78	54.51	47.66	41.97	37.21	33.21	29.82	26.95	19
20	97.19	82.84	71.11	61.47	53.50	46.90	41.38	36.76	32.86	29.56	26.74	20
21	94.24	80.59	69.39	60.15	52.50	46.13	40.79	36.30	32.51	29.28	26.53	21
22	91.35	78.38	67.69	58.85	51.49	45.35	40.19	35.84	32.15	29.00	26.31	22
23	88.51	76.19	66.01	57.55	50.49	44.57	39.58	35.37	31.78	28.71	26.08	23
24	85.73	74.04	64.34	56.25	49.48	43.79	38.97	34.89	31.40	28.42	25.85	24
25	83.01	71.93	62.69	54.97	48.48	43.00	38.35	34.40	31.02	28.12	25.61	25
26	80.34	69.84	61.06	53.69	47.47	42.21	37.73	33.91	30.63	27.81	25.37	26
27	77.73	67.79	59.45	52.42	46.47	41.41	37.10	33.41	30.23	27.49	25.11	27
28	75.17	65.77	57.85	51.15	45.46	40.62	36.47	32.90	29.83	27.17	24.85	28
29	72.67	63.79	56.27	49.90	44.46	39.82	35.83	32.39	29.42	26.84	24.59	29
30	70.22	61.83	54.71	48.65	43.46	39.01	35.18	31.87	29.00	26.50	24.31	30
31	67.82	59.91	53.17	47.40	42.46	38.20	34.53	31.34	28.57	26.15	24.03	31
32	65.47	58.01	51.64	46.17	41.46	37.40	33.87	30.81	28.13	25.79	23.74	32
33	63.16	56.15	50.13	44.94	40.46	36.58	33.21	30.26	27.69	25.43	23.44	33
34	60.91	54.31	48.63	43.72	39.47	35.77	32.54	29.72	27.24	25.06	23.13	34
35	58.70	52.51	47.15	42.51	38.47	34.95	31.86	29.16	26.78	24.68	22.82	35
36	56.54	50.73	45.69	41.30	37.47	34.12	31.18	28.59	26.31	24.29	22.49	36
37	54.42	48.98	44.24	40.10	36.48	33.30	30.49	28.02	25.83	23.89	22.16	37
38	52.35	47.26	42.81	38.91	35.49	32.47	29.80	27.44	25.34	23.48	21.81	38
39	50.32	45.57	41.40	37.73	34.49	31.64	29.10	26.85	24.85	23.06	21.46	39
40	48.33	43.90	40.00	36.55	33.50	30.80	28.40	26.26	24.35	22.63	21.10	40
41	46.38	42.26	38.61	35.38	32.51	29.96	27.69	25.65	23.83	22.20	20.73	41
42	44.48	40.64	37.24	34.22	31.53	29.12	26.97	25.04	23.31	21.75	20.34	42
43	42.61	39.06	35.89	33.06	30.54	28.28	26.25	24.42	22.78	21.29	19.95	43
44	40.79	37.49	34.55	31.92	29.55	27.43	25.52	23.79	22.24	20.82	19.55	44
45	39.00	35.96	33.23	30.78	28.57	26.58	24.79	23.16	21.69	20.35	19.13	45
46	37.26	34.45	31.93	29.65	27.59	25.73	24.05	22.52	21.13	19.86	18.71	46
47	35.55	32.97	30.64	28.53	26.62	24.88	23.30	21.87	20.56	19.36	18.27	47
48	33.88	31.51	29.37	27.42	25.64	24.03	22.56	21.21	19.98	18.86	17.83	48
49	32.25	30.08	28.11	26.31	24.67	23.18	21.81	20.55	19.40	18.34	17.37	49
50	30.66	28.68	26.87	25.22	23.71	22.32	21.05	19.88	18.81	17.82	16.90	50
51	29.10	27.30	25.65	24.14	22.75	21.47	20.29	19.20	18.20	17.28	16.42	51
52	27.58	25.94	24.44	23.06	21.78	20.61	19.52	18.52	17.59	16.73	15.93	52
53	26.08	24.61	23.25	21.99	20.83	19.75	18.75	17.83	16.97	16.17	15.43	53
54	24.63	23.30	22.07	20.93	19.87	18.89	17.98	17.13	16.34	15.60	14.91	54
55	23.20	22.01	20.91	19.88	18.92	18.03	17.20	16.42	15.69	15.02	14.38	55
56	21.81	20.75	19.76	18.83	17.97	17.16	16.41	15.70	15.04	14.42	13.84	56
57	20.45	19.50	18.62	17.80	17.02	16.30	15.62	14.98	14.38	13.81	13.28	57
58	19.11	18.28	17.50	16.77	16.08	15.43	14.82	14.25	13.70	13.19	12.71	58
59	17.80	17.07	16.39	15.74	15.13	14.56	14.02	13.50	13.02	12.56	12.12	59
60	16.52	15.88	15.29	14.72	14.19	13.68	13.20	12.75	12.32	11.91	11.52	60
61	15.26	14.71	14.20	13.71	13.24	12.80	12.38	11.98	11.60	11.24	10.89	61
62	14.03	13.56	13.12	12.70	12.30	11.92	11.56	11.21	10.88	10.56	10.26	62
63	12.83	12.43	12.06	11.70	11.36	11.04	10.72	10.42	10.14	9.86	9.60	63
64	11.65	11.33	11.01	10.71	10.43	10.15	9.89	9.63	9.39	9.16	8.93	64
65	10.50	10.24	9.98	9.73	9.50	9.27	9.05	8.84	8.63	8.43	8.24	65
66	9.38	9.16	8.96	8.76	8.57	8.38	8.20	8.03	7.86	7.70	7.54	66
67	8.28	8.11	7.95	7.79	7.64	7.49	7.35	7.21	7.07	6.94	6.81	67
68	7.19	7.07	6.94	6.82	6.70	6.59	6.48	6.37	6.27	6.17	6.07	68
69	6.13	6.04	5.95	5.86	5.77	5.69	5.60	5.52	5.44	5.37	5.29	69
70	5.08	5.01	4.95	4.89	4.83	4.77	4.71	4.66	4.60	4.55	4.49	70
71	4.04	4.00	3.96	3.92	3.88	3.85	3.81	3.77	3.73	3.70	3.66	71
72	3.02	3.00	2.97	2.95	2.93	2.91	2.89	2.86	2.84	2.82	2.80	72
73	2.01	2.00	1.99	1.98	1.97	1.96	1.95	1.94	1.93	1.92	1.91	73
74	1.00	1.00	1.00	0.99	0.99	0.99	0.99	0.98	0.98	0.98	0.98	74

Table 15 Multipliers for loss of pension commencing age 50 (males)

Age at date of trial	Multiplier calculated with allowance for projected mortality from the 2008-based population projections and rate of return of											Age at date of trial
	–2.0%	–1.5%	–1.0%	–0.5%	0.0%	0.5%	1.0%	1.5%	2.0%	2.5%	3.0%	
0	179.64	121.70	83.09	57.16	39.61	27.64	19.42	13.74	9.78	7.00	5.04	0
1	176.24	120.05	82.40	56.99	39.70	27.85	19.67	13.99	10.01	7.20	5.21	1
2	172.05	117.83	81.32	56.54	39.59	27.92	19.83	14.17	10.19	7.37	5.36	2
3	167.93	115.64	80.24	56.09	39.49	27.99	19.98	14.35	10.37	7.54	5.51	3
4	163.90	113.48	79.16	55.63	39.37	28.06	20.13	14.53	10.56	7.72	5.67	4
5	159.97	111.36	78.10	55.18	39.26	28.12	20.28	14.72	10.75	7.89	5.83	5
6	156.12	109.27	77.05	54.73	39.14	28.19	20.43	14.91	10.94	8.08	5.99	6
7	152.36	107.22	76.01	54.28	39.03	28.25	20.59	15.10	11.14	8.26	6.16	7
8	148.69	105.21	74.99	53.83	38.91	28.32	20.74	15.29	11.33	8.45	6.34	8
9	145.10	103.23	73.98	53.39	38.80	28.38	20.90	15.48	11.54	8.65	6.52	9
10	141.59	101.28	72.97	52.95	38.68	28.44	21.05	15.68	11.74	8.84	6.70	10
11	138.17	99.37	71.98	52.51	38.56	28.51	21.21	15.87	11.95	9.05	6.89	11
12	134.83	97.50	71.01	52.07	38.44	28.57	21.36	16.07	12.16	9.26	7.08	12
13	131.57	95.66	70.04	51.64	38.33	28.63	21.52	16.28	12.38	9.47	7.28	13
14	128.40	93.86	69.10	51.21	38.21	28.70	21.68	16.48	12.60	9.69	7.48	14
15	125.31	92.10	68.16	50.79	38.10	28.76	21.85	16.69	12.82	9.91	7.69	15
16	122.29	90.37	67.24	50.38	37.99	28.83	22.01	16.90	13.05	10.14	7.91	16
17	119.35	88.68	66.34	49.96	37.88	28.89	22.17	17.12	13.29	10.37	8.13	17
18	116.49	87.02	65.46	49.56	37.77	28.96	22.34	17.34	13.53	10.61	8.36	18
19	113.71	85.41	64.59	49.16	37.67	29.03	22.52	17.56	13.77	10.86	8.60	19
20	111.01	83.83	63.74	48.78	37.57	29.11	22.69	17.79	14.02	11.11	8.85	20
21	108.37	82.28	62.90	48.39	37.46	29.18	22.87	18.02	14.28	11.37	9.10	21
22	105.78	80.76	62.06	48.00	37.36	29.26	23.04	18.25	14.53	11.63	9.36	22
23	103.25	79.25	61.24	47.62	37.26	29.33	23.22	18.49	14.80	11.90	9.62	23
24	100.79	77.78	60.42	47.24	37.16	29.40	23.40	18.73	15.06	12.18	9.90	24
25	98.39	76.35	59.63	46.86	37.06	29.48	23.58	18.97	15.34	12.46	10.18	25
26	96.06	74.95	58.85	46.50	36.96	29.56	23.77	19.22	15.62	12.76	10.47	26
27	93.80	73.57	58.08	46.14	36.87	29.64	23.96	19.47	15.90	13.06	10.77	27
28	91.57	72.22	57.32	45.77	36.77	29.71	24.14	19.72	16.19	13.36	11.08	28
29	89.39	70.88	56.56	45.41	36.68	29.79	24.33	19.98	16.49	13.67	11.39	29
30	87.27	69.58	55.82	45.06	36.58	29.87	24.52	20.24	16.79	13.99	11.72	30
31	85.23	68.32	55.10	44.71	36.50	29.96	24.72	20.51	17.10	14.33	12.05	31
32	83.24	67.09	54.41	44.38	36.42	30.05	24.93	20.79	17.42	14.67	12.40	32
33	81.32	65.90	53.73	44.06	36.35	30.15	25.14	21.07	17.75	15.02	12.77	33
34	79.44	64.72	53.05	43.74	36.27	30.24	25.35	21.36	18.08	15.38	13.14	34
35	77.60	63.57	52.39	43.42	36.20	30.34	25.56	21.65	18.42	15.75	13.52	35
36	75.82	62.44	51.74	43.11	36.13	30.44	25.78	21.95	18.77	16.13	13.92	36
37	74.08	61.34	51.09	42.81	36.06	30.54	26.00	22.25	19.12	16.51	14.32	37
38	72.37	60.25	50.46	42.50	35.99	30.64	26.22	22.55	19.49	16.91	14.74	38
39	70.70	59.18	49.83	42.19	35.92	30.74	26.45	22.86	19.85	17.32	15.17	39
40	69.07	58.13	49.21	41.89	35.85	30.85	26.67	23.18	20.23	17.74	15.62	40
41	67.49	57.11	48.61	41.60	35.79	30.96	26.91	23.50	20.62	18.17	16.08	41
42	65.95	56.11	48.01	41.31	35.73	31.07	27.14	23.83	21.01	18.61	16.55	42
43	64.46	55.14	47.44	41.03	35.68	31.18	27.39	24.16	21.42	19.07	17.04	43
44	63.01	54.19	46.87	40.76	35.63	31.30	27.63	24.51	21.84	19.54	17.55	44
45	61.60	53.26	46.32	40.49	35.58	31.42	27.89	24.86	22.26	20.02	18.07	45
46	60.22	52.36	45.77	40.23	35.54	31.55	28.14	25.22	22.70	20.52	18.62	46
47	58.88	51.47	45.24	39.98	35.50	31.68	28.41	25.59	23.15	21.03	19.18	47
48	57.59	50.62	44.73	39.73	35.47	31.83	28.69	25.97	23.62	21.56	19.76	48
49	56.34	49.79	44.23	39.50	35.46	31.98	28.97	26.37	24.10	22.11	20.37	49
50	55.14	48.99	43.76	39.29	35.45	32.14	29.27	26.78	24.60	22.69	21.01	50

Table 16 Multipliers for loss of pension commencing age 50 (females)

Age at date of trial	Multiplier calculated with allowance for projected mortality from the 2008-based population projections and rate of return of											Age at date of trial
	–2.0%	–1.5%	–1.0%	–0.5%	0.0%	0.5%	1.0%	1.5%	2.0%	2.5%	3.0%	
0	199.59	134.37	91.19	62.37	42.98	29.85	20.87	14.70	10.42	7.43	5.33	0
1	195.74	132.49	90.40	62.16	43.07	30.06	21.13	14.95	10.65	7.64	5.51	1
2	191.18	130.11	89.25	61.69	42.97	30.15	21.30	15.16	10.85	7.82	5.67	2
3	186.71	127.75	88.10	61.23	42.87	30.24	21.48	15.36	11.05	8.00	5.83	3
4	182.34	125.44	86.97	60.76	42.77	30.32	21.65	15.56	11.26	8.19	6.00	4
5	178.06	123.16	85.85	60.30	42.67	30.41	21.82	15.77	11.46	8.39	6.17	5
6	173.88	120.92	84.74	59.84	42.56	30.49	22.00	15.97	11.67	8.58	6.35	6
7	169.79	118.72	83.65	59.38	42.46	30.58	22.17	16.18	11.89	8.78	6.53	7
8	165.80	116.55	82.56	58.92	42.36	30.66	22.35	16.40	12.10	8.99	6.72	8
9	161.89	114.43	81.49	58.47	42.25	30.75	22.53	16.61	12.33	9.20	6.91	9
10	158.08	112.34	80.43	58.02	42.15	30.83	22.70	16.83	12.55	9.42	7.11	10
11	154.36	110.29	79.39	57.57	42.04	30.92	22.89	17.05	12.78	9.64	7.31	11
12	150.73	108.28	78.36	57.12	41.94	31.00	23.07	17.27	13.01	9.86	7.52	12
13	147.17	106.30	77.34	56.68	41.83	31.08	23.25	17.50	13.25	10.09	7.73	13
14	143.71	104.36	76.34	56.24	41.73	31.17	23.43	17.73	13.49	10.33	7.95	14
15	140.33	102.45	75.35	55.81	41.62	31.25	23.62	17.96	13.74	10.57	8.18	15
16	137.02	100.58	74.37	55.38	41.52	31.34	23.81	18.20	13.99	10.82	8.41	16
17	133.80	98.75	73.41	54.95	41.42	31.42	24.00	18.44	14.25	11.07	8.65	17
18	130.66	96.95	72.46	54.53	41.32	31.51	24.19	18.68	14.51	11.33	8.90	18
19	127.60	95.19	71.52	54.11	41.22	31.60	24.38	18.92	14.78	11.60	9.16	19
20	124.61	93.47	70.61	53.70	41.12	31.69	24.58	19.18	15.05	11.87	9.42	20
21	121.70	91.78	69.70	53.30	41.03	31.78	24.78	19.43	15.32	12.15	9.69	21
22	118.85	90.11	68.80	52.89	40.93	31.87	24.97	19.69	15.61	12.44	9.97	22
23	116.05	88.47	67.91	52.48	40.82	31.96	25.17	19.94	15.89	12.73	10.25	23
24	113.32	86.85	67.03	52.08	40.72	32.05	25.37	20.21	16.18	13.03	10.54	24
25	110.66	85.27	66.16	51.68	40.62	32.14	25.57	20.47	16.48	13.33	10.85	25
26	108.06	83.73	65.31	51.28	40.53	32.23	25.78	20.74	16.78	13.65	11.16	26
27	105.53	82.21	64.47	50.89	40.43	32.32	25.99	21.02	17.09	13.97	11.48	27
28	103.06	80.72	63.64	50.50	40.33	32.41	26.19	21.29	17.40	14.30	11.81	28
29	100.65	79.26	62.82	50.12	40.24	32.50	26.41	21.58	17.72	14.64	12.14	29
30	98.30	77.82	62.02	49.74	40.15	32.60	26.62	21.86	18.05	14.98	12.49	30
31	96.01	76.42	61.23	49.37	40.06	32.69	26.84	22.15	18.38	15.33	12.85	31
32	93.78	75.05	60.46	49.00	39.97	32.79	27.06	22.45	18.73	15.70	13.22	32
33	91.61	73.71	59.69	48.64	39.88	32.89	27.28	22.75	19.07	16.07	13.61	33
34	89.48	72.38	58.93	48.28	39.79	32.99	27.50	23.05	19.43	16.45	14.00	34
35	87.39	71.08	58.18	47.92	39.70	33.09	27.73	23.36	19.79	16.84	14.40	35
36	85.37	69.81	57.45	47.57	39.62	33.19	27.96	23.68	20.16	17.24	14.82	36
37	83.40	68.57	56.73	47.22	39.54	33.29	28.19	24.00	20.53	17.65	15.25	37
38	81.47	67.35	56.02	46.87	39.45	33.40	28.43	24.32	20.92	18.07	15.69	38
39	79.59	66.15	55.31	46.53	39.37	33.50	28.66	24.65	21.31	18.50	16.14	39
40	77.75	64.97	54.62	46.19	39.29	33.61	28.90	24.99	21.71	18.95	16.61	40
41	75.96	63.82	53.94	45.86	39.22	33.72	29.15	25.33	22.11	19.40	17.10	41
42	74.22	62.69	53.27	45.54	39.14	33.83	29.40	25.67	22.53	19.87	17.60	42
43	72.53	61.59	52.62	45.22	39.07	33.95	29.65	26.03	22.96	20.35	18.11	43
44	70.88	60.52	51.98	44.90	39.01	34.07	29.91	26.39	23.40	20.84	18.64	44
45	69.28	59.47	51.35	44.60	38.94	34.19	30.17	26.76	23.85	21.35	19.19	45
46	67.72	58.45	50.74	44.30	38.89	34.32	30.44	27.14	24.31	21.87	19.76	46
47	66.20	57.45	50.14	44.01	38.83	34.45	30.72	27.53	24.78	22.41	20.35	47
48	64.73	56.48	49.56	43.73	38.79	34.59	31.01	27.93	25.27	22.97	20.96	48
49	63.31	55.54	48.99	43.46	38.76	34.74	31.30	28.34	25.77	23.54	21.59	49
50	61.93	54.62	48.44	43.20	38.73	34.90	31.61	28.76	26.29	24.14	22.25	50

Table 17 Multipliers for loss of pension commencing age 55 (males)

Age at date of trial	Multiplier calculated with allowance for projected mortality from the 2008-based population projections and rate of return of											Age at date of trial
	–2.0%	–1.5%	–1.0%	–0.5%	0.0%	0.5%	1.0%	1.5%	2.0%	2.5%	3.0%	
0	165.74	111.07	74.94	50.90	34.80	23.94	16.57	11.54	8.08	5.69	4.02	0
1	162.56	109.52	74.30	50.73	34.87	24.11	16.78	11.74	8.26	5.85	4.16	1
2	158.64	107.46	73.29	50.31	34.76	24.17	16.90	11.89	8.41	5.98	4.27	2
3	154.79	105.43	72.29	49.89	34.65	24.22	17.02	12.04	8.56	6.12	4.39	3
4	151.03	103.43	71.30	49.47	34.54	24.27	17.15	12.19	8.71	6.26	4.52	4
5	147.35	101.46	70.32	49.05	34.43	24.31	17.27	12.34	8.86	6.40	4.64	5
6	143.76	99.52	69.35	48.63	34.32	24.36	17.39	12.49	9.02	6.54	4.77	6
7	140.25	97.62	68.39	48.22	34.20	24.41	17.52	12.64	9.17	6.69	4.90	7
8	136.83	95.76	67.44	47.80	34.09	24.45	17.64	12.80	9.33	6.84	5.04	8
9	133.48	93.92	66.51	47.39	33.97	24.50	17.77	12.96	9.50	7.00	5.18	9
10	130.21	92.11	65.58	46.98	33.86	24.54	17.89	13.11	9.66	7.15	5.32	10
11	127.02	90.34	64.67	46.57	33.74	24.59	18.02	13.27	9.83	7.32	5.47	11
12	123.91	88.61	63.77	46.17	33.63	24.63	18.14	13.44	10.00	7.48	5.62	12
13	120.87	86.91	62.88	45.77	33.51	24.68	18.27	13.60	10.18	7.65	5.78	13
14	117.91	85.24	62.00	45.37	33.40	24.72	18.40	13.77	10.35	7.82	5.94	14
15	115.03	83.61	61.14	44.98	33.29	24.77	18.53	13.94	10.53	8.00	6.10	15
16	112.22	82.01	60.30	44.60	33.17	24.81	18.66	14.11	10.72	8.18	6.27	16
17	109.49	80.45	59.47	44.22	33.06	24.86	18.79	14.28	10.90	8.37	6.45	17
18	106.83	78.92	58.65	43.84	32.96	24.91	18.93	14.46	11.10	8.56	6.63	18
19	104.24	77.42	57.85	43.47	32.85	24.96	19.07	14.64	11.29	8.75	6.81	19
20	101.73	75.97	57.07	43.11	32.75	25.02	19.21	14.82	11.49	8.95	7.00	20
21	99.28	74.54	56.29	42.76	32.65	25.07	19.35	15.01	11.70	9.16	7.20	21
22	96.87	73.13	55.52	42.40	32.55	25.12	19.49	15.19	11.90	9.37	7.40	22
23	94.52	71.74	54.76	42.04	32.45	25.17	19.63	15.38	12.11	9.58	7.61	23
24	92.23	70.38	54.02	41.69	32.34	25.23	19.77	15.58	12.33	9.80	7.82	24
25	90.00	69.05	53.28	41.34	32.24	25.28	19.92	15.77	12.54	10.02	8.04	25
26	87.84	67.76	52.56	41.00	32.15	25.34	20.07	15.97	12.77	10.25	8.27	26
27	85.73	66.49	51.86	40.67	32.06	25.40	20.22	16.17	13.00	10.49	8.50	27
28	83.67	65.24	51.16	40.33	31.96	25.45	20.37	16.38	13.23	10.73	8.74	28
29	81.64	64.01	50.46	39.99	31.86	25.51	20.52	16.58	13.46	10.97	8.98	29
30	79.68	62.81	49.78	39.66	31.76	25.56	20.67	16.79	13.70	11.23	9.24	30
31	77.78	61.65	49.12	39.35	31.68	25.63	20.83	17.01	13.95	11.49	9.50	31
32	75.95	60.52	48.48	39.04	31.60	25.69	20.99	17.23	14.20	11.76	9.77	32
33	74.17	59.42	47.86	38.74	31.52	25.77	21.16	17.46	14.46	12.03	10.05	33
34	72.42	58.34	47.24	38.44	31.44	25.84	21.33	17.69	14.73	12.32	10.34	34
35	70.72	57.27	46.62	38.15	31.36	25.91	21.50	17.92	15.00	12.61	10.64	35
36	69.07	56.24	46.03	37.86	31.29	25.98	21.68	18.16	15.28	12.90	10.94	36
37	67.45	55.22	45.44	37.57	31.22	26.06	21.85	18.40	15.56	13.21	11.26	37
38	65.87	54.22	44.85	37.29	31.14	26.13	22.03	18.65	15.85	13.52	11.58	38
39	64.33	53.23	44.27	37.00	31.07	26.21	22.21	18.89	16.14	13.84	11.91	39
40	62.82	52.27	43.70	36.72	31.00	26.28	22.38	19.14	16.44	14.17	12.26	40
41	61.36	51.33	43.15	36.45	30.93	26.36	22.57	19.40	16.74	14.50	12.61	41
42	59.93	50.41	42.60	36.18	30.86	26.45	22.76	19.66	17.06	14.85	12.98	42
43	58.55	49.51	42.07	35.92	30.80	26.53	22.95	19.93	17.38	15.21	13.36	43
44	57.21	48.64	41.55	35.66	30.74	26.62	23.15	20.21	17.71	15.57	13.75	44
45	55.90	47.78	41.04	35.41	30.69	26.71	23.35	20.49	18.04	15.95	14.15	45
46	54.63	46.95	40.54	35.16	30.64	26.81	23.55	20.77	18.39	16.34	14.57	46
47	53.39	46.14	40.05	34.93	30.59	26.91	23.76	21.06	18.74	16.74	15.00	47
48	52.20	45.35	39.58	34.70	30.55	27.01	23.98	21.37	19.11	17.15	15.45	48
49	51.04	44.58	39.12	34.48	30.52	27.12	24.20	21.68	19.49	17.58	15.92	49
50	49.93	43.85	38.68	34.27	30.50	27.25	24.44	22.00	19.88	18.03	16.40	50
51	48.86	43.14	38.26	34.08	30.49	27.38	24.69	22.34	20.29	18.49	16.91	51
52	47.83	42.46	37.86	33.91	30.49	27.53	24.95	22.69	20.72	18.98	17.44	52
53	46.84	41.81	37.48	33.74	30.50	27.68	25.22	23.06	21.16	19.48	17.99	53
54	45.90	41.19	37.12	33.60	30.53	27.86	25.51	23.44	21.62	20.01	18.57	54
55	44.99	40.60	36.79	33.47	30.58	28.04	25.81	23.85	22.11	20.56	19.18	55

Table 18 Multipliers for loss of pension commencing age 55 (females)

Age at date of trial	Multiplier calculated with allowance for projected mortality from the 2008-based population projections and rate of return of											Age at date of trial
	–2.0%	–1.5%	–1.0%	–0.5%	0.0%	0.5%	1.0%	1.5%	2.0%	2.5%	3.0%	
0	185.47	123.56	82.90	56.01	38.10	26.08	17.97	12.46	8.69	6.09	4.30	0
1	181.85	121.80	82.16	55.81	38.16	26.26	18.19	12.68	8.88	6.26	4.44	1
2	177.57	119.58	81.09	55.37	38.06	26.33	18.33	12.84	9.05	6.41	4.57	2
3	173.37	117.38	80.03	54.94	37.96	26.40	18.48	13.01	9.21	6.56	4.69	3
4	169.26	115.23	78.98	54.51	37.86	26.47	18.62	13.18	9.38	6.71	4.83	4
5	165.25	113.10	77.94	54.08	37.76	26.54	18.76	13.35	9.55	6.87	4.97	5
6	161.33	111.01	76.92	53.65	37.66	26.60	18.91	13.52	9.72	7.03	5.11	6
7	157.49	108.96	75.90	53.22	37.56	26.67	19.05	13.69	9.89	7.19	5.25	7
8	153.74	106.95	74.89	52.79	37.45	26.73	19.20	13.87	10.07	7.36	5.40	8
9	150.08	104.96	73.90	52.37	37.35	26.80	19.35	14.04	10.25	7.53	5.55	9
10	146.51	103.02	72.92	51.95	37.24	26.86	19.49	14.22	10.44	7.70	5.71	10
11	143.02	101.11	71.95	51.53	37.14	26.93	19.64	14.41	10.63	7.88	5.87	11
12	139.61	99.24	71.00	51.12	37.04	26.99	19.79	14.59	10.82	8.06	6.04	12
13	136.29	97.39	70.05	50.71	36.93	27.06	19.94	14.78	11.01	8.25	6.21	13
14	133.04	95.59	69.12	50.30	36.83	27.12	20.09	14.97	11.21	8.44	6.38	14
15	129.87	93.82	68.21	49.90	36.72	27.19	20.25	15.16	11.41	8.63	6.56	15
16	126.78	92.08	67.30	49.50	36.62	27.26	20.40	15.35	11.61	8.83	6.75	16
17	123.76	90.37	66.41	49.10	36.52	27.32	20.55	15.55	11.82	9.03	6.94	17
18	120.82	88.70	65.53	48.71	36.42	27.39	20.71	15.75	12.03	9.24	7.13	18
19	117.96	87.07	64.67	48.32	36.32	27.46	20.87	15.95	12.25	9.46	7.34	19
20	115.17	85.47	63.82	47.94	36.23	27.53	21.03	16.16	12.47	9.68	7.54	20
21	112.45	83.90	62.98	47.56	36.13	27.60	21.20	16.37	12.70	9.90	7.76	21
22	109.78	82.35	62.15	47.19	36.03	27.67	21.36	16.58	12.93	10.13	7.98	22
23	107.16	80.82	61.33	46.81	35.93	27.73	21.52	16.79	13.16	10.37	8.20	23
24	104.61	79.32	60.51	46.43	35.83	27.80	21.68	17.00	13.40	10.61	8.43	24
25	102.12	77.86	59.71	46.06	35.73	27.87	21.85	17.22	13.64	10.85	8.67	25
26	99.70	76.42	58.92	45.69	35.63	27.94	22.02	17.44	13.88	11.10	8.92	26
27	97.34	75.01	58.15	45.33	35.54	28.01	22.19	17.67	14.13	11.36	9.17	27
28	95.02	73.63	57.38	44.97	35.44	28.08	22.36	17.89	14.39	11.62	9.43	28
29	92.77	72.27	56.62	44.61	35.34	28.15	22.53	18.12	14.65	11.89	9.70	29
30	90.58	70.94	55.88	44.26	35.25	28.22	22.71	18.36	14.91	12.17	9.97	30
31	88.45	69.65	55.15	43.92	35.16	28.29	22.88	18.60	15.18	12.45	10.26	31
32	86.37	68.38	54.44	43.58	35.07	28.37	23.06	18.84	15.46	12.74	10.55	32
33	84.34	67.13	53.73	43.24	34.98	28.45	23.24	19.09	15.74	13.04	10.85	33
34	82.35	65.90	53.03	42.90	34.89	28.52	23.43	19.33	16.03	13.35	11.16	34
35	80.41	64.70	52.34	42.57	34.80	28.60	23.61	19.59	16.32	13.66	11.48	35
36	78.53	63.52	51.66	42.24	34.72	28.67	23.80	19.84	16.62	13.98	11.80	36
37	76.69	62.37	51.00	41.92	34.63	28.75	23.99	20.10	16.92	14.30	12.14	37
38	74.89	61.24	50.34	41.60	34.55	28.83	24.18	20.37	17.23	14.64	12.49	38
39	73.14	60.13	49.69	41.28	34.46	28.91	24.37	20.64	17.55	14.98	12.85	39
40	71.43	59.04	49.05	40.97	34.38	29.00	24.57	20.91	17.87	15.34	13.22	40
41	69.76	57.97	48.43	40.66	34.30	29.08	24.77	21.19	18.20	15.70	13.60	41
42	68.14	56.93	47.81	40.35	34.23	29.17	24.97	21.47	18.54	16.07	13.99	42
43	66.56	55.91	47.21	40.05	34.15	29.25	25.17	21.76	18.88	16.45	14.39	43
44	65.03	54.92	46.62	39.76	34.08	29.35	25.38	22.05	19.23	16.84	14.81	44
45	63.54	53.95	46.04	39.48	34.02	29.44	25.60	22.35	19.60	17.25	15.24	45
46	62.09	53.00	45.47	39.20	33.95	29.54	25.82	22.66	19.97	17.66	15.68	46
47	60.68	52.07	44.91	38.93	33.89	29.64	26.04	22.97	20.35	18.09	16.14	47
48	59.31	51.18	44.38	38.66	33.84	29.75	26.27	23.30	20.74	18.53	16.62	48
49	57.99	50.31	43.85	38.41	33.80	29.87	26.51	23.63	21.14	18.99	17.12	49
50	56.70	49.46	43.35	38.17	33.76	29.99	26.76	23.97	21.56	19.46	17.63	50
51	55.46	48.63	42.85	37.93	33.73	30.12	27.01	24.32	21.99	19.95	18.16	51
52	54.25	47.83	42.37	37.70	33.70	30.25	27.27	24.68	22.43	20.45	18.71	52
53	53.08	47.05	41.90	37.49	33.68	30.40	27.54	25.06	22.88	20.97	19.29	53
54	51.95	46.30	41.45	37.28	33.68	30.55	27.83	25.44	23.35	21.51	19.88	54
55	50.86	45.57	41.02	37.09	33.68	30.71	28.12	25.84	23.84	22.07	20.51	55

Table 19 Multipliers for loss of pension commencing age 60 (males)

Age at date of trial	Multiplier calculated with allowance for projected mortality from the 2008-based population projections and rate of return of											Age at date of trial
	–2.0%	–1.5%	–1.0%	–0.5%	0.0%	0.5%	1.0%	1.5%	2.0%	2.5%	3.0%	
0	150.59	99.76	66.49	44.58	30.06	20.38	13.89	9.52	6.56	4.54	3.16	0
1	147.63	98.33	65.89	44.41	30.10	20.52	14.06	9.69	6.70	4.66	3.26	1
2	144.02	96.44	64.97	44.02	30.00	20.55	14.16	9.80	6.82	4.77	3.35	2
3	140.47	94.58	64.06	43.63	29.89	20.59	14.26	9.92	6.94	4.88	3.44	3
4	137.00	92.74	63.15	43.25	29.78	20.62	14.35	10.04	7.06	4.98	3.54	4
5	133.61	90.93	62.25	42.86	29.67	20.65	14.45	10.16	7.18	5.10	3.63	5
6	130.29	89.16	61.36	42.47	29.56	20.68	14.54	10.28	7.30	5.21	3.73	6
7	127.06	87.42	60.49	42.09	29.45	20.71	14.64	10.40	7.42	5.32	3.83	7
8	123.91	85.71	59.63	41.71	29.34	20.74	14.74	10.52	7.55	5.44	3.94	8
9	120.82	84.03	58.77	41.33	29.22	20.77	14.84	10.65	7.68	5.56	4.05	9
10	117.81	82.38	57.93	40.95	29.11	20.80	14.93	10.77	7.81	5.68	4.16	10
11	114.87	80.76	57.09	40.58	29.00	20.82	15.03	10.90	7.94	5.81	4.27	11
12	112.01	79.17	56.27	40.21	28.88	20.85	15.13	11.03	8.07	5.94	4.39	12
13	109.22	77.62	55.46	39.84	28.77	20.88	15.23	11.16	8.21	6.07	4.50	13
14	106.50	76.10	54.67	39.48	28.66	20.91	15.33	11.29	8.35	6.20	4.63	14
15	103.85	74.61	53.88	39.12	28.55	20.94	15.43	11.42	8.49	6.34	4.75	15
16	101.27	73.15	53.11	38.77	28.44	20.96	15.53	11.55	8.63	6.48	4.88	16
17	98.76	71.72	52.36	38.42	28.33	20.99	15.63	11.69	8.78	6.62	5.02	17
18	96.32	70.32	51.61	38.07	28.23	21.03	15.74	11.83	8.93	6.77	5.15	18
19	93.94	68.96	50.88	37.74	28.12	21.06	15.84	11.97	9.08	6.92	5.30	19
20	91.64	67.63	50.17	37.41	28.02	21.09	15.95	12.11	9.24	7.08	5.44	20
21	89.39	66.33	49.47	37.08	27.92	21.13	16.06	12.26	9.40	7.23	5.59	21
22	87.18	65.04	48.77	36.75	27.82	21.16	16.17	12.41	9.56	7.40	5.74	22
23	85.02	63.77	48.08	36.42	27.72	21.19	16.28	12.55	9.72	7.56	5.90	23
24	82.92	62.54	47.40	36.09	27.62	21.23	16.39	12.70	9.89	7.73	6.06	24
25	80.88	61.33	46.73	35.78	27.52	21.26	16.50	12.86	10.06	7.90	6.23	25
26	78.91	60.15	46.08	35.46	27.42	21.30	16.61	13.01	10.23	8.08	6.40	26
27	76.98	59.00	45.44	35.16	27.33	21.34	16.73	13.17	10.41	8.26	6.58	27
28	75.09	57.86	44.80	34.85	27.23	21.37	16.84	13.33	10.59	8.45	6.76	28
29	73.23	56.74	44.17	34.54	27.13	21.41	16.96	13.49	10.77	8.63	6.95	29
30	71.44	55.65	43.55	34.24	27.04	21.44	17.08	13.65	10.96	8.83	7.14	30
31	69.70	54.59	42.95	33.95	26.95	21.48	17.20	13.82	11.15	9.03	7.34	31
32	68.02	53.56	42.37	33.66	26.86	21.53	17.32	13.99	11.35	9.23	7.54	32
33	66.40	52.56	41.80	33.39	26.79	21.58	17.45	14.17	11.55	9.45	7.75	33
34	64.81	51.58	41.24	33.12	26.71	21.63	17.58	14.35	11.76	9.66	7.97	34
35	63.25	50.61	40.68	32.84	26.63	21.67	17.71	14.53	11.96	9.89	8.20	35
36	61.74	49.67	40.14	32.58	26.55	21.72	17.85	14.72	12.18	10.11	8.43	36
37	60.27	48.75	39.60	32.31	26.47	21.78	17.98	14.90	12.40	10.35	8.66	37
38	58.83	47.84	39.07	32.05	26.40	21.83	18.12	15.09	12.62	10.58	8.91	38
39	57.42	46.95	38.55	31.79	26.32	21.88	18.25	15.28	12.84	10.83	9.16	39
40	56.04	46.07	38.03	31.53	26.24	21.93	18.39	15.48	13.07	11.08	9.42	40
41	54.71	45.22	37.53	31.28	26.17	21.98	18.53	15.68	13.31	11.33	9.68	41
42	53.42	44.38	37.04	31.03	26.10	22.03	18.67	15.88	13.55	11.60	9.96	42
43	52.16	43.57	36.55	30.79	26.03	22.09	18.82	16.09	13.80	11.87	10.24	43
44	50.93	42.78	36.08	30.55	25.97	22.15	18.97	16.30	14.05	12.15	10.54	44
45	49.74	42.01	35.62	30.32	25.91	22.22	19.12	16.51	14.31	12.44	10.84	45
46	48.58	41.25	35.16	30.09	25.85	22.28	19.28	16.73	14.57	12.73	11.15	46
47	47.46	40.51	34.72	29.87	25.79	22.35	19.44	16.96	14.84	13.03	11.48	47
48	46.37	39.80	34.29	29.65	25.74	22.42	19.60	17.19	15.12	13.35	11.81	48
49	45.32	39.10	33.87	29.45	25.70	22.50	19.77	17.43	15.41	13.67	12.16	49
50	44.30	38.43	33.47	29.26	25.66	22.59	19.95	17.68	15.71	14.01	12.52	50
51	43.33	37.79	33.09	29.07	25.64	22.69	20.14	17.94	16.03	14.36	12.90	51
52	42.39	37.17	32.72	28.91	25.62	22.79	20.34	18.21	16.35	14.72	13.30	52
53	41.49	36.58	32.37	28.75	25.62	22.91	20.55	18.49	16.69	15.11	13.71	53
54	40.63	36.01	32.04	28.61	25.63	23.04	20.77	18.79	17.04	15.50	14.14	54
55	39.81	35.48	31.73	28.48	25.65	23.18	21.01	19.10	17.41	15.92	14.60	55
56	39.03	34.97	31.45	28.37	25.69	23.33	21.26	19.43	17.80	16.36	15.07	56
57	38.29	34.49	31.18	28.28	25.74	23.50	21.52	19.77	18.21	16.82	15.57	57
58	37.56	34.02	30.92	28.20	25.80	23.68	21.79	20.12	18.63	17.29	16.09	58
59	36.86	33.56	30.67	28.12	25.86	23.86	22.07	20.49	19.06	17.79	16.64	59
60	36.17	33.12	30.42	28.04	25.92	24.04	22.36	20.86	19.51	18.30	17.20	60

Table 20 Multipliers for loss of pension commencing age 60 (females)

Age at date of trial	Multiplier calculated with allowance for projected mortality from the 2008-based population projections and rate of return of											Age at date of trial
	−2.0%	−1.5%	−1.0%	−0.5%	0.0%	0.5%	1.0%	1.5%	2.0%	2.5%	3.0%	
0	169.99	112.01	74.27	49.55	33.26	22.45	15.24	10.40	7.14	4.92	3.41	0
1	166.62	110.38	73.58	49.35	33.30	22.59	15.42	10.58	7.30	5.06	3.52	1
2	162.64	108.33	72.60	48.95	33.20	22.65	15.53	10.71	7.43	5.17	3.62	2
3	158.74	106.30	71.62	48.55	33.10	22.70	15.65	10.85	7.56	5.29	3.72	3
4	154.93	104.31	70.66	48.15	33.00	22.75	15.77	10.98	7.69	5.41	3.83	4
5	151.21	102.36	69.71	47.75	32.90	22.80	15.88	11.12	7.83	5.54	3.93	5
6	147.57	100.43	68.76	47.36	32.80	22.85	16.00	11.26	7.97	5.66	4.04	6
7	144.01	98.54	67.83	46.96	32.70	22.89	16.11	11.40	8.11	5.79	4.16	7
8	140.54	96.68	66.91	46.57	32.60	22.94	16.23	11.54	8.25	5.92	4.27	8
9	137.14	94.85	65.99	46.18	32.49	22.99	16.35	11.69	8.39	6.06	4.39	9
10	133.83	93.06	65.09	45.79	32.39	23.03	16.47	11.83	8.54	6.20	4.51	10
11	130.60	91.31	64.21	45.41	32.29	23.08	16.59	11.98	8.69	6.34	4.64	11
12	127.45	89.58	63.33	45.02	32.18	23.13	16.71	12.13	8.84	6.48	4.77	12
13	124.36	87.89	62.47	44.65	32.08	23.17	16.83	12.28	9.00	6.63	4.90	13
14	121.36	86.23	61.62	44.27	31.98	23.22	16.95	12.43	9.16	6.78	5.04	14
15	118.43	84.60	60.77	43.90	31.88	23.27	17.07	12.58	9.32	6.93	5.18	15
16	115.57	83.00	59.95	43.53	31.78	23.31	17.19	12.74	9.48	7.09	5.32	16
17	112.78	81.44	59.13	43.16	31.67	23.36	17.32	12.90	9.65	7.25	5.47	17
18	110.06	79.90	58.33	42.80	31.58	23.41	17.44	13.06	9.82	7.42	5.62	18
19	107.41	78.40	57.53	42.45	31.48	23.46	17.57	13.22	9.99	7.58	5.78	19
20	104.83	76.93	56.76	42.10	31.38	23.51	17.70	13.38	10.17	7.76	5.94	20
21	102.32	75.49	55.99	41.75	31.29	23.56	17.83	13.55	10.35	7.93	6.11	21
22	99.85	74.07	55.23	41.40	31.19	23.61	17.96	13.72	10.53	8.12	6.28	22
23	97.44	72.67	54.48	41.05	31.09	23.66	18.09	13.89	10.71	8.30	6.45	23
24	95.08	71.29	53.73	40.70	30.99	23.70	18.22	14.06	10.90	8.49	6.63	24
25	92.79	69.95	53.00	40.36	30.89	23.75	18.35	14.24	11.09	8.68	6.82	25
26	90.55	68.63	52.28	40.03	30.79	23.80	18.48	14.41	11.29	8.88	7.01	26
27	88.37	67.34	51.57	39.69	30.70	23.85	18.62	14.59	11.49	9.08	7.20	27
28	86.24	66.07	50.87	39.36	30.60	23.90	18.75	14.77	11.69	9.29	7.41	28
29	84.17	64.83	50.18	39.03	30.51	23.95	18.89	14.96	11.90	9.50	7.61	29
30	82.15	63.61	49.50	38.71	30.41	24.00	19.03	15.15	12.11	9.71	7.83	30
31	80.18	62.43	48.84	38.39	30.32	24.05	19.17	15.34	12.32	9.94	8.04	31
32	78.27	61.26	48.19	38.08	30.23	24.11	19.31	15.53	12.54	10.16	8.27	32
33	76.40	60.12	47.54	37.77	30.14	24.16	19.45	15.72	12.76	10.40	8.50	33
34	74.57	59.00	46.90	37.46	30.05	24.22	19.60	15.92	12.99	10.64	8.74	34
35	72.79	57.90	46.27	37.15	29.96	24.27	19.74	16.12	13.22	10.88	8.99	35
36	71.05	56.82	45.66	36.85	29.88	24.33	19.89	16.33	13.45	11.13	9.24	36
37	69.36	55.77	45.05	36.55	29.79	24.38	20.04	16.53	13.69	11.38	9.50	37
38	67.71	54.73	44.45	36.26	29.71	24.44	20.19	16.74	13.94	11.65	9.77	38
39	66.10	53.72	43.86	35.97	29.62	24.50	20.34	16.96	14.19	11.92	10.04	39
40	64.53	52.73	43.28	35.68	29.54	24.56	20.50	17.17	14.44	12.19	10.32	40
41	63.00	51.75	42.70	35.39	29.46	24.62	20.65	17.39	14.70	12.47	10.62	41
42	61.51	50.80	42.14	35.11	29.38	24.68	20.81	17.62	14.97	12.76	10.92	42
43	60.06	49.87	41.59	34.84	29.30	24.74	20.97	17.85	15.24	13.06	11.23	43
44	58.65	48.97	41.06	34.57	29.23	24.81	21.14	18.08	15.52	13.36	11.55	44
45	57.28	48.08	40.53	34.31	29.16	24.88	21.31	18.32	15.80	13.68	11.88	45
46	55.95	47.21	40.01	34.05	29.09	24.95	21.48	18.56	16.09	14.00	12.22	46
47	54.65	46.37	39.50	33.79	29.02	25.02	21.65	18.81	16.39	14.33	12.57	47
48	53.40	45.55	39.01	33.55	28.97	25.10	21.84	19.06	16.70	14.67	12.94	48
49	52.19	44.75	38.54	33.32	28.92	25.19	22.03	19.33	17.01	15.03	13.32	49
50	51.01	43.98	38.07	33.09	28.87	25.28	22.22	19.60	17.34	15.39	13.71	50
51	49.86	43.22	37.62	32.87	28.83	25.38	22.42	19.87	17.67	15.77	14.11	51
52	48.76	42.49	37.17	32.65	28.79	25.47	22.62	20.16	18.02	16.16	14.53	52
53	47.68	41.78	36.75	32.45	28.76	25.58	22.83	20.45	18.38	16.56	14.97	53
54	46.65	41.09	36.34	32.26	28.74	25.70	23.06	20.76	18.74	16.98	15.43	54
55	45.65	40.43	35.94	32.08	28.73	25.82	23.29	21.07	19.13	17.41	15.90	55
56	44.69	39.79	35.57	31.91	28.73	25.95	23.53	21.40	19.52	17.86	16.39	56
57	43.76	39.18	35.20	31.75	28.73	26.09	23.78	21.74	19.93	18.33	16.91	57
58	42.86	38.57	34.85	31.59	28.74	26.24	24.04	22.09	20.35	18.81	17.44	58
59	41.98	37.99	34.50	31.44	28.76	26.39	24.30	22.44	20.79	19.31	17.99	59
60	41.12	37.41	34.16	31.30	28.78	26.55	24.57	22.81	21.24	19.83	18.57	60

Table 21 Multipliers for loss of pension commencing age 65 (males)

Age at date of trial	Multiplier calculated with allowance for projected mortality from the 2008-based population projections and rate of return of											Age at date of trial
	–2.0%	–1.5%	–1.0%	–0.5%	0.0%	0.5%	1.0%	1.5%	2.0%	2.5%	3.0%	
0	134.16	87.81	57.78	38.22	25.41	16.98	11.40	7.69	5.21	3.54	2.42	0
1	131.46	86.50	57.23	38.06	25.44	17.08	11.53	7.82	5.32	3.64	2.50	1
2	128.17	84.80	56.40	37.70	25.33	17.10	11.60	7.91	5.41	3.72	2.57	2
3	124.95	83.11	55.57	37.35	25.23	17.12	11.67	8.00	5.50	3.80	2.64	3
4	121.80	81.45	54.76	37.00	25.12	17.14	11.75	8.09	5.59	3.88	2.71	4
5	118.72	79.82	53.95	36.64	25.01	17.15	11.82	8.18	5.68	3.97	2.78	5
6	115.71	78.22	53.15	36.29	24.90	17.17	11.89	8.27	5.78	4.05	2.85	6
7	112.78	76.65	52.36	35.95	24.80	17.18	11.96	8.36	5.87	4.14	2.93	7
8	109.92	75.11	51.59	35.60	24.69	17.20	12.03	8.46	5.97	4.23	3.01	8
9	107.13	73.60	50.82	35.26	24.58	17.21	12.11	8.55	6.07	4.32	3.09	9
10	104.40	72.11	50.06	34.91	24.47	17.22	12.18	8.65	6.17	4.41	3.17	10
11	101.74	70.65	49.31	34.57	24.36	17.23	12.25	8.74	6.27	4.51	3.26	11
12	99.15	69.23	48.57	34.24	24.25	17.25	12.32	8.84	6.37	4.60	3.34	12
13	96.62	67.83	47.84	33.91	24.14	17.26	12.39	8.94	6.47	4.70	3.43	13
14	94.16	66.46	47.13	33.58	24.03	17.27	12.47	9.04	6.58	4.80	3.52	14
15	91.77	65.12	46.43	33.25	23.92	17.28	12.54	9.14	6.68	4.91	3.62	15
16	89.44	63.81	45.74	32.93	23.82	17.30	12.62	9.24	6.79	5.01	3.71	16
17	87.17	62.53	45.06	32.61	23.71	17.31	12.69	9.34	6.90	5.12	3.81	17
18	84.97	61.27	44.39	32.30	23.61	17.33	12.77	9.45	7.02	5.23	3.91	18
19	82.83	60.05	43.74	32.00	23.51	17.34	12.85	9.55	7.13	5.34	4.02	19
20	80.75	58.86	43.10	31.70	23.41	17.36	12.93	9.66	7.25	5.46	4.13	20
21	78.72	57.69	42.47	31.40	23.31	17.38	13.01	9.77	7.37	5.58	4.24	21
22	76.73	56.54	41.84	31.10	23.21	17.39	13.09	9.88	7.49	5.70	4.35	22
23	74.79	55.40	41.22	30.80	23.11	17.41	13.17	9.99	7.61	5.82	4.47	23
24	72.90	54.29	40.61	30.51	23.01	17.42	13.25	10.11	7.74	5.95	4.59	24
25	71.06	53.21	40.01	30.22	22.91	17.44	13.33	10.22	7.87	6.08	4.71	25
26	69.28	52.16	39.43	29.94	22.82	17.46	13.41	10.34	8.00	6.21	4.83	26
27	67.55	51.13	38.86	29.66	22.73	17.48	13.50	10.46	8.13	6.34	4.97	27
28	65.85	50.11	38.29	29.38	22.63	17.50	13.58	10.58	8.26	6.48	5.10	28
29	64.18	49.10	37.72	29.10	22.53	17.51	13.66	10.69	8.40	6.62	5.23	29
30	62.57	48.13	37.17	28.82	22.44	17.53	13.75	10.82	8.54	6.76	5.38	30
31	61.01	47.18	36.64	28.56	22.35	17.55	13.83	10.94	8.68	6.91	5.52	31
32	59.50	46.27	36.12	28.30	22.26	17.58	13.93	11.07	8.83	7.07	5.67	32
33	58.05	45.38	35.61	28.06	22.18	17.61	14.02	11.20	8.98	7.22	5.83	33
34	56.62	44.50	35.11	27.81	22.10	17.63	14.12	11.34	9.14	7.38	5.99	34
35	55.23	43.64	34.61	27.56	22.02	17.66	14.21	11.47	9.29	7.55	6.15	35
36	53.87	42.80	34.13	27.32	21.94	17.69	14.31	11.61	9.45	7.72	6.32	36
37	52.56	41.97	33.65	27.08	21.87	17.72	14.41	11.75	9.61	7.89	6.49	37
38	51.26	41.16	33.18	26.84	21.79	17.75	14.50	11.89	9.78	8.07	6.67	38
39	50.00	40.37	32.71	26.60	21.71	17.77	14.60	12.03	9.95	8.24	6.85	39
40	48.77	39.59	32.25	26.36	21.63	17.80	14.70	12.18	10.12	8.43	7.04	40
41	47.58	38.83	31.80	26.13	21.55	17.83	14.80	12.32	10.29	8.62	7.24	41
42	46.42	38.09	31.36	25.91	21.48	17.86	14.90	12.47	10.47	8.81	7.44	42
43	45.30	37.36	30.93	25.69	21.41	17.90	15.01	12.63	10.65	9.01	7.64	43
44	44.21	36.66	30.51	25.47	21.34	17.93	15.12	12.78	10.84	9.21	7.86	44
45	43.15	35.97	30.09	25.26	21.27	17.97	15.23	12.94	11.03	9.43	8.08	45
46	42.11	35.30	29.69	25.05	21.21	18.01	15.34	13.10	11.22	9.64	8.30	46
47	41.11	34.64	29.29	24.85	21.15	18.05	15.46	13.27	11.42	9.86	8.54	47
48	40.14	34.01	28.91	24.65	21.09	18.10	15.57	13.44	11.63	10.09	8.78	48
49	39.20	33.39	28.53	24.46	21.04	18.15	15.70	13.62	11.84	10.33	9.03	49
50	38.29	32.79	28.18	24.28	20.99	18.20	15.83	13.80	12.07	10.58	9.29	50
51	37.42	32.22	27.83	24.11	20.96	18.27	15.97	13.99	12.29	10.83	9.56	51
52	36.58	31.67	27.50	23.96	20.93	18.34	16.11	14.19	12.53	11.10	9.85	52
53	35.78	31.14	27.19	23.81	20.91	18.41	16.26	14.40	12.78	11.37	10.15	53
54	35.01	30.64	26.89	23.67	20.90	18.50	16.42	14.62	13.04	11.66	10.46	54
55	34.28	30.15	26.61	23.55	20.90	18.60	16.59	14.85	13.31	11.97	10.78	55
56	33.59	29.70	26.35	23.44	20.91	18.71	16.78	15.09	13.60	12.29	11.13	56
57	32.92	29.27	26.10	23.35	20.94	18.83	16.97	15.34	13.90	12.62	11.49	57
58	32.28	28.85	25.87	23.26	20.97	18.95	17.18	15.60	14.21	12.97	11.86	58
59	31.65	28.44	25.64	23.17	21.00	19.08	17.38	15.87	14.53	13.32	12.25	59
60	31.03	28.04	25.41	23.09	21.03	19.21	17.59	16.14	14.85	13.69	12.65	60
61	30.43	27.65	25.19	23.01	21.07	19.35	17.81	16.43	15.19	14.08	13.07	61
62	29.87	27.28	24.99	22.94	21.12	19.50	18.04	16.73	15.55	14.48	13.51	62
63	29.34	26.94	24.81	22.90	21.20	19.67	18.29	17.05	15.93	14.91	13.98	63
64	28.85	26.63	24.65	22.88	21.29	19.86	18.56	17.39	16.33	15.37	14.49	64
65	28.40	26.37	24.54	22.90	21.42	20.08	18.87	17.77	16.77	15.86	15.03	65

Table 22 Multipliers for loss of pension commencing age 65 (females)

Age at date of trial	Multiplier calculated with allowance for projected mortality from the 2008-based population projections and rate of return of											Age at date of trial
	−2.0%	−1.5%	−1.0%	−0.5%	0.0%	0.5%	1.0%	1.5%	2.0%	2.5%	3.0%	
0	153.09	99.71	65.31	43.01	28.47	18.95	12.67	8.52	5.75	3.90	2.66	0
1	149.98	98.22	64.68	42.82	28.50	19.06	12.81	8.66	5.87	4.00	2.74	1
2	146.34	96.35	63.78	42.45	28.40	19.10	12.90	8.76	5.98	4.09	2.82	2
3	142.77	94.51	62.90	42.08	28.30	19.13	12.99	8.87	6.08	4.19	2.90	3
4	139.29	92.70	62.02	41.72	28.21	19.16	13.08	8.98	6.18	4.28	2.98	4
5	135.88	90.92	61.16	41.36	28.11	19.20	13.17	9.08	6.29	4.38	3.06	5
6	132.55	89.17	60.30	40.99	28.01	19.23	13.26	9.19	6.40	4.47	3.14	6
7	129.30	87.45	59.46	40.63	27.91	19.26	13.35	9.30	6.51	4.57	3.23	7
8	126.13	85.76	58.62	40.27	27.81	19.29	13.45	9.41	6.62	4.68	3.32	8
9	123.03	84.10	57.80	39.92	27.70	19.32	13.54	9.53	6.73	4.78	3.41	9
10	120.00	82.48	56.98	39.56	27.60	19.35	13.63	9.64	6.85	4.89	3.50	10
11	117.06	80.89	56.18	39.21	27.50	19.38	13.72	9.75	6.97	4.99	3.60	11
12	114.18	79.32	55.39	38.87	27.40	19.41	13.81	9.87	7.08	5.11	3.69	12
13	111.37	77.79	54.61	38.52	27.30	19.44	13.90	9.99	7.20	5.22	3.79	13
14	108.63	76.28	53.84	38.18	27.20	19.47	14.00	10.11	7.33	5.33	3.90	14
15	105.96	74.81	53.08	37.84	27.10	19.50	14.09	10.23	7.45	5.45	4.00	15
16	103.35	73.36	52.33	37.50	27.00	19.53	14.19	10.35	7.58	5.57	4.11	16
17	100.81	71.94	51.59	37.17	26.90	19.56	14.28	10.47	7.71	5.70	4.23	17
18	98.33	70.55	50.86	36.84	26.80	19.59	14.38	10.60	7.84	5.82	4.34	18
19	95.92	69.19	50.15	36.52	26.71	19.62	14.47	10.72	7.97	5.95	4.46	19
20	93.58	67.87	49.45	36.20	26.61	19.65	14.57	10.85	8.11	6.09	4.58	20
21	91.29	66.56	48.76	35.88	26.52	19.69	14.67	10.98	8.25	6.22	4.71	21
22	89.05	65.28	48.07	35.56	26.42	19.72	14.77	11.11	8.39	6.36	4.84	22
23	86.86	64.01	47.39	35.24	26.32	19.74	14.87	11.24	8.53	6.50	4.97	23
24	84.71	62.77	46.72	34.93	26.23	19.77	14.97	11.38	8.68	6.65	5.11	24
25	82.63	61.55	46.06	34.62	26.13	19.80	15.07	11.51	8.83	6.79	5.25	25
26	80.60	60.37	45.41	34.31	26.03	19.83	15.17	11.65	8.98	6.94	5.39	26
27	78.62	59.20	44.77	34.01	25.94	19.86	15.27	11.79	9.13	7.10	5.54	27
28	76.69	58.06	44.14	33.71	25.84	19.89	15.38	11.93	9.29	7.26	5.69	28
29	74.81	56.94	43.52	33.41	25.75	19.93	15.48	12.07	9.44	7.42	5.84	29
30	72.98	55.84	42.91	33.12	25.66	19.96	15.58	12.21	9.61	7.58	6.00	30
31	71.20	54.77	42.32	32.83	25.57	19.99	15.69	12.36	9.77	7.75	6.17	31
32	69.46	53.73	41.73	32.54	25.48	20.03	15.80	12.51	9.94	7.92	6.34	32
33	67.77	52.70	41.15	32.26	25.39	20.06	15.91	12.66	10.11	8.10	6.51	33
34	66.12	51.69	40.58	31.98	25.30	20.09	16.02	12.81	10.28	8.28	6.69	34
35	64.50	50.70	40.01	31.70	25.21	20.13	16.13	12.97	10.46	8.47	6.88	35
36	62.93	49.73	39.45	31.43	25.13	20.16	16.24	13.12	10.64	8.66	7.06	36
37	61.41	48.78	38.91	31.15	25.04	20.20	16.35	13.28	10.83	8.85	7.26	37
38	59.91	47.85	38.37	30.89	24.95	20.23	16.47	13.44	11.01	9.05	7.46	38
39	58.46	46.94	37.84	30.62	24.87	20.27	16.58	13.61	11.20	9.25	7.67	39
40	57.04	46.05	37.32	30.36	24.79	20.31	16.70	13.77	11.40	9.46	7.88	40
41	55.66	45.17	36.80	30.10	24.70	20.35	16.81	13.94	11.60	9.67	8.10	41
42	54.31	44.32	36.30	29.84	24.62	20.38	16.93	14.11	11.80	9.89	8.32	42
43	53.01	43.48	35.81	29.59	24.54	20.43	17.05	14.29	12.00	10.12	8.55	43
44	51.74	42.67	35.33	29.35	24.47	20.47	17.18	14.46	12.22	10.35	8.79	44
45	50.50	41.88	34.85	29.11	24.40	20.51	17.31	14.65	12.43	10.58	9.04	45
46	49.30	41.10	34.39	28.87	24.32	20.56	17.44	14.83	12.65	10.83	9.29	46
47	48.13	40.34	33.93	28.64	24.26	20.61	17.57	15.02	12.88	11.08	9.55	47
48	47.00	39.61	33.49	28.42	24.19	20.66	17.70	15.22	13.11	11.33	9.82	48
49	45.91	38.89	33.06	28.20	24.14	20.72	17.85	15.42	13.35	11.60	10.10	49
50	44.85	38.20	32.64	27.99	24.08	20.78	17.99	15.62	13.60	11.88	10.40	50
51	43.82	37.52	32.23	27.79	24.03	20.85	18.14	15.83	13.85	12.16	10.70	51
52	42.82	36.86	31.84	27.59	23.99	20.92	18.29	16.05	14.12	12.45	11.01	52
53	41.85	36.22	31.45	27.40	23.95	20.99	18.45	16.27	14.38	12.75	11.33	53
54	40.92	35.60	31.08	27.22	23.91	21.07	18.62	16.50	14.66	13.06	11.67	54
55	40.02	35.01	30.73	27.05	23.89	21.16	18.80	16.74	14.95	13.39	12.02	55
56	39.16	34.44	30.38	26.89	23.87	21.26	18.98	16.99	15.25	13.73	12.38	56
57	38.32	33.88	30.05	26.74	23.86	21.36	19.17	17.25	15.56	14.08	12.76	57
58	37.51	33.34	29.73	26.59	23.86	21.46	19.36	17.51	15.88	14.44	13.16	58
59	36.72	32.81	29.42	26.45	23.85	21.57	19.56	17.78	16.21	14.81	13.56	59
60	35.94	32.29	29.10	26.31	23.85	21.68	19.76	18.06	16.54	15.19	13.98	60
61	35.18	31.78	28.80	26.17	23.85	21.79	19.97	18.34	16.89	15.59	14.42	61
62	34.46	31.29	28.51	26.04	23.86	21.91	20.18	18.63	17.25	16.00	14.87	62
63	33.76	30.83	28.23	25.93	23.88	22.05	20.41	18.94	17.62	16.43	15.35	63
64	33.10	30.39	27.98	25.83	23.92	22.20	20.66	19.27	18.02	16.89	15.86	64
65	32.50	29.99	27.76	25.77	23.98	22.38	20.93	19.63	18.45	17.38	16.40	65

Table 23 Multipliers for loss of pension commencing age 70 (males)

Age at date of trial	Multiplier calculated with allowance for projected mortality from the 2008-based population projections and rate of return of											Age at date of trial
	–2.0%	–1.5%	–1.0%	–0.5%	0.0%	0.5%	1.0%	1.5%	2.0%	2.5%	3.0%	
0	116.52	75.30	48.89	31.89	20.90	13.76	9.09	6.04	4.02	2.69	1.81	0
1	114.10	74.13	48.39	31.74	20.91	13.83	9.19	6.13	4.11	2.76	1.87	1
2	111.17	72.62	47.66	31.42	20.81	13.84	9.24	6.20	4.17	2.82	1.91	2
3	108.30	71.12	46.93	31.10	20.70	13.84	9.29	6.27	4.24	2.88	1.96	3
4	105.50	69.65	46.20	30.78	20.60	13.85	9.34	6.33	4.31	2.94	2.02	4
5	102.76	68.21	45.49	30.47	20.50	13.85	9.39	6.40	4.37	3.00	2.07	5
6	100.08	66.80	44.78	30.16	20.39	13.85	9.44	6.46	4.44	3.06	2.12	6
7	97.48	65.41	44.09	29.84	20.29	13.85	9.49	6.53	4.51	3.13	2.18	7
8	94.95	64.05	43.40	29.54	20.19	13.85	9.54	6.60	4.58	3.19	2.23	8
9	92.47	62.71	42.72	29.23	20.08	13.85	9.59	6.67	4.65	3.26	2.29	9
10	90.04	61.40	42.05	28.92	19.97	13.85	9.64	6.74	4.73	3.33	2.35	10
11	87.69	60.11	41.39	28.62	19.87	13.85	9.69	6.81	4.80	3.39	2.41	11
12	85.39	58.86	40.74	28.32	19.76	13.85	9.74	6.88	4.87	3.46	2.47	12
13	83.16	57.63	40.10	28.02	19.66	13.85	9.79	6.95	4.95	3.54	2.54	13
14	80.98	56.42	39.47	27.73	19.56	13.85	9.84	7.02	5.02	3.61	2.60	14
15	78.87	55.24	38.85	27.44	19.45	13.85	9.89	7.09	5.10	3.68	2.67	15
16	76.81	54.09	38.25	27.15	19.35	13.85	9.94	7.16	5.18	3.76	2.74	16
17	74.80	52.96	37.65	26.87	19.25	13.85	9.99	7.24	5.26	3.84	2.81	17
18	72.86	51.86	37.06	26.59	19.15	13.85	10.05	7.31	5.34	3.92	2.88	18
19	70.97	50.79	36.49	26.32	19.06	13.85	10.10	7.39	5.43	4.00	2.95	19
20	69.13	49.74	35.93	26.05	18.96	13.85	10.15	7.47	5.51	4.08	3.03	20
21	67.34	48.71	35.38	25.79	18.87	13.85	10.21	7.55	5.60	4.17	3.11	21
22	65.59	47.70	34.82	25.52	18.77	13.85	10.26	7.63	5.69	4.25	3.19	22
23	63.88	46.71	34.28	25.25	18.67	13.85	10.31	7.70	5.77	4.34	3.27	23
24	62.22	45.74	33.75	24.99	18.58	13.85	10.37	7.78	5.86	4.43	3.36	24
25	60.60	44.79	33.22	24.74	18.48	13.86	10.42	7.87	5.96	4.52	3.44	25
26	59.04	43.87	32.71	24.48	18.39	13.86	10.48	7.95	6.05	4.62	3.53	26
27	57.52	42.97	32.21	24.24	18.30	13.86	10.54	8.03	6.14	4.71	3.63	27
28	56.02	42.07	31.71	23.99	18.21	13.86	10.59	8.12	6.24	4.81	3.72	28
29	54.56	41.20	31.22	23.74	18.11	13.86	10.65	8.20	6.34	4.91	3.82	29
30	53.15	40.34	30.73	23.49	18.02	13.87	10.70	8.29	6.44	5.01	3.92	30
31	51.78	39.52	30.27	23.26	17.93	13.87	10.76	8.38	6.54	5.12	4.02	31
32	50.46	38.72	29.81	23.03	17.85	13.88	10.82	8.47	6.64	5.23	4.12	32
33	49.19	37.94	29.37	22.81	17.77	13.89	10.89	8.56	6.75	5.34	4.23	33
34	47.94	37.18	28.93	22.59	17.69	13.90	10.95	8.66	6.86	5.45	4.35	34
35	46.72	36.43	28.50	22.37	17.61	13.91	11.02	8.75	6.97	5.57	4.46	35
36	45.54	35.70	28.08	22.15	17.53	13.92	11.08	8.85	7.08	5.69	4.58	36
37	44.39	34.98	27.66	21.94	17.45	13.93	11.15	8.95	7.20	5.81	4.70	37
38	43.26	34.27	27.24	21.72	17.37	13.94	11.21	9.04	7.32	5.93	4.82	38
39	42.16	33.58	26.84	21.51	17.30	13.95	11.28	9.14	7.43	6.06	4.95	39
40	41.09	32.90	26.43	21.30	17.22	13.95	11.34	9.24	7.55	6.19	5.08	40
41	40.05	32.24	26.04	21.10	17.14	13.97	11.41	9.35	7.68	6.32	5.22	41
42	39.04	31.60	25.66	20.90	17.07	13.98	11.48	9.45	7.80	6.46	5.36	42
43	38.06	30.97	25.28	20.70	16.99	13.99	11.55	9.56	7.93	6.60	5.50	43
44	37.11	30.36	24.92	20.51	16.92	14.01	11.62	9.67	8.06	6.74	5.65	44
45	36.18	29.76	24.56	20.32	16.85	14.02	11.69	9.78	8.20	6.89	5.80	45
46	35.28	29.18	24.20	20.13	16.79	14.04	11.77	9.89	8.33	7.04	5.96	46
47	34.41	28.61	23.86	19.95	16.72	14.06	11.85	10.01	8.47	7.19	6.12	47
48	33.57	28.06	23.52	19.77	16.66	14.08	11.92	10.13	8.62	7.35	6.29	48
49	32.75	27.52	23.19	19.60	16.60	14.10	12.01	10.25	8.77	7.52	6.46	49
50	31.96	27.01	22.88	19.43	16.55	14.13	12.09	10.38	8.92	7.69	6.64	50
51	31.21	26.51	22.58	19.28	16.51	14.17	12.19	10.51	9.08	7.87	6.83	51
52	30.48	26.03	22.29	19.13	16.47	14.21	12.28	10.65	9.25	8.05	7.02	52
53	29.79	25.57	22.01	19.00	16.43	14.25	12.39	10.79	9.42	8.24	7.23	53
54	29.12	25.13	21.75	18.87	16.41	14.30	12.50	10.94	9.60	8.44	7.44	54
55	28.48	24.71	21.50	18.75	16.39	14.36	12.61	11.10	9.79	8.65	7.66	55
56	27.88	24.32	21.27	18.65	16.39	14.43	12.74	11.27	9.99	8.88	7.90	56
57	27.30	23.94	21.05	18.55	16.39	14.51	12.88	11.45	10.20	9.11	8.15	57
58	26.74	23.58	20.84	18.46	16.40	14.59	13.02	11.63	10.42	9.35	8.40	58
59	26.19	23.22	20.63	18.38	16.40	14.68	13.16	11.82	10.64	9.59	8.67	59
60	25.65	22.86	20.42	18.29	16.41	14.76	13.30	12.01	10.86	9.85	8.94	60
61	25.13	22.52	20.22	18.20	16.42	14.84	13.44	12.20	11.10	10.11	9.23	61
62	24.63	22.19	20.03	18.13	16.44	14.94	13.60	12.41	11.34	10.38	9.52	62
63	24.16	21.88	19.86	18.07	16.47	15.04	13.77	12.63	11.60	10.67	9.84	63
64	23.72	21.60	19.71	18.03	16.52	15.17	13.95	12.86	11.87	10.98	10.18	64
65	23.33	21.35	19.59	18.01	16.59	15.31	14.16	13.12	12.17	11.32	10.54	65
66	22.97	21.14	19.50	18.02	16.69	15.48	14.39	13.40	12.50	11.68	10.93	66
67	22.66	20.96	19.44	18.06	16.81	15.68	14.65	13.71	12.86	12.07	11.36	67
68	22.38	20.82	19.40	18.12	16.96	15.90	14.93	14.05	13.24	12.50	11.82	68
69	22.13	20.70	19.40	18.21	17.13	16.15	15.24	14.42	13.66	12.96	12.31	69
70	21.91	20.60	19.41	18.32	17.32	16.41	15.58	14.81	14.10	13.44	12.84	70

Table 24 Multipliers for loss of pension commencing age 70 (females)

Age at date of trial	Multiplier calculated with allowance for projected mortality from the 2008-based population projections and rate of return of											Age at date of trial
	−2.0%	−1.5%	−1.0%	−0.5%	0.0%	0.5%	1.0%	1.5%	2.0%	2.5%	3.0%	
0	134.74	86.70	56.06	36.43	23.78	15.60	10.28	6.80	4.52	3.01	2.02	0
1	131.93	85.35	55.49	36.25	23.79	15.68	10.38	6.91	4.61	3.09	2.08	1
2	128.66	83.68	54.69	35.92	23.69	15.70	10.45	6.99	4.69	3.16	2.14	2
3	125.45	82.03	53.90	35.58	23.60	15.72	10.52	7.07	4.77	3.23	2.20	3
4	122.32	80.42	53.12	35.25	23.50	15.74	10.58	7.15	4.85	3.30	2.25	4
5	119.26	78.83	52.35	34.93	23.41	15.76	10.65	7.23	4.93	3.37	2.32	5
6	116.28	77.27	51.59	34.60	23.31	15.77	10.72	7.31	5.01	3.44	2.38	6
7	113.36	75.74	50.83	34.27	23.21	15.79	10.78	7.39	5.09	3.52	2.44	7
8	110.51	74.23	50.09	33.95	23.11	15.80	10.85	7.48	5.18	3.59	2.51	8
9	107.73	72.75	49.35	33.63	23.01	15.82	10.92	7.56	5.26	3.67	2.57	9
10	105.03	71.30	48.63	33.31	22.92	15.83	10.98	7.65	5.35	3.75	2.64	10
11	102.39	69.89	47.92	33.00	22.82	15.85	11.05	7.73	5.43	3.83	2.71	11
12	99.81	68.49	47.21	32.68	22.72	15.86	11.12	7.82	5.52	3.92	2.79	12
13	97.30	67.13	46.52	32.37	22.62	15.87	11.18	7.91	5.61	4.00	2.86	13
14	94.85	65.79	45.83	32.07	22.53	15.89	11.25	8.00	5.71	4.09	2.94	14
15	92.46	64.48	45.16	31.76	22.43	15.90	11.32	8.09	5.80	4.17	3.01	15
16	90.13	63.19	44.49	31.46	22.33	15.92	11.39	8.18	5.89	4.26	3.09	16
17	87.86	61.93	43.84	31.16	22.24	15.93	11.46	8.27	5.99	4.36	3.18	17
18	85.65	60.70	43.19	30.86	22.14	15.95	11.53	8.36	6.09	4.45	3.26	18
19	83.51	59.49	42.56	30.57	22.05	15.96	11.60	8.46	6.19	4.55	3.35	19
20	81.42	58.32	41.94	30.29	21.96	15.98	11.67	8.55	6.29	4.64	3.44	20
21	79.38	57.16	41.33	30.00	21.86	15.99	11.74	8.65	6.40	4.74	3.53	21
22	77.38	56.02	40.72	29.72	21.77	16.01	11.81	8.75	6.50	4.85	3.62	22
23	75.43	54.90	40.12	29.43	21.67	16.02	11.88	8.85	6.61	4.95	3.72	23
24	73.52	53.80	39.52	29.15	21.58	16.03	11.95	8.94	6.71	5.06	3.82	24
25	71.67	52.72	38.94	28.87	21.48	16.05	12.03	9.04	6.82	5.16	3.92	25
26	69.86	51.67	38.37	28.60	21.39	16.06	12.10	9.14	6.93	5.28	4.03	26
27	68.11	50.64	37.80	28.32	21.30	16.07	12.17	9.25	7.05	5.39	4.13	27
28	66.39	49.63	37.25	28.05	21.21	16.09	12.24	9.35	7.16	5.50	4.24	28
29	64.72	48.64	36.70	27.79	21.11	16.10	12.32	9.46	7.28	5.62	4.36	29
30	63.09	47.68	36.16	27.52	21.03	16.12	12.39	9.56	7.40	5.74	4.47	30
31	61.51	46.73	35.63	27.27	20.94	16.13	12.47	9.67	7.52	5.87	4.59	31
32	59.98	45.81	35.11	27.01	20.85	16.15	12.55	9.78	7.65	6.00	4.72	32
33	58.48	44.91	34.60	26.76	20.76	16.16	12.62	9.89	7.77	6.13	4.84	33
34	57.02	44.02	34.10	26.51	20.68	16.18	12.70	10.00	7.90	6.26	4.97	34
35	55.59	43.14	33.60	26.26	20.59	16.20	12.78	10.12	8.03	6.39	5.10	35
36	54.20	42.29	33.11	26.01	20.50	16.21	12.86	10.23	8.16	6.53	5.24	36
37	52.85	41.45	32.63	25.77	20.42	16.23	12.94	10.35	8.30	6.67	5.38	37
38	51.53	40.64	32.16	25.53	20.33	16.25	13.02	10.46	8.44	6.82	5.53	38
39	50.24	39.83	31.69	25.29	20.25	16.26	13.10	10.58	8.57	6.97	5.67	39
40	48.99	39.05	31.23	25.06	20.17	16.28	13.18	10.70	8.72	7.12	5.83	40
41	47.77	38.28	30.78	24.82	20.08	16.30	13.27	10.83	8.86	7.27	5.98	41
42	46.58	37.53	30.34	24.60	20.00	16.32	13.35	10.95	9.01	7.43	6.14	42
43	45.43	36.80	29.90	24.37	19.93	16.34	13.44	11.08	9.16	7.59	6.31	43
44	44.31	36.08	29.48	24.15	19.85	16.36	13.52	11.21	9.31	7.76	6.48	44
45	43.23	35.39	29.06	23.94	19.78	16.39	13.61	11.34	9.47	7.93	6.66	45
46	42.17	34.70	28.65	23.73	19.70	16.41	13.70	11.47	9.63	8.11	6.84	46
47	41.14	34.04	28.25	23.52	19.63	16.44	13.80	11.61	9.80	8.29	7.03	47
48	40.14	33.39	27.86	23.32	19.57	16.47	13.89	11.75	9.97	8.47	7.22	48
49	39.18	32.77	27.49	23.12	19.51	16.50	13.99	11.90	10.14	8.67	7.42	49
50	38.25	32.16	27.12	22.93	19.45	16.54	14.10	12.05	10.32	8.86	7.63	50
51	37.34	31.56	26.76	22.75	19.39	16.57	14.20	12.20	10.51	9.07	7.84	51
52	36.46	30.99	26.41	22.57	19.34	16.62	14.31	12.36	10.69	9.28	8.06	52
53	35.61	30.43	26.07	22.40	19.29	16.66	14.42	12.52	10.89	9.49	8.30	53
54	34.79	29.89	25.74	22.23	19.25	16.71	14.54	12.69	11.09	9.72	8.53	54
55	34.00	29.36	25.43	22.08	19.21	16.77	14.67	12.86	11.30	9.95	8.78	55
56	33.24	28.86	25.12	21.93	19.19	16.83	14.80	13.04	11.52	10.19	9.04	56
57	32.51	28.37	24.83	21.79	19.16	16.89	14.93	13.23	11.74	10.44	9.31	57
58	31.79	27.90	24.54	21.65	19.14	16.96	15.07	13.42	11.97	10.70	9.59	58
59	31.10	27.43	24.26	21.51	19.12	17.03	15.21	13.61	12.21	10.97	9.88	59
60	30.41	26.97	23.98	21.37	19.10	17.10	15.35	13.81	12.44	11.24	10.17	60
61	29.74	26.52	23.71	21.24	19.08	17.17	15.49	14.01	12.69	11.52	10.48	61
62	29.10	26.09	23.44	21.11	19.06	17.25	15.64	14.22	12.94	11.81	10.80	62
63	28.48	25.67	23.19	21.00	19.06	17.33	15.80	14.43	13.21	12.11	11.13	63
64	27.90	25.28	22.96	20.90	19.07	17.43	15.97	14.67	13.49	12.43	11.48	64
65	27.36	24.92	22.75	20.82	19.10	17.55	16.17	14.92	13.79	12.78	11.86	65
66	26.86	24.60	22.58	20.77	19.15	17.69	16.38	15.19	14.12	13.15	12.26	66
67	26.40	24.30	22.43	20.74	19.22	17.85	16.61	15.49	14.47	13.54	12.69	67
68	25.97	24.04	22.30	20.73	19.32	18.03	16.87	15.81	14.84	13.96	13.15	68
69	25.57	23.79	22.19	20.74	19.43	18.23	17.14	16.15	15.24	14.40	13.64	69
70	25.19	23.57	22.10	20.76	19.55	18.44	17.43	16.50	15.65	14.87	14.15	70

Table 25 Multipliers for loss of pension commencing age 75 (males)

Age at date of trial	Multiplier calculated with allowance for projected mortality from the 2008-based population projections and rate of return of											Age at date of trial
	–2.0%	–1.5%	–1.0%	–0.5%	0.0%	0.5%	1.0%	1.5%	2.0%	2.5%	3.0%	
0	97.81	62.36	39.93	25.68	16.58	10.74	6.99	4.57	2.99	1.97	1.30	0
1	95.69	61.34	39.49	25.52	16.56	10.79	7.06	4.63	3.05	2.02	1.34	1
2	93.15	60.03	38.85	25.24	16.47	10.79	7.09	4.68	3.10	2.06	1.37	2
3	90.66	58.74	38.22	24.97	16.37	10.78	7.12	4.73	3.15	2.10	1.41	3
4	88.23	57.47	37.59	24.69	16.28	10.77	7.16	4.77	3.19	2.14	1.44	4
5	85.86	56.23	36.98	24.41	16.18	10.76	7.19	4.82	3.24	2.19	1.48	5
6	83.55	55.01	36.37	24.14	16.08	10.75	7.22	4.86	3.29	2.23	1.52	6
7	81.31	53.82	35.77	23.86	15.98	10.74	7.25	4.91	3.33	2.27	1.55	7
8	79.12	52.65	35.18	23.59	15.88	10.73	7.28	4.95	3.38	2.32	1.59	8
9	76.97	51.50	34.59	23.32	15.79	10.72	7.31	5.00	3.43	2.36	1.63	9
10	74.89	50.37	34.02	23.06	15.69	10.71	7.34	5.05	3.48	2.41	1.67	10
11	72.85	49.27	33.45	22.79	15.59	10.70	7.37	5.09	3.53	2.46	1.71	11
12	70.88	48.19	32.89	22.53	15.49	10.69	7.40	5.14	3.58	2.50	1.76	12
13	68.96	47.14	32.34	22.27	15.39	10.67	7.43	5.19	3.63	2.55	1.80	13
14	67.09	46.10	31.80	22.02	15.29	10.66	7.46	5.23	3.68	2.60	1.84	14
15	65.27	45.10	31.27	21.76	15.20	10.65	7.49	5.28	3.74	2.65	1.89	15
16	63.50	44.11	30.75	21.51	15.10	10.64	7.52	5.33	3.79	2.71	1.94	16
17	61.78	43.15	30.24	21.27	15.01	10.63	7.55	5.38	3.85	2.76	1.98	17
18	60.12	42.21	29.74	21.03	14.92	10.62	7.58	5.43	3.90	2.81	2.03	18
19	58.50	41.29	29.25	20.79	14.82	10.61	7.61	5.48	3.96	2.87	2.08	19
20	56.93	40.40	28.77	20.55	14.74	10.60	7.65	5.53	4.02	2.92	2.13	20
21	55.40	39.52	28.29	20.32	14.65	10.59	7.68	5.59	4.08	2.98	2.19	21
22	53.90	38.66	27.82	20.09	14.55	10.58	7.71	5.64	4.13	3.04	2.24	22
23	52.44	37.81	27.36	19.86	14.46	10.57	7.74	5.69	4.19	3.10	2.30	23
24	51.02	36.99	26.90	19.63	14.37	10.55	7.77	5.74	4.25	3.16	2.35	24
25	49.64	36.18	26.46	19.41	14.28	10.54	7.81	5.80	4.31	3.22	2.41	25
26	48.31	35.40	26.02	19.19	14.20	10.53	7.84	5.85	4.38	3.29	2.47	26
27	47.02	34.64	25.60	18.98	14.11	10.52	7.87	5.91	4.44	3.35	2.53	27
28	45.74	33.88	25.17	18.76	14.02	10.51	7.90	5.96	4.51	3.42	2.60	28
29	44.50	33.14	24.75	18.54	13.93	10.50	7.94	6.01	4.57	3.48	2.66	29
30	43.30	32.41	24.34	18.33	13.85	10.49	7.97	6.07	4.64	3.55	2.73	30
31	42.14	31.71	23.94	18.13	13.76	10.48	8.00	6.13	4.70	3.62	2.79	31
32	41.02	31.04	23.56	17.93	13.69	10.48	8.04	6.19	4.77	3.69	2.86	32
33	39.94	30.38	23.18	17.74	13.61	10.47	8.08	6.25	4.85	3.77	2.94	33
34	38.89	29.74	22.81	17.54	13.53	10.47	8.12	6.31	4.92	3.84	3.01	34
35	37.86	29.10	22.44	17.35	13.45	10.46	8.15	6.37	4.99	3.92	3.09	35
36	36.86	28.49	22.08	17.16	13.38	10.46	8.19	6.43	5.07	4.00	3.16	36
37	35.88	27.88	21.73	16.98	13.30	10.45	8.23	6.50	5.14	4.08	3.24	37
38	34.93	27.29	21.38	16.79	13.23	10.44	8.27	6.56	5.22	4.16	3.33	38
39	34.00	26.71	21.03	16.61	13.15	10.44	8.31	6.62	5.30	4.24	3.41	39
40	33.10	26.14	20.69	16.43	13.07	10.43	8.34	6.69	5.38	4.33	3.49	40
41	32.22	25.58	20.36	16.25	13.00	10.43	8.38	6.75	5.46	4.42	3.58	41
42	31.38	25.04	20.04	16.07	12.93	10.42	8.42	6.82	5.54	4.51	3.67	42
43	30.55	24.51	19.72	15.90	12.86	10.42	8.46	6.89	5.62	4.60	3.77	43
44	29.75	24.00	19.41	15.73	12.79	10.42	8.50	6.96	5.71	4.69	3.86	44
45	28.98	23.50	19.10	15.57	12.72	10.41	8.55	7.03	5.79	4.79	3.96	45
46	28.22	23.01	18.80	15.41	12.65	10.41	8.59	7.10	5.88	4.88	4.06	46
47	27.49	22.53	18.51	15.25	12.59	10.41	8.63	7.17	5.97	4.99	4.17	47
48	26.78	22.07	18.23	15.09	12.52	10.41	8.68	7.25	6.07	5.09	4.28	48
49	26.10	21.62	17.95	14.94	12.46	10.42	8.73	7.33	6.16	5.20	4.39	49
50	25.44	21.18	17.68	14.80	12.41	10.43	8.78	7.41	6.26	5.31	4.50	50
51	24.80	20.77	17.43	14.66	12.36	10.44	8.83	7.49	6.37	5.42	4.62	51
52	24.20	20.37	17.18	14.53	12.31	10.45	8.89	7.58	6.48	5.54	4.75	52
53	23.61	19.98	16.95	14.41	12.27	10.47	8.96	7.67	6.59	5.67	4.88	53
54	23.05	19.61	16.72	14.29	12.23	10.50	9.02	7.77	6.70	5.80	5.02	54
55	22.52	19.26	16.51	14.18	12.20	10.53	9.09	7.87	6.83	5.93	5.16	55
56	22.01	18.93	16.31	14.08	12.18	10.56	9.17	7.98	6.96	6.08	5.31	56
57	21.53	18.61	16.12	13.99	12.17	10.60	9.26	8.10	7.09	6.23	5.47	57
58	21.06	18.30	15.94	13.91	12.16	10.65	9.34	8.21	7.23	6.38	5.64	58
59	20.60	18.00	15.76	13.82	12.15	10.69	9.43	8.33	7.38	6.54	5.81	59
60	20.15	17.70	15.58	13.73	12.13	10.74	9.52	8.45	7.52	6.70	5.98	60
61	19.71	17.41	15.40	13.65	12.12	10.78	9.61	8.58	7.67	6.87	6.16	61
62	19.29	17.13	15.23	13.57	12.12	10.84	9.71	8.71	7.83	7.04	6.35	62
63	18.89	16.86	15.08	13.51	12.12	10.89	9.81	8.85	7.99	7.23	6.55	63
64	18.52	16.62	14.94	13.45	12.13	10.96	9.92	8.99	8.16	7.42	6.76	64
65	18.18	16.40	14.82	13.41	12.16	11.05	10.05	9.16	8.35	7.63	6.99	65
66	17.87	16.21	14.73	13.40	12.21	11.15	10.20	9.34	8.56	7.86	7.23	66
67	17.60	16.04	14.65	13.40	12.28	11.27	10.36	9.53	8.79	8.11	7.50	67
68	17.35	15.90	14.60	13.42	12.37	11.41	10.54	9.75	9.03	8.38	7.78	68
69	17.12	15.78	14.56	13.46	12.47	11.56	10.73	9.98	9.30	8.67	8.09	69

continued

Table 25 Multipliers for loss of pension commencing age 75 (males) ***continued***

Age at date of trial	Multiplier calculated with allowance for projected mortality from the 2008-based population projections and rate of return of											Age at date of trial
	–2.0%	–1.5%	–1.0%	–0.5%	0.0%	0.5%	1.0%	1.5%	2.0%	2.5%	3.0%	
70	16.92	15.67	14.54	13.51	12.58	11.72	10.94	10.23	9.58	8.97	8.42	70
71	16.72	15.57	14.53	13.57	12.70	11.90	11.17	10.49	9.87	9.30	8.77	71
72	16.53	15.48	14.52	13.64	12.83	12.08	11.40	10.77	10.18	9.64	9.14	72
73	16.36	15.40	14.52	13.71	12.97	12.28	11.64	11.05	10.51	10.00	9.53	73
74	16.19	15.33	14.53	13.80	13.12	12.49	11.90	11.36	10.86	10.39	9.95	74
75	16.04	15.27	14.56	13.90	13.29	12.72	12.19	11.70	11.24	10.81	10.40	75

Table 26 Multipliers for loss of pension commencing age 75 (females)

Age at date of trial	Multiplier calculated with allowance for projected mortality from the 2008-based population projections and rate of return of											Age at date of trial
	–2.0%	–1.5%	–1.0%	–0.5%	0.0%	0.5%	1.0%	1.5%	2.0%	2.5%	3.0%	
0	114.99	73.05	46.61	29.87	19.22	12.42	8.06	5.25	3.43	2.25	1.48	0
1	112.51	71.86	46.09	29.69	19.21	12.48	8.13	5.33	3.50	2.31	1.53	1
2	109.64	70.40	45.40	29.40	19.12	12.48	8.18	5.38	3.56	2.36	1.57	2
3	106.83	68.96	44.71	29.10	19.02	12.49	8.23	5.44	3.61	2.41	1.61	3
4	104.08	67.55	44.02	28.81	18.93	12.49	8.27	5.50	3.67	2.46	1.65	4
5	101.41	66.16	43.35	28.52	18.84	12.49	8.32	5.56	3.73	2.51	1.69	5
6	98.79	64.80	42.69	28.23	18.75	12.50	8.36	5.62	3.79	2.56	1.74	6
7	96.24	63.47	42.03	27.94	18.65	12.50	8.41	5.67	3.84	2.61	1.78	7
8	93.75	62.16	41.38	27.66	18.56	12.50	8.45	5.73	3.90	2.67	1.83	8
9	91.32	60.87	40.74	27.37	18.46	12.50	8.50	5.79	3.97	2.72	1.88	9
10	88.95	59.61	40.11	27.09	18.37	12.50	8.54	5.85	4.03	2.78	1.92	10
11	86.65	58.38	39.49	26.82	18.28	12.50	8.59	5.92	4.09	2.84	1.97	11
12	84.41	57.17	38.88	26.54	18.18	12.51	8.63	5.98	4.15	2.90	2.03	12
13	82.21	55.99	38.27	26.26	18.09	12.51	8.68	6.04	4.22	2.96	2.08	13
14	80.08	54.83	37.68	25.99	18.00	12.51	8.72	6.10	4.28	3.02	2.13	14
15	78.00	53.69	37.09	25.73	17.91	12.51	8.77	6.16	4.35	3.08	2.19	15
16	75.98	52.58	36.52	25.46	17.81	12.51	8.81	6.23	4.42	3.14	2.24	16
17	74.00	51.48	35.95	25.20	17.72	12.51	8.86	6.29	4.49	3.21	2.30	17
18	72.08	50.42	35.39	24.94	17.63	12.51	8.90	6.36	4.55	3.27	2.36	18
19	70.22	49.37	34.84	24.68	17.54	12.51	8.95	6.42	4.63	3.34	2.42	19
20	68.41	48.36	34.31	24.43	17.45	12.51	9.00	6.49	4.70	3.41	2.48	20
21	66.64	47.36	33.78	24.18	17.36	12.51	9.05	6.56	4.77	3.48	2.55	21
22	64.91	46.38	33.26	23.93	17.27	12.51	9.09	6.63	4.85	3.55	2.61	22
23	63.22	45.41	32.73	23.68	17.18	12.51	9.14	6.69	4.92	3.63	2.68	23
24	61.56	44.46	32.22	23.43	17.09	12.51	9.18	6.76	4.99	3.70	2.75	24
25	59.96	43.53	31.71	23.18	17.00	12.51	9.23	6.83	5.07	3.78	2.82	25
26	58.40	42.63	31.22	22.94	16.91	12.51	9.28	6.90	5.15	3.85	2.89	26
27	56.88	41.74	30.73	22.70	16.82	12.51	9.32	6.97	5.23	3.93	2.97	27
28	55.40	40.87	30.25	22.47	16.74	12.50	9.37	7.04	5.31	4.01	3.04	28
29	53.96	40.02	29.78	22.23	16.65	12.50	9.42	7.12	5.39	4.10	3.12	29
30	52.56	39.19	29.32	22.00	16.56	12.50	9.47	7.19	5.47	4.18	3.20	30
31	51.20	38.38	28.86	21.78	16.48	12.50	9.52	7.26	5.56	4.27	3.28	31
32	49.88	37.59	28.42	21.55	16.39	12.51	9.57	7.34	5.65	4.35	3.37	32
33	48.59	36.82	27.98	21.33	16.31	12.51	9.62	7.42	5.73	4.44	3.45	33
34	47.33	36.05	27.55	21.11	16.23	12.51	9.67	7.49	5.82	4.54	3.54	34
35	46.10	35.30	27.12	20.89	16.14	12.51	9.72	7.57	5.91	4.63	3.63	35
36	44.91	34.57	26.70	20.68	16.06	12.51	9.77	7.65	6.00	4.73	3.73	36
37	43.75	33.86	26.29	20.47	15.98	12.51	9.82	7.73	6.10	4.82	3.82	37
38	42.62	33.16	25.88	20.26	15.90	12.51	9.87	7.81	6.19	4.92	3.92	38
39	41.52	32.48	25.48	20.05	15.82	12.51	9.92	7.89	6.29	5.02	4.02	39
40	40.44	31.81	25.09	19.84	15.73	12.51	9.97	7.97	6.39	5.13	4.13	40
41	39.40	31.15	24.70	19.64	15.66	12.51	10.03	8.05	6.49	5.23	4.23	41
42	38.38	30.51	24.32	19.44	15.58	12.52	10.08	8.14	6.59	5.34	4.34	42
43	37.40	29.89	23.95	19.24	15.50	12.52	10.13	8.22	6.69	5.45	4.46	43
44	36.44	29.28	23.59	19.05	15.43	12.52	10.19	8.31	6.80	5.57	4.57	44
45	35.52	28.69	23.23	18.86	15.35	12.53	10.25	8.40	6.90	5.69	4.69	45
46	34.61	28.10	22.88	18.68	15.28	12.53	10.31	8.49	7.01	5.81	4.82	46
47	33.73	27.54	22.54	18.49	15.21	12.54	10.36	8.58	7.13	5.93	4.94	47
48	32.89	26.99	22.21	18.32	15.14	12.55	10.43	8.68	7.24	6.06	5.07	48
49	32.07	26.46	21.88	18.15	15.08	12.56	10.49	8.78	7.36	6.19	5.21	49
50	31.27	25.94	21.57	17.98	15.02	12.58	10.56	8.88	7.48	6.32	5.35	50
51	30.50	25.43	21.26	17.81	14.96	12.59	10.62	8.98	7.61	6.46	5.49	51
52	29.75	24.94	20.96	17.65	14.90	12.61	10.69	9.09	7.74	6.60	5.64	52
53	29.03	24.47	20.67	17.50	14.85	12.63	10.77	9.20	7.87	6.75	5.80	53
54	28.33	24.01	20.39	17.35	14.80	12.66	10.84	9.31	8.01	6.90	5.96	54
55	27.66	23.56	20.12	17.21	14.76	12.69	10.92	9.43	8.15	7.06	6.12	55
56	27.02	23.14	19.86	17.08	14.72	12.72	11.01	9.55	8.30	7.22	6.30	56
57	26.39	22.72	19.60	16.95	14.69	12.75	11.10	9.67	8.45	7.39	6.48	57
58	25.78	22.32	19.36	16.83	14.66	12.79	11.19	9.80	8.60	7.56	6.66	58
59	25.19	21.92	19.11	16.70	14.62	12.83	11.28	9.93	8.76	7.74	6.85	59
60	24.61	21.53	18.87	16.57	14.59	12.86	11.37	10.06	8.92	7.92	7.05	60
61	24.04	21.14	18.63	16.45	14.55	12.90	11.46	10.19	9.08	8.11	7.25	61
62	23.49	20.77	18.40	16.33	14.52	12.94	11.55	10.33	9.25	8.30	7.46	62
63	22.96	20.41	18.17	16.22	14.50	12.99	11.65	10.47	9.43	8.50	7.68	63
64	22.46	20.07	17.97	16.12	14.48	13.04	11.76	10.63	9.62	8.71	7.91	64
65	22.00	19.76	17.78	16.04	14.49	13.11	11.89	10.79	9.82	8.94	8.16	65
66	21.56	19.48	17.62	15.97	14.51	13.20	12.03	10.98	10.03	9.19	8.42	66
67	21.16	19.22	17.48	15.93	14.54	13.30	12.18	11.17	10.27	9.45	8.71	67
68	20.79	18.98	17.36	15.90	14.59	13.41	12.35	11.39	10.51	9.72	9.01	68
69	20.44	18.76	17.25	15.88	14.65	13.54	12.53	11.61	10.78	10.02	9.33	69

continued

Table 26 Multipliers for loss of pension commencing age 75 (females) *continued*

Age at date of trial	Multiplier calculated with allowance for projected mortality from the 2008-based population projections and rate of return of											Age at date of trial
	–2.0%	–1.5%	–1.0%	–0.5%	0.0%	0.5%	1.0%	1.5%	2.0%	2.5%	3.0%	
70	20.11	18.55	17.15	15.87	14.72	13.67	12.72	11.85	11.05	10.33	9.66	70
71	19.78	18.35	17.05	15.87	14.79	13.81	12.91	12.09	11.34	10.65	10.01	71
72	19.46	18.14	16.95	15.86	14.86	13.95	13.11	12.34	11.63	10.98	10.38	72
73	19.13	17.93	16.84	15.84	14.93	14.08	13.31	12.59	11.93	11.32	10.75	73
74	18.80	17.72	16.74	15.83	15.00	14.23	13.51	12.86	12.24	11.68	11.15	74
75	18.48	17.53	16.64	15.83	15.08	14.38	13.74	13.14	12.58	12.06	11.58	75

Table 27 Discounting factors for term certain

Factor to discount value of multiplier for a period of deferment

Term	–2.0%	–1.5%	–1.0%	–0.5%	0.0%	0.5%	1.0%	1.5%	2.0%	2.5%	3.0%	Term
1	1.0204	1.0152	1.0101	1.0050	1.0000	0.9950	0.9901	0.9852	0.9804	0.9756	0.9709	1
2	1.0412	1.0307	1.0203	1.0101	1.0000	0.9901	0.9803	0.9707	0.9612	0.9518	0.9426	2
3	1.0625	1.0464	1.0306	1.0152	1.0000	0.9851	0.9706	0.9563	0.9423	0.9286	0.9151	3
4	1.0842	1.0623	1.0410	1.0203	1.0000	0.9802	0.9610	0.9422	0.9238	0.9060	0.8885	4
5	1.1063	1.0785	1.0515	1.0254	1.0000	0.9754	0.9515	0.9283	0.9057	0.8839	0.8626	5
6	1.1289	1.0949	1.0622	1.0305	1.0000	0.9705	0.9420	0.9145	0.8880	0.8623	0.8375	6
7	1.1519	1.1116	1.0729	1.0357	1.0000	0.9657	0.9327	0.9010	0.8706	0.8413	0.8131	7
8	1.1754	1.1285	1.0837	1.0409	1.0000	0.9609	0.9235	0.8877	0.8535	0.8207	0.7894	8
9	1.1994	1.1457	1.0947	1.0461	1.0000	0.9561	0.9143	0.8746	0.8368	0.8007	0.7664	9
10	1.2239	1.1632	1.1057	1.0514	1.0000	0.9513	0.9053	0.8617	0.8203	0.7812	0.7441	10
11	1.2489	1.1809	1.1169	1.0567	1.0000	0.9466	0.8963	0.8489	0.8043	0.7621	0.7224	11
12	1.2743	1.1989	1.1282	1.0620	1.0000	0.9419	0.8874	0.8364	0.7885	0.7436	0.7014	12
13	1.3004	1.2171	1.1396	1.0673	1.0000	0.9372	0.8787	0.8240	0.7730	0.7254	0.6810	13
14	1.3269	1.2356	1.1511	1.0727	1.0000	0.9326	0.8700	0.8118	0.7579	0.7077	0.6611	14
15	1.3540	1.2545	1.1627	1.0781	1.0000	0.9279	0.8613	0.7999	0.7430	0.6905	0.6419	15
16	1.3816	1.2736	1.1745	1.0835	1.0000	0.9233	0.8528	0.7880	0.7284	0.6736	0.6232	16
17	1.4098	1.2930	1.1863	1.0889	1.0000	0.9187	0.8444	0.7764	0.7142	0.6572	0.6050	17
18	1.4386	1.3126	1.1983	1.0944	1.0000	0.9141	0.8360	0.7649	0.7002	0.6412	0.5874	18
19	1.4679	1.3326	1.2104	1.0999	1.0000	0.9096	0.8277	0.7536	0.6864	0.6255	0.5703	19
20	1.4979	1.3529	1.2226	1.1054	1.0000	0.9051	0.8195	0.7425	0.6730	0.6103	0.5537	20
21	1.5285	1.3735	1.2350	1.1110	1.0000	0.9006	0.8114	0.7315	0.6598	0.5954	0.5375	21
22	1.5596	1.3944	1.2475	1.1166	1.0000	0.8961	0.8034	0.7207	0.6468	0.5809	0.5219	22
23	1.5915	1.4157	1.2601	1.1222	1.0000	0.8916	0.7954	0.7100	0.6342	0.5667	0.5067	23
24	1.6240	1.4372	1.2728	1.1278	1.0000	0.8872	0.7876	0.6995	0.6217	0.5529	0.4919	24
25	1.6571	1.4591	1.2856	1.1335	1.0000	0.8828	0.7798	0.6892	0.6095	0.5394	0.4776	25
26	1.6909	1.4814	1.2986	1.1392	1.0000	0.8784	0.7720	0.6790	0.5976	0.5262	0.4637	26
27	1.7254	1.5039	1.3117	1.1449	1.0000	0.8740	0.7644	0.6690	0.5859	0.5134	0.4502	27
28	1.7606	1.5268	1.3250	1.1507	1.0000	0.8697	0.7568	0.6591	0.5744	0.5009	0.4371	28
29	1.7966	1.5501	1.3384	1.1565	1.0000	0.8653	0.7493	0.6494	0.5631	0.4887	0.4243	29
30	1.8332	1.5737	1.3519	1.1623	1.0000	0.8610	0.7419	0.6398	0.5521	0.4767	0.4120	30
31	1.8706	1.5976	1.3656	1.1681	1.0000	0.8567	0.7346	0.6303	0.5412	0.4651	0.4000	31
32	1.9088	1.6220	1.3793	1.1740	1.0000	0.8525	0.7273	0.6210	0.5306	0.4538	0.3883	32
33	1.9478	1.6467	1.3933	1.1799	1.0000	0.8482	0.7201	0.6118	0.5202	0.4427	0.3770	33
34	1.9875	1.6717	1.4074	1.1858	1.0000	0.8440	0.7130	0.6028	0.5100	0.4319	0.3660	34
35	2.0281	1.6972	1.4216	1.1918	1.0000	0.8398	0.7059	0.5939	0.5000	0.4214	0.3554	35
36	2.0695	1.7230	1.4359	1.1978	1.0000	0.8356	0.6989	0.5851	0.4902	0.4111	0.3450	36
37	2.1117	1.7493	1.4504	1.2038	1.0000	0.8315	0.6920	0.5764	0.4806	0.4011	0.3350	37
38	2.1548	1.7759	1.4651	1.2098	1.0000	0.8274	0.6852	0.5679	0.4712	0.3913	0.3252	38
39	2.1988	1.8030	1.4799	1.2159	1.0000	0.8232	0.6784	0.5595	0.4619	0.3817	0.3158	39
40	2.2437	1.8304	1.4948	1.2220	1.0000	0.8191	0.6717	0.5513	0.4529	0.3724	0.3066	40
41	2.2894	1.8583	1.5099	1.2282	1.0000	0.8151	0.6650	0.5431	0.4440	0.3633	0.2976	41
42	2.3362	1.8866	1.5252	1.2343	1.0000	0.8110	0.6584	0.5351	0.4353	0.3545	0.2890	42
43	2.3838	1.9153	1.5406	1.2405	1.0000	0.8070	0.6519	0.5272	0.4268	0.3458	0.2805	43
44	2.4325	1.9445	1.5561	1.2468	1.0000	0.8030	0.6454	0.5194	0.4184	0.3374	0.2724	44
45	2.4821	1.9741	1.5719	1.2530	1.0000	0.7990	0.6391	0.5117	0.4102	0.3292	0.2644	45
46	2.5328	2.0042	1.5877	1.2593	1.0000	0.7950	0.6327	0.5042	0.4022	0.3211	0.2567	46
47	2.5845	2.0347	1.6038	1.2657	1.0000	0.7910	0.6265	0.4967	0.3943	0.3133	0.2493	47
48	2.6372	2.0657	1.6200	1.2720	1.0000	0.7871	0.6203	0.4894	0.3865	0.3057	0.2420	48
49	2.6911	2.0971	1.6363	1.2784	1.0000	0.7832	0.6141	0.4821	0.3790	0.2982	0.2350	49
50	2.7460	2.1291	1.6529	1.2848	1.0000	0.7793	0.6080	0.4750	0.3715	0.2909	0.2281	50
51	2.8020	2.1615	1.6696	1.2913	1.0000	0.7754	0.6020	0.4680	0.3642	0.2838	0.2215	51
52	2.8592	2.1944	1.6864	1.2978	1.0000	0.7716	0.5961	0.4611	0.3571	0.2769	0.2150	52
53	2.9175	2.2278	1.7035	1.3043	1.0000	0.7677	0.5902	0.4543	0.3501	0.2702	0.2088	53
54	2.9771	2.2617	1.7207	1.3109	1.0000	0.7639	0.5843	0.4475	0.3432	0.2636	0.2027	54
55	3.0378	2.2962	1.7381	1.3174	1.0000	0.7601	0.5785	0.4409	0.3365	0.2572	0.1968	55
56	3.0998	2.3312	1.7556	1.3241	1.0000	0.7563	0.5728	0.4344	0.3299	0.2509	0.1910	56
57	3.1631	2.3667	1.7733	1.3307	1.0000	0.7525	0.5671	0.4280	0.3234	0.2448	0.1855	57
58	3.2277	2.4027	1.7913	1.3374	1.0000	0.7488	0.5615	0.4217	0.3171	0.2388	0.1801	58
59	3.2935	2.4393	1.8094	1.3441	1.0000	0.7451	0.5560	0.4154	0.3109	0.2330	0.1748	59
60	3.3607	2.4764	1.8276	1.3509	1.0000	0.7414	0.5504	0.4093	0.3048	0.2273	0.1697	60
61	3.4293	2.5141	1.8461	1.3577	1.0000	0.7377	0.5450	0.4032	0.2988	0.2217	0.1648	61
62	3.4993	2.5524	1.8647	1.3645	1.0000	0.7340	0.5396	0.3973	0.2929	0.2163	0.1600	62
63	3.5707	2.5913	1.8836	1.3713	1.0000	0.7304	0.5343	0.3914	0.2872	0.2111	0.1553	63
64	3.6436	2.6308	1.9026	1.3782	1.0000	0.7267	0.5290	0.3856	0.2816	0.2059	0.1508	64
65	3.7180	2.6708	1.9218	1.3852	1.0000	0.7231	0.5237	0.3799	0.2761	0.2009	0.1464	65
66	3.7938	2.7115	1.9412	1.3921	1.0000	0.7195	0.5185	0.3743	0.2706	0.1960	0.1421	66
67	3.8713	2.7528	1.9608	1.3991	1.0000	0.7159	0.5134	0.3688	0.2653	0.1912	0.1380	67
68	3.9503	2.7947	1.9806	1.4061	1.0000	0.7124	0.5083	0.3633	0.2601	0.1865	0.1340	68
69	4.0309	2.8373	2.0007	1.4132	1.0000	0.7088	0.5033	0.3580	0.2550	0.1820	0.1301	69
70	4.1132	2.8805	2.0209	1.4203	1.0000	0.7053	0.4983	0.3527	0.2500	0.1776	0.1263	70

continued

Table 27 Discounting factors for term certain *continued*

Factor to discount value of multiplier for a period of deferment

Term	–2.0%	–1.5%	–1.0%	–0.5%	0.0%	0.5%	1.0%	1.5%	2.0%	2.5%	3.0%	Term
71	4.1971	2.9243	2.0413	1.4275	1.0000	0.7018	0.4934	0.3475	0.2451	0.1732	0.1226	71
72	4.2827	2.9689	2.0619	1.4346	1.0000	0.6983	0.4885	0.3423	0.2403	0.1690	0.1190	72
73	4.3702	3.0141	2.0827	1.4418	1.0000	0.6948	0.4837	0.3373	0.2356	0.1649	0.1156	73
74	4.4593	3.0600	2.1038	1.4491	1.0000	0.6914	0.4789	0.3323	0.2310	0.1609	0.1122	74
75	4.5503	3.1066	2.1250	1.4564	1.0000	0.6879	0.4741	0.3274	0.2265	0.1569	0.1089	75
76	4.6432	3.1539	2.1465	1.4637	1.0000	0.6845	0.4694	0.3225	0.2220	0.1531	0.1058	76
77	4.7380	3.2019	2.1682	1.4710	1.0000	0.6811	0.4648	0.3178	0.2177	0.1494	0.1027	77
78	4.8347	3.2507	2.1901	1.4784	1.0000	0.6777	0.4602	0.3131	0.2134	0.1457	0.0997	78
79	4.9333	3.3002	2.2122	1.4859	1.0000	0.6743	0.4556	0.3084	0.2092	0.1422	0.0968	79
80	5.0340	3.3504	2.2345	1.4933	1.0000	0.6710	0.4511	0.3039	0.2051	0.1387	0.0940	80

Table 28 Multipliers for pecuniary loss for term certain

Multiplier for regular frequent payments for a term certain at rate of return of

Term	-2.0%	-1.5%	-1.0%	-0.5%	0.0%	0.5%	1.0%	1.5%	2.0%	2.5%	3.0%	Term
1	1.01	1.01	1.01	1.00	1.00	1.00	1.00	0.99	0.99	0.99	0.99	1
2	2.04	2.03	2.02	2.01	2.00	1.99	1.98	1.97	1.96	1.95	1.94	2
3	3.09	3.07	3.05	3.02	3.00	2.98	2.96	2.93	2.91	2.89	2.87	3
4	4.17	4.12	4.08	4.04	4.00	3.96	3.92	3.88	3.85	3.81	3.77	4
5	5.26	5.19	5.13	5.06	5.00	4.94	4.88	4.82	4.76	4.70	4.65	5
6	6.38	6.28	6.18	6.09	6.00	5.91	5.82	5.74	5.66	5.58	5.50	6
7	7.52	7.38	7.25	7.12	7.00	6.88	6.76	6.65	6.54	6.43	6.32	7
8	8.68	8.50	8.33	8.16	8.00	7.84	7.69	7.54	7.40	7.26	7.12	8
9	9.87	9.64	9.42	9.21	9.00	8.80	8.61	8.42	8.24	8.07	7.90	9
10	11.08	10.80	10.52	10.25	10.00	9.75	9.52	9.29	9.07	8.86	8.66	10
11	12.32	11.97	11.63	11.31	11.00	10.70	10.42	10.15	9.88	9.63	9.39	11
12	13.58	13.16	12.75	12.37	12.00	11.65	11.31	10.99	10.68	10.39	10.10	12
13	14.87	14.37	13.89	13.43	13.00	12.59	12.19	11.82	11.46	11.12	10.79	13
14	16.18	15.59	15.03	14.50	14.00	13.52	13.07	12.64	12.23	11.84	11.46	14
15	17.52	16.84	16.19	15.58	15.00	14.45	13.93	13.44	12.98	12.54	12.12	15
16	18.89	18.10	17.36	16.66	16.00	15.38	14.79	14.24	13.71	13.22	12.75	16
17	20.28	19.38	18.54	17.75	17.00	16.30	15.64	15.02	14.43	13.88	13.36	17
18	21.71	20.69	19.73	18.84	18.00	17.22	16.48	15.79	15.14	14.53	13.96	18
19	23.16	22.01	20.94	19.93	19.00	18.13	17.31	16.55	15.83	15.17	14.54	19
20	24.64	23.35	22.15	21.04	20.00	19.03	18.14	17.30	16.51	15.78	15.10	20
21	26.16	24.71	23.38	22.15	21.00	19.94	18.95	18.03	17.18	16.39	15.65	21
22	27.70	26.10	24.62	23.26	22.00	20.84	19.76	18.76	17.83	16.97	16.17	22
23	29.28	27.50	25.88	24.38	23.00	21.73	20.56	19.48	18.47	17.55	16.69	23
24	30.88	28.93	27.14	25.50	24.00	22.62	21.35	20.18	19.10	18.11	17.19	24
25	32.53	30.38	28.42	26.63	25.00	23.50	22.13	20.87	19.72	18.65	17.67	25
26	34.20	31.85	29.71	27.77	26.00	24.38	22.91	21.56	20.32	19.19	18.14	26
27	35.91	33.34	31.02	28.91	27.00	25.26	23.68	22.23	20.91	19.71	18.60	27
28	37.65	34.86	32.34	30.06	28.00	26.13	24.44	22.90	21.49	20.21	19.04	28
29	39.43	36.40	33.67	31.21	29.00	27.00	25.19	23.55	22.06	20.71	19.47	29
30	41.24	37.96	35.01	32.37	30.00	27.86	25.94	24.20	22.62	21.19	19.89	30
31	43.10	39.54	36.37	33.54	31.00	28.72	26.67	24.83	23.17	21.66	20.30	31
32	44.99	41.15	37.74	34.71	32.00	29.58	27.41	25.46	23.70	22.12	20.69	32
33	46.91	42.79	39.13	35.89	33.00	30.43	28.13	26.07	24.23	22.57	21.08	33
34	48.88	44.45	40.53	37.07	34.00	31.27	28.85	26.68	24.74	23.01	21.45	34
35	50.89	46.13	41.95	38.26	35.00	32.12	29.56	27.28	25.25	23.43	21.81	35
36	52.94	47.84	43.37	39.45	36.00	32.95	30.26	27.87	25.74	23.85	22.16	36
37	55.03	49.58	44.82	40.65	37.00	33.79	30.95	28.45	26.23	24.26	22.50	37
38	57.16	51.34	46.28	41.86	38.00	34.62	31.64	29.02	26.70	24.65	22.83	38
39	59.34	53.13	47.75	43.07	39.00	35.44	32.32	29.58	27.17	25.04	23.15	39
40	61.56	54.95	49.24	44.29	40.00	36.26	33.00	30.14	27.63	25.42	23.46	40
41	63.83	56.79	50.74	45.52	41.00	37.08	33.67	30.69	28.08	25.78	23.76	41
42	66.14	58.66	52.26	46.75	42.00	37.89	34.33	31.23	28.52	26.14	24.06	42
43	68.50	60.56	53.79	47.99	43.00	38.70	34.98	31.76	28.95	26.49	24.34	43
44	70.91	62.49	55.34	49.23	44.00	39.51	35.63	32.28	29.37	26.83	24.62	44
45	73.36	64.45	56.90	50.48	45.00	40.31	36.27	32.80	29.78	27.17	24.88	45
46	75.87	66.44	58.48	51.74	46.00	41.10	36.91	33.30	30.19	27.49	25.15	46
47	78.43	68.46	60.08	53.00	47.00	41.90	37.54	33.80	30.59	27.81	25.40	47
48	81.04	70.51	61.69	54.27	48.00	42.69	38.16	34.30	30.98	28.12	25.64	48
49	83.70	72.59	63.32	55.54	49.00	43.47	38.78	34.78	31.36	28.42	25.88	49
50	86.42	74.70	64.96	56.82	50.00	44.25	39.39	35.26	31.74	28.72	26.11	50
51	89.20	76.85	66.62	58.11	51.00	45.03	40.00	35.73	32.10	29.00	26.34	51
52	92.03	79.03	68.30	59.41	52.00	45.80	40.60	36.20	32.47	29.28	26.56	52
53	94.92	81.24	69.99	60.71	53.00	46.57	41.19	36.66	32.82	29.56	26.77	53
54	97.86	83.48	71.71	62.01	54.00	47.34	41.78	37.11	33.17	29.82	26.97	54
55	100.87	85.76	73.44	63.33	55.00	48.10	42.36	37.55	33.51	30.08	27.17	55
56	103.94	88.08	75.18	64.65	56.00	48.86	42.93	37.99	33.84	30.34	27.37	56
57	107.07	90.43	76.95	65.98	57.00	49.61	43.50	38.42	34.17	30.59	27.56	57
58	110.27	92.81	78.73	67.31	58.00	50.36	44.07	38.84	34.49	30.83	27.74	58
59	113.53	95.23	80.53	68.65	59.00	51.11	44.63	39.26	34.80	31.06	27.92	59
60	116.85	97.69	82.35	70.00	60.00	51.85	45.18	39.67	35.11	31.29	28.09	60
61	120.25	100.18	84.19	71.35	61.00	52.59	45.73	40.08	35.41	31.52	28.26	61
62	123.71	102.72	86.04	72.71	62.00	53.33	46.27	40.48	35.70	31.74	28.42	62
63	127.25	105.29	87.91	74.08	63.00	54.06	46.81	40.88	36.00	31.95	28.58	63
64	130.85	107.90	89.81	75.46	64.00	54.79	47.34	41.26	36.28	32.16	28.73	64
65	134.53	110.55	91.72	76.84	65.00	55.52	47.86	41.65	36.56	32.36	28.88	65
66	138.29	113.24	93.65	78.23	66.00	56.24	48.39	42.02	36.83	32.56	29.02	66
67	142.12	115.97	95.60	79.62	67.00	56.95	48.90	42.40	37.10	32.75	29.16	67
68	146.03	118.75	97.57	81.03	68.00	57.67	49.41	42.76	37.36	32.94	29.30	68
69	150.02	121.56	99.56	82.44	69.00	58.38	49.92	43.12	37.62	33.13	29.43	69
70	154.10	124.42	101.57	83.85	70.00	59.09	50.42	43.48	37.87	33.31	29.56	70

continued

Table 28 Multipliers for pecuniary loss for term certain *continued*

Multiplier for regular frequent payments for a term certain at rate of return of

Term	−2.0%	−1.5%	−1.0%	−0.5%	0.0%	0.5%	1.0%	1.5%	2.0%	2.5%	3.0%	Term
71	158.25	127.32	103.61	85.28	71.00	59.79	50.91	43.83	38.12	33.48	29.68	71
72	162.49	130.27	105.66	86.71	72.00	60.49	51.41	44.17	38.36	33.65	29.80	72
73	166.82	133.26	107.73	88.15	73.00	61.19	51.89	44.51	38.60	33.82	29.92	73
74	171.23	136.30	109.82	89.59	74.00	61.88	52.37	44.85	38.83	33.98	30.03	74
75	175.74	139.38	111.94	91.04	75.00	62.57	52.85	45.18	39.06	34.14	30.15	75
76	180.33	142.51	114.07	92.50	76.00	63.26	53.32	45.50	39.29	34.30	30.25	76
77	185.02	145.69	116.23	93.97	77.00	63.94	53.79	45.82	39.51	34.45	30.36	77
78	189.81	148.92	118.41	95.45	78.00	64.62	54.25	46.14	39.72	34.60	30.46	78
79	194.69	152.19	120.61	96.93	79.00	65.29	54.71	46.45	39.93	34.74	30.56	79
80	199.68	155.52	122.83	98.42	80.00	65.97	55.16	46.75	40.14	34.88	30.65	80

Table 27: discounting factors for term certain @ –0.75%

Table 28: multipliers for pecuniary loss for term certain @ –0.75%

Years	Table 27	Table 28
0.5	1.0038	0.501
1	1.0076	1.004
1.5	1.0114	1.509
2	1.0152	2.015
2.5	1.0190	2.524
3	1.0228	3.034
3.5	1.0267	3.547
4	1.0306	4.061
4.5	1.0345	4.577
5	1.0384	5.095
6	1.0462	6.138
7	1.0541	7.188
8	1.0621	8.246
9	1.0701	9.312
10	1.0782	10.386
11	1.0863	11.468
12	1.0945	12.559
13	1.1028	13.657
14	1.1112	14.764
15	1.1195	15.88
16	1.1280	17.004
17	1.1365	18.136
18	1.1451	19.277
19	1.1538	20.426
20	1.1625	21.584
21	1.1713	22.751
22	1.1801	23.927
23	1.1890	25.111
24	1.1980	26.305
25	1.2071	27.507
26	1.2162	28.719
27	1.2254	29.94
28	1.2347	31.17
29	1.2440	32.409
30	1.2534	33.658
31	1.2629	34.916
32	1.2724	36.184
33	1.2820	37.461
34	1.2917	38.748
35	1.3015	40.044
36	1.3113	41.351
37	1.3212	42.667
38	1.3312	43.993

Years	Table 27	Table 28
39	1.3413	45.329
40	1.3514	46.676
41	1.3616	48.032
42	1.3719	49.399
43	1.3823	50.776
44	1.3927	52.163
45	1.4032	53.561
46	1.4138	54.97
47	1.4245	56.389
48	1.4353	57.819
49	1.4461	59.26
50	1.4570	60.711
51	1.4681	62.174
52	1.4792	63.647
53	1.4903	65.132
54	1.5016	66.628
55	1.5129	68.135
56	1.5244	69.654
57	1.5359	71.184
58	1.5475	72.726
59	1.5592	74.279
60	1.5710	75.844
61	1.5828	77.421
62	1.5948	79.01
63	1.6069	80.611
64	1.6190	82.224
65	1.6312	83.849
66	1.6436	85.486
67	1.6560	87.136
68	1.6685	88.798
69	1.6811	90.473
70	1.6938	92.16
71	1.7066	93.86
72	1.7195	95.574
73	1.7325	97.299
74	1.7456	99.039
75	1.7588	100.791
76	1.7721	102.556
77	1.7855	104.335
78	1.7990	106.127
79	1.8125	107.933
80	1.8262	109.752

Multipliers at 2.5% discount **Table A5 Compound interest only** **Discount rate 2.50%**

	Single payment	Continuous loss	Frequency of payments in years 1	2	3	4	5	6	7	8	10	12	15	20
n														
1	0.976	0.99	0.98											
2	0.952	1.95	1.93	0.95										
3	0.929	2.89	2.86		0.93									
4	0.906	3.81	3.76	1.86		0.91								
5	0.884	4.70	4.65				0.88							
6	0.862	5.58	5.51	2.72	1.79			0.86						
7	0.841	6.43	6.35						0.84					
8	0.821	7.26	7.17	3.54		1.73				0.82				
9	0.801	8.07	7.97		2.59									
10	0.781	8.86	8.75	4.32			1.67				0.78			
11	0.762	9.63	9.51											
12	0.744	10.39	10.26	5.07	3.34	2.47		1.61				0.74		
13	0.725	11.12	10.98											
14	0.708	11.84	11.69	5.77					1.55					
15	0.690	12.54	12.38		4.03		2.36						0.69	
16	0.674	13.22	13.06	6.45		3.14				1.49				
17	0.657	13.88	13.71											
18	0.641	14.53	14.35	7.09	4.67			2.25						
19	0.626	15.17	14.98											

	Single payment	Continuous loss	Frequency of payments in years											
			1	2	3	4	5	6	7	8	10	12	15	20
20	0.610	15.78	15.59	7.70		3.75	2.97				1.39			0.61
21	0.595	16.39	16.18		5.26				2.14					
22	0.581	16.97	16.77	8.28										
23	0.567	17.55	17.33											
24	0.553	18.11	17.88	8.83	5.82	4.31		2.80		2.05		1.30		
25	0.539	18.65	18.42				3.51							
26	0.526	19.19	18.95	9.36										
27	0.513	19.71	19.46		6.33									
28	0.501	20.21	19.96	9.86		4.81			2.65					
29	0.489	20.71	20.45											
30	0.477	21.19	20.93	10.34	6.81		3.98	3.28			1.87		1.17	
31	0.465	21.66	21.40											
32	0.454	22.12	21.85	10.79		5.26				2.50				
33	0.443	22.57	22.29		7.25									
34	0.432	23.01	22.72	11.22										
35	0.421	23.43	23.15				4.40		3.07					
36	0.411	23.85	23.56	11.63	7.66	5.67		3.69				1.71		
37	0.401	24.26	23.96											
38	0.391	24.65	24.35	12.02										
39	0.382	25.04	24.73		8.04									
40	0.372	25.42	25.10	12.40		6.05	4.78			2.87	2.24			0.98
41	0.363	25.78	25.47											

	Single payment	Continuous loss	Frequency of payments in years											
			1	2	3	4	5	6	7	8	10	12	15	20
42	0.354	26.14	25.82	12.75	8.40			4.04	3.42					
43	0.346	26.49	26.17											
44	0.337	26.83	26.50	13.09		6.38								
45	0.329	27.17	26.83		8.72		5.10						1.50	
46	0.321	27.49	27.15	13.41										
47	0.313	27.81	27.47											
48	0.306	28.12	27.77	13.72	9.03	6.69		4.35		3.18		2.01		
49	0.298	28.42	28.07						3.72					
50	0.291	28.72	28.36	14.01			5.40				2.53			
51	0.284	29.00	28.65		9.31									
52	0.277	29.28	28.92	14.28		6.97								
53	0.270	29.56	29.19											
54	0.264	29.82	29.46	14.55	9.58			4.61						
55	0.257	30.08	29.71				5.65							
56	0.251	30.34	29.96	14.80		7.22			3.97	3.43				
57	0.245	30.59	30.21		9.82									
58	0.239	30.83	30.45	15.04										
59	0.233	31.06	30.68											
60	0.227	31.29	30.91	15.26	10.05	7.44	5.88	4.84			2.76	2.24	1.72	1.21
61	0.222	31.52	31.13											
62	0.216	31.74	31.35	15.48										
63	0.211	31.95	31.56		10.26				4.18					

	Single payment	Continuous loss	Frequency of payments in years											
			1	2	3	4	5	6	7	8	10	12	15	20
64	0.206	32.16	31.76	15.69		7.65				3.64				
65	0.201	32.36	31.96				6.08							
66	0.196	32.56	32.16	15.88	10.46			5.03						
67	0.191	32.75	32.35											
68	0.187	32.94	32.54	16.07		7.84								
69	0.182	33.13	32.72		10.64									
70	0.178	33.31	32.90	16.25			6.26		4.36		2.94			
71	0.173	33.48	33.07											
72	0.169	33.65	33.24	16.41	10.81	8.00		5.20		3.80		2.41		
73	0.165	33.82	33.40											
74	0.161	33.98	33.57	16.58										
75	0.157	34.14	33.72		10.96		6.42						1.88	
76	0.153	34.30	33.88	16.73		8.16								
77	0.149	34.45	34.03						4.51					
78	0.146	34.60	34.17	16.87	11.11			5.35						
79	0.142	34.74	34.31											
80	0.139	34.88	34.45	17.01		8.30	6.55			3.94	3.08			1.35
81	0.135	35.02	34.59		11.25									
82	0.132	35.15	34.72	17.15										
83	0.129	35.28	34.85											
84	0.126	35.41	34.97	17.27	11.37	8.42		5.48	4.63			2.54		
85	0.123	35.53	35.10				6.68							

	Single payment	Continuous loss	Frequency of payments in years											
			1	2	3	4	5	6	7	8	10	12	15	20
86	0.120	35.65	35.22	17.39										
87	0.117	35.77	35.33		11.49									
88	0.114	35.89	35.45	17.50		8.54				4.06				
89	0.111	36.00	35.56											
90	0.108	36.11	35.67	17.61	11.60		6.79	5.58			3.18		1.99	
91	0.106	36.22	35.77						4.74					
92	0.103	36.32	35.87	17.72		8.64								
93	0.101	36.42	35.98		11.70									
94	0.098	36.52	36.07	17.81										
95	0.096	36.62	36.17				6.88							
96	0.093	36.71	36.26	17.91	11.79	8.73		5.68		4.15		2.63		
97	0.091	36.81	36.35											
98	0.089	36.90	36.44	18.00					4.83					
99	0.087	36.98	36.53		11.88									
100	0.085	37.07	36.61	18.08		8.82	6.97				3.27			1.43

Multipliers at –0.75% discount

Discount rate –0.75%

	Single payment	Continuous loss	Frequency of payments in years											
			1	2	3	4	5	6	7	8	10	12	15	20
n														
1	1.008	1.00	1.01											
2	1.015	2.02	2.02	1.02										
3	1.023	3.03	3.05		1.02									
4	1.031	4.06	4.08	2.05		1.03								
5	1.038	5.10	5.11				1.04							
6	1.046	6.14	6.16	3.09	2.07			1.05						
7	1.054	7.19	7.21						1.05					
8	1.062	8.25	8.28	4.15		2.09				1.06				
9	1.070	9.31	9.35		3.14									
10	1.078	10.39	10.43	5.23			2.12				1.08			
11	1.086	11.47	11.51											
12	1.095	12.56	12.61	6.33	4.23	3.19		2.14				1.09		
13	1.103	13.66	13.71											
14	1.111	14.76	14.82	7.44					2.17					
15	1.120	15.88	15.94		5.35		3.24						1.12	
16	1.128	17.00	17.07	8.57		4.32				2.19				
17	1.137	18.14	18.20											
18	1.145	19.28	19.35	9.71	6.50			3.29						
19	1.154	20.43	20.50											

	Single payment	Continuous loss	Frequency of payments in years											
			1	2	3	4	5	6	7	8	10	12	15	20
20	1.162	21.58	21.67	10.87		5.48	4.40				2.24			1.16
21	1.171	22.75	22.84		7.67				3.34					
22	1.180	23.93	24.02	12.05										
23	1.189	25.11	25.21											
24	1.198	26.30	26.40	13.25	8.87	6.68		4.48		3.39		2.29		
25	1.207	27.51	27.61				5.61							
26	1.216	28.72	28.83	14.47										
27	1.225	29.94	30.05		10.09									
28	1.235	31.17	31.29	15.70		7.91			4.57					
29	1.244	32.41	32.53											
30	1.253	33.66	33.78	16.96	11.35		6.86	5.74			3.49		2.37	
31	1.263	34.92	35.05											
32	1.272	36.18	36.32	18.23		9.18				4.66				
33	1.282	37.46	37.60		12.63									
34	1.292	38.75	38.89	19.52										
35	1.301	40.04	40.20				8.16		5.87					
36	1.311	41.35	41.51	20.83	13.94	10.49		7.05				3.60		
37	1.321	42.67	42.83											
38	1.331	43.99	44.16	22.16										
39	1.341	45.33	45.50		15.28									
40	1.351	46.68	46.85	23.51		11.85	9.51			6.01	4.85			2.51
41	1.362	48.03	48.21											

	Single payment	Continuous loss	Frequency of payments in years											
			1	2	3	4	5	6	7	8	10	12	15	20
42	1.372	49.40	49.58	24.89	16.65			8.42	7.24					
43	1.382	50.78	50.97											
44	1.393	52.16	52.36	26.28		13.24								
45	1.403	53.56	53.76		18.06		10.92						3.78	
46	1.414	54.97	55.18	27.69										
47	1.425	56.39	56.60											
48	1.435	57.82	58.04	29.13	19.49	14.67		9.86		7.45		5.04		
49	1.446	59.26	59.48						8.69					
50	1.457	60.71	60.94	30.58			12.37				6.30			
51	1.468	62.17	62.41		20.96									
52	1.479	63.65	63.89	32.06		16.15								
53	1.490	65.13	65.38											
54	1.502	66.63	66.88	33.57	22.46			11.36						
55	1.513	68.14	68.39				13.89							
56	1.524	69.65	69.92	35.09		17.68			10.22	8.97				
57	1.536	71.18	71.45		24.00									
58	1.547	72.73	73.00	36.64										
59	1.559	74.28	74.56											
60	1.571	75.84	76.13	38.21	25.57	19.25	15.46	12.93			7.87	6.61	5.35	4.08
61	1.583	77.42	77.71											
62	1.595	79.01	79.31	39.80										
63	1.607	80.61	80.91		27.17				11.82					

	Single payment	Continuous loss	Frequency of payments in years											
			1	2	3	4	5	6	7	8	10	12	15	20
64	1.619	82.22	82.53	41.42		20.87				10.59				
65	1.631	83.85	84.16				17.09							
66	1.644	85.49	85.81	43.07	28.82			14.57						
67	1.656	87.14	87.46											
68	1.668	88.80	89.13	44.73		22.54								
69	1.681	90.47	90.81		30.50									
70	1.694	92.16	92.51	46.43			18.78		13.52		9.57			
71	1.707	93.86	94.21											
72	1.720	95.57	95.93	48.15	32.22	24.25		16.29		12.31		8.33		
73	1.732	97.30	97.67											
74	1.746	99.04	99.41	49.89										
75	1.759	100.79	101.17		33.98		20.54						7.11	
76	1.772	102.56	102.94	51.67		26.03								
77	1.785	104.33	104.73						15.30					
78	1.799	106.13	106.53	53.46	35.78			18.09						
79	1.813	107.93	108.34											
80	1.826	109.75	110.17	55.29		27.85	22.37			14.14	11.39			5.91
81	1.840	111.59	112.01		37.62									
82	1.854	113.43	113.86	57.14										
83	1.868	115.29	115.73											
84	1.882	117.17	117.61	59.03	39.50	29.74		19.97	17.18			10.21		
85	1.896	119.06	119.51				24.26							

	Single payment	Continuous loss	Frequency of payments in years											
			1	2	3	4	5	6	7	8	10	12	15	20
86	1.911	120.96	121.42	60.94										
87	1.925	122.88	123.34		41.42									
88	1.940	124.81	125.28	62.88		31.67				16.08				
89	1.954	126.76	127.24											
90	1.969	128.72	129.20	64.85	43.39		26.23	21.94			13.36		9.07	
91	1.984	130.70	131.19						19.17					
92	1.999	132.69	133.19	66.84		33.67								
93	2.014	134.69	135.20		45.41									
94	2.029	136.72	137.23	68.87										
95	2.045	138.75	139.28				28.28							
96	2.060	140.80	141.34	70.93	47.47	35.73		24.00		18.14		12.27		
97	2.076	142.87	143.41											
98	2.091	144.96	145.50	73.02					21.26					
99	2.107	147.06	147.61		49.57									
100	2.123	149.17	149.73	75.15		37.86	30.40				15.49			8.03

New tables for A1

–0.75 per cent discount tables 'at a glance' — MALE

Age at date of trial	Table 1 Pecuniary loss for life	Table 3 Loss of earnings to age 50	Table 5 Loss of earnings to age 55	Table 7 Loss of earnings to age 60	Table 9 Loss of earnings to age 65	Table 11 Loss of earnings to age 70	Table 13 Loss of earnings to age 75	Table 15 Loss of pension from age 50	Table 17 Loss of pension from age 55	Table 19 Loss of pension from age 60	Table 21 Loss of pension from age 65	Table 23 Loss of pension from age 70	Table 25 Loss of pension from age 75
0	128.73							68.85	61.71	54.40	46.96	39.47	32.00
1	127.21							68.46	61.34	54.05	46.64	39.16	31.73
2	125.07							67.74	60.68	53.44	46.08	38.67	31.30
3	122.92							67.02	60.01	52.83	45.53	38.18	30.87
4	120.79							66.30	59.34	52.22	44.98	37.69	30.45
5	118.67							65.59	58.68	51.62	44.43	37.21	30.03
6	116.57							64.88	58.03	51.02	43.89	36.73	29.61
7	114.49							64.18	57.38	50.42	43.36	36.25	29.20
8	112.42							63.48	56.74	49.84	42.83	35.78	28.79
9	110.36							62.79	56.10	49.25	42.30	35.32	28.39
10	108.32							62.10	55.46	48.67	41.78	34.86	27.99
11	106.29							61.42	54.84	48.10	41.26	34.40	27.60
12	104.29							60.75	54.22	47.54	40.76	33.95	27.21
13	102.30							60.09	53.61	46.98	40.25	33.50	26.83
14	100.33							59.44	53.00	46.43	39.76	33.07	26.45
15	98.38							58.79	52.41	45.88	39.27	32.64	26.08
16	96.45	38.30	44.63	51.11	57.67	64.24	70.74	58.15	51.82	45.35	38.79	32.21	25.71

Age at date of trial	Table 1 Pecuniary loss for life	Table 3 Loss of earnings to age 50	Table 5 Loss of earnings to age 55	Table 7 Loss of earnings to age 60	Table 9 Loss of earnings to age 65	Table 11 Loss of earnings to age 70	Table 13 Loss of earnings to age 75	Table 15 Loss of pension from age 50	Table 17 Loss of pension from age 55	Table 19 Loss of pension from age 60	Table 21 Loss of pension from age 65	Table 23 Loss of pension from age 70	Table 25 Loss of pension from age 75
17	94.55	37.02	43.31	49.73	56.23	62.76	69.20	57.53	51.24	44.82	38.31	31.79	25.35
18	92.66	35.75	41.99	48.36	54.82	61.28	67.67	56.91	50.67	44.30	37.85	31.38	24.99
19	90.80	34.50	40.69	47.01	53.41	59.83	66.16	56.30	50.11	43.79	37.39	30.98	24.65
20	88.96	33.25	39.40	45.67	52.02	58.38	64.66	55.71	49.57	43.29	36.94	30.58	24.31
21	87.14	32.02	38.12	44.34	50.64	56.95	63.17	55.12	49.02	42.80	36.50	30.19	23.97
22	85.33	30.79	36.84	43.02	49.27	55.53	61.69	54.54	48.48	42.31	36.05	29.80	23.63
23	83.53	29.57	35.58	41.71	47.92	54.12	60.23	53.96	47.95	41.82	35.61	29.41	23.30
24	81.75	28.37	34.33	40.41	46.57	52.72	58.77	53.38	47.42	41.34	35.18	29.03	22.97
25	79.99	27.17	33.09	39.12	45.23	51.33	57.33	52.82	46.90	40.86	34.76	28.65	22.65
26	78.25	25.98	31.85	37.85	43.91	49.96	55.91	52.27	46.39	40.40	34.34	28.29	22.34
27	76.52	24.80	30.63	36.58	42.59	48.60	54.49	51.73	45.89	39.95	33.93	27.93	22.03
28	74.81	23.63	29.42	35.32	41.29	47.24	53.09	51.18	45.39	39.49	33.52	27.57	21.72
29	73.11	22.47	28.21	34.07	39.99	45.90	51.69	50.64	44.89	39.03	33.11	27.21	21.41
30	71.43	21.31	27.02	32.84	38.71	44.57	50.31	50.11	44.41	38.59	32.72	26.86	21.11
31	69.77	20.17	25.84	31.61	37.44	43.25	48.95	49.60	43.93	38.16	32.33	26.52	20.82
32	68.14	19.04	24.67	30.40	36.19	41.95	47.60	49.10	43.48	37.74	31.96	26.19	20.54
33	66.54	17.92	23.51	29.20	34.94	40.67	46.27	48.62	43.03	37.34	31.59	25.87	20.27
34	64.94	16.80	22.36	28.01	33.71	39.39	44.95	48.14	42.59	36.93	31.23	25.55	20.00
35	63.36	15.70	21.21	26.83	32.49	38.12	43.63	47.66	42.15	36.53	30.87	25.24	19.73
36	61.80	14.60	20.08	25.65	31.28	36.87	42.33	47.19	41.72	36.14	30.52	24.93	19.46
37	60.25	13.51	18.95	24.49	30.07	35.62	41.05	46.73	41.29	35.75	30.17	24.62	19.20

Age at date of trial	Table 1 Pecuniary loss for life	Table 3 Loss of earnings to age 50	Table 5 Loss of earnings to age 55	Table 7 Loss of earnings to age 60	Table 9 Loss of earnings to age 65	Table 11 Loss of earnings to age 70	Table 13 Loss of earnings to age 75	Table 15 Loss of pension from age 50	Table 17 Loss of pension from age 55	Table 19 Loss of pension from age 60	Table 21 Loss of pension from age 65	Table 23 Loss of pension from age 70	Table 25 Loss of pension from age 75
38	58.71	12.43	17.84	23.34	28.88	34.39	39.76	46.28	40.87	35.37	29.83	24.32	18.94
39	57.18	11.36	16.73	22.19	27.69	33.16	38.49	45.82	40.45	34.99	29.48	24.02	18.68
40	55.66	10.29	15.63	21.05	26.52	31.94	37.23	45.37	40.04	34.61	29.15	23.72	18.43
41	54.16	9.23	14.53	19.92	25.35	30.73	35.98	44.94	39.63	34.24	28.82	23.43	18.18
42	52.68	8.18	13.45	18.80	24.19	29.54	34.74	44.51	39.24	33.88	28.49	23.15	17.94
43	51.22	7.13	12.37	17.69	23.04	28.35	33.52	44.09	38.85	33.53	28.18	22.87	17.70
44	49.77	6.10	11.30	16.59	21.91	27.18	32.30	43.68	38.47	33.18	27.87	22.60	17.47
45	48.34	5.06	10.24	15.49	20.78	26.01	31.10	43.28	38.10	32.85	27.56	22.33	17.24
46	46.92	4.04	9.19	14.41	19.66	24.86	29.91	42.88	37.74	32.51	27.26	22.06	17.01
47	45.52	3.02	8.14	13.33	18.55	23.72	28.73	42.50	37.38	32.19	26.97	21.81	16.79
48	44.14	2.01	7.10	12.27	17.45	22.58	27.56	42.13	37.04	31.87	26.69	21.56	16.58
49	42.78	1.00	6.07	11.21	16.37	21.46	26.41	41.78	36.71	31.57	26.41	21.31	16.37
50	41.44		5.05	10.16	15.29	20.36	25.27	41.44	36.39	31.28	26.15	21.08	16.17
51	40.12		4.03	9.12	14.22	19.26	24.14		36.09	31.00	25.90	20.86	15.98
52	38.82		3.01	8.08	13.17	18.18	23.03		35.81	30.74	25.66	20.64	15.80
53	37.55		2.01	7.06	12.12	17.11	21.93		35.55	30.49	25.43	20.44	15.62
54	36.30		1.00	6.04	11.08	16.05	20.85		35.30	30.26	25.22	20.25	15.45
55	35.07			5.02	10.05	15.00	19.78		35.07	30.05	25.02	20.07	15.30
56	33.87			4.01	9.03	13.96	18.72			29.86	24.84	19.91	15.15
57	32.69			3.01	8.01	12.93	17.67			29.68	24.68	19.76	15.02
58	31.52			2.00	7.00	11.91	16.63			29.51	24.52	19.61	14.88

Age at date of trial	Table 1 Pecuniary loss for life	Table 3 Loss of earnings to age 50	Table 5 Loss of earnings to age 55	Table 7 Loss of earnings to age 60	Table 9 Loss of earnings to age 65	Table 11 Loss of earnings to age 70	Table 13 Loss of earnings to age 75	Table 15 Loss of pension from age 50	Table 17 Loss of pension from age 55	Table 19 Loss of pension from age 60	Table 21 Loss of pension from age 65	Table 23 Loss of pension from age 70	Table 25 Loss of pension from age 75
59	30.35			1.00	5.99	10.89	15.60			29.35	24.36	19.47	14.75
60	29.19				4.98	9.87	14.57			29.19	24.21	19.32	14.62
61	28.05				3.98	8.87	13.55				24.06	19.18	14.50
62	26.92				2.99	7.87	12.55				23.94	19.05	14.38
63	25.82				1.99	6.88	11.55				23.83	18.94	14.27
64	24.74				1.00	5.90	10.57				23.74	18.85	14.17
65	23.70					4.92	9.60				23.70	18.78	14.10
66	22.68					3.94	8.64					18.74	14.04
67	21.69					2.96	7.68					18.73	14.01
68	20.73					1.98	6.73					18.75	14.00
69	19.78					0.99	5.78					18.79	14.00
70	18.85						4.83					18.85	14.02
71	17.92						3.88						14.04
72	17.00						2.93						14.07
73	16.07						1.96						14.11
74	15.15						0.99						14.16
75	14.22												14.22
76	13.32												
77	12.44												
78	11.58												
79	10.77												

Age at date of trial	Table 1 Pecuniary loss for life	Table 3 Loss of earnings to age 50	Table 5 Loss of earnings to age 55	Table 7 Loss of earnings to age 60	Table 9 Loss of earnings to age 65	Table 11 Loss of earnings to age 70	Table 13 Loss of earnings to age 75	Table 15 Loss of pension from age 50	Table 17 Loss of pension from age 55	Table 19 Loss of pension from age 60	Table 21 Loss of pension from age 65	Table 23 Loss of pension from age 70	Table 25 Loss of pension from age 75
80	9.99												
81	9.27												
82	8.61												
83	7.99												
84	7.42												
85	6.89												
86	6.38												
87	5.90												
88	5.44												
89	5.00												
90	4.59												
91	4.21												
92	3.85												
93	3.52												
94	3.22												
95	2.96												
96	2.74												
97	2.55												
98	2.37												
99	2.21												
100	2.06												

A1: –0.75 per cent discount tables for retirement ages 66 to 69 — MALE

	Loss of earnings to age 66	Loss of earnings to age 67	Loss of earnings to age 68	Loss of earnings to age 69		Loss of pension from age 66	Loss of pension from age 67	Loss of pension from age 68	Loss of pension from age 69
16	58.97	60.27	61.59	62.91	16	37.53	36.24	34.93	33.58
17	57.52	58.82	60.13	61.44	17	37.07	35.79	34.49	33.15
18	56.09	57.38	58.68	59.98	18	36.61	35.35	34.06	32.73
19	54.68	55.95	57.24	58.53	19	36.16	34.91	33.63	32.32
20	53.27	54.54	55.81	57.10	20	35.72	34.47	33.20	31.91
21	51.89	53.14	54.40	55.67	21	35.28	34.04	32.78	31.50
22	50.51	51.75	53.00	54.26	22	34.85	33.63	32.37	31.10
23	49.14	50.37	51.61	52.86	23	34.43	33.21	31.97	30.70
24	47.78	49.00	50.23	51.47	24	34.00	32.80	31.57	30.31
25	46.43	47.65	48.87	50.10	25	33.59	32.40	31.18	29.93
26	45.10	46.30	47.51	48.73	26	33.18	31.99	30.79	29.55
27	43.78	44.97	46.17	47.38	27	32.78	31.60	30.40	29.18
28	42.46	43.64	44.83	46.03	28	32.38	31.21	30.02	28.80
29	41.16	42.34	43.51	44.70	29	31.99	30.84	29.65	28.44
30	39.87	41.04	42.21	43.38	30	31.60	30.46	29.29	28.08
31	38.59	39.75	40.91	42.08	31	31.22	30.09	28.93	27.74
32	37.33	38.48	39.63	40.79	32	30.85	29.72	28.58	27.40
33	36.07	37.21	38.36	39.51	33	30.49	29.37	28.23	27.07
34	34.83	35.96	37.10	38.24	34	30.14	29.02	27.89	26.73
35	33.60	34.72	35.85	36.98	35	29.79	28.68	27.56	26.41

	Loss of earnings to age 66	Loss of earnings to age 67	Loss of earnings to age 68	Loss of earnings to age 69		Loss of pension from age 66	Loss of pension from age 67	Loss of pension from age 68	Loss of pension from age 69
36	32.38	33.49	34.61	35.74	36	29.44	28.35	27.23	26.09
37	31.17	32.27	33.38	34.50	37	29.10	28.01	26.90	25.77
38	29.97	31.06	32.16	33.27	38	28.77	27.68	26.58	25.46
39	28.77	29.86	30.95	32.05	39	28.43	27.36	26.27	25.15
40	27.59	28.67	29.75	30.84	40	28.11	27.04	25.96	24.85
41	26.42	27.49	28.56	29.64	41	27.78	26.73	25.65	24.55
42	25.25	26.31	27.38	28.46	42	27.47	26.42	25.35	24.26
43	24.10	25.15	26.21	27.28	43	27.15	26.11	25.06	23.97
44	22.95	24.00	25.05	26.11	44	26.85	25.82	24.76	23.69
45	21.82	22.86	23.91	24.96	45	26.56	25.53	24.48	23.41
46	20.69	21.73	22.77	23.81	46	26.26	25.24	24.20	23.14
47	19.58	20.61	21.64	22.68	47	25.98	24.97	23.93	22.88
48	18.48	19.50	20.53	21.55	48	25.70	24.70	23.67	22.62
49	17.39	18.40	19.42	20.44	49	25.44	24.44	23.42	22.38
50	16.30	17.32	18.33	19.34	50	25.18	24.19	23.17	22.14
51	15.23	16.24	17.25	18.25	51	24.93	23.95	22.94	21.91
52	14.17	15.17	16.18	17.18	52	24.70	23.72	22.71	21.69
53	13.12	14.12	15.12	16.11	53	24.48	23.50	22.50	21.48
54	12.08	13.07	14.07	15.06	54	24.27	23.30	22.30	21.29
55	11.04	12.03	13.02	14.01	55	24.07	23.10	22.12	21.11
56	10.01	11.00	11.99	12.98	56	23.88	22.92	21.94	20.94
57	8.99	9.98	10.96	11.95	57	23.71	22.74	21.77	20.77

	Loss of earnings to age 66	Loss of earnings to age 67	Loss of earnings to age 68	Loss of earnings to age 69		Loss of pension from age 66	Loss of pension from age 67	Loss of pension from age 68	Loss of pension from age 69
58	7.98	8.96	9.94	10.93	58	23.55	22.58	21.60	20.62
59	6.97	7.95	8.93	9.91	59	23.40	22.43	21.45	20.46
60	5.97	6.95	7.93	8.90	60	23.26	22.29	21.30	20.31
61	4.97	5.95	6.93	7.90	61	23.12	22.16	21.17	20.18
62	3.97	4.96	5.93	6.90	62	23.00	22.04	21.05	20.06
63	2.98	3.97	4.94	5.91	63	22.90	21.94	20.95	19.95
64	1.99	2.98	3.96	4.93	64	22.81	21.85	20.87	19.87
65	1.00	1.99	2.97	3.95	65	22.75	21.80	20.81	19.81
66		1.00	1.99	2.97	66	18.96	21.76	20.78	19.77
67			1.00	1.98	67		14.22	20.77	19.76
68				0.99	68			9.48	19.78
69					69				4.74

–0.75 per cent discount tables 'at a glance' — FEMALE

Age at date of trial	Table 2 Pecuniary loss for life	Table 4 Loss of earnings to age 50	Table 6 Loss of earnings to age 55	Table 8 Loss of earnings to age 60	Table 10 Loss of earnings to age 65	Table 12 Loss of earnings to age 70	Table 14 Loss of earnings to age 75	Table 16 Loss of pension from age 50	Table 18 Loss of pension from age 55	Table 20 Loss of pension from age 60	Table 22 Loss of pension from age 65	Table 24 Loss of pension from age 70	Table 26 Loss of pension from age 75
0	135.52							75.34	68.08	60.62	52.96	45.17	37.29
1	133.87							74.89	67.66	60.22	52.59	44.82	36.97
2	131.69							74.13	66.95	59.57	52.00	44.29	36.51
3	129.52							73.38	66.25	58.93	51.42	43.77	36.05
4	127.36							72.63	65.56	58.29	50.83	43.25	35.60
5	125.21							71.88	64.87	57.65	50.26	42.73	35.14
6	123.07							71.14	64.18	57.02	49.69	42.22	34.70
7	120.96							70.41	63.50	56.40	49.12	41.72	34.25
8	118.85							69.68	62.83	55.78	48.56	41.21	33.81
9	116.77							68.96	62.16	55.16	48.00	40.72	33.38
10	114.70							68.25	61.50	54.56	47.45	40.23	32.95
11	112.65							67.54	60.84	53.96	46.91	39.74	32.53
12	110.62							66.84	60.20	53.36	46.37	39.26	32.11
13	108.60							66.15	59.55	52.77	45.83	38.78	31.69
14	106.60							65.47	58.92	52.19	45.31	38.32	31.28
15	104.62							64.79	58.29	51.62	44.79	37.85	30.88
16	102.65	38.53	44.98	51.60	58.38	65.26	72.17	64.12	57.67	51.05	44.27	37.39	30.48
17	100.71	37.25	43.65	50.22	56.94	63.77	70.62	63.46	57.06	50.49	43.76	36.94	30.08
18	98.78	35.98	42.33	48.85	55.52	62.29	69.09	62.80	56.45	49.93	43.26	36.49	29.69

Age at date of trial	Table 2 Pecuniary loss for life	Table 4 Loss of earnings to age 50	Table 6 Loss of earnings to age 55	Table 8 Loss of earnings to age 60	Table 10 Loss of earnings to age 65	Table 12 Loss of earnings to age 70	Table 14 Loss of earnings to age 75	Table 16 Loss of pension from age 50	Table 18 Loss of pension from age 55	Table 20 Loss of pension from age 60	Table 22 Loss of pension from age 65	Table 24 Loss of pension from age 70	Table 26 Loss of pension from age 75
19	96.88	34.72	41.02	47.49	54.11	60.82	67.56	62.16	55.86	49.39	42.77	36.05	29.31
20	94.99	33.46	39.72	46.14	52.71	59.37	66.05	61.53	55.27	48.85	42.28	35.62	28.94
21	93.12	32.22	38.43	44.80	51.32	57.92	64.55	60.90	54.69	48.32	41.80	35.20	28.57
22	91.26	30.99	37.15	43.47	49.93	56.49	63.06	60.27	54.11	47.79	41.33	34.77	28.20
23	89.41	29.76	35.87	42.15	48.56	55.06	61.58	59.65	53.54	47.26	40.85	34.35	27.83
24	87.58	28.54	34.61	40.84	47.20	53.65	60.12	59.03	52.97	46.74	40.37	33.93	27.46
25	85.76	27.34	33.36	39.54	45.85	52.25	58.66	58.43	52.40	46.22	39.91	33.51	27.10
26	83.97	26.14	32.12	38.25	44.52	50.86	57.22	57.83	51.85	45.72	39.45	33.11	26.75
27	82.19	24.95	30.89	36.97	43.19	49.48	55.78	57.24	51.30	45.22	39.00	32.71	26.40
28	80.42	23.78	29.66	35.70	41.87	48.11	54.36	56.65	50.76	44.72	38.55	32.31	26.06
29	78.68	22.61	28.45	34.45	40.56	46.76	52.96	56.07	50.23	44.23	38.11	31.92	25.72
30	76.95	21.45	27.25	33.20	39.27	45.41	51.56	55.50	49.70	43.75	37.68	31.53	25.39
31	75.24	20.30	26.05	31.96	37.98	44.08	50.17	54.94	49.18	43.28	37.25	31.16	25.06
32	73.54	19.15	24.87	30.73	36.71	42.76	48.80	54.39	48.67	42.81	36.83	30.78	24.74
33	71.86	18.02	23.69	29.51	35.45	41.44	47.44	53.84	48.17	42.35	36.42	30.42	24.42
34	70.20	16.90	22.53	28.30	34.19	40.14	46.09	53.30	47.67	41.89	36.00	30.05	24.11
35	68.54	15.78	21.37	27.10	32.95	38.85	44.75	52.76	47.17	41.44	35.60	29.69	23.79
36	66.91	14.67	20.22	25.91	31.71	37.57	43.42	52.24	46.68	40.99	35.19	29.34	23.49
37	65.29	13.57	19.09	24.73	30.49	36.30	42.10	51.72	46.20	40.56	34.80	28.99	23.19
38	63.69	12.48	17.96	23.56	29.28	35.05	40.80	51.20	45.73	40.12	34.41	28.64	22.89
39	62.10	11.40	16.84	22.40	28.07	33.80	39.50	50.70	45.26	39.70	34.02	28.30	22.59

Age at date of trial	Table 2 Pecuniary loss for life	Table 4 Loss of earnings to age 50	Table 6 Loss of earnings to age 55	Table 8 Loss of earnings to age 60	Table 10 Loss of earnings to age 65	Table 12 Loss of earnings to age 70	Table 14 Loss of earnings to age 75	Table 16 Loss of pension from age 50	Table 18 Loss of pension from age 55	Table 20 Loss of pension from age 60	Table 22 Loss of pension from age 65	Table 24 Loss of pension from age 70	Table 26 Loss of pension from age 75
40	60.52	10.33	15.72	21.25	26.88	32.56	38.22	50.19	44.80	39.27	33.64	27.96	22.30
41	58.96	9.26	14.62	20.11	25.70	31.33	36.95	49.70	44.34	38.86	33.27	27.63	22.02
42	57.42	8.20	13.53	18.98	24.52	30.12	35.69	49.22	43.90	38.45	32.90	27.31	21.74
43	55.90	7.15	12.44	17.85	23.36	28.91	34.44	48.74	43.46	38.05	32.54	26.99	21.46
44	54.39	6.11	11.36	16.74	22.20	27.72	33.20	48.28	43.03	37.65	32.18	26.67	21.19
45	52.90	5.08	10.29	15.63	21.06	26.53	31.97	47.82	42.61	37.27	31.84	26.37	20.93
46	51.42	4.05	9.23	14.53	19.93	25.36	30.76	47.38	42.19	36.89	31.50	26.06	20.67
47	49.96	3.03	8.18	13.45	18.80	24.20	29.56	46.94	41.79	36.52	31.16	25.77	20.41
48	48.53	2.01	7.13	12.37	17.69	23.05	28.37	46.52	41.40	36.16	30.84	25.48	20.16
49	47.11	1.00	6.09	11.30	16.59	21.91	27.19	46.11	41.02	35.81	30.52	25.20	19.92
50	45.71		5.06	10.24	15.50	20.78	26.03	45.71	40.65	35.47	30.22	24.93	19.69
51	44.33		4.04	9.19	14.41	19.67	24.88		40.29	35.14	29.92	24.66	19.46
52	42.97		3.02	8.14	13.34	18.56	23.73		39.94	34.82	29.63	24.40	19.23
53	41.62		2.01	7.10	12.27	17.46	22.61		39.61	34.52	29.35	24.15	19.01
54	40.29		1.00	6.07	11.22	16.38	21.49		39.29	34.22	29.08	23.91	18.80
55	38.99			5.05	10.17	15.30	20.38		38.99	33.94	28.82	23.68	18.60
56	37.70			4.03	9.12	14.24	19.29			33.67	28.57	23.46	18.41
57	36.43			3.01	8.09	13.18	18.20			33.41	28.34	23.25	18.23
58	35.17			2.01	7.06	12.13	17.13			33.16	28.11	23.04	18.04
59	33.92			1.00	6.04	11.08	16.06			32.92	27.88	22.84	17.86
60	32.68				5.02	10.05	15.00			32.68	27.66	22.63	17.68

Age at date of trial	Table 2 Pecuniary loss for life	Table 4 Loss of earnings to age 50	Table 6 Loss of earnings to age 55	Table 8 Loss of earnings to age 60	Table 10 Loss of earnings to age 65	Table 12 Loss of earnings to age 70	Table 14 Loss of earnings to age 75	Table 16 Loss of pension from age 50	Table 18 Loss of pension from age 55	Table 20 Loss of pension from age 60	Table 22 Loss of pension from age 65	Table 24 Loss of pension from age 70	Table 26 Loss of pension from age 75
61	31.45				4.01	9.02	13.95				27.44	22.43	17.50
62	30.24				3.00	8.00	12.91				27.24	22.24	17.33
63	29.04				2.00	6.98	11.88				27.04	22.06	17.16
64	27.88				1.00	5.98	10.86				26.88	21.90	17.01
65	26.74					4.98	9.85				26.74	21.76	16.88
66	25.63					3.98	8.86					21.65	16.77
67	24.55					2.99	7.87					21.56	16.68
68	23.49					1.99	6.88					21.50	16.61
69	22.45					1.00	5.90					21.45	16.55
70	21.41						4.92					21.41	16.49
71	20.39						3.94						16.44
72	19.35						2.96						16.39
73	18.31						1.98						16.33
74	17.27						0.99						16.28
75	16.23												16.23
76	15.20												
77	14.19												
78	13.21												
79	12.27												
80	11.39												
81	10.56												

Age at date of trial	Table 2 Pecuniary loss for life	Table 4 Loss of earnings to age 50	Table 6 Loss of earnings to age 55	Table 8 Loss of earnings to age 60	Table 10 Loss of earnings to age 65	Table 12 Loss of earnings to age 70	Table 14 Loss of earnings to age 75	Table 16 Loss of pension from age 50	Table 18 Loss of pension from age 55	Table 20 Loss of pension from age 60	Table 22 Loss of pension from age 65	Table 24 Loss of pension from age 70	Table 26 Loss of pension from age 75
82	9.78												
83	9.06												
84	8.39												
85	7.76												
86	7.16												
87	6.59												
88	6.05												
89	5.53												
90	5.05												
91	4.60												
92	4.18												
93	3.81												
94	3.48												
95	3.20												
96	2.96												
97	2.75												
98	2.56												
99	2.38												
100	2.21												

A1: –0.75 per cent discount tables for retirement ages 66 to 69 — FEMALE

	Loss of earnings to age 66	Loss of earnings to age 67	Loss of earnings to age 68	Loss of earnings to age 69		Loss of pension from age 66	Loss of pension from age 67	Loss of pension from age 68	Loss of pension from age 69
16	59.74	61.10	62.48	63.86	16	42.95	41.61	40.23	38.83
17	58.29	59.64	61.01	62.38	17	42.46	41.12	39.76	38.36
18	56.85	58.20	59.55	60.91	18	41.97	40.64	39.29	37.91
19	55.43	56.76	58.10	59.46	19	41.48	40.17	38.83	37.46
20	54.02	55.34	56.67	58.01	20	41.00	39.70	38.37	37.01
21	52.61	53.92	55.25	56.58	21	40.53	39.23	37.91	36.57
22	51.22	52.52	53.83	55.16	22	40.07	38.78	37.46	36.13
23	49.84	51.13	52.43	53.74	23	39.60	38.33	37.02	35.70
24	48.47	49.75	51.04	52.34	24	39.14	37.88	36.59	35.27
25	47.11	48.38	49.66	50.95	25	38.68	37.43	36.15	34.85
26	45.77	47.03	48.29	49.57	26	38.23	36.99	35.72	34.43
27	44.43	45.68	46.94	48.20	27	37.79	36.56	35.30	34.02
28	43.10	44.34	45.59	46.85	28	37.36	36.13	34.88	33.61
29	41.79	43.02	44.25	45.50	29	36.93	35.71	34.47	33.21
30	40.48	41.70	42.93	44.17	30	36.50	35.30	34.07	32.82
31	39.19	40.40	41.62	42.84	31	36.08	34.89	33.67	32.43
32	37.90	39.10	40.31	41.53	32	35.67	34.48	33.28	32.04
33	36.63	37.82	39.02	40.23	33	35.26	34.08	32.89	31.66
34	35.37	36.55	37.74	38.94	34	34.86	33.69	32.50	31.29
35	34.11	35.29	36.47	37.66	35	34.46	33.31	32.12	30.92

	Loss of earnings to age 66	Loss of earnings to age 67	Loss of earnings to age 68	Loss of earnings to age 69		Loss of pension from age 66	Loss of pension from age 67	Loss of pension from age 68	Loss of pension from age 69
36	32.87	34.03	35.21	36.39	36	34.07	32.92	31.75	30.56
37	31.64	32.79	33.96	35.13	37	33.68	32.54	31.38	30.20
38	30.42	31.56	32.72	33.88	38	33.30	32.17	31.02	29.84
39	29.20	30.34	31.49	32.64	39	32.92	31.80	30.66	29.49
40	28.00	29.13	30.27	31.41	40	32.55	31.44	30.30	29.14
41	26.81	27.93	29.06	30.19	41	32.19	31.08	29.95	28.80
42	25.63	26.74	27.86	28.98	42	31.83	30.73	29.61	28.47
43	24.46	25.56	26.67	27.79	43	31.47	30.39	29.28	28.14
44	23.30	24.39	25.49	26.60	44	31.13	30.05	28.95	27.82
45	22.15	23.23	24.33	25.43	45	30.79	29.71	28.62	27.50
46	21.01	22.09	23.17	24.26	46	30.46	29.39	28.30	27.19
47	19.88	20.95	22.03	23.11	47	30.13	29.07	28.00	26.89
48	18.76	19.82	20.89	21.97	48	29.81	28.76	27.69	26.60
49	17.65	18.71	19.77	20.84	49	29.50	28.46	27.40	26.31
50	16.55	17.60	18.66	19.72	50	29.20	28.16	27.11	26.03
51	15.46	16.50	17.56	18.61	51	28.91	27.88	26.83	25.76
52	14.38	15.42	16.46	17.51	52	28.63	27.60	26.56	25.49
53	13.31	14.34	15.38	16.42	53	28.35	27.34	26.30	25.24
54	12.24	13.27	14.31	15.34	54	28.09	27.08	26.05	24.99
55	11.19	12.21	13.24	14.27	55	27.83	26.83	25.80	24.75
56	10.14	11.16	12.19	13.21	56	27.58	26.58	25.56	24.53
57	9.10	10.12	11.14	12.16	57	27.35	26.35	25.33	24.30

	Loss of earnings to age 66	Loss of earnings to age 67	Loss of earnings to age 68	Loss of earnings to age 69		Loss of pension from age 66	Loss of pension from age 67	Loss of pension from age 68	Loss of pension from age 69
58	8.07	9.08	10.10	11.11	58	27.12	26.12	25.11	24.09
59	7.05	8.05	9.06	10.07	59	26.90	25.90	24.89	23.87
60	6.03	7.03	8.03	9.04	60	26.69	25.69	24.68	23.66
61	5.01	6.01	7.02	8.02	61	26.48	25.49	24.48	23.46
62	4.00	5.00	6.00	7.00	62	26.28	25.30	24.29	23.27
63	3.00	4.00	5.00	5.99	63	26.10	25.13	24.12	23.10
64	2.00	3.00	3.99	4.99	64	25.94	24.97	23.97	22.94
65	1.00	2.00	2.99	3.99	65	25.79	24.83	23.83	22.81
66		1.00	2.00	2.99	66	25.67	24.71	23.72	22.70
67			1.00	1.99	67		24.61	23.62	22.61
68				1.00	68			23.54	22.54
69					69				22.48

15 Fatal claims

Tracy Head

Co-author: Robert Corrigan

- Law Reform (Miscellaneous Provisions) Act 1934
- Fatal Accidents Act 1976
- Bereavement damages
- Dependency claims: multiplicand and multiplier
- Costs of attending an inquest

Fatal claims

Introduction

Damages for death are dealt with differently to personal injury damages generally.

Where a person has been killed in an accident caused by another's wrongdoing, under the Law Reform (Miscellaneous Provisions) Act 1934 (the 1934 Act) the right to sue for damages vests in their estate.

If the deceased has left dependants who have suffered a loss as a result of the death, they may bring a claim under the Fatal Accidents Act 1976 (the 1976 Act).

There can be duplication of claims between the two Acts. If a claim under the 1934 Act duplicates a claim under the 1976 Act, the second claim cannot be pursued. This avoids double compensation.

Note that the rules in relation to contributory negligence apply to fatal claims in the same way as to any other claim, and so contributory negligence can be alleged.

Law Reform (Miscellaneous Provisions) Act 1934

The deceased's personal representatives (the executors or administrators) can seek compensation under the 1934 Act.

There are broadly three possible heads of claim under the 1934 Act:

- **Pain, suffering and loss of amenity (PSLA) suffered by the deceased between the date of the accident and the date of death:** For obvious reasons, if the accident and death occur almost simultaneously there may be no (or negligible) damages recoverable under this head. If, however, the accident caused injuries from which the deceased died some time later, and in the interim the deceased remained aware of their injuries, then compensation will be recoverable.

In *Kadir v Mistry and others* [2014], a case involving a delayed diagnosis of cancer, the Court of Appeal declined to award damages for PSLA where the deceased would have suffered the same symptoms in any event. However, an award was allowed for mental anguish on the basis that the deceased feared on good objective grounds that her life had been, or may have been, curtailed by the defendants' negligence.

- **Special damages:** If the deceased suffered a loss of earnings between the date of the accident and date of death, or suffered any damage to property in the accident, the estate can claim for this. This may include past losses and expenses to date of death, such as medical expenses, loss of earnings and travel expenses.
- **Funeral expenses:** The estate can recover the reasonable costs of a funeral and headstone. Costs for a wake, mourning clothes and a monument have previously failed.

Fatal Accidents Act 1976

The 1976 Act has been amended by the Administration of Justice Act 1982.

A claim can be brought under the 1976 Act by dependants of the deceased who have been deprived of the support (financial or otherwise) of the deceased. It is common to see such a claim brought by the executors or administrators of the estate in conjunction with a claim under the 1934 Act.

The following categories of people are able to claim as dependants:

- Spouses and civil partners.
- Former spouses or civil partners.
- Cohabitants, provided they had been living with the deceased immediately before death, and had been for at least two full years prior to death, as husband, wife or civil partner.

- Children or persons treated as children of the family in the case of any marriage or civil partnership, or other descendants.
- Parents, or persons treated as parents, or other ascendant.
- Brother, sister, uncle or aunt or any issue thereof.

A relationship of marriage/civil partnership is treated as a relationship of blood. A half-relation or step-relation is treated as a full relation. An illegitimate child is treated as the legitimate child of the mother and their 'reputed' father.

In each case, the person claiming must be able to show that they were dependent on the deceased, financially or otherwise. There must be a reasonable expectation of the benefit by the dependant.

There is no entitlement under the 1976 Act for dependants to claim damages for psychological loss, emotional distress or PSLA.

> Claims under the 1976 Act fall under three headings:
>
> - Bereavement damages
> - Funeral expenses
> - Loss of dependency.

Bereavement damages

Bereavement damages are awarded in the sum of £10,000 for causes of action accruing before 1 January 2008, £11,800 between 1 January 2008 and 1 April 2013 and £12,980 from 1 April 2013.

They are recoverable by people who fall into the following categories:

- A surviving spouse or civil partner.
- Parents of a deceased legitimate child who was under the age of 18 at the time of death and was not married/had a civil partner.

- The mother of a deceased illegitimate child under the age of 18 at the time of death.

In a recent development, the Court of Appeal in *Smith v Lancashire Teaching Hospitals NHS Trust and Others* [2017] found that Section 1A of the Fatal Accidents Act 1976 was incompatible with Article 14 (prohibition of discrimination), in conjunction with Article 8 (right to respect for private and family life) of the ECHR, to the extent that it excluded cohabitees of over two years from being able to recover bereavement damages. However, until Parliament amend the Fatal Accidents Act, there remains no obligation for Defendants to pay bereavement damages to a surviving cohabitee.

Former spouses or civil partners cannot generally recover bereavement damages. Children cannot claim bereavement damages for the death of a parent.

If there is more than one person who has been bereaved and who falls into the categories set out above, then the bereavement damages sum is shared.

Dependency claim: multiplicand

As in other personal injury cases, the multiplicand is the annual value of the loss, in this case the dependency. It will be based on the annual value of the pre-death dependency.

Some rules of thumb apply in claims under the 1976 Act, based on ascertaining the amount of the deceased's income they would have been likely to spend on themselves. The following are starting points:

- For a deceased breadwinner leaving a spouse and no children, the multiplicand will generally be two-thirds of the deceased's annual income (on the basis around one-third of their income would be spent on themselves).
- For a deceased breadwinner leaving a spouse and two children, the multiplicand will generally be three-quarters of the deceased's annual income (on the basis 25% of their income would be spent on themselves).

These are only rules of thumb and can be varied in particular circumstances, for example if the deceased worked away for long periods and would not have the opportunity to spend as much money on themselves as a result – see, for example, *Coward v Comex Houlder Diving Ltd* [1988].

Claimants' lawyers will often adopt another approach. They may deduct the deceased's personal living expenses from their annual income. That calculation should result in a multiplicand equating to the financial contribution made by the deceased for their family and children.

Some spouses will continue to earn after the deceased's death. This will require the joint income to be considered before any deductions are made.

> The loss of dependency is not limited solely to strict financial loss. The deceased may have provided services in other areas. For example, they may have carried out DIY, car maintenance, gardening, housework and/or childcare. The value of such services needs to be valued on a commercial basis. The same principles will apply as in personal injury cases.

The total of each head set out above can then be assessed as a multiplicand.

Dependency claim: multiplier

The multiplier will be the number of years for which the dependency would be expected to have lasted had the deceased not died. Multipliers for the various heads of claim will be:

- The multiplier in respect of dependency claims was previously fixed at the date of death, in accordance with *Cookson v Knowles* [1978] and *Graham v Dodds* [1983], and was then adjusted by subtracting from this multiplier the number of years between death and the date of trial. These decisions however pre-dated the Ogden tables, and it was argued for some time by claimants that this approach wrongly applied a discount for accelerated receipt to losses incurred pre-trial, i.e. wrongly applied a discount to past losses also.
- This issue was recently resolved by the Supreme Court in the matter of *Knauer v Ministry of Justice* [2016], which held that the correct approach for calculating such losses was to assess the multiplier at the date of trial, and not the date of death.
- For lost earnings the multiplier will have to take into account the age of the deceased at trial, the anticipated date of retirement and the appropriate Ogden tables. It is calculated from the date of trial.
- Multipliers for other services will vary. They will be calculated from the date of trial and will take into account the claimant's age. Different services will have different multipliers, depending upon when they could reasonably have expected to cease to have been given by the deceased to their dependants in any event. For example, it may be reasonable to argue that the deceased would not have been able to continue gardening and decorating beyond, say, the age of 75 (perhaps for health reasons that are established during the course of investigation).

Costs of attending an inquest

To what extent are the costs of the legal representation of the claimants at the inquest recoverable in the civil claims brought against the defendant?

The decision in *Lynch v Chief Constable of Warwickshire Police and others* [2014] provided some much needed and useful guidance. The court decided that, in assessing the recoverable inquest costs in subsequent civil proceedings, the court is tasked with assessing and determining what elements of the inquest costs are reasonable and proportionate costs of the civil proceedings.

Therefore, the court's focus is on the relationship between the inquest costs and the subsequent proceedings, rather than looking at the inquest costs in isolation. Costs incurred in relation to the inquest should be of benefit to the civil claim.

In *Lynch*, Collette Lynch was murdered by her former partner, Mr Wright, in 2005. The defendants were aware of the deteriorating mental health problems of Mr Wright and were sued by the claimants on behalf of Ms Lynch's estate. The inquest took place in 2009 and lasted three and a half months. Settlement of the civil claim was reached in May 2012. The family sought the costs of attending the inquest, which were estimated by the defendants at over £700,000 – a figure which represented between 40% and 50% of the total bill of £1.5 million.

The costs judge found the claimants' costs to be globally disproportionate and held it:

> "inconceivable, in my judgment, that the approach adopted by the Claimants in this case would be upheld as a proportionate method of bringing these claims to a civil hearing. No case managing judge would allow sums of the magnitude claimed here to be spent in the working up of the claim before the close of pleadings in the court proceedings."

Examples of costs incurred which were not recoverable included:

- Time spent that was irrelevant to the civil claim, such as attending the opening of the inquest, jury questions and waiting for the jury.
- Time spent listening to witness statements being read.

Following the decision in *Lynch*, and given the more recent shift towards a robust approach to managing costs, we anticipate that the justification of inquest costs will be subject to greater scrutiny than previously.

Other issues

- Benefits that have accrued or may accrue to any person from the estate or otherwise are disregarded. This would most typically include a life insurance policy.
- The fact that a widow or widower has remarried or may remarry is also disregarded.
- If a surviving spouse and infant children bring claims, the awards must be apportioned. Most of the monies will be paid to the surviving spouse to allow for provision for the future care of the children. The calculation is the responsibility of the claimants' solicitor.
- The court will need to be asked to approve any part of the claim relating to children's dependency. Without such approval, any settlement will be invalid.

16 Periodical payments

Christopher Malla

- The legal framework: reasonably secure and variation
- The Annual Survey of Hours and Earnings (ASHE)
- Standardising the approach to PPOs: practical considerations
- Calculating the annual increase
- Reclassification, change in methodology and practical guidance

Periodical payments

Introduction

Periodical payment orders (PPOs) are no longer a mode of settlement in high-value National Health Service (NHS) clinical negligence claims only. This form of award is invariably 'on the table' in most catastrophic personal injury claims. While PPOs may present difficulties for some defendants, there is no doubt they can be good news for the victim.

As PPOs are gaining in popularity, this chapter examines both the legal framework governing this form of award and recent developments in PPO jurisprudence.

Background

Damages for personal injury have traditionally taken the form of a lump sum award. Section 2(1) of the Damages Act 1996, as amended by s.100 of the Courts Act 2003, empowered the courts to make a PPO for damages for "future pecuniary loss" in personal injury cases. Section 2(1)(b) of the 1996 Act gives the courts a statutory obligation to consider making a PPO and they may impose a PPO even if the parties do not consent.

A PPO will include a retained lump sum to finance the purchase of capital assets and allow for any future contingencies and, usually annual, periodical payments to meet a claimant's annual costs. A PPO is flexible and can be paid immediately. The most common periodical payment provides the claimant with an income throughout their lifetime, regardless of how long they survive. Periodical payments can also be deferred to begin after a given date. A contingent deferred PPO may also be agreed where the periodical payments will not become payable until an event occurs, for example, a claimant's care regime is no longer funded by their local authority. At that stage the periodical payment becomes payable and the sums to be paid annually are already identified and set out in the order.

The majority of the maximum severity clinical negligence cases involving the NHS settle by way of PPO. These maximum severity cases usually involve brain-injured children whose parents seek the comfort of annual periodical payments to fund their child's future care, particularly when they are no longer alive.

It was accepted practice in NHS clinical negligence claims that all heads of loss are capitalised, with only care and case management paid by annual periodical payments. The capitalising of all heads of loss, save care and case management, allows claimants to purchase a new property and provides for future contingencies. Prior to the reduction in the discount rate to –0.75%, claimants would also request future loss of earnings and other heads of loss to be paid by periodical payments.

During recent years, claimants in non-NHS catastrophic personal injury cases have been increasingly interested in seeking PPOs. We expect claimants' financial advisors are advising their clients to seek a PPO rather than a lump sum award, in particular following the Court of Appeal's landmark judgment in *Thompstone v Tameside & Glossop Acute Services NHS Trust and RH v United Bristol Healthcare NHS Trust* [2008]. Kennedys acted on behalf of the defendant NHS trust in *RH.*

Legal framework

Civil Procedure Rules (CPR) Part 41.5(1) provides that each party "may" state in its statement of case whether it considers a PPO or a lump sum award more appropriate. Part 41.5(2) and (3) of the CPR grant the courts the power to order a party to set out its preference as to the structure of the award and provide details.

Part 41.7 of the CPR provides that the courts shall have regard to all the circumstances of the case when considering whether to make a PPO and, in particular, the form of award that best meets the claimant's needs. Practice Direction 41B sets out the factors to be considered:

- The scale of the annual payments, taking into account any deduction for contributory negligence.
- The reason for the claimant's preference for a periodical payment.
- The nature of any financial advice received by the claimant on the form of award.
- The defendant's preferred form of award and reason for that preference.

Reasonably secure

Section 2(3) of the Damages Act 1996 states the court may only make a PPO if the court is satisfied that the continuity of the periodical payment is "reasonably secure".

Bearing in mind periodical payments are likely to be paid for the duration of a claimant's lifetime, this is both an uncertain and potentially long period if the claim involves a young adult or child. A court must be satisfied that a defendant can meet the terms of any PPO for the claimant's lifetime, regardless of how long that may be. In the recent economic climate, this may be of greater importance to any judge approving a PPO where the source of payments is not a government body.

Section 2(4) provides that the continuity of payment will be reasonably secure where:

- It is protected by a ministerial guarantee under s.6 of the 1996 Act. This covers public sector bodies where a minister has specifically guaranteed those payments. It is our understanding that no such guarantees have been provided.

- It is protected by a scheme under s.213 of the Financial Services and Markets Act 2000. This provision covers payments made by authorised insurers who are able to self-fund and make payments direct to the claimant. It also includes payments made by a life insurer. A defendant, defendant insurer or a defence organisation may have purchased the annuity.
- The source of the payments is a government or health service body. This covers PPOs entered into by government or health service bodies. The Damages (Government and Health Service Bodies) Order 2005 lists the bodies that are designated as government and health services bodies for this purpose. Once a body is designated, the need to satisfy the court on a case-by-case basis that the continuity of payments is "reasonably secure" is removed. Although NHS trusts in England are not covered by the Order, the NHS Litigation Authority (NHS LA) is a designated health service body. In addition, claimants receiving periodical payments from the NHS LA have the added protection that s.70 of the National Health Service Act 2006 provides a statutory obligation on the Secretary of State for Health to ensure all the NHS LA's liabilities are appropriately dealt with in the event it ceases to exist.

> The real difference between defendants who self-fund and those who purchase an annuity is that the self-funded defendant will not know the total loss until the claimant's death. The self-funded defendant is taking an educated and informed risk as to the claimant's life expectancy.

Defendants who are not deemed automatically "reasonably secure" will either need to prove they are "reasonably secure" or will need to purchase an annuity to meet the obligations of any PPO.

The loss for a defendant who purchases an annuity crystallises at the point of settlement. The annuity insurer will usually charge the defendant a very significant premium for taking on the risk. The cost of purchasing an annuity is likely to be significantly higher than the actual award on a traditional lump sum basis.

An additional obstacle is that there are no annuity products currently on the market that provide payments linked to an earnings-based index, and certainly not to the Annual Survey of Hours and Earnings (ASHE) 6115. The very limited annuities available are linked to the Retail Price Index (RPI) plus a fixed percentage, e.g. RPI plus 2%. Insurers who are serious about offering periodical payments self-fund as the costs of purchasing an annuity are currently prohibitive. Claimants are likely to wish to have any periodical payment linked to an earnings-related index and not the RPI plus a certain percentage.

Variation

The Damages (Variation of Periodical Payments) Order 2005 provides that:

> 2) If there is proved or admitted to be a chance that at some definite or indefinite time in the future the claimant will:
>
> > a) as a result of the act or omission which gave rise to the cause of action, develop some serious disease or suffer some serious deterioration; or
> >
> > b) enjoy some significant improvement, in his physical or mental condition, where that condition had been adversely affected as a result of that act or omission, the court may, on the application of a party, with the agreement of all the parties, or of its own initiative, provide in an order for periodical payments that it may be varied.

Section 7 of the Order states that:

> “A party may make only one application to vary a variable order in respect of each specified disease or type of deterioration or improvement.”

It can be seen from these provisions that the power to make variable orders is limited in a similar way to the power to make orders for provisional damages. As far as we are aware, only a very limited number of PPOs that include provision for variation have been agreed. Examples from our own cases include two claims involving minors with significant care needs. In each case the PPO provided that the defendant could apply to vary the periodical payments in the event that the claimant's condition improved such that their care needs reduced and they only needed a 'sleep-in' carer at night rather than a 'waking' night carer.

Annual Survey of Hours and Earnings

The ASHE is published by the Office of National Statistics (ONS) and has replaced the New Earnings Survey. It is a snapshot of earnings of employees taken in one particular week each year in April within industries, occupations and regions. The survey is broken down into hundreds of standard occupational codes (SOCs). ASHE 6115 is the SOC that records wages paid to care assistants and home carers.

In *Thompstone*, the Court of Appeal accepted the appropriate index to use to calculate the annual increase of periodical payments for care and case management is ASHE 6115 and not the RPI. The Court of Appeal considered that an index that tracked the earnings of carers was more appropriate than the RPI, which measures the change of prices of a basket of goods and services thought to be typical of the majority of households and includes items such as food, drink, clothing, housing and transport.

Although the ASHE survey is undertaken in April each year, the results are not published until November/December of the same year. Even this is a provisional figure, described as "first release", and may be amended 12 months later when the following year's survey is

Table 16.1 – ASHE 6115: hourly rates

Year	Median	Mean	10%	20%	25%	30%	40%	60%	70%	75%	80%	90%
2004 First release	6.57	7.13	4.85	5.38	5.59	5.77	6.13	7.11	7.69	8.10	8.62	9.98
2004 Revised	6.56	7.12	4.85	5.37	5.58	5.77	6.12	7.11	7.68	8.09	8.60	9.97
2005 First release	6.88	7.40	5.10	5.58	5.82	6.05	6.42	7.42	8.03	8.47	8.95	10.30
2005 Revised	6.90	7.40	5.10	5.59	5.82	6.07	6.44	7.43	8.03	8.47	8.96	10.30
2006 First release	7.12	7.59	5.33	5.80	6.02	6.22	6.62	7.67	8.27	8.67	9.14	10.58
2006 Revised (2005 method)	7.13	7.61	5.35	5.81	6.03	6.23	6.63	7.67	8.28	8.69	9.16	10.58
2006 Revised (2007 method)	7.15	7.64	5.37	5.84	6.05	6.24	6.65	7.70	8.33	8.71	9.25	10.67
2007 First release	7.53	8.07	5.66	6.14	6.36	6.55	7.02	8.11	8.79	9.21	9.79	11.36
2007 Revised	7.53	8.07	5.66	6.15	6.36	6.55	7.01	8.12	8.80	9.21	9.79	11.38
2008 First release	7.71	8.26	5.85	6.29	6.48	6.69	7.19	8.32	9.11	9.55	10.11	11.68
2008 Revised	7.72	8.27	5.85	6.30	6.49	6.70	7.20	8.33	9.12	9.56	10.11	11.68
2009 First release	7.93	8.57	6.00	6.48	6.68	6.91	7.42	8.52	9.34	9.82	10.36	12.11
2009 Revised	7.93	8.57	6.00	6.47	6.68	6.90	7.42	8.51	9.33	9.82	10.36	12.10

continued...

...continued

Year	Median	Mean	10%	20%	25%	30%	40%	60%	70%	75%	80%	90%
2010 First release	8.07	8.63	6.05	6.53	6.80	7.03	7.50	8.70	9.45	9.91	10.44	12.18
2010 Revised	8.07	8.64	6.06	6.55	6.80	7.04	7.50	8.70	9.45	9.91	10.44	12.16
2011 First release	7.93	8.57	6.09	6.51	6.75	6.98	7.40	8.52	9.32	9.80	10.33	12.03
2011 Revised	7.83	8.52	6.05	6.44	6.65	6.87	7.28	8.45	9.17	9.67	10.22	11.92
2012 First release	7.90	8.57	6.21	6.55	6.78	7.00	7.42	8.50	9.19	9.69	10.24	11.98
2012 Revised	7.92	8.57	6.21	6.57	6.80	7.00	7.44	8.51	9.21	9.69	10.25	11.97
2013 First release	7.91	8.58	6.30	6.61	6.80	7.00	7.40	8.50	9.21	9.73	10.29	12.02
2013 Revised	7.91	8.58	6.30	6.61	6.80	7.00	7.40	8.50	9.22	9.73	10.29	12.02
2014 First release	8.00	8.58	6.41	6.74	6.94	7.12	7.53	8.55	9.23	9.72	10.21	11.94
2014 Revised	8.00	8.58	6.41	6.74	6.94	7.12	7.53	8.55	9.23	9.72	10.21	11.95
2015 First release	8.18	8.80	6.64	6.98	7.11	7.30	7.72	8.73	9.45	9.88	10.38	12.21
2015 Revised	8.18	8.79	6.63	6.98	7.10	7.29	7.72	8.73	9.44	9.88	10.38	12.21
2016 First release	8.51	9.21	7.20	7.36	7.50	7.70	8.08	9.02	9.77	10.20	10.76	12.55
2016 Revised	8.50	9.20	7.20	7.36	7.50	7.70	8.08	9.02	9.76	10.18	10.75	12.50
2017 First release	8.85	9.55	7.50	7.76	7.93	8.07	8.42	9.36	10.05	10.50	11.04	12.91

published. A final hourly rate is published 18 to 20 months after each survey is undertaken, and is described as the "revised" hourly rate. This delay enables the ONS to maximise the accuracy of the data.

The ASHE survey is split into percentiles. The percentiles represent the hourly rates paid at regular intervals, if those rates were placed in ascending order. Accordingly, if a sample of 10,000 carers within ASHE 6115 responded to the ASHE survey, the ASHE (10) (i.e. the 10th percentile) figure would be the wage paid to the 1,000th person from the bottom of the list, if placed in ascending order. Likewise, ASHE (80) (i.e. 80th percentile) would be the wage paid to the 8,000th person from the bottom.

For the purpose of PPOs, and in particular calculating the annual increase, the focus is on gross hourly pay. Set out in Table 16.1 are the historic and most up-to-date gross hourly rates for all percentiles of ASHE 6115 from 2004 to the 2017 first release.

In October 2017, the ONS released the 2017 first release data. This shows an increase across all percentiles, meaning claimants' periodical payments will increase from last year. The highest annual increase of 5.7% was at the 25th percentile. Interestingly, the lowest annual increase of 2.7% was at the 80th percentile.

The Court of Appeal selected ASHE 6115 in *Thompstone* as the appropriate index to calculate annual increases to periodical payments for care and case management as it closely matched carers' earnings, which is the main expenditure of any care package. If, as the ASHE data has shown over the last few years, the gross hourly rates of carers are not rising then this should be reflected in a claimant's annual periodical payments.

In addition to care and case management, loss of earnings started to emerge as another head of loss that is paid by periodical payments, prior to the discount rate reduction of –0.75%. Loss of earnings are usually index-linked to ASHE median and, in particular, gross annual pay for all male or female full-time employees.

Again prior to the discount rate reduction to –0.75%, claimants would also seek periodical payments for other heads of loss, including therapies and deputyship costs. Claimants sought therapies to be index-linked to the RPI and a deputy's annual costs to a variety of indices of ASHE. To date we have agreed no more than three different indices for different heads of loss, as in Table 16.2.

Table 16.2: Indices agreed for heads of loss

Head of loss	Index
Loss of earnings	AHSE median
Care	ASHE 6115
Therapies and deputyship costs	RPI

We have opposed any attempt, during negotiations, to index-link heads of loss to other indices. We have argued the above indices have been 'road tested' and are fit for purpose. Agreeing too many indices makes administering PPOs even more complex.

Standardising the approach to PPOs: practical considerations

Although not the named defendant, the insurer, NHS Resolution or the medical defence organisation (MDO) makes the periodical payment to the claimant. Accordingly, PPOs give claimants a direct right to enforce the terms of the order against the insurer, the NHS Litigation Authority (NHS Resolution's legal entity) or MDO.

There are a number of issues that should be taken into account when considering a PPO.

Standard model order

Self-funding insurers should adopt a unified approach to ensure the future administration of PPOs is efficiently managed. For the purposes of consistency, it is recommended that defendants considering self-funding PPOs should adopt a standard model order.

To that end, adoption of the NHS model schedule to the PPO (the model schedule) is advised. The formulae have been road-tested by a statistician, accountant and financial advisor to ensure that they are fit for purpose and have been judicially approved. NHS Resolution has used the formulae since 2008 to calculate the annual uplift of hundreds of claimants' periodical payments, and meet the desired objective. It is not advisable to depart from these judicially approved formulae without first obtaining specialist financial and statistical advice on the wisdom of doing so.

Calculation/payment date

The parties must agree on the date for payment of the periodical payment. This could be monthly, quarterly or annually. The model schedule is based on the claimant receiving their periodical payment annually and in advance on 15 December of each year. The 15 December date was chosen as this is four to six weeks after the ASHE data is published by the ONS and enables NHS Resolution to undertake the calculations and arrange payment.

> It is certainly far easier from an administrative perspective if all calculations are undertaken and payments made at the same time each year. Of course, the downside of one single payment date is this may have cash flow implications, and this will need to be taken into account.

If, however, a date is agreed on which to calculate the uplift, there is no reason why the annual sum could not be paid quarterly over the 12-month period. This would reduce the impact on cash flow. Quarterly payments would not increase the administrative burden, as automatic BACs payments can be arranged. It is unlikely a claimant will agree to monthly payments, as it will limit their ability to manage their affairs.

A calculation and/or payment date soon after the publication of the latest ASHE data is both logical and practical. It also ensures the claimant receives the benefit of the latest data as soon as it is available. Individual insurers have different objectives and priorities. For example, payments being made at the end or beginning of a particular financial year may be significant. This needs to be taken into account at a very early stage to ensure these objectives can be achieved.

Timing of first escalation

If a self-funding compensator has agreed that it will adopt one date for payment of a periodical payment, it must then decide whether it will adopt a unified and consistent approach as to the timing of the first escalation.

If the periodical payment relates to care and case management, the intended purpose of any annual increase is to allow the claimant to have sufficient funds year on year to purchase their care. Accordingly, if a claim is being settled in 2017 and the parties are relying on current care rates, the annual increase to the periodical payment should not take place until the following year. To do otherwise would provide a windfall to the claimant if they get the benefit of two increases in hourly rates in the same year.

A defendant should always argue that the first escalation should take place the year after settlement. This does not mean the claimant will not receive a periodical payment the first year. The claimant receives a periodical payment that is not index-linked. This is, however, a matter of negotiation.

Standard percentile

The hourly rates reported within ASHE 6115 reflect different skills, responsibilities, types of care and terms and conditions of employment. This distribution of skills and qualifications in the care sector matches, in broad terms, the different levels of hourly earnings at the different percentiles of the ASHE 6115 distribution. In any care package, carers are paid at different hourly rates. To enable the calculation of the annual increase of a periodical payment a percentile of ASHE 6115 needs to be adopted.

It is not the hourly rate itself that is of significance. When the uplifting calculation is undertaken, it is the annual increase in the gross hourly rate of carers that is used and not the actual rate. There is no real bias to either party as to which percentile is chosen, save it is accepted economic theory that those on higher earnings have greater annual increases.

Unless the care rates justify ASHE (90), it is recommended it be avoided. ASHE (90) is at the end of the earnings distribution and considered to be susceptible to greater volatility. As there is limited bias to either party on choice of percentile of ASHE 6115, it is advisable to adopt a standard percentile for all claims. This will assist when the uplifting process is undertaken. In practice, most parties now agree to ASHE (80).

Pro rata payment

If a defendant is paying all PPOs on a particular date, claimants will usually seek a pro rata periodical payment from the date of settlement to payment of the first periodical payment. So, by way of example, if a claim settles on 31 January, but the first periodical payment is not until 15 December, a claimant will usually seek a pro rata periodical payment from 1 February to 14 December. This should be resisted.

During negotiations, or within the terms of any Part 36 offer, it should be made clear to a claimant that the pro rata periodical payment is included in the retained lump sum. This is now almost standard practice in NHS cases.

Stepped payments

In the majority of catastrophic personal injury cases, there is a single payment that is agreed and paid throughout the duration of a claimant's life.

In, for example, birth injury or road traffic accident claims involving minors, a periodical payment can increase or decrease over the duration of a claimant's lifetime, depending on their needs. The schedule to the model order accommodates stepped payments so, for example, payments in a claim involving a child may increase at age 12 and post-19 years of age.

It has been common practice with RPI-linked PPOs for stepped payments to be centred on a claimant's birthday. If an insurer has decided to adopt a particular payment date, e.g. 15 December each year, all experts should assess the claimant's needs to and from the payment date, rather than focusing on a claimant's birthday.

By way of illustration, a claimant's birthday is on 30 July, and on 30 July 2017 they reach age 12, when their care regime increases from £50,000 pa to £100,000 pa. If the insurer has chosen 15 December as the date of payment, should the increase take place on 15 December 2017 after the claimant's 12th birthday, which would benefit the defendant; or should the increase take place on 15 December 2016, before the claimant's 12th birthday, which would be more advantageous to the claimant?

Defendants should consider carefully when stepped payments are triggered and ensure it is after the claimant's relevant birthday.

If the claimant is to receive a single annual payment throughout the duration of their life, and not stepped payments, the schedule to the model order for NHS cases will need to be amended as the model anticipates stepped payments.

Proof of life

The PPO should also state the claimant will provide written proof of life to facilitate continuing payments.

Proof of life should be provided by the claimant's deputy, if a professional deputy, or their general practitioner (GP). The PPO should require either the deputy or the GP to provide written confirmation, which should be based on having seen the claimant recently. If proof of life is not provided, payment should be suspended until provided.

Claimants should also be reminded there is no payment for the proof of life letter.

See the commentary on *Wallace v Follett* [2013] under the heading "Practical issues" below.

Standard Part 36 offer

If a unified approach is to be taken to the administration of PPOs, this needs to be clearly reflected in any standard Part 36 periodical payment offer. The Part 36 offer must state:

- Retained lump sum: to include all interim payments and recoverable benefits.
- Annual sum to be paid by periodical payment.
- Payment period: set out stepped payment dates, if appropriate, by dates and not birthdays.
- Index: ASHE 6115 for care and case management. Offer ASHE (80) or any other percentile but avoid ASHE (90).
- If offering periodical payments for other heads of loss, consider ASHE median for loss of earnings and RPI for therapies and deputyship costs. Avoid other untested indices.
- Payment date: the date chosen for all periodical payments to be paid.

- First escalation date: will the first payment also be index-linked? Ideally this should be avoided.
- Confirm whether a pro rata periodical payment is payable or, preferably, included in the retained lump sum.

Standardising the approach to PPOs: checklist for compensators

- ✓ Consider how best to manage PPOs and whether the model schedule should be adopted.
- ✓ Agree on a payment date of the periodical payment, taking into account the publication date of ASHE data. Should a single payment date apply to all periodical payments? Would quarterly payments be helpful to reduce the impact on cash flow?
- ✓ Consider approach to timing of first escalation. Argue that first escalation should not apply to first periodical payment made.
- ✓ Decide which percentile of ASHE 6115 should apply to the uplifting process.
- ✓ Resist arguments that a pro rata periodical payment should be made for the period from settlement to the first periodical payment date.
- ✓ Resist other indices for other heads of loss, save ASHE median and RPI.
- ✓ Consider potential impact of stepped payments. Should experts assess the claimant's needs based on the designated payment date?
- ✓ Ensure the PPO states that the claimant will provide written proof of life to facilitate continuing payments.
- ✓ Ensure that Part 36 offers include the necessary information in relation to the PPO.

Calculating the annual increase

As an example, consider a claim settled in July 2015 by way of annual periodical payments of £100,000. The periodical payments are for care and case management only and the index is ASHE 6115 at the 80th percentile. The compensator selected a payment date of 15 December each year. The parties agreed the first payment on 15 December 2015 would not be index-linked. The settlement was based on 2015 hourly rates for carers, introduced in April 2015.

To provide an annual uplift in December 2015 would be a windfall to the claimant. The first index-linked payment was made on 15 December 2016.

The model schedule sets out the computations necessary to calculate the annual uplift of a claimant's periodical payment.

First year of escalation

When calculating the annual increase in the first year, the following formula, as set out at paragraph 3 of the model schedule, is used to calculate the annual increase:

$$PP = C \times \frac{NP}{A}$$

PP = the new amount payable by way of periodical payment each year.

C = the original annual periodical payment.

NP = the first release hourly gross rate published by the ONS for the relevant percentile in the year the escalation is being undertaken.

A = the most recent revised hourly gross rate published by the ONS at the time the first escalation is being calculated for the relevant percentile. This remains unchanged each year the calculation is undertaken, until reclassification or discontinuity.

Using the ASHE data published in October 2016, the calculation is as follows:

$$PP = £100{,}000 \times \frac{£10.76}{£10.38} = £103{,}660.88$$

Explanatory note

£10.38 is the ASHE (80) revised gross hourly rate for 2015 and published in 2016 (A) and remains unchanged from the first year of calculation. It is used for all calculations until reclassification or discontinuity.

£10.76 is the ASHE (80) first release gross hourly rate for 2016 and published in 2016 (NP).

Subsequent years of escalation

The calculation for every year thereafter, until reclassification or change in methodology, is undertaken in accordance with the following formula, as set out at paragraph 4 of the model schedule:

$$PP = C \times \frac{NP + (NF - OP)}{A}$$

NF = the revised hourly gross rate for the relevant percentile published by the ONS for the year prior to the calculation being undertaken.

OP = the first release hourly gross rate for the relevant percentile published by the ONS for the year prior to the calculation being undertaken.

This calculation takes into account any differential between the first release and revised hourly rates of the previous year, represented by NF – OP in the above formula. The calculation for the second year, until reclassification or discontinuity, using the example above, will take place in December 2017, and using the ASHE data published in October 2017, based on ASHE (80), is:

$$PP = £100{,}000 \times \frac{£11.04 + (£10.75 - £10.76)}{£10.38} = £106{,}262.04$$

Explanatory note

£10.38 is the ASHE (80) revised gross hourly rate for 2015 and published in 2016 (A) and remains unchanged from the first year of calculation. It is used for all calculations until reclassification or discontinuity.

£11.04 is the ASHE (80) first release gross hourly rate for 2017 and published in 2017 (NP). This part of the formula calculates the annual increase of the annual periodical payment.

£10.75 is the ASHE (80) revised gross hourly rate for 2016 and published in 2017 (NF). £10.76 is the first release ASHE (80) gross hourly rate for 2016 and published in 2016 (OP). This part of the formula calculates any differential between the first release and revised gross hourly rates. In 2016/2017, the gross hourly rate went down from the first release of £10.76 to £10.75 when revised.

It would be wrong to assume that hourly care rates only rise and that, accordingly, a claimant's index-linked periodical payment for care and case management will increase annually. The ASHE 6115 data for 2011 illustrates that, in fact, care rates went down and this was reflected in claimants' annual periodical payments.

Reclassification

The ONS periodically reclassifies occupations to ensure that the workforce is measured accurately. We understand that, when the ONS considered a reclassification of ASHE 6115, the intention was to split those carers in a residential-based environment from those providing home-based care. Potentially, this would have meant that there would have been greater accuracy in the calculation of a claimant's care package.

Instead, in 2010, the ONS split ASHE 6115 into ASHE 6145 – "care workers and home carers" – and ASHE 6146 – "senior care workers". ASHE 6115 was based on 831,000 jobs in 2011, with ASHE 6146 only having 28,000 jobs within its occupation classification in the same year. Accordingly, ASHE 6146 is not statistically reliable. While ASHE 6145 is statistically robust, with almost 700,000 jobs within its classification, it is questionable whether it is a better match to ASHE 6115, bearing in mind it does not include "senior carers".

As we predicted, claimants have still not sought reclassification from ASHE 6115 to either ASHE 6145 (which excludes senior carers and is not, therefore, an accurate match to a care package) or to ASHE 6146 (which is statistically unreliable).

Time will tell what future changes are made to these SOCs, which could result in their use in future when index-linking a claimant's annual payments for care and case management.

Change in methodology

After the reclassification referred to above, and bearing in mind the importance of ASHE 6115 to periodical payments and personal injury claims generally, the ONS agreed to continue publishing ASHE 6115 for the foreseeable future, notwithstanding the reclassification. ASHE 6115 data published in November 2011 was used to index-link periodical payments made in December 2011.

On 22 November 2012, the ONS published the revised ASHE 6115 data for 2011 and the first release ASHE 6115 data for 2012.

There had been a change in methodology as the 2011 first release data was weighted on SOC 2000, and the 2011 revised data on SOC 2010. The two sets of data are not directly comparable and the 2011 first release and 2011 revised data showed significant discrepancies. Historically, between 2006 and 2011, and across all percentiles, the highest variation, both upwards and downwards, in first release and revised gross hourly rates has been only two pence.

The model schedule anticipated changes in methodology, and contained formulae to address this eventuality. The change in methodology provisions required 'AF', defined in the model schedule as the final published revised hourly gross wage rate for the relevant percentile of the previously applied SOC for "all" employees. This is the hourly gross wage rate for ASHE 6115 based on the SOC 2000 methodology. There was, however, a problem as AF was not available. The ONS had published the 2011 revised hourly rate of ASHE 6115, based on SOC 2010 methodology and not on the SOC 2000 methodology.

A number of compensators make periodical payments in December each year. In December 2012, they were unable to calculate the annual increase to claimants' periodical payments due to the missing data. In accordance with Paragraph 8 of Part 1 of the model schedule, many compensators paid claimants the sums paid the previous December. They confirmed a balancing payment would be made once the issue was resolved.

NHS Resolution had, as at December 2012, over 640 cases index-linked to ASHE 6115. It selected *RH v University Hospitals Bristol NHS Foundation Trust* [2013] as a test case to obtain judicial approval for the proposed solution of replacing AF with 'OPF' when applying the change in methodology formulae. NHS Resolution instructed Kennedys to represent the defendant NHS trust.

OPF is defined in the model schedule as the final first release hourly gross wage rate for the relevant percentile of the previously applied SOC for "all" employees. Rather than applying AF (the revised gross hourly wage rate based on SOC 2000 methodology, which was not available), it was proposed that OPF (the first release gross hourly wage rate based on 2000 methodology) would be used to apply the change in methodology provisions in the model schedule.

A hearing took place on 11 February 2013 and Mrs Justice Swift handed down her judgment on 1 March 2013. Swift J took a pragmatic approach to the problem:

- She approved the solution of replacing AF with OPF when applying the change in methodology formulae.
- She approved amendments to the model schedule in NHS cases to address this problem, should it reoccur.
- She strongly encouraged claimants and deputies to accept this solution, if the same issues had arisen in their cases, and adopt the amendments to the schedule.
- She warned of possible cost consequences if claimants objected to the solution without good reason.
- She confirmed the solution does not require court approval in cases involving protected parties for the purposes of CPR Part 21.10(1) or formal amendments to PPOs in cases not involving protected parties.
- She urged other non-NHS compensators to apply the same solution, if appropriate.

To date, claimants have accepted the solution set out in the *RH* test case and no cases have been individually listed that address this issue.

Practical issues

As PPOs provide a stream of annual payments for the duration of a claimant's life, there is a continuing relationship between claimant and compensator. In his judgment in *Wallace v Follett*, Lord Justice Leveson referred to Mr Justice Mackay's judgment in *Long v Norwich Union Insurance Ltd* [2009] in which he observed that, where settlements include PPOs, there is a balance of benefits and burdens for both sides.

In *Wallace*, the claimant suffered catastrophic injuries in a road traffic accident. Liability was accepted subject to a discount of 30% for contributory negligence. An agreement was subsequently reached on the basis of the payment of a lump sum and periodical payments. However, a dispute arose over two issues in relation to the terms of the PPO:

- Whether it was reasonable to permit the insurer to require the claimant to undergo medical examinations to obtain an up-to-date life expectancy figure for the purpose of calculating reserves. In previous cases, a provision had been inserted in the event that insurers wished to find an annuity provider.
- The consequences of the claimant failing to provide written confirmation from his GP, prior to the commencement of each payment year, that he was still alive.

At first instance, His Honour Judge McKenna found in favour of the claimant on these issues. The defendant appealed to the Court of Appeal. Leveson LJ allowed the defendant's appeal:

- A medical examination should be allowed for the purpose of purchasing an annuity or to review reserves, but limited to once every seven years.
- An insurer is entitled to be reassured that a claimant receiving PPOs is alive as at the date on which a payment is to be made. There was no reason why written confirmation should not be made available on an annual basis. The task should be made as straightforward as possible and the insurer should provide a reminder of the obligation. There was no virtue in requiring the insurer to return to court before suspending payments.

It is interesting that the Court of Appeal accepted that it was appropriate for it to resolve these discrete terms of PPOs where the parties had failed to reach agreement.

Discount rate

The Lord Chancellor, Liz Truss, pursuant to the power set out in the Damages Act 1996, dramatically reduced the discount rate on 27 February 2017 from 2.5% to –0.75%. The Ministry of Justice has issued draft legislation to address the methodology for setting the discount rate and the process for doing so.

For the moment the discount rate remains at –0.75%. Defendants can circumvent the discount rate reduction by actively promoting PPOs. Defendants can seek to pay a number of future heads of loss annually index linked to an inflationary index, rather than paying a lump sum award calculated using a –0.75% multiplier. Rather than limiting periodical payments to care and case management (index linked to ASHE 6115) as is general practice, PPOs could be extended to compensate a claimant for future loss of earnings (index linked to ASHE median) and various therapies and non-earnings related future losses (index linked to RPI).

The reality is the reduction in the discount rate has not seen any real change in practice – NHS cases settle by way of PPO and those funded by insurers largely by lump sum award. Depending on the stage of proceedings, and particularly if settlement is achieved in the pre-action stage, settlements are based on a 1% discount rate. Claimants appreciate this low discount rate environment is unlikely to remain.

Conclusion

Periodical payments are certainly increasing in popularity amongst claimants, and not just in claims involving NHS defendants. Claimants' financial advisors continue to promote the benefits of PPOs.

> The benefits to a claimant of an annual, tax-free, index-linked payment for the duration of life must be taken seriously, despite the significant reduction in the discount rate to –0.75%.
>
> The cash flow advantages to a defendant must also be considered.

It will be interesting to see whether the ONS continues to publish ASHE 6115 or decides to reclassify ASHE 6145 and 6146, which may prompt calls for an alternative SOC to be used when index-linking PPOs for care and case management.

17 Compensation Recovery Unit

Paul Morris

- Registering the claim with the CRU
- How much to repay and when?
- Offsetting benefits: worked examples
- CRU and Part 36 offers
- Payment of NHS charges
- Review and appeal

Compensation Recovery Unit

Introduction

The Compensation Recovery Unit (CRU) is part of the Department for Work and Pensions (DWP).

Individuals who are injured or disabled are entitled, in certain circumstances, to receive government benefits. Some benefits derive from the claimant's inability to work and some from a need for care and assistance with everyday living or getting about. Such benefits may run for the rest of an individual's life (if permanently disabled) or simply while that person recovers from their injuries.

The person paying the compensation must repay to the CRU certain benefits that relate to an injury for which the injured person receives compensation. That person is known as the compensator and is typically an insurance company or self-insured company.

In addition, the compensator is obliged to repay the CRU a specified amount of money towards the cost of NHS treatment expended on the injured person as a result of the injury.

The idea behind the repayments is to recover money for the government from the compensator as opposed to that money coming solely out of the public purse.

Registering the claim with the CRU

> It is the responsibility of the compensator to register each claim with the CRU.

A claim is registered by filling in a CRU1 registration form and sending it to the CRU. The form requires basic details about the claimant, the nature of their claim, the compensator and its representatives.

In addition, details must be provided about any NHS hospitals attended for inpatient or outpatient treatment and whether the claimant was taken to hospital by NHS ambulance as a result of the accident.

This form enables the compensator to obtain a certificate of benefits and a certificate of NHS charges, both of which should be obtained as soon as the letter of claim is received. A certificate of NHS charges is usually valid for the lifetime of a claim, whereas a certificate of benefits is only valid for a limited period of several months.

On expiry (or up to seven days in advance) the compensator should ask for an updated certificate of benefits from the CRU, so that as far as possible a valid certificate of benefits (and, if necessary, a certificate of NHS charges) is maintained.

If a claim is settled and compensation is paid to a claimant without the claim being registered with the CRU, the compensator will lose the chance to make reductions in the compensation paid to take account of equivalent benefits the claimant has received. The compensator will, however, still have to repay the full amount of benefits shown on the certificate, thereby overpaying.

It is, therefore, crucial that the compensator takes steps to register the claim with the CRU as soon as a letter of claim is received.

How much to repay and when?

The amounts of benefits that must be repaid are those shown on the certificate of benefits that are related to the injury and were paid within the relevant period.

The relevant period begins on the date of accident or, if a disease claim, when the claimant first claims benefits in respect of that disease and ends five years later, or on payment of final damages, if sooner.

It follows that the sooner following an injury that final compensation is paid, the fewer benefits will become repayable, for example, if the claim is settled and paid within 12 months of the accident, only 12 months' worth of benefits will have to be repaid.

It is a common misconception that the relevant period ends at the date of agreement of a claim, an order or a judgment.

It is, therefore, crucial that compensation is paid as quickly as possible where the relevant period has not ended.

The trigger for the obligation to repay benefits and NHS charges is when final damages are paid or on the making of an interim payment. However, remember that benefits may well continue to increase and need to be repaid after making an interim payment up until the relevant period ends.

Offsetting benefits

The compensator is, in certain circumstances, entitled to withhold/offset from the claimant's compensation a sum equivalent to the benefits that have to be repaid to the CRU.

No sum can be offset against damages for pain, suffering and loss of amenity (PSLA) or against any claims for future losses and they are said to be 'ringfenced'.

Only certain benefits can be offset against certain past heads of claim. The relevant heads of claim are loss of earnings, care and assistance and loss of mobility. Table 17.1 shows what benefits can be offset against each head of compensation.

Table 17.1: Offsetting benefits

Head of compensation	Benefits that can be offset
Past loss of earnings	Universal Credit Employment and Support Allowance (ESA) Incapacity Benefit Industrial Injuries Disablement Benefit Income Support Invalidity Pension Invalidity Allowance Jobseeker's Allowance (JSA) Reduced Earnings Allowance Severe Disablement Allowance Sickness Benefit Statutory Sick Pay paid before 6 April 1994 Unemployability Supplement Unemployment Benefit Disability Working Allowance
Past care and assistance	Living Component of Personal Independence Payment (PIP L) Care Component of Disability Living Allowance (DLAC) Attendance Allowance Disablement Pension increase for Constant Attendance Allowance Exceptionally Severe Disablement Allowance
Past loss of mobility	Mobility Component of Personal Independence Payment (PIP M) Mobility Component of Disability Allowance (DLAM) Mobility Allowance

Benefits can be offset only up to the value of the head of compensation against which that benefit can be offset. Examples are set out at Tables 17.2 to 17.4.

Table 17.2: First example

Item of calculation	Amount
Loss of earnings awarded	£7,000
Benefits (ESA)	£5,000
Offset	£5,000
Net sum to claimant after offset	£2,000

Table 17.3: Second example

Item of calculation	Amount
Loss of earnings awarded	£7,000
Benefits (ESA)	£7,000
Offset	£7,000
Net sum to claimant after offset	£0

Table 17.4: Third example

Item of calculation	Amount
Loss of earnings awarded	£7,000
Benefits (ESA)	£10,000
Offset	£7,000
Net sum to claimant after offset	£0

Remember that regardless of what offset is made, the obligation on the compensator is still to repay the entirety of the benefits shown on the benefits certificate.

As a general rule of thumb, a compensator should aim to offset as many benefits as possible as this will reduce to a minimum the amount of any settlement.

Working example

The following example assumes that the claimant and defendant have been able to agree quantum as set out in Table 17.5.

Table 17.5: Agreed figures for quantum

Head of compensation	Gross award
General damages	£5,000
Loss of earnings	£3,000
Pre-accident vehicle value	£3,500
Cost of care	£4,000
Taxi and bus fares (due to loss of mobility)	£500
Total damages	£16,000

The benefits in this case to the date of settlement are as set out in Table 17.6.

Table 17.6: Benefits to date of settlement

Benefits	Amount
ESA	£2,000
JSA	£1,500

Benefits	Amount
PIP L	£2,000
PIP M	£2,000
Total benefits paid to CRU	£7,500

The total value of the claim is £16,000. Benefits paid by the DWP to the claimant as a result of the accident total £7,500.

It is wrong simply to reduce the overall claim by £7,500, giving a net sum to the claimant of £8,500: see Table 17.1.

The claimant will receive a total of £10,500, as set out in Table 17.7.

Table 17.7: Receipts by claimant

Head of compensation	Net award
General damages (ringfenced)	£5,000
Loss of earnings	
(£3,000 less £2,000 ESA and £1,500 JSA)	£0
Pre-accident vehicle value	£3,500
Cost of care	
(£4,000 less £2,000 PIP L)	£2,000
Taxi/bus fares	
(£500 less £2,000 PIP M)	£0
Total net damages	£10,500

The compensator will pay a total of £18,000, as set out in Table 17.8.

Table 17.8: Payments by compensator

Item of calculation	Amount
Damages paid to claimant (as above)	£10,500
Benefits paid to CRU	£7,500
Total	£18,000

It is worth noting that although the total value of the claim is £16,000, that is not the maximum that the compensator is obliged to pay.

As shown in Tables 17.6 to 17.8, the loss of earnings figure of £3,000 will be cancelled out by ESA of £2,000 and JSA of £1,500 (a total of £3,500). Both those benefits relate to the claim for loss of earnings.

The surplus £500 cannot be deducted from any other aspect of the claimant's claim, but still has to be paid to the CRU, along with the other benefits on the certificate.

Similar principles apply to PIP L, which is fully offset with no surplus, and PIP M, which has a £1,500 surplus.

CRU and Part 36 offers

The subject of offers under Part 36 of the Civil Procedure Rules (CPR) is dealt with in more detail in Chapter 8.

No valid certificate

You may encounter a situation where a compensator wishes to make a Part 36 offer, but does not have a valid benefits certificate in its possession as it has expired or a fresh one is awaited from the CRU. Part 36.22(7) of the Civil Procedure Rules (CPR) allows a defendant to make a Part 36 offer, but to reserve the right to offset benefits once the fresh certificate is received.

When making the offer, the defendant should refer to Part 36.22(7) of the CPR and make it clear that a benefits certificate is awaited.

The defendant must then clarify the offer within seven days of receiving the benefits certificate by specifying in the usual manner:

- The total amount represented by the Part 36 offer (the gross compensation).
- The name and amount of any deductible benefit by which that gross amount is reduced (the offset).
- The net amount being paid after the deduction of the appropriate amount of benefit (the net compensation).

Late acceptance by claimant when benefits have increased

If a defendant's Part 36 offer is accepted outside the relevant period (21 days), where the benefits certificate shows benefits have increased since the original offer was made, Part 36.22(9) of the CPR makes it clear that the claimant will require the court's permission to accept the offer, unless the compensator agrees.

This allows the court to order, or the compensator to negotiate, a higher offset of benefits in return for allowing the claimant to accept the offer late. The effect of this is to maintain the gross offer, increase the sum offset and reduce the net offer to the claimant, but without losing the costs protection afforded by the initial offer.

Payment of NHS charges

Part 3 of the Health and Social Care (Community Health and Standards) Act 2003 allows the NHS to recover some of the cost of treating an accident victim from the party who pays compensation to that victim.

Prior to 29 January 2007, only National Health Service (NHS) charges incurred following a road traffic accident were repayable. After this date, NHS charges are repayable for all personal injury claims, except for disease claims, in other words in respect of employers' and public liability accidents.

The NHS charges recoverable include the cost of NHS ambulance trips after this date.

The NHS has a tariff that it applies to compensators. This alters each year via the Personal Injuries (NHS Charges) (Amounts) Amendment Regulations.

The tariff comprises outpatient, inpatient and ambulance charges. There is also an overall maximum amount that can be charged. The amount of NHS charges to be repaid will depend on the date of the accident.

Table 17.9: NHS charges since 2005

Accident date	Daily amounts to be repaid	Maximum amount to be repaid
01.04.06 – 28.01.07	Outpatient £505 Inpatient £620 per day	£37,100
29.01.07 – 31.03.08	Ambulance £159 Outpatient £505 Inpatient £620 per day	£37,100
01.04.08 – 31.03.09	Ambulance £165 Outpatient £547 Inpatient £672 per day	£40,179
01.04.09 – 31.03.10	Ambulance £171 Outpatient £566 Inpatient £695 per day	£41,545
01.04.10 – 31.03.11	Ambulance £177 Outpatient £585 Inpatient £719 per day	£42,999
01.04.11 – 31.03.12	Ambulance £181 Outpatient £600 Inpatient £737 per day	£44,056

Accident date	Daily amounts to be repaid	Maximum amount to be repaid
01.04.12 – 31.03.13	Ambulance £185 Outpatient £615 Inpatient £755 per day	£45,153
01.04.13 – 31.03.14	Ambulance: £189 Outpatient: £627 Inpatient: £770 per day	£46,046
01.04.14 – 31.03.15	Ambulance: £192 Outpatient: £637 Inpatient: £783 per day	£46,831
01.04.15 – 31.03.16	Ambulance: £195 Outpatient: £647 Inpatient: £796 per day	£47,569
01.04.16 – 31.03.17	Ambulance: £201 Outpatient: £665 Inpatient: £817 per day	£48,849

The NHS can demand almost £50,000 for NHS charges. It is critical, therefore, that when reserving a claim, claims handlers allow for NHS charges, as well as for surplus benefits that cannot be offset.

NHS charges – contributory negligence

At the same time as extending recoverable NHS charges to other types of personal injury claims after 29 January 2007, the new rules permit the compensator to reduce the NHS charges by the same proportion as the finding on contributory negligence.

For example, if NHS charges were originally £1,000 and 25% contributory negligence is agreed, this would reduce the NHS charges to £750.

> In order to reduce the NHS charges on the grounds that the claimant was contributorily negligent, the compensator should seek a review of the NHS charges certificate after settlement of the whole claim. The compensator does not need to repay NHS charges before seeking such a review, but could if it wished send payment for the net amount of the NHS charges on the assumption that the review will succeed.

The compensator must provide evidence of the liability split to the CRU to achieve the reduction in the NHS charges. This will take the form of either of the following:

- Correspondence between the parties (including from the claimant) evidencing the liability split; or
- A copy of a court order or judgment.

Review and appeal – benefits

The benefits certificate shows the benefits that the CRU believes are attributable to the injuries in question and which have to be repaid by the compensator at the date of settlement.

However, there are cases where the CRU is incorrect and some or all of the benefits listed on the certificate should not be repayable by the compensator.

The DWP may be unaware of relevant facts, may have wrongly assessed the claimant's entitlement to a benefit, or the payment of a benefit may be due to factors other than the injury caused by the compensator.

To challenge a benefits certificate, a compensator will have to seek a review before settlement of a claim and/or submit an appeal after settlement of a claim and payment of the full benefits shown on the certificate.

Examples of circumstances where a review or appeal should be considered include:

- Where a claimant had a pre-existing medical condition. The accident may only be responsible for a small period of exacerbation or the claimant may have recovered from the accident-related injuries after a short time, leaving only the pre-existing medical condition. Some or all of the benefits may relate to the claimant's pre-existing condition and not be recoverable.
- Where the claimant may have a pre-existing condition that has been accelerated by the accident in question by a specific period. In those circumstances, the benefits that are directly attributable to the accident are those paid over the period of acceleration. Benefits that fall outside of that period would not be attributable to the accident and it would not be reasonable for the compensator to be responsible for repaying them.
- Where the claimant is exaggerating or malingering and, as a result, the DWP has been fooled into paying additional benefits. It would not be reasonable for the compensator to be responsible for repaying those benefits.
- Where the claimant should not have been awarded the relevant benefit in the first place as they should not have been assessed as meeting the criteria for receiving that benefit, the compensator should not be responsible for paying those benefits.

Benefits review

A request for a review of the benefits certificate should be made in writing, accompanied by all relevant evidence. It should state concisely why it is felt that one or more benefits should not be recoverable.

Reviews can be repeated, but only once per certificate, so if a review fails, you must await a fresh certificate before seeking a further review.

The three grounds for a review of benefits are:

- An obvious mistake has been made in preparing the certificate.
- The amount of benefits on the certificate is wrong.
- A ground of appeal would be satisfied.

The grounds on which a review will succeed are, therefore, quite narrow. A review may well fail for the simple reason that the claimant claimed and the CRU awarded benefits due to the accident; in other words, there was no obvious mistake. This may well be plainly wrong on the evidence, but will be sufficient for the CRU to turn down the review request.

In general, a compensator should not hesitate to appeal after settlement of the case where there are good grounds, even on the same grounds as a review, as this often leads to a successful appeal where a previous review has failed.

Benefits appeal

An appeal can only be made after settlement of the claim and after full repayment of benefits.

An appeal of the benefits certificate should be made direct to HM Courts & Tribunals Service (HMCTS) using the dedicated benefits appeal form, but only after prior steps have been taken. We strongly suggest that the form is accompanied by more detailed reasons why the appeal should succeed and a copy of all relevant evidence.

The procedure provides that an appeal is made by first submitting the evidence and grounds of appeal to the CRU and requesting a Mandatory Reconsideration Notice (MRN) be issued. This must be done within one month after the date that the compensator makes full payment of benefits to the CRU. The time limit is strictly applied.

The CRU will respond to the request and may make a full or partial refund or confirm the certificate via the MRN. This will normally happen within a few months of submitting the request for an MRN.

On receipt of an MRN, if the compensator still wishes to appeal, it should submit a benefits appeal form (available from the HMCTS website) with all relevant evidence, including the grounds of appeal, direct to HMCTS. This must be done within one month of the date of the MRN. The time limit is strictly applied.

The grounds for an appeal of benefits are:

- The amount, rate or period of benefits shown on the certificate is wrong.
- The certificate shows benefits not paid as a result of the accident, injury or disease.
- Benefits have been included that the claimant should not have been awarded.
- The compensation was not paid as a consequence of the accident, injury or disease.

The HMCTS will notify the CRU, which will then prepare a written response to the appeal before referring the case back to HMCTS to list and hear the appeal. It is possible for the CRU to reconsider making a refund at this stage, but much less likely. All appeals are heard by HMCTS, which is independent of the CRU.

The compensator has to decide at the outset when submitting the appeal form whether to elect for a paper or oral hearing before an HMCTS panel. Assuming the grounds for appeal are sound and it is commercially viable to do so, it is strongly recommended that an oral hearing is sought.

Review and appeal – NHS charges

The NHS charges certificate shows the NHS charges that the CRU believes are attributable to the injuries in question and that have to be repaid by the compensator at the date of settlement.

However, there are cases where the CRU is wrong and some or all of the charges listed on the certificate should not be repayable by the compensator.

The DWP may be unaware of relevant facts or may have made an incorrect assessment of what caused the charges to be incurred.

To challenge an NHS charges certificate, a compensator should seek a review before settlement of a claim and/or submit an appeal after settlement of a claim and payment of the full charges shown on the certificate.

NHS charges review

A request to review the NHS charges certificate should be made in writing, accompanied by all relevant evidence. It should state concisely why it is felt that certain of the charges should not be recoverable.

It can be made at any time before settlement of the claim or within three months of the payment of damages or receipt of the NHS charges certificate, if after that time.

The three grounds for a review of NHS charges are:

- An obvious mistake in preparing the certificate
- The amount of charges on the certificate is wrong
- A ground of appeal would be satisfied.

A compensator should not hesitate to make an appeal after settlement of the case, even if the NHS charges review fails, as an appeal may succeed where a previous review has failed.

NHS charges appeals

An appeal of the NHS charges certificate should be made direct to HMCTS using the dedicated NHS charges appeal form. We strongly suggest that the form is accompanied by more detailed reasons why the appeal should succeed and a copy of all relevant evidence.

An appeal can only be made after settlement of the claim and after full repayment of NHS charges.

An appeal must be made within three months of the payment of damages or receipt of the NHS charges certificate if after that time. The time limit is strictly applied.

The CRU will be asked to respond to the appeal by preparing a written response and may make a full or partial refund or change the certificate. This will normally happen within three months of submitting the appeal form.

The grounds for an appeal of NHS charges are:

- The amount of the NHS charges is incorrect.
- The NHS charges certificate shows non-NHS treatment.
- The NHS charges certificate shows NHS charges incurred not as a result of the accident or injury.
- The ambulance was a non-NHS ambulance.
- The NHS charges certificate issued does not relate to a compensation payment.

The procedure followed is then identical to that of an appeal against a benefits certificate.

Checklist

- ✓ Has the claim been registered with the CRU? If not, arrange for it to be registered as soon as possible and obtain a certificate of benefits and NHS charges.
- ✓ Ensure an updated certificate of benefits (and, if necessary, a certificate of NHS charges) is requested when the current one expires.
- ✓ Which benefits can be offset against which heads of claim?
- ✓ Remember that making an interim payment will trigger payment of benefits and NHS charges.

- ✓ When making a Part 36 offer, set out in detail within the offer:
  - ✓ Gross sum offered.
  - ✓ Total benefits offset.
  - ✓ Which benefits are offset, in what amounts and against which heads of claim.
  - ✓ Net offer to the claimant after offset of benefits.
- ✓ Should a review or appeal of the certificate of benefits and/or the certificate of NHS charges be requested?
- ✓ Consider what evidence you will need for an appeal before settling the claim.
- ✓ Ensure that you comply with the strict time limits for requesting an MRN and submitting an appeal.
- ✓ On payment of final damages, arrange for recoverable benefits and any NHS charges to be paid, bearing in mind the deadlines for requesting an MRN and submitting an appeal.

18 Subsidence

Andrew Caplan

- Subsidence vs general movement
- Causes of subsidence
- Investigating a subsidence claim and the role of experts
- Recovery from a third party: foreseeability and causation
- Claimants' contributory negligence/failure to mitigate
- Industry agreements and protocols
- Tree preservation orders (TPOs)

Subsidence

Introduction

The online Oxford Dictionaries define subsidence as: "The gradual caving in or sinking of an area of land."

The crucial element of subsidence is a downward movement.

Before the early 1970s, subsidence as a risk was not included in domestic household insurance policies. Many homeowners who would now claim that their houses have subsided would have simply filled cracks and redecorated their homes themselves. Minor, and some moderate, cracking would have been acceptable.

Insurers now need to be able to identify subsidence and, with input from engineers, arrange for the repair of any damage that has been caused as a result in a proportionate way.

Underpinning is by no means always necessary. Indeed, some engineers believe that the partial underpinning of a building can simply lead to future problems. Underpinning can also cause problems for a homeowner on sale or remortgage of the property.

Insurers should always be alive to the alternative possibility of vegetation management and/or simple repair being the most cost-effective solution. Of course, such alternatives will not always be possible and, in serious cases, underpinning will be required.

Subsidence vs general movement

Subsidence is not caused by the weight of the building compressing the ground on which it stands. Any downward movement caused by the weight of the building is known as settlement. This invariably has ceased within a few years of construction although longer-term problems relating to extensions often occur.

Subsidence can be caused by, for example, moisture being extracted from the soil beneath the building by vegetation, or the drying out of the soil beneath the building during a particularly dry spell.

In either case, when moisture is extracted the volume of the soil below a building is reduced, causing the whole, or a particular part, of the building to drop lower into the soil.

> If the whole building drops slowly and at the same rate, then no damage is likely to arise. If, however, the building drops rapidly, if different parts drop at different rates or if only part of the building subsides, cracks will appear.

Are all cracks caused by subsidence?

The simple answer to this is no. New buildings, for example, often settle. Cracks will appear in plaster because the plaster dries out over a period of time.

Similarly, in the same way that subsidence can be caused by the extraction of moisture from the soil, a sudden addition of moisture to soil can cause the soil to swell and the building standing on the soil to be pushed up. This is known as heave and should be distinguished from upward recovery (that is where movement is purely seasonal and the previous level is achieved). In contrast, heave is where movement is ongoing and of an upward nature so that a progressive damage can be seen over a number of years. Heave claims are much rarer but often lead to much larger individual claims as remedial schemes tend to be far more expensive.

Causes of subsidence

There are a number of causes of subsidence. Most, if not all, relate to the movement of soil below the depth of the foundations. Any soil movement that occurs only between ground level and the bottom of the foundations will not affect the property.

The following are the main causes of subsidence a claims handler will encounter. (There are other causes of subsidence that need not be dealt with in this guide.)

Subsidence due to soil drying/shrinkage

This is currently the most common cause of subsidence. It will affect clay or clay-based soils. The Thames Valley and South East England generally have clay soils and suffer particularly from this type of subsidence. As the clay soil dries, its volume decreases and it therefore shrinks:

- In the winter, soil dries through normal evaporation. However, winter rainfall tends to replace the moisture lost through evaporation. The volume of the soil will, therefore, remain constant and buildings standing on it will stay level.
- However, in the summer months, particularly in droughts (known as event years), there will be insufficient rainfall to counteract the effects of evaporation and drying. The volume of the soil will decrease. Buildings will subside if the soil below the foundations is affected.

Drying is also caused by vegetation. Vegetation will extend its roots and continuously extract moisture from the soil. The volume of the soil will be reduced as the moisture is extracted. If the roots extend under part of the foundations of a property the soil there may shrink and subsidence can occur.

Burst drains, pipes, etc.

The escape of water from pipes, drains or water mains, etc. will, over a period of time, cause subsidence. Heave may well occur as the natural consequence of water being discharged into the soil. However, the discharge of water into the soil over a period of time can wash away small particles of soil from between the larger particles. This reduces the volume of the soil, causing it to be further compacted. Again, subsidence will occur, as buildings standing on such an area of soil will drop in level.

Investigating a subsidence claim

Claims handlers must first ascertain whether the damage claimed for is of a type covered by the insurance policy in question. The policy may cover subsidence, but may not cover settlement or a situation where the building is sinking because of disintegrating foundations. Therefore, a proper diagnosis of subsidence is necessary.

Proper investigations are also vital if insurers have any intention of seeking to recover the cost of remedial works from the owners of a neighbouring property or another party. Insurers may be able to do so if an effective cause of the subsidence is vegetation outside the boundaries of the insured's own property.

The legal landscape in relation to making a recovery has changed significantly since 2012, and a number of important recent decisions are highlighted under the heading "Recovery from a third party" below.

Loss adjuster

The loss adjuster coordinates investigations into the cause of the damage. They will often instruct an engineer to investigate the problem and provide a diagnosis.

Having received the engineer's report, the adjuster can arrange for contractors to tender for remedial works and coordinate works.

> The adjuster also plays an important role in assessing the damage caused by subsidence, including assessing whether any part of the remedial works could amount to betterment. Their reports often contain helpful background information about the policyholder/third party as the loss adjuster will often be the only person in contact with the policyholder and any potential third party.

The adjuster usually prepares a number of interim reports. The claims handler should obtain disclosure of all the interim reports. These are often a useful source of evidence of alternative causes.

Engineer

The engineer is arguably the most important member of a claims handler's team during the investigation stage.

The engineer can carry out the following tasks:

- Prepare a plan and photographs of the building. This will highlight vegetation on the insured property and on neighbouring land that may be affecting the building. Photographs will provide evidence of the damage that exists before any remedial works are carried out.
- Dig trial pits to a depth below the property's foundations to identify the type of soil on which the property is standing. Trial pits will also assist in identifying whether any roots are present from vegetation underneath or near to the foundations. Soil can be analysed to determine whether it is drier than it should be (i.e. it has been desiccated) in order to establish if moisture is being lost to any roots that are found.
- Dig a control pit in a location where the implicated vegetation is beyond the zone of influence, to test whether the soil is desiccated in any event. It is accepted that London clay, in particular, has a propensity to dry out while other soils do not. Foreseeability will be an important issue (see below). Owners of property/vegetation on London clay will struggle to argue foreseeability in relation to soil type. However, non-London clay areas may have a foreseeability defence.
- If a recovery against a third party is a possibility, safely keep any roots found in a manner that will prevent deterioration. They should be analysed immediately to accurately identify their species. This will allow any appropriate remedial action to be determined. Often roots are tested for starch to ascertain whether they were live when extracted.
- Survey the property. The engineer/surveyor will check drains and water mains, etc. for leaks or damage.

- Monitor cracks over a period of time. For example, if cracks widen during the summer months and close during the winter months, seasonal variations in the water content of the soil are the most likely cause of the damage. Vegetation near the property is usually the cause of such variations. Results over at least one year are advisable to analyse a pattern consistent with moisture extraction by vegetation.

Once the engineer has diagnosed the problems, the solutions they can recommend include:

- Simple vegetation management and repair of the property. The vegetation can be removed or cut back if the engineer concludes that the damage to the property is being caused by the effects of vegetation. The insured property can then be repaired and the damage should not occur again, as long as the vegetation is kept in check. Repairs should be carried out after the moisture content of the soil has stabilised. Vegetation management on the insured property should not present a problem. This may involve pollarding trees, cutting back vegetation or removing trees and vegetation completely. Tree root barriers can be installed in an attempt to prevent roots reaching the foundations of the affected building. It should be noted that some engineers question the effectiveness of using root barriers. They are also expensive. There could be difficulties if the vegetation to be managed is on a neighbouring property.

- Underpinning. If just carrying out vegetation management is not an option, and if the reason for the subsidence is not one that can be readily reversed, underpinning may be recommended. Underpinning involves the excavation of the soil from below the foundations of a property in order to underpin the property. This effectively increases the depth of the foundations. It allows damage to the property to be repaired and prevents the subsidence reoccurring.

- Partial underpinning. If only part of the property has subsided, partial underpinning may be recommended. For example, if an old scullery in an Edwardian house has subsided, it may be decided that only that part of the building should be underpinned. Some engineers are wary of partially underpinning a property. Generally, the whole property will rise and fall with the seasons, steadily and at the same rate. This minimises stresses on the structure and prevents major damage. If partial underpinning makes only part of the property more stable, additional damage can be caused because the part that has been underpinned will move less than the part of the building that has not.

Recovery from a third party

Insurers often find that damage caused to an insured property that has subsided has been caused by roots that have encroached from a neighbouring property.

Recovery from the neighbour/their insurers is often referred to as an action based on 'tree root trespass' as the roots have trespassed upon the insured property. The action will be founded in the tort of negligence or nuisance, which are to all intents indistinguishable from each other in this context (see chapters on negligence, Chapter 2, and nuisance, Chapter 3).

If roots encroach onto property and cause damage, the owner of the damaged property (and their insurers) may be able to obtain compensation for that damage. It must be emphasised that while proving causation is an essential requirement to obtain compensation, it is not alone sufficient. A claim for compensation is likely to succeed:

- If the owner of the land from which the roots are encroaching knew or should have known of the encroachment and the damage caused by it; and

- it was reasonably foreseeable that the encroachment would cause the damage, i.e. it must be shown that there was a causative breach of duty, which means showing that there was a 'real' (not merely a theoretical) risk and that there was a negligent failure to act and that this caused or materially contributed to the damage.

Foreseeability: private homeowner

It may be difficult to prove that a private homeowner should have foreseen damage to a neighbour's property.

Historically, it was highly unusual for insurers to seek recovery against domestic neighbours. This was not least because most insurers were signatories to the Association of British Insurers' Domestic Subsidence Tree Root Claims Agreement (ABI Agreement). In addition, it was considered difficult to expect or prove a domestic neighbour to have foreseeable knowledge of potential damage to a neighbouring property.

This position has changed as a result of *Khan and Khan v Harrow Council and Kane* [2013]. Mrs Kane owned property neighbouring the claimants, Mr and Mrs Khan. The claimants alleged that the defendant's cypress hedge had caused subsidence damage to their property. The claimants' insurers were not signatories to the ABI Agreement. It was determined that the hedge caused the damage as alleged.

The defendant's defence was one of foreseeability as an ordinary private individual of a domestic property. In addition, the claim was resisted on the grounds of breach of duty and contributory negligence, as well as a failure by the claimants to mitigate their losses.

The High Court applied foreseeability not subjectively but with reference to "the reasonably prudent landowner". The judge held:

- The defendant did not have knowledge of the risk of damage to the neighbours' property.

- However, a reasonably prudent landowner would have been aware of the real risk of danger of damage from the hedge.
- To impart a standard akin to that of an arboriculturist would be too high, but there was widespread coverage of problems of tree-related subsidence damage in clay soils.
- The foreseeability of damage caused by the hedge, which was close to the defendant's property and prominent, should be distinguished from the oak tree in the corner of the defendant's property. The oak tree was considerably older and the defendant was less likely to be aware of its presence. The arboricultural evidence had initially not identified the oak tree as having materially influenced the damage caused to the claimants' property.
- Contributory negligence could be applied to a nuisance claim. The judge considered the influence of the claimants' own vegetation, and the delay between identifying the influence of the defendant's vegetation and the request for removal (between 2007 and 2009). Having dismissed the sum claimed for the oak tree (as unforeseeable) and making allowance for the claimants' own vegetation, damages were reduced by 15% for contributory negligence.

Foreseeability: non-domestic neighbour

Historically, it has been relatively easy to satisfy the foreseeability test against a non-domestic neighbour, such as a local highway authority. Local authorities are likely to be deemed to have knowledge of soil conditions within their boundaries; this is a relevant factor but is not in itself determinative as to liability.

In *Paterson and another v Humberside County Council* [1995], the claimants sought damages against the council for subsidence damage to their home. They claimed in nuisance, negligence and breach of statutory duty. They alleged that the council's tree was drying out the soil under their property and that the soil was of a type that was likely to shrink.

The High Court allowed the claim. The council's knowledge about the soil type meant that it was foreseeable that there was a risk of damage being caused by its tree's roots. Therefore, the council was liable in nuisance and negligence.

A string of cases has followed this decision, for example *Eiles v Southwark London Borough Council* [2006] and *Hilda's Montessori Nursery Ltd v Tesco Stores Ltd* [2006], which have resulted in most claims against local authorities, where trees are planted in London clay and within a zone of influence, being settled. In these cases arguments focused on causation and quantum, rather than foreseeability.

However, the legal landscape changed with the Court of Appeal decision in *Berent v Family Mosaic Housing and London Borough of Islington* [2012]. The claimant was the owner of a property in a road lined with plane trees in Islington. Essentially the case against the local authority was a failure to maintain the trees in the street outside the claimant's property, which led to structural damage.

At first instance, the judge dismissed the claim, concluding:

- At the relevant time, there was no basis on which the defendants should have appreciated that there was a "real risk" that their trees would cause damage to the property, either alone or in conjunction with other factors.
- Upon this basis there had been no breach of duty.
- Removal of the trees would have been the only reliable way of eliminating the risk they might cause. However, given the defendants' knowledge as to the damage caused there was no breach in failing to remove the trees before autumn 2010.
- Failure to pollard, crown, or otherwise manage the trees would only serve to stimulate growth. This was not a realistic method of preventing tree root activity.

The Court of Appeal upheld the decision. It looked carefully at the expert evidence, in particular the evidence of the claimant's arboricultural expert, Mr Kelly:

- The London Borough of Islington had a tree maintenance programme. This included assessing risks, taking into account the claims history for the area and the nature of the trees and trying to identify hot spots.
- There was no evidence that the area generally, or particularly outside the affected property, had a relevant history.
- There was no evidence that the trees had posed a risk before 2003–2004 requiring action by the council over and above their tree maintenance programme.

Practical considerations arising out of this case are:

- Reasonable foreseeability is very much a live issue.
- If it can be established that a council has an active tree maintenance programme, implemented by properly qualified experts, it may have a defence.
- It may be unreasonable to remove all vegetation, when balancing the competing interests of stakeholders and reflecting the history of claims patterns.
- Historical records and tree maintenance programmes are important.
- Consider relevant claims in the neighbourhood.
- Consider what reasonable action could have been taken, given the reasonable foreseeability of damage.

The considerations in *Berent* were followed quickly in *Robbins v London Borough of Bexley* [2013].

The claimant's property backed on to Danson Park, owned by the defendant. A row of poplar trees grew in the park. The closest one was 30 metres from the rear of the claimant's property. Tree root damage occurred to the property in 2003 and 2006. At first instance, the judge made the following findings, which were upheld by the Court of Appeal:

- Damage to the property was caused by the poplar trees.
- From 1998, the risk of damage was reasonably foreseeable. This risk had been foreseen by the council as there had been similar claims in the road where damage had been caused by the same trees.
- The council carried out some crown reduction works but it should have carried out additional works.

Robbins makes it clear that in tree root cases proper consideration of the duty of care, breach of duty and causation is still essential.

Interestingly, one of the key arguments put forward by the council was in relation to the distance of the poplars from the property and, therefore, the zone of influence. However, because of similar past claims from properties at a similar distance from the trees it was difficult to argue the risk was not foreseeable.

In *Solloway v Hampshire County Council* [1981], the claimant was a homeowner. It was shown that a tree in the highway, owned by the council, was causing damage to the claimant's home. Its roots were extracting moisture from beneath the foundations of the claimant's home, causing it to subside.

It was shown in court that the tree would not normally have caused damage, but did so on this occasion because of a small pocket of clay soil on which the claimant's home stood. This could not have been seen on a geological survey.

The claimant's case was successful at first instance. However, on appeal the council argued successfully that the damage was not foreseeable because it did not know that the claimant's home was standing on a particularly susceptible type of soil. The Court of Appeal agreed and dismissed the claimant's action. It is essential to understand the factual matrix in the *Solloway* decision. The overall geology of the area indicated that it did not comprise shrinkable subsoils. It was, therefore, inherently less likely that subsidence would arise and upon the same basis it was far less likely that a '*real risk*' was reasonably foreseeable. Therefore, the factual background to *Solloway* was unusual and so is less likely to be relevant when considering claims that more typically arise in South East England, especially in areas predominantly comprising London clay.

Causation

The claimant will need to prove that the roots trespassing onto their land are causing the damage.

Paterson and another v Humberside County Council [1995] concerned lime trees that were approximately 10 metres from the claimant's house. The house was built in 1882 on a clay soil site. The trees were over 100 years old at the date of the trial in 1995.

The question for the High Court was whether the lime trees caused the subsidence. The judge held:

- It was enough to show that the tree roots were an effective and substantial cause of the damage to the house, although not the sole cause.
- Although the house had shallow foundations, which made the damage more likely, the defendants remained liable because "the roots take their victim as they find it".

Notification prior to substructure work

In *Delaware Mansions Ltd and others v Westminster City Council* [2001], the issue of causation in subsidence cases came before the House of Lords. The key point arising from the *Delaware* decision is the importance of providing notification to a third party before any substructure abatement work is carried out. The superstructure damage in *Delaware* was only valued at around £14,000; the eventual claim for remedial costs, which succeeded, was in the region of £500,000. Even if a defence of reasonable foreseeability had arisen for the early superstructure damage, once the council was on notice of actual damage, especially once site investigations and monitoring had been provided, a finding of liability was far more likely for the cost of abating the ongoing nuisance, i.e. the cost to the claimant of substructure works that would render the property immune from the effects of the tree which remained in place. The decision is therefore important from both perspectives. It is essential for a claimant to carry out proper investigations, and then to disclose these, together with details of the likely remedial scheme, and allow sufficient time for the third party to consider these before proceeding with substructure works. Conversely, from the third party's perspective, once they were on notice it was incumbent upon them to act and failure to do so resulted in liability for a very large claim.

The House of Lords had to determine whether the cost of repairing damage to the claimants' property, which had apparently occurred before the claimants acquired ownership of that property, could be recovered from the local authority responsible for the offending tree.

In his leading judgment, Lord Cooke stated:

- “It matters not that further cracking of the superstructure may not have occurred after [the date the claimants acquired ownership]. The encroachment of the roots was causing continuing damage to the land by dehydrating the soil and inhibiting rehydration. Damage consisting of impairment of the load-bearing qualities of residential land is, in my view, itself a nuisance.”

- “Having regard to the proximity of the plane tree to Delaware Mansions, a real risk of damage to the land and the foundations was foreseeable on the part of Westminster.”
- “I see *Solloway v Hampshire County Council* as important as a salutary warning against imposing unreasonable and unacceptable burdens on local authorities or other tree owners. If reasonableness between neighbours is the key to the solution of problems in this field, it cannot be right to visit the authority or owner responsible for a tree with a large bill for underpinning without giving them notice of the damage and the opportunity of avoiding further damage by removal of the tree. Should they elect to preserve the tree for environmental reasons, they may fairly be expected to bear the cost of underpinning or other reasonably necessary remedial works; and the party on whom the cost has fallen may recover it, even though there may be elements of hitherto unsatisfied pre-proprietorship damage or protection for the future. But, as a general proposition, I think that the defendant is entitled to notice and a reasonable opportunity of abatement before liability for remedial expenditure can arise.”
- “In the end, in my opinion, the law can be summed up in the proposition that, where there is a continuing nuisance of which the defendant knew or ought to have known, reasonable remedial expenditure may be recovered by the owner who has had to incur it.”

The House of Lords has laid down the following principles:

- The cost of repairs for damage arising over a period of time as a consequence of a continuing nuisance can be recovered. This can be so even if damage has arisen before a claimant owned the damaged property.

- The owner of the vegetation causing the damage must be given a reasonable opportunity to remedy the situation and properly avoid further damage being caused.
- If the owner of the vegetation, having been given such an opportunity, does nothing or does not do enough, the claimant can recover damages for reasonable remedial expenditure.

In *Loftus-Brigham and another v London Borough of Ealing* [2003], the Court of Appeal considered whether the claimant had to show that the defendant's trees were a dominant cause of the damage to the claimant's property in order to succeed.

Lord Justice Chadwick held that:

> “The question that [the trial judge] should have asked himself was ... whether desiccation from the tree roots materially contributed to the damage.”

The Court was also asked to consider the issue of apportionment between the parties, on the basis that the claimant's own vegetation was also contributing to the damage in question. Chadwick LJ stated:

> “A recurrent suggestion on the part of the claimants was that this court might cut the Gordian knot by simply apportioning the loss amongst the parties, on the basis that since both had caused the damage both should bear some part of the cost of that damage ... the Court has no power to take that step. Apportionment in law has to be based on liability, not simply on causation. Since the judge found that the claimants were not contributorily negligent – a finding that has not been appealed – they were not liable in law for any part of the damage, whether caused by them or not. [The defendant] has to take its victim as it finds it.”

Here, the Court of Appeal laid down the following principles:

- The claimant has to show only that the defendant's vegetation is materially contributing to the damage, not that it is a dominant cause.
- The amount that the claimant can recover will be reduced if the claimant has acted in a contributorily negligent manner and if that contributory negligence has also resulted in damage to the claimant's property.

It cannot be stated too often that neither the mere presence of tree roots nor the proximity of trees to a building proves a claim. Evidence must be viewed as a whole and there can be a tendency on both sides to pick out one convenient '*strand*' and to ignore the overall evidential picture.

> Oak trees are a persistent culprit (their roots grow unusually deep) but it should not simply be assumed that a particular tree is responsible. Many oak trees exist near buildings without causing problems. About 90% of damage from oak trees occurs where the trees are at distances up to 18 metres from buildings. In 50% of cases the distance is less than 9.5 metres. However, the maximum distance recorded is 30 metres. Nevertheless, even for oak trees at less than 9.5 metres from buildings, it is thought that less than 1% of oak trees located in clay soils cause damage. (See *Tree Roots and Buildings* by Cutler and Richardson (1989)).

Other examples of successfully defended cases include:

- *Siddiqui and another v Hillingdon London Borough Council* [2003]. Based on expert evidence, the council proved that subsidence was not caused by roots of trees in a neighbouring wood but by heave resulting from rehydration of the ground after removal of trees and root systems from the site. In particular, the judge was persuaded by evidence that the level of the house had risen thereby indicating a continual process of rehydration in the subsoil.
- The *Siddiqui* decision is principally known for the supposed 'foundations defence' – see paragraph 82 of the judgment of His Honour Judge Seymour. It was found that a defendant would have been entitled in any event to assume that a modern house, from, say, the 1980s onwards, had complied with modern building regulations and would have sufficiently robust foundations to withstand movement. This is, however, seen as a controversial judicial statement and has not been widely relied upon or followed. In particular, it will not apply where there has been a previous occurrence of damage at a particular property or once a council has been notified of damage occurring and the need for remedial works then arising. As has been seen, the *Robbins* decision also placed emphasis upon the occurrence of claims nearby.
- *Lumb v United Utilities Water Ltd* [2001]. Damage was attributed to blasting during nearby sewer construction and not to the action of trees on the surrounding subsoil.

Claimant's contributory negligence/failure to mitigate

Often subsidence cases involve competing causes of damage, for example, where both the claimant's and the defendant's trees are considered causative. However, as confirmed by the Court of Appeal in *Loftus-Brigham and another v London Borough of Ealing* [2003], apportionment must sound in liability, not causation alone and it is very rare that an argument of contributory negligence will succeed to reduce damages against a claimant whose trees have also been causative.

Following *Loftus-Brigham* it is hard for defendants to make headway with arguments about competing causes of damage. However, such arguments should not be ruled out. The courts have not overruled older authorities such as *Murray and others v Hutchinson* [1955], in which it was held that the defendant tree owner was 25% responsible for damage that could be attributed to faulty construction, general settlement in the area, dry summers and war damage.

While the duty is on the claimant to prove the claim, a defence that incorporates a credible alternative cause for the damage stands a better prospect of success. *Berent* is now the starting point for any successful defence of tree root subsidence cases.

In *Khan*, the claimant's own vegetation was found to be 15% responsible for the damage. In addition, in situations where a claimant is aware of damage caused by a neighbour's vegetation, but delays asking them to remedy the situation, the claimant has failed to mitigate their loss.

> The courts require the claimant to give the defendant an opportunity to abate the nuisance before undertaking expensive underpinning works. An easy early intervention could result in the removal of implicated vegetation, and no need for underpinning, thereby limiting the claim to only some cosmetic redecoration.

A claimant who underpins without giving a defendant the opportunity to abate the nuisance runs the risk of not recovering the costs of underpinning, unless they can prove that, in any event, the defendant would not have taken any action *(L.E. Jones (Insurance Brokers) Ltd v Portsmouth City Council* [2002]).

Historically, councils were reluctant to remove trees for biodiversity policy reasons. Since the advent of budgetary restraints, most councils will now, on production of satisfactory evidence, agree to remove vegetation and replant less water-demanding species of vegetation. However, this is not universally so and a failure to act especially once notified or following other claims in the surrounding area can be a costly error on the part of a local authority.

Quantum

Most claims for damages will focus on the cost of repairs. Where underpinning is required, this will include the superstructure and structural repairs generally. Claims will also be for the costs of experts, project management, and investigation fees. Care needs to be taken to ensure that claims handling fees are not included as part of the claim for expert fees.

> Often claims will include the costs of ground works to drains and CCTV investigation. However, most engineers (not only those that are instructed by defendants) accept that tree roots will only enter drainage systems if the systems are already compromised, and therefore, these elements of claims should be resisted.

Expert engineering evidence on larger-value claims should comment on the value of the structural repairs.

Diminution in value

A possible measure of damage to land is the diminution in the value of the land caused by the damage.

However, it is conventional in tree root cases to award the cost of the repair works as being equivalent to the diminution in value. This approach was recognised by the House of Lords in *Delaware Mansions*. A defendant should be alert to any arguments that the cost of the reinstatement exceeds the diminution in value.

Where defendants have not removed the cause of the damage and only superstructural repairs have been carried out, diminution in value claims have still been brought. Valuation evidence will be required if a diminution in value claim is to be made out. In urban centres such as London a claim for diminution in value where the tree remains can be very high. This amounts to a strong incentive to local authorities to cooperate at the mitigation phase, which will both avoid the claimant incurring far more substantial remedial costs where the tree remains and also leave a much smaller claim to be pursued where a reasonable foreseeability defence may have greater strength.

Unforeseeable extent

Even in cases where expensive underpinning works are required, the defendant can argue that the full extent of the damage was not foreseeable.

The normal rule is that if damage of a particular type was foreseeable, damages are recoverable for its full extent, even if that extent exceeded what could have been foreseen. However, *Holbeck Hall Hotel Ltd and another v Scarborough Borough Council* [2000] casts some doubt on the operation of this principle.

A landslip was caused by negligent removal of support on adjacent land. The defendant had failed to take appropriate remedial steps. The Court of Appeal distinguished the normal rule on the basis that the damage had been caused by nonfeasance. The Court of Appeal held that the duty in such cases is much more restricted. Lord Justice Stewart Smith stated:

> “I do not think justice requires that a defendant should be held liable for damage which, albeit of the same type, was vastly more extensive than that which was foreseen or could have been foreseen without extensive further geological investigation; and this is particularly so where the defect existed just as much on the claimant’s land as on their own.”

It was held that, in a case such as this, the scope of a defendant's duty may be limited to warning claimants of such risk as they were aware of or ought to have foreseen.

Unnecessary works

The most important question is whether the works, in particular underpinning, are necessary.

Often landowners will make arrangements for major works because they are advised that they are required urgently, and then seek to recover the costs from another party/the defendant. This raises two questions:

- Was the defendant given an opportunity to abate the nuisance, as required in *Delaware Mansions*?
- Were the works actually necessary? The defendant may be able to prove, with expert evidence from engineers/arboriculturists, that tree management, i.e. pruning, felling etc., would have been sufficient to curtail the problem.

Defendants will have to convince the court that, had they been given the opportunity to manage the tree, they would have done so. For example, in *Delaware Mansions*, the council had the opportunity to fell the tree and failed to do so.

In *L.E. Jones (Insurance Brokers) Ltd v Portsmouth City Council*, the defendant argued that the claimant had failed to mitigate its loss as it had not asked the defendant to manage the tree. The court rejected this argument, even though it was agreed that tree management would have been a satisfactory solution. The defendant was notified of the claim before the claimant was committed by contract to underpinning. In the absence of any assurance from the defendant that the tree would be managed, the claimant was entitled to proceed with underpinning. A critical factor in the *L.E. Jones* decision in this context was that the defendant sought to deny causation and to argue that it would have acted to remove the tree.

These are generally seen as inconsistent positions. A 'failure to notify' defence is more likely to be credible where a defendant at least admits causation once it has been provided with relevant evidence.

It is, therefore, advisable for defendants at an early stage to set out in writing:

- The options that may be available to abate the nuisance.
- Their wish to investigate the problem so as to decide which (if any) solution is necessary.
- Their willingness to implement whichever solution is found to be reasonable, if the matter can be shown to be their responsibility.

Given the added financial pressure placed on local authorities following the Comprehensive Spending Review they may be amenable to tree removal programmes to prevent large claims for underpinning.

ABI Domestic Subsidence Tree Root Claims Agreement

The ABI Agreement is a contract between those insurers who subscribe to it. It relates to disputes between neighbouring domestic property owners.

Insurers who have subscribed to the ABI Agreement have contracted not to pursue insurers of domestic owners of neighbouring trees that have caused damage to the insured property.

This agreement operates as follows:

- It takes effect from 1 October 1997
- It applies to domestic property only
- The defendant must be insured.

This is an inter-insurer agreement very much like the knock-for-knock agreement operated by motor insurers.

It does not prevent policyholders from pursuing one another for uninsured losses, such as their policy excess, which is usually £1,000.

Joint Mitigation Protocol

The Joint Mitigation Protocol applies mainly to London local authorities. It was the result of much hard work by the London Tree Officers Association, working in conjunction with arboriculturists, engineers, domestic insurers and local authorities' insurance departments.

The aim is to try to agree minimum evidential standards that will be provided by domestic insurers seeking to reclaim monies from local authorities. Historically, the London tree officers have been dissatisfied with the lack of evidence provided by local authorities to argue for the removal of vegetation and compensation. The parties to the Protocol have agreed to a formula for valuing the alleged offending tree.

The claimant's insurers notify the local authority of the implicated tree. The local authority supplies a valuation (low, medium or high). Depending on the valuation, the insurers agree to supply a certain level of evidence.

Historically, household insurers were only prepared to accept removal of vegetation as an acceptable solution. However, under the Protocol there is an acceptance that, in certain circumstances, pruning may be considered an alternative management option.

The Protocol does not form part of the court-sanctioned pre-action protocols. However, it provides enough incentive to both sides to sign up to the Protocol and adopt its principles. The advantage to insurers includes much speedier resolution of claims.

Investigations and actions under the Protocol are carried out on a without prejudice basis, although evidence gathered will, more likely than not, be used in subsequent recovery claims.

On a practical point, it is worth checking whether the defendant is a signatory to the Protocol.

Injunction/Other action

It is often the case that the cause of the subsidence is situated on land over which the policyholder has no control. The insurer can carry out remedial works to the policyholder's property. However, if the cause of the damage is not removed, damage may well occur again, causing further expense to the insurer and inconvenience to the policyholder.

In those circumstances, it is open to the insurer, in its policyholder's name, to pursue additional remedies as well as seeking repayment of costs incurred. These remedies are abatement and injunction, both of which are considered in the chapter on nuisance (Chapter 3).

It is in practice rare for a mandatory injunction requiring tree root removal to be ordered, especially at the interim stage (that is, prior to a full trial on the facts). A court would need to be persuaded to a very high degree as to causation and any arguable dispute would likely be an insurmountable barrier to an interim mandatory injunction being ordered. It must also be borne in mind that any injunction is a discretionary remedy and only likely to be ordered where damages are not a sufficient remedy. This might be the case where a real risk of collapse is imminent, and such instances are in practice rare.

Party Wall etc. Act 1996

As the name of this Act suggests, it affects neighbours on either side of a party wall.

If a party wall is subsiding, the Act obliges parties on either side of the wall to bear a proportion of the cost to remedy the situation, relative to their use of that wall.

If there are only two parties involved, for example in a semi-detached house, they (or their insurers) will each bear one half of the cost of the works.

Latent Damage Act 1986

The Latent Damage Act 1986 (the 1986 Act) modified the limitation period for negligence (but not nuisance) in non-injury cases.

The 1986 Act:

- Retains the six-year limitation period from the date on which the cause of action accrued.
- In the alternative, it allows a claimant three years to issue proceedings from the date on which they 'knew' they had an action. Therefore, a claimant now has three years from the date they became aware of damage, even if the damage was caused by a negligent act or omission of a neighbour many years before. In this context 'knowledge' includes constructive knowledge, i.e. not restricted to what a claimant actually knew but what they ought reasonably to have known (including the knowledge of their advisors, who would include loss adjusters).
- Imposes a maximum limitation period of 15 years from the original breach of duty. A claimant, therefore, has a maximum of 15 years from the date the cause of action accrued within which to issue proceedings.

Previous subsidence damage/change of insurer

An insurance policy is a contract between an insurer and policyholder that generally lasts for a year. It can, of course, be renewed. The contract of insurance will generally only cover damage arising within the life of the policy.

Consider the position of a homeowner who has owned their property for 20 years. In that period, they may have changed their insurers five times and most recently perhaps only one year ago. Since having changed their insurer a year ago, they have discovered subsidence damage in their home.

Engineers instructed by their current insurers may determine that the damage arose over a number of years. Their insurers may argue that they should not be responsible for the total cost of repairs under the policy, some of the damage having arisen outside the life of that policy.

As a result of this potential difficulty, insurers have agreed between themselves how to share the expenses of the claim between them in such circumstances. Most insurers have subscribed to the ABI's Domestic Subsidence/Heave/Landslip "Change of Insurer" Claims Agreement.

The Agreement, however, will not normally bridge a change of ownership. If subsidence is present when a policyholder buys a property, they may not be covered for the full cost of repairs under their policy. That is one reason why a structural survey is so important when a property is purchased.

Aside from obtaining a structural survey, it may be worthwhile checking that sufficiently careful pre-contract enquiries were made and if so, whether these were accurately answered. There are occasional instances of vendors becoming liable for misrepresentation if they seek to conceal a history of damage. While this is a possible right of enquiry for recoveries, it is comparatively rare and may not be covered by public liability insurance.

Tree preservation orders (TPOs)

It is essential to understand the significance of TPOs in connection with subsidence claims.

TPOs derive from planning legislation originally in the 1940s; both the legislation and accompanying regulations need to be understood and have been varied on several occasions since originally being promulgated.

The primary legislation is now found in the Town & County Planning Act 1990 as amended and especially s.202E. The relevant legislation and orders are as follows:

- Part VIII of the Town and Country Planning Act 1990 as amended by the Planning Act 2008.
- Town and Country Planning (Tree Preservation) (England) Regulations 2012 (SI 2012 605).

The existence of a TPO is likely to have implications for both mitigation and recovery.

Own tree

If the tree is on the land of a damaged property then complications can arise in achieving mitigation. There are substantial criminal sanctions arising for unauthorised work upon a protected tree and it is, therefore, essential to obtain the relevant consent but also to communicate effectively with the local tree officers. In practice most tree contractors will be fully aware of this and have good relations with the relevant officials, which can assist in progressing matters where a situation is potentially urgent.

Statutory compensation

If consent is refused then a claim for statutory compensation can arise. These are referred to as 'Section 203 claims' by reference to the original 1990 Act provisions, but now arise under s.202E of the revised legislation. Strictly speaking, a claim is not made under the Act itself, which only provides for the power for compensation to be payable under the terms of a particular TPO. A common pitfall is that a claim must be notified in writing to the Local Planning Authority (LPA) within 12 months of any refusal of consent or imposition of conditions (this can be extended where an appeal is pursued from the refusal of consent). The question of what constituted valid notice was considered in the decision of *Keates v Haringey LBC* [2011]. The local authority's argument that an invalid notification had been made was rejected, but ideally full details should be given.

Adjoining land

Where the tree is situated on adjoining land additional complications can arise and will sometimes be utilised by a wilfully recalcitrant third party dealing with their responsibilities as tree owner/controller. Where this is the case it can be possible for encouragement or cooperation to be obtained but ultimately a third party can unwittingly render themselves liable for compensation if they fail to act, which may mean a requirement for them to make an application for consent and once this has been granted, to take action in relation to the tree. It can be pointed out to a third party that any failure on their part reasonably to cooperate can result not only in liability arising, but also in an insurer seeking to decline indemnity, thereby leaving them potentially exposed to an uninsured liability.

There are, on occasions, misunderstandings on the part of a local authority as to when a claim for compensation arises – it is not a defence that consent was 'not negligently' refused. In *Wright v Horsham DC* [2011] it was held that the claimants had been entitled to proceed with underpinning rather than being required to seek to mitigate by making a second application for consent (as was argued by the local authority).

In all cases any party affected by a refusal of consent can bring a claim against the relevant local planning authority for losses arising. Providing the relevant 12 month notice has been given, the limitation period is six years from the date of refusal, and proceedings are commenced in the Upper Tribunal rather than in the county court.

Good engineering evidence along with sound investigations are vital to show that losses arose from a refusal, and this can even be the case where damage occurred before the request for consent.

Under the relevant regulations the evidential threshold required for a valid application for consent is higher than was hitherto the case and experienced arboricultural consultants will be able to ensure that these have been complied with. As with all subsidence claims, supposed 'savings' upon evidence can result in subsequent problems, and this is especially so with a TPO. LPAs' decisions are made effectively publicly and are likely to have regard to varying and sometimes conflicting interests. It is far quicker and cheaper to obtain the necessary consent than to be forced to pursue a recovery following expensive remedial works.

Summary

Whenever a TPO is found to exist in relation to a subsidence claim, it is essential to obtain prompt and expert advice from suitably qualified consultants to ensure that the necessary evidence is obtained and all relevant requirements and timelines are complied with. If a refusal of consent to works has been made, ensure that notice has been given to the relevant LPA of a claim to be made. Failure in any respect can result in claims becoming exacerbated both in time and quantification and/or prejudice possibly recovery avenues.

Experts

Experts play a crucial role in subsidence cases. Their evidence is frequently decisive on many of the main issues, which include:

- Species of the trees and their propensity to cause damage (their zone influence).
- Species and condition of tree roots present in the soil.
- Type of soil and its susceptibility to desiccation.
- Extent of damage caused and probable causes of that damage.
- Foreseeability of damage, what precautions might have been taken and the reasonableness of any tree maintenance programme.
- Choice of remedial measures and associated risks.
- Cost of remedial measures.

Arboriculturist

An arboriculturist will advise about the tree or trees. Frequently, more than one tree is potentially implicated in the damage. The arboriculturist is best qualified to comment on:

- What the roots of a particular tree are likely to do
- How thirsty the tree will be
- Whether pruning is sufficient or whether the tree needs to be removed
- The health and viability of the tree.

Engineer

An engineer will consider matters such as:

- Foundation depths
- Soil studies
- Level monitoring and crack monitoring results
- Issues of desiccation.

A structural engineer will also be able to consider proposed remedial works and the reasonableness of the tenders submitted.

Overall, the engineer is the expert most frequently turned to when considering whether subsidence is occurring to the property. The structural engineer's evidence will form the basis of any case put forward by the defendant that the damage has arisen from causes other than the trees.

Soil scientist

The soil scientist interprets and evaluates the soil and soil-related information to understand how soil resources contribute to the effects of tree roots in different types of soil.

The soil scientist can provide specialist evidence of what is underneath a house, having examined the results of the trial pits and borehole samples. Usually their evidence forms part of the overall report completed by the engineer.

Checklist

- ✓ Is it subsidence? What is the engineer's diagnosis?
- ✓ Is it covered by the policy?
- ✓ What is the cause?
- ✓ Can the cause be removed permanently? If so how?
- ✓ Is the claimant seeking an injunction for the removal of the vegetation?
- ✓ If the cause is removed, will simple repairs be sufficient?
- ✓ If the cause cannot or will not be removed, consider injunction or abatement.
- ✓ If the cause can be removed and simple repairs are not likely to be sufficient, what is the most proportionate way to rectify the problem?
- ✓ Is there a possible third-party recovery? Collate evidence and make claim:
  - ✓ Engineer's report with opinion as to cause of damage
  - ✓ Tender documents, quotations, estimates and invoices
  - ✓ Evidence of payments made
  - ✓ Who is the recovery against?
  - ✓ Will foreseeability be a problem?
  - ✓ ABI Domestic Subsidence Tree Root Claims Agreement?
  - ✓ ABI Domestic Subsidence/Heave/Landslip "Change of Insurer" Claims Agreement?
- ✓ Contributory negligence?

19 Highways claims

Ron Ruston and Andrew Caplan

- Highways: essential elements
- Highways maintainable at public expense
- Highway authorities' powers and duties:
  - Winter maintenance
  - Water and other substances on the highway
  - Accident prevention
- Supporting a special defence under the Highways Act 1980
- Code of practice: inspections and intervention levels
- Carrying out the policy: establishing liability
- Common law liability
- Lighting
- Statutory undertakers and contractors
- Evidence

Highways claims

Highways: essential elements

A highway is not simply a road or street or footpath. It is a way over which there exists a public right of passage. The essential elements of this are that:

- It must be a regular way and not simply a piece of open land over which the public can go where they like.
- All members of the public have the right to use it. Its use is not restricted to certain sections of the public, for instance visitors to properties located along the way.
- The public may use the highway at any season of the year.
- The public may use it freely and at their will to pass and repass without let or hindrance.

Limitations and types

While there can be no limitation as to who may use a highway or when it may be used, there may be limitations as to what class of traffic may use the highway. For example, a footpath may be a highway but it is only for pedestrians.

There are three kinds of highway:

- Carriageway
- Bridleway
- Footpath.

The public have rights of passage over a carriageway with vehicles, on and with beasts of burden and by foot. Rights of passage over a bridleway exclude the use of vehicles and sometimes the right to drive cattle, but include the other rights of passage, as well as the use of a bicycle.

A footpath is restricted to passage by foot.

Dedication

At common law, the fact that a way is a highway is established by proving dedication of the way and the public's acceptance of it as a highway. The dedication can be presumed from the landowner's action of permitting the public to pass over the way and the acceptance by the public can be presumed from the simple fact that the public use that way.

By virtue of the Rights of Way Act 1932 (now repealed), public use of a way for a period of 20 years may give rise to a presumption that a way is a highway unless there is sufficient evidence that there was no intention to dedicate the way a highway. This presumption is now governed by s.31 of the Highways Act 1980.

Highways maintainable at public expense

Until 1835, all highways were maintainable by the inhabitants at large; that is, the inhabitants of a parish were bound to repair the highways within their area. That responsibility continued for highways that were in existence in 1835 but any new highways brought into existence after 1835 were not maintainable by the inhabitants at large unless they were specially adopted.

In 1960, with the coming into force of the Highways Act 1959, the concept of repair by the inhabitants at large was replaced by the concept of highways maintainable at public expense and the duty of highway authorities to maintain the highways in their area. All the highways maintainable at that time by the inhabitants at large became highways maintainable at public expense.

By virtue of the National Parks and Access to the Countryside Act 1949, highways that were footpaths or bridleways in 1949 became repairable by the inhabitants at large and subsequently, therefore, became highways maintainable at public expense.

Other ways of becoming maintainable

Other highways created between 1835 and the present day have become highways maintainable at public expense in a number of ways:

- They have been adopted by the highway authority.
- They have been constructed by the highway authority.
- They have been constructed by a council within its own area under the Housing Act 1985.
- They are a highway that is a footpath or bridleway created in consequence of a public path creation or a public path diversion order, or under an order under town and planning legislation or dedicated in pursuance of a public planning agreement.
- They are a footpath or bridleway created under a rail crossing diversion order or under an order made under certain powers relating to transport.

However, there are a number of highways that have come into being since 1835 and are not maintainable at public expense, and it may well be that no one has a duty to maintain them.

Maintainable or not?

The simple way of establishing whether a highway is maintainable at public expense is to refer to the list that each county, metropolitan district and London borough council must maintain of streets within its area that are highways maintainable at public expense.

However, such lists are not definitive. If there is doubt as to whether a highway is truly maintainable at public expense, and if so to what level, then a search into the history and use of the highway will be needed.

The council responsible for maintaining the list will be the best source for documents necessary for the search.

Highway authorities

The main legislation relating to highways is the Highways Act 1980. The Act sets out which bodies are highway authorities.

The Secretary of State for Transport is the highway authority in respect of motorways and trunk roads.

Outside London, the highway authority in respect of all other highways maintainable at public expense is the county council or metropolitan district council. Within London, the highway authority is the relevant borough council.

However, the position was modified in April 1998 when a number of unitary authorities were set up, which, since that date, have replaced county councils as the highway authority within their area, and in 2000, when Transport for London, which is the highway authority for 580 km of main roads in London, was set up.

District councils

District councils are not highway authorities under the Act. It is possible under s.42 of the Highways Act 1980 for district councils to assume responsibility for maintenance of certain roads within their area. These roads must not be classified and they must have a speed limit of 30 mph or less.

It is not uncommon for district councils to act as agents for the highway authority in respect of the maintenance of other highways within the district council's area.

> The role of the district council can cause confusion. Under no circumstances, unless it has become a unitary authority, will the district council be the highway authority for a particular highway. If a claim goes into litigation then it would be sensible for the claimant to sue the highway authority as it has the duty to maintain the highway.

However, in the pre-litigation stage there will be a difference in respect of roads claimed by the district council under s.42 and the remainder of highways:

- In the case of roads claimed by the district council, the highway authority will almost certainly have provided an indemnity to the county council in respect of any claims arising from these roads. The claimant will be dealing with the district council, its claims handlers and insurers.
- In the case of other highways, while the claimant may well find themselves initially in contact with the district council, ultimately they should deal with the highway authority itself, its claims handlers or its insurers. It is important at an early stage to establish in what capacity a district council is acting so that time is not wasted by prolonged correspondence with the district council only to find that the matter is then referred to the county council as highway authority.

Powers

The Highways Act 1980 gives a large number of powers to highway authorities, mainly to do with the improvement of the highway.

It is important to remember that these are powers and not duties. Failure to exercise these powers will not render the highway authority liable to a person who has suffered an accident that would probably have been averted if those powers had been used.

The House of Lords, in *Stovin v Wise and Norfolk County Council* [1996], clarified this position. The claimant was injured when his motorcycle collided with a car driven by the defendant at a junction. An earth bank on the railway land adjacent to the road obscured the claimant's view of the side road from which the defendant emerged. Norfolk County Council, the highway authority, was aware that the presence of the bank made the junction dangerous. It had approached the railway authority with an offer to remove the bank and pay the cost. At the time of the accident no further action had been taken. At first instance the judge found that the highway authority was in breach of its common law duty of care, though not in breach of its statutory duty. The judge found it 30% to blame for the accident. The Court of Appeal dismissed an appeal by the highway authority. However, the House of Lords allowed the appeal.

Lord Hoffmann disposed of the argument that the council could be held responsible as occupier, referring with approval to the judgment in *McGeown v Northern Ireland Housing Executive* [1994]:

> “It therefore seems clear that if Station Road and Cemetery Road had been highways over private land which happened to be owned and occupied by the Norfolk County Council instead of being repairable at the public expense, there would have been no liability. The analogy of an occupier is therefore insufficient for the purpose of imposing liability.”

Lord Hoffmann went on to deal with the distinction between policy and operations. Following the speech of Lord Wilberforce in *Anns and others v Merton LBC* [1977], the Court took the view that an authority's statutory powers could be divided into policy (or 'discretion') and an operational area that was concerned with the practical execution of policy decisions. Lord Wilberforce said:

> " It can safely be said that the more 'operational' a power or duty may be, the easier it is to superimpose upon it a common law duty of care. "

Following that doctrine, the judge at first instance and the Court of Appeal held that, the decision to move the bank having been taken, they were simply dealing with the operational question of when the work should be done. Lord Hoffmann felt that this distinction between policy and operation was an inadequate tool. The decision when the work should be done was as much a part of the council's discretion as was the question of whether it should be done at all.

Lord Hoffmann went on to find that, even if the council should have in the past removed the bank, there was no legislative intent that the council should pay compensation for damage arising because of that failure. He also found that it was not in the public interest that there should be such a duty, as it would distort the priorities of local authorities spending more on road improvements to the disadvantage of other areas.

In summary, Lord Hoffmann's view was:

> " I think that the minimum preconditions for basing a duty of care upon the existence of a statutory power, if it can be done at all, are, first, that it would in the circumstances have been irrational not to have exercised the power, so that there was in effect a public law duty to act, and secondly, that there are exceptional grounds for holding that the policy of the statute requires compensation to be paid to persons who suffer loss because the power was not exercised. "

In *Gorringe v Calderdale Metropolitan Borough Council* [2002], Lord Hoffmann seemed to go even further:

> "I find it difficult to imagine a case in which a common law duty can be founded simply upon the failure (however irrational) to provide some benefit which a public authority has power (or a public law duty) to provide."

In the light of these cases it would seem impossible to found a claim against a highway authority on the basis of a failure to carry out a power.

Gorringe was applied in *Valentine v Transport for London and another* [2010]. The claimant's husband was killed when his motorcycle skidded on gravel and debris at the side of the road. On a preliminary application for summary judgment by both defendants, the Court of Appeal held that the removal of surface lying material (transient defects) was not required by s.41 of the Highways Act.

However, a claim for common law negligence was allowed to proceed against the local authority only. The Court of Appeal held there was no common law duty requiring the local authority to act. However, the Court had to distinguish between a situation where the local authority had done nothing at all and a situation where action had been taken that was either insufficient or negligently carried out.

In this case, the sweeping regime had failed to collect the debris on a small portion of the junction where the claimant had lost control of his motorbike. The Court of Appeal remitted the case back to the lower court to determine the substantive issue of whether, in failing to sweep the sliver of road, the council had created a trap. That would be a positive negligent act. The lower court found that a trap had not been created.

Where a local authority has acted negligently in taking a positive step it may be held to have breached its common law duty to users of the highway. In *Yetkin v Mahmood and another* [2010], the local authority had planted some shrubs on the central reservation. While crossing the road the claimant pedestrian was hit by a car. The local authority had failed to trim the shrubs, which reduced the visibility for pedestrians crossing the road. The Court of Appeal held that as the local authority had designed and maintained the junction, including the planting of shrubs, it had created a duty of care to use reasonable care in exercising its powers. Unfortunately, the shrubs had been left to grow to a height that posed a risk to road users. Accordingly, the local authority had breached its duty of care to road users. There was a finding of 75% contributory negligence on the part of the claimant.

Duties

The principal duty relevant to accident claims is the duty of the highway authority to maintain the highway. This is currently established under s. 41(1) of the Highways Act 1980, which states quite simply that:

> The authority who are for the time being the highway authority for a highway maintainable at the public expense are under a duty ... to maintain the highway.

No standard of maintenance is set by the Act. The standard adopted by the courts is that the highway must not be dangerous.

Until the decision of the House of Lords in *Goodes v East Sussex County Council* [2000], it was felt that the duty to maintain the highway went beyond simply repairing the surface. It would include removing snow, ice, mud, obstructions and draining the highway. However, it would now seem that 'maintenance' is to be interpreted as being restricted to keeping the structure in good repair, and that extraneous substances on the surface of the highway will not render the highway authority in breach of its duty under s. 41; nor would the repainting of a worn-out sign on the surface of the highway constitute maintenance of the structure of the highway – see *Gorringe*.

But what if the extraneous matter is more permanent? In *Thomas v Warwickshire County Council* [2011], the High Court held that a spillage of concrete that had become so affixed to the road surface that it was likely to be permanent, or at least long lasting, was sufficient to bring it within s.41. By contrast, in *Rollinson v Dudley MBC* [2015] the High Court held on appeal that the duty under s.41 did not extend to the removal of moss and algae, and therefore did not agree with the decision at first instance that it had become part of the surface of the highway.

Is the highway dangerous?

It cannot be emphasised too strongly that there is no mechanistic approach to determining what constitutes a danger on the highway.

Probably the most famous section of any judgment on a highway claim is in the judgment of Mr Justice Cumming-Bruce in *Littler v Liverpool Corporation* [1968]:

> “Uneven surfaces and differences in level between flagstones of about an inch may cause a pedestrian temporarily off balance to trip and stumble, but such characteristics have to be accepted. A highway is not to be criticised by the standards of a bowling green.”

Many people have made the assumption that a one-inch trip hazard is the standard by which dangerousness is judged. If a trip hazard of an inch is dangerous, less than an inch is not. However, that misconstrues the judgment. Earlier in his judgment, Cumming-Bruce J said:

> “It is a mistake to isolate and emphasise a particular difference in levels between flagstones unless that difference is such that a reasonable person who noticed and considered it would regard it as presenting a real source of danger.”

There is a widely held belief that trip hazards of less than three-quarters of an inch to one inch are not dangerous and trip hazards in excess of that level are. This is not the approach of the courts.

Test applied by the courts

The test applied by the courts is whether a reasonable person would consider that a particular defect had rendered the road dangerous. Of course the reasonable person is inevitably the judge themselves.

In *Rider v Rider* [1972], Lord Justice Lawton said:

> “[W]hether part of a highway is a danger for traffic is a question of fact, and the answer to the question will depend upon the evaluation of the evidence by the judge ... in a common sense way.”

In *Mills v Barnsley Metropolitan Borough Council* [1992], Lord Justice Steyn said:

> “For my part I find it a sterile exercise to make a comparison between the facts of reported decisions in tripping cases and the facts of the present case.”

In the more recent case of *Lawrence v Kent County Council* [2012], the elderly claimant tripped over a manhole cover which protruded above the surrounding pavement by at least 15 mm. The judge at first instance was influenced by witnesses who in evidence described the defect as “dangerous”.

On appeal to the High Court, Mr Justice Eady agreed the protrusion created a risk but that was insufficient to amount to a liability on the part of the council. This decision was upheld by the Court of Appeal. In his judgment, Eady J restated the need to conduct a balance between private and public interest, as the expenditure of public funds on highways has to be prioritised. Highway authorities cannot achieve perfection. Defendants should take heart from the fact that, even though the council arranged to repair the defect after the accident, this did not prove a breach of duty.

Mr Justice Eady commented that it was not for lay witnesses to comment on or apply the test of dangerousness:

> “[T]he judge should not have taken into account other people's views of what was “dangerous” and, therefore, by implication of what was or was not a breach of statutory duty. He had to carry out the balancing exercise himself.”

Character of road and traffic

Clearly, each case has to be judged on its own facts: the size of the defect, its position in the highway, the volume and type of traffic that might be expected to encounter it.

The character of the road and the character of the traffic using it are important considerations. In *Rider*, Lawton LJ said:

> “A stretch of uneven paving outside a factory probably would not be a danger for traffic, but a similar stretch outside an old people's home, and much used by the inmates to the knowledge of the highway authority, might be.”

In *Mills*, Steyn LJ gave a warning that the courts should not impose an unreasonably high burden on highway authorities. Allowing the appeal, he said:

> “[T]he judge impliedly set a standard which, if generally used in the thousands of tripping cases which come before the courts every year, would impose an unreasonable burden upon highway authorities in respect of minor depressions and holes in streets which in a less than perfect world the public must simply regard as a fact of life.”

In *Dalton v Nottingham County Council* [2011], a 49-year-old claimant tripped over a wobbling paving slab that protruded approximately 20mm.

Dismissing the council's appeal, Lord Justice Tomlinson stated:

> “We have no doubt that the condition of the block on 20 October 2006 was dangerous in the sense that, in the ordinary course of human affairs, danger may reasonably have been anticipated from the continued use of that area by the

public. The block was loose, unstable, wobbling, proud of its neighbours and moreover its height relative to its neighbours was capable of being altered. This was not therefore a case in which the danger lay only in a difference in level between two adjacent surfaces. It was also a block which had the potential to wobble underfoot and cause a pedestrian to overbalance. ”

Danger created by highway authority

It should be noted, however, that if the danger was actually created by the highway authority the courts may well apply higher standards.

In *Pitman v Southern Electricity Board* [1978], the court found that a metal plate, only an eighth of an inch thick, placed on the highway nonetheless constituted a danger because it was unexpected.

Special defence

If a highway is dangerous and damage ensues, then the highway authority may still be able to avoid liability on the basis of the special defence provided under s.58(1) of the Highways Act 1980.

Defence in relation to s.41

It must be noted, however, that s.58 only comes into play if it is shown that the highway authority is in breach of s.41 of the Act. Steyn LJ stressed this in *Mills*:

“ [T]he plaintiff must prove that:

a) the highway was in such a condition that it was dangerous ...

b) the dangerous condition was created by the failure to maintain or repair the highway; and

c) the injury or damage resulted from such a failure.

Only if the plaintiff proves these *facta probanda* does it become necessary to turn to the highway authority's reliance on the special defence. ”

Considerations under s.58(2)

In practice it is often difficult to disentangle the two sections. Section 58(2) sets requirements that the court has to take into consideration in respect of the s.58 defence:

> For the purposes of a defence under subsection (1) above, the court shall in particular have regard to the following matters:
>
> a) the character of the highway, and the traffic which was reasonably to be expected to use it;
>
> b) the standard of maintenance appropriate for a highway of that character and used by such traffic; and
>
> c) the state of repair in which a reasonable person would have expected to find the highway.

These are all matters that the court will have to consider when deciding whether there has been a breach of s.41. It is important that the court and the parties realise that, before going on to consider any other parts of s.58, it must first of all be established that there has been a breach of s.41.

Causation

Section 58(1) of the Highways Act 1980 states:

> In an action against a highway authority in respect of damage resulting from their failure to maintain a highway maintainable at public expense it is a defence ... to prove that the authority had taken such care as in all the circumstances was reasonably required to secure that the part of the highway to which the action relates was not dangerous for traffic.

On the face of it, the requirements seem to be no more than a statement that the highway authority should not be negligent. There is, in fact, an important difference and it relates to the question of causation, and is perhaps best explained by example.

Let us assume that a deep pothole has formed over which a claimant has tripped. If we consider the matter in negligence, putting aside the defence of nonfeasance, it would be necessary for the claimant to show that a lack of care on the part of the highway authority had caused the pothole to form or, perhaps more likely, the failure to see and repair the pothole quickly enough. If the authority could show, although it had no regular system of maintenance for that road, that nonetheless it had perhaps by chance looked at that road only a week before and that the road appeared to be in perfectly good condition, then the claimant might well have a struggle to make their case.

Under the Act, however, the position is different. The authority is already on the back foot as it is clearly in breach of s.41. It must, therefore, base its defence on s.58. In those circumstances, it is not sufficient for it to say that it had looked at the highway a week before and it seemed in good condition then. It must show that it has a proper system of inspection and maintenance and that it has properly carried out that system of inspection and maintenance. If it had, for example, missed three inspections in a row and then carried out the inspection immediately before the accident, although those missed inspections may well have not been causative of the accident, they probably would lead the court to find that the authority had not fulfilled its duties and therefore could not depend on the s.58 defence.

Section 58(2) sets out the matters that the court has to take into consideration when deciding whether or not the highway authority has taken the care required of it by s.58(1). Subsections (a), (b) and (c) are quoted above. The remainder of s.58(2) requires the court to consider:

d) whether the highway authority knew, or could reasonably have been expected to know, that the condition of the part of the highway to which the action relates was likely to cause danger to the users of the highway;

e) where the highway authority could not reasonably have been expected to repair that part of the highway before the cause of the action arose, what warning notices of its condition had been displayed;

f) but for the purposes of such a defence it is not relevant to prove that the highway authority had arranged for a competent person to carry out or supervise the maintenance of the part of the highway to which the action relates unless it is also proved that the authority had given him proper instructions with regard to the maintenance of the highway and that he had carried out the instructions.

In determining whether or not the highway authority has taken such care as in all the circumstances is reasonably required we look to s. 58(2), to what the general standards are and to what has been found to be reasonable in the past.

Section 58 defence in practice

In order to support a s.58 defence, a highway authority has to establish two things:

- It has a reasonable maintenance policy
- The policy has been properly carried out.

The main elements of a reasonable maintenance policy are:

- A reasonable inspection policy
- Reasonable timescales for repair.

The main elements of an inspection policy are:

- Road/footway hierarchy – the roads and footways within a highway authority area should be categorised according to the importance of the road and the amount of traffic that each carries (compare this with s 58(2)(a)).
- The frequency of inspection set for each category of road and footway.
- The way in which the inspection is to be carried out.
- The intervention levels set, i.e. how bad the defect has to be before it warrants repair. These intervention levels will differ depending on whether the defect is in the road or footway.

As to the repair policy, the important elements are:

- A reasonable timescale for repair should be set according to the severity of the defect.
- Where a repair cannot be effected immediately, proper steps are taken to render the highway safe by signing or other appropriate means (compare this with s.58(2)(e)).

Code of practice

The Local Authority Association (LAA) for some years produced a Code of Good Practice for Highway Maintenance, setting out a basic road hierarchy and suggesting inspection intervals both for safety inspections and service inspections. It also set out guidelines for intervention levels.

This was superseded by "Delivering Best Value in Highway Maintenance", published in July 2001 by the Institution of Highways and Transportation. This in turn was superseded in July 2005 by "Well-maintained Highways" (the code), published by the Stationery Office.

In so far as the highway authority's policy coincides with the practice proposed by the code it would be hard for a court to find that the highway authority's policy was unreasonable.

TR v Devon County Council [2013] concerned a defect at the edge of the carriageway. The inspection regime was every six months although the code recommendation was monthly. At first instance, the judge held that, because the authority had no written risk assessment as to its deviation from the code, it had to fail in its s.58 defence argument.

The Court of Appeal held that the judge's decision on this particular issue was erroneous. The code is guidance and not mandatory. It does not place a duty on a highway authority to carry out a risk assessment if it deviates from the code, and it is important not to overrate the importance of the code. The advice to give explicit reasons for adopting a different policy was wise, but it was not a rule. While adherence to the code will always be strong evidence of good practice, local authorities had to exercise their own judgement. In this case, there was sufficient evidence for the judge to conclude that the particular road needed more regular inspections and as such there was no good reason to interfere with the first instance decision.

> In practice, if a local authority has deviated from the code in terms of inspection frequencies and it does not have a written risk assessment it will need to show that its actions were reasonable, perhaps using data from other authorities that use a similar frequency as a comparison.

However, note that in *Wilkinson v City of York Council* [2011], a highway authority that had deviated from the code because of budgetary considerations could not rely on a s.58 defence.

On 28 October 2016 the UK Roads Liaison Group published the first edition of its Code of Practice "Well-managed Highways Infrastructure" (the new code) which is to replace the code. Again, the new code provides guidance but is not mandatory. It moves away from specific guidance and recommendations towards a risk-based approach. This risk-based approach is to be determined by each highway authority, which will involve analysis, development and the gaining of approval through the authorities' executive processes. The new code is said to provide guidance for highway authorities to consider when developing their approach in accordance with local needs, priorities and affordability. It will be interesting to see how this affordability point is considered by the courts in light of the decision in *Wilkinson*. The new code can be adopted by highway authorities straightaway, or they have until October 2018 to adopt a risk-based approach.

Inspections

Safety inspections will look for defects that are dangerous or are likely to become dangerous in the very near future. Service inspections are more detailed inspections tailored to the requirements of particular highway elements.

> When looking at the adequacy of inspection frequencies it is important not only to compare the highway authority's frequency of inspection with that proposed by the code, but also to consider whether or not the road in question has been correctly categorised within the hierarchy.

Inspection frequencies in line with the code will also not assist a highway authority if it knows that there is a special problem on the road that will cause more rapid deterioration and therefore warrants more frequent inspection: *Jacobs v Hampshire County Council* [1984].

Intervention levels

An intervention level is the degree to which a section of highway must be out of maintenance in order to trigger some form of remedial action by the highway authority.

Given the wide variety of defects that can occur, the detail of intervention levels is too wide a subject for this chapter. The important thing about an intervention level is that it should be set lower than the level at which the highway authority believes that the highway or footway is rendered dangerous, the aim being to prevent the highway from becoming dangerous. The code refers to Category 1 and Category 2 defects. Traditionally, Category 1 defects are those that require prompt attention because they represent an immediate or imminent hazard or because there is a risk of short-term deterioration. Category 2 encompasses all other defects.

The code has introduced a risk matrix that balances the probability of an accident happening against its likely impact if it does.

Category 1 defects are those with a high probability of causing an accident and a high impact if an accident occurs. Category 2 defects are divided into low, medium and high priority.

A trip on the footway is the most common form of highway accident, but the code is unspecific as to what the intervention level should be in relation to footway defects. Many authorities have, however, settled on a change in height of 20 mm as being the level at which they will order an urgent repair. A court's reluctance to set minimum standards and wish to treat each case on its own merits needs to be borne in mind. To that end, a sensible highway authority will not set rigid guidelines for its highway inspectors but give them authority to deal urgently with any defect they find that they believe to be dangerous or believe to be on the verge of becoming dangerous.

Timescale for repairs and/or making safe

The code recommends four response times to match the four categories of risk:

Category 1	Make safe or repair within 24 hours
Category 2 (high)	Make safe or repair within five working days
Category 2 (medium)	Repair within four weeks
Category 2 (low)	Repair during next available programme, schedule more detailed inspection, or review condition at next inspection, based on an assessment of the risk of deterioration before next visit

The code adds that if a defect with potentially serious consequences for network safety is made safe by means of temporary signing or repair arrangements then there should be special inspections to check the integrity of the signing or temporary repair until the permanent repair is carried out.

Consideration will need to be given to whether the repair and/or make safe timescales can be met if the defect is reported out of hours or over the weekend. In *Crawley v Barnsley MBC* [2017] a defect was reported by a member of the public on a Friday, and this was not due to be inspected until the Monday in line with the defendant's policy to inspect on the next working day. On the Saturday the claimant was out jogging when he fell on the pothole that had been reported on the Friday. The Court of Appeal dismissed the appeal by the local authority on the basis that the only justification for failing to inspect the next working day, where the accident was on a Friday, must have been due to resources, and that lack of resources is not a relevant consideration as demonstrated in *Wilkinson*. The need to train staff taking the calls to assess the seriousness of the defect, and the possibility of forwarding such reports to an on-call highway inspector was considered.

Carrying out the policy

Assuming that it is established that the highway authority's maintenance policy is reasonable, the next question is whether it has carried out that policy correctly. Important points to consider are:

- Have there been any missed inspections? One missed inspection may not condemn the highway authority, providing it is not the one immediately before the accident. Several missed inspections may cause the s.58 defence to fail, even though it can be shown that those missed inspections were not causative of the accident.
- Were the inspections carried out appropriately? It is suggested that a court would not be convinced that a footway in a busy pedestrian area could be adequately inspected from a slow-moving motor vehicle.
- Was the highway inspector who carried out the inspections sufficiently well trained and competent to carry them out? It is all very well if the highway authority has an excellent maintenance policy, but no use at all if it does not communicate it to its highway inspectors.

- Could it be that the highway inspector, while carrying out an inspection, simply missed a defect that already existed? It may be that there will be witnesses who will say that they were aware of the defect prior to the last safety inspection before the accident. It should be borne in mind, however, that such witnesses will be open to the attack that they did not consider the defect dangerous, otherwise they would have reported it.

A common feature of highway claims, however, is that the highway inspector did not notice the defect until the claimant brought it to their attention. It is important, therefore, to see the inspection report for the routine inspection post-accident as well as for the one before the accident. If the defect is not spotted in a post-accident inspection, then the implication is that the highway inspector may have also missed it in the pre-accident inspection.

Common law liability

It is common for claims against the highway authority to be pleaded as not only a breach of its duty under s.41 of the Highways Act, but also in negligence and nuisance.

It is also occasionally pleaded that the local authority is in breach of its common law duty of care under the Occupiers' Liability Act 1957.

It could be argued that none of these common law duties extend the duty of the highway authority beyond that stated in the Highways Act 1980.

Negligence

The position remains that the highway authority is only liable in negligence where the actions of the highway authority itself have brought about a dangerous state of affairs on the road (misfeasance). It is not liable under the common law for nonfeasance, which is where the road has become dangerous because of its failure to act.

With regards to a highway authority's potential liability as occupier of the highway, it is suggested that as members of the public are not visitors to the highway they cannot acquire rights as visitors. They are on the highway by right; they do not have to be invited or permitted to go onto the highway – see *Whiting v Hillingdon London Borough Council* [1970] and *Holden v White* [1982].

> It has to be borne in mind that if the definition of the highway is restricted to its structure, then ancillary items such as street furniture, which are occupied by or are the responsibility of the highway authority, will not enjoy the same privileged position as regards nonfeasance. If a highway authority fails to maintain a bollard, which becomes defective and causes injury, while the highway authority cannot be in breach of s.41 of the Highways Act, it can be found to be negligent – see *Shine v Tower Hamlets London Borough Council* [2006].

Nuisance

If someone else created the danger and the highway authority did not deal with it, it would be nonsense if they were deprived of the special defence enacted by statute simply because the case was pleaded in nuisance.

It is unlikely that the courts would be prepared to look at a highways claim in that way nor are there any cases in which they have. Clearly, the highway authority can be guilty of nuisance. One example would be trespass from a tree on a highway causing damage to a neighbouring property. However, that is clearly a different matter from dangers on the highway.

Lighting

There is no duty on a highway authority to light a highway. Section 97 of the Highways Act 1980 gives the highway authority power to light the highway. It was established in *Sheppard v Glossop Corporation* [1921] that there was no common law duty to light the highway even if the highway was dangerous when unlit.

Interestingly, the power under s.97 the Highways Act 1980 is to construct and maintain. It would appear that, therefore, having lit a highway, a highway authority has no duty to maintain that lighting, merely the power to do so. Following *Stovin*, it would not be liable if that power were not exercised.

However, in *Farrell v Northern Ireland Electricity Service* [1977] there was held to be a duty to maintain:

> “In my opinion if the defendants decide to carry out lighting to a certain standard in any particular place or for the duration of any particular period they are exercising a statutory discretion and in doing so they assume an obligation to exercise it with reasonable care. This involves the proposition that they ought to keep the lighting up to standard by means of the regular inspections that they conduct.”

It should be borne in mind, however, that this is a Northern Ireland decision and that it precedes the House of Lords' decision in *Stovin*.

There will, however, be a duty to maintain lighting where a highway authority creates a danger on the highway and makes it safe by lighting: *Polkinghorn v Lambeth Borough Council* [1938].

Polkinghorn was confirmed by the decision of *Chester County Court in McCabe v Cheshire West and Chester Council and another* [2014]. The claimant fell down a flight of steps on a public footpath. He alleged that a streetlight intended to illuminate the steps was not working at the time. His Honour Judge Halbert held that, in the circumstances, the council owed no duty of care to the claimant.

Winter maintenance

Approach prior to 2000

The duty of the highway authority to maintain the highway under the Highways Act 1980 was interpreted from 1978 to 2000 to include the duty to remove ice and snow from the surface of the highway: *Haydon v Kent County Council* [1978].

During this period, courts took the attitude that as ice and snow was likely to occur over a large section, if not the whole of a highway authority's network at the same time, it would be unrealistic to expect it to clear the entire network instantly. A highway authority's defence, therefore, was similar to a defence under s.58 in that it had a reasonable policy in force and that it carried out that policy correctly. An important element of the policy was the priority that it attributed to each of the roads within its area.

Highway authorities reasonably took the view that, both in terms of economic damage and health and safety, it was vital to keep open the most strategically important and most heavily travelled roads. That meant that minor roads and footways were not dealt with for some considerable time. Indeed, it was not uncommon for them not to be dealt with at all, but simply to await the thaw.

A court was likely to approve the highway authority's actions as long as the authority applied its principles reasonably and sensibly – see *Cross v Kirklees Metropolitan Borough Council* [1997]; *Wilcox v East Riding of Yorkshire District Council* [1998].

Approach from 2000 to 2003

The position changed radically in June 2000 with the House of Lords' decision in *Goodes v East Sussex County Council.* The House of Lords decided that Lord Denning, who had been in the minority in *Haydon* in finding that maintenance of the highway did not include the removal of snow and ice, was in fact correct.

The House of Lords found that the Highways Act 1959 and its successor in 1980 had not extended the duty to maintain beyond what was imposed by the common law prior to the passing of those acts. It held that the duty to maintain prior to 1959 had clearly not included the duty to remove ice and snow, and still less to prevent them falling on the road.

That also led to a view that, given that s.41 imposed an absolute duty to maintain the highway, it was illogical to include within that duty a duty to keep the highway free of snow and ice. No highway authority could avoid, from time to time, being in breach of that duty. It took the view that the Court of Appeal in its decision in *Haydon* had got itself into difficulty because, by including the removal of ice and snow from the road within the duty to maintain, it had been forced to water down the absolute nature of that duty.

While Lord Hoffmann, in the leading speech in *Goodes*, largely restricts himself to the question of whether or not the removal of ice and snow is included within the definition of maintenance, Lord Clyde's speech, also finding for the council, makes it clear that there are wider ramifications. First, he is firm in his view that the duty of maintenance does not extend beyond matters of repair; and second, that if the highway was made unsafe by the presence of extraneous material upon it, that, likewise, did not constitute a failure to maintain.

Current approach

There was within Lord Hoffmann's speech an open invitation to the government to consider legislation in order to make actionable a failure by a highway authority to take reasonable steps to keep the highway clear of snow and ice. The government responded by amending s.41 of the Highways Act 1980 to include s.41(1A), which came into force on 31 October 2003:

> In particular, a highway authority is under a duty to ensure, so far as is reasonably practicable, that safe passage along a highway is not endangered by snow or ice.

> A highway authority will have to satisfy a court that it took reasonable steps to obtain warnings of snow and ice and had a reasonable plan for dealing with them in terms of gritting and ploughing. The key constituent will be the gritting of routes. The timing of gritting, the density of grit used, and the system used for receiving, recording and dealing with isolated reports of ice will be important. Finally, it will have to show that it carried out that policy efficiently, for example that the gritters were working efficiently and covering the whole road.

The first case to consider the duty under s.41(1A) was *Pace v The City and County of Swansea* [2007], heard in Swansea County Court in July 2007 following an accident on 17 January 2004. In that case it was found that there was ice on the road and that it caused the claimant to lose control. The road had been gritted but patches of ice had still formed. The council's winter maintenance plan was in line with the Department of Transport's Code of Practice for Maintenance Management and was found to be adequate.

The claimant's main lines of attack were on implementation of the plan, that the spread rate of salt was too low and that the driver did not, in fact, cover the relevant section of the route. The judge rejected both these contentions as matters of fact.

The judge held that the council had an adequate and proper policy for salting and that the policy was implemented. The claim was dismissed. The judge also held that if he had found against the council he would have found that there was 60% contributory negligence on the part of the claimant.

In the more recent case of *Rockliffe v Liverpool City Council* [2013], heard in Liverpool County Court, the claimant slipped on ice while walking along a footway identified by the local authority as a "priority one prestige walking zone". The local authority had not salted or gritted the footway. The policy was to only salt, grit and clear footways if snow was also present. The court held that the local authority had the manpower and supplies to grit or salt the footway. It was practicable for it to have safeguarded the area and it was unreasonable for it not to have done so.

It should be remembered that only a duty in respect of snow and ice has been reintroduced by this legislation. There remains no duty on the highway authority to remove other extraneous materials, such as mud or leaves as demonstrated by *Valentine*, or moss and algae as demonstrated by *Rollinson*.

Water and other substances on the highway

Lord Clyde, in *Goodes v East Sussex County Council*, expressed the view that maintenance did not go beyond repair and that the duty to maintain did not extend to the removal of extraneous matter from the surface of the highway. Consequently, mud or leaves or oil on the road would not found a case for breach of s.41.

Flooding of the road, however, was found to be a different matter in *Department for Transport, Environment and the Regions v Mott MacDonald Ltd and others* [2006]. Here the Court of Appeal found that maintenance of the highway included maintenance of the highway drains and extended to the unblocking of drains as well as the repair of their structure. Therefore, if the highway became dangerous by reason of a failure to maintain the highway drains, then the highway authority would be liable under s.41 for the ensuing injury, loss and damage.

In *Vernon Knight Associates v Cornwall Council* [2013], the Court of Appeal held that the council was in breach of its duty under s.41 for flood damage caused to a property when drains it had installed in a road known to be a high flood risk had become blocked. Its system to prevent such blockages was adequate, based on action normally undertaken by a road maintenance contractor on his own initiative. However, there was no adequate explanation for why he had not followed his normal practice on the occasions of the two floods in question.

Accident prevention

Section 39 Road Traffic Act 1988 imposes a duty to carry out studies into road traffic accidents. The authority must:

> in the light of those studies, take such measures as appear to the authority to be appropriate to prevent such accidents, including ... the construction, improvement, maintenance or repair of

roads ... and other measures taken in the exercise of their powers for controlling, protecting or assisting the movement of traffic on roads.

Although this is expressed as a duty, it should be noted that the authority only has to take measures that appear to it to be appropriate.

The Court of Appeal considered the extent of a highway authority's duty under s.39 in *Larner v Solihull Metropolitan Borough Council* [2000]. The court decided that the duty under the section could properly be described as a "target" duty, which required the council to do no more than exercise its powers in the manner that it considered appropriate. The Court went on to express the view that although a common law duty of care might in exceptional circumstances be imposed on the statutory duty of s.39, it would have to be shown that the default of the relevant authority fell outside the ambit of the discretion given to the authority by that section, for example where the authority had acted wholly unreasonably. The Court of Appeal followed that finding in *Gorringe*.

In *Larner*, the claimant alleged that greater advance warning of a road junction should have been provided. In *Gorringe*, a slow sign, which had disappeared, should have been repainted to give warning of a dangerous section of road. The essential points that emerge from these judgments are:

- An action will have to be founded on a common law duty arising out of the duty under the Act, rather than directly on breach of duty under the Act itself.
- A court will have to find that the highway authority has acted wholly unreasonably in not taking steps under the Act.
- It will only be in very exceptional circumstances that a court will so find.

Statutory undertakers

Statutory undertakers are companies and agencies with statutory rights or duties to install, inspect, maintain, repair or replace apparatus in or under the street.

Many bodies have the need to place equipment in or under the highway. For example, water, gas, telephone and electricity companies. Their powers and duties in respect of this are dealt with under the New Roads and Street Works Act 1991.

Section 65 deals with the safety measures that they must take, s.70 deals with their duty to reinstate and s.71 deals with the standard of reinstatement and the maintenance period.

Reinstatement

Unlike s.41 of the Highways Act, which includes no definition of the standard of highway maintenance, standards of reinstatement are set out in a Code of Practice, and approved by the Secretary of State for Transport under the New Roads and Street Works Act 1991. There is insufficient space to go into the technical details of the standard of reinstatement. However, section 1.2.1 of the third edition of the Code, published in 2010, should be particularly noted:

> The Undertaker shall ensure that the interim reinstatement conforms to the prescribed standards until the permanent reinstatement is completed, and that the permanent reinstatement conforms to the prescribed standards throughout the guarantee period.

The Code goes on to say that the permanent guarantee will begin on completion of the permanent reinstatement and will run for two years, or three years in the case of "deep openings", which are excavations and trenches in which the depth of cover over the buried apparatus is greater than 1.5 m.

If a highway defect is the result of the failure of a statutory undertaker's reinstatement, then the highway authority would be entitled to refer any claim to the statutory undertaker if the accident occurred within the guarantee period.

Equipment

Where a statutory undertaker's equipment is located on the surface of the highway, the undertaker is responsible for maintaining the apparatus. The undertaker does not have the common law defence of nonfeasance that is available to the highway authority.

A statutory undertaker is entitled to rely on the highway inspections carried out by the highway authority, but is deemed to have the same knowledge as the highway authority as to the state of its highway equipment. It is not a defence, therefore, for an undertaker to say that the highway authority had not informed it of a defect in its equipment.

The duty to maintain the highway remains with the highway authority. If the highway is dangerous because of the defective equipment of a statutory undertaker both the undertaker and the highway authority can be jointly and severally liable. In these circumstances it is highly likely that liability will be apportioned 50:50 between them as in *Nolan v Merseyside County Council and another* [1982].

Contractors

Much of the work that is carried out by highway authorities is now contracted out. It is important to appreciate that the highway authority cannot rely on the defence that it has discharged its duty by employing a competent contractor. The duty of the highway authority is non-delegable. If the highway is dangerous because of the fault or failure of the contractor, the highway authority will remain liable. The highway authority may well have a right to indemnity or contribution from the contractor, but the injured party's cause of action will lie against the highway authority.

Evidence

The essential evidence that needs to be gathered in the majority of cases is as follows.

Section 41

- Photographs and dimension of the defect.
- Evidence of the type of traffic that uses that particular highway. It may be important (for example) to consider whether a high proportion of older people use a particular footway. It may, for certain types of defects, be important to establish whether the section of road in question is used by cyclists and motorcyclists who can be endangered by ridges and ruts running along the length of the carriageway rather than across it, in a way which would not inconvenience a pedestrian or a motorist.

Section 58

There is guidance in the standard disclosure list attached to the Pre-Action Protocol for Personal Injury Claims that stipulates disclosure of the following documents for a period of 12 months prior to the accident:

- Records of inspection of the relevant stretch of highway.
- Maintenance records, including records of independent contractors working in the relevant area.
- Records of the minutes of highway authority meetings where maintenance or repair policy has been discussed or decided.
- Records of complaints about the state of the highways.
- Records of other accidents that have occurred on the relevant stretch of the highway.

It would be prudent to see the following documents:

- Records of inspection for the period immediately post-accident, to see whether the defect was noticed at the next routine highway inspections after the accident took place. If it was not, and the defect had not already been repaired, then the chances are that it was overlooked at the pre-accident routine inspection.
- Any repair documents relating to repairs ordered as a result of the inspections in the 12 months preceding the accident. It is important to establish whether these repairs were carried out. It may be that the accident occurred because of a long-standing defect that had been identified but not yet repaired. It is also important to establish whether the highway authority generally repairs defects in line with reasonable timescales.
- The document that sets out the highway authority's policy regarding highway maintenance. This may not have been discussed at highway authority meetings within the 12 months prior to the accident.

A highway authority trying to establish a s.58 defence should consider the following points:

- The burden is on the defendant to make out the defence. They will need to produce relevant records and witness evidence from those responsible for policy setting and pre- and post-accident inspections.
- The evidence should refer to how the code of practice has been applied.
- It may be relevant to refer to the policies of bordering or similar local authorities.
- Complaints relating to the area under review should be explored.

Checklist

- ✓ Is the highway maintainable at public expense?
- ✓ Is the condition of the highway dangerous? One must, when considering this point, bear in mind the amount and type of traffic using that particular highway.
- ✓ If the highway is in a dangerous condition, can the highway authority, nonetheless, rely on the defence under s.58 of the Highways Act 1980? Points to consider in this regard are:
  - ✓ Is its policy for highway maintenance adequate? How does it compare with the code?
  - ✓ Has the policy been fully carried out? Is there, for example, evidence that a defect was missed at an inspection or that it was not repaired in the timescale set by the highway authority's own policy?
  - ✓ Were there any special factors known to the highway authority that made their maintenance policy inadequate in these circumstances? An example would be the frequent subsidence of the road surface due to the washing away of the subsurface.

20 Sexual abuse claims

Helen Snowball

- Defending claims
- Vicarious liability
- Areas of investigation: disclosure of documents and insurance history
- General damages
- Compensation schemes

Sexual abuse claims

Introduction

Claims of sexual abuse involve individuals whose lives may have been severely damaged by the trauma that they have experienced. Consequently, insurers should adopt an approach that is sensitive, expeditious and mindful of the vulnerability of those making such claims.

Sadly, claims involving sexual abuse will typically concern assaults perpetrated on children or vulnerable individuals who were subject to supervision, whether in care or in some other capacity. This may involve a range of institutions, including local authorities, schools, churches and youth organisations. The events under scrutiny will usually have occurred many years and sometimes decades ago.

The allegations will typically be on the basis of:

- Failure to remove abused/neglected children into care
- Failure to protect "looked after" children
- Vicarious liability for the conduct of third-party perpetrators of the abuse.

Defending claims

The historical nature of most abuse claims creates, in effect, a unique type of claim which needs careful handling. When investigating defence options regarding such claims, the types of issues normally under consideration will include:

- Failure to remove cases: Pursuant to the case of *CN & GN v Poole Borough Council* [2017] no duty of care is owed by a social service authority in the exercise of its child protection functions, to investigate and take action to prevent significant harm to children, whatever its source. It follows that the local authority does not owe a child living at home a duty of care, even if the family are receiving social service support. The case may however be appealed to the Supreme Court.

- Limitation. Some claims for sexual abuse will inevitably fail at this initial hurdle. (*JL v Bowan (1) and Scout Association (2)* [2017]).
- The absence of a duty of care in the particular circumstances of the pleaded claim. While this area of the law remains significantly underdeveloped, appropriate factual context should be explored.
- The absence of a relationship of vicarious liability between the insured and the alleged perpetrator. This will come down to issues of fact.

Vicarious liability

Vicarious liability is also considered in the Negligence chapter of this book (Chapter 2). We comment here on the aspects most relevant to sexual abuse claims.

The courts have extended the boundaries of vicarious liability over recent years, and the parameters within which an organisation will be held to be vicariously liable for the conduct of an abuser are now reasonably well settled.

The following principles may be derived from recent authorities, as helpfully summarised by Mr Justice Macduff in *JGE v The English Province of Our Lady of Charity and The Trustees of the Portsmouth Roman Catholic Diocesan Trust* [2011]:

- The doctrine imposes a type of strict liability. This recognises that those who profit from the activities of their employees should compensate those who are injured by such activities, even when performed negligently. The employer is able to spread the risk through pricing and insurance and is better organised and able to bear that risk.
- The issue of vicarious liability will be determined with reference to the "closeness of connection" test, which requires a determination of "whether the [employee's] torts were so closely connected with his employment that it would be fair and just to hold the employer vicariously liable".
- In this context, the trial judge is required to investigate the employee's specific duties and determine whether they gave rise to "special opportunities" for wrongdoing.
- The doctrine has regard to the desirability for an employer to put in place systems designed to encourage employees to do their jobs properly and safely. This is a deterrent factor: to deter from appointing the wrong person and to deter from adopting a 'devil-may-care' approach to safe systems of working.

Armes v Nottinghamshire County Council [2017] is a further extension of vicarious liability, this time in relation to foster carers. In summary:

- While the local authority is not under a non-delegable duty of care to ensure that reasonable care is taken for the safety of children in the care and control of foster parents, the court did impose vicarious liability for the acts of foster parents on the following basis:
    - The nature of the activity – the foster parents carrying out an activity on behalf of the defendant local authority and being integral to their organisation.
    - Risk creation – the placement of the child creates a relationship of authority and trust between foster parent and child. If the local authority considers it advantageous to place the child in foster care they should compensate the unfortunate child for whom the risk materialises.
    - Control – the local authority exercised a significant degree of control over the foster parents.
    - Means to pay – it was deemed a relevant consideration that local authorities could more easily compensate the victims.
- The decision has considerable implications for social care administered by local authorities and has wider implications for foster agencies in situations where they place children on behalf of local authorities.

Areas of investigation

As mentioned above, the historic nature of these claims raises specific considerations in a number of areas of investigation.

Locating and identifying documents and witnesses

These investigations are crucial to evaluate the evidential basis of the allegations made, which are likely to involve detailed assertions spanning long periods of time.

Disclosure of documents/redaction

Guidance was given in *Dunn v Durham County Council* [2012], where the Court of Appeal considered a local authority's duty in respect of the disclosure of records.

The claimant alleged he had been assaulted by staff at a centre for young people. His letter of claim requested disclosure of documents under the provisions of the Data Protection Act 1998 (DPA). The defendant provided copies of redacted files with the names of some children (other service users) and adults (staff) removed.

The claimant requested unredacted files pursuant to s.35 of the DPA. This allows a party to be exempt from the provisions of the DPA where litigation is intended or in the context of proceedings.

The district judge refused this application. The claimant appealed on the basis that, under s.35, unredacted disclosure was necessary. The circuit judge allowed the appeal on the grounds that the claimant had established that unredacted documents were necessary. The other residents might be material witnesses and their names should be disclosed.

The Court of Appeal held that the circuit judge had made the correct decision but for the wrong reasons. The correct test was to balance the Civil Procedure Rules (CPR) duties of disclosure with the European Convention on Human Rights (ECHR), as enacted into English law in the Human Rights Act 1998. Lord Justice Maurice Kay made a number of helpful observations:

- It was "unfortunate that this dispute about disclosure has been prolonged and distorted by references to the DPA".
- Obligations in relation to disclosure and inspection arise only when the test of relevance under Part 31 of the CPR is satisfied. This is a matter of fact, degree and proportionality: requests that are merely 'fishing expeditions' would not satisfy this test.
- Any dispute in relation to disclosure falls to be determined having regard to the right to a fair trial, at common law and under Article 6 of the ECHR, and the right of an opponent or non-party to privacy and confidentiality under Article 8.
- Withholding disclosure must be limited to circumstances where this is strictly necessary. The onus of establishing necessity is on the party refusing to provide disclosure or inspection. The circuit judge had been wrong to place the burden on the claimant rather than the defendant.
- Any order should include provisions that the identities of non-parties in the records are not disclosed beyond the parties to the proceedings and their legal advisors and that the documents are to be used solely for the purpose of those proceedings.
- Social work records and similar categories of documents may still attract public interest immunity, for example a document recording the identity of informers. This will be case specific and will not arise automatically because of the status of the documents.

The upshot of this guidance in practical terms is that careful thought will have to be given to whether:

- Documents are relevant and therefore disclosable
- If so, whether any redaction is considered to be necessary.

If documents are disclosed in a redacted format, the disclosing party will have to be prepared and able to justify such redactions with reference to the above guidance in order to meet any subsequent challenge.

Where documents are properly disclosed in the context of a civil claim, the relevant authority would have a defence to any claim for breach of the DPA pursuant to s.35. Where there is uncertainty about the extent of any proposed redactions, the safest course would be to require the claimant to make an application to the court.

Insurance history

The following is explained against the background, as stated above, of the need to adopt an approach that is sensitive and mindful of the vulnerability of those making abuse claims.

It will be necessary to consider what insurance contract policy issues might be available when contemplating indemnity issues.

A number of points will arise for consideration, which should be explored on a case by case basis. Those points will probably include issues surrounding the wording of individual policies, including, for example, apportionment of liability among successive insurers:

- The time at which the damage materialises for the purposes of invoking liability under the insurance policy, i.e. what is the relevant event that triggers liability under the policy?

- Where the sexual abuse has occurred over a period of time, the point(s) in time at which damage has occurred within the meaning of the policy. In particular, should it be defined as a single event or as a series of events? Are there any implications for the excess arising from such an interpretation?
- Can the damage be defined as divisible or indivisible? How might this approach affect the apportionment of liability amongst successive insurers?
- Are there common factors unifying the damage and losses, such as abuse by the same person or different persons?
- Do the facts fall within an exception stipulated within the policy, e.g. injury or damage resulting from a deliberate act or omission of the insured?
- Is late notification a condition precedent to insurers' liability? Can late notification in respect of any particular claim justify repudiation under the insurance policy?
- Was there material non-disclosure (at the inception of the policy)? For example, notice on the part of the relevant establishment of a particular incident of abuse having occurred and/or knowledge of a history of abuse on the part of a particular employee, together with a failure to bring such matters to the attention of the insurer.
- Has there been a breach of warranty, based on the insured's duty to make disclosure of such issues as may have been stipulated within the contract of insurance as being relevant to the insured risk?
- Has there been a breach of the insured's continuing duty of good faith to make disclosure of any circumstances relevant to the insured risk?

General damages

Perhaps surprisingly, the majority of claims for sexual abuse attract relatively low awards for general damages.

> The main component of injury in sexual abuse claims is typically psychiatric damage, although the award will also reflect and be commensurate with the physical aspects of the abuse.

The following table gives an overview of the range of awards likely to be made in particular cases, although it is important to note that all assessments will be fact specific. There is not always a direct correlation between the type or nature of the abuse in issue and the effects of such abuse. For these and other reasons it is not possible to work on a tariff basis as such.

Table 20.1: Overview of general damages awards

Band	Description	Range
1	Isolated or intermittent acts of physical and/ or sexual abuse	Up to £12,500
2	Non-penetrative physical and/or sexual physical acts including emotional abuse, e.g. depersonalisation and/or generating a climate of fear and apprehension	£12,500–£25,000
3	Rape and/or prolonged aggravated physical and/or sexual abuse: lower bracket	£18,750–£33,750
4	Rape and/or prolonged physical and/or sexual abuse: higher bracket	£31,250–£75,000
5	Rape and/or prolonged physical and/or sexual abuse with aggravating features	£75,000–£95,000

Compensation schemes

A number of compensation schemes for sexual abuse have been implemented over the years where it has been possible to identify claimants as finite cohorts. An example of such a scheme is the States of Jersey Historic Abuse Redress Scheme.

Important considerations in claims handling

1) Be mindful of reputational risk.
2) Promote early engagement with third-party solicitors to narrow issues in dispute and consider alternative forms of dispute resolution.
3) Provide cost-effective and pragmatic advice.
4) Adopt a sensitive, proactive and professional handling of claims throughout.
5) Where appropriate, suggest early intervention by way of rehabilitation and recommend an apology is offered for historic failings.

21 Housing disrepair

Andrew Caplan

- Causes of action
- Governing legislation: the Landlord and Tenant Act 1985, Defective Premises Act 1972 and Occupiers' Liability Act 1957
- Dampness and condensation
- Notice of defect
- The usual remedies for disrepair
- The Pre-Action protocol for Housing Disrepair cases: the parties' responsibilities
- Experts and time limits

Housing disrepair

Introduction

This chapter deals with claims brought by tenants against their landlords for breach of covenants, either expressly stated in the tenancy agreement or implied by statute.

Claims are subject to a pre-action protocol that governs the pre-action behaviour between the parties. As with other protocols, the overriding objective is to resolve claims without recourse to litigation. There are a variety of remedies open to tenants, including an application for an injunction to remedy continuing breaches of landlords' repairing obligations. The most common remedies will be for damages and orders for repairs to be carried out.

Causes of action

Most claims for disrepair are brought under s.11 of the Landlord and Tenant Act 1985 (LTA).

Section 11(1) of the LTA

Under s.11(1), the two aspects of the landlord's responsibility are:

- To keep in repair the structure and exterior of the house.
- To keep in repair and working order the installations in the house.

Do the complaints give rise to a liability? Guidance is provided by the following case law:

- *Brown v Liverpool Corporation* [1969] – the claimant fell on steps that were in a state of disrepair and leading to a path that gave access to a house. The question for the Court of Appeal was whether the steps and pathway were an integral part of the building. The court held that the question was one of degree and fact. On the evidence, the judge at first instance was entitled to reach the conclusion that, in all the circumstances, the steps formed part of the building.
- *Hopwood v Cannock Chase District Council* [1974] – normal access was from the front of the house, although there was a yard at the rear of the premises. The claimant tripped on a paving stone in the yard. The Court of Appeal distinguished *Brown* on the basis that the yard was not necessary to the house as the means of access to it. This may seem an artificial distinction, and it is noteworthy that the Court was influenced by the fact that in *Brown* the Corporation knew about the defective step, had known about it for some time and had promised to mend it.
- *Welsh v Greenwich London Borough Council* [2000] – condensation and mould were conceded not to be disrepair. However, a term in the tenancy agreement increased the landlord's obligation beyond that normally understood by repair to render it liable.
- *Cresswell v Sandwell Metropolitan Borough Council* [2000] – outbuildings consisting of a garden shed, a coal store and WC were not "structure and exterior" for the purposes of s.11.
- *Southwark London Borough Council v McIntosh* [2001] – the landlord was not under an obligation to warn the tenant not to dry clothes in a heated cupboard.
- *Lee v Leeds City Council; Ratcliffe and others v Sandwell Metropolitan Borough Council* [2002] – on the facts, the Court of Appeal held that defects in design do not fall under s.11.

- *O'Connor and others v Old Etonian Housing Association Ltd* [2002] – the Court of Appeal provided guidance as to the meaning of the s.11 phrase "keep in ... proper working order" in relation to water pipes. The issue was whether the landlord was liable for the failure in water supply due to a fall in pressure of the supply, coupled with the pipes fitted by the landlord being too small. The Court of Appeal held that an installation for the supply of water, gas and electricity will be in proper working order if it is able to function under those conditions of supply that it is reasonable to anticipate will prevail.
- *Sam-Yorke v Jawad* [2002] – failure to service a gas fire was a breach of duty under s.11(1)(c). However, with no evidence of any inconvenience caused by the breach, no damages were awarded.
- *Montoya v London Borough of Hackney* [2004] – an expert assessed the defects as commensurate with the age and type of property and so not disrepair under s.11. However, the judge at first instance held the landlord liable. On appeal it was held that there was no evidence to support that decision and the appeal was allowed.

Defective Premises Act 1972

When dealing with housing disrepair claims, claims handlers should also be aware of s.4 of the Defective Premises Act 1972 (DPA).

Section 4(1) states:

> Where premises are let under a tenancy which puts on the landlord an obligation to the tenant for the maintenance or repair of the premises, the landlord owes to all persons who might reasonably be expected to be affected by defects in the state of the premises a duty to take such care as is reasonable in all the circumstances to see that they are reasonably safe from personal injury or from damage to their property caused by a relevant defect.

The landlord's duties under this statute are, therefore, extended to include third parties, such as the tenant's visitors.

The duty is owed if the landlord knows (whether as the result of being notified by the tenant or otherwise), or if they ought in all the circumstances to have known, of the relevant defect. This contrasts with the provision under s.11 of the LTA where the landlord's obligation only begins once the tenant has given notice of a defect.

Occupiers' Liability Act 1957

It should be noted that s.2 of the Occupiers' Liability Act 1957 (OLA) does not apply to landlords. Section 4 of the OLA 1957 previously defined a landlord's duty, which was replaced by s.4 of the DPA. In *Drysdale v Hedges* [2012], the High Court held:

> “Whilst Section 2 of the 1957 Act would appear general in application a landlord's duty was defined by Section 4 of that Act. I cannot think that Parliament intended both sections to define a landlord's duty. Section 4 of the 1957 Act has been replaced by Section 4 of the Defective Premises Act 1972 which is in similar, although not identical, terms to Section 4 of the 1957 Act. I consider therefore that it is to Section 4 of the 1972 Act that one has to look, in the first place, to find the extent of the landlord's duty in tort.”

Dampness and condensation

A large majority of disrepair claims arise from some form of damp in the property. Where the dampness has been caused by condensation there is often a dispute as to whether the dampness is caused by a defect to the structure of the property or poor usage/design.

As the cases highlighted below demonstrate, it should be remembered that the fact that there is extensive damp in a property will not, of itself, be enough to found a disrepair action. The damp has to be in the plasterwork and has to be enough to cause a physical deterioration in the plasterwork.

- *Quick v Taff Ely Borough Council* [1985] – the claimant was a council tenant whose property suffered from severe condensation caused by a combination of window lintels, metal frame windows and inadequate heating and ventilation. The Court of Appeal rejected the argument that anything defective or inherently inefficient for living in or ineffective to provide the conditions of ordinary habitation is to be considered an aspect of disrepair. In other words, just because there was a problem affecting the habitation of the property or the design, it did not automatically follow that there was a failure to repair.

- *Staves and Staves v Leeds City Council* [1990] – the landlord alleged that the dampness in the property was caused by condensation. Three years after the complaints the landlord cured the condensation problem. The landlord was not helped by a letter from its chief housing officer referring to the plaster as being so saturated that it required replacement. The test, so far as the Court of Appeal was concerned, was as set out in the judgment of Lord Justice Dillon in *Quick*: "In my judgment, the key factor in the present case is that disrepair is related to the physical condition of whatever has to be repaired." In *Staves*, the physical condition of the plaster was such that renewal was required. As a matter of ordinary language, what was done was a repair.

- *Irvine's Estate v Moran* [1990] – the High Court held that the term "structure of the dwelling-house" had a more limited meaning than the overall building itself. It consisted of those elements of the overall dwelling house that give it its essential appearance, stability and shape. "Internal wall plaster is more in the nature of a decorative finish" (but see *Grand v Gill* on the next page).

- *Welsh v Greenwich London Borough Council* [2000] – the tenant conceded that condensation leading to mould was not disrepair.

- *Southwark London Borough Council v McIntosh* [2001] – damp in itself did not evidence a breach of s.11 of the LTA. It was up to the tenant to establish that the damp was caused by a breach of covenant by the landlord.
- *Lee v Leeds City Council; Ratcliffe and others v Sandwell Metropolitan Borough Council* [2002] – damp caused by a defect in design did not fall under s.11 of the LTA.
- *Ball and Ball v Plymouth City Council* [2004] – the tenants failed to prove causation in relation to dampness. The dampness must be caused by an actionable defect.
- In *Grand v Gill* [2011] – the Court of Appeal finally decided, in unequivocal terms, that internal plasterwork does form part of the structure of the premises for the purpose of s.11 of the LTA. Lord Justice Rimer held that the decision in *Irvine's Estate* provided a good working definition of "the structure ... of the dwelling-house", but said that:

> " I am respectfully unconvinced by his [judge at first instance] holding that the plaster finish to an internal wall or ceiling is to be regarded as in the nature of a decorative finish rather than as forming part of the 'structure' ... I would also regard plasterwork generally, including that applied to external walls, as being ordinarily in the nature of a smooth constructional finish to walls and ceilings, to which the decoration can then be applied, rather than a decorative finish in itself. I would therefore hold that it is part of the 'structure'. "

Notice

The landlord's obligations under the LTA will not arise until they have been given notice of the defect (except where it occurs in any common parts of a building, such as a shared entrance hall or stairway). Notice, for the purposes of s.11 of the LTA, does not need to be in any specific form; it may be written or oral.

> A tenant may be required to prove they have given notice of disrepair if they decide to pursue a claim. Usually a tenant would be expected to produce copy letters or, if verbal notice was given, copy letters from the landlord agreeing to execute works.

Note the following case law:

- *Sykes v Harry and another* [2001] – under s.11 of the LTA the landlord must have notice of a defect to be in breach. This is in contrast to s.4 of the DPA under which, in this case, the landlord was found liable for a defective gas fire.
- *Jeffers v West Lancashire District Council* [2002] – it was reasonable for the local authority to expect the tenants to report any disrepair (Occupiers' Liability Act 1984).

> As soon as the landlord has received notice of the defect, the repairs must then be completed within a reasonable time. "Reasonable time" will be judged by several factors, including the type and extent of the disrepair and the nature of the tenancy. The tenant must demonstrate unreasonable delay. In cases where the landlord has the right of entry to the property the landlord still has to be put on notice of the defect.

In *Morris v Liverpool City Council* [1987], the fire brigade had to force entry to a property, as a result of which the front door had to be replaced. However, before the council had an opportunity to replace the front door, the property was burgled. The Court of Appeal held that the duty of the court was to explore the reasonableness of the delay. In this case, factors included difficulty in obtaining and fitting the door, including the council's workload and steps taken to secure the property. The tenant failed to show that a failure to carry out a permanent repair within a week was unreasonable.

Remedies

The usual remedies for disrepair will be:

- Damages for inconvenience and discomfort
- Special damages
- Interim injunction
- Damages for personal injury
- Damages for diminution in value
- Specific performance.

General issues

- *Welsh v Greenwich London Borough Council* [2000] – the parties agreed an award of £9,000 damages for disrepair during four years' residence in a council flat.
- *Mitchell v Barnsley Metropolitan Borough Council* [2003] – general damages of £300 per year for two years were awarded.
- *English Churches Housing Group v Shine* [2004] – the Court of Appeal confirmed that when making an award of damages under s.11 of the LTA the guidance given in *Wallace v Manchester City Council* [1998] should be applied or clear reasons given for departing from that guidance.

Damages for inconvenience and discomfort

The development of case law is set out below, with a key decision being *Wallace v Manchester City Council* [1998]:

- *Calabar Properties Ltd v Stitcher* [1983] – the disrepair had been over a five-year period, during which there had been substantial water penetration affecting the tenant's health. The Court of Appeal upheld an award of £3,000 made for the five-year period (£600 per year) for this element of the claim.

- *Elmcroft Developments Ltd v Tankersley–Sawyer* [1984] – the Court of Appeal upheld an award of £2,600 for a two-year period (£1,300 per year) where the property was affected by severe rising damp. The Court took into account that the flat was in an expensive and fashionable part of London.
- *Chiodi v De Marney* [1988] – the Court of Appeal dismissed an appeal against an award of £5,460 for inconvenience and distress, on the basis of £30 per week. There had been no hot water and there were electrical problems and damaged windows in the property.
- *Wallace v Manchester City Council* [1998] – the Court of Appeal recognised an unofficial tariff of between £1,000 and £2,750 per year for each year the property was considered to be in a state of disrepair.
- *Mulligan v Halton Borough Council* [1999] – damages of £1,750 per year were awarded in relation to inconvenience and discomfort.
- *Peirce v City of Westminster* [2001] – the property was affected by subsidence. The court held that although the interference with enjoyment of the property was low there had been real disruption to the claimant's life. Damages of £5,450 were awarded, representing between £500 and £1,000 per year.
- *English Churches Housing Group v Shine* [2004] – any award for stress and inconvenience should be related to the fact that the tenant is not getting value for the rent being paid. The award is for breach of contract, not tort.

- *Earle v Charalambous* [2006] – the tenant's property was inundated with water through up to 20 holes, causing the ceiling to collapse. The landlord argued that the tenant's compensation should be limited to the *Wallace v Manchester* tariff or to the (nominal) ground rent. The Court of Appeal upheld damages equivalent to 50% of the rent the tenant would have received had the flat been available for rent on the open market in good repair (£6,000 per annum).

The limitation period for claims under this heading is six years.

Special damages

In *Mitchell v Barnsley Metropolitan Borough Council*, £70 was awarded in relation to repairs.

Repairs usually include the following types of items:

- Redecoration costs
- Extra heating costs
- Replacement furniture
- Other personal belongings.

Receipts should be produced for all items claimed. There may be an issue of betterment to be considered.

Interim injunction

In cases where the tenant alleges continuing breach of the landlord's repairing obligations, the tenant may apply to the court for an interim injunction compelling the landlord to carry out repairs to stop a continuing breach. The courts recognise that, by the very nature of an injunction, the granting of an injunction is an onerous obligation and will usually involve a landlord in outlay. The courts are therefore reluctant to grant this remedy. For an injunction to be granted:

- The work required must be agreed between the parties, or it must be clear what needs to be done, i.e. there should not be a substantial dispute between the surveyors.

- The circumstances must be exceptional, e.g. there is an immediate risk to health and safety.

Personal injury

Damages will usually be on the low side, although claims for minors will be higher. Claims will need to be substantiated with medical evidence. It is worth checking the medical records as the claimant may have suffered from the condition irrespective of the accident, or the claim might be limited to an exacerbation of an existing condition. Common claims for personal injury include pneumonia, depression, asthma and bronchitis. Examples include:

- *Mulligan v Halton Borough Council* – aggravation of pre-existing asthma led to an award of £1,000 for a one-and-a-half-year period.
- *Conroy v Hire Token Ltd* [2001] – claim brought under s.4 of the DPA for two children's chest conditions. No treatment was ever sought nor any diagnosis of asthma obtained, but general damages of £650 for each child were awarded.
- *L (a child) v Empire Estates* [2002] – a six-year-old girl's asthma was exacerbated by damp conditions. General damages of £1,750 were awarded.
- *C (A Child) v Empire Estates* [2002] – a baby boy developed asthma while living in a damp property. Although it was felt that he would have been likely to develop it anyway later in life due to the family history, general damages of £8,500 were awarded.

Diminution in value

In *Hassib v Hackney London Borough Council* [2002], it was held that the guidelines in *Wallace v Manchester City Council* were more useful in assessing damages than diminution in value. In *Wallace*, the Court of Appeal stated that there is no requirement to calculate this loss separately from damages for inconvenience and discomfort.

If the claim is pleaded separately, expert evidence from a surveyor will be necessary to formulate the difference in the value of the property in the state of disrepair against the usual rental value. For example, for a three-roomed flat where only two rooms are habitable, the formulation would be a value of a two-roomed as opposed to a three-roomed flat.

Specific performance

An order for specific performance would force the landlord to carry out the terms of the tenancy agreement. An order must be clear, and in normal circumstances one would expect the surveyor or experts to draw up a schedule of works, to be agreed between the parties if possible, together with a realistic timescale.

Failure to comply with an order for specific performance can lead to committal proceedings for contempt of court. The court order can be served on a suitable officer of the local authority, who may be committed for that breach.

Human Rights Act 1998

Lee v Leeds County Council; Ratcliffe and others v Sandwell Metropolitan Borough Council discussed the effect of the Human Rights Act 1998 (HRA) on landlords' obligations under s.11 of the LTA. The landlord was under no obligation to rectify design faults as a result of the HRA 1998.

Pre-Action Protocol for Housing Disrepair Cases

The pre-action protocol (PAP) governs the pre-litigation behaviour of the parties. Specific objectives of the PAP are:

- Avoiding unnecessary litigation.
- Promoting the speedy and appropriate carrying out of any repairs that are the landlord's responsibility.

- Ensuring that tenants receive any compensation to which they are entitled as speedily as possible.
- Promoting good pre-litigation practice, including the early exchange of information, and giving guidance about the instruction of experts.
- Keeping the costs of resolving disputes down.

Areas covered by the protocol

The PAP states that a disrepair claim is a civil claim arising from the condition of residential premises and may include a related personal injury claim.

Key components of the protocol

The PAP will be triggered by writing:

- An early notification letter, or
- A letter of claim.

The PAP envisages first writing an early notification letter, but either type of letter may be received.

The parties' responsibilities

There is a helpful flowchart at Annex D of the protocol outlining each party's responsibilities. These include:

Tenant

- As soon as possible, a notification letter is sent to the landlord. This may not be necessary if the repair is urgent.
- The letter should give basic details, request disclosure from the landlord and propose an expert.

Landlord

- Respond to early notification letter within 20 working days of receipt of the first letter from the tenant.
- Disclose all relevant documents, including tenancy agreement and all records relating to notice of disrepair and inspection reports.
- Confirm whether or not the expert is agreed.

Experts

It will not always be necessary for a tenant to instruct an expert if, for example, only damages are in issue.

If required, the expert should be instructed to report on all items of disrepair about which the landlord will reasonably need to know. The expert should provide a schedule of works, an estimate of costs of repair and a separate list if any urgent works are required.

The tenant will have proposed an expert in either the early notification letter or the letter of claim. The landlord can object to the expert, but if they fail to do so within 20 working days the tenant can proceed to instruct the proposed expert as a single joint expert. If no agreement is reached on the proposed expert the parties should try to agree an alternative expert.

Time limits

The property should be inspected within 20 working days of the date that the landlord responds to the tenant's first letter. Where there is a joint inspection, the experts should produce an agreed schedule of works detailing:

- The defects and required works that are agreed and the timetable for the agreed works.
- The areas of disagreement and the reasons for disagreement.

The agreed schedule should be sent to both the landlord and the tenant within 10 working days of the joint inspection.

If there is a single joint expert, a copy of the report should be sent to both the landlord and the tenant within 10 working days of the inspection. Either party can ask relevant questions of the expert.

Other options

Alternatives should be considered before the application of the PAP. The claimant should be encouraged to pursue other avenues.

For council tenants these include:

- Local authorities' repairs and complaints procedures
- The Right to Repair Scheme
- The Local Government Ombudsman.

With private landlords, tenants should consider:

- The Independent Housing Ombudsman
- Local authority environmental health officers.

Checklist

- ✓ Do the complaints give rise to liability under s.11 of the LTA:
  - ✓ What is included in the structure and exterior of the house?
  - ✓ Has there been a failure to keep in repair and working order?
- ✓ Consider the potential impact of the DPA.
- ✓ In cases involving damp, is the damp in the plasterwork and is it enough to cause a physical deterioration in the plasterwork?
- ✓ In a claim under the LTA, has the tenant given notice of the defect?

- ✓ What damages are appropriate for inconvenience and discomfort? Consider the unofficial tariff set out in *Wallace v Manchester City Council* [1998].
- ✓ Have receipts been provided for all items claimed for special damages? Is there an issue of betterment?
- ✓ Are claims for personal injury substantiated by medical evidence? Remember that awards for personal injury are generally on the low side.
- ✓ Be alert to the timetable set out in the pre-action protocol. Consider whether expert evidence will be required.
- ✓ Are there suitable alternatives to the pre-action protocol that will assist in resolving the issues?

22 Road Traffic Act 1998: third-party liabilities

Richard West

- Who must insure?
- What risks must the insurance cover?
- Certificates of insurance
- Avoidance of certain exceptions in policies
- Duty of insurers to satisfy judgments
- Entitlement of insurer to recover sums paid under s.151 Road Traffic Act 1988
- Points of special difficulty:
  - Employees
  - Definition of a road/other public place
  - European law
- Driverless cars

Road Traffic Act 1998: third-party liabilities

Introduction

The main requirements regarding compulsory insurance or security against third-party risks are contained in sections 143 to 159 of the Road Traffic Act 1988 (RTA 1988), which are summarised in Table 24.1.

Table 24.1 – Summary of main requirements regarding compulsory insurance

Section	Issues covered
143	Establishes the requirement to insure against third-party risks.
144	Provides the alternative of depositing a sum with the Accountant General of the Senior Courts. Also provides exemptions from the need to insure to local government, the police, the armed forces and the National Health Service, although in practice most of these bodies will carry insurance.
145	Specifies who may issue a policy of insurance and what the policy must cover.
146	Specifies requirements in respect of securities.
147	Deals with the issue and need for continuous availability of certificates of insurance.
148	Greatly restricts the ability of an insurer to avoid liability to third parties by reason of breach of policy condition.
149	Prohibits the avoidance of liability to passengers by agreement.
150	Aims to prevent restrictions in the use of the vehicle under the insurance policy by preventing the vehicle from being used in a car-sharing scheme.

Section	Issues covered
151	Deals with the duty of insurers to satisfy judgments against persons insured under its policies.
152	Sets out the circumstances in which insurers would not have to meet such judgments.
153	Preserves the rights of third parties to claim against insured parties who have become bankrupt.
154	Establishes the duty of a person against whom a claim is made to provide details of their insurance.
155	Deals with deposits.
156	Deals with the duty to provide details of insurance when applying for a vehicle excise licence.
157 to 159	Deal with medical treatment following an accident.

Who must insure?

Subject to the exceptions set out in s.144 and summarised above, any person who uses or causes or permits any other person to use a motor vehicle on a road or other public place must have insurance. "Use" does not simply mean driving but can include having a car laid up on a road. The duty to insure lies not simply on the owner but also on the user.

If the owner of a vehicle permits another person to drive the vehicle while there is no insurance in force, both would be guilty of a criminal offence.

The case of *Vnuk v Zavarovalnica Triglav* [2014] ruled that cars driven solely on private property are required to be insured, as set out in the Motor Insurance Directive. This case has prompted a government consultation to consider amendment to the EU Directive, which first commenced on 20 December 2016. While the UK is part of the EU, it must take steps to comply with this Directive.

In July 2017 the European Commission opened a four-week consultation on the scope of the Motor Insurance Directive in relation to the *Vnuk* ruling. The consultation is expected to run until the end of March 2018. At the date of publication of this edition, the principles set out by the decision of the European Court in VNUK has yet to be brought into English law.

Who can issue an insurance policy?

Only an authorised insurer can issue an insurance policy. That is any person or body of persons carrying on a motor vehicle insurance business in Great Britain that is authorised under the Financial Services and Markets Act 2000. The authorised insurer must also be a member of the Motor Insurers' Bureau (MIB).

What risks must the insurance cover?

Insurance must cover liability:

i) For death of, or bodily injury to, any person

ii) For damage to property limited to £1 million

iii) Incurred in respect of emergency treatment

caused by, or arising out of, the use of the vehicle on a road or other public place in Great Britain.

The policy must also provide insurance cover in respect of any liability that may be incurred in respect of the use of the vehicle, and of any trailer whether or not coupled, within the territory of each of the other Member States of the European Union (EU), up to the standards set by the law on compulsory insurance within the state in which the vehicle is being used, or up to the standard set by the RTA 1988, whichever is higher.

> The requirement to cover liability for damage is restricted to £1 million, and that is the sum of all liabilities arising out of one accident. There is no requirement to cover liability in respect of damage to the vehicle itself, goods carried for hire or reward within the vehicle or goods that are within the custody or the control of the insured person or any contractual liability.

In respect of personal injury, exceptions that relate to employees are complex and are dealt with separately.

Certificates of insurance

For certificates of insurance issued before 30 June 2015, the certificate of insurance was a vitally important document. The policy of insurance was of no effect unless and until the certificate was delivered by the insurer to the person by whom the policy was effected. It was the delivery of the certificate that established an insurer's obligations under the RTA 1988. If the policy was cancelled, s.147 set out how the certificate was to be surrendered, such that an insurer's liability ceased under the RTA 1988.

For insurance policies issued on or after 30 June 2015, the policy commences on the date of inception and recording of the policy on the Motor Insurance Database (MID). The policy must be delivered by the insurer to the person by whom the policy is effected. Section 147 provides for the certificate to be delivered electronically or made available to a policyholder continuously on a website, in addition to any delivery by any other means.

Section 9(4) of the Deregulation Act 2015 amends s.147 so that holders of insurance policies are no longer obliged to return their certificate of insurance if a policy or security is cancelled mid-term and after inception on 30 June 2015. Therefore, insurers are no longer required in such circumstances to ensure the return of certificates.

As of 30 June 2015, for the insurer's liability to cease and in order to gain the necessary protection, an insurer must amend the MID to show that they are no longer on cover.

Changes brought about by the Insurance Act 2015 apply to all insurance policies issued, renewed or varied on or after 12 August 2016. The fundamental changes include:

- Redefined duty of utmost good faith to duty of fair presentation
- Changes to the consequences of a breach and new proportionate remedies
- Potential to 'contract out' of the new duty and remedies in certain limited circumstances
- Technical amendments to the Third Parties (Rights Against Insurers) Act 2010 to permit the 2010 Act to come fully into force.

Avoidance of certain exceptions in policies

It is quite likely that an insurer will have conditions in its policy regarding the user of the vehicle, the condition of the vehicle and the use of the vehicle. It is quite reasonable that an insurer should do so. An insurer may not want to cover an 18-year-old driving a powerful car. It will certainly not want a car driven in an unroadworthy condition.

After 12 August 2016, the Insurance Act 2015 (the 2015 Act) brings about a new duty of fair presentation of the risk to non-consumer contracts, which requires:

- Disclosure of every material circumstance that the insured knows or ought to know; or
- Disclosure of sufficient information to put the prudent insurer on enquiry.

Where such disclosure is made, the presentation will be fair if:

i) It is made in a manner which is reasonably clear and accessible to a prudent insurer,

ii) the facts as represented are substantially correct, and

iii) the representations as to expectation or belief are made in good faith.

An insurer will also have conditions in its policy as to what must be done in the event of an accident. There will no doubt be a requirement for the reporting of the accident and again it is quite reasonable that this should be so.

Nonetheless, s.148 of the 2015 Act prevents an insurer from avoiding its liability to a third party who has suffered injury or damage by reason of the insured person's breach of certain conditions. The conditions in question are as follows:

a) The age or physical or mental condition of the persons driving the vehicle.

b) The condition of the vehicle.

c) The number of persons that the vehicle carries.

d) The weight or physical characteristics of the goods that the vehicle carries.

e) The time at which, or the areas within which, the vehicle is used.

f) The horsepower or cylinder capacity or value of the vehicle.

g) The carrying on the vehicle of any particular apparatus.

h) The carrying on the vehicle of any particular means of identification, other than any means of identification required to be carried by or under the Vehicle Excise and Registration Act 1971.

i) Conditions relating to requirements of some specified thing being done or omitted to be done after the happening of the event giving rise to a claim under the policy.

In non-consumer insurance contracts renewed, incepted or varied on or after 12 August 2016, an insurer will only have a remedy against the insured for a breach of the duty of fair presentation if the insurer shows that, but for the breach, the insurer:

a) Would not have entered into the contact of insurance at all; or

b) Would have done so only on different terms.

Either of the above are referred to as a 'qualifying breach'.

If the qualifying breach is deliberate or reckless, the insurer may avoid the contract, refuse all claims and retain the premium paid.

If the qualifying breach is not deliberate or reckless, the insurer must show that but for the breach it would not have entered into the contract at all, or would only have done so on different terms.

Where the insurer has had to meet claims only by reason of the provisions of s.148, it is entitled to recover the money from its insured. In respect of the first eight conditions referred to above, the right to recover lies in s.148(4).

Where it relates to the last condition, then s.148(6) permits the insurer to have a policy condition that requires the repayment of the monies.

Duty of insurers to satisfy judgments

Section 151(5) requires an insurer to meet judgments where:

- A certificate of insurance has been delivered under s.147 to the person effecting the insurance.
- A judgment has actually been obtained.
- The judgment is in respect of a liability that is required to be covered by a policy of insurance under s.145 (see above).
- It is a liability covered by the terms of the policy.

- The vehicle is being used in a way that is not excluded under the terms of the policy or, if it is excluded, the exclusion falls into one of the categories deemed to be of no effect by s.148.

Despite the fact that the insurer may be entitled to avoid or cancel the policy, and indeed may already have avoided or cancelled the policy, if all the other conditions are met, the insurer must, nonetheless, meet the judgment.

These conditions, if they stood alone, would still permit the insurer to avoid liability if the vehicle was being used by someone who was not permitted to use the vehicle under the policy or did not hold a driving licence.

However, s.151(3) prevents the insurer from avoiding payment if the user of the vehicle does not hold a driving licence. In addition, s.151(2)(b) provides that as long as the liability is not an excluded liability, the policy will be treated as covering all persons. Therefore, the insurer will have to satisfy a judgment obtained against any person using the vehicle, whether or not their liability is covered under the policy.

Excluded liability

In this context, an excluded liability means a liability in respect of the death of, or bodily injury to, or damage to the property of, any person who, at the time of the use which gave rise to the liability, was allowing themselves to be carried in or upon the vehicle and knew, or had reason to believe, that the vehicle had been stolen or unlawfully taken.

If, however, the person concerned only became aware that the vehicle had been unlawfully taken after the commencement of their journey, and could not then have reasonably been expected to alight from the vehicle, it will not be an excluded liability.

Calculations of sums payable under judgment

In respect of death and personal injury, the sum payable is the total amount of damages, interest and costs. In respect of damage, there is a more complex calculation, because the insurer is entitled to restrict its liability to pay claims for property damage to £1 million for all claims for property damage arising out of the same incident. Where the total of claims arising out of one incident for property damage is less than £1 million, then the insurer clearly has to pay the full amount of the judgment.

Where the total of claims exceeds £1 million there are two means of calculation. The first formula is:

> Amount payable = judgment + interest × £1 million/total amounts payable in respect of one incident

The second formula applies to the situation where all the other claims have already been paid. The sum payable is £1 million, less the total of any amounts already paid. Interest on that sum is calculated using the formula:

> Interest awarded on judgment × amount payable of damages by insurer/damages awarded in judgment

The insurer is entitled to make payment in these circumstances on whichever of the two bases produces the lower figure.

The effect of sections 148 and 151

The combined effect of sections 148 and 151 means that in most circumstances, if a person is injured, or their property damaged, as a result of an incident involving a vehicle that is insured, and in respect of which a certificate of insurance has been delivered by the insurer to the person effecting the insurance, that insurer will be obliged to meet a judgment.

This applies even in the following circumstances:

- The policy has been avoided or cancelled, subject to what is said below about s.152.

- The person driving the vehicle is a person not permitted to drive under the terms of the insurance or did not have a driving licence.
- The vehicle is not roadworthy, is carrying more people than it can safely do so or has been fitted with a more powerful engine than the insurer believed to be the case.

One area, however, where the ability of the insurer to exclude its liability is not affected is in respect of the use of the vehicle. If the insurer restricts its cover to social, domestic and pleasure use, it would still be able to avoid liability if the vehicle is used for business use, for example as a taxi. Likewise, if the insurer excludes racing, it can exclude its liability if the incident that gives rise to the judgment happens in the course of a race.

Avoiding the duty to meet a judgment by reason of s.152

Section 152 provides four other important ways in which the insurer can avoid the obligation to meet judgments imposed on it by s.151.

One of these is simply that an insurer does not have to meet any judgments where execution on the judgment is stayed pending an appeal. That is really a postponement rather than an avoidance of the liability. The other three are more important.

Duty to give notice of proceedings

A judgment is only enforceable against an insurer if before, or within seven days after, the commencement of the proceedings in which the judgment was given, the insurer is given notice of the bringing of the proceedings.

Courts have become rather liberal as to what constitutes notice, but the fact remains that if the claimant does not comply with this provision they will not be able to require the insurer to meet the judgment. The provision is, of course, only of use to the insurer if it is not indemnifying its insured. If it is indemnifying its insured and its insured has a judgment against them, then it will have to meet that judgment in order to fulfil its contractual obligation to its insured.

Cancellation of the policy

The second important provision relates to the cancellation of the policy within its normal term, either by the insured, the insurer or by consent of both parties. Following the implementation of s.9 of the Deregulation Act 2015, the steps previously imposed on the insurer by s.147 for their liability to cease once a policy had been cancelled have been removed. When an insurer cancels a policy it is not now necessary for the policyholder to acknowledge the cancellation by returning the certificate or making a statutory declaration to that effect.

Cancellation occurs when the appropriate notice under the policy has been given. Even though the policy has been cancelled, the insurer still generally remains liable to meet judgments unless and until the MID is amended to show that the insurer is no longer on cover.

Avoidance by reason of misrepresentation or non-disclosure

The final provision relates to a situation where the insurance has been obtained on the basis of non-disclosure of a material fact or by misrepresentation and the insurer is, therefore, entitled to avoid the policy from the outset. The situation may be that the insurer has already purported to avoid the policy or it may be that it has not yet done so, having only just discovered the non-disclosure or misrepresentation, and wishes to do so.

In either case the insurer must bring proceedings against its insured for a declaration from the court that it is or was so entitled to avoid the policy. To successfully avoid liability to meet a judgment the insurer must:

- State that the avoidance of the policy is on the basis of non-disclosure or misrepresentation and not on the basis of any policy condition.

- Begin proceedings for the declaration before or within three months of the commencement of the proceedings in which the judgment that it is seeking to avoid was given.
- Give notice to the claimant of the proceedings within seven days of the commencement of its proceedings for a declaration, specifying in that notice the non-disclosure or false representation upon which it proposes to rely.

The three-month and seven-day time limits referred to above are vital and any declaration from the court will not avail the insurer if it does not comply with them.

Entitlement of insurer to recover sums paid under s.151

As is already noted, s.148 entitles the insurer to recover from its insured such sums it has had to pay to the claimant where there has been a breach of its policy condition or where it would be entitled to rely on an exception under the policy but for s.148.

> Section 151 has added to insurers' problems by preventing them from avoiding liability even when the person driving the vehicle is not one permitted under the policy or where the person driving the vehicle did not hold a driving licence.

Section 151 gives the insurer the right to recover its outlay from a person insured under the policy but who does not hold a driving licence and whose liability would not have had to be met but for its provisions.

Likewise, where the insurer has had to meet the liability of a person who would not be permitted to drive under the policy, it may recover its outlay either from that person or from a person insured under the policy, if that person caused or permitted the use of the vehicle that gave rise to the liability.

In *Churchill Insurance Company Ltd v Fitzgerald and Wilkinson; Evans v Cockayne & Equity Claims Ltd* [2012], the Court of Appeal considered the application of s.151.

In *Wilkinson*, the insured named driver, Mr Wilkinson, allowed Mr Fitzgerald to drive the car. Mr Fitzgerald lost control of the car and collided with another vehicle, causing Mr Wilkinson, who was the passenger, to suffer severe injuries. The insurer accepted that, by virtue of s.151(5), it had to compensate Mr Wilkinson as the passenger. However, it argued that under s.151(8) it could reclaim the compensation on the basis that Mr Wilkinson had caused or permitted the use of the vehicle.

The facts of *Evans* were essentially the same. Ms Evans allowed Mr Cockayne to drive the motorcycle as an uninsured driver while she travelled as a pillion passenger. He drove into the back of a lorry and Ms Evans sustained serious injuries.

The Court of Appeal referred the matter to the Court of Justice of the European Union (CJEU) for a preliminary hearing. The CJEU found that EU law must be interpreted as precluding national rules where the effect is to omit automatically the requirement that the insurer should compensate an insured passenger who is injured as a result of giving permission to an uninsured driver.

The Court of Appeal accepted that when the insured is the injured passenger, the effect of s.151(8) is to limit the extent of insurance cover and, as such, has to be consistent with EU law. The Court indicated that s.151(8) should be interpreted as notionally adding the following words: "save that where the person insured by the policy may be entitled to the benefit of any judgment to which this section refers, any recovery by the insurer in respect of that judgment must be proportionate and determined on the basis of the circumstances of the case."

Further restrictions on insurers' ability to rely on exceptions in the policy

Sections 149 and 150 make provisions that also have a bearing on the restrictions on the insurer's ability to rely on exceptions in the policy.

Under s.149, any agreements made with passengers that they will not be able to hold the user of the vehicle liable for injury or damage, or that they will only be able to do so on the fulfilment of certain conditions, are of no effect.

Section 150 seeks to prevent car-sharing schemes falling foul of any exclusion of business use under the policy.

Duty to give information as to insurance or security where claim is made

The person against whom a claim is made in respect of death or bodily injury or damage arising out of the use of a vehicle on the road must provide the following information:

- Whether or not they were insured.
- Whether or not they would have been insured but for the fact that their insurer has avoided or cancelled the policy.
- If they were insured, such particulars as are specified in the certificate of insurance.
- Where no certificate was delivered, give the following particulars: the registration mark, the number of the policy, the name of the insurer and the period of the insurance cover.

Failure to provide this information is an offence. There is no reason why a claimant or a claimant's insurer should not lay an information against a person who has failed to provide this information.

Points of special difficulty

Employees

There is, under s.145, provision that a motor policy does not have to cover an employer's liability for the death of, or a personal injury to, an employee arising out of and in the course of their employment. Such liability was required to be covered under an employers' liability insurance.

However, as a consequence of the EC Directive 90/232/EEC, the Motor Vehicles (Compulsory Insurance) Regulations 1992 were brought into force and a new subsection (4A) was added to s.145 on 31 December 1992. This stated that the exception in respect of employees did not apply unless that liability was in fact insured under an employers' liability insurance.

The situation was altered further by the Employers' Liability (Compulsory Insurance) Exemption (Amendment) Regulations 1992, which came into effect on 1 July 1994. These no longer required the employer to cover their liability to an employee, who was being carried on or upon a vehicle, or was entering or getting onto or alighting from a vehicle, under their employers' liability insurance.

The new s.145(4A) of the RTA 1988 left some uncertainty regarding the position of drivers injured in the course of their employment because it referred to "a person (a) carried in or upon a vehicle, or (b) entering or getting on to, or alighting from, a vehicle", which a layman would certainly interpret as including drivers. The position was clarified by Mr Justice Popplewell in *R v Secretary of State for the Department of Transport ex parte National Insurance Guarantee Corporation plc* [1996]. He concluded that the section did not apply to drivers.

AXA Insurance UK Plc v Norwich Union Insurance Ltd [2007] has further refined the meaning of a person "carried in or upon a vehicle". It was held that "carried" is to be understood to be a person being transported. So an employee working in an elevated bucket affixed to the bed of a stationary vehicle was not deemed to be carried in or upon the vehicle. His claim was accordingly outside s.145(4A) and fell to be dealt with by the employers' liability insurer.

> It is important to note that the transfer of responsibility from the employers' liability insurer to the RTA 1988 insurer is only in respect of "passengers". There has been no such transfer in respect of employees killed or injured as pedestrians. That risk still remains with the employers' liability insurer, as does the risk in respect of employees killed or injured as drivers.

Definition of a road/other public place

The comments set out in this section are subject to the developing impact of a ruling of the CJEU in September 2014 (see below).

Section 145 makes insurance obligatory in respect of the use of a vehicle on a road in Great Britain. The difficulty is to decide what actually constitutes a road. A road is not synonymous with a highway, so a road to which the public has access, even though it is not a highway or a highway maintainable at public expense, would still be a road for the purposes of the RTA 1988. However, a road within a factory to which the public did not have access would not be considered a road for the purposes of the RTA 1988: *O'Brien v Trafalgar Insurance Company Ltd* [1945].

The law has tended to push the definition of a road ever wider. For example, a forecourt, which was clearly in private ownership, but that was nevertheless used by the public as a shortcut, has been found to be a road: *Bugge v Taylor* [1940]. On the other hand, in *Clarke v General Accident Fire and Life Assurance Corporation Plc* [1998] and *Cutter v Eagle Star Insurance Company Ltd* [1998], the House of Lords held that, on the facts of two cases, a car park was not a road.

On 3 April 2000, the Motor Vehicles (Compulsory Insurance) Regulations 2000 came into effect and added the term "or other public place" after "road" in sections 143 and 145 of the RTA 1988.

This amendment brought these sections into line with those sections dealing with dangerous driving and driving under the influence of drugs and alcohol.

Clearly, the term "other public place" is wider than road. An accident in a public car park would now certainly fall under the terms of the RTA 1988. The test is whether the public have access not simply by right but also by permission or even acquiescence of the owner. In the Scottish case of *Rodger v Normand* [1994], the defendant was charged with dangerous driving in the grounds of a secondary school. It was held that this was a public place. Even though the public had no official right of access, the public did regularly use it as a leisure park outside school hours and this was tolerated or acquiesced in by the education authority.

However, for an area to constitute a public place, that permission, toleration or acquiescence must be extended to the public at large. In *Director of Public Prosecutions v Coulman* [1992], Lord Justice Mann referred to the earlier decision in *Director of Public Prosecutions v Vivier* [1991]. He stated:

> "It would appear from the analysis in that decision that the inquiry is as to whether those who are permitted to use the Lanes in this case are so permitted because of some special characteristic or reason personal to themselves, which is not possessed by the public at large. If they are not, then it is a place to which the public has access. If they are, then it is not."

Guests or visitors using a private road or a private car park are persons with special characteristics or reasons personal to themselves. They do not render such private roads or private car parks a public place (*R v Director of Public Prosecutions ex parte Taussik* [2000] and *Young v Carmichael* [1990]).

CJEU decision: September 2014

EC Directive 72/166/EEC addresses the approximation of the laws of Member States relating to insurance against civil liability in respect of the use of motor vehicles.

Vnuk v Zavarovalnica Triglav [2014] concerned an accident in Slovenia that occurred when a tractor, to which a trailer was attached, reversed into a farmyard, striking a ladder on which the claimant had climbed, causing him to fall. The CJEU held as follows:

- The definition of the concept of "vehicle" within the meaning of the Directive is unconnected with the use that is made, or may be made, of the vehicle in question. As a result, the fact that a tractor may be used as an agricultural machine has no effect on the finding that such a vehicle corresponds to that concept of "vehicle".
- The concept of "use of vehicles" in the Directive cannot be left to the assessment of each Member State. The concept covers any use of a vehicle that is consistent with the normal function of that vehicle. That concept may, therefore, cover (as in this decision) the manoeuvre of a tractor in a farmyard in order to bring the trailer attached to that tractor into a barn. Whether it did in fact cover this was a matter for the national court to determine.

The full implications of this decision remain to be considered. However, it may be necessary for the RTA 1988 to be amended to extend the requirement to insure to any place, as opposed to only "a road or other public place".

Some commentators have suggested that, as a result of this decision, a motorised lawnmower used on UK private land that runs down a visitor may now need to be insured. This area of law is currently developing , not least having been clarified to some degree by the decision of the same court in *Rodrigues de Andrade v Salvador and another* [2017].

Driverless cars

The Modern Transport Bill was announced in the Queen's Speech in May 2016, with the aim of putting the UK "at the forefront of technology for new forms of transport, including autonomous and electric vehicles".

Soon after, the Department for Transport published a Consultation Paper on the 'Pathway to Driverless Cars: Proposals to support advanced driver assistance systems and automated vehicle technologies.' It is clear that such change is at the forefront of the government's mind.

Automated vehicle technology (AVT) testing has already begun in the UK; testers have been provided with a Code of Practice to ensure compliance with UK law.

Further proposals include the review of the domestic regulatory issues, including immediate changes to primary legislation to ensure that suitable insurance products are available, changes to the Highways Code and the Road Vehicle (Construction and Use) Regulations.

In response to the consultation, Kennedys have submitted written evidence to the House of Lords Science and Technology Committee, stating that innovation is to be embraced as long as the right checks and balances are in place. Kennedys have also referenced the wider industry call for urgent direction from the government on what good driving will look like, in regards to autonomous vehicles, and reinforced the point that the government needs to have a full handle on the impact of cyber risk.

The consultation ran until 23 November 2016, following which the government published the Vehicle Technology and Aviation Bill (formally known as the Modern Transport Bill), which had its first reading on the 22 February 2017.

The Automated and Electric Vehicles Bill was announced in the Queen's Speech in June 2017. It is intended that the Bill will:

- Allow the regulatory framework to keep pace with the fast – evolving technology for electric cars, helping improve air quality.
- Provide for the installation of charging points for electric and hydrogen vehicles.
- Extend compulsory motor vehicle insurance to cover the use of automated vehicles, to ensure that compensation claims continue to be paid quickly, fairly, and easily, in line with longstanding insurance practice.

The impact of such drastic changes to the current transport system in relation to negligence and civil liability is unknown; however, there is likely to be some overlap with product liability.

Checklist for insurers

Sections 148 and 151 of the RTA 1988 make it difficult for an insurer to avoid having to meet judgments, even when there has been clear breach of its policy conditions or where it has cancelled the policy. However, before deciding that it must definitely meet a judgment, an insurer who has refused indemnity to its insured for whatever reason should consider:

- ✓ Is this a liability that is required to be covered under s.145? If it concerns death, bodily injury or damage it almost certainly is, but consider the following:
  - ✓ Did the incident take place on a road or other public place? Have the principles, set out in the case of VNUK, now been brought into UK law?
  - ✓ Is the claimant an employee not being carried as a passenger, or working on a stationary vehicle?
  - ✓ If the vehicle was stolen, is the claimant a passenger who knew or had reason to believe it was stolen?

- ✓ Is the breach of condition being questioned one that, under s.148, it is not allowed to take into account or does it, for example, relate to a use of the vehicle that is not an excluded exception?
- ✓ Was notice given either before the commencement of proceedings or within seven days of the commencement of proceedings as required by s.151?
- ✓ Once it cancelled the policy, was the MID amended successfully?
- ✓ Has there been non-disclosure or misrepresentation involved in the obtaining of the policy of insurance? If so, it can bring proceedings for a declaration within three months of the commencement of the claimant's own proceedings. If so, it must remember to give the claimant notice of the commencement of the proceedings within seven days of their commencement, and also to provide them with details of the non-disclosure or misrepresentation as alleged.
- ✓ What is the effect of Insurance Act 2015, and the operation of the customer's duty of fair presentation?

Article 75

Lying between insurers' obligations under the RTA 1988 and the MIB's obligations are the obligations of what used to be termed the "insurer concerned" under the MIB's Article 75.

This was most recently updated on 31 March 2017.

The obligations on the claimant as regards notice are more onerous than under the RTA 1988 and the insurer does not have to deal with subrogated claims from insurers.

The purpose of this section is to highlight those circumstances in which an insurer, while having no obligation under RTA 1988, would have a liability under the Article 75.

The terms of Article 75 have been updated to reflect the change in the cancellation procedure (policies cancelled after 30 June 2015) introduced by s.9 of the Deregulation Act 2015. Article 75 now confirms that an insurer will cease to have an Article 75 liability from the date the policy is cancelled, so long as the MID is properly updated.

Article 75(2)(a)

Defines the "Article 75 Insurer" as the member who at the time of the accident that gave rise to the RTA 1988 liability was providing any insurance in respect of the vehicle from the use of which the liability of the judgment debtor arose.

Article 75(2)(a)(1)

The insurer is the Article 75 Insurer notwithstanding that:

- The insurance has been obtained by fraud, misrepresentation, non-disclosure of material facts or mistake.
- Cover has been backdated.
- Use of the vehicle is other than that permitted under the policy.

Article 75(2)(a)(2)

The insurer ceases to be the Article 75 Insurer on the expiry of the policy. Subsections (i) to (iii) define when this will be the case. If the policy is cancelled mid-term, the insurer only ceases to be the Article 75 Insurer when the certificate has been surrendered to the insurer by the policyholder (if cancelled before 30 June 2015); or the MID had been amended to confirm the cancellation (if cancelled after the 30th June 2015).

The insurer is not the Article 75 Insurer if:

- It obtains a court declaration that the policy is void or unenforceable before the date on which the RTA 1988 liability was incurred.
- The insurance has ceased to operate by reason of a transfer of interest in the vehicle involved in the accident, which transfer is proved by evidence.
- The certificate has been stolen and its theft reported to the police within 30 days of discovery of the theft.
- The certificate has been forged by someone other than the member or its intermediary or an officer, employee or agent of either.

The differences between Article 75 liability and RTA 1988 liability are:

- Before RTA 1988 liability starts, an insurance certificate must be issued, as explained above. That is not the case under Article 75.
- Under the RTA 1988 it is possible to apply to the court for a declaration that a policy is void by reason of non-disclosure or misrepresentation. Proceedings for such a declaration can be brought up to three months after proceedings are commenced by the injured party (s.152). However, the insurer would remain liable as the Article 75 Insurer unless it had obtained that declaration before the accident that is the subject matter of the claim had taken place.
- As is already stated, showing that the use of the vehicle is other than that permitted by the policy does permit the insurer to avoid liability under the RTA 1988 but it does not allow it to avoid its liability under Article 75.

- Where a policy has been issued for less than 12 months, to avoid liability as insurer after the insurance period has terminated, the insurer must show that it had no intention to renew and no renewal documents were issued, and that no new insurance for the same policyholder had incepted within a period of 15 days of the date of expiry. Clearly, if renewal documents were issued but not taken up by the policyholder, the insurer could find itself still the Article 75 Insurer even though the insurance had expired. Much also depends on what is contained on the MID.
- Under s.152 of the RTA 1988, if an insurer cancels a policy it can protect itself against continued RTA 1988 liability by bringing proceedings in respect of the failure to surrender the certificate of insurance within 14 days of the cancellation or amending the MID. That is not the situation under Article 75 where this step must have been taken before the accident took place.

It can be seen from this that where a policy is cancelled mid-term, or avoidance is sought because of misrepresentation or non-disclosure, there are a number of possibilities for who should deal with the matter and how:

- If a policy has been cancelled mid-term, but the certificate was not surrendered and no proceedings were brought in this regard within 14 days, or the MID not amended, then the liability remains with the insurer as the RTA 1988 insurer.
- If a policy has been cancelled mid-term but the certificate was not surrendered, but the insurer has brought proceedings in this regard within the 14-day period, then it is the Article 75 Insurer.
- If the certificate was surrendered before the accident, or MID properly amended, then the matter falls to be dealt with by the MIB (see below).

- If the insurer seeks to avoid the policy on the basis of misrepresentation or non-disclosure, but does not do so within three months of the claimant commencing proceedings and/or does not give seven days' notice of its proceedings for the declaration to the claimant, then the insurer remains the RTA 1988 insurer. If the insurer brings proceedings for a declaration within three months of the claimant's own proceedings, but after the accident, then it is the Article 75 Insurer. Note here, again, that an insurer that cancels a policy thereby affirms that policy and so may not then seek also to avoid that policy.
- If the insurer obtains its declaration that it is entitled to avoid the policy on the basis of misrepresentation or non-disclosure prior to the accident, then the claim falls to be dealt with by the MIB.

The insurer is relieved of liability if it can prove there has been a transfer of interest in the vehicle prior to the accident, even though the policy has not been cancelled and the certificate of insurance surrendered.

There are two changes to a previous version of Article 75, which also appear to limit the liability of the insurer. Formerly, when an insurer had issued a certificate covering "any vehicle", it was deemed to be the Article 75 Insurer in respect of each and every vehicle owned, leased or in the custody or control of the policyholder in the same taxation class as that insured. This provision has gone.

It is replaced by Article 75(2)(d): "Where, after 1 January 2002, a record is held on the Motor Insurance Database (MID), the existence of such a record covering the date of an accident shall, unless there is documentary evidence to the contrary, be sufficient to establish the existence of 'insurance' for the purpose of this Article".

Direct right of action against motor insurer

On 19 January 2003 the European Communities (Rights Against Insurers) Regulations 2002 came into force. These and other motor insurance directives now form part of the codified Directive 2009/103/EC (the Regulations). The Directive required EC nationals living outside the home country of the defendant motorist to have the right to sue the motor insurer directly. The Regulations went beyond this by permitting UK resident claimants also to bring proceedings directly against the UK-based motor insurer of the party they hold responsible for the accident. If they are successful, the insurer will be directly liable to them.

The advantage for the claimant is that, while it may be difficult to find and serve proceedings on the driver, the insurer is easy to find. Also, the insurer will immediately be liable to pay any judgment, and there is no need for further proceedings if the insurer does not pay. The claimant can simply enforce the judgment against the insurer.

> What the Regulations do not do is enable the claimant to sue the insurer where they cannot identify the driver. For the Regulations to apply, there has to be an "insured person". An insured person has been issued with a policy of insurance, which is in force, which covers their use of the vehicle on a road or other public place and fulfils the requirements of s.145 of the RTA 1988.

In addition, the Regulations do not enable the claimant to successfully sue the insurer when the insurer is not obliged to indemnify the driver. The insurer is only liable to the claimant to the extent that it is liable to the insured person.

It would seem to be unwise for a claimant to sue the insurer where the insurer is entitled to refuse indemnity to its insured. That would give the insurer a defence that the insured themselves would not have and might well defeat the claim.

It would equally be unwise for an insurer to settle a claim where the insurer was sued directly but was entitled to refuse an indemnity. That is because the judgment would not be one to which sections 148 or 151 of the RTA 1988 applied and there would, consequently, be no right of recovery against the insured.

MIB Agreements

The application of The Uninsured Drivers' Agreement 2015, as supplemented in 2017, and The Untraced Drivers' Agreement 2017 lies outside the day-to-day experience of most claims handlers as generally the MIB or its instructed agents will deal with these Agreements. It is important to be aware of the Agreements, however, in that they do impact on the handling of claims against insured drivers. Of particular importance is the requirement that where there is a meaningful degree of negligence on the part of an insured driver involved in an accident, their insurer will deal with the claims arising in full without contribution from the MIB.

23 Assessing RTA negligence

Niall Edwards

- Causation and liability in negligence
- Witness evidence
- Police Accident Report
- Criminal charges and convictions
- Medical evidence
- Contributory negligence
- Accidents involving; roundabouts, failure to wear a seatbelt, rear shunts, overtaking, vehicles emerging from a side road, misleading signals, motorbikes or cyclists, pedestrians, children, parked vehicles, alcohol, and involuntary acts
- Useful cases

Assessing RTA negligence

Introduction

Nearly everyone considers themselves the "King or Queen of the Road" and policyholders or their drivers are no exception to this rule. However, when something goes wrong and road users collide, and when third-party road user claims are intimated, the claims handler will quickly need to assess fault for the collision. While early admissions of liability can sometimes be reversed, this initial assessment can have profound consequences for the way a third-party claim is handled, often into litigation or even to a civil trial.

There is a danger in focusing too rigidly upon existing case law (reported court decisions) negligence when assessing fault. In this chapter, rather than providing an academic analysis of the law and the case reports (which often contradict one another), the focus is upon providing a practical guide for handlers. This chapter seeks to cover no more than the basics of assessing liability in negligence in motor claims.

Most civil motor claims first come to the handler's attention in the RTA Portal in Stage 1. The alleged details of a road accident and why the third party holds the policyholder (or their driver) at fault are set out, in brief, in a claim notification form (CNF). Unfortunately, the details of the time and location of the accident and mechanisms of the collision(s) are rarely set out clearly. The handler has only a brief period then to collate information and evidence and reach a decision on whether to contest liability for the collision, whether to raise seatbelt issues or whether to simply concede liability.

So, how to go about assessing fault for a motor accident?

The "reasonable" road user?

Road users include not only the policyholder or driver, but also other car drivers, drivers of other vehicles like lorries or buses, motorbike riders, cyclists, pedestrians and even horse riders and so forth.

In assessing whether each or any of the road users involved in an accident was negligent, the first question to consider for each road user is "what would the reasonable road user have done in those circumstances?".

Every road user owes every other road user a duty of care.

They must use the roads (and pavements, parking areas, etc.) in a reasonable manner in all the circumstances. So, if a reasonable driver would have driven to a higher standard in the circumstances of an accident, the road user in question *may* have driven negligently. For a driver, the minimum standard of care they must show to other road users is that of a 'reasonable' driver in similar circumstances.

If a road user has driven unreasonably, has breached their duty of care to other road users, is liable in negligence to an extent, has that negligence caused the loss or injury that is now being alleged?

Causation and liability in negligence

It is important to make this point at the outset. Even if the policyholder or driver has driven negligently, that negligence may not have caused the losses or injuries now being claimed by the claimant.

By way of example, the driver may have driven at excessive and ultimately negligent speed in *all the circumstances*, but speed may not in itself have caused the injury to that pedestrian. They may have stepped directly into the side of the driver's passing vehicle and so, whatever speed the vehicle was travelling, it may be that the injury would have occurred in any event.

The third-party driver may have driven at speed into the rear of the stationary vehicle ahead. The insured driver may have then collided with the rear of the third-party vehicle but not propelled it again into the rear of the vehicle in front of it. The insured driver is likely negligent for driving into the rear of the third-party vehicle and that negligence will have caused the rear-end damage to the third-party vehicle. However, the 'rear shunt' will not have caused the damage to the front of the third-party vehicle and associated proportionate repair costs. Furthermore, if the third party is injured it may be that, dependent on the medical evidence, some, most or all of that injury was caused by the third party driving into the vehicle in front.

The Highway Code

The Highway Code is a starting point for the claims handler in assessing liability in negligence as set out in s.38(7) of the Road Traffic Act 1988. The rules of the Highway Code are key to establishing the baseline standards for road users. The driving test is firmly based on these rules. The Highway Code focuses a great deal on proper consideration and protection of other road users and, in particular, pedestrians, children, cyclists, motorcyclists and the disabled. In fact, the first 88 rules of the Highway Code are directed solely to this aim.

The substance of the rules touching on how road users should behave on the road are set out in rules 103 to 203 and particularly in rules 159 to 203.

This Code is *required reading* for any handler who deals with motor claims. At the time of writing, the current version of the Highway Code, published on 9 November 2016, is readily accessible online and can be found at: http://www.highwaycodeuk.co.uk.

It is important to understand that it is a *code* and that, in the context of civil motor claims, a breach of any provision in the Highway Code does not in itself establish negligence (or indeed a criminal liability), but it can be relied upon as *tending to establish* who is liable in negligence. Reference to provisions in the Highway Code are persuasive but not conclusive and need to be read in the context of the other facts and circumstances of the accident. Ideally, the handler needs to consider them while drawing upon their personal experience as a driver and road user.

Assessing RTA negligence is fact sensitive!

There is a real danger of wrongly assessing RTA negligence if focusing too heavily on one or more rules in the Highway Code or, indeed, on case law being quoted by the claimant's solicitors. Rarely does a reported case fit exactly with the circumstances of the RTA under consideration, and rules of the Highway Code can invariably be interpreted and applied in different ways by the opposing parties in a civil motor claim. Some rules of the Highway Code may support the driver's position; others may support the third-party claimant.

All available facts and *all* available evidence surrounding the incident in question must be carefully assessed and weighed up. The rules and case law may assist in interpreting those facts and that evidence, as will the handler's own experience.

Of course, it may prove impossible to obtain and consider all the potentially available evidence before a decision must be reached on liability in negligence. For instance, the Police Accident Report may take some time to arrive, and almost certainly not prior to the date when a decision on liability in an RTA Portal case must be made.

Below is a summary of potentially useful evidence to consider when assessing liability in negligence in a motor claim:

- **Witness evidence** of the road users involved.
- **Vehicle damage documentation** in relation to the vehicles involved.
- **Accident location details**, including the road layout, lane markings and so forth.
- **Calculated speed** of the vehicles involved with reference to skid marks and the Highway Code tables, in addition to consideration of prevailing road conditions and corresponding safe speeds.
- **Police Accident Report** and police statements, police reconstruction reports and other documents.

- **CCTV** evidence, for instance in car parks, petrol stations or supermarkets or at key road junctions can be obtained – but you need to move quickly to obtain it. This form of evidence is often overlooked.
- **Dashcam footage** from car windscreens or public transport vehicles, or indeed from helmets of cyclists and motorcyclists, is becoming more prevalent and can be invaluable in establishing how road collisions occur. It is often worth asking for it, just in case.
- **Telematics and Event Data Recorders (EDR) in vehicle data** can be referenced to establish how collisions have occurred, where they have occurred, the speed of the vehicles, whether seatbelts were in place, whether airbags were deployed, the forces and impacts involved and so forth. However, expert reports covering such evidence can be costly and disproportionate when handling lower-value claims.
- **Criminal charges and convictions** of any of the road users involved.
- **Coroner's inquest and facts** established at that hearing.
- **Medical evidence** in personal injury motor claims and other indirect documents in which the third party may have set out an account of the road accident.
- **Accident reconstruction expert's report(s)** in cases of significant value or complexity.

Some of these sources of evidence are dealt with below in a little more detail.

Witness evidence

The evidence of witnesses, their description of what they say happened in a road accident and why, perhaps, they consider a certain road user at fault, can come in many forms.

Handlers might first review the incident report form filled in by the insured driver. That incident report form may give details of other potential witnesses. The handler might follow up and then obtain more detailed statements from both the driver and any witnesses.

Where liability (in negligence) is in dispute, evidence of truly independent witnesses can be very persuasive. Independent witnesses are people who witnessed the road accident but have no personal connection to any of the parties involved. Passenger witnesses are usually not independent and they are usually friends or family members. However, it is quite possible to obtain evidence from a passenger as an independent witness in, say, a taxi.

Bear in mind that pedestrians and other road users who are not in the vehicles involved may have a very useful perspective on what occurred in the road accident.

Potential witnesses can be identified from other sources too. They can be found in the pages of Police Accident Reports (see below), or upon a review of social media or press coverage of the road accident, or when attending related criminal proceedings or coroner's inquests to take notes. They can also be ascertained through modern intelligence gathering techniques like geofencing (pulling in tweets and similar online social messaging relating to the road accident in the location of the accident).

While independent witnesses are most helpful, it is often still worth obtaining statements from family members who may have witnessed the accident, usually as passengers. They may have had a better or a useful or unique view of how the accident unfolded.

Incident report forms and brief handwritten descriptions of road accidents can be misleading and it is best to obtain more detailed information from witnesses over the phone or by email and, ultimately, obtain more detailed statements from witnesses.

For instance, when completing incident report forms drivers rarely set out accurate details of the accident location, the areas of damage to any of the vehicles involved, whether they themselves were injured or when they first saw the other road users involved in the accident.

The credibility of witnesses is also crucial in weighing up how persuasive their evidence is. Consider if their account of the accident circumstances has been consistent throughout? Is there other or related evidence of fraudulent activity on their part? Does their account of the accident tally with the vehicle damage documentation? Have they accurately described the road accident location? Is their evidence vague in any way? How committed are they to attending court if necessary? Is there any contemporaneous evidence from the witness (i.e. in a police accident report)? Often, evidence given nearer the time of a road accident is more accurate, as a person's perception of what happened can change or be skewed over time.

In accidents involving fleet vehicles, an agency driver may need to be located and a witness statement obtained, and they are often hard to trace. If the driver witness is untraceable, unwilling or unable to attend trial (if necessary) or provide a statement, it will prove a challenge to successfully argue the third-party driver was negligent to any extent, even if they were.

While witness evidence is critical to the assessment of negligence in an RTA, always bear in mind that how witnesses will give their evidence in court, should the matter run to a liability trial, is just as critical. If any particular witness is a poor communicator, inconsistent or unreliable, unnecessarily florid or aggressive in their account of the accident, this has to be another factor to take into account when assessing RTA negligence.

Vehicle damage documentation

Vehicle damage documentation can include a repair estimate, engineer's or assessor's report, photographic images taken by the engineer or assessor and photographic images taken at the scene of the accident by either the police or one of the road users involved. Indirectly, it could also include descriptions of areas of damage to the vehicles involved as set out in any incident report form or in the Police Accident Report.

It is most useful to have vehicle damage documentation in relation to all other vehicles involved in the road accident and not just the driver's documentation. Witnesses can prove highly subjective in their account of road accidents and their assessment of who is at fault also tends to be understandably biased. Vehicle damage documentation is rather more objective evidence and judges at trial make good use of it for this reason. They use it as a useful comparator to and corroborator of the evidence of the witnesses.

For instance, if Driver A says they emerged from the side road and had completed a right turn onto the main road before the collision with Driver B who had come from the left on the main road, why then is the damage to Car A down the offside and the damage to Car B directly to the front?

Inspection and images of the damage to the vehicles are also very useful in this regard. Repair or engineering documents can be slightly misleading in terms of the force, area and direction of impact to the vehicles involved. However, images can help clarify that and often reference to them alone can quickly provide a feel for how a road accident truly occurred.

Accident location

In the past, handlers and their investigators would visit the site of a road accident, take measurements and photographs and draw up scaled plans to obtain a better understanding of the accident location. While this resource and level of attention is sometimes still warranted on cases of sufficient value or complexity, nowadays handlers have access to Google Streetview images of the accident location. It can sometimes be tricky ascertaining where exactly the accident occurred when on Streetview, but a review of the accident location using this web service usually proves invaluable.

Details of the accident location, including the road layout, road markings, road signage and so forth, are useful when weighing up the accounts of how the accident occurred, the credibility of the witnesses and the accuracy of descriptions of the accident and location.

Handlers should be wary though. Road layouts, lane markings and signage change over time. Google Streetview images may be time-sensitive. Happily, it is often possible to select a different date or timeframe on Streetview to obtain a more accurate idea of the accident location at the time the accident occurred. This is not always the case though and the traditional investigator visit to the accident location may still be warranted.

Photographs taken at the scene of the accident are often very helpful in both placing the position of the vehicles after the collision (if they had not by then been moved), verifying the witnesses present at the scene, noting skid marks on the road (see below) and noting where debris is on the road. Often the position of debris on the road can help the handler deduce precisely where on the road the collision occurred.

Calculated speed of the vehicles involved

While travelling above or below the speed limit for a road may suggest a criminal offence, the speed of a vehicle is not of itself decisive evidence of negligence in civil motor claims but may be suggestive of negligence in all the circumstances of the particular case. Simply travelling at excessive speed may not have caused the accident and loss and may sometimes, therefore, not be considered negligent. Equally, a driver cannot necessarily establish they were not negligent simply because they were travelling within the speed limit for a road. A driver travelling just under the stipulated speed limit of 30mph on a road may be driving at a negligent speed if they are driving in an area alongside a primary school, at home time, with children crossing the road at various points and numerous parked cars on either side of the road.

It remains useful to ascertain the speed of the vehicles involved in a road accident in the moments prior to the collision. Obviously, if there are two vehicles involved on the same stretch of road, but one is driving at a far higher speed than the other and perhaps over the speed limit, it is more likely that they have made the driver error.

If the speed of vehicles can be established, the braking distance may be roughly calculated by reference to the Highway Code. Using this ready-reckoner can provide assistance when deciding on liability.

Skid marks (visible on contemporaneous accident location photographs) can be used to ascertain not only whether vehicles were driving at excessive speed, but also the position of the vehicles both prior to and after collision. From this, the handler may be able to ascertain which vehicle might have crossed lanes, lost control or come over onto the wrong side of the road.

Police Accident Report

Even when the police attend an accident scene or the accident is reported to the police, and they either take statements at the scene or do so later, a full Police Accident Report may not exist. However, if there is police involvement in the road accident and if there was injury, particularly if serious, as a result of the accident, it is likely the police will in due course generate a full Police Accident Report rather than a shorter document simply listing the vehicles and road users involved. A Police Accident Report may be generated if criminal charges are laid.

It will usually be impossible to obtain a copy of any Police Accident Report while the criminal investigation is ongoing, and in more serious cases this may take some months.

A fee is normally paid when obtaining a Police Accident Report or other documentation from the relevant police service. The Report will be located and provided more quickly if the police/crime reference number and/or the collar number for the police officer(s) attending the scene of the accident is provided.

If there is time to obtain them, Police Accident Reports are very useful documents to consider when assessing negligence in a motor accident. Police traffic officers attending the scene are considered (in court) to be road traffic experts. Anything they set out in the report indicating potential fault on the part of one driver or another is useful. Police reports usually contain contemporaneous sketches of the accident location and circumstances, details of whether drivers were wearing seatbelts (see below), areas of damage to the vehicles involved and, most importantly of all, they can include contemporaneous statements taken from the witnesses and perhaps notes of interviews with the witnesses too.

Criminal charges and convictions

If one of the drivers involved in the accident has already been convicted of a relevant motoring offence, such as careless driving, dangerous driving, death by careless driving or death by dangerous driving, that criminal conviction suggests negligence on that driver's part, which then leads to a presumption of civil negligence on that driver's part in any civil claim.

Often, evidence of such a criminal conviction leads to the view that the relevant driver is entirely at fault (100% negligent) in the context of the civil claim.

However, the presumption of negligence can be overturned if the criminal act is not causative of the loss in the civil claim and, though very rarely, if the evidence in the civil claim completely overturns the presumption.

Where the policyholder or driver has been charged with a criminal offence, or even as early as when they are first to be interviewed by the police under caution, it is worthwhile for the handler to arrange the attendance of a legal representative for the court hearing or interview. Legal representation at that early stage, as well as in criminal proceedings, may mean the difference between a criminal conviction leading to a presumption of civil liability in negligence and no such criminal conviction.

Coroner's inquest

Coroner's inquests occur in road accident cases that, unfortunately, involve one or more fatalities. Such cases will not be dealt with in the RTA Portal and tend to be longer running.

It is well worth the handler/insurer sending along a representative to a coroner's inquest. The coroner does not attribute fault for accidents, but rather embarks on a fact-finding mission. Useful evidence may be elicited, and useful findings of fact can occur at an inquest. It may be that the insurer will arrange for representation for the family of the deceased policyholder at the inquest or it may be that they are separately represented and the insurer sends a 'noting brief' to garner the evidence introduced at the inquest and the coroner's findings of fact.

Medical evidence

While the reports of medical experts are principally there to assist the parties and, ultimately, the trial judge in assessing the potential value of any injury claim, they are also useful to review from an RTA negligence perspective.

The claimant's history and account of the road accident and the mechanics of how they came to be injured, are also worth reviewing for consistency with other evidence and statements and to check that what is said to the medical expert (often more contemporaneously) tallies with what is later said in witness evidence, what has already been said to the police or what is indicated by vehicle damage documentation. This can also go to the credibility of the injured claimant.

Accident reconstruction expert's report

For claims of sufficient value or complexity it can be worth obtaining an accident reconstruction expert's report.

Such reports can be costly to obtain (from £1,500 to £6,500), so their use is usually restricted to road accidents involving injury claims that are large or catastrophic in nature or very complex road accidents involving multiple vehicles. Where there is sufficient evidence available in relation to the accident from other sources then even on high-value or complicated cases the use of such experts is not justified.

Contributory negligence

Many cases where liability (in negligence) is disputed are not clear cut. Sometimes liability can be apportioned between the various road users involved.

Claims taken to court involving roundabout accidents often result in the trial judge apportioning liability between the two drivers on a 50:50 basis (see below). Of course, there can be 100% of liability for the accident on the part of any party. The handler must consider how liability is likely to be apportioned in the particular case based on the evidence, the Highway Code, case law and by drawing on the handler's experience as a road user.

The Civil Liability (Contribution) Act 1978 can entitle the defendant driver to claim a contribution against the claimant driver on the basis the claimant has contributed to the accident because of their own negligence.

In theory, the claimant bringing the claim could be found to bear up to 100% contributory negligence (which would leave the defendant completely not at fault), but this rarely occurs.

Failure to wear a seatbelt

The need to wear seatbelts in vehicles (save for drivers in certain vehicles like taxis) is mandated by ss.14 and 15 of the Road Traffic Act 1988.

If the claimant in a road accident claim is claiming for injury but it comes to light that the claimant failed to wear a seatbelt, and that failure to wear a seatbelt was causative of the injury, an argument can usually be made for a reduction of between 15% (if the wearing of the seatbelt would have reduced the injury) to 25% (if the wearing of the seatbelt would have prevented the injury) in the total figure claimed for that injury and related losses.

'Classic' crashes – things to consider

Some of the leading court decisions on RTA negligence are set out at the end of this chapter. However, this is done with the heavy caveat that while this case law and the Highway Code can provide the handler with a great deal of guidance and confidence in assessing liability, the facts of and evidence in the particular accident remain key to their assessment.

Below is set out a helpful summary of the most typical road accident types and the sorts of factors a handler may wish to consider when assessing RTA negligence for those accident types.

Rear shunt accidents

These claims are usually straightforward. If the non-fault vehicle has damage to its rear and the fault vehicle has damage to its front, there is no other unexplainable vehicle damage and no other vehicles involved, then it is most likely that total liability in negligence will attach to the driver of the fault vehicle. The fault vehicle should have maintained a safe braking distance and clearly did not.

In very few cases, it may be that the vehicle in front came to an unnaturally sudden stop because it failed to maintain a safe braking distance and collided with a stationary vehicle or immovable object in front of it. In such rare circumstances, some portion of liability may attach to the vehicle in front.

Roundabout accidents

Trial judges do often follow the easiest course and often find on a 50:50 split liability basis in road accident cases involving two cars on a roundabout.

Factors that can sway the view of a trial judge (and any assessment of liability) include:

- Which vehicle had cause to change lanes before the collision? Which vehicle straddled lanes? It is often the vehicle in the lane closest to the centre of the roundabout. The vehicle that had cause to change lanes is more likely to be found at fault.
- Which vehicle was in front? Which vehicle would have been least likely to note the presence of the other vehicle? The vehicle that was in front was less likely to note the presence of the other vehicle and therefore more likely to be found at fault.
- Where were the areas of damage to the vehicles involved? Does the vehicle damage documentation place one of the vehicles ahead of the other? (See above.)
- Did one vehicle emerge onto the roundabout and was the other vehicle already established on the roundabout? If so, the onus is on the vehicle emerging onto the roundabout to do so safely and to give way to vehicles already on the roundabout. The emerging vehicle is more likely to be found at fault.

Accidents involving overtaking manoeuvre

The onus is very much on the vehicle attempting to overtake another vehicle to ensure this can be done safely. This onus increases if that vehicle is seeking to undertake the other vehicle (pass down the nearside). In most such cases where a collision then ensues, liability or primary (most) liability attaches to the overtaking/undertaking vehicle.

In a few cases, the vehicle being overtaken may in fact attempt a U-turn or to turn right. If that vehicle commits to that manoeuvre after the overtaking vehicle has begun to overtake, then the vehicle being overtaken may bear primary liability. If the vehicle being overtaken does not signal first and moves to the right, again it may bear primary liability. The overtaking vehicle should never seek to overtake where the vehicle in front is behaving unusually, is at a junction or is signalling its intention to turn.

Quite often a claim is brought by an overtaking vehicle when the other vehicle, apparently, pulls over to the left side of the road but then suddenly swings out to the right. How liability will be apportioned will depend upon factors such as when or if the vehicle that pulled over to the left came to a stop, whether it was signalling to the right and whether it was adjacent to a junction to the right.

Accidents involving vehicles emerging from a side road

The onus is on the vehicle emerging from a side road to do so safely. If a collision ensues it is most likely the vehicle emerging from the side road will be at fault. Sometimes the emerging vehicle driver suggests they had successfully completed a manoeuvre before being hit. Again, details of vehicle damage to both vehicles will either support or contradict this. If emerging and turning right, then the emerging vehicle should not have damage to its nearside, save perhaps for the very front or very rear nearside, if it had emerged successfully and was in lane. Similarly, if the emerging vehicle had already emerged left and was in lane before the collision, damage to the offside would be unexpected, except perhaps to the rear offside corner.

Misleading signal accidents

If a vehicle emerges from a side road, placing reliance on seeing a vehicle approaching from the right on the main road that was signalling to the left, but the vehicle on the main road carries straight on and collides with the emerging vehicle, liability is normally apportioned on a 1/3 to 2/3 basis in favour of the vehicle on the main road. In other words, the driver on the main road is found to be have been 33% responsible for making that misleading signal. However, the emerging driver, even then, bears 66% liability.

If the vehicle on the main road was intending to turn left just after the turning from which the other vehicle was emerging, then it may be that the emerging vehicle will be found entirely at fault. The same may be the case if, say, independent witnesses place the vehicle on the main road, well away from the side of the main road, when approaching the side road in question. However, if the vehicle on the main road was found to have 'flashed' the emerging vehicle, the liability pendulum swings back in favour of the emerging vehicle.

If the main road has two lanes in either direction and the vehicle in the first lane is signalling to turn left, the onus is still on the emerging vehicle to ensure it is safe before crossing over the second lane on the main road if it intends to turn right.

Accidents involving motorbikes or cyclists

Drivers must, according to the Highway Code, pay particular care and attention to other road users who are at more risk, such as motorbikes, cyclists, pedestrians and children.

Drivers should realise it is entirely possible that motorbikes will undertake or overtake other vehicles in lane as well as overtaking across other lanes. Special care is required because motorbikes (as with cyclists and pedestrians) are harder to see on the road.

On the other hand, a motorcyclist filtering past a line of stationary or slow-moving traffic is performing a manoeuvre that is potentially fraught with danger. In the leading case on motorbikes filtering past traffic, *Powell v Moody* [1966], liability was apportioned on an 80:20 basis in favour of the driver emerging from a side road. However, in another significant case, *Williams v Walter Frederick* [1993], the driver of an emerging vehicle was found entirely at fault for colliding with a motorbike overtaking a lorry that was indicating to turn left immediately before the emerging vehicle. The speed and caution of the emerging vehicle is critical always to the apportionment on liability here.

Sometimes, at trial, the apportionment on liability between a motorcyclist or cyclist and a motor car depends upon which party had the best opportunity to take avoiding steps before the collision occurred.

As ever, each case needs to be assessed on its own, very specific, facts.

In cases where motorcyclists or cyclists have either failed to wear an appropriate bike helmet or have failed to wear reflective clothing at night, it may be possible to obtain a reduction in their claim of between 5% and 25% on the basis of their contributory negligence. Failure to wear a helmet cases rarely attract more than a 15% reduction on the claim.

Accidents involving pedestrians

In the leading reported case in relation to pedestrians, *Eagle v Chambers* [2004], one of the appellate judges asserted that cases in which a pedestrian might be found more liable for the accident than the driver would be "exceptional".

While this holds true generally, things that might sway a claims handler's assessment of less liability on the part of the driver and more contributory negligence on the part of the pedestrian might include accidents where:

- The pedestrian could have safely crossed the road at a pedestrian crossing but instead chose to cross at a different point nearby.
- The pedestrian stepped out into the road directly into the path of the driver, leaving the reasonable driver no realistic opportunity to brake or avoid a collision.
- The pedestrian ran in a haphazard or diagonal fashion across traffic.
- The pedestrian fell into the road.
- The pedestrian walked backwards into the road or simply did not look left or right or had their head down (a fact that independent witness evidence supports) when stepping into the road.

As with motorcyclists and cyclists, a reduction on a claim on the grounds of contributory negligence may be obtained if a pedestrian at night has failed to wear sufficient reflective clothing when on the road (in unlit areas and when this failure to wear high-visibility clothing has definitely led in some way to the collision itself).

Accidents involving children

If a child, usually a pedestrian or cyclist, is involved in an RTA their age is a key factor to be taken into account when deciding whether they are at fault for the accident to any extent and whether they bear any contributory negligence.

There is no minimum age at which a child cannot be found, to an extent, negligent. It is more a question of what 'mental processes', road sense and experiences a child of a specific age could reasonably be expected to have. If a child of that particular age should know not to, say, cycle out between two parked cars or run diagonally across an A road at an unsafe place rather than at a pedestrian crossing, then they may be found to be contributorily negligent. That being said, it is rare for a child of six or younger to be found to be at fault for an RTA to any extent.

It is possible for a driver to be held entirely not at fault for colliding with a child on the road – but only if it is abundantly clear in the circumstances that no reasonable driver in similar circumstances could have been expected to avoid the collision.

It is clear that trial judges need a lot of persuading to find the driver entirely faultless in such cases and leave the injured child with no party to sue for compensation for injury.

Accidents involving a parked vehicle

In such cases, liability in negligence will normally attach to the vehicle that struck the parked vehicle. This is because that parked vehicle was there to be seen and the other vehicle could have taken an avoiding manoeuvre to avoid the collision. In some very rare cases, it may be possible to attribute some negligence to the user of the parked vehicle, but only if they left the vehicle in a position on the road that was inherently dangerous to other road users and, in particular, other cars, motorbikes and cyclists – such as parking the car just over the brow of a hill or just around a blind corner. It is not enough to show that a vehicle is parked illegally, as that in itself will not have led to the collision in question.

Accidents involving alcohol

With pedestrians, cyclists and motorcyclists, the fact that they are drunk when the collision occurs helps to explain how they came to be where they were, but being drunk is not of itself negligent. It is better to simply view them against the standard of a reasonable (and sober) road user in their situation. Would such a road user have done what they did?

Passengers who are involved in road accidents in which their driver was, on the facts, drunk (over the legal limit) may be considered to have volunteered and consented to the risk of injury. Of course, the drunkenness of their drivers will need to be obvious and the more extreme the obvious drunkenness the more likely that a trial judge would ultimately find that the passenger had consented to be driven by a quite-obviously drunk driver.

Ex turpi causa

These are accidents where the Latin maxim *ex turpi causa non oritur* action might apply. They are very few and far between. Essentially, the courts are reluctant to award a claimant damages where their claim is directly founded upon their own illegal or immoral act. In such cases it is conceivable that, even if the defendant is at fault in negligence, the court may still refuse to allow the claim to proceed, instead applying the above maxim.

For instance, in one case, *Agheampong v Allied Manufacturing* [2009], the claimant was driving uninsured, unlawfully, and had no intention of arranging compulsory insurance for his vehicle. The court held that the claimant was not allowed to claim in those circumstances.

Accidents involving an involuntary act

To be found to be negligent the fault driver needs to have been in proper control of their mental faculties leading up to the accident.

Where a driver was unaware and rendered insensate it might be possible to argue that they cannot have been negligent. Such cases are exceptional.

The London Markets Authority and numerous other insurers are, as a matter of policy, unwilling to raise a defence in a civil claim on this basis, but many are.

Such a defence is only possible in civil claims where it can be shown that the driver had no indication of or precursor to the condition that then rendered them unconscious and could have done nothing consciously or even subconsciously to avoid the ensuing collision.

Trial judges are averse to allowing such defences to succeed. If it can be shown that the defendant driver had failed to sleep or eat sufficiently prior to the accident, or had failed to take their medication if they knew about their medical condition but were allowed to drive, or if they had any precursor or indication that they were medically unfit to drive in the hours or even weeks or months prior to the accident, a trial judge is likely to use this fact to deny this defence.

List of useful cases

Although the need to only be guided by case law in the context of the Highway Code, the evidence in every particular case and the handler's own experience as a road user has been repeatedly highlighted in this chapter, it may be helpful in any event to highlight some of the leading cases on RTA negligence.

You will find that case law in relation to RTA negligence is often seemingly contradictory.

Failure to wear a seatbelt

Froom v Butcher [1975]

Stanton v Collinson [2010]

Rear shunt accidents

Sharp v MOD [2007]

Emerging from a side road accidents

Smith v Goss [1996]

Farley v Buckley [2007]

Misleading signal accidents

Wadsworth v Gillespie [1978] (n.b. decided on 'particular facts of the case')

Accidents involving motorbikes or cyclists

Capps v Miller [1989] (failure to wear helmet)

Powell v Moody [1966] (motorbike filtering past traffic, car emerging from side road) but see...

Williams v Walter Frederick [1993]

Accidents involving pedestrians

Eagle v Chambers [2004]

Wormald v Ahmed [2014]

Accidents involving children

Jackson v Murray [2015] (Scottish Supreme Court)

Paramasivan v Wicks [2013]

Wells v Trinder [2002]

James v Farley [2002]

Ex turpi causa accidents

Pitts v Hunt [1991]

Agheampong v Allied Manufacturing [2009]

Involuntary act accidents

Mansfield v Weetabix [1998]

24 Low-value personal injury claims: road traffic accidents

Ian Davies

- Stage 1: claim notification and defendant's account
- Stage 2: medical evidence, consideration period and reaching settlement
- Stage 3: proceedings pack
- Interim payments
- Fixed recoverable costs: for settled claims and those which exit the Protocol
- Other basic points: including limitation, understated claims and fraud
- Proposed future changes

Low-value personal injury claims: road traffic accidents

Introduction

The original Pre-Action Protocol for Low Value Personal Injury Claims in Road Traffic Accidents (RTAs) was implemented on 30 April 2010. The protocol has been amended on a number of occasions to extend and vary the rules since that date with the process now well embedded into the claims handling strategy of all operating in the motor arena.

The extended RTA Protocol (the Protocol) goes hand in hand with a revised fixed recoverable costs (FRC) regime for claims that are settled within the process and those which exit it. There are costs consequences of a claim leaving the Protocol. The economics of keeping claims within the Protocol are persuasive and most insurers seek, where it is appropriate to do so, to retain claims within the portal process. The management of Protocol claims is supported by an online portal system, provided by Claims Portal Ltd. In other words, the Protocol sets out the process and the portal is the system used by all parties to conduct the claims within it.

The Protocol has similarities to the Protocol for Low Value Personal Injury (Employers' Liability and Public Liability) Claims – see Chapter 25. For ease of reference, given that claims handlers may deal only with specific types of claims, some issues are covered in both chapters.

The Protocol defines the "defendant" as the insurer of the person who is subject to the claim under the Protocol. In this chapter we will refer to the defendant, but in practice this will mean the claims handler with responsibility for the claim at the defendant's insurer.

We have also adopted the Protocol's definition of a "day" meaning "business day".

General points

The RTA Protocol applies where the claimant's injuries arise out of an RTA on or after 30 April 2010.

The process has three stages.

The value of the claim is calculated on a full liability basis by reference to general and special damages. While the cost of repairs and credit hire are included within portal claims they are excluded for the purposes of valuation. The Protocol works slightly differently if the claimant is a child. The Protocol does not apply to claims in relation to:

- Motor Insurers' Bureau (MIB) Untraced Drivers' Agreement.
- Breach of duty by a person who is not a road user.
- Defendant's vehicle not registered in the UK.
- Either the claimant or defendant is deceased.
- The claimant is bankrupt.
- The claimant or defendant is a protected party as defined in Part 21.1(2) of the Civil Procedure Rules (CPR).

Historic Protocol amendments

The process was introduced in April 2010 and limited to claims between £1,000 and £10,000. In July 2013, the upper limit was increased to £25,000. Amendments in October 2014 and April 2015 regulated medical fees and confirmed that reports should be sourced through approved Association of Medical Reporting Experts (AMRO) experts. The costs permitted within the process have also been amended and reduced, and success fees not permitted after April 2013.

Whiplash defined

The Protocol (RTA PAP 1.1 (16A)) defines a soft tissue injury claim as:

> “a claim brought by an occupant of a motor vehicle where the significant physical injury caused is a soft tissue injury and includes claims where there is a minor psychological injury secondary in significance to the physical injury.”

Stage 1: claim notification

Table 24.1 – Stage 1: claim notification

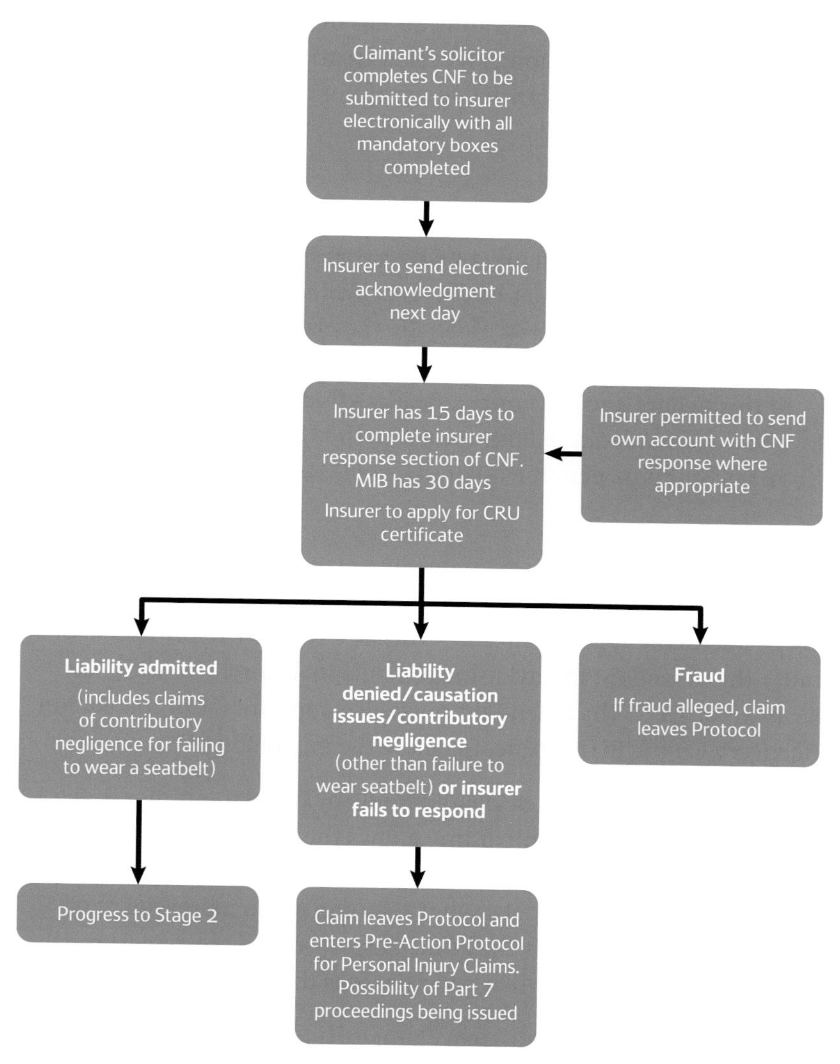

Notification

The claimant should complete all mandatory fields in the claim notification form (CNF), including details of injury, time off work and, if the absence is ongoing, whether treatment was sought. The defendant must acknowledge receipt of the CNF the next business day.

> The claimant must make a reasonable attempt to complete the CNF. If the defendant considers that inadequate mandatory information has been provided, that will be a valid reason for the defendant to decide the claim should leave the process (if the defendant wishes to exercise that option). If this occurs and the court considers that the claimant provided inadequate information in the CNF, the claimant may incur cost penalties (Part 45.24 of the CPR).

Where an admission is made, unless the claimant is a child, the defendant must pay Stage 1 fixed costs within 10 days of receiving the Stage 2 settlement pack (Part 45.18 of the CPR). The court may also order the defendant to pay disbursements in accordance with Part 45.19 of the CPR. The defendant must also apply for a Compensation Recovery Unit (CRU) certificate before the end of Stage 1.

Failure to ensure receipt of cleared funds by the claimant for Stage 1 fixed costs within that time frame allows the claimant to give notice to exit the Protocol. The claimant may attempt to argue that the claim is out of the Protocol so that they can claim increased fixed costs. However, to do this they must serve written notice within 10 days after the last date when payment was due.

Other reasons that will lead to a claim exiting the Protocol are:

- The defendant does not respond within 15 business days.
- Liability is denied.
- Contributory negligence is alleged for anything other than failing to wear a seatbelt.

There is no opportunity to re-enter the Stage 1 process once the claim leaves it, unless the claimant has sent the CNF to the wrong insurer and the process has to commence again. Any claim that falls out of the Protocol at Stage 1 should proceed under the existing Pre-Action Protocol for Personal Injury Claims. The three-month investigation period should be calculated from the date of the CNF, assuming that sufficient information was provided for it to be treated as a letter of claim.

> It is important for the defendant to keep copies of an inadequate CNF (and any associated documentation). Should the claim proceed to be litigated, such information may well support a defence that the claim was suitable to be resolved in the Protocol and that the claimant costs should be limited to those permitted in the portal.

Children

Claimants' solicitors must ensure that the person providing instructions on behalf of a child is an 'appropriate person' and the CNF must state if the claim is for an injury to a child or an adult.

Note that there is no provision for an interim payment to be made to a child under the age of 18 years. If there is a reasonable requirement for an interim payment, Part 7 proceedings must be commenced, accompanied by an application for an interim payment. If the court does not approve the award, the claim will exit the process. The hearing fee will then form part of the costs to be recovered by the claimant at the conclusion of the matter.

Decision on liability in absence of instructions

The period of 15 days to determine liability within Stage 1 is particularly tight. Where it is not possible to obtain instructions from the insured in time, careful consideration needs to be given if conceding liability.

Remember: conceding liability could affect the insured in relation to any uninsured loss claim they wish to pursue.

Contributory negligence: non-seatbelt related

Where liability is admitted within the 15-day time period, the defendant must, in the response section of the CNF, set out reasons for alleging contributory negligence. The claim will then leave the Protocol.

Contributory negligence: seatbelt related

If the claimant completes the CNF and admits to not wearing a seatbelt, the claim will remain in the process if liability is admitted within 15 days (at Stage 1). The defendant must then, in the Stage 2 settlement pack, suggest a percentage reduction in respect of the seatbelt issue.

Defendant's account

When denying liability, the defendant must give brief reasons in the CNF response. The claim should then proceed under the Pre-Action Protocol for Personal Injury Claims, which provides the defendant with three months to investigate liability. Tactically, it is prudent to allow the claim to simply time out of the portal process, thereby allowing the defendant a full three months to investigate liability and present a detailed liability position outside the restrictions of the portal.

The claimant must provide the account as part of the instructions to the medical expert for the sole purpose of asking the expert to comment on the impact, if any, on diagnosis and prognosis if either the claimant's or insurer's account is found to be true. There is also the opportunity for the defendant to provide their account to the medical expert, should they believe the accident circumstances give rise to an issue around contributory negligence. Again, in practice, most insurers choose not to provide any additional information.

If liability is admitted, the claim progresses to Stage 2.

Signatures

The statement of truth in the CNF must be signed by the claimant or by their legal representative where the claimant has authorised the legal representative to do so. It will be the responsibility of the claimant's legal representative to ensure that the CNF has been approved and to retain evidence of this. The electronic copy will simply have a confirmation on it to be completed by the claimant's solicitor as to its accuracy.

Stage 2: settlement pack

Table 24.2 – Stage 2: settlement pack

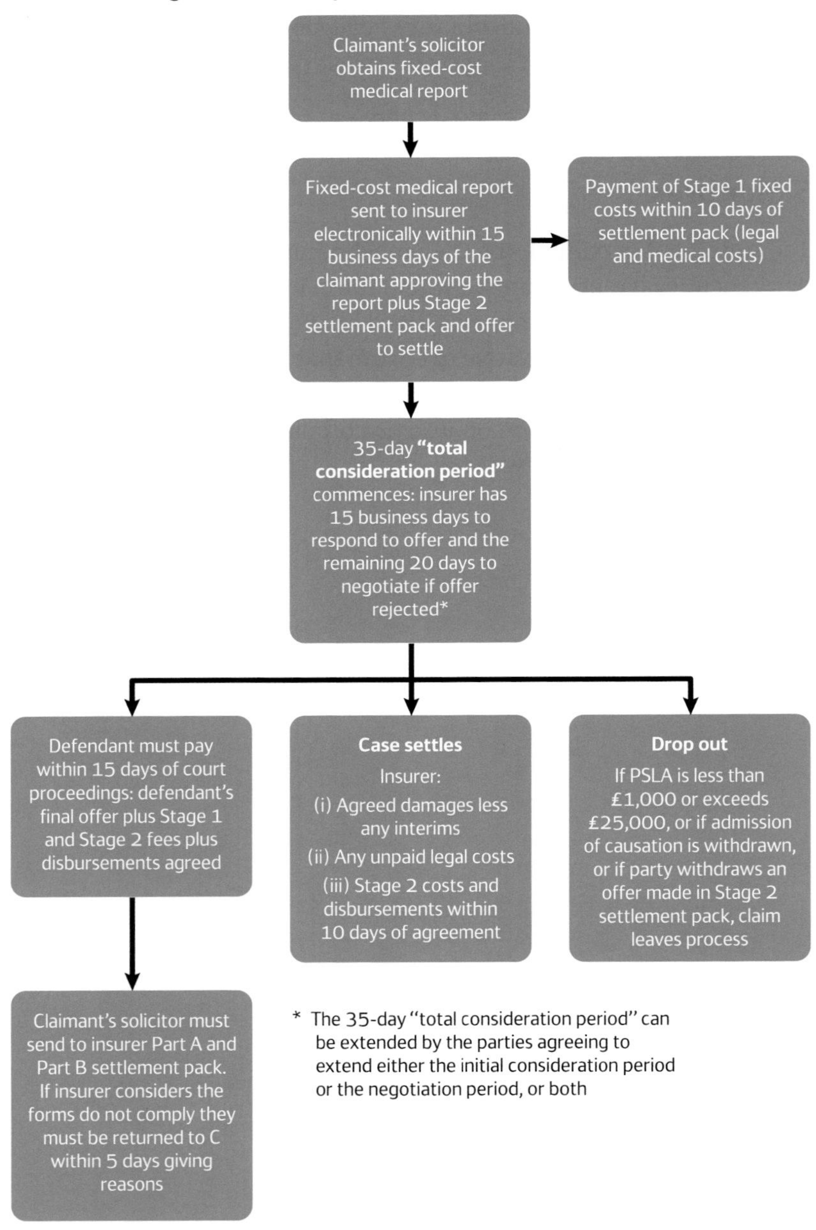

Claimant's solicitor obtains fixed-cost medical report
Fixed-cost medical report sent to insurer electronically within 15 business days of the claimant approving the report plus Stage 2 settlement pack and offer to settle
Payment of Stage 1 fixed costs within 10 days of settlement pack (legal and medical costs)
35-day "total consideration period" commences: insurer has 15 business days to respond to offer and the remaining 20 days to negotiate if offer rejected*
Defendant must pay within 15 days of court proceedings: defendant's final offer plus Stage 1 and Stage 2 fees plus disbursements agreed
Case settles
Insurer:
(i) Agreed damages less any interims
(ii) Any unpaid legal costs
(iii) Stage 2 costs and disbursements within 10 days of agreement
Drop out
If PSLA is less than £1,000 or exceeds £25,000, or if admission of causation is withdrawn, or if party withdraws an offer made in Stage 2 settlement pack, claim leaves process
Claimant's solicitor must send to insurer Part A and Part B settlement pack. If insurer considers the forms do not comply they must be returned to C within 5 days giving reasons
* The 35-day "total consideration period" can be extended by the parties agreeing to extend either the initial consideration period or the negotiation period, or both

Stage 2 is the critical stage of the process as it gives the defendant the opportunity to put forward their best quantum arguments in response to the claim. If settlement is not agreed at Stage 2 and the case moves into Stage 3, no further evidence is permitted before the court.

Medical evidence

It is for the claimant to obtain medical evidence and there is no deadline for obtaining the report. The claimant must check the factual accuracy of the medical report as they will not be able to challenge the accuracy of the report after it has been sent to the defendant.

The majority of first reports are from a general practitioner (GP), who is not the claimant's own GP. It is expected that only one report will be required. A subsequent report – whether from the first expert or an expert in a different discipline – will only be justified in "exceptional circumstances" and where it is recommended in the first report and that first report has been disclosed to the defendant.

A number of claimant firms have adopted the tactic of disclosing their medical evidence in one go, even if multiple reports are obtained. There is nothing within the rules that can force a claimant to disclose a report pre-litigation much to the frustration of the defendant.

If subsequent medical reports or non-medical reports are required, the parties should agree a suitable stay.

Save in exceptional circumstances, no medical expert should have a connection with the treatment of the claimant – be it previous or proposed treatment.

The expert must state if medical records have been reviewed. In practice for claims below £10,000 medical records are rarely reviewed.

If the claimant was not wearing a seatbelt at the time of the accident the report must contain sufficient detail of the injuries the claimant has sustained as a result of not wearing the seatbelt to allow the defendant to calculate the appropriate reduction for contributory negligence.

Rehabilitation

The claimant must set out details of rehabilitation in the CNF. The Rehabilitation Code should be considered at all stages of the process.

Witness evidence

In most cases, witness statements are not expected from the claimant or other individuals as liability has been admitted. Only where witness evidence is reasonably needed to value the claim should it be considered necessary, such as a brief statement from a gratuitous carer.

Consideration period

The defendant has 15 business days to accept or reject the claimant's offer (the initial consideration period) or the claim will leave the process and the claimant will be at liberty to commence proceedings under Part 7 of the CPR. If a counter-offer is made the parties have a further 20 days to negotiate. Time periods for consideration of offers can be varied by agreement.

If either party makes an offer with less than five days of the total 35-day consideration period remaining there will be a further period of five days added to the end of the window with the aim of preventing either party being ambushed into settlement.

Defendants should be alive to the possibility of an unrealistic offer being made in the initial consideration period, followed by a sensible offer towards the end of the timeframe, leaving a defendant with only five days for consideration. While negotiations can take place outside the Protocol process (by way of telephone and email), many claimant firms resist any attempt to do so and have a standard practice of requesting "all offers are made within the portal".

Defendants should also be alive to the possibility that experts of various backgrounds may not be properly qualified to comment on whether a claimant has a recognisable psychiatric injury, if they reach that far in their diagnosis.

Equally so, in their diagnosis, such experts may be drawn into mentioning psychological "problems" that do not amount to recognisable psychiatric injury. Doing so may add value to the injury claim.

Additional damages

It is possible for the claimant to introduce claims for vehicle repair or hire between Stages 2 and 3. The Stage 2 settlement period may then be extended by a further 15 days and the claimant has to send an updated settlement pack.

The defendant can then make a further offer. If a sizeable hire claim is introduced the defendant should consider including references to applicable leading credit hire cases and detailed arguments on the relevant points. Or, many insurers prefer to attempt to remove the claim from the portal and accept the higher costs recovered by the claimant for the opportunity to make the detailed credit hire arguments.

If the claimant has indicated on the CNF that a replacement vehicle has not been hired, there is an opportunity for the defendant to intervene by offering an alternative vehicle.

Credit hire

Credit hire claims are included within the portal process, unless there are arguments as to the validity of the agreement when the claim should exit the portal process to allow the defendant sufficient scope to make the more technical arguments.

With large credit hire claims, the claimant may seek to exit the process so that fixed costs will not apply. Clearly, it is in the interests of the defendant to keep the entire claim within the Protocol and to be aware of such attempts.

Reaching settlement

When making an offer, the defendant must propose an amount for each head of claim and, where relevant, must explain why they have offered less than the amount claimed. In essence, the Stage 2 response of the defendant is their counter-schedule, and care should be taken to ensure the response is as detailed as the portal allows. The defendant can exhibit documents in support of any arguments put forward, for example relevant case law.

If settlement is reached the claimant must have actually received cleared funds in respect of the damages (less any deductible amount payable to the CRU and any previous interim payment), plus costs and disbursements within 10 days (plus a 12.5% success fee if under a pre-1 April 2013 conditional fee arrangement (CFA)). Relevant invoices should have been included in the settlement pack.

If the claimant does not receive payment of damages and costs within 10 days, they can make an application to court for payment of the damages and associated costs.

If any party withdraws an offer made in the Stage 2 settlement pack after the total consideration period including any further period agreed, the claim will no longer continue under the Protocol. The claimant may then start proceedings under Part 7 of the CPR.

Sanctions

If the claimant obtains a medical report that is a non-fixed-cost medical report, the cost of that report will not be recoverable and the Stage 2 settlement pack will have no effect (Part 45.19(1) of the CPR). If the claim exits the portal, the court must only allow a fixed-cost report (Part 45.29B of the CPR).

Further, an offer to settle made by either party before a fixed-cost medical report has been obtained and disclosed will have no adverse costs consequences until after the report has been disclosed. This rule is aimed at discouraging 'pre-medical' offers. The proposed 'whiplash reforms' announced in the Queen's Speech in 2017 will prohibit the making of 'pre-medical offers' in any event.

Interim payments

The claimant can request an interim payment of £1,000 by submitting an interim settlement pack and initial medical report in support. Such requests are more likely where the claimant's symptoms are ongoing and a further medical report is sought.

If requested, the payment must be made within 10 days of receipt of the interim settlement pack.

If requesting more than £1,000, the claimant must specify the heads of damage and reasons for the request. Usually, vehicle-related damage will be dealt with outside the Protocol process. However, if the claimant has paid for vehicle-related damage this may be included. The defendant may pay a sum higher than £1,000 but less than requested but must explain why the full amount is not paid. Payment is calculated by deducting any relevant CRU.

If no payment is received within the relevant time periods the claimant can give notice and the claim will exit the Protocol.

Where an interim payment is requested for a child, Part 7 proceedings must be commenced and an application for an interim payment can be made within the proceedings. No payment relating to a child is valid without court approval.

> Where the defendant does not have a CRU certificate that will remain in force for at least 10 days from the date of receiving the interim settlement pack, they should apply for one as soon as possible and make the interim payment within 30 days of receiving the interim settlement pack.

It is possible for more than one interim payment to be requested, but this is rare in practice.

Limitation

Where limitation is due to expire, the claimant can issue proceedings and then request a stay so that the claim can be dealt with within the Protocol. The opportunity to continue to negotiate with the claimant's solicitors within the Protocol and the application of lower fixed costs is appealing, but care should be taken in simply agreeing to the stay.

Many stays are granted for 12 months, essentially providing the claimant with a four-year period to prepare the case. Often the stay will be requested with only the original medical report attached. There is no requirement for the claimant to update the defendant during the stay on what evidence they are obtaining.

As the portal process evolves and the 'book' of claims within the process ages, an increasing number of claims are being presented with a request for a stay.

When the claimant wants to restart the Stage 3 procedure, the claimant should make an application to the court to lift the stay (PD 8B paragraph 16.5). It is the claimant's responsibility to amend the claim form and file related documents with the court. A paper or oral hearing can then take place.

Stage 3: proceedings pack

Table 24.3 – Stage 3: proceedings pack

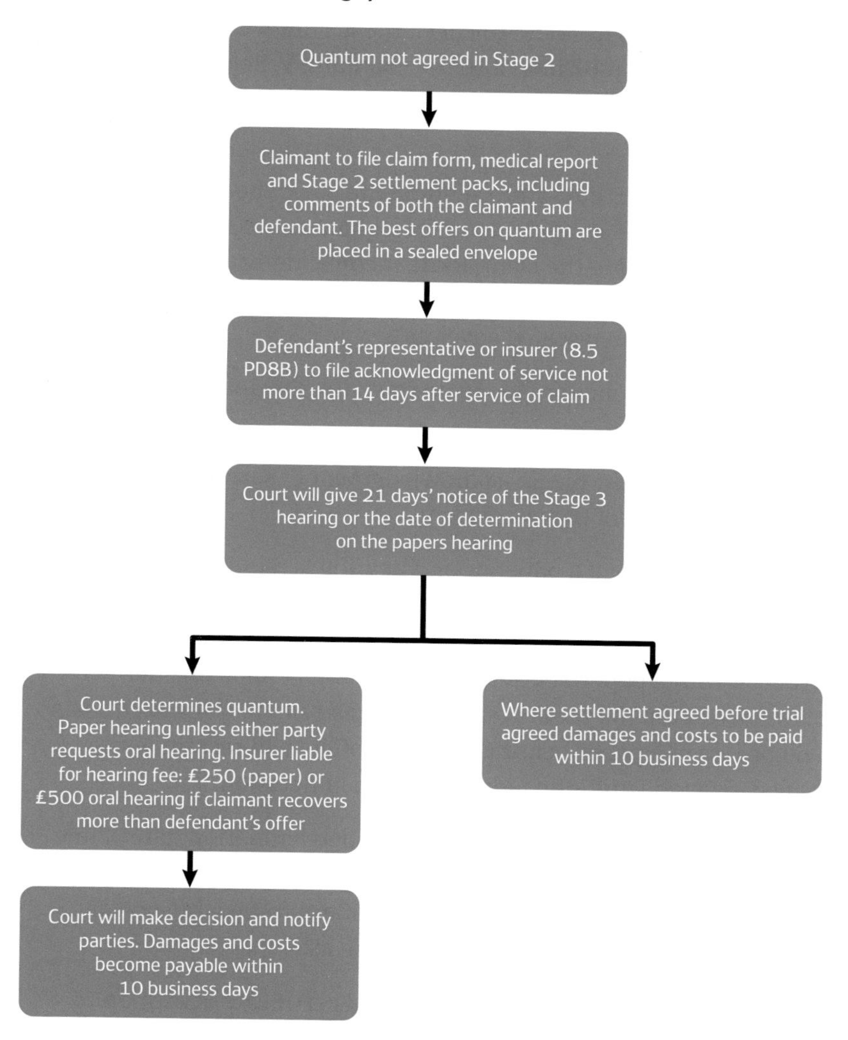

Where the parties do not reach agreement, the claimant must prepare the court proceedings pack (Part A and Part B) form and submit this to the defendant with details of both parties' final offers. The defendant has five days to check the accuracy and provide comments before returning it to the claimant. Where the defendant intends to nominate solicitors to accept service it must do so in the Part A form.

After a period of 10 days from sending the pack, the claimant's solicitor will make an application for a quantum hearing (Part 8 proceedings), filing the claim form, medical report and court proceedings pack at the time of issuing the application. Details of any offers will be in a sealed envelope.

If the claimant's solicitor fails to do this then the defendant may do so.

The defendant must file an acknowledgment of service within 14 days of service of the claim form.

The parties specify if a paper or oral hearing is required in the court proceedings pack (claimant) and acknowledgment of service (defendant). Oral hearings are the norm and if a claimant elects to proceed with a paper hearing the defendant should consider why they have taken the tactical step of doing so as the claimant's costs will be less in a paper hearing. The final offers will remain in the sealed envelope until the judge makes their decision.

The court will give 21 days' notice of the determination date. Some of the North West courts have lengthy waiting lists for hearings with some of the courts popular with the claimant fraternity, such as Birkenhead, having a nine-month waiting list.

The defendant must ensure that the CRU certificate is kept up to date and valid at the time of the final hearing. If further CRU benefits have accrued after the final offer made, the defendant must file a valid CRU certificate at least five days before the hearing date (PD 8B paragraph 11.3).

Does a solicitor have to be instructed at Stage 3?

The rules provide for paper hearings to be handled by the defendant themselves (PD 8.5). The insurer may complete the acknowledgment of service and must remember to ensure it is fully completed with the signed statement of truth.

Appeals

Once the decision is made, if a party wishes to appeal they will have 21 days to lodge an appeal.

Payment

If settlement is not reached, the defendant must pay the full amount of its best offer (less CRU) within 10 days of receiving the court proceedings pack form, together with any unpaid Stage 1 costs, Stage 2 costs and disbursements. The claimant must have received cleared funds by this date as failure to do so entitles the claimant to give written notice that the claim will no longer continue under the Protocol and to commence CPR Part 7 proceedings. If, after the court proceedings pack has been sent to the defendant, but before the proceedings are issued under Stage 3, a settlement is reached, the Stage 1 and Stage 2 fixed costs will also include the Stage 3 Type A fixed costs (£250).

Time period for payments

Reference to a time period for a payment means the time by which the claimant must receive cleared funds. Any failure to pay will give the claimant the right to exit the Protocol. However, unless written notice is sent to the defendant within 10 working days of the breach, the claim will continue under the Protocol.

If cheques are sent by post, then the rules of service dictate that they must be sent out on the eighth day, at the absolute latest, in order to reach the claimant in time.

Claimant fails to follow Protocol

The court proceedings pack form cannot contain anything that was not raised in the Stage 2 settlement pack. If the case is not going to settle, defendants must ensure at Stage 2 that they give full reasons why a head of damage is not accepted or has been reduced, together with all grounds for rejecting/reducing heads of damage, as the court will look at this if the case proceeds to Stage 3.

The rules provide for the claim to be dismissed where the defendant opposes the claim because:

- The claimant has not followed the procedure set out in the Protocol; and/or
- The claimant has filed and served additional or new evidence with the claim form that had not been provided under the Protocol.

If the defendant considers that the court proceedings pack form does not comply with the Protocol, it can be returned to the claimant within five days of receipt with a suitable explanation as to why it does not comply.

However, should the claim be dismissed at this stage, it may leave the claimant open to start proceedings under Part 7 of the CPR. It is prudent to seek guidance in these circumstances to explore whether a challenge is available, including seeking a cost sanction in the form of awarding fixed recoverable Protocol costs only.

A party may seek the court's permission to withdraw a Protocol offer at Stage 3. Permission will only be given on the basis there is "good reason" for the claim not to continue under the Stage 3 procedure. Where permission is granted, the claim will no longer continue under Stage 3 and the court will give directions as to future conduct of the case (PD 8B paragraph 10.1).

Fixed recoverable costs: claims settled within the Protocol

The following table is included in Part 45.18 of the CPR:

Fixed costs in relation to the RTA Protocol			
Where the value of the claim for damages is not more than £10,000		Where the value of the claim for damages is more than £10,000, but not more than £25,000	
Stage 1 – fixed costs	£200	Stage 1 – fixed costs	£200
Stage 2 – fixed costs	£300	Stage 2 – fixed costs	£600
Stage 3 – Type A fixed costs	£250	Stage 3 – Type A fixed costs	£250
Stage 3 – Type B fixed costs	£250	Stage 3 – Type B fixed costs	£250
Stage 3 – Type C fixed costs	£150	Stage 3 – Type C fixed costs	£150

Table 24.4 – Stage 3: Protocol costs

Type		Amount
Type A	Legal representative's fixed costs for the hearing.	£250
Type B	Additional advocate's costs for conducting a Stage 3 hearing.	£250
Type C	Specialist advice required to value to the claim. This will usually be where the claim is valued at over £10,000.	£150

Specialist legal advice on quantum

In some cases additional advice from a specialist solicitor or counsel may be justified where it is reasonably required to value the claim. The claimant can claim an additional fee of £150.

If an offer to settle is made, it will also be an agreement in principle to pay this additional fee. If a need for specialist advice is not accepted, the defendant will have to provide reasons why it is not justified.

The Protocol does not currently define 'specialist lawyer'. However, we anticipate this will relate to the advice of a senior lawyer in cases that involve, for example, care claims or complex loss of earnings claims involving self-employment or loss of pension calculations.

The court has discretion to award the additional fee where the:

- Claim is issued and is resolved at a hearing.
- Court considers that it was reasonable for such advice to have been sought.
- Claimant's solicitor is entitled to costs, where the defendant's offer has been beaten in accordance with Part 36.

Where payment is not made, the claimant will be able to seek a remedy by issuing costs-only proceedings (under Part 44.12A of the CPR) and it will be at the discretion of the judge whether the fee for a specialist lawyer's advice is payable.

Medical costs

With effect from 1 October 2014, the only sums that are recoverable in respect of the cost of obtaining a fixed-cost medical report or medical records are fixed by virtue of a schedule of the CPR (Part 45.19(2A)). The report must be from an accredited medical expert selected via the MedCo Portal.

Table 24.5: Medical costs

Fixed costs in relation to the cost of medical report/records		
Fee for first medical report		£180
Fees for secondary medical report	Consultant orthopaedic surgeon	£420 (*see footnote)
	Accident & emergency consultant	£360
	GP/physiotherapist	£180
Medical records		£30 plus direct cost from records holder (**see footnote)
Addendum report on medical records		£50
Answer to Part 35 questions		£80

* The fee for the secondary report by an orthopaedic surgeon includes the cost of an addendum report on medical records

** Limited to £80 in total for each set of records required

VAT/uplift

The fixed costs included in the tables above are exclusive of VAT.

The claimant is entitled to a 12.5% uplift on the above Stage 1, Stage 2 and Stage 3 Type A costs where the claimant lives or works and instructs a solicitor in London or the following country court districts:

Barnet, Bow, Brentford, Central London, Clerkenwell and Shoreditch, Edmonton, Ilford, Lambeth, Mayor's and City of London, Romford, Wandsworth, West London, Willesden, Woolwich and (outside London) Bromley, Croydon, Dartford, Gravesend, Uxbridge.

Fixed recoverable costs: claims that exit the Protocol

From 31 July 2013, where an RTA claim started under the Protocol leaves the process and moves into the Pre-Action Protocol for Personal Injury Claims, an FRC regime also applies.

The FRC regime applies to matters started under:

- The RTA Protocol – i.e. where the CNF is submitted on or after 31 July 2013 (Part 45.29A(1)(a) of the CPR); or
- The Protocol for Low Value Personal Injury (Employers' Liability and Public Liability) Claims – i.e. where the accident occurs on or after 31 July 2013 (Part 45.29A(1)(b) of the CPR),

but which no longer continue under the relevant Protocol or the Stage 3 Procedure in Practice Direction 8B.

Which cases are not covered?

Industrial disease claims started under the Employers' Liability (EL) and Public Liability (PL) Protocol are excluded from the FRC regime (Rule 45.29A(2)). Such cases that exit the portal will move into standard basis costs.

Medical evidence

The Protocol defines a medical expert as a person registered with the General Medical Council, General Dental Council or a psychologist or physiotherapist registered with the Health and Care Professions Council.

There is no fixed timetable for the claimant to obtain a report. Given the low-value nature of Protocol claims, the initial medical report should typically be provided by a GP. The expectation is that one report will suffice.

A subsequent medical report – whether from the first expert or from an expert in another discipline – must be justified.

If the defendant wants to question or deny causation, the claim will leave the Protocol. Questions can then be put to experts.

Costs of medical records will only be allowed as a disbursement where the medical expert has identified a need for them. If medical records have been reviewed by the expert, the claimant must disclose them with the medical report.

Amount

The regime separates the costs for RTA, EL and PL matters. The costs are fixed for each stage of the claim starting from pre-issue through to trial. Whether the claim settles pre-proceedings or the claimant issues proceedings, recoverable costs are set on the basis of the value of the claim at settlement, based on a fixed value plus a percentage of damages and the stage at which the claim settles (before or after issue).

The following table is in Part 45.29C of the CPR.

Fixed costs where a claim no longer continues under the RTA Protocol			
A. If parties reach a settlement prior to the claimant issuing proceedings under Part 7			
Agreed damages	At least £1,000, but not more than £5,000	More than £5,000, but not more than £10,000	More than £10,000, but not more than £25,000
Fixed costs	The greater of – (a) £550; or (b) the total of – (i) £100; and (ii) 20% of the damages	The total of – (a) £1,100; and (b) 15% of damages over £5,000	The total of – (a) £1,930; and (b) 10% of damages over £10,000
B. If proceedings are issued under Part 7, but the case settles before trial			

Fixed costs where a claim no longer continues under the RTA Protocol			
Stage at which case is settled	On or after the date of issue, but prior to the date of allocation under Part 26	On or after the date of allocation under Part 26, but prior to the date of listing	On or after the date of listing but prior to the date of trial
Fixed costs	The total of – (a) £1,160; and (b) 20% of the damages	The total of – (a) £1,880; and (b) 20% of the damages	The total of – (a) £2,655; and (b) 20% of the damages
C. If the claim is disposed of at trial			
Fixed costs	The total of: (a) £2,655; and (b) 20% of the damages agreed or awarded; and (c) the relevant trial advocacy fee		

D. Trial advocacy fees				
Damages agreed or awarded	Not more than £3,000	More than £3,000, but not more than £10,000	More than £10,000, but not more than £15,000	More than £15,000
Trial advocacy fee	£500	£710	£1,070	£1,705

Part 36

Where a claim exits the Protocol and the claimant accepts a Part 36 offer made by the defendant before the defendant receives a fixed cost medical report, adverse costs consequences will only apply if the claimant accepts the offer more than 21 days after the defendant received the report (Part 36.10A(5A) of the CPR).

Disbursements

Part 45.29I of the CPR also provides for the extent of any disbursements allowed, such costs being limited to:

- The cost of obtaining medical records and expert medical reports as provided for in the Protocol (i.e. fixed medical costs as above).
- The cost of any non-medical expert reports as provided for in the Protocol.
- The cost of any advice from a specialist solicitor or counsel as provided for in the Protocol.
- Court fees.
- Any expert's fee for attending the trial where the court has given permission for the expert to attend.
- Expenses that a party or witness has reasonably incurred in travelling to and from a hearing or in staying away from home for the purposes of attending a hearing.
- A sum not exceeding the amount specified in Practice Direction 45 for any loss of earnings or loss of leave by a party or witness due to attending a hearing or to staying away from home for the purpose of attending a hearing.
- Any other disbursement reasonably incurred due to a particular feature of the dispute.

VAT/uplift

As above, the fixed costs are exclusive of VAT. The claimant is entitled to a 12.5% uplift where the claimant lives or works and instructs a solicitor in London or the following county court districts:

Barnet, Brentford, Central London, Clerkenwell and Shoreditch, Edmonton, Ilford, Lambeth, Mayor's and City of London, Romford, Wandsworth, Willesden, Woolwich and (outside London) Bromley, Croydon, Dartford, Gravesend, Uxbridge.

Tactical considerations

Understated claim

Defendants should be alive to a number of situations where the claimant may attempt to understate a claim. The claimant may, for example, understate the circumstances of the accident in order to secure a denial of liability, only for it to later transpire that evidence was available that would have meant that liability should have been admitted. The claimant will not then be bound by the new fixed-costs regime.

In addition, claims for pain, suffering and loss of amenity that are truly worth less than £1,000 – and therefore not subject to any costs – may be inflated to go through the Protocol.

Objections related to costs should be raised at the earliest opportunity.

Where the claimant reasonably believes that the claim is valued at between £1,000 and £25,000 (and so seeks to pursue the claim through the RTA Protocol), but it subsequently becomes apparent that the value of the claim is less than £1,000, the claimant is still entitled to the Stage 1 and (where relevant) Stage 2 fixed costs.

Fraud

The Protocol makes an attempt to introduce counter-fraud safeguards and thereby overcome the scope for fraudulent claims that the tight timelines, in particular, can create. These include:

- Mandatory provision of full particulars of claim, including personal details of the claimant (as compared to the previous drip-feed of information).
- Provisions of details of passenger claims at the outset.
- Disclosure by the claimant's solicitor of the source of their work, in order to help identify accident management companies.

- Although this is not mandatory, failure to answer this question may give defendants cause for suspicion.
- Requirement at Stage 2 for the claimant to check the medical report for factual accuracy before sending it to the defendant. There will be no further opportunity for the claimant to challenge the report. It is hoped that it will be more difficult for the claimant to provide a convincing explanation in the event that inconsistencies are revealed after disclosure of the medical report.

If there is any concern that a claim is fraudulent, it is advisable to consider removing the claim from the Protocol rather than risk being pressured into making the wrong decision.

Conclusion

The portal works well and enables insurer and claimant lawyers to process claims swiftly with maximum operational efficiency. Insurers should compensate genuine injured claimants quickly to take advantage of cost savings. At the same time, they should be alert to those cases that should, quite properly, exit the Protocol.

The Future

The *Whiplash Reforms* of 2017, as led by Sir Rupert Jackson, have introduced amongst other measures a matrix for low-value whiplash claims. It has been proposed that the matrix would apply for all injuries of less than two years in duration. No practical guidance or draft rules have at the time of this edition been provided. It is clear that to implement the changes there must be an amendment to the existing portal process.

The reforms also propose that for these low-severity whiplash claims the process be made more claimant friendly, enabling lay litigants to progress the claim themselves without the need for the assistance of a lawyer. This will require structural change to the portal process, which is also currently not defined.

25 Low-value personal injury claims: employers' and public liability

Tracy Head

Co-author: Robert Corrigan

- Stage 1: claim notification and defendant's account
- Stage 2: medical evidence, consideration period and reaching settlement
- Stage 2: interim payments
- Stage 3: proceedings pack
- Fixed recoverable costs: for settled claims and those which exit the Protocol
- Disbursements and uplift
- Other basic points: including limitation, success fees and fraud

Low-value personal injury claims: employers' and public liability

Introduction

The Pre-Action Protocol for Low Value Personal Injury (Employers' Liability and Public Liability) Claims (the Protocol) applies to:

- Employers' liability (EL) and public liability (PL) claims valued between £1,000 and £25,000 where the accident occurred on or after 31 July 2013.
- EL disease claims where no letter of claim was sent to the defendant prior to 31 July 2013.

The Protocol poses a number of key challenges for claims handlers. In particular, there are costs consequences of a claim leaving the Protocol. The economics of keeping claims within the Protocol are persuasive – but not always.

The following claims are excluded from the Protocol:

- PL claims against an individual.
- EL disease claims with more than one defendant.
- All PL disease claims.
- Where the defendant or claimant is deceased or is a protected party.
- Where the accident or breach of duty occurred outside England and Wales.
- Abuse, mesothelioma and clinical negligence claims.
- Where the claimant is bankrupt.
- Where the defendant is insolvent and uninsured.

Claims can exit the Protocol in the following cases:

- Damages value increases above £25,000 (before interest).
- Defendant considers that the claim is worth less than £1,000.
- Liability is denied.
- Contributory negligence is alleged.
- Fraud is alleged.
- On failure to meet certain Protocol deadlines.
- Defendant considers that claimant has provided insufficient information on the claim notification form (CNF).
- Defendant withdraws its admission of causation.
- A party withdraws an offer made after the end of the Stage 2 consideration period.

The management of Protocol claims is supported by an online portal system (the portal), provided by Claims Portal Ltd. In other words, the Protocol sets out the process, and the portal is the means by which it is carried out.

The EL/PL Protocol has similarities to the Pre-Action Protocol for Low Value Personal Injury Claims in Road Traffic Accidents – see Chapter 24. For ease of reference, given that claims handlers may deal only with specific types of claims, some issues are covered in both chapters.

The "defendant" is defined in the Protocol as including, where the context indicates, the defendant's insurer or legal representative. This chapter uses the term "defendant", but in practice this will often mean the claims handler with responsibility for the claim at the defendant's insurer.

The definition in the Protocol of "a day" meaning "business day" has also been adopted for the purposes of this chapter.

Stage 1: claim notification

Table 25.1 – Stage 1: claim notification

EL claims

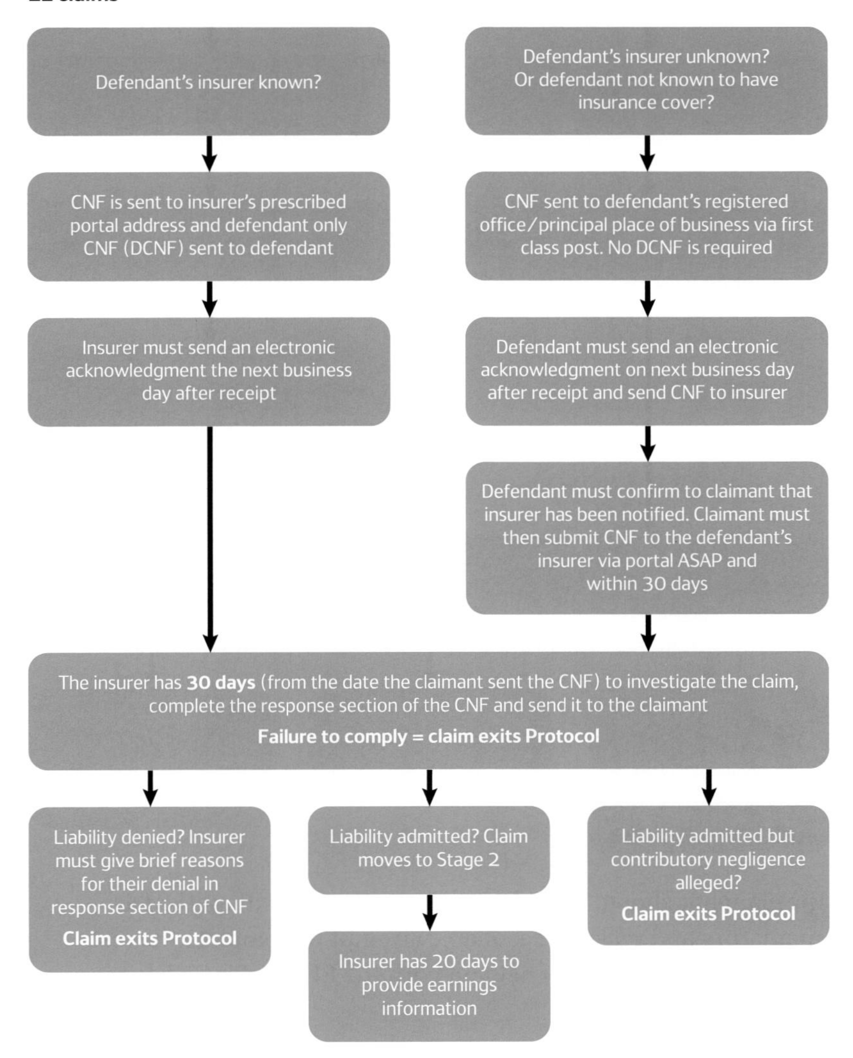

PL claims

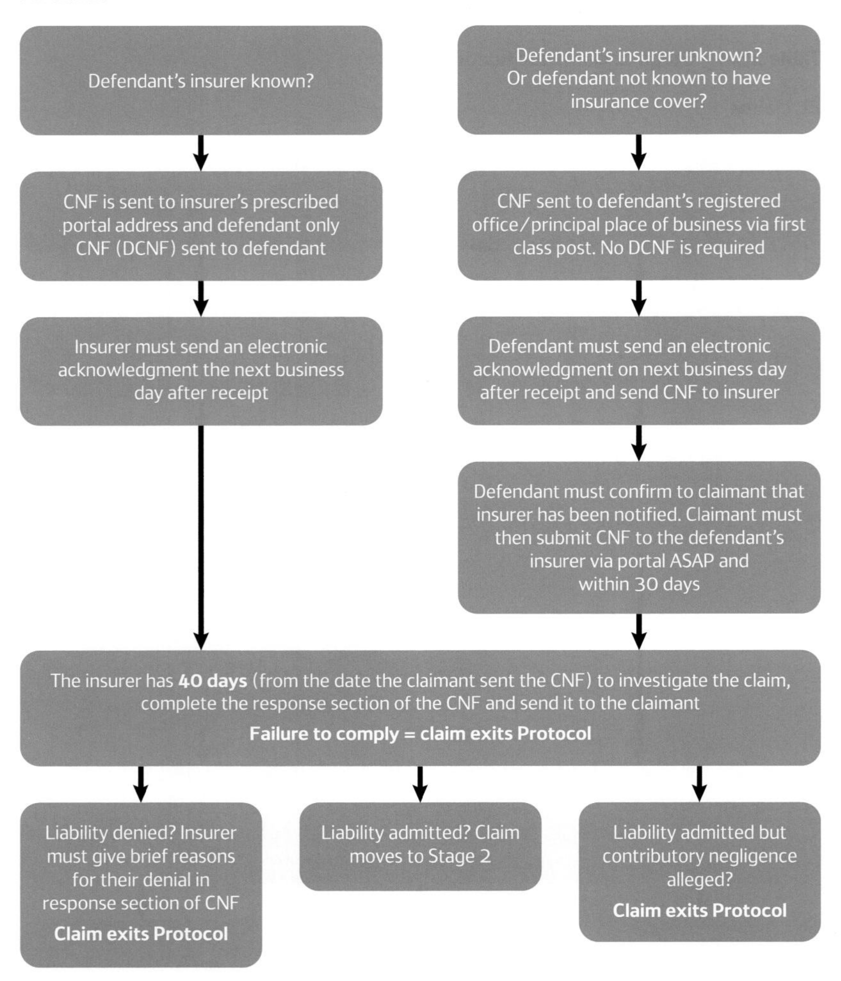

The claimant should complete all boxes in the CNF marked as mandatory and make a reasonable attempt to complete the rest. The only non-mandatory field on both the EL and PL CNF is the defendant's address.

> If the defendant considers that inadequate mandatory information has been provided, that is a valid reason for the claim to exit the Protocol. If the claim exits the Protocol because of the claimant's failure to complete the CNF properly, there is a good argument that the claimant should only be entitled to Protocol costs if the claim subsequently settles outside the Protocol before proceedings commence (Part 45.24 of the Civil Procedure Rules (CPR)). It may, therefore, be sensible to argue that the claim should exit the Protocol for this reason.

In both EL and PL claims the claimant must make a reasonable attempt to identify the defendant's insurer. For EL matters, the claimant must carry out a search through the Employers' Liability Tracing Office.

If the claimant is unrepresented, on receipt of the CNF the defendant must explain to the claimant the period within which a response is required, and that the claimant may obtain independent legal advice.

If a claim exits, it will continue under the Pre-Action Protocol for Personal Injury Claims and the CNF will stand as the letter of claim (unless insufficient information has been provided). The defendant will then have three months from the date the CNF was acknowledged to investigate liability and provide full disclosure in the event that liability is denied.

Claims which exit the Protocol cannot re-enter.

Compliance with deadlines

Failure to comply with the deadlines for investigating and making a decision on liability will result in the claim leaving the Protocol. The sanction for failure to provide next-day acknowledgment of the CNF is not specified in the Protocol. However, case law from before the time of the extended Protocol held that failure to provide next-day acknowledgment does not mean that either the claim exits the procedure automatically or the claimant has the right to elect to discontinue. Should the claimant discontinue, it may put them at risk with regard to costs liability (should they issue Part 7 proceedings) on the basis that their conduct was unreasonable and not in the spirit of the Protocol.

The sanction (if any) for the claimant's failure to resubmit the CNF to the insurer within 30 days where it is first issued to the defendant is also not specified.

> It is best practice to obtain the claimant's BACs details at the offset. This should ensure that the claimant receives any payments within the specified timeframes.

If Stage 1 costs are not paid within 10 working days of receipt of the Stage 2 settlement pack the claimant can give notice of their intention to exit the Protocol. However, if the claimant fails to give notice within 10 days of the expiry of the specified period the claim will continue under the Protocol.

> The defendant must before the end of Stage 1 apply for a Compensation Recovery Unit (CRU) certificate. This ensures that the defendant has a valid CRU certificate when the matter reaches Stage 2. Best practice would be to apply for a CRU certificate after acknowledging the CNF. Given the tight Protocol timescales, there is unlikely to be an opportunity to request a review of the CRU certificate. If the CRU figure is disputed it will probably be better to satisfy the CRU in full and appeal later.

Admission of liability

An "admission of liability" under the Protocol means that the defendant admits an accident occurred and was caused by their breach of duty. The defendant thereby admits that they caused the claimant some loss and damage, the nature and extent of which is not admitted. The defendant must also admit that they have no accrued defence to the claim under the Limitation Act 1980.

> An admission that the breach of duty caused the claimant some loss can later be withdrawn up until the end of the initial consideration period in Stage 2. This is because at Stage 1 (when making the admission), no medical evidence will have been served. It may transpire that, in fact, the claimant did not sustain any injury as a result of the accident, or the medical records reviewed may cast doubt over whether the accident even took place. After the initial consideration period has expired (15 days), the defendant can only withdraw an admission that the claimant sustained a loss with the consent of the other party or with permission of the court if proceedings have been issued.

If a breach of duty is admitted, for Protocol savings to be made it will be important to consider whether alleging contributory negligence is likely to be successful or worthwhile, taking into account the value of the claim. Generally speaking, it will require a successful agreement of 15% to 25% contributory negligence to make dropping out of the Protocol economically worthwhile on smaller claims. This decreases to under 10% contributory negligence for claims worth over £11,000.

While a commercial view may exist for not alleging contributory negligence in some cases due to the cost-to-benefit ratio, one should be alive to the fact that in some cases there may be good reason to argue that contributory negligence should apply, for example, to send a message to an insured's workplace that certain employee practices are not acceptable.

If liability is denied, or contributory negligence is alleged, the claim will exit the Protocol. Therefore, a limited admission, such as "we admit a breach of duty but are unable to admit that the accident occurred as alleged", or admitting "primary liability" will cause the claim to exit the Protocol.

Medical reports

The medical report must be provided by the claimant with the Stage 2 settlement pack. There is no fixed timescale for the claimant to obtain a medical report.

It is anticipated that most claims will be resolved with just one medical report. Indeed, looking to the Protocol for low-value road traffic accident (RTA) claims, there is a specific assumption that only one report will be required. Nevertheless, additional reports may be obtained where the injuries require reports from more than one medical discipline. The claimant must explain in the Stage 2 settlement pack why additional reports were obtained.

The Stage 2 settlement pack should be sent to the defendant within 15 days of the claimant approving the final medical report and agreeing to rely on the prognosis in that report, or any non-medical expert report, whichever is later.

If a final medical report is not served by the claimant with the Stage 2 settlement pack, the parties should agree for the claim to be stayed within the Protocol and reinstated once a final report has been received. If a stay is agreed, the claimant can apply for an interim payment.

Should the claimant seek to obtain a subsequent medical report, the report must be justified, for example:

- The expert recommends further time before providing a final prognosis.
- The claimant is receiving continuing treatment.
- The claimant has not recovered as expected in the original prognosis.

The claimant may also obtain a non-medical report if it is reasonably required to value the claim, for example, counsel's advice.

Medical records

There is no obligation for the claimant's expert to consider the claimant's medical records, but the expert should confirm whether they consider the medical records to be relevant to the claim and whether they have been reviewed. The claimant must disclose any medical records that the expert considered relevant, along with any photographs of the claimant's injury relied on.

Stage 2: settlement pack

Table 25.2 – Stage 2: settlement pack

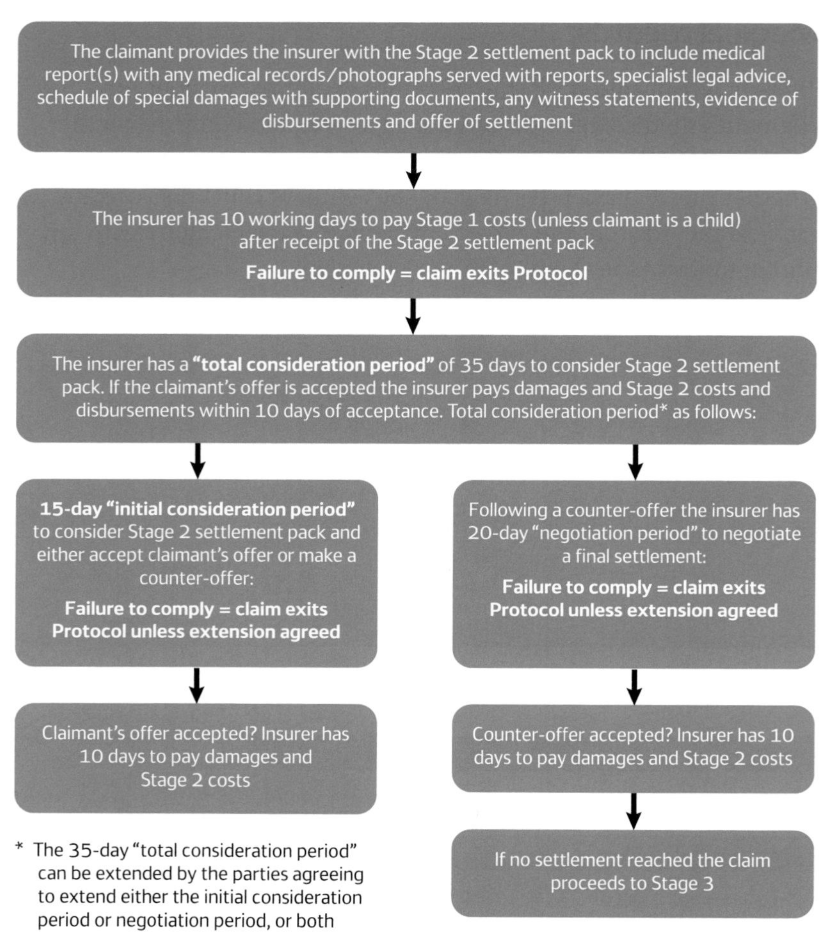

The claimant provides the insurer with the Stage 2 settlement pack to include medical report(s) with any medical records/photographs served with reports, specialist legal advice, schedule of special damages with supporting documents, any witness statements, evidence of disbursements and offer of settlement
The insurer has 10 working days to pay Stage 1 costs (unless claimant is a child) after receipt of the Stage 2 settlement pack
Failure to comply = claim exits Protocol
The insurer has a "total consideration period" of 35 days to consider Stage 2 settlement pack. If the claimant's offer is accepted the insurer pays damages and Stage 2 costs and disbursements within 10 days of acceptance. Total consideration period* as follows:
15-day "initial consideration period" to consider Stage 2 settlement pack and either accept claimant's offer or make a counter-offer:
Failure to comply = claim exits Protocol unless extension agreed
Following a counter-offer the insurer has 20-day "negotiation period" to negotiate a final settlement:
Failure to comply = claim exits Protocol unless extension agreed
Claimant's offer accepted? Insurer has 10 days to pay damages and Stage 2 costs
Counter-offer accepted? Insurer has 10 days to pay damages and Stage 2 costs
If no settlement reached the claim proceeds to Stage 3
* The 35-day "total consideration period" can be extended by the parties agreeing to extend either the initial consideration period or negotiation period, or both

The claimant must check the factual accuracy of their medical report(s) as they will not be able to amend it once submitted. Within 15 days of the claimant confirming that the report is factually correct the report should be sent to the defendant with the Stage 2 settlement pack.

> The defendant should identify in the Stage 2 settlement pack any expert reports or specialist legal advice for which they will not pay and explain why they will not pay for that report or advice. This could include, for example, where specialist legal advice is obtained in a low-value matter (usually under £10,000) and which is considered unreasonable given the simplicity of the issue in question, or where an irrelevant medical report is obtained.

When making a counter-offer the defendant must propose an amount for each head of damage and must explain why they have offered less than the claimant's offer. A counter-offer must state the type and amount of any CRU deductible benefits.

Withdrawal of admission

If within the 15-day initial consideration period (or any agreed extension) the defendant withdraws its admission that the claimant sustained some loss, or considers that if proceedings were started the matter would be allocated to the small claims track, the claim will exit the Protocol. Therefore, on receipt of the Stage 2 settlement pack it is important to check within the 15-day initial consideration period that:

- The claim is likely to be a fast track matter, i.e. the claimant is likely to recover £1,000 or more for pain, suffering and loss of amenity; and
- There are no concerns as to whether the accident in question caused the claimant some loss.

Non-medical expert reports are allowed if reasonably required to value the claim. This is unlikely to be the case for any claims worth under £10,000.

The Part 36 indemnity provisions do not apply in the Protocol. Therefore, if the claim does exit the Protocol it is likely that the claimant will make a Part 36 offer as soon as possible. If the claimant entered into a conditional fee agreement on or after 1 April 2013, this will entitle them to recover a 10% uplift on damages should they later receive judgment of equal or higher value.

Consideration period

Failure to comply with the deadlines within the consideration period will result in the claim leaving the Protocol unless an extension has been agreed. The 35-day "total consideration period" can be extended by the parties agreeing to extend either the initial consideration period or negotiation period, or both.

Within the 15-day initial consideration period and when reviewing the medical evidence, it is important to consider causation and value, and, if necessary, withdraw an admission that the accident in question caused the claimant a loss, or advise the claimant that you consider that the matter would usually be allocated to the small claims track.

Where a party makes an offer five days or less before the end of the total consideration period (including any agreed extension) there will be a further period of five days after the end of the period for the relevant party to consider the offer. During this period no further offers can be made by either party. Tactically, the claimant may make a counter-offer on the last day of the total consideration period (i.e. on day 34, unless an extension has been agreed) to give the defendant minimal time to consider the offer and proceed to Stage 3.

If a party withdraws an offer made at Stage 2 after the total consideration period, or further consideration period, the claim will exit the Protocol and the claimant may start Part 7 proceedings.

Reaching settlement

If settlement is reached, the claimant must receive their damages, costs and disbursements within 10 days of settlement being agreed.

Where the parties subsequently agree settlement for more than the sum offered by the defendant during the total consideration period, or further consideration period, after the court proceedings pack has been sent to the defendant, but before Stage 3 proceedings have been issued, the defendant must pay damages, costs and disbursements under Stage 2 plus fixed late settlement costs under Part 45.23 of the CPR (Stage 3 Type A fixed costs).

If settlement is not reached, the defendant must ensure that the claimant receives the full amount of their best offer (less any CRU repayment) within 15 working days of receiving the court proceedings pack, together with Stage 2 costs and disbursements. Hence, it is important to obtain the claimant's payment details at the outset. The defendant will have 30 working days to make this payment if there are fewer than 10 days on the current CRU certificate. If this is the case the defendant must request a new CRU certificate and advise the claimant that they have done so.

Interim payments

Table 25.3 – Interim payments

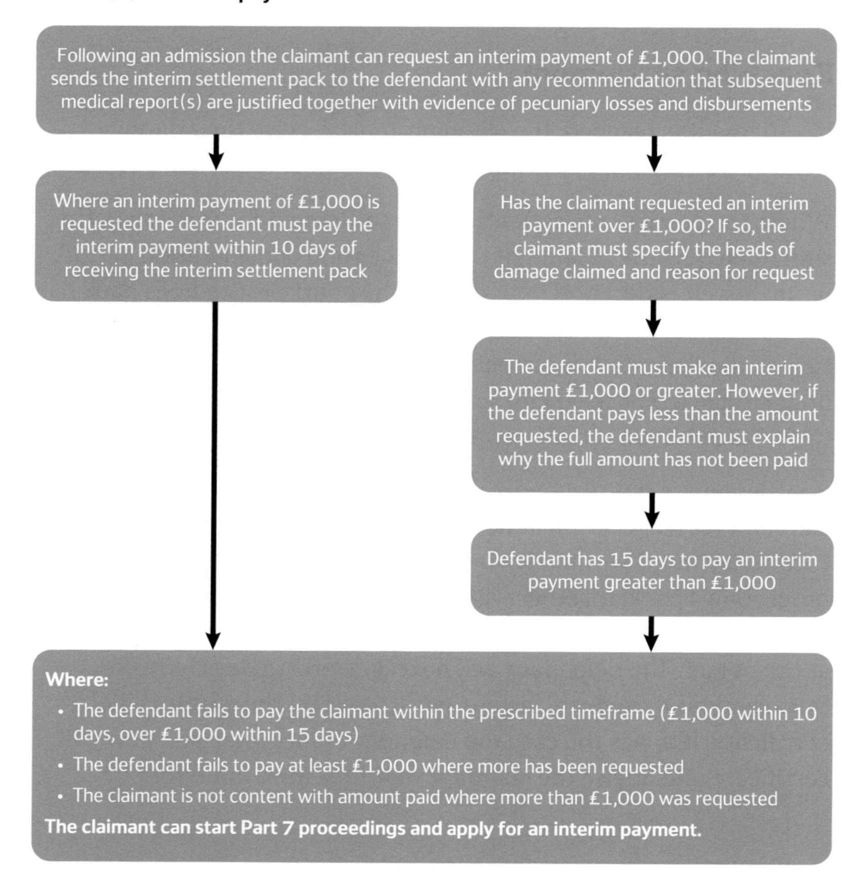

Following an admission the claimant can request an interim payment of £1,000. The claimant sends the interim settlement pack to the defendant with any recommendation that subsequent medical report(s) are justified together with evidence of pecuniary losses and disbursements
Where an interim payment of £1,000 is requested the defendant must pay the interim payment within 10 days of receiving the interim settlement pack
Has the claimant requested an interim payment over £1,000? If so, the claimant must specify the heads of damage claimed and reason for request
The defendant must make an interim payment £1,000 or greater. However, if the defendant pays less than the amount requested, the defendant must explain why the full amount has not been paid
Defendant has 15 days to pay an interim payment greater than £1,000
Where:
• The defendant fails to pay the claimant within the prescribed timeframe (£1,000 within 10 days, over £1,000 within 15 days)
• The defendant fails to pay at least £1,000 where more has been requested
• The claimant is not content with amount paid where more than £1,000 was requested
The claimant can start Part 7 proceedings and apply for an interim payment.

There is no opportunity for the defendant to challenge the claimant's entitlement to a £1,000 interim payment if the claim remains in the Protocol.

The claimant can start Part 7 proceedings and apply for an interim payment if they are dissatisfied with the interim payment made by the defendant. However, the court will order the defendant to pay no more than Stage 2 fixed costs if it does not award the claimant an interim payment greater than that offered by the defendant.

The claimant must give the defendant notice of their intention to start Part 7 proceedings within 10 days of the expiry of the prescribed time limit for the interim payment to be paid: £1,000 requires 10 days' notice and £1,000 or more requires 15 days' notice. If the claimant fails to provide notification, the claim will remain in the Protocol.

Where an interim payment is requested for a child, Part 7 proceedings are required. Any payment to a child requires court approval.

Where the defendant does not have a CRU certificate that will remain in force for at least 10 days from the date of receiving the interim settlement pack, they should apply for one as soon as possible, advise the claimant of this and make the interim payment no more than 30 days from receipt of the interim settlement pack.

Where the claim is valued at more than £10,000, the claimant may request more than one interim payment.

Stage 3: proceedings pack

Table 25.4 – Stage 3: proceedings pack

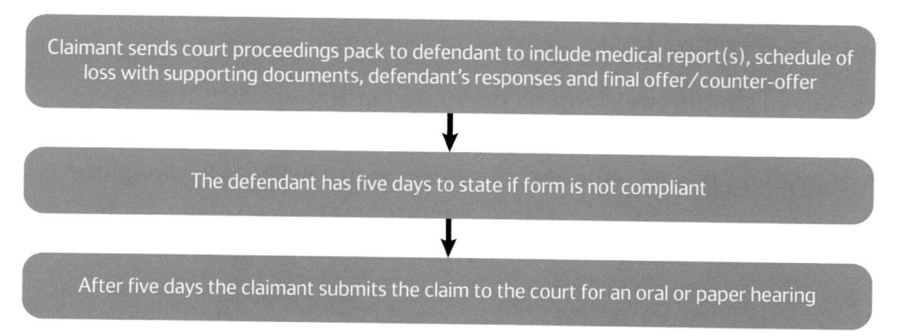

Claimant sends court proceedings pack to defendant to include medical report(s), schedule of loss with supporting documents, defendant's responses and final offer/counter-offer
The defendant has five days to state if form is not compliant
After five days the claimant submits the claim to the court for an oral or paper hearing

Where a settlement is not agreed, the claimant sends the court proceedings pack to the defendant with details of both parties' final offers. The defendant has five days to check the accuracy and provide any comments to the claimant – the Part A and Part B forms of the Stage 3 proceedings pack cannot contain anything that was not raised in the Stage 2 settlement pack.

After 10 days from sending the court proceedings pack to the defendant, the claimant must file the court proceedings pack with the court and make an application for a quantum hearing. Details of both parties' offers will be sent to the court in a sealed envelope.

The defendant will receive notification of the claim and must file an acknowledgment of service within 14 days.

The rules provide for the claim to be dismissed where the defendant opposes the claim because:

- The claimant did not follow the procedure set out in the Protocol; and/or
- The claimant filed and served additional or new evidence with the claim form that was not provided under the Protocol.

If the defendant considers that the court proceedings pack form does not comply with the Protocol, it can be returned to the claimant within five days with a suitable explanation as to why it does not comply.

However, should the claim be dismissed at this stage, it may leave the claimant open to start proceedings under Part 7 of the CPR. It is prudent to seek guidance in these circumstances and explore whether a challenge is available, including seeking a cost sanction in the form of awarding fixed recoverable Protocol costs only.

> A party may withdraw an offer at Stage 3 if there is "good reason" to do so, but only with the court's permission. The claim will then no longer continue under the Protocol and the court will give directions for the future conduct of the case (PD 8B paragraph 10.1).

There is a presumption that the hearing will be a paper hearing unless either party requests an oral hearing. Final offers will remain in a sealed envelope until the judge makes their decision.

The court will give 21 days' notice of the determination date. Once the decision is made, if the claimant wishes to appeal they will have 21 days to lodge an appeal if it was an oral hearing, or 23 days if it was a paper hearing.

Fixed recoverable costs: claims settled within the Protocol

The following table is included in Part 45.18 of the CPR:

Fixed costs in relation to the EL/PL Protocol			
Where the value of the claim for damages is not more than £10,000		Where the value of the claim for damages is more than £10,000, but not more than £25,000	
Stage 1 fixed costs	£300	Stage 1 fixed costs	£300
Stage 2 fixed costs	£600	Stage 2 fixed costs	£1300
Stage 3 – Type A fixed costs	£250	Stage 3 – Type A fixed costs	£250
Stage 3 – Type B fixed costs	£250	Stage 3 – Type B fixed costs	£250
Stage 3 – Type C fixed costs	£150	Stage 3 – Type C fixed costs	£150

VAT/uplift

The fixed costs included in the tables above are exclusive of VAT.

The claimant is entitled to a 12.5% uplift on the above Stage 1, Stage 2 and Stage 3 Type A costs where the claimant lives or works and instructs a solicitor in London, or the following county court districts:

Barnet, Bow, Brentford, Central London, Clerkenwell and Shoreditch, Edmonton, Ilford, Lambeth, Mayor's and City of London, Romford, Wandsworth, West London, Willesden, Woolwich and (outside London) Bromley, Croydon, Dartford, Gravesend, Uxbridge.

Fixed recoverable costs: claims which exit the Protocol

From 31 July 2013, where an EL/PL claim started under the Protocol leaves the process and moves into the Pre-Action Protocol for Personal Injury Claims, a fixed cost regime also applies.

The fixed recoverable costs (FRC) regime applies to matters started under:

- The Protocol for Low Value Personal Injury (Road Traffic Accident) Claims, i.e. where the CNF is submitted on or after 31 July 2013 (CPR Part 45.29A(1)(a)); or
- The Protocol for Low Value Personal Injury EL and PL Claims, i.e. where the accident occurred on or after 31 July 2013 (CPR Part 45.29A(1)(b)),

but which no longer continues under the relevant Protocol or the Stage 3 Procedure in Practice Direction 8B.

Which cases are not covered?

Industrial disease claims started under the EL/PL Protocol are excluded from the FRC regime (CPR Part 45.29A(2)). When such cases exit the portal, they move into standard basis costs.

Amount of fixed recoverable costs

The regime separates the costs for RTA, EL and PL matters and the costs are also fixed for each stage of the claim, starting from pre-issue through to trial. Whether the claim settles pre-proceedings or the claimant issues proceedings, recoverable costs are set on the basis of the value of the claim at issue, based on a fixed value plus a percentage of damages and the stage at which the claim settles (before or after issue).

The following table is included in Part 45.29E of the CPR:

Fixed costs where a claim no longer continues under the EL/PL Protocol – employers' liability claims

A. If parties reach a settlement prior to the claimant issuing proceedings under Part 7

Agreed damages	At least £1,000, but not more than £5,000	More than £5,000, but not more than £10,000	More than £10,000, but not more than £25,000
Fixed costs	The total of: (a) £950; and (b) 17.5% of the damages	The total of: (a) £1,855; and (b) 12.5% of damages over £5,000	The total of: (a) £2,500; and (b) 10% of damages over £10,000

Fixed costs where a claim no longer continues under the EL/PL Protocol – employers' liability claims

B. If proceedings are issued under Part 7, but the case settles before trial

Stage at which case is settled	On or after the date of issue, but prior to the date of allocation under Part 26	On or after the date of allocation under Part 26, but prior to the date of listing	On or after the date of listing but prior to the date of trial
Fixed costs	The total of: (a) £2,630; and (b) 20% of the damages	The total of: (a) £3,350; and (b) 25% of the damages	The total of: (a) £4,280; and (b) 30% of the damages

C. If the claim is disposed of at trial

Fixed costs	The total of: (a) £4,280; (b) 30% of the damages agreed or awarded; and (c) the relevant trial advocacy fee

D. Trial advocacy fees

Damages agreed or awarded	Not more than £3,000	More than £3,000, but not more than £10,000	More than £10,000, but not more than £15,000	More than £15,000
Trial advocacy fee	£500	£710	£1,070	£1,705

Fixed costs where a claim no longer continues under the EL/PL Protocol – public liability claims

A. If parties reach a settlement prior to the claimant issuing proceedings under Part 7

Agreed damages	At least £1,000, but not more than £5,000	More than £5,000, but not more than £10,000	More than £10,000, but not more than £25,000
Fixed costs	The total of: (a) £950; and (b) 17.5% of the damages	The total of: (a) £1,855; and (b) 10% of damages over £5,000	The total of: (a) £2,370; and (b) 10% of damages over £10,000

B. If proceedings are issued under Part 7, but the case settles before trial

Stage at which case is settled	On or after the date of issue, but prior to the date of allocation under Part 26	On or after the date of allocation under Part 26, but prior to the date of listing	On or after the date of listing but prior to the date of trial
Fixed costs damages	The total of: (a) £2,450; and (b) 17.5% of the damages	The total of: (a) £3,065; and (b) 22.5% of the damages	The total of: (a) £3,790; and (b) 27.5% of the damages

C. If the claim is disposed of at trial

Fixed costs	The total of: (a) £3,790; (b) 27.5% of the damages agreed or awarded; and (c) the relevant trial advocacy fee

Fixed costs where a claim no longer continues under the EL/PL Protocol – public liability claims

D. Trial advocacy fees

Damages agreed or awarded	Not more than £3,000	More than £3,000, but not more than £10,000	More than £10,000, but not more than £15,000	More than £15,000
Trial advocacy fee	£500	£710	£1,070	£1,705

Disbursements

CPR Part 45.29I also provides for the extent of any disbursements allowed, such costs being limited to:

- The cost of obtaining medical records and expert medical reports as provided for in the Protocol (i.e. fixed medical costs as above).
- The cost of any non-medical expert reports as provided for in the Protocol.
- The cost of any advice from a specialist solicitor or counsel as provided for in the Protocol.
- Court fees.
- Any expert's fee for attending the trial where the court has given permission for the expert to attend.
- Expenses that a party or witness has reasonably incurred in travelling to and from a hearing or in staying away from home for the purposes of attending a hearing.

- A sum not exceeding the amount specified in Practice Direction 45 for any loss of earnings or loss of leave by a party or witness due to attending a hearing or to staying away from home for the purpose of attending a hearing.
- Any other disbursement reasonably incurred due to a particular feature of the dispute.

VAT/uplift

As above, the fixed costs are exclusive of VAT. The claimant is entitled to a 12.5% uplift where the claimant lives or works and instructs a solicitor in London or the following county court districts:

Barnet, Bow, Brentford, Central London, Clerkenwell and Shoreditch, Edmonton, Ilford, Lambeth, Mayor's and City of London, Romford, Wandsworth, West London, Willesden, Woolwich and (outside London) Bromley, Croydon, Dartford, Gravesend, Uxbridge.

Other basic points

Children

The claimant's solicitor must ensure that the person providing instructions on behalf of the child is an "appropriate person" and the CNF must state if the claim is for an injury to a child.

Where an interim payment is required for a child, Part 7 proceedings must be issued.

The court must approve any settlement agreed in relation to a child.

Claimant's reasonable belief of value of claim

Where the claimant reasonably believes the claim is valued between £1,000 and £25,000 and it subsequently becomes apparent the claim is worth less than £1,000, the claimant is still entitled to Stage 1 and (where relevant) Stage 2 fixed costs. The claim will, however, drop out of the Protocol. It is sensible to be alive to claimants' solicitors seeking to put what are clearly small claims into the Protocol. That being said, it will rarely be economic for defendants to challenge borderline small claims.

CNF

On receipt of a CNF it will be important to:

- Ensure the mandatory fields have been completed by the claimant.
- Form an opinion of the approximate value of the claim.
- Ensure the claim is not limitation barred.
- Check the claimant is not insolvent.
- Check the defendant is not insolvent.
- Check you are the correct insurer for the defendant.
- If the CNF is compliant, register the matter with CRU as soon as possible.
- If the CNF is compliant, obtain the claimant's payment details as soon as possible.
- Contact the insured and advise them of the 30-day or 40-day deadline to provide a response to the claim.
- For EL claims, request the claimant's earnings information from the insured.

Costs of expert medical and non-medical reports and specialist legal advice

Where the claimant obtains more than one expert report or advice from a specialist solicitor or counsel:

- The defendant may at the end of Stage 2 refuse to pay; or
- The court may at Stage 3 refuse to allow the costs of these.

Failure by claimant to provide adequate mandatory information on CNF

Where the defendant considers that inadequate mandatory information has been provided, this is a valid reason for the defendant to decide that the claim should exit the Protocol.

If the court agrees, then it should order that the defendant pay no more than the fixed costs and disbursements that the claimant would have recovered pursuant to the Protocol.

Limitation period

Where limitation is due to expire, the claimant can issue Part 7 proceedings and apply for a stay while the parties then take steps to follow the Protocol.

Litigants in person

The fixed fees are only payable where the claimant has a legal representative.

Part 36

If the matter falls out of the Protocol, tactically a claimant's solicitor is likely to make a Part 36 offer at the earliest opportunity. This is because, in accordance with the decision in *Broadhurst v Tan* [2017], if a claimant 'beats' a Part 36 offer they make on a claim where fixed costs apply, they are entitled to fixed costs up until the relevant stage applicable at the end of the relevant period, and costs on an indemnity basis (on an hourly rate basis) from thereafter. Tactically therefore there is a greater cost incentive than usual on such cases, for claimants to make Part 36 offers.

Specialist legal advice

In most cases, it is expected that the claimant's legal representative will be able to value the claim. In some cases with a value of more than £10,000, additional advice from a specialist solicitor or counsel may be justified where it is reasonably required to value the claim. It is expected that claimants' solicitors will attempt to claim for additional specialist advice on most claims valued over £10,000 as it is unlikely to be economical for a defendant to challenge the justification for providing the specialist advice.

Success fees

Success fees for EL/PL claims submitted via the Protocol are not recoverable from a losing defendant. However, in EL disease claims where the claimant entered into a conditional fee agreement (CFA) before 1 April 2013 that provides for a success fee, a success fee may be recoverable. This, however, is unlikely, as claimants' solicitors who entered into a CFA prior to 1 April 2013 will most probably have sent a letter of claim before 31 July 2013 to avoid the need to follow the new Protocol.

Withdrawal of offer after consideration period

If a party withdraws an offer made in the Stage 2 settlement pack after the consideration period or further consideration period, the claim will exit the Protocol and the claimant may start Part 7 proceedings.

Fraud

The Protocol attempts to introduce counter-fraud safeguards and thereby overcome the scope for fraudulent claims that the tight timelines, in particular, can create. These include:

- Mandatory provision of full particulars of claim, including personal details of the claimant.
- Disclosure by the claimant's solicitors of the source of their work, in order to help identify accident management companies. Although this is not mandatory, failure to answer this question may give defendants cause for suspicion.
- Requirement at Stage 2 for the claimant to check the medical report for factual accuracy before sending it to the defendant. There will be no further opportunity for the claimant to challenge the report. It is hoped that it will be more difficult for the claimant to provide a convincing explanation in the event that inconsistencies are revealed after the medical report has been disclosed.

If there is any concern that a claim is fraudulent, it is advisable to consider removing the claim from the Protocol, rather than risk being pressured into making the wrong decision.

Conclusion

Insurers should compensate genuine injured claimants quickly to take advantage of cost savings. At the same time, they should be alert to those cases that should, quite properly, exit the Protocol.

Substantial savings can be made on claims that would have been subject to assessed costs prior to the Protocol extension. The maximum solicitor's fee (excluding disbursements) now recoverable under the Protocol is £2,100 (plus VAT) where, at an oral hearing, the claimant successfully recovers an award greater than the defendant's offer. This applies even if the claimant recovers the 'specialist advice' fee of £150.

Compare this to a case settled at £20,000 before the extension; the fee payable would likely have been many times this sum, even where an early settlement was achieved. Therefore, insurers should be alive to attempts to remove claims from the Protocol in an attempt to build costs recovery.

Although the Protocol has been in effect for a relatively short period of time, certain behaviours are already being seen that suggest deliberate attempts to exit or avoid the process and, no doubt, seek to enjoy enhanced costs. This includes disease claims that are not currently subject to a fixed costs regime outside the Protocol. Examples of such behaviours include submission of CNFs without completion of mandatory fields, such as national insurance details, or, in the case of disease claim, asserting that there are multiple defendants.

Overall, the introduction of the Protocol means that insurers need to review the way in which claims are handled. There needs to be increased emphasis on the front end of the process, including educating policyholders about the importance of prompt notification.

26 Credit hire

Niall Edwards

- What is a credit hire agreement?
- The Association of British Insurers' General Terms of Agreement (GTA)
- Outside the GTA: entitlement to recover the hire claim:
  - Genuine need
  - Is the hire agreement enforceable?
  - Subrogated claims and insurance
  - Offer of an alternative vehicle
  - Third-party intervention
  - Period of hire and impecuniosity
  - Failure to mitigate
  - Other arguments
- Flowchart for credit hire claims

Credit hire

Introduction

Since the later 1990s, the battle between defendants and the credit hire industry has waxed and waned. The subject is as relevant today as it was 20 years ago.

Recently, credit hire claims have again been very much under the spotlight both in court and, earlier, as part of the Competition and Markets Authority's (CMA) review of the private motor market. The CMA report had very little impact on the motor market but the final implementation of the 'Whiplash reforms' may very well further impact on credit hire claims.

The last year has seen a change, with the higher courts siding with the paying motor insurer rather than the credit hire organisations (CHOs), who have pursued claims for recovery of the credit hire costs as subrogated claims through claimants in civil litigation.

The same year has also seen a number of insurers and then some CHOs unsubscribe from the ABI GTA (see below) and attempt to reach bilateral agreements instead to avoid the significant costs of litigation and further reduce friction and lifecycle in resolving these claims.

This chapter ends with some comment on these recent developments and an overview of the current state of play in relation to credit hire claims. A helpful flowchart of credit hire claims handling is also provided.

At the time of writing, the motor industry is awaiting the final outcome and implications of some recent appeal cases on credit hire and these cases are also mentioned at the end of this chapter.

What is a credit hire agreement?

A credit hire agreement is an agreement entered into between a third party, or their representative, and a CHO.

The CHO provides a replacement vehicle when the third party's own vehicle is damaged in an incident. The period of hire should commence from when the damaged vehicle is being repaired and/or waiting to be declared a total loss.

The vehicle will be provided to the third party on a credit basis. Once the hire period has ended, the CHO will seek to recover the credit hire charges from the at-fault party or their insurer. While the third party is technically liable for the costs of the hire, these charges are never actually paid by them. The at-fault party will pay them directly to the CHO.

A credit hire agreement is not a regulated agreement pursuant to the Consumer Credit Act 1974 (1974 Act). Instead, the normal contractual principles, such as offer and acceptance, apply. The decisive factor is whether the third party has read and understood the terms and conditions of hire.

Resolution of claims

Insurers and CHOs will try to resolve credit hire claims before they litigate, if at all possible.

Prior to litigation, a large number of credit hire claims have historically been dealt with under the Association of British Insurers' (ABI) General Terms of Agreement (GTA). A smaller number of credit hire claims are dealt with prior to litigation outside the GTA because the insurer or opposing CHO, or both, are not signatories to the GTA.

If credit hire claims are litigated, the GTA no longer applies.

Whether a hire claim is dealt with within or without the GTA is significant as different issues will apply.

When considering the benefits of the GTA, the impact of *Stevens v Equity Syndicate Management Ltd* [2015] and subsequent cases should be considered.

In *Stevens* the Court of Appeal held that, in litigated claims, the basic hire rate (BHR) should be based on the lowest reasonable rate quoted by a mainstream supplier. If this decision is consistently applied in the lower courts (as it should be), it will be necessary to review whether proceeding under the GTA is economically sound.

The ABI GTA

The ABI GTA is redrafted from time to time. The latest version of the GTA (at the time of going to print) is dated 13 February 2017 and can be downloaded from the ABI GTA website.

> Paragraph 1.1 of the GTA states:
>
> > These terms of Agreement (GTA) set out the arrangements between subscribers for the provision of replacement vehicles to third party motorists (referred to as customers throughout), and, where appropriate, the undertaking of repairs. Whilst intended to provide comprehensive guidelines, these are entirely voluntary between the subscribers involved, who may elect to un-subscribe from the GTA at any time. The GTA was introduced to promote better communication and settlement and to avoid escalating litigation and legal costs between insurers and CHOs. Over time, and until 2016, it was very much the 'Marmite' solution.

However, as from 2016 insurers can take wildly different views of the GTA. Some are vehemently opposed to it; others are still supporters of it. With proper application and a case management and diary system, insurers can limit escalating costs of third-party credit hire. Conversely, CHOs can have some element of certainty in recovery of credit hire costs, while everyone also avoids costly litigation.

Unfortunately, signatory CHOs often hold the view that insurers abuse the GTA, and vice versa. It can be very lucrative for CHOs to introduce enough uncertainty into a credit hire claim presented under the GTA to allow the claim to slip into the penalty periods (see below) and thus increase their recovery and their profits.

The GTA does not apply when either party (insurer or CHO) is not a signatory. This can be very significant.

The GTA is only intended to apply to situations where a CHO considers the third party has prospects of full recovery against an at-fault driver's insurer. All subscribers are required to follow the GTA in such cases. In all other cases (i.e. those where full recovery is not anticipated), the subscribers may elect to follow the same principles, provided that they comply with the spirit and terms of the GTA, including the application of the relevant settlement rates.

The wording of the GTA changes from time to time. This section is based on the GTA effective 1 January 2013 but revised recently in late 2017. Claims handlers should check that this is still the current GTA.

Where the GTA is applied, it can be used to negotiate:

- Daily rates of hire.
- Hire period.
- Unreasonable delays.
- Class of vehicle (as well as ordinary vehicles; this includes private hire/taxis, motorcycles and commercial vehicles).
- The necessity for a prestige vehicle.

Daily rates and what can be recovered

The applicable maximum daily rates are available on the ABI website. Signatory CHOs can only claim the maximum rates for various classes of vehicle and the signatory insurers need pay no more than those rates (although they may incur additional costs and penalty charges).

Maximum rates are provided for car hire, commercial vehicle hire, private hire/taxi and for motorbikes. Different maximum rates are set for different groups (classes) of vehicle within each category.

The maximum hire rates are reset from time to time. So, for instance, the maximum hire rates for hire agreements entered into on or after 25 May 2016 are different from those entered into before that date. There are several sets of historic maximum rates.

In respect of hires started on or after 15 June 2012, the insurer will pay the CHO a fee of £37 per hire and the relevant daily hire rate, which will be below the maximum rate mentioned above. This fee and lower fees for hires started before that cut-off date are set out in paragraph 5.2 of the GTA.

CHOs can also recover additional charges, on either a daily basis or as a lump sum, for example where the vehicle is an automatic, dual control, for top boxes and panniers, and so forth. These are set out in paragraphs 5.4 and 5.5 of the GTA.

Timeframes: period and delays

The insurer must respond to the CHO's New Claim Advice Form within five days of receipt, confirming the correct handling centre and claims reference number. If an insurer fails to do so, it will be responsible for any delays resulting from exchange of notification documents (paragraph 4.2 of the GTA).

The hire period commences when the third party both needs and takes delivery of the replacement vehicle. Where it is reasonable for the third party to believe that the damaged vehicle is unusable and/ or unroadworthy, but the engineer subsequently confirms the vehicle to be usable, the hire will be paid up to the date the disagreement is resolved.

The hire period should end no later than 24 hours after repairs to the third party's vehicle have been completed (paragraph 4.8).

The CHO should monitor the hire period throughout, and in particular:

- Ensure that repairs have been commenced within three working days of the damaged vehicle going in for repairs.
- Make a further check with the garage after the lesser of five working days or three working days before the hire should have ended (paragraph 4.10).

The insurer should be informed of all "unreasonable" delays. If the repair is further delayed, the CHO should undertake checks every five working days after the original hire period should have ended. Any further delays should be notified to the at-fault driver's insurer (paragraph 4.11).

> An "unreasonable" delay is defined as "delays that are at least two working days longer than expected or over 20% more than the estimated hire period notified to the CHO".

Provided that the CHO has correctly monitored the repairs, it will not be held responsible and the hire period will not be reduced if an engineer fails to liaise with the at-fault driver's insurer if a significant delay is likely for required parts (paragraph 4.13). Consideration may, however, be given to bringing contribution proceedings outside the ABI GTA at a later point (*Clark v Ardington Electrical Services* [2003]).

Where the third party's vehicle is deemed a total loss, the CHO should check, within 10 working days of the hire commencing, that the vehicle has been inspected and an offer has been made to the third party. If an offer has not been made, the CHO should inform the insurer. The 10-working-day period can be extended by up to four working days where the CHO's procedures provide for an offer being agreed with the third party. The CHO should inform the insurer of any dispute on the pre-accident value (PAV) so the insurer can consider appropriate action. The hire may continue until seven calendar days after receipt of the final settlement cheque by the third party. The insurer should advise the CHO, on request, as soon as possible of the date on which the total loss settlement cheque is issued (paragraph 4.14).

Where delays result from the insurer not receiving documentation from the CHO, proof of sending will be accepted by the insurer as the appropriate start date from which penalty payments apply (paragraph 6.6).

Mitigation

The CHO must advise their customers (the third party from the insurer's perspective) of their duty to mitigate their losses before and throughout the period of hire, e.g. an overseas holiday without the need for the hire vehicle. The third party must complete a mitigation questionnaire/statement of truth form as part of the payment pack (paragraph 4.3).

Class of vehicle

The CHO will normally provide the third party with a hire vehicle in the same class as their own vehicle. The insurer must be consulted in the event of a dispute about entitlement. The third party may opt for a higher-class vehicle or an extension of the hire period at their own cost (paragraph 4.4).

Prestige vehicles

Where the vehicle owned by the third party is a prestige vehicle, the CHO should make enquiries with the third party to ensure they have need for such a vehicle. Where the prestige vehicle is over six years old, it is only in exceptional circumstances that a similar prestige replacement is required. Need will be determined by reference to the make, model, value and use of the vehicle (paragraph 4.5).

Payment packs

The CHO must submit a payment pack in support of its payment request to the insurer as soon as full documentation is available.

The pack should include a covering letter that sets out all the charges due, with documentation and supporting evidence. This should include a mitigation questionnaire/statement of truth form signed by the third party, new claims form and hire period validation form, where necessary. If appropriate, an engineer's report, repair authorisation details and details of storage and recovery fees should be included (paragraphs 6.1, 6.2 and 6.3).

Penalty payments

Failure to settle the payment pack within one calendar month of the **full** payment pack being sent to the insurer's correct handling centre will result in increases to the total invoice (paragraph 6.8) (see Tables 26.1, 26.2 and 26.3). However, for hires commencing after 1 May 2016 and settled within that 30 days (just hires, not repairs) a paying insurer should get a 2% discount on the amount claimed (see paragraphs 6.8.3 and 6.8.4).

Table 26.1: Penalty payments for hires that start before 15 June 2012

	Hire	Repair (if included in payment pack)
Up to one calendar month (from date of hire pack being sent to the correct address)	None	None
Between one and two calendar months	7.5% penalty	2.5% penalty
Between two and three calendar months	15% penalty	5% penalty

Table 26.2: Penalty payments for hires that start on or after 15 June 2012 but before 1 May 2016 (there is a discrepancy in the wording of the GTA here)

	Hire	Repair (if included in payment pack)
Up to one calendar month	None	None
Between one and two calendar months	12.5% penalty	2.5% penalty
Between two and three calendar months	20% penalty	5% penalty

Table 26.3: Penalty payments for hires that start on or after 1 May 2016

	Hire	Repair (if included in payment pack)
Within 30 days	Insurer entitled to 2% discount	None
Between 31 and 60 days	15% penalty	2.5% penalty

If an insurer wishes to raise issues on liability between the hirer/claimant and the other driver, notice should be given to the CHO within 21 days of the payment pack being sent to the correct insurer handling centre. CHOs and insurers should aim to resolve liability issues in any event within three months.

After three months from the date the payment pack is sent, the CHO (not the insurer) may elect to deal with the claim for hire outside the GTA and claim a full commercial rate, whatever that turns out to be.

Problems with payment packs and penalty payments

Because CHOs may send payment packs to one of several addresses for the insurer, the insurer needs to be entirely clear about their correct handling centre.

CHOs may miss certain key information from the payment pack. Dates of engineer's inspections and repairs, etc. may, in fact, be contradictory. An insurer should flag any missing information or documentation to the CHO within 30 days of receiving the payment pack. This is critical.

The above penalty payment percentages are not cumulative. Some CHOs may nevertheless add 12.5% to the hire at just over one month and then take that total figure and add a further 15% or 20% after three months. That is incorrect.

More recently, some CHOs (for hire packs sent on or after 1 May 2016) may fail to accept payment 'in full' where a 2% discount is applied for payment by the insurer within 30 days. Indeed the full amount and then with the discount applied may be unclear on the face of the payment pack.

Resolving disputes

The GTA technical committee (which includes representatives from both CHOs and insurers) deals with complaints, addresses bad conduct under the GTA and resolves disputes between insurers and CHOs.

Insurers and CHOs can email conduct issues and complaints to a representative of the technical committee. If a particular CHO is, for instance, continually miscalculating penalty charges or failing to provide a complete hire pack, insurers can log all such behaviour and submit details to the technical committee. This may discourage such behaviour in the future. Unfortunately, the technical committee has no real powers to castigate or penalise insurers or CHOs that continuously fail to comply with the GTA.

Outside the GTA: entitlement to recover the hire claim

The remainder of this chapter addresses claims where the GTA does not apply.

A claims handler should first of all be satisfied that the third party is the registered keeper and/or a registered driver of the damaged vehicle. For example, if a husband was the registered keeper of the vehicle that his wife was driving at the time of the collision, as long as the wife was a registered driver she may bring a claim for the recovery of credit hire charges.

In order to establish who the registered keeper is, a copy of the V5 should be requested from the third party. If the V5 is not produced, it can be obtained directly from the DVLA for a minimal fee.

For the third party to bring a claim for recovery and hire, the damaged vehicle should have been on the road legally at the time of the relevant accident. This can be proved by obtaining from the third party copies of:

- MOT certificate.
- Certificate of insurance (which can be verified by carrying out a Motor Insurance Database search).
- Driving licence.

Genuine need

Need is not conclusive. The third party must prove their need to hire a replacement vehicle (*Giles v Thompson* [1993]). In reality, the burden of proof is easily satisfied.

The third party should complete a mitigation questionnaire to confirm their need for a hire vehicle by reference to:

- Occupation
- Mileage

- Family/personal circumstances
- Social commitments
- Other available vehicles.

When dealing with claims by taxi drivers, a claims handler should request a copy of the licence granted by the local authority authorising carriage of passengers. If the third party does not produce the licence, enquiries of the relevant local authority should be made.

> Also relevant to the question of need is whether the third party has access to any other vehicles, such as family vehicles or vehicles within a fleet/pool. The relevant consideration is whether such an arrangement would cause unreasonable inconvenience to the party who permits use of a vehicle to the third party (*Beechwood Birmingham Ltd v Hoyer Group UK Ltd* [2010]).

For example, consider a wife whose vehicle is damaged and requires repair. The only other family car is her husband's, which he uses to drive to work, and the absence of which would require him to make alternative travel arrangements. It is unlikely to be considered a reasonable sacrifice for him to make to allow his wife to use the vehicle.

Is the hire agreement enforceable?

In order for a credit hire agreement to be enforceable the third party must be made aware of the terms and conditions before they enter into the agreement.

Doorstep Regulations (agreements entered into before 13 June 2014)

The Cancellation of Contracts made in a Consumer's Home or Place of Work etc. Regulations 2008 (Doorstep Regulations) came into force on 1 October 2008 and apply to all contracts with a total payment of more than £35, and set the cooling-off period to a minimum of seven calendar days. If a credit hire company does not comply with these Regulations the credit hire agreement may be unenforceable.

These Regulations do not apply to credit hire agreements entered in to on or after 13 June 2014 when the Consumer Contracts (Information, Cancellation and Additional Charges) Regulations 2013 came into force. For such credit hire agreements the arguments below fall away. Nonetheless, many credit hire agreements that were entered in to before 13 June 2014 may still fall foul of the Doorstep Regulations.

The location where the credit hire agreement is entered into is relevant to determine whether the Doorstep Regulations apply. The Regulations are aimed at traders who enter into a contract with a consumer at their home or workplace. However, they also cover contracts made at another individual's home or on an excursion organised by the trader away from their business premises. The Regulations will not apply if the third party is not a consumer, e.g. uses the vehicle during the course of employment.

The Regulations require cancellation rights to be clearly and prominently displayed in any written contract, or provided in writing if there is no written contract. Failure to do so is a criminal offence (Regulation 7). The notice must:

- Be dated.
- Indicate the right of the consumer to cancel the contract within the cancellation period.
- Be easily legible.
- Contain the information set out in Schedule 4, Part I, and a cancellation form in the form set out in Schedule 4, Part II be provided as a detachable slip and completed by or on behalf of the trader in accordance with the notes.

- Indicate, if applicable, that:
  - The consumer may be required to pay for the goods or services supplied if the consumer decides to have work done, or to receive goods, within the seven-day cooling-off period.
  - A related credit agreement will be automatically cancelled if the contract for goods or services is cancelled.

The written notice must also contain (Schedule 4, Part I):

- The identity of the trader including trading name, if any.
- The trader's reference number or other details to enable the contract or offer to be identified.
- A statement that the consumer has a right to cancel the contract if they wish and that this right can be exercised by delivering or sending (including by email) a cancellation notice to the person mentioned in the next paragraph at any time within the seven-day cooling off period, starting with the day of receipt of a notice in writing of the right to cancel the contract.
- The name and address (including any email address, as well as the postal address) of a person to whom a cancellation notice may be given.
- A statement that notice of cancellation is deemed to be served as soon as it is posted or sent to a trader or, in the case of an electronic communication, on the day it is sent to the trader.
- A statement that the consumer can use the cancellation form provided if they wish.

If the third party is not made aware of the right to cancel in accordance with the Doorstep Regulations, the entire credit hire agreement is unenforceable. However, in this situation, the third party may be able to recover the equivalent of basic hire rates by way of a general damages award (*Wei v Cambridge Power and Light Ltd* [2010]).

Be aware: third-party representatives have developed certain tactics to avoid enforceability arguments. These include the provision of a witness statement to confirm that the third party knew the terms of the agreement and was aware of their right to cancel before they signed the agreement.

Electronic signature of agreements

Many credit hire agreements are endorsed at the time the hire vehicle is delivered to the third party by the third party signing for safe receipt on an electronic handheld device. It is not uncommon for these signatures to be transposed to the relevant signature sections on the credit hire agreement.

The concern here is that the third party has not been made aware of the credit hire terms and conditions before signing the agreement. Even though the credit hire provider will probably argue that the agreement is enforceable because the agreement is signed, was the third party aware of what they were signing?

Indicators of status of the agreement/third-party awareness include:

- Is the signature obviously electronically transposed?
- Do the signatures look identical on the receipt document and the agreement (i.e. consideration of size and matching letter characteristics)?
- Is there a defined shading around the signature?

See *Dixon v Arriva* [2007] and *Tyrell v Staniforth* [2009].

Other discrepancies

Another practice surrounding creation of the agreement is to refer the third party to online terms and conditions. The concern is knowing whether the third party has actually viewed and agreed to these online. There have been cases where the terms and conditions have apparently been agreed by the third party at a location where it is unrealistic or unlikely they would have been. Such a discovery can be achieved by cross-referencing the locations with the unique IP address of the computer on which the terms and conditions have been agreed.

> In addition to obvious geographic inconsistencies, the date and time of the purported agreement should be looked at closely, to ensure that they are feasible.

For example, a third party residing in Newcastle is provided with a hire vehicle from the credit hire provider's Newcastle branch. However, after carrying out a search of the IP address of the computer on which the terms and conditions were viewed and agreed, it transpires that the terms and conditions were in fact agreed to in Plymouth. This is unlikely to be possible unless the third party had reason to be in Plymouth.

The location of the computer by reference to the IP address can be identified by searching for "IP address locator" and using any search engine. However, these searches may not be accurate.

Contractual provisions

While a credit hire agreement is not a regulated agreement for the purposes of the Consumer Credit Act 1974, the normal contractual provisions apply with regard to enforcement:

- Was the third party made aware of the terms and conditions prior to entering into the agreement?
- Did they actually sign it?

If either of these provisions is not satisfied the credit hire agreement is unenforceable.

Public policy

Other situations where a credit hire agreement may not be enforceable relate to public policy issues:

- When the credit hire vehicle is used in the commission of an illegal act.
- When the third party drives their vehicle at the time of the collision without insurance or a valid driving licence. (The third party would still be able to bring a claim for personal injury.)

Subrogated claims and insurance

As with vehicle damage claims, credit hire providers will seek to recover credit hire charges by way of a subrogated claim brought in the third party's name. The right to do so is normally set out in the terms and conditions of hire.

It is now common to have separate insurance premiums in place running alongside the credit hire agreement. These pay the outstanding credit hire charges in full on behalf of the third party, thereby discharging them from liability for the charges. The insurance provider will, in turn, seek to recover this payment from the at-fault party.

> If the existence of a separate insurance policy can be proven, it is a sound way of sidestepping the cancellation notice arguments (*W v Veolia Environmental Services (UK) plc* [2011]).

There is nothing wrong with the credit hire then being paid within and under an insurance policy. Even though the hirer would be fully indemnified for the cost of hire, they would hold that sum for the benefit of their paying insurer (*Bee v Jenson* [2007]). In such circumstances, the hirer is entitled to recover a "reasonable rate of hire", which essentially means a "basic hire rate" (see below).

Where a policy paying off the hire is produced – 'conveniently' – when the enforceability of the hire is challenged, it can be worthwhile to request sight of sufficient policy documentation (the policy paying the hire) to tie the policy to the specific hire agreement, specific hirer and/or specific hire vehicle. If the policy is not sufficiently tied to the relevant hire, it may be ineffective.

Validating a credit hire claim: checklist

There are various steps claims handlers can take to validate a credit hire claim to ensure it is at least arguably viable:

- ✓ Check that the claimant is entitled to recover for the hire.
- ✓ Check enforceability points.
- ✓ Check the "loss of use" dates provided by the CHO – these are all the relevant dates when things have happened and where notifications have been provided surrounding the dates of hire. Loss of use dates that are contradictory or unusual can point to incorrect information from the CHO, a potentially excessive period of hire or even a fraudulent hire.
- ✓ Consider employing engineers to review repair invoices or engineers' reports to check that the period over which repairs were taken was reasonable, or indeed that a third-party vehicle said to be a commercial write-off was one, and was not repairable.

Offer of an alternative vehicle

To avoid the third party incurring credit hire charges, the insurer should be in a position to offer them an alternative vehicle at no cost. The cost to the insurer is likely to be at BHR or less. This is commonly known as 'capture' or 'third-party intervention' (*Copley v Lawn; Maden v Haller* [2009]).

Any offers of an alternative vehicle made by the insurer should be made before the third party enters into a credit hire agreement and should:

- Be in writing.
- Be addressed to the third party and copied to the third party's insurer.
- Be clear as to the cost of the vehicle to the third party as well as to the insurer.
- Be sufficiently clear that the third party can readily compare what is being offered with what it might cost the third party to hire a similar vehicle with a hire company.
- Offer a like-for-like vehicle.
- Be made in a non-threatening and non-aggressive tone.

If a third party fails to consider an offer of an alternative vehicle they risk an argument against them for failing to mitigate their loss. This could include where there are two periods of hire and the offer of an alternative vehicle was made after the first period of hire but before the second.

However, even if the third party has unreasonably rejected the offer, it is likely that they will be able to recover BHRs. Therefore, it is essential that the offer of an alternative vehicle follows the guidance set out above and is made early. In addition, if the resultant credit hire claim is then litigated, the insurer opposing the hire should ensure that they have some good BHRs evidence to hand, even if they succeed in their failure to mitigate loss arguments.

Third-party intervention

To assist in keeping the hire period to a minimum, the insurer can consider whether any intervention by them could assist. The following are examples of where it would be appropriate to intervene:

- Offering to inspect the third-party vehicle at the outset.
- Arranging an alternative garage to carry out repairs, if for some reason the instructed garage is delayed/unable to perform the repairs.
- Offering to source and deliver parts if there is a delay by the repairing garage to obtain parts.
- Offering to provide the third party with an alternative vehicle.
- Arranging a holiday for the third party, which would bring to an end their need to hire an alternative vehicle.

If these attempts are made by the insurer but are not agreed to by the third party, there may be an argument that the third party has failed to mitigate their loss.

Period of hire

The period of hire will have a significant impact on the value of all credit hire claims. Most arguments in relation to the period of hire stem from delays caused by various factors, which can occur in isolation or in conjunction with other reasons, and include delays in:

- The third party or their representative advising the insurer of the collision.
- The third party instructing an engineer to inspect the damaged vehicle.
- The insurer instructing an engineer to inspect the damaged vehicle when the third party has third-party cover only.
- The third party sending the engineer's report to the insurer.

- The insurer sending out payment for the PAV of the damaged vehicle when the third party has third-party cover only.
- The third party authorising repairs.
- Repairing garages commencing work, e.g. due to work backlog.
- Repairs, because of delay in the delivery of parts.
- The third party providing vehicle documents where relevant, e.g. V5, MOT certificate and driving licence.
- The third party collecting the repaired vehicle or signing the satisfaction note.

If it is impossible to show that the third party *personally* (or through their agents) prolonged a period of hire, the insurer is likely to be liable for the whole period of hire. Third parties often rely on *Clark v Ardington Electrical Services* [2003] to argue this point.

Contribution claims

Where it is possible to show that the delay was caused by another party, such as the repairing garage or the credit hire provider, the option of bringing a claim for contribution may be considered.

However, with reference to cases like *Mason v TNT UK Ltd and another* [2009], the cold reality is that it is very difficult, if not impossible, to bring a later contribution claim against a third-party insurer, repairer or engineer who may have caused the period of hire to be prolonged through their actions.

Ironically, in pre-litigation it is often possible to persuade the third-party insurer to agree to a contribution to the total cost of their insured's credit hire where their actions have led to the hire period becoming overly protracted. Not all insurers will countenance this though.

Like-for-like vehicle

A party should be put back into the position they would have been in had the collision not occurred. They will not be entitled to a better class of hire vehicle than their own. For this purpose, reference should be made to the grouping of vehicles within the GTA agreed maximum settlement rates. CHOs follow this structure, but the grouping categories are often labelled differently.

CHOs will sometimes provide a third party with a better class of vehicle than their own but charge at the daily rate for the third party's own vehicle class, which is acceptable practice.

Impecuniosity

The third party must prove that they needed to hire a replacement vehicle on a credit basis and did not have the financial means otherwise to fund the hire of an alternative vehicle.

The burden of proof is on the third party to establish that they were impecunious at the time of the collision and had no other option but to hire a vehicle on a credit basis. However, the insurer has the overall burden of proving that the third party could not have hired at a basic hire rate (*Lagden v O'Connor* [2003]).

> A prudent insurer will recognise that third parties and/or their representatives are not always willing to assist in providing evidence of impecuniosity at the outset. It is, therefore, advisable for insurers to begin shifting the burden of proof to the third party by obtaining BHR evidence early on. This may be by way of Internet rates or a pre-litigation rates report from a preferred rates evidence provider. This report can then also be used for the purpose of litigation and negotiation (if need be).

In order to establish the third party's financial position, the claims handler should request:

- Bank statements, including details of any overdraft facility (ideally for a period three months before and three months after the collision).
- Credit card statements.
- Savings accounts statements (including any joint accounts).
- Details of any loans.
- Wage slips.
- Tax returns.
- Profit and loss accounts.
- Details of any credit reference problems, e.g. county court judgments.
- Details of any unreasonable sacrifice that would arise from hiring at basic hire rates.

Impecuniosity arguments can relate to both the rate and the period of hire claimed. Even an impecunious third party can fail to mitigate their losses in keeping the hire period to a reasonable minimum (*Opoku v Tintas* [2013]). This is especially the case when the total hire claim cost is out of all proportion to the cost of repairs, or the PAV of the vehicle damaged in the accident if it is a commercial write-off.

As long as the insurer indicates whether or not it is going to inspect, and whether or not it is going to fund repairs or a replacement vehicle, a claimant who has the funds to repair or replace their vehicle damaged in the accident must get on and do so within a reasonable period of time (*Umerji v Zurich Insurance PLC* [2014]).

As was pointed out in *Lagden*, impecuniosity and whether or not one is in funds is a question of priorities.

Therefore, for the insurer opposing a hire claim, it makes good sense to take a view on whether to inspect a third-party vehicle or not and confirm the insurer's view to the third party (and whether the insurer can also provide a replacement vehicle) as soon as possible.

Failure to mitigate

The third party is always under a duty to mitigate their loss and this includes both the rate of hire per day and the period of hire then claimed. Examples of ways they can do this are:

- Using public transport.
- Borrowing/sharing a vehicle from a friend or family member.
- Arranging hire at BHRs from providers such as Enterprise, Europcar, Hertz, Avis.
- Using a courtesy car from the repairing garage.
- Continuing to drive the damaged but roadworthy vehicle up until the point of repair.
- Returning a credit hire vehicle while not in use, e.g. during a holiday.
- Hiring a vehicle that is in the same or lower class than the damaged vehicle.
- Giving genuine consideration to offers of a replacement vehicle from all parties involved in the collision and their representatives.
- Responding to all parties involved in the collision and their representatives promptly.
- Ceasing hire promptly when repairs are completed or when the PAV cheque is received.

The failure to do the above can be used to argue that the hire period or rate should be reduced or that the third party should not have hired a vehicle on credit at all.

The *Stevens, Umerji* and *Opoku* cases are all subject to constant challenge in the courts by the CHOs. The CHOs seek to argue that basic hire rates evidence provided by insurers is evidentially insufficient because it does not relate to a sufficiently like-for-like vehicle, is not from a hire company sufficiently local to the claimant or is not comparable as it does not contain similar terms (no excess waiver or reduced waiver or so forth). In other words, the CHOs want the courts to take a very subjective approach.

Case law in 2016 in the lower courts broadly suggests a lack of judicial favour with these arguments but decisions in local courts do vary.

Basic hire rate

If the third party is unable to prove that they were impecunious at the time of the hire, then the appropriate daily rate of hire should be limited to the market rate. This is otherwise known as the BHR (*Bent v Highways and Utilities Construction Ltd* [2011]).

The BHR is the rate at which the third party should have been able to obtain a vehicle on a non-credit hire basis. The appropriate BHR is for the following:

- Like-for-like vehicle
- Hire from somewhere geographically near the third party
- Hire for the same length of time
- Hire at the same date.

As indicated above, in *Stevens* the Court of Appeal held that the BHR should be based on the lowest reasonable rate quoted by a mainstream supplier or, if there is no mainstream supplier, by a local reputable supplier.

While not impossible, it can be difficult to obtain BHR evidence for taxis, motorcycles and commercial vehicles. Again, the above criteria should be applied.

The third party may still be able to recover credit hire rates even if they are not impecunious and can demonstrate there was no other option but to hire on a credit hire basis. Examples would be if they had driving convictions or were under the age of 25.

CHOs have taken to challenging BHR evidence (see above as well) by attempting to introduce rebuttal evidence or by forcing hire rates witnesses to attend court in litigated matters. Again, this has received little judicial favour in recent years but local courts do take markedly different approaches to this tactic as well.

Additional extras

It is not uncommon for CHOs to include additional charges. These may include items such as:

- Collision damage waiver
- Underbody waiver
- Windscreen waiver
- Theft excess waiver
- Young driver excess
- Additional driver surcharge
- High mileage charge
- Satellite navigation charge
- Automatic vehicle charge
- Road tax
- Additional insurance
- Dual control charge (driving instructor).

Assessment of whether additional items such as these are recoverable should be considered on a case-by-case basis. For example, if a third party had an automatic vehicle and was 18 years old at the time of the collision, they will be entitled to recover a young driver's excess and automatic vehicle charge.

However, many of these items are not recoverable under the credit hire agreement and should be removed for calculation purposes, as they constitute additional benefits that can only be seen as betterment.

The situation in relation to additional extras differs from credit hire claims under the GTA where certain additional charges are allowed.

Engineer's fee

Any engineer's fee that is claimed by the third party where the CHO also arranged the repairs is not a recoverable head of loss as it is considered an additional benefit (*Clark v Ardington Electrical Services* [2011]).

Interest

In litigation, and sometimes before litigation, contractual interest and/or statutory interest (if litigated) is claimed on credit hire charges, but is not recoverable. The point is that interest cannot be claimed on charges that are not yet paid (*Pattni v First Leicester Buses Ltd* [2011]).

Tactics

Without prejudice payments

Whether a third-party vehicle is damaged beyond economical repair or is repairable, a without prejudice payment to settle the PAV or cost of repairs should be made in order to cease the hire. These payments should be made even if liability is in dispute, as they can be recovered if the third party admits being, or is held to be, fully or partially at fault.

Review the agreement

The credit hire agreement should contain information about the third party's age, occupation and driving licence endorsements. This information may allow a claims handler to make assumptions in relation to the financial status of the third party and their potential ability to hire a vehicle at BHRs. This should always be clarified by questions to the third party (or their representative).

Offers and interim payments

It is advisable to make offers to settle the third party's credit hire claim as soon as possible. The CHO will often accept a reduced sum to that claimed in total in order to conclude matters swiftly.

In addition, an early interim payment, and offer, towards hire may allow the insurer's solicitors to later argue for a lower court track if the matter then litigates – this reduces the costs that can be recovered in litigation.

With hire claims worth £10,000 or more (which are above the current small claims track limit), it is worthwhile making a Part 36 offer towards the hire claim before proceedings are issued. This will apply some pressure on the CHO to settle the hire claim before litigation.

Obtaining evidence

Any offers of settlement should be supported with evidence from a BHRs provider, Internet research or ABI-based calculations. Obtaining evidence as near to the collision date as possible is important to help ensure accuracy.

In less valuable credit hire claims it is rare for a formal statement on hire rates to be obtained from a hire rates provider. In such cases, insurers tend to instead refer to equivalent hire rates obtainable on the Internet.

Challenging rates evidence

When the third-party representative or CHO presents their own evidence, this should be challenged as soon as possible if there is merit in doing so, and may include challenging the following:

- Independence of the evidence, for example evidence provided by subsidiaries of the CHO.
- Comparability of the evidence, by reference to vehicle class, hire period, location or time of hire.

In court, where the hire rates evidence is critical, the judge will prefer most accessible and most easily understood hire rates evidence. The hire rates that are the most like-for-like, contemporaneous and local are more likely to sway the judge.

Period

A realistic approach should be taken when advancing arguments in relation to the period of hire.

Any arguments challenging the hire period on the basis of delays not caused by the third party directly are unlikely to be successful. If there are arguments that others caused the delay, including the repairing garage, third party's insurer, CHO or accident management company, they may need to be joined to any court proceedings. However, careful consideration should be given before joining others, for reasons of costs, and this should only be done if the delays caused are significant.

Summary and review

The CMA's final report was more aspirational than effective or relevant and the status quo seems to have remained between insurers and CHOs following publication of the report. On the one hand, the CHOs were at first calling on all insurers to join the GTA, and even to help fund a GTA electronic portal. On the other hand, many insurers were hailing the CMA's final report as heralding the final 'death throes' of that same GTA. There has been recent friction between subscribing insurers and CHOs under the GTA such that certain large CHOs and insurers are no longer subscribers and instead have sought to reach bilateral agreements as an alternative means to avoid litigation.

At the time of writing there is also a reasonable possibility of the new government implementing changes to how third-party credit hire claims are resolved through civil reform on the back of the 'Whiplash reforms'.

We await the outcome of the most recent CHO challenges in court to the appeal cases of *Stevens*, *Umerji* and *Opoku*. It is unlikely the CHOs will relent – they are most likely to continue to seek ways of challenging the current raft of cases – of seeking to find reasons to persuade the judiciary to ignore lower or lowest basic hire rates, of seeking to push for sequential exchange of hire rates witness evidence and so forth.

It only seems certain that more litigious CHOs will continue to advance grossly inflated credit hire claims, in terms of both rate and hire. Hopefully, the contents of this chapter will assist in combating such claims.

Flowchart

Table 26.4: Flowchart for credit hire claims

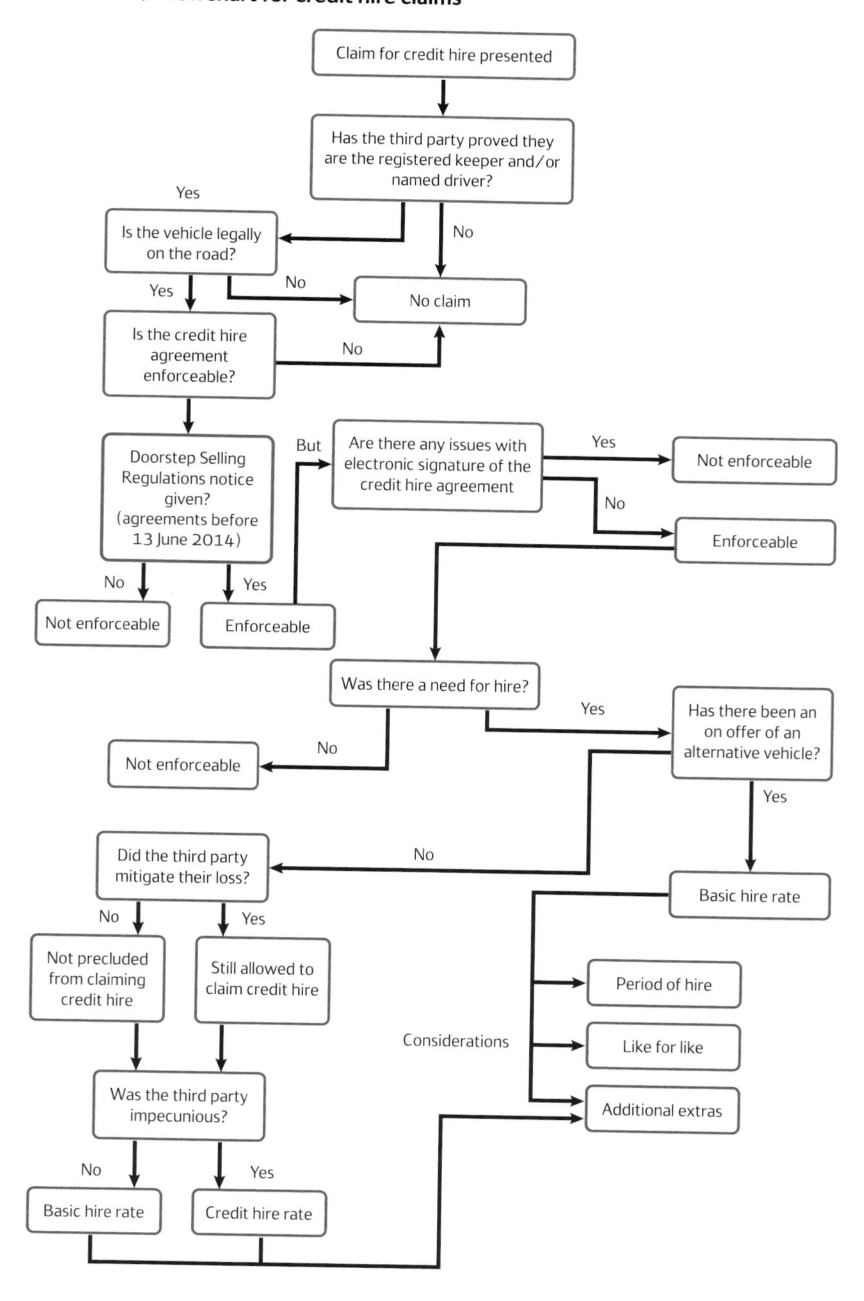

27 Product liability

Shane Sayers

Co-author: Karishma Paroha

- Current law: the PL Directive, EU Directives and the Consumer Protection Act 1987
- Who can be liable?
- Products covered and meaning of defective product
- Criteria for assessing defects
- Defences and limitation
- Pending EU law: Consumer Products Safety Regulations (CPSR) and Market Surveillance for Products Regulations (MSR)
- Recent cases

Product liability

Introduction

Manufacturers increasingly ship products worldwide and their insurance policies cover multi-jurisdiction claims. As a result, there is undoubtedly an increasing number of cross-border and cross-jurisdictional claims being brought against global manufacturers and suppliers. This has been encouraged by legislation, including European Union (EU) product regulation.

This chapter considers the current law applicable to product claims, with particular emphasis on claims in the EU. In so doing, we will consider the European Commission Council Directive 85/374/EEC (the PL Directive) adopted in the various Member States by their own legislation, as well as the Consumer Protection Act (CPA) 1987, which implements the PL Directive.

It is important to note that a product liability claim can be brought under the grounds of contract, negligence and/or strict liability under the PL Directive. However, for the purposes of this chapter the focus is on strict liability product claims only.

Current law

PL Directive

The PL Directive adopted on 25 July 1985 was born out of the Thalidomide tragedy in the late 1960s to provide a new European Community-wide law for consumer protection. Under the PL Directive, a "producer" is strictly liable for personal injury, death or damage to a consumer's property caused by defective products. However, although fault is not a requirement, consumers must still prove defect, injury and a causal link between the two.

Under the PL Directive, an injured person can usually take action against the manufacturer of the product or, in the case of raw materials, the person who obtained them. An injured person can also pursue an action against an importer into the EU and suppliers who put their own name on the product and portray themselves as the producers. The European Court of Justice has ruled that, in principle, liability for defective products, as regulated by the PL Directive, lies with the manufacturer, and will rest on the importer and distributor of the product only in limited cases (i.e. when the manufacturer is not identified). Retailers are not liable unless they fail to identify the producer, importer or 'own-brander' if asked to do so by an injured person.

Under the PL Directive, "product" means any moveable goods or electricity, including items incorporated into something else (whether moveable or not), either as components or as raw materials. Under Article 6 of the PL Directive, a product is defective when it does not provide the safety that a person is entitled to expect, taking all circumstances into account. Article 6 provides three examples that may be relevant to this issue:

- The presentation of the product, i.e. its marketing, description and the information and warnings with which it was supplied
- The use to which it could reasonably be expected to be put
- The time when the product was put into circulation.

The PL Directive provides a limited number of statutory defences. The most important of these is that the state of scientific and technical knowledge at the time of circulation did not permit the producer of the products to discover the defect (known as the development risks defence).

> It is important to note that limitation of liability may vary amongst the EU Member States. For example, in the UK the total liability is limited to €70 million under Article 16 of the PL Directive. However, in Germany it is limited to €85 million.

Other specific Directives

The General Product Safety Directive (2001/95/EC) (the GPS Directive) is intended to ensure a high level of product safety throughout the EU for consumer products. It complements other sector-specific EU directives, such as the Cosmetics Directive (76/768/EEC), Toy Safety Directive (88/378/EEC), Low Voltage Directive (73/23/EEC) and Personal Protective Equipment Directive (89/686/EEC). A more detailed consideration of the GPS Directive is beyond the scope of this chapter.

It is also important to note that, within the EU, medical and pharmaceutical products are subject to extensive and elaborate licensing arrangements. The requirements of individual states in respect of licensing vary considerably. It should be noted, however, that the mere act of obtaining a licence for a product does not make it 'safe' in the eyes of the law. Mere compliance with such a regulation, while indicative of some product assessment, does not preclude, nor limit, the prospects of the claimant succeeding under the PL Directive and GPS Directive.

After obtaining the licence or 'marketing approval', the manufacturer remains liable for the product's continued safety. It is not enough for a manufacturer to consider a product carefully and then market it for a number of years without further review. It is essential that it continues to carefully consider information that is forthcoming in respect of the product. This includes staying up to date on all relevant published studies. In this respect the manufacturer will be assisted and further regulated by a number of government agencies.

UK Law – Consumer Protection Act (CPA) 1987

The PL Directive was implemented in the United Kingdom by the CPA. Part 1 CPA, which is particularly relevant to product liability claims, came into force on 1 March 1988.

In the UK, the supplier must identify the producer within a reasonable period from when the identification request was made.

Who can be liable?

Section 2(2) states that liability for damage may apply to:

a) the producer of the product;

b) any person who, by putting his name on the product or using a trade mark or other distinguishing mark in relation to the product, has held himself out to be the producer of the product;

c) any person who has imported the product into a member State from a place outside the member States in order, in the course of any business of his, to supply it to another.

However, these provisions must be read in conjunction with s.1(3), which states:

> “For the purposes of this Part a person who supplies any product in which products are comprised, whether by virtue of being component parts or raw materials or otherwise, shall not be treated by reason only of his supply of that product as supplying any of the products so comprised.”

Thus, an injured person can usually take action against the manufacturer or the party that obtained the raw materials. An injured person can also pursue an action against:

- An importer into the EU
- A supplier that puts its name on a product and represents itself as the producer.

Retailers are not liable unless they fail to identify the producer, importer or 'own-branding' supplier when asked to do so by an injured person.

Liability under the CPA is joint and several, so a potential claimant can sue all potential defendants.

Products covered

Section 1(2) defines a "product" as:

> "any goods or electricity and (subject to subsection (3) below) includes a product which is comprised in another product, whether by virtue of being a component part or raw material or otherwise."

The CPA applies to all consumer products, including food. It extends to components and raw materials, and it is generally accepted that human blood and blood components are also products.

The definition of "producer" in s.1(2) sheds further light on the meaning of the term "product" under the CPA. It suggests that a product must have been "manufactured, won or abstracted", or that its "essential characteristics [must be] attributable to an industrial or other process". Thus, it is arguable that even human tissues or organs that have been abstracted for transplant or implant may be regarded as products under the CPA.

Meaning of defective product

Section 3(1) states that:

> "Subject to the following provisions of this section, there is a defect in a product for the purposes of this Part if the safety of the product is not such as persons generally are entitled to expect; and for those purposes "safety", in relation to a product, shall include safety with respect to products comprised in that product and safety in the context of risks of damage to property, as well as in the context of risks of death or personal injury."

Section 3(2) identifies other factors to consider, which include:

a) the manner in which, and purposes for which, the product has been marketed, its get-up, the use of any mark in relation to the product and any instructions for, or warnings with respect to, doing or refraining from doing anything with or in relation to the product;

b) what might reasonably be expected to be done with or in relation to the product; and

c) the time when the product was supplied by its producer to another.

Section 3 further states that "nothing in this section shall require a defect to be inferred from the fact alone that the safety of a product which is supplied after that time is greater than the safety of the product in question".

This list of relevant matters is not exhaustive and the courts have wide discretion. They will take into account other factors, including:

- The value of the products supplied
- The availability of alternative products
- The choice of features between competing products
- Relative prices.

For example, a court might be entitled to infer that a more expensive and therefore more heavily researched or tested product is likely to have undergone more extensive safety testing than a cheaper, less sophisticated product. With regard to established, well-known products, the court might well find that the public is entitled to expect a considerable degree of safety.

Criteria for assessing defects

Presentation

This includes the product's get-up, marketing and warnings. The courts will consider how products are marketed, as well as their description and the information and warnings supplied with them. Expectations in relation to safety may be limited to the extent that labelling or public information is made available.

Cigarettes have attracted much attention and, for a number of years, their packaging has incorporated extensive warnings regarding health risks. The courts will take account of:

- The clarity of such warnings and the extent to which they comply with health regulations
- Warnings on packaging produced by other manufacturers, including warnings on packets manufactured by the same company in other countries.

As has always been the case when looking at the question of warnings, the courts will consider the question of how effectively the gravity of the risk is brought to the consumer's attention. For example, if a new type of toothbrush were invented with soft metal bristles that carried a very small risk of causing a life-threatening gum infection, the courts would take into account:

- The way in which the product was advertised and marketed and the extent to which the public might assume from the marketing or advertising that the product was entirely safe.
- The extent to which alternative products could be used. If brushes with ordinary bristles were found to produce very similar results without risk, the court might find the product to be unsafe, given that its use conferred no additional benefit.
- The effectiveness of warnings in relation to the risk.

Assessing the effectiveness of a warning includes considering the extent and gravity of the risk and the way in which the risk is presented. For instance, if reference to a risk were made only in packaging inserts, rather than being explicitly referenced in bold print on the outside of the packaging, a court might be less willing to find that the risk had been sufficiently brought to the public's attention.

Anticipated use

Any use that might reasonably be expected will be taken into account in determining whether a product is defective. For example, if a bottle manufacturer were to produce a bottle of carbonated drink with a stiffly fitting cap, consumers might have to use a pair of pliers or their teeth to remove the cap. Although this might be an obvious misuse of the bottle or the cap, a court might find that the producer should have ensured that the bottle cap was easily detachable. It might even be argued that the manufacturer should have anticipated that the lid might be damaged as a result of efforts to remove it.

Time of supply

Consideration must be given to the date on which a product was supplied. This requirement relates to warnings, indications and other information given in respect of a product. If a product has subsequently been improved or made safer, the court will not take this into account – the concept of "safety" is seen as relative, not absolute.

A product may not be defective if it becomes dangerous only after extensive use or after its reasonable or stated life. In some circumstances, a product that is liable to become less safe with time may be defective when put into circulation, unless it is supplied with an adequate time warning or statement of its shelf life. Thus, a producer is not necessarily liable if a consumer uses a product after its clearly marked expiry date.

Type of damage covered

Section 5 provides that "damage" means death or personal injury or any loss or damage to private property (including land), provided that the amount of loss or damage is £275 or more.

Defences

A claimant must prove that damage has been suffered, that the product was defective and that the damage was caused by the defect. However, a defendant can avoid liability under s.4 if it can show that:

- It did not supply the product to another party (e.g. the product was stolen or a fake).
- The defect did not exist in the product when it was supplied (e.g. the product became defective as a result of the retailer's or user's careless handling).
- The product was not supplied in the course of business (e.g. it was supplied for charity purposes or sold at a car boot sale).
- The defect was caused by the defendant's compliance with the law (in which case the defendant must show that the defect was the inevitable result of such compliance).
- It is a producer of a component and the defect was due to the design of the finished product or to defective specifications provided by the producer of the finished product.
- The state of scientific and technical knowledge at the relevant time was not such that a producer of products of the same description as the product in question might be expected to have discovered the defect if it had existed in its products while they were under its control.

The last of these defences is known as the "development risks" defence and has been examined in a number of leading cases, and is beyond the scope of this chapter.

Limitation

A claimant must issue proceedings against a defendant within three years of the date of the cause of action or the date of knowledge, whichever is later. However, under s.4(2) of the CPA and s.11A(3) of the Limitation Act 1980, a claimant cannot sue under Part 1 CPA if 10 years have elapsed since the defective product was first supplied by the producer.

Pending EU law

In February 2013 the European Commission adopted a Product Safety and Market Surveillance Package (the Package) which was initially expected to apply from 2015. It is unclear when it will actually come into effect due to a deadlock between the European Parliament and the European Council in respect of the issue of country of origin marking of consumer products. The Package includes proposals for new Regulations on:

- Consumer Products Safety (the CPSR), repealing and replacing the GPS Directive
- Market Surveillance for Products (the MSR), replacing previous provisions on market surveillance.

The idea behind the Package is to strengthen the confidence of consumers and businesses in the internal market that products are safe. This would be achieved by providing businesses with "clearer rules, lower compliance costs and more level-playing field for legitimate business". The main areas for revision include new rules for traceability of products, better and more efficient use of standardisation, and better coordination of national market surveillance activities.

Consumer Products Safety Regulations (CPSR)

The CPSR (like the GPS Directive) seek to impose a general safety requirement on all non-food consumer products, with the exception of a specific list of excluded products, e.g. antiques and medicines. The CPSR:

- Seeks to ensure identification and traceability of products by requiring them to be marked with a batch and lot number, the identity of the manufacturer and importer, as well as the product's place of origin.
- Places an obligation on distributors to check that these elements are present on the products.
- Places an obligation on economic operators to keep details of the direct entity above and below them in the supply chain.
- Provides the European Commission with the power to bring in specific product traceability schemes.
- Places a new, and onerous, obligation on manufacturers to draw up technical documentation for their products. This includes undertaking risk analysis and risk management by showing what standards have been applied, what testing methods have been used and what the results were. This technical documentation must then be kept available for the authorities for compliance checks and risk assessment.
- Places an obligation on economic operators to notify the authorities, and take corrective measures, if they have reason to believe that a product they have made available is not safe or is otherwise not in conformity with the legislation.
- Places new obligations on distributors to check the work of the manufacturer or importer and to ensure corrective action if necessary.

Market Surveillance Regulations (MSR)

- The MSR aim to improve cross-border cooperation and action between Member States.
- They codify the powers of the market surveillance authorities and increase their obligations to monitor products to ensure that surveillance is effective.
- Under the MSR, the European Market Surveillance Forum (an overarching guiding body of Member States' market surveillance authorities) will facilitate information exchange and joint testing.
- The Rapid Alert System for dangerous non-food products (RAPEX) will continue under the MSR and will be increasingly used to report all risk types, rather than just significant risks to health and safety.

The overall Package specifically seeks to:

- Enhance the level of conformity assessment of products, via more robust requirements for notification of conformity assessment bodies (including inspection of laboratories, testing, certification and accreditation).
- Improve market surveillance rules to better protect both consumers and professionals from unsafe products (particularly those that can be hazardous to health or the environment), including imports from third countries.
- Increase the credibility of CE marking, by providing a clearer definition for its application and providing CE marking protection as a trademark, which will give competitors and authorities the right to sue where there is misuse.

Manufacturers, importers and distributors are advised to ensure that:

- Their products comply with all requirements under the Package before they are distributed
- They have contracts in place which clearly specify the duties of each contracting party should non-compliance be detected
- They have effective procedures in place to ensure product and component traceability.

Recent cases

Mr Justice Hickinbottom's landmark decision in favour of the defendant in *Wilkes v DePuy International Limited* [2016], where Kennedys acted for the defendant, will provide manufacturers with some comfort that the CPA does not impose a standard of absolute safety where claimants sustain injury and/or damage in all circumstances, for example when, as in the case above, a known but rare side effect or complication arising from the use of a product occurs where that risk had been warned about and the overall benefits outweigh the small risk.

Wilkes involved a claim made by the recipient of a hip replacement who said that part of the prosthesis, the femoral hip stem, was defective under the CPA because it fractured three years after implantation, requiring surgery to remove and replace the prosthesis. It was manufactured by DePuy.

Hickinbottom J said: "In considering whether a product suffered from a defect, the court must assess the appropriate level of safety, exercising its judgment, and taking into account the information and the circumstances before it, whether or not an actual or notional patient or patients, or indeed other members of the public, would in fact have considered each of those factors and all of that information."

He stressed that safety is "inherently and necessarily a relative concept" and there cannot be a "sensible expectation that any medicine or medicinal product is entirely risk-free".

Among the key factors were the regulatory approval, which while not of itself providing a complete or automatic defence, the judge considered to be "powerful evidence that a product provided the level of safety persons were entitled to expect". There was also the risk-benefit analysis that must attach to certain products: i.e. do the benefits sufficiently outweigh the risks? The court also took into account the warnings that were supplied with the product which, crucially, warned of the risk of fracture.

Hickinbottom J concluded that the loading to which the stem was exposed was "clearly greater" than it could withstand, and for which it had been tested, but this was the result of "a constellation of factors, each variable, which came together in a manner such that the neck of the stem fractured".

Crucially, this was not down to a defect in the stem at the time it was put on the market. The claimant had failed to convince the court that its safety was not such as persons generally were entitled to expect.

The court's decision will also guide claimants to consider the merits of claims made against manufacturers of products where those products have obtained regulatory approval and have met appropriate standards, which in turn should reduce and deter the number of speculative claims brought under the CPA.

On 5 March 2015, the Court of Justice of the European Union (CJEU) delivered its ruling on product liability in joined cases, *Boston Scientific Medizintechnik GmbH v AOK Sachsen-Anhalt – Die Gesundheitskasse, Betriebskrankenkasse RWE (Boston Scientific)* following a reference from the Bundesgerichtshof (German Federal Court of Justice).

This judgment is highly important for manufacturers of high-risk products and/or their related components and for their insurers.

The joined cases concerned:

- Pacemakers where the sealing component might gradually deteriorate leading to premature battery depletion, resulting in loss of pacing output without warning.
- Implantable cardioverter defibrillators where a magnetic switch might stick in the closed position and could prevent the treatment of ventricular or atrial arrhythmias.

The CJEU considered whether a person's medical implant could be held to be 'defective', if the product batch had been recalled due to higher than expected failure rates for a specific reason, even if that person's particular implant seemed to be functioning properly. The CJEU held that it could.

This is a landmark decision in that it suggests that a product could be held defective under the CPA even if it has not failed, but is subject to a product recall. In addition, it is evident that the public is entitled to have a very high expectation in respect of their medical implants due to their particular vulnerability.

Mr Justice Stewart delivered a landmark decision in the High Court case of *Allen and others v DePuy International Limited* [2014] for all those engaged in product liability with an international perspective, in which Kennedys represented the successful defendant manufacturer.

Claimants from outside the EU brought claims against DePuy International Ltd for alleged personal injuries arising out of the insertion of prosthetic hip implants manufactured in England. Each claimant alleged that English law should apply to their claims and that they should be entitled to rely on the CPA.

DePuy asserted that the "local law" applied to each claimant, either being the country in which each claimant first suffered their injury, or the country in which the claimant received their implant, none of which were England. The question of when the "event" giving rise to injury occurred arose in each case. The preliminary issues before the Court were:

- Whether the event giving rise to damage to each claimant arose before or after 11 January 2009 (thus falling under Article 31 of the Rome II Regulation).
- If the event occurred before 11 January 2009, what factors should be taken into account when determining the applicable law under the Private International Law (Miscellaneous Provisions) Act (PILA) 1995.
- What law was to be applied to each individual claim.
- If English law applied to any of them, whether the claimants could pursue a claim under the PL Directive/CPA.

The Court held:

- The provisions of Rome II did not apply as all of the claimants had received their prostheses before January 2009.
- The relevant date of the event giving rise to damage was the dispatch of the product from DePuy's warehouse, but if that was incorrect it was the date of original implant operation.

- PILA governed the determination of applicable law.
- The PL Directive and the CPA were not intended to harmonise redress worldwide in respect of products manufactured in the European Economic Area (EEA).
- Manufacturers within the EEA are not liable to consumers suffering injuries outside the EEA under the PL Directive (nor are UK manufacturers under the CPA for injuries suffered outside the UK).
- Accordingly, in respect of individuals who suffer injury outside the EEA, due to a product manufactured in the UK, while they have the right in principle to sue the manufacturer in its home country, even if a court was to decide that English law should apply (as an exception to the general position in PILA or Rome II), there is no right to sue under the CPA.

This decision has far-reaching implications for non-EU claimants, who suffered their injuries abroad but attempt to sue a UK manufacturer in England or Wales.

Kingspan Environmental Ltd and others v Borealis A/S and another [2012] (the "*Borealis* litigation") concerned the sale by Borealis of a polymer product, Borecene, which was used by customers globally for the manufacture of various types of products and by Kingspan for the manufacture of oil storage tanks for domestic and commercial use. Kingspan claimed that the ultraviolet stability of Borecene was inadequate for use in external fuel storage tanks and that Borealis had made misrepresentations in relation to Borecene that had induced Kingspan to purchase the product. Kingspan claimed damages for losses said to arise from the fact that many of its fuel tanks made from Borecene had cracked while in service.

...continued

...continued

The court found in favour of Borealis and dismissed the £101 million claim by Kingspan in its entirety. Mr Justice Christopher Clarke found that the failure of Kingspan's oil tanks in service was the result of poor tank design, deficient manufacturing and inadequate quality control. The judge held that Kingspan had, in effect, caused its own loss. The judge further found that the contractual claim was governed by Danish law and subject to Borealis' standard terms and conditions. In the circumstances, even had Kingspan succeeded, its claim would have been limited to the value of the product purchased by it.

The *Borealis* litigation serves as a reminder for parties involved in product liability claims to streamline the basis of their case and the evidence they are relying on, rather than spreading the net wide and then failing to establish liability.

O'Byrne v Aventis Pasteur MSD Ltd [2010] concerned a claimant who had received a unit of a vaccine at a surgery in November 1992. He subsequently suffered brain damage, which he claimed was caused by a defect in the vaccine. In November 2000, the claimant (suing through his mother and litigation friend) brought a personal injury action under the CPA against Aventis Pasteur MSD Ltd, in the mistaken belief that it was the manufacturer of the vaccine. In October 2002, the claimant brought an action against Aventis Pasteur SA, which defended the action on the grounds that the claim was time barred. In March 2003, after the expiry of the 10-year period referred to in Article 11 of the PL Directive, the claimant applied for an order that Aventis Pasteur SA be substituted for Aventis Pasteur MSD as the defendant in the action begun in November 2000. The question of whether the substitution was permitted came before the CJEU.

In February 2006, the CJEU held that it is for national law to determine the conditions under which one party may be substituted for another party in such an action, but that national courts must have regard to the personal scope of the PL Directive (i.e. with reference to the term "producer" as defined by Articles 1 and 3(1)).

The Court of Appeal ordered the substitution of Aventis Pasteur SA, which applied to the House of Lords requesting that the point be referred back to the CJEU. The House of Lords sought a preliminary ruling from the CJEU on whether it is consistent with the PL Directive for national legislation to provide for the substitution of a new defendant after the expiry of the 10-year period in circumstances where the only person to have been named as a defendant in proceedings instituted within the period does not fall within Article 3 of the Directive.

In December 2009, the CJEU ruled as follows:

- Article 11 does not allow a producer of allegedly defective goods to be substituted as the defendant if the proceedings in question were not issued within the 10-year period against a person that is a producer under Article 3.
- However, if the action is brought against a wholly owned subsidiary of the producer supplying the goods, the national court may find that the supplier must have known the identity of the producer and may treat that supplier as the producer.
- Where a person injured by an allegedly defective product is not reasonably able to identify the producer before exercising their rights against the supplier, the latter is to be treated as a producer for these purposes, particularly if it failed to inform the injured person – promptly and on its own initiative – of the identity of the producer or its own supplier. This issue is for the national court to determine in the circumstances of the case.

Considering the CJEU's second judgment, the Supreme Court allowed the appeal and set aside the order of the High Court.

This case arguably provides UK manufacturers with greater certainty in relation to the period in which they may face liability under the CPA and the PL Directive. It also helps to prevent potential defendant manufacturers from being indefinitely exposed to legal actions for allegedly defective products. Nevertheless, the CJEU has left scope for a UK court to permit substitution outside the 10-year period in certain, admittedly limited, factual circumstances.

Conclusion

The European Commission, in 2006, in its third report on the PL Directive, accepted that the prospect of "total harmonisation" of product liability laws "is not only unrealistic, but also not necessary in view of the limited impact (if any) that its absence would have on the Internal Market".

Despite the fact that the PL Directive achieves considerable harmonisation of the laws of Member States, it remains true that several aspects of product liability-related claims differ under different EU Member States' legal systems, including their litigation practices and procedures in contract, negligence and strict liability. This inevitably increases the complexity and litigation costs of cross-border products claims.

Recent case law under the CPA/the PL Directive in the UK has made it easier for consumers to prove that a product is defective and less easy for a manufacturer to prove the safety of their products. However, there are fewer decided cases in the EU, and those that have been decided demonstrate a more relaxed judicial approach.

> However, the single biggest hurdle that a claimant must overcome is proving causation, i.e. that the damage/injury complained of was caused by the relevant product. This has meant that many claims fail even to commence, notably the failed MMR and organophosphates litigation.

There are also considerable funding problems that claimants increasingly face. Certainly, the funding bodies require a potential claimant to go further in establishing the potential of successfully pursuing a claim than ever before. These funding problems are a happy coincidence for manufacturers and insurers alike. However, where a potential claim looks strong on causation, there are many claimant law firms that are prepared to take claimants on under conditional fee agreements (CFAs), so manufacturers cannot ignore this risk.

Manufacturers should have in place comprehensive risk management procedures/systems. The importance of continuing to invest in research on existing as well as new products is also seen in the case of *XYZ and others v Schering Health Care Ltd and others* [2002], where such research won the case for the drug companies involved.

Consideration should be given to the use of a settlement protocol in the event of an international group action where the employment of this could save manufacturers and/or their insurers substantial time and costs, as well as help to protect their global reputation and profitability.

Considerations for insurers

In light of the increase in the number of product liability claims and their high value, companies may look for their product liability policies to address some of the likely costs they may incur. It is important to keep policy wording and premiums under review. For example, the availability and cost of a product liability policy will necessarily depend upon how well prepared the company is for a product recall. If it has developed a recovery plan and has quality control systems in place it may be entitled to benefit from lower premiums.

28 Travel

Claire Mulligan and Justin Collins

- Package Travel, Package Holidays and Package Tours Regulations 1992
- General liability
- Reasonableness test: local standards
- Defences
- Key issues
- Deaths on holiday

Travel

Introduction

When compared to other areas of liability, such as employers' liability, the prospects of successfully defending a tour operator liability claim are good.

Beware of claimants suggesting that the Occupiers' Liability Act applies to accidents involving tour operators overseas. The Act has no relevance to these claims.

When defending tour operator liability claims, the claims handler should look at the terms and conditions of the holiday contract, the operator's duty of care and whether the Package Travel, Package Holidays and Package Tours Regulations 1992 (the Regulations) apply.

The cases in the highlighted panels below have all been defended by the Kennedys travel team, whether at Kennedys or at a previous firm.

Package Travel, Package Holidays and Package Tours Regulations 1992

The Regulations only govern contracts that are defined as packages.

A package is defined as the pre-arranged combination of at least two of the following components when sold, or offered for sale, at an inclusive price and when the service covers a period of more than 24 hours or includes overnight accommodation:

- Transport
- Accommodation
- Other tourist services not ancillary to transport or accommodation and accounting for a significant proportion of the package.

Initially, there was significant debate as to the exact scope of this definition, until *Association of British Travel Agents Ltd v Civil Aviation*

Authority [2006] settled the debate for good. The Court of Appeal held that the words 'inclusive' and 'pre-arranged' are vital for a package to have been sold.

It is worth noting that:

- The vast majority of traditional package holidays sold by the likes of Thomas Cook and TUI Group are packages because they include transport and accommodation and are sold on an all-inclusive price basis.
- Genuine flight-only arrangements are not covered by the Regulations.
- Accommodation rentals, such as French gîtes or Airbnb, are not covered by the Regulations.

In *Moore v loveholidays.com* [2016] the claimants raised various complaints with the defendant about the quality of accommodation provided by them at a hotel. The claim was defended on the basis that loveholidays.com acted as an agent, as was clearly stated in the booking documentation and their terms and conditions. Evidence was provided of the telephone call in which the holiday was sold by the defendant to the claimant. The court agreed that the Regulations did not apply as the holiday was sold on an agency basis, and the claim was dismissed.

If the Regulations do not apply, the claimant will have to rely on more general areas of law such as the Misrepresentation Act 1967, the Unfair Contract Terms Act 1977, possibly the Consumer Rights Act 2015 and common law breach of contract.

Liability is imposed against a tour operator in three ways:

- General liability when things go wrong
- Descriptions of holidays
- Changes to arrangements.

General liability

Regulation 15 provides that the tour operator is liable to the consumer for the proper performance of the obligations under the contract. This is irrespective of whether these obligations are to be performed by the tour operator or by the suppliers of the services.

It therefore makes no difference whether the breach of contract is caused by the tour operator itself or one of its suppliers, for example, the hotelier. The operator stands in the shoes of its supplier.

A few examples are:

- Food served at the hotel restaurant is of poor quality
- Food served in the hotel causes salmonella food poisoning
- Swimming pool is closed
- Swimming pool is inadequately maintained and the water causes illness
- Customer falls from a balcony when the railing gives way
- Playground equipment has viciously sharp edges, injuring children
- Mildew on the bedroom wall
- Tour operator's representative (rep) fails to do anything about a problem and is completely offhand
- Security guard assaults a customer.

Not all these examples will result in liability on the part of the tour operator. It is necessary to consider the individual circumstances. However, in many cases these examples will constitute improper performance of the contract and the tour operator will be liable, even though in most cases the matters will be beyond its control.

There are, of course, many other suppliers for which the tour operator can be liable, for example, airlines, coach transfers, ski instructors, ski equipment providers, indeed anything that is sold as part of the package. Usually liability for excursions falls outside the Regulations. However, it is necessary to check the terms and conditions in the booking form as some tour operators accept liability for excursions.

Starting point

- The starting point for dealing with any claim is to ascertain the actual obligations under the contract. To do this, the claims handler should read the booking conditions for the actual holiday.
- It is then necessary to decide whether there has been proper performance of these obligations by the tour operator and/or its supplier.
- The standard to apply is the local standard in the country where the accident occurred.

Breach of contract

A tour operator has a non-delegable implied contractual obligation that all reasonable care will be exercised in the carrying out of the services the tour operator is contracted to provide to the customer, provided that the language of the contract demonstrates that the tour operator had undertaken to provide those services.

It is therefore necessary to look at the language of the contract, the brochure and the literature.

This implied contractual obligation is not the same as warranting the consumer's safety; neither is it a contractual duty to ensure that the consumer will be reasonably safe (*Wong Mee Wan v Kwan Kin Travel Services Ltd* [1995]). A term is implied into the contract that services will be carried out with reasonable care and skill whoever carries out the service. This is of enormous benefit for consumers, and has potential application in respect of:

- All forms and modes of transport
- Excursions organised by the tour operator
- Food and hygiene standards.

Reasonableness test

The standard to be invoked in judging whether or not reasonable skill and care has been exercised is the standard applicable at the place of destination, that is, not UK standards.

It is for the claimant to show that the hotel (or other provider of services) did not comply with relevant local standards.

The leading decision in this area is *Wilson v Best Travel Ltd* [1991], which concerned a Greek hotel with glass patio doors fitted with ordinary, not safety, glass. The windows were compliant with Greek safety standards. Despite the claimant's assertion that the hotel should comply with English safety standards in relation to the type of glass used, it was held that the tour operator's duty was simply to check that local safety regulations were complied with.

More recently, in *Lougheed v On The Beach Ltd* [2014], the Court of Appeal dismissed a claim involving a slip on stairs. Lord Justice Tomlinson commented:

> “Standards of maintenance and cleanliness vary as between countries and continents and indeed what is reasonably to be expected in a five star hotel in a Western European capital differs from what is reasonably to be expected in a safari lodge ... An Englishman does not travel abroad in a cocoon.”

In a postscript to his judgment, Tomlinson LJ provides a reminder that holidaymakers can take out travel insurance to insure against the risk of personal injury. He commented that to find against tour operators in claims such as this one would no doubt result in an increase in the costs of holidays.

Examples from the experience of the Kennedys travel team include the following:

- *Codd v Thomson Tour Operations Ltd* [2000] – the claimant sought to argue that a lift in Majorca was not safe because it did not comply with English safety standards. The Court of Appeal rejected this approach.
- *Potter v TUI UK Ltd* [2006] – the claimant slipped and fell on moss on a tennis court in Spain. He alleged that the very presence of the moss proved his case. His claim was dismissed as he adduced no evidence to prove that a tennis court at a private villa in Spain had to be kept to such a high standard that all moss should be removed from it.
- *Dunmore v TUI UK Ltd* [2006] – the claimant, who was 86 at the time of the accident, fractured her hip and leg after falling down stairs in Mallorca. The handrail on the stairs did not extend to the bottom of the steps, leaving at least two steps without a handrail. The claimant failed to prove breach of local standards. In addition, the defendant showed high volumes of guests – over 9,000 a year – with no other reported accidents. Her claim was dismissed.

continued...

...continued

- *Lilley v First Choice Holidays and Flights Ltd* [2008] – the claimant slipped on a wet floor in a hotel corridor where a maid had just mopped. A warning sign was in place. At first instance the judge found for the claimant, on the basis that there were insufficient warning signs and the hotel had not done enough to alert the claimant to the wet floor. The judge regarded this as a breach of the contractual duty to exercise reasonable care and skill. On appeal, the claim was dismissed. The claimant had failed to adduce any evidence of local standards. The court was bound to dismiss the case in the absence of this.
- *Wilson v TUI UK Ltd* [2015] – the claim involved a trip on some stairs/a ramp in Bodrum, Turkey, as the claimant was shown to his room on the evening of his arrival at the hotel. The issues in the claim related to the level of lighting, whether or not there should have been a handrail and whether the bellboy should have verbally warned the claimant of the presence of the stairs/ramp. The claim was dismissed, with the judge finding that the hotel complied with Turkish local standards. The claimant's experts were heavily criticised by the judge.

Defences

Regulation 15 specifically excludes liability in three scenarios:

- Where the failure of the performance of the contract was the consumer's own fault, for example turning up late at the airport or getting drunk and jumping off a balcony.
- Where the failure was attributable to a third party unconnected with the contract and was unforeseeable or unavoidable, for example a motorist driving into the side of a transfer bus from a side street.
- Unusual/unforeseeable circumstances or an event that the tour operator could not prevent.

Where the circumstances were unforeseeable and unusual, the tour operator must also be able to show that the consequences could not have been avoided even if all due care had been exercised.

Foster v My Travel [2006] is an example of a statutory defence being successfully applied. The claimant travelled to Cancun in Mexico. The day after arrival it was clear there was a lot of activity in the hotel, with windows being boarded and furniture moved. They learnt from another holidaymaker that the resort was expected to be hit by a hurricane. The claimant was sent to the local hurricane shelter where he stayed for a number of days. There was a limited supply of food and water, and sanitary conditions at the end of the time in the shelter were appalling.

The claimant claimed the operator should have warned him of the potential of adverse weather conditions before he flew to Mexico so he could decide whether to cancel. Evidence was presented to the court that the hurricane had not proceeded in the way expected. As a result, the impact of the hurricane could not have been foreseen or forestalled and the case was dismissed.

Key issues

A number of issues appear repeatedly in travel law cases, as summarised below.

Alcohol

The consumption of alcohol, often to extremes, plays a part in many accidents and subsequent claims. It is not unusual to find claimants denying that drink was consumed or played any part in their accident.

Medical records from the resort provide useful evidence of alcohol consumption, as do contemporaneous accident reports, bar bills and witness evidence. Of course, in many cases it is difficult to imagine the accident occurring in the absence of alcohol.

> *Martens v Thomson Holidays Ltd* [2001]
>
> The claimant had drunk 21 rum cocktails, as proved by his bar bill. He then decided to leave a campsite, in the dead of night, to find more driftwood to feed a bonfire. He fell down an unguarded well outside the campsite gates. While the well was off-site, and so not under the control of the campsite owners, the court held that it was a known hazard, and very dangerous, especially at night. Therefore, warnings should have been provided, and the claimant's case succeeded on primary liability. However, the claimant's damages were reduced by 60% for contributory negligence relating to his alcohol consumption.

Williams v First Choice Holidays & Flights Ltd [2001]

While on an 18–30-style holiday in Greece the claimant attended an excursion to a local tavern. Free wine and plate smashing accompanied a Greek meal. To avoid the risk of injury from flying shards of crockery, plaster of Paris plates were provided. On the coach, guests were advised that the plate smashing would be supervised by the reps, plaster plates would be used and guests were only to smash them in a certain area. The claimant accepted she was "tipsy" at the time plate smashing commenced. One of her friends used a normal dessert plate rather than a plaster plate and a shard entered the claimant's ankle.

The claimant alleged that drunkenness was encouraged and that paper plates should have been used for the dessert. The court dismissed the claim. It accepted that to use paper plates was too high a burden, given that no other accidents had occurred, warnings were given and reps were supervising.

Logue v Flying Colours Ltd [2001]

The claimant had been out all night drinking and came back to his hotel at 06:00. He attempted to go to the toilet and fell over with his feet tangled in bedclothes. This caused him to fall out of the patio window. The claim was brought for failure to mark the patio window with a warning sticker and failure to use safety glass. The court dismissed the claim. The claimant had failed to prove breach of local standards. In addition, a sticker would have made no difference. If there had been a primary liability, the court would have found contributory negligence at 75%.

Clough v First Choice Holidays & Flights Ltd [2006]

The claimant slipped and fell from a wall by a swimming pool in Lanzarote, breaking his neck. He had drunk a significant amount of alcohol. The judge found that the claimant slipped from a surface that should have been, but was not, coated with non-slip paint. However, other guests had used the wall safely in the past, and even if non-slip paint had been applied, the wall would probably not have been slip free. The inference was that the claimant would probably have been able to avoid his fall, even if he had slipped, had he not been drunk. The Court of Appeal dismissed his claim.

Crime and civil unrest

As the world becomes a more dangerous place, we expect that claims arising from crime and civil unrest at destinations will increase. This will be especially so in claims arising from the impact of terrorist attacks.

Beales v Airtours Plc [1994]

The claimants were mugged in their Algarve resort. The claim was dismissed and the Court of Appeal refused permission to appeal. There was no evidence that tourists were the particular target of this criminal activity. A duty to warn could have arisen if there was evidence to show that tourists were the particular target.

Wilkinson and others v First Choice Holidays & Flights Ltd [2008]

The claimants flew out on holiday to Kenya on 30 December 2007, just as Kenyan election results were announced, which were followed by civil unrest. The claimants complained that they had been flown into a war zone, been accompanied on their transfer coach by armed guards and confined to the hotel like prisoners for one week of their holiday. The defendant relied on the fact it had followed Foreign & Commonwealth Office advice, which, at the date of departure, did not advise against travel to Kenya. The court found in favour of the defendant. The political upheaval was an event that could not have been foreseen or forestalled.

XVW and YZA v Gravesend Grammar Schools for Girls and Adventure Life Signs Ltd [2012]

While on a gap year trip to Belize, two pupils were attacked in their accommodation one evening. A claim was brought against the school and the organisers of the trip. The attacker was employed locally. The case was dismissed. For the tour operator to be liable for the attack, the unlawful act had to be much more than a mere possibility.

Excursions

Many tour operators offer excursions. Some are offered for sale and purchased as part of the package transaction. The majority are offered and purchased in resort. The range and type of excursions vary significantly, often dictated by local attractions. Examples of excursions include trips to local markets or nearby ancient ruins, toboggan runs, sailing days – the list is endless.

Where excursions are purchased in resort, they do not form part of the package, and therefore are not covered by the Regulations. Even so, when things go wrong on an excursion, claims are often made against the tour operator.

To determine whether there is liability on the part of the tour operator it is necessary to consider the nature of the sale, the terms and conditions and issues of agency.

Shaffer v Scantours Ltd [2008]

While on a snowmobile trip to dine at an ice hotel, the claimant slipped on ice on an embankment. He alleged:

- The areas of snow and ice were not adequately lit, signposted nor warned of
- He was not given the right boots
- A guide should have escorted the guests at all times
- Ropes or handholds should have been provided.

Evidence was provided that there had been no other accidents since 2004, for 34,000 guests. The claim was dismissed. The court held that ice is obvious in such a location and it is not for a tour operator to identify every possible hazard.

continued...

...continued

Parker v TUI UK Ltd [2009]

The claimant was on a ski holiday in Austria, purchased from the defendant. When in resort she purchased a night toboggan ride from one of the defendant's reps. At the end of the toboggan run, the claimant decided to carry on in her toboggan to the car park, and in doing so, ignored warnings to stop and walk. She suffered significant injury when she hit hay bales by the car park, which were frozen solid. She brought her claim against the tour operator.

The Court of Appeal held that there was no contractual relationship between the claimant and the tour operator. The facts showed that the tour operator had acted as agent for the excursion provider and not as principal for that contract. However, because reps went on the excursion, the Court accepted that the tour operator owed the claimant a duty of care in tort. That duty had been discharged by the checks carried out by the tour operator prior to the excursion.

Contrast the *Parker* judgment with that of *Moore v Hotelplan Ltd* (below) where the tour operator's excursion documentation did not match the allegation that it acted as agent. This is a pertinent reminder that you need to ensure your documentation follows the assertion you operate as agent and names the principal supplier to the contract, so it is clear who a claimant should sue.

Moore v Hotelplan Ltd [2010]

This case is at the other end of the spectrum to *Parker* in relation to an excursion purchased locally in resort. The claimant went on a skidoo excursion, which did not form part of the package holiday. She lost control of the skidoo, crashed it into a car and suffered catastrophic injury. The defendant denied the claim made against it on the basis that it acted as agent for the excursion provider.

On the facts it was held that the defendant's rep had not made it clear to the claimant that it was acting as agent for a third-party provider. On this basis, it was found to be the principal to the contract. As the defendant's standard terms and conditions for the holiday contract accepted liability for the negligence of its suppliers, it was liable to the claimant.

The negligence arose from the failure of the third party to properly instruct the claimant in the use of the skidoo. The agency argument failed because the defendant did not make clear in its ticketing or information provided to the claimant that it was selling the excursion as agent for a third party.

Falls

Falls are common problems on holidays. Exposed edges are not necessarily fenced or protected, as they may be in the UK. Local standards are relevant to such claims.

Lockwood v TUI UK Ltd [2007]

The claimant fell off the edge of terracing at a hotel overlooking the sea, having lost his footing on a small step on the terracing. The hotel had placed sunbeds on the terrace, but did not own the terrace. The drop was unfenced and neither the hotel nor the tour operator had undertaken any risk assessment of this area. After the accident, signage was placed in the area to warn of the drop.

The case was dismissed as the judge held the step and drop were there to be seen. The claimant had successfully negotiated the area before. It was likely he had stepped backwards from his sunbed without realising the drop was behind him. The judge accepted that the area should have been risk assessed, but found it would not have prevented the accident, which was caused by the claimant's failure to pay attention and look where he was going. The judge did not accept that the warning notices put up after the accident implied an admission of liability.

Hotels, pools and other hazards

Inevitably, most accidents on holiday happen in hotels or their surroundings, particularly swimming pools. The following cases illustrate the number of issues arising in these cases, and emphasise the importance of evidence, including expert evidence of local standards.

Codd v Thomson Tour Operations Ltd [2000]

The 10-year-old claimant and his two sisters were injured when using a lift in Mallorca. The lift featured an outer hinged door and an inner sliding door that closed automatically. The lift doors failed to close, seeming to have jammed, so the claimant put his hand around the door and pulled it towards him. It shut quickly, trapping his finger and causing serious injury. The claim was brought on the basis that the lift did not comply with UK standards. The evidence showed that the lift complied with local Spanish standards. As a result, the claim was dismissed at first instance and by the Court of Appeal.

Purcell v Thomson Holidays Ltd [2003]

The claimant slipped in the shower and hit her head, suffering serious injuries including concussion. She had difficulties remembering the incident. It was claimed that the bath was unusually narrow and her movements were very cramped. The court accepted that hotel bathrooms are often cramped compared to those at home. Evidence was also provided from the manufacturer confirming compliance with European Union Kitemark standards. The claimant had used the bath without incident for nine days. While it was held that a bathmat might have prevented the accident, there was no requirement on the hotel to provide one. The case was dismissed.

continued...

continued...

Buckley v TUI UK Ltd [2004]

The hotel provided five-a-side football games for guests at the hotel. The claimant participated in these every day while on holiday. The games were organised by a qualified referee employed by the hotel. The pitch doubled as a volleyball pitch and the hotel covered the holes for the volleyball net when the pitch was used for football. The claimant alleged he sustained injury when his foot was caught in one of the holes that had become uncovered. The defendant disputed the location of his fall. The contemporaneous report of the injury made no reference to the hole and the claimant did not complain at the time about the hole. The judge described his evidence at trial as unreliable and his claim for damages was dismissed.

Barlow v Thomson Holidays Ltd [2005]

The claimant was on a 'Young at Heart' holiday. She fractured her wrist when the automatic closing doors at the hotel closed on her. There had been no previous incidents but clearly there was a defect with the door at the time of her accident. Expert evidence for the defendant showed that the doors complied with local standards and that the defect must have been an intermittent fault. The case was dismissed.

Godfreys v Thomson Holidays Ltd [2006]

The claimant stated she sustained injury when she stood on a child's bed in her hotel room to turn on an air conditioning unit. The hotel gave evidence that it was not necessary to stand on the bed to turn on the air conditioning. It was accepted by the court that the claimant's evidence was not credible. The case was dismissed as the claimant failed to show breach of duty, and the risk of injury should have been obvious.

continued...

...continued

McDonald v Diamond Resorts International [2013]

The claimant decided to wash her feet by placing one of her feet in the sink of the bathroom; the sink was adjacent to the bath. As she did so, the sink fell from the wall and injured her leg. She alleged the clips that held the sink to the wall had corroded. She blamed the defendant for failing to inspect the sink. The defendant provided evidence of inspections. It denied the claim on the basis it was not foreseeable that a person would use the sink to wash their feet when there was a bath beside the sink. The court agreed with the defendant and dismissed the claim.

Hurley v TUI UK Ltd [2014]

The claimant was injured when descending a waterslide in Egypt. He claimed that in the course of his descent the design of the slide flipped him upside down, meaning that instead of exiting feet first, he exited head first and hit his head on the bottom of the pool. The defendant asserted that the claimant had entered the slide head first and caused his own accident. The court dismissed the claim. It found that the slide complied with relevant standards, the flow of water was safe and there was no flaw in its design. The judge held that the claimant must have deliberately altered his position at some point during the course of his descent.

Illness and injury

Sickness claims are common, time consuming and expensive to defend. They tend to involve large class actions. While these actions may include those who were genuinely ill, there can be a suspicion of claimants jumping on the claims bandwagon.

Well-run and well-managed hotels should be able to produce documents recording food hygiene procedures, pool monitoring, cleaning, auditing, etc., which can all help to establish that there was no breach of duty by the hotel.

Martin v Thomson Tour Operations Ltd [1999]

The claimant became ill on a Nile cruise. He sought to argue that a strict duty of care applied for food provided on the vessel, and claimed he had not consumed food at any other time while on holiday, so the ship had to be the source of his cryptosporidium. The defendant showed that no one else had complained of sickness. It also provided evidence of an outbreak of cryptosporidium in Wales where the claimant had been camping a week before his cruise. The claim failed on the basis that the claimant had not proved causation.

Nicholl v TUI UK Ltd [2007]

The claimant cruised from Sharm el-Sheikh. About 5% of passengers on the cruise reported gastric symptoms. The claimant had no formal diagnosis of illness. He pointed to the large number of people being ill as evidence of a foodborne pathogen rather than a viral infection (for which there could be no liability). It was alleged that the hygiene procedures on board the ship were not carried out effectively. A number of hygiene shortcomings were highlighted in an expert report.

The case was defended on the basis that the claimant, in all probability, contracted a viral illness. In addition, the proportion of passengers affected was not particularly large. The court held it was more probable than not that the claimant had suffered viral symptoms and so the case was dismissed.

Loss of enjoyment/diminution in value

When damages are claimed, they often include a claim for loss of enjoyment and/or diminution in value. The levels sought (and awarded) can vary. The nature of the holiday and its purpose are often important factors. Significant anniversaries and weddings are considered to be special events; other events such as birthdays are considered less important.

Damages for loss of enjoyment and diminution in value are linked, but different in nature. Diminution in value is linked into the value of the holiday while loss of enjoyment is not. For example, when considering a claim for loss of enjoyment, a lover of sailing may suffer loss of enjoyment if all the sailing boats are out of action, while their partner may not do so as they just enjoy reading by the pool.

Milner and Milner v Carnival Plc [2010]

The claimants booked onto the inaugural round-the-world cruise of the *Queen Victoria* with Cunard. The cost of the holiday was just under £60,000. The cruise was to last 106 days. The claimants had a number of reasonable complaints about their cabin and were moved to a number of different cabins. Eventually they left the cruise after about 30 days. They received compensation of around £48,000. They returned to the UK on board a different cruise ship. The cost was deducted from their compensation, leaving them with around £35,000.

continued...

continued...

They sued and, at first instance, were each awarded £2,500 for diminution in value and £7,500 for distress and disappointment. Mrs Milner was awarded £2,000 for wasted expenditure on clothes. On appeal, the Court of Appeal considered that the damages awarded were too high. The total damages award was reduced from £22,000 to £8,500. Commenting on earlier case law, Lord Justice Ward stated:

> “The run of the mill award even for the honeymoon cases or other special occasion cases, not to mention ordinary family holidays, may seldom reach £2,000 and the highest awards to which we have been referred are over £4,000 where a planned marriage on holiday was frustrated.”

Deaths on holiday

Unfortunately, tragic accidents involving holidaymakers can occur.

Coroners have begun to increase their scrutiny of the role travel operators play in ensuring the safety of customers overseas. Since 2014, we have seen a marked increase in tour operators being called to give evidence at inquests.

If a customer of a tour operator, or one of its employees, dies unexpectedly as a result of an accident overseas, then an inquest will be held in the UK to establish the following facts:

- Who died
- How they died
- Where they died
- When they died.

While an inquest is a court hearing, it is not a process designed to apportion blame but to establish facts.

It is routine now for coroners to compel tour operators to provide disclosure of relevant documents, including health and safety documentation, risk assessments, accident reports, witness statements and any internal investigations into deaths. In addition, the coroner is likely to require a representative from the company to attend the inquest to answer questions about the death.

Inquests are usually held in public. In addition to the family of the deceased, the press and members of the public are likely to be in attendance.

Other interested parties, including the family of the deceased, police, enforcing authorities or public bodies, such as the Health and Safety Executive and fire authorities, are entitled to question a witness.

> It is important that travel companies seek proper assistance and guidance throughout this process. It is necessary to fully understand the legal obligations of the directors and managers of the business to ensure appropriate documentation is provided and to properly prepare for the inquest process and hearing.

Where evidence at an inquest indicates that similar fatalities might occur in the future, the coroner has to draw this to the attention of any person or organisation who may be able to take steps to prevent further fatalities. The coroner will do this in the form of a 'report to prevent future deaths'. Over 500 of these reports were issued in 2015.

Anyone who receives such a report, such as a tour operator or an organisation such as the Association of British Travel Agents, must send the coroner a written response. The reports and the responses to them are copied to all interested persons and to the Lord Chancellor.

Recent reports have addressed the following:

- Evacuation process on being alerted to a drowning in a pool
- Provision of adequate lifesaving equipment at pools

- Protection against carbon monoxide and gas risk assessments of properties
- Training of lifeguards at hotel pools
- Provision of warnings about dangerous seas and rip tides, etc.

Not all these reports result in action being taken or rules and regulations being changed. However, they do highlight areas of concern that coroners will explore when seeking to establish why someone has died.

Checklist for tour operators

- ✓ Do you follow the due diligence and risk management processes set out in your health and safety manuals? If not, amend your processes and manuals.
- ✓ Ensure you can demonstrate that your suppliers comply with local laws and standards and have appropriate licences.
- ✓ Immediately alert your insurers/legal advisors if you are contacted by a coroner following the death of a guest or employee overseas.
- ✓ Decide who in your organisation would represent the company if required to give evidence.

29 Marine

Christopher Chatfield

- Where do I find the contract of marine insurance?
- Coverage considerations
- Marine property losses
- Hull insurance
- Sea transport
- Air transport
- Road transport
- Marine casualties
- Freight forwarders' liability
- Road Haulage Association Limited's Conditions of Carriage 2009 (RHA)

Marine

Introduction

What is marine insurance?

For the purposes of English law, ss.1–4 of the Marine Insurance Act 1906 (MIA 1906) contain the definition of marine insurance. In broad terms, marine insurance provides cover to insureds for loss, damage and liability caused by maritime perils, which are the risks inherent to navigation at sea. Marine insurance can also include shipbuilding, risks on inland waters and land risks incidental to any sea voyage (such as storage and transit).

An insured must of course have an insurable interest in the subject matter of the insurance. A legal or equitable interest in a marine venture or to property at risk in such a venture, under which the insured may benefit from the safety or due arrival of that property or be prejudiced by its loss or damage, or be exposed to a liability, will suffice. In marine insurance the insured need only have such interest at the time of the loss.

Commercially, marine insurance is essential. Banks and others who finance ships and trade will usually require their customers to obtain insurance. Buyers of goods may require the sellers to procure cargo insurance, such as under Cost, Insurance and Freight (CIF) contracts. Other commercial contracts regarding the operation of ships may require the parties to insure.

Marine insurance encompasses several product lines, which we have grouped for the purposes of this Guide into the following classes.

1) Hull and machinery

   Related products such as Increased Value (IC), Loss of Hire (LOH) and Builder's Risk insurance are also available.

2) Cargo and goods in transit

    This includes Project Cargo/DSU, Stock Throughput, Fine Art and Specie.

3) Marine liability

    This includes Protection and Indemnity (P&I), Charterers Liability, Freight Forwarders/Freight Services Liability, Marine Trades, Ports and Terminals Operators Liability, Ship Owners Liability, Ship Repairers Liability, Warehouse Keepers Liability. It also includes errors and omissions cover for marine professionals such as pilots, designers, surveyors, valuers and classification societies.

4) Marine war

    Standard hull and cargo policies exclude war and strikes perils and so separate insurance is required from the war market.

5) Yachts and pleasure craft

    More detail on claims handling in relation to these product lines is contained in later sections of this chapter. First, it may help to provide some comment, from the perspective of English law, on general principles applicable to all marine insurance.

Where do I find the contract of marine insurance?

Many marine insurance contracts are in the form of a slip policy, prepared by the broker. A slip policy is in law evidence of the contract of insurance. The slip contains the main details of the risk and other relevant matters, and will often incorporate standard marine insurance wordings by reference.

For cargo and liability risks, the insurance may be by way of open covers or broker facilities. Insurers are bound by declarations within the relevant period of the facility or open cover. Each conforming declaration will represent a different insurance contract, on the specific terms of the declaration and the terms of the facility/open cover.

Cargo insurers may be required to issue insurance certificates, especially where the insured intends to sell the cargo while in transit. A certificate is evidence of the contract of insurance. Transfer of the certificate to the buyer operates to assign to the buyer the benefit of the contract of insurance.

Applicable law and jurisdiction

When considering policy coverage, it is important to understand what law applies to the policy. Chapter 41 of this Guide explains the concepts of applicable law and jurisdiction in more detail.

Many marine insurance contracts will be subject to English law. This may be because of an express choice of law in the policy or by way of implication, applying rules of international law. The MIA 1906 remains the main source of English law as it applies to marine insurance.

However, due to the international nature of marine risks, and in some cases because of overseas regulations, many marine insurance contracts written in the London market will not be subject to English law.

A choice of law is not the same thing as a choice of jurisdiction. Many marine insurance contracts also contain a clause by which the insurer and insured agree that the English High Court is to determine any disputes. However, again, many contracts will provide for the courts of another country to have jurisdiction.

Where England and Wales is the appropriate jurisdiction in which policy coverage disputes are to be resolved, the Commercial Court, a part of the English High Court of Justice, has jurisdiction over marine insurance policy disputes. The Mercantile Court can handle simpler cases.

Coverage considerations

Many of the same legal principles apply to marine and non-marine insurance – for these please refer to Chapter 41.

There are also specific rules applicable only to marine insurance. For example, Schedule 1 to the MIA 1906 contains definitions of some perils and policy terms.

Marine warranties

The contract of insurance may contain express warranties. Typical warranties applicable to specific types of cover (such as hull and cargo) are discussed in the sections of the Guide dealing with those products. In considering policy coverage, check for express warranties in the policy wording, but remember that there may be implied warranties too.

- In a voyage policy there is an implied warranty that at the commencement of the voyage the ship will be seaworthy for the adventure insured (s.39(1) MIA 1906). In practice, cargo insurers usually waive this warranty and apply an exclusion for unseaworthiness to which the insured is privy (see e.g. Clause 5, Institute Cargo Clauses).
- In a time policy, there is no implied warranty that the ship will be seaworthy, but if the insured sends the ship to sea knowing it is unseaworthy the insurers are not liable for any loss caused by that unseaworthiness (s.39(5) MIA 1906).
- In a voyage policy on cargo there is an implied warranty that at the commencement of the voyage the carrying ship is seaworthy in itself and reasonably fit to carry the cargo to destination (s.40(2) MIA 1906). In practice, cargo insurers usually waive this warranty and apply an exclusion for unseaworthiness to which the insured is privy (see e.g. Clause 5, Institute Cargo Clauses).

- In all marine insurance contracts, there is an implied warranty that the marine adventure insured is lawful and will be carried out lawfully (s.41 MIA 1906). This was traditionally relevant to prohibitions on trading with enemies of state but in modern times is relevant in relation to international sanctions, although most policies will contain express sanctions clauses.

Legal advice may be required as to whether the insured has breached an express or implied warranty and if so what the consequences are. The effect of a breach may differ depending on whether or not the Insurance Act 2015 applies to the contract and on what type of warranty it is: see Chapter 41.

Many marine policies will include a 'held covered' clause under which insurers agree to continue cover in the event of a breach of warranty subject to the insured paying any additional premium and agreeing any additional terms imposed by insurers. They may also contain an 'errors and omissions clause', which might prevent insurers relying on late notice provisions.

Proximate cause and excluded losses

Marine insurance policies can be on either a 'named perils' or 'all risks' basis. Under an all risks policy, the insured need only prove accidental loss. Under a named perils policy, the insured must prove loss proximately caused by a named peril (s.55(1) MIA 1906). The proximate cause is the effective cause, not necessarily the most recent in time.

There may be more than one proximate cause of the loss. If each proximate cause is a covered peril then the insured will recover under the policy. If one cause is an insured peril, and one is a peril that is not covered (but not excluded), the insured will recover under the policy. If one cause is an insured peril, and the other an excluded peril then the exclusion will be effective and the insured will not recover under the policy (*The Miss Jay Jay* [1985]).

The policy may contain express exclusions, such as that for war and strikes risks in standard hull or cargo policies.

Section 55(2) of the MIA 1906 also excludes certain types of loss, such as loss due to wilful misconduct, delay, wear and tear and inherent vice, subject to anything to the contrary in the contract of insurance.

Marine property losses

Total loss, including constructive total loss

Total loss may be actual or constructive.

There is an actual total loss when the insured is irretrievably deprived of the property insured or where the property is destroyed (s.57 MIA 1906). In the event of an actual total loss the insured is entitled to recover the insured (or agreed) value of the property.

The concept of a constructive total loss (CTL) is unique to marine insurance. A CTL is a partial loss but one which the insured may elect to treat as a total loss for the purposes of indemnity under the policy. Section 60 of the MIA 1906 sets out various types of CTL. In broad terms, there is a CTL where the insured is deprived of possession of the property and its recovery is unlikely within a reasonable time or where the actual or estimated cost of recovery and repair of the property exceeds 100% of its value when repaired. Policy terms treat the repaired value as the insured (or agreed) value.

When an insured wants to claim a CTL then in most cases it will be necessary for the insured to indicate that it is willing to relinquish all its rights and interest in the ship to the insurer by giving insurers a notice of abandonment (NOA). If an insured fails to give NOA sufficiently promptly or when required, it can recover only as for a partial loss.

If insurers accept the NOA they take over all proprietary interest in and responsibility for the ship. This means they are entitled to the proceeds of sale of the ship. But they would also become responsible for such liabilities as wreck removal expenses. In most cases insurers will decline to accept the NOA. This does not mean they are declining the claim.

In law, to recover as for a CTL, the insured must prove that the property was a CTL at the time NOA is given and (in the event of a dispute) at the time when legal proceedings against the insurer are begun. Restoration of the property insured prior to legal proceedings would extinguish any loss. Therefore when giving NOA the insured may ask insurers to agree a 'writ clause' if the NOA is declined, to put the insured in the same position as if legal proceedings against insurers had been issued on the date of the NOA.

Partial losses

Section 69 of the MIA 1906 sets out the measure of indemnity for a partial loss, subject to any express terms of the policy. If the insured effects a full repair, the measure of indemnity is the reasonable costs of repair, less any customary deductions. However, the indemnity cannot exceed the agreed (or insured) value. A full repair restores the ship to its pre-casualty condition, as far as it is reasonably possible to do so. Most policies now include a 'new for old' provision, which negates any customary or other potential deduction in the claim for betterment.

However, an insured is under no obligation to its insurers to repair or remediate damaged property. If the insured does a partial repair, the insured can recover the reasonable costs of the repair, plus depreciation in the value of the property (if any) resulting from the unrepaired damage. The aggregate of these claims cannot exceed the reasonable costs of a full repair. If none of the damage is repaired by the end of the policy period, the insured can claim depreciation (if any) in the value of the property resulting from the unrepaired damage, not exceeding the reasonable costs of a full repair.

Salvage and general average

Standard hull and cargo insurance will also include cover for contributions due in salvage, salvage charges and general average (GA). The Casualty section of this chapter explains these concepts in more detail.

Collisions

Those navigating ships at sea have a duty to do so with reasonable care and must comply with the International Regulations for the Prevention of Collisions at Sea 1972 (as amended). Hull insurance may therefore also include a proportion of any legal liability arising from a collision with other ships or structures.

Under English law and where the Collision Convention 1910 applies, liability for any damage caused by a collision will be agreed or determined by a court by reference to each ship's proportionate degree of fault. In the UK, the Admiralty Court is competent to determine claims arising out of collisions, the Court being able to draw on advice from the Elder Brethren of Trinity House on technical nautical matters. The claims will be set off against each other so there is one payment. There is a two-year time limit for recourse claims (s.8, Maritime Conventions Act 1911).

Other countries apply a different approach to apportionment of liability and as to how cross-claims are treated.

Hull insurance

Introduction

Hull insurance provides cover against total or partial loss of or damage to a ship's hull and machinery, sue and labour expense, and the ship's proportion of salvage and GA. It may include a proportion of the ship's legal liability to third parties for damage caused by way of collisions and can be on a voyage or time basis. Voyage cover insures the ship at and from one location to a named destination. A time policy insures the ship for a specific period, often 12 months.

More limited cover is available to suit an insured's needs – such as for port risks (where a vessel is laid up), or against total loss only, or against total loss but with limited partial loss cover.

Contracts may be in respect of an individual ship or in respect of vessels within a fleet, in which case there will be separate contracts of insurance in respect of each ship.

The contractual ownership and operation of ships is often complex. Typically, there will be a special purpose corporate registered legal owner of the ship. A bank mortgage will finance the purchase. The legal owner will lease the vessel on a long-term basis to a bareboat charterer, which will be responsible for the technical and commercial management of the ship. The bareboat charterer may choose to sub-contract aspects of management. The bareboat charterer (or sub-contracted commercial managers) will hire the vessel out to time charterers for a specified time. The time charterers will pay for and take over fuel on board and decide how to employ the ship. They may enter into contracts for the carriage of goods with shippers and receivers in return for receiving freight; or they may hire the vessel out to voyage charterers, with the voyage charterers entering into contracts of carriage with the shippers and receivers.

Anyone with an insurable interest in the ship can insure against hull risks. Policies will usually insure the registered shipowner, any bareboat charterer/operator, the technical and commercial managers and sometimes the mortgagee bank, each for their respective rights and interests. Mortgagee banks may have an assignment of the benefit of the insurances and be named as a loss payee, in addition or alternatively to being named as an insured. Time and voyage charterers can insure freight and bunkers at risk, but will not have an insurable interest in the ship itself.

Various standard London market hull insurance wordings are in common use, including Institute Time Clauses (Hulls) 1.10.83 and 1.11.95 and Institute Voyage Clauses (Hulls) 1.10.83 and 1.11.95. These insure against loss or damage to the subject matter insured proximately caused by named perils. For an additional premium, the insured can obtain extended cover under the Institute Additional Perils Clauses – Hulls.

Other wordings in common use in the London market are the Nordic Plan, the German ADS-DTV, and the American Institute Hull Clauses. The Nordic Plan and the ADS-DTV are 'all risks' covers, rather than named perils.

These policies cover ships once built. Cover for shipbuilders for loss of or damage to ships under construction is available by way of Builder's Risk insurance.

Losses covered under standard hull policies

Clause 6.1 ITC Hulls gives cover against risks of physical loss or damage proximately caused by named marine perils, including perils of the sea, fire and explosion.

Clause 6.2 ITC Hulls gives cover against risks of physical loss and damage due to machinery breakdown, latent defect, and negligence of ship's crew, pilots, repairers and charterers. This cover is not available if insurers can prove that the loss resulted from the negligence of the insured's senior personnel, the owners or the managers, or superintendents (the latter only under ITC Hulls 1.11.95). Most claims in practice tend to be the result of negligent navigation or negligent operation (or maintenance) of machinery.

Hull policies will exclude cover for violent theft (Clause 6.1.3), piracy (Clause 6.1.5) and barratry (Clause 6.2.4 ITC Hulls 1.11.95/6.2.5 ITC Hulls 1.10.83) by virtue of Violent Theft, Piracy and Barratry Extension; this cover is available from war risks insurers instead.

The insured can, by paying an additional premium, extend the basic cover under Clause 6 ITC Hulls through the Institute Additional Perils Clauses (IAPC). These clauses provide cover for any accidental loss and negligence of any persons, but subject to the same due diligence requirement as in Clause 6.2 ITC Hulls. Extending cover in this way makes the cover very similar to an 'all risks' cover.

Clause 8 ITC Hulls provides cover for legal liabilities arising out of collisions. This is usually limited to 3/4 of any liability, with the remaining 1/4 of the liability being insured with P&I insurers.

Clause 11 ITC Hulls 1.10.83 (Clause 10 ITC Hulls 1.11.95) gives cover for salvage and GA. The time and expense of collecting GA can sometimes be uneconomic. Many policies now include a (small) GA absorption clause allowing the insured to recover GA expense in full from hull insurers. Sometimes the policy will also cover 'ballast general average'. This treats ballast voyages as if they were laden ones, so that, despite there being no common adventure, the insured can recover certain types of expense as if they were GA expense.

There is at Clause 13 ITC Hulls 1.10.83 (Clause 11 ITC Hulls 1.11.95) an express obligation on the insured to sue and labour, which would arise anyway under s.78 of the MIA 1906, and a right of the insured to an indemnity for such expense properly and reasonably incurred in avoiding or minimising loss covered by the insurance.

Hull policies exclude claims for delay. There are also standard exclusions for war and strikes risks and malicious acts in Clauses 23–25 ITC Hulls 1.10.83 (Clauses 24–26 ITC Hulls 1.11.95). The insured can obtain cover for these risks from the war market.

Hull claims handling

A lead insurer or reinsurer exercising claims control will need to ensure that they obtain the necessary information to assess coverage, adjust the claim, and consider potential recourse rights.

The insured's brokers will usually inform insurers of a potential incident that may give rise to a claim. It is likely that insurers will need to appoint marine surveyors and other technical experts to attend the casualty, investigate and report on the damage, and its possible cause. Complex casualties may require lengthy attendance. Likewise, it may be necessary depending on the facts to consider the instruction of additional expertise (such as fire investigators, naval architects or metallurgists).

Occasionally the surveyors and experts may be required to sign an indemnity, for example as a condition of allowing the surveyor access to the ship. In rare cases, it may be necessary to apply for a court order to enable the surveyor to get on board.

Repairs may involve a need for towage of the ship to a suitable repair facility. Other than in an emergency, towage without the insurers' consent may be a breach of the towage warranty in Clause 1 ITC Hulls. Normally insurers agree to allow towage to a repair yard for a small additional premium and subject to a towage warranty surveyor's approval of the proposed tug, towing arrangements and the route and speed.

The insured should draw up a repair specification, and obtain repair quotes and submit those to the insurers' appointed surveyors for approval (often done 'for cost only', in other words without confirming coverage or that the repairs were necessary or reasonable). Some policies give a right to insurers to reduce the indemnity where the insured fails to do this. Some give a right to insurers to obtain repair tenders themselves.

In considering repair estimates, claims handlers and surveyors should bear in mind that the test is what is reasonable from the perspective of a prudent uninsured shipowner who is in the position of the actual insured. Commercial issues such as financing, trading and crew nationality may all have to be considered as well as availability and condition of spares or second-hand parts, lead times for manufacture of parts, types and grades of steel and location and availability of repair facilities.

The insurers' appointed surveyors may need to attend the repair yard during repairs and on completion of repairs to review and approve the repair accounts.

The insured (or in some cases the insurer) may appoint an adjuster to draw up a particular average adjustment, for example where some work may be routine maintenance and that work is carried out in dry-dock at the same time as casualty-related work. The adjuster will apply law, custom and practice, including the Average Adjusters Association Rules of Practice, in determining which items are for the insurers' account as particular average and which are for the insured's account (remainder). The adjuster's fees are included in the adjustment.

Similarly, the insured will appoint an average adjuster in the event of a GA incident. However, the insurer may wish to consider taking advice from another adjuster in such cases, and in relation to claims under GA absorption clauses or under ballast GA clauses.

Coverage questions

The first thing for an insurer to do is to check it has the full and complete terms of the insurance, including any amendments by way of endorsements. The insurer will also need details of the loss by way of the brokers' advices, survey reports, repair costs or estimates.

Then the insurer may need to do some or all of the following.

- Check that the date of loss (when the loss or damage occurs) is within the period of insurance.
- Check that the ship was within any navigational limits in the policy at the time of loss.
- Check that there is no exclusion of the particular cargo or trade.
- Check for Confirmation of Class (a certificate given by the ship's classification society confirming that the ship was in class at the time of the casualty). If the ship was not in class at the time, this may afford a defence to any claim by way of breach of warranty.
- Check for any potential undisclosed changes of the vessel's management during the policy period that might have operated to terminate the insurance prior to the loss.
- Check for compliance with any express warranties in the policy, such as the towage warranty in Clause 1 ITC Hulls, or a requirement for the insured to obtain a condition survey within 30 days of policy inception.

- Check the placing file to see what information the underwriters received about the risk at the time they agreed to write it, in case issues of non-disclosure or misrepresentation arise. The insured has the same duty (of good faith or fair presentation) in relation to variations to the policy by way of endorsements. It is important also to check what information the underwriters received at the time of any relevant endorsements.
- Check the policy for any conditions precedent to liability. These are rare in hull insurance, but coverage for collision liability damages may be on terms that require the insured to have paid the claim against it first before it is entitled to an indemnity.

If there is a chance of a potential coverage defence, it is worth issuing a short reservation of rights. This is because exercising an insurer's rights under the policy or making a part payment on account could be inconsistent with and so prevent any subsequent denial of coverage.

If no issues arise which might entitle insurers to avoid or terminate cover, it is then necessary to consider whether the loss is due to a peril insured by the policy and if so what indemnity the insured is entitled to.

- Has the insured proved its loss? Does the underwriters' surveyor concur with the insured's allegation of cause? Are there other potential proximate causes of the loss, and are any of those excluded by the policy?
- Has the insurers' surveyor agreed the repair costs as fair and reasonable?
- If the claim is for unrepaired damage, has the insured provided evidence of depreciation? It may be necessary for the insurer to obtain its own expert assessment of the extent of any depreciation.

In a CTL claim for deprivation of possession the usual issue is whether at the time of giving NOA there is a realistic prospect of recovery of the ship. If there is, the ship is not a CTL: see *Masefield v Amlin* [2011].

In a CTL claim based on the estimated costs of recovery and repair exceeding the agreed value, the insured is entitled to include many different kinds of expense in the calculation, such as salvage expenses (incurred or anticipated), as well as the estimated costs of repair. The insured will also benefit from a generous (5–10%) allowance to take into account the uncertainties inherent in any repair costs estimate: *The Brillante Virtuoso* [2015].

The measure of indemnity

Almost all hull policies are agreed value policies. In the event of a total loss (actual or constructive) the agreed value is paid. Hull insurers can theoretically pay up to three times the agreed value in respect of property damage claims: once for loss and damage, once for sue and labour expense, and once for salvage/GA.

On a full repair, the policy pays the reasonable costs of repair, less any applicable deductible. This is not necessarily limited to the actual costs of permanent repairs. It can include the costs of a temporary repair for example, where this enables deferment of permanent repairs to the next routine dry-docking or it is necessary to enable the vessel to get to a repair yard.

Most hull policies now exclude the application of the principle of betterment (giving credit to the insurer for the insured property being in a better position than it was before the loss) by inclusion of a ‘new for old’ clause. Contrary to what many insureds think, this does not entitle them automatically to replace damaged parts with new parts. If reconditioned or second-hand parts are available and it would be reasonable to use those instead, the insured should be indemnified by reference to that cost rather than the cost of new parts.

If there is an unrepaired partial loss and a subsequent total loss during the policy period, the partial loss claim merges into the total loss claim, and only the latter is paid.

If at the end of the policy period, there is no repair or an incomplete repair, the insured has an unrepaired damage claim. The insured can recover the actual depreciation in the market value of the ship (if any) which is caused by the unrepaired damage, but not exceeding the reasonable cost of repairing the unrepaired damage. The provisions of Clause 18 ITC Hulls will override s.69 of the MIA 1906, where the two are inconsistent.

Some machinery repair claims can create issues as to whether a repair that is approved by class as a permanent repair, and that restores the vessel to an operational condition, is a full or a partial repair. To avoid disputes later it is always worth insurers asking their surveyor not just to advise whether the repair is a permanent repair but also whether it is a full repair – has the repair restored the ship to its pre-casualty condition so far as it is possible to do so?

Recoveries

By way of subrogation, insurers can benefit from the insured's rights of recourse, to the extent of the insurers' payment. From first notification of a loss, insurers should be considering the possibility of a recovery from a third party in order to ensure that they obtain any necessary documents and evidence, and to ensure that potential rights are preserved.

In the case of hull damage, there may be opportunities for recovery from a wider range of contractual or third parties:

- The ship builder in respect of construction defects.
- Designers, in respect of design defects.
- Ship repairers, for negligent repair work.
- The former owners of the ship in respect of undisclosed defects which pre-existed the sale.

- Pre-purchase surveyors.
- Engine, equipment or coating manufacturers and suppliers.
- Another vessel in respect of damage sustained in a collision.
- Charterers, for damage arising out of the carriage of dangerous cargo, or caused by stevedores, or from the vessel proceeding to an unsafe port or berth.
- Port or terminal operators, for damage sustained where the port or berth is unsafe.

The usual time limit under English law is six years for claims for breach of contract or negligence. However, contracts between the insured and the relevant third party may impose a shorter time limit. If the recourse action is not subject to English law, different time limits will apply.

Insurers should check the policy for waivers of subrogation and consider whether the potential target is a co-insured under the policy.

Insurers should also ask for and check the insured's contracts with the third party for waivers of subrogation and 'knock-for-knock' agreements under which the insured agrees not to pursue its contract partner for loss of or damage to the insured's property.

These contracts may also contain limitations and exclusions of liability, and the potential recovery target may be entitled by law to limit liability for the loss in question.

Third parties with whom the insured has no contract may be able to rely on disclaimers of liability.

Legal advice may be required on the effectiveness of waivers of subrogation and contractual limitations and exclusions of liability, and the ability of the third party to limit liability under law or international convention.

Finally, with any recovery, the target must be worth pursuing. Insurers should consider whether the recovery target has insurance or funds to pay a claim, where and how to pursue any claim, and how a successful claim might need to be enforced.

The third party's liability insurance might be on 'pay to be paid' terms, which would preclude recovery against the third party's insurer in the event of the third party's insolvency. The Third Parties (Rights against Insurers) Act 2010 makes pay to be paid clauses unenforceable but contains an exemption from that for policies of marine insurance where the claim against the third party is one for property damage or financial loss.

Insurers should also check the policy for any terms that deal with allocation of recoveries, such as Clause 12 ITC Hulls. This allows the insurer to recover in priority to any uninsured loss in the form of a deductible. However, hull insurers cannot share in any recovery of uninsured loss of a kind not insured under the policy, such as loss of hire, for example.

Related insurances

Increased Value

Increased Value (IV) insurance was originally designed to provide insurance against the insured's loss of income from long-term contracts for the use of the ship as the result of a total loss of the ship, limited to 25% of the value of the hull insurance. Now, it is quite common for insureds to arrange their insurance on the basis that the hull policy covers 80% of the overall insured value of the ship and an IV policy covers the remaining 20%. This may save on the insurance premium and helps to bring standard London market coverage into line with alternatives such as the Nordic Plan.

IV insurers are obliged to pay where the hull insurers have settled a claim on the hull policy as an ATL or a CTL, or to settle (in proportion) where the hull insurers have compromised a total loss claim on the hull policy.

If the claim on the hull policy has been settled as for a partial loss, there is usually no basis for a claim on the IV policy.

To consider claims under an IV policy, the claims handler will need to ensure that there is evidence that hull insurers have agreed to settle a total loss under the hull policy. This evidence may be in the form of a signed settlement agreement between the insured and hull insurers. The claims handler will need to check that the proximate cause of loss is one which was covered by the hull policy (and the IV), and will need to check the terms of the settlement agreement carefully. If, as part of the settlement, the insured abandons its CTL claim, there is no basis for any recovery against IV insurers.

Disbursements and Excess Liabilities

These policies protect the insured in the event of a total loss where under-insurance results in a reduction of the hull policy indemnity.

Loss of Hire

These policies cover the ship owner for loss of income consequent upon loss or damage to the ship by named perils set out in the policy or by reference to the hull insurance on the ship. Cover is often for an agreed rate per day, subject to a 14-day deductible and an overall aggregate limit of cover, per event or annually. LOH insurers sometimes agree to follow the settlements of the hull insurers so that decisions on proximate cause are binding on LOH underwriters, to save the insured having to prove this twice.

Mortgagee's Interest Insurance (MII)

A mortgagee bank also faces a specific financial risk that something the ship owner does or fails to do may invalidate the terms of the ship owner's hull, war risks or liability insurance, rendering any assignment of the policy ineffective and meaning the mortgagor cannot discharge the mortgage. A similar risk arises even where the mortgagee is a co-insured if the ship's owner has scuttled the ship.

MII insurance meets these risks. Often the cover will be on the Institute Mortgagees' Interest Clauses, which set out specific insured perils, supplemented by bespoke terms. There are express warranties, such as that the hull, war and P&I insurances are in place and maintained. There are exclusions from cover if those insurers terminate the ship owner's policy for non-payment of premium, and exclusions in respect of other purely financial risks. Policy indemnity will usually be for the lower of the insured's net loss under the loan agreement(s) or the amount not recovered under the relevant owner's policy, capped at the sum insured.

Builder's Risks Insurance

Builder's Risk Insurance covers ships under construction against the risks of loss and damage, usually on an all risks basis. In addition, there is cover for salvage, GA and collision liability on coastal sea trial voyages.

War risks

In broad terms, war risks insurance on ships covers loss of or damage to the ship, salvage and GA, proximately caused by named perils. War and strikes perils include war, civil war, various types of civil unrest, terrorism and politically motivated violence, malicious damage, strikes and labour disturbances, and riots. War perils also currently include violent theft, piracy and barratry.

The detention perils include capture, seizure, arrest, restraint and detainment, confiscation and expropriation. Cover will typically exclude arrest for ordinary commercial trade debts owed by the insured and for detention in connection with actual or alleged breaches of customs and trading regulations or from criminal activities.

One of the difficulties with CTL claims for detention perils is establishing when the insured was deprived of the ship with no likely prospect of its return within a reasonable time. War policies therefore often deem a CTL to have occurred where the detention of the ship (by a covered peril) is for a continuous period of 12 months.

Yachts and pleasure craft

Hull and war risks insurance on yachts and pleasure craft is similar to that on commercial ships, and many of the comments made above will apply. However, there are some key differences. Yacht insurance may be on a stand-alone basis, or as part of personal lines High Net Worth insurance. Insurance on yachts and pleasure craft owned by private individuals is often consumer insurance.

Policy forms and cover provided

Many insurers have their own specific policy terms and conditions for yachts. Standard market wordings include the Institute Yacht Clauses 1.7.87 (IYC) and the American R12 Form.

The IYC cover is for named perils and subject to English law. The scope of cover is similar to ITC Hulls but some perils (theft and explosion) are subject to the due diligence requirement. Clause 10 IYC contains exclusions from cover of property and of certain perils. Clause 22 IYC excludes war perils.

The R12 Form is all risks and subject to US law, unless otherwise agreed.

Both wordings include cover for hull damage while the yacht is both in commission (at sea) and out of commission (laid up) including lifting and hauling ashore and launching. Both wordings include cover for salvage and salvage charges, and if required third-party liability cover. Typically, yacht covers also include P&I liability cover under the same property.

Cover does not extend to shipping the yacht as cargo, such as from the Mediterranean to the Caribbean, and vice versa, for the winter and summer sailing seasons.

There may be exclusions for loss, damage and liability while participating in regatta races.

A pleasure craft's gear and equipment, personal effects and outboard motors are highly vulnerable to theft, so cover for theft is often restricted. Many covers only offer protection if there is evidence of "forcible and violent entry", but in practice, where English law applies, this may not be a difficult hurdle for the insured to overcome.

Claims handling and coverage

Where the yacht insurance is consumer insurance, this will affect obligations of disclosure by the insured and the insurers' remedies for non-disclosure and breach of warranty. Under the Consumer Insurance (Disclosure and Representations) Act 2012, the consumer has to take the reasonable care that a reasonable consumer would take not to make misrepresentations to the insurer in answering any questions. This applies upon entering into a new insurance contract, upon renewal or upon any contract variation.

Insurers should check any navigational, professional master, crewing and private use warranties for the yacht carefully. The effect of a breach of warranty may be different dependent upon whether the insurance is consumer insurance or not, and upon whether the Insurance Act 2015 applies.

For theft claims, insurers should check whether the loss falls outside the scope of any restrictions on cover, and whether the insured has complied with conditions of cover regarding protection against theft, and that the circumstances of the loss fit any "forcible and violent entry" requirement. The insurer will want to see the police report filed by the insured.

The R12 Form requires the insured to file a sworn proof of loss within 90 days of the loss. The form also makes compliance with the policy terms a condition precedent to insurers' liability. Under English law, this means that a failure to file the sworn proof of loss within 90 days can deprive the insured of any recovery (at least in non-consumer cases).

As with commercial vessels, the time limit for collision damage claims by persons on board or the owners of the colliding vessel against the insured arising out of a collision will often be two years. Time limits for personal injury claims by those on board the insured's vessel will be subject to a three year-limit, even if they arise out of a collision. Time limits for recourse action against the insured by third parties (other than collision claims) will be three years for personal injury claims and six years for other claims. However, where the claim is in the nature of a contribution claim governed by the Civil Liability Contribution Act 1978, the time limit will be two years from the date on which the liability arose.

For liability claims, insurers should remember that the owners of yachts and some pleasure craft may be able to limit liability to third parties under national law or international convention by reference to the size of the yacht.

Repairs and the measure of indemnity

Owners trade commercial ships for profit. They sail yachts for enjoyment. The appearance of a yacht is often very important to the insured. The reasonable costs of repair for a yacht may therefore be very different to those of a commercial ship, especially as regards repairs to paintwork and hull.

Recoveries

The Collision Regulations will still apply to yachts while racing, but the terms of entry may affect rights of recourse in respect of collision between participating yachts.

Cargo claims handling

Cargo damage

The first thing that needs to be established is the cause, nature and extent of the alleged damage to the cargo – not only to determine whether any claim for that damage is covered under the policy of insurance, but also in relation to any recovery.

It is wise to instruct a suitable surveyor as quickly as possible upon notification of the damage/loss. Speed is especially important when dealing with a large loss involving multiple parties as it is likely that the firm or individual one would wish to instruct is also on somebody else's list. Interested parties/potentially interested parties to any major loss thus move very quickly to retain their 'preferred' surveyor (even on a precautionary basis) following an incident.

The next stage is to ensure that one has the necessary documentation in order to assess the claim.

Whether the transit has been by sea, road, rail or air, there will usually be certain documentation issued by the entity receiving the goods for transport when the cargo is delivered into their care.

The documentation varies between each mode of transport but the 'core' information contained in the document should be the same, in that it should state:

i) A description of the cargo.

ii) The period that the cargo is in the care of the issuer of the document.

iii) The identity of the issuer of the document.

iv) The shipper of the cargo.

v) The receiver of the cargo.

vi) The terms and conditions under which the cargo is transported by the issuer of the document.

We shall look at each mode of transport in turn. This is often contained within a consignment note but the information may also be available in other documents.

Sea transport

Usually either a bill of lading or a sea waybill is issued by a sea carrier.

Bills of lading vs sea waybills

There are two types of bill of lading: a 'straight' bill of lading and a 'negotiable' bill.

A 'negotiable' bill of lading is the 'classic' bill of lading. It will state 'To order' in the 'receiver' field enabling the bill to be endorsed to a third party. The 'endorsement' is stated on the reverse of the bill (usually by means of a stamp that may or may not be legible).

A 'straight' bill of lading will state a named shipper and a named consignee and will either contain no words importing transferability or contain words negating transferability.

A sea waybill is a receipt for the cargo. It will usually, however, make reference to the standard terms of carriage and identify the parties to the contract. 'Straight' bills of lading are similar to sea waybills insofar that delivery under them has to be made to the named consignee. However, with a 'straight' bill of lading, production of an original is necessary whereas this is not usually the case with a sea waybill!

Bill of lading

The most important document in any marine cargo claim is the bill of lading and, if one has been issued, a copy should be requested at the outset. Always request a copy of the front *and* the back of the bill (we explain why this is important below). Beware of using the internet to try and ascertain the bill of lading terms and conditions of a particular carrier. The bill of lading actually used may be a different/older version than that found on a carrier's website.

This document has been in existence in one form or another for several hundred years and (as one may expect) has been the subject of much litigation in English law over that time; the law surrounding bills of lading is complex and fraught with pitfalls.

The guide below should provide a way to navigate through the initial stages of a claim. However, if there is any doubt upon the documentation presented, advice should be obtained.

It will be useful to highlight what to look for with a reference to each of the following functions.

A receipt for the goods

A bill of lading is a declaration by the carrier stating what was received and when. There is no 'standard format' bill and nearly all carriers have their own version (although there are various 'templates' provided by different trade bodies, such as BIMCO).

However, regardless of the version, every bill will state (i) what the cargo is (ii) where the cargo was being carried to/from (be it a location such as a premises or a port) and (ii) the date the bill was issued.

In addition, the 'description' section on the front of the bill (and sometimes continuation sheets) will contain any remarks that the carrier wishes to make upon the condition of the goods upon loading (such as whether the cargo was in any way damaged). If there are no remarks, the bill is said to be 'clean'. If there are any remarks then the bill is said to be 'claused'.

If the bill is 'claused', check the nature of the clausing carefully. It is usually only possible to recover against the carrier for damage that occurred while the cargo was in their care and for which the carrier was responsible.

The contract of carriage

Strictly speaking, the bill of lading is only *evidence* of the contract of carriage because the terms of the *actual* contract can be contained in one or more additional documents.

It may be that all the terms of the contract (save for those 'imported' as per (b) below) under which the cargo has been carried are set out on the bill, and these are usually set out on the reverse, but key terms can also be contained on the front. The entire document must be considered.

The terms on the reverse of the bill are usually the issuing carrier's standard terms and conditions and vary according to the carrier.

As a general rule there are three 'types' of terms:

a) Express terms that are printed on the bill (such as the carriers' standard terms and conditions).

b) Terms that are 'imported' into the contract by reference (such as a charterparty).

c) Terms that are incorporated by statute and cannot be derogated from.

All express terms and all the 'imported' terms need to be available for study.

Charterparty

Often the terms of a given charterparty will be incorporated into a bill of lading. If there is any reference to a charterparty on the bill a copy must be obtained.

Although the shipper/receiver on the bill may be bound by the terms of the charterparty and have a right to see the charterparty, it is often the case that the shipper/receiver does not have a copy of the document and has never asked for it. The rules are very different if the shipper is also the *charterer* under the charterparty incorporated in or referred to on the bill. In that event the charterparty is the contract of carriage and not the bill of lading. This area of law is complicated and if there is any doubt as to whether a party to the charterparty is also a charterer, expert advice should be sought.

Conventions

Conventions set out the rights and responsibilities of both the shipper and the carrier as well as key issues such as limitation periods and limitation amounts (package limitation). Each convention will specify the circumstances in which it will apply to a given bill of lading.

For ocean carriage, the Hague and Hague-Visby Rules will apply if the goods are shipped from a contracting country but may also be incorporated contractually into the agreement. These contain limits of liability, defences and exceptions to liability and set out the obligations of the parties. Most of the international conventions deal with such issues. They also contain provisions for notification of claims and time bars.

We set out the key provisions of each convention below.

	When does it apply?		Time bar	Notification of claims	Limit of liability
Hague-Visby Rules	(a) Bill of lading issued in a contracting state (b) carriage from a contracting state (c) contract of carriage expressly applies Rules **(Article X)**	**Loss / damage**	1 year from date of delivery or when delivery should have taken place **(Article III, Rule 6)**	Written notice within 3 days – but at time of delivery if loss apparent **(Article III, Rule 6)**	The higher of 2 SDRs* per kg or 666.67 SDRs per package/unit **(Article IV, Rule 5)** * SDR is the Special Drawing Right of the IMO
		Delay	As above.	Within 3 days **(Article III, Rule 6)**	As above
Hague Rules	Applies to bills of lading	**Loss / damage**	'Suit' must be brought within 1 year from date of delivery or when delivery should have taken place **(Article III, Rule 6)**	Written notice within 3 days – but at time of delivery if loss apparent **(Article III, Rule 6)**	£100 per package or unit unless value declared and inserted in the bill of lading. The £100 limit per package has been held to amount to £100 gold value where the appropriate wording is used (*The Rosa S* [1988] 2 Lloyd's Rep. 574) **(Article IV, Rule 5)**
		Delay	As above	Within 3 days **(Article III, Rule 6)**	As above

	When does it apply?		Time bar	Notification of claims	Limit of liability
Hamburg Rules	(a) the port of loading is in a contracting state, or (b) the port of discharge is in a contracting state, or (c) one of the optional ports of discharge is the actual port of discharge and such port is in a contracting state, or (d) bill of lading issued in a contracting state, or (e) contract of carriage expressly applies Rules **(Article 2)**	**Loss/ damage**	2 years from date of delivery or the last day upon which the carrier has delivered the goods or part thereof or, in cases where no goods have been delivered, on the last day on which the goods should have been delivered **(Article 20)**	Written notice to carrier (i) by the working day following delivery; or (ii) within 15 days of delivery where damage not apparent **(Article 19)**	The higher of 2.5 SDR per kg or 835 SDRs per package/unit **(Article 6)**
		Delay	As above	Within 60 days of delivery **(Article 19)**	As above

The below 'first stage' checklist should assist:

(i) Notification of claims

Ascertaining whether any notification provisions have been or need to be complied with should be a first priority. If the cargo owner fails to notify the carrier of its intention to claim, this may prejudice the claim. In some instances, it may preclude a claim altogether. In others, it may create a presumption which can be difficult to rebut. It must be established if there is a contractual time for notifying claims and whether there is any convention which contains compulsory claims notification periods.

(i) Time bar

If the limitation period has expired, any claim for a recovery against the carrier may be effectively 'dead'.

Often the term specifying the limitation period will be printed on the reverse of the relevant carriage document. However, where a convention applies, the period stated in the convention may supersede any written term on the bill.

However, a trap for the unwary lies where no convention applies. If no bill of lading is issued or the carriage is from a state that doesn't contract to a particular convention, this may arise.

In that event, English law permits the parties to agree a limitation period. Either the bill can contain a clause incorporating a particular convention or a bill can contain a 'stand-alone' term. A bill can, for example, specify that any claim under the bill will be time barred unless proceedings are commenced within nine months from the date of delivery AND the carrier is advised in writing of proceedings having been commenced within that nine-month period.
If proceedings are commenced but the carrier is not notified, the claim will be time barred.

The default provision under English law is a limitation period of six years from the 'breach' of the contract of carriage (Limitation Act 1980, s.5) but this cannot be assumed. If in doubt, seek advice.

(ii) Law and jurisdiction

It is essential at an early stage to determine under which law the terms of the contract will be construed (as with time bar provisions etc.) and which court has jurisdiction to ensure that any suit is brought in the correct jurisdiction. The law and jurisdiction provisions will almost always be found on the reverse of the bill of lading so requesting a copy of the reverse is essential at the outset. The applicable law may determine whether any conventions compulsorily apply or whether any other terms will be applicable to the contract.

(iii) Package limitation

The same rules apply here in relation to conventions as with the time bar. There will often be a compulsory limit of liability set out in the relevant convention. Where, under the relevant convention, the package limit is referred to, this usually refers to the packages as enumerated on the bill of lading.

The table above sets out the package limitation provisions of each convention.

(iv) Identity of the carrier

There will usually be a clause on the reverse of the bill identifying the issuing carrier. Sometimes this clause is missing or contrasts with the name or carrier's logo on the front of the bill. The law in England determining the identity of the carrier in that event can be complex. An erroneous assumption as to the identity of the carrier can be potentially fatal to any claim (for example, bringing a claim against a 'wrong' party just before a time bar expires). If there is any doubt, seek advice. However, as a general rule the contractual carrier should be identified objectively and "in the way in which a reasonable person, versed in the shipping trade would read the bill" (*The Starsin* [2003] UKHL 12). They will usually be identified as carrier on both the front and reverse of the bill.

Air and road transport

The above checklist is an equally useful guide to follow in relation to both air and road transport claims.

If the above checklist is followed, at the outset it should be possible to quickly ascertain

i) The identity of the carrier

ii) The jurisdiction in which the claim should be brought

iii) The law applicable to the claim

iv) Any limitation date

v) Whether any package limitation applies.

The following sections address issues specific to both air transport and road transport claims.

Air transport

Documentation

An air waybill (AWB) is similar in function to that of a bill of lading in that it is both a receipt of goods by an airline (carrier) and a contract of carriage between the shipper and the carrier. An AWB will usually set out the conditions of carriage upon the reverse of the document. Unlike a bill of lading, an AWB is a non-negotiable instrument.

There are several conventions that apply to air carriage. In order to determine which applies, the place from which the aircraft takes off and the destination must be established; consider which is the most recent convention to apply between the two.

The key provisions of each applicable convention are set out below:

	When does it apply?		Time bar	Notification of claims	Limit of liability
Montreal Convention	All international carriage of persons, baggage or cargo performed by aircraft for reward. Also gratuitous carriage by aircraft performed by an air transport undertaking **(Article 1)**	**Loss/damage**	2 years from the date of arrival, when the aircraft ought to have arrived or on which carriage stopped **(Article 35)**	Written notice 'forthwith' after discovery of damage and at the latest within 14 days from receipt of cargo and within 7 days from the date of receipt in the case of checked baggage. In the case of delay, within 21 days from the date on which the baggage or cargo have been placed at disposal **(Article 31.2)**	19 SDRs per kg for cargo (unless value declared for carriage) **(Article 22.3)**
		Delay	As above	As above	As above

Warsaw Convention

When does it apply?		Time bar	Notification of claims	Limit of liability
All international carriage of persons, baggage or goods performed by aircraft for reward. Also gratuitous carriage by aircraft performed by an air transport undertaking **(Article 1)**	**Loss/damage**	2 years from the date of arrival, when the aircraft ought to have arrived or on which carriage stopped **(Article 29)**	Written notice 'forthwith' after discovery of damage and at the latest within 14 days from receipt of cargo and within 7 days from the date of receipt in the case of checked baggage. In the case of delay, within 21 days from the date on which the baggage or cargo have been placed at disposal **(Article 26.2)**	17 SDRs per kg for cargo (unless value declared for carriage) **(Article 22)**
	Delay	As above	As above	As above

Road transport

Documentation

For the international carriage of goods by road throughout Europe, much of the Middle East and some of Africa, the contract of carriage will be subject to the compulsory application of the Convention on the Contract for the International Carriage of Goods by Road (the CMR). This convention contains provisions which impose obligations on the parties to the contract and which determine their liability in the case of loss, damage or delay.

Usually the carrier will issue a consignment note which contains the information that is required by the CMR. This consignment note is known as a CMR note. The CMR note will list the contracting parties, provide details of the goods accepted for carriage and contain any special instructions or any notes on the cargo which might be relevant to the carriage. The CMR note is a receipt and acts as confirmation that a contract of carriage exists between the shipper and carrier. The absence of such a document will not prevent the CMR convention provisions from being applied to the contract. Unlike a bill of lading, a CMR note is not a document of title.

There is frequently a long list of carriers and sub-contractors involved and one of the most difficult issues can be to identify a carrier against whom a claim can be brought. This issue is discussed in more detail in the freight forwarders' liability section.

We set out the key provisions of the CMR convention below:

	When does it apply?	Time bar	Notification of claims	Limit of liability	Time bar
CMR	To every contract for the carriage of goods by road in vehicles for reward when the place of taking over the goods and the place of designated delivery are situated in two different countries of which at least one is a contracting party **(Article 1)**	**Loss/damage**	1 year from: (a) the date of delivery (partial loss, damage or delay); (b) 30th day after the expiry of agreed time limit (total loss) or if no agreed limit, 60th day from when the goods were taken over by the carrier; and 3 years for wilful misconduct **(Article 32)**	If apparent, reservation must be sent at time of delivery. If not, 7 days after delivery **(Article 30)**	8.33 SDRs per kg of gross weight short. (Article 23(3)) plus carriage charges, customs duties and other charges **(Article 23(4))** No limit for wilful misconduct **(Article 29)**
		Delay	1 year from the date of delivery **(Article 32)**	21 days from time goods placed at disposal **(Article 30)**	Damages shall not exceed the carriage charges **(Article 23(5))**

Marine casualties

Introduction

The way in which cargo is transported on the high seas and the sheer volume of cargo being traded on a daily basis means that shipping casualties are a certainty, on an almost daily basis. Marine casualties can take many forms and can occur at any point during the maritime adventure. When marine casualties occur they are often expensive and can impact the relevant cargo insurer.

The most common form of marine casualties are:

- Fire.
- Grounding
- Collision with another vessel
- Engine breakdown giving rise to salvage services and/or a declaration of general average (GA)
- Heavy weather damage
- Shift of cargo
- Actual or constructive total loss of ship and/or cargo.

In this chapter, an introduction is provided to salvage and GA, focusing on the steps that need to be taken by the prudent cargo interest (whether the owner or the insurer) in a case where a fire has occurred on board a multi-interest container carrier giving rise to a declaration of GA. The position following engine breakdown, leading to immobilisation and thereafter a grounding that has resulted in salvage services being rendered under the provisions of Lloyd's Open Form salvage agreement (LOF), is also considered.

Salvage

Salvage can take two forms. There is contract salvage, such as where a tug is engaged on a lump sum or daily rate to tow a vessel that has broken down to an agreed location. The cost of this may be recoverable by an express provision in the policy or as a sue and labour expense, or in appropriate circumstances may form part of GA (see below).

There is also maritime salvage. This describes the reward payable to persons, known as salvors, who, acting voluntarily, successfully preserve property (ship, cargo, bunkers, freight and stores) at sea from the risk of danger. This is 'no cure, no pay' salvage.

The obligation to contribute to maritime salvage may arise at common law or under terms such as Lloyd's Open Form (LOF). LOF salvage is administered by the Lloyd's Salvage Arbitration Branch (LSAB) and in accordance with the Lloyd's Standard Salvage and Arbitration Clauses.

Salvors have a maritime lien over the property saved and, on completion of the services, property interests will have to provide security to the salvors for the salvage contributions due. The International Salvage Union (ISU) has approved guarantee wordings for this purpose.

The amount of the salvage reward is, in most cases, assessed by reference to the criteria set out in Article 13 of the International Convention on Salvage 1989. Each property interest contributes to an Article 13 award by reference to its salved (not sound) value as a proportion of the total salved values (known as the salved fund).

The contributions to a common law or LOF salvage award due from each property interest are, for marine insurance purposes, treated as a loss caused by the peril from which the property was saved (s.65 MIA 1906): see *The Vergina* [2001].

Article 14 of the International Convention on Salvage 1989 entitles the salvors to special compensation for efforts to prevent damage to the environment where the Article 13 award is insufficient to cover the salvor's expenses. Such compensation is payable by the owners of the ship, and is a P&I risk. An industry agreement known as SCOPIC allows the salvors to opt to recover lump sum rates instead of Article 14 special compensation.

Under LOF the amount of the salvage award will be agreed between the parties or determined by a specialist arbitrator appointed by LSAB. Insurers of property required to contribute in salvage will customarily appoint lawyers to represent them in the arbitration proceedings. Most LOF salvage claims are settled amicably. The Admiralty Court (part of the Commercial Court) has jurisdiction to determine common law salvage claims and this will be considered in more depth below.

General average

General average (GA) is a long-standing practice of maritime law of the carriage of goods by sea. It enables the sharing of extraordinary costs or expenses voluntarily incurred by one party to safeguard the common maritime adventure such as where a ship carrying cargo needs to put into a port of refuge for temporary repairs.

The circumstances and expenses that qualify for this purpose, and the amount of each party's contribution, are usually determined in accordance with the York-Antwerp Rules. Qualifying expenses may include some salvage payments, other than special compensation payable in accordance with Article 14 of the Salvage Convention, and sums payable under SCOPIC.

When a maritime casualty gives or may give rise to GA expense it is customary for one party, usually the ship's owners, to 'declare' GA. Appointed adjusters will collect GA security from interested parties. They review and allocate the expenses equitably in the form of a written GA adjustment. This will set out the amount due from each interested party.

Major containership casualties often give rise to very long-drawn-out and complex GA adjustments because of the number of different interests involved.

One good example of a GA expense would be a ransom payment made to secure the release of a ship and cargo seized by pirates. Such expenses certainly are recoverable in GA.

Expenses incurred for the safety of ship or cargo alone are not ordinarily general average expenses but may constitute special charges under the contract of carriage. For marine insurance purposes, such expense is termed 'particular charges' and may be recoverable under the policy as a sue and labour expense.

Fire and general average (GA)

For the purpose of this section the example of a fire originating in a sea container mid-voyage is considered.

If a fire takes hold on board a container carrier the first objective of the crew is to extinguish the fire as quickly and safely as possible. If the crew cannot extinguish the fire of their own accord it is likely that the owners of the vessel will have to engage fire-fighting tugs to render assistance to the vessel and her cargo. In these circumstances, the owners of the vessel are likely to declare GA in order to recover extraordinary costs incurred while in a position of peril to safeguard the common maritime adventure.

In circumstances where a containership has suffered a fire and the owners of the ship have declared GA, there are a number of important steps that should be taken in order to ensure that the position of the cargo underwriters is in no way prejudiced.

These steps, among others, include the following:

1) First, establish who insures the cargo laden on board the containership that has suffered the fire and the value of the cargo in question. Frequently, vessel owners and/or carriers will send out notices to shippers and receivers of cargo advising that a fire has taken hold and that GA has been declared. The earlier that notification of the casualty is given, the more time is available to consider the steps to be taken.

2) Determine the condition of the cargo and whether it has suffered any losses. A container carrier that has suffered a fire may well be towed to a port of refuge where cargo will be offloaded and surveyed (frequently a GA surveyor will be appointed to survey cargo for the good of the maritime community involved). The surveyors must try and ascertain whether the cargo was damaged by fire or by the use of water in extinguishing the fire as the latter may give rise to a sacrificial claim in GA. A sacrificial loss is one which is incurred in the operation to preserve the maritime property. For example, if a cargo is damaged by water due to the efforts to extinguish the fire in order to preserve the maritime adventure then such losses will be considered a sacrificial loss. Sacrificial losses will be made good in GA, less their original liability in GA. However, the indemnity for a sacrificial loss will be reduced to take into consideration the contribution which that party would otherwise have made in GA.

3) If vessel owners declare GA they will, at a very early stage, appoint GA adjusters who will be responsible for collecting GA security. Once a cargo is surveyed and is found to be sound, the vessel owners can exercise their maritime lien over the cargo. In such circumstances they will demand that GA security is provided to their satisfaction prior to on-forwarding of any cargo. GA security ordinarily comes in the form of a GA guarantee (to be provided by the cargo insurer) and a GA bond (to be provided by the owner of the cargo).

4) Prior to the issuance of any GA security, there are several obstacles to be overcome in order to ensure that the cargo underwriter's position is protected. First, it must be established that the cargo is sound or at the very least has residual value against which a GA claim can be progressed. Ordinarily, GA will be adjusted based on the sound arrived market value of cargo. Therefore, if cargo is a total loss there is no need to issue GA security as the vessel owners do not have a claim in GA against cargo that is a total loss. Further, the insurer must be satisfied it is on risk for GA and actually insures the cargo in question that

was on board the casualty at the time of the GA incident. Once the insurer is satisfied with the above, the wording of the security must be considered.

5) The wording of the security being demanded by the vessel owners must be carefully reviewed and considered before any security is provided. Frequently the vessel owners will seek security for GA monies "properly due". This prejudices the cargo underwriter. Under such wording, once GA monies are ascertained to be due by an adjuster, they are seen as legally due and become immediately payable, notwithstanding any defence which may be available to the cargo interests in relation to payment of GA. The case of the *Maersk Neuchatel* [2014] highlighted the importance of GA security wording.

6) Once the cargo underwriter is happy with the wording of the GA security, the recovery aspect of the case must be considered. The insurer of the cargo that suffered damage must establish the party against whom they may have a recovery claim, be it in contract (ordinarily against the contractual carrier who has issued the bill of lading) or in tort (ordinarily against the vessel owner and/or the operator of the containership).

7) There are many considerations that come into play when considering the recovery aspect if cargo has suffered damage. What is the quantum of loss? What caused the damage? Who are the likely recovery targets? Is it economically viable to pursue a recovery? Should security be obtained for a recovery claim? All these aspects need to be dealt with as soon as a casualty has occurred and once the cargo insurers are exposed to claims under their policy or policies.

8) If cargo has been unaffected by the fire and/or extinguishing operation, the cargo insurer must ascertain at an early stage the likely exposure to GA in order to consider the options available. In many cases a ship and/or cargo will have suffered significant damage and/or sacrificial losses that are recoverable in GA. This may mean that cargo that is sound will have to pay a considerable sum in GA, possibly in exceptional circumstances

up to the value of the cargo in question. Therefore, the cargo insurer must carefully consider the appointment of a fire expert in order to investigate the cause of the fire.

9) The fire expert will investigate how the fire was caused, which will assist in identifying potential avenues of recovery available to the cargo insurer. Further, it will assist in ascertaining whether the fire occurred as a result of the unseaworthiness of the vessel, which, in turn, could mean that the cargo insurer can defend any claim for GA. The claim by the vessel owners for GA may be defended if the fire occurred as a result of causative unseaworthiness that was discoverable by due diligence on the part of the owners of the vessel. Any such defence to GA is brought under Rule D of the York-Antwerp Rules, commonly known as a Rule D defence. It is imperative that documents surrounding causation are obtained from the vessel owners at the earliest opportunity so that investigations can commence at the earliest possible stage.

10) Once it has been decided that a fire expert should be appointed, access to the casualty has to be obtained. Vessel owners will frequently deny access to a casualty and her crew. In these circumstances, advice should be taken from local lawyers in order to establish the options available to gain access on board a vessel and access to her papers. For example, in Singapore an application can be made to the local court for immediate access to a casualty for a fire expert to attend on board to commence investigations as to causation, and such an order will often be granted immediately by the local court.

11) Once a GA security has been provided, cargo has been on-forwarded, and investigations have commenced, usually the vessel owners will pass documents to the GA adjusters, who will be responsible for drafting the GA adjustment.

12) The GA adjustment will be drafted in accordance with the York-Antwerp Rules, which govern the claims and allowances in GA. The York-Antwerp Rules will be written into each contract of affreightment. The most commonly seen version is the 1994

version of the Rules, notwithstanding the fact that two newer versions have come into force, namely the 2004 Rules and the 2016 Rules.

In summary, when a fire casualty occurs and vessel owners of a casualty declare GA, the cargo insurers are faced with a significant number of very important issues to consider quickly in order that their position isn't in any way prejudiced. Of particular importance is the obtaining of documents from the vessel owners in relation to causation and further to commence investigations as soon as is practically possible.

Engine breakdown, grounding and LOF salvage services

When a vessel suffers a peril such as an engine breakdown and salvage services are rendered under Lloyd's Open Form salvage agreement, the cargo insurer can be faced with a number of claims and counter claims. To illustrate, we shall use the example of a bulk carrier that is suffering engine breakdown, grounding and subsequently receives LOF salvage services.

The engine breakdown

When considering a bulk cargo, such as wheat, soya bean or aluminium pellets, it is likely that the value of the consignment will be high, which, in turn, means that any financial exposure arising as a result of a casualty could be significant.

In the situation where a bulk carrier suffers an engine breakdown the crew may try to rectify the problem in order to restore motive power. If the crew cannot restore power, the vessel owners may have to seek salvage assistance under either a commercial salvage agreement (the vessel owners may then declare GA in order to recover cargo interests' proportion of the costs incurred to safeguard the common maritime adventure) or the vessel owners may engage professional salvors to render assistance under the provisions of an LOF salvage agreement, which will be discussed further in this section.

It is possible that a vessel may be unfortunate enough to suffer an engine breakdown, thereby rendering her immobilised, while transiting close to rocks or in shallow waters, which increases the danger of her running aground. Clearly, in such circumstances, the risks and dangers to vessel, the cargo and her crew are increased and therefore the vessel owners have to act quickly and decisively in order to try and ensure the ship and her cargo are not lost.

Lloyd's Open Form salvage agreement (LOF)

LOF salvage agreement was developed in the late nineteenth century/early twentieth century when the Council of Lloyd's appointed Sir Henry Johnson of Waltons & Morse to draft a suitable salvage contract. As such, the first LOF contract for use in marine salvage was published in 1908.

The essence of the contract is based on a 'No Cure – No Pay' principle in order to ensure that professional salvors are remunerated for the salvage services that they perform in salving a ship and her cargo.

Once salvors are engaged by the owners of a vessel in peril, the LOF contract will be agreed between the owners of the vessel and the salvors and the LOF contract will be signed by the master. Importantly, the master of the vessel has the ability to contract with the salvors on behalf of all property interests involved, including cargo, container interests and bunkers. Thereafter, once the LOF is signed the salvors will be contractually obliged to use their best endeavours to salve the casualty and her cargo.

Often, salvage services can be long in duration, will be rendered in difficult weather and seas and can be extremely hazardous in nature. Once the casualty has been successfully salved the salvors will, frequently, nominate a port of refuge where the ship will be delivered back to her owners. Under the provisions of LOF the salvage services are considered to be ongoing until the ship and her cargo are at an agreed place of safety. Once the casualty has reached the agreed port of refuge the salvors will re-deliver the ship to her owners and a re-delivery certificate will be signed.

LOF salvage security

Upon the successful completion of salvage services, the salvors have a lien over the salved property, including cargo. Prior to any delivery or on-forwarding of the cargo, the salvors are entitled to demand security to their satisfaction in order to safeguard their claim against the cargo and release their lien. The responsibility for collecting salvage security rests with the Lloyd's Salvage Arbitration Branch, who are based in the Lloyd's building in London. It is at this point that the cargo insurers will be exposed to a liability under the policy in relation to salvage costs.

The salvors will usually quantify their demand for security taking into account the nature of the salvage services rendered, the costs incurred in the rendering of the salvage services and the likely level of remuneration they will receive. At this point the security demand will be issued and cargo insurers will be called upon to provide salvage security, to be lodged with the Lloyds' Salvage Arbitration Branch. The value of the security provided must not exceed the value of the cargo salved. In practice the salvors will not demand security above the value of the cargo salved. Any security lodged must always be lodged with the caveat that security is lodged under protest as to quantum.

Cargo survey

Once salvage security is provided and the cargo is released, it is extremely important that the cargo is surveyed at the earliest possible opportunity. If there appears to be significant damage, surveyors acting on behalf of salvors, ship interests and P&I interests must be invited to attend a joint survey. Under LOF, property interests contribute to salvage remuneration based on the salved values as at termination of the cargo services. The cargo insurer must, therefore, obtain evidence as quickly as possible in order to determine the salved value of the cargo. The appointment of surveyors at the earliest opportunity is essential.

Salvage remuneration

Following the provision of salvage security, the salvors will then wish to progress their claim for reward, or remuneration, for the salvage services rendered to the casualty. While the salvage services are rendered under the provisions of LOF, it is Article 13 of the 1989 Salvage Convention that dictates the parameters against which remuneration is adjudged.

Article 13 of the Salvage Convention states that, when consideration is given as to the quantum of remuneration, the following must be taken into account:

1) The value of the salved property.
2) The skill and efforts of the salvors in minimising the damage to the environment.
3) The measure of success obtained by the salvor.
4) The nature and degree of the danger.
5) The skill and effort of the salvor in salving the vessel.
6) The time and expenses incurred by the salvors or their equipment.
7) The risk of liability and other risks run by the salvor.
8) The promptness of the services rendered.
9) The availability of alternative assistance.
10) The state of readiness and efficiency of the salvors' equipment and value thereof.

The salvors will, at a very early stage, appoint an arbitrator who, in the absence of amicable settlement of the salvors' claim will hear the salvors' claim by way of private submission to arbitration. LOF contains an English law and arbitration clause. Thereafter, once the arbitrator has heard the salvors' case and the case of the property interests, they will publish the award determining how much the salvors should be paid for the salvage services rendered.

The award can be appealed on grounds of quantum or on a point of law and, once the appeal award is published, cargo interests will be liable for salvage under the award. At this point, ordinarily, the cargo insurer will be called to settle the sums due in salvage and, once paid, the salvage security must be returned for cancellation.

Causation investigation

Immediately a cargo interest and/or a cargo insurer is notified of LOF salvage services to a casualty with an interest in or insurance of cargo laden on board, immediate consideration must be given to investigation. As with fire and GA, the cargo interest/cargo insurer must consider whether to appoint an expert to investigate what happened.

In the case of LOF, the cargo insurer may have a third-party salvage indemnity claim (the money paid to the salvors for the salvage services rendered to the ship and cargo) to pursue. The Hague and the Hague-Visby Rules, which govern many contracts of carriage, state that the owners must provide a seaworthy vessel at the commencement of the voyage. If not, then cargo interests may have a strong claim to recover any monies paid in salvage against the vessel owners.

The prudent cargo interest or prudent cargo insurer should consider the following at a very early stage:

1) What is the value of the cargo insured on board the casualty?
2) What are the nature, extent, risks, dangers and financial outlay of the salvage services?
3) What is the likely exposure the cargo owner may have to salvage?
4) Is there any indication as to the cause of the engine breakdown?
5) Would it be prudent to try and obtain access for an expert to investigate causation?
6) Is it economically viable to appoint an expert to investigate?

7) Against whom do cargo interests have a potential recovery claim, for example the bill of lading issuer or the vessel owner?

8) Is the vessel in a jurisdiction that is favourable to applications for access should the vessel owners refuse to grant access amicably?

9) What options are available for obtaining security for any claim? Is the security offered in an acceptable format and backed by an adequately rated insurer or P&I Club?

These are the principal questions that the cargo insurer must consider as soon as it appears likely that salvors may have to be paid for salvage services rendered and to also consider the pursuit of a salvage indemnity claim.

Summary

There are many different facets to a casualty case and no two cases are the same. When a shipping casualty arises, cargo interests face a number of complex and challenging issues. Very early on the cargo interests must consider investigation into cause and the possible appointment of experts. Moreover, consideration must be given to the provision of security for the claim in GA or salvage and to the obtaining of security for the possible subsequent indemnity claim.

Freight forwarders' liability

Introduction

The term 'freight forwarder' is often used with no real consideration as to what that term means. So, what is a freight forwarder?

In practice, the words 'freight forwarder' may describe parties providing a wide range of services and, under English law, the expression has no legal definition. A freight forwarder can perform a number of roles, such as a carrier, an agent or even as a contractor for a particular service only, such as customs clearance.

It is important to establish the role of the freight forwarder in any particular transport as the role performed will have an effect upon its liabilities under not only an agreed contract, but also under the various conventions that may be applicable.

Identifying whether a party is contracted as an agent or carrier

In the case of *Tetroc Ltd v Cross-Con (Int) Ltd* [1981] the court laid down a number of tests in order to establish whether a party is an agent or a carrier. Questions that are to be considered are, among others:

a) Did the forwarder move the goods?

   A person who contracts to carry the goods will still be a carrier even if the actual performance of the whole of the carriage is sub-contracted to someone else.

b) How were the pricing arrangements agreed?

   If a forwarder provides an 'all in' quote, this is likely to indicate that the forwarder acted as a carrier, rather than an agent.

c) What were the terms of the contract?

   Words like "arrange" within the contractual documents hold little weight. Further, a forwarder can still be deemed to be a carrier, even if not named in any contractual documents, such as a consignment note. Consider what the parties have agreed in terms of services.

d) Was the customer kept informed of the arrangements in place?

   For example, was the customer informed of the instructions sent from a forwarder to a sub-contractor? If not, the court is more likely to lean towards the forwarder acting as a carrier.

e) Overall review of the carriage documents, such as CMR consignment note, bills of lading, air waybills etc.

   The court will look at the overall picture presented in the contractual documents, together with the real intention of

> the parties. Words such as "forwarding agent" and "freight forwarder" only go some way towards establishing the role of the forwarder.

There are additional considerations that a court may look to, such as any previous course of dealings. However, the court's decision is "a matter of impression, what impression the evidence forms" (*Hair & Skin Trading Co. Ltd v Norman Air Freight Carriers and World Transport Agencies Ltd* [1974]).

Contractual terms and a forwarder's liability

There are numerous standard terms and conditions that parties may incorporate, all with varying liability regimes.

Below are considered a number of industry standard terms and conditions and the potential liability of a forwarder under those terms and conditions.

It is also relevant to consider that forwarders are now providing many 'add-ons' as services, such as warehousing and customs clearance, ancillary to the carriage itself. With those ancillary services come additional liabilities.

British International Freight Association Standard Trading Conditions 2005A (BIFA)

Many forwarders in the UK are trading members of BIFA. BIFA conditions envisage that a forwarder will provide a variety of services beyond carrying out or arranging the carriage of goods.

Clause 2(A) states,

> "Subject to sub-paragraph (B) below, all and any activities of the Company in the course of business, whether gratuitous or not, are undertaken subject to these conditions."

There are a number of clauses that are worthy of note and are often the subject of dispute between a forwarder and its customer. Both the rights and liabilities of the forwarder need to be considered at the outset when dealing with any dispute. For example, while a forwarder may be liable for a particular failure under BIFA, similarly, there are limits and defences that a forwarder can rely upon within BIFA.

a) Clause 8 – Rights of lien

> “ 8. Subject to Sub-Clause (B) below,
>
> The Company:
>
> i) Has a general lien on all Goods and documents relating to Goods in its possession, custody or control for all sums due at any time to the Company from the Customer and/or Owner on any account whatsoever, whether relating to the Goods belonging to, or services provided by or on behalf of the Company to the Customer or Owner. Storage charges shall continue to accrue on any Goods detained under lien; ”

The general lien (which is wider than a specific or particular lien) granted by Clause 8 of BIFA attaches in respect of sums due from the customer and/or owner of the cargo. This can be particularly useful where, for example, a forwarder has offered an ‘add-in’ to warehouse the goods. This may provide the forwarder with the possibility of exercising a lien over the goods, for example, for non-payment of carriage charges or storage costs.

At common law, a party wishing to exercise a lien must possess the goods. In the current BIFA conditions, the word “possession” is supplemented by the words “custody or control”. Moreover, the common law lien has no right of sale. BIFA confers a contractual right of sale.

b) Clauses 17 and 18 – Customer warranties and dangerous goods

> “ 17. The Customer warrants:
>
> (A)(i) that the description and particulars of any Goods or information furnished, or services required, by or on behalf of the Customer are full and accurate … ”

The warranty contained within Clause 17 protects a forwarder where they may not be fully informed as to the nature and characteristics of the goods. This is particularly relevant if the forwarder is arranging for carriage of goods that may be dangerous or harmful.

Clause 18 goes on to state:

> “18. Without prejudice to any rights under Clause 15, where the Customer delivers to the Company, or causes the Company to deal with or handle Goods of a dangerous or damaging nature, or Goods likely to harbour or encourage vermin or other pests, or Goods liable to taint or affect other goods, whether declared to the Company or not, he shall be liable for all loss or damage arising in connection with such Goods ... ”

The warranty at Clause 17(A) provides an obligation upon the customer to provide relevant information and, upon sufficient notification, the risk is placed on the forwarder. Clause 18, however, applies regardless of any notification and/or fault on the part of the customer. The contradiction between Clauses 17 and 18 can be rather confusing. However, in summary, the burden is upon the customer and the forwarder can rely upon Clause 18 in defence to any such claims.

c) Clause 24 – Exclusion of liability

> “24. The Company shall be relieved of liability for any loss or damage, if, and to the extent that, such loss or damage is caused by:
>
> ...
>
> (B) any cause or event which the Company is unable to avoid, and the consequences of which the Company is unable to prevent by the exercise of reasonable diligence. ”

Clause 24(B) is of particular interest as many disputes centre on the interpretation of actions that a company is "unable to prevent" and the "exercise of reasonable diligence". The test under Clause 24 will need to be assessed on a case-by-case basis.

Example

A warehouse fire caused the loss of a significant amount of stock belonging to over 50 cargo interests. The fire was a result of a leaking gas valve on a forklift truck that was stored in a warehouse overnight. After obtaining reports and expert evidence, it was found that the damage to the gas valve was such that the damage would not have been visible to the naked eye. Further, the leak appeared to have been continuing for five days, with the forklift truck working at full power for those five days. The forwarder completed a checklist every day that indicated that the forklift truck had been working as normal with no signs of damage. The forwarder put forward a defence under Clause 24(B), in that the forwarder had exercised all reasonable diligence and was unable to prevent the consequences of the fire. In the above example, it appears that the forwarder may be able to demonstrate that it has exercised all reasonable skill and care in its maintenance and dealings with the equipment. The documentary evidence demonstrating this will be important. As such, the defence has a reasonable prospect of succeeding here.

The situation may, however, have been different if the forklift truck was due for a service or there was no evidence of regular maintenance checks.

There is, therefore, quite a fine line as to when a forwarder may be able to rely upon this defence.

It is also worth noting that a forwarder can be vicariously liable for the actions of its employees under BIFA. For example, where it is proved that a theft is an 'inside job', a forwarder may not be able to rely upon Clause 24(B) where the forwarder has failed to act diligently. For example, where a forwarder provided all employees with the alarm code and some employees broke in overnight to steal the goods, the forwarder was not able to rely upon such a defence (*Frans Maas (UK) v Samsung Electronics (UK) Ltd*) [2004].

d) Clause 26 – Limitation of liability

If a claim does not fall within the exclusion set out in Clause 24, a forwarder may limit its liability under Clause 26. Clause 26 may limit liability in respect of claims for loss or damage, claims for delay, and other general claims that may come under BIFA conditions. Sub-clause (A) deals with loss or damage to goods, and Sub-clause (B) deals with loss or damage as a result of failure to deliver goods within a reasonable time.

Loss or damage to goods

When considering limits of liability for loss or damage to goods, a forwarder can limit its liability to the value of the loss or damage, or a sum at the rate of 2 SDR per kilo of the gross weight of the goods lost or damaged, whichever is the lower. Therefore, if the goods are particularly light, a forwarder can significantly limit its liability.

Errors and/or omissions

In respect of errors and/or omissions, the relevant limit is the lesser of the loss incurred or 75,000 SDRs in the aggregate of any one trading year.

Delay

Where the company's liability is as a result of failing to deliver the goods within a reasonable time, such liability shall not exceed a sum "equal to twice the amount of the company's charges in respect of the relevant contract".

The majority of claims are, from experience, dealt with under the limits stipulated for loss or damage to goods. However, there appears to be no reason why, where goods arrive damaged and late, there cannot be a claim for both applicable limits for each claim applied together. A forwarder must ensure they are not caught by this and so are exposed to a higher claim limit than anticipated.

e) Clause 27 – Limitation of action

> “27. Notwithstanding the provisions of sub-paragraph (A) above, the Company shall in any event be discharged of all liability whatsoever and howsoever arising in respect of any service provided for the Customer, or which the Company has undertaken to provide, unless suit be brought and written notice thereof given to the Company within nine months from the date of the event or occurrence alleged to give rise to a cause of action against the Company.”

Clause 27 provides an overall time bar of nine months from the date of the event or occurrence alleged to give rise to a cause of action. Note, this is not the date of delivery or the date of discovery of the damage.

It should also be noted that in accordance with Clause 27(A) a claim must be notified to the company “within 14 days of the date upon which the customer became, or ought reasonably to have become, aware of any event or occurrence alleged to give rise to such claim…”.

However, the courts will consider each case on its own facts, and relevant factors such as the bargaining power of each of the parties will be taken into account.

Parties also need to be aware of the additional requirement to provide “written notice” of the suit issued within the nine-month time bar. This is a particular procedural requirement that many parties fall foul of. Most other terms and conditions stipulate a time bar in which proceedings must be commenced; however, they usually do not require notice of those proceedings to be provided within that same time bar.

Road Haulage Association Limited's Conditions of Carriage 2009 (RHA)

The RHA conditions are, as the name would suggest, drafted specifically with hauliers in mind. However, Clause 6(2) states:

> “6(2)Transit shall (unless otherwise previously determined) end when the consignment is tendered at the usual place of delivery ... ”

This suggests that, if agreed, the “transit” can continue while the goods are being temporarily stored at a warehouse, and the RHA conditions may apply to such storage. It would not be sufficient for a carrier to assume that those services are covered under some separate agreement, unless specified.

a) Clause 9 – Liability for loss and damage

Clause 9(2) states that the carrier shall only be liable if the loss is proved to be due to the negligence of the carrier, its servants, agents or sub-contractors. Such liability will only arise during “transit” and will not continue after the transit has ended within the meaning of Clause 6(2). Therefore, it is important to clarify what the “usual place of delivery” is and when the parties intend for the obligations under RHA conditions to cease.

A carrier could easily find itself liable under the RHA conditions even after the physical carriage aspect has ended.

A carrier may wish to incorporate different terms and, for example, different limits of liability, for any services carried out before (such as customs clearance or insurance) or after the carriage has ‘ended’. This will need to be explicitly agreed in order to provide certainty to the forwarder's liability.

b) Clause 11 – Limits of liability

If the carrier is liable under Clause 9, according to Clause 11(a) (b) and (c) that liability is limited to the lesser of the value of the goods lost/damaged, the costs of repairs to the goods, or the sum calculated at the rate of £1,300 per tonne on the gross weight of the goods. This is lower than the limit of liability under BIFA conditions, which equates to £1,839.30 per tonne, but significantly greater than the limits provided under the UKWA conditions, which is £100 per tonne.

Under Clause 11(1)(iv), however, the parties can agree to a higher limit of liability. Any agreement to increase the limit of liability will, however, be subject to an agreement for the carrier to increase the carriage charges raised. This is something to watch out for as carriers can inadvertently agree higher limits without realising the impact upon their liability should damage occur.

Clause 11(2) does provide for the recovery of indirect or consequential loss. Clause 11(2) states:

> “11(2) The liability of the Carrier in respect of claims for any other loss whatsoever (including indirect or consequential loss or damage and loss of market), and howsoever arising in connection with the Consignment, shall not exceed the amount of carriage charges in respect of the Consignment or the amount of the Claimant's proved loss, whichever is the lesser, ...”

c) Clause 13 – Time limits for claims

> “13(2) The carrier shall in any event be discharged from all liability whatsoever and howsoever arising in respect of the consignment unless suit is brought and notice in writing thereof given to the Carrier within one year of the date when transit commenced.”

The RHA conditions provide a slightly longer period in which to commence proceedings than the BIFA conditions. It is important to note that the one-year time bar runs from the date when carriage commenced, rather than from the date of damage. There is, however, the same requirement as under the BIFA conditions where notice must also be given of the commencement of proceedings within one year. There is no requirement for the claim form to be served.

Clause 13 further states that the claim must be notified to the carrier within seven days and a claim must be made in writing within 14 days in respect of physical loss, mis-delivery or non-delivery. This is extended to 28 days and 42 days respectively in respect of "any other loss".

d) Clause 14 – Lien

Clause 14 provides that the company has the right to exercise a general and specific lien.

> "14(1) The carrier shall have:
>
> a) a particular lien on the Consignment, and
>
> b) a general lien against the Trader for sums unpaid on any invoice, account or Contract whatsoever."

This may be a useful tool for a forwarder to rely upon.

Convention on the Contract for the International Carriage of Goods by Road (CMR)

a) Article 1 – When does the CMR apply?

The CMR applies to the international carriage of goods by road. Article 1 states,

> "1. This convention shall apply to every contract for the carriage of goods by road in vehicles for reward, when the place of taking over of the goods and the place designated for delivery, as specified in the contract, are situated in two different countries, of which at least one is a contracting country, irrespective of the place of residence and the nationality of the parties."

While the parties are free to agree certain contractual terms, such as BIFA and RHA as referred to above, the parties cannot derogate from the CMR (Article 41). The CMR applies by statute throughout much of Europe, and even some states in Asia and North Africa. However, parties are free to agree that the CMR will apply to a particular contract, even if the shipment is domestic only.

b) Article 23 – Liability

> “23(1) When, under the provisions of this Convention, a carrier is liable for compensation in respect of total or partial loss of the goods, such compensation shall be calculated by reference to the value of the goods at the place and time at which they were accepted for carriage.
>
> ...
>
> (3) Compensation shall not, however, exceed 8.33 units of account per kilogram of gross weight short.”

A forwarder may rely on the limits set out in Article 23 of the CMR if it is a carrier of goods by road. However, it is important to bear in mind that if goods are particularly heavy, the limit set out above can easily be exceeded. Equally, where goods are very light but expensive, the limit can significantly reduce any recovery.

The limits of liability can be increased by special agreement in accordance with Articles 24 and 26.

It would seem from the wording of Article 23 that the CMR covers carriage only, not a breach of ancillary services. If ancillary obligations are breached, there would be nothing to prevent a forwarder relying upon its own standard terms and conditions to limit liability. However, if the forwarder is relying on the CMR to limit liability and has not incorporated other limits of liability, it may be exposed to far greater liability than anticipated insofar as ancillary services are concerned.

c) Article 29 – Wilful misconduct

> “29(1) The carrier shall not be entitled to avail himself of the provisions of this chapter which exclude or limit his liability or which shift the burden of proof if the damage was caused by his wilful misconduct or by such default on his part as, in accordance with the law of the court or tribunal seized of the case, is considered as equivalent to wilful misconduct.
>
> (2) The same provision shall apply if the wilful misconduct is committed by the agents or servants of the carrier or by any other persons of whose services he makes use for the performance of the carriage, when such agents, servants or other persons are acting within the scope of their employment. Furthermore, in such a case such agents, servants or other persons shall not be entitled to avail themselves, with regard to their personal liability, of the provisions of this chapter referred to in paragraph 1.”

If wilful misconduct is established in accordance with Article 29, the carrier cannot rely on the limits of liability in the CMR. However, Article 29 is interpreted very differently throughout Europe with different jurisdictions being considered ‘cargo friendly’ or ‘carrier friendly’. Such considerations will be important when it comes to forum shopping, which is addressed in the Jurisdiction section below.

Each case must be considered on its own facts; however, it is not, on the whole, easy to break limits using Article 29 in England.

d) Article 32 – Time bar

> “32(1) The period of limitation for an action arising out of carriage under this Convention shall be one year. Nevertheless, in the case of wilful misconduct, or such default as in accordance with the law of court or

> tribunal seized of the case, is considered equivalent to wilful misconduct, the period of limitation shall be three years. ”

It is important to ensure that the one-year time bar is considered not only in respect of receiving a claim, but also with protecting a forwarders' recovery position against a sub-contractor. It is also important to assess when the one year time bar commences and whether it has been suspended by an appropriate claim.

If a forwarder pays a claim in accordance with the CMR, under Article 37 of the CMR, he is entitled to recover such sums paid, together with interest and costs, from the carrier responsible for the loss. Such a recovery action must be brought within one year from the date of the final judicial decision or actual date of payment. This is not, however, uniformly applied in different jurisdictions and it is best to enquire about recovery before one year from the date of the loss.

e) Article 31 and 39 – Jurisdiction

Article 31 allows the parties to bring proceedings in the courts or tribunals of a contracting country designated by agreement between the parties.

> “ 31 In legal proceedings arising out of carriage under the Convention, the plaintiff may bring an action in any court or tribunal of a contracting country designated by agreement between the parties and, in addition, in the courts or tribunals of a country within whose territory:
>
> a) The defendant is ordinarily resident, or has his principal place of business, or the branch or agency through which the contract of carriage was made, or
>
> b) The place where the goods were taken over by the carrier of the place designated for delivery is situated
>
> And in no other courts or tribunals."

It is important to note that if the parties contractually agree a jurisdiction, the country chosen must have contracted to the CMR. The parties cannot seek to exclude the CMR by agreeing jurisdiction in a non-contracting country. Article 31 is worded to suggest that any choice of jurisdiction by the parties is not exclusive. Rather, the choice is to be additional to the bases of jurisdiction set out in Article 31. To try and exclude the other heads of jurisdiction specified in Article 31 would be to derogate from Article 31 and would therefore be null and void as per Article 41. An exclusive arbitration agreement may be allowed.

As might be expected of an international convention which affects a number of parties in a number of different jurisdictions, the CMR contains detailed provisions on the issue of jurisdiction. Article 31 governs claims by cargo interests whereas Article 39.2 covers claims between successive carriers. To a forwarder, the successive carriage provisions are likely to be very relevant. If the forwarder is deemed to be acting as a carrier and thus has a liability for loss or damage suffered by the goods, the forwarder will be looking to pass on that liability.

> “39(2) A carrier wishing to take proceedings to enforce his right of recovery may make his claim before the competent court or tribunal of the country in which one of the carriers concerned is ordinarily resident, or has his principal place of business or the branch or agency through which the contract of carriage was made. All the carriers concerned may be made defendants in the same action.”

While the principle of 'forum shopping' exists under the CMR, the choice of jurisdiction for an indemnity action by a forwarder will be limited by Article 39(2).

In the case of *British American Tobacco Switzerland SA v H Essers Security Logistics BV* [2015], the Supreme Court held that although the first carrier could be sued in England (by reason of its English domicile and/or exclusive jurisdiction clause), this was not sufficient to found jurisdiction against subsequent, non-English, carriers and to allow them to be joined to the same proceedings. If consignees wish to be able to proceed in England against all carriers, they will need to ensure that express jurisdiction clauses are included in all consignment notes passed between successive carriers or that England is the place designated for collection or delivery of the goods.

United Kingdom Warehousing Association Conditions of Contract (UKWA)

As a forwarder, warehousing services can often be included with other services. If the parties choose, these may be governed by UKWA despite the carriage element being the dominant purpose of the agreement.

a) Clause 3 – Company's liability for goods and other losses

At Clause 3, a forwarder's liability is excluded, unless

> “3(ii) If and to the extent that Loss is directly caused by neglect or wilful act or default of the company, its employees (acting in furtherance of their duties as employees) or sub-contractors (acting in furtherance of their duties as sub-contractors) ...”

Further, that liability is limited under Clause 3(v) to £100 per tonne. This limit can be increased by agreement in writing; however, notice of the increase needs to be provided to the forwarder at least seven days before the increased limit is to be operative. The customer must also pay an additional amount for the increased costs in insuring against the increased liability.

In the case of *Sonicare International Ltd v East Anglia Freight Terminal Ltd* [1997] the court found that the £100 per tonne limit contained in the UKWA conditions was reasonable on the facts as found in the case but the judge expressed concern at the limit. However, this limit may be open to challenge in some circumstances under the Unfair Contract Terms Act 1977, particularly given the time elapsed since that judgment.

There is also a nine-month time bar at Clause 3(vii)(b), which states:

> “(b) No legal proceedings may be brought against the Company unless they are issued and served, and no counterclaim may be raised unless full written details are received by the Company within 9 months of the event giving rise to the Claim.”

Parties must remember that the proceedings must be served, as well as issued, within the nine-month time bar. Again, the requirement to not only issue but also serve proceedings may be subject to challenge on the terms of reasonableness.

In addition, UKWA terms and conditions state that a company shall not be liable for any claim unless it has received written notice of the claim from the customer within 21 days (seven days in the case of sub-contract carriage) of the cause of the claim coming to the customer's knowledge or of the goods being delivered by the company to or to the use of the customer, whichever is the later.

Conclusion

It is essential to remember time bars and claims notice periods. If a claim is not brought within the relevant stipulated time bars, a claimant may be barred from bringing a claim.

While the various industry standard terms and conditions provide for a number of liabilities and defences, a forwarder must also confirm that any referenced terms and conditions have been incorporated. Checking email signatures and references on invoices, etc. can assist with establishing incorporation of terms. In addition, some conventions, such as the CMR, will apply by statute and such mandatory conventions must also be considered when assessing a forwarder's liability.

30 Environmental claims

Joe McManus and Carole Vernon

Co-author: David Wright

- Tort
- Legislation
- Regulatory enforcement
- Policy coverage

Environmental claims

Private civil law claims and statutory enforcement

Introduction

Although the UK has had environmental laws in place for many years, it is over the last 20 years that they have begun to enjoy a much higher profile. This is, in part, due to greater political and public pressure to clean up the environment, much of which has been driven by EU legislation.

There are a variety of regimes in place to protect the environment covering different areas including:

- Contaminated land
- Water pollution
- Common law nuisance
- Waste.

Environmental law encompasses a range of environments including pollution of land and water as well as biodiversity damage.

Environmental torts

Where environmental damage has occurred, four torts can theoretically be used to impose liability on those responsible:

- Negligence
- Nuisance
- The rule in *Rylands v Fletcher* [1868]
- Trespass.

Negligence

Liability in negligence exists where one person falls short of the standard of conduct that is expected towards another person and injury or property damage ensues. This would include a company carelessly releasing pollutants into the local environment leading to damage to the local environment or those nearby becoming ill.

Three elements must be present to establish negligence.

- The defendant must owe a duty of care to the claimant.
- That duty must have been breached.
- Personal injury or damage to property must have been suffered by the claimant.

Nuisance

Common law nuisance can be subdivided into two categories:

- Private nuisance
- Public nuisance.

Private nuisance

Private nuisance is a tort based on the interference by one occupier of land with the right of enjoyment of land by another. The damage or interference with the enjoyment of the neighbour's land must be "substantial or unreasonable".

Nuisance can arise from a single incident or a continuing state of affairs.

The House of Lords in the case of *Cambridge Water Company v Eastern Counties Leather Plc* [1994], confirmed that:

- There is no liability in nuisance for damage that is not reasonably foreseeable.
- A private nuisance generally involves an ongoing or repeated harm.

- Loss can be categorised as either actual physical harm, such as contaminating a neighbour's soil or unreasonable interference with the property rights of a neighbour causing loss; examples of this include smell or noise pollution to neighbours.
- The longer the period over which the act occurs the more likely it is to amount to a nuisance. A one-off event is less likely to amount to a nuisance.
- The fact that the defendant may have planning permission or other permits for the activity causing the nuisance is not a defence in itself to a common law nuisance claim.

Defence to nuisance proceedings – the reasonable user

- Liability for nuisance is generally regarded as strict and there is no need to prove carelessness (negligence) by the defendant. However, if the use of the land is reasonable, the party causing the nuisance will not be liable for consequent harm to the neighbour's enjoyment of land. If use is unreasonable, the party causing the nuisance will be liable even if they exercised reasonable care and skill to avoid it.

Public nuisance

Public nuisance occurs when a party's actions materially affect the lives, comfort or property of the general public. Public nuisance is not only a tort, but also a crime. A large range of issues can be dealt with as public nuisance, including picketing on a road or sewage leaking into rivers. Court proceedings for public nuisances are generally instigated by local authorities in the magistrates' court and more serious cases can be resolved in the Crown Court. Damages for personal injury can be claimed in public nuisance claims.

Rylands v Fletcher

Rylands v Fletcher [1868] established that a defendant is strictly liable for damage caused by the escape from his land of things which he has accumulated in the course of a "non-natural" use of the land and which will cause damage if they escape. Under the rule, damages for death or personal injury are not recoverable, nor is it necessary to establish the defendant's negligence. In practice, the *ratio* in *Rylands v Fletcher* is frequently referred to but rarely tested in court. In the case of *Transco Plc v Stockport MBC* [2003], Lord Hoffmann expressed surprise that counsel could not find one case since the Second World War in which anyone had succeeded in a claim under the rule.

Trespass

Trespass to land is the voluntary, direct and unjustified intrusion by one person onto the land of another.

The leading case on the issue is *Coventry and others v Lawrence and another* [2014]. The Supreme Court stated that at first sight the remedy for the successful claimant is an injunction to restrain the defendant from committing a similar nuisance in the future. It was stressed that the public interest needs to be carefully considered and, furthermore, that the existence of planning permission that expressly or inherently authorises carrying on an activity in such a way as to create a nuisance can be a factor in the court refusing an injunction and compensating with damages instead.

Damages

The object of damages is to place a claimant in the position they would have been in had the nuisance not occurred. The measure of damages for the interference with a proprietary interest is generally the diminution in value of the claimant's property as a result of the nuisance. The court has a discretionary power to award damages in lieu of an injunction against the continuance of a wrongful act.

Environmental torts – shortcomings

In many environmental cases, tort is largely reactive rather than pro-active and in order to address this situation a series of statutory regimes have been created to address the shortcomings of tort in relation to environmental liability. These are set out in the table below.

Statutory regime

Ever since the UK joined the EU in 1972, European environmental legislation and its enforcement by UK regulators has become increasingly influential. Over time, single issue Directives have been replaced by framework Directives with a more integrated approach. It is now difficult to find an area where environmental regulations do not apply. Despite the breadth of their reach, however, and successive reviews aimed at simplification, many of them are still very detailed, technical and overly complicated.

A table summarising key environmental legislation and regulators is set out below.

Environmental area	Legislation	Provisions
Air	Clean Air Act 1993	Powers for local authorities to: designate and police smoke control areas – applies to most major UK towns and cities; approve new non-domestic boilers and height of certain chimneys; control dark smoke and fumes from industrial premises; and compel disclosure of air pollution information via service of notices.

Environmental area	Legislation	Provisions
	Environmental Permitting (England & Wales) Regulations 2010	Permitting regime designed to be integrated and wide ranging, primarily policed by the Environment Agency (EA) (in England), Natural Resources Wales (NRW) and Scottish Environment Protection Agency (SEPA) (Pollution Prevention and Control (Scotland) Regulations 2012 (PPC)). Local authorities also regulate small industries that must obtain environmental permits setting out air quality under the Industrial Emissions Directive.
	Statutory Nuisance – Part III Environmental Protection Act 1990 (EPA)	Duty on local authority to serve abatement notice if noise, odour or other nuisance "prejudicial to health or a nuisance" occurs, with the potential for civil and criminal sanctions.
Water	Environmental Permitting (England & Wales) Regulations 2010	Offence to cause (strict liability) or knowingly permit water discharge activity or groundwater activity (without environmental permit/exemption).

Environmental area	Legislation	Provisions
		Main regulators are EA, NRW and SEPA (PPC Regulations); also local authorities, water companies and Drinking Water Inspectorate.
Land	Contaminated land regime for remediation of land that causes unacceptable level of risk – Part IIA EPA 1990	Local authority/EA/NRW/SEPA serves remediation notice on "appropriate persons", i.e. those who caused or knowingly permitted contamination, or current owner/occupier.
	Environmental Damage Regulations 2015	Local authority/EA/NRW/SEPA serves remediation notice on "appropriate persons", i.e. those who caused or knowingly permitted contamination, or current owner/occupier. Aim is to prevent damage to water, protected species, natural habitats and land and to increase the responsibility of operators to address such damage. 'Polluter pays' principle, but not retrospective. EA/local authority serves notice or uses step-in powers to remediate. Of 30,000 cases of damage every year, only about 1% covered by the Regulations and little enforcement impact seen so far.

Environmental area	Legislation	Provisions
	s. 34 EPA 1990 – waste	General duty of care: Anyone who produces, imports, keeps, stores, transports, treats or disposes of waste must take all reasonable steps to ensure waste managed properly, including checking others' waste licences, storing safely and securely, and describing waste in writing and preparing/retaining transfer notes.
	Wildlife and Countryside Act 1981	Many plants, animals and habitats protected by a range of regulators, including police, Natural England and local authorities.

With Brexit on the horizon, businesses are now wondering if some of these regulations will disappear. Very little change is likely to take place in the short term and the longer-term prognosis is unclear, but, either way, if UK manufacturers wish to continue to trade with European partners, clients and consumers then it seems likely they will have little choice but to continue to comply with the relevant EU legislation.

In the meantime, environmental issues continue to feature ever more prominently in the boardrooms of major businesses, as awareness of environmental risk grows and environmental controls are increasingly viewed as part and parcel of corporate governance. Smaller businesses too are touched by these developments, but often at a more practical level.

Environmental enforcement trends in the UK

Tougher enforcement by regulators, including much larger fines, has played a part in UK industry's increased awareness of environmental risk. So too has the trend in environmental and other areas of regulation towards mandatory corporate transparency in the form of self-reporting, not only of ongoing performance, but also of breaches.

Self-reporting has now developed to the extent that it applies to even relatively minor, technical non-compliances as well as significant pollution events. By way of example, the EU's Restriction of Hazardous Substances (RoHS) Directive requires manufacturers and others to take remedial measures (including recall if appropriate) and immediately inform the relevant regulator where they have "reason to believe" their product has breached RoHS limits on the use of certain substances. In the UK, it is a strict liability criminal offence not to do so.

Subject to the impact of Brexit, analogous duties to remedy and self-report are being included in a wide range of consumer product regimes as part of the EU's drive towards harmonisation.

In some circumstances, the legal obligation to self-report may not be the primary driver for doing so. The enforcement policies and practices of most regulators recognise that early, voluntary flagging and admission of breach, followed by prompt steps to correct the situation and improve systems and procedures for the future, should result in more lenient sanctions. Should criminal prosecution nevertheless ensue, such actions are equally valuable mitigation in the criminal courts (see below). On an individual level, board directors and other senior managers who can show that they had a hand in the decision to self-report will be able to rely on this should a criminal investigation begin. While there is often, but not always, benefit to be had in admitting fault before anyone else finds out, this may not fit with an insurer's preferred approach to a case.

As well as the rise of self-reporting, many new environmental reporting regimes have come into force over the past few years. Indeed, the burden and complexity of reporting emissions, such as the Carbon Reduction Commitment, reporting energy efficiency via the Energy Savings Opportunity Scheme, greenhouse gas reporting for UK quoted companies, and various other statutory reporting duties, has finally driven the UK government to consult on a new, streamlined framework. While the product of consultation may be a simpler system, it is unlikely that the extent and degree of data to be gathered and reported by business will decrease.

In the courts, the level of fines imposed on UK business that fall foul of environmental legislation has been rising steeply since the introduction in 2014 of a new sentencing guideline for such offences, particularly for larger organisations. The guideline can be found here:

https://www.sentencingcouncil.org.uk/wp-content/uploads/Final_Environmental_Offences_Definitive_Guideline_web1.pdf

(Correct as at 4 January 2018)

In January 2016, the first £1m fine was imposed against Thames Water, for the pollution of the Grand Union canal in Hertfordshire. In an earlier, unrelated case against Thames Water, the Court of Appeal had made it clear that in the worst cases the appropriate level of fine might amount to as much as an organisation's pre-tax profits for the year, and that for "very large" companies this could quite conceivably mean fines in excess of £100m. While Thames Water has not been the only environmental offender to feel the force of the courts as they apply the new guideline's tougher approach, its cases have continued to hit the headlines. Most recently, the £20.3m fine imposed on Thames Water in March 2017 broke all previous records and attracted considerable media attention. Having heard submissions from the EA and Thames Water about a series of discharges of untreated sewage into the Thames from sewage treatment works and pumping stations in 2013 and 2014, the sentencing judge at Aylesbury Crown Court referred to what he considered to be "a shocking and disgraceful state of affairs". Referring to the company's "continual failure to report incidents" and "history of non-compliance", he went on to say that he had "to make the fine sufficiently large that they get the message".

In light of this developing enforcement landscape, insurers' and insureds' interests are not always as aligned as they once were and it is all the more important for close communication to take place from the earliest stage.

Investigating environmental claims

- Review the insurance policy and the cover provided.
- Consider who might be best placed to investigate (insured/loss adjuster/solicitor) and whether steps should be taken to extend legal professional privilege to any investigation and expert material that may be generated.
- Is expert input required? If so, which experts have the correct specialism and the right practical and forensic experience?
- Establish how long the problem has existed: is it a one-off or a regular occurrence?
- What measures had the company put in place to deal with the problem prior to the issue arising, and afterwards?
- Have there been repeated complaints and has the local environmental health officer (EHO) or the EA investigated previously? Consider the possibility of obtaining a copy of the authorities' papers, via simple request, Freedom of Information Act request or otherwise.

Environmental coverage issues

A more general discussion of policy coverage is at Chapter 35, so this section concentrates on common issues specific to environmental coverage.

Standard public liability (PL) policies cover many forms of third-party liability. They are subject to the important limitation that they generally cover only liability at law to pay damages or compensation. That means that they exclude two significant forms of loss: costs incurred in preventing pollution damage and costs incurred in cleaning up pollution damage where the costs have been incurred on the instruction of a regulatory authority rather than arising out of a private claim (see *Bartoline v RSA* [2006]).

It is also the case that PL policies generally do not cover claims that can be brought only in contract and typically they contain pollution exclusions that limit cover only to “sudden and unexpected” damage claims as opposed to damage caused by gradual pollution, including seepage. This has led to the development of specialist policies designed to indemnify the insured against the vast potential liabilities that may arise in relation to environmental matters.

Major risks will often be insured under tailor-made policies covering the potential liabilities in question and taking into account the law applicable to any claims against the insured in the relevant jurisdiction. Such policies, referred to as environmental impairment liability (EIL) policies, are generally written on a “claims made” basis (in contrast to the standard occurrence type wording for PL polices) and will cover seepage and gradual pollution liabilities in addition to remediation and clean-up costs. They may also cover some first party property losses such as remedial work to the insured’s own land.

EIL policies themselves are not unlimited in scope. In particular, the general law precludes recovery for criminal fines and claims arising from conduct that is deliberately designed to cause the loss in question, or which is reckless in that regard. This type of policy often excludes cover for criminal defence costs arising out of prosecutions by the EA or in relation to regulatory issues that do not relate to clean up, e.g. suspension notices.

As always the policy wording governs the scope of the cover, which can vary from insurer to insurer and is case specific.

Lack of coverage under PL policies for clean-up and regulatory enforcement

There are very broadly two types of third-party claims that result in environmental losses. The first are private law civil claims (often nuisance claims) brought by neighbours. When it is a one-off event, these are usually claims for compensation for what has already happened. The second are claims brought by the EA as environmental regulator.

The rule of thumb is that civil claims by neighbours may be covered by a standard PL policy (subject to the "sudden and unexpected" requirement) whereas claims arising out of regulatory action are generally not covered under such a policy.

The courts have decided that statutory claims by the EA and other regulators do not give rise to liability for damages, within the meaning of the typical insuring clause.

In the *Bartoline* case, a fire at Bartoline's factory caused contamination of a stream, and led the EA to spend over £600,000 in clean-up costs, which they attempted to reclaim from Bartoline under s.161 of the Water Resources Act 1991. Bartoline spent nearly £150,000 on complying with an EA works notice. Bartoline claimed on its PL policy, a claim that was declined by its insurers. Bartoline sued its insurers to recover both sums. The judge held that neither sum was recoverable. The liability to pay the £600,000 was not a liability to pay damages; it was a liability to pay a debt under a statute. Equally, Bartoline's expenditure on works that it carried out itself could not amount to a liability to pay "damages".

Pertinent sections from the judgment are:

> " **Para. 125** – The relevant clause of the Policy must be read as a whole. When read as a whole, it seems quite clear that the indemnity which it confers extends only to legal liability for damages in respect of certain types of tortious claim. Even if some latitude were permissible in construing these provisions in such a way as to bring within their scope some form of statutory liability which was essentially co-extensive with

> such tortious liability at common law, it seems to me that the liability of Bartoline under the relevant provisions of the 1991 Act is so different in its nature and scope as to preclude such an approach to the liability in question. ”

> “ **Para. 128** – I conclude, therefore, that it would be wrong to construe the relevant provisions of the Policy in such a way as to bring within the scope of the indemnity a liability pursuant to statute which is, in my judgment, analytically separate and distinct from the liability for damages in respect of breaches of tortious duty at common law which it is so plainly designed to cover. ”

Bartoline, as a first instance decision (High Court of Justice, Queen's Bench Division, Manchester District Registry, Mercantile Court), is not by itself binding on any other first instance judge. However, the main principles underlying the decision do come from authority in the Court of Appeal, and for all practical purposes, the law is settled unless and until a case reaches the Supreme Court on the point.

There are some fairly obvious anomalies in the *Bartoline* result. If pollutants from a factory escape and contaminate a privately owned river, its owner may clean up and then sue the factory owner for damage to both river and land. If this happens, the factory owner can claim on their PL policy. But if the EA steps in and carries out urgent river decontamination works before reclaiming the money under statute, the factory owner will not have cover under their PL policy.

The *Bartoline* case led to insurers giving *extensions* to general PL policies to cover this type of liability under a so-called Bartoline extension to PL coverage (such liability could also be insured under an environmental liability policy).

Is the incident sudden and unexpected?

In order to be covered under a PL policy for third-party losses it is generally necessary for the third-party damage to have been caused by a sudden and unexpected occurrence and usually there will be a pollution exclusion with a "carve out" for sudden and unexpected occurrences.

In the *Bartoline* case, the wording of the exclusion to the PL policy was: "The indemnity will not apply to legal liability ... caused by or arising out of pollution or contamination ... unless the pollution or contamination is caused by a sudden identifiable unintended and unexpected incident which takes place in its entirety at a specific moment in time and place during any Period of Insurance; provided that all pollution or contamination which arises out of one incident shall be considered by [the insurer] for the purposes of this policy to have occurred at the time such incident takes place."

What does "sudden" and "unexpected" mean?

"Sudden"

There is a lack of English authority on the meaning of the standard wordings of pollution exclusions so it is relevant to look at other jurisdictions.

The Australian judgment of Flanagan J in *Matton Developments Pty Ltd v CGU Insurance Ltd (No 2)* [2015] considers the meaning of the commonly used phrase "accidental, sudden and unforeseen" damage in respect of a property insurance policy.

The court referred to *Visy Packaging Pty Ltd v Siegwerk Australia Pty Ltd* [2013], a tort case reversed on appeal on other grounds, where it was noted that "sudden" might imply a temporal restriction or it might just mean unexpected. Australian insurance authority has, for the most part, adopted the latter view. The better view may be in a considerable body of authority from New Zealand and Singapore on the matter, not referred to by the Australian court in *Matton* Developments. Although the cases do conflict, there is certainly support in them for the proposition that "sudden" means immediate and without warning: see *Pacific Chemicals Pte Ltd v MSIG Insurance (Singapore) Pte Ltd* [2012] (where it was pointed out that if "sudden" meant no more than accidental and unforeseen, it would be superfluous in a clause of the type used in *Matton Developments*).

The High Court of Singapore ruling in *Pacific Chemicals Pte Ltd v MSIG Insurance (Singapore) Pte Ltd* had to consider in a property insurance policy whether damage was "unforeseen and sudden". It was held that the word "sudden" did not mean the same as "unforeseen", and was to be contrasted with "gradual". Synonyms were "abrupt" and "quick".

"Unexpected"/"Unforeseen"

A dictionary definition of "unexpected" is "not expected; unforeseen; surprising".

Flanagan J, in *Matton Developments*, accepted that "unforeseen" overlapped considerably with "accidental" although it did add to "unintended". It was noted that in *Federation Insurance Ltd v R Banks* [1984] the word "accident" was assumed to encompass "unforeseen".

Is the test of unforeseen loss objective or subjective? The better approach would, in our view, appear to be a combination of the two. Was the incident unexpected from the point of view of the insured? The objective qualifications to the subjective test appear to be:
(a) where an insured gambles or courts a risk or takes a calculated risk with knowledge of its potential outcome, that is classed as a deliberate acceptance of that risk and is not unexpected; or
(b) where an insured voluntarily embarks on a foolhardy venture from which the loss or damage that resulted was the almost inevitable consequence, that cannot be said to be unexpected.

PL policy cover and EIL covers compared

Policies will give cover based on their specific wordings, which will vary, but it is possible to give some general comparisons (see the table below as a guide). EIL wordings might be split into sections covering third-party and first-party cover.

Comparisons between PL, property and EIL coverage:

Coverage	PL	Property	EIL
Sudden & accidental pollution	Yes	No	Yes
Gradual pollution	No	No	Yes
Historic pollution	No	No	Yes
Statutory clean-up	No	No	Yes
On-site first-party clean-up	No	No	Yes
Environmental liability directive	No	No	Yes
Environmental damage	No	No	Yes
Loss mitigation	No	No	Yes

31 Aviation

Mark Welbourn

Co-author: Sam Mason

- International Framework – The Warsaw/ Montreal System
- Baggage claims
- Passenger claims
- Cargo claims
- Major losses
- Outside the Conventions – general aviation

Aviation

Introduction

Aviation is by its very nature an international industry and covers a wide scope of different activities from General Aviation (private flights and smaller commercial operators) and domestic carriage, through to major international carriers operating fleets of aircraft numbering in the hundreds. The International Civil Aviation Organization (ICAO) has 191 member states and the International Air Transport Association (IATA) represents the interests of 272 airlines across 117 countries. The international nature of aviation claims will often bring the claims handler into contact with a variety of customs, practices and legal systems in a variety of jurisdictions. While claims can cover a variety of subjects, this chapter will focus on the broad topics of:

- Baggage claims
- Passenger claims
- Cargo claims.

Although this guide will focus on international carriage by air for reward, 'general aviation' (covering a wide range of activities from hang-gliding to business jets) in fact covers a majority of air traffic and includes a large number of claims.

In order to deal with the international nature of aviation, a system of conventions and treaties has developed to deal with claims arising from international carriage by air, beginning with the Warsaw Convention in 1929. This is now largely (but not entirely) superseded by the Montreal Convention of 1999. While the provisions of these two conventions are 'exclusive' (in that there should be no other remedy available than the ones they provide) and binding upon the countries that have ratified them, the extent to which their provisions are followed in practice varies considerably from jurisdiction to jurisdiction.

This requires a degree of pragmatism in handling aviation claims as provisions of domestic law and legal tradition can play a considerable role in determining the outcome of cases that should (in theory) be covered entirely by the terms of these conventions. Nevertheless, the Warsaw/Montreal system does provide a framework for passenger, baggage and cargo claims and it is important to understand its provisions.

Legal framework – the Warsaw/ Montreal system

Commercial aviation began to expand in the early part of the twentieth century and shortly after the First World War countries around the world were beginning to commit to an international system of aviation regulation aimed at putting an end to "conflicts of law" issues between different jurisdictions and providing a stable and predictable legal environment for fledgling international passenger and cargo operators.

This process led to the Convention for the Unification of Certain Rules relating to International Carriage by Air at Warsaw in 1929 (more commonly known as the Warsaw Convention). This established a uniform system of rules relating to the rights of passengers and the owners of goods in transit and defined the scope of liability for the carrier. While the Warsaw Convention was amended at various times (most notably by the Hague Protocol in 1955 and the 4th Montreal Protocol (MAP4) in 1975), it was not until the Convention for the Unification of Certain Rules relating to International Carriage by Air (the Montreal Convention) was signed in Montreal in 1999 that major changes were introduced. Together, these international conventions provide the framework for a carrier's legal liability in international (and domestic in many jurisdictions) commercial air transport.

Although not all countries have signed either the Warsaw Convention or the Montreal Convention, there are 120 signatories of the Montreal Convention (including the EU as a whole), meaning that the majority of claims will be subject to one or other of the international conventions.

For example, the provisions of the Montreal Convention are enacted into UK law by s.1(1) of the Carriage by Air Act 1961 (as amended) in relation to non "Community Carriers" and by Regulation 2027/97 as amended by Regulation 889/2002 in relation to Community Carriers.

The terms and conditions of carriage adopted by most international airlines tend to mirror the provisions of the Warsaw and Montreal conventions (depending on which applies). While an airline cannot 'contract out' of the provisions of the applicable convention (Articles 23 and 33 of the Warsaw Convention and Article 47 of the Montreal Convention), it can provide more generous terms to its passengers by means of contract, and this still occurs, in some instances, by reason of the IATA Inter-Carrier Agreement. Care should always be taken to examine the relevant contractual provisions as well as the applicable convention.

The international conventions apply a regime of strict liability to carriers for damage to passengers, their baggage and cargo, but this is subject to certain conditions being met. Importantly, the international conventions also provide that, while the carrier is burdened with strict liability in some circumstances, their liability can be subject to financial limits.

Documentary requirements

Aside from the provisions relating to liability in the international conventions, the conventions also set out the basic requirements for tickets and air waybills (in the case of cargo).

While failure to provide proper documentation does not lead to a claim avoiding the provisions of the Montreal Convention (in cases that are subject to it, pursuant to Articles 3 and 8 of the Montreal Convention), the provisions of the Warsaw Convention are somewhat different. Failure to provide an air waybill in carriage governed by the Warsaw Convention in such circumstances would not lead to the carrier being unable to avail itself of the protections of the Convention (Article 5 of the Warsaw Convention). However, the failure to provide a passenger with a proper ticket with a notice explaining the provisions of the Warsaw Convention or a proper baggage check will mean that a carrier is not entitled to the protections provided by the limits on its liability contained in Article 22 of the Warsaw Convention (which are explained in more detail below).

It is for this reason (as well as administrative ease) that ticketing documentation often refers to the Warsaw Convention, even in cases of flights between two countries that have already adopted the Montreal Convention.

In any event, the carrier will be liable for any damages caused by the failure to provide adequate documentation in accordance with the international conventions.

Exclusivity

One of the most useful provisions in the Warsaw and Montreal conventions is that they provide an 'exclusive' cause of action and sole remedy. That means that, in relation to a claim dealt with by the conventions, if the cause of action claimed by a passenger or owner of goods against a carrier is not provided for in the relevant convention, they will not be entitled to recover damages.

This principle is contained in Article 29 of the Montreal Convention (as it was in Article 24 of the Warsaw Convention). The courts in England and Wales ruled on this in *Sidhu v British Airways Plc* [1997] and, more recently, in *Stott v Thomas Cook Tour Operators Ltd* [2014] (a case that dealt with a claim by a disabled passenger for breach of European disability legislation and in which Lord Toulson JSC (reiterating Lord Hope of Craighead's comments in *Sidhu*) stated that the purpose of the Montreal and Warsaw conventions was to:

> “prescribe the circumstances – that is to say, the only circumstances – in which a carrier would be liable to the passenger for claims arising out of international carriage by air. To permit exceptions whereby the passenger could sue

> outside the Convention for losses sustained during the course of international carriage by air, would distort the whole system, even for cases for which the Convention did not create any liability on the part of the carrier. ”

Claims that do not fall within the terms of the international conventions (e.g. claims for stress, inconvenience or discomfort) are not recoverable in England and Wales (*Cowden v British Airways Plc* [2009]). The Convention causes of action are considered in greater detail below but, as mentioned above, case law in different jurisdictions differs on what is recoverable under the international conventions.

Jurisdiction

Before considering in detail any claim in respect of international carriage by air, it is important to consider where the potential claimant has jurisdiction to bring a claim. Apart from the practical considerations as to where a claim can be pursued, the level of damages that can be awarded to a claimant and the extent to which legal costs can be recovered vary dramatically from country to country. It is for this reason that 'forum shopping' is popular for claimant lawyers and should always be a consideration when looking at a new claim.

The Warsaw Convention provided four alternatives for where a claim can be pursued. The claimant can choose to bring a claim in the courts of a High Contracting Party to the Warsaw Convention where:

1) The carrier is ordinarily resident
2) The carrier has its principal place of business
3) The carrier has an establishment through which the contract is made
4) The place of destination.

The Montreal Convention added a fifth jurisdiction for claims relating to the death or personal injury of a passenger only:

5) In the territory of a state party to the Montreal Convention where the passenger has their principal and permanent residence.

These jurisdictional 'gateways' can lead to arguments (particularly in cases where jurisdiction can have a significant financial benefit to either the claimant or the carrier) in cases where, for example, a contract is formed over the internet (*Transvalue Inc. v KLM Royal Dutch Airlines* [2008] and *Polanski v KLM Royal Dutch Airlines* [2005] or when the ticket is booked on behalf of a passenger by their employer or through a third-party travel agent. It can be increasingly difficult to identify the physical location of the formation of a contract and in some instances this will need to be examined on the facts of a particular case and the answer may differ depending on the jurisdiction in question.

Determining which convention applies

The Warsaw and Montreal conventions are distinct legal regimes and apply to all international carriage for reward between two contracting states or within one contracting state with an agreed stopping place in another state (whether or not that other state is a party). For example:

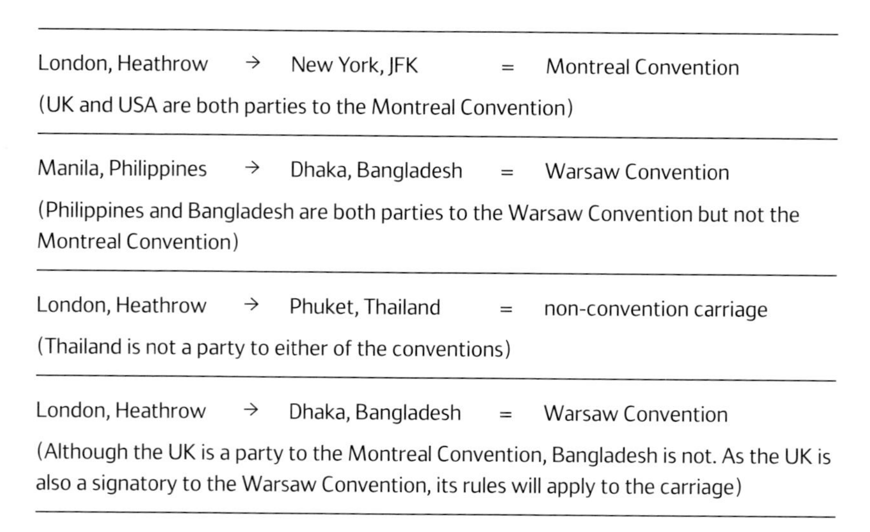

London, Heathrow → New York, JFK = Montreal Convention

(UK and USA are both parties to the Montreal Convention)

Manila, Philippines → Dhaka, Bangladesh = Warsaw Convention

(Philippines and Bangladesh are both parties to the Warsaw Convention but not the Montreal Convention)

London, Heathrow → Phuket, Thailand = non-convention carriage

(Thailand is not a party to either of the conventions)

London, Heathrow → Dhaka, Bangladesh = Warsaw Convention

(Although the UK is a party to the Montreal Convention, Bangladesh is not. As the UK is also a signatory to the Warsaw Convention, its rules will apply to the carriage)

Where a contract for carriage is from one country to another and a return to the first country, the fact that there is an agreed stopping place in the carriage is not relevant when considering which of the conventions applies (*Grein v Imperial Airways* [1937]).

Therefore:

London, Heathrow → Phuket, Thailand → London Heathrow = Montreal Convention

(Even though Thailand is not a party to either convention)

If there is no international convention that governs the carriage, then the claim will be governed by the laws of the country where the claim is being heard (subject to its own internal rules relating to jurisdiction, service of proceedings and assessment of loss).

Non-international carriage

The Warsaw and Montreal conventions only apply to international carriage and would not, absent domestic legislation, apply to domestic carriage, for example on a flight from Edinburgh to London. In the UK, in respect of non-Community Carriers, the provisions of the Montreal Convention are applied to domestic carriage by the Carriage by Air Acts (Application of Provisions) Order 2004.

However, it cannot be assumed that other countries have adopted a similar approach; many have their own laws setting out provisions for domestic carriage in which the conventions have no relevance.

Limits of liability

In exchange for strict liability under the international conventions, carriers benefit from limitations on their liability in many circumstances. This can (but does not always) place a financial cap on the carrier's liability.

These are in the form of either Convention Francs (also called Poincare Francs, in the case of the Warsaw Convention) or Special Drawing Rights (SDR) (in the case of the Montreal Convention and subsequent amendments of the Warsaw Convention). These are not currencies in their own right but units used to calculate financial values that apply across different countries. The SDR is a basket of currencies and its value fluctuates with movements in currency markets. The Convention Franc was its predecessor and was based on the value of 65.5 milligrams of gold of millesimal fineness (0.900). Calculating its value can be complex and how it is done varies from jurisdiction to jurisdiction. A specific statutory instrument in the UK defines its value: The Carriage by Air Act (Sterling Equivalents) Order 1999 (SI 1999/2881), but the approach varies in different countries.

The limits on liability provided by the international conventions are not automatic entitlements to damages. Damages are subject to proof of loss, although this issue is not always appreciated in all jurisdictions.

The Montreal Convention provides for periodic review of limits of liability; the last review took place in 2009.

Baggage claims

The most numerous type of claim received by airlines relate to baggage (either checked baggage carried in the aircraft's hold or unchecked baggage carried with the passenger in the cabin). The term "baggage" is not defined, but is taken to be any item checked or carried by a passenger that is not consigned for carriage as cargo under an airway bill.

The vast majority of these claims are not litigated and are dealt with directly between passenger and airline. As set out below, the provisions of the international conventions as well as the value of such claims tend to mean that they are not handled by lawyers, but there are nevertheless a (relatively) small number of claims that do require the involvement of lawyers, because the claimant either decides to issue proceedings without first contacting the airline or is unwilling to accept the provisions of the applicable convention or conditions of carriage; thus, these cases can provide their own challenges.

The position under the international conventions

Checked baggage

A carrier's liability for damage to checked baggage is strict – it will be liable for all destruction of, loss of or damage to any checked baggage, provided that the damage, loss or destruction complained of occurred while the bag was in the course of carriage by air (Article 18 of the Warsaw Convention) or where the baggage was in the charge of the carrier (Article 17(2) of the Montreal Convention). The carrier is also liable for any damage caused by delay to baggage (Article 19 of the Warsaw Convention and Article 19 of the Montreal Convention). Under the Warsaw Convention Article 18(3) states that:

> “The period of the carriage by air does not extend to any carriage by land, by sea or by river performed outside an aerodrome. If, however, such a carriage takes place in the performance of a contract for carriage by air, for the purpose of loading, delivery or transshipment, any damage is presumed, subject to proof to the contrary, to have been the result of an event which took place during the carriage by air.”

Whereas, Article 17 of the Montreal Convention only applies for the period:

> “when checked baggage was in the charge of the carrier”

This means that if, for example, the damage were to have occurred during the course of transport by road from the airport to a passenger whose bag had been mislaid, the liability provisions of the international conventions would still apply. The relevant periods clearly differ.

Defences

The Warsaw Convention provides a defence to claims relating to damage to baggage under Article 20:

> “The carrier is not liable if he proves that he and his servants or agents have taken all necessary measures to avoid the damage or that it was impossible for him or them to take such measures.”

In practice, this is a very limited defence as it is very difficult to establish that a carrier took “all necessary measures” to avoid damage. It is a very high evidential burden to overcome.

There is also a defence available to the carrier under Article 20(2) of the unamended Warsaw Convention for any damage occasioned by negligent pilotage or navigation of the aircraft (and that in all other respects the carrier's servants or agents took all reasonable measures to avoid the damage). This defence is rarely (if ever) used and was removed by the Hague Protocol 1955.

Of more use is the defence under Article 21 of the Warsaw Convention, Article 20 of the Montreal where there is contributory negligence on the part of the person claiming compensation. Therefore, where a passenger's baggage suffered damage because of, for example, rough treatment by the passenger themselves, or where the bag was unsuitable for carriage, the carrier may be wholly or partially exonerated from liability. The availability of this defence will clearly depend on the facts, and the available evidence (which may be minimal).

The Montreal Convention (Article 17(2)) provides that a carrier will not be liable to the extent that the damage resulted from an “inherent defect, quality or vice of the baggage”. This defence is more often associated with claims relating to cargo carried by air (rather than baggage), but it is still available in cases concerning checked baggage carried under the provisions of the Montreal Convention. The phrase's meaning is discussed in greater depth in relation to cargo claims below, but it would allow a carrier to avoid liability caused by 'normal' incidents of flight. For example, damage caused by a leaking pen in a bag could potentially qualify as resulting from an "inherent vice" of that baggage. The availability of this defence is fact specific.

As will be apparent, while there are certain defences available to a carrier, they are often of little practical use in defending baggage claims.

Notice periods

The international conventions provide strict time limits to notify the carrier of damage. This is to allow the carrier to preserve the relevant evidence related to a claim and to give it proper notice of the claim being pursued against it.

In the case of checked baggage, a person looking to bring a claim against a carrier must give written notice of their intent to bring a claim within:

- seven days from the date of receipt of the baggage, in cases concerning damage to baggage; or
- 21 days from the date of receipt in cases related to delayed baggage (Article 26(2) of the Warsaw Convention/Article 31(2) of the Montreal Convention).

Neither convention deals with a situation where a passenger's baggage is lost for an indefinite period of time. This is often provided for in carriers' terms and conditions of carriage and, provided that there is no conflict with or derogation from the provisions of the relevant international convention, there is nothing prohibiting a carrier from doing so.

Unchecked baggage

Although the Warsaw Convention did not specifically deal with a carrier's liability for unchecked baggage, it is clear from the limits of liability contained in Article 22 that a carrier would be liable for loss or damage to unchecked baggage. However, the drafting of the Warsaw Convention is not clear on the nature and scope of this liability (given that it is not specifically addressed in the text).

Unlike checked baggage, unchecked baggage is, by its very nature, never in the sole charge of the carrier as it remains with the passenger. When dealing with claims of this nature, the courts have sought to apply the terms of the Warsaw Convention in different ways. For example, the court in *Baker v Landsell Protective Agency Inc.* [1984 (US)] saw it as an extension of the carrier's liability for personal injury (as set out in Article 17 of the Warsaw Convention). While different approaches have been adopted elsewhere, in view of the relatively small number of such claims involving the Warsaw Convention this does not warrant detailed discussion.

In any event, the issue was clarified in the Montreal Convention, which deals more explicitly with the carrier's liability for unchecked baggage. Article 17 of the Montreal Convention provides that a carrier will be liable for damage to unchecked baggage where this results from its fault, or that of its servants or agents. A simple example of this would be a drink negligently spilled onto a laptop causing damage (*Sue v Korean Air Lines Co. Ltd* [2008]).

Defences

Under the Warsaw Convention, the same defences would be available as in respect of checked baggage, namely:

- The carrier took all necessary measures to avoid the damage or it was impossible for them to do so (Article 20 of the Warsaw Convention); and
- Contributory negligence on the part of the injured party.

The difference between the Warsaw Convention and the Montreal Convention is that, for the latter, in order for liability to be attributed to the carrier, the damage must have been caused by a negligent act or omission of a servant or agent of the carrier. Therefore, damage to a mobile phone that slips into the base of a seat in business class and is crushed when the passenger reclines their seat would not be recoverable under these provisions.

Limits of liability

In respect of checked baggage:

Convention texts	Limit of liability
Unamended Warsaw Convention	250 Convention Francs per kg of baggage
Warsaw Convention as amended by the Hague Protocol (including where MAP4 has been adopted)	250 Convention Francs per kg of baggage
Montreal Convention	1,131 SDR

In respect of unchecked baggage, the Warsaw Convention provided a separate limit of 5,000 Convention Francs, but the Montreal Convention does not have separate limits for checked or unchecked baggage.

A passenger can also make a "special declaration of interest in delivery at destination", effectively notifying the carrier of particularly valuable items in their luggage and increasing the limit of liability. In practice this rarely happens and most carriers have clauses in their conditions of carriage that purport to prevent passengers from carrying valuables in their checked baggage. The extent to which this can be enforced varies in different jurisdictions.

The liability limits can be exceeded if:

1) There is a failure to provide a proper baggage check (Article 4(2) of the Warsaw Convention).
2) The damage was caused by a negligent act or omission (on the part of the carrier or their servant or agent), done with intent to cause damage, or recklessly with the knowledge that damage would probably result (Article 25 of the Warsaw Convention, Article 22(5) of the Montreal Convention).

In the absence of clear evidence of intent, it can be difficult to establish that a carrier (or its agents) acted recklessly with the knowledge that a bag would be damaged, at least in the UK. Other jurisdictions can be more liberal as to how they define "recklessness", and some reverse the burden of proof in this regard (notably Germany).

Summary

In the case of checked baggage, a carrier is strictly liable for damage to baggage during the course of carriage by air for the period the baggage is in the care of the carrier.

1) There is a distinction between checked and unchecked baggage.
2) Limited defences – "All necessary measures" (Warsaw Convention) or contributory negligence on the part of the passenger.
3) Strict notice periods under the international conventions for written notification of an intention to bring a claim.
4) It is important to consider the international conventions in conjunction with the carrier's own conditions of carriage. Although these cannot directly contradict the international conventions or reduce their limits of liability, they can still be useful in defending claims.
5) Limits of liability – can be broken.

Passenger claims

Liability for death or bodily injury

Aside from providing a regime for dealing with claims relating to a passenger's baggage, the international conventions also provide that the carrier will be strictly liable for damages arising from a passenger's death or bodily injury caused by an accident on board an aircraft or in the course of embarkation or disembarkation. There is no requirement for negligence. (Article 17 of the Warsaw Convention/Article 17(1) of the Montreal Convention.)

The inclusion of this provision is historically related to the recognition that an aviation accident could very easily cause the death of all passengers on board, with potentially significant difficulties in determining the cause of the accident and the party responsible. Without the provisions of the Warsaw Convention, the surviving family of a victim of a disaster would have been faced with an uphill struggle to prove negligence on the part of the carrier, the aircraft's manufacturer or a third party.

While accident investigation (and safety generally) has improved immeasurably since the early days of aviation, the provisions remained unchanged in the more recent Montreal Convention. Liability is also subject to the available defences under the international conventions.

Meaning of an "accident"

The occurrence of an "accident" is a prerequisite to liability under both the Warsaw and Montreal conventions. However, the term is not defined in either text. Therefore, much case law (particularly in the UK, Australia and the USA) has defined the scope of the term. While that case law may be persuasive in other jurisdictions, it is important to remember that other courts can (and do) apply their own definitions.

While a literal reading of the term would define this as something that happens without the fault of another, the definition adopted by courts around the world (and particularly in common law jurisdictions) differs from the meaning of "accident" in common parlance.

Annex 13 to the Chicago Convention on Civil Aviation 1944 (which deals with aviation accident investigation) defines an "accident" in an aviation context as:

> "an occurrence associated with the operation of an aircraft."

This was a definition referred to in *Saks v Air France* [1985]. In this case a passenger claimed damages relating to an incident that caused her permanent deafness in her left ear. It was alleged that the injury was caused by the negligent maintenance of the aircraft's pressurisation system, although no defect was found. The court found that in order for liability to be found under Article 17 of the Warsaw Convention, the injury must have been caused by an "unexpected or unusual event or happening that is external to the passenger, and not where the injury results from the passenger's own internal reaction to the usual, normal and expected operation of the aircraft".

The reference to an "unusual" event in *Saks* needs to be treated with caution as a large number of incidents that could not possibly be said to be unusual (given their relatively common frequency, for example, a passenger being struck by baggage falling from an overhead locker or a burn caused by a coffee spill) will still be treated as "accidents" for the purposes of the international conventions. See for example the case of *El Al v Tseng* [1999 (US)], where a passenger sued for damages for assault and false imprisonment arising from an intrusive security search.

In this instance, the court adopted the approach that the international conventions did not seek to place strict liability onto the carrier for damages for routine operating procedures that, although potentially inconvenient or embarrassing, were necessary for the safe operation of commercial aviation. A similar approach was adopted in the UK in *Barclay v British Airways Plc* [2008], where the claimant was prevented from recovering damages as the result of slipping on a strip embedded in the aircraft's floor. Similarly, the famous deep vein thrombosis litigation *(Deep Vein Thrombosis and Air Travel Group Litigation* [2005]) found that an accident must be an event external to the passenger, not an event resulting from their own internal reaction to the normal operation of an aircraft.

Events that have been held by courts to be an accident include:

- Hijackings, terrorist attacks and bomb threats (see e.g. *Evangelinos v Trans World Airlines Inc.* [1976], where passengers were victims of an attack by terrorists armed with automatic weapons, while waiting in line at a security checkpoint).
- Dehydration caused by being forced to remain in a transit lounge for three days while documents were inspected (*Uwagbai v Alitalia Airlines* [1994]).
- Heavy landings causing neck or back injuries.
- Particularly severe turbulence.
- Food poisoning.
- Sexual molestation of an unaccompanied minor (*Morris v KLM* [2001]).

Injury caused by an injection administered by a well-meaning medical professional attending to a medical issue was found not to be an "accident" in *Ford v Malaysia Airline Systems Berhad* [2013].

It is important to examine each case relating to the interpretation of the international conventions on its own particular facts, rather than seeking to develop categories of incident that will always be considered to be an "accident". When dealing with claims it is important to gather information (e.g. reports from cabin crew members, accident logs, maintenance and defect logs and witness evidence from other passengers) as soon as possible. Witnesses (both airline employees and other passengers) can be reluctant to come forward and time is against the carrier in looking to build their case. While an injured passenger can be a very plausible witness (although not always), an airline employee whose recollection of events is dulled by the passage of time and the number of flights they are responsible for often does not present as a sympathetic witness to a court. This is not the case in every incident, but should be considered when forming a defence strategy.

The other point that bears consideration in dealing with claims for death or bodily injury is that the accident must have occurred during the course of carriage by air or in the course of the operations of embarkation or disembarkation. The classic example of this is a slip on stairs leading up to an aircraft. Again, there is much discussion as to what constitutes the operations of embarking or disembarking an aircraft in case law (given the growth of airport facilities), but one must look to examine the place where the incident occurred and whether it is a place where the passenger was required to be while embarking or disembarking an aircraft. The degree of control exercised by a carrier may also be a factor (*Adatia v Air Canada* [1992] and *Phillips v Air New Zealand* [2002]).

What is a "bodily injury"?

The next point to consider when examining a claim for injuries sustained on board an aircraft is whether or not the passenger has suffered "bodily injury".

This phrase was used in the original versions of the Warsaw Convention and discussed in the travaux preparatoires (notes of the meetings of the representatives who framed the Warsaw Convention) and was carried over to the Montreal Convention. It is clear from the early discussions on the issue that some nations favoured a definition that included a "mental" injury (i.e. psychiatric) whereas the term "personal" injury was considered to open the door to claims for libel, slander, fright, discrimination or shock.

Courts in the UK and elsewhere have examined this area of law in detail. While this is a complex area, the consensus is that a "bodily" injury must be either a physical injury (caused by the accident), including psychological sequelae of that bodily injury, or a physical manifestation of a psychological injury (e.g. stomach ulcers) that flows from an accident.

The key case from a US perspective is *Eastern Airlines v Floyd* [1991] (a case that concerned a flight from Miami to the Bahamas, which had to turn back because of engine trouble, risking a ditching in the Atlantic. Ultimately, the aircraft landed safely back in Miami, but several passengers sued for the distress caused by the incident). The court decided that there could be no recovery for "psychic" injury unless accompanied by physical injury.

The most important decision on the issue from the UK perspective is *King v Bristow Helicopters Ltd* [2002]. The case of *King* [2002] (a Scottish case) was joined with a separate claim, *Morris v KLM Airlines* [2001] (an unpleasant set of facts concerning a 15-year-old passenger who was indecently assaulted on board an aircraft by a fellow passenger. Although she suffered no physical injury, she developed clinical depression). When the appeals were heard, the House of Lords found that while Mr King could recover damages for a peptic ulcer that developed from the psychological trauma of a helicopter accident (but not the psychological trauma itself), Ms Morris could not as she had not suffered any physical injury.

The distinction is quite fine and, again, claims need to be examined on their individual facts. Medical evidence is very important.

However, it is worth noting here that not all jurisdictions will apply this case law or reasoning. For example, Israel has long recognised the recoverability of psychological damage and other jurisdictions (particularly those based on Sharia law) will routinely award 'moral' damages in a wide variety of cases, as well as damages for purely psychological injuries, even without proof of loss. Specialist local advice should always be sought.

Defences

As in the case of baggage, the Warsaw Convention (Article 20) provides for an "all necessary measures" defence to claims by passengers for bodily injury. However, as noted above, there are practical difficulties in succeeding with this defence. Similarly, the defence of negligent pilotage is of little practical assistance to carriers.

These defences are not available in respect of the Montreal Convention, leaving an argument of contributory negligence on the part of the passenger injured as the only realistic assistance to a carrier.

Limits of liability

Convention text	Limit of liability
Unamended Warsaw Convention	125,000 Convention Francs
Warsaw Convention (as amended by the Hague Protocol)	250,000 Convention Francs
Montreal Convention	113,100 SDR

However, it is important to remember that these are not firm limits of liability. In the case of a claim brought under the Montreal Convention, they can be exceeded unless a carrier can prove:

1) That the damage was not caused as the result of negligent or wrongful acts or omissions on its part or its servants or agents; or

2) That the damage was solely caused by the negligent or wrongful acts or omissions of a third party.

(Article 21(2) of the Montreal Convention.)

As is apparent, this is a particularly high evidential hurdle to overcome and in practice (particularly in the case of deaths resulting from a crash), it will often not be possible to rely on the limits of liability.

As in the case of baggage, the Warsaw Convention limits can be breached if the damage was caused by a negligent act or omission (on the part of the carrier or their servant or agent), done with intent to cause damage, or recklessly with the knowledge that damage would probably result (Article 25 of the Warsaw Convention).

Summary

A carrier is strictly liable for bodily injuries caused by an accident while a passenger is on board the aircraft or in the course of embarking or disembarking.

- "Accident" – must be an unusual event external to a passenger. Arguably, the normal operation of an aircraft could not cause an "accident".
- "Bodily injury" does not include purely psychological injuries. If the bodily injury arises from a psychological one, the carrier may be liable.
- Limited defences – "all necessary measures" (Warsaw Convention) or contributory negligence on the part of the passenger.
- Limits of liability – can be broken. The Montreal Convention allows the limits to be exceeded.

Delays

Both conventions provide that a carrier can be liable for damage caused by delay to passengers, baggage or cargo (Article 19 of the Warsaw Convention, Article 19 of the Montreal Convention).

While the cause of action exists, in the case of passengers it is relatively uncommon to see claims arising from delay brought under the international conventions. A simple reason for this is that any claim would be subject to proof of loss and many jurisdictions do not award general damages for delay.

A claim would be subject to the defence that the carrier took all reasonable measures to avoid the damage (or that it was impossible to do so). The limit of liability for delay under the Warsaw Convention is not separated from the limits for damages, but under the Montreal Convention the separate limit of liability for delay is 4,694 SDR.

Cargo claims

The international conventions also provide that a carrier will be liable for damage caused to cargo (including damage caused by delay) due to an "occurrence" during the course of carriage by air (Article 19 of the Warsaw Convention, Article 18 of the Montreal Convention).

Again, there is no need for negligence on the part of the carrier. Provided that the damage occurred due to an "occurrence" during the course of carriage by air, the carrier is liable.

There is no guidance in the international conventions as to what constitutes cargo, but in principle, anything that can be shipped would be considered "cargo". This includes a wide range of commodities from live animals (ranging from bees to sea lions) to valuable commodities such as coins, bank notes and jewellery, to foodstuffs and flowers and valuable pharmaceuticals.

Given the wide variety of goods involved, there are many different requirements relating to carriage. Temperature-sensitive cargo must be stored at the correct temperature at all times during its carriage and fragile and delicate cargo (including live animals), as well as dangerous goods, require careful packaging to ensure that they are protected during transit. The responsibility for these requirements varies and there are a multitude of regulations (published by IATA) that deal with the correct way to handle certain types of cargo. The result is the development of large-scale logistics operations that cater (at a price) for the needs of the aviation industry.

However, it is important to consider what information is given to the carrier regarding any special handling requests. Although a consignor of cargo may have informed their agent that the consignment had to be carried under particular conditions, that does not guarantee that the carrier will be informed of those conditions.

The one exception to the provisions of the international conventions is the carriage of mail (Article 2 of the Warsaw Convention, Article 2 of the Montreal Convention). There are specific provisions relating to the carriage of mail internationally, which are beyond the scope of this guide.

In the course of "carriage by air"

The definition of "carriage by air" under the international conventions is the same as that used in the case of baggage. That is, the carrier is liable for damage that occurs while baggage is in the care of the carrier, whether or not it is in an aerodrome (Article18(2) and (3) of the Warsaw Convention, Article 18(3) and (4) of the Montreal Convention).

However, the process of storing and importing cargo into a country can make this a more complex question to consider. For example, in *Swiss Bank Corpn and others v Brink's-MAT Ltd and others* [1986] (a case relating to the infamous Brink's-MAT robbery at London Heathrow), a consignment of bank notes was in the process of being checked in for carriage (with two of three consignments having been checked and weighed for carriage by the carrier and its agents) when the robbers struck. The court (at first instance) found that the consignments did not come into the charge of the carrier until they had been checked, weighed and accepted by the carrier. Accordingly, the carrier in this instance did not have charge of two of the three consignments at the time of the robbery.

However, there are often several stages to the carriage chain, involving freight forwarders, consolidators and other agents. It is important to consider the point at which damage occurred and that the obligation is on the claimant to prove (on the balance of probabilities) that the damage occurred during the time that the consignment was in the care of the carrier.

In some cases this will be clear. For example, in cases where temperature-sensitive cargo spoils during the course of carriage and where there is no evidence that the captain of the aircraft was informed (by a Notice to Captain (NOTOC), which is given to the aircraft commander to inform them of special cargo and other points to note about the flight they are due to operate), it is likely that there was an error on the part of the carrier.

Many freight forwarders (who handle cargo on behalf of exporters) will use temperature loggers with temperature-sensitive cargo or "tip 'n tells" that show when containers that should be stored upright have been mishandled. These devices can show clearly that cargo may have been handled improperly, but it can still be difficult to conclusively show at what point the damage occurred.

Once cargo has been delivered many carriers require agents to sign declarations confirming that they have received a consignment in good order, but occasionally damage cannot be ascertained until the cargo is examined more closely.

However, the scope of a carrier's liability could extend to liability for goods stored in a warehouse pending delivery. Thus, a carrier could be liable for damage sustained in a flooded warehouse or one destroyed in an explosion during an armed attack (subject to the defences set out below).

Party entitled to claim

One issue that can arise in respect of cargo claims is which party is entitled to bring a claim against a carrier. While in cases of injuries to passengers or damage to baggage it is straightforward to determine whether a claim can be pursued, in terms of cargo, determining which party has a right to sue can be more complex.

The contract between the airline and the person contracting for the carriage of cargo is evidenced in the air waybill (often referred to as the master air waybill (MAWB)), which contains important information regarding the place of destination, agreed stopping places, special handling conditions and the weight and nature of the cargo. The reverse of the air waybill contains the terms and conditions under which a consignment is carried. These are standard terms and conditions published by IATA (Cargo Services Conference Resolution (32) 600b) and should therefore be adopted by all members of IATA. The air waybill also contains the name of the consignor of the cargo and the name of the consignee. While that should make identifying the party able to claim easy, it is not always conclusive.

A situation that often arises is where an air waybill is issued with the names of the consignor and the consignee being listed as the same freight forwarder (often one of the larger organisations, such as DHL, who purchase blocks of space on cargo-carrying aircraft for their customers). The freight forwarder does not have a legal right to the cargo and in principle suffers no loss if it is damaged or destroyed. Nevertheless, the contractual relationship is between them and the airline, and the conventions give the consignor and consignee a right of action

This situation was resolved by the UK Court of Appeal in *Western Digital Corpn and others v British Airways Plc* [2001]. In this case the court held that the terms "consignor" and "consignee" (which are used in both the Warsaw and Montreal conventions) are not the only parties entitled to claim under the conventions. A claim could be brought by the party with the right to immediate possession of the goods.

In ascertaining who has title to the goods and can, therefore, sue, it is important to look beyond the air waybill to other contractual documentation, particularly the "house air waybill" (i.e., an air waybill drawn up by the freight forwarder), which will list the actual consignor and consignee. Invoices can also be important, given they often contain "Incoterms" that set out the point at which risk for a shipment transfers.

Incoterms are pre-defined commercial terms published by the International Chamber of Commerce and often used in international commercial transactions. They set out clearly (and simply) the obligations of the parties to the transaction and which party assumes the risks of transport; they also set out the requirements relating to insurance.

For example, a consignment that is shipped under a CPT Incoterm requires the seller/consignor to pay the costs of carriage up to a named destination, but the goods are considered to be delivered once they have been handed over to the first or main carrier. Goods that are damaged in transit should, therefore, only be the subject of a claim by the consignee on the basis that they would be the party with a right to immediate possession (per *Western Digital* [2001]).

Defences

There are significant differences between the treatment of cargo claims under the Warsaw Convention (including countries which have adopted the Hague Protocol) and claims that fall within the Montreal Convention (including the relatively limited number of claims where the claim will be governed by the Warsaw Convention as amended by MAP4).

Under the Warsaw Convention (and the Warsaw Convention as amended by the Hague Protocol), the only defences available to a claim in respect of damage to cargo will be:

- The carrier took all necessary measures to avoid the damage or it was impossible for them to do so (Article 20 of the Warsaw Convention); and
- Contributory negligence on the part of the injured party.

While the "all necessary measures" defence is often difficult to establish, an allegation of contributory negligence is certainly a useful tactic to be deployed (particularly in cases where a consignor's agent has failed to inform an airline of special handling conditions, for example).

However, under the Montreal Convention (and MAP4), the defences available to a carrier are much more extensive.

In addition to the defence of contributory negligence, a carrier is also exempt from liability to the extent that it proves that damage to cargo was caused by:

- An inherent defect or vice of that cargo.
- Defective packaging performed by a person other than the carrier or its agent.

- An act of war or armed conflict.
- An act of a public authority carried out in accordance with the entry, exit or transit of the cargo.

(Article 21(2) of the MAP4, Article 18(2) of the Montreal Convention.)

The term "inherent defect or vice" is not defined but can be used to describe something about the nature of cargo that means it will decay or suffer damage during carriage by otherwise normal means. The classic example is cut flowers that decay by virtue of a disease in the flowers themselves (*Eastern & Global (NZ) Ltd v Air New Zealand Ltd* [2004]). It would not, however, extend to the simple fact that a live animal transported by air could die.

Cases of defective packaging are often more easily quantifiable; IATA publishes a series of guidelines for the correct packaging of a wide range of commodities (e.g. Live Animal Regulations and Perishable Cargo Regulations). These guidelines are aimed at ensuring that packaging is, as far as possible, standardised. The guidelines can be seen as 'best practice' guidelines, and a shipper that does not comply with them can be open to criticism. However, it is important to remember that this defence is only applicable to packaging performed by a person other than the carrier or its agents. Agents of a carrier that (for example) accidentally cover a consignment, thereby causing heat to build up within the packaging, will not be entitled to a defence.

The defence that cargo was destroyed by an act of war or armed conflict is easily understood, although again there is no definition of what is meant by "armed conflict". In turbulent political times, what is an "armed conflict" is potentially an open question.

Similarly, while it is clear that providing a carrier with a means to exempt itself from liability for the acts of a public authority suggests that it was intended to exclude liability for damage caused while a consignment is undergoing a customs inspection or while a consignment is improperly delayed by the acts of a public authority, there is no definition of what is covered by Article 21(2) of the MAP4 and 18(2) of the Montreal Convention.

It should be noted that the obligation is on the carrier to prove that damage was caused by one of the circumstances listed in Article 21(2) of the MAP4 and Article 18(2) of the Montreal Convention. This can be a high hurdle, particularly in some jurisdictions (Germany, in particular).

Notice periods

As in the case of baggage, there are strict time limits for a party to notify a carrier of their intention to bring a claim. Receipt of cargo without complaint is prima facie evidence of delivery in good condition.

In the case of damage to cargo, the time periods for notice to be given to the carrier are forthwith on discovery of the damage and, in any event, within:

- Seven days in the case of the unamended Warsaw Convention; and
- 14 days in the case of the Warsaw Convention (as amended by the Hague Protocol), MAP4 and the Montreal Convention.

(Article 26(1) of the Warsaw Convention, Article 31 of the Montreal Convention.)

In cases of delay, the international conventions provide that notice must be given within:

- 14 days in the case of the unamended Warsaw Convention; and
- 21 days in the case of the Warsaw Convention (as amended by the Hague Protocol), MAP4 and the Montreal Convention.

In each case, the period is calculated from the date on which the consignment is placed at the disposal of the party entitled to delivery.

It should be noted that the terms and conditions on the reverse of an air waybill provide that in cases of non-delivery, complaint must be made within 120 days of the date of the air waybill or the date on which the cargo was delivered to the carrier. This guards against the possibility that a consignment could be missing indefinitely by providing a long stop date for notices to be given in instances where a consignment cannot be located.

Limits of liability

Convention	Limit of liability
Unamended Warsaw Convention	250 Convention Francs per kg of cargo
Warsaw Convention as amended by Hague Protocol	250 Convention Francs per kg of cargo
MAP4	17 SDR per kg of cargo
Montreal Convention	19 SDR per kg of cargo

A consignee can give a special declaration of value, fixing a higher limit (which does occasionally happen in relation to particularly valuable cargo), although that is still a limit, not an entitlement to recover a fixed sum.

The terms and conditions on the reverse of an air waybill fix the limit at 19 SDR per kg of cargo irrespective of which international convention applies (and the parties are free to contract at a higher limit of liability than provided by the applicable convention). This makes the limits applicable under the Warsaw Convention largely irrelevant.

What is relevant is that, under the Warsaw Convention, the limits of liability can be broken if the claimant can prove wilful misconduct or recklessness on the part of the carrier. The Montreal Convention removes this provision, and cargo carried under the Montreal Convention is subject to an "unbreakable limit".

The international conventions provide that the weight to be considered is the actual weight of the pieces of cargo damaged (i.e. if four pieces out of a total consignment of five are damaged, it is the weight of those four pieces that is used to calculate the carrier's limit of liability). In cases concerning cargo transported from the USA, the weight to be used in that calculation is the chargeable weight of the goods (as listed on the air waybill), not the gross weight, which is the usual means of calculating the limit of liability.

However, if the value of a consignment is affected by the loss or damage of one part, then the weight to be taken into account is the weight of the entire consignment. Thus, a consignment that consisted of several packages comprising parts of a machine that can only function once all parts are together could be subject to a limit of liability based on the weight of all packages (see e.g. *China Airlines Ltd v Philips Hong Kong Ltd* [2002]).

Summary

A carrier is strictly liable for damage to cargo during the course of carriage by air.

- It is important to closely examine the air waybill and other shipping documents in order to determine the obligations of the carrier.
- The party entitled to claim may not be immediately obvious.
- There are defences available, particularly under the Montreal Convention.
- The international conventions apply strict time periods for notice to the carrier of an intention to bring a claim.
- The reverse of the air waybill contains terms and conditions, including amendments to the applicable limit of liability.
- Carriers often also have their own terms and conditions of carriage for cargo.
- Limits of liability – under the Montreal Convention these are "unbreakable".

Major losses

Major aviation accidents provide scope for large numbers of complex claims against carriers and their insurers. By their very nature, these incidents can be the source of immense shock and anguish, naturally enough, from the relatives of victims, but also from the staff of the carrier itself (many of whom may know crew who are victims of an incident). The immediate aftermath of a major incident can be chaotic and fraught. These events often involve deep and lasting damage to the reputation of the carrier involved.

Because of the individual circumstances of each incident it is hard to pick out many individual recommendations, save that early instruction of lawyers with expertise is critical, as is establishing clear lines of communication and control of information.

In cases involving accidents within the EU, there is a requirement that a carrier makes a payment of not less than 16,000 SDR within 15 days of the identification of the person entitled to compensation. This is to cover the immediate economic needs of relatives. Different jurisdictions have different requirements and local advice may be required (EC Regulation 889/2002).

The process of identifying those entitled to compensation can be difficult and emotional for those involved, and care must be taken to handle claims sensitively. It is also worth noting that there are many claimant law firms with expertise in handling such claims. Many will attempt to bring claims in the jurisdiction that is most beneficial to their clients and may seek avenues to pursue claims of product liability against aircraft or parts manufacturers, particularly in certain states of the US.

Annex 13 of the Chicago Convention sets out the provisions relating to the investigation of an accident. Investigators can and will take possession of aircraft wreckage in order to carry out their investigation. While an investigation report can provide useful evidence as to the causes of an accident (for all parties), the report is (or at least should be) written impartially with the aim of improving aviation safety, not apportioning blame. A fairly recent decision in the UK, the case of *Rogers v Hoyle* [2013], found that the report of the UK Air Accidents Investigation Branch could be used in the context of civil proceedings relating to the crash of a Tiger Moth vintage aircraft, but the underlying documents created by or for the investigation are protected from disclosure in criminal or civil proceedings.

Once the investigating authority releases wreckage, care should be taken to properly preserve it so as to avoid claims relating to spoliation of evidence (i.e. intentional, reckless, or negligent withholding, hiding, altering, fabricating or destroying of evidence relevant to a legal proceeding), particularly in cases with a US element.

Aside from claims arising from passengers in relation to major losses, one must also consider the prospects of claims for damage to property on the ground (including property belonging to airports), which may extend to environmental contamination. Under UK law, liability for such damage is strict by virtue of the provisions of s.76(2) of the Civil Aviation Act 1982, but local provisions may vary.

Outside the conventions – general aviation and domestic carriage

The term "general aviation" is not uniformly defined, but generally refers to all civil aviation operations other than scheduled or non-scheduled flights by an air transport undertaking (Air Operator Certificate holder). In the aviation insurance market it extends to commercial operation of aircraft with a passenger seating capacity of less than 70. It covers a large number of aircraft operated by private pilots for pleasure and the operation of helicopters and other "aircraft" by the police or other rescue agencies or by industry, such as aircraft serving offshore oil rigs.

Hot-air balloons and helicopters qualify as "aircraft" under the international conventions, However, the conventions do not apply to non-international carriage for reward. Therefore, carriage within the territory of one state (e.g. from London to Edinburgh) is not directly covered by the international conventions.

However, UK and EU legislation incorporates and applies the provisions of the Montreal Convention to carriage. In the case of

UK domestic carriage for reward, other than by a "Community Carrier", the Carriage by Air Acts (Application of Provisions) Order 2004 applies, with some minor modifications, the provisions of the Montreal Convention to domestic carriage. The provisions of the Montreal Convention cover passengers on domestic flights in the UK where those flights are operated for reward. In fact, English courts adopt an expansive interpretation of the term "aircraft" to encompass even hang-gliders. If carriage is not performed by a Community Carrier, or is not otherwise subject to the provisions of the Montreal Convention, regard must be had to domestic causes of action, such as negligence, breach of contract, bailment, etc. Likewise, other jurisdictions will apply their own domestic law, and specialist advice in respect of the applicable law will be required in cases of domestic carriage and carriage other than by a passenger aircraft.

32 Directors' and officers' liability insurance

Jenny Boldon

Co-author: Dónal Clark

- Potential insureds under a D&O policy
- Duties owed by Directors
- Potential sources of liability
- Examples of D&O exposures
- Typical D&O policy coverage considerations
- Claims handling framework for considering D&O claims

Directors' and officers' liability insurance

Introduction

This chapter provides an overview of directors' and officers' (D&O) liability insurance.

D&O insurance can provide valuable protection to those in a managerial role at a company who are the subject of an official investigation or legal proceedings.

This type of cover is of particular importance in the London market, both in terms of the provision of direct insurance and the reinsurance of D&O policies issued in other jurisdictions.

The operation of D&O cover can be complex and involve a myriad of issues that are outside the scope of this text. This chapter seeks to give an overview of typical insureds under a D&O policy, duties owed by directors, potential sources of liability and examples of remedies. It also identifies common coverage issues and sets out a claims handling framework for considering D&O claims.

Potential insureds under a D&O policy

The question of who is covered under a D&O policy will generally be governed by the definition of 'insured' (or similar term) in the policy wording. Guidance can also be drawn from the Companies Act 2006 (CA 2006), as set out below, and by searching Companies House, which provides a public record of appointed directors for registered companies.

In addition to D&Os, modern policies frequently extend cover to company employees acting in a managerial capacity, even if that person is not formally a director or officer, as well as those involved with the management of partnerships and not-for-profit organisations.

Directors

Section 250 of the CA 2006 defines a director as:

> "any person occupying the position of Director, by whatever name called."

This definition is of limited assistance, although it makes it clear that the title a person holds is not necessarily determinative of whether they are a director. Rather, the test is functional and the definition is such that it provides the court with flexibility. A company's constitution, in particular its Articles of Association, will usually set out the powers of the director(s) to take decisions on behalf of the company, and a person exercising such powers will be indicative of them being a director.

A director must be 16 years of age or over and not be disqualified from being a director.

There are different types of directors, including:

- **De jure director** – a person validly appointed as a director.
- **De facto director** – a person appointed as a director, but with a defect in their appointment, or an unappointed person treated as a director by the Board.
- **Shadow director** – someone not appointed as a director but "a person with whose directions or instructions the Directors of the company are accustomed to act" (per s.251 of the CA 2006).

A distinction can also be drawn between individuals who act as executive directors and those who act as non-executive directors. The former are generally employed by the company and are involved with managing its affairs on a full-time basis, whereas the latter tend to be appointed due to a particular skill or knowledge and may be part-time.

Officers

Section 1173 of the CA 2006 defines an "officer" as a position that:

> "in relation to a body corporate, includes a Director, manager or secretary."

Other potential insureds

Depending on the precise terms of the policy, cover may extend to individuals who are employees of the company who act in a managerial or supervisory capacity.

This can be a valuable extension of cover, particularly to those potentially subject to investigation by regulatory bodies, which often involves an assessment of conduct by non-director employees who hold managerial or supervisory positions. Some policies are even broad enough to cover all employees.

Duties owed by directors

The CA 2006 codified a number of general duties owed by directors based on common law rules and equitable principles, but regard should be had to such rules and principles when interpreting and applying the statutory duties. It follows that while the CA 2006 provides a helpful overview of general duties owed by directors, an extensive body of court judgments regarding duties owed by directors remains relevant.

It is important to note that broader duties can be owed than those in the CA 2006. In particular, directors are obliged to consider or act in the interests of creditors in certain circumstances, depending on the solvency of the company.

Companies Act 2006

The duties below are owed by a director to the company (s.170(1)) and, therefore, it is the company that is able to enforce them.

- **Duty to act within powers (s. 171)** – i.e. to act in accordance with the company's constitution (including its Articles of Association) and company resolutions and to only exercise powers for the purposes for which they are conferred.
- **Duty to promote the success of the company for the benefit of its members (s. 172)** – i.e. a director should have regard to (among other matters):
    - The likely consequences of any decision in the long term.
    - The interests of the company's employees.
    - The need to foster the company's business relationships with suppliers, customers and others.
    - The impact of the company's operations on the community and the environment.
    - The desirability of the company maintaining a reputation for high standards of business conduct.
    - The need to act fairly as between the members of the company.

This duty is subject to any specific requirement or enactment or rule of law requiring directors in certain circumstances to consider and act in the interests of creditors of the company (s.172(3)) (see further below).

- **Duty to exercise independent judgment (s.173)** – a director must exercise their powers independently, without subordinating their powers to the will of others. Appropriate delegation authorised by the company's constitution is permissible and this duty does not prevent a director from relying on advice, so long as the director exercises their own judgment on whether or not to follow the advice.

- **Duty to exercise reasonable care, skill and diligence (s.174)** – a director must exercise the care, skill and diligence exercised by a reasonably diligent person with both:

  i) the general knowledge, skill and experience that may reasonably be expected of a person carrying out the same functions as are carried out by that director (an objective test); and

  ii) the general knowledge, skill and experience that that director has (a subjective test).

It follows that not only must a director meet the objective test, but also where the director has specialist knowledge, skill and experience, the higher subjective standard must additionally be met. In assessing these standards, regard will be had to all the circumstances of the company–director relationship.

Generally, the courts are reluctant to interfere with business decisions, irrespective of how prudent the judgement of a director may appear with the benefit of hindsight.

As part of complying with the duty to exercise diligence, a director will be expected to keep themselves informed about the company's affairs. This duty will not prevent a director from relying on others or from delegating, so long as it is reasonable to do so and the director does not relinquish all responsibility.

- **Duty to avoid conflicts of interest (s.175)** – a director must not place themselves in a position where there is a conflict, or possible conflict, between duties owed to the company and either their personal interests or other duties owed to a third party.

This duty applies in particular to the exploitation of property, information or opportunity, irrespective of whether the company could take advantage of it. It is also irrelevant whether the director was aware of such a duty existing. If a conflict of interest exists, this duty may be circumvented if appropriate consent is obtained.

- **Duty to not accept benefits from third parties (s.176)** – a director must not accept any benefit from a third party which is conferred because of:

  i) their being a director, or

  ii) doing or not doing anything as a director.

The word 'benefit' is not defined in s.176. Its ordinary meaning is a favourable or helpful factor, circumstance, advantage or profit.

- **Duty to declare any interest in a proposed transaction or arrangement with the company (s.177)** – a director should declare to other directors the nature and extent of any interest, direct or indirect, in a proposed transaction or arrangement with the company.

Significantly, the director need not be a party to the proposed transaction in order for the duty to apply. Also, a director will not be in breach of this duty if they act in accordance with the company's constitution as regards conflicts of interest.

Fiduciary duties

A fiduciary is a person acting for or on behalf of another in a particular matter or situation that gives rise to a relationship of trust and confidence. The distinguishing obligation of a fiduciary is the obligation of loyalty.

Directors owe fiduciary duties to the company. As set out above, particular fiduciary duties owed by a director are now codified in the CA 2006.

Duties to creditors

A director's duty to promote the success of the company for the benefit of its members under s. 172 of the CA 2006 is subject to any legal duty or requirement requiring directors in certain circumstances to consider or act in the interests of creditors of the company (s.172(3) of the CA 2006).

Where the company is in danger of insolvency, or is insolvent, a director should consider the position of creditors, and may be obliged to preserve the assets of the company and act in the interests of the general class of creditors.

This provision builds on common law duties owed by directors to creditors in an insolvency situation and exists alongside the provisions of the Insolvency Act 1986 (IA 1986). Failure to comply may expose the director to allegations of wrongful trading or fraudulent trading (as to which, see further below).

Potential sources of liability

Action by the company

English law recognises a company as a legal person, independent of the person or persons that incorporated it and who manage it.

A D&O may be pursued by the company in respect of conduct that is not capable of being ratified by the company's shareholders in the form of a derivative action. A derivative action is based on the notion that a wrong has been done to the company by those in control of it.

The standing to bring a derivative action is vested in the company's shareholders. Such an action is brought in the name of the company and it is the company (rather than the shareholders) that would have the benefit of any recovery.

Action by a shareholder

A D&O may be the subject of a petition for unfair prejudice by a minority shareholder. Such an action can be made pursuant to s.994 of the CA 2006. In order to succeed with an unfair prejudice action, the burden is on the petitioner to prove that the manner in which the company's business has been carried out is unfairly prejudicial to their interests.

The remedy available under s.994 is against the company rather than against the directors, and what is generally sought by a petitioner is an order from the court regulating the future conduct of the company or imposing an obligation on the majority shareholder(s) to buy the petitioner's shareholding at a particular price.

For D&O insurers, it will be necessary to assess whether such an action involves an allegation of wrongdoing by an individual in their capacity as an insured, as opposed to as a shareholder.

Action by a liquidator

Upon the insolvency of a company, a liquidator has a duty to consider the conduct of the directors as part of the liquidation process and any possible rights of action that the company or liquidator may have against third parties, including D&Os.

The IA 1986 provides a basis for liability on the part of a director, in particular regarding:

- Misfeasance (s.212)
- Fraudulent trading (s.213)
- Wrongful trading (s.214).

Pursuant to s.212 of the IA 1986, if in the course of a winding-up of a company it appears that a D&O has misapplied any of the company's money or other property, the D&O can be compelled to restore such money or property or be ordered to compensate the company.

Under s.213, if business of the company has been carried on with the intent to defraud creditors, or for any fraudulent purpose, a person who knowingly carried out such business may be guilty of fraudulent trading.

Wrongful trading occurs, pursuant to s.214, where a company continues to trade when there is an awareness that the company does not have a reasonable prospect of avoiding liquidation. In cases of wrongful trading, a director may be forced to contribute to the company's assets for the benefit of the company's creditors. A defence is available to a director if it can be shown that after knowing the company was in financial difficulties, all reasonable steps were taken to minimise creditors' losses.

Regulatory actions/investigations

Depending on the nature and activities of a company, D&Os may be the subject of a variety of investigations by official bodies, for example the Secretary of State / the Insolvency Service in relation to a director's conduct generally falling short, or the Serious Fraud Office (SFO) in connection with allegations under the Bribery Act 2010.

D&Os acting in the regulated financial services sector should be mindful of the powers of the Financial Conduct Authority (FCA) and legislation under which personal liabilities can arise, such as the Financial Services and Markets Act 2000 and individual accountability under the FCA's Senior Managers Regime, which requires senior managers to be responsible for a regulated firm's activities.

All D&Os should have regard to health and safety, with the possibility of action by the Health and Safety Executive (HSE) following personal injury/death, and indeed criminal prosecution.

Liquidator's report/Insolvency Service

In the event of a company entering into liquidation, the appointed liquidator has a reporting responsibility as regards the conduct of the director(s) under the Company Directors Disqualification Act 1986 (CDDA 1986).

In addition, upon a company entering into formal insolvency proceedings, the Insolvency Service may investigate the conduct of a director. If there is evidence of wrongdoing or unfit conduct, the director may be disqualified from holding the office of a director in the event of proceedings being brought pursuant to the CDDA 1986.

Examples of D&O exposures

Depending on the nature of any established wrongdoing by a D&O, a personal exposure to the company or a third party may arise. Examples of potential exposures faced by D&Os include:

- Damages or compensation, where the company has suffered loss.
- Restoration of the company's property.

- An account of unlawful profit made by the D&O.
- Rescission of a contract where the D&O failed to disclose an interest.

D&O claims can vary in size enormously and settlements tend to be confidential. Nevertheless, major D&O settlements have been reported, including in the US where multi-million-dollar actions have been brought against insured individuals.

The 2008/2009 financial crisis led to an escalation in D&O claims, with actions brought in relation to subprime losses and the Madoff scandal.

The trend of increased numbers of claims against D&Os is continuing with ever more legislation creating potential liabilities for directors. For example, the Criminal Finances Act 2017 (CFA 2017) came into force in September 2017 and imposes a new criminal liability on UK and non-UK businesses that fail to prevent the facilitation of tax evasion by an 'associated person'. The CFA provides a significant overhaul of money laundering and proceeds of crime legislation.

Typical D&O policy coverage considerations

Coverage issues generally are considered in Chapter 35. In addition, like professional indemnity policies considered in Chapter 11, D&O policies are usually written on a 'claims made' basis. We do not repeat the comments on those issues here, but they should be borne in mind in considering any D&O claim.

Pre-inception issues

With the enactment of the Insurance Act 2015 on 12 August 2016, insureds under a D&O policy that incepts after that date are under a duty to make a "fair presentation of the risk". As considered elsewhere, a breach of this duty results in new proportionate remedies being available to insurers.[1]

From a D&O perspective, it is important to note that cover is usually composite in nature, i.e. the policy is treated in such a way that,

[1] http://www.kennedyslaw.com/article/the-insurance-act-2015-what-you-need-to-know/

in effect, each insured has a separate contract of insurance with insurers. Therefore, if one insured fails to comply with the duty to make a fair presentation of the risk, for example, the rights of the other, innocent co-insureds are likely to be unaffected.

Notification

A D&O policy will generally prescribe how a notification should be made to insurers, for example by way of a 'Notice and Reporting' provision. Compliance, or otherwise, with such a provision may impact the response of the policy.

The policy may draw a distinction between notification of i) a 'claim' and ii) a circumstance.

In respect of a 'claim', cover is generally restricted to a claim first made during the policy period or an applicable discovery period, i.e. a set period of time following the expiration of a policy that is not renewed, during which a notice of a claim can be provided.

Some wordings impose an obligation on the insured to notify insurers of a 'claim' within a certain timescale, though it is more common to see an obligation to notify insurers "as soon as practicable", or words to similar effect. Where such an obligation is a condition precedent to insurers' liability under the policy, a delay in notifying a matter to insurers may provide a coverage defence for insurers. If it is not a condition precedent, insurers' rights will be limited to the extent its position has been prejudiced by the delay in notification.

With regards to a circumstance, some policies allow notification of a circumstance which 'may' give rise to a claim, while others require there to be a circumstance which is 'likely' to give rise to a claim. As considered further in Chapter 35, 'may' is a lower threshold than 'likely', with the latter having been held to require there to be at least a 50% chance of a claim.

Where a circumstance has been notified validly to insurers, a subsequent 'claim' arising out of the circumstance will attach back for consideration under the terms of the policy, irrespective of whether the claim materialises after the expiration of the policy period.

Insuring clause

Assuming there are no pre-inception issues that provide insurers with a coverage defence, the starting point in determining coverage under a D&O policy is whether an insuring clause has been triggered.

Some D&O policies contain two insuring clauses, commonly known as Side A and Side B. Side A provides cover for individual insureds, typically where the company is unable or unwilling to provide an indemnity to the insured itself. Side B offers reimbursement to the company to the extent that the company has reimbursed the insured. Some policies also contain a Side C or entity cover, whereby cover is available to the company, typically in relation to US securities actions. Different deductibles will generally apply depending on whether cover is sought under Side A, Side B or Side C.

In determining cover under any insuring clause, an assessment must be made as to whether the notified matter satisfies the criteria prescribed in the wording, usually by reference to defined terms. This will be a fact-specific assessment.

Typically, a D&O insuring clause will oblige the insurer to pay the 'loss' of an 'insured person' arising from a 'claim' for a 'wrongful act' first made during the policy period and reported to the insurer as required by the policy.

The definition of a 'claim' can vary in breadth. For example, there may be a requirement for a written demand for monetary compensation alleging a 'wrongful act' or a civil, regulatory or administrative proceeding (such as disqualification proceedings) against an insured person. Other wordings may provide cover for non-monetary or injunctive relief.

The term 'loss' will generally include 'defence costs' as well as damages, adverse awards of costs and settlements that an insured is legally liable to pay resulting from a claim.

Some wordings are sufficiently broad that cover is also available for costs associated with fighting proceedings to confiscate a director's property or to freeze their assets, as well as to fund school fees, mortgage and utility payments in circumstances where assets are frozen.

Cover may also be available for retired directors for claims against them alleging wrongful acts while acting as a director, even if their successors do not maintain D&O cover.

Investigation costs cover

The D&O market has developed such that cover is now routinely available for the costs of legal representation in relation to an official investigation.

Usually such cover is dependent on the insured being identified as a target of investigation by an 'official body', or similar, for example investigations by the FCA, Insolvency Service, etc. It follows that cover may not be available for internal investigations, depending on the nature of the investigation and the precise wording of the policy.

Outside directorship liability cover

Depending on the nature of a company and its operations, outside directorship liability (ODL) cover may be obtained in addition to standard D&O cover.

ODL cover is relevant where D&Os of a company are likely to hold outside directorships, for example, in the private equity sector where an individual may be placed on an outside board to assist with the management of the outside entity.

Typically, ODL cover is provided as an extension or endorsement to the D&O policy and sits in excess of any D&O cover available to the outside entity. If the outside entity does not have D&O cover, or if such cover has been eroded, cover will be available under the ODL cover, subject to its terms.

Exclusions

A D&O policy will usually contain exclusions that restrict the scope of cover available under the policy. The precise wording of the exclusion will determine its operation.

Below are examples of exclusions that might be contained in a D&O policy.

Conduct

Cover is typically excluded for loss arising out of, based upon or attributable to the gaining of profit or advantage to which an insured is not legally entitled or for the committing of any dishonest or fraudulent act. The scope of such an exclusion can be restricted, for example by requiring there to be an intentional breach of the law.

Usually, such an exclusion is only applicable where the relevant conduct is established by a final adjudication or formal written admission by the insured. In such circumstances, unless and until there is a final adjudication or admission, the exclusion will not apply and insurers will be obliged to advance 'defence costs', subject to the terms of the policy.

When considering this type of exclusion it is important to analyse whether there is a requirement that the relevant conduct be established in the underlying action or if it is open to insurers to seek a declaration of such conduct in order to provide a basis for the application of the exclusion.

This kind of exclusion reflects the position at common law that a director cannot recover from insurers for a liability resulting from dishonest conduct. In the event of a relevant finding or admission, the policy may provide for the insured to repay any defence costs advanced on their behalf.

Prior claims and circumstances

Cover may be excluded where loss arises from a 'claim' or a circumstance of which notice has been given under an earlier policy.

This exclusion ties in with the 'claims made' nature of a D&O policy and the typical subjectivity within the insuring clause of a claim being first made during the policy period.

Contract

Understandably, D&O insurers tend to seek to exclude cover for liabilities voluntarily undertaken pursuant to the terms of a contract. Normally the exclusion is limited in scope to a liability that is derived exclusively from a contract, such that a concurrent tortious liability will not fall within the scope of the exclusion.

Professional services

Cover may be excluded for claims arising out of the provision of, or failure to provide, professional services.

Broadly, the effect of the exclusion is to provide that a claim relating to the provision of professional services is directed to the company's professional indemnity/errors and omissions insurance policy, with the D&O policy in place to cover wrongful acts committed by a D&O in an insured capacity.

The operation of such an exclusion can be complex and the scope of the exclusion will depend on the precise wording of the policy and the nature of the claim.

Bodily injury/property damage

Generally, a D&O policy is not intended to provide cover for actions relating to bodily injury or damage to property. Such risks are more usually insured by general liability/employers' liability cover.

Defence costs

The cover available under a D&O policy for 'defence costs' can be crucial to an insured. Without such cover, the cost of defending legal proceedings may be prohibitive or have devastating financial consequences.

Normally, the policy requires insurers' consent to costs incurred on behalf of an insured, with such consent not to be unreasonably withheld.

Typically, 'defence costs' are defined by reference to 'reasonable' costs incurred in the defence of a claim. Some wordings also require the costs to be 'necessary'.

There is scope for different views to exist about what amounts to 'reasonable' and 'necessary' costs, so the response of the policy to costs incurred on behalf of an insured can be a contentious issue. It is advisable for D&O insurers to obtain details of the insured's proposed lawyers at an early stage, particularly their hourly rates and estimated costs, with a view to resolving issues in that regard as early on as possible.

In assessing the reasonableness and necessity of costs, much is likely to depend on the nature of the claim, the complexity of the issues, the sums at stake and the potential adverse consequences to the insured if the claim is successful.

Where a dispute arises between insurers and the insured regarding the reasonableness of costs, some policies prescribe a resolution procedure, such as determination by an independent QC.

Allocation

Where a claim is made jointly against an insured and a jointly represented party that is not insured, and/or the claim involves both matters which are covered and those which are not covered.

Often a D&O policy will contain an 'allocation' provision that governs such scenarios. Typically, such a provision will provide for the insured and the insurer to use reasonable efforts to determine a fair and equitable allocation of loss. Sometimes the wording refers to an allocation on the basis of established judicial principles that take into account the legal and financial exposures and the relative benefits obtained by the respective parties.

In some cases, it may be practicable for a defence firm to distinguish between work done for an insured and an uninsured party and/or work relating to insured claims and uninsured claims. In cases where there is no overlap in these respects, it is not necessary to determine an allocation.

If a D&O policy does not contain an allocation provision, the approach taken by the courts has been to develop what has been coined the "reasonably related defence costs test", by which defence costs are regarded as 'reasonably related' to the defence of covered claims if it can be shown that those costs would have been incurred if the proceedings had been brought only against the D&Os and not an uninsured party. If the defence costs are 'reasonably related', then they are payable in their entirety, irrespective of the fact that they may also benefit uninsured parties.

Claims handling framework for considering D&O claims

- We suggest the following framework for considering D&O claims. The framework is in two parts:

    i) Coverage investigation

    ii) Monitoring considerations.

(i) Coverage investigation

Stage of Coverage Investigation	Matters to consider (examples only)
Preliminary assessment	Is further information required in order to assess coverage? If appropriate, consider whether to comment without prejudice to policy coverage, making it clear that there is no waiver of insurer's rights.

Stage of Coverage Investigation	Matters to consider (examples only)
Matters pre-dating inception of policy	Does the notification concern matters that pre-date the inception of the policy? If so, has the insured complied with the duty of disclosure/fairly presented the risk? If appropriate, review the proposal form and obtain evidence from the underwriter. Consider consequences of breach depending on whether the Insurance Act 2015 is applicable or pre-existing law (the Insurance Act 2015 will apply to policies that incepted on or after 12 August 2016).
Notification	Is the matter notified a claim or a circumstance? Has the matter been notified in accordance with the provisions in the policy? Has adequate detail been provided in the notification?
Trigger of insuring clause	Is there a claim first made during the policy period? Have policy definitions within the insuring clause been met? E.g. is there an allegation of a 'wrongful act' against an insured? Does the matter involve a D&O in an insured capacity?
Exclusions	Do any policy exclusions apply? Does the claim involve insured and excluded claims that may give rise to allocation issues?
Limit/deductible	Is cover sought under Side A or Side B? Do different deductibles apply? Is the policy limit in the aggregate or any one claim? Have other claims eroded the policy limit?

(ii) Monitoring considerations

Issue	Matters to consider (examples only)
Defence firm	Has the insured proposed a firm to be their legal representative? If so, does that law firm have appropriate expertise? Would the defence firm represent more than one party, be that another insured or an uninsured? If so, consider scope for a conflict situation, as well as whether an allocation of costs is appropriate.
Defence costs	What are the insured's lawyers' hourly rates? How do these compare to market rates/court guideline rates? Are the rates reasonable? What work do the insured's lawyers propose to undertake? What estimated costs would such work involve? Can the defence firm provide an estimate of costs for their recommended next steps and/or the lifetime of the matter?
Defence strategy	What is the insured's defence strategy? What steps can be taken on behalf of the insured to protect the insured's position/defend a claim/manage an investigation? Is an application justified/tactically advantageous, e.g. to strike out the claim or seek security for costs? Is some kind of alternative dispute resolution (ADR) procedure such as mediation appropriate? If so, at what stage? If an insured is subject to a regulatory investigation, can undertakings be negotiated to resolve matters at an early stage? Will the insured need to make any concessions in respect of their conduct?

Issue	Matters to consider (examples only)
Merits of action against insured	What is the defence firm's assessment of the merits of the claim against the insured? What information or evidence is required to form a view if a merits advice cannot be provided by the defence firm? Do some aspects of the claim have more merit than others, in particular, does the position differ between insured and uninsured claims?
Settlement	Is the alleged liability insured under the policy? Would a liability give rise to coverage issues, such as the application of a conduct exclusion/public policy considerations? If a liability would not be covered under the policy, consider to what extent any settlement contribution is appropriate, e.g. one based on saved costs. Is the insured prepared to fund/contribute to a potential settlement?

33 Motor prosecutions and coroner's inquests

Naomi North

- The role of the police and their powers
- The importance of police interview and the caution
- The difference between being a suspect and a witness
- Common offences
- An overview of court procedure
- Evidence and disclosure
- Coroners inquests

Motor prosecutions and coroner's inquests

The scene

A driver involved in a road traffic accident (RTA) resulting in serious injury or death will often be distressed and disorientated. It is therefore important, especially with professional drivers, that they have a nominated contact who can, if at all possible, offer some rationality to what can be a terrifying situation. The driver can be reminded of their rights and entitlements and, most importantly, instructed to undertake any practicalities such as securing witness details and taking photographs of the scene. This information can prove useful later and minimise the risks of prosecution.

This chapter deals with the early stages of a collision, including what may happen at the scene and during any initial police interview right through to criminal proceedings.

The role of the police

The police will attend any serious injury or fatal collision to investigate what happened and secure evidence. Where there is a multi-agency response to a collision, the police have primacy.

The role of the police at the scene is to gather and preserve the evidence, to try to establish what happened and to identify potential witnesses and suspects. In serious collisions, a dedicated unit of specially trained officers will attend, usually known as the *collision investigation unit*. A senior investigating officer (SIO) will usually be appointed to lead and manage the investigation.

If there is any suggestion that a party might be criminally liable the police will usually obtain an initial account under caution from them at the scene. The police will make a contemporaneous note, writing out verbatim what is said. Just because a driver is not under arrest does not mean that they cannot be treated as a suspect.

Before speaking with a suspect, the police should read the caution. The caution states:

> "You do not have to say anything but it may harm your defence if you do not mention when questioned something that you later rely on in court. Anything you do say may be given in evidence."

Whenever a person is interviewed under caution they are entitled to free and independent legal advice. It does not matter whether they are under arrest at the time, or at a police station, their home or in hospital. It is important to remember that anything that is said after caution may be used in evidence at a future date either in a criminal or civil court. Any person being interviewed by the police should speak to a solicitor. Most people are in a certain degree of shock after even the most minor of incidents and may say things that do not fully represent the truth of what happened. This can create problems as often the police will rely on any initial account and it can form the most compelling evidence during any court proceedings.

Two common areas that the police will ask about when obtaining an account from a suspect relate to speed and timings. These two areas are sometimes crucial elements in any collision and unfortunately are the most difficult to judge. The thing to remember is that any account is likely to come under close scrutiny, not only by the police, but also potentially by a court. Those initial statements can make or break a case and can be an influencing factor for the Crown Prosecution Service (CPS) when considering the evidence and importantly the decision whether to prosecute. Therefore, while it is important to cooperate with the police to avoid being arrested, it is also important to secure prompt legal advice (if at all possible).

Seizure and retention of vehicles

It is usual for police to seize vehicles at the scene, thereby enabling forensic examination. This can of course have a significant impact, both on domestic drivers and, in particular, on smaller fleets.

Most police forces operate a policy where the vehicle is retained until a decision regarding prosecution is made. Seizure can extend (in cases involving a prosecution) to the resolution of the trial. While it is possible to make representations regarding the release of the vehicle, the police ultimately make the decision and usually demonstrate an unwillingness to deviate from force policy.

In cases involving a fatality the police are required to allow a potential suspect the opportunity to have an independent examination of the vehicle. This formality was established in the case of *R v Beckford* [1996]. An examination can prove useful in assessing whether any defects exist that could have caused or contributed to the collision and may also reveal a lot about the dynamics of the collision.

Arrest

Following a collision, the police will consider whether a suspect needs to be arrested. The primary source of authority is the Police and Criminal Evidence Act 1984 (PACE) and the Codes of Practice.

The main power of arrest is contained within ss.24 and ss.24 A of PACE. The powers of arrest were reshaped by the Criminal Justice Act 2003 and the Serious Organised Crime and Police Act 2005, which made extensive amendments to PACE. One key change was that all offences are now arrestable providing that certain conditions are fulfilled. The police have the power to arrest in the following circumstances:

1) Where a person is about to commit an offence or where a person whom they have reasonable grounds to suspect is about to commit an offence.

2) Where a person is in the act of committing an offence or where they have reasonable grounds to suspect a person is committing an offence.

3) Where they have reasonable grounds for suspecting that an offence has been committed and where they have reasonable grounds to suspect a person is guilty of it.

Even if the conditions set out above are satisfied, the arrest must still be necessary. Code G of PACE, introduced on 12 November 2012, set out the law around the necessity of arrest. This followed a number of decisions in which the courts clarified the law on the necessity to arrest. The changes were driven by a number of cases where the police were criticised by the courts and found to have acted unlawfully. The most significant of those cases was *Richardson v The Chief Constable of West Midlands Police* [2011]. Here, the High Court decided that Mr Richardson's arrest had been unlawful, and in making that decision clarified the law on the necessity of arrest. The same issues were considered in the case of *Hayes v Chief Constable of Merseyside* [2011], which outlined a two-stage test. Stage one required the police to be satisfied that there were reasonable grounds for suspecting that an arrestable offence had been committed and stage two required them to demonstrate that it was necessary to arrest in order to allow the prompt and effective investigation of the offence. As a result, the police must always consider whether a voluntary interview would be appropriate as an alternative to arrest. Given most drivers will demonstrate a willingness to co-operate with the police, that in itself will usually steer the police towards a voluntary interview conducted at a later date. This enables legal advice to be organised.

If a driver is, however, arrested, they will be driven to a local police station and booked into custody. They will usually be detained until after an interview has taken place. They will often then be released from custody pending the investigation. The process of arrest is therefore very different to a driver attending the station on a voluntary basis. While both persons are permitted to have a solicitor present, an individual attending the police station on a voluntary basis is entitled to leave at any point, although the police could, at that stage, consider whether to detain the individual by arresting them.

Whether attending as a volunteer or while under arrest, there is a right to seek legal advice. A legal representative can be nominated or indeed appointed under the duty solicitor scheme. All representation under this scheme is entirely free and independent.

At the police station

The role of the duty solicitor

If a suspect is arrested the solicitor/legal representative will attend the police station and will secure disclosure from the police prior to interview. This usually consists of an outline of the collision circumstances and a summary of any witness accounts. All consultations with a solicitor/legal representative are subject to legal privilege. The police cannot be present for those private discussions. The solicitor/legal representative will secure full instructions from the suspect and advise them how best to proceed during interview. The suspect may be advised to answer all questions put to them, to submit a prepared statement or indeed answer 'no comment' to questions.

Being represented during a police interview has a number of benefits. It can minimise the prospects of a prosecution or indeed prevent prejudicial comments being made. Additionally, the interview can be an important tool for gathering intelligence about the collision, the injured party and any witnesses. This information can help a claims handler form an early view on liability and quantum.

The caution

At the outset of the interview, the police will caution the suspect:

> "You do not have to say anything but it may harm your defence if you do not mention when questioned something that you later rely on in court. Anything you do say may be given in evidence."

The caution is extremely important.

- The first part, "you do not have to say anything", emphasises a person's right to remain silent: to decline to answer the questions or to answer "no comment".
- The second part, "but it may harm your defence", means that if the suspect chooses to remain silent and later provides an account at court or indeed the account provided changes at court, the jury or indeed the magistrates deciding on the issue of guilt may be less inclined to believe the suspect. This is known as an 'adverse inference'.
- The third part, "Anything you do say may be given in evidence", essentially means the tapes or DVD can be played, or a transcript read, during the course of any trial.

A police interview is a small part of the police investigation, but it can be the most important. What is said in interview can shape the remainder of the police investigation.

After the interview, the police will continue to speak with witnesses, prepare any collision reports and once their file is complete pass it to the CPS for a decision whether to prosecute.

If at any stage the police take the view no offences have been committed they may proceed to simply deal with the matter by taking a formal witness statement.

Being treated as a witness

The police may take the view that a driver has not committed any offences and may decide to deal with them as a witness only.

This decision can be made at the scene or indeed at a later stage. In those circumstances the police will almost certainly take a witness statement. A witness statement is a document recording the evidence of a person, which is signed by that person to confirm that the contents of the statement are true. Most statements are provided voluntarily and in compliance with s.9 of the Criminal Justice Act 1967.

The statement contains a declaration by the maker that it is true to the best of their knowledge and belief and that it is made knowing that, if it were tendered in evidence, the maker would be liable to prosecution if they wilfully stated in it anything which they knew to be false or did not believe to be true (which is known as a perjury declaration).

It is important to remember that if the police take an initial view that someone should be treated as a witness, that does not preclude the individual becoming a suspect should they make prejudicial comments or admissions when the witness statement is being taken. An example may be admitting (during the statement process) that they were using their mobile phone or travelling at excessive speed. The police may not have been aware of this information and it may cause them to change their their views regarding how to deal with the driver. If the witness becomes a suspect the police should stop the procedure and confirm that the individual has the right to seek legal advice. Arrangements should be made for the individual to be interviewed as a suspect.

It is therefore important that claims handlers are alive to this common misunderstanding and, if at all possible, speak with a solicitor so that a determination can be made as to whether the driver is at risk of prejudicing their position. It may be cost effective to engage an independent solicitor to advise the insured during the witness statement process.

Quick checklist for claims handlers:

1) Following notification of the incident ensure all details are taken including potential witness information.

2) Check potential conflict between insured and driver (usually applicable for professional drivers).

3) Instruct claims inspector to undertake scene visit/secure photos.

4) Instruct a solicitor to make contact with driver and secure initial account. This will ensure legal privilege is preserved. Note: discussions between drivers and claims inspectors will not necessarily be protected and could be disclosable.

5) Make contact with police to ascertain likely next steps. Ensure driver has representation for any interview.

6) Make social media enquiries, including newspaper reports for intelligence gathering.

7) If driver is to be treated as a witness only, carry out checks to ensure that the driver will not prejudice his position. A solicitor can attend if necessary during the witness statement process.

Decision-making stage

Once the investigation is complete, either a senior police officer or a CPS lawyer will decide whether the case should go to court or whether another disposal may be appropriate. In recent years, the injured party in any collision or their family are involved in the decision-making process. It is now a regular occurence for prosecutors to meet with families to discuss the case and their respective views.

Role of the CPS

The CPS is a government agency responsible for prosecuting individuals (and occasionally institutions such as companies) for breaking the law. It works closely with the police but is in fact a completely separate institution. It is important to remember that while a decision to charge may be made, there is nothing to prevent the defence from making representations or presenting fresh evidence, such as expert evidence, in order to seek a review of the case. The CPS has an ongoing duty to review the case.

Before commencing a prosecution the CPS and/or the police will apply the full code test set out below:

The full code test has two stages: (i) the evidential stage, followed by (ii) the public interest stage.

The CPS must first be satisfied that there is sufficient evidence to provide a realistic prospect of conviction. It must consider what the defence case may be, and how it is likely to affect the prospects of conviction. The CPS is obliged to consider the admissibility of the evidence and the reliability and credibility of witnesses. A case that does not pass the evidential stage must not proceed, no matter how serious or sensitive it may be.

Once satisfied that the case meets the evidential test, the CPS must then consider whether it is in the public interest to bring the prosecution. This will include consideration of factors such as the severity of the offence, the culpability of the suspect and the harm caused to any victim. In cases involving serious injury or a fatality, this test will almost certainly be satisfied.

Death in driving cases where the victim is a close friend or relative of the driver

It is a sad reality that drivers are sometimes involved in collisions where a loved one loses their life. Historically, there was a reluctance to prosecute in these cases; however, there now seems to be a greater willingness to take these cases to court, perhaps motivated by the need to ensure the safety of other road users. If there is evidence to suggest that an individual may present a continuing danger to other road users, the usual view adopted by the CPS is that a prosecution should proceed.

In cases where the degree of culpability of the driver is low and there is no evidence they present a continuing danger to other road users, it is less likely that a prosecution will be in the public interest.

No further action

If the investigation indicates that there is no fault on the part of the driver or the full code test is not met, the CPS should not prosecute and will confirm that no further action is being taken. It is important to remember that if further evidence comes to light at a later stage, providing there are no time limits barring a prosecution, the case could still proceed to court.

National Driver Alertness Course

The police may take the view that there is sufficient evidence to prosecute but may feel the driver would benefit from attending the National Driver Improvement Scheme (also known as the National Driver Alertness Course).

The scheme aims to provide training and guidance to drivers who have been involved in a collision. It is an alternative to prosecution. If the course is not attended or fully completed, the police are advised and can then consider whether to prosecute the driver. The course lasts between 1 and 1.5 days and costs around £150.

To be eligible for the course the driver must accept some culpability for the collision. Therefore, while it is not recorded as a criminal conviction, from a civil perspective it is still likely to be relevant and regarded as an admission of guilt. These courses are only offered to drivers involved in incidents where the type of poor driving evidenced is of a low level and no serious injury or death has been caused.

Common offences and terms explained

Definition of a "motor vehicle"

The term "motor vehicle" is defined in s.185(1) of the Road Traffic Act 1988 and s.136(1) of the Road Traffic Regulation Act 1984 as "a mechanically propelled vehicle, intended or adapted for use on roads". At its most basic level, it is a vehicle that can be propelled by mechanical means.

Definitions of "road" and "road or other public place"

The term "road" is defined at s.142 of the Road Traffic Regulation Act 1984 as any length of highway or other road to which the public has access, and includes bridges over which a road passes.

The expression "on a road or other public place" is frequently referred to in road traffic legislation. A public place is a place to which the public, or part thereof, have access. A car park may be a road or it may be a public place and the two may have different meanings for different offences.

Careless driving

Careless driving or driving without due care and attention is defined as driving which falls below the standard expected of a competent driver; or driving that does not show reasonable consideration for other persons. Examples may include inattention or misjudgement, perhaps inadvertently driving through a red light or colliding with the rear of the vehicle ahead, which stopped suddenly.

Dangerous driving

Dangerous driving is where the standard of driving falls far below the standard of a careful and competent driver and the driving would be regarded as dangerous to a competent and careful driver.

Examples of dangerous driving include competitive driving, excessive speed for the road conditions, driving while knowingly suffering from a medical condition such as impaired eyesight or driving when fatigued or unwell. Dangerous driving will also include situations where a person knowingly drives a vehicle with a dangerous defect or uses a hand-held mobile phone to compile a text message.

Causing the death of – causation

The manner of the defendant's driving must have been a cause of the death. The defendant's driving need not be the sole, principal or even a substantial cause of the death. The defendant's driving must have played a part.

Common offences

Causing death by dangerous driving

Section 1 of the Road Traffic Act 1988

"A person who causes the death of another person by driving a mechanically propelled vehicle dangerously on a road or other public place is guilty of an offence."

- Triable on indictment
- Maximum sentence of 14 years imprisonment
- Obligatory disqualification – minimum two years
- Compulsory extended retest.

Causing serious injury by dangerous driving

Section 1A of the Road Traffic Act 1988

"A person who causes serious injury to another person by driving a mechanically propelled vehicle dangerously on a road or other public place is guilty of an offence." The test for dangerous driving is as above, although the offence requires the driving to result in another person suffering a serious injury. Serious injury is defined as "physical harm which amounts to grievous bodily harm for the purposes of the Offences Against the Person Act 1861". Examples have included serious multiple injuries, paralysis, several broken bones and serious head injuries.

- Triable either way.
- Maximum sentence is six months' imprisonment and/or fine on summary conviction.
- Maximum sentence on indictment is five years' imprisonment and/or fine.
- Obligatory disqualification – minimum two years.
- Compulsory extended retest.

Dangerous driving

Section 2 of the Road Traffic Act 1988

"A person who drives a mechanically propelled vehicle dangerously on a road or other public place is guilty of an offence." The test is whether the standard of driving falls far below that of a competent and careful driver and it would be obvious to a competent and careful driver that driving in that way would be dangerous.

- Triable either way.
- Maximum sentence is six months' imprisonment and/or a fine on summary conviction.
- Maximum sentence of two years' imprisonment on indictment and/or a fine.
- Obligatory disqualification – minimum 12 months.
- Compulsory extended retest.

Causing death by careless driving

Section 2B of the Road Traffic Act 1988

"A person who causes the death of another person by driving a mechanically propelled vehicle on a road or other public place without due care and attention, or without reasonable consideration for other persons using the road or place, is guilty of an offence."

- Triable either way
- Maximum sentence is six months' imprisonment and/or fine on summary conviction.
- Maximum sentence on indictment is five years' imprisonment and/or fine.
- Obligatory disqualification of a minimum of one year.
- Discretionary retest.

Careless driving

Section 3 of the Road Traffic Act 1988

"If a person drives a mechanically propelled vehicle on a road or other public place without due care and attention, or without reasonable consideration for other persons using the road or place, he is guilty of an offence." The legal test is whether the standard of driving falls below that of a competent and careful driver. In determining what is to be expected of a competent and careful driver, the court must consider not only the circumstances of which the driver could be expected to be aware, but also any circumstances shown to have been within the driver's actual knowledge. The test of whether the standard of driving has fallen below the required standard is objective.

- Triable summarily.
- Maximum fine of £5,000.
- Discretionary disqualification.
- Licence endorsement of three to nine penalty points.

Starting proceedings

There are three main ways of commencing proceedings:

1) The police arrest a suspect without a warrant at the scene and take them to the police station. After questioning, the police formally charge the driver with an offence and a nominated

court date is provided while the driver is in custody. For reasons dealt with above in the chapter, this route is rare in road traffic collisions.

2) The police lay the information before a magistrate or magistrates' clerk alleging that the driver has committed the offence specified in the information. On the basis of the information a summons is issued under the Magistrates' Court Act 1980 (MCA 1980) and then served. The summons requires the driver to attend the magistrates' court on a specific day.

3) The prosecution may issue a written charge requiring the defendant to attend court. The written charge and requisition must be served on the defendant. A copy of both the written charge and requisition must also be served on the court specified in the requisition. This is known as a postal requisition.

Category of offences

Summary only offences can only be heard and tried in the magistrates' court. The most common summary only offences include careless driving, failing to stop at the scene of a road traffic accident and excess alcohol offences.

While there are generally no statutory time limits for prosecuting indictable offences, under the MCA 1980 there is a time limit imposed for summary only offences. A magistrates' court may not try a defendant for a summary offence unless the information was laid within six months of the date of the commission of the offence. Failure to observe these statutory time limits will mean the CPS is time-barred from commencing proceedings. In calculating the limitation period, the day on which the offence was committed is not included. It is also important to note that, providing the information is laid at the court within the six-month time limit, the summons will not be defective if it is served outside the six-month timeframe.

Indictable only offences are deemed so serious that only the Crown Court can deal with them. One example is causing death by dangerous driving. Other than one short administrative hearing in the magistrates' court all other hearings will take place in the Crown Court.

Triable either way offences can be dealt with in either the magistrates' court or Crown Court. Examples are causing death by careless driving and dangerous driving. At the first hearing the court will go through the 'plea before venue' procedure where the defendant will be asked to indicate a plea of guilty, not guilty or make no indication of plea at all. If the defendant pleads guilty, then the court will have to decide if its powers of sentence are sufficient to deal with the case. If it thinks that it has insufficient sentencing powers then it will send the case to the Crown Court.

If the defendant pleads not guilty or gives no indication, then the court will decide which court is the most appropriate venue to hear the case. The court will consider the seriousness of the allegations and the case complexity. If it thinks that the case is capable of being retained in the magistrates' court, then the defendant will be offered the right to have the case tried in the magistrates' court or elect a Crown Court trial.

The different courts

Lay magistrates sit in the magistrates' court. Their work is unpaid although they can claim allowances for travel. Lay magistrates have no legal qualifications and are appointed by the Lord Chancellor on behalf of and in the name of Her Majesty.

District judges also sit in the magistrates' court. They are professional salaried members of the judiciary. They are appointed by the Queen upon the recommendation of the Lord Chancellor from among barristers, solicitors or legal executives of at least seven years' standing.

A district judge can try a case sitting alone whereas at least two magistrates must sit together for the purposes of a summary trial. The magistrates are assisted by a legally trained clerk.

In summary only cases, the defendant considers the evidence provided by the prosecution and is usually compelled to enter a plea at the first hearing. If a guilty plea is entered, the court will proceed to sentence. If a not guilty plea is entered then there will have to be a trial. It is usual to fix a trial date at the first hearing. Most road traffic cases in the magistrates' court are resolved in one day. The case is decided by the magistrates who are the judges of both fact and law. The magistrates are entitled to seek advice from the clerk or legal advisor on matters of law, evidence and procedure but the decision on these matters is solely that of the magistrates. Legal advisors are qualified lawyers and, in addition to their duties advising the magistrates, they play an important role in administering the court.

The Crown Court deals with more serious criminal cases. In the Crown Court the trial takes place before a jury. The trial is presided over by a salaried judge who is or has been a practising barrister, solicitor or legal executive. The judge adjudicates on all matters of the law including admissibility of evidence and other legal arguments. The jury decides matters of fact. The jury consists of laypersons drawn at random from the community. They are usually summonsed for a period of two weeks. They must accept and apply the law as it is explained to them by the judge in the summing-up at the end of the case. They alone decide questions of fact and find the defendant guilty or not guilty.

The burden of proof

In the three jurisdictions of the UK there are only two standards of proof in trials.

The criminal standard is described as "beyond reasonable doubt". That standard remains, and the words commonly used, though the Judicial Studies Board guidance is that juries are to be told that to convict they must be persuaded "so that you are sure".

The civil standard is "the balance of probabilities", often referred to in judgments as "more likely than not".

Entering a plea

Before deciding whether to plead guilty or not guilty it is essential the defendant is properly advised about the strength of the evidence and the implications of pleading guilty or not guilty. It is important to note that the Advance Information Rules apply only to triable either way offences. This means that for summary only offences, such as careless driving, the CPS is under no obligation to provide details of its case prior to trial. In reality, providing early contact is made with the relevant CPS unit, there is a willingness by the CPS to provide some disclosure in an effort to assist the smooth running of proceedings. It is important the legal representative adopts a proactive approach to securing disclosure as this will ensure proper time can be taken to consider the defendant's options.

In relation to triable either way offences, the rules relating to advance disclosure are set out in Part 8 of the Criminal Procedure Rules. The prosecution is obliged to provide the defence with either copies of the statements and documents upon which the prosecution is based or, at the very least, a summary of the facts and matters which will be adduced during the prosecution case. These details must be provided as soon as practicable but certainly no later than the beginning of the day of the first hearing. This information in turn assists the defence in deciding key issues such as plea and mode of trial.

Pleading guilty

Pleading guilty means that there will not be a trial and that the facts of the case as presented by the prosecution are accepted. In summary only offences, it may be possible to plead guilty by post; however, if the court is considering disqualification, the defendant will usually need to be present. In summary only offences, the defendant will usually be sentenced at the first hearing.

If the defendant faces an either way offence and pleads guilty, the court will hear representations from the CPS and the defence and will consider whether it has sufficient powers to pass sentence or whether the case should be sent to the Crown Court for sentence.

Pleading guilty can be advantageous for a number of reasons:

1) A plea at the first opportunity will lead to a one-third reduction of sentence. This credit for a guilty plea is reduced on a sliding scale until the trial, but can be significant.

2) Costs sought by the CPS will also be significantly reduced if an early guilty plea is entered. In summary only matters, costs in the region of £85 are awarded if matters are disposed of on the first date. Should the matter progress to trial, requests for costs in excess of £1,000 are not uncommon.

3) The defendant's advocate is also able to demonstrate their client's remorse if the client has accepted responsibility for their actions.

It is possible to plead guilty but dispute certain aspects of the CPS case. For example, the Crown may say that the collision occurred due to the defendant driving 30 mph over the speed limit or following a prolonged course of bad driving. If this is disputed, it may be possible to plead guilty on a limited basis, which can have a significant impact on the eventual sentence passed. In this scenario, a solicitor will negotiate with the CPS to draft a formal document called a 'basis of plea', which outlines the exact basis upon which guilt is accepted. A basis of plea can be a useful tool in formalising any points that would assist in relation to sentence and potentially any civil claim going forwards.

Basis of plea and Newton hearings

General guidance about the procedure to be adopted where the defendant pleads guilty on a different factual basis (than the CPS case) has been set down in the case of *R v Underwood* [2005]. Essentially, it is the responsibility of the defence to alert the prosecution to areas of dispute.

On ascertaining there is a dispute there are three options:

1) The prosecution may accept and agree the defendant's account. If so, the respective positions should be reduced to writing and signed by both advocates.

2) If the prosecution rejects the defence position, the areas of dispute should be identified in writing and aired before the sentencing judge.

3) The prosecution may lack the evidence to positively dispute the defence account. This does not mean that the prosecution must accept the account. Even where the facts relied on by the defendant arise from the defendant's own personal knowledge the prosecution should not normally accept them unless it is supported by other material.

After submissions from the parties, the magistrates or judge will decide how to proceed. They may approve the basis of plea and sentence according to its contents or indeed may order a Newton hearing.

If the prosecution does not accept the defendant's account, the areas of dispute should be set out in writing. A Newton hearing may be required to resolve those areas. The hearing will take place in front of the judge or magistrates who will consider the specific issues in dispute. Having heard the evidence, the magistrates or judge will decide which version of events the defendant should be sentenced on. Few defendants decide to proceed with a Newton hearing, not least because if the decision goes against them their credit for an early guilty plea is compromised.

Special reasons

For a special reasons argument to be successful the defendant will need to demonstrate that while they were technically guilty of an offence the circumstances are so exceptional that there is good reason for the court not to impose points or a disqualification. The legal argument must be directly connected with the commission of the offence and one that the court should to take into consideration when imposing punishment. Examples of cases where a special reasons argument may be applicable include where the defendant drove someone to hospital while over the alcohol limit or drove over the limit after their drink was spiked. Before deciding whether special reasons are found, the court will consider a number of factors such as the reason for driving, the duration of driving time and the risk to other road users. The onus of establishing special reasons lies on the defence, and the standard is that of the balance of probabilities. It is important to remember that a conviction does still stand albeit no points or indeed a disqualification is imposed.

Exceptional hardship application

During a sentencing exercise, the court may consider imposing a period of disqualification. It may be the offence attracts a discretionary disqualification or indeed the driver has existing points on his licence. Disqualification for a minimum of six months must be ordered if a driver incurs 12 penalty points or more within a three-year period. The minimum period may be increased if the driver has been disqualified within the three preceding years. Totting-up disqualifications erase all penalty points. The period of a totting-up disqualification may be reduced or avoided for exceptional hardship,

An exceptional hardship application can be made to explain why the loss of a driving licence will cause hardship to the driver beyond that which can usually be expected from losing the ability to drive. It is rarely sufficient to demonstrate that the driver alone will suffer; the hardship must have a direct impact on other people, such as employees who would also lose their jobs or family members who rely on the driver.

If the application is successful it is not possible to make a further application within three years.

Pleading not guilty

Where a not guilty plea is entered, the case will be contested and resolved by trial.

Depending upon the classification (summary only, either way or indictable only) and seriousness of the offence, the trial may take place in either the magistrates' or the Crown Court. In the magistrates' court trials usually take place within three months of the first hearing, but it very much depends on the location as some court centres have significant delays. If the offence is triable either way the magistrates' court will consider mode of trial and if the magistrates accept jurisdiction of the case, the defendant has the right to elect a Crown Court trial. Crown Court trials take longer to be listed due to a lack of court time and witness availability.

An acquittal in a criminal trial can assist the civil case as it prevents the claimant's solicitor pleading a conviction. It also allows the prosecution, and by extension the claimant's, evidence to be challenged and tested and key witnesses observed. Sometimes very helpful evidence can be given during a trial, which can shape the civil case thereafter.

Additionally, by entering a not guilty plea, the prosecution is obliged to disclose any information they hold that undermines their case or is capable of assisting the defence. By securing access to this material, it can increase a defendant's prospects in successfully defending an allegation. For example, the disclosure exercise may reveal details of helpful witnesses or perhaps helpful comments made by witnesses at the scene. With a guilty plea, there is no obligation to disclose this material. For obvious reasons, this information can prove helpful for claims handlers dealing with any civil claim.

If a defendant is found not guilty, the court may make a defence costs order allowing the recovery of the costs incurred in defending the case. There has been a dramatic overhaul of the costs rules since the Legal Aid, Sentencing and Punishment of Offenders Act 2012. A defendant is now only eligible to recover costs at legal aid rates in magistrates' court cases. In the Crown Court, legal costs are also limited to legal aid rates but only where a defendant has applied for and been rejected for legal aid.

The trial process

In the magistrates' court, the trial will usually be heard before three lay magistrates who are not legally qualified. They will be advised on the law by the clerk who is usually a solicitor or barrister.

The magistrates, subject to advice, will decide on any factual or legal issues in the case, such as admissibility of bad character evidence, and will then reach a verdict. To find a defendant guilty, the magistrates will need to be satisfied that they are sure the offence has been committed. Sometimes a legally qualified magistrate, known as a district judge, will hear the case.

In the Crown Court, the trial will take place before a judge and 12 jurors. The judge will give guidance on the law; a judge should not offer opinion on the evidence. The jurors are responsible for hearing the evidence and deciding guilt.

Initially, all the jurors will need to agree on a verdict, which is known as a unanimous verdict. If, however, after at least two hours this has not been possible, the judge may give a majority direction, meaning that the court can accept a decision on which at least 10 jurors (or 9 if only 10 jurors remain) agree.

Trial on indictment vs summary trial

For any triable either way offence the defendant has a choice of trial on indictment in the Crown Court or summary trial in the magistrates' court.

Summary trial is less expensive and is usually resolved more quickly than a trial in the Crown Court. The prosecution costs associated with a Crown Court trial are usually around two to three times that of a summary trial. The traditional view is that trial by jury offers a better prospect of acquittal. Not only is there a reluctance by jurors to convict, but it is often harder for all jurors to reach a unanimous or majority verdict. Also, in the Crown Court, a judge presides over the case and will hear legal arguments in the absence of the jury. This means that the jury is not privy to prejudicial information such as the defendant's bad character unless it is ruled admissible. Magistrates are required to decide whether to admit bad character evidence and if they decide it is inadmissible, put it out of their minds. Cases in the Crown Court are generally better prepared and there are additional rules surrounding disclosure, which usually results in more information being provided to the defence.

Disclosure and evidence

In criminal cases, material is generated during the investigation. Some of it will be evidential and some will not. The material that does not form part of the prosecution case is called 'unused' material.

In simple terms, the meaning of disclosure is the obligation of the prosecution to serve on the defence unused material that may reasonably be capable of undermining the prosecution case or assisting the defence.

Disclosure by the prosecution must be done in a timely manner so as to provide the defence with a proper opportunity to consider it. The rules around disclosure are set out in the Criminal Procedure and Investigations Act 1996 (CPIA).

Material provided to the defence either before or at the first hearing will usually be limited to the Initial Details of the Prosecution Case (IDPC); in other words, the evidence that is said to support the prosecution. This information should be sufficient for pleas to be taken or to decide mode of trial. The prosecution's initial duty of disclosure (under s. 3 of the CPIA) will arise should the defendant enter a not guilty plea. If there is no such material in existence, the prosecution must confirm this in writing. Prosecution disclosure obligations continue through to trial.

Defence Case Statement

In the magistrates' court, once the prosecution has provided a schedule of any unused material the defendant may serve a Defence Case Statement (DCS), the content of which is prescribed in s.6A of the CPIA. The DCS must be served within 14 days of the day on which the prosecutor complies or purports to comply with the initial duty of disclosure and must set out the nature of the defence, matters on which the defendant takes issue with the prosecution and why, and must raise any points of law the defendant wishes to take, such as admissibility of evidence. In the magistrates' court, a DCS is discretionary. In the Crown Court, a DCS must be served within 28 days of the day on which the prosecutor complies or purports to comply with the initial duty to disclose. This timescale can be extended with the permission of the court.

At the end of the DCS the defendant can request specific material it is believed the prosecution may hold that may assist the defence case, such as contact details of helpful witnesses, details of convictions of the other party involved, first accounts of witnesses and so on. In a road traffic case, the defendant can request information from the police, such as highway data or accident statistics, which again can prove helpful in defending a case. The DCS is therefore a useful tool which can assist both the criminal and civil case.

The service of a DCS also strengthens and protects the defendant's legal position if problems arise in obtaining disclosure from the prosecution. Section 8 of the CPIA only permits defendants who have served a DCS to apply to the court for an order requiring the prosecution to disclose prosecution material that has not previously been supplied.

Hearsay evidence

Hearsay in criminal proceedings is a statement not made in oral evidence in the proceedings that is evidence of any matter stated. As a general rule, hearsay evidence is inadmissible in criminal cases.

Part 20 of the Criminal Procedure Rules sets out the rules relating to hearsay evidence. The Rules were introduced following the Criminal Justice Act 2003. The same rules apply in both the magistrates' court and the Crown Court. Where a prosecutor wishes to introduce hearsay evidence, notice must be given not more than 14 days after the defendant pleads not guilty in the Crown Court or 28 days after a not guilty plea in the magistrates' court.

Where the defendant wishes to introduce hearsay evidence, a notice must be served as soon as reasonably practicable.

A party must serve a notice to introduce hearsay evidence and the application may be opposed.

Only certain categories of hearsay evidence require a notice:

a) Hearsay evidence admissible because the witness is unavailable;

b) Multiple hearsay;

c) Evidence to be admitted at the discretion of the court;

d) Evidence in a statement prepared for the criminal proceedings.

In road traffic matters, examples of hearsay evidence could be comments made by a now deceased witness, or an account provided by an untraceable witness.

When considering whether to permit hearsay evidence, the court will consider the following:

- How much probative value the statement has in relation to the issue in the proceedings;
- The circumstances in which the statement was made;
- How reliable the statement-maker appears to be;
- Whether it is in the 'interests of justice' to be admissable.

Evidence of bad character

In criminal proceedings, bad character means "evidence of a disposition towards misconduct". Misconduct means the commission of an offence or other reprehensible conduct. There is no definition of what constitutes reprehensible conduct but it could include (in road traffic cases) evidence of the defendant having undertaken a Speed Awareness Course following being caught allegedly driving in excess of the speed limit. The rules governing the admissibility of bad character evidence are set out in ss.98–113 of the Criminal Justice Act 2003.

If the prosecution wishes to adduce bad character evidence in relation to the defendant they must serve a formal notice outlining that evidence and the reasons it is admissible and relevant to the case.

In some circumstances the defendant may wish to adduce bad character evidence relating to a non-defendant. An example would be the defendant who alleges that the motorcyclist they struck was speeding. If the motorcyclist had a history of speeding endorsements or motoring convictions an application would be needed (unless the prosecution consented) to put this evidence before the court. The defendant must be able to demonstrate the following:

1) It has substantial probative value in relation to a matter that is in issue in the proceedings; and
2) Is of substantial importance in the context of the case as a whole.

Submission of no case to answer

Once the prosecution has closed its case, the defence can make a submission of no case to answer. This cannot be done in every case as it depends upon the strength of the prosecution evidence, or rather the lack of it. If successful, the case is dismissed, avoiding the defendant giving evidence.

The case of *R v Galbraith* [1981] set out the test for the court to consider when hearing a submission that there is no case to answer. The court must consider whether the evidence that has been adduced, taken at its highest, is such that a reasonable jury, properly directed, could convict. If the answer is no, then the case should stop. If not, then the case will proceed, and any evidence that the defence wishes to put forward should be heard.

Sentence

If the defendant has pleaded guilty or is found guilty following trial, dependent upon the severity of the offence, the case may be adjourned for the preparation of a pre-sentence report. This happens where the court is considering disposals such as community orders or custody.

The Probation Service undertakes a pre-sentence report. This report is used by the court when passing sentence and will address key issues such as remorse, risk of re-offending and risks to the public. The report will also consider the various sentencing options available to the court.

At the sentencing hearing, the court will have regard to the conclusion of any pre-sentence report but also any aggravating or mitigating factors.

Aggravating factors include:

- More than one person is killed or injured
- Previous convictions for motoring offences
- Prolonged case of bad driving

Mitigating factors include:

- Offender injured as a result of the collision
- Good driving record
- A third party/victim contributed to the collision.

Appeals

There are two types of appeals: against conviction and against sentence.

If a defendant is convicted in the magistrates' court they have 21 days from the date of the sentence hearing to lodge an appeal against either the conviction or the sentence. An appeal should be lodged with the magistrates' court that heard the case. A defendant does not need to seek permission to appeal and the appeal will be heard in the Crown Court before a judge and two lay magistrates.

Pending the appeal being heard in the Crown Court, an application may be made to suspend any disqualification from driving or for bail should the sentence have been one of imprisonment.

An appeal against the conviction will involve the evidence being called again including any witnesses. If successful, the conviction will no longer stand and any sentence imposed by the magistrates' court will also be removed.

At an appeal against sentence, it will be necessary to show that the sentence imposed was wrong in law, wrong in principle or manifestly excessive.

Appealing from the Crown Court is more difficult. An appeal against either conviction or sentence must be lodged within 28 days. Appeals are lodged using a specific form and must be accompanied by a document setting out the grounds of appeal; usually this is drafted by the advocate who represented the defendant.

It is not possible to appeal against a conviction in the Crown Court simply because the defendant disagrees with the decision to convict. It is necessary to show that the conviction was in some way unsafe. Usually, appeals against convictions are based upon an error of law or the jury being incorrectly directed by the judge. It may be possible to appeal after the 28-day period if new evidence comes to light, although it will be necessary to show that swift action was taken as soon as the new evidence became known.

Any appeal from the Crown Court against sentence must show that the sentence was manifestly excessive or wrong in law.

Appeals from the Crown Court are made to the Court of Appeal and permission must first be granted by a single judge before the appeal can be heard in full. The single judge will assess the merits of the application and if it is felt that there is no prospect of success, the appeal will be rejected at that point. If an appellant at that stage decides to still proceed there can be costs implications but also, should the appeal be considered by the court to be without merit the full court can give a "loss of time" direction. This means that in the event of a custodial sentence having been imposed by the Crown Court, the Court of Appeal can direct that a certain portion of the prison sentence already served does not count against the total to be served, effectively increasing the length of the custodial sentence.

Under s.155 of the Powers of Criminal Courts (Sentencing) Act 2000, the Crown Court can alter a sentence up to 56 days after it was first imposed. The usual reason for altering the sentence is that further information relevant to the sentence has become available to the court; or the court has overlooked some statutory provisions limiting its powers. Applications can be made to the Crown Court inviting the court to consider altering the sentence imposed and, if successful, this can often be quicker than appeal to the Court of Appeal. It is best to approach the court as quickly as possible to exercise its powers to ensure that if the Crown Court refuses to review the sentence then any appeal to the Court of Appeal can be lodged in time.

Coroner's inquests

The coroner is expected to open an inquest where there is reasonable suspicion that the deceased has died from a violent or unnatural death, where the cause of death is unknown or if the deceased died while in custody or state detention. On that basis, it naturally follows that whenever a death occurs as a result of a road traffic collision, the coroner will be notified.

Coroners are independent judicial officers, appointed by the local authority. They are either doctors or lawyers responsible for investigating the cause of deaths.

In 2013, the coronial system underwent significant changes with the implementation of the Coroners and Justice Act 2009 and the Coroner's Rules 2013. These rules were introduced to improve the efficiency of the coronial process and as a consequence coroners are working hard to hear inquests more quickly.

Following a road traffic collision, the coroner will request a post mortem to be carried out by a pathologist to determine the cause of death. The coroner may also give any potential suspect involved in the collision an opportunity to obtain a second post mortem. The second post mortem examination will allow the coroner to release the body and retain the report for use by the defence if, in due course, a prosecution is pursued. In reality, it is rare for a second post mortem to be requested by the defence. One may be considered where there are issues around causation, for example, whether the death occurred as a result of the collision or indeed by way of an underlying medical problem unrelated to it.

In deaths arising from a road traffic collision, the coroner will usually open the inquest and adjourn it. This enables the police enquiry to proceed. The coroner will then continue to liaise with the police until a final decision is made regarding prosecution. Periodically, the coroner will fix hearings to monitor the progress of the investigation. These hearings are called pre-inquest reviews. Interested persons and their representatives can attend these hearings. They can be a useful intelligence gathering tool enabling enquiries to be undertaken about the status of the police investigation and likely next steps. Information can also be secured about the personal circumstances of the deceased, which can help the claims handlers with reserving strategies.

The general rule is that the coroner will adjourn any inquest until the outcome of any criminal proceedings is finalised. If a criminal prosecution is pursued (for offences such as causing death by careless or dangerous driving) the coroner may not hold an inquest at all.

If the coroner does decide to hold an inquest, the hearing is intended to allow the coroner to deal with several key questions:

1) who the deceased was;
2) how, when and where the deceased came by his or her death; and
3) the particulars (if any) required by the Births and Deaths Registrations Act 1953 to be registered concerning the death.

Before an inquest takes place, the coroner must review the evidence and determine who, if anyone, should be formally identified as an 'interested person'.

An interested person has the opportunity to:

- Be more involved in the inquest process
- Be legally represented
- Receive a copy of the evidence in advance of the inquest
- Ask questions of other witnesses at the inquest.

A deceased's spouse, parent or child has a right to be identified as an interested person. Any person whose act or omission, in the opinion of the coroner, may have caused or contributed to the death will also be identified as an interested person. This means that the driver of a vehicle involved in an accident could well find themselves being identified as an interested person, even if a police investigation took place and they were not prosecuted.

As set out above, going on record as an interested person has important consequences for both a driver directly involved in the collision and indeed his/her respective insurer. Being an interested person will ensure disclosure is provided prior to the inquest.
In cases involving a road traffic collision, this will include witness statements, a copy of the post mortem report and even a copy of any collision report. Early review of this material (which otherwise may not have been available) can assist the claims handler determining liability and quantum.

For example, the witness evidence or collision report may assist with arguments of contributory negligence. The post-mortem evidence may also reveal key information around the deceased's health pre-accident and this can be relevant when defending dependancy claims.

The coroner is also obliged to provide a witness list setting out which witnesses will be attending to give evidence and which statements will be read. The coroner's decisions about these issues can be challenged by way of written representations ahead of the inquest. In deaths arising from a road traffic collision the hearing usually takes place in front of the coroner. Jury inquests are incredibly rare.

Bearing in mind that one of the objectives of an inquest is to identify how a person died, anyone who is an interested person — especially someone who was directly involved in the collision — should approach the inquest process with seriousness and caution. An inquest is often the first and only time when evidence can be tested by an interested person. Coroners recognise the importance of this for those involved and are increasingly willing to allow detailed questioning of witnesses at an inquest (particularly from the representatives of the deceased's family). While inquest hearings are not meant to be about apportioning blame, the reality can often be very different, especially if you are the one being questioned. While the coroner should prevent inappropriate questioning, it is often the legal representative for the interested person who is first to raise concerns.

Effective questioning of witnesses (such as the attending police officers or witnesses to the collision) may prove key in influencing how the evidence is viewed and the coroner's conclusion and/or the content of any narrative judgement. Also, it can be a useful mechanism to shape the evidence which can, ultimately have a bearing on any civil claim going forwards. For example, a coroner's narrative conclusion can be documented and used during the civil claim. The inquest can also be used as an opportunity to assess witnesses and how they perform when giving evidence. Witnesses (in particular police collision investigators) can be challenged by way of questioning and their evidence be referred to during negotiations within civil proceedings. The evidence given by all witnesses will assist the coroner in dealing with the key questions set out above and importantly determine how, when and where the deceased came by their death. The most common conclusions are 'accidental death, road traffic collision' or indeed the coroner may give a narrative conclusion. The coroner or jury can reach one of these conclusions once satisfied of the necessary facts to the required standard of proof. The civil standard is used, namely 'on the balance of probabilities', except for conclusions of unlawful killing and suicide where the criminal standard of 'beyond all reasonable doubt' applies.

Finally, the coroner has a number of key powers. Perhaps the most significant to a driver directly involved in a collision is the ability to refer a case back to the CPS for a review regarding prosecution. Good representation can minimise the risks of this occurring helping to ensure the driver does not prejudice his position and indeed the civil case.

Checklist

- ✓ Identify the correct coroner (usually the coroner is responsible for the area where the death occurred).
- ✓ Check whether a second post-mortem is being offered.
- ✓ Seek advice reference a second post-mortem.
- ✓ If a driver is required to give evidence at the inquest consider providing representation, enabling disclosure to be secured.

34 First-party property claims

Will Brown

- Types of property insurance
- What they cover
- Defining and measuring loss
- Aggregation
- Notification
- Contribution

First-party property claims

Types of insurance

At its simplest, property insurance provides cover for damage to a building (houses, commercial buildings, etc.) and its contents (personal possessions, stock, business assets).

Property policies, particularly those insuring commercial entities, are often extended to cover consequential losses, such as 'business interruption'.

There are two main types of property policy, namely 'specified perils' and 'all risks'.

Specified perils

These types of policies expressly set out the risks that the policy will respond to. Under a property policy, these normally include, as a minimum, damage to property caused by fire, flood and storm.

The onus is on the insured to prove its loss/damage was caused by an insured risk.

All risks

These policies by contrast remove from the insured the need to demonstrate the precise cause of its loss. Instead, the burden is on the insured to prove that some loss or damage has occurred during the period of cover. It is then for the insurer to show the cause is either excluded or was not fortuitous.

A common type of all risks insurance is contractors all risks (CAR).

As all risks policies are the most common type of commercial risks policy, this is the focus of this chapter.

Schedule and wording

The policy schedule usually sets out the key information upon which the policy operates: the identity of the insured, the property insured, sum insured and premium.

While policy wordings will vary, as a minimum, the insuring clause will confirm that the policy will respond in respect of "loss of or damage to the insured property" during the period of the policy, or contain words with the equivalent effect.

Insured

The first issue when faced with a claim is to consider whether the person or corporate entity claiming under the policy falls within the definition of "insured" in the policy. Where parties are expressly named the position is generally straightforward.

Policies can extend to cover a class of insured parties (such as a subcontractor or supplier) or a person who has the benefit of an obligation by the main insured to provide it with cover under the policy. As a result, consideration of the underlying contractual position may be necessary.

Insured property

The "insured property" will almost always be defined, usually in the schedule.

Cover can be in respect of named properties or sites or sometimes classes of properties, e.g. "all properties owned by the insured at the time cover incepted". Here it is worth noting that the word "property" (which is used in the insuring clause) is normally restricted to physical property rather than other forms of property such as intellectual property rights or electronic data.

While CAR insurance primarily seeks to cover physical damage to the contract works, it is often extended to cover additional categories of insurance, such as damage to construction plant, equipment and machinery as well as third-party liability.

Has there been damage?

A policy that covers all risks of "loss of or damage to" the insured property responds only to physical loss of, or damage to, such property. "Loss" therefore means physical deprivation.

Something is damaged when it has suffered some event, or process, that has caused an adverse physical change but this doesn't need to be permanent. There can be damage even if the condition of the property can be restored without great cost. For example, this has been held to include cleaning away dust (*Hunter v Canary Wharf Ltd* 1996).

Damage should not be confused with a defect. Something is 'defective' if it does not function as it should. This is a static concept.

Financial loss is not included as "loss and damage" under an all risks policy. The insured must point to actual loss of, or physical damage to, the insured property, as opposed to a trading or commercial loss, within the period of the policy.

Likewise, where there is separate business interruption cover, there is generally a requirement that the loss arises out of damage to property, though again this will depend on the precise wording.

Timing of loss

The loss must occur during the policy period, otherwise it is not covered (unless the policy indicates otherwise) even if a future loss seems likely.

CAR policies often expire on practical completion of the works or may include a period of maintenance after completion.

Providing an insured can show some loss or damage within the policy period then the burden shifts to the insurer to show the cause was not fortuitous or is excluded.

Fortuity

Despite their name, all risks policies do not cover all eventualities.

The very nature of insurance implicitly creates the requirement that a loss is accidental or occurred by chance to be a covered loss under an insurance policy. Therefore, the requirement of fortuity applies, namely the loss (rather than the act itself) must be accidental, unintended and not inevitable as per Aikens J in *Seashore Marine S.A. v Phoenix Assurance plc and others ("The "Vergina") (No. 2)* [2001].

Sometimes cover will be limited to "unforeseen" or "sudden" damage. The latter is intended to prevent insurers being liable for progressive damage and goes together with the restriction on wear and tear (see below).

Likewise, there is no cover under an all risks policy for loss or damage caused by the "wilful misconduct" of the insured. Wilful misconduct is wider than deliberate sabotage by the insured and extends to the reckless running of risks. Courts are careful, when considering recklessness, to avoid eroding the principle that an insured's negligence is covered, which is one of the key reasons for having insurance.

Losses caused by wilful misconduct of third parties is, by contrast, fortuitous.

Wear and tear

Wear and tear is not a fortuitous happening, but part of the processes of nature. Therefore, even if there is not an express exclusion it is impliedly excluded from cover unless there is some provision to the contrary. Wear and tear is only relevant where it is the proximate cause of the loss.

The meaning of "wear and tear" needs to be viewed in the context of the policy exclusion. However, normally the deterioration of the property must be ordinary or natural. Therefore, where the property has been subject to some unusual or inappropriate use, which results in damage, the damage will not be excluded.

When considering this issue, life expectancy may also be relevant. For example, where the damage occurs towards the end of the natural life expectancy of the product, this may be a good indication that the loss has resulted from wear and tear.

Corrosion

This is often, but not always, expressly excluded within an all risks policy.

The key issue is how the corrosion occurred. For example, corrosion caused by atmospheric conditions, chemical reactions or weather causing some deterioration is normally excluded as it is not accidental.

However, where corrosion is caused by an accidental and fortuitous event it would be covered, subject to the terms of the policy. For example, the bursting of a tank resulting in a spillage of chemicals that in turn corrodes the surrounding metal work would be covered.

Again, the scope of the exclusion will depend on the precise wording.

Excluding risks

In addition to the implied requirement of fortuity/non-inevitable damage, underwriters will seek, through the use of excluding clauses, to define the risk that the policy covers so they are not left open to covering risks that were not contemplated. These exclusions will be expressly stated in the policy.

There are several commonly excluded risks, namely wear and tear, civil commotion, war, terrorism, loss due to ionising radioactive contamination or damage caused by pressure waves from aircraft travelling at sonic or supersonic speeds, and damage caused by pollution. In addition, many policies contain an express exclusion in respect of "defective or faulty material workmanship and design".

The scope of the exclusion will vary, so it is essential to carefully consider the wording.

In CAR policies there are what are known as DE (design exclusion) clauses that range from DE1, being an outright defect exclusion (it excludes any and all damages due to a property in a defective condition), through to DE5, being a design improvement exclusion (it covers all damage except additional costs of improvements to design/materials, etc.).

As mentioned above, it must be remembered that, generally, the negligence of the insured is not a bar to recovery (as that is what insurance policies are intended to cover), so exceptions must be looked at with care as courts will try to avoid giving exceptions a meaning that will prevent the insured from recovering where they have been merely negligent.

Appropriate measure of loss

Assuming the damage is covered, it is necessary to consider the appropriate measure of loss. Again, this will depend on the policy wording but usually the following general principles apply.

Buildings

A policy of indemnity will pay to the insured the amount of loss in accordance with the provisions of the insurance. The starting point is always likely to be the financial cost of repair or reinstatement.

Absent repair/reinstatement, the normal measure of loss is diminution in market value (i.e. difference in market value before and after the insured incident).

Difficulties will arise if the cost of repair is greater than the value of the property before the loss or greater than the cost of replacement. In such cases, courts will usually only allow the cost of repair if: (a) the insured genuinely intends to repair; and (b) such a course is not eccentric or absurd *(Dodd Properties (Kent) Ltd v Canterbury CC* [1980]).

Where there is no clause in the policy requiring reinstatement, the insurer cannot require the property to be reinstated.

If the indemnity is going to be calculated by reference to the diminution in value caused by the damage, then the date of damage is most likely to be the appropriate date to use when calculating the diminution of value. Where, however, the indemnity is calculated by reference to the cost of repairs, the indemnity will normally be calculated by reference to the cost of repairs when they are carried out.

If an insured fails to carry out necessary repairs for no good reason and the cost or content of the repairs is thereby increased, it is open to insurers to maintain that the increased cost is attributable to the unwarranted delay rather than to initial damage. It is commonly provided that reinstatement works must be commenced and carried out with reasonable despatch and that no payment (or no payment beyond what would otherwise be payable) is to be made until the cost of reinstatement has actually been incurred.

However it is now comparatively common for property policies to pay the cost of reinstatement of property destroyed or damaged.

Betterment

In relation to existing structures there is likely to be an element of betterment, as the old structure is being replaced with a new structure.

Betterment is frequently excluded by policy terms. For example, if there is an option to reinstate in the policy, and that option is exercised, it is difficult to see how insurers could properly demand a cash settlement from the insured representing the increased value of the property.

Chattels (contents)

The general rule is that the measure of damages is the difference between the value of the chattel before the damage and its value once it is damaged.

In the case of a partial loss, the measure of damages will usually be the cost of repairing the chattel, together with any depreciation in value, which is the difference between the value of the chattel, when repaired, and the value before the damage, less any increase in value owing to the substitution of new for old material.

Where a chattel is completely destroyed or so damaged that it is not worth repairing, the usual measure of damages is the market value, or the cost of replacement.

Even if the repair or replacement cost exceeds the market value of the chattel it can still be reasonable to claim the repair or replacement cost as damages if the chattel has a particular quality, rarity or special character that warrants replacement and the owner intends to replace or reinstate the property. In principle, the insured is required to credit the insurer for any betterment.

For example, in *Dominion Mosaics and Tile Co Limited v Trafalgar Trucking Co Ltd* [1990] the claimant's machines suffered irreparable damage in a fire. The machines had been purchased a few months prior to the fire at a bargain price of £13,500, but cost £65,000 to replace. Taylor LJ considered that where goods were not available on the second-hand market "and the only way the owner of the destroyed chattels can replace them is by buying new ones, the measure of damages is the cost of doing that, unless the result would be absurd". However, the Court of Appeal did note that, had it been argued some discount from the £65,000 should have been allowed to reflect the depreciation of the machines in their few months of service, the point would have merited consideration.

However, it is common for policies on goods to be written on a "new for old" basis so that any attempt to deduct sums for betterment is inconsistent with the insurer's obligation to provide an indemnity by giving the insured the benefit of new goods.

Average

Many policies contain an average clause, which applies where the insured is underinsured.

The principle underpinning average is that the insured is their own insurer for the difference between the sum insured and the true value of the subject matter and is liable for a proportionate amount of the loss.

Average has no role to play in the case of a total loss.

Consequential loss/business interruption

This cover may form part of a material damage policy, or may be a separate insurance that relates to a material damage policy.

Usually such cover will only respond where "insured property" has sustained "damage". Furthermore, the damage must generally occur during the currency of the policy.

Some wordings do not specify that the property that has been damaged has to belong to the insured or is covered by material damage insurance, and it may be that it is sufficient that property used by the insured in the course of the business has been damaged.

Business interruption insurance is most commonly written on a loss of "gross profits" basis. Whilst the precise basis of cover will be defined in the policy, in summary this covers the insured for the loss of net profit following a reduction in turnover as well as fixed expenses. Such policies can also cover increased cost of workings (ICWs), namely additional costs incurred by the insured in order to prevent a further reduction in turnover, for example staff overtime. An alternative, although less common, form of business interruption insurance is written on a loss of gross revenue basis. Such policies cover the reduction in turnover following a loss. They usually also cover any increased cost of workings. These are suited to industries with fewer variable costs such as the service industry.

Policies normally have a maximum indemnity period for business interruption losses, which can extend beyond the period of policy cover. The period is often 12 or 24 months, so as to cap insurers' liability.

Aggregation

Policies often have an aggregation clause. The most common aggregation wordings are "series of related acts or omissions", "arising from one event" and "arising from one original cause". The latter two wordings have different meanings.

An event is "something which happens at a particular time, at a particular place, in a particular way". (*Axa Reinsurance (UK) Plc v Field* [1996]). It is a narrower concept than a "cause", in that a cause can embrace a state of affairs or an omission to act.

Often, the occurrence of the peril that brought about the entire damage (i.e. the fire, the flood or the hurricane, etc.) will undoubtedly qualify as an event.

Notification

All risks is an occurrence-based rather than claims-made policy, meaning that the insurer will cover the occurrence of an event that arises during the period of insurance, as opposed to simply covering claims made during the period of insurance.

For this reason there is normally a requirement (often a condition precedent to liability) that the insured must notify insurers of any potential claim "as soon as possible" or "as soon as practicable" or within a specified number of days. When notified of a claim it is important for insurers to consider at the outset whether the insured has abided by the policy requirements.

Contribution and non-contribution

An insured may enjoy coverage in respect of the same loss under more than one policy. This can often arise where an insured has a global or master policy but is also insured under a contract specific policy.

Policies will frequently contain "contribution" or "non-contribution" clauses, which serve to clarify how the policy will respond in circumstances of multiple insurance policies. Typically, a contribution clause provides that where other insurance responds to the same loss or damage, the insurer's liability is limited to a specified or calculable amount.

A non-contribution clause usually provides that the insurance is not to be called upon and will not respond to any claim in respect of which there is other valid and collectable insurance that will respond to the loss. On the other hand, the clause may stipulate that the current policy will operate in excess of and not contribute to any such insurance.

Where both policies contain the same non-contribution clause then the usual effect is to cancel each other out, enabling the insured to claim under either policy in full. It is then left to the insurer whose policy has responded to seek an equitable contribution from the other insurer.

Third-party liability

Finally, it is not unusual for all risks policies to provide public liability cover. This will indemnify the insured in respect of its legal liability to third parties for damage to third-party property, personal injury or death.

35 Policy coverage: employers' liability and public liability claims

Roger Jones

- Interpretation of the policy: ordinary meaning of words and other considerations
- Warranties, conditions precedent and conditions
- Formation of the insurance contract and duty of utmost good faith
- Non-disclosure and misrepresentation
- Reservation of rights
- Claims procedure: including notice, coverage and defending the claim
- What happens if the insured becomes insolvent?
- Joint retainer of solicitors by insurer and insured
- Which is the right policy for the claim?

Policy coverage: employers' liability and public liability claims

Introduction

The interpretation of insurance policies has been discussed and debated since Edward Lloyd's Coffee House became the focal point for the gathering of merchants in the late seventeenth century. While originally based on case law, insurance law became partly codified in the Marine Insurance Act 1906 (MIA 1906) which, despite its name, has been applied to all contracts of insurance since it embodies the common law. However, there has recently been substantial reform effected by the Insurance Act 2015 (the 2015 Act), which applies to all contracts of insurance commenced, amended or renewed from 12 August 2016.

This chapter is intended to assist the claims handler in obtaining some insight of insurance law both pre and post the 2015 Act, since historical claims will continue to be notified (particularly those involving disease). It is therefore important that the claims handler has some knowledge of the coverage issues under both regimes when dealing with employers' and public liability insurance policies.

Employers' liability (EL) and public liability (PL) insurance policies deal with:

- the provision of an indemnity by an insurer to an insured
- on the happening of an event stated within the policy
- which results in injury, damage or loss arising from third-party risks
- for which the insured is covered by the insurer.

They are contracts between the insurer and the insured. The policy will set out various contractual terms agreed between the insurer and insured. In order to consider whether the insured is entitled to an indemnity under the policy it is necessary to consider the terms of the policy.

> Policy cover and interpretation of the applicable terms are important issues to consider in every claim presented to an insurer. They must be considered before any steps are taken in relation to a claim, otherwise taking any action could potentially waive or affirm the insurer's rights, or estop the insurer from enforcing those rights.

A successful avoidance of cover, or exclusion of a claim under the policy, will lead to some, or all, of the loss being rejected and therefore result in a direct saving for insurers.

Conversely, a hasty or poorly considered policy interpretation, resulting in the insurer making an incorrect avoidance, repudiation or declinature, could be costly for the insurer in terms of legal fees. Perhaps more importantly, such a decision may be detrimental to the commercial relationship between the insured and the insurer, or the insured's broker and the insurer. Therefore careful thought should be given not only to the insurance issues, but also to the commercial factors involved, which should be discussed with the underwriter.

Insurance contracts are contracts of the utmost good faith between an insurer and its insured. The courts will enforce them on that basis. Since decisions about policy cover are contractual, and are governed by insurance law and the duty of the utmost good faith, a court is likely to make its decision in a detached manner.

What follows is an overview of the main points to consider in EL and PL policies.

Interpretation of the policy

The courts have adopted various rules to assist with policy construction and interpretation over the years. In *Investors Compensation Scheme Ltd v West Bromwich Building Society and others* [1997] Lord Hoffmann restated the principles which should be used in the modern age:

- The aim of the court is to ascertain what a reasonable person would have concluded, having all the background knowledge which would reasonably have been available to the parties in the situation they were in at the time of the contract.
- Previous negotiations of the parties and their declarations of subjective intent are to be excluded, save for the purpose of rectification.
- However, the court should not ignore the possibility that the parties may have misunderstood what the words used actually meant. As occasionally happens in real life, the court could conclude that the parties must have used the wrong words or syntax.
- Finally, in considering the background facts of which the parties were aware, the court is not obliged to attribute to the parties an intention which they plainly could not have had.

It is clear that the intention of the parties in entering the contract is paramount and that the document as a whole should be considered, rather than simply the individual words used. The court should adopt a construction that makes good commercial sense.

This commercial approach to policy construction was reinforced in *Sirius International Insurance Company (Publ) v FAI General Insurance Limited and others* [2004].

The normal guiding principles of policy interpretation should be considered with the above decisions in mind.

Ordinary meaning of words

Generally the words used in a policy are to be given their natural and ordinary meaning, since people do not usually make linguistic mistakes. It may be helpful to check the dictionary definition of a word. However, where the word has a specific technical or legal meaning then that meaning should usually be adopted.

Similarly, the meaning of a word or phrase may be affected not only by the immediate context in which it appears but also by the general context of the policy as a whole, and the circumstances prevailing at the time the policy was entered into.

Other considerations

The court will consider if the phrase or form of words in issue has been construed before. If so it will either be bound, or strongly persuaded, by such construction.

Other documents may also be incorporated into the contract by way of reference and these must also be considered. The proposal form or statements of fact, and any declarations they contain, should be considered.

The court will reject any absurd interpretations of words or phrases if a more reasonable alternative is available.

Contra proferentem rule

If a word or phrase is unclear and there is a true ambiguity between two different competing interpretations, the court will construe the meaning on the '*contra proferentem*' basis. This means that it will be interpreted against the party who drafted the particular clause.

The reason for this rule is that the party who drafted the offending part should not benefit from any ambiguity contained therein. Since insurance contracts are usually drafted by insurers, this will mean that any ambiguity is found in favour of the insured. However, occasionally clauses may be drafted by an insured's broker to express the particular needs of its client and, in such circumstances, the insurer will gain the benefit.

Warranties, conditions precedent and conditions

Warranties

A warranty in normal contract law is usually regarded as a relatively minor term which, when breached, only entitles the innocent party to damages. However in insurance law a warranty has an entirely different effect. This is because it involves a promise (a warranty) by the insured that a particular state of affairs exists at a particular time.

A warranty is intended to reduce the risk to the insurer to an acceptable level and consequently compliance with the warranty is fundamental to the decision by the insurer to accept the risk.

However under the 2015 Act, while warranties still remain important, the impact for a breach of warranty has been lessened.

Position before the 2015 Act

The essential characteristics of a warranty in insurance law were that it had to be a term of the contract; the matter warranted did not need to be material to the risk; the term had to be strictly complied with and that a breach of the warranty automatically entitled the insurer to terminate the contract, even if the breach did not have any connection with the loss.

A warranty can be either express or implied. Simply because the term is not described in the policy as a warranty does not prevent it from being held to be one. No particular form of words is required to create a warranty. However, in *HIH Casualty and General Insurance Ltd v New Hampshire Insurance Company and others* [2001] the Court of Appeal suggested three alternative tests for deciding whether a term was a warranty:

- Is it a term which goes to the root of the transaction?
- Is it descriptive of, or bears materiality to, the risk?
- Would damages be an unsatisfactory or inadequate remedy?

Since warranties were so fundamental to the risk insured, if a warranty was breached, it entitled the insurer to discharge the contract.

In *Bank of Nova Scotia v Hellenic Mutual War Risks Association (Bermuda) Ltd (The Good Luck)* [1991] the House of Lords held that the breach of warranty automatically discharged the insurer from any liability in accordance with the literal meaning of the words in s.33(3) of the Marine Insurance Act 1906.

Position following the 2015 Act

Warranties have been dramatically changed by the 2015 Act.

Firstly, section 9 abolished what were known as 'basis of contract' clauses. These clauses usually arose when, prior to entering the contract a prospective insured completed a proposal form or statement of facts, declaring the answers provided are correct and shall form the basis of the contract. The policy wording usually also stated that the proposal form or statement of facts would be incorporated into, and thus formed the basis of, the insurance contract, thereby turning these representations into warranties.

The prohibition of converting such representations into warranties brings non-consumer contracts in line with consumer contracts, which outlawed using the basis of contract clause by the Consumer Insurance (Disclosure and Representations) Act 2012, which has been in force since 6 April 2013.

Secondly, section 10(1) abolished the right of the insurer to discharge the contract if a warranty is breached.

Further, under the remainder of section 10, the insurer's liability to provide cover under the policy is suspended from the date of the insured's breach of warranty until that breach is remedied.

Therefore, subject to what is said in the two following paragraphs, if the loss takes place during the period of the breach the insurer is not liable to provide cover, but if the loss arises before the breach occurs, or after it has been remedied, then the insurer will still have to provide cover.

However, if the warranty ceases to be applicable to the circumstances of the contract, or is rendered unlawful by any subsequent law, or is waived by the insurer, then the insurer is still liable to provide cover.

If the insured can prove that the non-compliance with the warranty did not increase the risk of the loss arising for the insurer, in either the kind, location, or time of the particular loss, then the insurer will not be able to rely upon the breach to exclude or limit its liability.

Conditions

Conditions are terms of the insurance policy which are potentially of less significance than warranties, but which remain important. They can cover all manner of things but the three common types are:

- Conditions precedent, which impose obligations on the insured
- Conditions which give rights to insurers
- Mere conditions.

The policy will usually contain a number of general conditions, which give rights to an insurer. These conditions often provide the insurer with greater rights than it would have had under common law. Examples of such conditions include a right to cancel the policy, to conduct the claim in the manner it wishes and to exercise rights of subrogation in the name of the insured.

Conditions precedent

- A 'condition precedent to the insurance' is a condition that a state of affairs must be fulfilled before the insurance policy comes into existence. The insured must prove that it has met the condition before it is entitled to make a valid claim under the policy.
- Prior to the 2015 Act, if there was a breach of condition precedent to the insurance then the insurer probably never came on risk. However under the 2015 Act, if the insured can show that the breach of condition precedent to insurance was not material to the loss suffered, the insurer must still provide cover.
- A 'condition precedent to liability' is a state of affairs the insured must satisfy before the insurer becomes liable to deal with a claim made under the policy. A typical example of a condition precedent to liability clause is a notification clause once an event has occurred, which may give rise to a claim under the policy.
- If there is a breach of condition precedent to liability then, whilst the insurer is still on risk in terms of the policy generally, it is not on risk in relation to that particular claim.

Simply because a condition is described as a condition precedent does not mean that it will be held to be one. For example, where the policy attempts to make every term a condition precedent, a court is very unlikely to accept this as being sufficient to create an effective condition precedent unless the individual term merits it.

Exclusion clauses

Policies may also contain certain exclusion clauses. These are different from warranties since, whilst they both limit the cover provided by the insurer, they operate in different ways. Where there is a breach of warranty the cover is suspended. Where there is an exclusion clause which operates in respect of the claim, the cover will not apply.

Mere conditions/innominate terms

If a term of the policy is neither a warranty, condition precedent, nor an exclusion clause, then it will be a mere condition or an innominate term. Breach of such a condition by the insured will only give rise to an action for damages by the insurer.

Formation of the insurance contract

Insurance contracts follow the usual rules concerning contracts. There must be offer and acceptance, agreement, consideration and an intention to create legal relations.

A prospective insured will usually complete a standard proposal form prepared by the insurer. This can be done on paper, online or by telephone depending on the insurer's system. In Lloyd's policies the proposal form can be replaced by a 'slip' and the binding contract is concluded once the slip is initialled (or 'scratched') by the underwriter.

The proposal form contains information sought about the prospective insured and the type and nature of the business that it wishes to be insured. It seeks details about the risk, such as the number of employees or turnover of the business involved, the number of previous claims made, the period and the date from when the cover is sought.

Where the insured acts through a broker this does not prevent the prospective insured from being responsible for ensuring that the answers on the proposal form are true and that all material facts have been disclosed.

> The parties must agree on the material terms of the insurance, which must include the identity of the insured, the nature of the risk insured against, the duration of the insurance, the limits of the indemnity provided and the premium.

Material non-disclosure and the duty of fair presentation

Duty of utmost good faith

Contracts of insurance are governed by the principle of '*uberrimae fidei*' or the duty of utmost good faith. The reason for this was explained by Lord Mansfield over 250 years ago in *Carter v Boehm* [1766]:

> "Insurance is a contract upon speculation. The special facts, upon which the contingent chance is to be computed, lie most commonly in the knowledge of the insured only: the under-writer trusts to his representation, and proceeds upon confidence that he does not keep back any circumstance in his knowledge, to mislead the under-writer into a belief that the circumstance does not exist… The keeping back such circumstance is a fraud, and therefore the policy is void. Although the suppression should happen through mistake, without any fraudulent intention; yet still the under-writer is deceived and the policy is void; because the risque run is really different from the risque understood and intended to be run, at the time of the agreement."

This duty of the utmost good faith was codified in section 17 of the MIA 1906 which states: "A contract of marine insurance is a contract based upon the utmost good faith, and, if the utmost good faith be not observed by either party, the contract may be avoided by the other party."

The trouble with this was that, in practice, it proved significantly more onerous for the insured rather than the insurer.

Position before the 2015 Act

The rules of disclosure were codified under the MIA 1906 with section 18(1) providing that, "Subject to the provisions of this section the assured must disclose to the insurer, before the contract is concluded, every material circumstance which is known to the assured, and the assured is deemed to know every circumstance which, in the ordinary course of business, ought to be known by him. If the assured fails to make such disclosure, the insurer may avoid the contract."

This was supported by section 20 MIA 1906, which stated, "Every material representation made by the assured or his agent to the insurer during the negotiations for the contract, and before the contract is concluded, must be true. If it be untrue the insurer may avoid the contract."

What facts are "material"?

A material fact is every circumstance which would influence the judgement of a prudent insurer in fixing the premium or determining whether it will take the risk. The opinion of the prospective insured as to the materiality of a fact was not taken into account.

However, whilst the view of the insurer concerned will be relevant in determining what is a material fact, the insurer's opinion is not conclusive. The insurer will have to obtain an opinion from an expert underwriter to prove that the reasonably prudent underwriter would have wanted to know of the relevant fact.

Only those facts which are material at the time when the policy was incepted are relevant. Once the policy has been incepted there is no duty on the insured to keep the insurer informed, although the insured will be under the same duty to disclose all material facts when the policy comes up for renewal.

Physical and moral hazard

Unsurprisingly, the burden of proving non-disclosure of a material fact or misrepresentation by an insured falls upon the insurer. The question of whether a non-disclosed fact is material is a question of law and for determination by the trial judge. However, some facts are more obviously material than others. These more obvious ones tend to fall into two categories:

- Facts that are relevant to the physical hazard
- Facts that are relevant to the moral hazard.

Those that relate to the physical hazard will influence the probability of the particular risk occurring to the subject matter of the insurance. An example in liability policies would include a bad accident or loss record (see *New Hampshire Insurance Company v Oil Refineries Ltd* [2002]).

> With regard to moral hazard, the facts usually relate to the policyholder's character and tendency to make claims. Examples would include having a history of dishonesty, disqualification as a director, bankruptcy, previous insurance claims, avoidance or cancellation of policies by previous insurers or the refusal by any insurer to insure or renew a policy.

Material facts the insured need not disclose

Under section 18(3) of the MIA 1906, where an insured is aware of certain facts, it did not have to disclose them if:

- The information diminished the risk
- The information was known or presumed to be known to the insurer. The insurer was presumed to know matters of common notoriety or knowledge, and matters which it ought to know in the ordinary course of its business
- The insurer waived its right to the information
- The information was superfluous to disclose because of an express or implied warranty.

An example of express waiver is where the insurer only seeks the number of claims which the insured has had within the last five years. This expressly waives the insurer's right to details of the claims made more than five years ago.

The manner in which the questions are asked on the proposal form will effectively limit the insured's duty of disclosure. For example, if the insurer only asks whether individual directors of a business have ever been declared bankrupt, it is impliedly waving its disclosure of material facts relating to the liquidation/insolvency of companies with which the directors have previously been involved.

Inducement

In *Pan Atlantic Insurance Co Limited v Pine Top Insurance Co Limited* [1994] the House of Lords established the principle that, where an insurer seeks to rely on a material non-disclosure or misrepresentation by an insured, it has to show:

- The fact in question was a fact that a reasonably prudent underwriter would have considered material, though it need not be decisive, and
- had the actual underwriter been aware of the fact then the insurer would not have written the risk on those terms.

If there is a dispute, a statement is required from the actual underwriter concerned confirming the insurer would have either rejected the risk, not written it on the same terms or would have charged a higher premium. In addition, expert evidence is often required to confirm that the undisclosed or misrepresented fact was material to a prudent underwriter when considering the risk.

Problems with the old regime

The trouble with the MIA 1906 was that there was only one remedy, namely avoidance 'ab initio' which was draconian and usually highly prejudicial to the insured.

Further, insureds and their brokers often had difficulty in understanding their duty of disclosure especially since what one underwriter may consider material to the risk might be different from another underwriter.

Position since the 2015 Act

Fair presentation

The 2015 Act introduced the new concept of 'fair presentation' by the insured. Under section 3 of the 2015 Act the insured now has to provide disclosure of every material circumstance which the insured knows, or ought reasonably to know, or which gives a prudent insurer sufficient information to make further enquiries to reveal those material circumstances.

Every material fact is to be substantially correct, and every material representation as to matters of expectation or belief must be made in good faith.

The insured also must provide the disclosure in a manner that is reasonably clear and accessible to a prudent insurer.

What is a material circumstance?

Section 7(3) of the 2015 Act explains that a circumstance is material if it would influence the judgement of a prudent insurer in determining whether to take the risk and, if so, on what terms.

What then constitutes things that are material to the risk? This would include:

- Special or unusual facts relating to the risk
- Any particular concerns which led the insured to seek cover for the risk
- Anything which an insurer familiar with the class of insurance concerned would generally understand to be dealt with in a fair presentation of that risk.

Further, section 3(5) of the 2015 Act confirms that, in the absence of enquiry by the insurer, the insured is not required to disclose a circumstance if:

- It diminishes the risk
- The insurer knows it

- The insurer ought to know it
- The insurer is presumed to know it
- It is something about which the insurer has waived information.

Who has what knowledge?

Where the insured is an individual, their knowledge is only that which is known to them, or known to one or more of the individuals responsible for the insured's insurance.

If the insured is not an individual (e.g. a partnership or company) then the insured's knowledge is limited to the knowledge of those who are part of the insured's senior management, or responsible for the insured's insurance.

Under section 4(6) of the 2015 Act the insured, whether an individual or not, ought to know what should have been revealed upon a reasonable search of information available to the insured.

The insurer is deemed to know something only if it is known to one or more of the individuals who participate in the insurer's decision to accept the risk. In addition, the insurer ought to know something if an employee or agent of the insurer should have passed such information on. This second element might encompass a claims department at the insurer passing on information to the insurer considering the risk at renewal.

Remedies

This is an area where the 2015 Act brings in a fundamental change from the old regime. Now, where the insured has breached its duty of fair presentation, the insurer has different remedies available depending on the situation. This brings non-consumer insurance into line with what has been in place with consumer insurance contracts since 6 April 2013.

In a similar way to the old regime, the insurer now must show that, absent the breach, it would not have entered into the contract, or that it would only have done so on different terms. If there has been such a breach it is referred to as a 'qualifying breach'.

A qualifying breach is either:

- Deliberate or reckless, or
- Neither deliberate nor reckless.

Section 8(5) of the 2015 Act explains that a qualifying breach is deliberate or reckless if the insured knew that it was in breach of the duty of fair presentation, or did not care whether it was in breach or not. The onus on proving whether a qualifying breach was deliberate or reckless falls upon the insurer.

If the qualifying breach was deliberate or reckless then the insurer can avoid the contract, refuse all claims and keep the premium(s) paid.

If the qualifying breach was neither deliberate nor reckless and the insurer would not have entered into the contract on any terms, it may avoid the contract, refuse all claims, but it must return the premiums(s) paid.

If the insurer would have entered into the contract but on different terms (terms not relating to premium), for example, with the imposition of an exclusion clause, then the contract is to be treated as if entered into on those terms.

If the insurer would have entered into the contract but charged a higher premium, then the insurer may reduce proportionately the amount to be paid out. The formula for calculating this reduction is set out in Schedule 1 of the 2015 Act.

Affirmation, waiver and estoppel

Insurers must exercise great care when they find themselves in a position of potential avoidance or repudiation for breach of warranty, as it is relatively easy to affirm the contract or waive the breach.

To affirm the contract:

- The insurer must have actual knowledge of the non-disclosed fact or misrepresentation prior to inception. Mere constructive knowledge is insufficient.
- The insurer has to know that the non-disclosure created a right to avoid.
- The insurer has had a reasonable period of time in which to decide what to do.
- There must be an unequivocal communication to the insured, by words or conduct, that the insurer has made an informed choice to affirm the policy.
- Whether such a communication will be found depends on how a reasonable person in the insured's position would interpret the insurer's words or conduct.
- Mere delay or inactivity is not sufficient to demonstrate an intention to waive the insured's breach. However, it would affect the insurer's position if the insured was prejudiced by the delay or was led to believe that it was because the insurer was affirming the policy.

Some examples of conduct which could amount to affirmation would include:

- Dealing with a claim on behalf of the insured
- Paying a claim under the policy
- Making an interim payment regarding a claim
- Cancelling the policy (as opposed to expressly avoiding it)
- Renewing the policy
- Relying on a condition of the policy to reject the claim on other grounds.

Even if the insurer is not aware that it has a right to avoid the policy, it can still find itself estopped from avoiding the policy. This will occur where:

- By words or conduct the insurer makes an unequivocal representation to the insured that the policy remains in force.
- The insured can show that it has relied on that representation to its detriment.

In light of the above it is crucial that, if the claims handler suspects there might have been a non-disclosure, a reservation of rights is sent immediately to the insured. The insurer should then carry out its investigation regarding the possibility of non-disclosure as soon as possible.

Regulation

The business of insurers is regulated by the Financial Conduct Authority (FCA). One of its key policies is that, where dealing with consumers, the insurer adopts the practice of treating customers fairly (TCF). This includes providing the consumer insured with clear information and communications and dealing with any complaints fairly and within a reasonable time. The guiding principles behind this are contained within the FCA's 'Insurance: Conduct of Business sourcebook' (or ICOBS as it is known).

The Financial Ombudsman Service (FOS) will consider complaints where particular categories of insureds are aggrieved about a decision made by an insurer. The categories are:

- An individual
- A micro enterprise (which has fewer than 10 staff and an annual turnover of less than €2m)
- A charity with an annual income of less than £1m
- A trust with net assets of less than £1m.

The financial limits apply at the time when the complaint is made.

The complaint must be made to the FOS within six months of the insurer making its final decision. The FOS cannot consider a complaint referred to it more than six years after the event complained of, or (if later) more than three years from the date on which the complainant became aware (or ought reasonably to have become aware) that it had cause for complaint. These limitation periods can be extended in certain circumstances.

The decisions of the FOS are not based solely on insurance law, but on delivering fair and reasonable outcomes. Consequently, these will often favour the complainant rather than the insurer. If the FOS upholds a complaint, the maximum award it can make that is binding on an insurer is £100,000. This is intended to compensate the insured for the losses suffered as a result of the insurer's conduct.

Reservation of rights

A reservation of rights is a communication by an insurer to an insured following the notification of a claim, which makes it clear that the insurer's rights are reserved. As a result, the insured cannot interpret any activity or inactivity on the part of the insurer as meaning that it is waiving its rights to either avoid the policy or decline the claim.

> The purpose of a reservation of rights is to allow the insurer time to consider and investigate the claim. The reservation of rights should be clear. The insurer should endeavour to complete its enquiries into the avoidance or policy response within a reasonable period and notify the insured of its decision.

The contents of the reservation of rights letter are important and should be tailored to each situation. It is not enough merely to state that the insurer's rights are reserved. The letter should state what the issue, or potential issue, is and what is being done.

The reservation is not open-ended. The insurer has a duty to conduct its investigations and make a decision which is notified to the insured within a reasonable timeframe.

Claims procedure

Liability policies invariably contain conditions (typically described in the policy as being conditions precedent to the liability of the insurer) which:

- Impose a number of obligations on the insured regarding when notice of a loss is required to be given to the insurer.
- Specify what claims procedures the insured should follow.

If they are genuinely conditions precedent, then breach of them may entitle the insurer to avoid liability for that particular loss.

If not conditions precedent then the clause is a mere condition (or innominate term). In these circumstances, if the insured fails to notify the insurer in accordance with the condition, the insurer will only be able to claim damages for such loss as it has suffered arising from the breach, which will usually be difficult to prove.

Notice

The precise wording of a notification clause should be carefully considered. Generally, in third-party claims, they appear in roughly similar terms to:

> “The insured shall give immediate notice to the insurer of any circumstance which is likely to give rise to a claim being made against the insured for which there may be liability under this insurance.”

In determining what constitutes “likely” the courts have held that this means there is at least a 50% chance of a claim (*Layher Ltd v Lowe* [1996]).

An alternative wording refers to "may give rise to a claim". Here, the test applied is substantially lower than the "likely" test. However, there must be a real, as opposed to a fanciful, risk of the insurer having to indemnify the insured. The court will apply an objective test, taking into account the knowledge the insured possessed at the time. It will determine the extent to which it was aware of, and hence capable of giving notification of, occurrences which may give rise to a claim (*J Rothschild Assurance Plc v Collyear and others* [1998]).

Occasionally the words "as soon as possible" are also mentioned in terms of notification of an event but, as the Court of Appeal has recently found, without additional clarification, such words do not place a duty of enquiry on an insured to ascertain whether an event has occurred, and they simply specify how soon after the event such notice must be given (*Maccaferri v Zurich Insurance Plc* [2016]).

Time limits

Usually there is a requirement for the insured to give immediate notice of any claims arising to the insurer or its agents.

While there is some uncertainty as to what "immediate" means, it has been held to mean "with all reasonable speed considering the circumstances of the case" (*Re Coleman's Depositories Ltd* [1907]).

The courts have held this to mean that notice within five days was appropriate, but one week and nine days have both been held as being too long.

Waiver and estoppel

The notification of claims during the claims procedure is a highly contentious area. The insured is likely to argue that the insurer is, in some way, prevented from relying on a breach of condition precedent. However, in *Kosmar Villa Holidays Plc v Trustees of Syndicate 1234* [2008] the Court of Appeal held that breaches of conditions precedent could not be waived by election (as in the case of a breach of warranty) but could only be waived by an estoppel.

Cover

The claim made against the insured must be one that is covered by the policy. It is necessary to consider the substance of the claim, rather than its form, in order to establish whether the policy will respond. Simply because a claimant may plead a claim in a certain manner does not mean to say that the facts of the claim match the pleading.

Admission of liability and defence

There is usually a standard term in liability policies similar to the following:

> "No admission of liability or offer or promise of payment, whether expressed or implied, shall be made without written consent of the insurer."

Such a condition is a precedent to cover being provided. It is therefore possible that a breach of this condition precedent will allow the insurer to avoid the claim.

Defending the claim

The insurer's coverage of a liability policy extends to any first-party and third-party costs incurred by the insured in defending the third-party claim. Insurers will generally also have a claims control clause in the policy, similar to the following:

> "The insurer shall be entitled at its own discretion to take over and conduct in the name of the insured the defence to or settlement of any claim."

This empowers the insurer to deal with the claim as it sees fit, even if this is against the wishes of the insured. However, often the wishes of the insured are an important factor for the insurer to take into consideration, bearing in mind their commercial relationship.

Payment

Payment becomes due under a liability policy when the third party establishes both the liability of the insured and the quantum of the damages payable by the insured. It is at this point that the limitation period for any action against the insurer is deemed to accrue.

For all policies taken out or renewed from 4 May 2017 the insurer now has a duty to pay the claim within a reasonable time (under an implied term brought in by the Enterprise Act 2016) or potentially face paying any additional losses suffered by the insured.

What to look for on notification of a claim

The full policy wording must be obtained so the claims handler can review the context to understand the overall meaning, including the policy schedule and any endorsements. The wording will determine the majority of the cover, but other documents can incorporate terms. It is possible to incorporate other terms by the consent of both parties, although this is unlikely to be a significant issue in the majority of claims.

Once these have been obtained, it is vital to consider all the basics of the policy in relation to the specifics of the claim made. It is possible that the insured or the insured's broker has presented a claim that is not covered:

- Insured: the definition of the insured in the policy and proposal form should be checked. Where the insured is a registered company, if the name of the defendant making the notification is not the same as that contained on the policy schedule there may be an issue, given that each company is a separate legal entity.
- Policy period: this is normally expressly defined in times and dates. Check whether the accident falls within this period. If it does not, then explain this to the insured or its brokers.

- Policy wording: ensure that the correct version of the policy wording is obtained. There may have been several renewals before and after the accident and the wordings may have been updated or changed during this time. It is possible that the relevant year could have a helpful exclusion or condition that does not appear in the other wordings.
- Policy schedule/certificate: what cover did the insured take? Although some policies contain a number of different risks, such as combined commercial cover, the insured may not require all of the cover. If they have not taken out the PL cover section in a combined policy, for example, then a PL loss will not be covered under that policy.
- Policy conditions: has the incident been notified in accordance with the notification clause?
- Endorsements and warranties: the policy schedule also usually notes relevant endorsements or exclusions that could affect whether the loss is covered, but the specific wording will need to be checked.
- Premium: has the premium been paid? There is no strict rule in liability insurance that if the premium has not been paid then the policy is not binding. Therefore, the terms of the insurance must be obtained to see whether there is any condition regarding payment of the premium. If there is, then it should be checked that there has been compliance by the insured. If not, it is unlikely that the failure to pay the premium will release the insurer from providing cover.
- Proposal form and underwriting file: what has the insured said on the proposal form and is that information correct? Check for file notes and representations relevant to cover and the insured's specific contract to establish whether there has been a fair presentation of the risk.

What happens if the insured becomes insolvent?

Where an insured becomes bankrupt or goes into liquidation, usually a claimant would have little prospect of obtaining any damages. However, where the insolvent insured has a policy of insurance which covers third-party liability applicable to that claim then, if the insured becomes insolvent and incurs a liability to a third party before 1 August 2016, under the Third Parties (Rights Against Insurers) Act 1930 (the 1930 Act), the claimant has a potential right of action against the insurer.

Unfortunately, the 1930 Act had various deficiencies which sometimes made it difficult for the third party to pursue insurers. In order to address these issues, and the various changes to the insolvency laws since the 1930 Act, the Third Parties (Rights Against Insurers) Act 2010 (the 2010 Act) was introduced, and became effective for claims where the insured became insolvent and incurred a liability from 1 August 2016.

Since both regimes are still effective, it is necessary to explain the procedures under each.

The 1930 Act

Section 1 of the 1930 Act does not give a claimant the right to pursue recovery against the insurer until a judgment has been obtained against the insured. Consequently, the third-party claimant needs to pursue the insured first. If it is a dissolved company, the claimant will have to restore the company to the Companies Register first before proceedings can be commenced. The claimant should then obtain a judgment or settlement against the insured. Only once this has been done can the claimant then seek recovery against the insurers.

Even once a claimant has obtained judgment against the insured it does not always mean the insurer has to pay the claim. The 1930 Act does not place the claimant in any better position than the insured would have been in. It simply transfers to the claimant the rights of the insured under the contract of insurance. Therefore, if the insurer can defeat a claim to provide an indemnity because, for example, it has a right to avoid the policy for material non-disclosure or misrepresentation then, providing the insurer can prove this, it will not have to pay the claim.

In addition, any claimant will be bound by the limitations of the policy itself regarding the indemnity provided. If there is appropriate wording in the policy so that the insured itself would have to pay a specific sum as an excess before the insurer has to provide the indemnity, then the insurer should only have to pay the remaining balance.

If there is a condition requiring claims to be notified which could not be complied with because the insured was a company which went into liquidation before a claim could be notified, then such a clause is not effective, since compliance would have been impossible.

It is a fairly usual condition in insurance policies that the insurer can step into the shoes of the insured and conduct the litigation itself. A claimant's solicitor pursuing an insolvent insured would prefer to deal with the insurer direct. In many cases the insurer may wish to become involved, particularly where the insurer will ultimately have to provide an indemnity, more so where there is a potential defence on liability. The reason for this is that the insolvent insured (or its liquidator/receiver) will prove unconcerned about a judgment and in all likelihood will not take any action to defend the claim.

Rather than leaving the claimant to obtain an uncontested judgement against the insolvent insured and then having to indemnify the claimant, the insurer might prefer to step into the insured's shoes at an early stage, and play an active role in either defending the claim, or minimising the quantum which it may ultimately have to pay.

However, if the insurer considers there is a valid breach of warranty or condition precedent, or that the policy will not respond because of a relevant exclusion, the insurer may not wish to incur the costs of becoming involved at an early stage.

If the claimant's solicitors have been advised that the policy has been avoided, or will not respond, they will often attempt to ascertain the basis and reasons for such a decision, together with a copy of the relevant policy documents. This is to enable the claimant's solicitor to assess whether the insurer's arguments are valid, before money is invested in attempting to obtain a judgment against the insolvent insured, and possibly pursuing the insurer.

Under s.2(1) of the 1930 Act a claimant can obtain details of the insurance provisions of an insolvent insured from the trustee in bankruptcy or the liquidator/receiver, and under s.2(2) of the 1930 Act the insurer is also under an obligation.

Originally, it was thought that the obligation to provide information only arose when the claimant had obtained a judgment against the insured. However, in *Re OT Computers (in administration)* [2004] the Court of Appeal held that it was not necessary to obtain a judgment first before the information had to be provided. The trigger to obtaining the insurance information occurred on the insured's insolvency.

The problem for a claimant's solicitor is when an insured is solvent but is likely to become insolvent once a judgment is obtained. In such circumstances the claimant's solicitor is usually anxious to establish what insurance provisions the insured has and whether the policy will respond. The insurer is under no obligation to provide any such information or documentation to a claimant's solicitors under CPR 31.16, since it is highly unlikely to be relevant material simply because the solvent insured might become insolvent and the claimant might then have a claim against insurers. This was confirmed by *Peel Port Shareholder Finance Company Ltd v Dornoch Limited* [2017].

Once a claimant has obtained judgment against an insolvent insured, if the insurer has avoided the policy or declined cover, the claimant can bring declaratory proceedings against the insurer disputing the avoidance or declinature by effectively stepping into the insured's shoes.

The 2010 Act

The 2010 Act rectifies a considerable number of deficiencies with the 1930 Act.

The definitions of insolvent individuals and companies have been updated to bring them into line with modern insolvency laws.

The third-party claimant no longer has to establish the insolvent insured's liability to it before it can litigate against the insurer. The claimant can now issue proceedings under section 2(2) seeking a declaration as to the insolvent insured's liability to the claimant and/or the insurer's potential liability to the claimant.

A claimant who reasonably believes (s)he has a right of action under the 2010 Act is entitled by Schedule 1 to obtain information about the rights transferred both before and after the issue of proceedings. If the claimant can establish that there is a contract of insurance that covers, or might reasonably be expected to cover, the supposed liability, the claimant can obtain information on:

- The identity of the insurer.
- The terms of the insurance.
- Whether there are (or have been) proceedings between the insurer and the insured in respect of the supposed liability.
- Whether there is an aggregate limit of indemnity (and if so, how much) and whether there are any fixed charges which would apply to any sums paid out.

A person who receives a notice requesting information is obliged, within 28 days of receipt of the notice, to provide as much of the information specified as they can "without due difficulty". If it cannot be provided, the person must state why and provide details of any other person who might be able to supply it.

The 2010 Act also retains the general approach of the 1930 Act in that the rights transferred to the claimant will be subject to the defences which the insurer could have used against the insured such as avoidance, breach of warranty, declinature etc.

However, the 2010 Act limits the insurer's defences in three key regards for an insured's failure to comply with policy conditions. These are:

- Anything done by the claimant which, if done by the insured, would have amounted to effective compliance with the condition is to be treated as if done by the insured.
- A failure of the insured to provide information or assistance where the insured is an individual who has died or a company which has been dissolved.
- The transferred rights to the claimant are not subject to a 'pay to be paid' clause requiring the prior discharge by the insured before the insurer is obliged to indemnify.

Joint retainer of solicitors by insurer and insured

Insurers often reserve the right to appoint solicitors to act on behalf of their insured in defending claims made against the insured. However, some insurers, particularly where the claim has only been notified to them very late in the day, also instruct solicitors to accept service of proceedings, or go on the court record in order to protect their insured's position initially, or act for the insured in some way. This creates a joint retainer of the solicitor by both the insurer and the insured.

The insurer has a financial interest in the outcome of the claim against the insured, and the insured usually has a financial interest since it may be subject to a deductible or excess. There are also other reasons why the insured may have an interest in the claim, such as business reputation, which may well be affected by the manner in which the litigation is conducted.

Due to the joint retainer a potential conflict of interest is created for the solicitor. Normally this is not an issue. However, what does cause a problem is if the insurer then asks the same solicitor to provide advice on policy matters. While it is understandable for the insurer to want to avoid paying two sets of legal fees, unfortunately dealing with matters this way creates a conflict of interest for the solicitor.

The better way of dealing with this kind of scenario is for the insurer to instruct the solicitor on a sole basis initially and obtain the coverage advice. If it transpires that there are no coverage issues arising and the insurer confirms cover, the solicitor can then be instructed on behalf of the insured as well.

Matters specific to EL policies

While the rules of general liability insurance are applicable to EL policies, there are some important areas where the rules governing EL policies differ and cause employers' policies to respond in a slightly different way.

Why is EL different?

The emergence of trade unions and their demand for protection of the health, safety and welfare of employees by legislation meant that, with such legislation, there was a corresponding increase in the number of successful personal injury claims against employers.

Employers sought financial protection from these claims, and the insurance industry provided cover through workmen's compensation insurance. However, the least safety conscious employers did not take out insurance. When the successful claimants obtained judgments, if the employer became bankrupt or went into liquidation, there was nothing the injured employee could do to enforce the judgment.

Employers' Liability (Compulsory Insurance) Act 1969

To rectify this harshness, the Employers' Liability (Compulsory Insurance) Act 1969 (the 1969 Act) was introduced. It came into effect on 1 January 1972. The 1969 Act states:

> “every employer carrying on any business in Great Britain shall insure, and maintain insurance ... with an authorised insurer ... against liability for bodily injury or disease sustained by his employees, and arising out of and in the course of their employment in Great Britain in that business, but except in so far as regulations otherwise provide not including injury or disease suffered or contracted outside Great Britain.”

Sections 3(1)(a) and (b) of the 1969 Act exempt some employers from insurance. The 1969 Act does not require local authority employers and employers under a statutory body under national ownership or control to have insurance cover. This includes, amongst others, most local councils, NHS trusts, primary care trusts, national park authorities, as well as any police authority.

Broken down, the 1969 Act only applies to:

- Employers carrying on business in Great Britain
- Whose employees sustain bodily injury or disease
- Arising out of and in the course of their employment
- In Great Britain.

It is important to remember that, as mentioned in chapter 22, as a result of the Employers' Liability (Compulsory Insurance) Exemption (Amendment) Regulations 1992, EL policies no longer have to cover an employer for liability arising due to his employees being carried in or upon, entering or getting onto or alighting from a vehicle.

The minimum level of cover required is currently £5m for any one or more of an insured's employees arising out of any one occurrence (Regulation 3 of the Employers' Liability (Compulsory Insurance) Regulations 1998), although most insurers currently usually provide £10m of cover or more. This financial limit does not relate to each injury to each employee but is an aggregate figure for each occurrence. For example if there was a mining disaster resulting in hundreds of employee casualties, given that all the injuries arise out of a single occurrence, the insurer would only have to pay out overall to the £10m maximum amount under the policy, before its cover was exhausted.

Employers' Liability (Compulsory Insurance) Regulations 1998

While an EL policy often has some similar terms to a general liability policy, there are four conditions which are prohibited by Regulation 2(1) of the Employers' Liability (Compulsory Insurance) Regulations 1998. An insurer cannot refuse to pay compensation purely because of a breach of these conditions:

- "some specified thing is done or omitted to be done after the happening of the event giving rise to a claim under the policy".

  For instance where there is a notification clause that the employer will notify the insurer of a claim immediately or within a specified number of days upon the happening of any occurrence that may give rise to a claim.

- "the policy holder does not take reasonable care to protect his employees against the risk of bodily injury or disease in the course of their employment".

  Notwithstanding this provision, the meaning of which is self-evident, reasonable care clauses have, independently of the above provision, been held by the courts to be limited to recklessness.

- "the policy holder fails to comply with the requirements of any enactment for the protection of employees against the risk of bodily injury or disease in the course of their employment".

This might apply where an employer fails to carry out a risk assessment or provide personal protective equipment and consequently the employee is injured. The insurer cannot rely on the employer's failure to comply with the enactment to avoid paying under the policy.

- "the policy holder does not keep specified records or fails to provide the insurer with or make available to him information from such records".

  This might include the maintaining of risk assessments or accident records.

While these four aspects prevent an EL insurer from avoiding cover, they do not prevent the insurer from seeking to recoup its outlay in dealing with the claim direct from the employer, providing there is a term within the policy allowing it to do so.

While the purpose of EL cover is intended to provide a more secure place for employees, the actual insurance regime is fairly limited when compared to the Road Traffic Act 1988. For example:

- There is no body set up to meet the liabilities of uninsured employers (such as the Motor Insurers' Bureau).
- There is no system whereby the injured employee can recover directly from their employer's insurance company. This is unless the employer become insolvent, when the employee will have the powers granted by the 1930 Act and the 2010 Act.
- There are no restrictions on the right of an insurer being able to avoid cover for non-disclosure, misrepresentation or breach of warranty, although this has been ameliorated to some degree by the 2015 Act.
- Where an employer does not obtain the relevant insurance, there is no recourse for the injured employee to pursue the directors of the employing company direct.

Which is the right policy for the claim?

The crucial difference between an EL policy and a PL policy is that the EL policy focuses on the relevant relationship and activities between the employer and the employee, whereas the PL policy relates to the insured's relationships and activities affecting everyone else.

An insured's broker should check which policy is the likely one to respond and submit the claim to the correct insurer. In most cases it is clear whether an injured person is an employee of the insured or not. However, the claims handler should still check whether its policy is the correct one to respond. In some cases it may be necessary to check the definition of "employee" under the policy, which may contain some assistance in determining whether the EL or PL policy responds.

Who is an employee?

Generally, the courts take an elastic approach to the definition of employee because there is a public interest in recognising the employer/employee relationship in the context of health and safety. The distinction can often be blurred and in some cases where someone would usually be thought of, in the normal sense of the word, to be self-employed, they may be held to be an employee.

This issue is considered in more detail in chapter 5.

The reason why the distinction is so important is that, as indicated above, if a person is held to fall within the definition of an employee within an EL policy, then they will have considerably more protection from legislation, than if held to fall within the PL policy definition.

Caused/sustained wording in policies

Some insurers have slightly different policy wordings when it comes to considering whether an injury was caused or sustained. This has created difficulties, especially in disease claims for conditions like mesothelioma, where the actual exposure to asbestos which causes the injury takes place many years before the symptoms of the disease manifest themselves.

This frequently resulted in difficulty where the employer became insolvent and/or was no longer existent and the insurer declined to deal with the claim, arguing it was not the insurer on risk when the disease manifested itself. The problem was resolved by the Supreme Court in *Durham v BAI (Run Off) Ltd* [2012] (the EL policy trigger litigation). It held that, even if the disease only manifests itself later, the triggering date for the policy was when the individuals were exposed to the asbestos.

For further detail see chapter 9.

Transfer of liabilities

When dealing with EL claims, an issue arises where an employee is injured in the course of their employment due to fault on the part of the employer, but where the employee is subsequently transferred to another employer under the Transfer of Undertakings (Protection of Employment) Regulations 1981 (TUPE): who is responsible for the claim?

This issue was considered in *Bernadone v Pall Mall Services Group and another* [1999]. The High Court held that, under TUPE, liability in tort passes from the original employer to the new employer. Therefore while the claimant's right of action lies against the new employer, the old employer's right to an indemnity under its EL policy also passes to the new employer. These liabilities will only transfer to the new employer if the claimant was still employed by the original employer at the time of the transfer.

Checklist for claims handlers when receiving a new claim

- ✓ Obtain the full underwriting file including the policy schedule, proposal form and notification documents.
- ✓ Check the name of the insured on the policy against the name of the potentially liable/notifying party. Do they tally?
- ✓ Is the policy a 'claims made' or a 'claims occurring' wording?
- ✓ Does the accident/event fall within the period of cover?
- ✓ Is the claim covered under the policy?
- ✓ Do any exclusions/warranties apply which are material to the incident?
- ✓ When was the notification made? Check the notification provisions of the policy. Has the insured complied with these? Has there been a delay in notifying the accident? Has any explanation for such delay been provided?
- ✓ If there has been a late notification, which is a condition precedent, then ensure that no steps are taken to waive the insurer's rights to rely upon the breach, and send a suitable reservation of rights letter to the insured while investigating this.
- ✓ If there is a potential avoidance or other policy issue then send a clear and relevant reservation of rights letter to the insured as soon as possible while this is considered.
- ✓ If, during the course of investigations, it is revealed there has been a breach of the duty of fair presentation, then ensure that no steps are taken that could affirm the policy or waive the insurer's rights.
- ✓ Speak to the relevant underwriter to ascertain whether the breach of fair presentation is a qualifying breach.

- ✓ Was the qualifying breach deliberate or reckless? (Remember, it is for the insurer to prove this.) If so, consider avoiding the contract and refusing all claims. There is no need to return the premium(s) paid.
- ✓ If the qualifying breach was neither reckless nor careless, then:
    - ✓ If the insurer would not have entered the contract on any terms, consider avoiding the policy and returning all the premium(s).
    - ✓ If the insurer would have entered the contract, but on different terms (other than premium), ascertain what the impact of this would be and treat the contract as if entered into on that basis – but explain this to the insured.
    - ✓ If the insurer would have entered into the contract but for a higher premium, ascertain what the proportionate repose by the insurer would be – and explain this to the insured.
- ✓ When construing policy wording, base the decision on what a reasonable insured would have concluded having the relevant background knowledge available to the parties. Consider the ordinary meaning of the words in the context on the insurance is placed.
- ✓ If there is any ambiguity in the policy then, provided the relevant clause was drafted by the insurer, it is likely to be interpreted against the insurer, on the contra proferentem basis, in favour of the insured.

36 Subrogation

Will Brown

Co-author: Felicity Ingram

- Meaning of subrogation
- When does the right of subrogation arise?
- Obstacles to pursuing a successful recovery
- Practical considerations

Subrogation

Introduction

Where an insurer has paid out money to an insured, subrogation enables the insurer to recoup all or some of that money from a third party who caused or contributed to the loss.

In construction matters claims will often be against a professional who has insurance under a professional indemnity cover, but in some other cases it will be against a contractor who has cover under public liability (PL) insurance. Or it could be against a wide range of other categories of target that may or may not be insured, whether individuals, partnerships or companies.

One of the most important practical points for claims handlers to understand is that for some subrogation claims the target party may not have responsive insurance cover in place. For example a claim against a contractor for damage caused by design defects, as it may only have PL cover that would not respond to such a claim.

What exactly is subrogation?

In an insurance context, it is an insurer's right to take over the claim of its insured against a third party responsible for the loss (and, in claims governed by the law of England and Wales, pursue that claim in the name of the insured), so as to recover the insurer's outlay. It is only available for policies of indemnity insurance; benefit policies, such as life and personal accident policies are excluded from the right to subrogate.

The nineteenth-century case of *Castellain v Preston* [1883] confirmed that insurers are entitled to "the advantage of every right of the assured". Subrogation therefore provides insurers with a powerful tool to potentially enable a recovery of part or possibly all of an indemnity paid out under a policy.

When can the right be exercised?

While the right of subrogation vests in the insurer as soon as the policy is entered into, it is a contingent right and cannot be exercised unless and until insurers have made a payment under the policy.

The reality is that many policy wordings will seek to modify the prerequisite of payment and allow insurers to take steps to pursue a recovery before the insured has been fully indemnified. However, in the 2013 first instance case of *Rathbone Brothers v Novae* [2014] Burton J did not accept that such a clause would, in fact, be effective in allowing insurers to exercise the right before payment.

Obstacles to pursuing a recovery

Insurers can only ever acquire the rights of their insured. Accordingly, if an insured has no right to claim against a culpable third party, an insurer will similarly be prevented from pursuing a recovery against that third party.

Take, for example, a contract between the insured (X) and a supplier (Y), pursuant to which Y supplies widgets to X. The contract excludes liability on the part of Y for breach of contract, breach of statutory duty or liability in tort for material damage or consequential loss. X suffers a fire as a result of Y supplying widgets that are not fit for purpose, which constitutes both a breach of contract and negligence. X claims on its property insurance but, because of the exclusion of liability in the contract (assuming it is held to be valid and enforceable), insurers cannot seek a recovery of their outlay from Y.

The insurance policy itself may also contain a limitation on insurers' rights of recovery. Pressure brought to bear by insureds whose accounts are highly valuable might result in underwriters waiving any rights to pursue entities connected to those insureds.

Furthermore, joint names policies, common in the context of contractor's all risks (CAR) policies are likely to limit insurers' rights of subrogation. Even in circumstances where such a joint names policy does not contain an express bar or waiver of subrogation, the law will imply into the policy a term that where two or more insureds (let us say, A and B) are covered in respect of the same loss or damage that has occurred (for example, fire damage), the insurer will not pursue a recovery from B of the outlay which they (insurers) have paid to A. To do so would conflict with the insurer's agreement to insure B against the fire damage.

Practical considerations

The obstacles discussed above should not, however, be a deterrent to considering the prospects of subrogation: successful recoveries are frequently pursued.

The following (non-exhaustive) pointers should assist in considering prospects and pursuing a successful recovery:

- In which country did the loss occur? Statutory limitation periods in foreign jurisdictions may be far shorter than those in England and so swift action may be needed to preserve rights of recovery.
- What is the choice of law and jurisdiction in respect of any underlying contract? While the loss may have occurred in England, the contract, breach of which has led to the loss, may be governed by the law of another country, in which case the claim will need to be pursued under that law.
- Has physical and documentary evidence been preserved? This may be key to proving blame, so, to the extent evidence can be retained, it should be.
- Have witnesses been identified? Memories fade with time so recording witness evidence at an early stage will help in piecing together the case against the third party.

- Does the corporate insured remain a live entity? If it has become insolvent, steps must be taken to avoid it being struck off the register of companies (dissolved) as the claim will need to be pursued in the insured's name. Should this occur then an application will need to be made to restore the company to the register. An alternative may be for the insured to assign its rights to the insurer.
- Does the recovery target remain a live entity? If not, consider whether an action against the target's insurers pursuant to the Third Parties (Rights Against Insurers) Act 2010 might be possible.
- Each loss will undoubtedly bring with it its own unique considerations and merits. However, the possibility of making a recovery in respect of the indemnity outlay with the attendant improvement in the insurers' bottom line is reason enough to consider such a prospect.

We set out below a further example of a loss that is likely to give rise to a subrogated recovery and the considerations that may come into play.

Facts

A fire occurs at the premises of X during the course of extension works being carried out by a contractor (Y) under contract with X. The fire (thought to be caused by Z, one of Y's subcontractors carrying out hot works) causes physical damage to the existing building, contents, the extension works and consequential losses given that X is incapable of carrying on its business until the damage has been addressed.

Under the contract with Y, X had taken out joint names contractors all risks insurance "for their respective rights and interests" in respect of the extension works. This policy has an exclusion in respect of consequential loss.

Following the fire, X makes a claim on, and is paid out under, its property policy for the damage to the existing building and contents, and, under the business interruption section of that policy, for loss of revenue. The property policy has an exclusion in respect of damage to construction works.

X also makes a claim on the joint names CAR policy in respect of damage to the extension works.

Analysis

The property policy insurers can subrogate against Y in contract and possibly Z in tort (given that there is no contractual relationship between X and Z) in respect of the sums it has paid out. Consideration will, however, need to be given to whether any sums paid to X under the property policy are over and above what would be recoverable against Y in contract and/or Z in tort. For example, the property policy may provide new for old cover in respect of a piece of machinery damaged by the fire, but in the subrogated claim, insurers will only be able to claim the difference between the value of the pre-damaged machinery and that following the fire, or the cost of a piece of machinery, equivalent in terms of age and deterioration to the piece of machinery prior to the fire.

Y and Z are likely to have a PL policy covering their liability for damage to third-party property (i.e. X's existing building and contents). They may or may not have cover for liability for consequential losses. If not, it should be considered whether Y and Z have the requisite funds themselves to meet a subrogated claim in respect of the amounts paid out by property policy insurers in respect of loss of revenue. Also some PL policies contain a hot works warranty. If this has been breached, and that breach led to the fire, the policy may not respond.

Finally, the CAR policy insurers are unlikely to be able to subrogate against Y, given that Y is also insured under the joint names CAR policy. Consideration will need to be given as to whether Z is also an insured such as to preclude a recovery being pursued by the CAR policy insurers.

37 Fraud

Martin Stockdale

Co-author: Katherine Totty

- What is fraud?
- Fraud risks matrix
- Fraud detection including key fraud indicators
- Investigation: desktop searches, surveillance and other evidence
- Challenging fraud: when to show your hand
- Fundamental dishonesty
- Deterrence: criminal and civil sanctions

Fraud

Introduction

More than anything else, fraud is a behaviour. It is:

- **Covert:** a fraudster does not present their claim as a fraudulent claim.
- **Fluid:** fraudsters adapt and change in response to tactics used to detect and defend claims.
- **Often unique:** how fraud affects an organisation will depend on the nature of the liability risk, customer profile, claims processes and more.

Fraud is an attack on the weaknesses within the claims process. For example, claims submitted via an online portal and reduced periods for decisions on liability restrict the time so often required for any claims handler to stand back and assess potential fraud issues.

All of the above makes fraud particularly challenging to deal with.

Fraud is a fast moving area of claims and one that has seen recent developments in terms of legislation, civil procedure and judicial decisions. It is correct to say that defendants are as well protected as they ever have been, but more still needs be done to make liability claims less fertile ground for fraud.

In this chapter are some of the key principles required to understand and respond to fraud in liability claims.

What is fraud?

Legally defined

Fraud is not new. It has existed and thrived for many years, both in respect of liability claims and in wider society.

Derry and others v Peek [1889]

> "Fraud is proved when it is shewn that a false representation has been made knowingly, or without belief in its truth, or recklessly, careless whether it be true or false."

Agapitos and another v Agnew and others [2002]

> "A fraudulent claim exists where the insured claims, knowing that he has suffered no loss, or only a lesser loss than that which he claims (or is reckless as to whether this is the case)."

Fraud Act 2006

Section 2: Fraud by false representation

1) A person is in breach of this section if he —
   a) dishonestly makes a false representation, and
   b) intends, by making the representation —
      i) to make a gain for himself or another, or
      ii) to cause loss to another or to expose another to a risk of loss.

continued...

...continued

2) A representation is false if —
    a) it is untrue or misleading, and
    b) the person making it knows that it is, or might be, untrue or misleading.
3) "Representation" means any representation as to fact or law, including a representation as to the state of mind of —
    a) the person making the representation, or
    b) any other person.
4) A representation may be express or implied.
5) For the purposes of this section a representation may be regarded as made if it (or anything implying it) is submitted in any form to any system or device designed to receive, convey or respond to communications (with or without human intervention).

Section 3: Fraud by failing to disclose information

1) A person is in breach of this section if he —
    a) dishonestly fails to disclose to another person information which he is under a legal duty to disclose, and
    b) intends, by failing to disclose the information —
        i) to make a gain for himself or another, or
        ii) to cause loss to another or to expose another to a risk of loss.

continued...

...continued

Section 4: Fraud by abuse of position

1) A person is in breach of this section if he —
   a) occupies a position in which he is expected to safeguard, or not to act against, the financial interests of another person,
   b) dishonestly abuses that position, and
   c) intends, by means of the abuse of that position —
      i) to make a gain for himself or another, or
      ii) to cause loss to another or to expose another to a risk of loss.
2) A person may be regarded as having abused his position even though his conduct consisted of an omission rather than an act.

Fraud in liability claims

Remember that fraud is a changing phenomenon. Therefore, it is important to be alive to new behaviours.

A summary of fraud risks in liability claims is set out in Table 37.1.

Exaggerated claims

When does exaggeration become a fraudulent act? Most claims handlers will recognise the inflation of claims as part of the negotiation of quantum. Not all exaggeration is necessarily fraudulent. However, where a loss is presented in such a way as to deceive, it is likely that the principles set out above in the courts and legislation will apply.

Table 37.1: Fraud risk matrix

<table>
<tr><th colspan="2"></th><th colspan="4">Risk</th></tr>
<tr><th colspan="2"></th><th>Highways</th><th>Motor</th><th>Public liability</th><th>Employers' liability</th></tr>
<tr><td rowspan="8">Fraud</td><td rowspan="2">Contrived Event</td><td colspan="4">Accident did not occur
No injury/damage
Injury/damage caused by other incident
Fictitious losses (e.g. loss of earnings, care)
Organised fraud – targeting open risks</td></tr>
<tr><td>Paper-based highway claims
(e.g. slip/trip, cycle)
Deliberately created defects</td><td>Contrived RTAs
Phantom passengers
Deliberate damage</td><td>Slip/trip on premises
Trespass claims</td><td>Manual handling/back claims
RSI claims
Stress claims</td></tr>
<tr><td rowspan="2">Deliberate/ Staged Event</td><td colspan="4">Incident occurs by design/deliberate
Organised fraud</td></tr>
<tr><td>Highway defect slip/trip claims
Deliberately created defects</td><td>Induced/deliberate accidents
Staged
Deliberate driving over potholes
Deliberate/increased damage</td><td>Slip/trip on premises
Trespass claims</td><td>Manual handling/back claims
Workplace hazard claims
Workplace slip/trip claims</td></tr>
<tr><td rowspan="2">Exaggeration</td><td colspan="4">Extent/causation of injury/damage
Loss of earnings
Special damage losses
Malingering (e.g. recovery, return to work)
Deliberate/self-serving medical attention sought</td></tr>
<tr><td></td><td>Deliberately exaggerated vehicle damage
Increased credit hire
Low speed impact claims</td><td></td><td></td></tr>
<tr><td rowspan="2">False Evidence</td><td colspan="4">False witnesses – liability
Falsified witness documentation (e.g. witness questionnaire)
Falsified loss of earnings evidence (e.g. payslips, witness evidence)
Organised fraud – professional enablers
Falsified other special damages – property losses, care claims, future losses (e.g. witnesses, witness statements, receipts, documents)
Photographs
Medical reports/evidence</td></tr>
<tr><td></td><td>Repair documents
Engineer reports</td><td></td><td></td></tr>
</table>

In order for an exaggerated claim to be considered fraudulent, two elements need to be present:

- There must be an intention to obtain an advantage or put someone else at a disadvantage. Courts often draw a distinction between conscious and unconscious exaggeration. An individual exaggerates consciously when they deliberately (or recklessly) maintain their injuries/losses are worse than they are. Conversely, unconscious exaggeration takes place when an individual falsely but unknowingly claims for an extent of loss that is not the true case. For example, a claimant may be suffering from anxiety or chronic pain syndrome, which makes them believe the loss they have suffered is worse than it actually is. In such circumstances a court will not usually find the claim to be fraudulent.

- The amount claimed must be more than a bargaining position. A claim may be exaggerated but not fraudulent if the claimant is merely taking a bargaining position, as opposed to intending to recover more than that to which they are entitled. For instance, in *Nsubuga v Commercial Union Assurance Co Plc* [1998] Mr Justice Thomas commented:

  > “[O]ne has to accept as a matter of commercial reality that people will often put forward a claim that is more than they believe that they will recover. That is because they expect to engage in some form of "horse trading" or other negotiation. It would not generally in those circumstances be right to conclude readily that someone had behaved fraudulently merely because he put forward an amount greater than that which he reasonably believed he would recover. He would have to put forward a claim that was so far exaggerated that he knew that in respect of a material part of it, there was no basis whatsoever for the claim.”

Therefore, where a claim merely involves a degree of overvaluation, it is unlikely to be considered fraudulent. The greater the exaggeration however, the greater the likelihood there is of a finding of fraud.

The issue of fraudulent exaggeration is complex and has evolved significantly in recent years. Some of the more prominent cases are considered below.

Ul-Haq and others v Shah [2008]

The defendant caused a genuine accident when she drove into the rear of the claimants' stationary car at traffic lights. Three claims were brought.

At trial, Mr Recorder Parkes QC held that one of the claimants, Mrs Khatoon, was not in the car at the time of the accident. The defendant sought to have all three claims struck out, notwithstanding that two of them were genuine, arguing:

- There was clearly a fraud by the other two claimants in supporting the dishonest claim of Mrs Khatoon.
- The court had a discretion to strike out a genuine claim under Part 3.4(2) of the Civil Procedure Rules (CPR), even at the end of the hearing.

The Court of Appeal held that the courts did not have the power to reject a genuine claim on the basis of fraudulent exaggeration or where a claimant had supported a dishonest claim. Any genuine claim would remain payable, with parties sanctioned in costs where applicable.

Many insurers considered it anomalous that although a small exaggeration by the insured is enough to forfeit an entire claim under an insurance policy, they would have to pay third-party claims even where the claimant attempted to deceive.

The result was an environment that appeared to many to encourage fraudulent claims as there would be little or no consequence were the fraud discovered.

This area of law has now developed and the concept of 'fundamental dishonesty' must routinely be considered. Fundamental dishonesty is discussed later in more detail, but the following exaggeration cases helped establish the principle.

Summers v Fairclough Homes Ltd [2012]

This is the leading exaggeration case, which went to the Supreme Court.

Mr Summers claimed over £800,000 in damages against his employer. He alleged that he was permanently disabled, in a permanent state of pain and unable to work. However, surveillance evidence showed him living a normal life, including working in a job, walking without crutches and even playing football. At trial his claim was reduced to £88,000.

After the trial the defendant applied to have the entire claim struck out due to the claimant's "deliberate, gross and dishonest exaggeration".

The application was appealed to the Supreme Court, which overruled *Ul-Haq and others v Shah*. It held that the courts do have the power to strike out an entire claim, but only in circumstances where it would be "just and proportionate" to do so.

The judgment established that in cases that were fundamentally dishonest it would be appropriate to strike out a claim.

Fari v Homes for Haringey [2012]

Mrs Fari sued Homes for Haringey for more than £750,000 after she tripped on a paving stone and hurt her knee.

In the first application of the *Summers* decision, the claim was struck out at trial after surveillance footage and medical evidence revealed "a complete gross exaggeration of the symptoms by Mrs Fari, aided and abetted by her husband". His Honour Judge Mitchell found that Mrs Fari had suffered a minor injury worth no more than £1,500.

continued...

...continued

Permission was subsequently granted to bring contempt of court proceedings. Mrs Fari received a sentence of three months' imprisonment. Mr Fari was sentenced to two months' imprisonment (suspended for 12 months).

Plana v First Capital East Ltd [2013]

Kennedys defended this claim, which arose from an incident in 2007.

The claimant alleged that he had suffered a traumatic brain injury, such that he needed constant supervision and was unable to drive or work. Liability was admitted on a 90:10 basis in the claimant's favour and interim payments made totalling £125,000.

Surveillance evidence showed the claimant to have grossly exaggerated his symptoms and their impact on him. For example, during the course of the footage, the claimant was seen to be working at a car wash business and able to drive. The defendant made an application before trial to strike out the claim.

His Honour Judge Collender QC struck out the claim as it amounted to an abuse of process. The judge made reference to *Summers*, concluding that even though the accident was likely to have been genuine, he was still able to make a finding of fraud against the claimant. The genuine element of the claim represented a mere fraction of the presented claim value.

The claimant was also ordered to repay the interim payments and to pay the defendant's costs.

Dealing with claims fraud

Stopping fraud is the responsibility of an entire claims department. How can a dedicated counter-fraud team tackle problem cases if suspected fraudulent claims are not channelled to them? A system for organising a response to this problem is encouraged. A fraud strategy can be broken into the following component parts:

Detect
fraud risk through system automation and trained judgement
Validate
genuine claims and reduce false positives
Investigate
by building the evidence to defend and reject dishonest claims
Challenge
effectively, commercially and robustly
Deter
future fraud by ensuring consequence to dishonesty

In this section the key aspects of dealing with suspect and fraudulent claims are considered.

Detect

The first element of any fraud response is to detect the issue. Insurers, rightly, see themselves in the business of paying genuine claims, but fighting dishonest ones. The detection of a fraud risk is a necessary trigger to take a claim out of the normal process that aims to settle a claim quickly and fairly.

Fraud exists in many shapes and guises and is not restricted to any one particular section of the community. In addition, it is rare for two fraud cases to be identical. This makes fraud detection more complex.

Early fraud detection is possible, however, through the application of 'fraud indicators'. These are common profiles or aspects of a claim that indicate fraud might be present. The indicators are supported by data-mining technology from both internal and external data sources.

How many indicators are needed as a trigger for a case to be considered high risk will depend on the process and strategy of an organisation. Typical key fraud indicators are set out in Table 37.2.

Table 30.2: Key fraud indicators

<table>
<tr><th rowspan="2" colspan="2">Aspect</th><th colspan="4">Claim Type</th></tr>
<tr><th>Highways</th><th>Motor</th><th>Public liability</th><th>Employers' liability</th></tr>
<tr><td rowspan="2">Aspect</td><td rowspan="2">Accident</td><td colspan="4">■ No contemporaneous report of incident
■ Unlikely/implausible accident circumstances
■ Unlikely/implausible accident location
■ No independent witnesses
■ Witnesses (suspected) linked/known to claimant
■ Accident occurred in remote/isolated area</td></tr>
<tr><td>■ Location/specific defect in 2 or more claims</td><td>■ Employee driver states claimant stopped for no reason
■ Accident occurred on entry to roundabout
■ Vehicle has 3 or more passengers
■ Employee driver unaware of a collision
■ Accident occurs at low speed
■ Employee driver keen to accept liability</td><td></td><td></td></tr>
<tr><td rowspan="2">Aspect</td><td rowspan="2">Claimant/Claim</td><td colspan="4">■ Relevant accident history
■ Claimed losses not compatible with claimant lifestyle
■ Injuries entirely subjective
■ Claimant some distance from own solicitor/accident claims company involvement
■ Claimant eager to compromise/seeks early settlement
■ Claimant has financial problems
■ Quick/early instruction of solicitor
■ Self-serving medical attention
■ Pattern of involvement in number of claims (claimant, families, solicitors, experts)</td></tr>
<tr><td></td><td>■ Claimant description does not match ID supplied
■ Credit hire period 89 days or more
■ Credit hire prolonged
■ Claimant seeks cash in lieu of repair
■ Claimant/vehicle uninsured</td><td></td><td>■ Employee/claimant on short-term contract
■ Claim made shortly after end of employment
■ Employee/claimant has poor employment/ attendance record</td></tr>
</table>

continued...

Table 37.2: Key fraud indicators (continued)

<table>
<tr><th rowspan="2">Aspect</th><th colspan="4">Claim Type</th></tr>
<tr><th>Highways</th><th>Motor</th><th>Public liability</th><th>Employers' liability</th></tr>
<tr><td>Claimant/Claim</td><td></td><td>■ Claimant vehicle in first or last month of insurance
■ Little/no damage to claimant vehicle
■ Damage inconsistent with accident circumstances
■ Damage between vehicles inconsistent</td><td></td><td></td></tr>
<tr><td>Discrepancies</td><td colspan="4">■ Inconsistent accounts from claimant re. circumstances
■ Inconsistent accounts from claimant re. injury/loss
■ Inconsistent accounts between claimant and supporting witnesses</td></tr>
<tr><td>Documents</td><td colspan="4">■ Appears altered
■ Only poor copies available
■ Basic documents missing/unavailable/not disclosed
■ Invoices early sequential number references
■ Aspects of documents retain same information to other documents from same source
■ Similarities in documents from different sources
■ Common handwriting on different documents/from different sources
■ Documents omit key/important information</td></tr>
<tr><td rowspan="2">Miscellaneous</td><td colspan="4">■ False/misleading information provided
■ Non-disclosure of relevant information</td></tr>
<tr><td>■ Relevant Freedom of Information Act request
■ Relevant entry on pothole website service</td><td></td><td></td><td></td></tr>
</table>

This is not to say that an incident must be fraudulent purely because it involves one or more of these indicators. However, by using a system of fraud indicators, the at-risk insurer has the opportunity to properly investigate a claim before any payments are made.

Of course, indicators are only of limited assistance when dealing with exaggerated genuine claims, which comprise the highest proportion of fraudulent claims. In these cases, the detection of fraud often rests with the ability of the claims handler to spot the exaggeration. This involves observing anomalies, inconsistencies, patterns of behaviour and the recognition of claimant characteristics to identify claims requiring further scrutiny. The ability to detect fraud through a mixture of good process, experience and instinct in such cases becomes crucial.

Claims handlers see genuine claims every day; they know claims and, therefore, have developed (whether they realise or not) a valuable instinct or gut feel. If a claim doesn't feel right, then it probably is not.

Investigate

Once a possible fraud is detected (and that detection is validated), it is necessary to investigate to build the evidence to repudiate a claim. Many organisations have dedicated investigation and intelligence teams with specialist skills in data analytics and access to numerous data sources and investigation tools. These departments consider a number of lines of enquiry when engaging in early investigation of fraudulent claims.

Credibility

Like most liability claims, fraud cases ultimately succeed or fail on the credibility of the claimant. A pleading of fraud against an individual claimant can have grave consequences for them given the cost consequences and potential criminal liability that could follow.

A court may be reluctant to make a finding of fraud against an individual unless it can be established that enough questions have been raised about a claimant's character to enable it to conclude that they acted dishonestly. If the claimant can portray themselves as an honest, credible character then it is conceivable their claim will succeed. This can often be the outcome notwithstanding the many concerns raised in connection with the incident.

Armstrong and another v First York [2005]

A dispute arose as to whether the claimants could have sustained personal injury following a minor impact with one of the defendant's buses. The single joint expert in the matter, a forensic motor vehicle engineer, gave evidence that the damage sustained to the second claimant's car was so minimal that it would not have moved at all, let alone jolt sufficiently to cause injury. The claimants called no technical evidence to challenge the expert's view.

Although the Court of Appeal could find no fault with the expert evidence, it was not prepared to dismiss a claim in circumstances where the claimants were otherwise found to be entirely credible. The claim therefore succeeded. Lord Justice Brooke commented:

> “In my judgment there is no principle of law that an expert's evidence in an unusual field – doing his best, with his great experience, to reconstruct what happened to the parties based on the secondhand material he received in this case – must be dispositive of liability in such a case and that a judge must be compelled to find that, in his view, two palpably honest witnesses have come to court to deceive him in order to obtain damages, in this case a small amount of damages, for a case they know to be a false one.”

The deciding factor for a court is whether it can believe in the honesty of a claimant. Otherwise, as observed by Lord Justice Longmore, “It would mean that cases were decided by experts rather than by judges”.

It is absolutely essential therefore that the defence is able to make inroads into the claimant's credibility. Factors to be considered are:

- What does the claimant's accident history say about them? For example, have they shown a propensity for fraud? Do they admit the full extent of this history? Are there striking similarities in the way the accidents occurred?
- Has the claimant given a consistent account of the incident throughout the course of the case? How does the description of the incident in the claim notification form (CNF) compare to the reporting of the accident to the claimant's GP/medical expert/insurer? Does the claimant remain consistent in their witness evidence and answers to Part 18 questions? If the account has changed then why is this the case? Is the claimant attempting to tailor their evidence?
- Has the claimant remained consistent with regards to the nature of their symptoms and the mechanism of injury? Are the symptoms revealed in the CNF broadly consistent with those reported in the medical records and medico-legal examination? Has the claimant remained consistent as to how the injury was caused, for example, in a road traffic accident, whether the impact propelled the claimant forward and backward or side to side in the seat, the speed of impact and how far the claimant's vehicle was shunted?
- Has the claimant demonstrated that they are prepared to lie on oath to advance their claim by signing a false statement of truth? If so, then how can a judge discount the possibility that they are equally likely to lie under cross-examination?

A fraud case is ever evolving. It is crucial that a claims handler regularly revisits the evidence to determine whether the claimant will appear dishonest in cross-examination. If an insurer's investigations call the claimant's honesty into sufficient question then the prospects of a successful defence in a fraud case will improve markedly. If at the end of an investigation, however, the claimant's credibility remains intact then it would be a major risk to defend the matter to trial.

Desktop searches

The ability to collate, in a meaningful way, a large amount of data brings with it a number of immediate advantages. Not only can it act as a deterrent to repeat offenders, but it also offers an insurer an array of information about the claimant that can be used to test them throughout the course of the case.

Through desktop investigations insurers look to answer the following types of questions:

- Can the parties' addresses be authenticated?
- Can the parties be linked to other risk addresses?
- Can the parties be linked to one another?
- Have any of the vehicles been involved in other accidents? Were these vehicles suitably repaired? Where required, was a vehicle inspection check completed?
- Do the parties have a claims history? If so, has the insured declared this at inception and the claimant during the course of the proceedings?
- Have any of the parties been investigated for fraud before? Can any similar fact evidence be ascertained from previous investigations?
- Who were the vehicles registered to? Are there grounds to request a full keeper history? Can any adverse links be identified?
- Do any of the parties have an adverse financial history, offering a potential motive to participate in a fraud?
- Can evidence be found that contradicts the accident circumstances or alleged injuries?
- Are there potential adverse links to any companies, particularly those that will benefit in the claim?

Data protection

It is important that the principles of data protection are adhered to and an organisation's processes and policies are abided by at all times.

Below is a summary of the Data Protection Principles detailed in Part 1 of the Data Protection Act 1998 (the DPA):

1) Personal data should be processed fairly and lawfully and shall not be processed unless at least one of the conditions in Schedule 2 are met (see below).

2) Personal data should be obtained only for specified and lawful purposes and should not be processed in any way incompatible with those purposes.

3) Personal data being processed should be adequate, relevant and not excessive in relation to those purposes.

4) Personal data processed shall be accurate and where necessary kept up to date.

5) Personal data should only be kept for as long as it is necessary for the purposes.

6) Processing of personal data should always be done in accordance with the rights of the data subject.

7) There should be appropriate technical and organisational measures taken to prevent unauthorised or unlawful processing and/or the accident loss or damage of personal data.

8) Personal data should not be transferred to a country or territory outside the EEA unless that country ensures an adequate level of protection for the rights of data subjects.

Schedule 2 of the DPA provides conditions that need to be present to satisfy the first data protection principle. The most relevant in the handling of claims and fraud investigation would be:

1) The data subject has provided consent.

6) (1) The processing is **necessary** for the purposes of your **legitimate interests** or those third parties to whom data may be disclosed.

Consent may (currently) be implied or explicitly provided. A fair processing notice will provide the basis for the implied consent and satisfy the second data protection principle in third-party claims. Most organisations include fair processing notices in a number of ways including on their websites, as part of their telephone systems and on correspondence in the early stages of a claim. The Claim Notification Form (CNF) also provides a fair processing notice as part of the statement of truth signed by (or on instruction of) the claimant at the outset of proceedings. The CNF fair processing notice is below:

> “Your personal information will only be disclosed to third parties, where we are obliged or permitted by law to do so. This includes use for the purpose of claims administration as well as disclosure to third-party managed databases used to help prevent fraud, and to regulatory bodies for the purposes of monitoring and/or enforcing our compliance with any regulatory rules/codes.”

In first-party claims, consent and fair processing notices are usually part of the policy terms which form the insurance contract.

General Data Protection Regulation (GDPR)

Data protection is changing in response to the changes in the way in which data is now generated by data subjects and captured by organisations. Since the DPA, the internet, social media and data management have revolutionised the world of personal data.

The GDPR's main focus and goal is to strengthen the rights of the data subject and build consumer trust. There is a focus on the issue of consent, which will raise the bar to a higher standard around consent with a requirement for it to be provided explicitly.

The GDPR will come into effect in May 2018, but the ICO are conducting (at the time of writing) an ongoing consultation before issuing final guidance to data controllers in the United Kingdom.

Sharing data and information

Sharing data and information is vital in the fight against fraud. Where data is not fully or properly shared, fraudsters thrive. The basis of sharing data is established within the data protection principles and relevant conditions in Schedule 2 of the DPA.

In addition, there two important exemptions to the provisions discussed above and/or the duty not to disclose personal data to others:

- s.29 (1) (a) DPA allows the processing of personal data for the purpose of the prevention and detection of crime.
- s.35 (2) DPA permits the disclosure of personal data where that disclosure is necessary for the purpose, or in connection with, any legal proceedings, including prospective legal proceedings, or obtaining legal advice.

Following a project carried out by the Chartered Insurance Institute New Generation Group there is now an industry sponsored best practice guide to sharing data under the s.29 exemption. This guidance is available to download from the Insurance Fraud Bureau (IFB) website at https://www.insurancefraudbureau.org/dpa-29-3-best-practice.

The IFB maintain the guidance documentation and manage the register of organisations who have adopted the guidance and relevant the single point of contact (SPOC).

Witness statements

It is vital that all potential witnesses are interviewed at the first available opportunity. Regardless of whether the witness is engaged in fraud, memories will fade and accounts become vague.

The initial interview of a witness is sometimes the only opportunity an insurer will have to speak to that individual. Ensuring that a credible claims investigator is utilised is, therefore, crucial. Key points include the following:

- It is essential that the investigator is well prepared and fully understands the witness/claim they are dealing with.
- If the witness' first language is not English, then the statement should be taken in their own language and then translated by a professional translator. This will avoid potential admissibility questions later in the proceedings.
- It is important that a statement is in the witness's own words. It can be hugely damaging if a witness statement contains 'facts' that are later revealed to be the words of the claims handler or investigator rather than the witness.
- The claims handler should determine whether the account given is coherent. If not, then an unreliable account provided shortly after the accident could give rise to a suspicion of fraud, or at least an understanding that the witness cannot be relied upon. Check the statement against previous accounts of the incident to ensure it remains consistent. Be prepared to revisit it should further information materialise.

A witness is hugely valuable when defending a claim. It is important that any witness is contacted regularly to ensure contact details remain current and they know they are still required. Often, good witness evidence is lost because contact with the individual is not maintained.

In cases where the evidence of any witness needs to be tested, it is sensible to hold a conference where it is also possible to test their resolve. If a witness is not willing to make the effort to meet in conference, why should they be any more willing to attend a day-long trial, particularly given they may have nothing personally to gain from doing so?

Part 18 questions

It is often advisable to use Part 18 of the CPR to put questions to a claimant in a fraud case. These questions are a valuable tool to clarify aspects of the case that are not known to the insurer (particularly in circumstances when an indemnity is not being offered to the policyholder). They can also fix the claimant to a specific assertion or position, such as establishing an admitted accident history. Part 18 responses are verified by a statement of truth and can be hugely damaging to a claimant's case if they are proven to be incorrect. They may provide the opportunity for contempt proceedings later.

An application to compel a response under Part 18 can only be made when proceedings have been issued, but that is not to say a request for information cannot be made before proceedings. The request may elicit a response or, at the very least, pave the way for a formal Part 18 request/application in litigation.

Questions put to the claimant should be concise and specific. The Practice Direction to Part 18 states that "A Request should be concise and strictly confined to matters which are reasonably necessary and proportionate to enable the first party to prepare his own case or to understand the case he has to meet." Pro forma questions are often challenged by those acting for the claimant, and the courts rarely indulge fishing exercises.

Medical records

A claimant's medical records are a valuable source of information and can often assist in undermining the veracity of a claimant's case. For instance they may reveal that the claimant:

- Did not seek medical attention following the accident, despite advising the medical expert to the contrary.
- Did seek medical attention, but not immediately after the accident as reported in the CNF but a significant while later (often having already sought legal advice).
- Reported an entirely different version of the accident circumstances to the GP than those reported elsewhere.
- Reported entirely different symptoms or cause of injury.
- Had a history of pre-accident symptoms not disclosed to the medical expert.

- Attended their GP several times following the accident without mentioning any alleged ongoing accident-related symptoms.
- Attended their GP on several occasions prior to the accident date for the same or similar ailments as those alleged to have been caused by the accident.
- Was offered the possibility of physiotherapy courtesy of the NHS but did not take this up.
- Has been involved in other accidents not disclosed in the proceedings.

Should a claimant seek to argue that disclosure of their medical records would be disproportionate, an insurer does have a number of arguments in response. Subject to the issues in the case, it could be argued that the issue of relevance should not be restricted to the claimant's specific injury or accident but should be considered in terms of the claimant's credibility as a whole. This is especially pertinent where causation, previous or subsequent claims and medical history are relevant.

Forensic engineering evidence

The assessment of damage to vehicles can prove pivotal to a successful repudiation of a suspect motor claim. Forensic engineering evidence can be particularly useful when determining whether two particular vehicles have collided and, if so, whether such a collision could have occurred in the manner alleged. Forensic engineers can also be instructed to offer an opinion on the likely speed of impact and, consequentially, the likelihood of occupant movement within the vehicle.

It should be noted that defendants face judicial resistance to the use of forensic engineering evidence in low-speed impact cases.

If a party wishes to rely on a report from a forensic engineer then they should seek to instruct the engineer at the earliest opportunity. Vehicles are not always available for inspection, especially when time has passed since the accident. A report will be given more weight by a court if the engineer has physically inspected both vehicles involved in the accident. If an inspection of a vehicle is frustrated, then a party should consider making a pre-action application for inspection of property. Correspondence and file/telephone notes (from both the claims handler and the engineer) should be kept to demonstrate attempts made to inspect and reasons why this has not been possible.

If one or more of the vehicles are not available for inspection an engineer can still be instructed to provide a desktop opinion using images of the vehicles. As mentioned above, such reports are given less evidential weight by the courts. A credible vehicle examiner should therefore take high-quality digital images of the vehicle, displaying all areas of damage as well as the vehicle registration, vehicle identification number, model and mileage.

If a situation arises where the third-party inspection report refers to images, but these are not disclosed by the other side, there is scope to make an application under Part 31 of the CPR for disclosure of the images as "relevant documents".

It is normally the case that two vehicles involved in a collision will share similar damage profiles. However, when considering images, it must be remembered that this is not always true.

Judges will often accept that the true extent of damage to a vehicle may not be readily displayed by images. For instance, it may well be the case in a low-speed-type impact that an inspection of images displays no visible damage at all. However, it is possible that on impact the bumper of a vehicle deformed and caused damage to the components behind, before returning to its original shape.

In addition, in a rear-end "shunt" the design difference between the front and rear of modern vehicles may result in the front of the fault vehicle being badly damaged with little obvious corresponding damage to the non-fault vehicle. The temptation is often to conclude that the damage is not consistent, and caution is urged before jumping to a conclusion. Also, the comparative size and robustness of the two vehicles must be borne in mind when determining the level of damage to each.

When instructing an engineer, remember that instructions may become disclosable, as well as any documents provided to the expert. It is therefore important to keep the instructions neutral and only refer to documents where disclosure will cause no difficulty.

Electronic document disclosure

Most documents are now created in electronic form. This means that any document provided in support of a claim is itself only a copy of the electronic original.

The original document is potentially rich in valuable metadata that describes and provides attributes about the data (or document) of primary interest. For example, the metadata of a photograph will tell you, amongst other things, the date, time, device and (in GPS enabled devices such as smartphones) the location where that photograph was taken. Most other electronically created documents contain similarly wide-ranging metadata.

When seeking disclosure of documents from a claimant you may wish to ask for the document in its 'Native Format', i.e. a copy of the document in its original electronic form. Be careful to guard against attempts to disguise or remove original metadata, such as photographs embedded in a word document or pdf files or documents which have been received by email, saved by the claimant's representative and sent on.

Surveillance

While obtaining surveillance evidence can often be expensive and it may prove inconclusive, it can be of real benefit in cases where it is suspected the claimant is exaggerating the extent of their loss or where losses are said to be ongoing. Examples include:

- Significant claims that are reliant on the questionable disability

- Ongoing loss of earnings
- Care claims
- Credit hire validation.

The obtaining of video evidence and its disclosure raises the following two key issues for compensators:

- The obtaining of surveillance evidence in light of the Human Rights Act 1998. This Act incorporates Articles 6 and 8 of the European Convention on Human Rights with regard to the right to a fair trial (which applies equally to claimants and defendants) and the right to respect for an individual's private and family life. In *Jones v University of Warwick* [2003], the Court of Appeal had to consider the issue of video evidence obtained in a manner contrary to Article 8. It held that the evidence would be allowed. However, it penalised the defendant in costs by making it pay for having to apply for permission to rely on the surveillance video and for the two subsequent appeals. Also, it made it clear that the admission of such evidence should not amount to trial by ambush. The reason the evidence was permitted was because its content was regarded as having sufficient probative value to the issues in the proceedings.
- The requirement for public bodies to consider the authorisation framework of the Regulation of Investigatory Powers Act 2000, which requires directed surveillance to be authorised by a senior officer/person and for the specific purpose of detecting or preventing crime.

As a matter of best practice, all surveillance should limit unnecessary capture of third parties who are not the subject of the investigation (also known as 'collateral capture'). Skilled surveillance operatives should be aware of this and carry out a risk assessment in advance of undertaking surveillance investigation.

Challenge

Having completed the investigation, what are the next steps? Where does all the investigative material and evidence lead? Consider some of the key issues to appraise when challenging fraudulent claims.

Disclosure

Perhaps the most challenging area of handling fraudulent claims is making the call as to when to detail the defendant's case against the claimant. The desire to do so early and achieve an early repudiation is obvious. However, how many times does a claimant simply change the story to fit? When is there sufficient information to show a claim is fraudulent without the claimant committing their position formally?

Where a claimant is given room to change a story they will often be permitted to do so by a judge, who must always remain impartial and balanced. If there is insufficient evidence to support allegations then how can a judge be expected to decide a case in that way?

It is important to fix the claimant to their story before revealing evidence that disproves it. Where possible, obtain a detailed account of circumstances relevant to the claim and alleged losses and require a claimant to provide the account in documents that require a statement of truth. Above all else, it is important to leave the claimant with nowhere else to go or any other explanation. For example, ask the claimant to confirm:

- Whether they already knew the defendant, before providing evidence of friendship lasting many years.
- The full extent of physical capacity, on good and bad days, before disclosing surveillance footage of sporting and DIY exploits.

In *Uttley v Uttley* [2001], the High Court held that it was reasonable for the defendant to delay disclosure of surveillance evidence until after the claimant had disclosed his medical evidence and updated his witness statement supporting his physical limitations. More recently *Hayden v Maidstone & Tunbridge Wells NHS Trust* [2016] confirmed this, with the defendant being given permission to rely upon surveillance evidence, despite it being disclosed just two weeks before trial. Foskett J made it clear in his judgment that the application must, however, be made promptly after the claimant has "pinned his sail to the mast".

There are two schools of thought as to the best approach when repudiating a claim:

- Full, detailed, disclosure presented with a particularised argument as to the position in that claim. The purpose here is to convince the claimant and/or their solicitors (as well as any other professional enablers) that their claim has been significantly undermined and that it has no real prospect of success. Furthermore, by presenting the issues in this way there is the opportunity to pass any litigation risk to the claimant.
- No material disclosure or detailed reasoning as to why the claim is denied. The claimant (or solicitor) does not know what is known. It is not always appropriate to disclose all evidence, as the investigation (into that specific claim and/or others) may be ongoing.

There is no right or wrong way and these strategies are often interchangeable. Remember, the primary goal is to deny the claim, close the file and remove the reserve. The CPR also encourages pre-action disclosure and behaviour that narrows the issues in a case. Therefore, once the claimant is fixed to an account of their claim, the full disclosure of overwhelming repudiatory evidence is preferable.

Should fraud be pleaded?

Alleging fraud can be a serious matter, with consequences for those who are the subject of allegations and those who make them. When defending a claim, a positive allegation of fraud will need to be properly proven at trial.

In *Medcalf v Mardell and others* [2002], Lord Bingham commented that there must be "reasonably credible material establishing a prima facie case of fraud".

However, a defendant may need to advance a positive case in the defence, especially where this is necessary to run certain lines of cross-examination at trial. It can be inappropriate and insufficient to attack the credibility of a claimant when the defence does little more than require the claimant to prove the claim.

Part 16.5 of the CPR requires a defendant to:

- State which allegations the claimant is required to prove
- Deny allegations and give reasons
- State their own version of events.

Further guidance is derived from case law, which has developed over time.

Kearsley v Klarfeld [2005]:

- A defendant does not need to include a substantive allegation of fraud when dealing with a low-velocity impact claim.
- A defendant should set out the full facts from which they would be inviting the court to infer that the claimant could not have been injured.

Hussain v Amin and Charters Insurance Ltd [2012]:

- It is not sufficient or appropriate to plead that the presented claim gives rise to "significant concerns" or defend a claim by insinuation.
- If a defendant wishes to plead fraud they must do so in "clear and unequivocal terms and with proper particulars."

...continued

...continued

Howlett v Davies and Ageas Insurance Ltd [2017]:

- Riding back on *Hussain v Amin*, the Court of Appeal confirmed that an express allegation of fraud or fundamental dishonesty is not required.
- "... the District Judge was entitled to find that the claim was "fundamentally dishonest" and, hence, that CPR 44.16(1) applied. The relevant points were, as it seems to me, adequately foreshadowed in Ageas' defence and sufficiently explored during the oral evidence."

Table 37.3 sets out the pros and cons of pleading fraud.

Table 37.3: Pros and cons of pleading fraud

Pros	Cons
• Fulfils the requirement to plead a positive case. • Can be taken into account in case management directions. • Impact on the claimant and their representatives. • Qualified one-way costs shifting (QOCS) protection can be removed and costs orders can be enforced against the claimant.	• Finding of fraud may invalidate the claimant's funding arrangements (which may frustrate attempts to recover defence costs). • Obligation to prove positive case. • Allocation to multi-track may lead to increased costs.

Fundamental dishonesty

In the second edition of this book this area was identified as one in which to expect significant change and development. There was no clear definition of fundamental dishonesty with lawmakers looking for judicial interpretation. It was considered that a universal definition of fundamental dishonesty would be difficult to arrive at, which appears to have been accurate.

This difficulty arises from there being two principal areas of fundamental dishonesty: firstly, the QOCS fundamental dishonesty in the CPR; and, secondly, s.57 of the Criminal Justice and Courts Act 2015 (CJCA). The way in which fundamental dishonesty is considered by each are different: the CPR looks at the claim, whereas s.57 CJCA considers the actions of the claimant.

What constitutes fundamental dishonesty?

Gosling v Screwfix Direct and another [2014]

The claimant was found to have exaggerated both his ongoing pain and the limitations to his mobility following an operation to his knee. In considering whether this exaggeration constituted fundamental dishonesty, His Honour Judge Moloney QC held:

> “a claimant should not be exposed to costs liability merely because he is shown to have been dishonest as to some collateral matter or perhaps as to some minor, self-contained head of damage. If, on the other hand, the dishonesty went to the root of either the whole of his claim or a substantial part of his claim, then it appears to me that it would be a fundamentally dishonest claim: a claim which depended as to a substantial or important part of itself upon dishonesty.”

continued...

...contnued

In assessing the extent of that dishonesty, HHJ Moloney considered that the claimant had sought to increase the value of his claim by approximately 50% from its true value. The claimant's dishonesty was therefore found to be fundamental as it related to a "very substantial element of his claim".

However, it should not be inferred that 50% exaggeration automatically means a claim is fundamentally dishonest. A court will assess each case on its own merits and may require evidence of a greater or lesser amount of exaggeration.

Creech v Apple Security Group Limited & others [2015]

The issue of fundamental dishonesty in this case arises from the evidence and allegations as to the facts relating to the happening of the accident. Quite simply, the claimant's alleged version of events was not true. The claimant alleged he had fallen over a pile of mats, but the court preferred the evidence of three witnesses who said the mats were not there at the time of the accident. District Judge Rogers said:

> " It is not a case of a court hearing witnesses from both sides and deciding that Car A had strayed further over to one side of the road than the driver of Car A remembered, and having decided the two competing versions on the basis of mistaken recollections. "

This is important in cases where a claimant lies about how an accident occurred so as to attempt to create a favourable position on liability that would not otherwise exist.

Olympic and Paralympic Games (In Liquidation) v Sinfield [2018]

The leading case on the definition of fundamental dishonesty was heard in the High Court on an appeal brought by Kennedys. London Organising Committee for the *Olympic and Paralympic Games (In Liquidation) v Sinfield* [2018] has widened the scope of fundamental dishonesty to dishonest actions which "substantially affect" the presentation of the claim, and in a departure from Moloney HHJ's reasoning, said that the fact that the greater part of the claim may have been genuine was not relevant in determining whether the dishonesty was fundamental.

The dishonesty arose from a claim for gardening services of £15,000, comprising 42% of the special damages claim (and a smaller proportion of the overall claim, which included personal injury). The claimant admitted fabricating invoices and changed his account to admit that he had previously used the gardener but that was a choice; now it was necessary due to his injuries. The Judge at first instance found that the gardening claim had been presented in a muddled, confused and careless way and so the dishonesty did not taint the whole claim.

On appeal, the High Court (Knowles J) disagreed and dismissed the entire claim under Section 57 of the Criminal Justice and Courts Act. He found that the claimant had knowingly made dishonest misrepresentations which could have resulted in the defendant's insurer, Aviva, paying out more than if honest evidence had been presented.

continued...

...continued

In his judgment he stated that fundamental dishonesty pursuant to S57 (1)(b) will be shown if "..the defendant proves on the balance of probabilities that the claimant has acted dishonestly... and that he has thus substantially affected the presentation of his case, either in respect of liability or quantum..." He went on to define "substantially affects" as being "...the same idea as the expressions 'going to the root' or 'going to the heart' of the claim.

He made it clear that findings of fundamental dishonesty will remain fact and claim specific but this provides the first binding definition and has widened the scope to beyond the mathematical interpretation of "fundamental dishonesty" used in *Gosling*.

Practical application of fundamental dishonesty

It remains the case that judges take differing approaches to applications for a finding of fundamental dishonesty and many will be fact-specific. Some judges will list the matter for a directions hearing, with evidence to be served and a mini trial taking place to hear the evidence. Increasingly, however, the approach in *Rouse v Aviva* is being taken with inferences being drawn and findings being made on assessment of the papers.

Rouse v Aviva Insurance Limited [2016]

In this case the court considered whether a finding of fundamental dishonesty could be established without a full trial and hearing evidence.

The claimant had discontinued his claim in the shadow of trial. In doing so he was seeking to take advantage of the costs protection provided by QOCS.

continued...

...continued

On appeal, it was held that an adverse inference could be drawn against the claimant for failing to contest an application for a finding of fundamental dishonesty and that, absent the claimant's engagement in the process, a court could make such a finding on consideration of application on paper and without a hearing.

In a case recently handled by Kennedys an application for fundamental dishonesty was dealt with on the papers by the judge in the absence of the claimants. The judge inferred from their failure to attend that the reason for their discontinuance of their claim shortly after a defence was filed pleading fundamental dishonesty was that the claims were, indeed, dishonest. She set aside the effect of QOCS.

Khan v Rahman & Haven Insurance Limited [2016]

It was held that a finding of fundamental dishonesty could be made within the court's consideration of an application for summary judgment; without a trial of the evidence.

In this Kennedys case the court agreed that any requirement on the defendants to make a separate application under CPR 44.16 would be disproportionate. The judge entered summary judgment based on the written evidence and made a fundamental dishonesty finding permitting the enforcement of an order for costs against the claimant.

Claimants' solicitors frequently come off the court record before the hearing and so we recommend asking them to confirm whether they are instructed to deal with the application and advise them that, in the absence of a response, we will serve their client direct. Filing a certificate of service reduces the risk that a judge will adjourn a hearing if a claimant fails to attend or his solicitors come off the record at the 11th hour. It is also important to ensure that your witnesses are ready to give oral evidence at the first hearing, unless listed as a directions hearing, as that was also a factor in the Kennedys case listed above. Being demonstrably clear and fair to the claimant will be of increasing importance with the number of litigants in person expected to rise and the Supreme Court considering whether the Rules (and penalties for breach) should be considered differently.

Legal mechanisms of fundamental dishonesty

QOCS CPR 44.16

Following the introduction of QOCS, a defendant will recover costs against the claimant in fraud cases where:

- The claim is struck out because the claimant has disclosed no reasonable grounds for bringing the proceedings, the proceedings are an abuse of the court's process, or the conduct of the claimant or a person acting on their behalf (with the claimant's knowledge of such conduct) is likely to obstruct the just disposal of the proceedings (Part 44.15 of the CPR).
- The claim is found on the balance of probabilities to be fundamentally dishonest (Part 44.16 of the CPR).

Part 44.16 of the CPR states that orders for costs made against the claimant may be enforced to the full extent of such orders with the permission of the court where the claim is found on the balance of probabilities to be fundamentally dishonest.

It is an important distinction that the focus of the court is on whether **the claim** is fundamentally dishonest, not specifically the claimant.

s.57 Criminal Justice and Courts Act 2015 (CJCA)

Personal injury claims: cases of fundamental dishonesty

1) This section applies where, in proceedings on a claim for damages in respect of personal injury ("the primary claim")—

   a) the court finds that the claimant is entitled to damages in respect of the claim, but

   b) on an application by the defendant for the dismissal of the claim under this section, the court is satisfied on the balance of probabilities that the claimant has been fundamentally dishonest in relation to the primary claim or a related claim.

2) The court must dismiss the primary claim, unless it is satisfied that the claimant would suffer substantial injustice if the claim were dismissed.

3) The duty under subsection (2) includes the dismissal of any element of the primary claim in respect of which the claimant has not been dishonest.

4) The court's order dismissing the claim must record the amount of damages that the court would have awarded to the claimant in respect of the primary claim but for the dismissal of the claim.

5) When assessing costs in the proceedings, a court which dismisses a claim under this section must deduct the amount recorded in accordance with subsection (4) from the amount which it would otherwise order the claimant to pay in respect of costs incurred by the defendant.

Section 57 of the CJCA came into force on 13 April 2015 and applies to all claims where proceedings have been issued after that date. It permits a court, in a personal injury claim, where it is established that there is some element of genuine loss, to strike out a claimant's entire claim where a finding of fundamental dishonesty has been made "unless it is satisfied that the claimant would suffer substantial injustice".

When making such an order the court will assess the damages that would have been awarded to the claimant, but for the fundamental dishonesty finding. The claimant will be ordered to pay the defendant's costs less the sum assessed by the court for the genuine element of their claim.

As with the CPR fundamental dishonesty, the CJCA does not define fundamental dishonesty. Legislators have left the specific interpretation to be developed by the courts. The same lack of certainty surrounds the issue of "substantial injustice".

How section 57 works

Consider the following example:

- Following a road traffic accident a claim is presented for personal injury damages (minor whiplash, lasting 12 months) and loss of earnings (totalling £50,000). Defence investigation reveals that the claim for loss of earnings is entirely false.
- A successful application is made to strike out the claim. The court awards £10,000 in defence costs and assesses the genuine whiplash claim at £3,500.
- The claimant receives no compensation, the claim having been struck out.
- The defendant is entitled to receive £6,500 from the claimant (£10,000 minus £3,500, being the value of the genuine claim).

The focus of the CJCA is whether **the claimant** has been fundamentally dishonest in respect of the primary claim or any related claim. This is useful when dealing with issues such as bogus occupancy where the claimant (who, it may be accepted, was present in the vehicle) supports the ("related") claim of someone who was not. This can also be applied in claims of exaggerated loss, credit hire, etc. where the claimant is demonstrably and fundamentally dishonest.

It was anticipated that as s.57 CJCA operates as a defence in law to a genuine loss, then such matters would be expected to be pleaded by the party seeking to exercise that statutory right.

However, this is also a developing area where the courts are prepared to accept that fraudulent behaviour, being covert, does not always allow the defendant to present this type of case at the stage that pleadings are settled. This has recently been endorsed by the Court of Appeal in *Howlett v Davies & Ageas* [2017] in relation to a finding of fundamental dishonesty in respect of the application of CPR 44.16. Insofar as s.57 is concerned, there are two cases of interest in respect of the Act's application:

Hanif v Patel [2016]

In this case the court did not require the defendant to have pleaded fundamental dishonesty or that the sanction as prescribed by the CJCA would be sought:

> "... I recognise that the defendant's insurers have not expressly pleaded fraud and they have not taken it upon themselves any onus of providing it. However, if on proper assessment of the evidence, it leads me to the clear conclusion that the claimant has attempted to lie to me and mislead the court and present bogus evidence as part of his statement (and I am satisfied that it does) it must in my judgment lead the court to striking out his claim."

Hughes, Kingdon & Jones v KGM [2016]

Another case where the scope has been widened for defendants. The judge was happy to accept an oral application after the trial had been completed and the judgment given and to provide a finding of fundamental dishonesty.

Two of the claimants were found to have suffered minor injuries valued at £750 from what was only a very minor incident (the third having been procedurally struck out before trial). These injuries were at odds with those presented in the claimants' cases.

The claims were struck out with costs for the defendant, less the offset for the genuine aspects of the claim.

It should be noted that s.57 will only be relevant where there is a genuine loss suffered by the claimant. If the claim is entirely fabricated (i.e. no accident ever occurred) and there is no loss, then the issue of whether the claim or claimant is "fundamentally dishonest" is superfluous. It is simply fraudulent. Existing provision within the CPR, supported by the principles established in case law such as *Summers*, would be the basis for striking out and defeating such a claim.

Not every claim where there are contradictory cases will be fundamentally dishonest. Litigants will often hold positions in cases where both versions of events cannot be true. As a matter of best practice, going back to the definitions of fraud set out at the beginning of this chapter will assist in drawing the distinction between an honest dispute over facts to one where there is a deliberate and false representation intending to benefit that person to the detriment of another.

Deter

A number of measures are now in place that act as a deterrence to the problem of insurance fraud. These are designed to be both preventative (e.g. data-sharing) and punitive (criminal and civil sanctions).

Insurance Fraud Register

The Association of British Insurers, in conjunction with the Insurance Fraud Bureau, introduced the Insurance Fraud Register (IFR) in November 2013. This is the first industry-wide database of known insurance fraudsters. The IFR lists the individuals who have been detected acting fraudulently toward insurers, whether in the process of applying for/renewing insurance cover or when making a claim.

The IFR is designed to help insurers identify whether individuals have committed insurance fraud. They can then take appropriate action at the point of sale, the renewal of a policy or when a claim is made, with the intention of stopping fraud as early as possible.

Criminal sanctions

Insurance Fraud Bureau (IFB)

The IFB was established as a member levy, funded cross-industry, for insurers to share intelligence and undertake collaborative investigation of organised motor insurance fraud.

The remit and membership of the IFB has expanded with fraud investigation and intelligence relevant to multiple lines of business undertaken and with members from insurance, corporates and legal and investigation supply chain, via the Affiliate Membership scheme. Kennedys are IFB Affiliate members.

Since its inception up to the end October 2017, the IFB have contributed to 1,229 arrests resulting in 498.3 years of prison time.

Insurance Fraud Enforcement Department (IFED)

The IFED was set up in 2012. It comprises a specialist police unit dedicated to tackling insurance fraud, is funded by ABI members and is based at the City of London Police Economic Crime Directorate. IFED comprises a team of detectives and financial investigators who act with operational independence while sharing information with insurers.

In August 2014, IFED reported that its investigations had resulted in 500 arrests since its establishment.

Perjury

Perjury is governed by the Perjury Act 1911. Section 1 states:

> “If any person lawfully sworn as a witness or as an interpreter in a judicial proceeding wilfully makes a statement material in that proceeding, which he knows to be false or does not believe to be true, he shall be guilty of perjury… ”

Perjury relates to sworn evidence by a party or witness at trial. A deliberate attempt to give false evidence is a criminal offence that carries a maximum sentence of seven years' imprisonment.

Contempt of court

Part 32.14 of the CPR allows for a person to be prosecuted where they make, or cause to be made, a false statement in a document verified by a statement of truth, in circumstances where they do not have an honest belief in its truth.

In order to succeed, the applicant must prove contempt to the criminal standard. They must prove beyond all reasonable doubt, in respect of each statement:

- The falsity of the statement in question.
- The statement has, or if persisted in would be likely to have, interfered with the course of justice in some material respect.

- At the time it was made, the maker of the statement had no honest belief in the truth of the statement and knew of its likelihood to interfere with the course of justice.

The process of bringing proceedings for contempt of court has been streamlined under Part 81 of the CPR. The sanctions include both fines and imprisonment (up to two years).

While contempt of court proceedings can sometimes be expensive, courts are showing a real willingness to impose custodial sentences in circumstances where there is compelling evidence that a claimant has signed a false statement of truth.

Private prosecutions

Insurers also have the ability to commence private prosecutions, rather than leaving this to the police or Crown Prosecution Service. This right is preserved by s.6 of the Prosecution of Offences Act 1985.

While there are a number of offences that require the prior specific consent of the Director of Public Prosecutions or the Attorney General to prosecute, offences under the Fraud Act 2006 or Theft Act 1968 do not require specific permission and might therefore be attractive to insurers.

All Fraud Act offences can be tried by either the Crown Court or the magistrates' court. The maximum sentence that the magistrates are able to pass is six months for one offence and a total of 12 months for two offences.

If the matter is heard at the Crown Court, the maximum sentence is 10 years' imprisonment. However, much would depend upon the extent of the fraud and whether any mitigating or aggravating factors are present.

A party bringing a private prosecution will normally not face any costs liability. If the prosecution fails, costs can normally be recovered from central funds. Conversely, if the prosecution succeeds, the prosecuting party may seek recovery of its costs (including investigation costs) directly from the criminal defendant, and in default, central funds. In cases where monies have been fraudulently received and/or where the criminal act was part of a criminal enterprise or lifestyle, recovery of monies can be pursued by way of a compensation order or under the Proceeds of Crime Act 2002.

Civil sanctions

Adverse costs orders

It is an unfortunate fact that many individuals who pursue fraudulent insurance claims are not wealthy. Few will have significant assets and many will not find it easy to meet an adverse costs order.

Most fraudsters will pursue their claim on a no-win no-fee basis, believing that if it does not succeed, the defendant's costs will be paid by the after-the-event (ATE) insurer. However, a defence pleading fraud often causes the ATE provider to withdraw indemnity. This leaves the claimant with no protection should the case fail.

Fraud cases often see considerable costs incurred. Insurers understandably view success without recovery in such cases to be a somewhat pyrrhic victory.

Some insurers use recovery actions as a form of deterrent. Being visited by bailiffs, surrendering assets, facing bankruptcy and having charging orders placed over property can have a devastating impact on an individual and sends out a strong message that fraud will not be tolerated.

A claim in the tort of deceit

Bringing a claim for damages in the tort of deceit can present a tactical advantage to an insurer. The damages recoverable if the claim succeeds can be considerable and do not require the claimant to have issued proceedings. The losses for which compensation can be sought include:

- **Repayment of sums already paid:** an action against the claimant for repayment of interim payments, including where payment is made to another who is not party to the original claim.

- **Exemplary damages:** such damages are intended to be punitive. They are a punishment to the claimant and significant sums can be awarded. In *Rookes v Barnard* [1964] Lord Devlin commented:

  > “Exemplary damages are essentially different from ordinary damages. The object of damages in the usual sense of the term is to compensate. The object of exemplary damages is to punish and deter ... Exemplary damages can properly be awarded whenever it is necessary to teach a wrongdoer that tort does not pay ... In a case in which exemplary damages are appropriate, a jury should be directed that if, but only if, the sum which they have in mind to award as compensation ... is inadequate to punish him for his outrageous conduct, to mark their disapproval of such conduct and to deter him from repeating it, then it can award some larger sum.”

- Costs of defending the claim: these are the costs incurred in maintaining the repudiation and/or settling of certain parts of the claim before the deceit was uncovered.

- Internal investigation costs: it is often the case that insurers have dealt with the case for some time and investigated the claim to show the claimant's deceit.

Re-opening a claim and setting aside settlements

Fraud is covert. Uncovering fraud can happen at any stage, even after a claim has been concluded.

Unpicking a compromise or the contract that is formed when parties settle a claim is possible, but only in specific circumstances. One of these is where the contract is established on the misrepresentations of one of the contracting parties and those misrepresentations are relied upon to the detriment of the receiving party.

Hayward v Zurich Insurance Company plc [2016]

This case was decided by the Supreme Court and is the leading case in setting aside a compromised claim.

In this case the insurer suspected that the claim may have been fraudulent but felt that this could not be proven at trial. The claim was settled and subsequently evidence of the fraud came to light.

In finding for the defendant the Supreme Court held that there is no need for the insurer to have believed that the claim was genuine when they settled it; it was entitled to set aside the settlement because it did not know that it was false.

Suspicion or a qualified belief that a misrepresentation had been made did not prevent the insurer from setting aside the award. Toulson LJ stated that the question of whether the insurer was induced by the misrepresentation to settle the claim was fact-specific. It was accepted by the court that the insurer was induced to make the settlement by the risk that the misrepresentation may have been believed by the court.

These cases will always turn on their own facts. The court ruled that had they known that the claimant had lied when they settled the case, the insurer would not have been allowed to set the award aside.

It is always important therefore to be able to demonstrate that the evidence being relied upon to prove fraud has only become available after the settlement of the claim.

Conclusion

Fraud is a complex and highly strategic area of claims process and handling. The response to fraud is multifaceted, involving ever-advancing technology, tools and thinking.

However, what has been, and will always be, at the heart of a fraud strategy is the skill, experience and wit of claims handlers. The need to understand fraud, at least to some degree, is required whatever an individual's role in claims handling.

38 Evidence gathering and negotiation

Evidence gathering: Laura Siddall
Negotiation: Greg Woods

- Gathering evidence effectively
- What makes good evidence?
- Basic principles behind effective negotiation
- The key stages of negotiation
- Best alternative to a negotiated settlement

Evidence gathering

A large part of handling claims is assessing the evidence to reach a decision on liability and quantum, but before the evidence can be assessed it must be obtained.

While most clients will provide some basic evidence at the outset (such as the accident report form) this will, in most cases, be insufficient to make an informed decision on liability and quantum.

In this chapter we aim to:

- Explain the importance of gathering evidence
- Provide some guidance about the type of evidence to gather
- Give some helpful tips and advice on how to go about collecting evidence
- Explain how the evidence will be used (by opponents, solicitors and the court)
- Explain what constitutes the 'best evidence'.

Why is evidence important?

It is highly unlikely that a claims handler will have first-hand knowledge of the circumstances that give rise to a claim and may have little more than the letter of claim or claim notification form (CNF). This ought to provide a basic statement of circumstances, from the claimant's point of view, but there will rarely be any evidence provided to support the claimant's description of the accident (or issue) giving rise to the claim.

The first reason why it is important to gather evidence is, therefore, to provide further information to assess liability.

In almost all defendant claims, one of the pre-action protocols that supplement the Civil Procedure Rules will apply. These set out timeframes in which the claimant's solicitors must be provided with a decision on liability. Since the introduction of the Pre-action

Protocol for Low Value Personal Injury Claims in Road Traffic Accidents and the Pre-action Protocol for Low Value Personal Injury (Employers' Liability and Public Liability) Claims the timeframe for providing decisions on liability in claims under those protocols is very short:

- 15 days for road traffic accident (RTA) claims
- 30 days for employers' liability claims
- 40 days for public liability claims.

Other protocols provide varying time limits in which to provide a response but it is still essential that the process of gathering evidence is commenced as soon as possible after receipt of a letter of claim or CNF.

Once the evidence is gathered, a decision on liability must be made and the claimant's solicitors informed of the decision. If liability is denied then this must be justified to the claimant's solicitors.

Each of the pre-action protocols requires the parties to "disclose key documents relevant to the issues in dispute" to allow them to:

- Understand each other's position
- Make decisions about how to proceed
- Try to settle the issues without proceedings.

It is, therefore, essential that evidence is gathered not only to assist in making a decision on liability, but also because the Civil Procedure Rules require disclosure of such evidence to the claimant's solicitors.

Failure to provide relevant documentation could result in an application for pre-action disclosure. Further failure to provide relevant documentation, or any explanation for why that documentation is not available to the court, is likely to lead to an order for that documentation be served within a short period of time (usually 14 days) and an order to pay the costs of the claimant's application.

The person who asserts a fact must provide evidence to prove it (unless that fact is admitted by their opponent). It is, therefore, essential to take the obligation to gather and exchange evidence seriously. It is insufficient to accept what the client says at face value. The court and claimant will require the defendant to prove any assertion.

What evidence should be sought?

Relevant evidence in any case will be fact dependent. It is, therefore, not possible to provide a comprehensive list of documents that will be relevant to every given case.

However, for those dealing with personal injury claims the Pre-action Protocol for Personal Injury Claims includes helpful lists of the types of documents that might be relevant in different types of claims. The lists are available at:

http://www.justice.gov.uk/courts/procedure-rules/civil/protocol/prot_pic#C

These lists are not exhaustive (although they are extensive) and it is important to consider the facts of each case when reflecting upon what other documents might be relevant in the circumstances. Consider, in particular, whether it would assist all parties to have a plan, photographs or even a video of the accident location or the relevant process to understand the accident circumstances better.

How to gather evidence – starting point

The starting point should be the letter of claim or CNF and the accident investigation report prepared by the defendant.

It may be helpful to produce a table or flow chart to help consider:

- What assertions or allegations have been made by either the claimant or defendant
- What documents might prove or disprove those assertions
- What witnesses might help to investigate those assertions.

Example 1

Following receipt of a CNF in which the claimant alleges that she was a customer visiting the defendant's cash and carry warehouse when she slipped on a wet floor, the investigation table may look something like this:

Assertion or statement of fact made	Documents which might be relevant	Witnesses I might want to speak to
The claimant says she was visiting the defendant's premises on 1 October 2016.	• Accident Report/First Aid Report. Did the claimant report the accident immediately? • Visitor's book. If the accident was not reported at the time, is there other evidence that the claimant was there? • CCTV. Does this show the accident or the claimant entering the warehouse?	• Staff working on the day of the alleged accident. Did they see the accident or did they see the claimant in the warehouse?
• The claimant says the floor was wet.	• Accident Report/ Investigation. Does that record that the floor was wet? • Cleaning records. Had the floor just been cleaned, could it have still been wet as a result?	• Person who carried out the accident investigation. Did they check the floor themselves to see if it was wet? • First aider. What did the claimant tell them about the accident circumstances? Did the claimant mention the wet floor immediately after the accident or did they say something else about why they fell?

The insured say they have a reasonable system of cleaning and inspection.	• Risk assessments/systems of work for cleaning/housekeeping. Do they cover the task in question? Were they in force at the time of the accident? • Cleaning records for the day of the accident. Are they fully completed? Who completed them? Do they show that the system had been adhered to? • Training records for the housekeeper/cleaner. Is there evidence that the cleaner had been trained to follow the system?	• The warehouse manager. What is the system for cleaning and inspection? • The cleaner/housekeeper who is responsible for cleaning/inspecting the shop floor. What exactly did they do on the day in question? If they can't remember what they did on the day are they able to confirm what they would ordinarily do/what system they adopt?

It is important to identify which piece or pieces of evidence will make the difference between defending the claim and admitting liability. If that crucial piece of evidence is missing, then there is little point in wasting time searching for ancillary evidence since liability will still have to be conceded.

How to gather evidence – consider what has been received

Ensure that all documents received from the defendant are carefully considered. This may be stating the obvious, but it is important to consider whether these documents open up new lines of enquiry such as:

- Do they refer to other, as yet unseen, documents?
- Do the dates on the documents indicate that they were in force at the time of the accident? Cases often rely upon a safe system of work or risk assessment that postdates the accident. The post-accident risk assessments and safe systems of work may well be relevant (to evidence changes that have been made post-accident), but the version that was in force at the time of the accident is important and must be obtained.
- Do the documents identify potential witnesses who have not yet been spoken to?

How to gather evidence – drilling down

It is important to drill down into the evidence. Do not take statements made in an accident investigation or any other document at face value.

Example 2

A customer claims that they slipped on a wet floor at the defendant's retail premises at 2.30 p.m. The accident investigation report says: "The floor was cleaned at 2 p.m. – half an hour before the accident." It may appear that you have good grounds for denying liability but when drilling down into that statement things may prove less straightforward. There are a number of potential scenarios here:

1) A copy of the cleaning log and conversation with the cleaner confirms that he cleans the shop floor and immediately completes the cleaning log. He is happy to provide a statement about how he carries out the cleaning.

2) The person who completed the accident investigation report says that he saw the cleaner cleaning the area in question at 2 p.m.

3) The person who completed the accident investigation report tells you that another member of staff has told them that they saw the cleaner carrying out the cleaning.

4) The person who completed the accident investigation report says that they presume that the cleaner would have cleaned the floor at 2 p.m. because that is what time it is usually cleaned, but there is no cleaning log to confirm this and the cleaner has now left (even if the cleaner is still employed he is unlikely to be able to recall accurately what time he cleaned the floor months or even years earlier).

5) A copy of the cleaning log is provided and the cleaner is still employed but he states he always completes the cleaning log at the end of the day and estimates what time he carried out the cleaning.

6) A copy of the cleaning log is provided which records that the floor was cleaned at 2 p.m. but the cleaner was subsequently dismissed for falsifying his cleaning logs.

...continued

...continued

Of the above six scenarios, scenario 1 is the most compelling in terms of proving that the cleaning was carried out at 2 p.m. since both the contemporaneous cleaning log and a witness statement support the contention.

Even better would be a combination of scenarios 1 and 2, as this would provide first-hand evidence from the cleaner who completed the contemporaneous log and corroborative evidence from other witnesses who saw him doing the cleaning.

Scenario 3 is, at present, hearsay evidence. It is one person reporting what someone else told them they saw. A statement from the person who saw the cleaner carrying out the cleaning at 2 p.m. is reasonably strong evidence. However, if that person is no longer contactable then there is only a second-hand account of whether and when the cleaning was carried out.

Scenarios 4 and 5 are not compelling since the evidence involves individuals making assumptions or guesses about when the cleaning was carried out. Faced with these scenarios, liability can be denied but consideration given to making an offer to reflect the litigation risk.

Scenario 6 is likely to create a struggle to convince the claimant's solicitors or the court that the cleaning was in fact carried out at 2 p.m. (or at all) since it casts doubt on the credibility of the individual who created the document and in turn the credibility of the document itself.

Example 3

A claim is received from an employee. The claimant claims that he injured his back while lifting heavy boxes and that he had not received any manual handling training. The defendant maintains that the claimant had received manual handling training and it is appropriate to speak to the claimant's supervisor. The scenarios could be:

1) The claimant's supervisor is adamant that all staff are trained. There are no documents to prove this and he can't remember when exactly the claimant received his manual handling training but he is pretty sure it was before the accident and he is prepared to provide a statement to that effect.

2) The claimant's supervisor provides a sheet of paper headed "manual handling training" which the claimant has signed. The supervisor states that staff are asked to sign the piece of paper after they have had their training. The piece of paper is the only evidence of the training. It is not dated. The person who provided the training has left.

3) The claimant's supervisor provides a sheet of paper headed "manual handling training" which the claimant has signed. The document is dated 10 years before the accident. The supervisor provided the training and is prepared to provide a statement to confirm that he provided the training to the claimant.

4) The claimant's supervisor provides a sheet of paper headed "manual handling training". It lists an initial manual handling training session 10 years before the accident and annual refresher training. It is signed by the claimant. In addition the claimant's supervisor provides a copy of the handouts provided to the claimant during that training and a copy of the video shown to the claimant during the training.

...continued

...continued

In terms of proving that the claimant had received suitable and sufficient manual handling training prior to the accident, scenario 4 is clearly the strongest evidence since it demonstrates that the claimant has received regular training, the dates he received the training and evidences what the training consisted of.

Scenario 3 is weaker in that it proves the claimant received some training many years ago but it is unlikely that reliable, detailed evidence about what the training consisted of is available.

Scenarios 1 and 2 are very weak evidentially and are unlikely to persuade a judge that the claimant had received suitable and sufficient manual handling training.

The above examples illustrate how a simple statement, such as "The floor was cleaned prior to the accident" or "The claimant had received training", could mean a number of different things and may or may not stand up to scrutiny. It is essential that such bald statements are not taken at face value and that they are properly investigated to establish what is meant by such statements and what evidence is available to corroborate those statements.

Best evidence

When collating evidence it is important to consider what will be the best evidence of the facts in support of the defendant's case:

- Contemporaneous documents are more persuasive than documents prepared weeks, months or even years after the event. Looking at Example 2 above, a cleaning log prepared by the cleaner as he goes along is likely to be much more reliable as evidence of the time cleaning took place than a statement from the cleaner prepared six months later.

- Do not rely on hearsay evidence. Hearsay in simple terms is second-hand evidence where the witness is not telling what they know personally but what others have said to them. The court will only consider hearsay evidence if the party wishing to rely upon the hearsay evidence serves notice that they intend to rely upon it. In addition, hearsay evidence is generally given less weight by the court than first-hand evidence. Consider the following examples:
    - "I put out wet floor signs." This is a first-hand account of what the person making the statement did. Not hearsay.
    - "I saw the cleaner put out wet floor signs." This is a first-hand account of what the person making the statement saw someone else do. Not hearsay.
    - "When I completed my accident investigation I asked the cleaner if he had put out wet floor signs and he told me that he had." This is first-hand evidence of the content of the conversation with the cleaner, but hearsay evidence that the signs had actually been put out.
    - "When I completed my accident investigation I spoke to the store manager and she told me that she had spoken to the cleaner and the cleaner had told her that he had put out wet floor signs." This is second-hand hearsay evidence. It is one person's account of a conversation that they were not a party to.

The first two examples here are good evidence about whether wet floor signs were put out or not. The third and fourth examples are hearsay evidence about whether signs were put out or not and are unlikely to be given any weight by the judge. You should always attempt to obtain direct evidence of the facts. Hearsay evidence will always be less credible than direct evidence. Be careful to establish what type of evidence is being presented. Is it genuinely direct evidence?

- Opinion evidence. The general rule is that only suitably qualified expert witnesses may give opinion evidence. However, under the Civil Evidence Act 1972 a non-expert witness can give opinion evidence which, "if made as a way of conveying relevant facts personally perceived by him, is admissible as evidence of what he perceived". Consider the following examples:
  - A non-expert witness says: "The floor didn't seem to be slippery when I walked across it moments before the accident." This is evidence of what the witness perceived.
  - Contrast that with a non-expert witness saying: "The floor has a high slip-resistance when wet." This is expert evidence and would only be allowed from a qualified engineer who has carried out formal slip testing of the flooring. It is not evidence of what the witness perceived at the time.

How to address concerns regarding data protection

Companies are often concerned about falling foul of the Data Protection Act 1998 (DPA) and may refuse to provide documents from the claimant's personnel or occupational health file without a signed form of authority.

While it may be possible to obtain a signed form of authority from the claimant this will inevitably cause delay and is unnecessary.

Section 35 DPA states that:

"(1) Personal data are exempt from the non-disclosure provisions where the disclosure is required by or under any enactment, by any rule of law or by the order of a court.

(2) Personal data are exempt from the non-disclosure provisions where the disclosure is necessary—

(a) for the purpose of, or in connection with, any legal proceedings (including prospective legal proceedings), or

(b) for the purpose of obtaining legal advice,

or is otherwise necessary for the purposes of establishing, exercising or defending legal rights."

Therefore, where the disclosure is required for the purposes of legal proceedings, prospective legal proceedings or to obtain legal advice, it is not necessary for the client to obtain the employee's consent to disclose the personal information. However, only information which is relevant to the legal proceedings/prospective legal proceedings/legal advice should be disclosed.

A client who is concerned about disclosing documents without a form of authority should be referred to s. 35 DPA and reassured that they are able to disclose documents that are relevant to the claimant's claim (including in relation to causation of the injuries).

Occupation health professionals employed by the defendant are often highly reluctant to release occupational health records, believing that a signed form of authority from the claimant is always required, whatever the circumstances. It is possible that their professional body has advised them that this is the case. While we do not believe that is correct, in light of s. 35 DPA, practically speaking, the records may simply not be released without a signed form of authority.

It is, therefore, sensible to send forms of authority out to the claimant (via their solicitor) at the outset to avoid potential delays caused by a refusal to release records without the claimant's authority.

Privilege

The meaning and application of so-called legal professional privilege would require its own chapter. Here, focus is on the creation of documents made "in contemplation of litigation".

If a claims inspector is instructed by the claims handler to go to the site, take photographs and obtain statements, the claims inspector's report and any documents they produce will have been prepared in contemplation of litigation; i.e. the claims inspector has only produced them because a claim has been made (or it was anticipated that a claim was about to be made) and with the intention of assisting the claims handler to assess liability.

Because these documents have been "prepared in contemplation of litigation" they do not have to be disclosed to the claimant (or any other party to the litigation). The documents are "privileged from inspection".

It may be that the documents that have been produced, in particular photographs, plans or witness statements, support your denial of liability and a decision may, therefore, be made to send the claimant's solicitors a copy of those documents. This is known as waiving privilege. However, once privilege has been waived it is impossible to later claim privilege over that document. Waiving privilege is, therefore, an important decision that should be carefully made.

In summary

- Consider what is needed to be prove to successfully defend the claim, then consider what evidence might be available to prove that.
- Consider what the crucial piece of evidence will be. If that is missing, consider whether there is any point in continuing the search for other ancillary evidence or whether liability should be conceded immediately.
- Read the documents provided. Do they refer to other documents, witnesses or lines of enquiry not previously identified? Were the documents relevant/in force at the time of the incident in question?
- Drill down into the evidence provided. Speak to the individuals who created the documents you have been provided with. Are the documents clear and unambiguous or are they open to interpretation? If open to interpretation, investigate further.

- Is there a contemporaneous document or statement to support the assertions being made by the defendant or to disprove the assertions being made by the claimant?
- Do not rely on hearsay evidence. Wherever possible, speak to the person who is able to provide a first-hand account of events.
- Avoid opinion evidence from anyone other than an expert witness instructed pursuant to Part 35 of the Civil Procedure Rules.
- Be aware of the provisions of the DPA, in particular, the exception provided by s. 35 of the Act.
- Consider whether the documents received have been prepared "in contemplation of litigation". Consider whether withholding disclosure of those documents is legitimate. Consider carefully whether to disclose them anyway and "waive privilege".

Effective negotiation

Introduction

This book is designed to be a guide for claims handlers. Its chapters cover many aspects of the law and it is intended to help handlers understand core legal principles and apply that knowledge to their work effectively across a range of legal scenarios.

Whatever type of claim is being dealt with, at some point the claims handler will be called upon to negotiate. In fact, negotiation forms a central part of the claims handler's role.

Some consider that "effective negotiation" is not something that can be taught. Most recognise, however, that some people are better negotiators than others. If so, why is that? What techniques are employed, consciously or unconsciously, that enable them to reach better results in the negotiation of claims than others?

Negotiation is part of life

We all negotiate. Which channel should the family watch? When should the central heating be put on? What pay rise do I think I am entitled to? Negotiation is woven into everyone's daily life and people have different styles of negotiation:

- Aggressive
- Collaborative
- Empathetic
- Short-sighted
- Strategic.

This is not an exhaustive list. Negotiation style is influenced by personality and experience. Different styles may be adopted in different contexts and at different times.

Good negotiators are able to recognise their personal style, understand their opponent's style and learn what works and what doesn't through experience.

Claims negotiation

The techniques discussed in this chapter are not exclusive to the negotiation of claims, but will, of course, focus on that particular context.

We will consider, firstly, some basic principles to bear in mind when entering negotiation.

We will then map the stages of negotiation.

Finally, we list some 'top tips' for effective negotiation.

Basic principles

- **Your opponent is a person**

Your opponent is still more likely to be a human being than a computer algorithm. That means they will come to the negotiation with 'baggage'. They will have a boss and a client they may want to impress. They may have a particular style or approach that they use in all negotiations. They may take the view that, as a claimant's solicitor, they are 'on the side of the angels' and the defendant's representatives are the opposite. They will have targets to meet. They may have cash flow issues. They may be aggressive, patronising, poorly prepared, tired or overworked.

It is important to separate the 'person' issues from the substance of the negotiation. This is true both because 'person' issues can be a distraction and because a better understanding of your opponent, as a human being, may reveal opportunities for settlement which would otherwise be undisclosed, or may cause you to alter your strategy. Is there, for example, particular pressure on the opponent to settle claims at a particular point in the litigation cycle? Is your opponent one who simply won't address their mind to properly valuing the claim until counsel provides an advice? Are they impossible to have a constructive discussion with such that a mediation might prove more effective?

Try to avoid allowing an opponent's temperament to distract focus away from the substance of the negotiation. Don't react to emotional outbursts, which can easily push negotiations off track and delay resolution.

It can be helpful to allow them to 'let off steam' – they may be frustrated by a perceived delay in dealing with a claim, or simply not understand why their demands are not being agreed to. It can be very effective to listen quietly, without responding to their attacks, encouraging your opponent to 'get it all out' rather than leave issues to fester. This approach may reveal misunderstandings on the part of your opponent that can be addressed (for example: our recommended OT provider is genuinely independent; the data to be able to agree loss of earnings is currently unavailable, but is being obtained). It should also show your opponent that you are a calm individual keen to negotiate on the substance of the claim rather than be distracted by 'fireworks'.

We all have a tendency to hear what we want to hear and filter out what we do not. Good communication lies at the heart of effective negotiation. Develop the skills of a good listener. That involves taking good notes, clarifying ambiguity ("do you mean...?) and asking sensible questions ("who is providing the care you say your client needs?", "What precisely is it about your client's injuries that mean he is unable to continue as a warehouseman?").

A negotiator who is both a good listener and focused on substance rather than personality will:

- Encourage the opponent to believe there is scope for constructive negotiation.
- Identify those issues which genuinely divide the parties.

- Stand a better chance of understanding the unspoken motivations of their opponent (is the claimant more interested in returning to work than maximising compensation?).
- Be better able to build a working relationship that endures throughout the claim and on other shared cases.
- Reach a mutually acceptable resolution more quickly.

- **Conduct negotiations ethically.**

Negotiations should always be conducted on an ethical basis.

Precisely what that means in practice is worth considering, given that there is a shared understanding between those negotiating a claim, where both are professionals acting on behalf of a client, that a negotiation may involve a degree of misdirection and that comments made will likely fall short of being a 'warts and all' presentation of their case.

It is easier to start with the obvious. An ethical negotiator does not lie. Even that statement bears further consideration, however.

Compare these two statements:

- *"The defendant has told us that your client's position in the company is secure"* (when the company has advised that they intend to terminate his employment as soon as the claim is settled).
- *"Your claim is worth no more than £35,000"* (when you think that it could be worth £75,000).

The first statement is a clear lie about a factual issue. The second could be characterised as a lie, but falls more in the realms of opinion. There may be a credible explanation as to why £35,000 is an equitable settlement, even though you believe a court may allow a higher figure. You might think a court could award more, but it falls into a range of possible valuations.

There is a shared understanding, between professional representatives, that a negotiation involves advancing settlement figures that may not reflect the party's final position or even be what they consider to be a realistic position, although advancing unrealistic proposals is unlikely to be an effective negotiation strategy.

Furthermore, an ethical approach to negotiation does not mean volunteering potentially adverse information.

Never allow a natural desire to secure a negotiated settlement that is better than your 'bottom line' figure to tempt you to mislead your negotiating partner with false information. Far better, in the long run, to develop a reputation as an honest and ethical negotiator than to sacrifice that reputation for the sake of short-term gain. It is possible to want to 'win' too much.

- **Consider the underlying interests**

In a well-regarded book on negotiation, *Getting to Yes* by Roger Fisher and William Ury (Random House Business Books 2012), the authors encourage negotiators to focus on the parties' interests rather than their positions:

"Your position is something you have decided upon. Your interests are what caused you so to decide."

They give an example: imagine two men quarrelling in a library. One wants the window open and the other wants it closed. The librarian asks one why he wants the window open: *"to get some fresh air."* She asks the other why he wants it closed: *"To avoid a draught."* After thinking for a minute, she opens wide a window in the next room, bringing in fresh air without a draught.

The stated positions were irreconcilable. One wanted it open and the other wanted it closed. It was only when their interests were clarified that a resolution could be achieved.

The same approach should be adopted in negotiation. For example, the stated position of the claimant's solicitor may be that his client wants £250,000 to settle the claim. The claimant's interests, however, may be in rapid recovery from, or diminution of, symptoms sufficient to permit a return to work. Liability may be in dispute, but modest expenditure on therapy at an early stage might address the underlying interests of both sides.

Of course, both sides may have multiple interests underpinning their stated positions. Focusing on 'interests' rather than 'positions' moves the negotiation away from the zero-sum 'win/lose' game, to the mutual search for a solution that satisfies both parties' interests.

The stages of negotiation

Preparation

Remember the old army maxim: PPPPP ("Proper Preparation Prevents Poor Performance" is one version; there is another, less printable, one)? It is as true in the context of negotiation as it is in any other walk of life.

Here is a suggested approach to your preparation:

- **Facts, law and procedures**

Ensure that you have a thorough knowledge of the facts in dispute, the relevant law and procedures.

Think: what is the legal context? What are the legal duties my client owed the claimant? Do I understand them clearly? If not, is assistance from a senior colleague necessary or perhaps some research (or consult this book!). Are there facts to clarify by further investigation, before I can understand the legal position properly (and before launching into negotiation)?

When negotiating a personal injury claim, it is essential to consider the authorities carefully (eg. JC Guidelines, Kemp) and have them to hand. Ensure that you understand how to compute past and future losses under the various heads of loss. Is there sufficient information to calculate pre-accident average earnings? If not, can that information be obtained easily? If not, what estimate is appropriate and on what basis? If dealing with future losses, are you comfortable applying the Ogden Tables? Can you manipulate multipliers and adjustment factors appropriately? Helpful software may carry out the calculations, but not understanding the process creates *vulnerability* in negotiation.

The aim here is to understand the legal context in which the claim sits properly and to be able to reach a sensible, defensible valuation of the claim. If challenged, what evidence can be relied upon to justify that position? Be clear in your own mind what that is.

Some heads of loss may be capable of agreement with little difficulty. It may simply be a question of ensuring that both sides have done the maths correctly. Others will be open to dispute and it is in these spaces that skilful negotiators operate.

Identify those elements, whether relating to liability or quantum, which are open to reasonable debate. Begin to formulate credible 'best' and 'worst' case positions, the worst case position being that which, if not agreed, will result in a breakdown in the negotiation (of which more below).

Despite the fact that almost all claims settle at some point without going to trial, *the claims handler must attempt to anticipate what view a judge would take of the evidence and what value that judge would place on the claim.*

Research thoroughly!

Strengths and weaknesses

Before picking up the telephone, draw up a list of the strengths and weaknesses of both side's cases. This can help negotiation considerably.

It is not unusual for people to overestimate their strengths and underestimate their weaknesses. What is required here is a sober analysis. It can help to consider the position from the perspective of your opponent, looking at your case from outside. What would concern you? How would you seek to undermine your own valuations?

You may already have a reasonable idea of the claim that is being advanced by the claimant. Consider each element of the claim and test it. Probe for weaknesses.

Take a claim for care and assistance. Consider, for example:

- Does it appear overstated?
- Is it supported by the medical evidence?
- Is the rate applied in line with the Local Authority Spinal Point 8 Rates (as conveniently set out in the latest edition of Sweet & Maxwell's *"Facts and Figures – Tables for the Calculation of Damages"*).
- Has a discount been applied to reflect the fact that the care was provided on a non-commercial basis, by members of the family? (Typically 20–25%)
- Does it fail to reflect evidence of recovery, in medical evidence or witness statements, or the medical expert's prognosis?

Take a claim that the claimant was not provided with training before using the work equipment. Consider, for example:

- Is there documentary evidence to the contrary?
- How compelling is it? Is it a training record signed by the claimant and dated? Is it clear from the document that the training covered the equipment being used at the time of the accident?
- If documentary evidence is lacking, is there witness evidence that contradicts the claimant's account? How persuasive is it?

The 'strengths and weaknesses' appraisal involves a marshalling of evidential resources and a clear-eyed assessment of each side's position.

- **Develop a negotiation plan**

Having done your research, understood the legal context and assessed the strengths and weaknesses of each party's position, next develop a negotiation plan ahead of any discussion with the other side.

Set out below is *one* approach to preparing a negotiation plan. It should help focus your thinking and achieve an acceptable outcome, but it is just a suggestion. It may appear too detailed, and there will certainly be some simple negotiations that require minimal preparation, but the more it is followed, the more its steps become habitual.

- **List of issues:** prepare a list of the issues that need to be covered.
- **Interests:** assess each side's underlying interests, or consider questions to be asked to determine your opponent's interests as clearly as possible.
- **Best, fall-back and worst case positions:** identify the best and worst case scenario for each issue. Consider fall-back positions on each issue (not your worst case scenario, but a credible alternative position to your best case). Be able to defend your positions on each point. Does each position have a credible narrative behind it? What is it?
- **Defence and attack:** how will you defend your weaknesses and exploit the other side's?
- **Concessions:** identify concessions that you will be prepared to make. They may be genuine concessions, in the sense that you believe the initial point is reasonable but you are prepared to cede ground to reach an overall settlement. They may be *"pseudo-concessions"*, i.e. movement from 'initial positions' that you do not, in reality, hold, to give the *impression* of movement without losing any significant ground. That will be easier if you feel that your opponent has overvalued the head of loss in question, or underestimated the weakness of your liability position.

- **Consider multiple options:** there is unlikely to be only one acceptable resolution. Consider alternative options.
- **Sequence:** it is worth considering, ahead of the negotiation, whether to address the least controversial elements first, to get them out of the way, or the most contentious. It may not matter, but having a clear plan of attack in mind will help ensure everything is covered. It may be that addressing the least contentious issues first will help get the discussion off to a positive start and demonstrate a willingness to be sensible that will encourage a greater willingness to engage on the more difficult elements.

Be prepared to be flexible with your plan. To adopt another military maxim, no plan survives engagement with the enemy. While not always entirely true, it is a reminder to stay flexible. *Each discussion may reveal new information that will create a need to review and recalibrate your strategy.*

Exchange of Information

Before any negotiation can take place, there must be an exchange of information between the parties.

It is important to consider carefully what to disclose at each stage.

It may be that the law requires obtaining and disclosing a raft of documentation, for example pursuant to the Pre-Action Protocol for Personal Injury Claims. You will need to ensure that your client has provided you with full disclosure sufficient to discharge their obligations under the Protocol.

There may be certain information that has been obtained in circumstances that mean it need not be disclosed. For example, an investigation report prepared by a loss adjuster or claims investigator in contemplation of litigation and for the (dominant) purpose of obtaining legal advice (therefore a "privileged" document). Witness statements may have been obtained on the same basis. If there is no need to disclose them, consider whether it is nevertheless in the client's interests to do so.

Whatever documentation is exchanged, make sure that it is clear on the file exactly what has been sent to the other side. Do not simply write a letter which says, "Please find enclosed our witness statements", for example. Which witnesses? Dated when? Be clear. Be specific. Itemise each document in your correspondence.

The negotiation

The aim is to achieve a compromise acceptable to both sides.

You will have prepared for the initial discussion and there will have been at least some exchange of information.

You will have a plan. You will know your best case position, your fall-back position and your worst case position. You will have identified acceptable concessions.

Bear the following in mind:

- Developing a constructive rapport with your opponent certainly helps. That may mean 'overlooking' (or not reacting to) unhelpful earlier communications. Remember the key principles and the purpose of the negotiation.
- Introduce yourself and who you represent (e.g. the insurer and the insured).
- Confirm your desire to discuss (liability/quantum/the claim) on a 'without prejudice' basis. That will make it clear from the outset that both sides are free to make concessions, or offers, that they will not be bound to. It allows for a free exchange of proposals rather than each side simply re-stating their best case positions.
- Set out the factual circumstances – those points that are agreed, or largely agreed. They form the framework within which the negotiation will take place.

- Follow your negotiation plan (but be prepared to be flexible) – are there less contentious elements to be identified and addressed first? Are there concessions you are willing to make early on to demonstrate your willingness to reach an agreement? Will these be held back, anticipating resistance on certain points and offering them up in response? As a general rule, you will want to hold any material concessions back initially, but there may be modest concessions that it would be tactically sensible to make at the outset, couched in terms that make it clear you are attempting to be sensible and constructive, and are making the concessions on that basis.
- If you have prepared well you will already know what your opponent is going to say about some or all of the points in contention, and will have prepared a response. Often, however, the initial discussion will reveal something new: a piece of information that was not previously disclosed; an update on the claimant's condition that undermines your calculations; a clearer understanding of what really matters for your opponent and what doesn't matter so much. Listen carefully. Make a clear note.
- Be prepared to suggest that certain issues be 'parked' for further consideration by you in light of the new information, or simply because they cannot be agreed upon at this stage, and focus on what remains.
- One discussion does not have to conclude everything. More often than not, both parties will need time to consider what the other has said, with a view to re-engaging in negotiation at a later date. Proposals may have been made which lie outside of a party's authority to agree to without further discussion with a third party (supervisor; the insured; the claimant; the opponent's supervisor).

- Remember the 'big picture' – people sometimes become obsessive about one element of the negotiation which, if they reflected a little, they would recognise was not of overriding importance, and certainly not something they should allow to jeopardise the negotiation. If the overall deal is acceptable, there is no need to win that single issue. Consider also the time and effort spent arguing that one point. Is any saving you might make completely overshadowed by the increased costs the other side will incur, and the time you have spent on it?

- Be prepared to terminate the negotiation if it is clear that no compromise that is better than the worst case scenario is likely (but bear in mind the 'best alternative to a negotiated agreement' (BATNA) – see below).

- Don't forget the key principles during the course of the negotiation: separate the 'person' issues from the 'substance' issues; be a good listener; be ethical; expose and focus on the underlying issues.

- If settlement is not reached on that occasion, conclude the discussion positively. Thank your opponent for their time; thank them for any positive contributions/concessions made. Ensure that both sides are in agreement as to what has been agreed, what is not agreed and what (if anything) has been parked for further consideration/discussion with a third party.

- Make a clear note of the discussion.

Best alternative to a negotiated agreement (BATNA)

The Fisher and Ury book *Getting to Yes* was referred to when discussing the importance of identifying the underlying interests behind a party's stated position.

Another helpful insight from that book relates to the strategy to adopt if negotiations break down.

Remember, the reason for negotiation is to produce something better than the results achievable without negotiating.

Consider what those results would be:

"What is the alternative? What is your BATNA – your best alternative to a negotiated agreement? That is the standard against which any proposed agreement should be measured. That is the only standard that can protect you from both accepting terms that are too unfavourable and from rejecting terms it would be in your interest to accept.....instead of ruling out any solution that does not meet your bottom line, you can compare a proposal with your BATNA to see whether it satisfies your interests." (Getting to Yes, 2012 edition, p.102).

In the claims context, consider what you will need to do, and what your opponent will likely do, if a negotiated settlement cannot be reached at that point. Will further medical evidence be required? Will there need to be a joint site visit? Will your client need to undertake a much deeper search for documentation? What will be the time/cost implications of those steps?

Having reflected on what may need to be done, reconsider the best offer made. Is it still unacceptable?

In conclusion – some top tips

1) Good preparation is key – ensure you understand the law and the factual circumstances.
2) Be prepared to support your case, at each point, with credible and persuasive argument.
3) Practice the art of good listening.
4) Focus on interests rather than positions.
5) Be prepared to compromise, but be clear about what is being conceded and why.
6) Prepare a negotiation plan.
7) Remember the Big Picture. Don't allow arguments over trivial points to defeat a successful negotiation.
8) Don't be intimidated by an aggressive negotiator. Remain focused on substance. Good preparation breeds confidence and will overcome the aggressive and the ill-prepared.
9) Have a clear idea of what you hope to achieve in the negotiation – your best case, fall-back case and worst case positions, but also be clear what your BATNA is!
10) Be a principled negotiator. It is not about winning at all costs. You may well have to negotiate with the same person again. Develop a reputation as someone who is firm and well-prepared, but reasonable to deal with.

39 Crisis management

Claire Mulligan

- What is a 'crisis'?
- The risk of civil claims
- Crisis management plan
- Communication strategy
- Evidence
- Liability of third parties
- Insurers
- Identify key witnesses
- Manage the regulatory investigation

Crisis management

This chapter considers crisis management and the key steps that should be considered in the aftermath of a serious incident.

It is important for all those involved in responding to a crisis to react swiftly and carefully to seek to ensure the safety of individuals and to minimise the negative short- and long-term impact on the insured's business.

What is a 'crisis'?

The definition of a crisis will often vary according to each insurer's policy wording; however, typically it will include:

> "Any incident which has the potential to affect short or long term confidence in a company, or its products, or which can interfere with its ability to continue operating normally."

Such incidents are likely to involve members of the public, clients, or employees where a loss of life or a major threat to safety or the environment has occurred, or instances where there is an impact on general safety and/or travel arrangements.

Other definitions may include wording along the following lines:

> "Crisis shall mean any event which involves:
>
> - Death or serious injury which is life threatening or involves emergency hospitalisation.
> - Kidnap or hijack and where the company considers there to be a risk to the business as a consequence or adverse press, publicity or other media attention."

Why is it necessary to respond effectively to a crisis?

A badly managed crisis can ruin an otherwise successfully performing business, while a well-managed crisis will reduce the impact, protect (and even enhance) the insured's reputation and brand, and secure customer and employee loyalty.

Doing the right thing, be it for employees, customers or the public, is in our view the best way to manage an incident with a view to seeking to ensure it does not develop into a crisis with potentially devastating long-term consequences.

However, one also needs to carefully consider the potential for civil and criminal proceedings which can flow from a crisis, especially one where serious harm has occurred.

The risk of civil claims

Any accident now, whether motor, at work or in a public place, is likely to result in a civil claim for compensation, in addition to criminal proceedings. Appropriate engagement and sensible management from as early as is practicable after a crisis can help to minimise damage. The ever present possibility of the civil claim means that early evidence and witness gathering is critical to how they can be dealt with,

Depending upon the nature of the incident, there may be a number of different regulatory bodies involved in carrying out in-depth investigations to gather evidence, assess whether criminal offences have been committed and whether criminal proceedings are likely to be brought. These investigations can also bring with them the closure of work sites, the quarantining or seizure of equipment, impounding of vehicles and other action which can hamper and seriously disrupt continued operations and production.

If there has been a fatality arising out of or in connection with work, the police will usually lead the criminal investigation but they will do so in accordance with the Work-related Death Protocol, which provides that the investigation should be conducted jointly with other relevant bodies such as the Health and Safety Executive (HSE). The police will investigate whether there have been any homicide related offences and will normally establish the circumstances surrounding the death to assist with the coroner's investigation. The HSE (or other relevant regulatory body) has a parallel duty to investigate and consider whether any health and safety offences may have been committed in connection with the incident.

Non-fatal incidents can also lead to potential criminal proceedings for breach of health and safety, food safety and/or environmental legislation. Such proceedings can lead to substantial fines being imposed on businesses and custodial sentences for individuals in the most serious cases. It is therefore critical that the regulatory investigations are carefully managed and monitored to protect the insured's position and to seek to minimise the prospect of enforcement action being taken.

Brand protection is also key and those managing the crisis need to work closely with those responsible for the insured's public relations and media profile. An organisation's reputation takes years to build and yet it can be rapidly eroded in the event of a badly managed crisis.

Crisis management plan

In practice, the businesses who tend to respond most effectively to a crisis are those who have already identified the key risks to their organisation and have developed a clear and workable multi-disciplinary crisis management plan which has been effectively communicated. Such a plan should be to hand, be revised from time to time and be ready to deploy in the event of a crisis. One of the best forms of preparation is to run a crisis simulation where only one or two of the stakeholders realise the crisis is a simulation, as it enables you to test your organisation's ability to respond to a crisis and prompts those with roles to play to understand their responsibilities and what is required of them in the event of a real crisis.

When a serious incident takes place, it should be rapidly decided who will form part of the crisis management team and what roles and responsibilities each of these individuals will assume. We would always recommend where there is likely to be involvement from a regulatory body, that one person or a small tight-knit team assumes the role of the 'single point of contact' to facilitate and keep a careful record of the flow of information, and coordinate the crisis management response.

Communication strategy

The communication strategy engaged by the insured or insurer should be swift, clear and decisive. Organisations should consider the need for holding statements to be prepared, appoint a public relations representative and ensure that information is being disseminated to the right people, in the right place, at the right time. The mediums for dealing with communication need to be considered; there will be a need for an internal alert and brief to staff so they are aware of the crisis and issues involved, and then external responses to the media, and customers affected and customers not involved but with whom the company will have an ongoing relationship who will seek reassurance.

Lawyers are often criticised for warning those involved in a crisis never to apologise or say sorry. However, a failure to express empathy for those involved in a horrific, terrifying, or frightening ordeal is ill-advised, and can lead to widespread condemnation in the media, or entrenched views in subsequent litigation. The public acknowledgment of the incident by the organisation and an acceptance that investigations are necessary and are in hand can be very effective in damage limitation.

Nowadays it is commonplace after an incident to see the CEO or senior official from the insured making a public statement to express remorse and regret. In most cases we actively endorse and support such an approach.

Successful crisis management

The key to successful crisis or incident management is speed of response in line with a well-prepared crisis management plan. It used to be the case that one had a good 12 or 24 hours to respond to a crisis, as, in the days before mobile phones and immediate visual downloads, there was always a time lag between the crisis or incident occurring and it being picked up and followed by the media. This is no longer the case.

Now we witness crises as they happen in real time thanks to downloads from eyewitnesses who capture the event on their mobile phones. The speed of your response and how you respond to the crisis as it unfolds is therefore critical.

The principles of effective crisis management include:

Attendance at scene

If it is probable that significant claims will arise or that there is a strong likelihood of a regulatory investigation, it is helpful to ensure the right experts attend the scene at the earliest opportunity.

Who should attend will very much be dictated by the type and nature of the incident. It could include adjusters, lawyers, and trauma response counsellors, together with experts whose evidence may be needed later in any claim.

Sometimes where there has been a very serious incident, the site will be sealed off as a 'scene of crime' and access for the insured and experts will be restricted. The regulator will take control of the scene and preserve any evidence and it is important for insureds to liaise closely with the regulators to facilitate the process.

Evidence

Those attending the scene will be responsible for gathering and securing evidence be it via witness evidence, photographs, plans, maps, video footage, geofencing of social media data, or collecting real evidence such as food or product samples, inspecting machinery or vehicles etc..

The purpose will be not only to enable you to understand how the incident occurred, and why, and to enable the insured to learn lessons and avoid a reoccurrence of the situation, but also to prepare and best protect the insured against any potential regulatory investigation. It should also facilitate an early decision on civil liability, and to protect and retain evidence that may be essential for the defence of future litigation or claims.

Establishing facts

Getting to the cause of the incident and establishing the facts is essential to enable the crisis to be managed effectively and to allow insureds to work to reduce the impact of the crisis on their business. It is for this reason that the decision as to who to send to the scene is so important. They will be your eyes and ears on the ground, feeding you information and updates and enabling you to make considered decisions about how to react to the incident. Ideally they will be experts in their field as it is clearly not ideal to be learning the ropes while in the midst of crisis management.

Mitigation of injury/losses

Managing a crisis well enables you to assist those affected immediately with consideration being given to what can be done to assist, be it provision of a form of treatment or rehabilitation usually in the form of trauma response to those psychologically affected by an incident or relocating those affected in a property disaster of some description. This has the additional benefit of securing the gratitude of those affected and thus their goodwill which is likely to reduce the inclination to bring a claim down the line, or at least mitigates losses incurred and therefore any potential outlay.

It also allows you to work directly with potential claimants to resolve claims without them having to go down the litigation route, should that be your desired outcome.

Carefully worded customer care letters, if necessary, expressing remorse and perhaps (if applicable) offering recourse to trauma counselling or other forms of assistance, can also work to diffuse a claims mentality.

Liability of third parties

When something goes badly wrong, thought always turns to who is to blame and responsible for the incident. Successful crisis management not only incorporates protection of the insured's employees, customers, business and brand, but also thinks ahead about liability and potential recovery opportunities. Therefore investigating who might be responsible and securing evidence that will assist in any contribution proceedings or recovery action is essential.

Insurers

It might be obvious, but it is surprising how many insureds actually forget to notify their insurers when they are in the midst of managing a crisis. Clearly, it is vital to ensure that the appropriate insurers are notified. Not only will they have notification requirements, but often they will contribute to the management of any incident.

Third-party insurers who may also be involved in an incident need to be put on notice of potential claims, and often there will be overlap between insurers responding to an incident, on behalf either of different insureds, or in respect of the different classes of insurance involved. Clear communication between insurers and their teams is necessary to guard against duplication and to ensure balls are not dropped when managing the crisis.

We would strongly recommend that notification of insurers and reinsurers is a part of the crisis management response plan.

Identify key witnesses

As part of the early attendance at scene and incident response, one needs the gift of foresight to ensure all key witnesses are located and statements taken, together with contact details to enable follow-up investigations later down the line. There is no substitute for contemporaneous evidence obtained from eyewitnesses, and footage they have on their mobile phones and similar devices.

Real care should be exercised when taking written witness accounts and statements if the criminal authorities are also actively investigating. Such statements, if poorly worded and not subject to legal professional privilege, can sometimes form an important part of the evidence used against an organisation in a subsequent prosecution.

Detailed witness accounts should be taken, if possible, at the scene and if more details are needed, then such evidence can be expanded upon in witness statement form. When securing contact information, consider that you may be seeking to make contact two, three or more years down the line if proceedings are later served so ensure you have the fullest contact details possible.

In motor accidents the insured or insured's driver may well be interviewed, or, more uncommonly, arrested at the scene.
An appropriate crisis management response is key. We would strongly recommend a plan that enables the rapid presence of an expert motor prosecution lawyer to liaise with both driver and police to manage effectively the interview process. All too often the driver's first advice and representation at the police station for the interview is from the duty solicitor who will not have any subsequent involvement in the case or proceedings (criminal or civil), knowledge of the insured/insurer or reason to seek to defer the interview.
We think that it is very important for the driver and the business to have the immediate support of an expert who can guide them through such a daunting process and offer a continuation of support from criminal to civil proceedings, if necessary.

Early involvement at this stage allows an early assessment of the likely claims and an informed approach.

Assess likely areas and extent of liability

Sometimes the best example of a well-managed crisis is one where an early decision as to potential liability can be made because there has been an opportunity to investigate at an early stage. Insurers can reduce their exposure to costs and claims inflation by making admissions where appropriate and settling claims at the earliest stage. Alternatively, a clear letter of response with persuasive case law in support of a denial of liability may deter those claims where liability arguments are weak. Similarly, early notification to third-party insurers with a well-set-out letter laying out the facts and evidence supporting a claim may secure an early settlement.

Manage the regulatory investigation

Following an incident the key is to get the right balance between being seen to cooperate with the regulator without incriminating the insured company or any individual and without increasing any culpability.

The police and other regulatory bodies will want to take copies of documents, inspect and remove items of equipment, take statements and establish what has happened since the incident. A protocol should be established with the regulator so that all communications are through the 'single point of contact'. A detailed log should be maintained of all discussions with the regulator and all information provided to them. There should be a complete audit trail of all documentation requested and supplied.

The regulators have certain powers to enter premises and compel information to be provided to them about the incident. The HSE and local authority Environmental Health Officers can also serve formal enforcement notices requiring certain action to be taken and it is an offence to fail to comply with such notices. It is essential that insureds are mindful that the regulator does not have to restrict their visit and investigation to the location and circumstances of the incident itself. They may, and often do, undertake wider-ranging investigation, taking in a variety of safety management systems, procedures and arrangements.

It is important to consider whether any pre- or post-incident documents might be legally privileged and therefore protected from disclosure to the enforcement authorities. Legal privilege is not considered in detail in this chapter, but insureds should be aware that post-incident internal emails and accident investigation documents could be vulnerable to disclosure and therefore extreme care should be taken when documents are prepared post-incident. All communications should be kept as factual as possible and should be circulated on a 'need to know' basis. If it is intended that the internal investigation should be subject to the protection of legal privilege, which is most often a sensible course, legal advice should be sought at an early stage to ensure that the relevant legal tests are met.

The regulatory bodies may also seek to take statements from witnesses and conduct interviews with those suspected of having committed offences. The timing of such interviews will vary considerably but the key point to note is that insureds who are invited to attend what is commonly referred to as a PACE interview should seek immediate legal advice on the options available to them. It is essential that the insured is aware of the nature of the offences suspected of being committed and whether the proposed interview relates to them as an individual in their personal capacity or as a representative of an organisation.

40 Funding methods

Martin Cox

- Conditional fee agreements
- After-the-event insurance
- Before-the-event insurance
- Ordinary private client retainer
- Legal aid
- Damages-based agreements

Funding methods

Introduction

There are various methods available to claimants to fund personal injury claims. The different options:

- Have an impact on the potential costs for which a defendant will be liable if the claim is successful;
- Have an impact on the potential costs a defendant can recover if the claim is successfully defended;
- Mean that there are tactical considerations as to how a claims handler should deal with the claim.

Indemnity principle

The starting point for understanding the various funding methods is the indemnity principle. This is a concept in legal costs where the receiving party cannot recover from the paying party more than the receiving party is liable to pay their own solicitor.

Jackson reforms

The Jackson reforms, implemented in April 2013, brought in wide-reaching reforms to civil litigation funding and costs in England and Wales. The reforms concerned the way that civil claims are funded and the costs involved in such claims. The principal piece of legislation that was required to achieve these reforms came into effect on 1 April 2013 – Part 2 of the Legal Aid, Sentencing and Punishment of Offenders Act 2012 (LASPO).

The reforms apply across all civil litigation but have a particular impact in personal injury cases, where no-win no-fee conditional fee agreements (CFAs) are frequently used. The key changes under LASPO include:

- No-win no-fee CFAs remain available in civil cases. However, subject to limited and prescribed exceptions, the additional costs involved (success fees and after-the-event insurance premiums) are no longer payable by the losing party.
- Wide ranging fixed costs are payable in fast track matters for EL, PL and RTA claims. For more detail on these costs, see Chapters 24 and 25.

For more detail on the Jackson reforms, see Chapter 8 on the Civil Procedure Rules.

Types of funding

Conditional fee agreements

A CFA, or a collective conditional fee agreement (CCFA), is an agreement whereby a party's solicitor's fees are payable only in circumstances agreed with the client, i.e. the fee payable by the client is *conditional* upon agreed outcomes of the claim.

Although there are a number of potential ways for these agreements to work, the most common method used by claimant solicitors is that if the claim is lost, the solicitor makes no charge. However, if the claim is won the solicitor charges their normal costs plus a percentage uplift (success fee) on those fees, explaining why such arrangements are typically referred to as no-win no-fee agreements.

CCFAs were introduced to enable the bulk purchase and provision of legal services and were designed for bodies such as trade unions. There is a long tradition of trade unions funding personal injury claims for their members, usually against their employers. The trade union pays for their members' legal fees and agrees to indemnify the member for any adverse costs orders made against them.

CCFAs enable such bodies to enter into a single agreement with solicitors to govern the way its members' claims will be managed and funded. These cases are treated in a similar fashion to those run under a CFA. However, individual CFAs do not have to be prepared and signed for by each claimant whose case is run under the agreement.

For CFAs/CCFAs entered into between 1 April 2000 and 31 March 2013, the success fee is recoverable from the losing party in the dispute.

For CFAs entered into on or after 1 April 2013, or where legal advice has been supplied for the first time after 1 April 2013 under a pre-April 2013 CCFA, the success fee is no longer recoverable from the losing party to the litigation. The exceptions to this are where a claim relates to publication and privacy proceedings or a mesothelioma claim, where the success fee remains payable by the losing party in such cases.

We are now at a stage where the majority of claims are being brought under CFAs which post-date 1 April 2013 and recoverable success fees are being consigned to history. Under these CFAs, solicitors will still usually insist upon a success fee but this is now sought from their own client and is paid for out of damages awarded. In personal injury matters this is capped to a maximum of 25% of damages, inclusive of VAT, and with future losses being ringfenced.

The quid pro quo for the abolition of recoverable success fees from losing parties was the introduction of qualified one-way costs shifting (QOCS), which protects claimants seeking damages for personal injury from the threat of having to pay any adverse costs orders should they lose their claim, save in prescribed exceptional circumstances. For more details on QOCS, see Chapters 24 and 25.

After-the-event insurance

In matters where QOCS does not apply, the risk to an unsuccessful claimant extends beyond failing to recover their own costs. They are also at risk of having to pay the other side's legal fees.

To protect a claimant from the risk of paying an adverse costs order, a number of insurance providers developed and marketed policies designed to cover that risk. These are known as after-the-event

(ATE) insurance policies because they are entered into after the accident (event) has occurred and when a claim is being contemplated. This type of policy is to be distinguished from before-the-event (BTE) policies mentioned below.

Where a claim is successful, the recoverability of the premium depends on the date the ATE policy was entered into:

- Between 1 April 2000 and 31 March 2013: the premium is recoverable from the losing party, subject to reasonableness and proportionality;
- On or after 1 April 2013: the premium is not recoverable from the losing party, save for the exceptions below.

The exceptions to ATE policies entered into on or after 1 April 2013 are where the claim relates to publication and privacy proceedings or damages for the contraction of diffuse mesothelioma. In these exceptional cases the premium remains payable by the losing party. In addition, in clinical negligence claims, that part of the ATE premium that relates to the risk associated with the cost of the liability and causation reports necessary during the investigation into the merits of a claim remains recoverable.

Before-the-event insurance

Many claims are funded through a legal expenses insurance policy purchased before an accident occurs. Such policies are referred to as before-the-event (BTE) insurance.

Many people have BTE insurance as part of their existing motor insurance policies, home insurance policies or even through their credit cards. In the event of a policyholder having an accident and desiring to bring a claim, the insurance company will normally refer the matter to one of its panel solicitors. The policy will usually indemnify the claimant in respect of their own legal costs and those of the other side if the claim is lost.

The cost of these premiums is not recoverable from the other side if the claim is successful.

Ordinary private client retainer

The traditional way to fund a claim is for a client to instruct a solicitor on a private basis and agree to pay a certain sum per hour, or a fixed fee, for the solicitor's time. The client is liable to pay these costs whatever the outcome of the claim:

- If successful, they will usually be able to recover most of these costs from the other side;
- If unsuccessful, they will usually become liable for the other side's costs as well as their own.

This method of funding is practically non-existent in the personal injury sector but remains the most common method of funding in commercial litigation.

Legal aid

Historically, many personal injury claims were publicly funded through the legal aid system. However, in April 2000, public funding was withdrawn for the vast majority of personal injury claims.

Part 1 of LASPO made further changes to the legal aid system. Civil legal aid was retained only for a limited number of case types. These include:

- The care, supervision and protection of children or vulnerable adults;
- Abuse of powers by a public authority (including a breach of rights under the European Convention on Human Rights);
- Children who have suffered severe disability due to a neurological injury sustained during the mother's pregnancy, the child's birth or the first eight weeks of the child's life.

Damages-based agreements

A DBA is a form of CFA arrangement where a solicitor:

- Is not paid if their client loses, but
- May take as their fee a percentage of the damages recovered for their client if the claim is successful.

Before 1 April 2013, DBAs could not be used in civil litigation although they were commonplace in other areas, for example employment tribunals where recovery of costs between the parties was limited. The DBA Regulations 2013 came into force as from 1 April 2013, allowing the use of DBAs in civil litigation.

However, those Regulations have come under considerable criticism, being described as unworkable, such that in October 2014 the Ministry of Justice asked the Civil Justice Council (CJC) to consider how to improve the Regulations. In September 2015 the CJC published its report setting out 45 recommendations designed to make the statutory regime relating to DBAs simpler and clearer, with a view to encouraging the uptake of this method of funding.

At the time of publishing this guide, there has been no sign of the drafting of any revised regulations and the take-up of DBAs remains practically non-existent in civil litigation matters.

41 Jurisdiction and applicable law

Rachel Moore

- European regime:
  - Brussels I/Brussels Regulation recast
  - Conventions
- Traditional rules and national law:
  - Jurisdictional gateways
  - *Forum non conveniens*
  - Submission to the jurisdiction and objection
- Applicable law: Private International Law (Miscellaneous Provisions) Act 1995 and Rome II
- Brexit

Jurisdiction and applicable law

Introduction

Liability claims handlers will frequently face claims involving a foreign element. For example, a party may be based overseas or the accident may have taken place overseas.

Decisions about whether the English courts have jurisdiction over such a claim, and if so whether English law will be applied to the dispute, will fundamentally affect both the way the case is handled and its ultimate value.

This chapter provides an overview of the key rules that determine jurisdiction and applicable law, and assumes that the claim is being brought in the English courts. In this chapter, "jurisdiction" refers to the power of a court to hear and decide a case; "applicable law" refers to the legal principles that the court will apply to the facts to decide the case.

Jurisdiction

Many English claimants will prefer to bring their claim in England, even if their accident occurred overseas. It will enable them to instruct an English lawyer, conduct proceedings in English and have the matter concluded by a local court.

However, if the defendant is based overseas then any judgment may have to be enforced overseas, relevant documents and witnesses may be overseas and, in some cases, the damages awarded may be higher and/or the costs of bringing the claim lower. In addition, limitation periods can differ from country to country, as can the length of time a case takes to reach a final hearing. There are, therefore, a number of factors that any claimant needs to consider when deciding where to bring a claim, and, from the defendant's perspective, when deciding whether to challenge the jurisdiction of the English court.

There are two sets of general rules that determine whether the courts of England and Wales have jurisdiction to deal with a claim:

- The European regime (Brussels I/Brussels Regulation recast, Lugano Convention and Brussels Convention).
- The traditional rules under national law, which mainly apply to defendants domiciled outside Europe.

European regime

The European regime generally applies in matters where the defendant is domiciled in one of the 28 Member States of the European Union (Austria, Belgium, Bulgaria, Croatia, Republic of Cyprus, Czech Republic, Denmark, Estonia, Finland, France, Germany, Greece, Hungary, Ireland, Italy, Latvia, Lithuania, Luxembourg, Malta, Netherlands, Poland, Portugal, Romania, Slovakia, Slovenia, Spain, Sweden and the UK) or a 2007 Lugano Convention state (Iceland, Norway and Switzerland). It is expected that similar rules will be adopted by the UK following its exit from the EU but no further information is currently available.

Brussels I/Brussels Regulation recast

For European Union (EU) Member States, Regulation (EC) No 44/2001 on jurisdiction and the recognition and enforcement of judgments in civil and commercial matters (Brussels I) applied to proceedings issued on or after 1 March 2002.

Regulation (EU) 1215/2012 (Brussels Regulation recast) applies to legal proceedings instituted on or after 10 January 2015. From that date, Regulation 44/2001 has been repealed, save that it will continue to apply to judgments given in proceedings instituted before 10 January 2015. The references below are to the Brussels Regulation recast.

General position

Defendants should be sued in the courts of their domicile, i.e. the Member State in which they are domiciled (Article 4).

The rules that determine domicile are different for an individual and a company:

- An individual's domicile is determined by national law (Article 62). An individual is domiciled in the UK if they reside in the UK and if the nature and circumstances of their residence indicate that they have a substantial connection with the UK. Residence for three months is deemed to be a substantial connection, unless the contrary is proved (paragraph 9, Schedule 1, Civil Jurisdiction and Judgments Order 2001).
- A company is domiciled at the place where it has its statutory seat (registered office), central administration or principal place of business (Article 63).

In addition, a defendant could be sued in another Member State:

- Contract: in relation to sale of goods, the Member State where the goods were delivered or should have been delivered. In relation to supply of services, the Member State where the services were provided or should have been provided (Article 7(1)).
- Tort: in the courts for the place where the harmful event occurred (Article 7(2)).

Where there are a number of defendants and the claims are so closely connected that it is expedient to determine them together to prevent irreconcilable judgments, a defendant can be sued in the Member State of any of the defendants (Article 8).

Where there are third-party proceedings, a claimant may bring proceedings in the court seised of the original proceedings (Article 8(2)).

Agreement as to jurisdiction

If the parties, regardless of their domicile, have agreed in writing that the courts of a particular Member State(s) are to have jurisdiction to settle any disputes, those courts shall have exclusive jurisdiction unless the parties agree otherwise (Article 25).

Insurance

An insurer domiciled in a Member State can be sued:

- In the courts of the Member State where the insurer is domiciled.
- In the case of actions brought by the policyholder, the insured or a beneficiary, in the courts of the Member State where the claimant is domiciled (Article 11). It is worth noting the Court of Appeal's decision in *Hoteles Pinero Canarias SL & MAPFRE v Keefe* [2015] in relation to the applicability of Article 11 for matters relating to insurance and how this is interpreted as not only being limited to disputes relating to the meaning or effect of an insurance policy. It should be noted that the decision in Keefe that there is no logical reason not to apply the insurance provisions to the policyholder has been appealed to the Supreme Court (heard 7 March 2017) and judgment is awaited.

A liability insurer can also be sued in the courts for the place where the harmful event occurred (Article 12).

The above principles also apply to direct actions brought by an injured person against an insurer, where such direct actions are permitted (Article 13).

These Articles do not confer the direct right itself. It is, therefore, important to confirm whether or not a direct right of action exists when considering whether the claimant has the ability to sue in their home court. The claimant will have such a direct right in road traffic claims as the Fourth Motor Insurance Directive (2009/103/EC) required all Member States to create such a direct right.

The principle that a claimant as beneficiary can sue in their domicile was confirmed in *FBTO Schadeverzekeringen NV v Odenbreit* [2007], in which the European Court of Justice (ECJ) ruled that a German national injured in the Netherlands was entitled to sue the defendant's insurers, domiciled in the Netherlands, in his home court in Germany. This decision was based on the old Article 9(1)(b), but the same principle applies to the new Article 11(1)(b).

Conventions

The Brussels Convention regulated jurisdiction as between the (then) 15 Member States of the EU up to 1 March 2002. It was superseded by Brussels I and now only has very limited applicability.

The Lugano Convention binds the current EU Member States with Switzerland, Norway and Iceland. The general principle is that defendants should be sued in the state where they are domiciled (Article 2). The position as regards claims in contract or tort is identical to those in the Brussels Regulation recast. Therefore, in contract cases, a Swiss defendant can be sued in England (as well as in Switzerland) if the obligation was to be performed in England.

The Hague Convention on Choice of Court Agreements 2005 came into force on 1 October 2015. The aim of the Hague Convention 2005 is to ensure the effectiveness of choice of court agreements. The Hague Convention 2005 is largely similar to the regime under the Brussels Regulation recast. However, there are occasional differences. The relationship between the Hague Convention 2005 and Brussels Regulation recast is regulated by Article 26 of the Convention. Depending on the specific circumstances, one gives precedence to the other.

The Civil Jurisdiction and Judgments (Hague Convention on Choice of Court Agreements 2005) Regulations 2015 facilitate the application of the Hague Convention 2005 in the UK, by amending domestic legislation. In particular, the Civil Jurisdiction and Judgments Act 1982 and Part 6 of the Civil Procedure Rules 1998 have been amended.

Traditional rules: national law

Where the European regime does not apply, because the defendant is based outside a EU Member State or Lugano Convention state, the relevant national law rules will apply.

The national law in England provides that the English court has jurisdiction over a defendant not domiciled in a European regime state through service of process on the defendant outside of the jurisdiction, subject to obtaining permission of the court.

It is also important to note that establishing jurisdiction under these traditional rules is at the court's discretion.

However, an English court's jurisdiction may still be challenged and a stay granted on the basis that there is a more appropriate forum. This is the concept of *forum non conveniens*, which will be covered below in this chapter.

Under the national law of England and Wales, if the defendant is based outside the jurisdiction, the claimant must seek the permission of the court to serve proceedings on them. To obtain such permission, the claimant must show:

- The claim falls within one of the jurisdictional gateways laid out in Practice Direction (PD) 6B 3.1 of the Civil Procedure Rules (CPR).
- The claim has a reasonable prospect of success (Part 6.37(1)(b) of the CPR).
- England is the most appropriate forum to bring the claim (Part 6.37(3) of the CPR).

Jurisdictional gateways

The jurisdictional gateways are set out in PD 6B 3.1. The ground most frequently used in personal injury cases following accidents abroad is that at PD 6B 3.1.9. This provides that the claimant may serve a claim form out of the jurisdiction where a claim is made in tort and the damage was sustained within the jurisdiction, or the damage sustained resulted from an act committed within the jurisdiction.

The definition of damage and whether it has been sustained within the jurisdiction is the subject of much case law. Earlier cases show that the court will interpret damage widely. For example:

- *Booth v Phillips and others* [2004]: financial loss suffered by a dependent wife in England following the death of her husband in Egypt was held to be damage sustained in England.
- *Cooley v Ramsey* [2008]: claimant's loss of income in England following an accident in Australia was sufficient.

This approach was followed in *Wink v Croatia Osiguranje DD* [2013]. Ongoing effects, such as loss of earnings and treatment for injuries after repatriation, appear to be sufficient to be classed as damages sustained within the jurisdiction, and enable the claim to pass through that particular jurisdictional gateway.

In *Wink*, an English claimant was injured when he was knocked off his bicycle while cycling on holiday in Croatia. The defendant was the insurer of a Croatian national. The claim was made before Croatia became part of the EU. The claimant suffered multiple injuries and was repatriated to England after 15 days. The High Court held that England was the appropriate forum. The claimant suffered much of the physical and mental effects of his injuries within the jurisdiction once he had returned to England, and had sustained and continued to sustain ongoing loss of earnings and other special damages in the jurisdiction.

continued...

...continued

However, on 3 July 2015 the Court of Appeal handed down judgment in *Brownlie v Four Seasons Holdings Incorporated* [2015]. This decision clarifies that any damage sustained in the jurisdiction for the purposes of the jurisdictional gateway in PD 6B 3.1.9 must be direct damage. *Brownlie* was heard by the Supreme Court in May 2017, with judgment handed down in December 2017. The Supreme Court unanimously agreed that the defendant was not the correct defendant because there was no contract between it and the claimant. As a result, comments on the jurisdictional gateway point are obiter. By a majority of 3:2 it was held that a claim in tort can be brought in England if damage is suffered here as a result of personal injuries inflicted abroad. Lady Hale said that *"it is quite clear that damage can be suffered by the same person in more than one place, just as the wrongful acts can be committed in more than one place"*. For the time being though, the Court of Appeal judgment remains good law on the point. The earlier first instance decisions of *Booth v Phillips and others* [2004] and *Cooley v Ramsey* [2008], where indirect and consequential damage was held as sufficient for the purposes of PD 6B 3.1.9, have not yet been overruled. However, an earlier Court of Appeal decision, *Erste Group Bank AG, London Branch v JSC 'VMZ Red October' and others* [2015], had already cast doubt on whether the tort jurisdictional gateway extended to consequential loss, but reached no final conclusion.

Forum non conveniens

The court has discretion to decline jurisdiction even where one of the gateways applies and the claim has a reasonable prospect of success.

The claimant in their application to serve out of the jurisdiction under Part 6.36 of the CPR needs to satisfy the court that England is the most appropriate forum. The court will, therefore, consider the question of *forum non conveniens*.

The basic principle of *forum non conveniens* was set out by Lord Goff in *Spiliada Maritime Corporation v Cansulex Ltd* [1986]. It was confirmed that a stay will only be granted on the ground of *forum non conveniens* where the court is satisfied that there is some other available forum with competent jurisdiction and that it is the appropriate forum for the trial of the action.

> The discretion to decline jurisdiction is a general discretion of the court. The court will take into account the facts, such as the domicile of the majority of the parties, location of witnesses and even the governing law applicable.

Submission to the jurisdiction

A defendant can submit to the jurisdiction of the English courts if they take a step that amounts to a submission. This is assessed by reference to the procedural law. For example, it could be by acknowledging service, filing a defence or taking any step that could be considered inconsistent with a jurisdictional challenge. A defendant will be considered as having consented to the court's jurisdiction if they do not:

- File an acknowledgment of service that solely states that they intend to challenge the jurisdiction of the English court; and
- Make an application to challenge the jurisdiction within 14 days after filing the acknowledgment of service.

An application or request for an extension of time for filing a defence could be classed as submitting to the jurisdiction. It is, therefore, of considerable importance that any potential challenge to jurisdiction is considered at the outset.

Objection to jurisdiction

The procedure is set out in Part 11 of the CPR. However, it is important to recognise that there is a restricted time in which to contest jurisdiction.

Part 11(4) of the CPR provides that an application must be made within 14 days after service of an acknowledgment of service. If an application is not made in time, the defendant is treated as having accepted jurisdiction. As stated above, the acknowledgment of service must solely state that the defendant intends to challenge the jurisdiction of the English court.

Pre-emptive steps

Where a defendant may be liable to the claimant, it is worth considering seeking a negative declaration of liability in order to establish jurisdiction in the court of their choosing and, thus, be able to exercise some control over proceedings.

Applicable law

When it comes to considering what law would be applicable in a matter involving the law of tort with a foreign element, there are two regimes:

- Private International Law (Miscellaneous Provisions) Act 1995 (the 1995 Act).
- Rome II.

For torts committed prior to 11 January 2009, the law applicable is governed by the 1995 Act. The 1995 Act also applies post 11 January 2009 to torts outside of the scope of Rome II and between parts of the UK.

For torts committed on or after 11 January 2009, Rome II is applicable.

1995 Act

The general rule is set out under s.11(1). This provides that the applicable law is that of the country in which the events constituting the tort occurred.

This general rule can be displaced by the exceptions under s.12, which state that if it appears:

> that it is substantially more appropriate for the applicable law for determining the issues arising in the case, or any of those issues, to be the law of the other country, the general rule is displaced and the applicable law for determining those issues or that issue (as the case may be) is the law of that other country.

For the exception under s.12 to apply, many factors would be considered by the court in order to decide whether it is "substantially more appropriate". Indeed, case law shows that English courts have in the past been reluctant to displace the general rule in s.11.

Scope of applicable law

It is important also to consider the scope of the relevant applicable law. This was dealt with in *Harding v Wealands* [2006].

This case involved a road traffic collision in Australia. The claimant was a passenger in a vehicle being driven by his Australian girlfriend. Both parties were living in England. This was held insufficient for the rule in s.11 to be displaced. The applicable law was held to be that of Australia (New South Wales). Following an appeal, the House of Lords held that substantive law issues, such as liability and heads of loss, are matters governed by the applicable law, i.e. the law of the place where the accident happened. However, procedural law issues, such as the quantification of damages, were a question for the law of the forum, in this case England.

In *Cox v Ergo Versicherung AG* [2014], the Supreme Court ruled that in a case brought in England and where German law applied to liability, the Fatal Accidents Act 1976 could not be used to assess damages payable to the widow of the deceased, an army major who had been killed while cycling in Germany in 2004. The Act was a substantive matter and not a procedural matter. Therefore, the applicable German law had to be used to determine liability and the heads of loss, with English law only applying to quantification. The finding meant that the claimant had to give credit for a war widow's pension, which under English law would have been irrelevant.

Rome II

The rules that determine the governing law of non-contractual obligations in civil and commercial matters have been set out in Regulation (EC) 864/2007 (Rome II). The purpose of the Regulation was to implement a uniform approach when determining applicable law throughout the EU Member States. It replaces the previous choice of law rules contained in the 1995 Act as detailed above for cases after 11 January 2009.

Initially there was some debate over when Rome II came into force. However, in *Homawoo v GMF Assurances SA* [2011], the ECJ clarified that Rome II applies to matters where the events giving rise to the damage occurred after 11 January 2009.

Rome II has what is known as universal application. The rules of Rome II will therefore apply to non-contractual matters, even if it means that the substantive law of a non-member state is applied. For example, Rome II would still apply to proceedings brought in England in relation to an accident in Australia, with Australian law being applied by the English courts.

General rule: Article 4(1)

The general rule provides that the applicable law will be the law of the country in which the damage occurs. The law of the country in which the event giving rise to the damage occurred or in which the indirect consequences of an event occurred is specifically excluded. The applicable law will, therefore, generally be the law of the country where the accident took place. The fact that the claimant subsequently suffers indirect or ongoing losses in another country should not be relevant (*Jacobs v Motor Insurers Bureau* [2010]).

Exception: Article 4(2)

Where the person claimed to be liable and the person sustaining damage both have their habitual residence in the same country at the time when the damage occurs, the law of that country shall apply.

It should be noted that there is no definition of "habitual residence" in Rome II. Cases are frequently brought where habitual residence is pleaded in order to try to establish the most desirable applicable law. In *Winrow v Hemphill and Ageas Insurance Ltd* [2014]:

- The claimant passenger was involved in a road traffic accident in Germany. She pursued her claim against the driver of the vehicle and her insurer.
- Both the claimant and the driver were UK residents but the claimant had been living in Germany for over eight years at the time of the accident. The driver had also been living in Germany for up to two years before the accident.
- The basic rule under Article 4(1) would generally lead to a finding that German law should apply, being the law of the country where the damage occurred. However, the claimant sought to persuade the High Court that Article 4(2) should displace the basic rule and that English law should apply as both the claimant and the driver were habitually resident in England.

- It was held that the law indicated by Article 4(1) was not displaced and that the law applicable to the claim was German, despite the claimant and the driver having returned to live in England since the accident. What was important was their habitual residence at the time of the accident.

Escape clause: Article 4(3)

The general rule is displaced if the tort is "manifestly more closely connected" with another country. A manifestly closer connection with another country might be based, in particular, on a pre-existing relationship between the parties, such as a contract, that is closely connected with the tort in question.

This exception will allow for displacement of either the law of the place of damage (Article 4(1)) or the law of the place of mutual habitual residence (Article 4(2)).

However, the use of the word "manifestly" is intended to convey the exceptional nature of this exception.

See *Gillian Marshall v MIB and others; Christopher Pickard v MIB* [2015] where the judge considered whether English or French law governed Marshall's claim against Pickard under Rome II, and found that Art 4(3) displaced the law identified by Art 4(2) as it was clear from the circumstances of the case that the tort was manifestly more closely connected to France. This was on the basis that Marshall and Pickard were hit by a French national driving a French car on a French road and French law governed claims against the driver and against the recovery vehicle. Consequently, Marshall's claim against Pickard was also governed by French law.

Scope of applicable law: Article 15

Once the applicable law is established it is important to establish its scope. For example, it will govern:

- Basis and extent of liability.
- Grounds for exemption from liability, restriction of liability or any contributory negligence.

- Existence, nature and assessment of damages claimed.
- Rules of limitation.

Evidence and procedure

Article 1(3) makes it clear that Rome II will not apply to "evidence and procedure". These matters should be governed by the law of the forum, i.e. where the claim is heard.

There has been much debate over what constitutes evidence and procedure. In particular, should the judicial practices used for assessing damages, such as expert evidence to assess damages, come under the practices of the law of the forum or that of the applicable law?

Guidance on this was eventually provided by the case of *Wall v Mutuelle de Poitiers Assurances* [2014], where the Court of Appeal held that questions of what expert evidence the court should order was a matter of procedure and would fall out of the scope of Rome II. It should, therefore, be determined by the law of the forum.

Brexit

On 23 June 2016, the UK voted to leave the EU with the UK notifying the European Council of its intention to leave pursuant to Article 50 of the Lisbon Treaty on 29 March 2017. This decision will have significant implications on issues of jurisdiction and applicable law in the future. However, the extent of the changes will depend on the terms of any future UK/EU relationship, which are currently unknown.

What is clear is that the current rules on jurisdiction, applicable law, service, and reciprocity and enforcement of judgments across EU Member States will remain in force until the UK formally leaves the EU. This will be a maximum of two years from 29 March 2017, i.e. March 2019.

Jurisdiction after Brexit

As soon as the UK is no longer a member of the EU, the Brussels Regulation recast will cease to apply in the UK, unless similar provisions are adopted by the UK. The post-Brexit rules on jurisdiction are currently uncertain.

Applicable law after Brexit

Again, once the UK ceases to be a member of the EU, Rome II will no longer apply to the UK, unless similar provisions are adopted by the UK. The default position with regard to applicable law will therefore be the Private International Law (Miscellaneous Provisions) Act 1995 unless some alternative agreement is reached with the EU.

Brexit will also see an end to the recognition and enforcement of UK judgments in EU Member States, unless an alternative agreement is reached with the EU.

The EU service regulations will also no longer apply, meaning that parties will need to obtain permission to serve proceedings on a party in an EU Member State, adding cost and delays to proceedings, unless a bilateral/multilateral agreement is agreed with the EU.

Conclusion

This chapter only scrapes the surface of what is a very technical interweaving of European and other legislation and common law. It is a complicated and evolving area of law with many uncertainties over the position of the rules on jurisdiction and applicable law following the UK's withdrawal from the EU.

Priority must be given to consideration of these issues at the outset. The management and value of a claim could vary hugely depending on what is the relevant jurisdiction and applicable law.

42 Other jurisdictions

Amanda Wylie, Rory Jackson and Marian Brennan

Co-authors: Louise Houliston and Martina O'Mahoney

- Northern Ireland
- Scotland
- Ireland

Northern Ireland

Introduction

Northern Ireland is a small jurisdiction comprising six counties with a population of around 1.8 million people. It was not affected by the Civil Procedure Rules (CPR) or Jackson reforms but follows England and Wales legislatively and in terms of case law generally.

Historically, there has been the perception that litigating in Northern Ireland is a laborious process. However, strict case management provisions now ensure that parties move actions along expeditiously. The one issue that does continue to frustrate is legally aided cases, given the backlog in the Legal Services Commission. There are ongoing discussions as to the future of litigation funding, which will impact access to justice.

Institutions

The court system in Northern Ireland is divided into civil and criminal matters. Criminal matters are dealt with in the magistrates' courts and Crown Court. Civil jurisdiction is covered by the High Court and county courts.

The Court of Judicature, comprising the High Court, Crown Court and Court of Appeal, is in Belfast. The Court of Judicature was constituted by the Judicature (Northern Ireland) Act 1978.

The High Court has three divisions: Queen's Bench, Chancery and Family. The Queen's Bench Division deals with personal injury actions with a value above £30,000.

The Commercial List is within the Queen's Bench division. This is a specialist commercial litigation court that is case managed by the Commercial Judge. It deals with all commercial disputes, professional negligence matters, and breach of contract and coverage disputes.

Chancery deals with estate disputes and wills, partnership disputes and land disputes as well as administrative law.

The Court of Appeal is Northern Ireland's highest court. Appeal from the Court of Appeal is to the Supreme Court.

The county courts are the main regional civil courts. County court judges hear claims valued up to £30,000. The senior county court judges in Belfast and Londonderry are called recorders; the others are simply county court judges. County courts deal with all manner of claims, including personal injury, contractual disputes, equity civil bills, land/property disputes and debt.

District judges hear claims valued up to £10,000 as well as small claims arbitrations.

Personal injury matters are excluded from the small claims court (jurisdiction up to £3,000 at present).

Terminology

Terminology used in Northern Ireland can confuse. If you remember that Northern Ireland is pre-CPR this should assist. Common terms are set out below.

Table 1 – Terminology

England and Wales	Northern Ireland
Claimant	Plaintiff
Claim form	Civil bill or writ of summons
Statement of case	Statement of claim
Disclosure	Discovery
Part 36	No equivalent in Northern Ireland
Acknowledge service	Enter an appearance

England and Wales	Northern Ireland
No equivalent	Remittal: the process by which a claim issued in the High Court is transferred down to the county court jurisdiction. Removal: the process by which a claim is transferred up to the High Court from the county court.

Pre-action procedure

Pre-action protocols for personal injury matters have existed in the High Court since 1 April 2008 and in the county court since 25 February 2013. Other pre-action protocols include those for cases in the Commercial List, defamation actions, clinical negligence actions, possession cases and judicial review.

Personal injury

The pre-action protocol for personal injury matters requires parties to act in accordance with the overriding objective, set out at Order 1 Rule 1A of the Rules of the Court of Judicature (Northern Ireland) 1980 (the Rules). This states that the "overriding objective of these Rules is to enable the Court to deal with cases justly" by:

- Ensuring the parties are on an equal footing.
- Saving expense.
- Dealing with the case in a way that is proportionate to the amount of money involved, the importance of the case, the complexity of the issues and the financial position of each party.
- Ensuring that the case is dealt with expeditiously and fairly.
- Allotting to it an appropriate share of the court's resources, while taking into account the need to allot resources to other cases.

A pre-action letter should include:

- A clear summary of the facts
- Details of financial loss
- Compensation Recovery Unit details
- An indication of the injuries
- A request for documents.

The defendant should acknowledge receipt within 21 days and provide a detailed response and decision on liability within three months. If liability is denied, an explanation with sufficient clarity should be given so the plaintiff is aware of the case being made by the defence, including any allegation of contributory negligence. Any documents that are relevant to the action should be enclosed.

If there is no response to the pre-action letter, the plaintiff may issue proceedings.

Offers to settle

Where liability is admitted, the plaintiff should serve medical evidence together with a schedule of special damages and supporting documentation. A defendant can then make a written offer to settle within 21 days. The plaintiff has a further 21 days to make a counter-offer, which the defendant has 21 days to accept or reject.

Non-compliance

There are currently no formal costs sanctions for non-compliance with the pre-action protocol. However, in *Monaghan v The Very Reverent Graham sued on behalf of the Trustees of Milltown Cemetery* [2013] the judiciary showed how it may apply the protocol in practice.

continued...

...continued

In this case the defendant's insurers failed to provide pre-action discovery. As a consequence, the plaintiff's solicitors brought an application for pre-action discovery. Mr Justice Stephens, finding for the plaintiff, stated,

"[at] a fundamental level the pre-action protocol is an articulation of fairness. Before proceedings are issued the plaintiff should give proper information to allow a view to be formed by the defendant. A similar obligation rests on the defendant."

Costs were awarded against the defendant's insurers in relation to the application.

So, what can you do if a plaintiff's solicitor does not comply?

- Remind them of the pre-action protocol.
- Threaten to stay any proceedings prematurely issued.
- Put them on notice that you will raise the non-compliance when costs are being awarded.
- Refuse any pre-action discovery request until they have complied with the protocol.

Court procedure

High Court

The procedure for personal injury claims issued in the Queen's Bench Division is as follows:

- A writ of summons is the pleading that formally starts a claim.
- The defendant has 14 days to enter an appearance, or 21 days if the defendant is outside the jurisdiction.

- Once an appearance has been entered, the defendant requests that a statement of claim be served, together with all medical evidence under Order 25 of the Rules within six weeks.
- A statement of claim must state specifically the relief or remedy that the plaintiff claims, but costs need not be specifically claimed.
- The defence must be served within six weeks of receipt of the statement of claim, along with any notice for particulars asking for better information regarding the claim.
- The case will come before the High Court senior Queen's Bench judge one year after issue of the writ and at least six weeks before a trial date. The judge will check whether the case is ready for hearing and that all interlocutory matters have been dealt with to the satisfaction of the court and the parties. The judge may direct a meeting between the parties a few weeks prior to trial to discuss without prejudice resolution to avoid trial. This is particularly relevant to clinical negligence matters.
- The master will review a case nine months after the entering of an appearance. Often this takes place before the case is mentioned before the judge. The master will make directions as to case management and fix the trial date.

Offers

> There is no equivalent to a Part 36 offer in Northern Ireland. A defendant in a personal injury matter has the option of making a payment into court or a Calderbank offer.

Payments into court

The rules about payments into court are set out in Order 22 of the Rules. In summary, a defendant can make a payment into court:

- Before close of pleadings (i.e. 21 days after service of the reply to the defence);
- Not later than 14 weeks after this date; or
- Within four weeks of disclosure of the plaintiff's medical evidence under Order 25.

The plaintiff has 21 days after receipt of the notice of payment to accept the offer by serving the requisite notice. After this time, they can only do so with the express consent of the defendant. The interest on any monies paid into court is paid out to the defendant if the plaintiff accepts the lodgement. There are penalties in costs for a plaintiff who does not 'beat' the lodgement, i.e. achieve an award of damages higher than the figure paid in.

Calderbank offer

At any stage during the proceedings a defendant can write a Calderbank letter, in which it either makes a reasonable offer in relation to the claim and costs or offers to bear its own costs should the action be discontinued. This is intended to put the plaintiff at risk of costs.

Defence tactics

- If the plaintiff is not progressing the matter expeditiously a review before a master or a judge can be requested at any time.
- If the plaintiff does not deal with the pleadings in accordance with the Rules the defendant can make an application to strike out the plaintiff's case for non-compliance.
- It is also possible to apply to dismiss a claim for 'want of prosecution' if two years have passed without any further pleadings being served.

- A defendant can also seek to remit the proceedings to the county court.

County court

County court claims are commenced by way of a civil bill and can deal with a wide range of disputes.

The general procedure under the County Court Rules (Northern Ireland) 1981, as amended, (the County Court Rules) is as follows:

- Once a civil bill has been issued and served, a defendant has 21 days to enter a notice of intention to defend. Judgment can be entered by the plaintiff in default of a notice being served, but seven further days – the service period – should be allowed before they do so.
- At the same time as serving a notice of intention to defend, the defendant serves a notice to produce, a notice for discovery and a notice for further and better particulars. These notices should be served within 14 days of the notice of intention to defend.
- The plaintiff must then serve their replies to the notice for further and better particulars within 14 days of receiving the notice, along with any medical evidence.
- An exchange of lists of discoverable documents should occur between the parties once replies are received.
- The plaintiff can then serve a certificate of readiness, which should be prepared with the defendant's input, although this is not always the case. Once served, the certificate of readiness enables a trial date to be fixed.
- If a certificate of readiness is not served within six months of issue of a civil bill the case automatically comes before a judge for review. The judge will either make appropriate orders or fix a date for hearing.

Time limits for payments into court in the county court differ from those in the High Court:

- Where a case started life in the High Court but is then transferred to the county court (i.e. remitted), a payment into court must be made within eight days of the date of the order of remittal.
- In any other action, a payment into court must be made within 28 days of service of the plaintiff's medical evidence or within 28 days of service of the notice of intention to defend in non-personal injury matters.

Key features of claims in Northern Ireland

Alternative dispute resolution

- **Personal injury:** formal mediation in personal injury matters is not common in Northern Ireland. Instead, without prejudice informal settlement discussions take place. As it is a small jurisdiction, the lawyers generally know each other.
- **Other claims:** all forms of alternative dispute resolution are practised in non-personal injury matters, and include adjudication, mediation, expert determination and arbitration. Many commercial matters are resolved through these processes. In addition, the Commercial List is seen as being progressive in its use of 'hot tubbing' of witnesses and mini-trials, where a judge will give a preliminary (and non-binding) view after hearing the evidence of key witnesses.

Costs

The costs of the successful party are borne by the unsuccessful party.

In the High Court the Belfast Solicitors' Guide to High Court Costs is used. The court has some discretion in relation to costs, for example where a pre-action protocol has not been complied with, experts have been retained for no good reason or there has been delay on the part of the plaintiff.

In the county court, costs are dealt with by way of a statutory scale for solicitors and counsel under the County Court Fees (Amendment) Order (Northern Ireland) 2017. The plaintiff will base their costs on the amount of the settlement and/or award. Defendants claim costs in line with the amount claimed in the civil bill.

For example, consider a case involving a civil bill claiming £30,000. It settles for £17,500. The plaintiff will base their costs on the scale figure applicable to £17,500. The defendant will base their costs on the scale figure applicable to £30,000.

> Costs are not front-loaded in Northern Ireland. Conditional fee agreements and after-the-event insurance are not used. Costs are fixed and therefore certain. Whereas claimant firms in England and Wales may incur sizeable costs at an early stage on pre-action investigations, disclosure and witness statements, in Northern Ireland the scale fee is fixed regardless of the amount of time spent by the solicitor before and after issue of proceedings.

Local conventions provide that any matter that is settled before proceedings has costs allowed at two-thirds of the scale figure applicable to the settlement. Where proceedings have been issued, but resolved before a certificate of readiness is served, then costs are three-quarters of the scale figure.

Once fixed for trial the full scale figure will apply. This makes it very economical to litigate in the county court in Northern Ireland as fixed fees apply up to and including trial.

The case of *Tomasz Baranowski (by his mother and next friend Anna Baranowski) v Michael* [2014] set the precedent for costs in Northern Ireland in which the defendant has been successful.

By way of background, the plaintiff's claim was dismissed by the court and the plaintiff was ordered to pay the defendant's costs.

The defendant's insurance company had appointed a defence panel solicitor under a costs agreement. This agreement stipulated that the defence solicitor would provide a discount on the County Court Scale; however, if the defendant was successful, then the full fee would apply. The plaintiff appealed the costs order and Mr Justice Stephens held that sums due under a conditional normal fee agreement were irrecoverable, on public policy grounds.

The implication is that cases in which there is a discount costs agreement and the defendant is successful, the recoverable sum will be that of the costs agreement.

Documentary evidence

Order 24 of the Rules deals with discovery of documents in the High Court. This is automatic after a defence has been served, reply to defence received and the pleadings closed. A list of documents that are relevant or material to any question arising in the action must be drawn up and served on/exchanged with all the parties in the action. If discovery is inadequate then a specific discovery application can be brought.

There is no automatic discovery in the county court. A notice for discovery must be served. If the plaintiff does not comply with this, an order can be sought ex parte under Order 15 of the County Court Rules. Generally, discovery should not be applied for until replies to particulars are received. A list of documents gives the right of inspection of the documents that are stated to be discoverable as between the parties.

Enterprise Act 2013

It is arguable that section 69 of the Enterprise and Regulatory Reform Act 2013 does not extend to Northern Ireland. This section provides that breach of a health and safety regulation shall not be actionable except to the extent that subsequent regulations might provide. There has been no case law to date on the point and it is anticipated that clarification will be sought in the future, so watch this space.

Funding

While legal aid is still available in Northern Ireland for civil claims, this is under review. The Department of Justice is proposing that civil legal aid be withdrawn from personal injury cases. This is subject to an exception for claims relating to alleged clinical negligence resulting in brain damage to babies. Alternatives, including conditional fee agreements (CFAs), are being considered.

However, at present, CFAs are not applicable in Northern Ireland. The position at this stage is fluid as discussions are ongoing.

Quantum

Awards of general damages for personal injuries are determined with reference to the guidelines published by the Judicial Studies Board for Northern Ireland, known as the 'Green Book'. The guidelines for specific categories of injuries are broad in their application and range and so are of limited assistance. The guidelines should only be seen as a general guide as each personal injury case is nuanced.

Compared to England and Wales, general damages tend to be higher in Northern Ireland but care costs are generally lower. In addition, claims for care are not as prevalent.

Recess

The High Court goes into recess for July and August. There are no trials listed during this period and a limited number of dates are available for masters' courts to process applications. There is always an emergency rota of judges available for injunctions and emergency applications but the general run-of-the-mill cases will not be dealt with during this time.

The county courts are more flexible and hold trials throughout the summer.

Witness statements

There is generally no exchange of witness statements in Northern Ireland as evidence is given orally. There are provisions under the Civil Evidence (Northern Ireland) Order 1997, in restricted circumstances, for the admissibility of witness statements.

Scotland

Introduction

Scotland's court system was, broadly speaking, preserved in the Acts of Union 1707. The creation of the Scottish Parliament in the late 1990s and differing political approaches north and south of the border have contributed to an increasingly divergent system. Substantial court reforms are ongoing.

Institutions

> An All-Scotland Sheriff Personal Injury Court was established in September 2015 to deal with employers' liability claims valued at £1,000 upwards and other personal injury claims valued at more than £5,000. The specialist court is based in Edinburgh.

Pursuers retain the option of litigating at their local sheriff court under either summary cause (actions up to £5,000) or ordinary cause (actions over £5,000) procedures, which have contained specialist personal injury provisions for some time.

Non-personal injury claims will continue to be dealt with at local sheriff courts. Sheriff courts have exclusive jurisdiction for any dispute where the sum sought is up to £100,000. There is no upper limit on sheriff court jurisdiction. However, where the sum sought is above £100,000 it is open to a pursuer to bring proceedings in the Court of Session, which is Scotland's highest civil court (although appeal to the Supreme Court is possible).

Terminology

Table 2 – Terminology

England and Wales	Scotland
Claimant	Pursuer (or claimant for some procedures)
Defence	Answers/Defences
Defendant	Defender
Lodge/file at court	Enrol
Schedule of special damages	Valuation
Trial	Diet of proof

Pre-action procedure

New compulsory pre-action protocol

> The new compulsory protocol takes effect in relation to cases where the accident, or the circumstances giving rise to the claim for damages, occurred on or after 28 November 2016.
>
> The new protocol applies to personal injury claims (with some exceptions) up to a value of £25,000 in both the local sheriff courts and the All-Scotland Sheriff Personal Injury Court. It amends the existing court rules so that parties are required to comply with the compulsory protocol before commencing proceedings.

The protocol requires the pursuer (known as the claimant for the purposes of the protocol) to issue a claim form and progress the claim through to the settlement stage. If the defender declines to make an offer, only then is the claimant entitled to raise proceedings.

If an offer is made, the claimant must either accept this or issue a reasoned response, explaining why it has been rejected. A period of 14 days then follows to allow final settlement negotiations.

Importantly, the compulsory protocol provides the courts with an express power to make an award of expenses against a party who either:

- Fails to comply with the protocol, or
- Unreasonably fails to accept a settlement offer, which is then lodged as a tender once proceedings are raised.

The protocol also sets out the expenses to be paid to the claimant. These are based on a fixed amount, plus a percentage of the damages and VAT.

Voluntary pre-action protocols

There are also voluntary pre-action protocols in place for other personal injury, professional negligence and disease claims. For the purposes of this chapter, the focus is on the current voluntary personal injury pre-action protocol. This is usually used when the accident occurred before 28 November 2016.

The hint is in the name: both parties must voluntarily agree to abide by the protocol. The pursuer's letter of claim should provide information, including their full name, address, date of birth and national insurance number, and should set out details of what happened, where it happened, alleged breaches of common law/ statutory duties, injuries sustained and treatment received. A three-month investigation period follows.

If liability is not admitted, the insurer should reply giving reasons for the denial, including any alternative version of events relied on and all available documents supporting its position.

If liability is admitted:

- The admission is normally binding unless subsequently there is evidence that the claim was fraudulent.
- The pursuer must instruct a medical expert within five weeks. The report should follow a standard format.
- Within five weeks of receipt of the medical report the pursuer's agents must disclose the medical report along with a valuation of the claim confirming all heads of claim and the value attributable to each.
- The insurer/defender has five weeks to provide a counter-schedule of valuation.
- The pursuer has a further five weeks to say whether the counter-schedule is accepted or not.
- If an agreement is reached then damages and expenses must be paid within five weeks of settlement.

If the parties agree, there can be flexibility in the process. However, some firms will proceed to litigation quickly in the event of any default.

Where the pre-action protocol is agreed to and settlement is achieved, costs are calculated on a set scale, based on an instruction fee and an additional completion fee, which is a percentage of the settlement sum.

Court procedure

Table 3 provides an overview of the timetable for a claim proceeding through the Court of Session or the sheriff courts.

Court of Session

A Court of Session action commences with a summons, which is served on the defender or their nominated solicitors and subsequently lodged at court 'to call':

- The summons in a personal injury action must be lodged at court to call within three months of the date of service.
- In non-personal injury matters, the time limit for lodging is generally a year and a day from service.
- The summons cannot be lodged to call until 21 days after service on the defender.

A calling list is published as part of the court rolls, which are updated daily online. While it is good etiquette for a pursuer's agents to inform nominated defence solicitors that they have lodged the summons to call, this is not a universal practice. Accordingly, a summons that is served should be passed to agents as soon as possible to avoid a calling being missed.

After the summons calls, agents for the defenders must enter appearance within three court days. This tells the court that agents are appointed. Defences must be lodged within seven court days of the summons calling. Accordingly, time can be very tight.

On the lodging of a defence the court procedure will commence.

Personal injury

The court will issue a timetable, which sets out the procedural deadlines for the case. The rules require that a number of steps take place. Those steps must occur within the timescales outlined in the rules.

Parties can apply to the court to vary the timetable/procedure, but must provide some justification for doing so. The timetable dates will vary according to court holiday periods and other factors. The total duration of a timetable is generally approximately nine months. The timetable makes an allowance for a four-day diet of proof. Hearings only take place from Tuesday to Friday. If a six- or eight-day hearing is required then the first available dates are likely to be 18 months to two years from the time the record is lodged.

Table 3 – Overview of court timetable

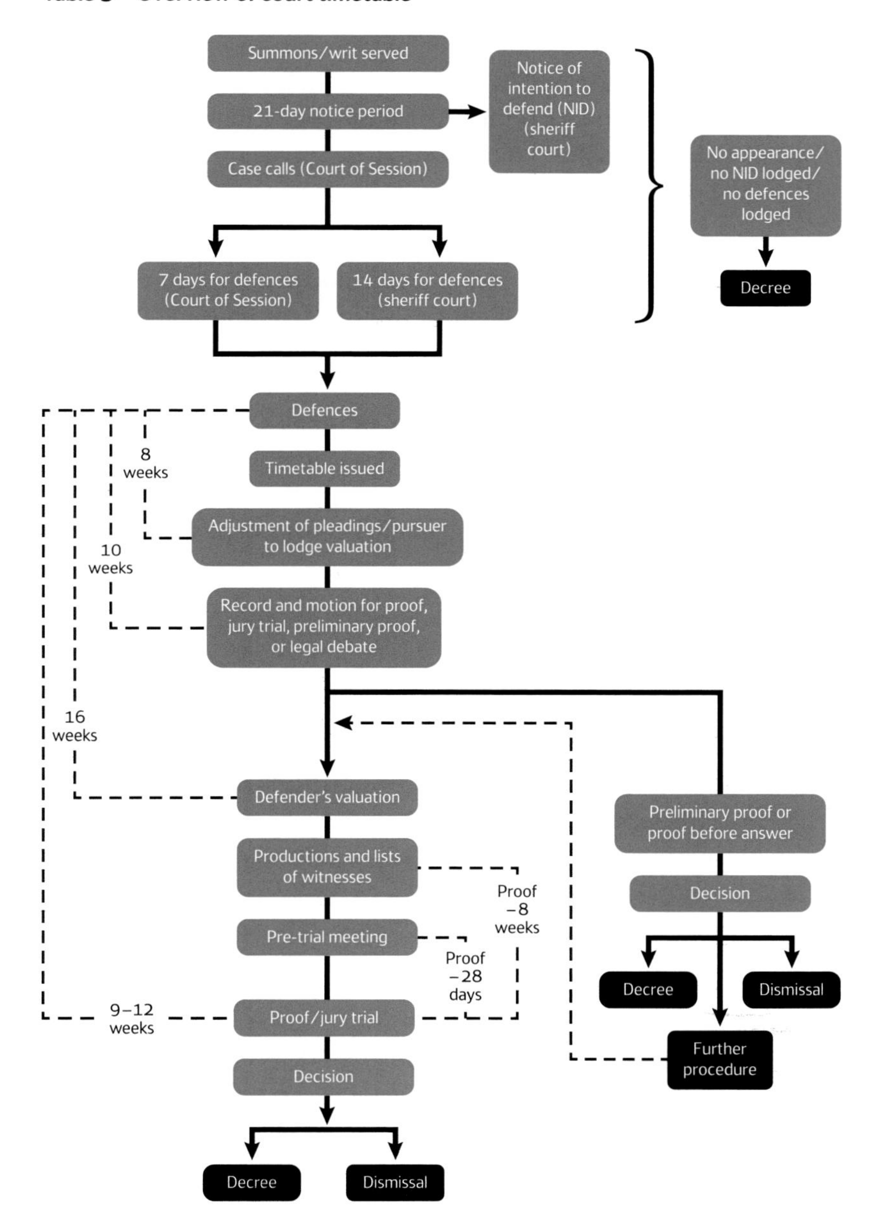

Key stages in the process include the following:

- The first deadlines are, where relevant, to enrol a motion to withdraw the claim (by the pursuer) or bring in a third party (by the defender). Bringing in a third party requires a revision of the timetable to allow them to be served and then to enter the process. The timetable will then begin again.
- On raising the action the pursuer is granted a specification of documents to recover essential documents such as medical records, accident records and earnings information. The theory is that this will ensure that the key information is obtained early in the process. A commission is held at a later stage to investigate any documentation that has not been produced. In theory, the pursuer's agents should then lodge all documentation at court to allow both sides to focus the issues. This deadline is frequently ignored in practice.
- The adjustment period refers to the time for alteration. i.e. revising the written pleadings in the case. Pleadings in personal injury actions are less technical and detailed than previously. However, there does need to be fair notice of both sides' cases.
- When the adjustment period ends, the pursuer is required to lodge a statement of valuation of claim. This sets out the heads of claim and the interest sought. Valuations will ignore issues of liability and contributory negligence, but issues of medical causation can be addressed. It is a requirement to list any documentary evidence being relied on in support of the valuation.
- The pursuer is then required to prepare a composite document of the summons and defence(s). That document is called the record and it is lodged with a motion and a certified estimate of the number of days required for the proof. Unless there is something contentious, the court will generally proceed to fix the proof dates previously contained in the timetable.

- The defender has a period to consider the pursuer's statement of valuation of claim before lodging a counter-statement of valuation of claim.
- The next stage in the process is the deadline for lodging lists of witnesses that each side intends to call and lodging any remaining documents they wish to rely on. This deadline is critical to the progress of the action and any party will find themselves in very significant difficulty if they fail to comply with it.
- The final timetabled requirement before the proof is the lodging of a pre-trial minute. This is prepared following a joint pre-trial meeting of the parties' representatives to explore settlement, which is similar to a joint settlement meeting in England. The minute is completed by both sides and sets out what, if anything, can be agreed and what remains in dispute. One critical feature of the minute is the opportunity for the defender to take a different view on proof duration. If that happens then the minute may not be signed and a procedural hearing, called a 'by order hearing' will be triggered so the court can be addressed on that issue. The pre-trial meeting often achieves settlement as both sides are required to have access to someone who can give instructions.

The court's view on the strictness of the timetable has changed over time. When this procedure was introduced in 2003, there was a relaxed approach to timetable deadlines. In the past few years there has been an increasing unwillingness to allow any derogation from the deadlines. It is necessary to provide reason for failure to meet the requirements of the timetable.

All-Scotland Sheriff Personal Injury Court

Based in the Edinburgh sheriff court, the All-Scotland Sheriff Personal Injury Court has jurisdiction to hear personal injury actions from across Scotland. There are six specialist sheriffs appointed to deal with cases. The intention is that the specialist sheriffs will manage and drive the progress of actions.

The court procedure is broadly similar to the Court of Session procedure. However, the precise interpretation of rules and expected practices are still developing.

The court provides the option of a jury trial. The first jury trial took place on 9 May 2017. It is the pursuer's automatic right unless cause can be shown that the case is not appropriate for a jury, for example if there are complex issues of medical negligence or in relation to quantification.

Sheriff courts

In the sheriff courts, personal injury cases will follow either summary cause personal injury procedure or ordinary cause personal injury procedure. There are very few differences between these procedures, which are also similar to those used in the Court of Session. Table 3 sets out an overview of the procedure.

Simple procedure

A new 'simple procedure' came into force on 28 November 2016. This applies to claims up to £5,000.

The approach of the court in simple procedure cases is to be as informal as is appropriate, taking into account the nature and complexity of the matter. Sheriffs have wide powers and may take any steps or make any order necessary to encourage negotiation or alternative dispute resolution, or to decide the case.

continued...

> *...continued*
>
> Within the rules, there is a reference to a 'portal' on the Scottish Courts and Tribunals Service website. This will be introduced in two phases. Phase 1 introduces a case tracker and will be available in March 2018.

Making a claim

To begin a simple procedure case, the pursuer (known as the claimant for the purposes of this procedure) must complete a claim form and send this to court. This sets out the parties, the essential facts, what the claimant wants, why they should succeed, and the steps already taken to resolve the dispute.

The sheriff's clerk checks this and registers the claim. A timetable is then issued and the claim form is served on the defender (known as the respondent). The timetable sets out the last date for service and the last date for a response.

Responding to a claim

If the response form indicates that the respondent admits the claim and will settle it, the sheriff may then do one of three things:

- Dismiss the claim
- Award some or all of what is asked for
- Order the claimant to come to court to discuss matters.

If no response form is received by the court the sheriff may make a decision awarding the claimant some or all of what was requested in the claim form or dismiss the claim.

If the respondent disputes the claim, the sheriff must consider the case in private and then send the parties the first written orders within two weeks from the date the court received the response form. The orders may do any of the following:

- Refer the parties to alternative dispute resolution
- Arrange a case management discussion
- Arrange a hearing
- Indicate that the sheriff is considering making a decision without a hearing
- Use their powers to dismiss a claim or decide a case.

The hearing

The purpose of the hearing is to help the sheriff resolve the dispute.

The sheriff may refer parties to alternative dispute resolution, and if the sheriff thinks a negotiated settlement is possible, the sheriff must help the parties to do so. If no negotiated settlement is possible, the sheriff must resolve the dispute by deciding it at the hearing.

At the end of the hearing, the sheriff may either make an immediate decision or reserve judgment. In any event, the sheriff must set out the decision in the case in a decision form. Once a claim has been resolved the sheriff must make an order about expenses.

Key features of claims in Scotland

Asbestos

Damages (Asbestos-related Conditions) (Scotland) Act 2009

In *Rothwell v Chemical & Insulating Co Ltd and another* [2006], the House of Lords held that asymptomatic asbestos-related conditions caused as a result of employment were not compensable in negligence.

continued...

...continued

In light of *Rothwell*, the Scottish Parliament passed the Damages (Asbestos-related Conditions) (Scotland) Act 2009. In practice, this reversed the *Rothwell* decision in Scotland and provided that asymptomatic pleural plaques did in fact constitute harm and injury.

Since then, there have been a number of cases that have provided guidance in relation to appropriate assessments of quantum. The following are examples:

- *WW v Advocate General for Scotland* [2015]: Lord Pentland considered that the bracket in England and Wales for provisional damages for asymptomatic pleural plaques with associated moderate anxiety would have fallen between £5,500 and £9,000 if *Rothwell* had not happened. He awarded provisional damages of £8,500, on the basis that the pursuer had suffered a greater level of anxiety than the average pleural plaques sufferer.
- *Harris v Advocate General for Scotland* [2016]: Lord Boyd agreed with this bracket. In this case, where the pursuer did not suffer from the same level of anxiety, he considered an award of provisional damages of £7,500 was appropriate. The pursuer's agents put forward a formula for calculating full and final damages based on the potential loss of expectation of life should the pursuer develop a more serious condition, for example, mesothelioma. That formula was viewed favourably by Lord Boyd and is now used by pursuer firms when negotiating settlements and valuing cases.

Framework agreement

Following the introduction of the 2009 Act, a framework agreement was negotiated between various pursuer agents and the insurance industry. This provided agreed levels of damages for:

- Final damages, on a sliding scale of between £1,500 and £8,000, dependent upon the age of the pursuer.
- Provisional damages in the fixed sum of £4,000, with agreed return conditions.

The framework agreement also includes provisions for interest on damages and expenses.

The awards in *WW* and *Harris* represent increases in the level of damages when compared to the framework agreement. As at August 2016, it is understood that pursuer firms are endeavouring to renegotiate the framework agreement in line with these awards.

Recovery of Medical Costs for Asbestos Diseases (Scotland) Bill

The Recovery of Medical Costs for Asbestos Diseases (Scotland) Bill was lodged at the Scottish Parliament in January 2015, following in the footsteps of a similar bill in Wales. Scottish National Party MSP Stuart McMillan, who has a long history with Clydeside Action on Asbestos, proposed it as a Member's bill.

It proposed that the costs incurred by the National Health Service in relation to diagnosing and treating asbestos-related conditions should be recoverable from those responsible for compensating the victim.

The Bill was ultimately not successful. However, there have since been proposals to put forward a new bill in similar terms.

Documentary evidence

Scotland has no formal disclosure procedure. However, there is provision under which documentation can be recovered.

As indicated above, a pursuer may append a specification of documents to their summons or writ. This seeks the recovery of medical and employment information, together with accident reports and witness statements, etc.

Once the summons is signed or the writ warranted (this being when the court has given authority to serve the proceedings on the defender), the specification of documents can be served on those likely to be in possession of documents, known as 'havers', along with the relevant order. Typically, the identified havers are the pursuer's GP, treating hospital(s) and employer. Strictly speaking, a haver only has seven days to produce the documentation, but compliance is not frequent.

If the order is not complied with by a particular haver, a commission can be fixed. At this hearing, the haver is examined to identify what steps have been taken to secure and/or recover documentation.

Confidential documents are sent to the court (rather than the party who served the order) in a sealed envelope.

Any pursuer seeking to fix a commission in relation to a specification of documents served alongside a writ/summons must do so within 28 days of defences being lodged at court.

Further specifications may be lodged at court throughout an action. However, to justify a specification, there must usually be pleadings on record in relation to the particular documents sought. Specifications are often opposed on the grounds that they are too wide and amount to a 'fishing expedition'.

Fatal claims

The valuation of claims for wrongful death in Scotland is starkly different to other jurisdictions in the United Kingdom.

The deceased's relatives are broadly defined in the Damages (Scotland) Act 2011 to include the deceased's partner, parents, children, grandchildren and siblings. They are entitled to claim for 'loss of society', that is, distress, grief and loss of any 'non-patrimonial' (non-monetary) benefit they might have been expected to derive from the deceased's society and guidance had they not died.

Awards are dependent on the particular impact suffered by the family. When defending claims it can be difficult to pick apart the nature of the relationship between the deceased and the relative; by necessity, awards made are arbitrary. There are no specific rules about calculation of this type of damages or fixed awards. The value of loss of society awards has varied wildly over the years but the trend has been for increased awards by both judges and juries. The awards are far greater than in other parts of the United Kingdom.

There is a generally recognised hierarchy of awards for relatives, depending on their relationship with the deceased. Spouses and parents of young adult children are at the top of the scale. Table 4 sets out examples of awards made to relatives in recently decided cases.

Table 4 – Examples of awards to relatives

Year	Summary	Relative	Award
2010	21-year-old male RAF serviceman killed in Nimrod crash in Afghanistan in 2006 (jury award)	Single mother (54)	£90,000
		Sibling (29): first sibling award in Scotland	£60,000
2013	82-year-old male former shipyard worker died of mesothelioma caused by asbestos exposure (jury award)	Widow	£40,000
		Son and daughter	£25,000 each
		Two grandchildren (14)	£8,000 each
		Grandchild (7)	£4,000
		Grandchild (2)	£1,500
		Brother	£8,000
2014	60-year-old male pedestrian killed when standing at rear of his parked vehicle (judge award)	Granddaughter (5)	£18,000
		Granddaughter (3)	£16,000
		Grandson (born five months after death)	£14,000

Year	Summary	Relative	Award
2016	Deceased was a 64-year-old female passenger, killed instantly in a head on collision	Widower Sons Granddaughter (13) Two granddaughters (both mid-teens)	£120,000 £50,000 each £20,000 £15,000 each

It is also likely there will be loss of support claims by relatives. These are currently subject to a maximum of 75% of the deceased's net annual income. The deceased's spouse or partner and any dependent children are automatically entitled to claim loss of support as a result of s.7 of the 2011 Act. Other relatives are entitled to claim for any actual loss of support that they can evidence.

Under s.6 of the 2011 Act, relatives are also entitled to claim in respect of loss of services. They may claim a reasonable sum for personal services that would have been rendered to them by the deceased.

Jury awards

The launch of the All-Scotland Sheriff Personal Injury Court introduced civil jury trials at sheriff court level. Previously, the use of a civil jury was restricted to Court of Session matters.

Juries have historically been much more favourable to pursuers and tend to award higher sums. Jury awards in Scotland, particularly in fatal cases, have had a decidedly upward trend in recent years.

Civil jury procedure in Scotland was revised as a result of the judgment of the Court of Session in *Hamilton v Ferguson Transport (Spean Bridge) Ltd* and *Thomson v Dennis Thomson Builders Ltd* [2012], the appeals of which were heard together. Following this decision, counsel for each party addresses the judge as to the appropriate level of compensation, and the judge then puts a spectrum of awards to the jury. However, the jury is not bound to keep to that spectrum.

A detailed review of recent jury awards is outside the scope of this chapter. However, it is worth noting the unreported case of *Anderson and others v Brig Brae Garage Ltd* [2015]. The fiancée, father and baby daughter of a man killed in the course of his employment sought damages.

The spectrum of awards put to the jury in respect of the fiancée was £100,000 to £140,000, and £50,000 to £80,000 for the father and the baby. The jury made a total award to the fiancée of £140,000. This is currently the highest fatal award in Scotland, and is more than double the second highest comparable award. The father and the daughter were both awarded £80,000.

It should, therefore, be borne in mind that juries are likely to be sympathetic to pursuers and much more generous in terms of the awards made.

Witness statements

It is important to note that for most civil cases in Scotland there are no written witness statements. All witnesses are required to attend court, give oral evidence and be subject to examination and cross-examination. Until the list of witnesses is lodged, it can be unclear to either party who is going to be in attendance at the proof as a witness for their opponent. The general rule is that witnesses can speak without documents but documents cannot speak for themselves.

Ireland

Introduction

Ireland is a jurisdiction comprising 26 counties with a population of approximately 4.5 million people. The courts are governed by legislation but also by a written constitution, Bunreacht na hÉireann.

There is a perception that litigating in Ireland is a slow process. Damages are significantly higher in personal injury matters than in other European jurisdictions.

In recent years the courts are, however, very alert to exaggeration of injury and fraud.

Institutions

The Irish courts comprise the Supreme Court, the Court of Appeal, the High Court, the Commercial Court (the fast track division of the High Court for high-value cases of a commercial nature), the Circuit Court and the District Court.

The Supreme Court is the highest court in the state and its primary function is a court of appeal. It hears appeals against judgments and orders of the High Court. It also hears certain applications on points of law referred from the lower court. It deals with all important legal points or constitutional challenges.

The Court of Appeal was established in 2014 and deals with the majority of appeals in tort matters as a result of a Constitutional Referendum and was incorporated into the judicial system by SI 485/2014 RSC (Court of Appeal Act 2014). Its purpose was to facilitate the Supreme Court and alleviate the pressure on its appeals list. It is an appellate court and is governed by Order 86A RSC.

The High Court consists of 36 judges each of whom sit alone. The High Court sits continuously in Dublin with the exception of a long vacation, which is during the months of August and September.

Sittings occur throughout the year at provincial venues of Dundalk, Sligo, Galway, Limerick, Cork, Waterford and Kilkenny. The High Court is the Court of Appeal from the Circuit Court.

The Circuit Court consists of the President of the Circuit Court and sits in each county throughout the country and, for administrative purposes, the Court Service has divided it into eight circuits. The Circuit Court only sits continually throughout the legal term in Dublin and Cork and sits periodically on other circuits. The Circuit Court is the Court of Appeal from the District Court.

The District Court is a court of more limited jurisdiction than the Circuit Court or the High Court. The island is divided into a large number of District Court areas and the plaintiff normally brings proceedings in the area where the defendant resides or ordinarily carries on business. The majority of claims in the District Court relate to material damage, breach of contract, debt recovery and family law matters together with some certain licensing matters. However the Court also deals with minor Personal Injuries Assessment Board (PIAB) cases where damages sought are under the monetary limit of €15,000.

The Circuit Court is the Court of Appeal from the District Court.

Terminology

Ireland	England & Wales	Scotland
Plaintiff	Claimant	Pursuer (or claimant for some procedures)
Defence	Defence	Answer
Defendant	Defendant	Defender
Lodge/file at court	Lodge/file at court	Enrol
Schedule of Special Damages	Schedule of Special Damages	Valuation
Trial/hearing	Trial	Diet of proof

Pre-action

Personal injury cases

The Civil Liability & Courts Act 2004 introduced pre-action procedures in personal injury matters (with the exception of injuries arising out of clinical negligence claims).

- Section 8 provides that a letter of claim must be issued within two months of the date of the accident. Courts interpret this provision loosely and do not hold plaintiffs to the same.
- Section 12 provides that the plaintiff can call upon the defendant to preserve relevant evidence and if the defendant fails to undertake to do so, the plaintiff can apply to the courts by way of injunction proceedings which often prove costly for the defendant.

The Personal Injury Assessment Board Act 2003 provides:

- Section 11 – that the plaintiff completes an application form known as Form A and sends it with a medical report to the Injuries Board.
- Section 13 – that the Injuries Board sends the application to the respondent allowing the respondent 90-days to respond. (It is important to note that if the defendant or its insurer does not respond within the 90 day period, the matter is deemed to be one for assessment only.)
- Section 17 – that the Injuries Board may use its discretion not to assess the claim where for example the interaction of other injuries makes assessment too complex, for example, when there is a large psychological element to the injury or when it is unlikely that an award will be made within the statutory timeframe due to an uncertain prognosis.

- Section 14 – that if the respondent declines to allow the Injuries Board to deal with the matter, or in circumstances where the Injuries Board declines to assess the claim using its discretion, an authorisation is issued allowing the plaintiff to proceed to the courts.
- If assessment proceeds, the Injuries Board arranges medical appointments for the plaintiff (which the respondent pays for) and also calls on the plaintiff to furnish details of any special damages.
- The Injuries Board will assess the amount of damages payable within nine months of receipt of the plaintiff's application form. However, they can extend this period by a further six months by informing all parties.
- Once assessment has been made the plaintiff has 28 days to accept or reject the award. If the plaintiff fails to respond, the award is deemed to be rejected.
- The respondent has only 21 days to accept or reject the award, and if they fail to respond, the award is deemed to be accepted.

It is important to note that if the respondent fails to respond to the Injuries Board within the earlier 90-day deadline, the assessment by the Injuries Board will proceed by default. However the respondent can still reject the award and proceed to fully defend the matter.

Throughout the PIAB procedure parties can if they are both agreeable proceed to negotiations and notify the Injuries Board if the matter settles.

Costs

Prior to October 2007, no costs were awarded by PIAB when making an award, with the exception of cases requiring ruling before the court. Since October 2007, PIAB has changed its policy and now will award costs in cases in which it deems the claimant as "vulnerable". A "vulnerable" claimant has yet to be defined in either the legislation or in common law and, accordingly, it is open to the claimant to make such an application for costs to PIAB in every case. While it is likely that most will be refused, the exact policy of PIAB in dealing with these applications remains unclear.

It is also important to note that further to Section 51 of the Personal Injuries Board Amendment Act 2007, when an assessment has been made by the Injuries Board which the plaintiff rejects but the respondent accepts, this assessment will act as a tender in the proceedings going forward.

PIAB procedure at a glance

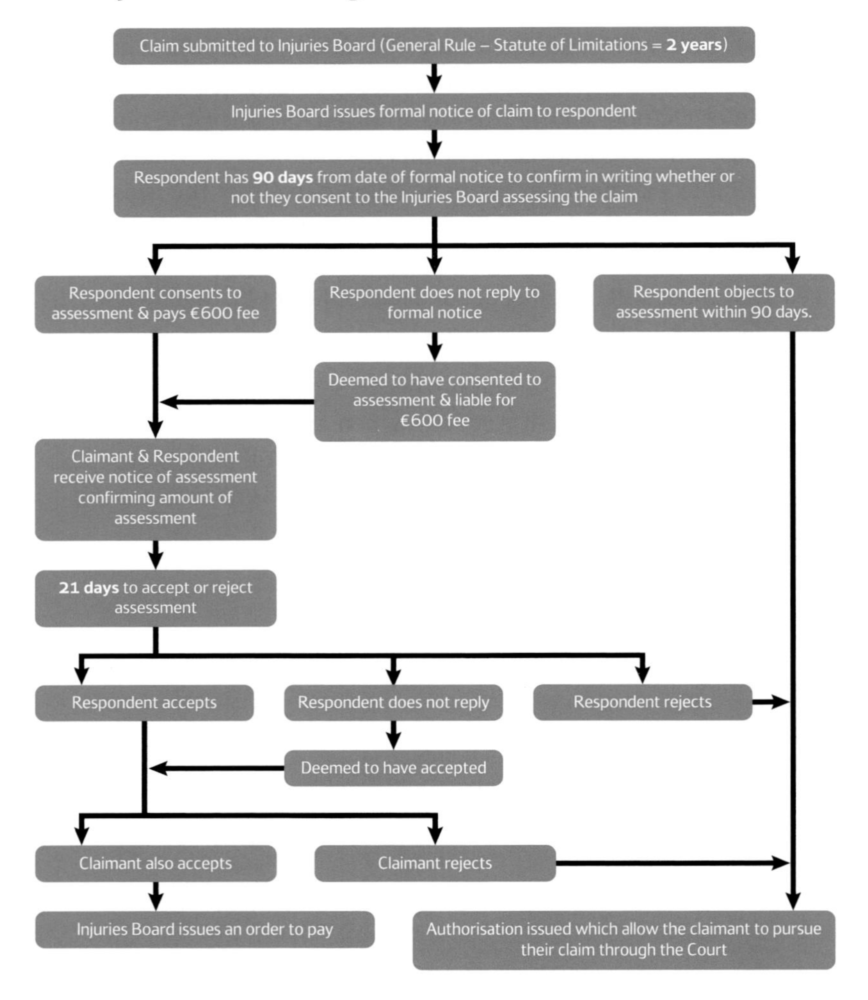

Court procedure

The time limits for pleadings, but not the procedures, differ between the Circuit and the High Court.

- Jurisdiction of the Circuit Court for personal injury claims is valued between €15,000 and €60,000 and for non-personal injury matters €75,000.

- The Circuit Court is the Court of Appeal for the District Court.
- The High Court has unlimited jurisdiction.
- The High Court is the Court of Appeal for the Circuit Court.

  In both courts:

  - A personal injuries summons is issued on production of an authorisation from PIAB. The personal injuries summons must include:
  - The person's personal details
  - Their public service number
  - The defendant's details
  - The injuries the plaintiff is alleged to have suffered
  - The particulars of special damage
  - The acts of negligence and wrongdoing against the defendant.

The personal injuries summons must be accompanied by an affidavit verifying the contents of all pleadings in the summons but also all advices to expert witnesses.

The defendant enters an Appearance and raises a notice for further particulars.

The plaintiff responds and it then falls to the defendant to file a defence.

In terms of the defence where liability is in issue, the defendant must swear an affidavit verifying that each individual denial and allegation of contributory negligence are true. Filing an incorrect defence and swearing a false affidavit can lead to criminal prosecution. This results in early investigations with defendants and their insurers and means that a full defence can only be filed based on known evidence and expert reports in this jurisdiction. Since the introduction of this procedure in 2004 a blanket defence cannot be filed unless the defendant can stand over the denials. It is at defence stage that a notice of lodgement or tender, as discussed below, must be filed. Only following a defence can a plaintiff or a defendant request discovery of documents.

It is open to either party to then set the case down for trial. There is no disclosure provision in the Circuit Court but it is usual for parties to attempt to agree medical evidence.

In the High Court, disclosure of all expert reports must be made to include any memo of a consultation with an expert witness. Witnesses as to fact must also be disclosed by both parties prior to a hearing date being assigned.

The separate time limits for both courts are set out on the following pages.

Overview of Circuit Court procedure: (for claims €15,000 to €60,000 in personal injuries cases)

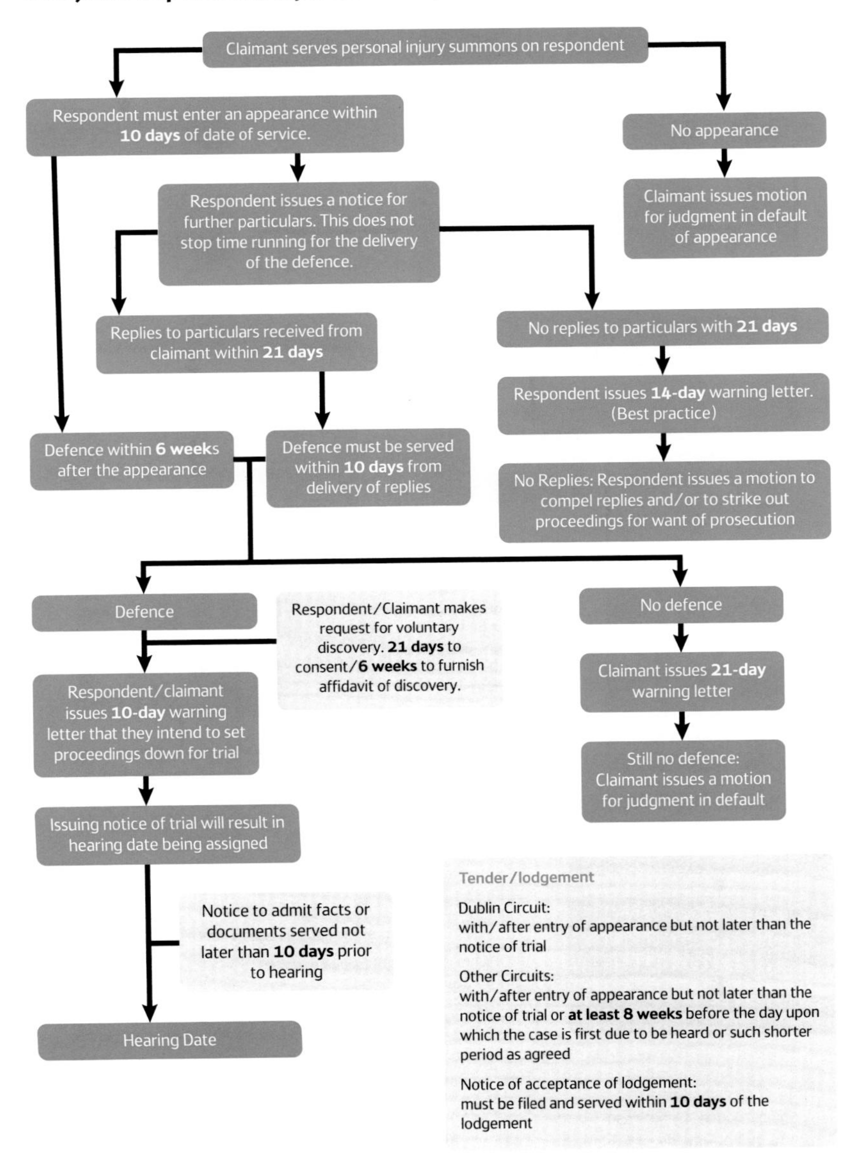
Claimant serves personal injury summons on respondent
Respondent must enter an appearance within **10 days** of date of service.
No appearance
Claimant issues motion for judgment in default of appearance
Respondent issues a notice for further particulars. This does not stop time running for the delivery of the defence.
Replies to particulars received from claimant within **21 days**
No replies to particulars with **21 days**
Respondent issues **14-day** warning letter. (Best practice)
Defence within **6 weeks** after the appearance
Defence must be served within **10 days** from delivery of replies
No Replies: Respondent issues a motion to compel replies and/or to strike out proceedings for want of prosecution
Defence
Respondent/Claimant makes request for voluntary discovery. **21 days** to consent/**6 weeks** to furnish affidavit of discovery.
No defence
Claimant issues **21-day** warning letter
Respondent/claimant issues **10-day** warning letter that they intend to set proceedings down for trial
Still no defence: Claimant issues a motion for judgment in default
Issuing notice of trial will result in hearing date being assigned
Notice to admit facts or documents served not later than **10 days** prior to hearing
Hearing Date
Tender/lodgement
Dublin Circuit:
with/after entry of appearance but not later than the notice of trial
Other Circuits:
with/after entry of appearance but not later than the notice of trial or **at least 8 weeks** before the day upon which the case is first due to be heard or such shorter period as agreed
Notice of acceptance of lodgement:
must be filed and served within **10 days** of the lodgement

Overview of High Court procedure: (for claims exceeding €75,000, save for personal injuries cases – claims in excess of €60,000)

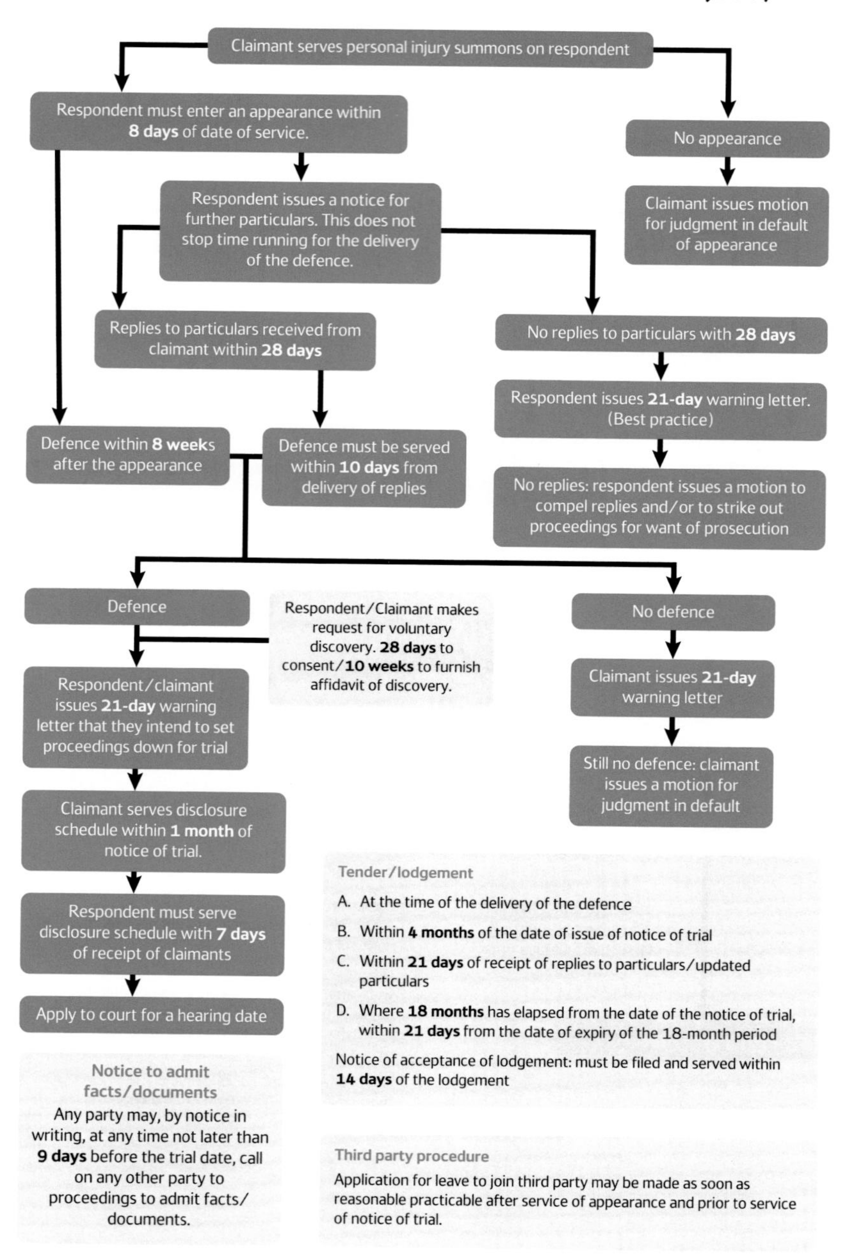
Claimant serves personal injury summons on respondent
Respondent must enter an appearance within 8 days of date of service.
No appearance
Claimant issues motion for judgment in default of appearance
Respondent issues a notice for further particulars. This does not stop time running for the delivery of the defence.
Replies to particulars received from claimant within 28 days
No replies to particulars with 28 days
Respondent issues 21-day warning letter. (Best practice)
No replies: respondent issues a motion to compel replies and/or to strike out proceedings for want of prosecution
Defence within 8 weeks after the appearance
Defence must be served within 10 days from delivery of replies
Defence
Respondent/Claimant makes request for voluntary discovery. 28 days to consent/10 weeks to furnish affidavit of discovery.
No defence
Claimant issues 21-day warning letter
Still no defence: claimant issues a motion for judgment in default
Respondent/claimant issues 21-day warning letter that they intend to set proceedings down for trial
Claimant serves disclosure schedule within 1 month of notice of trial.
Respondent must serve disclosure schedule with 7 days of receipt of claimants
Apply to court for a hearing date
Tender/lodgement
A. At the time of the delivery of the defence
B. Within 4 months of the date of issue of notice of trial
C. Within 21 days of receipt of replies to particulars/updated particulars
D. Where 18 months has elapsed from the date of the notice of trial, within 21 days from the date of expiry of the 18-month period
Notice of acceptance of lodgement: must be filed and served within 14 days of the lodgement
Notice to admit facts/documents
Any party may, by notice in writing, at any time not later than 9 days before the trial date, call on any other party to proceedings to admit facts/documents.
Third party procedure
Application for leave to join third party may be made as soon as reasonable practicable after service of appearance and prior to service of notice of trial.

Key features of claims in Ireland

Statute of Limitations

It should be noted that Section 50 of the Personal Injuries Assessment Board Act 2003 stops the clock running in respect of the limitation periods from the date of acknowledgment by PIAB of the plaintiff's Form A application and for a period of six months after the issuing of the Authorisation.

At this point the clock will start to run again.

Personal injury actions

Such actions shall not be brought after the expiration of two years from the date:

a) on which the cause of action accrued; or

b) when the plaintiff first had the requisite knowledge as defined in s.2 of the Statute of Limitation (Amendment) Act 1991.

It is important to note that this two-year limitation period does not apply to the personal injury actions based on assault and battery.

Fatal injuries claims

Such action shall not be brought after the expiration of two years from the date of death or the date of knowledge of the person for whose benefit the action is brought whichever is the later. Date of knowledge is defined in Section 2 of the above mentioned 1991 Act.

Assault

An action claiming damages for personal injuries from assault and battery has a limitation period of six years from the date of accrual of the cause of action.

Defamation

Actions for defamation have a limitation period of one year from the date of the cause of action accrued or two years from the date, if the court so directs.

Claims for latent damage (other than personal injury)

In such cases the limitation period is six years from the date of accrual of the right of action, and such limitation period begins to run when the damage has been caused by the defendant's wrongful acts even where the damage is latent and therefore the plaintiff is unaware of it and their right of action.

Contract

Such actions shall not be brought after the expiration of six years from the accrual of the cause of action. In contract the cause of action accrues when the breach of contract occurs not from the damages suffered since the essence of the action for breach of contract is a breach and not a resulting damage suffered.

Debt/acknowledgment and part payment

Claims for liquidated sums are based on contracts subject to the limitation period of six years calculated from the date on which the sum became due. However, this starting date can be altered if the debtor acknowledges the debt after it becomes due or if the debtor makes part payment.

Section 56 of the 1957 statute provides that where a right of action has accrued to recover a debt and the debtor acknowledges the claim, the right of action shall be deemed to have accrued on and not before the date of acknowledgment. Similarly s.65 of the 1957 statute provides that if the debtor makes any part payment in respect of the debt, the right of action for recovery on the balance is deemed to have accrued on, and not before, the date of such part payment. This applies to whether or not the statutory period has expired when the acknowledgment or part payment is made.

Claims for defective motor vehicles

These such actions shall not be brought after the expiration of two years from the date on which the cause of action accrued.

Defective products

Strict liability for defective products was introduced by the Liability for Defective Products Act 1991. Section 7(1) provides that an action for the recovery of damages under this Act shall be brought within three years from: (a) the date of accrual of the cause of action; or (b) the date (if later) on which the plaintiff became aware, or should reasonably have become aware, of the damage, the defect, and the identity of the producer.

A further limitation period (commonly known as the "longstop" is provided at s.7(2)(a), which states that the right of action under the Liability for Defective Products Act 1991 shall be extended until the expiration of 10 years from the date on which the producer puts into circulation the actual product which caused the damage, unless the injured person has issued proceedings against the producer within that period.

Recovery of Benefits and Assistance Scheme

The Recovery of Benefits and Assistance Scheme is comparable to the CRU process undertaken by the Department of Communities in the UK. It was introduced in Ireland on the 1 August 2014 legislating for certain categories of social welfare payments to become deductible from the loss of earnings element of a plaintiff's claim for special damages.

The categories of deductible social welfare payments are:

- Illness benefit
- Disability allowance
- Partial capacity benefit
- Injury benefit

- Incapacity supplement
- Invalidity pension
- Increase in disablement benefit.

The scheme puts the onus on insurers to directly reimburse the deductive social welfare payments to the Department of Social Protection. The refund payable to the Department of Social Welfare is limited to a period of five years' social welfare benefits, or the total payments up to the date of compensation, whichever is the smaller amount. The defendant requests a Statement of Recoverable Benefits from the department once a case is identified as suitable for settlement or one which is advancing to hearing. Once issued, this statement is valid for three months.

It is important to note that the legislation requires that the defendant/its insurer discharge the amount specified in the Statement of Recoverable Benefits to the department prior to paying any compensation to the plaintiff.

Motions

As each pleading falls due, there are time limits as set out in the previous diagrams. This jurisdiction has no procedures for automatic judgments if the time limits are missed by either party to the proceedings. A warning letter must be furnished to the defaulting party allowing them an extension of 21 days to comply with the court rules. If they fail to do so, a motion on notice is brought before the court based on a grounding affidavit.

Traditionally courts allow significant leeway and while they are tightening up timeframes, it is likely that the defaulting party will either succeed in having the motion adjourned or be granted an extension of six weeks to file the pleading.

Therefore time limits are not strict.

Third-party procedure

Strict time limits are applied in Ireland in respect of the joinder of third parties to proceedings. While the Statute of Limitations does not provide a deadline for joining a third party to proceedings' court rules state that it must happen "as soon as reasonably practicable". This has been interpreted in the Circuit and High Court to the effect that a defendant who wants to join a third party should be in a position to do so at the time their defence is due.

It is not uncommon therefore for a third-party joinder to be challenged on the basis of delay.

Time limits for joinder of third parties are tighter still in the District Court, which provides that the third party notice must be served within 10 days of the service of the claim of that notice.

Once the potential third party is identified, the defendant issues a notice of motion seeking leave to issue and file a third party notice. This is an ex-parte application but once the third party notice is filed, the grounding affidavit must be provided if requested to the third party. Time limits for serving a third party notice are strict in the Circuit and High Court at 28 days following the date upon which the notice of motion was heard.

In practice it is usual for the trial of the main action and the third party issue to take place together.

It is open to a plaintiff to join a proposed third party as a co-defendant and if they are within the statutory time limits and/or were unaware pursuant to the 1991 Act, of the potential to sue the third party. Then no challenge can be brought by the third party to their joinder as a co-defendant. This regularly operates as a remedy where there has been delay on the part of a defendant but is subject to the plaintiff seeking to join them also.

Exaggerated claims

Sections 25 and 26 of the Civil Liability & Courts Act 2004 provided a statutory basis for a court to strike out a claim in a personal injury action where the plaintiff had exaggerated their injury. In circumstances where a plaintiff exaggerates any aspect of their injury or special damage it is open to the court to strike out the entire action if they believe this would not do an injustice to the plaintiff. This has led to numerous actions where minor injuries were involved being struck out by the court but in the more serious injuries a court tends to strike out only a portion of the claim, for example what they believe to be an exaggerated loss of earnings.

Discovery

Discovery in Ireland is ordered in respect of documents which are in "power, possession or procurement". It tends therefore to afford parties wider discovery than they would obtain in other jurisdictions.

It is made either voluntarily or by court order pursuant to a format set out in the court rules. It is unusual outside mass product recall for discovery to take place in favour of either party prior to a defence being served.

Settlement tools for defence litigators

Pre-litigation written offers, Calderbank letter

The general rule in Ireland is that *costs follow the event.* A Calderbank letter is a written offer made to the plaintiff on a without prejudice basis but which can be relied upon before the court in relation to costs.

Where a Calderbank offer is not accepted, and the judgment is for less, the costs are at the discretion of the court.

Lodgement

A defendant can lodge in court a sum of money in full and final settlement of the plaintiff's claim. Such lodgement can be made with or without an admission of liability. Lodgements can be made in the District Court, Circuit Court and High Court.

If the plaintiff does not accept the lodgement and obtains a judgment greater than the lodgement, the plaintiff:

a) Has to bear their own costs for the date of lodgement; and

b) Discharge the defendant's costs for the date of the lodgement.

If a plaintiff accepts the lodgement, their costs up to the date of the lodgement can be taxed in the normal way unless the lodgement was costs inclusive.

District Court time limits for lodgements

In a District Court matter, the money must be lodged into the Court's accountancy office and notice of lodgement served on the claimant at any time after the entry of appearance and up to the filing of the defence. Outside of these time limits, the permission of the Court is required to make a lodgement. If the claimant amends their claim notice an amended lodgement may be made.

A claimant has 28 days to accept a lodgement. After 28 days, they will need to obtain the consent of the defendant to accept the lodgement.

Circuit Court time limits for lodgements

In a Circuit Court matter, money must be lodged with the Court's accountancy office and a notice of lodgement served on the claimant at any time after the entry of appearance and before the notice of trial is served. The defendant can make one additional lodgement inside this time limit.

The claimant has 10 days to accept the lodgement. After 10 days, the claimant will need to obtain the consent of the defendant to accept the lodgement.

Lodgements in High Court non-personal injury matters

In a High Court matter, money can be lodged and a notice of lodgement served at any time after the memorandum of appearance up to the matter being set down for trial. Once the matter is set down for trial, a defendant must seek the Court's permission to make a lodgement. A defendant can make a top-up lodgement up to three months before a case is listed for hearing.

A plaintiff has 14 days to accept the lodgement, otherwise the plaintiff will require the consent of the defendant.

Lodgements in High Court personal injury matters

In personal injury matters there is a separate set of time limits for making a lodgement. A lodgement of money and serving a notice of lodgement on the plaintiff can be made at any time after a memorandum of appearance has been entered and within a period of four months from the date of the notice of trial.

A defendant may also make a lodgement outside of this time period, without seeking leave of the Court; where:

a) The plaintiff delivers a reply to the notice of particulars or additional particulars are delivered, the defendant has 21 days to make a lodgement; and

b) 18 months has passed since the notice of trial has been issued, the defendant has 21 days following the expiring of the 18 months to make a lodgement.

A plaintiff has 14 days to accept a lodgement made in a personal injury matter, otherwise the consent of the defendant is required.

A minor or person of unsound mind

A court ruling is required before acceptance of a lodgement or a tender for a minor or a person of unsound mind.

Tenders

Certain 'qualified indemnifiers' approved by the state along with insurance undertakings authorised to carry on business in the state, can serve a notice of tender instead of making a lodgement of money into court. The same rules and time limits apply to making a tender as making a lodgement.

Personal injury matters, formal offers/ Section 17 offers

In a personal injury matter, a defendant and plaintiff must make an offer to the other party no later than 14 days after the service of the notice of trial. The plaintiff's offer must state what they are willing to accept and a defendant's offer must state what they are willing to offer to settle or that they do not wish to settle.

The relevant letters of offer must be filed in the appropriate Courts Office. Should the matter not settle and proceed to full hearing, a judge may consider the reasonableness of said offers when making a costs order.

Costs

Taxation of costs refers to the manner in which costs are measured and this function is normally carried out by the Taxing Master (High Court) and the local County Registrar (Circuit Court).

Three principal categories exist under which legal costs may be measured:

1) Party and party costs (payable by one party to an action to another).

2) Solicitor client costs (payable by one party to an action to another but on a more generous scale).

3) Solicitor and own client costs (payable to the client's own solicitor as a matter of contract).

Table 5 – District Court costs

The District Court operates on a fixed claim scale set by statute as follows:

SOLICITORS' COSTS IN CONTRACT, BREACH OF CONTRACT AND TORT PROCEEDINGS AND IN CLAIMS FOR DAMAGES UNCONNECTED WITH CONTRACT				
Amount due at the date of issue of claim notice or, (as the case may be) the amount decreed for debt	Costs if settled without necessity for appearance	Costs of judgment (decree) if case not defended	Costs of judgment (decree) if case defended (assessment of damages)	Costs of judgment (decree/ dismiss) if case defended (liability)
	€	€	€	€
Not exceeding €3,000	300	500	650	750
Exceeding €3,000 and not exceeding €6,000	600	1,000	1,300	1,500
Exceeding €6,000 and not exceeding €9,000	900	1,500	1,950	2,250
Exceeding €9,000 and not exceeding €12,000	1,200	2,000	2,600	3,000
Exceeding €12,000 and not exceeding €15,000	1,500	2,500	3,250	3,750

The above scale of costs (2):

- is in every instance exclusive of and in addition to all actual and necessary outlay;
- applies to actions for wrongful detention brought by virtue of section 33(3) of the Courts (Supplemental Provisions) Act 1961, according to the value of the goods as determined by the Court;
- applies to actions for wrongful detention arising out of a hire-purchase transaction.